T0180364

Lecture Notes in Computer Science 1101

Edited by G. Goos, J. Hartmanis and J. van Leeuwen

Advisory Board: W. Brauer   D. Gries   J. Stoer

Springer
Berlin
Heidelberg
New York
Barcelona
Budapest
Hong Kong
London
Milan
Paris
Santa Clara
Singapore
Tokyo

Martin Wirsing   Maurice Nivat (Eds.)

Algebraic Methodology and Software Technology

5th International Conference, AMAST '96
Munich, Germany, July 1-5, 1996
Proceedings

Springer

Series Editors

Gerhard Goos, Karlsruhe University, Germany

Juris Hartmanis, Cornell University, NY, USA

Jan van Leeuwen, Utrecht University, The Netherlands

Volume Editors

Martin Wirsing
Ludwig-Maximilians-Universität München, Institut für Informatik
Oettingenstr. 67, D-80538 München, Germany

Maurice Nivat
LITP, Université Paris XII - Denis Diderot
2, Place Jussieu, F-75005 Paris, France

Cataloging-in-Publication data applied for

Die Deutsche Bibliothek - CIP-Einheitsaufnahme

Algebraic methodology and software technology : 5th
international conference ; proceedings / AMAST '96, Munich,
Germany, July 1 - 5, 1996. Martin Wirsing ; Maurice Nivat
(ed.). - Berlin ; Heidelberg ; New York ; Barcelona ; Budapest ;
Hong Kong ; London ; Milan ; Paris ; Santa Clara ; Singapore ;
Tokyo : Springer, 1996
  (Lecture notes in computer science ; Vol. 1101)
  ISBN 3-540-61463-X
NE: Wirsing, Martin [Hrsg.]; AMAST <5, 1996, München>; GT

CR Subject Classification (1991): F.3-4, D.2, C.3, D.1.6, I.2.3, H.2.1-4

ISSN 0302-9743
ISBN 3-540-61463-X Springer-Verlag Berlin Heidelberg New York

© Springer-Verlag Berlin Heidelberg 1996
Printed in Germany

Typesetting: Camera-ready by author
SPIN 10513306   06/3142 – 5 4 3 2 1 0   Printed on acid-free paper

Preface

This volume contains the contributions of invited speakers, refereed papers, and reports on system presentations of the Fifth International Conference on Algebraic Methodology and Software Technology (AMAST '96) held in Munich, July 1-5, 1996. The previous four editions of AMAST took place at the University of Iowa (USA) in 1989 and 1991, at the University of Twente (The Netherlands) in 1993, and at the University of Montreal (Canada) in 1995.

The major goals of the AMAST conferences are to put software development technology on a firm, mathematical foundation. Particular emphasis is given to algebraic and logical foundations of software technology. An eventual goal is to establish algebraic and logical methodology as a practically viable and attractive alternative to the prevailing ad hoc approaches to software engineering.

As in the previous years the first day of AMAST '96 was dedicated to the education of software engineers. The theme this year was on applications of formal methods in industrial software development showing the use of mathematics-based methods to give support for requirement analysis, formal specification, and design.

In response to the call for papers, 67 papers were submitted. We invited six speakers for the education day, six speakers for the conference days, and one speaker for the banquet. The Program Committee met on January 29 and accepted 25 papers, complemented by an almost equal number of 23 system demonstrations.

The distinguished invited speakers are André Arnold, Jan Bergstra, Gérard Berry, Manfred Broy, Arie van Deursen, José Fiadeiro, John Fitzgerald, Eric Hehner, Bernd Krämer, Dino Mandrioli, Sriram Sankar, and Douglas Smith. We are also fortunate to have F.L. Bauer as our banquet speaker.

The accepted papers cover the major conference themes: algebraic and logical foundations, concurrency, software technology, and logic programming. The subjects of these papers include a wide variety of methods, notations, semantics, and proofs contributing to an advancement and rigorous development of software systems. The reports on system presentations describe ongoing research efforts to implement algebraic and logical methods and to apply formal methods in software technology.

On behalf of the Program Committee I would like to thank all those who submitted papers and system presentations and the referees who helped to evaluate the papers. The support of DFG (Deutsche Forschungsgemeinschaft),
Münchener Universitätsgesellschaft,
sd&m,
Versicherungskammer Bayern/Bayen-Versicherung,
Siemens AG
is gratefully acknowledged. Rolf Hennicker, Christian Baur, Alexander Kurz, Luis Mandel, Bernhard Reus, Weishi Zhang, Marianne Diem, Agnes Szabo-Lackinger, Thomas Lackinger, and several other members of the department provided invaluable help throughout the preparation and organization of the conference. I also would like to thank Alfred Hofmann at Springer-Verlag for his excellent cooperation concerning the publication of this volume.

Munich, April 1996   Martin Wirsing

Program Chair: Martin Wirsing

General Chair: Maurice Nivat

Program Committee
Martin Abadi (USA)
V.S. Alagar (Canada)
Egidio Astesiano (Italy)
Didier Begay (France)
Gregor Bochmann (Canada)
Chris Brink (South Africa)
Bruno Buchberger (Austria)
Kokichi Futatsugi (Japan)
Harald Ganzinger (Germany)
Armando Haeberer (Brazil)
Nicolas Halbwachs (France)
Yasuyoshi Inagaki (Japan)
Paola Inverardi (Italy)
Mike Johnson (Australia)
Helene Kirchner (France)
Tom Maibaum (UK)
Jan Maluszynski (Sweden)
Josè Meseguer (USA)
Peter Mosses (Denmark)
Rocco De Nicola (Italy)
Anton Nijholt (The Netherlands)
Fernando Orejas (Spain)
R. Ramanujam (India)
Charles Rattray (UK)
Teodor Rus (USA)
Giuseppe Scollo (The Netherlands)
R.K. Shyamasundar (India)
Andrzej Tarlecki (Poland)
Herbert Weber (Germany)

Organizing Committee
Chair: Martin Wirsing (Germany)

Tools and Demos:
Christian Baur (Germany)

Publicity:
Charles Rattray (UK)
V.S. Alagar (Canada)
Michel Bidoit (France)
Jacques Printz (France)
Teodor Rus (USA)
Giuseppe Scollo (The Netherlands)

Local Arrangements:
Rolf Hennicker (Germany)
Marianne Diem (Germany)

Subreferees

The program committee members and a number of external referees refereed all submitted papers and helped in the selection of papers from among the many excellent submissions received. Their invaluable timely reports and assistance during the selection process made it possible to bring the proceedings to its present form.

A. Arnold
D. Basin
H. Baumeister
B. Berthomieu
P. Bhaduri
A. Bockmayr
A. Borusan
A.M. Borzyszkowski
A. Bouajjani
G. Boudol
J. Boye
P. van den Broek
R. Buckland
L. Campora
M. Carlsson
P. Caspi
I. Castellani
P. Casteran
C. Castro
I. Claßen
D. Craigen
P. Degano
S.M. Eker
G. Ferrari
M. Fokkinga
P. Freedman
B. Gramlich
A. Griffault
H. Hong
S.B. Jones
J-P. Katoen
F. Khendek
A. Khoumsi
M. Klar
B. Konikowska

R. Kubiak
K.N. Kumar
J. Kuper
R-D. Kutsche
A. Labella
Y. Lakhnech
R. Langerak
B. Le Saec
P. Lincoln
K. Lodaya
G. Malcolm
O. Maler
C. Marché
R. Mateescu
C. Meo
S.K. Mohalik
M. Mukund
T. Naoi
M. Nesi
F. Nickl
W. Pawlowski
M. Peixoto
A. Petrenko
A. Pierantonio
M. Poel
F.P. Presicce
C. Priami
R. Pugliese
M.R.K. Krishna Rao
G. Reggio
G. Richard
F. Rossi
M. Rusinowitch
T. Sakabe
L. Scott

M. Sighireanu
R. de Simone
S. Sokolowski
S. Tai
P.S. Thiagarajan
E. Tronci
P.A. Wacrenier
S. Wasserroth
D. Wolz
S. Yuen
M.V. Zilli
E. Zucca
J. Zwiers

Table of Contents

Education Day: Industrial Applications of Formal Methods

Conference

Session 1: Theorem Proving

Session 2: Algebraic Specification

Two Industrial Trials of Formal Specification

J. S. Fitzgerald

Centre for Software Reliability, University of Newcastle upon Tyne, NE1 7RU, UK

Abstract. Formal methods are gradually making their way onto the "shop floor" of software engineering. As part of this process, industrial software developers are conducting trials of formal techniques in realistic projects. This paper describes two such studies: one each from the nuclear and aerospace industries. Both projects stressed the importance of formal specification as a modelling tool in the early stages of system development, but they differed in their approaches to specification validation.

The specification styles and validation activities in the two studies will be compared. Finally the conclusions which can be drawn from projects such as these are discussed.

1   Introduction

In common with other branches of software engineering, there is only limited empirical evidence about the quality of software developed or the costs of development using formal methods. The software engineering manager considering applying formal techniques in a new development project would wish to gather evidence about the choice of techniques, the best way to employ them, what the costs and benefits might be. In the absence of results from large-scale formal experiments, the adoption of a novel approach tends to be governed by experience in small-scale trials, either in industry or in research laboratories with industrial collaboration.

This paper compares two projects based on formal techniques. The first, from the nuclear industry, concerns the development of a formal model for the tracking of nuclear waste through the stages of a reprocessing plant. A substantial formal specification was developed and subjected to conventional inspection. A study into the value of proof in checking the consistency of the specification and validating safety properties raised a number of issues surrounding the use of proof in the validation of large specifications. The specification and proof work was done by researchers under guidance from domain experts from industry.

The second study was carried out in industry and concerned the development of a secure message processing system. The specification produced in this trial was much smaller than the tracking manager specification, and was validated largely by testing rather than proof.

Section 2, reports on the tracking manager project, including a discussion of the findings of the proof activity. Section 3 provides a brief review of the trusted gateway development, which is already widely reported elsewhere. The two studies are compared in Section 4. Some concluding remarks on the gathering and interpretation of evidence from studies of this sort are included in Section 5.

2 The BNFL Tracking Manager Study

As nuclear material passes through the various stages of processing in a commercial plant, it is important keep track of each container and its fissile content to ensure, for example, that there is not a build-up of fissile material in one stage of processing, and that no material goes missing. A novel approach to tracking has been proposed, based on a topology of communicating *tracking managers*. Each tracking manager is responsible for monitoring, recording and providing advisory permission on the movement of material through one part of the plant. The study reported here investigated the use of formal modelling in clarifying the requirements for the tracking manager architecture and contributing to the safety case for the plant.

Informal requirements for a specific demonstrator plant illustrating the use of the tracking manager architecture were determined in collaboration with domain experts at British Nuclear Fuels Engineering (BNFL). Certain properties of the plant were considered to be related to its safe operation. These distinguished properties, called *safety properties*, were stated informally. A formal model of the demonstrator plant, incorporating the safety properties was developed by a team of researchers at The University of Manchester, UK. The model was presented in VDM-SL [ABH+95] using SpecBox [BFM89] and the IFAD VDM-SL Toolbox [ELL94] for syntax- and type-checking. Although the latter tool permits execution of executable parts of a specification for test-based validation, this facility was not used. As a validation exercise, two formal reviews were conducted and an investigation of the use of proof in checking the specification's consistency, including respect for safety properties, took place.

A full discussion of the formal model is not possible in this short paper. Instead, Section 2.1 describes in outline the structure of the model while Section 2.2 describes some of the findings of the proof activity which are of interest beyond the confines of this particular study.

2.1 The Formal Model of the Demonstrator Plant

A VDM-SL specification is typically built around a model of the system state. Possible modifications to the state are mediated via operations specified using pre-/post-conditions to denote relations between states (and input and result values). There is an obligation to show that each operation is *satisfiable* in the sense that, for every state satisfying the precondition, there is a state related to it via the postcondition. In discharging the satisfiability obligation, the bulk of the proof is typically devoted to showing that a candidate "after" state satisfies the invariant conditions attached to the state in its definition.

The formal model of the demonstrator plant was developed by Spink [FS96] from informal descriptions supplied by domain experts in BNFL. The three main components of the model can be seen in the state definition from the formal specification:

> **state** *System* **of**
>   *tms* : *TMId* $\xrightarrow{m}$ *TM*
>   *phases* : *PhaseId* $\xrightarrow{m}$ *Phase*
>   *containers* : *ContainerId* $\xrightarrow{m}$ *Container*
>   ⋮
>
>   **inv mk-***System* (...) $\triangleq$ ...
>   **init** *System* $\triangleq$ *sys* = **mk-***System* (...)
> **end**

In a conventional plant, material is passed through a number of phases (state component *phases*), which may themselves consist of a sequence of sub-phases. Material is held in containers (state component *containers*), each of which is uniquely identified. At the end of the sequence of phases, the packaged processed material is put into store prior to long-term storage or shipping to the customer.

The tracking managers (state component *tms*) added in the proposed demonstrator architecture are uniquely identified, each one being responsible for monitoring the position of containers in a given phase or sub-phase, and for granting permission for a container to move from one phase to the next. The tracking managers are connected in the same hierarchy as the phases and sub-phases of the plant, so that, to determine the position of a container, it is sufficient to send a request to a "root" tracking manager.

The state invariant (**inv mk-***System* ...) is a conjunction of clauses which constrain the state space. Some clauses ensure consistency between the state components, for example that the *phases* mapping is closed over phase identifiers. Other clauses capture the safety properties provided by domain experts, for example that the maximum fissile content of a drum (a type of container) must be less than a defined limit.

A characteristic of the specification is its mixture of generic aspects and material specific to the particular demonstrator architecture. For example, the structure for phases and tracking managers shown in the system state is quite independent of the particular number of phases and sub-phases chosen for the demonstrator. The instantiation of the general phase structure takes place in the separate state initialisation clause (**init** *System* ...), where the *phases* state component is set to the specific collection of phases and phase identifiers laid down for the demonstrator.

Containers are also represented as a generic type. However, for the specific demonstrator architecture, only five kinds of container are permitted: drums, packages, liners and pucks. This restriction is recorded in the invariant on the type *Container* (not shown here), and not in the initialisation clause. Strict rules, also recorded in the invariant, govern the kind of material which may be stored in a container. Certain types of container may stored within other types of container, e.g. a drum may contain some packages, a stillage may only contain precisely four drums.

The operations in the formal model also reflect this mixture of the generic and specific. Some operations characterise actions which are invoked at various points in the plant, for example packing and unpacking containers. The operation shown in part below describes the generic packing of a new container with a number of other containers (the *contents* parameter). This adds the new container to the *containers* state component:

$$Pack\text{-}Container\,(cid : ContainerId, ctype : ContainerType,$$
$$conttype : ContentsType \mid ContainerType,$$
$$contents : ContainerId\text{-}\textbf{set})$$
$$\textbf{ext wr } containers : ContainerId \xrightarrow{m} Container$$
$$\textbf{wr } history : Transformation^*$$
$$\textbf{post } (cid \notin \textbf{dom } containers \land contents \subseteq \textbf{dom } containers \;\Rightarrow$$
$$containers = \overleftarrow{containers} \dagger$$
$$\{cid \mapsto \textbf{mk-}Container\,(ctype, conttype, contents, \textbf{nil }\,)\} \land$$
$$\ldots)$$

Other operations describe the actions associated with each phase in the plant, for example generating assay data or describing the compaction of certain containers.

This mixture of the generic and particular affected the proofs performed in the study, particularly through the use of the initialisation clause to record information required in satisfiability arguments. The following section describes the main findings from the proofs undertaken.

2.2 Main findings

The specification produced in the formal modelling activity was substantial, containing 42 value definitions, 16 type definitions, seven state components, 24 function definitions and 28 operation specifications. The proof work undertaken [FJ96] was therefore illustrative rather than comprehensive. The total effort invested in specification and proof together is recorded as being about four person-months. Three Proofs were conducted at a range of levels of rigour, from largely informal proofs mixing formulae and natural language, through rigorous proofs (structured Natural Deduction proofs in the style of [Jon90]) to the fully formal, using the proof theory in [BFL$^+$94]. This provided an informal evaluation of the relative value of different levels of rigour in contributing to the validation of the formal model.

One conjecture concerned the demonstrator-specific operation describing the effects of compacting certain kinds of container. The conjecture was stated informally, and somewhat imprecisely, as "It should not be possible to compact liquor". Put more formally, the assertion stated that the compaction operation should not apply to liners containing any containers which hold liquor. Its proof revealed that it relied on an aspect of the system state set up in the **init** clause, namely that the compaction phase only accepts liners as input. Consequently, a proof of the conjecture would rely on an induction over all reachable states, rather than a proof based only around the operation specification and state invariant, as is normally the case in VDM. This serious complication is a consequence of the mixture of genericity and demonstrator-specific aspects in the specification.

The use of formal proof was valuable in raising and resolving a number of deficiencies in the specification, for example insufficiently strong preconditions in some operations (including the container packing operation shown above). The potential contribution of a formal model with proof to the plant safety case was established. However, the proof work raised a number of issues about the way proof should be exploited during the development of large specifications. These are summarised below.

In the tracking manager project, the proof work was treated as a review activity which took place after the completion and inspection of the formal model of the demonstrator plant. A number of issues raised by the proof work (e.g. the use of the initialisation clause to instantiate generic parts of the specification) could have been resolved earlier had intermediate reviews been incorporated containing an element of rigorous proof. This would allow a later proof phase to concentrate on the discovery of more subtle problems and showing preservation of safety properties to a higher level of rigour or formality.

There is an issue of the scope of the system being specified. The tracking manager system was intended as an advisory rather than a process control system. Nevertheless, note the liquor compaction assertion above: the formal model of the tracking manager system cannot in itself ensure that liquor is not compacted. The proofs of safety properties constructed in the project do not have any ramifications beyond the formal model over which they were constructed. The connection between the tracking manager model (whether an advisory or control system) and the physical processes on containers must be established through a suitable hazard analysis.

The model of the demonstrator architecture was intended to be specific to a given plant consisting of a fixed structure of phases. However, the specification is more generic in certain aspects, notably the definition of generic operations and the general phase structure. It was felt during the proof work that the proofs themselves might have been more straightforward to construct had the specification actually included rather less genericity. In the longer term, a modular form of the specification encapsulating separate theories of generic components could potentially assist in producing the safety case for instances of the tracking manager architecture at particular plant.

3 The ConForm Project

In contrast with the tracking manager study, which highlighted some of the benefits and difficulties of applying proof in the analysis of a large-scale formal model, the ConForm project concentrated on the modest application of formal specification validated by testing rather than proof. This study has been widely reported elsewhere [BFL96, LFB96], so it will not be reported in detail here.

The ConForm project was carried out by British Aerospace (Systems & Equipment) Ltd. and involved applying VDM-SL to the description of the security policy for a secure message-processing device known as a trusted gateway. A stream of messages is received at the gateway's input. The classification of each message is determined by the gateway and the message routed to an output port appropriate to the classification. The security policy is simply that messages should not be sent to lower-classification output ports than appropriate.

The system design was represented using the Yourdon structured method with Ward & Mellor's extensions. VDM-SL was used in the data dictionary and process specifications of the data-flow model central to the design. Again, the IFAD VDM-SL Toolbox was used to syntax- and type-check the formal specification. In contrast to the tracking manager project, however, the specification, being executable, was tested extensively. The tests applied to the formal specification were added to the system test plan so that the final product could be tested against the same data.

Comparison of the trusted gateway's development using VDM-SL with a parallel development not using the formal language suggested that the process was assisted in the analysis of the customer requirement by the use of an appropriate formalism. The test sets developed in the path using VDM-SL highlighted a deficiency in the requirements analysis of the conventionally-developed product, which would not normally have been revealed until the product was in service. A report from the external assurance authority indicated that the use of VDM-SL was sufficient to allow the product to be certificated to higher security criteria than would otherwise be the case.

As a result of the study, the company also concluded that the cost of applying the formal technique was not excessive and justified the higher level of external assurance which could be placed in the developed software as a result.

4   Comparing the Tracking Manager and ConForm Trials

The two studies reported here share a common specification language, and both concern the assurance of a system model. However, there the similarity ends. The specifications produced were of very different sizes, were produced by practitioners of different levels of expertise and, perhaps most importantly, took different approaches to achieving the assurance required: the tracking manager specification was used as the basis of an exercise in proof, while the trusted gateway specification was tested extensively.

The question of using proof and testing in the validation of model-oriented specifications is connected to the executability of specifications. Although the value of executable specification has been debated [HJ89, Fuc92], the choice of an executable style in the trusted gateway development was governed by pragmatic concerns, particularly the relatively low cost of testing in terms of training and tool support and the stress on testing in the BASE development process, rather than on the production of any equivalent of the safety case used in the nuclear industry.

A significant difference between the two projects is the level of ambition for the formal models produced. In BASE, formal specification was being introduced for the first time, while those participating in the BNFL study were experts. If it is a longer-term goal for BASE to develop systems to still higher assurance levels, proof may become an area of concern, as it is for developers of high-integrity systems in other sectors (e.g. safety-related defence equipment conformant to UK Defence Standard 00-55). Modest introduction of easily testable specifications can be seen as an effective route of entry into formal methods.

The tracking manager project, although it exploited proof, did not have access to machine support for proof, particularly for rigorous or semi-formal proof of the kind advocated for intermediate reviews. Nevertheless, its list of findings emphasises the extent to which proof can expose deficiencies which may elude a generated test set.

The ConForm work has been criticised for its non-exploitation of proof which, it is sometimes argued, is the *raison d'être* for formal methods. Without proof, could one not simply do prototyping in a very high level programming language? In answer, it is worth noting that formal specification languages are mandated because their semantics are well worked-out and form a solid basis for analysis of specifications whether by the developer, customer or external assurance authority. Further, they provide the potential for proof in future, even if that potential is not immediately realised.

5   Concluding remarks

An examination of the range of industrial applications of formal methods in the Formal Methods Applications Database[1] suggests that the extent of the differences between these two studies is not unusual. Formal methods applications vary greatly in technical ambition and the level of monitoring of commercial issues such as cost-effectiveness. Given such variety, it is hard to draw general conclusions about the effectiveness of formal methods or one method over another. Indeed, it would be unwise to allow excessive claims about formal techniques to be made on the basis of small-scale trials, as these tend only to discredit the methods being advocated.

Software engineering practitioners are likely to draw conclusions about formal techniques based on experience closely related to their own area of work. For example, a developer of real-time avionics systems would not draw many conclusions from either example reported here. However, the recorded experience of other practitioners may encourage a local study which is directly relevant to a company's needs and which could itself contribute to the evidence available to others. Practitioners involved in local trials of formal techniques should be encouraged to record their conclusions and make these available widely through such media as the applications database.

---

[1] Nico Plat (ed.): *The Formal Methods Applications Database*, accessible in the World-wide Web via URL http://www.cs.ncl.ac.uk/research/csr/FME

References

[ABH⁺95] D.J. Andrews, H. Bruun, B.S. Hansen, P.G. Larsen, N. Plat, et al. *Information Technology — Programming Languages, their environments and system software interfaces — Vienna Development Method-Specification Language Part 1: Base language*. ISO, 1995.

[BFL⁺94] J. C. Bicarregui, J. S. Fitzgerald, P. A. Lindsay, R. Moore, and B. Ritchie. *Proof in VDM: A Practitioner's Guide*. FACIT. Springer-Verlag, 1994. ISBN 3-540-19813-X.

[BFL96] T. M. Brookes, J. S. Fitzgerald, and P. G. Larsen. Formal and informal specifications of a secure system component: final results in a comparative study. In *Proceedings of FME'96*, Lecture Notes in Computer Science. Springer-Verlag, 1996.

[BFM89] Robin Bloomfield, Peter Froome, and Brian Monahan. SpecBox: A toolkit for BSI-VDM. *SafetyNet*, (5):4–7, 1989.

[ELL94] René Elmstrøm, Peter Gorm Larsen, and Poul Bøgh Lassen. The IFAD VDM-SL Toolbox: A Practical Approach to Formal Specifications. *ACM Sigplan Notices*, September 1994.

[FJ96] J. S. Fitzgerald and C. B. Jones. Proof in the Validation of a Formal Model of a Tracking System. Technical report, Dept. of Computer Science, University of Manchester, 1996. In preparation.

[FS96] J. S. Fitzgerald and M. A. Spink. Formal Modelling of a Tracking System for a Nuclear Plant. Technical report, Dept. of Computer Science, University of Manchester, 1996. In preparation.

[Fuc92] N. E. Fuchs. Specifications are (preferably) executable. *Software Engineering Journal*, pages 323–334, September 1992.

[HJ89] I. J. Hayes and C. B. Jones. Specifications are not (necessarily) executable. *Software Engineering Journal*, pages 330–338, November 1989.

[Jon90] Cliff B. Jones. *Systematic Software Development Using VDM*. Prentice-Hall International, Englewood Cliffs, New Jersey, second edition, 1990. ISBN 0-13-880733-7.

[LFB96] Peter Gorm Larsen, John S. Fitzgerald, and Tom Brookes. Applying formal specification in industry. *IEEE Software*, May 1996.

Acknowledgements The author is grateful to the organisers and programme committee of AMAST'96 for the opportunity to prepare this short paper. Many colleagues have contributed to the studies reported here. The original tracking manager demonstrator architecture model is largely due to Martyn Spink, while the proof work was shared with Cliff Jones. Much of the guidance during the BNFL project was afforded by Ian Cottam of Adelard, Bill Neary & Paul Vlissidis of BNFL. The ConForm project was led by Tom Brookes and carried out in collaboration with Peter Gorm Larsen of IFAD. The author acknowledges the support of the UK Engineering and Physical Sciences Research Council under the terms of a Research Fellowship and research grant GR/K/26769.

Industrial Applications of ASF+SDF

Mark van den Brand,[1] Arie van Deursen,[2] Paul Klint,[1,2]
Steven Klusener,[2,4] and Emma van der Meulen[3]

[1] University of Amsterdam, Kruislaan 403, 1098 SJ Amsterdam
[2] CWI, P.O. Box 94079, 1090 GB Amsterdam
[3] MeesPierson, Rokin 55, Amsterdam
[4] CAP Volmac, P.O. Box 2575, 3500 GN Utrecht

Email: arie@cwi.nl; URL: http://www.cwi.nl/~arie/

Abstract. In recent years, a number of Dutch companies have used the algebraic
specification formalism ASF+SDF. Bank MeesPierson has specified a language
for describing interest rate products, their translation into COBOL, and their
generation from interactive questionnaires. A consultancy company has specified
a language to represent the company's object-oriented models, and the compilation
of this language into Access. Bank ABN-AMRO has started investigating the use
of algebraic specifications for renovating legacy COBOL systems. We discuss the
implications of such projects for teaching algebraic specifications and software
engineering, and the role students have been playing in these projects.

1 Introduction

Day to day automation in trade and industry makes little or no use of formal methods.
Instead, software construction and maintenance in the real world deals with COBOL,
PL/I, IMS or Fortran, and at best with SQL, C++, graphical user interfaces, or CORBA-
like middleware. Of all software running in the world, the fraction developed using
formal methods is practically equal to zero.

In spite of that, many computer science departments training their students to become
professional software engineers, have included formal method courses in their curricula.
The reason for this is not only that such courses help to understand the foundations
of computing; most departments strongly believe that the use of formal methods will
greatly enhance the software development process. But we should ask ourselves whether
teaching these classes is not simply a waste of time and energy. Is it not so that students,
once they have found a software engineering job in industry, will find it almost impossible
to spot opportunities for applying their formal methods skills?

If we take these questions seriously, we have to teach students how to apply their
knowledge in practice. We must train them to recognize which situations may be ripe
for formalization, and when the cost of using formal techniques will not outweigh the
benefits. We have to show students how we tried to use formal methods, how our business
partners reacted, and which techniques we mainly used. Wherever possible, we have to
involve students in our collaboration with industry, and make them participate actively.

In this paper, we address such questions in the context of the algebraic specification
formalism ASF+SDF. We report on our experiences with the use of ASF+SDF in Dutch
industry, and on the role students have been playing in these.

1.1 Language Prototyping

Languages are ubiquitous in software engineering: they are used for specification and implementation, as interfaces between components, to access databases, to build user interfaces, and so on. Many software systems are centered around one or more *domain-specific* languages, which are tailored to the specific needs of the system in question and which can be used to extend a system easily with new application software.

It is the aim of ASF+SDF to assist during the design and further development of such languages [2, 14, 7]. It consists of a formalism to describe languages and of a Meta-Environment to derive tools from such language descriptions. Ingredients often found in an ASF+SDF language definition include the description of the (1) context-free grammar, (2) context-sensitive requirements, (3) transformations or optimizations that are possible, (4) operational semantics expressing how to execute a program, and (5) translation to the desired target language. The Meta-Environment turns these into a parser, type checker, optimizer, interpreter, and compiler, respectively.

1.2 ASF+SDF

The Formalism The language ASF+SDF grew out of the integration of the Algebraic Specification Formalism ASF and the Syntax Definition Formalism SDF [2]. An ASF+SDF specification consists of a declaration of the functions that can be used to build *terms*, and of a set of equations expressing *equalities* between terms.

If we use ASF+SDF to define a language L, the grammar is described by a series of functions for constructing abstract syntax trees. Transformations, type checking, translations to a target language L', etc., are all described as functions mapping L to, respectively, L, Boolean values, and L'. These functions are specified using conditional equations, which may have negative premises. In addition to that, ASF+SDF supports so-called *default*-equations, which can be used to "cover all remaining cases", a feature which can result in significantly shorter specifications for real-life situations [7]. Specification in the large is supported by some basic modularization constructs.

Terms can be written in arbitrary user-defined syntax. In fact, an ASF+SDF signature is at the same time a context-free grammar, and defines a fixed mapping between sentences over the grammar and terms over the signature. Thus, an ASF+SDF definition of a set of language constructors specifies the concrete as well as the abstract syntax at the same time. Moreover, concrete syntax can be used in equations when specifying language properties. This smooth integration of concrete syntax with equations is one of the factors that makes ASF+SDF attractive for language definition.

The Meta-Environment The role of the ASF+SDF Meta-Environment [14] is to support the development of language definitions, and to produce prototype tools from these. It is best explained using Figure 1. A modular definition of language L, generates *parsers*, which can map L-programs to L-terms, *rewriters*, which compute functions over L-programs by reducing terms to their normal form, and *pretty printers*, which map the result to a textual representation. In the Meta-Environment, the generators are

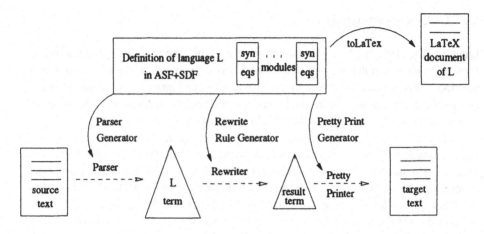

Fig. 1. A language definition for L in the ASF+SDF Meta-Environment.

invisible, and run automatically when needed. The derived pretty printer can be fine-tuned, allowing one to specify compilers to languages in which layout is semantically relevant (e.g., COBOL) [6].

This pattern gives rise to a series of language processors, with a functionality as specified in the language definition. Basic user-interface primitives can be used to connect the processors to an integrated L-specific environment.

The ToLaTeX facility of the ASF+SDF Meta-Environment encourages the language designer to write his or her definition as a *literate* specification.

2 Applying ASF+SDF in Practice

The typical industrial usage of ASF+SDF is to support the design of a domain-specific language. The formalism is used to write a formal language definition, and the Meta-Environment is used to obtain prototype tools. Once the language design is stable and completed successfully, the prototype tools can be re-implemented in an efficient language like C, although there are also examples in which the generated prototype is satisfactory, and re-implementation is not even considered.

The underlying observation is that language design is both critical and difficult, and that it should not be disturbed by implementation efforts in a language like C. At the same time, prototype tools are required during the design phase to get feedback from language users. ASF+SDF helps to obtain these tools with minimal effort, by executing the language definitions, and by offering a number of generation facilities.

This requires an extra investment during the design phase, since ASF+SDF enforces users to write a thorough language definition. The assumption is that this investment will pay for itself during the implementation phase, an assumption confirmed by the various projects carried out so far, such as the ones discussed below.

2.1 Structure Definition in Compiler Production

An example of the use of ASF+SDF for the development of a successful industrial language is the "full Structure Definition Language" (fSDL) [13]: a language for data structure descriptions, developed in the ESPRIT compiler generation project COMPARE. It has been used by Associated Computer Experts B.V. to develop their commercially available CoSy Compiler Suite. Using the primitives of fSDL, a compiler developer can define complex data types such as lists, tables, and graphs, together with functions for manipulating these. fSDL definitions are compiled to C.

During the design of fSDL, a *flattener* and the compilation to C were specified using ASF+SDF. The language design phase was a ponderous process, with various parties involved, during which a series of changes and language releases were issued. The ASF+SDF code describing the language took approximately 3000 lines, corresponding to roughly one person-year. However, once the design was completed, the final C implementation could be written very easily, and required no significant changes in fSDL.

2.2 Interlocking in Railway Applications

An example of the use of ASF+SDF for prototyping tools comes from the safety guaranteeing systems as used by the Dutch Railways (NS) [11]. To ensure that signals along railway yards are turned to green only when this is safe, devices called *Vital Processor Interlockings* (VPIs) are used. VPIs are programmed using the *Vital Logic Code* language (VLC). In collaboration with Utrecht University and NS, a project was carried out to verify safety properties of VPIs by expressing VLC in process algebra. Several tools were prototyped using ASF+SDF, mostly for transforming VLC programs, or for translating them to propositions that can be given as input to a tautology checker. The ASF+SDF specifications, covering a total of 400 lines of code, were used as the basis for an efficient implementation in C. An interesting observation is that NS had initially estimated that building a complete implementation would cost them one person year. Using ASF+SDF, a full functional prototype was constructed in only seven person-days.

2.3 RISLA: A Specification Language for Financial Products

RISLA is a language for describing *financial products* such as *mortgages, interest rate swaps*, etc. It has been developed by Bank MeesPierson and software house Cap Volmac. In principle, a product defines a scheme of agreements between a bank and its customers. A product may have several parameters, such as the principle amount, the interest rate, whether or not irregular redemptions are allowed, etc. An instance of such a scheme is called a *contract*. Several software systems running in the bank, such as the financial administration or the risk analysis programs, require information about the various financial contracts established. For a large part, this information is characterized by the *cash flows* each product generates. A cash flow is a list of (payment, date) pairs.

Originally, a product was described informally by a financial engineer, and then implemented in COBOL by the software engineer. However, products are subject to changes, and new products are introduced on a regular basis. This involved a severe maintenance effort. Moreover, it was difficult to guarantee the correspondence between the informal description and the implementation. Therefore, in 1992, the software engineers involved with interest rate products started to think about the specification language RISLA; a language that should be readable by financial experts on the one hand, and that should permit automatic COBOL-code generation on the other hand.

A first version of RISLA The starting point for RISLA was the observation that all elementary operations could be defined as functions in a COBOL library. The first step was the semi-formal description of several existing products in terms of these functions.

Using ASF+SDF a formal language definition for RISLA has been extracted from these example descriptions [1]. Furthermore, some ideas about information hiding and structuring have been formulated in an object-oriented manner.

Since then a product has been regarded as an object. It has an internal state, and is parameterized by its *contract data*, which are given a value upon contract creation. *Information methods* can be defined to retrieve data from a contract; *registration methods* can be used to update the state of a contract (for example, to register a redemption). Auxiliary methods can be defined, which are invisible for the outside world, and methods can be parameterized. At present, recursion is not allowed.

RISLA product descriptions can be translated to COBOL. The current compiler is written in C, although the COBOL generator has also been specified in ASF+SDF as part of a M.Sc. project [16].

By now about 40 financial products have been defined in RISLA. Their generated COBOL code is in daily operation. The product descriptions, however, have become longer and longer; low level computations are specified in great detail for each product again. This showed that the specifications were not yet at the right abstraction level. As a consequence, only a small group of RISLA experts could read them, and the communication with the financial experts still occurred on the basis of the informal descriptions.

Modular RISLA In order to solve this problem the *Upgrade RISLA* project was started in the summer of 1995. The project team consisted of people from various disciplines: accountants, software consultants and people who knew about ASF+SDF.

To reduce the size of RISLA specifications, RISLA was extended with modularization features to construct products from separate *components*. Like a product, a component has contract data and methods. Components represent common notions such as interest payment schemes. Products and components can import other components, and, if necessary, rename the contract parameters or the method names.

The import/renaming mechanism has been provided with a semantics by an *expansion* function translating a modular specification into a *flat* one. The specification of the syntax of RISLA, the syntax of the modularization mechanisms, a type checker and the expansion procedure takes about 100 pages of ASF+SDF. The obtained flat form can be compiled further to COBOL using the existing RISLA to COBOL compiler.

Currently, a library of components has been developed, and about 10 products have been specified in terms of these components. A financial expert can use the components as simple building blocks to construct new products.

Risquest: A Language for Questionnaires The RISLA-environment should also support the smooth introduction of new products. Therefore the language Risquest has been developed, which can be used to specify a *questionnaire*, i.e., a list of interactive questions by which information about the new product is extracted in a structured manner from a user. While filling in a questionnaire, a first product specification is built up by *selecting* components from the library corresponding to the answers given. Comments are gathered as free text, in case the questions are not sufficiently detailed. After answering the questions, the resulting product description can be fine-tuned; the comments can be formalized by, for example, adapting renamings of certain components. Currently, approximately 20 Risquest procedures have been implemented at MeesPierson.

To run the questionnaire, Risquest is translated into TCL/TK. The specification of the syntax of Risquest, some type checking, part of the syntax of TCL/TK, and the translation takes about 40 pages of ASF+SDF. The pretty printer generator [6] was used to conform to TCL/TK's strict layout conventions.

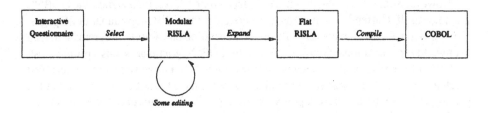

Fig. 2. From Questionnaire via RISLA to COBOL.

Assessment In Figure 2 an overview is given of the environment that combines the questionnaire formalized in Risquest, the modular RISLA obtained from selecting the components according to the answers given, the corresponding flat RISLA, and the resulting COBOL. This environment for financial products meets its requirements; financial engineers can construct their own product specifications, from which COBOL can be generated. Software experts are only needed for the maintenance of the environment (the library of components, the compiler to COBOL, etc.), but are not needed as intermediary between the users and the RISLA specifications.

Only a small part (about one third, or 6 person-months) of the work of the *Upgrade RISLA* team was dedicated to the development of the environment using ASF+SDF. For a great deal these 6 months were spent on engineering matters that come with the use of the ASF+SDF Meta-Environment on a problem of such a large scale, and were caused by the fact that also for the ASF+SDF-experts many aspects were rather new.

The modeling of the financial knowledge itself, such as the definition of the component library and the concrete questionnaire, took most of the effort.

2.4   Renovating Legacy Systems

Unlike the work described in the other sections of this paper, application of ASF+SDF to the renovation of software systems should be labeled as *work in progress* rather than as work already completed. However, we have just (January 1996) embarked on a large project dealing with this subject, in collaboration with several industrial partners including the Dutch ABN-AMRO bank, and we feel that this application is too interesting to leave undiscussed in a paper on industrial applications of ASF+SDF.

The problem at hand involves the analysis, cleaning-up and reconstruction of a large suite (25,000 programs, 30M LOC) of mainframe-based COBOL applications. The two main problems currently studied are conversions between COBOL dialects and identification and correction of software errors related to the "year 2000."

In principle, all techniques available in the ASF+SDF Meta-Environment can be applied to these renovation problems. More specifically, we intend to develop new techniques and tools to support impact analysis, data flow analysis, parsing, pretty printing, code uniformization, goto-elimination, etc.

However, some size problems have to be tackled first. Take, for instance, the COBOL grammar itself. Currently, we have an SDF version of the COBOL grammar of 25 pages. Using this as the basis for any formally defined operation on COBOL programs will lead to unwieldy specifications. Simplification of the COBOL grammar is thus a primary task here. Clearly, applying formal techniques to COBOL is not an activity that has received much attention in the research community, hence we have to start from scratch. On the positive side, we already have a pretty printer for a COBOL subset and we expect that the documentation tools from [6] can be used to build typesetting tools for full COBOL.

Another size problem concerns the amount of information that can be gathered during program analysis. It may, for instance, turn out that program slicing (see [17]) cannot be applied due to the size of the programs to be analysed. We are currently investigating whether more traditional techniques for data flow analysis can be applied, although their results are less precise than those of slicing. A topic here is that we need insight in the data flow of complete applications, as opposed to a single program. This implies that we need to analysed not only individual COBOL programs but also the JCL scripts that combine these COBOL programs into a complete application.

In addition to these size problems, several research questions have to be addressed. Many renovation activities consist of an analyse-regenerate cycle: first information is gathered about a particular source module and then it is regenerated (with the purpose of performing some improvement, e.g., producing another dialect, repairing date-related problems, and the like). In all these activities the question arises how the link between the regenerated code and the original source code can be maintained. For transformations expressed using rewriting, such links can be derived fully automatically using origin tracking [8]. We will investigate which adaptations are necessary to apply origin tracking to the COBOL migration and year 2000 problems.

A last topic directly related to ASF+SDF deals with logging editing actions. Since the state of the art in system renovation is not a fully automated process, the standard mode of operation of a renovation system will be a mixture of fully automatic subtasks and human interventions. In order to enable the complete replay of the whole renovation process, all human interventions have to be captured in *editing scripts* that can be executed automatically later on. Currently, the ASF+SDF Meta-Environment does not support such an editor command language.

3 Concluding Remarks

Education The general pattern displayed in the various projects is the following. Domain-specific languages are important in industrial practice and the use of a formal method such as ASF+SDF helps a language developer to improve the language design significantly, and to obtain prototype tools in a fast and simple manner.

It is easy to convince students as well as potential industrial users of the validity of this claim. At the University of Amsterdam, ASF+SDF[5] has been used in various classes, covering such topics as algebraic specification, software engineering, and compiler construction. The industrial case studies are discussed in such classes, and help the students to recognize similar situations in which formal methods could be applied. Students are encouraged to do their M.Sc. project in the context of ASF+SDF. Many students express interest in carrying out a case study in industry, which has resulted in a series of practical results [1, 15, 10, 20, 5]. We will discuss one of these in more detail.

First Result Consultants (FRC), is a small software house specialized in the field of information systems. Together with two students, FRC initiated a research project investigating the opportunities for automatic code generation from the company's proprietary object-oriented design models (so-called *FRC Models*). These are expressed using a graphical modeling language. The students used ASF+SDF to describe the FRC Models formally and to develop a prototype of a code generator translating FRC Models to *Access* database commands [4]. Both FRC and the students were satisfied with the results and one of the students has been hired to build a production implementation in C++ on the basis of the ASF+SDF specification.

Industrial Participation Cooperation between industry and universities is not without its problems. Managers are under pressure to minimize the risks their companies take, whereas it is a researcher's job to try new and not-yet-proven technology. Moreover, there is a conflict between the company's desire to keep their competitors ignorant of improvements in technology it paid for, and the researcher's ambition to write a paper reporting on this interesting case study. Some of these cultural differences between academia and business partners are covered by [19]. Nonetheless, when these are overcome, industries may gain much more efficient software construction methods, and computer scientists will obtain an opportunity to identify the most relevant problems in their field of research – and to what extent their theories help to address these.

Returning to more ASF+SDF-specific issues, the main factor contributing to the acceptance of ASF+SDF is that the formalism is executable, and can be used to actually build something. In some cases, this was the main reason to start using ASF+SDF. Improving the efficiency of the derived prototype tools will increase the industrial applicability, and will lead to further cost reduction if it could eliminate the need to build the final re-implementation in a language like C.

---

[5] An account of the use of ASF+SDF for teaching formal methods is given in [9].

Another point is that in all projects the industries paid academic people to help them during language design or to write prototype tools. It is not (yet) the case that the companies train their own people to start using ASF+SDF. However, there are already several examples of companies hiring people specifically for their ASF+SDF expertise.

Research Questions Language design and tool building based on term rewriting technology has a high potential, and further research will help to increase the acceptance and industrial applicability. We mention two topics that need to be addressed:

- The efficiency of the prototypes is for a large part determined by the efficiency of the rewrite machinery used. Some results from functional programming can be used here, but the problem is both simpler – there is no need for dealing with λ-expressions – and more complicated – the pattern matching can be arbitrarily deep. Current research has led to a prototype ASF2C compiler [12].
  One technical problem is how and when to output the resulting term: for realistic specifications (such as the one for fSDL) the normal form may be several megabytes in size, and in order to keep the prototype's runtime memory small such results should be written to file as early as possible. But when can one be sure that part of a term is in normal form, and will not be changed later? It may be that results of combining rewriting with I/O are of help here [18].
- Another critical issue is the openness of the prototypes built. In an industrial setting, a tool never runs alone. Instead, it will require application-specific data from other components, or functionality available in libraries modeled in other languages. At present, we are investigating to what extent the ToolBus[6], a software bus based on process algebra [3], can help to address these problems.

Acknowledgments Thanks to T.B. Dinesh, Jasper Kamperman, Wilco Koorn, Eelco Visser, Machteld Vonk, and Pum Walters. The authors acknowledge Bank MeesPierson and the Centre of Excellence for Risk Management, Finance division Cap Volmac, for the set up of the Upgrade Risla project and their permission to publish the results of the project in Section 2.3. We thank Jan Boef from ABN-AMRO for his encouragement to publish the work described in Section 2.4.

References

1. B. R. T. Arnold, A. van Deursen, and M. Res. An algebraic specification of a language for describing financial products. In M. Wirsing, editor, *ICSE-17 Workshop on Formal Methods Application in Software Engineering*, pages 6–13. IEEE, April 1995.
2. J. A. Bergstra, J. Heering, and P. Klint, editors. *Algebraic Specification*. The ACM Press in cooperation with Addison-Wesley, 1989.
3. J. A. Bergstra and P. Klint. The ToolBus coordination architecture. In *Proceedings of the First International Conference on Coordination Models, Languages and Applications*, Cesena, Italy, April 15–17 1996. to appear.

---

[6] A demonstration of the ToolBus will be given during this AMAST conference.

4. F. Bonsu and R. Oudejans. Graphic generation language — automatic code generation from design. Master's thesis, Programming Research Group, University of Amsterdam, 1995.
5. M. van den Brand, S. M. Eijkelkamp, D. K. A. Geluk, H. Meijer, H. R. Osborne, and M. J. F. Polling. Program transformations using ASF+SDF. In M. van den Brand, A. van Deursen, T. B. Dinesh, J. F. Th. Kamperman, and E. Visser, editors, *ASF+SDF '95: A Workshop on Generating Tools from Algebraic Specifications*, Technical Report P9505, pages 29–52. Programming Research Group, University of Amsterdam, May 1995.
6. M. van den Brand and Eelco Visser. Generation of formatters for context-free languages. Technical Report P9506, Programming Research Group, University of Amsterdam, 1995. To appear in ACM Transactions on Software Engineering Methodology.
7. A. van Deursen, J. Heering, and P. Klint (eds.). *Language Prototyping, An Algebraic Specification Approach*, volume 5 of *AMAST Series in Computing*. World Scientific Publising Co., 1996. To Appear.
8. A. van Deursen, P. Klint, and F. Tip. Origin tracking. *Journal of Symbolic Computation*, 15:523–545, 1993. Special Issue on Automatic Programming.
9. T. B. Dinesh and S. M. Üsküdarlı (Eds.). Teaching formal methods using the ASF+SDF Meta-environment. Technical report, CWI and University of Amsterdam, July 1994. Proceedings of the NSF Workshop on Teaching Formal Methods, URL: ftp:// ftp.cwi.nl/ pub/gipe/drafts/ TFM.ps.Z.
10. J.N. Entken. A prototype of a simulator for hydraulic systems. Master's thesis, Programming Research Group, University of Amsterdam, 1993.
11. J. F. Groote, S. F. M. van Vlijmen, and J. W. C. Koorn. The safety guaranteeing system at station Hoorn-Kersenboogerd. Technical report, Department of Philosophy, Utrecht University, 1995.
12. J. F. Th. Kamperman and H.R. Walters. Lazy rewriting and eager machinery. In J. Hsiang, editor, *Rewriting Techniques and Applications, RTA'95*, volume 914 of *Lecture Notes in Computer Science*, pages 147–162. Springer-Verlag, 1995.
13. J. F. Th. Kamperman, T. B. Dinesh, and H. R. Walters. An extensible language for the generation of parallel data manipulation and control packages. In Peter A. Fritzson, editor, *Proceedings of the Poster Session of Compiler Construction '94*, 1994. Appeared as technical report LiTH-IDA-R-94-11, university of Linköping; Full version as CWI Report CS-R9575.
14. P. Klint. A meta-environment for generating programming environments. *ACM Transactions on Software Engineering and Methodology*, 2(2):176–201, 1993.
15. L.H. Oei. Pruning the search tree of interlocking design and application language operational semantics. Technical Report P9418, Programming Research Group, University of Amsterdam, 1994.
16. M. Res. A generated programming environment for RISLA, a specification language defining financial products. Master's thesis, Programming Research Group, University of Amsterdam, 1994.
17. F. Tip. A survey of program slicing techniques. *Journal of Programming Languages*, 3(3):121–189, 1995.
18. H. R. Walters and J. F. Th. Kamperman. A model for I/O in equational languages with don't care non-determinism. In *Workshop on Abstract Data Types ADT'95*, Lecture Notes in Computer Science. Springer-Verlag, 1996.
19. D. Weber-Wulff. Selling formal methods to industry. In J. C. P. Woodcock and P. G. Larsen, editors, *FME'93: Industrial Strength Formal Methods*, volume 670 of *Lecture Notes in Computer Science*. Springer-Verlag, 1993.
20. C. Zaadnoordijk. An ASF+SDF specification of a query optimizer for a RDBMS. Master's thesis, Programming Research Group, University of Amsterdam, 1994.

The Embedded Software of an Electricity Meter: An Experience in Using Formal Methods in an Industrial Project*

André Arnold[1], Didier Bégay[1], Jean-Pierre Radoux[2]

[1] LaBRI, Université Bordeaux 1
351, cours de la Libération
F-33405 Talence, France
[2] SERLI-Informatique,
avenue du Téléport
F-86960 Futuroscope, France

Abstract. This article releases an industrial experiment of using formal methods to conceive, design, develop and test an embedded software in a massproduced device.

1 Introduction

1.1 The Eurotri Project

The EUROTRI project was aimed by Schlumberger-Industries to define, conceive, design and develop a static electricity meter with large abilities of tariff programming and distant measuring. As short time of development and low cost of production (ie: use of components at frontier of their technical limits) were the challenges, it has been decided at the very beginning of the project to use formal methods in most steps of it, from feasability study to reception testing.

1.2 The partners

In this project the industrial party was twofold: an international industrial group that is leader in the measuring technics, which ordered the development to be done in its research center; and a software house which provided a part of the manpower, some expertise and the link with the team at LaBRI.

Schlumberger introduces itself in its Worlwide Web server in the following way at date of July the 30th, 1995:

There is a subsidiary of Schlumberger-Industries near Poitiers: a production plant dedicated to large scale production, and a development center including a small scale production line in Chasseneuil du Poitou. This subsidiary is part of the electricity branch and has long been used for the production of electromechanical electricity meters.

---

* This text is a shortened version of a text that will appear elsewhere.

Serli is a software society located near Poitiers, France. Its interests are in assisting societies in the area of center–west of France in data management and real-time systems developments. For both reasons Schlumberger-Industries is a major customer of Serli and has appreciated its abilities in software engineering. The teams at Serli amount to 40 people.

J.-P. Radoux is with Serli as a software engineer.

LaBRI The team in charge of the project was composed of seven researchers. In this paper, we present how the research team joined the industrial project and played its part; then how formal methods have been used at different levels, different times and in different ways; and finally, as a conclusion, the results of this process for every party.

Why using Formal Methods? This question relates to two important issues: what benefit is awaited from using formal methods, and why the choice of these peculiar ones?

Formal methods have been used in the main aim of avoiding backward steps in the development: as every step is mathematically verified there is no need to loop back to some previous erroneous step, and even to iterate. This ideal straighforward development is the big issue of formal methods, provided they are correctly applied.

Formal methods are just another tool to use in a development, and that means they have to be practicable by the engineers in charge of the project, who have already a lot of tools to control. In the case we present here, the basic common culture of them was electronics, and the readability of automata by electronic engineers, as well as the fundamentally synchronous approach of the Arnold-Nivat model[2] are easily assumed. The availability of a powerful model-checker, the MEC tool[3] settled it.

The formal approach to temporal aspects of the system, and more precisely the respect of every deadline, were since the beginning considered out of reach of the automata approach, as time could not be in no way unfolded in a so wide range of periods. A rate monotonic analysis[12] had been successfully used in a previous development, and it has been considered as suitable to ensure desired timing properties.

As it happened during the development, a coupling of both formal methods has been successfully studied and used to achieved a fine study of the loaded system.

2 Formal Methods at Work

Traditionnally at Schlumberger's the families of trades involved in such a project were marketing, industrialization and technics. In this case the technical part was composed of three teams: mechanics, electronics, software. Obviously the skills of Serli were dedicated to sustain the efforts of this last team, who was thus composed of engineers from Schlumberger and Serli.

As validation had to deal with electronics as well as software, and was directly involved in the reliability of the product, another team dedicated to validation, was created at LaBRI. The strong point of the Bordeaux team was its expertise on the MEC system already used in various domains, and its ability to tailor adhoc versions if necessary; the weak point was it consisted of part-time researchers, in a limited number. So all aspects of the projects would not be covered at the same time. Instead of scattering the forces, we proposed to focus on the kernel design and development with the dedicated team while another development team would do with the application, that was more classical matter for the people involved, and supposed to be more easily contained.

In order to spare time, two sub-teams of the software team developed simultaneously in a layer approach: one subteam had to deal with underlying electronics to provide some services used by the other team to achieve functionalities of the software as defined by the marketing team, and compatible with industrialization requirements.

2.1 The Embedded System

The new concept of electricity meter and its advanced functionalities implied the massive use of software, unlike previous generations which could be developped on an electromechanical or electronic basis.

Basic features of the meter were obvious: sampling signals (either power characteristics or signaling elements) and signal processing, keeping a database of tariffs and counters, managing protocols. Some other features are less obvious: safety of measure (whatever could happen on the metered lines, even drops of power), integrity of the system (protection against fraud), or low energy consumption of the meter itself. Another need was to design a family of products, and the different variants had to be derived afterwards in an easy and safe way.

2.2 Preliminary Study

It appeared that a single processor of the Texas Instruments 320C30 (for example) class could be a good candidate to support the features, excepted for the consumption of the meter. A low consumption could be achieved only with very lowlevel processors, and no single one could achieve all the features. The idea then was to use "more than one" low-level–low-consumption–low-price processors (such as the ones used in domestic applications), in order to meet the requirements.

To cover all features, two different processors have been chosen, one more dedicated to signal processing, and the other on controlling. But nearly every feature had to use both of them to be achieved. It was then necessary to conceive a system with a large use of communication between the processors, and that raised the question of fiability, leading to a need of a reliable software architecture, and thus to the use of some formal technics.

It was then decided to conceive in a layer approach a distributed kernel implementing a rendez-vous scheduler, offering services to a distributed application, and to verify this architecture using formal technics.

It has been part of the preliminary study to propose both the architecture and the ways to develop and verify it. So the formal methods have been considered as a companion for the project since the beginning of the design phase.

2.3 Aims of Formal Technics

The kernel had to offer such elaborated mechanisms as scheduling services, based on a very low level hardware. This gap made the software difficult to conceive with a high level of confidence.

On the other hand that meant that a verified description at some abstract level would be available for the engineers who had to implement the software system. And the readability of the description would be part of the reliability of the implementation.

Synchronized transition systems are very handy for expressing rendez-vous techniques, and this would allow an abstraction of the kernel, and thus a test of the rendez-vous architecture of the application layer. A description explicitely using automata happened to cover widely the different cultures of the people involved in the project, on software part, on hardware part (closely interfaced with the software) and on the validation part. Even if such systems as MEC can model up to millions of states systems, it was stated it would be out of reach to model in one time all aspects (from signals on interruption lines to a succession of nested rendez-vous calls); actually we stated this would be the wrong way to do. The validation of the kernel would be made layer by layer, abstracting lower and upper layers.

Explicit time expression is not easily done using transition systems, even if some academic experiments are very promising[13]. To model explicit time aspects, and more peculiarly deadlines meetings, we decided to use the Rate Monotonic Analysis model, that was well suited for the type of system to express whether or not the deadlines could be met. It happened this model could be coupled with the Synchronized Transition System one to determine where the bugs were hidden in the control and call structures.

As it happened later, the Formal Methods approach with the MEC tool was of some profit for both aspects of the project: ab initio for the kernel, and a posteriori for the application, leading to a good quality production, revealed by a surprisingly short time for industrial validation tests.

Even more surprisingly, this approach could be used to diagnose faulty behaviours observed at testing time, whose very low rate of appearance made the diagnostic tedious.

In the following we present these different aspects of the use of Formal nMethods in this development project.

3 Development of the Kernel

Formal methods have been used along this development.

The aim of the layer was to provide a cooperation mechanism between tasks as near as possible of the ADA concept of rendez-vous. For economical reasons, the hardware is of very low level and is composed of two processors communicating through a limited number of signals, without shared memory . The challenge of the development of the kernel is to fill the gap between the hardware constraints and the highlevel, implementation independant features of the kernel.

In order to divide and conquer difficulties, we adopted a layer-oriented architecture.

3.1 Hardware Description and Provided Services

The hardware is composed of two processors, a micro-controller (μc) and a DSP (dsp): the DSP sizes up to 2K instructions and 256 words of RAM, and the micro-controller goes up to 32K instructions and 1K bytes RAM, including registers. They are linked to some physical devices for measure and control, and connected through a serial line: links are signals. The DSP is badly suited for running a kernel: no interruption is associated with the line; moreover, the line is sensitive to noise altering messages and clock.

The kernel is designed to provide a distributed application with task calls and communication, either locally (same processor) or remotely, in a way analogous to ADA rendez-vous, in a severely restricted environment.

Actually four classes of rendez-vous have been designed: local strong rendez-vous, where the caller waits during the callee runs its rendez-vous code; local weak, where the caller does not wait and delivers the message in a mailbox, the upper layer being informed of the status of the rendez-vous ; distant strong rendez-vous, with the possibility of a blocking state; and distant weak rendez-vous, with a message handed to the other task through the physical link. The semantics of the rendez-vous have to be independant of the local–distant concept. This terminology is the one used in the project; only strong rendez-vous are real ones; others are message passings.

3.2 Rendez-Vous Scheduler

The difficulty was to ensure reliability of the scheduler, including blocking freeness, and efficiency of coding for space and computation consumption.

The functional description was used to specify behaviours of the components of the scheduler as transition systems; they are obvious enough and can be considered as elementary specifications: see figures 1 to 4.

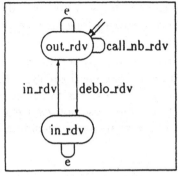

Fig. 1: Caller's interface

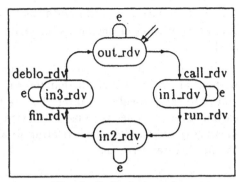

Fig. 2: Callee's interface

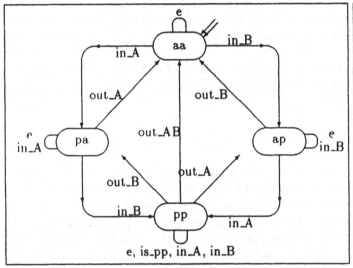

Fig. 3: Memory

Fig. 4: a mailbox

Differences between local and distant, or strong and weak rendez-vous have been expressed as different sets of synchronization constraints.

Another part of the functional description consists in the list of properties the system had to satisfy to be considered correct; actually we defined a list for the weak rendez-vous and another one for the strong rendez-vous, including absence of deadlock, or control of memory, or consistency of mailboxes and registers.

The main results of the study have been: obviously a validation of the functional architecture, but also quantitative gains, as only two bits were necessary per rendez-vous and some controls could be removed, strongly lowering memory use.

3.3 Presentation Layer

This layer stores the messages from the scheduler and transmits them one-by-one to the link layer; provided service is the transfer from upper to lower layers of frames, at a pace compatible with the flow between processors. A potential danger is the overflow of the local storage, or underflow due to a wrong management of this store.

In case of repeated weak rendez-vous calls, some information could be lost without any control. The link handles such situation in signaling the rendez-vous status to the presentation layer. This latter propagates the status to the application layer, in order to substitute extra calls (that would lose not yet treated messages) with a global call relating to a result of a global value, depending of the implied rendez-vous.

Functional Aspects are related to the underlying design principle, that is a critical section to protect a shared ressource.

So we model a scheduler, a status of frame, a number of messages, a service for the scheduler to request, an indication for the link to signal free, and the link.

This leads to a synchronized transition system of 17 states and 29 transitions, which reveals that a deadlock occurs only if the stack of rendez-vous overflows.

3.4 Link Layer

The aim of the link layer consists in guaranteeing that an emitted frame is correctly received, provided underlying layer ensures correct routing of bytes. Concerned properties include no-blocking, no-loss, no-duplication of bytes.

The solution is based on the well-known alternated bit protocol, as presented in [6]. It consists in adding to the payload information (number of rendez-vous, possible message) some extra structure information (an extra (alternated) bit, a byte count, and some redundancy through a CRC), working in a half-duplex way.

To ensure against an erroneous reception of the structure information, we need some watchdogs on both ends of the link. Unfortunately one of the processors is not equipped with such a device, and we make it of no use at this end by using fixed length frames in this direction and using watchdogs both for emission and reception on the other processor.

An expected problem for this layer was the non-instantaneous transfer at the physical level, where the data are exchanged in a full-duplex way. So we modeled both lignes in an abstracted way, and each link (left, right) also. The computations aimed to four blocking states, due to some uncontrolability of the events relating the link layer to the upper one; these states leaded to a loss of the beginning of some frame. This reflects the physical asynchronism of both underlying processors: one is ready to send, the other one is not yet ready to receive. Then a solution was designed, where the link layer prepared the begin of next frame (to be ready to receive) immediately before sending the previous one (and thus passing hand over). The MEC computations validated this solution.

3.5   Hardware Protocol

The aim of the protocol is to forward bytes from dsp to µc and vice-versa. The protocol must meet the following property: *no byte is lost on an hypothetical perfect line*.

We present here the protocol used for managing distributed control between both processors at the physical level. A representation of the physical structure can be found in figure 5.

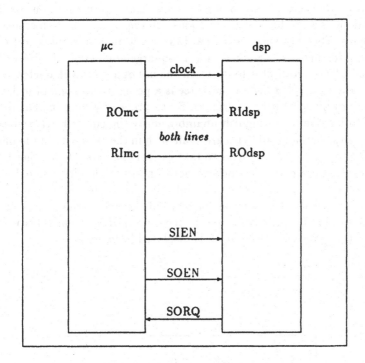

Fig. 5. Physical structure of the serial link

Data are exchanged along two serial lines sharing a common clock. The byte is the unit of information during the transfer. One line links the output register of the microcontroller (ROmc) to the input register of the dsp (RIdsp), the other one the output register of the dsp (ROdsp) to the input register of the microcontroller (RImc). Only the microcontroller is in charge of the clock signal. An extra signal, SORQ (Signal Output ReQuest) can be set by the dsp to ask for the clock and the microcontroller sets a SOEN (Signal Output ENable) signal to trigger the output by the dsp. An extra signal, SIEN (Signal Input ENable), set by the µc, allows RIdsp to receive data from line. Transfers of data to and from the registers of the microcontroller are controled through interrupts, and a special attention must be paid to the fact that the dsp supports no interrupt mechanism: data entering the input register must be polled regularly. Another feature of dsp registers is their structure; they are double sized shift-registers. The μc registers are one byte large.

Loss of data due to polling rate are definitely difficult to detect by statistical simulation. The only solution consists of a protocol that absolutely avoids this risk.

Loss or spontaneous creation of data on the line embodies the perturbation of line by interference, namely interference losing or creating tops on the clock of the synchronous serial lines by spikes. This will imply a desynchronization in the flow of bytes. The only solution is a hardware reset on a time-out condition after communication has been erroneous for a too-large number of bits. Nevertheless, the physical layer protocol is founded on the use of a special character, denoted "b"; alteration implying such a character is a potential occasion of lock of data flow or of misinterpretation of frames. So to prove anything in that direction we have to be able to distinguish unambiguously the emitted, transferred, and received bytes. Actually, all bytes are dealt with in the same way in the modeling --as in the real life-- and we have to take care of one byte. On another hand we have to deal with a common clock on both lines; this implies a signal must be considered on each line, providing the link with *false* bytes. So we consider only three different values of data to be transmitted through the link, "b", "X", "Y". We are then able to distinguish *one of them* from *all of them*. This transition system in the generic representation is displayed in figure 6.

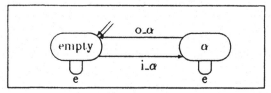

Fig. 6: Line

The physical objects we model are: the serial lines; the signals SORQ, SOEN, and the clock; and the four registers. As stated before, register management is a central point in the study. This is achieved using a protocol defined on each processor in the way shown figures 7 and 8. This protocol has been designed in an experimental way, every attempt being validated or not using the modeling.

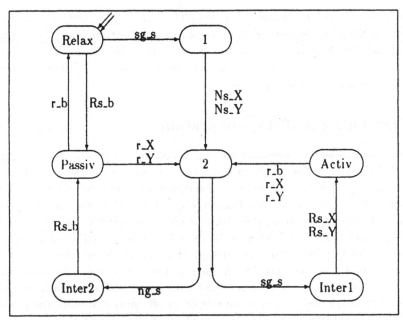

Fig. 7: Micro-controller part of the protocol

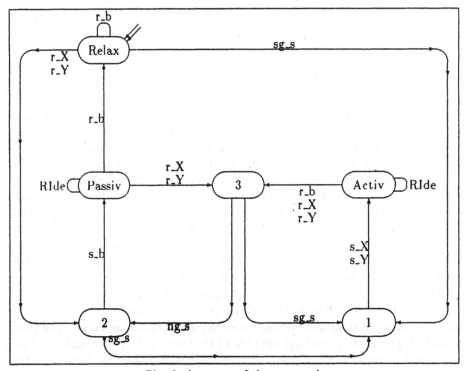

Fig. 8: dsp part of the protocol

In order to make sure every byte is correctly routed whatever has gone or is going on, the modeling has been completed by various sets of two testers generating arbitrary sequences of bytes, on one way or on both. In the most general case, both emitted a sequence of $X^*.Y.X^*$, and on the other side the Y neither lost nor duplicated. In that precise case, the modeling amounted to 60,737 states and 112,654 transitions.

4 Development of the Application

In a way very different from what had happened for the kernel, the application part of the software has not been developped using formal methods from the very beginning; this does not reflect a methodological position: the main reason for that is that human (academic) power was not available, and that we needed a sane and efficient kernel, at the border of electronics and software.

Unfortunately some difficulties arose in this part (application) of the project, and we had to step in at a detailed design phase of the development.

Formal methods have then been used in two ways: the first consisted to check the consistency of the calls of rendez-vous among tasks, specially in critical phases of the application, such as turning on or off, most of it when the power is cut while in the starting-up phase or comes back in the stoping phase; the second was related to the validation of respect of deadlines for every task, whatever could happen. This last point is a priori out of reach of the model used, but combined with Rate Monotonic Analysis technics it revealed efficient in handling this kind of temporal aspects.

4.1 Validating the call graph

In order to verify the mutual interlocking of the various tasks, those have been abstracted to their call structure, and the behaviour of each of them has been reduced to the control related to rendez-vous calls depicted in figure 11. The rendez-vous semantics has been expressed as a set of synchronization constraints.

Unfortunately it appeared that the synchronized product of these 36 tasks could not be built in a reasonable time (a couple of days) using a server as a workstation: the modeling amounted to too much states (more than 4 millions). Actually the modeling of the behaviour of starting-up phase was not fully built! So we decided to study the call graph using a partial and progressive approach: the initial states sets have been modified to model from this new point of the system, up to what was physically buildable. This way of doing left uncertain the fact that the whole modeling had been studied.

This process allowed detection of interlocking situation among rendez-vous calls, and thus early modification of the call architecture; it allowed as well detection of controls on some rendez-vous that were actually of no use, and thus could be suppressed. These bugs would not have happened if formal methods had been applied earlier in the conception stage. A minor default has been revealed after tests, in a part that had not been studied. In a way, this confirms that formal studies are both less practicable and less efficient when applied at then end of the project.

4.2   Dealing with deadlines

The model used did not basically handle quantitative temporal aspects, and the tools available at this time revealed to be unefficient to deal with so many tasks and a so large scale of time: some of the tasks had to be performed at a 50Khz rate, and another one had a period of more than 6 months!

On the other hand, the temporal properties we intended to verify had more to do with respect of deadlines than with exact timing validation for each instruction to be performed. So we moved to a study following the Rate Monotonic Analysis approach, as the prerequisites for its application were fulfilled (static tasks, static priorities ...) even if there was no proper theoretical scheduler in the system, but a rendez-vous manager. Let us recall than in this approach the static priority order is the period order.

The model as presented in [9] and [11] has been extended to take into account switching durations and real run-time priorities. The temporal characteristics of the circuits have been measured on the bench and the algorithm applied. It appeared that the deadlines were not met at all.

The first idea was then to modify the too long tasks, to artificially cut them into shorter ones, thus modifying the priority order. Then after some attempts, the algorithm could be run again on this new task organization.

The second idea was that this new set of tasks could be obtained with no code change (very few actually), and that this modification could not put the previous validation in danger. This has been made possible because the synchronized transition systems were an unifying tool between both models.

5   Testing and debugging

Formal methods are usually thought as code validation tools after detailed conception, or less often as an architecture validation tool at conception time, but their investigative power is supposed to be irrelevant with the testing step of the development: they are argued as shorting down this last step, but without any direct involvment in it.

The experiment we present here is a counter–example of this narrow way of seeing, as it emphazises the role of the investigative power of formal methods even in the testing phase.

This case refers to some lowlevel seldom mechanism driving a signal multiplexer. At a given time t, one among N analog signals is input in the measuring software, by the mean of a 1-in-n multiplexer, driven by an external (external to the software) counter. So we have two counters referring to the same value: an *external* (hardware) counter, selecting the input signal, an *internal* (software) counter, processing the input signal, both of them being controled by the same clock. The first problem we have to deal with is that parasites can impact the links between the common clock and both devices, and thus desynchronize both counters, making the software process erroneously input values.

This can be handled either by identifying each sample transmitted to the software or by periodically synchronizing both counters. The first solution was not relevant for technical reasons, and it has been designed that an output port would be used by the software counter to reset the hardware counter.

In such an embedded system as the electricity meter, various processes have to be activated to ensure the fiability of the apparatus. One of them is the OUCABO system. This system requires a device to be periodically activated and tested. The second problem is that the solution to first problem left no output port available to activate a secondary device required for fiability reasons, nor input port to test it. This situation has been handled using the leftmost carry bit of the hardware counter to activate the device : if the software counter does not reset the hardware counter in due time, there occurs an arithmetic overflow occurs and the device is activated; this had been conceived and implemented ignoring formal methods, as an electronic hack to answer a very simple, low-level problem.

This part of the system had been developped and implemented, and tested using laboratory testing devices to simultaneously measure same signals. Unfortunately, it happened that a very seldom measure difference occurred between testing and tested devices; at first glance, the origin could be hardware, software or a *testing protocol error*.

Testing such rare behaviours may last a long time, and in order to spare time, a model-checking approach was suggested. Then the system has been modeled using synchronized transition systems. The error and the error rate could be confirmed on a study of synchronized transitions, thus identifying the source of the erroneous behaviour. The bug was fixed in the model and after validation, the system could be efficiently and safely corrected.

6 Conclusion

This study has been an opportunity to test several cases of use of formal methods in a real industrial project, all along the project. From design to test, through detailed design and architecture, the synchronized transition systems, standing for a formal algebraic framework, played an active and efficient role in the development of the product. It helped to keep the development and production deadlines in a concurrential background; main consequences seem to be a better quality of product and a strong reduction of testing phase.

References

1. M. Alabau, D. Bégay, J.-P. Radoux. *Formal Methods and Real-Time: Design and Validation of a Real-Time Embedded System.* submitted to RTS'96.
2. A. Arnold. *Finite transition systems.* Prentice-Hall, 1994.
3. A. Arnold, D. Bégay, P. Crubillé. *Construction and analysis of transition systems with MEC.* World Scientific Pub., 1994.
4. A. Arnold, D. Bégay, J.-P. Radoux. *An example of use of formal methods to debug an embedded software.* submitted to FME'96.

5. D. Bégay, J. Dormoy, P. Félix. An experiment in developing real-time systems using Mec. In Teodor Rus and Charles Rattray, editors, *Theories and experiences for real-time system development*, volume 2 of *AMAST series in Computing*, chapter 14, pages 363–388. World Scientific Pub., 1994.
6. P. Crubillé. *Réalisation de l'outil Mec : spécification fonctionnelle et architecture*. PhD thesis, Université de Bordeaux I, nov. 1989.
7. A. Dicky. *Une approche algébrique et algorithmique de l'analyse des systèmes de transition*. PhD thesis, Université de Bordeaux I, feb. 1985.
8. A. Griffault, A. Ressouche. Synthesis of a rendez-vous based scheduler. In Didier Bégay and Marc-Michel Corsini, editors, *Models and Proofs, Bordeaux, 14-16 june '95*, LaBRI Université Bordeaux I, jun. 1995.
9. C.L. Liu, J.W. Layland. Scheduling algorithms for multiprogramming in a hard real-time environment. *Journal of the ACM*, 20(1):46–61. Jan. 1973.
10. J.-P. Radoux. *Utilisation de systèmes de transitions finis pour la conception et le développement d'un système embarqué*. PhD thesis, Université de Bordeaux I, mar. 1995.
11. L. Sha, J.B. Goodenough, J.P. Lehoczky. Priority inheritance protocols: an approach to real-time synchronization. *IEEE Transactions on Computers*, C-39(9):1175–1185. Sept. 1990.
12. L. Sha, M.H. Klein, J.B. Goodenough. Rate Monotonic Analysis for real-time systems. *Tech. report, CMU/SEI 91-TR-6*, Mar. 1991.
13. T. Henzinger, X. Nicollin, J. Sifakis et S. Yovine. *Symbolic model checking for real-time systems*. Information and Computation, 111, 2, 1994 pp. 193-244.

pure mathematical formalisms to catch many aspects that matter in practical applications; even the impact on final product correctness is often challenged.

This paper addresses the issue of practical usefulness of formal methods in the development of computer-based applications on the basis of author's experience. This experience has been developed for several years in the field of real-time systems. Author's group has been composed from the very beginning by researchers and "users" (i.e., industrial experts of the application domain)[3]. The core of the research consists of a formal specification language for real-time systems, TRIO, which is an extension of traditional temporal logic.

The language has been enriched by supporting tools (editors, interpreters, test-case generators, verifiers and, in a more general sense, manuals, seminars, and methods for its use) and has been applied to real industrial projects of increasing complexity. The three "processes", namely theoretical language development, tools construction, and application to real-life cases, have been and are being performed in parallel producing mutual feedbacks.

The paper is organised as follows: Section 2 provides a short introduction to TRIO: this includes a survey of language features and a brief description of related tools and methods; Section 3 reports on major past and present applications of TRIO to industrial projects. Section 4 reports on main lessons learned from such experiences. In Section 5 a few conclusions are derived: it is argued that, if we are able to learn from previous failures, new enthusiasm can be generated and useful indications can be obtained for hoping into greater success of formal methods in the future.

The presentation style of this paper is of tutorial type: only general principles and main features are addressed, avoiding technicalities. The interested reader will be referred to a more appropriate literature for a deep analysis of technical details. A little background on mathematical logic and on object-oriented terminology is assumed.

2 . TRIO's Basics

TRIO [GMM] (acronym for the italian words "Tempo Reale ImplicitO") is now a fairly general purpose specification language, although it is rooted in the application field of real-time systems – which are often highly demanding in terms of safety-critical requirements. TRIO's evolution has been driven by the following guidelines and major objectives:

- Attention was initially focused on the "high phases of the life-cycle" which are universally acknowledged as the most critical ones. It has always been kept in mind, however, that, eventually, a complete development methodology covering the whole life-cycle was needed.
- Requirement specifications should be as abstract as possible, i.e., should not bias – nor should they be biased by – implementation choices. This is mainly important in an application environment whose products often have a life of tens of years – and, therefore, must survive tumultuous technological evolution – and where often the product implementation is performed by a different organization than the one which defines requirements and uses the product.

  For this reason a specification language based on mathematical logic rather than on some kind of abstract machine has been chosen.
- A specifcation language to be used in practice must join the precision and rigor that are typical of mathematical formalisms with other factors that have a major impact

---

[3]Our main industrial partner is ENEL, the italian agency of energy.

Applying Research Results in the Industrial Environment: the Case of the TRIO Specification Language[1].

Dino Mandrioli[2]

Abstract

There are almost universal complaints that too much research effort goes wasted and never finds application in the industrial world. The complaints are raised symmetrically both by the academia and by the industrial world. This situation becomes even more frustrating in the case of application of formal methods to software engineering: despite formal methods are advocated as a useful tool to enhance software quality from more than thirty years, it is still quite controversial whether or not they can really have an impact on the industrial software development.

This paper addresses the above issue on the basis of author's experience. This experience has been developed for several years in the field of real-time systems. The core of the research is a formal specification language for real-time systems, TRIO, which is an extension of temporal logic. The language has been enriched by supporting tools and methods and has been applied to real industrial projects of increasing complexity.

In this paper, a short introduction to the TRIO language is provided; then the experience on its practical application is briefly reported; finally comments are given on the most important "lessons learned" from the above experience. It is argued that, on the basis of this and similar experiences, new enthusiasm and useful indications for hoping into greater success of formal methods can be generated.

1. Introduction

There are almost universal complaints that too much research effort goes wasted and never finds application in the industrial world. The complaints are raised symmetrically both by the academia and by the industrial world. This situation becomes even more frustrating in the case of application of formal methods to software engineering: despite formal methods are advocated as a useful tool to enhance software quality from more than thirty years, it is still quite controversial whether or not they can really have an impact on the industrial software development.

On the one hand, the literature reports many examples of unsatisfactory software quality. This inconvenience is most serious when software is embedded in *safety-critical systems*, such as avionics systems, plant control systems, etc. In these cases, it has been often reported that a software failure caused major disasters: see, e.g., the well documented case of the THERAC 25 accidents [LT]. In principle, the use of formal techniques promises major improvements in the overall quality of such products (see e.g. [MMM] for an in depth analysis of the THERAC 25 case). These promises have also been verified in a fairly rich set of prototypal applications to real-life cases.

On the other hand, still much skepticism is raised against a wide and generalized adoption of formal methods in practice. Usual complaints are about the excessive amount of mathematical skill that is needed to apply them; about the unsuitability of

1Work partially supported by CNR and partially by ENEL.
2Dipartimento di Elettronica e Informazione, Politecnico di Milano, Piazza L. Da Vinci 32, 20133, Milano, Email: mandriol@elet.polimi.it

on usability such as understandability, ability to manage large specifications in a modular and incremental way.

- The development of the conceptual bases of the language must proceed hand-in-hand with its experimentation on the field and with the construction of supporting tools, though prototypal in nature. For this reason, from the very beginning, the TRIO group consisted of academic researchers and industrial users. Both subgroups participated actively to the essential phases of all subactivities: typically industrial people did participate to language definition and academic people did participate to application developments.

The result of the whole activity, at the present state of the art, is the following picture, which still is named TRIO but includes several items besides the "pure language".

The basic logic language

TRIO's kernel is a first order logical language, augmented with *temporal operators* which permit to talk about the truth and falsity of propositions at time instants different from the current one, which is left implicit in the formula.

TRIO includes all typical elements of first order languages: variables, functions, predicates, propositional connectors, quantifiers, terms, formulas.

Unlike classic first-order theories, TRIO is a typed language. Among variable domains there is a distinguished one, called the *Temporal Domain*, which is numerical in nature: it can be the set of integer, rational, or real numbers. Functions and predicates representing the usual arithmetic operations and relations are predefined at least for values in the temporal domain.

Variables, functions, and predicates are divided into *time dependent* and *time independent* ones. This allows representing change in time. Time dependent variables represent physical quantities or configurations that are subject to change in time, and time independent ones represent values unrelated with time. Time dependent functions and predicates denote relations, properties, or events that may or may not hold at a given time instant, while time independent functions and predicates represent facts and properties which can be assumed not to change with time.

TRIO formulas are constructed in the classical inductive way. However, besides the usual propositional operators and the quantifiers, one may compose TRIO formulas by using *primitive and derived temporal operators*.

There is one primitive temporal operator, *Dist*, that allows the specifier to refer to events occurring in the future or in the past with respect to the current, implicit time instant. If F is a TRIO formula and t is a term of the temporal type, then $Dist(F, t)$ is a TRIO formula that is satisfied at the current time instant if and only if F holds at the distance of t time units from the current one. Based on the primitive temporal operator *Dist*, several derived operators can be defined. A sample thereof is given in Table 2.1.

Notice that the operators of classic temporal logic can be easily obtained as TRIO derived operators. Also, it can be easily shown that the operators of several versions of temporal logic (e.g., interval logic) can be defined as TRIO derived operators. This argues in favor of TRIO's generality since many different logic formalisms can be described as particular cases of TRIO.

Another useful short-notation provided by TRIO is the application of the temporal operators to a term rather than to a formula: for instance, Past(s,t) denotes the value of term s at the instant laying t time units in the past from the current one.

Futr(F, d)	$\stackrel{\text{def}}{=} d \geq 0 \wedge \text{Dist}(F, d)$	Future
Past(F, d)	$\stackrel{\text{def}}{=} d \geq 0 \wedge \text{Dist}(F, -d)$	Past
Lasts(F, d)	$\stackrel{\text{def}}{=} \forall d'(0 < d' < d \rightarrow \text{Dist}(F, d'))$	F holds over a period of length d
Alw(F)	$\stackrel{\text{def}}{=} \forall d \ \text{Dist}(F, d)$	F always holds
Within(F, d)	$\stackrel{\text{def}}{=} \exists d'(0 < d' < d \wedge \text{Dist}(F, d'))$	F will occur within d time units
UpToNow (F)	$\stackrel{\text{def}}{=} \exists \delta \ (\delta > 0 \wedge \text{Past}(F, \delta) \wedge \text{Lasted}(F, \delta))$	F held for a nonnull time interval that ended at the current instant
Becomes (F)	$\stackrel{\text{def}}{=} F \wedge \text{UpToNow}(\neg F)$	F holds at the current instant but it did not hold for a nonnull interval that preceded the current instant
NextTime (F, t)	$\stackrel{\text{def}}{=} \text{Futr}(F, t) \wedge \text{Lasts}(\neg F, t)$	the first time in the future when F will hold is t time units apart from the current instant

Table 2.1   A sample of derived temporal operators.

Example 2.1

We consider a small fragment of the specification of a digital energy and power meter. The meter is composed of a magnetic transducer that converts the energy flow through the line into the rotation of a disc. In the peripheral part of the disc transparent and opaque portions are evenly alternated, with the purpose of permitting the detection of the disc motion and its velocity (which are respectively proportional to energy and power consumption) by means of a photocell. Figure 2.1 displays one such instrument. To minimise its wear, the photocell is activated only for a small fraction of the total working time of the meter. Its activation is performed according to the diagram of Figure 2.2.

Once the photocell is activated, the acquisition of its signal must be postponed by a delay δ, to permit it to reach a stable state. The cell activation lasts only δ_1 time units, and it is repeated after δ_2 time units.

We formalize this description in the following way: first, we define two time dependent 0-ary predicates, *activation* and *acquisition*, with obvious meaning. Then, the next two formulas specify the timing constraints on the *activation* and *acquisition* predicates, respectively.

$$1) \quad \text{Becomes(activation)} \rightarrow \left(\begin{array}{c} \text{Lasts(activation, } \delta_1) \\ \wedge \\ \text{Futr(NextTime(activation, } \delta_2), \delta_1) \end{array} \right)$$

$$2) \quad \text{acquisition} \leftrightarrow \text{Past(Becomes(activation), } \delta)$$

At the instant of acquisition the photocell may be in one of two states which correspond to the detection of a transparent or opaque portion of the disc. We thus model the photocell state by a time dependent variable *position* ranging in the set {open, closed}.

Figure 2.1. A digital energy and power meter.

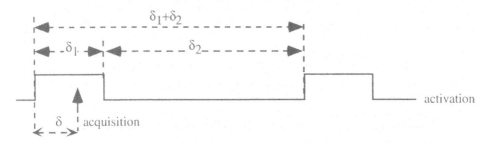

Figure 2.2. Timing diagram for the photocell activation.

The consumption of an energy quantum is detected when the disc moves from a transparent portion to an opaque one, or vice versa, and in the following formula it is modelled by the time dependent 0-ary predicate *quantum*, which may be true only at times when the acquisition takes place, if the current photocell state is different from the preceding one.

3) $\quad quantum \leftrightarrow \left(\begin{array}{c} \text{acquisition} \\ \wedge \\ position \neq Past(position,\ \delta_1 + \delta_2) \end{array} \right)$

Writing large specifications: the object-oriented version of TRIO

Pure logic formulas such as those exemplified in the previous section are totally unsuitable for managing large and complex specifications which are likely to be built incrementally through several refinements and corrections and will consist of hundreds or even thousands of pages of documentations. We assumed that managing large specifications is not far from managing several other types of large and complex documents, including design documentation. Thus, we adopted in TRIO the same principles and mechanisms that proved useful for "programming in the large" [MSP].

In particular, object-oriented (OO) paradigms have been "imported" in TRIO: this produced an "OO version of TRIO" that allows modularizing large specifications in several modules – or classes. Each module contains a number of TRIO axioms that formalize some system property. Modules can be further (de)composed in (smaller) larger modules both in a top-down and in a bottom up way. Other typical OO mechanisms such as genericity and inheritance are available in TRIO.

Furthermore, to improve understandability, TRIO is provided with a graphical interface which represents each class as a rectangular box and the items that belong to an instance of such a class as segments. The fact that a segment crosses or not a box boundary denotes whether or not the corresponding item is visible outside the class.

For instance, Figure 2.3 displays the TRIO structure of the class *EnergyMeter*. It represents the fact that each instance of such a class is composed of three elements: one instance of class disc, one of detector, one of totalizer, respectively.

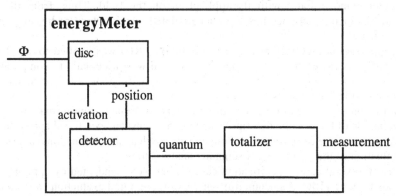

Figure 2.3. The graphic representation of the class *EnergyMeter*.

The detector module, whose behavior has been formalized in the previous section, shares with the disc component the activation predicate and the position variable; it produces the quantum – regulated by axiom 3) in Example 2.1 – to the totalizer module.

TRIO tools and methods.

A language usability (whether a specification, a design, or a programming language) highly depends on the tools and methods that guide its use. Ideally, in the case of a specification language such as TRIO, typical support tools should include:

- Editing tools for writing, updating, and managing complex specification documents.
- Analysis tools for validating specifications (e.g. through prototyping and/or (semi)automatic property proof).
- Tools supporting the transition from requirements specification to design and to lower phases.
- Tools supporting the verification phase: e.g., test case generators, or, more ambitiously, tools supporting correctness proofs.

Also necessary are a suitable collection of methodological guidelines and manuals that help the user in the creative but still rigorous and well disciplined process of going from initial, informal, and imprecise requirements through a precise formulation thereof and to a consistent design and verification.

In the case of TRIO only a few prototypal steps have been moved towards this goal. Presently, two tools are available:
- A graphical interactive editor, and
- A semantic tool based on a logic interpreter of the language that can be used both to prototype specifications and to generate test cases for the implementation [MMM]. Also, methodological guidelines and illustrating manuals are available.

This "TRIO environment", though still in a preliminary stage, allows writing specifications in a fairly understandable way. For instance, an appropriate use of comments and an incremental approach to the formalization process (i.e., starting with initial informal specifications and then refining them stepwise) makes a high portion – and the essential meaning – of specification documents understandable even to non TRIO experts.

3 . TRIO's Applications in Industrial Projects

As we stated above, the development of TRIO, of its methods, and of its tools was conducted hand-in-hand with its application on the field. Thus, from the very beginning, much experience has been accumulated which helped addressing further developments.

By applying an incremental approach, initially, TRIO was applied to small sized *case studies* extracted from real projects: their goal was principally to comparatively evaluate the new language from several viewpoints. In particular, we focused our attention on the following issues:
- Evaluation of the use of formal methods against informal or semiformal ones.
- Evaluation of the use of a descriptive approach against an operational approach.
- Evaluation of the use of an object-oriented approach against a functional approach.
- Evaluation of the usefulness of semantic analysis tools.

Thus, in several cases, specification case studies were conducted by applying other methods besides TRIO. A meaningful sample of these initial evaluation case studies is the following:
1. The specification of a digital energy and power meter – of which Example 2.1 constitutes a greatly simplified version.
3. The specification of monitoring a voltage signal by means of digital sampling. The requirements to be formally specified put a set of constraints on the absolute and relative times of the sampling measurements.
4. The specification of several complex hardware devices.
5. Other case studies were derived from a few typical benchmarks proposed in the literature [MMPSS].

All case studies confirmed major TRIO's strengths from the point of view of the above evaluation criteria. They were also used as training vehicles for industrial users[4].

Subsequently, TRIO has been applied to real industrial projects. This required taking into consideration the whole life cycle, not only the specification phase. By exploiting design methods that are based on OO paradigms as well as TRIO, the transition among

---

[4]As a side remark, introducing industrial people to descriptive style formal methods such as those based on logics, requires more training than operational formalisms such as Finite State Machines or Petri Nets. The extra effort, however, is well repaid by results in terms of abstraction, mainly when we wish to clearlky separate specifications from design.

the various phases did not cause serious problems, although no complete methodology involving the whole life cycle has been developed yet.

Some industrial projects have been (or are being) conducted in cooperation with ENEL, possibly with the support of some public funding (ESPRIT, ESSI, italian CNR). Others have been supported exclusively within the project budget. The most relevant projects that applied TRIO are:

- The ELSA project [BCMRS] which built the control system of a pondage power plant.
- The automation of a city traffic light system [GLMZ] (this project is still ongoing and TRIO has been applied only to a critical subset thereof.)
- The Opendreams project, which is a recently started Framework-4 project, aimed at building a CORBA-based platform and developing pilot projects based thereon.

4. Main Lessons Learned

Let us try to summarize the main lessons learned from TRIO experience. We feel that most of the comments below hold for the application of formal methods in general, though, certainly, we like to think that TRIO does have a few peculiar merits.

From a technical point of view we can strongly and safely claim that all major "challenges" have been "won". Not only TRIO produced recognized high quality specifications in small but critical examples, but even it confirmed that formal methods do indeed *scale-up* to large size industrial projects, provided that formalisms are complemented with modularity, incrementality, adequate training, etc. For instance, the final evaluation of the ELSA project reports that even in the first instance of application of the new method the extra-time and effort that was put in the specification phase were far compensated by the gain in the design and verification phases which were performed much more efficiently and safely than in other similar projects.

Nevertheless, we must acknowledge that we are still far from a complete success of the endeavor. By *complete success* we mean reaching a fairly well-established methodology which is satisfactorily adopted within several industrial environments in an *autonomous way* (after a reasonable training period).

All in all, we believe that major obstacles to achieve success are more of organizational and promotional nature than technical. Next we discuss the most relevant ones trying to suggest possible solutions.

1. A key issue is the deep and *effective cooperation* between research components (often from academic world) and industrial components. Also, it is fundamental that an incremental approach is pursued even in the strategic plans to develop and apply a new method in the industrial environment. From the research point of view this implies being ready to *give-up overambitious goals*. For instance, the academia uses to think that the major strength and objective of a formal method is the *proof* of design correctness. Instead, we believe that, initially, one should be happy enough if a "newcomer" reaches the ability of *writing* good formal specifications and *informally analyzing* them.

2. *Training* is a fundamental step in the adoption of a new method. We must admit that, in general, a formal method requires more training effort than informal ones. Unfortunately, industry managers tend to give low priority to training activity. This is often under-budgeted. Furthermore we experienced with frustration that often meetings scheduled for training on TRIO were canceled at the last moment because of overwhelming deadlines in the production activity. We have no magic solution to this problem: only try to be patient and accept flexibility (i.e., delays) on training plans.

There are also important psychological aspects in the training activity. Cooperation with symmetric exchange of experiences is much better than traditional "teaching"[5]. The ideal working group should be composed by some application expert and some method expert (usually the second type of person is young and recently graduated). If the ideal composition can not be achieved it is probably easier training the method expert in the application field than the opposite way, mainly if the involved person is not very young.

3. Diffusion and promotion of the results are at least as important as their technical quality. Recently, the academia learnt this lesson and much effort is presently devoted to the diffusion of new methods. Two clear examples of "pioneers" from this point of view are "Z" and "VDM". Certainly, (most of) the academia left its "ivory tower". The risk is falling in the opposite error. Perhaps, presently, too much time is devoted to quick and superficial presentation and too little effort is devoted to careful evaluation and deep development.

To favor TRIO's adoption we decided to make it *fully public domain*. All TRIO documentation and tools are freely available.

Still in the realm of promotion and evaluation, perhaps too much effort is put in developing "original" methods and claiming their superiority over the other ones and much less is put in general to convince the industrial world of the usefulness of formal methods in general, postponing the choice of a particular one to a more mature stage.

4. In the case of TRIO (we do not know how general is this experience) we suffered from what we called "the tool deadlock": on the one hand we needed good tools to convince potential partners to adopt TRIO. On the other hand, to obtain the necessary funds to produce acceptable tools we need a rich set of – at least potential – users. We are slowly recovering from this deadlock by applying stepwise developments and by trying to organize the prototype development mainly based on students' theses in an industrial-like fashion.

We also realized that it was a mistake delivering tool prototypes too early to the public: external users with no support by the developers were unable to overcome typical prototype inconveniences and were lead to reject the tool and sometimes even the conceptual aspects of the method.

5. Conclusions

Our TRIO adventure is now almost 10 years old. All in all we are fairly satisfied with the obtained results both from a scientific and from an industrial application point of view. We do not hide, however, that we are still far from a "final success" and we still have to overtake several major obstacles. These are definitely more of organizational and promotional type than technical.

In general, we believe that a certain amount of "stubbornness" is needed by the formal methods community if we still want to fight a war that has not yet been won after more than 30 years. Also, more cooperation within the community to reach a "critical mass" against oppositors is wished. A good way to achieve this goal still respecting the natural tendency towards scientific originality is to favor joint projects aimed at *integrating* different approaches (for instance, a cooperation is ongoing between NRL and ourselves to integrate TRIO tools with PVS [Jef]) and at applying several methods to real-life cases in a *comparative* (but *not competitive!*) way.

---

[5]There are also a few negative remarks on such psychological aspects but these perhaps belong to the exclusive personal experience of the author.

A good symptom for formal methods is the recent attention of some standardization institution (e.g., ISO) for them. We must also warn, however, against the risks of immature standardization (standardization implies slowing down development).

References

[BCMRS]   Basso M., Ciapessoni E., Crivelli E., Mandrioli D., Morzenti A., Ratto E., San Pietro P., "Experimenting a Logic-Based ApproAch to the Specification and Design of the Control System of a Pondage Power plant", Proceedings of the ICSE-17 Workshop on Formal Methods Application in Software Engineering Practice, 1995, pp. 174-181

[GLMZ]   Gargantini A., Liberati L., Morzenti A., Zacchetti C., "Specifying, Validating and Testing a Semaphore System in the TRIO Environment", submitted for publication, 1996.

[GMM]   Ghezzi C., Mandrioli D., Morzenti A., "TRIO a Logic Language for Executable Specifications of Real-time Systems", *Journal of Systems and Software*, June 1990

[Jef]   R.D.Jeffords, "An Approach to Encoding the TRIO Logic in PVS", Technical Report, Naval Research Laboratory, Wash.,D.C.,1995.

[LT]   Leveson, N, ans Turner, C., "An investigation of the Therac-25 accidents," *IEEE COMPUTER*, Vol.26, no.7, July 1993, pp.18-41

[MMM]   Mandrioli D., Morasca S., Morzenti A., "Generating Test Cases for Real-Time Systems from Logic Specifications", *ACM Trans. on Computer Systems*, November 1995.

[MMPSS]   Mandrioli D., Morzenti A., Pezzè M., San Pietro P. Silva S., "A Petri Net and Logic Approach to the Specification and Verification of Real Time Systems" in *Formal Methods for Real-Time Computing*, Heitmeyer C., Mandrioli D. (editors), John Wiley & Sons, March 1996

[MSP]   Morzenti, A. and SanPietro, P., An Object Oriented Logic Language for Modular System Specification. *ACM Transaction on Software Engineering and Methodology*, Vol.3, No.1, Jan. 1994.

Using Heterogeneous Formal Methods in Distributed Software Engineering Education

Bernd J. Krämer

FernUniversität, D-58084 Hagen, Germany
E-Mail: bernd.kraemer@fernuni-hagen.de
WWW: http://www.fernuni-hagen.de/DVT

Abstract. At FernUniversität we developed a new distance education course on Distributed Software Engineering especially designed for graduate students of the Electrical Engineering faculty. The course focuses on reactive software systems which are increasingly being used to monitor and control safety-related devices and high risk technical processes. Erroneous assumptions and insufficient foresight during requirements analysis and design activities are known as major causes of software safety problems. Therefore the course emphasizes development of adequate modeling ideas, precise descriptions of system functions and safety requirements, and careful analysis of design solutions. A simple production cell whose electromechanical components are controlled by individual processors is used as a patent case study. This paper describes some of the motivation behind the organization of the course, sketches the core contents of the course, and reports on experiences from its first run.

1 Introduction

The Computer Science (CS) Faculty of FernUniversität has offered a two-semester course in software engineering (SE) for years [1]. Occasionally students from the Faculty of Electrical Engineering (EE) applied for permission to include this course as a selective to their individual study plan. Some had recognized the value of a mature software engineering education for their future career in application areas where micro-electronic components, communications infra-structure, and software have grown together to a functional unit. Others, in their role as working professionals[1], had realized their incompetence in engineering software used, e.g., in digital telecommunications systems, computerized medical equipment, traffic control systems, or energy distribution systems. These and related application areas are predominantly occupied by EE graduates as they tend to have a good understanding of application-domain issues.

In 1994 we decided to develop new course material for the second term of the SE course to answer the growing demand of EE students [2]. The course contents is particularly adapted to three characteristics of many computer-based process control applications: *reactivity*, *distribution*, and *safety*. Most process control software must continuously react to actions in its physical environment

---

[1] Nearly 70% of our students are working full or part-time besides their study.

and should not terminate under normal operation. This requires a shift from relational to process-oriented specification models and delimits the value of testing as a means to validate the software due to the huge number of possible computation threads and the difficulty to provide realistic test conditions.

If the software is distributed across physically separated devices or spatially dispersed processing facilities, program components can act concurrently and their coordinated interaction requires a careful design of their communication behavior. Examples are computer-controlled exchanges in digital telephony, mobile communication systems, or pipeline-control software in petrol industry.

Since a few years, we observe a growing number of computer-based control systems being used in safety-related applications [3]. Their failure can cause dangerous situations or severe accidents including loss of life, injury or damage to the environment. These characteristics obligate the system developer to carefully elicit and document safety requirements and consider their satisfaction throughout the whole development process. Often safety-related applications must be certified by independent assessors before being licensed by the authorities.

With the new course we wanted to endow our students with core competence in the development of reactive distributed software used in safety-related applications. A simple production cell whose electromechanical components are controlled by a distributed program serves as a patent case study. In the stepwise development of this example we emphasize formal models and description techniques without claiming that they are necessary prerequisites for a disciplined software engineering approach. Rather we rely on their underlying concepts and use their notations to: train the recognition of realistic abstractions; illustrate the benefit of precise and unambiguous requirements and design documentation; and demonstrate the usefulness of rigorous safety analysis and verification procedures. The use of antagonistic formalisms such action structures [4] or Z [5] and Petri nets [6] or LOTOS [7] for requirements and design specification, respectively, aims at contrasting different modeling ideas and representation alternatives for the same application.

This paper presents the organization and core contents of the course. Section 2 introduces the production cell example. In Sect. 3 we sketch the process of formalizing requirements characterizing the intended system function and safety conditions imposed on the cell controller's operation. Section 4 discusses two alternative design solutions, while Sect. 5 touches upon the construction of a distributed control program from the validated design. We conclude with a brief report on experiences and an outlook on future developments.

2 The Case Study

The production cell case was first introduced in a study comparing the strengths and weaknesses of several formal methods for reactive systems [9]. The case study describes the operation of a real metal processing factory. Despite some simplifications made, it displays an example of realistic complexity. To allow for an asynchronous flow of material into and out of the cell, we have slightly modified the cell configuration as illustrated in Fig. 1.

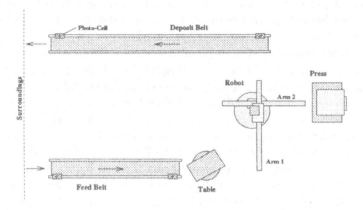

Fig. 1. Bird's eye view of the production cell

We assume an external gadget to deposit individual blanks on the left end of the feed belt in arbitrary time intervals. The belt conveys these blanks to the rotary table at the belt's other end. Once the blank has been passed over, the table moves up to bring the blank into a position from where robot arm 1 can pick it up. After loading arm 1, the robot rotates counter-clockwise into a position in which arm 1 points at the press to deposit the blank in the press. To increase the use of the press, the robot is equipped with a second arm. This arm picks up a shaped part cast-off in the press during the previous robot cycle, the robot rotates counter-clockwise until arm 2 points towards the deposit belt, and arm 2 unloads the piece of metal to the right end of the deposit belt. This belt moves processed parts to the other end from where they are removed one by one from a second gadget in the surroundings. Arm 1 and 2 are mounted on different vertical levels. They can operate their grippers and extend or retract independently but always rotate together as they are strongly coupled. Photo-cells monitor the load and unload zone of the conveyer belts, while switches and other types of sensors signal the actual horizontal or vertical position of robot arms, table, and press cheek.

3 Safety Analysis and Requirements Documentation

A salient characteristic of this case study is a multitude of safety requirements constraining the operation of the controller software. To elicit these requirements, application specialists, operators, and software developers typically would perform a careful system safety analysis [10]. Its purpose is to reveal all potential sources of safety hazards and ensure the safe operation of the entire system, even in the presence of failures of physical devices or human operators. Hence, safety conditions may include requirements that the embedded software is responsible for detecting hazardous system states and prevent the system to enter unsafe states by taking appropriate actions. Emergency shut-down systems for nuclear power plants provide a typical example for this kind of behavior [11].

System safety analysis for heterogeneous systems is an important but relatively new and underdeveloped field of research. We felt this topic too weighty to be crushed into a few pages of discourse in an SE course. Rather we decided to start our sample development process with a predefined list of informally described safety requirements and touch the issue of safety analysis during the practice days typically offered at the end of the term.

The safety requirements refer to four types of critical situations that can arise and must be avoided under all conditions: infringement of machine mobility, insufficient spatial separation of metal parts, and unloading of metal parts in unsafe areas. Besides safety requirements, a functional description of the whole manufacturing process and the operation of individual machine controllers is given. The task then is to develop a distributed control program consisting of five loosely coupled machine controllers for the two belts, the robot, the table, and the press, respectively. Their interaction must be designed in such a way that a maximum of metal parts moves through the pipeline of processing machines and is processed concurrently, while all safety requirements are observed.

The operation of the press, for example, is defined as the cyclic execution of the following three steps: *(1) range the movable cheek from its bottom into the middle position and wait until arm 1 has unloaded a blank in the press; (2) move the cheek up to shape the blank; (3) move the cheek down to the lowest position and wait until arm 2 has picked up the shaped metal piece.*

An example for a safety requirement prohibiting machine collision by requiring controllers of the two adjacent machines to synchronize their movements properly is:

Press-Robot: *The press may only move its cheek if no robot arm is positioned inside the press.*

The first constructive step demonstrated in the course is the formalization of functional and safety requirement. For this purpose we use action structures of the form $(E_p, \rightarrow_p, \alpha_p)$ [4]. They provide a causality-based formal model of non-sequential processes p by mapping the partially ordered set E_p of events through the total function α_p into a given set A of elementary atomic actions. The elements of E_p represent occurrences of actions in A, their partial ordering is defined by the relation $\rightarrow_p$. For illustration purposes we often use an obvious graphical notation of finite processes. To specify functional properties and safety conditions, we define a number of logical predicates characterizing a particular set of action structures modeling the permissible behavior of a distributed system. Examples for such predicates are $mutex(a, b, p)$ and $cyclic(a, b, p)$. For a given process p the former requires that all occurrences of a and b in p causally depend on each other, which means that they cannot occur concurrently. The second predicate states that the occurrences of a and b alternate in p starting with an occurrence of action a.

Having introduced the action sets

$$A_{robot} \stackrel{\text{def}}{=} \{extend(a), retract(a), rotate(d), load(a), unload(a), stop|$$
$$a \in \{arm1, arm2\}, d \in \{cc, cw\}\}$$
$$A_{press} \stackrel{\text{def}}{=} \{move(f, t)|f, t \in \{l, u, p\}, f \neq t\}$$
$$\ldots$$

modeling the interfaces of each machine, the intended cyclic behavior q of the press can be specified by the following predicate:

$$cycle(move(u, l), move(l, p), q) \quad \wedge \quad cycle(move(l, p), move(p, u), q) \quad \wedge$$
$$cycle(move(u, l), move(p, u), q)$$

Safety requirement **Press-Robot** can be formalized as follows with $a \in \{arm1, arm2\}, m \in A_{press}$:

$$mutex(extend(a), m) \quad \wedge \quad after\_unless(A_{press}, extend(a), retract(a), p)$$

with

$$after\_unless(A, a, b, q) \stackrel{\text{def}}{=} \forall d \in E_q|\alpha_q(d) = a \bullet$$
$$(\exists e \in E_q \bullet \alpha_q(e) \in A \wedge d \rightarrow_q e \Rightarrow$$
$$(\exists f \in E_q \bullet d \rightarrow_q f \wedge f \rightarrow_q e))$$

The second part of the predicate tells us that after an arm has been extended a retract action must occur before any press action is allowed. The first part ensures that critical actions may not occur concurrently. For simplicity reasons we have neglected the fact that this constraint only applies if the last rotate action of the robot prior to the arm extension rotated the robot in position in which the respective arm points at the press. To validate these specifications we propose to develop an alternative specifications check it for consistency with the first.

Experience has shown that this way of specifying behavioral requirements, is extremely difficult to understand and reproduce by our students. This is not only due to the fact that most EE students do not have a background in discrete mathematics[2] and thus lack experience with these mathematical concepts. The main difficulty seems to be the extreme abstraction embodied in this model, which just allows us to reason about actions and restrictions on their causal structure. But we deliberately chose this model as we believe that it helps to

- displace the predominant "sequential thinking" in the heads of our students by a partial order model of behavior,
- emphasize the special properties in the behavior of distributed software, and
- prevent early commitment to design solutions.

---

[2] We spend the equivalent of six hours of lecture time on basics in mathematical logic, set theory, functions and relations.

To contrast different specification paradigms, we also develop a model-based specification with Z^3. This formalism includes an explicit notion of state and allows us to refer to a component's state space when defining operations and safety invariants. We demonstrate how the confidence in a Z specification can be increased and ambiguous, conflicting, or incomplete requirements can be resolved by performing the standard consistency checks for Z (existence of an initial state, calculation of preconditions for operations, etc.).

A relationship between the two styles of requirements definitions is maintained through the use of identical operation names (modulo necessary notational adaptations). In addition, we illustrate some informal reasoning to determine whether the Z specification satisfies some of the predicates on action structures.

4 Software Architecture and Component Behavior

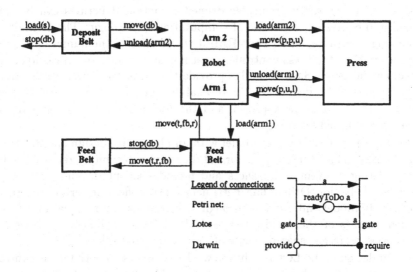

Fig. 2. Architecture of the production cell controller

After the formalized requirements have been validated, we introduce the design architecture depicted in Fig. 2 together with the pertinent concepts. As a first approach to a design solution, we develop a Petri net model of the behavior of individual components and their interaction. The Petri net model nicely combines a notion of distributed state with a notion of concurrent actions affecting local state changes. Like in action structures concurrency is based on a partial

---

[3] Z is not particularly suited for specifying distributed systems as it relies on a sequential computation model. Its use in this course is justified by the growing popularity of Z in industry and by the fact that our case study can be naturally decomposed into components that operate in a sequential mode.

order semantics. In fact, non-sequential observations of Petri nets, which can be represented by occurrence nets (i.e., acyclic nets with unbranched places [6]), can be related to action structures simply by forgetting the places.

Except for the robot, the behavior of all components is adequately modeled by state machine components cyclically relating the interface operations of each controller through intermediate places. If possible, we re-use the names of state variables of the Z specification to label the places. The interaction among adjacent machines can be adequately modeled as a producer-consumer interaction. Roughly, this leads us to interpret the arcs of the abstract architecture in Fig. 2 as places that are connected to appropriate transitions of the behavior nets of adjacent controllers. These places them model an asynchronous communication among interacting controllers.

With appropriate Petri net tools various types of analyses can be performed to detect design errors or formally verify that the nets are free of deadlocks and other undesired properties. To verify the satisfaction of given requirements, we illustrate how the safety predicates defined on action structures can be transformed into equivalent formulae of computational tree logic. The formula corresponding to requirement **Press-Robot** would refer to the names of places. It would state that the press controller must not move while an arm is loading or unloading the press. Such formulae provide the basis for formal verification of safety properties by inspecting the reachability graph of a net through model checking. This validation approach and the tool environment supporting this process are adapted from [12].

Again, we contrast the net model with an alternative design specification in basic LOTOS. This standardized formal description technique relies on a temporal ordering of event occurrences and provides an interleaving semantics of concurrent behavior. Other than Petri nets LOTOS offers powerful process constructors. It models interaction through synchronous communication. Viewing the components of the architecture model in Fig. 2 as LOTOS processes, the connections represent shared events of interacting controllers.

In our design of the LOTOS solution we define processes both for the controller behavior and the machine or sensor behavior. The machine behavior models all possible machine actions (at the given abstraction level, of course) including a crash in the case that the controler infringed the mobility constraints of the machine. The control processes for both arms, the machine processes, and the sensor processes are then run in parallel to obtain a black-box view of a composite component like the robot.

During our practice days we offer the students access to several LOTOS tools so that they can experiment with specification-based testing by means of test processes or interactive simulation. As basic LOTOS can be mapped into CCS, we also demonstrate the model checking technique for the LOTOS specification using the Concurrency Workbench. It supports CCS and includes a propositional modal logic. Two predefined macros built on that logic can directly be applied to express requirement **Press-Robot** in a form similar to predicate *after_unless*:

```
Allways ([extendArm1] (NotUnless {retractArm1} {moveUL,moveLP,movePL}))
```

The main objective of demonstrating these different techniques is to raise some awareness about the use of rigorous design analysis before building operational systems, at least in critical applications. But even if formal verification is not applied, we believe that much of the benefit of formalisms can be mediated already by applying disciplined and careful analysis procedures.

5 Distributed Programming

The Darwin notation is used for design specification at the distributed programming level [8]. It supports the automatic generation of program code which implements composite components and the binding between them. Cooperation is based on a client/server paradigm. With the current language binding of Darwin primitive components have to be implemented manually as single-threaded C++ objects.

The architecture in Fig. 2 is equivalent to the top level architecture of the Darwin design. Here the links denote bindings between provided and required services (operations) of server and client components, respectively.

As yet, verification of the program code against the requirements is a weak point of our development architecture. But at least for the Darwin designs tools are under construction at Imperial college that support model checking of hierarchical program architectures. For a subset of the Darwin language we have recently defined a mapping to the CORBA Interface Definition Language (IDL) and in [13] we have proposed concurrency annotations to IDL. Once implemented, the latter would allow us to relate formal requirements to such annotations mapped into automatically generated C++ code instrumenting these annotations.

6 Conclusions and Outlook

The course we have outlined in this paper emphasizes formal methods in the development of safety-critical distributed control applications. The description techniques and notations we use mainly serve as communication mechanisms. Rather than developing skills in their use, we try to mediate fundamental concepts of distributed software and develop skills in concept abstraction and careful analysis of design ideas. Feedback from students suggests that the use of a patent example is well received. Moreover it seems to render the range of formal modeling and description techniques easier to digest than a collection of incoherent examples.

During our study days at the end of the second term the students are faced with the re-development of a modification to the production cell configuration that introduces new safety requirements. The task is complicated by the constraint to re-use a maximum of specifications, design solutions, and code. Prior to this work we jointly perform a system safety analysis and inspect the solutions given in the course. As they was designed with respect to the given safety requirements, our controller specifications are unable to properly cope with certain hardware failures.

Currently, teaching software engineering from a distance means communicating ideas largely on paper. Practice days provide students a limited opportunity to interact closely with their teachers and thereby solidify their knowledge of central concepts. but for time and cost reasons the number of practice days cannot be extended. To overcome this barrier, we decided to exploit the potential of multi-media technology and started recently to develop parts of the course into an interactive multi-media form. We aim to include light versions of software specification, design and programming tools supporting the techniques used in different phases of the course. This will help students in getting feedback through trial use and error. The multi-media course will also include an animated visual representation of the production cell. We hope to provide a plug-in version of visual components that can linked the student's own control program. Parts of our course were recently taken over by the Open University. Currently we are discussing ways to join forces in the development of overlapping multi-media versions of our courses.

References

1. B.-U. Pagel and H.-W. Six. *Software Engineering – Band 1*. Addison-Wesley 1994.
2. B.J. Krämer. *Software Engineering II – Konstruktion verteilter Systeme*. Kurs 2521. FernUniversität 1995.
3. W.J. Cullyer, W.A.Halang, and B.J. Krämer. High integrity programmable electronic systems. Dagstuhl-Seminar-Report 107, D-66687 Wadern, 1995.
4. M. Broy. *Informatik: Eine grundlegende Einführung III*. Springer Verlag, 1994.
5. J.B. Wordsworth. *Software Development with Z*. International Computer Science Series. Addison-Wesley 1992.
6. W. Reisig. *Petri Nets, EATCS Monographs on Theoretical Computer Science*, 4. Springer Verlag 1985.
7. K.J. Turner. *Using Formal Description Techniques*. John Wiley & Sons, 1993.
8. J. Magee, N. Dulay, S. Eisenbach, and J. Kramer. Specifying distributed software architectures. In *Fifth European Software Engineering Conference (ESEC '95)*, Springer Verlag, 1995.
9. C. Lewerentz and T. Lindner, editors. *Formal Development of Reactive Systems – Case Study Production Cell*, LNCS 891. Springer Verlag, 1994.
10. N.G. Leveson. *Safeware – System Safety and Computers*. Addison-Wesley, 1995.
11. W.A. Halang, B.J. Krämer, and N. Völker. Formally verified building blocks in functional logic diagrams for emergency shutdown system design. *High Integrity Systems*, 1995.
12. M. Heiner and P. Deussen. Petri net based qualitative analysis. Reihe Informatik I-08/1995, Technische Universität Cottbuss, 1995.
13. G. Henze, T. Koch, and B.J. Krämer. Annotations for synchronization constraints in CORBA IDL. In *SDNE '96*, Macau, June 1996.

Introducing Formal Methods To Software Engineers Through OMG's CORBA Environment And Interface Definition Language

Sriram Sankar
Sun Microsystems Laboratories
2550 Garcia Avenue, MTV29-112
Mountain View, CA 94043
U.S.A.
sriram.sankar@sun.com
1-415-336-6230

Abstract

This paper talks about an ongoing project at Sun Microsystems Laboratories in which the interface definition language IDL of OMG's CORBA environment is extended with formal specification constructs. Tool support is provided to compile the specifications into code that can perform sanity checks to provide an added amount of security in a distributed system.

The software engineering industry has long been resisting formal methods as a means to improving software quality. This work attempts to maintain the current level of software quality while the complexity of software increases due to the presence of distributed objects. We hope that a means to maintain (rather than improve) software quality will be accepted more easily by the software engineering industry.

This paper motivates the need for formal methods in the CORBA environment and presents an overview of Borneo, the specification language extension of IDL.

For more detailed and uptodate information on Borneo, please send email to: borneo-help@asap.eng.sun.com.

1 Introduction

Software engineers in industry work in a time-pressured environment with incentives that usually direct them towards a rather ad hoc, quick and dirty approach to developing software rather than using a more formal approach. The resulting software is typically not perfect, and requires many revisions to make it more robust. However this approach is seen by management as the best way to improve the bottom line such as better earnings, revenues, stock price, etc.

Formal methods proponents look at this state of the industry and wonder how their ideas can really cause an impact. There is a common belief that a software related disaster is imminent which will affect the bottom line of the software industry (such as through law suits), and that at this point, industry will adopt a more formal approach to developing software. In our opinion, however, such disasters and resulting financial losses have already been considered by industry management and factored into their software development processes. In fact formal approaches are already being used today for applications with high costs of failures.

We believe that the complexity of software is increasing in a manner that today's software development techniques will soon prove inadequate to maintain current levels of software quality. We believe that introducing formal methods into the current software development techniques can compensate for the increased complexity of software hence maintaining the current level of software quality — thus enabling the use of formal methods in industry.

At Sun Microsystems, we have identified one piece of technology that enables the construction of these more complex and more heterogeneous systems. This technology is OMG's CORBA [2] (Common Object Request Broker Architecture) and IDL (Interface Definition Language) standard and more specifically, Sun Microsystem's own implementation of this standard — NEO^{TM} [4]. NEO provides the capability to build systems consisting of distributed objects that cooperate with each other in performing a common task. The interaction between these objects takes place through a well defined interface written in the IDL language.

IDL interfaces contain only signature information — similar to Ada package specifications or C++ classes. We have designed a language and associated tool support (*Borneo*) to extend IDL's capabilities with:

- A behavior specification capability using which one can describe the input-output behavior of object methods;

- A protocol specification capability using which one can describe relationships between events that occur in the distributed environment; *and*

- A design capability using which one can rapidly prototype object designs before their efficient implementation in a programming language.

Our tools provide the capability to automatically check conformance of implementations with respect to their specifications as well as to conveniently build early prototypes of distributed objects.

The work on Borneo is based on our earlier work on ADL (Assertion Definition Language) where we developed a general specification framework and applied it in the testing of C programs [1,3]. Borneo represents a significant improvement to ADL and provides tool support that is applicable to all aspects of the software development cycle rather than just testing.

We believe there is a good chance of industry acceptance of formal methods technology for CORBA, especially when compared to using formal methods with other programming environments. Some reasons are given below:

- An environment such as CORBA causes discomfort to software engineers. Many people feel disconcerted by the absence of anything more than signature information in the IDL interface. This feeling is, to some extent, psychological. But there are some real reasons too. For example, an object implementation may reside at a remote location and may be modified constantly without the client's knowledge.

- The overhead of checking specifications during program execution is not perceived to be a problem. This overhead is considered insignificant compared to the network traffic overhead. In fact, people seem to be perfectly happy about having these specifications checked permanantly.

- Our tools are added to the NEO tools in a manner transparent to the user. Hence the user simply has to learn how to write specifications.

- Issues in the area of "software architectures" are becoming very important in many circles, especially given the recent interest the US DoD has had in this area. Our specification and design capabilities will make it very easy to design and develop software architectures.

In this paper, we provide an overview of the Borneo language. We do not present details of the tool support. As mentioned earlier, the tool support is transparent to the NEO user — once the user has learned NEO, simply extending their interfaces with specifications provides automatic specification based consistency checking.

2 An Overview of OMG's CORBA and IDL

CORBA is a standard developed by OMG (Object Management Group) to facilitate the interaction between objects distributed over a network. CORBA includes the definition of IDL, a programming language independent interface definition language, which is used to describe the object interfaces for use in the CORBA environment. The objects may be implemented in any programming language and CORBA defines bindings between IDL entities and programming language entities to match IDL interfaces with their programming language implementations. Currently, bindings are defined for languages such as C and C++. Java^{TM} bindings are expected to be defined shortly.

In addition, CORBA also provides utilities such as to help users (clients) of objects to locate the objects they wish to use and then invoke them. An example of an IDL interface is:

```
interface StockBroker {

    long Cash_Balance(in long account);

    long Stock_Balance(in long account, in string symbol);

    void Buy(
        in long account,
        in string symbol,
        in long no_of_shares
    );

};
```

Interfaces in IDL are types that describe visible methods, attributes, and exceptions of objects that implement them. In the above example, the interface StockBroker describes three methods that may be called of any StockBroker object, namely, Cash_Balance, Stock_Balance, and Buy. Notice that IDL has its own type system to describe basic types such as integers and strings. Also note that all parameters are passed either in, out, or inout to reflect how they are really passed in a distributed environment.

The following scenario describes a simple use of the CORBA environment to create a stock broker object and use it across the network:

Step 1: Develop the interface. This results in the interface shown above.

Step 2: Compile the interface using an IDL compiler. In this step, we need to make a choice of programming language for the client (user of the object) and for the server (the object itself). Suppose we choose C++ for both client and server.
The IDL compiler produces a "skeleton" for the implementation of a C++ object that implements the stock broker interface. It also produces a make file to build the filled up skeleton into a CORBA object.
The IDL compiler also produces a header file for the client that contains definitions of Cash_Balance, Stock_Balance, and Buy. It also produces a make file to build the client.

Step 3: Fill up the object skeleton produced in step 2 and run the make file to compile and build the object. Then register the object with the CORBA naming service and start the object. This can also be achieved by running yet another make file. The object is now available to accept calls from across the network.

Step 4: Build a client that makes calls to the header file generated in step 2. The client must first get an object reference to the object generated in step 3 by calling the CORBA naming service and providing the same name as the object used when registering itself in step 3. Calls to the header file are made through this object reference that is implemented in C++ as a pointer to a class. Run make to create an executable for the client, and then run this executable. Obviously, the client and server may be run on different machines.

The result of the above four steps is a simple distributed client-server program. The advantage of using CORBA to do this is that everything in the above steps may be done at the programming language level. There is no need to learn detailed operating system commands such as RPC, etc. Figure 1 below illustrates the final result.

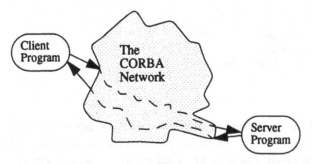

Figure 1. A simple distributed client-server system in CORBA

There are many more issues to be dealt with before a thorough introduction to CORBA can be completed, however, this introduction is sufficient for the purpose of this paper.

3 Adding Borneo Behavior Specifications To StockBroker

As an introduction to Borneo, we present an extension of the IDL interface of the stock broker with Borneo specifications:

```
interface StockBroker {

    auxiliary long price(in string symbol);

    inline long cost(in string symbol, in long no_of_shares) {
        no_of_shares * price(symbol);
    };

    long Cash_Balance(in long account);

    long Stock_Balance(in long account, in string symbol);

    void Buy(
        in long account,
        in string symbol,
        in long no_of_shares
    ) semantics {
        Cash_Balance(account) ==
            @Cash_Balance(account) - @cost(symbol, no_of_shares);
        Stock_Balance(account, symbol) ==
            @Stock_Balance(account, symbol) + no_of_shares;
    };

};
```

In this example, the stock broker interface is augmented with a description of the behavior of Buy. While Cash_Balance and Stock_Balance have been written in the standard IDL syntax, Buy has been written in the annotated operation declaration syntax. The two boolean expressions appearing within "semantics { ... }" describe legitimate behavior of the Buy operation. In these expressions, "@" is an unary operator (referred to as the *call state operator*) whose sole function is to evaluate its argument prior to the execution of the operation — by default all expressions are evaluated after the execution of the operation.

The first of these boolean expressions make use of the notion of "cost" of a stock purchase. This is implemented in the interface as an inline operation declaration. The inline operation declaration in turn requires the notion of the "price" of a particular share, and this is implemented as an auxiliary operation declaration. The main difference between inline and auxiliary operation declarations is that inline operation declarations are defined inline (at the point of the declaration), while auxiliary operation declarations are defined in a manner similar to the standard interface operations.

The syntax described above requires that Borneo constructs be inserted within IDL interfaces. In many cases, this may not be suitable. For example, one may wish to retain existing IDL interfaces as is (possibly to remain compliant to the CORBA standard). Borneo therefore provides an alternate syntax whereby the constructs introduced above may be placed outside the IDL interface, and possibly even in separate files that "#include" the file containing the interface. The earlier example is rewritten below using this alternate syntax (the IDL interface is omitted):

```
auxiliary long StockBroker::price(in string symbol);

inline long StockBroker::cost(in string symbol, in long
no_of_shares) {
   no_of_shares * price(symbol);
};

void StockBroker::Buy(
   in long account,
   in string symbol,
   in long no_of_shares
) semantics {
   Cash_Balance(account) ==
        @Cash_Balance(account) - @cost(symbol, no_of_shares);
   Stock_Balance(account, symbol) ==
        @Stock_Balance(account, symbol) + no_of_shares;
};
```

This alternate approach to describing the behavior of Buy has the same meaning. When steps 1–4 described in Section 2 are performed with this new interface (assuming Borneo has been installed), the same distributed client-server system as before is created, but with the added effect of specification checking during the network hop. Figure 2 illustrates this result. The rectangular black box does the specification checking and may be considered a firewall built into the communication path.

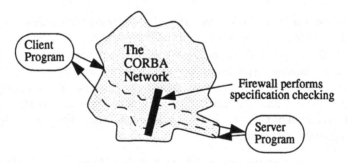

Figure 2. A Borneo firewall in CORBA

4 Protocol Specifications in Borneo

Borneo provides constructs to describe the behavior of a distributed system through specifying constraints on events that occur during the execution of this system. Events are activities of interest that occur in a system. Examples of events may be "file_opened", "email_sent", etc. An event may have attributes. For example, "file_opened" may have a string attribute called "file_name", and "email_sent" may have a string attribute called "receiver".

Borneo provides facilities for describing constraints on the occurrence of events and the time ordering between them. Events related by constraints may occur in different parts of the network and distributed time algorithms are used to determine time ordering between them.

The first thing to do while specifying constraints on events is to define the events. These are done using *event types*. Borneo defines a few standard event types that describe the invocation of methods of objects. In addition, Borneo provides facilities for defining user events. Once event types are defined, event constraints may be specified by grouping them together into a syntactic construct called the *protocol*. Protocols are encapsulations where constraints on events are described. These constraints are compiled into checks that report errors whenever they are violated by the implementation being monitored.

As an illustrative example, consider the following extended stock broker interface:

```
interface StockBroker {

   long Cash_Balance(in long account);

   long Stock_Balance(in long account, in string symbol);

   void Buy(
      in long account,
      in string symbol,
      in long no_of_shares
   );

   void PlaceLimitOrderToBuy(
      in long account,
      in string symbol,
      in long no_of_shares,
      in long limit_price,
      out long order_no
   );

   void LimitOrderExecuted(in long account, in long order_no);

   void QueryLimitOrderStatus(
      in long account,
      in long order_no,
      out boolean executed
   );

};
```

This interface has three new operations. PlaceLimitOrderToBuy and QueryLimitOrderStatus are used by the client of the stock broker to place and query the status of limit orders. The third operation LimitOrderExecuted is invoked by the trader when the limit order has just been executed. The following protocol specification partially describes the behavior of these new operations:

```
protocol LimitOrderConstraints {

    server_return(StockBroker::PlaceLimitOrderToBuy) place_order;
    server_return(StockBroker::LimitOrderExecuted) order_execd;
    server_return(StockBroker::QueryLimitOrderStatus) query_rslt;

    when place_order
    then order_execd
    before (query_rslt where query_rslt.executed);

    when place_order
    then not order_execd
    before (query_rslt where !query_rslt.executed);

};
```

This protocol starts with the declaration of three *event variables* place_order, order_execd, and query_rslt. These variables are declared to be of three different predefined event types. These event types describe events corresponding to the end of an operation execution at the server end. Following these declarations are two event constraints. The first event constraint says that whenever a place_order event occurs, then an order_execd event must occur before a query_rslt event occurs if the component "executed" (the out parameter of the corresponding call to QueryLimitOrderStatus) of query_rslt is true. The second event constraint says that whenever a place_order event occurs, then no order_execd event may occur before a query_rslt event occurs if the component "executed" of query_rslt is false.

Essentially this protocol describes the value returned by QueryLimitOrderStatus based on earlier events that have occurred. For the sake of brevity, we have omitted from this protocol specification the fact that the order numbers of all the events must be the same.

5 Borneo's Design Capabilities

The software engineering process starts with the requirements phase and then proceeds on to a phase of design. This is also referred to by other terms such as modeling, simulation, prototyping, etc. Most specification frameworks have focused on the software requirements phase and have tended to ignore the design phase. Our goal is to provide an advanced capability to quickly implement designs of a system so as to provide feedback to the software engineer on various issues relating to the particular choice of design. The Borneo design language is not yet complete. However, constructs already in Borneo such as inline declarations already permit an executable capability (which is crucial for a design facility). The goal then is to extend Borneo further with more executable constructs that may be used along with Borneo's specification constructs. To avoid having to design executable constructs from scratch, we may reuse the syntax of an existing high level language that has proven itself to be suitable for high level design.

6 Why Yet Another Specification Language?

This is an important question to answer given the multitude of specification languages available. Why did we not choose an existing specification capability? This section attempts to answer this question, and thereby tries to highlight some of the advantages of a Borneo-like language.

Our primary goal was to provide specification capabilities to average software engineers. Thus the specification capability had to be simple to learn and use, while at the same time providing a lot of returns to investment. All existing specification languages we considered had been designed in an attempt to address more fundamental issues of specification methodology, or were directed towards extremely sophisticated users willing to go through some significant training to convince themselves of the effectiveness of using these languages. While most of these other specification languages have achieved significant goals in their respective domains, it was our feeling that they would not be able to effectively address our intended audience — the average software engineer. To make the specification language simple to learn and use, we concluded that it must build upon the syntax of C expressions and also take on a similar semantic meaning. To achieve maximum returns on investment for the software engineer, we chose CORBA as our target audience.

The following is a summary of some of the advantages offered by Borneo to an average software engineer:

- Borneo is an extremely easy to learn and use language. Whenever possible, decisions have been made which are oriented towards more simplicity.

- The Borneo tools have been designed to seamlessly integrate with the NEO tools. Hence, a Borneo user simply has to learn the specification language, and be able to understand the error messages produced by the specification checking tools.

- Borneo specifications may be written separately from the IDL interface. This facilitates specification both during and after the development of the IDL interface. It also permits users to move between using Borneo and not using it for a particular IDL interface very easily.

- Borneo specifications may be partial — it is not necessary to completely specify an object before checking code can be generated.

- The choice of CORBA as a target environment offers obvious advantages to the software engineer who uses Borneo. These advantages are listed at the beginning of this paper.

7 Conclusions and Ongoing Activity

The Borneo tools are in the process of development. We anticipate early versions to be available to external (outside Sun) users sometime in the summer of this year. To be able to use the Borneo tools, one must have Sun's NEO which in turn requires a Sun workstation running Solaris™. For more information on Borneo please send email to borneo-help@asap.eng.sun.com.

References

[1]   *ADL Language Reference Manual* and *ADL Translator Design Specification.* "http://wwwsunlabs.com/research/adl/.

[2]   Common Object Request Broker: Architecture and Specification Revision 2.0. Available from the OMG.

[3]   Sankar, S. & Hayes, R. *Specifying and Testing Software Components using ADL.*, Sun Microsystens Laboratories Technical Report No. SML-TR-94-23.

[4]   SunSoft NEO External Web Page. "http://wwwsun.com/sunsoft/neo/.

Java™, NEO™, and Solaris™ are trademarks of Sun Microsystems, Inc.

Toward a Classification Approach to Design

Douglas R. Smith

Kestrel Institute, 3260 Hillview Avenue, Palo Alto, California 94304, USA
smith@kestrel.edu
18 March 1996

Abstract. This paper addresses the problem of how to construct refinements of specifications formally and incrementally. The key idea is to use a taxonomy of abstract design concepts, each represented by a *design theory*. An abstract design concept is applied by constructing a specification morphism from its design theory to a requirement specification. Procedures for propagating constraints, computing colimits, and constructing specification morphisms provide computational support for this approach. Although we conjecture that classification generally applies to the incremental application of knowledge represented in a taxonomy of design theories, this paper mainly focuses on algorithm design theories and presents several examples of design by classification.

1   Introduction

Mathematically-based techniques for software construction will play an increasing, if not critical, role in the future of software engineering. This paper is part of a broader research program to explore a mechanizable model of software development based on algebraic specifications and specification morphisms. An algebraic specification (or simply a *specification* or *theory*) defines a language and constrains its possible meanings via axioms and inference rules. Specifications can be used to express many kinds of software-related artifacts, including application domain models [22], formal requirements [1, 5, 14], abstract data types [7, 10], abstract algorithms [17], and programming languages [3, 9, 11]. A *specification morphism* (or simply a *morphism*) translates the language of one specification into the language of another specification in a way that preserves theorems. Specification morphisms underlie several aspects of software development, including the binding of parameters in parameterized specifications [4, 9], specification refinement and implementation [2, 15, 24], and algorithm design [12, 17, 25].

Despite years of research on specification languages and specification refinement, there has been relatively little work on formal techniques for constructing refinements, as opposed to verifying refinements that have been written manually. This paper addresses the following overall problem: given a specification S_0, construct a specification morphism $J : S_0 \rightarrow S_1$ that refines S_0 by using preexisting knowledge about standard generic designs.

Software often can be explained in terms of a relatively small collection of abstract design concepts. Examples of design abstractions include divide-and-conquer as an algorithm abstraction, heaps as a data structure abstraction, and a standard tracking architecture as a software system abstraction. An abstract design concept corresponds to a class of artifacts and the common structure of the class can be represented as a specification, called an *artifact theory*. Consider a class of related artifacts $\mathcal{A}$. Elements of $\mathcal{A}$ can be described via normal-form expressions in an appropriate artifact description language. Then, abstracting out those sorts and operations that vary over the elements we obtain the language of a *design theory* DT for $\mathcal{A}$ and an artifact scheme with free sort and operator symbols. The axioms of DT arise as conditions under which the sorts and operations can be instantiated in the artifact scheme to yield a correct concrete artifact. A specification AT containing the artifact scheme and parameterized on the design theory is called an *artifact theory*.

Greedy algorithms provide a particularly clear and well-known example of these concepts. Many algorithm design texts give a program scheme for greedy algorithms. If the free operators of the scheme have matroid structure, then the corresponding instance of the greedy scheme is provably correct with respect to its optimization objective [13]. Here, matroid theory is the design theory, and the artifact theory is parameterized on matroid theory and contains the greedy scheme.

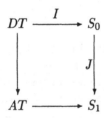

The diagram to the left shows how a design and artifact theory can be used to construct a refinement of a requirement specification S_0. The hard work in design is constructing a *classification arrow* (a morphism or interpretation between theories) I from the design theory DT to S_0, which explicates the $\mathcal{A}$-structure of S_0, or *classifies* S_0 as an $\mathcal{A}$-structure. Given I and $DT \longrightarrow AT$, then the refinement $J : S_0 \to S_1$ is automatically generated via a colimit construction which instantiates the parameter to AT.

In Section 3 a design theory for the algorithmic concept of divide-and-conquer is presented. Any particular divide-and-conquer algorithm corresponds to an interpretation from divide-and-conquer theory to a specification of the particular problem being solved. In particular, various interpretations from divide-and-conquer theory to a sorting specification correspond to various sorting algorithms, such as quicksort, mergesort or Batcher's sort. Given such an interpretation, a concrete sorting algorithm is obtained by instantiating a divide-and-conquer scheme with the translations of the symbols in divide-and-conquer theory.

Design theories can be arranged in a refinement hierarchy with specification morphisms providing the refinement links; e.g. a hierarchy of algorithm theories is presented in Figure 4 (see [17, 25]). *The main technical focus of this paper is showing how a refinement hierarchy of design theories supports incremental construction of refinements.*

The concepts and procedures described below are intended to improve the practicality of machine support for formal software development. This work is based on experience with algorithm design and optimization using KIDS (Kestrel Interactive Development System) which has been used to design over 70 algorithms from formal specifications [18]. Currently in KIDS, algorithm design is carried out by specialized procedures for each class of algorithms, called *design tactics* [17]. Classification allows us to duplicate and extend the functionality of the KIDS algorithm design tactics. Classification is being implemented in the successor to KIDS, called Specware [23]. We conjecture that classification will also support a much broader range of design tasks, such as the design of data structures, user interfaces, and software systems.

After reviewing basic concepts and notation in Section 2, the classification method is presented in Section 3. Two examples are presented in Section 4.

2 Basic Concepts and Notations

2.1 Specifications

As much as possible we adhere to conventional concepts and notation for first-order algebraic specification [6, 8, 26]. A *signature* $\Sigma = \langle S, \Omega \rangle$ consists of a set of sort symbols S and a family $\Omega = \langle \Omega_{v,s} \rangle$ of finite disjoint sets indexed by $S^* \times S$, where $\Omega_{v,s}$ is the set of operation symbols of rank $\langle v, s \rangle$. We write $f : v \to s$ to denote $f \in \Omega_{v,s}$ for $v \in S^*$, $s \in S$ when the signature is clear from context. As far as possible in this paper we treat truth-values as any other sort. Letting *boolean* be the sort symbol for truth values, then $\Omega_{v,boolean}$ is a set of predicate symbols for each $v \in S^*$. The usual logical connectives $\wedge$, $\vee$, $\neg$, $\Longrightarrow$, and $\Longleftrightarrow$ are treated as boolean operations. For any signature Σ, the Σ-*terms* are defined inductively in the usual way as the well-sorted composition of operator symbols and variables. A Σ-*formula* is a boolean-valued term built from Σ-terms and the quantifiers $\forall$ and $\exists$. A Σ-*sentence* is a closed formula. The generic term *expression* is used to refer to a term, formula, or sentence. A *specification* $T = \langle S, \Omega, Ax \rangle$ comprises a signature $\Sigma = \langle S, \Omega \rangle$ and a set of Σ-sentences Ax called *axioms*. Specification $T' = \langle S', \Omega', Ax' \rangle$ *extends* specification $T = \langle S, \Omega, Ax \rangle$ if $S \subseteq S'$, $\Omega_{v,s} \subseteq \Omega'_{v,s}$ for each $v \in S^*$, $s \in S$, and $Ax \subseteq Ax'$. Alternatively, we say T' is an *extension* of T. A *model* for T is a structure for $\langle S, \Omega \rangle$ that satisfies the axioms. We shall use modus ponens, substitution of equals/equivalents and other natural deduction *rules of inference* in T. A sentence e is a *theorem* of T, written $\vdash_T e$, if e is in the closure of the axioms under the rules of inference.

2.2 Morphisms

A *signature morphism* $I : \langle S, \Omega \rangle \to \langle S', \Omega' \rangle$ maps S to S' and Ω to Ω' such that the ranks of operations are preserved: if $f : v \to s$ in Ω and $v = v_1, \ldots v_n$ then $I(f) : I(v_1) \ldots I(v_n) \to I(s)$ in Ω'. A signature morphism extends in a unique way to a translation of expressions (as a homomorphism between term algebras) or sets of expressions. For Σ-expression e, let $I(e)$ denote its translation to a Σ'-expression. For a set of Σ-expressions E, let $I(E)$ denote the set of Σ'-expressions $\{I(e) \mid e \in E\}$. The notion of a signature morphism can be extended to a specification morphism by requiring that the translation preserve theorems. Let $T = \langle S, \Omega, Ax \rangle$ and $T' = \langle S', \Omega', Ax' \rangle$ be specifications and let $I : \langle S, \Omega \rangle \rightarrow \langle S', \Omega' \rangle$ be a signature morphism between them. I is a *specification morphism* if for every axiom $A \in Ax$, $I(A)$ is a theorem of T': $\vdash_{T'} I(A)$. It is straightforward to show that a specification morphism translates theorems of the source specification to theorems of the target specification.

Specifications and specification morphisms form a category. Colimits exist in this category and are easily computed.

The semantics of a specification morphism is given by a model construction. If $I : T1 \rightarrow T2$ is a specification morphism, then every model $\mathcal{M}$ of $T2$ can be made into a model of $T1$ by simply "forgetting" some structure of $\mathcal{M}$.

It will be convenient to generalize the definition of signature morphism slightly so that the translations of operator symbols are allowed to be expressions in the target specification and the translations of sort symbols are allowed to be constructions (e.g. products) over the target sorts. A symbol-to-expression morphism is called an *interpretation between theories* (or simply, an *interpretation*). An interpretation, notated $I : A \implies B$ or $A \overset{I}{\implies} B$, can be represented as a morphism into an extension by definitions of the target specification; i.e. as a pair of morphisms $A \rightarrow A\text{-}B \leftarrow B$. The specification $A\text{-}B$ is called the *mediator* of the interpretation. Composition of interpretations is straightforward.

2.3 Examples of Specifications and Morphisms

A *problem P* consists of a set of possible inputs $x \in D$ such that *input condition* $I(x)$ holds, and a set of outputs (also called *feasible solutions*) $z \in R$ such that some *output condition* $O(x, z)$ holds. A *problem specification* can be presented in the following format

> **Spec** *Problem-Theory*
>   **sorts** D, R
>   **op** $I : D \rightarrow Boolean$
>   **op** $O : D \times R \rightarrow Boolean$
> **end-spec**

A concrete problem can be presented via an interpretation from *Problem-Theory* into the specification of the problem. For example, consider the problem of sorting a bag of integers. A specification for sorting defines the concepts and laws necessary to support the definition of the sorting problem. The following domain specification is parameterized on a linear order — given any particular set S that is linearly ordered by $\leq$ we obtain a concrete sorting specification.

Spec *Sorting-Theory* $(\langle S, \leq \rangle :: Linear\text{-}Order)$
    imports *seq-over-linear-order*$(\langle S, \leq \rangle)$,
             bag-over-linear-order$(\langle S, \leq \rangle)$
      op *ordered* : $seq(S) \rightarrow boolean$
      op *bagify* : $seq(S) \rightarrow bag(S)$
      op *Sorting* $(x : bag(S) \mid true)$
          returns $(z : seq(S) \mid ordered(z) \wedge x = bagify(z))$
      axioms ... axioms defining the operations ...
end-spec

Here a program-like format is used for specifying problems:

    op $f\ (x : D \mid I(x))$
      returns $(z : R \mid O(x, z))$

which can be regarded as syntactic sugar for the following signature and axiom

    op $f : D \rightarrow R$
    ax $\forall (x : D)(I(x) \implies O(x, f(x)))$

We can present the sorting problem via an interpretation from *Problem-Theory* to *Sorting*:

$$
\begin{aligned}
D &\longmapsto bag(S) \\
I &\longmapsto \lambda(x)\, true \\
R &\longmapsto seq(S) \\
O &\longmapsto \lambda(x, z)\, (ordered(z) \wedge x = bagify(z)
\end{aligned}
$$

Again this interpretation is represented as a pair of morphisms. The mediator is a definitional extension to *Sorting-Theory* with the new symbols and definitional axioms

    op $I_m : seq(S) \rightarrow boolean$
    op $O_m : seq(S) \times bag(S) \rightarrow boolean$
    def $I_m(x) = true$
    def $O_m(x, z) = ordered(z) \wedge x = bagify(z)$

The morphism from *problem-theory* to the mediator is

$$
\begin{aligned}
D &\longmapsto bag(S) \\
I &\longmapsto I_m \\
R &\longmapsto seq(S) \\
O &\longmapsto O_m
\end{aligned}
$$

In the following we will present interpretations in the more convenient symbol-to-expression format.

3 Classification Approach to Design

The hard work in the classification approach to design lies in constructing interpretations from design theories to requirement specifications; that is, constructing classification arrows. There are two problems related to constructing classification arrows: (1) selecting an appropriate design theory, and (2) constructing an interpretation. Suppose that we have a refinement hierarchy of design theories with specification morphisms providing the refinement links. The refinement hierarchy provides a framework for solving the selection problem, and simultaneously providing a way to construct classification arrows incrementally. The stronger a theory is, the more structure that can be exploited in an artifact theory. Consequently, we want to construct an interpretation from the deepest possible theories in the hierarchy to the given requirement specification. This suggests an incremental procedure for accessing a hierarchic library of design theories and for constructing classification arrows. First, construct an interpretation from the root theory of the hierarchy. Then, iteratively, given an interpretation from design theory DT, try to construct an interpretation from DT's refinements in the hierarchy. If several succeed, then select one or keep several and repeat the process. If none succeed, then the current design theory exploits as much of the problem structure as possible (with respect to this classification hierarchy). A concrete design can be obtained by instantiating an artifact theory parameterized on the design theory.

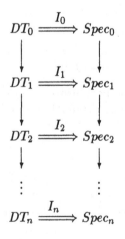

Ladder Construction

The process of incrementally constructing an interpretation is illustrated in the *ladder construction* diagram to the left. The left-hand side of the ladder is a path in a refinement hierarchy of design theories starting at the root. The ladder is constructed a rung at a time from the top down. The initial interpretation from problem theory to $Spec_0$ may be simple to construct. Subsequent rungs of the ladder are constructed by a constraint solving process that involves user choices, the propagation of consistency constraints, calculation of colimits, and constructive theorem proving [20].

Once we have constructed a classification arrow, then constructing a refinement of $Spec_0$ is straightforward. Elaborating a little on the presentation in the introduction, if we have a classification arrow $DT_n \stackrel{I_n}{\Longrightarrow} Spec_n$ represented by the pair of morphisms $DT_n \stackrel{M_n}{\longrightarrow} \text{DT-Spec}_n \stackrel{d_n}{\longleftarrow} S_n$, and an artifact theory AT_n that is parameterized on DT_n, then we can mechanically calculate a morphism that refines $Spec_n$ (by computing the pushout and then composing J_n and d_n):

$$DT_n \xrightarrow{M_n} DT\text{-}Spec_n \xleftarrow{d_n} Spec_n$$

$$\text{p.o.} \quad J_n \Big\downarrow \qquad \diagdown \ J_n \circ d_n$$

$$AT_n \longrightarrow AT\text{-}Spec_n$$

Finally, by composition we construct the refinement morphism

$$Spec_0 \longrightarrow AT\text{-}Spec_n$$

whose codomain contains the artifact specified in $Spec_0$.

The incremental situation in rung construction is this: given I_i and $DT_i \longrightarrow DT_{i+1}$

$$DT_i \xrightarrow{M_i} DT\text{-}Spec_i \xleftarrow{d_i} Spec_i$$

$$DT_{i+1} \cdots\cdots\blacktriangleright DT\text{-}Spec_{i+1} \blacktriangleleft\cdots Spec_{i+1}$$

with M_{i+1}

construct specifications $DT\text{-}Spec_{i+1}$ and $Spec_{i+1}$, and the dotted-line morphisms.

It is unlikely that a general automated method exists for constructing rungs. At present it seems that users must be involved in guiding the rung construction process. Our intent is to build an interface providing the user with various generic automated operations and libraries of standard components. The user applies various operators with the goal of filling out partial morphisms and specifications until the rung is complete. After each user-directed operation, various constraint propagation rules are automatically invoked to perform sound extensions to the partial morphisms and specifications in the rung diagram.

Strategies for rung construction vary according to the particular refinement $DT_i \rightarrow DT_{i+1}$. Different design theories call for different methods for constructing the morphism M_{i+1}. The construction of $Spec_{i+1}$ is mainly driven by the construction M_{i+1}. Typically $Spec_{i+1}$ is a conservative extension of $Spec_i$; however, in some cases arising during algorithm design (global search in particular), $Spec_{i+1}$ is a (conservative) extension of a colimit involving a refinement of $Spec_i$.

There are several obvious user-directed actions, including supplying translations for symbols and invoking a prover to verify that axioms translate to theorems. The user may translate a symbol into existing or new symbols, in which case the codomain specification $Spec_{i+1}$ is extended. The user may also elect to translate imported specifications via preexisting interpretations.

Constraint propagation rules are based on constraints that are generic to rung construction, such as commutativity of the rung diagram and preservation of operator rank under a morphism. Initially, we can propagate the symbol translations in I_i through $DT_i \xrightarrow{K_i} DT_{i+1}$. For example, if symbol a in DT_i is translated to b ($I_i : a \mapsto b$), then let $I_{i+1} : K_i(a) \mapsto b$. If two symbols of DT_i translate to the same symbol in DT_{i+1}, then they are effectively equated by the morphism, so the translation of either one will suffice.

The constraint that morphisms must preserve signatures under translations yields various propagation rules. If $I_i : f \mapsto g$ where $f : D \to R$ and $g : E \to S$, then propagation rules can add the translations $I_i : D \mapsto E$ and $I_i : R \mapsto S$.

There are several mechanizable techniques for constructing morphisms [20], one of which, called *unskolemization*, will be discussed here. The key idea in unskolemization is to use the axioms of the source specification as constraints on the translations of source symbols. Theorem-proving techniques are used to deduce symbol translations such that the source axioms are properly translated.

Skolemization is the process of replacing an existentially quantified variable z with a Skolem function over the universally quantified variables whose scope includes z. For example, the formula

$$\exists(w)\forall(x,y)\exists(z)\forall(u)H(w,x,y,z,u) \tag{1}$$

is skolemized to

$$\forall(x,y)\forall(u)H(a,x,y,f(x,y),u) \tag{2}$$

where f is a Skolem function of x and y and a is a Skolem function of no arguments – a Skolem constant. A *simple occurrence* of an operation symbol $g : v \to s$ in a sentence G is a subexpression of G of the form $g(x)$ where $x : v$ is a sequence of distinct variables that are universally quantified in G. Skolemization always replaces an existentially quantified variable with simple occurrences of a fresh operation symbol.

We are interested in the inverse process, *unskolemization*: given a sentence (such as (2)) containing identical simple occurrences of operation symbol g, say $g(x)$, replace g by a fresh existentially quantified variable in the scope of x (such as (1)).

Suppose that we are trying to complete a partial specification morphism σ from specification T to specification S. Let $f : v \to s$ be a function symbol of T that has no translation yet under σ. Suppose that F is a prenex normal form axiom in which all occurrences of f are identical and simple, and suppose that all other symbols in F are translatable under σ (i.e. the domain of σ includes all of the sort and operator symbols of F except for the function symbol f). To obtain a candidate translation for a function symbol f, we proceed as follows.

(1) *Unskolemize f in F yielding F'.* Since this has the effect of replacing each occurrence of f by a variable, each symbol in F' can be translated via σ.

(2) *Translate F'.* The translated sentence $\sigma(F')$ need not be an axiom of S. In order for σ to become a specification morphism we need an expression defining the translation of f in S. $\sigma(F')$ can be viewed as a constraint on the possible translations of f.

(3) *Attempt to prove $\sigma(F')$ in S.* A constructive proof will yield a (witness) expression $t(x)$ for f that depends only on the variables x. If the proof involves induction (resulting in a recursively defined witness), then we extend

the target specification with a fresh operator symbol and an axiom stating its recursive definition.

(4) *Extend the partial morphism σ by defining σ(f) to be t(x).* By construction this translation for f guarantees that σ properly translates the axiom F.

Other axioms that involve f may now be translatable, and if so, then we can attempt to prove that they translate to theorems. In this manner constructive theorem-proving can help to construct a specification morphism.

4 Examples

A partial taxonomy of algorithm classes that we have developed over the years is shown in Figure 4 [17]. Each algorithm theory is a refinement of *Problem-Theory.* The classification approach to algorithm design starts with the construction of an interpretation from *Problem-Theory* to the requirement specification; this interpretation makes explicit what problem is to be solved. Given the format for expressing requirements, this task is simple since it amounts to little more than parsing.

Ladder construction has the effect of making more structure explicit in the requirement specification so that appropriate problem-solving methods can be applied. For efficiency we want to find the strongest problem structure exhibited by the problem, so that the strongest problem-solving method can be applied.

Two examples are presented: Sorting and a Goods Distribution Problem (GDP). These are intended to clearly illustrate the concepts of this paper. They are not intended as complex or particularly challenging problems, nor are they presented in full detail. Sorting illustrates the use of classification in generating a new (divide-and-conquer) algorithm. The GDP example illustrates the synthesis of code to solve a problem by reducing it to an existing library code – it is necessary to set up the appropriate call to the code and to back-translate its results.

4.1 Sorting

The principle of divide-and-conquer is to solve small problem instances by some direct means, and to solve larger problem instances by decomposing them, solving the pieces, and composing the resulting solutions. Part of a specification for a simple divide-and-conquer design theory is given next. It provides the structure for a binary decomposition operator and corresponding composition operator. A general scheme for problem reduction theories (including divide-and-conquer) is given in [19].

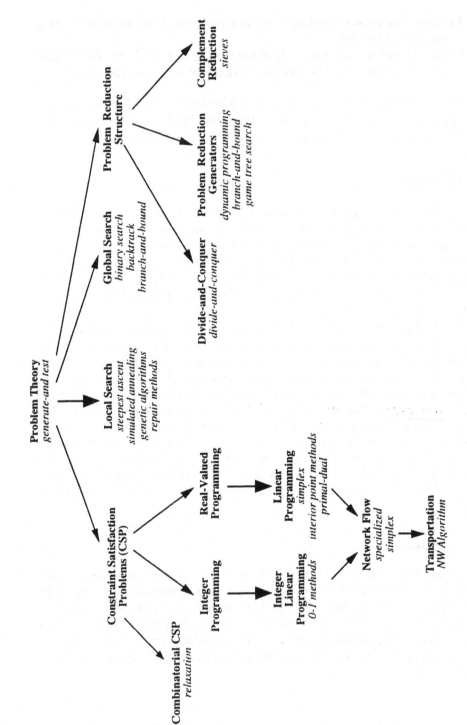

Fig. 1. Refinement Hierarchy of Algorithm Theories

Spec *Divide-and-Conquer*
Sorts

D	*input domain*
R	*output domain*

Operations

$I : D \rightarrow boolean$	*input condition*
$O : D \times R \rightarrow boolean$	*output condition*
$O_{Decompose} : D \times D \times D \rightarrow boolean$	*decomposition relation*
$O_{Compose} : R \times R \times R \rightarrow boolean$	*composition relation*
$primitive : D \rightarrow boolean$	*primitive predicate*

Axioms

$\forall(x_0, x_1, x_2 : D) \; \forall(z_0, z_1, z_2 : R)$	*Soundness axiom*

$$(I(x_0) \wedge O_{Decompose}(x_0, x_1, x_2)$$
$$\wedge \; O(x_1, z_1) \wedge O(x_2, z_2)$$
$$\wedge \; O_{Compose}(z_0, z_1, z_2)$$
$$\implies O(x_0, z_0))$$

...

end spec

The Soundness axiom relates O, $O_{Decompose}$, and $O_{Compose}$. It asserts that if (1) nonprimitive problem instance x_0 can decompose into two subproblem instances x_1 and x_2, (2) subproblem instances x_1 and x_2 have feasible solutions z_1 and z_2 respectively, (3) z_1 and z_2 can compose to form z_0, then z_0 is a feasible solution to input x_0. We omit the remaining axioms.

An artifact theory for divide-and-conquer is parameterized on divide-and-conquer (design) theory and contains a schematic definition for the top-level divide-and-conquer functions and schematic requirement specifications for subalgorithms *Directly-Solve*, *Decompose*, and *Compose*. For simplicity we omit well-foundedness constraints that ensure termination. With well-foundedness constraints in place, this theory can be shown to be consistent. That is, given any interpretation from *Divide-and-Conquer* and functions that satisfy the requirement specifications for the subalgorithms, the corresponding instance of the divide-and-conquer function satisfies its requirement specification (see [16]).

Spec *Divide-and-Conquer-Program (T :: Divide-and-Conquer)*

op *Directly-Solve* $(x : D \mid I(x) \wedge prim(x))$
    returns $(z : R \mid O(x, z))$

op *Decompose* $(x_0 : D \mid I(x_0) \wedge \neg prim(x_0))$
    returns $(\langle x_1, x_2 \rangle : D \times D \mid O_{Decompose}(x_0, x_1, x_2) \wedge I(x_1) \wedge I(x_2))$

op *Compose* $(z_1 : R, \; z_2 : R \mid I_{Compose}(z_1, z_2))$
    returns $(z_0 : R \mid O_{Compose}(z_0, z_1, z_2))$

def $F(x_0 : D \mid I(x_0))$
    returns $(z : R \mid O(x, z))$
    $= \textbf{if } prim(x_0)$
        then $Directly\text{-}Solve(x_0)$
        else $let(\langle x_1, x_2 \rangle : D \times D = Decompose(x_0))$
             $Compose(F(x_1),\ F(x_2))$

end spec

The development by classification of a divide-and-conquer algorithm for sorting begins with the construction of an interpretation from *Problem-theory* to *Sorting* theory (as described earlier):

$$
\begin{aligned}
D &\longmapsto bag(S) \\
I &\longmapsto \lambda(x)\ true \\
R &\longmapsto seq(S) \\
O &\longmapsto \lambda(x, z)\ ordered(z) \land x = bagify(z)
\end{aligned}
$$

Since the morphism from *Problem-theory* to *Divide-and-Conquer* is an inclusion, we can use straightforward propagation to obtain translations for the components of *Problem-theory* in *Divide-and-Conquer*:

$$
\begin{aligned}
D &\longmapsto bag(S) \\
I &\longmapsto \lambda(x)\ true \\
R &\longmapsto seq(S) \\
O &\longmapsto \lambda(x, z)\ ordered(z) \land x = bagify(z) \\
Primitive &\longmapsto\ ? \\
O_{Decompose} &\longmapsto\ ? \\
O_{Compose} &\longmapsto\ ?
\end{aligned}
$$

To complete the classification arrow we attempt to translate the remaining operators into expressions of *Sorting*. Alternative translations give rise to different sorting algorithms.

There are several ways to proceed. One tactic in KIDS is based on the choice of a standard decomposition operator from a library. The tactic then uses unskolemization on the soundness axiom to derive a specification for a composition operator. This approach allows the derivation of insertion sort, mergesort, and various parallel sorting algorithms [16, 21]. A dual approach is to choose a simple composition relation and use the Soundness axiom to derive a decomposition operator.

Suppose that we choose concatenation as a simple composition relation on the output domain $seq(integer)$. This gives us the partial signature morphism

$$D \longmapsto bag(S)$$
$$I \longmapsto \lambda(x) \; true$$
$$R \longmapsto seq(S)$$
$$O \longmapsto \lambda(x, z) \; ordered(z) \wedge x = bagify(z)$$
$$Primitive \longmapsto \; ?$$
$$O_{Decompose} \longmapsto \; ?$$
$$O_{Compose} \longmapsto \lambda(z_0, z_1, z_2) \; z_0 = concat(z_1, z_2)$$

The soundness axiom

$$\forall(x_0, x_1, x_2 : D) \; \forall(z_0, z_1, z_2 : R)$$
$$(I(x_0) \wedge O_{Decompose}(x_0, x_1, x_2)$$
$$\wedge O(x_1, z_1) \wedge O(x_2, z_2)$$
$$\wedge O_{Compose}(z_0, z_1, z_2)$$
$$\implies O(x_0, z_0))$$

cannot yet be translated into *Sorting* because of $O_{Decompose}$. However, unskolemization on operator symbol $O_{Decompose}$ replaces the occurrence of $O_{Decompose}$ by a variable:

$$\forall(x_0, x_1, x_2 : D) \; \exists(y : boolean) \; \forall(z_0, z_1, z_2 : R)$$
$$(I(x_0) \wedge y \wedge O(x_1, z_1) \wedge O(x_2, z_2) \wedge O_{Compose}(z_0, z_1, z_2)$$
$$\implies O(x_0, z_0)).$$

This formula can be translated via the partial signature morphism yielding:

$$\forall(x_0, x_1, x_2 : bag(integer)) \; \exists(y : boolean) \; \forall(z_0, z_1, z_2 : seq(integer))$$
$$(true \wedge y$$
$$\wedge ordered(z_1) \wedge x_1 = bagify(z_1)$$
$$\wedge ordered(z_2) \wedge x_2 = bagify(z_2)$$
$$\wedge z_0 = concat(z_1, z_2)$$
$$\implies ordered(z_0) \wedge x_0 = bagify(z_0))$$

A straightforward proof of this formula in *Sorting* results in a constructive definition of $O_{Decompose}$ (see [16]):

$$x_0 = x_1 \uplus x_2 \wedge x_1 \leq x_2$$

where $\uplus$ is bag-union and $x_1 \leq x_2$ means that each element of bag x_1 is less-than-or-equal to each element of bag x_2. This is, of course, a specification for a partition operation in a Quicksort. If we take this as the translation of $O_{Decompose}$, then we know that the soundness axiom translates to a theorem in *Sorting-theory* by construction.

The remaining steps in constructing this classification arrow include unskolemizing another axiom to obtain a translation for the *prim* predicate, and translating and proving other axioms. The resulting algorithm is a variant of Quicksort. Once the classification arrow is complete, *divide-and-conquer-program-theory* can be instantiated to obtain concrete code; see [16, 19] for details.

4.2 Distribution of Goods

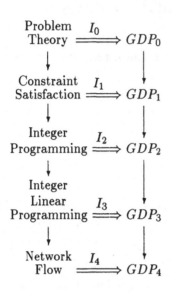

Problem
Theory $\xRightarrow{I_0}$ GDP_0

Constraint
Satisfaction $\xRightarrow{I_1}$ GDP_1

Integer
Programming $\xRightarrow{I_2}$ GDP_2

Integer
Linear
Programming $\xRightarrow{I_3}$ GDP_3

Network
Flow $\xRightarrow{I_4}$ GDP_4

GDP Ladder Construction

Suppose that a large organization needs to rationalize its distribution system and to lower its shipping costs. The distribution system comprises factories that produce goods, warehouses that store the goods, and outlets that sell the goods. There is a known cost for shipping goods from factory to warehouse and from warehouse to outlet. The problem is to find a least cost flow of goods from the factories through the warehouses to the outlets. The figure to the left shows the ladder construction that enables us to classify this problem as a network flow problem and generate code to solve it by invoking a pre-existing network flow code.

The natural first approach to modeling this problem domain is to introduce three sorts called *Factory*, *Warehouse*, and *Retail-Outlet*. A little further work on the nature of the problem constraints leads to the conclusion that these distinctions are cumbersome. The shipping routes from *Factory* to *Warehouse* are a distinct type from routes from *Warehouse* to *Retail-Outlet*. More seriously, factories and warehouses may coincide, similarly warehouses and retail outlets, and even factories and retail outlets. These observations suggest that we abstract a little and use a generalized sort called *depot*. Associated with each depot is a *supply* of goods. Depots that represent factories have a positive supply; retail outlets consume goods, so their supply is negative; and warehouses have zero supply since goods flow through them. A specification for this goods distribution problem appears in Figure 2. For simplicity we focus on the problem of finding a feasible distribution flow:

$$GDP\ (dpts : set(Depot),\ supply : map(Depot,\ Supply\text{-}quant)$$
$$|\ domain(supply) = dpts)$$
$$\textbf{returns}\ (flow : map(Channel,\ Flow\text{-}quant)$$
$$|\ domain(flow) = cart\text{-}product(dpts,\ dpts)$$
$$\wedge\ \forall(ch : Channel)\ (ch \in domain(flow) \implies 0 \leq flow(ch))$$
$$\wedge\ balanced\text{-}flow(dpts,\ supply,\ flow))$$

This problem specification is easily expressed as an interpretation from *Problem-Theory* to *DISTRIBUTION-SYSTEM*:

Spec *GDP*

imports *arithmetic, map, set, tuple*

sorts *Depot,*
       Channel = tuple(Depot, Depot),
       Supply-quant = integer,
       Flow-quant = integer

def *FLOW-OUT*
  (d : Depot, dpts : set(Depot), flow : map(Channel, Flow-quant)
  | d ∈ dpts ∧ domain(flow) = cart-product(dpts, dpts)) : Flow-quant
  = reduce(+, image(λ(e : Depot) flow(⟨d, e⟩), dpts))

def *FLOW-IN*
  (d : Depot, dpts : set(Depot), flow : map(Channel, Flow-quant)
  | d ∈ dpts ∧ domain(flow) = cart-product(dpts, dpts)) : Flow-quant
  = reduce(+, image(λ(e : Depot) flow(⟨e, d⟩), dpts))

def *BALANCED-FLOW*
  (dpts : set(Depot),
  supply : map(Depot, Supply-quant),
  flow : map(Channel, Flow-quant)
  | domain(supply) = dpts
    ∧ domain(flow) = cart-product(dpts, dpts)) : boolean
  = ∀(d : Depot)
    (d ∈ dpts
      ⟹ flow-out(d, dpts, flow)−flow-in(d, dpts, flow) = supply(d))

op *GDP(dpts : set(Depot), supply : map(Depot, Supply-quant)*
       | domain(supply) = dpts)
returns *(flow : map(Channel, Flow-quant)*
      | domain(flow) = cart-product(dpts, dpts)
        ∧ ∀(ch : Channel)(ch ∈ domain(flow) ⟹ 0 ≤ flow(ch))
      ∧ balanced-flow(dpts, supply, flow))

end-spec

Fig. 2. GDP Specification

$D \longmapsto set(Depot) \times map(Depot, Supply\text{-}quant)$
$I \longmapsto \lambda(dpts, supply)\ domain(supply) = dpts$
$R \longmapsto map(Channel, Flow\text{-}quant)$
$O \longmapsto \lambda(dpts, supply, flow)$
       $domain(flow) = cart\text{-}product(dpts, dpts)$
         $\wedge\ \forall(ch : Channel)\ (ch \in domain(flow) \implies 0 \leq flow(ch))$
         $\wedge\ balanced\text{-}flow(dpts, supply, flow)$

4.3 Constraint Satisfaction Problems

The goal now is to classify the structure of the goods-distribution problem (GDP) so that we can design a good algorithm for it. We try to classify the goods-distribution problem towards the classes of Operations Research algorithms in Figure 1.

The first step is to see if GDP can be classified as a Constraint Satisfaction Problem (CSP). Intuitively, the goal of a CSP is to produce an assignment of values to some finite set of variables subject to contraints on the assignments. A specification of CSP is:

> **Spec** *Constraint-Satisfaction-Problem*
> **imports** *Boolean, map, set*
> **sorts** *D, Var, Val*
> **op** $I : D \rightarrow boolean$
> **op** *Variables* $: D \rightarrow set(Var)$
> **op** *Legal-Val* $: D, Var, map(Var, Val) \rightarrow boolean$
> **op** *O-Constraint* $: D, map(Var, Val) \rightarrow Boolean$
> **op** *O-CSP* $: D, map(Var, Val) \rightarrow Boolean$
> **def** $O\text{-}CSP(x, vm) = (domain(vm) = Variables(x)$
> $\qquad\qquad\qquad \wedge\, \forall(v : Var)(v \in domain(vm)$
> $\qquad\qquad\qquad\qquad\qquad\qquad \implies Legal\text{-}Val(x, v, vm))$
> $\qquad\qquad\qquad \wedge\, O\text{-}constraint(x, vm))$
>
> **end-spec**

The intention is that sort D provides input data constrained by input condition I. Var and Val are the sorts of variables and values respectively. *Variables* computes the set of variables for a given input and *Legal-Val* constrains the values that can be assigned to a particular variable. The output sort is $map(Var, Val)$ and is subject to the further condition *O-constraint*. The view of CSPs as problems is carried by the refinement morphism from *Problem-Theory* to *Constraint-Satisfaction-Problem*:

$$
\begin{aligned}
D &\longmapsto D \\
I &\longmapsto I \\
R &\longmapsto map(Var, Val) \\
O &\longmapsto O\text{-}CSP
\end{aligned}
$$

To classify GDP as a CSP we perform propagation of the symbol translations from *Problem-Theory* $\xrightarrow{I_0}$ *GDP*, yielding the main translations in Figure 3. Identification of the *map* subspecification in *CSP* with the corresponding map in *GDP* triggers propagation rules that infer

$$
\begin{aligned}
Var &\mapsto Depot \times Depot \\
Val &\mapsto Flow\text{-}Quant
\end{aligned}
$$

i.e. that the variables are pairs of depots and the values being assigned to the variables are flow quantities. These translations are shown in small font inside

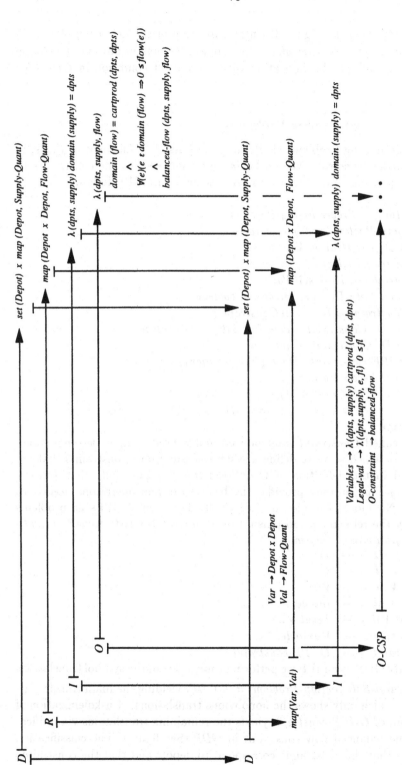

Fig. 3. Classifying GDP as a CSP

the main translations in Figure 3. Unskolemization of the definition of O-CSP on the operator symbols *Variables, Legal-val,* and *O-constraint* easily yields the remaining translations via unification with the output condition in GDP (See figure).

4.4 Integer Programming Problems

Integer Programming Problems (IPPs) are one possible refinement of CSPs, in that they further constrain *Vals* to be *integers,* and restrict the constraints to be a set of equations of a certain form. A specification of IPP follows:

> **Spec** *Integer-Programming-Problem*
> **imports** *Boolean, integer, map, set*
> **sorts** D, *Constraint, Var*
> **op** $I : D \rightarrow boolean$
> **op** $Variables : D \rightarrow set(Var)$
> **op** $Legal\text{-}Val : D, Var, integer \rightarrow boolean$
> **op** $Constraints : D \rightarrow set(Constraint)$
> **op** $H : D, Constraint, map(Var, integer) \rightarrow integer$
> **op** $b : D, Constraint \rightarrow integer$
> **op** $O\text{-}IPP\text{-}constraint : Dmap(Var, integer) \rightarrow boolean$
> **def** $O\text{-}IPP\text{-}constraint(x, vm)$
> $\qquad = \forall(c : Constraint)(c \in Constraints(x)$
> $\qquad\qquad\qquad \Longrightarrow H(x, c, vm) = b(x, c))$
> **end-spec**

A new sort called *Constraint* is introduced and is used to index two new functions H and b which serve to define a system of equational constraints that are encapsulated in the definition of *O-IPP-constraint.* Again, note that *Integer-Programming-Problem* only provides the basic sorts and operations needed to state IPPs. No more is needed at this point. The view of IPPs as problems is carried by the refinement morphism from *Constraint-Satisfaction-Problem* to *Integer-Programming-Problem:*

$$
\begin{array}{rcl}
D & \longmapsto & D \\
I & \longmapsto & I \\
Var & \longmapsto & Var \\
Val & \longmapsto & integer \\
Legal\text{-}Val & \longmapsto & Legal\text{-}Val \\
Variables & \longmapsto & Variables \\
O\text{-}constraint & \longmapsto & O\text{-}IPP\text{-}constraint
\end{array}
$$

To classify GDP as an IPP we perform propagation of the symbol translations from *Constraint-Satisfaction-Problem* $\xrightarrow{I_1}$ *GDP*, yielding the main translations in Figure 4 (which only shows the nonobvious translations). Unskolemization of the definition of *O-IPP-constraint* yields the remaining translations via unification with the balanced flow constraint in *GDP* (See figure). The classification arrow shows that the constraints correspond to depots and that the constraints check whether the flows in and out match the supply for each depot.

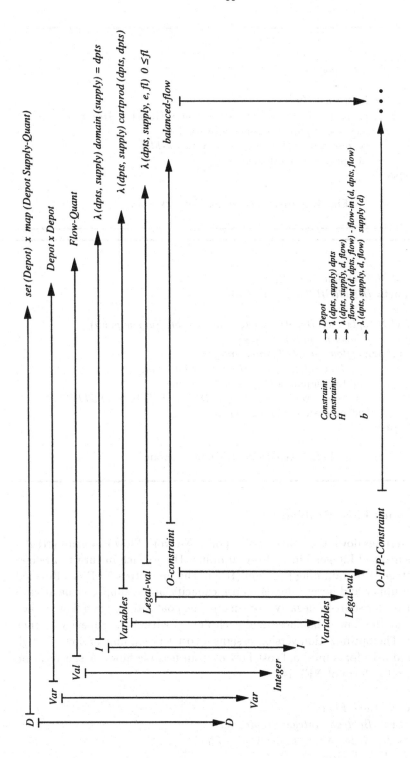

Fig. 4. Classifying GDP as an IPP

Spec *MODFLO-Solver* (*NF* :: *Network-Flow*)

  def *NF-solve*($x : D \mid I(x)$)
    returns (*flow* : *map*(*ARC*, *integer*) $\mid$ *domain*(*flow*) = *Arcs*(*x*) $\wedge$ ...)
    = ... code to compute a feasible network flow
          expressed over the symbols of *Network-Flow*
          and programming language *L* ...
end-spec

Fig. 5. Artifact Theory for Network Flow

Spec *MODFLO-Solver-for-GDP*
  imports *DISTRIBUTION-SYSTEM*

  def *GDP*(*dpts* : *set*(*Depot*), *supply* : *map*(*Depot*, *Supply-quant*)
      $\mid$ *domain*(*supply*) = *dpts*)
    returns (*flow* : *map*(*Channel*, *integer*)
        $\mid$ *domain*(*flow*) = *cart-product*(*dpts*, *dpts*) $\wedge$ ...)
    = ... code to compute a feasible network flow
          expressed over the symbols of *DISTRIBUTION-SYSTEM*
          and programming language *L* ...
end-spec

Fig. 6. Goods Distribution Program

4.5 Network Flow Problems

We skip two rungs down the ladder at this point. Network Flow Problems (NFPs) are a refinement of Integer Linear Programming (ILP) which in turn is a refinement of Integer Programming Problem (IPP). The input to a NFP is a directed graph with upper and lower bounds on arc capacity and a supply value at each node (positive for sources, negative for sinks). The goal is to assign a flow to each arc such that the flow is balanced and each flow is within the capacity bounds on the arc. The optimization version assigns a cost to each unit of flow through each arc and asks for a minimal cost flow over all feasible flows. A specification of the feasibility form of NFP is:

Spec *Network-Flow*
  imports *Boolean, integer, tuple, set*
  sorts *D, Node, Arc* = *tuple*(*Node, Node*)
  op *I* : *D* → *boolean*
  op *Nodes* : *D* → *set*(*Node*)

op $Arcs : D \rightarrow set(Arc)$
op $Arc\text{-}lb\text{-}capacity : D,\ Node,\ Node,\ integer \rightarrow boolean$
op $Arc\text{-}ub\text{-}capacity : D,\ Node,\ Node,\ integer \rightarrow boolean$
op $Supply : D,\ Node \rightarrow integer$
end-spec

Suppose that we have continued the ladder construction and finally managed to classify GDP as a Network Flow problem:

$$
\begin{aligned}
D &\longmapsto set(Depot) \times map(Depot, Supply\text{-}quant) \\
I &\longmapsto \lambda(dpts, supply)\ domain(supply) = dpts \\
Node &\longmapsto Depot \\
Nodes &\longmapsto \lambda(dpts, supply)\ dpts \\
Arc &\longmapsto Channel \\
Arcs &\longmapsto \lambda(dpts, supply)\ cart\text{-}product(dpts, dpts) \\
Arc\text{-}lb\text{-}capacity &\longmapsto \lambda(dpts, supply, d1, d2, i)\ 0 \leq i \\
Arc\text{-}ub\text{-}capacity &\longmapsto \lambda(dpts, supply, d1, d2, i)\ true \\
Supply &\longmapsto \lambda(dpts, supply, d : Depot)\ supply(d)
\end{aligned}
$$

Once we have a problem classified as a *NFP*, then the artifact theory (called a program theory) shown in Figure 5 can be used to obtain concrete code. The classification arrow from *NFP* to *GDP* binds the parameter in the program theory and a pushout calculation carries out the instantiation. The effect is to extend the GDP specification with the translated program scheme as shown in Figure 6.

The actual program theory in our system sets up a foreign function call to a FORTRAN network flow solver called MODFLO. In effect MODFLO has been wrapped in a well-defined interface, providing an example of how "legacy" code can be made to work in a formal software development process. An alternative approach to solving *GDP* using a network flow algorithm would be via problem reduction [16] which is a special case of a connection between specifications [20]. The necessary inferences would be difficult in general, whereas here we have achieved a similar result with a sequence of relatively easy propagation and unskolemization steps.

5 Concluding Remarks

The examples in this paper have shown how a refinement hierarchy of algorithm theories can be used to support algorithm design. We believe that the classification approach can usefully support a much broader range of design tasks, such as the design of data structures, user interfaces, and software systems. data structure design and software system design. For example, we conjecture that a hierarchy of software architecture theories could be used to support software system design. An architecture theory is parameterized on the interfaces to its component modules and its body specifies exported services, interconnections between components, system invariants, etc. More generally, we conjecture that classification is applicable to the design of any kind of artifact whose requirements can be specified and for which standard design abstractions can be expressed in a refinement hierarchy.

The ladder construction technique is being implemented in Specware [23], a specification-based development system at Kestrel Institute. We believe that this system will be much more flexible and easy to use than KIDS because a few general mechanisms support design directly from a taxonomic library of design theories without relying on complex, hard-to-write design tactics.

Acknowledgements

Discussions with Richard Jüllig, Junbo Liu, and Y.V. Srinivas helped to clarify the ideas presented above. This research was supported by the Air Force Office of Scientific Research under Contract F49620-91-C-0073, by the Office of Naval Research under Grant N00014-93-C-0056, and by ARPA and Rome Laboratories under Contracts F30602-91-C-0043 and F30602-95-10018.

References

1. ASTESIANO, E., AND WIRSING, M. An introduction to ASL. In *Program Specification and Transformation*, L. Meertens, Ed. North-Holland, Amsterdam, 1987, pp. 343–365.

2. BLAINE, L., AND GOLDBERG, A. DTRE – a semi-automatic transformation system. In *Constructing Programs from Specifications*, B. Möller, Ed. North-Holland, Amsterdam, 1991, pp. 165–204.

3. BROY, M., WIRSING, M., AND PEPPER, P. On the algebraic definition of programming languages. *ACM Transactions on Programming Languages and Systems 9*, 1 (January 1987), 54–99.

4. EHRIG, H., KREOWSKI, H. J., THATCHER, J., WAGNER, E., AND WRIGHT, J. Parameter passing in algebraic specification languages. In *Proceedings, Workshop on Program Specification* (Aarhus, Denmark, Aug. 1981), vol. 134, pp. 322–369.

5. EHRIG, H., AND MAHR, B. *Fundamentals of Algebraic Specification, vol. 2: Module Specifications and Constraints*. Springer-Verlag, Berlin, 1990.

6. ENDERTON, H. B. *A Mathematical Introduction to Logic*. Academic Press, New York, 1972.

7. GOGUEN, J. A., THATCHER, J. W., AND WAGNER, E. G. An initial algebra approach to the specification, correctness and implementation of abstract data types. In *Current Trends in Programming Methodology, Vol. 4: Data Structuring*, R. Yeh, Ed. Prentice-Hall, Englewood Cliffs, NJ, 1978.

8. GOGUEN, J. A., THATCHER, J. W., WAGNER, E. G., AND WRIGHT, J. B. Initial algebra semantics and continuous algebras. *Journal of the ACM 24*, 1 (January 1977), 68–95.

9. GOGUEN, J. A., AND WINKLER, T. Introducing OBJ3. Tech. Rep. SRI-CSL-88-09, SRI International, Menlo Park, California, 1988.

10. GUTTAG, J. V., AND HORNING, J. J. The algebraic specification of abstract data types. *Acta Inf. 10* (1978), 27–52.

11. HOARE, C. Varieties of programming languages. Tech. rep., Programming Research Group, University of Oxford, Oxford, UK, 1989.

12. LOWRY, M. R. Algorithm synthesis through problem reformulation. In *Proceedings of the 1987 National Conference on Artificial Intelligence* (Seattle, WA, July 13-17, 1987).

13. PAPADIMITRIOU, C. H., AND STEIGLITZ, K. *Combinatorial Optimization: Algorithms and Complexity.* Prentice Hall, Englewood Cliffs, NJ, 1982.

14. PARTSCH, H. *Specification and Transformation of Programs: A Formal Approach to Software Development.* Springer-Verlag, New York, 1990.

15. SANNELLA, D., AND TARLECKI, A. Toward formal development of programs from algebraic specifications: Implementations revisited. *Acta Informatica 25*, 3 (1988), 233-281.

16. SMITH, D. R. Top-down synthesis of divide-and-conquer algorithms. *Artificial Intelligence 27*, 1 (September 1985), 43-96. (Reprinted in *Readings in Artificial Intelligence and Software Engineering*, C. Rich and R. Waters, Eds., Los Altos, CA, Morgan Kaufmann, 1986.).

17. SMITH, D. R., AND LOWRY, M. R. Algorithm theories and design tactics. In *Proceedings of the International Conference on Mathematics of Program Construction, LNCS 375*, L. van de Snepscheut, Ed. Springer-Verlag, Berlin, 1989, pp. 379-398. (reprinted in *Science of Computer Programming*, 14(2-3), October 1990, pp. 305-321).

18. SMITH, D. R. KIDS - a semi-automatic program development system. *IEEE Transactions on Software Engineering Special Issue on Formal Methods in Software Engineering 16*, 9 (September 1990), 1024-1043.

19. SMITH, D. R. Structure and design of problem reduction generators. In *Constructing Programs from Specifications*, B. Möller, Ed. North-Holland, Amsterdam, 1991, pp. 91-124.

20. SMITH, D. R. Constructing specification morphisms. *Journal of Symbolic Computation, Special Issue on Automatic Programming 15*, 5-6 (May-June 1993), 571-606.

21. SMITH, D. R. Derivation of parallel sorting algorithms. In *Parallel Algorithm Derivation and Program Transformation*, R. Paige, J. Reif, and R. Wachter, Eds. Kluwer Academic Publishers, New York, 1993, pp. 55-69.

22. SRINIVAS, Y. V. Algebraic specification for domains. In *Domain Analysis: Acquisition of Reusable Information for Software Construction*, R. Prieto-Diaz and G. Arango, Eds. IEEE Computer Society Press, Los Alamitos, CA, 1991, pp. 90-124.

23. SRINIVAS, Y. V., AND JÜLLIG, R. Specware:[tm] formal support for composing software. In *Proceedings of the Conference on Mathematics of Program Construction*, B. Moeller, Ed. Springer-Verlag, Berlin, 1995. Lecture Notes in Computer Science, Vol. 947.

24. TURSKI, W. M., AND MAIBAUM, T. E. *The Specification of Computer Programs.* Addison-Wesley, Wokingham, England, 1987.

25. VELOSO, P. A. Problem solving by interpretation of theories. In *Contemporary Mathematics*, vol. 69. American Mathematical Society, Providence, Rhode Island, 1988, pp. 241-250.

26. WIRSING, M. Algebraic specification. In *Formal Models and Semantics*, J. van Leeuwen, Ed., vol. B of *Handbook of Theoretical Computer Science*. MIT Press/Elsevier, 1990, pp. 675-788.

Semantic Foundations for Embedding HOL in Nuprl

Douglas J. Howe

Bell Labs
600 Mountain Ave., Room 2B-438
Murray Hill, NJ 07974, USA.

Abstract. We give a new semantics for Nuprl's constructive type theory that justifies a useful embedding of the logic of the HOL theorem prover inside Nuprl. The embedding gives Nuprl effective access to most of the large body of formalized mathematics that the HOL community has amassed over the last decade. The new semantics is dramatically simpler than the old, and gives a novel and general way of adding set-theoretic equivalence classes to untyped functional programming languages.

1 Introduction

Nuprl [5] and HOL [9] are interactive theorem proving systems with a number of similarities: their logics are higher-order type theories, their approaches to automated reasoning are based on that of LCF [8], and their main application has been to formal reasoning about computation. However, the two logics are very different in a number of ways. Nuprl has a constructive type theory, based on a type theory of Martin-Löf[16]. The theory contains a programming language, and all objects have a computational interpretation. Programs are reasoned about directly in logic, and the constructivity of the theory means that programs can be synthesised from proofs. On the other hand, HOL's theory is classical, and the way mathematics is encoded is similar to the way ordinary mathematics is done in ZF set theory. Functions are built in, but all other objects, such as integers and lists, are given set-theory-like encodings with the aid of the "select operator" $@x \in T.\ P(x)$, which denotes some x of type T such that $P(x)$.

The HOL theory has proven to be well suited to formalizing much of the mathematics of computation. The system has attracted a large number of users (almost certainly more than any theorem-proving system), and a great deal of the effort in the HOL community has gone into building the libraries of formal mathematics needed for verifying hardware and software of practical interest. A good picture of the scope and extent of this work can be obtained from the proceedings of recent meetings of the annual HOL conference (for example, [2]).

Nuprl's type theory offers a number of advantages over HOL's logic.

- *Expressive power of the type system.* Nuprl has subtypes and dependent function types. Also, through the use of universes and "sigma" types, one can express modules of the kind found in Standard ML [18].

- *Constructivity.* Experience with Nuprl has shown that for the mathematics of ordinary programs, constructivity comes at essentially no cost. Thus it seems to be a strict loss that one cannot extract programs from formal proofs in HOL.
- *Writing programs.* Nuprl includes a programming language which, while primitive, includes many of the features, such as function definition by general recursion, of a conventional functional programming language.

Most of these features have been recognized in the HOL community as desirable for HOL. See, for example, [17, 15, 20].

There have been a number of substantial applications of Nuprl (see [14] for a recent example), but there has been nothing like the sustained effort of the HOL community in formalizing mathematics useful for verification.

There are two main motivations for the present work. The first is to make up for Nuprl's relative lack of libraries of mathematics. The proposed solution is to reconcile the semantics of the two logics so that most of the mathematics developed in HOL can be directly imported into Nuprl. The goal here is a practical one, to be able to effectively use HOL mathematics in Nuprl proofs. Just about any theorem-prover can embed the logic of any other simply by formalizing the syntax of proofs, but this is not effective. We need a strong connection between the mathematics developed in Nuprl and the mathematics imported from HOL, so that HOL facts will be applicable in Nuprl proofs, and furthermore will be applicable in such a way that Nuprl's automated reasoning programs can readily incorporate them. We also need to be careful not to let HOL's classical nature spill over and destroy the constructivity of Nuprl proofs.

All the work in reconciling the semantics is on the Nuprl side. We give a new semantics of Nuprl which combines set theory with the operational semantics of Nuprl's programming language. In this semantics one can find standard models of HOL's type theory.

The other main motivation for this work is to fix a long-standing and serious problem with the semantics of Nuprl's logic. The problem is the complexity of the semantics. The semantics is operationally derived: one starts with an untyped programming language presented as a set of terms together with an evaluation relation, and then inductively builds a type system. A type system is a partial function from terms to partial equivalence relations over terms ("PERS"), and the terms in the domain of the function are called types. Thus the meaning of a type is a set of terms together with an equivalence relation over the set.

Deriving the semantics of types from an operational semantics of an untyped programming language has several advantages. One is that the approach is fairly generic. For example, there is no difficulty in substituting a language like the functional part of Standard ML (ignoring ML's types) for Nuprl's current language. Another advantage is the flexibility and expressive power of the type system.

The main cost of this approach has been the use of PERs. The PER type system itself is not particularly complicated — the difficulties arise when one extends the semantics to sequents, or "hypothetical judgements" to use Martin-

Löf's terminology. Consider, for example, the rule

$$\frac{\Gamma, x{:}T_1 \vdash b \in T_2 \quad \Gamma \vdash T_1 \in U_1}{\Gamma \vdash \lambda x.\, b \in T_1 \to T_2}$$

Ignoring the second premise and the list Γ of typing assumptions, a naive reading of the rule would say that in order to show that $\lambda x.\, b$ has type $T_1 \to T_2$, it suffices to assume x has type T_1 and prove that b has type T_2. But this is not sufficient. In order for $\lambda x.\, b$ to have type $T_1 \to T_2$, it must map equal members of T_1 to equal members of T_2. Thus, for this rule to be valid, the truth of the first premise must guarantee this "functionality" of $\lambda x.\, b$.

This gives rise to a "functionality semantics" for sequents. A functionality semantics is given by Martin-Löf in [16]. This semantics is itself fairly complicated. However, for technical reasons having to do with several essential practical considerations, including reasoning about general recursive programs, and collapsing Martin-Löf's four forms on judgement into one, Nuprl requires a more refined notion of functionality. Chapter 8 of the Nuprl book [5] gives a sketch of this semantics. For a better idea of the complications involved, see Allen's PhD thesis [3]. Because of this complexity, many of the existing Nuprl rules have not been completely verified, and there is a strong barrier to extending or modifying the theory. In particular, it has been a barrier to changing Nuprl to have a programming language more like SML.

The new semantics completely does away with PERs and functionality. Instead, types are simply sets of terms, and sequents essentially have the naive semantics: the sequent

$$x_1{:}A_1, \ldots, x_n{:}A_n \vdash t \in T$$

will be true if t is a member of T whenever the x_i are terms such that x_i is a member of A_i for $1 \leq i \leq n$.

Section 2 gives the technical core of the paper. In it, we show how to add objects of set theory to the operational semantics of a programming language. These objects come from a universe V of sets, whose members include functions (represented as graphs), pairs, and so on, as well as sets of these objects and equivalence classes over these sets. The approach is to extend the evaluation relation of the programming language with rules for objects in V. The technical work is to make this coherent. Because of space considerations, Section 2 does not deal with all of Nuprl's (rather large) language.

The hardest part of making this semantics work is dealing with equivalence classes. These are included to account for Nuprl's quotient type, which is essential for implementing abstract data types in Nuprl. In Nuprl, an ADT is represented by a sigma type, each member of which is a tuple consisting of an implementation type together with implementations of the operators of the ADT. The operators must satisfy the equations of the ADT. Often a desired implementation type does not have the right equality. Consider, for example, the implementation of rational numbers as pairs of integers. In this case, a quotient must be used to give the implementation type the right equality.

A quotient type in Nuprl has the form $(x, y) : A//E$, where x and y bind in E. E represents an equivalence relation over the type A. In the PER model, this is easily explained. It is simply the type that has the same members as A, but whose equivalence relation is defined by E. In the new semantics, the type will contain equivalence classes, in the usual set theoretic sense, formed from A. Since we also want the quotient to be computationally meaningful, the type will also contain "polymorphic equivalence classes" that can be computed with.

A point worth emphasizing about the new semantics is that is not particular to any programming language. When constructing V, one needs to know what the possible forms of data values are (and the current construction covers most of the forms in existing programming languages), but almost all of the technical development is independent of the rest of the language. The approach to operational semantics builds on our work described in [12]. Evidence for the robustness of this approach with respect to changes in the programming language can be found, for example, in the adaptations of our approach by Pitts and Gordon, described in [19, 7].

In Section 3, we show how to apply this semantics to the Nuprl logic as described in [5]. This is done by adding, to the programming language, operators representing Nuprl's type constructors, together with rules specifying how to "evaluate" instances of these constructors to get a member of V representing the set of all members of a type. We have to make a small change to the Nuprl rules to accommodate the new semantics. In particular, the rules for the quotient type need to incorporate the new constructor for values of the type. Also, we need to slight modify the extensionality rule (which reduces proving $f \in A \to B$ to proving $f(x) \in B$ for all $x \in A$). These rule changes have no significant practical import for Nuprl. It should be easy to adapt old proofs to use the new rules.

In Section 4 we sketch how to use this new semantics to justify an embedding of HOL. We are currently in the process of actually using this embedding. The connection between HOL and Nuprl has been implemented, and we have begun the importation of HOL theories. The immediate goal is to use these theories in a project to use Nuprl to verify the SCI cache-coherency protocol [1]. Details on the embedding of HOL and its practical applications will be the subject of a future paper.

In the last section we discuss some related work and discuss some extensions of Nuprl justified by our semantics. The appendix gives a proof sketch postponed from the body of the paper.

2 Semantics

The semantics has an operational flavour. We start with the standard cumulative hierarchy of set theory. We modify encodings of objects like functions, equivalence classes and the sets that will be used to stand for types in the type theory, so that they are distinguishable via "tags". We then remove certain ill-behaved sets, calling the resulting universe of sets V.

We then construct a "programming" language based on V and the terms of Nuprl. The semantics of this language is given as a set of rules inductively defining an evaluation relation $\Downarrow$. These rules explain how to evaluate, for example, the application of a set theoretic function, represented as a graph, to an arbitrary term. We then define an operational preorder, $\leq$, for the resulting language. Intuitively, $e \leq e'$ if e approximates e'. In particular, if $e \leq e'$, and if $C[\cdot]$ is a program context (i.e. a term with a hole in it) such that $C[e]$ evaluates to an atomic value v (an integer, say), then $C[e']$ also evaluates to v. Some examples are given in Section 2.2.

The operational preorder will be used to give set theoretic meanings to terms. If $\alpha \in V$ and $\alpha \leq a$ then α will be a possible set-theoretic meaning of a. For some a there will be many possible values of α. However, because of the removal of "ill-behaved" objects, if $\gamma \in V$ stands for a type, then for all e there will be at most one $\alpha \in \gamma$ such that $\alpha \leq e$. Thus, relative to a given type γ, terms will have unique set theoretic meanings. Furthermore, for any given e there will be at most one $\gamma \leq e$. Thus a term e will represent at most one type γ.

2.1 The Set Theoretic Universe V

We first define Z to be a large chunk of the usual cumulative hierarchy of ZF set theory. In particular, define sets Z_σ, indexed by ordinals σ, by $Z_{\sigma+1} = Pow(Z_\sigma)$, where $Pow(X)$ is the power set of X, and $Z_\tau = \bigcup_{\sigma < \tau} Z_\sigma$ if τ is a limit ordinal. Now fix some ordinal σ_0, and let $Z = \bigcup_{\tau < \sigma_0} Z_\tau$. For $\alpha \in Z$, define the *rank* of α, denoted $rank(\alpha)$, to be the least ordinal $\tau < \sigma_0$ such that $\alpha \in Z_\tau$.

We now define $W \subset Z$ to be elements of Z that are tagged according to a certain scheme. Let I be some set. Pick distinct sets fn, set, eq and c_i, $i \in I$, and let (a, b), for $a, b \in W$, be the standard encoding of pairs in set theory. Inductively define $W \subset Z$ as follows.

1. $(set, \gamma) \in W$ if $\gamma \subset W$.
2. $(fn, \phi) \in W$ if $\phi \subset W \times W$ and for all $(x, y), (x', y') \in \phi$, $x = x'$ implies $y = y'$.
3. $(c_i, (x_1, \ldots, x_n)) \in W$ if $x_i \in W$ for all i.
4. $(eq, \xi) \in W$ if $\xi \subset W$.

We will usually identify (fn, ϕ) and ϕ, (eq, ξ) and ξ, (set, γ) and γ, and write $c_i(\overline{x})$ for $(c_i, \overline{x})$. We use the letters ϕ, γ, and ξ exclusively for objects introduced by clauses *1*, *2* and *4* above, respectively. We use the letters α and β for arbitrary members of W.

An object $c_i(\overline{e})$ is intended to represent a value built with the data constructor c_i; ϕ is intended to represent a set-theoretic function; ξ, an equivalence class; and γ, the collection of set-theoretic meanings of a type in the type theory.

The definition of $V \subset W$ is rather technical, and was chosen to meet two requirements. One requirement is the unique-meaning property described above. The other is that V be closed under the set constructors, such as generalized cartesian product, that correspond to Nuprl's type constructors.

$$\frac{f \Downarrow \phi \quad (\alpha,\beta) \in \phi \quad \alpha \lhd a}{f(a) \Downarrow \hat{\beta}} \, (ap_\phi) \qquad \frac{f \Downarrow \lambda x.\, b \quad b[a/x] \Downarrow v}{f(a) \Downarrow v} \, (ap_\lambda)$$

$$\frac{}{\hat{\alpha} \Downarrow \hat{\alpha}} \, (\alpha) \qquad \frac{}{\lambda x.\, b \Downarrow \lambda x.\, b} \, (\lambda) \qquad \frac{}{[e] \Downarrow [e]} \, (eq) \qquad \frac{}{c_i(\bar{e}) \Downarrow c_i(\bar{e})} \, (c_i)$$

$$\frac{a \Downarrow \xi \quad \forall \alpha \in \xi.\ \beta \lhd f(\hat{\alpha})}{f \cdot a \Downarrow \hat{\beta}} \, (ap_\xi) \qquad \frac{a \Downarrow [a_0] \quad f(a_0) \Downarrow v}{f \cdot a \Downarrow v} \, (ap_{eq})$$

Fig. 1. Evaluation rules.

To define V, we first need to introduce a notion of consistency between members of W. It will turn out that two members that are *not* consistent cannot approximate the same term.

Definition 1. Two elements $x, y \in W$ are *consistent* if $x \uparrow y$, where $\uparrow \subset W \times W$ is defined by rank induction as follows.

- $\gamma \uparrow \gamma$.
- $\phi_1 \uparrow \phi_2$ if for all $(\alpha_1, \beta_1) \in \phi_1$ and $(\alpha_2, \beta_2) \in \phi_2$, if $\alpha_1 \uparrow \alpha_2$ then $\beta_1 \uparrow \beta_2$.
- $c_i(x_1, \ldots, x_n) \uparrow c_i(x_1', \ldots, x_n')$ if for all j, $x_j \uparrow x_j'$.
- $\xi \uparrow \xi'$ if for some $\alpha \in \xi$ and $\alpha' \in \xi'$, $\alpha \uparrow \alpha'$.

Definition 2. Define $V \subset W$ by rank induction as follows.

- $\gamma \in V$ if $\gamma \subset V$ and for all $\alpha, \alpha' \in \gamma$, $\alpha \uparrow \alpha'$ implies $\alpha = \alpha'$.
- $\phi \in V$ if $\phi \subset V \times V$ and $\phi \uparrow \phi$.
- $c_i(x_1, \ldots, x_n) \in V$ if $x_j \in V$ for all j.
- $\xi \in V$ if $\xi \subset V$.

Note that $\alpha \uparrow \alpha$ for all $\alpha \in V$. Hencefore all uses of the letters $\alpha, \beta, \gamma, \phi$ and ξ will be restricted to V.

2.2 A Programming Language

In this section we give a "programming" language that combines V with Nuprl's term language. We are taking Nuprl's language to include two new operators, one for constructing members of quotient types, and one for destructing them. The changes in the Nuprl rules needed to accommodate these new operators will be discussed in Section 3.

The operators in Nuprl's term language are either canonical, and are used to construct values, or are non-canonical, and are used to build terms that require evaluation to obtain a value. For the new semantics, we reclassify Nuprl's operators for building types from canonical to non-canonical (this will be expanded on in the next section). We treat Nuprl's canonical operators generically, and omit

$$\frac{e \Downarrow v \quad \alpha \lhd v}{\alpha \lhd e} (\Downarrow\lhd) \qquad \frac{}{\alpha \lhd \alpha} (\alpha\lhd) \qquad \frac{\alpha \in \xi \quad \alpha \lhd a}{\xi \lhd [a]} (\xi\lhd)$$

$$\frac{\forall (\alpha,\beta) \in \phi. \ \beta \lhd b[\hat\alpha/x]}{\phi \lhd \lambda x. \, b} (\phi\lhd) \qquad \frac{\forall j. \ \alpha_j \lhd e_j}{c_i(\overline\alpha) \lhd c_i(\overline e)} (c_i\lhd)$$

Fig. 2. Approximation rules.

here all of its non-canonical operators except for function application. Extending the proofs to deal with the omitted operations is completely straightforward. In [12] we show how to define a general rule schema such that Theorem 6 holds whenever the underlying evaluation rules fit the schema, as is the case with the rules for the omitted operators.

The index set I used in the definition of V is chosen so that the c_i's can be put in one-to-one correspondence with the set of all canonical operators of Nuprl except for λ (which is the only canonical binding operator).

We build the set T of terms of our programming language by starting with an infinite set of variables and all $\gamma, \phi, \xi \in V$ as constants, and then closing under the following two rules. If f and a are terms, then $f(a)$, $f \cdot a$ and $[a]$ are terms. If $\overline e$ is a tuple of terms, then for all $i \in I$, $c_i(\overline e)$ is a term. If b is a term and x is a variable, then $\lambda x. \, b$ is a term.

The usual definitions of substitution, closed term, and so on, apply to this language. Let T_0 be the set of closed terms. Inductively define an injection i from V to T_0 as follows.

$$i[\alpha] = \begin{cases} c_i(i[\alpha_1], \ldots, i[\alpha_n]) & \text{if } e \text{ has the form } c_i(\alpha_1, \ldots, \alpha_n) \\ \alpha & \text{otherwise} \end{cases}$$

We will usually write $\hat\alpha$ for $i[\alpha]$.

We now give a form of operational semantics for this language by giving a set of inductive rules that simultaneously define binary relations $\lhd \subset V \times T_0$ and $\Downarrow \subset T_0 \times T_0$. $\Downarrow$ will be the evaluation relation of the language, and $\lhd$ will turn out to be a restriction of the operational preorder based on $\Downarrow$.

The rules for $\Downarrow$ and $\lhd$ are given in Figures 1 and 2. We first give the intuitive meanings of these rules, and then illustrate with a few examples. Consider first the evaluation rules (Figure 1). The first two rules are for evaluation of function applications. To evaluate a term $f(a)$, one first evaluates f. If the value is an abstraction $\lambda x. \, b$, then the value is the value of $b[a/x]$ (if any). If it is a constant $\phi \in V_{fn}$, then find an ordered pair $(\alpha, \beta) \in \phi$ such that α approximates a, and return $\hat\beta$.

The second line of rules in Figure 1 simply says that any expression built with a value constructor evaluates to itself. The last two rules are for computing with equivalence classes. The idea is that one computes with an equivalence class by computing with its members. To evaluate $f \cdot a$, first evaluate a. If the value is the "polymorphic" equivalence class $[a_0]$, then the result is simply the value of the function application $f(a_0)$. $[a_0]$ can be thought of as standing for any equivalence class that has a_0 as a member.

Rule (ap_ξ), covering the case where the value of f is the equivalence class ξ, is crucial. It is the reason why we can dispense with functionality in our semantics. Intuitively, the rule will force any function computing with equivalence classes to do a "run-time" check that it respects the equality represented by the classes. In particular, we want to force f to check that it returns the same value no matter what member of ξ it is applied to. Unfortunately, there is no appropriate global notion of "same value". So, this rule "guesses" a value $\beta \in V$ such that β approximates $f(\hat{\alpha})$ for all $\alpha \in \xi$, and returns $\hat{\beta}$.

Now consider the rules in Figure 2. Rule $(\xi \lhd)$ says that an equivalence class ξ approximates a polymorphic equivalence class $[a]$ if some member of ξ approximates a. Rule $(\phi \lhd)$ says that a graph ϕ approximates an abstraction $\lambda x. b$ if every α in the domain of ϕ, the value of ϕ at α approximates $b[\hat{\alpha}/x]$.

We now look at a few examples. In the full language, some of the c_i correspond to the integers, and there are non-canonical operators for addition etc. Let $\phi = \{(0, 4), (1, 5)\}$, $\phi' = \{(0, 2)\}$ and $\psi = \{(\phi, 17), (\phi', 18)\}$. We have

- $\hat{\phi}(0 + 0) \Downarrow 4$ because $0 \lhd 0 + 0$.
- $\hat{\phi} \lhd \lambda x. x + 4$, but not $\hat{\phi}' \lhd \lambda x. x + 4$.
- $\hat{\psi}(\lambda x. x + 4) \Downarrow 17$.

We now consider an example involving the quotient type. Let $\xi_1 = \{0, 2, \ldots\}$ and $\xi_2 = \{1, 3, \ldots\}$ (again ignoring tags). The type $(x, y) : N//even(x - y)$ will have as members $\hat{\xi}_1, \hat{\xi}_2$ and $[n]$ for $n \geq 0$. We have $\hat{\xi}_1 \lhd [2]$ but not $\hat{\xi}_2 \lhd [2]$. Also, if

$$f = \lambda x. \; if \; evenp(x) \; then \; 0 \; else \; 1$$

then $f \cdot [2] \Downarrow 0$ and $f \cdot \xi_2 \Downarrow \hat{1}$.

The evaluation relation $\Downarrow$ is idempotent, in the sense that if $e \Downarrow v$ then $v \Downarrow v$. We use the letters u and v exclusively for *values*, which are terms u such that $u \Downarrow u$. Note that, because of the rule (ap_ξ), $\Downarrow$ is not determinate: there is a term e and distinct v, v' such that $e \Downarrow v$ and $e \Downarrow v'$. However, Theorem 9 below says that this indeterminacy is inessential.

2.3 Operational Preorder and Meaning of Programs

All of the terms considered so far, except for λ-abstractions, can be written as $\tau(\bar{e})$ where τ is an operator and $\bar{e}$ is a (possibly empty) sequence of terms. Applications $f(a)$ can be thought of as having the form $ap(f, a)$. For η a binary relation on terms, define $e \langle \eta \rangle e'$ if $e = e' = x$, or if $e = \lambda x. b$, $e' = \lambda x. b'$ and $b \eta b'$, or if $e = \tau(e_1, \ldots, e_n)$, $e' = \tau(e'_1, \ldots, e'_n)$ and $e_i \eta e'_i$ for $1 \leq i \leq n$. Some of the Nuprl operators that we are omitting from the present account are binding operators. In the full account, the definition of $\langle \eta \rangle$ is extended to these operators in the obvious way.

We extend a relation $\eta \subset T_0 \times T_0$ on closed terms to a relation η° on open terms by defining $e \; \eta^\circ \; e'$ if $\sigma(e) \; \eta \; \sigma(e')$ for all substitutions σ such that $\sigma(e)$ and $\sigma(e')$ are closed.

The operational preorder is now defined as follows.

Definition 3. Let $\eta \subset T_0 \times T_0$. Define $[\eta] \subset T_0 \times T_0$ by $e \; [\eta] \; e'$ if $e \Downarrow u$ implies there exists u' such that $e' \Downarrow u'$ and one of the following holds.

1. $u \; \langle \eta^\circ \rangle \; u'$.
2. $u = \phi$, $u' = \lambda x. \; b'$ and for all $(\alpha, \beta) \in \phi$, $\hat{\beta} \; \eta \; b'[\hat{\alpha}/x]$.
3. $u = \xi$, $u' = [a']$ and for some $\alpha \in \xi$, $\hat{\alpha} \; \eta \; a'$.

Note that the mapping $\eta \mapsto [\eta]$ is monotone with respect to inclusion of relations. This allows us to make the following definition.

Definition 4. Define $\leq$ to be the largest relation $\eta \subset T_0 \times T_0$ such that $\eta \subset [\eta]$. Define $\sim$ to be the symmetric closure of $\leq$.

It is easy to show that the fixed-point equation $\leq \; = \; [\leq]$ holds. We will use this equation frequently (and implicitly, usually) in the rest of the paper.

As in [10, 11], it is straightforward to show that $\leq$ is a preorder (i.e. it is reflexive and transitive). This can be done by the principle of *coinduction*, which says that to prove $\eta \subset \; \leq$ it suffices to prove $\eta \subset [\eta]$.

Lemma 5. *For all $\alpha \in V$ and all closed terms e, $\alpha \lhd e$ if and only if $\hat{\alpha} \leq e$.*

Proof. The proof is a straightforward induction on the rank of α.

In what follows we will use $\alpha \lhd e$ and $\hat{\alpha} \leq e$ interchangeably.

The proof of the following theorem is too long to be included here. The details are not particularly interesting. The appendix gives a sketch of the proof.

Theorem 6. $\leq^\circ$ *is a precongruence: for all terms e and e', if $e \; \langle \leq^\circ \rangle \; e'$ then $e \leq^\circ e'$.*

An immediate consequence Theorem 6 is a substitutivity property: if $e \leq^\circ e'$ and $a \leq^\circ a'$ then $e[a/x] \leq^\circ e'[a'/x]$.

Proving the coherence theorem (Theorem 9 below) is straightforward because if a term e evaluates to both v and v', then v and v' are the same up to consistent constants. This is made precise in the following definition and lemma.

Definition 7. Define $e \bowtie e'$ if there is a term c with free variables $x_1, \ldots, x_n$ and some $\alpha_1, \ldots, \alpha_n \in V$ and $\alpha'_1, \ldots, \alpha'_n \in V$, such that $e = c[\overline{\alpha}/\overline{x}]$, $e' = c[\overline{\alpha'}/\overline{x}]$, and for each i, $1 \leq i \leq n$, $\alpha_i \uparrow \alpha'_i$.

Lemma 8. *1. If $e \bowtie e'$, $e \Downarrow v$ and $e' \Downarrow v'$, then $v \bowtie v'$.*
2. If $e \bowtie e'$, $\alpha \lhd e$ and $\alpha' \lhd e'$ then $\alpha \uparrow \alpha'$.

Proof. The proof is a straightforward induction on the definitions of $e \Downarrow v$ and $\alpha \lhd e$. We do only two cases; the remaining cases are similar.

Case (ap_ϕ). We must have $e' = f'(a')$ for some f', a'. Since $f \Downarrow \phi$ and $f \bowtie f'$, by part 1 of the induction hypothesis we cannot have $f' \Downarrow \lambda x.\ b'$ for any b', and so $f'(a') \Downarrow v'$ must be derived by an instance of rule (ap_ϕ). By part 1 of the induction hypothesis, $\phi \uparrow \phi'$, and by part 2, $\alpha \uparrow \alpha'$. By definition of $\phi \uparrow \phi'$, $\beta \uparrow \beta'$.

Case (ap_ξ). Proceeding as in the previous case, we have $e' = f' \cdot a'$ and $f' \cdot a' \Downarrow \beta'$ via (ap_ξ). By the induction hypothesis, $\xi \uparrow \xi'$, so there exist $\alpha \in \xi$ and $\alpha' \in \xi'$ such that $\alpha \uparrow \alpha'$. We have $f(\alpha) \bowtie f'(\alpha')$, so by the induction hypothesis $\beta \uparrow \beta'$.

Theorem 9. (Coherence.) *Suppose $e \in T_0$.*

1. *If $\gamma_1 \lhd e$ and $\gamma_2 \lhd e$ then $\gamma_1 = \gamma_2$.*
2. *For all $\gamma \in V$ and $\alpha_1, \alpha_2 \in \gamma$, if $\hat{\alpha_1} \lhd e$ and $\hat{\alpha_2} \lhd e$ then $\alpha_1 = \alpha_2$.*

Proof. For part 2, if $\alpha \lhd e$ and $\alpha' \lhd e$ for $\alpha, \alpha' \in \gamma$, then by Lemma 8, $\alpha \uparrow \alpha'$, and so $\alpha = \alpha'$ by the definition of V. The proof of part 1 is similar.

3 Nuprl

This section shows how to apply the semantic ideas of the previous section to a variant of Nuprl's type theory.

Nuprl has a large number of built-in type constructors and a very large number of inference rules (close to 100), so a complete account here is impossible. However, the semantics is sufficient simple that an interested reader would not have too much difficulty in verifying all the rules given in the Nuprl book [5], given the definitions and examples in this section, and assuming the results of Section 2.

To give the semantics for the type theory, we first need to extend the operational semantics to include evaluation rules for all the type constructors. It is easy to show that all the results of the previous section hold for this extension. We only give a few examples of such rules. Obvious variations work for the other type constructors.

To account for all of Nuprl, we have to make V sufficiently large. Nuprl has a hierarchy of universes $U_1, U_2, \ldots$ of types. Each U_i has to be closed under type constructors such as generalized cartesian product. This means that the set-theoretic meaning of each U_i has to be closed under the corresponding set constructors. This requires the use of *inaccessible cardinals*. These are defined in most set theory texts, and the reason for their use in this context is explained further in [11]. We choose the ordinal σ_0 in the definition of W to be the limit of a countable sequence $\tau_1 < \tau_2 \ldots$ of inaccessible cardinals. For each $i \geq 1$, let $\gamma^i = V \cap Z_{\tau_i}$. We add evaluation rules $U_i \Downarrow \widehat{\gamma^i}$ for each $i \geq 1$.

We give a rule for Nuprl's generalized cartesian product $x : A \to B$ as follows. If $\gamma \in V$ and, for each $\alpha \in \gamma$, $\gamma_\alpha \in V$, then let $\Pi \alpha \in \gamma . \gamma_\alpha$ denote the set of all

$\phi \in V$ such that the domain of ϕ is γ, and for each $(\alpha, \beta) \in \phi$, $\beta \in \gamma_\alpha$. Note that $(\Pi \alpha \in \gamma . \gamma_\alpha) \in V$. The evaluation rule is

$$\frac{A \Downarrow \hat{\gamma} \quad \forall \alpha \in \gamma . \ B[\hat{\alpha}/x] \Downarrow \widehat{\gamma_\alpha}}{x : A \to B \Downarrow i[\Pi \alpha \in \gamma . \gamma_\alpha]}$$

Nuprl has an equality type, similar to Martin-Löf's "I" type, which represents the proposition that two elements of the type are equal. Let γ_{true} be some one-element set, and let γ_{false} be the empty set. The rules for the equality type are as follows.

$$\frac{A \Downarrow \hat{\gamma} \quad \alpha \in \gamma \quad \alpha \lhd a_1 \quad \alpha \lhd a_2}{(a_1 = a_2 \in A) \Downarrow \widehat{\gamma_{true}}} \qquad \frac{A \Downarrow \hat{\gamma} \quad \alpha \neq \beta \in \gamma \quad \alpha \lhd a_1 \quad \beta \lhd a_2}{(a_1 = a_2 \in A) \Downarrow \widehat{\gamma_{false}}.}$$

Finally, we give a rule for the quotient type. If X is an equivalence relation over γ, then let $\gamma//X$ be the set of equivalence classes of X. In the rule below, let Q stand for $\{(\alpha, \beta) \in \gamma \times \gamma \mid \gamma_{\alpha, \beta} \neq \emptyset\}$.

$$\frac{A \Downarrow \gamma \quad \forall \alpha, \beta \in \gamma . \ E[\hat{\alpha}, \hat{\beta}/x, y] \Downarrow \widehat{\gamma_{\alpha, \beta}} \quad Q \text{ is an equivalence relation}}{(x, y) : A//E \Downarrow i[\gamma//Q].}$$

Having added the evaluation rules for all the type constructors, we can give the semantics of Nuprl's type system.

Definition 10. A closed term e is a *type* if there is a $\gamma \in V$ such that $e \Downarrow \hat{\gamma}$. Define $M_*[e] = \gamma$.

M_* is well-defined by Theorem 9 and the fact that $e \Downarrow \gamma$ implies $\gamma \lhd e$.

Definition 11. Let e and a be closed terms. Define $a \in e$ if e is a type and there exists $\alpha \in M_*[e]$ such that $\alpha \lhd a$. In the case α exists, define $M_e[a] = \alpha$.

M_e is well-defined by Theorem 9. We will write $M_\gamma[a]$ for $M_{\hat{\gamma}}[a]$. Note that if $e \in U_i$ then e is a type and $M_*[e] \in \gamma^i$.

The preceding definition gives the core idea of the semantics. With a type is associated a set γ, and the members of the type are all terms e which are approximated by some member of γ.

It is now easy to give the semantics of Nuprl sequents. Nuprl sequents have the form

$$x_1 : A_1, \ldots, x_n : A_n \vdash t \in T$$

where $t, T, A_1, \ldots, A_n$ are terms and for all i, $1 \leq i \leq n$, all of the free variables of t and T are among $x_1, \ldots, x_n$, and all of the free variables of each A_i are among $x_1, \ldots, x_{i-1}$. A *closing substitution* for the sequent is a substitution which has domain $x_1, \ldots, x_n$ and whose values are all closed terms.

Definition 12. The sequent

$$x_1 : A_1, \ldots, x_n : A_n \vdash t \in T$$

is *true* if $\sigma(t) \in \sigma(T)$ for all closing substitutions σ such that for all i, $1 \leq i \leq n$, $\sigma(x_i) \in \sigma(A_i)$.

Soundness of an inference rule is now defined as usual: the conclusion is true whenever the premises are.

Theorem 13. *The rules of Nuprl, with suitable modifications to the quotient and extensionality rules, are sound.*

We do not give the proof here, but just give a few representative cases. We also simplify the rules somewhat, for example by dealing only with the hypotheses that are introduced or analyzed by a rule (as opposed to the common prefix of hypotheses shared by the conclusion and premises).

We first do the "function intro" rule.

$$\frac{\vdash A \in U_i \quad x{:}A \vdash b \in B}{\vdash \lambda x.\, b \in x : A \to B}$$

By the first premise, there is a γ such that $M_*[A] = \gamma$. By the second premise, for each $\alpha \in \gamma$, $B[\hat{\alpha}/x]$ is a type, so for some γ_α, $M_*[B[\hat{\alpha}/x]] = \gamma_\alpha$. By the evaluation rule for the product type,

$$M_*[x : A \to B] = \Pi\alpha \in \gamma . \gamma_\alpha.$$

By the second premise, $b[\hat{\alpha}/x] \in B[\hat{\alpha}/x]$ for all $\alpha \in \gamma$. Let $\phi \in \Pi\alpha \in \gamma . \gamma_\alpha$ encode the mapping $\alpha \mapsto M_{\gamma_\alpha}[b[\hat{\alpha}/x]]$. To complete the verification of the rule, we only need to show that $\phi \leq \lambda x.\, b$, and this is immediate.

Next we do the "function elim" rule.

$$\frac{\vdash a \in A \quad \vdash f \in x : A \to B}{\vdash f(a) \in B[a/x]}$$

Let $M_A[a] = \alpha$ and $M_{x:A \to B}[f] = \phi$. Let β be such that $(\alpha, \beta) \in \phi$. By the evaluation rule for product, $B[\hat{\alpha}/x] \Downarrow \gamma$ for some γ such that $\beta \in \gamma$, so, using Theorem 6, $\gamma \leq B[\hat{\alpha}/x] \leq B[a/x]$ and hence $M_*[B[a/x]] = \gamma$. Since $\phi \leq f$, we have $\hat{\beta} \leq f(\hat{\alpha}) \leq f(a)$, so $f(a) \in B[a/x]$.

Some of the rules for Nuprl's quotient type need to be changed. We sketch these changes below. Verification of the rules is straightforward, and is omitted here. Let Q be $(x, y) : A//E$. The new "introduction" rule adds the constructor $[\cdot]$.

$$\frac{\vdash Q \in U_i \quad \vdash a \in A}{\vdash [a] \in Q}$$

The new "elimination" rule adds the non-canonical form for quotients.

$$\frac{\vdash e \in Q \quad x{:}A, y{:}A, z{:}E \vdash c_{true} \in (f(x) = f(y) \in T)}{\vdash f{\cdot}e \in T}$$

where c_{true} is the unique member of γ_{true}. In the second premise, the assumption $z{:}E$ merely asserts that E is true; the variable z is not allowed to occur free in f or T. Also, there is no need for a premise giving a type to f.

One other rule for quotients also needs to be changed. The changes are similar to the "intro" rule. Also, Nuprl's "direct computation" rule, which formalizes symbolic computation, must be updated to include the equivalence $f{\cdot}[e] \sim f(e)$.

4 HOL

In this section we first sketch how to use the semantics we have developed to justify an embedding of HOL. We then explain why this embedding is effective.

In order to embed HOL, we need to add an operator to Nuprl to represent HOL's "select" operator. The evaluation rule is as follows. Note that non-emptiness of a type is taken to represent truth of the corresponding proposition.

$$\frac{T \Downarrow \hat{\gamma} \quad \forall \alpha \in \gamma: \ P[\hat{\alpha}/x] \Downarrow \widehat{\gamma_\alpha} \quad \alpha_0 \in \gamma \ of \ minimum \ rank \ such \ that \ \gamma_{\alpha_0} \neq \emptyset}{@x \in T. \ P \quad \Downarrow \quad \widehat{\alpha_0}}$$

The base logic of HOL is a polymorphic version of the simply typed λ-calculus with two base types: *bool*, for the booleans, and *ind*, representing an infinite set. There are three constants

$$= : \ 'a \to \ 'a \to bool$$
$$==> : \ bool \to bool \to bool$$
$$@ : ('a \to bool) \to \ 'a$$

for equality, implication, and "select", respectively. The $'a$ is a type variable. The semantics of HOL is the standard set-theoretic one where function type is given the usual set-theoretic meaning.

Given Nuprl's select operator, it is trivial to give definitions in Nuprl for the base types and the constants. *ind* is defined to be Nuprl's type of natural numbers, and HOL's function type is interpreted as Nuprl's function type. We can prove in Nuprl that each of the (defined) constants has the appropriate type. For example, we can prove

$$\forall \ 'a \in HOL\_U. \ @ \in ('a \to bool) \to \ 'a$$

where HOL_U is the type of all members of the type universe U_1 that are non-empty, and *bool* is defined as the subtype $\{\, x \in Z \mid x = 0 \lor x = 1 \,\}$ of Nuprl's type Z of integers. In general, all HOL theorems and axioms have implicit outermost quantifiers for their type variables. These quantifiers are made explicit in the Nuprl interpretation.

Extensions to the HOL logic are made by creating *theories*. A theory consists of a set of new type constructors, and set of new constants with their types, some axioms involving the new constants and types, and a set of theorems proved using the axioms. To import this theory into Nuprl, we proceed as we did for the base logic: we find Nuprl objects to use in place of the new types and constants (these can usually be computed automatically from the theory's definitions), prove in Nuprl that the constants have their assigned types, and then prove that the axioms all hold. Once we have done this, the new semantics of Nuprl tells us that the set theoretic meaning of the Nuprl objects we introduced can be directly used to give a model of the HOL theory. The theorems are valid in this model, hence their translations into Nuprl are true.

The use of Nuprl objects to "instantiate" HOL theories is one reason why this embedding is effective. For example, we instantiate the HOL theories for the integers with Nuprl's integer type and Nuprl's built-in operations over the integers. All the HOL theorems about the HOL integers then become applicable to Nuprl integers.

A major concern here is the constructivity of Nuprl proofs. HOL formulas, when imported into Nuprl, have type *bool*. Nuprl's encoding of logic uses propositions-as-types, so, for example, Nuprl's universal quantification is represented using the generalized cartesian product type. We can prove, however, that the two ways of encoding logic are equivalent. Thus, for each HOL theorem imported, we can derive a version of the theorem that uses Nuprl's logical connectives. However, the proof of this derivation is non-constructive, and so the program synthesized from one of these new theorems might mention the non-computable select operator $\mathcal{O}$. If such a theorem is cited in another Nuprl proof, the program there might also be uncomputable.

The reason this is not a problem is because equalities in Nuprl have no computational content. So, for example, if a universally quantified equation is proved, then the program extracted from the proof is simply a constant function. This has two main consequences. First, if we are proving an equation (possibly under assumptions) in Nuprl, we can safely use any HOL theorem whatsoever. Second, no matter what we are proving, it is always safe to use HOL facts, such as universally quantified equations, that have no computational content. Fortunately, the vast majority of HOL theorems fit this category, and the vast majority of the work in proving any theorem about software involves computationally trivial facts (mostly equations and inequations). Most of the work in Nuprl proofs is done by term rewriting. All the programs that apply term rewriting can safely use any HOL theorem.

It is easy to modify the system to ensure that non-computable "programs" are not inadvertently extracted from proofs. For example, we can add a bit to each proof node, where a true bit means that the extracted program of the subproof rooted at the node must not contain the select operator. The user sets the bit at the root, and the system computes the bit when the proof is extended by refinement, setting it to false when the node being refined has a conclusion which is computationally trivial, and simply propagating it otherwise. Inference steps may not mention the select operator, or use lemmas whose top bit is false, if the bit at the node being refined is true.

Details on the actual HOL embedding and some of its practical applications will be given in a forthcoming paper.

5 Related Work, Discussion

In [4], Breazu-Tannen and Subrahmanyam give a logic for reasoning about programs using structural recursion over data types formed from constructors subject to some equations. Their idea, to make the meaning of a definition by structural recursion $\perp$ if it does not respect the equations, is somewhat similar to our treatment of $f \cdot t$, which tests to see if f respects equality as given by the equivalence class t.

It is straightforward to give a classical interpretation justifying the select operator for typed variants of Martin-Löf's type theory. Such an interpretation is given by Dybjer in [6]. Because these variants are based on a typed language, they do not enjoy some of the useful features of Nuprl, such as direct reasoning about the programming language used for realizers extracted from proofs, writing programs in a conventional style (e.g. general recursion), genericity with respect to programming language (e.g. using ML instead) and partial functions.

The idea of adding function oracles ϕ to an untyped programming language comes from our paper [11]. The semantics we gave there might give a model of Nuprl in which the select operator is definable, but we would have had to use the complicated PER semantics along the lines discussed earlier (the author gave up on doing this in disgust), and the embedding of HOL would be much harder to justify because of the PER/set mismatch in the respective semantics.

The idea for the proof of Theorem 6 first appeared in [10]. An expanded treatment of the proof method is in [11].

In [13] we gave a type theory that contained ZF set theory. Although that theory is in some respects similar to Nuprl, the programming language in the theory is typed in an essential way and hence the semantics cannot be applied to Nuprl. Also, there are no polymorphic equivalence classes in that work, and the semantics is much more complicated than the present one.

The new semantics justifies some useful extensions to Nuprl. It justifies extensional equality of types: two types are equal if and only if they have the same set of members. Currently, Nuprl's type equality is taken to be intensional, or structural, for technical reasons having to do with collapsing Martin-Löf's four forms of judgment to one, although there are no rules that exploit this. Other extensions include: the law of the excluded middle (an immediate consequence of the introduction of the @ operator), a power set constructor, and some impredicative constructs.

References

1. *Part IIIA: SCI Coherence Overview, 1995.* Unapproved draft IEEE-P1596-05Nov90-doc197-iii.

2. *Higher Order Logic Theorem Proving and Its Applications*, Lecture Notes in Computer Science. Springer, 1995.

3. S. F. Allen. *A Non-Type-Theoretic Semantics for Type-Theoretic Language.* PhD thesis, Cornell University, 1987.

4. V. Breazu-Tannen and R. Subrahmanyam. Logical and computational aspects of programming with sets/bags/lists. In *Automata, Languages and Programming: 18th International Colloquium*, Lecture Notes in Computer Science, pages 60–75. Springer-Verlag, 1991.

5. R. L. Constable, et al. *Implementing Mathematics with the Nuprl Proof Development System.* Prentice-Hall, Englewood Cliffs, New Jersey, 1986.

6. P. Dybjer. Inductive sets and families in Martin-Löf's type theory and their set-theoretic semantics. In *Proceedings of the B.R.A. Workshop on Logical Frameworks*, Sophia-Antipolis, France, June 1990.

7. A. Gordon. *Functional Programming and Input/Output*. Cambrige University Press, 1994.

8. M. J. Gordon, R. Milner, and C. P. Wadsworth. *Edinburgh LCF: A Mechanized Logic of Computation*, volume 78 of *Lecture Notes in Computer Science*. Springer-Verlag, 1979.

9. M. J. C. Gordon and T. F. Melham. *Introduction to HOL: A Theorem Proving Environment for Higher Order Logic*. Cambridge University Press, Cambridge, UK, 1993.

10. D. J. Howe. Equality in lazy computation systems. In *Proceedings of the Fourth Annual Symposium on Logic in Computer Science*, pages 198–203. IEEE Computer Society, June 1989.

11. D. J. Howe. On computational open-endedness in Martin-Löf's type theory. In *Proceedings of the Sixth Annual Symposium on Logic in Computer Science*, pages 162–172. IEEE Computer Society, 1991.

12. D. J. Howe. Proving congruence of bisimulation in functional programming languages. *Information and Computation*, 1996. To appear.

13. D. J. Howe and S. D. Stoller. An operational approach to combining classical set theory and functional programming languages. In *Theoretical Aspects of Computer Software*, Lecture Notes in Computer Science. Springer-Verlag, 1994.

14. P. B. Jackson. Exploring abstract algebra in constructive type theory. In A. Bundy, editor, *12th Conference on Automated Deduction*, Lecture Notes in Artifical Intelligence. Springer, June 1994.

15. B. Jacobs and T. Melham. Translating dependent type theory into higher order logic. In *Proceedings of the Second International Conference on Typed Lambda Calculi and Applications*, volume 664 of *Lecture Notes in Computer Science*, pages 209–229. Springer, 1993.

16. P. Martin-Löf. Constructive mathematics and computer programming. In *Sixth International Congress for Logic, Methodology, and Philosophy of Science*, pages 153–175, Amsterdam, 1982. North Holland.

17. T. Melham. The HOL logic extended with quantification over type variables. *Formal Methods in System Design*, 3(1–2):7–24, August 1993.

18. R. Milner, M. Tofte, and R. Harper. *The Definition of Standard ML*. MIT Press, 1990.

19. E. Ritter and A. Pitts. A fully abstract translation between a λ-calculus with reference types and Standard ML. In *Proceedings of the Second International Conference on Typed Lambda Calculi and Applications*, volume 902 of *Lecture Notes in Computer Science*, pages 397–413. Springer, 1995.

20. M. van der Voort. Introducing well-founded function definitions in HOL. In *Higher Order Logic Theorem Proving and Its Applications*, volume A-20 of *IFIP Transactions*, pages 117–131. North-Holland, 1993.

A   Proof of Precongruence

The proof of Theorem 6 in large part a straightforward extension of the method of [10, 12]. One of the main differences is that we use Lemma 14 for the cases for rules (ap_ϕ) and (ap_ξ).

Lemma 14. *If $\alpha \lhd e[\hat{\beta}/x]$ and $\beta \lhd e'$ then $\alpha \lhd e[e'/x]$.*

Lemma 14, while highly plausible, is in fact rather difficult to prove. The obvious inductive argument over the definition of $\lhd$ fails because of rules (ap_ϕ) and (ap_ξ). Our proof is rather complicated, and is omitted because of lack of space. All the complication resides in the well-founded relation that the inductive proof is based on.

We now sketch the remainder of the proof. We continue to omit any mention of operators not treated in Section 2. The key to the rest of the proof is the following definition.

Definition 15. Define the *precongruence candidate*, a binary relation $\hat{\leq}$ on terms, by induction on the size of its first argument: $e \hat{\leq} e'$ if there exists e'' such that $e \langle\hat{\leq}\rangle e''$ and $e'' \leq^\circ e'$.

It is straightforward to verify that the precongruence candidate has the following properties: it is reflexive; it is *operator respecting* in the sense that if $e \hat{\leq} e'$ then $C[e] \hat{\leq} C[e']$ for all contexts $C[\cdot]$; if $e_1 \hat{\leq} e_2 \leq e_3$ then $e_1 \hat{\leq} e_3$; if $v \hat{\leq} v'$ then $v [\hat{\leq}] v'$; and if $e \leq^\circ e'$ then $e \hat{\leq} e'$. We can also show that $\hat{\leq}$ is substitutive: if $e \hat{\leq} e'$ and $b \hat{\leq} b'$ then $b[e/x] \hat{\leq} b'[e'/x]$.

The following key lemma can be easily proved using co-induction on the definition of $\leq$.

Lemma 16. *Suppose that for all closed e, e' and v such that $e \Downarrow v$ and $e \hat{\leq} e'$, there exists v' such that $e' \Downarrow v'$ and $v \hat{\leq} v'$. Then $\leq$ is a precongruence.*

We can now prove Theorem 6.

Proof. By the preceding lemma, it suffices to prove by induction on the definitions of $\Downarrow$ and $\lhd$ that

1. If $e \Downarrow v$ and $e \hat{\leq} e'$ then $e' \Downarrow v'$ with $v \hat{\leq} v'$.
2. If $\alpha \lhd e$ and $e \hat{\leq} e'$ then $\alpha \lhd e'$.

We do a case analysis on rules. In each case, we use the following fact. Let $1'$ be property 1 above with $e \hat{\leq} e'$ replaced by $e \langle\hat{\leq}\rangle e'$. It is straightforward to show that for any particular e, e', v and v', $1'$ implies 1. An analogous statement holds for property 2.

We only consider a few representative cases. The remaining cases are either very similar or trivial.

Case (ap_ϕ). Suppose $f(a) \langle\hat{\leq}\rangle f'(a')$. $f' \Downarrow v'$ with $\phi \hat{\leq} v'$. By definition of $\hat{\leq}$, $\phi \leq v'$. Suppose $v' = \phi$. By part 2 of the induction hypothesis, $\alpha \lhd a'$, so $f'(a') \Downarrow \beta$. Suppose $v' = \lambda x.\, b$. Since $\beta \leq b'[\alpha/x]$, by Lemma 14 we have $\beta \leq b'[a'/x]$, so $b'[a'/x] \Downarrow v''$ with $\beta \leq v''$, and this implies $\beta \hat{\leq} v''$.

Case (ap_λ). Suppose $f(a) \langle\hat{\leq}\rangle f'(a')$. $f \Downarrow \lambda x.\, b$ so by the induction hypothesis there exists b' such that $f' \Downarrow \lambda x.\, b'$ and $b \hat{\leq} b'$. $b[a/x] \hat{\leq} b'[a'/x]$, so by the induction hypothesis $v \hat{\leq} v'$.

Case $(\phi\lhd)$. Suppose $\lambda x.\, b \langle\hat{\leq}\rangle e'$. Then $e' = \lambda x.\, b'$ where $b \hat{\leq} b'$. $b[\hat{\alpha}/x] \hat{\leq} b'[\hat{\alpha}/x]$, so $\beta \lhd b'[\hat{\alpha}/x]$ and $\phi \lhd \lambda x.\, b$.

Free Variable Tableaux
for a Many Sorted Logic with Preorders

A. Gavilanes,   J. Leach,   S. Nieva

Dept. de Informática. y Automática. Univ. Complutense Madrid.*

E-mail: {agav, leach, nieva}@dia.ucm.es

Abstract. We propose a sound and complete free variable semantic tableau method for handling many-sorted preorders in a first order logic, where functions and predicates behave monotonically or antimonotonically. We formulate additional expansion tableau rules as a more efficient alternative to adding the axioms characterizing a preordered structure. Completeness of the system is proved in detail. Examples and applications are introduced.

1   Introduction

The use of non-symmetric relations and in particular inequalities, has become an interesting work line in several fields of computer science. For instance, ordered sorts in equational and object-oriented programming [GM 92], constraints in declarative programming languages [JM 94], nondeterministic specifications [Hus 91], among many others, all of them consider the use of preorders on expressions. In these cases, the logical framework is usually a generalization of the equational logic which includes a specific handling of preorders. Among the several formal mechanisms proposed, we quote order-sorted algebras [GM 92], bi-rewriting [LA 93], chaining with superposition [BG 94] and the rewriting logic [Mes 92].

In this paper a classical many-sorted predicate logic with preorder is defined, where functions and predicates behave monotonically or antimonotonically in their arguments. We use a many-sorted language to improve the performance of a theorem proving system based on it, because in many-sorted calculi, reasonings with sorts are easily incorporated into the inference mechanism, allowing shorter deductions from smaller sets of hypothesis. For this logic a sound and complete tableau-based deduction system is presented, dealing efficiently with inequalities. The system has specific inequality rules for the monotonic and the antimonotonic case.

Although semantic tableaux are not the most efficient tool for automated theorem proving, first order tableaux can be extended to many nonclassical logics used in AI research [Fit 88],[GL 90],[LN 93]. Other advantages of the method are naturalness —not requiring any conversion to canonical forms–, easy definition of a simple control structure —allowing the introduction of heuristics and human interaction [OS 88]–, and possibility of generating counterexamples for non-theorems.

---

*This paper has been supported by Proyecto Precompetitivo PR 219/94 5564.

Our deduction system is based on the semantic tableaux proposed by Fitting [Fit 96] for adding equality to classical tableaux. His proposal improves classical semantic tableaux by using free variables as witnesses of universal quantifications; these variables are instantiated on demand when a branch is closed. In addition some specific rules are defined, expressing equality as a congruence relation and, at the same time, restricting the search space in order to obtain tableaux more suitable for mechanization. Following the ideas above, some specific versions involving free variables have been proposed (see, e.g. [HS 94], [BH 92]), they incorporate solvers for detecting obvious contradictions between formulas and it has been shown that equalities are so handled in a much more efficient way. Our aim is to introduce the use of the preorder relation in free variable semantic tableaux incorporating equality as a particular case of preorder.

The organization of the paper is as follows. In Section 2 a many-sorted first order logic with preorders is outlined and its basic semantic properties are shown. Section 3 extends the first order ground semantic tableaux to cope with preorders, for this purpose additional tableau expansion rules dealing with inequalities are formulated. Section 4 presents a more efficient system, such that the inequality expansion rules are defined in presence of γ and δ rules that use free variables instead of ground terms. The completeness of this system is shown by means of a Lifting Lemma. Examples of applications of the method are presented in Section 5. We finish with some conclusions and future work.

2 Syntax and Semantics

The *Logic with Preorder* we present (*LP*, for short) is a many-sorted predicate logic where preorders are expressed by sorted logical symbols $\sqsubseteq_s$, and functions and predicates behave monotonically or antimonotonically on their arguments.

Definition 1 *Given preorders* $(D_i, \sqsubseteq_{D_i})$, $1 \leq i \leq n$, *and* $(D, \sqsubseteq_D)$, *we say that a function* $f : D_1 \times \ldots \times D_n \to D$ *is monotonic (resp. antimonotonic) in the i-th argument if for every* $d_i, d'_i \in D_i$, $d_i \sqsubseteq_{D_i} d'_i \Rightarrow f(d_1, \ldots, d_i, \ldots, d_n) \sqsubseteq_D f(d_1, \ldots, d'_i, \ldots, d_n)$ *(resp. $\sqsupseteq_D$).*

A signature Σ for *LP* is composed of a set of primitive types (or *sorts*) $S = \{s_1, \ldots, s_m\}$, sets of symbols for sorted constants $C^s (s \in S)$, functions $F^{s_1, \ldots, s_l \to s} (s_1, \ldots, s_l, s \in S)$, and predicates $P^{s_1, \ldots, s_r} (s_1, \ldots, s_r \in S)$, and for every $f \in F^{s_1, \ldots, s_l \to s}$ a mapping $m(f)$ from $\{1, \ldots, l\}$ into $\{0, 1\}$ expressing in which arguments f will be interpreted as monotonic or antimonotonic $-m(f)(i) = 0$, $m(f)(i) = 1$, respectively–. Analogously a mapping $m(P)$ is supplied for every predicate symbol P.

Given a family of countable pairwise disjunct sorted sets of variables $X = (X^s)_{s \in S}$, we define the set of Σ-terms as follows.

Definition 2 *The set* $T(\Sigma)$ *of* Σ-terms *is the union of the family of sorted sets* $T(\Sigma, s)$, $s \in S$, *where the elements* t^s *of* $T(\Sigma, s)$ *are defined by the usual formation rules:*

$$t^s ::= x^s (\in X^s) \mid c (\in C^s) \mid f(t_1, \ldots, t_n) \ (f \in F^{s_1, \ldots, s_n \to s}; \ t_i \in T(\Sigma, s_i)).$$

We suppose that $T(\Sigma, s)$ is non-empty for every sort s and every signature Σ. We omit superscripts for sorts where they are not relevant.

Definition 3 *The set $F(\Sigma)$ of Σ-formulas is defined by the formation rules:*

$$\varphi ::= t^s \sqsubseteq_s t'^s \mid P(t_1, \ldots, t_n) \ (P \in P^{s_1, \ldots, s_n}; t_i \in T(\Sigma, s_i)) \mid \neg\varphi \mid \varphi \wedge \varphi' \mid \exists x^s. \varphi.$$

$\forall x^s \varphi, \varphi \vee \varphi', \varphi \rightarrow \varphi'$ will stand for $\neg\exists x^s \neg\varphi$, $\neg(\neg\varphi \wedge \neg\varphi')$ and $\neg\varphi \vee \varphi'$, respectively. We omit the subscript of $\sqsubseteq_s$ when it is not relevant.

Simultaneous substitution of terms t_i for the free occurrences of different variables x_i in a term t or in a formula φ are denoted $t[t_1/x_1, \ldots, t_n/x_n]$ or $\varphi[t_1/x_1, \ldots, t_n/x_n]$ respectively, avoiding the clashes by renaming bound variables.

The structures of *LP* contain preordered domains and interpret symbols of Σ as functions that for each argument are monotonic or antimonotonic.

Definition 4 *A Σ-structure is any system $\mathcal{D} = \langle \{(D^s, \sqsubseteq_s^{\mathcal{D}}) | s \in S\}, \{c^{\mathcal{D}} \in D^s | c \in C^s\}, \{f^{\mathcal{D}} : D^{s_1} \times \ldots \times D^{s_l} \to D^s | f \in F^{s_1, \ldots, s_l \to s}\}, \{P^{\mathcal{D}} : D^{s_1} \times \ldots \times D^{s_r} \to \{\underline{f}, \underline{t}\} | P \in P^{s_1, \ldots, s_r}\} \rangle$ such that $\sqsubseteq_s^{\mathcal{D}}$ is a preorder on $D^s \neq \emptyset$ and $f^{\mathcal{D}}$ is monotonic in the i-th argument if $m(f)(i) = 0$ and antimonotonic if $m(f)(i) = 1$, and analogously for $P^{\mathcal{D}}$.*[1] *As needed, we will use $\approx_s^{\mathcal{D}}$ for the equivalence relation induced by $\sqsubseteq_s^{\mathcal{D}}$: $d_1 \approx_s^{\mathcal{D}} d_2$ iff $d_1 \sqsubseteq_s^{\mathcal{D}} d_2$ and $d_2 \sqsubseteq_s^{\mathcal{D}} d_1$.*

A valuation ρ for $\mathcal{D}$ is a sorted set of applications $\rho = \{\rho^s | s \in S\}$, where for each sort $s \in S$, $\rho^s : X^s \to D^s$ is a valuation of the set X^s.

A Σ-interpretation is a pair $\langle \mathcal{D}, \rho \rangle$ such that $\mathcal{D}$ is a Σ-structure and ρ is a valuation for $\mathcal{D}$.

Note that a functional term or predicate formula behaves monotonically whenever we increase a subterm which is on the scope of an even number of antimonotonic arguments. As we will see later, some deduction rules will be founded on this fact.

Example 5 If we consider sets ordered by inclusion $\subseteq$, the operations union $\cup$ and intersection $\cap$ are monotonic in both arguments and complement $^{-}$ is antimonotonic. Then we have $A \subseteq B \Rightarrow \overline{C \cup (D \cap \overline{A})} \subseteq \overline{C \cup (D \cap \overline{B})}$ and note that the second A is on the scope of two complement operations. In this case we say that the position of A in $\overline{C \cup (D \cap \overline{A})}$ is monotonic in the sense that monotonicity is preserved. ■

Now we introduce some notation. Let $Pos(t)$ be the set of positions of t inductively defined by: $\{\varepsilon\}$, if t is a variable or a constant; $\{\varepsilon\} \cup \{i.p | p \in Pos(t_i), 1 \leq i \leq n\}$, if $t \equiv f(t_1, \ldots, t_n)$.

Given $p \in Pos(t)$, $t|_p$ is the subterm of t at the position p, and $t[t']_p$ is the result of substituting t' for $t|_p$ in t. If $p, q \in Pos(t)$ we say that $p \leq q$ if there is a $r \in Pos(t)$ such that $p.r = q$; in that case $q - p$ will denote r.

Let $root(t)$ be the root of the term t viewed as a tree. Given $p \in Pos(t)$, the function $Fun_{t,p} : \{q \in Pos(t) | q < p\} \to \mathbb{N}$ is defined by $Fun_{t,p}(q) = $ first digit of $p - q$. Note that $q \in dom(Fun_{t,p})$ if $t|_p$ is subterm of $t|_q$, and that $Fun_{t,p}(q)$ is the number of the argument of $t|_q$ in which $t|_p$ occurs as subterm. For simplicity, we will write Fun instead of $Fun_{t,p}$.

---

[1] The set of truth values $\{\underline{f}, \underline{t}\}$ is ordered by setting $\underline{f}$ less than $\underline{t}$.

Definition 6 *Given $t \in T(\Sigma)$ and $p \in Pos(t)$, we say that p is a monotonic position of t if $\sum_{q<p} m(root(t|_q))(Fun(q))$ is even. Otherwise p is an antimonotonic position of t. ε is a monotonic position of t.*

Given $P(t_1, \ldots, t_n)(\equiv A) \in F(\Sigma)$ and $p \in Pos(t_i)$, for some $1 \leq i \leq n$, we say that p is a monotonic position of A at i, if $\sum_{q<p} m(root(t_i|_q))(Fun(q)) + m(P)(i)$ is even. Otherwise p is an antimonotonic position of A at i.

The semantic value of a Σ-term t^s in a Σ-interpretation $\langle \mathcal{D}, \rho \rangle$ is given by an element $[\![t^s]\!]_\rho^\mathcal{D}$ of D^s and is defined as in classical logic.

Lemma 7 *Let $t \in T(\Sigma, s')$ and $\mathcal{D}$ a Σ-structure then:*

(i) *Coincidence Lemma for terms. If $\rho(x) \approx_s^\mathcal{D} \sigma(x)$, for all variable x of t and sort s, then $[\![t]\!]_\rho^\mathcal{D} \approx_{s'}^\mathcal{D} [\![t]\!]_\sigma^\mathcal{D}$.*

(ii) *Substitution Lemma for terms. $[\![t[t'/x]]\!]_\rho^\mathcal{D} \approx_{s'}^\mathcal{D} [\![t]\!]_{\rho[[\![t']\!]_\rho^\mathcal{D}/x]}^\mathcal{D}$.* [2]

(iii) *Monotonicity and antimonotonicity of terms. Let $p \in Pos(t)$ a monotonic (resp. antimonotonic) position of t such that $t|_p \equiv t_1^s$. If $[\![t_1]\!]_\rho^\mathcal{D} \sqsubseteq_s^\mathcal{D} [\![t_2]\!]_\rho^\mathcal{D}$ then $[\![t[t_1]_p]\!]_\rho^\mathcal{D} \sqsubseteq_{s'}^\mathcal{D} [\![t[t_2]_p]\!]_\rho^\mathcal{D}$ (resp. $[\![t[t_2]_p]\!]_\rho^\mathcal{D} \sqsubseteq_{s'}^\mathcal{D} [\![t[t_1]_p]\!]_\rho^\mathcal{D}$).*

The truth value $\underline{t}$ (for true) or $\underline{f}$ (for false) of Σ-formulas is defined as in classical logic except a special mention of the logical symbol $\sqsubseteq_s$.

Definition 8 *The truth value of a Σ-formula φ in a Σ-interpretation $\langle \mathcal{D}, \rho \rangle$ will be denoted by $[\![\varphi]\!]_\rho^\mathcal{D}(\in \{\underline{f}, \underline{t}\})$ and defined by the following rules:*

- $[\![t^s \sqsubseteq_s t'^s]\!]_\rho^\mathcal{D} = \begin{cases} \underline{t} & \text{if } [\![t^s]\!]_\rho^\mathcal{D} \sqsubseteq_s^\mathcal{D} [\![t'^s]\!]_\rho^\mathcal{D} \\ \underline{f} & \text{otherwise.} \end{cases}$

- $[\![P(t_1, \ldots, t_n)]\!]_\rho^\mathcal{D} = P^\mathcal{D}([\![t_1]\!]_\rho^\mathcal{D}, \ldots, [\![t_n]\!]_\rho^\mathcal{D})$.

- *For the rest of Σ-formulas the semantics is defined as in many-sorted logic.*

Lemma 9 *Let $\mathcal{D}$ be a Σ-structure then:*

(i) *Coincidence Lemma for formulas. If $\rho(x) \approx_s^\mathcal{D} \sigma(x)$, for all x free in φ and sort s, then $[\![\varphi]\!]_\rho^\mathcal{D} = [\![\varphi]\!]_\sigma^\mathcal{D}$.*

(ii) *Substitution Lemma for formulas. $[\![\varphi[t/x]]\!]_\rho^\mathcal{D} = [\![\varphi]\!]_{\rho[[\![t]\!]_\rho^\mathcal{D}/x]}^\mathcal{D}$.*

(iii) *Monotonicity and antimonotonicity of atomic formulas. Let $P(t_1, \ldots, t_n)(\equiv A) \in F(\Sigma)$ and $p \in Pos(t_i)$ a monotonic (resp. antimon.) position of A at i such that $[\![t_i|_p]\!]_\rho^\mathcal{D} \sqsubseteq_s^\mathcal{D} [\![t]\!]_\rho^\mathcal{D}$, then $[\![P(t_1, \ldots, t_n)]\!]_\rho^\mathcal{D} = \underline{t} \Rightarrow [\![P(t_1, \ldots, t_i[t]_p, \ldots, t_n)]\!]_\rho^\mathcal{D} = \underline{t}$ (resp. $[\![P(t_1, \ldots, t_i[t]_p, \ldots, t_n)]\!]_\rho^\mathcal{D} = \underline{t} \Rightarrow [\![P(t_1, \ldots, t_n)]\!]_\rho^\mathcal{D} = \underline{t}$).*

If the truth value of a Σ-formula φ in a Σ-interpretation $\langle \mathcal{D}, \rho \rangle$ is $\underline{t}$ we say that $\langle \mathcal{D}, \rho \rangle$ is a *model* of φ (or φ is *satisfiable* in $\langle \mathcal{D}, \rho \rangle$). Given a set of Σ-formulas Φ, we say that $\langle \mathcal{D}, \rho \rangle$ is a *model* of Φ if it is a model of ψ for all $\psi \in \Phi$, and φ is a *logical consequence* of Φ, written $\Phi \models \varphi$, if every model of Φ is a model of φ.

---

[2] $\rho[a/x]$ is the valuation that coincides with ρ in $y \neq x$ and $\rho[a/x](x) = a$.

3 A Ground Tableau System

This section presents an extension of first order semantic tableaux [Fit 96] to deal with preorders. Attempts of adding the axioms characterizing a preordered structure to the initial set of formulas do not lead to satisfying results, because of the huge increasing of the search space. It is better to formulate additional tableau expansion rules to capture the essential properties of preorders.

In the definition of the method we need to extend the signature Σ by countably infinite sets AC^s, $s \in S$, of new auxiliary constants. The new signature so obtained will be denoted by $\overline{\Sigma}$. The partition of $\overline{\Sigma}$-formulas in *Alpha, Beta, Gamma* and *Delta* classes is the usual in classical logic (cf. [Fit 96]). The *Basic* class is the set of atomic $\overline{\Sigma}$-formulas, $P(t_1, \ldots, t_n)$, $t \sqsubseteq_s t'$, and their complementaries $\neg P(t_1, \ldots, t_n)$, $\neg t \sqsubseteq_s t'$.

The expansion rules used during the construction of a tableau for a non-empty set Φ of Σ-sentences[3] are defined as follows:

α If $\mathcal{T}$ is a finite tableau for Φ, B is a branch of $\mathcal{T}$ and $\varphi \wedge \psi$ (resp. $\neg\neg\varphi$) is a sentence labeling some of its nodes then the tree resulting from enlarging B with nodes labeled by φ and ψ (resp. φ) is a finite tableau for Φ.

β If $\mathcal{T}$ is a finite tableau for Φ, B is a branch of $\mathcal{T}$ and $\neg(\varphi \wedge \psi)$ is a sentence labeling some of its nodes then the tree resulting from splitting B with two nodes labeled by $\neg\varphi$ and $\neg\psi$ is a finite tableau for Φ.

γ, δ If $\mathcal{T}$ is a finite tableau for Φ, B is a branch of $\mathcal{T}$ and $\neg\exists x^s\varphi$ ($\exists x^s\varphi$, for δ) is a sentence labeling some of its nodes, then the tree resulting from enlarging B with a node labeled by $\neg\varphi[t/x^s]$ ($\varphi[c/x^s]$, for δ), where $t \in T(\overline{\Sigma}, s)$ and ground, ($c \in AC^s$ and does not occur in B's nodes, for δ), is a finite tableau for Φ.

In If $\mathcal{T}$ is a finite tableau for Φ then the result of enlarging some branch B with a new node labeled by a $\varphi \in \Phi$, which is not yet in B, is a finite tableau for Φ.

Ref If $\mathcal{T}$ is a finite tableau for Φ then the result of enlarging some branch B with a new node labeled by $t \sqsubseteq t$, where t is a ground $\overline{\Sigma}$-term, is a finite tableau for Φ.

ζ_1, ζ_2 If $\mathcal{T}$ is a finite tableau for Φ, B is a branch of $\mathcal{T}$, $t \sqsubseteq_s t'$, ($t' \sqsubseteq_s t$, for ζ_2) $t_1 \sqsubseteq_{s'}$ $t_2[t]_p$ are sentences labeling two nodes of B, and p is a monotonic (antimonotonic, for ζ_2) position of t_2 then the tree resulting from extending B with a node labeled by $t_1 \sqsubseteq_{s'} t_2[t']_p$ is a finite tableau for Φ.

ξ_1, ξ_2 If $\mathcal{T}$ is a finite tableau for Φ, B is a branch of $\mathcal{T}$, $P(t_1, \ldots, t_i[t]_p, \ldots, t_n)(\equiv A)$, $t \sqsubseteq_s t'$ ($t' \sqsubseteq_s t$, for ξ_2) are sentences labeling two nodes of B, and p is a monotonic (antimonotonic, for ξ_2) position of A at i then the tree resulting from extending B with a node labeled by $P(t_1, \ldots, t_i[t']_p, \ldots, t_n)$ is a finite tableau for Φ.

Rules α—δ are classical first order expansion rules and are applied to sentences in classes *Alpha, Beta, Gamma* and *Delta*, respectively. Rules *Ref*, ζ_1, ζ_2, ξ_1, ξ_2 are the inequality extension rules.

---

[3]Σ-formulas without free variables.

Definition 10 *A tableau sequence for a non-empty set Φ of Σ-sentences is any sequence $T_0, T_1, T_2, \ldots$ where T_0 is a linear tree with a branch labeled by some sentences $\{\varphi_1, \ldots, \varphi_n\} \subseteq \Phi$. And T_{k+1} arises from T_k through one of the tableau rules α—ξ_2 above. An infinite tableau for a non-empty set of Σ-sentences Φ is defined as the limit of some tableau sequence.*

We say that a branch in a tableau is *closed*, and then it is neither enlarged nor split anymore, when an atomic contradiction is detected at its labels. That means, φ and $\neg\varphi$ (φ atomic) are on the branch. Otherwise the branch is *open*. A tableau is *closed* if all its branches are closed.

As we will prove, this tableau method is (refutationally) sound and complete.

Theorem 11 (Soundness) *For every set Φ of Σ-sentences, if Φ has a closed tableau, then Φ is non-satisfiable.*

Proof. It is based on the soundness of expansion rules in the sense that an extension of a branch that has a model also has a model. ζ_1, ζ_2 are sound due to Lemma 7 (iii) and transitivity of preorders. Soundness of ξ_1, ξ_2 uses Lemma 9 (iii). ∎

3.1 Completeness

The tableau method we have presented is refutationally complete in the sense expressed by the opposite direction in the previous theorem. We show that if a set of sentences Φ does not have a closed tableau, then we can obtain sufficient information from a systematically built tableau to define a model of Φ. This information is derived from the set of sentences **H** labeling an open branch having special saturation properties (w.r.t. the tableau expansion rules). The properties of **H** are defined in *Hintikka's* way.

Definition 12 (Hintikka set) *A set of $\overline{\Sigma}$-sentences **H** is a Hintikka set if it satisfies the following conditions:*

(1) If $\varphi_1 \wedge \varphi_2 \in \mathbf{H}$ then $\varphi_1, \varphi_2 \in \mathbf{H}$.

(2) If $\neg(\varphi_1 \wedge \varphi_2) \in \mathbf{H}$ then $\neg\varphi_1 \in \mathbf{H}$ or $\neg\varphi_2 \in \mathbf{H}$.

(3) If $\neg\neg\varphi \in \mathbf{H}$ then $\varphi \in \mathbf{H}$.

(4) If $\exists x^s \varphi \in \mathbf{H}$ then there exists a constant $c \in AC^s$ such that $\varphi[c/x] \in \mathbf{H}$.

(5) If $\neg\exists x^s \varphi \in \mathbf{H}$ then $\neg\varphi[t/x] \in \mathbf{H}$, for all ground $t \in T(\overline{\Sigma}, s)$.

(6) For all ground $t \in T(\overline{\Sigma}, s), s \in S, t \sqsubseteq_s t \in \mathbf{H}$.

(7) For any terms $t, t' \in T(\overline{\Sigma}, s), s \in S$:

(i) if $t \sqsubseteq_s t'$ (resp. $t' \sqsubseteq_s t$), $t_1 \sqsubseteq_{s'} t_2[t]_p \in \mathbf{H}$, and p is a monotonic (resp. antimonotonic) position of t_2, then $t_1 \sqsubseteq t_2[t']_p \in \mathbf{H}$,

(ii) if $t \sqsubseteq_s t'$ (resp. $t' \sqsubseteq_s t$), $P(t_1, \ldots, t_i[t]_p, \ldots, t_n)(\equiv A) \in \mathbf{H}$, and p is a monotonic (resp. antimonotonic) position of A at i, then $P(t_1, \ldots, t_i[t']_p, \ldots, t_n) \in \mathbf{H}$.

(8) **H** *is a coherent set of sentences, i.e. no atomic sentence belongs to* **H** *together with its negation.*

A term model for a Hintikka set **H** can be defined by ordering terms according to the information that **H** has about them.

Lemma 13 *The system* $\mathcal{D} = \langle \{(D^s, \sqsubseteq_s^{\mathcal{D}}) | s \in S\}, \{c^{\mathcal{D}}, f^{\mathcal{D}}, P^{\mathcal{D}} | c, f, P \in \Sigma\}\rangle$ *where:* $D^s = \{t | t \in T(\overline{\Sigma}, s), t \text{ ground}\}$; $t \sqsubseteq_s^{\mathcal{D}} t' \Leftrightarrow t \sqsubseteq_s t' \in \mathbf{H}$; *if* $f^{\mathcal{D}} : D^{s_1} \times \ldots \times D^{s_n} \to D^s$, *then* $f^{\mathcal{D}}(t_1, \ldots, t_n) = f(t_1, \ldots, t_n)$[4]; *if* $P^{\mathcal{D}} : D^{s_1} \times \ldots \times D^{s_n} \to \{\underline{t}, \underline{f}\}$, *then* $P^{\mathcal{D}}(t_1, \ldots, t_n) = \underline{t}$ *if* $P(t_1, \ldots, t_n) \in \mathbf{H}$, *and* $P^{\mathcal{D}}(t_1, \ldots, t_n) = \underline{f}$ *otherwise; is a* $\overline{\Sigma}$*-structure.*

Proof. $\sqsubseteq_s^{\mathcal{D}}$ is a preorder on D^s. Note that D^s is not empty because every sort is inhabited. For reflexivity, $t \sqsubseteq_s t \in \mathbf{H}$, by Definition 12.(6), then $t \sqsubseteq_s^{\mathcal{D}} t$, for any $t \in D^s$. For transitivity, if $t \sqsubseteq_s^{\mathcal{D}} t'$ and $t' \sqsubseteq_s^{\mathcal{D}} t''$ then $t \sqsubseteq_s t', t' \sqsubseteq_s t'' \in \mathbf{H}$, and $t \sqsubseteq_s t'' \in \mathbf{H}$, by Definition 12.(7)(i) since ε is a monotonic position of t'; therefore $t \sqsubseteq_s^{\mathcal{D}} t''$. On the other hand, if $m(f)(i) = 0$ then $f^{\mathcal{D}}$ is monotonic in the i-th argument. In fact, if $t_i \sqsubseteq_{s_i}^{\mathcal{D}} t_i'$, then $t_i \sqsubseteq_{s_i} t_i' \in \mathbf{H}$, so from Definition 12.(7)(i) and 12.(6) we can deduce $f(t_1, \ldots, t_n) \sqsubseteq_s f(t_1', \ldots, t_n') \in \mathbf{H}$, therefore $f^{\mathcal{D}}(t_1, \ldots, t_n) \sqsubseteq_s^{\mathcal{D}} f^{\mathcal{D}}(t_1', \ldots, t_n')$. We would reason analogously for $m(f)(i) = 1$ and $P^{\mathcal{D}}$. ∎

Theorem 14 *Every Hintikka set* **H** *has a model.*

Proof. We prove that for all $\overline{\Sigma}$-sentence φ, if $\varphi \in \mathbf{H}$ and $\mathcal{D}$ is the $\overline{\Sigma}$-structure of Lemma 13, then $[\![\varphi]\!]^{\mathcal{D}} = \underline{t}$.[5] It is immediate that $[\![t]\!]^{\mathcal{D}} = t$, for every ground $\overline{\Sigma}$-term t. Then proceed by induction on φ. Let us see some cases:

- If $\exists x^s \varphi \in \mathbf{H}$ then there exists $c \in AC^s$ such that $\varphi[c/x] \in \mathbf{H}$, by Definition 12.(4); by induction hypothesis $[\![\varphi[c/x]]\!]^{\mathcal{D}} = \underline{t}$, so by Lemma 9.(ii) $[\![\exists x^s \varphi]\!]^{\mathcal{D}} = \underline{t}$.

- If $\neg t_1 \sqsubseteq_s t_2 \in \mathbf{H}$ then $t_1 \sqsubseteq_s t_2 \notin \mathbf{H}$ by Definition 12.(8). If $[\![t_1 \sqsubseteq_s t_2]\!]^{\mathcal{D}} = \underline{t}$, then $[\![t_1]\!]^{\mathcal{D}} \sqsubseteq_s^{\mathcal{D}} [\![t_2]\!]^{\mathcal{D}}$ and, by definition of $\sqsubseteq_s^{\mathcal{D}}$, we would have $t_1 \sqsubseteq_s t_2 \in \mathbf{H}$. Therefore $[\![t_1 \sqsubseteq_s t_2]\!]^{\mathcal{D}} = \underline{f}$. ∎

We are interested in a method for building a tableau such that, if it does not become closed, then every open branch is a Hintikka set **H**. Then we will define the notion of *fair* tableau construction rule, as a suitable algorithm so that, every sentence occurring in an open branch will have the corresponding rule applied to it; that yields the conditions (1)-(5) and (7) of Definition 12 for **H**. Condition (6) is satisfied by simply supposing that the reflexivity of every term is eventually introduced onto every open branch.

Definition 15 *A ground tableau construction rule is a procedure* $\mathcal{R}$ *that given a finite tableau* $\mathcal{T}$ *produces as answer either a refusal if no continuation is possible, or a new tableau* $\mathcal{T}'$ *that results from the application of a ground tableau expansion rule to* $\mathcal{T}$. *A ground tableau construction rule* $\mathcal{R}$ *is fair if, for any tableau sequence* $\mathcal{T}_0, \mathcal{T}_1, \ldots$ *for a set of* Σ*-sentences* Φ *constructed according to* $\mathcal{R}$, *it verifies the following properties:*

---

[4]If f is a constant c then $c^{\mathcal{D}} = c$.

[5]Note that no valuation is needed because **H** does not contain free variables.

1. Every $\varphi \in \Phi$ is eventually introduced onto each open branch of some T_i.

2. Every non-Basic sentence occurrence in an open branch of any T_i eventually has the appropriate first order tableau expansion rule applied to it.

3. For any i, every occurrence of a sentence of class Gamma in an open branch in T_i has the γ-rule applied to it arbitrarily often.

4. $\mathcal{R}$ eventually introduces $t \sqsubseteq t$ onto each open branch of some T_i, for every ground $\overline{\Sigma}$-term t.

5. For any i, every occurrence of a pair of Basic sentences in an open branch in T_i, for which ζ_1, ζ_2, ξ_1 or ξ_2 rules can be used, eventually has the appropriate extension rule applied to it.

Theorem 16 (Completeness) *Let $\mathcal{R}$ be a fair ground tableau construction rule. If Φ is a non-satisfiable set of Σ-sentences then Φ has a closed tableau constructed according to $\mathcal{R}$.*

Proof. Assume that Φ has no closed tableaux. Let T be the tableau for Φ constructed according to $\mathcal{R}$. In particular this systematically built tableau is not closed. Even if T is infinite, and by König's Lemma has an infinite branch –that will be open because closed branches are finite–, we can assure that there exists a branch B with the saturation properties w.r.t. the tableau expansion rules inducing the definition of Hintikka sets. So the sentences labeling the nodes of B form a Hintikka set **H** including Φ. By Theorem 14, **H** has a model which in turn supplies a model for Φ. ∎

4 Free Variable Tableaux

Regarding implementation, the ground version of first order semantic tableaux is very inefficient, even more in presence of inequalities. A more efficient system may be defined using free variable quantifier rules, which introduce new free variables, instead of ground terms, substituting the quantified variable of a formula of class *Gamma*. Then these free variables will be instantiated on demand, either to close a branch or applying inequality rules to expand a branch.

We will assume that the extended signature $\overline{\Sigma}$ also contains a collection of countable sets $SF^{s_1,\ldots,s_l \to s}$, $s_1,\ldots,s_l,s \in S$, of Skolem function symbols, which are monotonic in all their arguments.

Following [BH 92], γ and δ rules are modified in the following sense:

γ', δ^+ If T is a finite tableau for Φ, B is a branch of T and $\neg \exists x^s \varphi$ ($\exists x^s \varphi$, for δ^+) is a formula labeling some of its nodes, then the tree resulting from enlarging B with a node labeled by $\neg \varphi[y^s/x^s]$ ($\varphi[f(x_1,\ldots,x_n)/x^s]$, for δ^+) is a finite tableau for Φ, where y^s is a new free variable, that is, it is not used for $\neg \exists x^s \varphi$ in B (where f is a new Skolem function symbol and $x_1,\ldots,x_n$ are the free variables in $\exists x^s \varphi$, for δ^+).

Using this new approach to first order tableaux, the inequality expansion rules may require substituting variables. Then the replacement rules ζ_1, ζ_2, ξ_1 and ξ_2 are redefined as follows:

ζ_1', ζ_2' If $\mathcal{T}$ is a finite tableau for Φ, $t \sqsubseteq_\bullet t'$, $(t' \sqsubseteq_\bullet t$, for $\zeta_2')$ and $t_1 \sqsubseteq_{\bullet'} t_2[t'']_p$ are formulas labeling two nodes of a branch B of $\mathcal{T}$, σ is the most general unifier of t and t'', and p is a monotonic (antimonotonic, for ζ_2') position of t_2, then the tree resulting from the tableau $\mathcal{T}\sigma$, extending the branch $B\sigma$ with a node labeled by $(t_1 \sqsubseteq_{\bullet'} t_2[t']_p)\sigma$, is a finite tableau for Φ.

ξ_1', ξ_2' If $\mathcal{T}$ is a finite tableau for Φ, $t \sqsubseteq_\bullet t'$, $(t' \sqsubseteq_\bullet t$, for $\xi_2')$ and $P(t_1, \ldots, t_i[t'']_p, \ldots, t_n)$ $(\equiv A)$ are formulas labeling two nodes of a branch B of $\mathcal{T}$, σ is the most general unifier of t and t'', and p is a monotonic (antimonotonic, for ξ_2') position of A at i, then the tree resulting from the tableau $\mathcal{T}\sigma$, extending the branch $B\sigma$ with a node labeled by $P(t_1, \ldots, t_i[t']_p, \ldots, t_n)\sigma$, is a finite tableau for Φ.

It is important to note that the most general unifier σ has to be applied not only to the involved formulas but to the whole tableau.

Dealing with free variables, in order to ensure completeness two new reflexivity rules are needed instead of Ref:

$Refv, Reff$ If $\mathcal{T}$ is a finite tableau for Φ then the result of enlarging some branch B with a new node labeled by $x \sqsubseteq x$ $(f(x_1, \ldots, x_n) \sqsubseteq f(x_1, \ldots, x_n)$, for $Reff)$, where x is new in B $(f$ is any function symbol of $\overline{\Sigma}$ and $x_1, \ldots, x_n$ are new in B, for $Reff)$, is a finite tableau for Φ.

Unification may as well become necessary for closing a branch as the following definition shows.

Definition 17 *A free variable tableau $\mathcal{T}$ with branches $B_1, \ldots, B_k$ is closed iff there is a grounding substitution σ such that, for every $1 \le i \le k$, there are two basic formulas φ_i and ψ_i labeling two nodes of B_i such that $\varphi_i\sigma$ and $\psi_i\sigma$ are complementary.*

The soundness of the new method can be established along the same lines as in the ground case, but using the arguments of Hähnle and Schmitt [HS 94] for the δ^+-rule. In the next subsection we prove that the method is complete even when some restrictions are placed on the tableau construction mechanism.

4.1 Completeness

The main result of this section is a Lifting Lemma that allows to show completeness of the free variable method leaning on the completeness of the ground case. The idea of this lemma is that any extension of a ground tableau can be lifted to an extension of a free variable tableau producing a similar effect.

Lemma 18 (Lifting Lemma) *Let $\mathcal{T}$ be a free variable tableau and τ be a grounding substitution whose domain is the set of free variables of $\mathcal{T}$. If $\mathcal{T}\tau$ can be closed applying Ref, ζ_1, ζ_2, ξ_1 and ξ_2 rules, then $\mathcal{T}$ can be closed using $Refv$, $Reff$, ζ_1', ζ_2', ξ_1' and ξ_2' rules.*

Proof. By induction on the number n of applications of *Ref*, ζ_1, ζ_2, ξ_1 and ξ_2 rules needed for closing $\mathcal{T}\tau$. If $n = 0$, then $\mathcal{T}\tau$ is closed and $\mathcal{T}$ is obviously also closed.

For the induction step, assume the goal for a number n of inequality extension rule applications, and suppose that $\mathcal{T}\tau$ needs $n + 1$ to be closed. Let $B_1, \ldots, B_l$ be the branches of $\mathcal{T}$, then there is some i, $1 \leq i \leq l$, such that $B_i\tau$ needs $m + 1$, $0 \leq m \leq n$, applications of *Ref*, ζ_1, ζ_2, ξ_1 and ξ_2 rules to be closed. Let B^* be the branch obtained from extending $B_i\tau$ with the first application of *Ref*, ζ_1, ζ_2, ξ_1 and ξ_2 rules. Then B^* can be closed in m steps. The idea of the proof is to transform $\mathcal{T}$ in $\mathcal{T}'$, with branches $B'_1, \ldots, B'_l$, –using the tableau rules allowed in the lemma– and to obtain a grounding substitution τ' such that $B'_j\tau' = B_j\tau$, $1 \leq j \leq l$, $j \neq i$, and $B'_i\tau' \supseteq B^{*6}$. That means that $\mathcal{T}'\tau'$ can be closed with n applications of the inequality rules. Therefore, by the induction hypothesis, we deduce that $\mathcal{T}$ can be closed applying only *Refv*, *Reff*, ζ'_1, ζ'_2, ξ'_1 and ξ'_2 rules.

Let us construct $\mathcal{T}'$ by case analysis depending on the rule that converts $B_i\tau$ in B^*. We avoid the subscript i in order to simplify the notation.

The case *Ref* is easy to prove using *Refv* in B with a new variable not appearing in $\mathcal{T}$. Suppose now that B^* is obtained by applying ξ_1 to some formulas of $B\tau$. We may assume that the branches B, $B\tau$ and B^* have the following scheme:

$\underline{B}$	$\underline{B\tau}$	$\underline{B^*}$	
$\vdots$	$\vdots$	$B\tau$	
$t \sqsubseteq t'$	$t\tau \sqsubseteq t'\tau$	$\mid$	
$P(t_1, \ldots, t_k)$	$P(t_1\tau, \ldots, t_k\tau)$	$P(t_1\tau, \ldots, t_i\tau[t'\tau]_p, \ldots, t_k\tau)$	$t_i\tau\vert_p = t\tau.$

As we will prove in the next lemma, there is $q \in Pos(t_i)$, $q \leq p$, such that B can be extended to a branch B'', with *Reff*, ζ'_1 and ζ'_2, in such a way that B'' contains B and also an inequality $s_q \sqsubseteq s'_q$ or $s'_q \sqsubseteq s_q$ for which there is a substitution τ' extending τ such that: (i) $s'_q\tau' = (t_i\tau\vert_q)[t'\tau]_{p-q}$, and (ii) τ' unifies s_q and $t_i\vert_q$.

Assuming this result, the desired branch B' is constructed from B'' applying ξ'_1 to $s_q \sqsubseteq s'_q$ (or ξ'_2 to $s'_q \sqsubseteq s_q$) and $P(t_1, \ldots, t_k)$. So $B' = B''\sigma \cup P(t_1\sigma, \ldots, (t_i[s'_q]_q)\sigma, \ldots, t_k\sigma)$, where σ is the mgu of s_q and $t_i\vert_q$. Then $B'\tau' \supseteq B^*$ as we show:

- $B''\sigma\tau' = B''\tau'$ (by (ii)) $\supseteq B\tau' = B\tau$ (because τ' agrees with τ in B).

- $P(t_1\sigma\tau', \ldots, (t_i[s'_q]_q)\sigma\tau', \ldots, t_k\sigma\tau') = P(t_1\tau, \ldots, t_i\tau[s'_q\tau']_q, \ldots, t_k\tau)$

    (because $(t_i\vert_q)\tau = t_i\tau\vert_q$, τ' agrees with τ in B and (ii))

    $= P(t_1\tau, \ldots, t_i\tau[(t_i\tau\vert_q)[t'\tau]_{p-q}]_q, \ldots, t_k\tau)$ (by (i)) $= P(t_1\tau, \ldots, t_i\tau[t'\tau]_p, \ldots, t_k\tau)$

    (since $(t_i\tau\vert_q)\vert_{p-q} = t_i\tau\vert_p$).

For the other branches $B'_j = B_j\sigma$ and $B'_j\tau' = B_j\tau$ trivially.

A similar reasoning is used for the cases ζ_1, ζ_2 and ξ_2. ∎

The next result says that the extension of $\mathcal{T}\tau$ can be lifted even in the case that the inequality rule were applied to a new subterm t introduced by τ. This will be possible by previously building an inequality containing a term unifying with t.

---

[6] The equality and inclusion refer to the sets of formulas labeling the nodes of the mentioned branches.

Lemma 19 *Using the notation and conditions of the preceding lemma, if $t_i \tau|_p = t\tau$ then there is a position q of t_i, $q \leq p$, such that T can be expanded using only Refl, ζ_1' and ζ_2' rules, in such a way that only B changes and is extended to a branch B' such that $B' \supseteq B$, and B' also contains, for each position r, $q \leq r \leq p$, an inequality $s_r \sqsubseteq s_r'$ ($s_r' \sqsubseteq s_r$) if r is a monotonic (resp. antimonotonic) position of $P(t_1\tau, \ldots, t_n\tau)$ at i, for which there is a substitution τ' extending τ such that:*

i) $s_r\tau' = (t_i\tau|_r)[t\tau]_{p-r}$ and $s_r'\tau' = (t_i\tau|_r)[t'\tau]_{p-r}$. ii) τ' is a unifier of s_q and $t_i|_q$.

Proof. Let q be the greatest position such that $q \leq p$ and $q \in Pos(t_i)$. If $p \in Pos(t_i)$ then $q = p$; otherwise $t_i|_q$ is a variable. Let us prove that in any case, q is the sought position.

By induction on the length of $p - q$. If $p - q = \varepsilon$ then $r = p = q$. Let $B' \equiv B$, $s_r \sqsubseteq s_r' \equiv t \sqsubseteq t'$ and $\tau' \equiv \tau$, then $s_q\tau' = t\tau = (t_i\tau|_q)[t\tau]_\varepsilon$ and $s_q'\tau' = t'\tau = (t_i\tau|_q)[t'\tau]_\varepsilon$, proving i). On the other side, $(t_i|_q)\tau = t_i\tau|_q = t_i\tau|_p = t\tau = s_q\tau$, proving ii).

For the induction step, assume the lemma for a length n and let $n + 1$ the length of $p - q$. Then there are B'' and τ'' verifying the goal, which implies the existence in B'' of an inequality for each r, $q < r \leq p$. Our present goal is to extend B'' in order to incorporate an inequality for q. Suppose $p - q = j.r'$ for some $j \in N$ and a chain r' of length n. Let r be the position $q.j$ and suppose that r is an antimonotonic position, then $p-r = r'$ and, by the induction hypothesis, the formula $s_r' \sqsubseteq s_r$ (†) is in B'' and i) is verified. Since $q.j$ is a position of $t_i\tau$, there is a function symbol f of a certain arity k, $k \geq j$, such that $t_i\tau|_q = f(u_1, \ldots, u_k)$ for some ground terms $u_1, \ldots, u_k$. Apply Refl to B'' extending the branch with the formula $f(z_1, \ldots, z_k) \sqsubseteq f(z_1, \ldots, z_k)$ (‡), being $z_1, \ldots, z_k$ new variables not appearing in T neither in B''. Next suppose that $m(f)(j) = 1$ and apply ζ_2' to (†) and (‡), using the substitution $[s_r/z_j]$. The extended branch will be:

$$B' = B'' \cup \{f(z_1, \ldots, z_{j-1}, s_r, z_{j+1}, \ldots, z_k) \sqsubseteq f(z_1, \ldots, z_{j-1}, s_r, z_{j+1}, \ldots, z_k),$$
$$f(z_1, \ldots, z_{j-1}, s_r, z_{j+1}, \ldots, z_k) \sqsubseteq f(z_1, \ldots, z_{j-1}, s_r', z_{j+1}, \ldots, z_k)(\S)\}.$$

The other branches do not change because z_j does not appear on them. Taking $\tau' = \tau'' \cup [u_1/z_1, \ldots, u_{j-1}/z_{j-1}, u_{j+1}/z_{j+1}, \ldots, u_k/z_k]$, a straightforward proof allows to deduce that (§) is the formula $s_q \sqsubseteq s_q'$ we were looking for. Other cases are similarly proved using ζ_1' when necessary. ∎

In practice, even using the free variable version, the implementation of the tableau method may result considerably inefficient if any order in the application of the rules is allowed. Let us impose some restrictions to the tableau construction mechanism in order to improve efficiency, without loss of completeness:

- For the application of γ', Refv and Refl rules, we enumerate the set of variables X as $x_1, x_2, \ldots$. Applying γ' to a formula φ of class *Gamma* on a branch B, φ is instantiated with the first free variable x_i^s of the enumeration not used for φ in B, where s is the sort of the quantified variable of φ. Similarly, applying Refv and Refl.

- We consider a limit $l \geq 1$ for the number of applications of γ'-rule to every occurrence of a formula of class *Gamma* on a branch.

- All the possible applications of first order expansion rules and *In* come before the applications of the inequality extension rules.

Definition 20 *The definition of free variable tableau construction rule is similar to the ground case. A free variable tableau construction rule $\mathcal{R}$ is fair with respect to a limit l for the application of γ'-rule if, for any tableau sequence $T_0, T_1, \ldots$ for a set of Σ-sentences Φ constructed according to $\mathcal{R}$, it verifies:*

1. *Every sentence $\varphi \in \Phi$ is eventually introduced onto each open tableau branch.*

2. *For any i, if T_i is open, every non-Basic formula occurrence in a branch of T_i, eventually has the appropriate first order tableau expansion rule applied to it.*

3. *For any i, if T_i is open, every occurrence of a formula of class Gamma in a branch of T_i has the γ'-rule applied to it l times.*

4. *$\mathcal{R}$ eventually introduces $x \sqsubseteq x$ and $f(x_1, \ldots, x_n) \sqsubseteq f(x_1, \ldots, x_n)$ onto each open tableau branch, for each new free variable x, and each function symbol f of $\overline{\Sigma}$ and all new free variables $x_1, \ldots, x_n$, respectively.*

5. *For any i, if T_i is open, every occurrence in a branch of T_i of a pair of Basic formulas for which $\zeta'_1, \zeta'_2, \xi'_1$ or ξ'_2 rules can be used, eventually has the appropriate extension rule applied to it.*

Actually we are assuming that the set of sentences for which a tableau is constructed is finite. If not, a limit for the application of *In*-rule on each branch should be fixed, and a completeness result could be proved similarly to the next one.

Theorem 21 (Completeness) *Let Φ be a non-satisfiable finite set of Σ-sentences. There is a limit $l \geq 1$ for which, if $\mathcal{R}$ is a fair free variable tableau construction rule with respect to l such that: a) the applications of all first order expansion rules and In come first, and b) all possible applications of inequality rules come next, then Φ has a closed free variable tableau constructed according to $\mathcal{R}$.*

Proof. Sketch. Consider an enumeration $t_1, t_2, \ldots$ of the ground $\overline{\Sigma}$-terms, where the sort of t_i is the sort of x_i, being x_i the i-th element of the enumeration of variables used by $\mathcal{R}$, and let σ be the substitution $[t_1/x_1, t_2/x_2, \ldots]$. It is possible to find a fair ground tableau construction rule $\mathcal{R}'$ similar to $\mathcal{R}$[7], but not considering any limit for the application of γ'-rule, in such a way that, if T' is constructed according to $\mathcal{R}'$, then there is a free variable tableau T for Φ constructed according to $\mathcal{R}$ such that $T' = T\sigma$.

Theorem 16 assures the existence of a closed ground tableau T_g for Φ constructed according to $\mathcal{R}'$. Let l be the greatest number of the applications of γ-rule to a sentence of T_g. Transform T_g by applying γ-rule until to reach the limit l, for every occurrence in T_g of a sentence of class *Gamma*, and moving the applications of inequality rules to the end[8]. Let T'_g be the part of the transformed tableau, before the application

---

[7] $\mathcal{R}'$ uses δ-rule for a sentence φ with a functional Skolem term $f(t'_1, \ldots, t'_n)$ instead of an auxiliary constant, being $t'_1, \ldots, t'_n$ the terms previously introduced in φ by some expansion rule. See [GLN 96] for details.

[8] This movement has no matter because the resulting sentences of *Ref*, ζ_1, ζ_2, ξ_1 and ξ_2 rules are *Basic*.

of the inequality extension rules. Let $\mathcal{T}_v$ be a free variable tableau for Φ constructed according to $\mathcal{R}$ such that $\mathcal{T}_v\sigma = \mathcal{T}_g'$. Using Lifting Lemma, since $\mathcal{T}_g'$ can be extended to a closed tableau applying Ref, ζ_1, ζ_2, ξ_1 and ξ_2 rules, $\mathcal{T}_v$ can be closed using inequality rules. ∎

5   Examples

Example 22 The free variable tableau system defined for PL can be used when working with an order sorted logic in which the set of sorts is partially ordered by $\leq$. In this case, sorts are considered in PL as terms of a new sort, ordered by the relation $\sqsubseteq$ that denotes the relation $\leq$ between sorts. The following example treated in [Wal 90] also with tableaux can be easily solved in our system.

(i) No used-car dealer buys a used car. (ii) Some people who buy used cars are absolutely dishonest. Conclude that (iii) some absolutely dishonest people are not used-car dealers.

Let s_1, s_2 and s_3 be sorts representing, respectively, people who buy used cars, absolutely dishonest people and used-car dealers. We axiomatize (ii) by defining s_4 as subsort of s_1 and s_2. We also say that s_2 is subsort of s_3, axiomatizing the negation of statement (iii). For (i) we establish that there is not a sort which is a subsort of s_3 and s_1. A closed tableau is found for this set of sentences.

$$1 : s_4 \sqsubseteq s_1$$
$$|$$
$$2 : s_4 \sqsubseteq s_2$$
$$|$$
$$3 : s_2 \sqsubseteq s_3$$
$$|$$
$$4 : \neg\exists x(x \sqsubseteq s_3 \wedge x \sqsubseteq s_1)$$
$$| \quad \gamma' \text{ to } 4$$
$$5 : \neg(x_1 \sqsubseteq s_3 \wedge x_1 \sqsubseteq s_1)$$

$$\beta \text{ to } 5$$

$$6 : \neg x_1 \sqsubseteq s_3 \qquad 7 : \neg x_1 \sqsubseteq s_1$$
$$| \ \zeta_1' \text{ to } 3,2 \qquad \sharp \text{ by } 1,7$$
$$8 : s_4 \sqsubseteq s_3$$
$$\sharp \text{ by } 6,8$$

The substitution $[s_4/x_1]$ allows to close the whole tableau.

Example 23 Interpreting $\sqsubseteq$ as the inclusion relation between sets, we prove the following inclusion of the De Morgan's law $x \cup y \sqsubseteq \overline{\overline{x} \cap \overline{y}}$ from basic properties of the involved operations $\cup$, $\cap$ and $^-$.

Let $\varphi_1 \equiv \forall x(x \sqsubseteq \overline{\overline{x}})$, $\varphi_2 \equiv \forall x\forall y\forall z(x \sqsubseteq z \wedge y \sqsubseteq z \rightarrow x \cup y \sqsubseteq z)$, $\varphi_3 \equiv \forall x\forall y(x \cap y \sqsubseteq x \wedge x \cap y \sqsubseteq y)$, and $\psi \equiv \forall x\forall y(x \cup y \sqsubseteq \overline{\overline{x} \cap \overline{y}})$. We prove that $\{\varphi_1, \varphi_2, \varphi_3, \neg\psi\}$ has a closed tableau. We present below part of the tableau. For simplicity, the initial linear tableau containing the sentences 1: φ_1, 2: φ_2, 3: φ_3 and 4: $\neg\psi$ does not appear. Note that the applications of rules ζ_2' and ζ_1' obtaining 16 and 17 would change the tableau by applying the substitutions $[y_2/w_1]$ and $[\overline{z}/y_2]$, respectively. Then taking into account these substitutions, and extending B_1 similarly to B_2, an extension of the substitution $\sigma = [a/x_1, b/x_2, \overline{a} \cap \overline{b}/x_3, \overline{a}/y_1, b/z]$ allows finally to close the tableau.

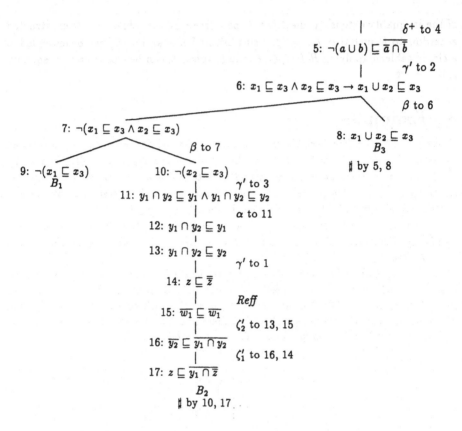

6 Conclusions and Future Work

In this paper we have presented a many-sorted first order logic for reasoning about preorders, where functions and predicates behave monotonically or antimonotonically on their arguments. We have defined a sound and complete semantic tableau method for this logic, characterizing preorders by expansion rules, in two versions; one for the ground case and another, more efficient, using free variables. The completeness of this second version is proved through a lifting lemma based on the completeness of the ground case.

We plan to investigate specific methods for solving the problems of unification of terms under inequalities allowing to recognize unsatisfiable formulas or sets of formulas, and then to close branches on which they occur, without applying the inequality expansion rules. We think these methods will critically improve the free variable semantic tableaux we have presented, in the same way as the free variable tableaux with equalities achieve it by means of E-unification.

References

[BG 94] L. Bachmair, H. Ganzinger. *Ordered Chaining for Total Orderings*. Proc. CADE-12. A. Bundy ed. LNAI 814, 435-450 Springer 1994.

[BH 92] B. Beckert, R. Hähnle. *An Improved Method for Adding Equality to Free Variable Semantic Tableaux*. Proc. CADE-10. M.E. Stickel ed. LNAI 607, 507–521. Springer 1992.

[Fit 88] M. Fitting. *First-Order modal tableaux*. Journal of Automated Reasoning 4, 191–213 1988.

[Fit 96] M. Fitting. *First-Order Logic and Automated Theorem Proving*. Springer, 2nd edition 1996.

[GL 90] A. Gavilanes-Franco, F. Lucio-Carrasco. *A first order logic for partial functions*. Theoretical Computer Science 74, 37–69, 1990.

[GLN 96] A. Gavilanes, J. Leach, S. Nieva. *Free Variable Tableaux for a Many Sorted Logic with Preorders*. Technical Report DIA 23/96 Univ. Complutense Madrid 1996.

[GM 92] J. A. Goguen, J. Meseguer. *Order-sorted algebra I: Equational deduction for multiple inheritance, overloading, exceptions and partial operations*. Theoretical Computer Science 105, 217–273, 1992.

[HS 94] R. Hähnle, P. H. Schmitt. *The liberalized δ-rule in free variable semantic tableaux*. Journal of Automated Reasoning. 13, 211-221, 1994.

[Hus 91] H.Hussmann. *Nondeterministic Algebraic Specifications*. PhD. thesis, Institut für Informatik, Technische Universität München, 1991.

[JM 94] J. Jaffar, M. J. Maher. *Constraint logic programming: A survey*. Journal of Logic Programming 19/20, 503–582, 1994.

[LA 93] J. Levy, J. Agustí. *Bi-rewriting, a term rewriting technique for monotonic order relations*. Proc. RTA'93. C. Kirchner ed. LNCS 690, 17–31. Springer 1993.

[LN 93] J. Leach, S. Nieva. *Foundations of a Theorem Prover for Functional and Mathematical Uses*. Journal of Applied Non-Classical Logics 3(1), 7–38, 1993.

[Mes 92] J. Meseguer. *Conditional rewriting logic as a unified model of concurrency*. Theoretical Computer Science 96, 73–155, 1992.

[OS 88] F. Oppacher, E. Suen. *HARP: A Tableau-Based Theorem Prover*. Journal of Automated Reasoning 4, 69–100, 1988.

[Wal 90] C. Walther. *Many Sorted Inferences in Automated Theorem Proving*. Proc. Workshop on Sorts and Types in Artificial Intelligence (1989). K.H. Bläsius, U. Hedtstück, C.-R. Rollinger eds. LNAI 418, 18–48. Springer 1990.

Automating Induction over Mutually Recursive Functions*

Deepak Kapur   M. Subramaniam

Computer Science Department
State University of New York
Albany, NY 12222
kapur@cs.albany.edu, subu@cs.albany.edu

Abstract. In order to automate proofs by induction a crucial problem that needs to be addressed is to decide on an induction scheme that leads to appropriate induction hypotheses for carrying out the proof. Boyer and Moore proposed in [5] the use of terminating function definitions for generating induction schemes. Inspired by Boyer and Moore's work, Zhang, Kapur and Krishnamoorthy introduced the cover set induction method for mechanizing induction for equational specifications in [14]. Both these approaches do not consider interaction among function definitions. Induction schemes are generated by considering function definitions in isolation, one at a time. In applications involving mutually recursive definitions, exploiting interactions among the definitions seems crucial. The cover set method implemented in the theorem prover *RRL* [13] as well as the methods implemented for induction in Boyer and Moore's theorem prover *Nqthm* based on the above approaches, do not perform well when the definitions involved are mutually recursive. Proving even very simple properties over such definitions by these methods requires some form of user intervention. We discuss how the cover set induction method implemented in *RRL* can be extended to automatically prove inductive properties of mutual recursive functions. An algorithm for generating cover sets from mutually recursive definitions is given. The proposed method has been implemented in the theorem prover *RRL* and has been extensively experimented with good results. The effectiveness of the method is illustrated using a nontrivial example of showing the equivalence of the call by value and call by name bottom-up evaluation of arithmetic expressions. A comparison of the method with those employed in *Nqthm* and also with an approach based on implicit induction [7, 3, 2] implemented in the theorem prover *Spike* is given.

1 Introduction

The importance of function definitions in mechanizing induction and on choosing an appropriate induction scheme was recognized by Boyer and Moore in [5]. In their prover *Nqthm*, definitions of function symbols appearing in a conjecture are typically considered as candidates for designing induction schemes.

---

* Partially supported by the National Science Foundation Grant no. CCR-9303394.

The soundness of an induction scheme so designed is based on a well-founded ordering used to show the termination of the function definition. In [14] Zhang, Kapur and Krishnamoorthy introduced a *cover set* induction method for designing induction schemes for automating proofs by induction from equations. The cover set induction method is implemented in the theorem prover *Rewrite Rule Laboratory(RRL)* [13] and has been used to prove many nontrivial theorems to reason about equational specifications and functional programs. Function definitions again play a crucial role in generating induction schemes in the cover set induction method. This method is based on the assumption that a function symbol is defined using a finite set of terminating (conditional or unconditional) rewrite rules; the left sides of the rules are used to design different cases of an induction scheme, and recursive calls to the function made in the right side are used to design appropriate instantiations for generating induction hypotheses.

The methods for automating induction currently employed in theorem provers such as *Nqthm*, *RRL*, *INKA*, etc., do not consider interaction among function definitions. Induction schemes are generated by considering function definitions in isolation, one at a time. However, in many situations, exploiting the interactions among function definitions seems crucial for designing appropriate induction schemes. We focus on one such application in this paper, proving inductive properties involving mutually recursive functions.

A variety of graph algorithms and many others from diverse application areas such as compilers, logic programming, rewriting techniques etc., that are based on data structures such as graphs or forest of trees, can be specified elegantly in terms of mutual recursive functions. For instance, it is common in many graph algorithms to define an attribute of a vertex v, specified by a function such as $attrib(v)$ in terms of the attribute values of its immediate descendants, $attriblist(descendants(v))$, which is in turn defined in terms of the attribute value of each descendant vertex v_i, $attrib(v_i)$. Similarly, in axiomatizing orderings such as the recursive path ordering, comparison of two terms s and t could be specified using a predicate such as $termorder(s, t)$. If the outermost function symbols of s and t are identical then $termorder(s, t)$ is defined to be the multiset comparison of the arguments of s and t, $mult\text{-}termorder(args(s), args(t))$, which in turn uses $termorder$ to compare the individual arguments of s and t.

Reasoning about such algorithms often involves proving inductive properties of mutually recursive functions. The cover set induction method in RRL as well as the methods for induction in *Nqthm*, that have been very successful in proving properties based on recursive definitions, do not perform well when the definitions are mutually recursive. Proving even very simple properties over such definitions by these methods requires significant manual intervention, either in terms of additional lemmas or in terms of user directed induction schemes.

In this paper we discuss how the cover set induction method can be extended to automatically prove inductive properties of mutual recursive functions. The main contribution of this paper is an algorithm for generating cover sets from mutually recursive definitions. Given two mutually recursive functions f and g, the basic idea that is used in the algorithm is to expand occurrences of the mutually recursive function g in the rules defining f by the rules defining g. The expanded rules are then used to generate a cover set for f. Such cover sets can be used to automatically generate induction schemes for proving properties of mutually recursive functions. The proposed method has been implemented in RRL and the results from the initial experiments carried out using this implementation are quite encouraging. It is hoped that the proposed method would enable us to apply RRL to reason about many of the above mentioned algorithms, that employ mutual recursive definitions, with minimal user intervention in terms of additional lemmas and other induction related suggestions.

We first provide an informal review of the cover set method in mechanizing induction using a simple example. For formal definitions of cover sets, induction schemes and other relevant material the reader may refer to [12, 11]. Then, we use another example to illustrate the problems that arise in the cover set method while proving properties of mutually recursive functions. This is followed by a brief review of the proposed solution.

1.1 Informal Overview of the Cover Set Induction Method

Consider the rules defining *append* and length *len* on lists built using the constructors *nl* denoting the empty list and *cons*. The function *s* below denotes the successor over natural numbers.

$$append(nl, x) \rightarrow x,$$
$$append(cons(x, y), z) \rightarrow cons(x, append(y, z)).$$
$$len(nl) \rightarrow 0,$$
$$len(cons(x, y)) \rightarrow s(len(y)).$$

A possible conjecture to prove is:

$$(C_1): \quad len(append(m, n)) = len(m) + len(n).$$

Using the cover set induction method, a base case corresponding to the first rewrite rule in the definition of *append* and an induction step case corresponding to the second rule in the definition of *append* are generated. The cover set based on the definition of *append* is:

$$(\mathcal{C}_{app}): \quad \{\langle\langle nl, y\rangle, \{\}, \{\}\rangle, \langle\langle cons(x, y), z\rangle, \{\langle y, z\rangle\}, \{\}\rangle\}.$$

For every rule in the definition, there is a triple in the cover set, whose first component is the tuple corresponding to the arguments of *append* in the left side, the second component is a finite set consisting of the arguments of all the recursive calls to *append*, if any, in the right side of the rule, and the third component is the finite set of conditions from the literals in the condition, if any, of the rule. A triple could have empty second and third components.

Induction scheme generated from $append(m, n)$ at position 1.1^2 based on its cover set is:

$$(\mathcal{I}_{app}): \{\langle\langle\{m \rightarrow nl, n \rightarrow y\}, \{\}, \{1.1 \leftarrow append(nl, y)\}\rangle, \{\}\rangle,$$
$$\langle\langle\{m \rightarrow cons(x, y), n \rightarrow z\}, \{\}, \{1.1 \leftarrow append(cons(x, y), z)\}\rangle,$$
$$\{\langle\{m \rightarrow y, n \rightarrow z\}, \{\}, \{1.1 \leftarrow append(y, z)\}\rangle\}\rangle\}.$$

An induction scheme is a finite set of tuples, each tuple corresponding to an induction case or subgoal. The first component of the tuple is used to generate the conclusion in the induction subgoal; the second component is used to generate

---

² A position is a sequence of nonnegative integers used to refer to a subterm in a term. An equation will be considered as a term with = as the binary predicate; a conditional equation will be considered as a term with = as the binary predicate whose second argument is an *if* term, where *if* is a considered as a binary function. In the above example, the position of $append(m, n)$ is 1.1.

the induction hypotheses, if any. The first component of the induction case is a 3-tuple, whose first component is a substitution to be made on the conjecture, the second component is a finite set of the conditions for which the induction case is applicable, and the third component is how the subterm being used for generating the induction scheme must be replaced so that the rule of the definition from which the induction case is generated, can be applied. The second component of the induction case is a finite set of 3-tuples for generating the induction hypotheses in the same way as the conclusion is generated.

For the above conjecture, the substitutions $m = nl$, $n = y$ from the the first tuple in the induction scheme lead to the base case: $len(append(nl, y)) = len(nl) + len(y)$. This formula simplifies to true using the definition of $+$ and the first rule in the definitions of $append$ and len.

The induction step case is obtained from the second tuple with the substitutions $m = cons(x, y)$, $n = z$ coming from the first component of the tuple leading to the conclusion: $len(append(cons(x, y), z)) = len(cons(x, y)) + len(z)$, and the substitutions $m = y$, $n = z$ coming from the second component of the tuple lead to the hypothesis: $len(append(y, z)) = len(y) + len(z)$. The conclusion simplifies by the definitions of $append$ and len to, $s(len(append(y, z))) = s(len(y)) + len(z)$, which reduces to true by the definition of $+$ and the hypothesis.

1.2 Problem in Dealing with Mutual Recursive Functions

Consider the following definitions of $evenlist$ and $oddlist$ that compute the elements occupying the even positions and those occupying the odd positions in a given list respectively. It is assumed in the following definitions that the first element of a non-empty list is at an odd position.[3]

$$evenlist(nl) = nl, \qquad evenlist(cons(x_1, x)) = oddlist(x).$$
$$oddlist(nl) = nl, \qquad oddlist(cons(x_1, x)) = cons(x_1, evenlist(x)).$$

The functions $evenlist$ and $oddlist$ are defined in terms of each other and are therefore, mutually recursive. Based on the above definitions consider proving the following conjecture,

$$(C_2): \quad len(evenlist(m)) \leq len(m).$$

In order to prove (C_2), the above equations are oriented into terminating rewrite rules (by using term orderings such as $rpos$ (recursive path ordering with status)[8] as implemented in RRL. This can be done by making the mutually recursively defined functions $evenlist$ and $oddlist$ equivalent in the precedence relation.) The cover sets corresponding to these definitions are then derived. The cover set corresponding to $evenlist$ is:

$$(C_{evenlist}): \quad \{\langle\langle nl\rangle, \{\}, \{\}\rangle, \langle\langle cons(x_1, x)\rangle, \{\}, \{\}\rangle\}.$$

---

[3] The definitions of $evenlist$ ($oddlist$) could be directly given without mutual recursion. We have chosen to define them mutually recursively for illustrating our algorithm in subsection 2.1. A direct definition can in fact be automatically generated by unrolling these mutually recursive definitions using this algorithm. However, unrolling is not sufficient to eliminate mutual recursion when functions f and g are defined in terms of both f and g. The functions exp and $exhelp$ in section 3 are such examples.

The second component of both the cover set triples in $(\mathcal{C}_{evenlist})$ is empty as there are no recursive calls to *evenlist* in the rules defining *evenlist*. The induction scheme obtained from the cover set $(\mathcal{C}_{evenlist})$ is:

$$(\mathcal{I}_{evenlist}) : \quad \{\langle\langle\{m \to nl\}, \{\}, \{\}\rangle, \{\}\rangle, \langle\langle\{m \to cons(x_1, x)\}, \{\}, \{\}\rangle, \{\}\rangle\}.$$

For conjecture (C_2), both induction cases obtained from the two tuples of $(\mathcal{I}_{evenlist})$ are base cases since the their second component is empty. The first base case is got from the first tuple (which comes from the first rule in the definition of *evenlist*) as: $len(evenlist(nl)) \leq len(nl)$, which follows from the definitions of *len* and *evenlist*.

The second base case (generated from the second tuple) is:

$$len(evenlist(cons(x_1, x))) \leq len(cons(x_1, x)),$$

which simplifies by the definition of *evenlist* and *len* to,

$$(C_3) : \quad len(oddlist(x)) \leq s(len(x)).$$

Since (C_3) cannot be simplified any further, the induction proof attempt is not successful. However, an inductive proof of (C_3) could be attempted. The cover set obtained from the definition of *oddlist* is identical to $(\mathcal{C}_{evenlist})$ and by symmetry, the inductive proof attempt of (C_3) leads to two base cases one of which is:

$$len(oddlist(cons(x_1, x))) \leq s(len(cons(x_1, x))),$$

which simplifies by the definitions of *len*, *evenlist* and $\leq$ to:

$$len(evenlist(x)) \leq s(len(x)).$$

The above formula is almost the same as (C_2), the conjecture that we started with. It is easy to verify that further inductions using the cover set induction method would not be successful as they would repeatedly involve proving conjectures which are almost identical to (C_2).

Such failure is not surprising and is common in almost all the inductive proof attempts where the cover sets are derived from mutually recursive definitions. In the cover set induction method the conclusion of an induction case is generated from the left hand side of a rule in the definition and the hypotheses are generated from the recursive calls to the function on the right hand side of the same rule. In case of mutually recursive definitions, the right hand side of a rule in the definition of a function such as *evenlist* contains a call to the *oddlist* and not to *evenlist*. So, such rules do not lead to the generation of any hypotheses. Consequently, the induction case generated from such rules has to be established without any hypotheses which leads to failure.

1.3 Unrolled Cover Set

Since mutually recursive functions are defined in terms of one another, to reason about any one of these functions, it is often necessary to reason about all of these functions together. For instance, a proof attempt of the conjecture (C_2) involving *evenlist* requires us to establish (C_3) involving the function *oddlist* which in turn requires us to establish a conjecture that is very similar to (C_2) involving *evenlist*.

An algorithm that overcomes this problem by considering all mutually recursive function definitions together to generate unrolled cover sets to be used for generating induction schemes is described in section 2. The main idea is to unroll the right side of of a rule in a function definition by instantiating occurrences of mutually recursive functions based on the left sides of their definitions. New expanded rules are thus obtained from which different elements of the cover set are generated. For *evenlist*, *oddlist* appears in the right side of its second rule; the left sides in the definition of *oddlist* are used to instantiate this occurrence of *oddlist* in the definition of *evenlist*. These instantiations give new rules: corresponding to the base case in the recursive definition of *oddlist*, there is an additional base case for *evenlist*; from the second rule of *oddlist*, an induction hypothesis is generated since *evenlist* appears in the right side. The working of the algorithm is first illustrated by proving some simple properties of *evenlist* and *oddlist* functions. Subsequently, a nontrivial case study exhibiting the equivalence of the *call by value* and *call by name* bottom-up evaluations of arithmetic expressions that was performed in *RRL* is described in section 3. A natural formalization of the two evaluation schemes in *RRL* involves mutually recursive function definitions. The equivalence of the two evaluation schemes was established in *RRL* by induction using the unrolled cover sets generated from the algorithm. We would like to emphasize that it is not possible to do this proof in *RRL* using the cover set method alone without considerable user intervention or without changing the formalization considerably.

A detailed comparison of the proposed method with the strategy employed in *Nqthm* for proving properties of mutual recursive functions and a method developed in [7, 2] based on implicit induction is given in section 4. In [2] a number of properties involving the predicates *even* and *odd*, defined mutually recursively, and a proof of the behavioral equivalence of two simple counters, formalized using mutually recursive functions, that were carried out using the theorem prover *Spike*, are presented. All of these properties including the behavioral equivalence of the two counters described in [2] can be easily established in *RRL* using the proposed method.

2 Mutual Recursive Definitions

An algorithm for producing an *unrolled cover set* for mutually recursive definitions is described. The key steps of the algorithm are first discussed in detail, followed by a complete description of the algorithm. The use of the algorithm to eliminate mutual recursion from *simple* mutual recursive functions such as *evenlist* is described. In many cases specifications involving such mutual recursive definitions might be preferred as such definitions improve the readability of the specifications by relating functions explicitly and also lead to more concise and elegant specifications. Automating induction over *inherently* mutually recursive definitions using unrolled cover sets is discussed in the next section.[4]

Definition 1 *Definitions D_f and D_g are mutually recursive iff there exists a rule $l_f \rightarrow r_f$ in D_f such that r_f contains the function symbol g and there exists a rule $l_g \rightarrow r_g$ in D_g such that r_g contains the function symbol f. Functions f and g are mutually recursive iff their definitions are mutually recursive.*

---

[4] For ease of exposition, we consider only those forms of mutual recursion where the function f is directly defined in terms of g and g is directly defined in terms of f. The proposed method is however applicable to the general case in which mutually recursive definitions of f and g can be given using other intermediate functions also.

2.1 Generating Cover sets for mutually recursive functions

Let f and g be any two mutual recursive functions with definitions D_f and D_g respectively. Consider proving a conjecture such as $\phi(\cdots, f(x_1, \cdots, x_n), \cdots)$ by induction using the induction scheme based on the cover set generated from the definition D_f, say. As mentioned earlier, an induction subgoal is generated corresponding to each rule $l_f \rightarrow r_f$ if $cond_f$ in the definition D_f. Consider a rule, $l_f \rightarrow r_f$, in D_f in which the right hand side contains g at position p, say; let u be the subterm of r_f at p. If r_f does not contain recursive calls to f, then the cover set triple corresponding to this rule generates a subgoal in which no induction hypothesis is available for use, i.e., the instance of the conjecture must be established without any hypotheses. Since this rule defines f in terms of g which, in turn, is defined in terms of function f, l_f is indirectly defined recursively in terms of function f. The induction case generated from the corresponding cover set triple is not likely to be established without the use of any induction hypotheses, and consequently, the inductive proof attempt of the conjecture is likely to fail.

The main proposal for addressing this problem of generating useful induction hypotheses is to use the definition of g. For every rule in the definition D_f of f in which g occurs, we further elaborate the corresponding cover set element by generating *expanded* rules in which those occurrences are instantiated using the definition D_g of g.

Given a rule $l_f \rightarrow r_f$ if $cond_f$ in D_f with a subterm u at p in r_f such that the outermost symbol of u is g, expanded rules are generated as follows: For every rule $g(s_1, \cdots, s_n) \rightarrow h_2(\cdots, v, \cdots)$ if $cond_g$ in D_g, u must match $g(s_1, \cdots, s_n)$ using a substitution γ, say. The expanded rule generated from this rule in D_g is $\gamma(l_f) \rightarrow \gamma(r_f[p \leftarrow h_2(\cdots, v, \cdots)])$ if $\gamma(cond_f) \wedge cond_g$. The expanded rules are used to generate an unrolled cover set of f.[5]

Expanded rules in the definition D_f of f may still have occurrences of g (in the next subsection, we define *simply* mutually recursive definitions in which expanded rules do not have any occurrence of g). In such cases, further unrolling or expansion is unlikely to eliminate occurrences of g. Our experience has suggested that often one level of unrolling is enough to generate sufficient cover set triples for producing induction hypotheses; of course, additional cover set triples leading to more induction hypotheses could be generated.

Expanded rules are used to generate elements of the cover set instead of the original rules in which g occurs. For an expanded rule of the form: $\gamma(l_f) \rightarrow \gamma(r_f[p \leftarrow h_2(\cdots, v, \cdots)])$ if $\gamma(cond_f) \wedge cond_g$, the first and the third component of the triple are generated as before. Generating the second component of the triple is done differently based on whether the outermost symbol of v is f or g. If the outermost function symbol of v is f, then the second component of the triple is the tuple corresponding the arguments to the recursive call to f.

If the outermost symbol of v is g, v is used to generate an induction hypothesis; the second component is specified as a *positional replacement* that leads

---

[5] If mutually recursive functions f and g are in terms of each other via other intermediate functions, further cross-products would be necessary. The method as implemented in RRL handles such cases also and the number of cross-products is bounded by the number of the intermediate functions in the path defining f and g mutually recursively.

to a hypothesis obtained by replacing in a conjecture, a subterm whose outermost function symbol is f with a subterm with the outermost function symbol g. A direct replacement of a subterm with outermost function symbol f by a subterm with outermost function symbol g is problematic both from syntactic and semantic considerations. The functions f and g could have different return types in which case such a replacement is not possible. Since the expanded rule relates f to g under a possibly nonempty, surrounding context (function symbols enclosing the subterm v in the right hand side of the expanded rule), it is likely that the property being established for f holds for g only within the surrounding context. This can be achieved using a uniform mechanism of positional replacement for specifying how induction hypotheses can be generated from the second component of the cover set triple: $\gamma(l_f) \leftarrow \gamma(r_f[p \leftarrow v])$. Examples of such positional replacements are given in the next section in terms of the functions exp and $exhelp$.

If the right hand side of the rule in D_g contains more than one subterm with the outermost function symbol g, each of these subterms leads to a hypothesis given by a positional replacement as described above.

The complete description of the algorithm is given below.

An algorithm for generating unrolled cover sets

- **Input** : Mutual recursive complete definitions D_f and D_g.
- **Output** : The unrolled cover set C_{uf} for f.
- **Method** :
  1. Let $C_{uf} = \{\}$. For each rule $f(t_1, \cdots t_n) \rightarrow r_f$ if $cond_f$ in D_f do:
     (a) $[f \notin funcs(r_f) \wedge g \notin funcs(r_f)]$: $C_{uf} = C_{uf} \cup \langle\langle t_1, \cdots, t_n\rangle, \{\}, cond_f\rangle$.
     (b) $[f \in funcs(r_f) \wedge g \notin funcs(r_f)]$: $C_{uf} = C_{uf} \cup \langle\langle t_n, \cdots, t_n\rangle, \{\cdots, \langle t_1^i, \cdots, t_n^i\rangle, \cdots\}, cond_f\rangle$ where $f(t_1^i, \cdots, t_n^i) \in subterms(r_f)$.
     (c) $[g \in funcs(r_f)]$: Let $r_f|_p = u = g(y_1, \cdots, y_n)$. For each rule $g(s_1, \cdots, s_k) \rightarrow r_g$ if $cond_g$ in D_g do:
        i. Let $\gamma(u) = l_g$ for some substitution γ.
        A. $[f \notin funcs(r_g) \wedge g \notin funcs(r_g)]$:
           $C_{uf} = C_{uf} \cup \langle\langle\gamma(t_1), \cdots, \gamma(t_n)\rangle, \{\cdots, \langle \gamma(t_1^i), \cdots, \gamma(t_n^i)\rangle, \cdots\}, \gamma(cond_f) \wedge cond_g\rangle$ where $f(t_1^i, \cdots, t_n^i) \in subterms(r_f)$.
        B. $[f \in funcs(r_g) \wedge g \notin funcs(r_g)]$:
           $C_{uf} = C_{uf} \cup \langle\langle\gamma(t_1), \cdots, \gamma(t_n)\rangle, \{\cdots, \langle\gamma(t_1^i), \cdots, \gamma(t_n^i)\rangle, \langle s_1^i, \cdots, s_n^i\rangle, \cdots\}, \gamma(cond_f) \wedge cond_g\rangle$ where $f(t_1^i \cdots t_n^i) \in subterms(r_f)$ and $f(s_1^i, \cdots, s_n^i) \in subterms(r_g)$.
        C. $[g \in funcs(r_g)]$:
           $C_{uf} = C_{uf} \cup \langle\langle\gamma(t_1), \cdots, \gamma(t_n)\rangle, \{\cdots, \langle\gamma(l_f) \leftarrow \gamma(r_f[p \leftarrow v_i])\rangle, \langle\gamma(t_1^i), \cdots, \gamma(t_n^i)\rangle, \langle s_1^i, \cdots, s_n^i\rangle, \cdots\}, \gamma(cond_f) \wedge cond_g\rangle$ where $f(t_1^i \cdots t_n^i) \in subterms(r_f)$ and $f(s_1^i, \cdots, s_n^i) \in subterms(r_g)$ and $v_i \in subterms(r_g)$ whose outermost function symbol is g.
  2. Return the unrolled cover set C_{uf}.

The completeness and soundness properties of an induction scheme are directly linked to those of the underlying cover set from which it was obtained. The completeness of the induction scheme generated from the unrolled cover set obtained from the above algorithm is ensured by the fact that it is generated from complete definitions D_f and D_g. Soundness follows because of a common well-founded reduction ordering $\succ$ used to prove the termination of mutually recursive definitions. Additionally, for ensuring the completeness of the unrolled cover set, each subterm u with outermost function symbol g appearing in the definition D_f of f must match with each of the left hand sides of the rules in the definition of g.[6] Otherwise, the induction schemes generated from the cover sets might be incomplete and unsound, and should not be used.[7] A proof sketch for the soundness and completeness properties of an induction scheme generated using the above algorithm is given in [12].

Eliminating Simple Mutual Recursion by Unrolling If the right hand sides of a definition D_f of f do not contain recursive calls to f (alternatively the right hand sides of D_g do not contain recursive calls to g) then the functions f and g are *simply* mutually recursive. In such cases, a recursive definition of g (f, respectively) can be generated that does not involve mutual recursion. The functions *evenlist* and *oddlist* are simply mutually recursive since their definitions do not contain recursive calls to *evenlist* or *oddlist*, respectively. Using the above algorithm, alternate definitions are automatically generated from simple mutual recursive definitions from which unrolled cover sets are computed.

For instance, consider *evenlist* defined in Section 1. Only the second rule in the definition of *evenlist*: $evenlist(cons(x_1, x)) \rightarrow oddlist(x)$, has an occurrence of *oddlist*. Two expanded rules are generated from it using the definition of *oddlist* consisting of two rules: $evenlist(cons(x_1, nl)) \rightarrow nl$ and $evenlist(cons(x_1, cons(y_1, y))) \rightarrow cons(y_1, evenlist(y))$. The first expanded rule is the result of applying the substitution $\{x = nl\}$ obtained by matching the subterm $oddlist(x)$ with the left hand side of the first rule $oddlist(nl) \rightarrow nl$ in the definition of *oddlist*. The second expanded rule is obtained by applying the substitution $\{x = cons(y_1, y)\}$ obtained by matching $oddlist(x)$ with the left hand side of the second rule $oddlist(cons(y_1, y)) \rightarrow cons(y_1, evenlist(y))$.

The unrolled cover set for *evenlist* is:

$$(\mathcal{C}_{uevenlist}): \{\langle\langle nl\rangle, \{\}, \{\}\rangle, \langle\langle cons(x_1, nl)\rangle, \{\}, \{\}\rangle,$$
$$\langle\langle cons(x_1, cons(y_1, y))\rangle, \{\langle y\rangle\}, \{\}\}.$$

We illustrate below how this unrolled cover set can be used to establish the conjecture (C_2): $len(evenlist(m)) \leq len(m)$ that could not be proved earlier using cover set induction method. The induction scheme suggested by the subterm $evenlist(m)$ generated using the cover set $\mathcal{C}_{uevenlist}$ is:

$$(\mathcal{I}_{uevenlist}): \{\langle\langle\{m \rightarrow nl\}, \{\}, \{\}\rangle, \{\}\rangle, \langle\langle\{m \rightarrow cons(x_1, nl)\}, \{\}, \{\}\rangle, \{\}\rangle,$$
$$\langle\langle\{m \rightarrow cons(x_1, cons(y_1, y))\}, \{\}, \{\}\rangle, \{\langle\{m \rightarrow y\}, \{\}, \{\}\rangle\}\rangle\}.$$

Note that the first rule in the definition of *evenlist* along with two expanded rules corresponding to the second rule in the definition constitute an alternate definition of *evenlist* that does not involve mutual recursion, and the above cover set corresponds to this definition.

---

[6] This requirement can, however, be relaxed. We do not discuss this extension because of lack of space.

[7] However, semantic unification could be used in such cases to generate complete cover sets and it is also possible to use such schemes to establish conjectures that are relativized with respect to the incomplete cover sets. Both these aspects are discussed in detail in [11].

A proof attempt of (C_2) based on the scheme $(\mathcal{I}_{evenlist})$ leads to two bases cases and an inductive step case all of which are easily established using the definitions and the hypotheses as illustrated below.

The first base case: $len(evenlist(nl)) \leq len(nl)$, is trivially reduced to true by the definitions of $evenlist$, len and $\leq$. The next base case: $len(evenlist(cons(x_1, nl))) \leq len(cons(x_1, nl))$, is similarly reduced to true by the definitions of len, $evenlist$ and $\leq$.

In the induction step case the conclusion is:

$$len(evenlist(cons(x_1, cons(y_1, y)))) \leq len(cons(x_1, cons(y_1, y))),$$

with the hypothesis: $len(evenlist(y)) \leq len(y)$. The conclusion simplifies by the definitions of len, $\leq$ and $evenlist$ to: $len(evenlist(y)) \leq s(len(y))$, which is reduced by the hypothesis and transitivity of $\leq$.

3 Equivalence of Two Forms of Expression Evaluation

We consider a nontrivial example of establishing the equivalence of *call by name* and *call by value* evaluation of arithmetic expressions with function calls. The basic building blocks for expressions are natural numbers and variables denoted by the constructors $nat(x)$ and $id(x)$ respectively. More complex expressions can be built from expressions recursively by the operator *plus* denoting addition of two expressions, and a ternary operator $apply(x, y, z)$ denoting a function call with expression x as the *body* of the function, variable y as the formal parameter and actual parameter z. The meaning of $apply(x, y, z)$ is to replace y by z in the body x.[8]

Arithmetic expressions are evaluated under a given *state* containing the bindings for the variables. The start state is given by the constructor *start*. The default binding for any variable in this state is assumed to be 0. Any other state can be constructed by updating a state with a variable and its associated binding using the constructor *update*. For instance, $update(x, y, z)$ updates the state z with expression y being bound to the variable x. *lookup* function defined below returns the binding associated with a variable.

$$lookup(x, start) = 0, \quad lookup(x, update(y, z, w)) = cond(x = y, z, lookup(x, w)).$$

In order to evaluate an expression e in a given state s we can first expand every function call $apply(x, y, z)$ in the expression e by uniformly replacing every occurrence of y in x by z and evaluate the resulting expression e' in s. This corresponds to *call by name* evaluation of e. The expansion of the function calls in a given expression is done bottom up by the functions exp and $exhelp$.

1. $exp(nat(x), y, z) = nat(x)$,
2. $exp(id(x), y, z) = id(x) \ if \ (not(x = y))$,
3. $exp(plus(x, y), z, w) = plus(exp(x, z, w), exp(y, z, w))$,
4. $exp(apply(x, y, z), z1, w) = exp(exp(x, y, z), z1, w)$.
5. $exp(id(x), x, z) = exhelp(z)$,
6. $exhelp(nat(x)) = nat(x)$,
7. $exhelp(id(x)) = id(x)$,
8. $exhelp(plus(x, y)) = plus(exhelp(x), exhelp(y))$,
9. $exhelp(apply(x, y, z)) = exp(x, y, z)$.

---

[8] We thank Michele Bidoit and Steve Garland for suggesting this example.

Note that the functions exp and $exhelp$ are mutually recursive. Alternatively, expression e can be evaluated by first evaluating the actual parameter in a given state s and binding the formal parameter with the evaluated value. The body can then be evaluated in the updated state. This corresponds to call by value evaluation of e carried out by the following function $eval$.

$$eval(nat(x), w) = x,$$
$$eval(id(x), w) = lookup(x, w),$$
$$eval(plus(x, y), w) = eval(x, w) + eval(y, w),$$
$$eval(apply(x, y, z), w) = eval(x, update(y, eval(z, w), w)).$$

The main theorem expressing the equivalence of the two forms of evaluation is:

$$(C_4): \quad eval(exp(u, v, t), s) = eval(u, update(v, eval(t, s), s)).$$

In order to use the cover set method to prove (C_4) the above definitions first have to be oriented into terminating rules. All the equations in the above definitions with the exception of $exp(apply(x, y, z), z1, w) = exp(exp(x, y, z), z1, w)$ can be oriented left to right using term orderings such as $rpos$ by making exp and $exhelp$ equivalent. A semantic argument that the number of formal parameters (number of variables y being substituted for) on the right hand side of the above problematic equation is strictly smaller than that on the left hand side can be used to orient this equation as a rewrite rule from left to right as well.

The cover sets associated with the functions are then computed from the definitions. Performing induction based on a scheme generated from the definition of exp alone leads to failure in a similar fashion as seen earlier in case of conjectures such as (C_2), that involve mutually recursive functions.

We now illustrate how the unrolled cover set for exp is generated and then used to prove (C_4) by induction. Only the fifth rule defining exp involves an occurrence of the mutually recursive function $exhelp$. The left sides of the rules defining $exhelp$ are used to generate the expanded rules corresponding to the rule 5 of exp. These expanded rules give 2 additional base cases for exp, generated from the two base cases in the definition of $exhelp$. Rule 9 gives an expanded rule $exp(id(x), x, apply(x_1, y_1, z_1)) = exp(x_1, y_1, z_1)$, which gives an additional element in the cover set of exp. Rule 8 gives an expanded rule $exp(id(x), x, plus(z_1, z_2)) = plus(exhelp(z_1), exhelp(z_2))$ leading to yet another additional element in the cover set of exp. The unrolled cover set of exp is:

$$(C_{uexp}): \quad \{\langle\langle nat(x), y, z\rangle, \{\}, \{\}\rangle, \quad \langle\langle id(x), y, z\rangle, \{\}, \{not(x = y)\}\rangle,$$
$$\langle\langle plus(x, y), z, w\rangle, \{\langle\langle x, z, w\rangle, \langle y, z, w\rangle\}, \{\}\rangle,$$
$$\langle\langle apply(x, y, z), z_1, w\rangle, \{\langle x, y, z\rangle, \langle exp(x, y, z), z_1, w\rangle\}\rangle,$$
$$\langle\langle id(x), x, nat(z)\rangle, \{\}, \{\}\rangle, \quad \langle\langle id(x), x, id(z)\rangle, \{\}, \{\}\rangle$$
$$\langle\langle id(x), x, plus(z_1, z_2)\rangle, \{\langle exp(id(x), x, plus(z_1, z_2)) \leftarrow exhelp(z_1)\rangle,$$
$$\langle exp(id(x), x, plus(z_1, z_2)) \leftarrow exhelp(z_2)\rangle\}, \{\}\rangle\rangle,$$
$$\langle\langle id(x), x, apply(x_1, y_1, z_1)\rangle, \{\langle x_1, y_1, z_1\rangle\}, \{\}\rangle.$$

As to be expected, the first four triples are generated from the first four rules in the definition of exp. The next four triples are generated from the expanded rules corresponding to the fifth rule of exp.

To prove (C_4), induction is performed using the scheme generated from (C_{uexp}). There are four bases cases and four induction step cases. The subgoals derived from the first four triples follow from the definitions of exp, $eval$ and $lookup$, and the hypotheses generated from these triples. These proofs are typical of proofs of different subgoals generated from a cover set. The remaining subgoals are obtained from the triples generated by the expanded rules corresponding to the rule 5 in the definition of exp, so we discuss them in more detail.

The subgoal corresponding to the first of these triples,

$$eval(exp(id(x), x, nat(z)), s) = eval(id(x), update(x, eval(nat(z), s), s)),$$

is reduced by the definition of exp, $eval$ and $lookup$ to: $eval(exhelp(nat(z)), w))$ $= nat(z)$, which reduces to true by the definition of $exhelp$ and $eval$. The subgoal generated from the second of these triples is similarly established.

The subgoal generated from the third triple is interesting; the conclusion is:

$$eval(exp(id(x), x, plus(z_1, z_2)), s) = eval(id(x), update(x, eval(plus(z_1, z_2), s), s)),$$

with the hypotheses: 1. $eval(exhelp(z_1), s) = eval(z_1, s)$, 2. $eval(exhelp(z_2), s) = eval(z_2, s)$. The conclusion simplifies by the definitions of exp, $eval$ and $lookup$ to, $eval(exhelp(plus(z_1, z_2)), s) = eval(plus(z_1, z_2), s)$, which reduces to true by the definitions of $exhelp$ and $eval$ and the application of the hypotheses.

In the subgoal generated from the last cover set triple the conclusion is: $eval(exp(id(x), x, apply(x_1, y_1, z_1)), s) = eval(id(x), update(x, eval(apply(x_1, y_1, z_1), s), s))$, with the hypothesis: $eval(exp(x_1.y_1, z_1), s) = eval(x_1, update(x_1, eval(z_1, s), s))$. The conclusion simplifies by the definitions of exp, $eval$, $exhelp$ and $lookup$ to the hypothesis. Therefore, (C_4) is proved.

4 Related work

The proposed approach based on the cover set induction method is closer in spirit to the methodology (*explicit induction*) supported by Nqthm for automating induction. We first discuss the proposed approach in the context of explicit induction approaches using Nqthm. A comparison with the approach implemented in Spike is subsequently given.

4.1 Handling Mutual Recursive Functions in Nqthm

In [6] Boyer and Moore discussed how mutually recursive function definitions can be admitted into Nqthm. A function definition can be admitted in Nqthm logic provided it is not already defined or referred to in any other definition. Since mutually recursive definitions violate this requirement it is not possible to admit such definitions directly in Nqthm. As a solution to this problem Boyer and Moore in [6] introduce a single combined function with the use of an auxiliary argument *flag*. The combined function calls either of the two mutually recursive functions based on the value of *flag*. For instance, the single combined function *eolist* corresponding to the mutually recursive functions *evenlist* and *oddlist* can be defined as follows.

$eolist(x, nl) = nl,$
$eolist('even, cons(x_1, x)) = eolist('odd, x),$
$eolist('odd, cons(x_1, x)) = cons(x_1, eolist('even, x)).$

In the above definition $'even$ and $'odd$ represent the two possible values of flag corresponding to the calls to *evenlist* and *oddlist* functions respectively. Inductive properties involving either (or both) of these functions can be easily expressed in terms of the single combined function. For instance, the conjecture (C_2) can be reformulated as:

$$(C_5): \quad len(eolist('even, m)) \leq len(m).$$

To prove inductive properties such as the above, the usual induction scheme generation heuristics implemented in $Nqthm$ are employed. A proof attempt of (C_5) directly from the definition of $eolist$ is not successful since in the step case, the conclusion is: $len(eolist('even, cons(x_1, x))) \leq len(cons(x_1, x))$, with the hypotheses: $len(eolist('even, x)) \leq len(x)$. The conclusion simplifies by the definitions to: $len(eolist('odd, x)) \leq s(len(x))$, which cannot be simplified any further since the hypothesis is not applicable. It can be easily verified that further inductions are futile as illustrated earlier for conjecture (C_2).

It is possible in Nqthm for the user to specify induction schemes that the prover should use, by a *hint* directive. An induction scheme such as $(\mathcal{I}_{evenlist})$ can be provided as a hint to Nqthm, using which (C_5) can be proved[4].

A more preferred approach according to [4] for dealing with conjectures such as (C_5), which again involves manual intervention, is to come up with stronger versions of the conjecture being attempted or to use intermediate lemmas that involve both the mutually recursive functions. For instance, in order to prove (C_5), a stronger version of (C_5), $len(eolist(x, y)) \leq len(y)$, can be proved. Similarly, in order to prove a conjecture such as (C_6) : $len(eolist('even, x)) \leq len(eolist('odd, x))$, an intermediate lemma such as $len(eolist(x, y)) \leq len(eolist(x, cons(y_1, y)))$ is necessary.

There does not seem to be a uniform strategy that could be used for formulating stronger conjectures and appropriate intermediate assertions as the above. Often, some amount of ingenuity is required in coming up with appropriate intermediate assertions as these depend upon the property being attempted. Discovering such lemmas usually entails careful analyses of failed proof attempts. For instance, in order to prove a conjecture such as $len(eolist('even, x)) + len(eolist('even, x)) \leq len(x)$, the intermediate lemma used for (C_6) is not helpful and alternate intermediate lemmas that are required are not obvious since a similar assertion, $len(eolist('odd, x)) + len(eolist('odd, x)) \leq len(x)$, over the odd elements of the list is not a theorem.

With the proposed method using unrolled cover sets, no manual intervention in terms of hint directive or additional intermediate lemmas are necessary for proving simple properties of such functions. Each of the above mentioned conjectures can be automatically proved in a straightforward manner.

4.2 Handling Mutual Recursive Functions in Spike

A method for performing mutual induction based on term orderings has been proposed in [7, 3, 2]. It has been implemented in the theorem prover *Spike* and has been used to reason about inductive properties over mutually recursive definitions. This method is motivated from the *implicit induction* approach described in [9] where completion based strategies are employed to prove inductive properties. Proof attempts by mutual induction are formalized as a sequence of transformations of pairs of the form (P, H) where P is a set of inductive propositions and H is a set of available induction hypotheses. A successful inductive proof is a sequence of transformations of the form $(P, \{\}) \rightarrow \cdots \rightarrow (\{\}, H)$, i.e., a sequence starting with a set of propositions P and an empty set of inductive hypothesis and ending with an empty set of propositions and a set of hypothesis H. Each step in the above sequence can be one of the following:

- *Expand*: $(P \cup \{p\}, H) \to (P \cup \{p_1, \cdots, p_n\}, H \cup \{p\})$ where each p_i, $i = 1$ to n is a subgoal corresponding to an induction case obtained using a cover set[9] This transition assumes the proposition p itself as a hypothesis.
- *Simplify*: $(P \cup \{p\}, H) \to (P \cup P', H)$ where p follows from the definitions and instances of elements P and P' that are not larger than p with respect to the term orderings. Instances of elements in H that are strictly smaller than p with term orderings could also be used to establish p.[10]

Conjectures, (C_2) : $len(evenlist(x)) \leq len(x)$ and (C_4) : $eval(exp(u, v, t), s)$ $= eval(u, update(v, eval(t, s)), s)$, were both attempted in the theorem prover $Spike$[1]. The proof of (C_2) requires an additional lemma: $x \leq s(y)$ if $(x \leq y)$. Such a lemma is not necessary in RRL. This is perhaps due to the built-in linear arithmetic decision procedure [10].

The proof of conjecture (C_4) in Spike is rather complicated. More importantly, it requires the user to suggest a crucial intermediate lemma:

$$eval(exhelp(x), y) = eval(x, y),$$

that establishes the desired property on the mutual recursive function $exhelp$. Based on [1], we believe that inductive reasoning about mutual recursive functions, in Spike might require considerable manual intervention. It might be necessary to prove intermediate lemmas establishing the desired property over each of the functions in a given set of mutual recursive functions, especially when the functions are inherently mutually recursive. On the other hand, the proof of (C_4) can be generated in RRL fully automatically using the proposed approach. This is because the proposed approach unlike Spike exploits the interaction among function definitions to obtain unrolled cover sets. And, the induction schemes generated from such cover sets contain all mutual recursive functions along with the context surrounding these functions in the definitions.

5 Concluding Remarks

The methods currently implemented for automating induction in provers such as RRL, $Nqthm$, do not consider the interaction among function definitions. In many applications exploiting the interactions among function definitions seems crucial for designing induction schemes. In this paper, we have focussed on one such application that involves proving inductive properties over mutually recursive functions. Specification involving mutually recursive functions naturally arise while dealing with graph algorithms or other algorithms in a variety of areas that operate on data structures such as graphs or forest of trees. The methods supported in automating induction in provers are not effective for proving inductive properties of such algorithms. Proving even very simple properties of mutual recursive functions using these provers requires considerable manual intervention in terms of induction hints or suggesting intermediate lemmas.

---

[9] In Spike, a set of irreducible ground terms called the *test set* is used in lieu of the cover set. And, the induction variables are heuristically chosen.

[10] Term orderings are extended to propositions in [7] to compare a hypothesis with a conjecture and a skolemized instance of the hypothesis is used for simplification. For more details, an interested reader might consult [7, 2].

A simple extension to the cover set method in terms of unrolled cover sets built by considering interaction among the definitions of mutually recursive functions can be successfully used to automate induction over mutually recursive functions, as discussed and illustrated in this paper. The method has been implemented in RRL and has been successfully used on several examples that could not be proved earlier in RRL without considerable user intervention in terms of intermediate lemmas and other induction related suggestions. The implementation is also quite simple and straightforward, requiring no additional book-keeping. It is hoped that the proposed method would enable RRL to reason about inductive properties of many diverse applications such as term orderings, search strategies over and-or trees etc., which are naturally axiomatized using mutually recursive functions.

Acknowledgments: We thank Adel Bouhoula for attempting the proofs of some of the conjectures in this paper on the theorem prover Spike.

References

1. A. Bouhoula, Private Communication, March 1996.
2. A. Bouhoula, "Using Induction and Rewriting to Verify and Complete Parameterized Specifications", To appear in *Theoretical Computer Science*, Dec. 1996.
3. A. Bouhoula and M. Rusinowitch, "Implicit induction in conditional theories", *Journal of Automated Reasoning*, 1995.
4. R.S. Boyer and M. Kaufmann, Private Communication, March 1995.
5. R.S. Boyer and J S. Moore, *A Computational Logic*. ACM Monographs in Computer Sc., 1979.
6. R.S. Boyer and J S. Moore, *A Computational Logic Handbook.* New York: Academic Press, 1988.
7. F. Bronsard, U. Reddy and R.W. Hasker, "Induction using term orderings," Proc. *12th International Conference on Automated Deduction (CADE-12)*, Nancy, France, July 1994.
8. N. Dershowitz, "Termination of rewriting," *J. of Symbolic Computation*, 3, 69-116, 1987.
9. D.Kapur and D.R. Musser, "Proof by Consistency", *AI Journal*, 31(2):125-157, Feb. 1987.
10. D. Kapur and X. Nie, "Reasoning about numbers in Tecton," Proc. of *ISMIS'94*, October 1994.
11. D. Kapur and M. Subramaniam, "Using linear arithmetic procedure for generating Induction Schemes," Proc. *Foundations of Software Technology and Theoretical Computer Science (FSTTCS-14)* (ed: Thiagarajan), LNCS, Dec. 1994.
12. Deepak Kapur and M. Subramaniam, " Automating Inductions over Mutual Recursive Functions", CS Dept. Tech. Report, March. 1996.
13. D. Kapur and H. Zhang, "An overview of Rewrite Rule Laboratory (RRL)," *J. of Computer and Mathematics with Applications*, 29, 2, 1995, 91-114. Earlier descriptions in CADE-88 and RTA-89.
14. H. Zhang, D. Kapur, and M.S. Krishnamoorthy, "A mechanizable induction principle for equational specifications," Proc. *Ninth International Conference on Automated Deduction (CADE-9)*, Argonne, IL, LNCS 310, 162-181, 1988.

Pushouts of Order-Sorted Algebraic Specifications

Anne Elisabeth Haxthausen[1]
Department of Information Technology,
Technical University of Denmark
2800 Lyngby, Denmark
e-mail: ah@it.dtu.dk

Friederike Nickl[2]
sd&m GmbH & Co. KG
Thomas-Dehler-Str. 27
81737 München, Germany
e-mail: Friederike.Nickl@sdm.de

Abstract. This paper investigates the existence of pushouts in the category of order-sorted algebraic specifications and specification morphisms. As a main result
it is shown that the existence can be guaranteed by imposing certain conditions
on the specification morphisms. This result is important as the pushout construction is one of the most widely used approaches to combine specifications.

1. Introduction

A specification language which is meant to support the specification of large software
systems must provide mechanisms for defining specifications in a modular way. Modularity aids in coping with the complexity of large systems and is a prerequisite for reusing
parts of a specification. To this aim different mechanisms for defining parameterized
specifications and for applying these to actual parameters have been considered (cf.
[ST85], [Hax88], [Wir90]). Moreover, concepts of algebraic module specifications and
of reusable components together with formal composition operations have been introduced (cf. [EM90], [HN94], [NN95]). One of the most widely used approaches to define
the semantics of the actualization of a parameterized specification or the composition of
module specifications is based on the pushout construction in the category of specifications. This approach was originally introduced for many-sorted algebraic specifications
(see e.g. [EM85] and [BG80]), but can (cf. [ST85] and [GB85]) be generalized to specifications in any institution for which the category of signatures is co-complete.

In this paper we are interested in how the pushout construction works for the order-
sorted approach to algebraic specification (see e.g. [GD94], [GM92] and [FGJM85]), as
this approach provides the possibility of specifying subsorts (i.e. subtypes) and thereby
for treating partially defined functions in a clean way. The existence of pushouts of order-sorted specifications depends on the existence of pushouts of the underlying signatures. Following [GM92] we require signatures to have a number of properties and hence
pushouts of signatures must preserve these properties. One of the properties we require
of the signatures is regularity, since this ensures that the term algebras are initial, as one
might expect. Another required property is locally upward filteredness which ensures
that equational satisfaction is closed under isomorphism. Unfortunately it turns out that
pushouts of signatures do not always preserve these properties[3] and therefore pushouts

---

1. The research by A.E.H. was supported by the Danish Technical Research Council
under the "Codesign" programme.
2. The work was carried out when F.N. was a member of the Institut für Informatik,
Ludwig-Maximilians-Universität München.
3. For the regularity property this has already been pointed out in [Poi90].

of specifications do not always exist. An interesting question is whether there exist conditions under which pushouts of signatures preserve the required properties. The aim of this paper is to answer that question.

Pushouts of order-sorted specifications have already been considered in [Poi90] in the context of parameterized specifications. In Poigné's approach it is not required that the signatures of specifications are regular and locally upward filtered as in our approach, but instead more conditions are imposed on order-sorted algebras. Therefore [Poi90] is not concerned with conditions which guarantee the preservation of regularity and locally upward filteredness of signatures by pushouts which is the central topic of our paper.

The paper is organized as follows. First, in section 2, we give basic definitions of order-sorted algebra and state desirable properties of signatures. Then, in section 3, we investigate the existence of pushouts in the category of order-sorted signatures and signature morphisms and we look for conditions that we can impose on signature morphisms to ensure that pushouts preserve the desirable properties. Finally, in section 4, a summary and a topic of future research are given. For full proofs of the results in this paper we refer to [HN96].

2. Order-Sorted Algebra
This section contains some well-known definitions and results on order-sorted algebra that we need for section 3. For a full treatment, see e.g. [GD94] or [GM92].

2.1 Signatures

Definition 1 An *(order-sorted) signature* is a triple $(S, \leq, OP)$ where $(S, \leq)$ is a partially ordered set (of sorts) and OP is an indexed family $OP = (OP_{w,s})_{w \in S*, s \in S}$ of operation symbols. ◆

Definition 2

a. An order-sorted signature $(S, \leq, OP)$ is *monotonic* iff for all $w1, w2, s1, s2$, op
   $$op \in OP_{w1,s1} \cap OP_{w2,s2} \text{ and } w1 \leq w2 \text{ imply } s1 \leq s2.$$
   (Here $\leq$ is extended to $S*$ using the componentwise ordering)

b. An order-sorted signature $(S, \leq, OP)$ is *regular* iff it is monotonic and for all
   $op \in (\cup_{w \in S*, s \in S} OP_{w,s})$ and all $w \in S^*$ the set
   $$R_{SIG}(op, w) := \{u \in S^*: w \leq u \text{ and } \exists s \in S. op \in OP_{u,s} \}$$
   is either empty or has a least element.

c. An order-sorted signature $(S, \leq, OP)$ is *locally upward filtered* iff $(S, \leq)$ is *locally upward filtered*, that is any two connected sorts, s1 and s2, have a common supersort.

d. An order-sorted signature $(S, \leq, OP)$ is *coherent* iff it is regular and locally upward filtered. ◆

In [GM92], the authors require in their definition of an order-sorted signature already the monotonicity condition. In this paper we are primarily interested in monotonic signatures, however, in the facts and theorems we present in section 3 about pushout con-structures we will not require signatures to be monotonic when the results hold also for non-monotonic signatures. Therefore, as in [GD94] we do not include the monotonicity condition in the definition of an order-sorted signature. Our definition of regularity is not exactly the one given in [GM92], but is equivalent to their definition, since in our definition of "regularity" also "monotonicity" is included (see also [GM92], Fact 2.4).

Our definition of coherence is exactly the one given in [GM92]. We would like the signatures to be coherent and the pushout constructions to preserve this property, as coherence of a signature SIG ensures (cf. fact 1 and 2 below) that the initial SIG-algebra can be defined as a term algebra and that equational satisfaction is closed under isomorphism.

2.2 Algebras

The definition of the notion of an order-sorted algebra is given as in [GD94].

Definition 3 Let SIG = $(S, \leq, OP)$ be an order-sorted signature.

a. An *(order-sorted) SIG-algebra* A is a many sorted (S, OP)-algebra such that $s \leq s'$ in S implies $A_s \subseteq A_{s'}$.

b. A SIG-algebra A is *monotonic* if $op \in OP_{w1,s1} \cap OP_{w2,s2}$ and $w1 \leq w2$ and $s1 \leq s2$ imply that

$$op^A_{w1,s1} : A_{w1} \rightarrow A_{s1} \text{ equals } op^A_{w2,s2} : A_{w2} \rightarrow A_{s2} \text{ on } A_{w1}. \qquad \blacklozenge$$

The definition of an order-sorted SIG-homomorphism is given as in [GM92], but we consider it more generally also for non-monotonic algebras:

Definition 4 Let SIG = $(S, \leq, OP)$ be an order-sorted signature and A, B be SIG-algebras. Then an *(order-sorted) SIG-homomorphism* h : A $\rightarrow$ B is a many sorted (S, OP)-homomorphism such that for all s, s' $\in$ S the following holds: $s \leq s'$ and $a \in A_s$ imply $h_s(a) = h_{s'}(a)$. $\qquad \blacklozenge$

For an order-sorted signature SIG, the category of SIG-algebras and SIG-homomorphisms is denoted by Alg(SIG) and the category of monotonic SIG-algebras and SIG-homomorphisms by MAlg(SIG).

2.3 Equations

Here we quickly review the definition of SIG-terms and SIG-equations over an order-sorted signature SIG as given in [GM92].

Definition 5 Let SIG = $(S, \leq, OP)$ be an order-sorted signature and let $X = (X_s)_{s \in S}$ be an S-sorted set of *variables*. The sets $T_s(SIG,X)$, $s \in S$ of *SIG-terms* of sort s with variables in X, are inductively defined by the following rules

    1. $x \in T_s(SIG,X)$, if $x \in X_s$

    2. $op \in T_s(SIG,X)$, if $op \in OP_s$

    3. $op(t1,...,tn) \in T_s(SIG,X)$, if $op \in OP_{s1...sn,s}$, $ti \in T_{si}(SIG,X)$ for $1 \leq i \leq n$

    4. $t \in T_s(SIG,X)$, if $t \in T_{s'}(SIG,X)$ and $s' \leq s$. $\qquad \blacklozenge$

Fact 1 For regular signatures, SIG, any SIG-term has a least sort and the initial SIG-algebra in MAlg(SIG) can be defined as a term algebra, cf. [GM92]. ♦

Definition 6 For a regular order-sorted signature, SIG = (S, ≤, OP), a *SIG-equation* is a triple <X,t1,t2> where X is an S-sorted set of variables, t1 and t2 are SIG-terms with variables in X such that the least sorts of t1 and t2 are in the same connected component of (S, ≤). ♦

For a definition of what it means for a monotonic SIG-algebra to satisfy a SIG-equation, see [GM92].

Fact 2 For coherent signatures, SIG, isomorphic SIG-algebras in MAlg(SIG) satisfy the same SIG-equations, cf. [GM92]. ♦

2.4 Signature Morphisms

Definition 7 Let SIG = (S, ≤, OP) and SIG' = (S', ≤', OP') be order-sorted signatures. An *(order-sorted) signature morphism* σ: SIG → SIG' is a pair (σ_S, σ_{OP}) such that
$\sigma_S : (S, \leq) \to (S', \leq')$ is a monotonic function and
$\sigma_{OP} = (\sigma_{w,s})_{w \in S*, s \in S}$ is a family of functions with $\sigma_{w,s} : OP_{w,s} \to OP'_{\sigma_{S^*(w)}, \sigma_{S(s)}}$.
In the sequel we will often write σ instead of σ_S. ♦

For a signature morphism σ: SIG → SIG' its reduct functor Mod(σ): Alg(SIG') → Alg(SIG) can be defined as in the many-sorted case: It is easily checked that due to the monotonicity of σ_S, Mod(σ)(A) thus defined is an order-sorted SIG-algebra for all order-sorted SIG'-algebras A and Mod(σ)(h) is an order-sorted SIG-homomorphism for all order-sorted SIG'-homomorphisms h.
However, if σ is a signature morphism, which does not preserve subtype polymorphism, then there exist monotonic algebras A, for which Mod(σ)(A) is not monotonic as shown by the following example:

Example 1 Consider the following order-sorted signatures SIG, SIG1 and SIG2 where
    SIG = **sorts** s1, s1', s2, s2'. **subsorts** s1' < s1, s2' < s2 .
    SIG1 = SIG + **ops** f : s1 -> s2 , f : s1' -> s2' .
    SIG2 = SIG + **ops** h : s1 -> s2 , g : s1' -> s2' .

Then every SIG2-algebra is monotonic. If we defined σ: SIG1 → SIG2 to be the identity on sorts and $\sigma_{s1,s2}(f) = g$ and $\sigma_{s1',s2'}(f) = h$, then for any SIG2-algebra A with $h^A(a) \neq g^A(a)$ for some $a \in A_{s1}$, the algebra Mod(σ)(A) is not monotonic. ♦

It is easily checked that for signature morphisms preserving subtype polymorphism the reduct functor Mod(σ) maps monotonic algebras to monotonic algebras. For the sake of simplicity, in this paper we do not restrict ourselves just to signature morphisms preserving subtype polymorphism, but to signature morphisms preserving overloading in general:

Definition 8 Let SIG, SIG' be as in Definition 7. A signature morphism σ: SIG $\rightarrow$ SIG' *preserves overloading* if for all w, w'$\in$ S*, s, s' $\in$ S and all op $\in$ $OP_{w,s} \cap OP_{w',s'}$ it holds $\sigma_{w,s}$ (op) = $\sigma_{w',s'}$ (op). ◆

Fact 3 If σ: SIG $\rightarrow$ SIG' is a signature morphism preserving overloading, then there is a function $\sigma_{\cup OP} : (\cup_{w \in S*, s \in S} OP_{w,s}) \rightarrow (\cup_{w' \in S'*, s' \in S'} OP'_{w',s'})$ such that for all w,s and op $\in$ $OP_{w,s}$ it holds $\sigma_{w,s}$(op) = $\sigma_{\cup OP}$ (op). ◆

Notation In the sequel, for a signature morphism σ: SIG $\rightarrow$ SIG' preserving overloading and some operation symbol op in SIG, we will often simply write σ(op) instead of $\sigma_{\cup OP}$(op).

In the kind of problems that we will use pushouts constructions on, the signature morphisms will typically be embeddings, and therefore several of our theorems in section 3 will assume that.

Definition 9 A signature morphism σ: SIG $\rightarrow$ SIG' preserving overloading is called an *embedding* if

i) σ_S is an order-embedding, i.e. s $\leq$ s' iff σ_S(s) $\leq$' σ_S(s') holds for all s, s' $\in$ S.

ii) $\sigma_{\cup OP}$ is injective. ◆

In particular it follows that if σ is an embedding, then σ_S is injective. Notice that the requirement that $\sigma_{\cup OP}$ is injective is stronger than the requirement that $\sigma_{w,s}$ is injective for all w, s.

2.5 Specifications and Specification Morphisms

Definition 10 An *(order-sorted) specification*, SPEC, is a pair, (SIG, E), consisting of a coherent order-sorted signature SIG and a set of SIG-equations E. ◆

Definition 11 Let SPEC1 = (SIG1,E1) and SPEC2 = (SIG2,E2) be order-sorted specifications.

a. A *specification morphism*, σ: SPEC1 $\rightarrow$ SPEC2, is a signature morphism, σ: SIG1 $\rightarrow$ SIG2, for which the following holds: for any e $\in$ E1, the translation, σ(e), of e by σ, must be provable from E2 with the order-sorted equational calculus of [GM92].

b. A specification morphism σ : SPEC1 $\rightarrow$ SPEC2 *preserves overloading* if σ: SIG1 $\rightarrow$ SIG2 preserves overloading. ◆

3. Pushout Constructions

The aim of this section is to establish some conditions on specification morphisms which guarantee the existence of pushouts in the category of order-sorted specifications. In a first step, we show that the category of order-sorted signatures with signature morphisms preserving overloading has pushouts. Then, we gradually establish conditions on signature morphisms which guarantee that the pushout preserves monotonicity, regularity and coherence of signatures. Finally, we investigate the applicability of the results.

3.1 Existence of Pushouts

Here we first state (without proof) the following well-known fact

Fact 4 The category of partially ordered sets and monotonic functions has pushouts.
♦

Since, as stated in section 2, we are mainly interested in signature morphisms which are embeddings, we now give a detailed description of the pushout construction in the category of partially ordered sets and order-embeddings:

Fact 5 Let $fi: (S0, \leq 0) \to (Si, \leq i)$ $(i = 1, 2)$ be order-embeddings and let their pushout in the category of partially ordered sets and monotonic functions be given by the following diagram:

$$
\begin{array}{ccc}
(S0, \leq 0) & \xrightarrow{\;f1\;} & (S1, \leq 1) \\
{\scriptstyle f2}\downarrow & & \downarrow{\scriptstyle g1} \\
(S2, \leq 2) & \xrightarrow{\;g2\;} & (S, \leq)
\end{array}
$$

Then the following holds:

1. The set S together with $g1, g2$ is a pushout of $f1$ and $f2$ in the category of sets. Since the fi are injective, the gi are injective and for all $x1 \in S1$, $x2 \in S2$ it holds that $g1(x1) = g2(x2)$ iff there is some $z \in S0$ such that $x1 = f1(z)$ and $x2 = f2(z)$.

2. The ordering $\leq$ on S is given as follows:
   Let $\check{i}$ denote $(i \bmod 2) + 1$ for $i \in \{1,2\}$. Then for $x, y \in S$ it holds
   $x \leq y$ iff
   there is some i such that $x, y \in gi(Si)$ and $gi^{-1}(x) \leq i\ gi^{-1}(y)$ or
   there is some i such that $x \in gi(Si)$ and $y \in g\check{i}(S\check{i})$, and there is some z in $S0$
   such that $gi^{-1}(x) \leq i\ fi(z)$ and $f\check{i}(z) \leq\check{i}\ g\check{i}^{-1}(y)$

3. $g1$ and $g2$ are order-embeddings.

Proof: We first show that a pushout of $f1$ and $f2$ with the properties 1., 2. and 3. can be constructed in the category of posets and monotonic functions:
Let S, $g1$ and $g2$ be as in 1. Since the fi are order-embeddings it can be checked that $\leq$ as defined in 2. indeed is a partial order and that $g1$ and $g2$ are order embeddings w.r.t this order. It is straightforward to check that S together with $g1$ and $g2$ is a pushout of $f1$ and $f2$ in the category of posets and monotonic functions.
Now if $g1': (S1, \leq 1) \to (S', \leq')$, $g2': (S2, \leq 2) \to (S', \leq')$ is another pushout of $f1$ and

f2, then by the universal property of the pushout there exists an order-isomorphism h: $(S, \leq) \rightarrow (S', \leq')$ with $gi' = h\ gi$ for $i = 1,2$. Hence it is easily checked that $(S', \leq')$ together with $g1'$ and $g2'$ also satisfy properties 1., 2., 3. above. Therefore these properties do not depend on the choice of the pushout.   ♦

The next Theorem states that pushouts exist in the category OSCAT of order-sorted signatures and signature morphisms preserving overloading:

Theorem 1
The category OSCAT has pushouts. Let $\sigma i : SIG0 \rightarrow SIGi$ (i=1,2) be signature morphisms preserving overloading where $SIGi = (Si, \leq i, OPi)$ for i=0,1,2. Then their pushout in OSCAT is given by the following diagram

$$
\begin{array}{ccc}
SIG0 & \xrightarrow{\ \sigma1\ } & SIG1 \\
\downarrow{\sigma2} & & \downarrow{\tau1} \\
SIG2 & \xrightarrow{\ \tau2\ } & SIG
\end{array}
$$

where SIG = (S, ≤, OP) and τ1, τ2 are given as follows:

1. $(S, \leq)$ together with $\tau1_S$ and $\tau2_S$ is a pushout of $\sigma1_S$ and $\sigma2_S$ in the category of partially ordered sets and monotonic functions.
2. $\tau1_{\cup OP}$ and $\tau2_{\cup OP}$ are obtained by the following pushout in the category of sets:

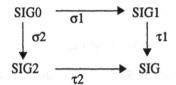

$$
\begin{array}{ccc}
\cup OP0 & \xrightarrow{\ \sigma1_{\cup OP}\ } & \cup OP1 \\
\downarrow{\sigma2_{\cup OP}} & & \downarrow{\tau1_{\cup OP}} \\
\cup OP2 & \xrightarrow{\ \tau2_{\cup OP}\ } & UOP
\end{array}
$$

3. $OP = (OP_{w,s})_{w \in S^*, s \in S}$ is obtained as follows:

$$OP_{w,s} = \{ \tau1_{\cup OP}(op) : \exists\ w1 \in S1^*, s1 \in S1.$$
$$w = \tau1_S^*(w1),\ s = \tau1_S(s1)\ and\ op \in OP1_{w1,s1} \}$$
$$\cup$$
$$\{ \tau2_{\cup OP}(op) : \exists\ w2 \in S2^*, s2 \in S2.$$
$$w = \tau2_S^*(w2),\ s = \tau2_S(s2)\ and\ op \in OP2_{w2,s2}\}$$

Obviously, UOP = ∪OP.

Proof: It is easily checked, that this indeed is a pushout in the category of signature morphisms preserving overloading. Moreover, using the universal property of the pushout, it is straightforward to see that 1., 2., and 3. do not depend on the choice of the pushout.   ♦

Remark 1 By Fact 5 and Definition 9 it follows from Theorem 1 that if σ1 and σ2 are embeddings, then τ1 and τ2 also are.   ♦

3.2 Preservation of Monotonicity

In this section we look for conditions that we can impose on signature morphisms to ensure that monotonicity of signatures is preserved by pushouts.

Fact 6 Monotonicity of signatures is not always preserved by pushouts in the category OSCAT. ♦

The proof of this fact is given by the following example of a pushout of two monotonic signatures yielding a non-monotonic signature

Example 2 For the following monotonic signatures

SIG0 = **sorts** u1, s1, t1, u2, t2, s2 .
        subsorts s1 < t1, t1 < u1, s2 < t2, t2 < u2 .
        ops   f : u1 -> u2 .

SIG1 = SIG0 + **ops** f : s1 -> t2 .   SIG2 = SIG0 + **ops** f : t1 -> s2 .

the pushout signature of the embeddings $\sigma 1 : \text{SIG0} \rightarrow \text{SIG1}$ and $\sigma 2 : \text{SIG0} \rightarrow \text{SIG2}$ is (up to isomorphism) SIG = SIG0 + **ops** f : s1 -> t2, f : t1 -> s2 . which is not monotonic.

Note how the requirement that signature morphisms preserve overloading implies the overloaded f operations in SIG1 should be mapped to two operations with the same name, $\tau 1(f)$, in SIG, and the two overloaded f operations in SIG2 should be mapped to two operations with the same name, $\tau 2(f)$, in SIG. As one of the f operations in SIG1 and one of the f operations in SIG2 are images (by $\sigma 1$ and $\sigma 2$, respectively) of the same operation, f, in SIG0, $\tau 1(f)$ and $\tau 2(f)$ must be identified, and therefore we get three operations with the same name in SIG. ♦

The signature morphisms $\sigma 1$ and $\sigma 2$ in the above example do not satisfy a property called *regular* which in the following we shall see is a sufficient condition for embeddings between regular signatures to ensure that the resulting pushout signature is monotonic:

Definition 12 Let SIG and SIG' be regular signatures, where SIG = $(S, \leq, OP)$. Let the sets $R_{SIG}(op, w)$, $R_{SIG'}(op', w')$ be defined as in Definition 2.
Then a signature morphism $\sigma : \text{SIG} \rightarrow \text{SIG'}$ preserving overloading is called *regular* if for all $w \in S^*$ and $op \in \cup OP$ the following holds:
If $R_{SIG'}(\sigma(op), \sigma^*(w))$ is not empty, then also $R_{SIG}(op, w)$ is non-empty and the least element of $R_{SIG'}(\sigma(op), \sigma^*(w))$ is determined by the equation
$$\min(R_{SIG'}(\sigma(op), \sigma^*(w))) = \sigma^*(\min R_{SIG}(op, w))$$
♦

In Example 2, $\sigma 1$ and $\sigma 2$ are not regular: For instance for $\sigma 1$ regularity does not hold since
$$\min(R_{SIG1}(\sigma 1(f), \sigma 1(s1))) = \min(R_{SIG1}(f, s1)) = s1 \neq u1 = \sigma 1(u1) = \sigma 1(\min(R_{SIG0}(f, s1)))$$

Theorem 2 (Preservation of monotonicity)
Let SIG0, SIG1 and SIG2 be regular signatures, and σi: SIG0 $\rightarrow$ SIGi be regular em-

beddings for i=1,2. Let SIG together with τi: SIGi $\rightarrow$ SIG (i=1,2) be their pushout in OSCAT. Then SIG is monotonic.

Proof: We have to check for all function symbols op in SIG that op $\in OP_{w1, s1} \cap OP_{w2, s2}$ with $w1 \le w2$ implies $s1 \le s2$. By Theorem 1 and the fact that the $\sigma i_{\cup OP}$ are injective we know that we only have to distinguish between the following two cases:

i) there is some $i \in \{1,2\}$, op' $\in \cup OPi$, $w1'$, $w2' \in Si^*$, $s1'$, $s2' \in Si$ such that op = $\tau i(op')$, $w1 = \tau i(w1')$, $w2 = \tau i(w2')$, $s1 = \tau i(s1')$, $s2 = \tau i(s2')$ and op' $\in OPi_{w1', s1'} \cap OPi_{w2', s2'}$. In this case the result follows from the monotonicity of SIGi together with the fact that τi is an embedding.

ii) there is op0 $\in \cup OP0$ such that op = $\tau 1(\sigma 1(op0)) = \tau 2(\sigma 2(op0))$ and there is $i \in \{1,2\}$, $w1' \in Si^*$, $s1' \in Si$, $w2' \in S\bar{i}^*$, $s2' \in S\bar{i}$ (where $\bar{i} = (i \bmod 2) + 1$) such that $w1 = \tau i(w1')$, $w2 = \tau \bar{i}(w2')$, $s1 = \tau i(s1')$, $s2 = \tau \bar{i}(s2')$, $\sigma i(op0) \in OPi_{w1', s1'}$ and $\sigma \bar{i}(op0) \in OPi_{w2', s2'}$. In this case, using Fact 5, we may conclude from $w1 \le w2$ that there is some $w \in S0^*$ such that $w1' \le_i \sigma i^*(w)$ and $\sigma \bar{i}^*(w) \le_{\bar{i}} w2'$. By regularity of SIG$\bar{i}$ and $\sigma \bar{i}$ we obtain that min $R_{SIG0}(op0, w)$ exists and $\sigma \bar{i}(w0) \le_{\bar{i}} w2'$ where w0:= min $R_{SIG0}(op0, w)$. Let s0$\in$ S0 such that op0 $\in OP0_{w0,s0}$. Since SIG$\bar{i}$, SIGi and σi are monotonic it can easily be concluded that $\sigma \bar{i}(s0) \le_{\bar{i}} s2'$ and $s1' \le_i \sigma i(s0)$ from which $s1 \le s2$ follows by Fact 5.$\blacklozenge$

3.3 Preservation of Regularity

The regularity condition on signature morphisms established in the previous section is not yet sufficient to guarantee that pushouts of regular embeddings preserve the regularity of signatures:

Fact 7 Regularity of signatures is not always preserved by pushouts of regular embeddings in OSCAT. $\blacklozenge$

To justify Fact 7 we present two examples:

Example 3a Consider the following regular signatures

SIG0 =	SIG1 = SIG0 +	SIG2 = SIG0 +
sorts t1, t2 .	sorts s .	ops f: t1 -> t1, f: t2 -> t2 .
	subsorts s < t1, s < t2 .	

Then the pushout signature of the regular embeddings $\sigma 1$: SIG0 $\rightarrow$ SIG1 and $\sigma 2$: SIG0 $\rightarrow$ SIG2 is (up to isomorphism) SIG = SIG2 + **sorts** s. **subsorts** s < t1, s < t2. which is not regular. The problem is that there are two sorts, t1 and t2, which do not have a lower bound in SIG0, but their images (by $\sigma 1$) have a lower bound, s, in SIG1. $\blacklozenge$

One of the signature morphisms ($\sigma 1$) does not satisfy a property called *single inheritance extension*. Informally, an embedding σ: SIG $\rightarrow$ SIG' is a single inheritance extension, if every s $\in$ S' which has an ancestor in $\sigma(S)$ has a least ancestor in $\sigma(S)$:

Definition 13 An embedding σ: SIG $\rightarrow$ SIG' is called a *single inheritance extension* iff for every s $\in$ S' the set $\{t \in S \mid s \le' \sigma(t)\}$ is either empty or has a least element in S. $\blacklozenge$

Let for a subset A of a poset $(S, \leq)$ its *downward closure* $DOC_S(A)$ in S is given by $DOC_S(A) = \{s \in S: \exists a \in A. \ s \leq a\}$. A is called *downward closed* in S if $A = DOC_S(A)$. It is immediate that every embedding $\sigma: SIG \rightarrow SIG'$ with $\sigma(S)$ downward closed in S' is a single inheritance extension.

The next example demonstrates that pushouts of regular single inheritance extensions still may fail to preserve the regularity of signatures:

Example 3b For the following regular signatures

SIG0 =	SIG1 = SIG0 +	SIG2 = SIG0 +
sorts u .	**sorts** s . **subsorts** s < u .	**sorts** t . **subsorts** t < u .
ops f : u u -> u .	**ops** f : s u -> s .	**ops** f : u t -> t .

the pushout signature of the regular single inheritance extensions $\sigma1: SIG0 \rightarrow SIG1$ and $\sigma2: SIG0 \rightarrow SIG2$ is (up to isomorphism)

SIG = SIG0 + **sorts** s, t .
subsorts s < u, t < u .
ops f : s u -> s, f : u t -> t .

which is not regular, since the set $R_{SIG}(f, s\ t)$ has no least element. The problem is, that the word s t is a lower bound of s u in $(S1)^*$ and u t in $(S2)^*$, which are not comparable in S^*. ◆

In order to overcome this problem we require one of the signature morphisms to be *strongly regular* as defined below.

Definition 14 Let SIG and SIG' be regular signatures. Then a regular signature morphism $\sigma: SIG \rightarrow SIG'$ is called *strongly regular* if for all $w \in DOC_{S'^*}(\sigma^*(S^*))$ and op $\in \cup OP$ the following holds:
If $\{w_k \in \sigma(S): 1 \leq k \leq |w|\} \neq \emptyset$ and $R_{SIG'}(\sigma(op), w) \neq \emptyset$ then $\min R_{SIG'}(\sigma(op), w) \in \sigma^*(S^*)$.
(Here w_k denotes the k-th component of the word w.) ◆

The signature morphism $\sigma1$ in Example 3b is not strongly regular, since s u $\in DOC_{S1^*}(\sigma1^*(S^*))$, but $\min R_{SIG1}(\sigma1(f), s\ u) = s\ u$ where $u \in \sigma1(S)$, but $s \notin \sigma1(S)$. For a similar reason, $\sigma2$ is not strongly regular.

If every operation symbol in SIG has the arity 1, then it is immediate that every regular signature morphism $\sigma: SIG \rightarrow SIG'$ is already strongly regular. Moreover, it is easily seen that if $\sigma(S)$ is downward closed in S' then σ is strongly regular iff it is regular.
The next Theorem states that regularity of signatures is preserved by pushouts of regular single inheritance extensions $\sigma1$ and $\sigma2$ provided that one of the σi is strongly regular:

Theorem 3 (Preservation of regularity)
Let SIG0, SIG1, SIG2 , $\sigma1$, $\sigma2$ and $\tau1$, $\tau2$ be as in Theorem 2. If $\sigma1$ and $\sigma2$ are single inheritance extensions, which are regular, and if $\sigma1$ or $\sigma2$ is strongly regular, then SIG is regular.

Proof Sketch (For a full proof we refer to [HN96].)

Let $\sigma 1$ and $\sigma 2$ be as required in the above Theorem. Then we have to show that for every op $\in \cup OP$ and every $w \in S^*$ the set $R_{SIG}(op, w)$ is either empty or has a least element.

Using Fact 5 it is easily seen that since the σi are single inheritance extensions the τi also have this property. Hence it is straightforward to check that for all $i \in \{1,2\}$, all op$i \in \cup OPi \setminus \sigma i(\cup OP0)$ and all $w \in S^*$ such that $R_{SIG}(\tau i(op i), w) \neq \varnothing$ it holds $R_{SIG}(\tau i(op i), w) = \tau i^*(R_{SIGi}(op i, \pi i(w))$ where $\pi i(w) := \min \{w' \in Si^* : w \leq \tau i^*(w') \}$. Since SIGi is regular, we can therefore conclude from the monotonicity of τi^* that $R_{SIG}(\tau i(op i), w)$ has a least element provided it is non-empty and op$i \notin \sigma i(\cup OP0)$.

Hence the interesting case is

$$op = \tau 1(\sigma 1(op0)) = \tau 2(\sigma 2(op0)) \text{ for some } op0 \in \cup OP0.$$

Here it suffices to consider such $w \in S^*$ for which it holds $\{w' \in Si^* : w \leq \tau i^*(w') \} \neq \varnothing$ for $i \in \{1,2\}$ (since otherwise it is obvious that $R_{SIG}(op, w)$ is either empty or has a least element.) Then it is straightforward to see that

$$R_{SIG}(op, w) = \tau 1^*(R_{SIG1}(\sigma 1(op0), \pi 1(w))) \cup \tau 2^*(R_{SIG2}(\sigma 2(op0), \pi 2(w)))$$

where, as above $\pi i(w) := \min \{w' \in Si^* : w \leq \tau i^*(w')\}$. Let us assume that it holds $R_{SIGi}(\sigma i(op0), \pi i(w)) \neq \varnothing$ for $i \in \{1,2\}$ (since otherwise the desired result follows immediately).

Since the σi are regular, it is easily checked that if $\pi i(w) \in \sigma i^*(S0^*)$ for some $i \in \{1,2\}$ then $R_{SIG}(op, w)$ has a least element: If $\pi i(w) \in \sigma i^*(S0^*)$ then by regularity of σi we have min $R_{SIGi}(\sigma i(op0), \pi i(w)) = \sigma i^*(w0)$ for some $w0 \in S0^*$, $s0 \in S0$ with $op0 \in OP0_{w0,s0}$. Then it follows $\tau i^*(\sigma i^*(w0)) \in \tau \tilde{i}^*(R_{SIG\tilde{i}}(\sigma \tilde{i}(op0), \pi \tilde{i}(w)))$ (where $\tilde{i} = (i \bmod 2) + 1$) and hence that $\tau \tilde{i}^*(\min(R_{SIG\tilde{i}}(\sigma \tilde{i}(op0), \pi \tilde{i}(w))))$ is a least element of $R_{SIG}(op, w)$.

It remains to consider the case where $\pi i(w) \notin \sigma i^*(S0^*)$ for $i \in \{1,2\}$. In this case it is straightforward to conclude from the definition of the $\pi i(w)$ that for $i \in \{1,2\}$ it holds

$$\pi i(w) \in DOC_{Si^*} (\sigma i^*(S0^*)) \text{ and } \{\pi i(w)_k \in \sigma i(S0) : 1 \leq k \leq |w| \} \neq \varnothing$$

Since $\sigma 1$ or $\sigma 2$ is strongly regular, it is easy to see that $R_{SIG}(op, w)$ also has a least element in this case. ♦

3.4 Preservation of Locally Upward Filteredness

In this section we look for conditions that we can impose on signature morphisms to ensure that locally upward filteredness of signatures is preserved by pushouts.

Fact 8 Locally upward filteredness of signatures is not always preserved by pushouts in OSCAT. ♦

Example 4 For the following locally upward filtered signatures

SIG0 = **sorts** Elem .
SIG1 = SIG0 + **sorts** List . **subsorts** Elem < List .
SIG2 = **sorts** Nat, Int . **subsorts** Nat < Int .

the pushout signature of the embeddings σ1: SIG0 → SIG1 and σ2: SIG0 → SIG2
with σ2(Elem) = Nat is (up to isomorphism)

    SIG = **sorts** Nat, List, Int . **subsorts** Nat < List, Nat < Int .

which is not locally upward filtered. The problem is that σ1(Elem) and List are connected
in S1, but do not have an upper bound in σ1(S0) and σ2(Elem) and Int are connected in
SIG2 without having an upper bound in σ2(S0). Therefore the sorts List and Int are
mapped to sorts (List and Int) in SIG that are connected without having an upper bound.

                                                                       ♦

The signature morphisms σ1 and σ2 in the above example do not satisfy a property called
locally upward dense which we in the following shall see is a sufficient condition to ensure that locally upward filteredness of signatures is preserved by pushouts of embeddings.

Definition 15
a. Let $(S, \leq)$ and $(S', \leq')$ be partially ordered sets. A monotonic function
   f: $(S, \leq) \rightarrow (S', \leq')$ is called *locally upward dense*, if for all $x \in S$, $y \in S'$ such that
   f(x) and y are connected, there is an upper bound of f(x) and y in f(S).
b. Let SIG and SIG' be order-sorted signatures, where SIG = $(S, \leq, OP)$, SIG'= $(S',$
   $\leq', OP')$. Then an order-sorted signature morphism σ: SIG → SIG' is called *locally
   upward dense*, if $\sigma_S : (S, \leq) \rightarrow (S', \leq')$ is locally upward dense.   ♦

The next Lemma (which we also state without proof) gives a characterization of locally
upward dense functions between locally upward filtered noetherian posets:

Lemma 1 Let $(S1, \leq1)$ and $(S2, \leq2)$ be locally upward filtered and noetherian posets.
Let max(Ci(x)) denote the maximum of the connected component generated by x in
$(Si, \leq i)$ for i = 1,2 (which exists by Proposition 2.20 in [GM 92]).
Then an order-embedding f: $(S1, \leq1) \rightarrow (S2, \leq2)$ is locally upward dense iff for all
$x \in S1$ the following holds: max $(C2(f(x))) = f(max(C1(x)))$.   ♦

Theorem 4 (Preservation of locally upward filteredness)
Let SIG0, SIG1 and SIG2 be locally upward filtered order-sorted signatures, and
σi : SIG0 → SIGi be embeddings for i=1,2. Let SIG together with τi : SIGi → SIG
(i=1,2) be their pushout in OSCAT. Then the following holds:
If σ1 or σ2 is locally upward dense, then SIG is locally upward filtered.   ♦

Theorem 4 is an easy consequence of the following Lemma (which is proved in [HN96])

Lemma 2 Let fi : $(S0, \leq0) \rightarrow (Si, \leq i)$ for i =1,2 be embeddings between locally upward filtered posets where f1 or f2 is locally upward dense. Let $(S, \leq)$ together with
gi: $(Si, \leq i) \rightarrow (S, \leq)$ (i=1,2) be their pushout in the category of posets and monotonic
functions. Then for all x, y ∈ S with a lower bound in S there is also an upper bound of
x, y in S.   ♦

144

3.5 Pushouts of Specifications

In this section we use the results on the preservation of regularity and locally upward filteredness of signatures to formulate our result on the construction of pushouts in the category of order-sorted specifications and specification morphisms.

Theorem 5 Let SPECi = (SIGi, Ei) be order-sorted specifications for i=0,1,2 and σi: SPEC0 → SPECi be specification morphisms such that the σi: SIG0 → SIGi are regular single inheritance extensions. If σ1 or σ2 is strongly regular and σ1 or σ2 is locally upward dense then their pushout in the category of specifications and specification morphisms preserving overloading exists and is given by the following diagram

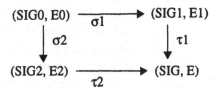

where (SIG, E) can be constructed as follows:

1. SIG together with τ1 and τ2 is a pushout of σ1 and σ2 in OSCAT.
2. E = τ1(E1) ∪ τ2(E1).

Proof: From the Theorems 1- 4 it follows that SIG is a coherent signature. Hence (SIG, E) is an order-sorted specification. From the choice of E it follows that τ1 and τ2 are specification morphisms. If SPEC'= (SIG', E') is a specification together with specification morphisms γi : SPECi → SPEC' preserving overloading, then it is easily checked that the uniquely determined signature morphism γ : SIG → SIG' preserving overloading such that γ τi = γi for i =1,2 is a specification morphism γ : SPEC → SPEC' . ♦

3.6 Application of the Theory

As mentioned in the introduction pushouts can be used to define specification building operations that combine specifications into new specifications. For example the union of two specifications SPEC1 and SPEC2 having a common subspecification SPEC0 can be defined as the pushout of the embeddings σ1 : SPEC0 → SPEC1 and σ2 : SPEC0 → SPEC2 of SPEC0 into SPEC1 and SPEC2, respectively. As another example, the actualization of a parameterized specification can be defined as the pushout of σ1 : SPEC0 → SPEC1 and σ2 : SPEC0 → SPEC2 where σ1 is the embedding of the formal parameter specification SPEC0 into the body specification SPEC1, and σ2 is the parameter passing morphism from the formal parameter specification to the actual parameter specification SPEC2. For the above mentioned specification building operations, Theorem 5 tells us that if the specification morphisms satisfy the given conditions then the result of their application is well-defined. Does this suggest that we should formulate our specifications in a special way?

For the case of actualization of parameterized specifications we propose that parameterized specifications are formulated such that the embedding (σ1) is a strongly regular single inheritance extension which is locally upward dense. Then, by Theorem 5, actualization of the parameterized specification will be well-formed for any actual parameter passing morphism σ2 which is a regular single inheritance extension. By investigating many existing parameterized specifications we have found that σ1 usually satisfies the above proposed conditions. σ1 is usually downward closed (cf. also [Poi90]) and regular, which implies that it is a strongly regular single inheritance extension. In a few examples σ1 was not locally upward dense because the body added a supersort (e.g. an errorsort) to a maximal parameter sort. However, the specifications can easily be rewritten such that σ1 becomes locally upward dense. For instance, in the example with the errorsort this can be achieved by moving the definition of the errorsort to the parameter specification; and in example 4, this can be achieved by removing the subsort relation Elem < List in SIG1 and introducing a coercion function from Elem to List (and actually we prefer this specification as there are implementations where there is an injection from elements to lists, but no inclusion). For parameter passing morphisms (σ2), the only condition we have found that could be restrictive is the embedding condition (which is a part of the single inheritance extension condition). It prohibits two different parameter sorts to be mapped to the same actual parameter sort.

In the following example we use Theorem 5 to investigate whether a specification of pictures with a move-operation can be constructed by actualizing a parameterized specification of lists with a specification of graphical elements.

Example 5 LISTf is parameterized specification of lists of elements with a canonical extension of a function on elements to a function on lists of elements.

```
ELEMf =
  sorts Elem, Par . ops  f : Elem Par -> Elem .

LISTf = ELEMf +
  sorts NeList, List . subsorts NeList < List .
  ops
    nil : List,
    append : Elem List -> NeList,
    top : NeList -> Elem,
    pop : NeList -> List,
    f  : List Par -> List,
    f  : NeList Par -> NeList .
  vars e : Elem, l : List, p: Par .
  eqns
    top(append(e, l)) = e,
    pop(append(e, l)) = l,
    f(nil, p) = nil,
    f(append(e,l), p) = append(f(e,p), f(l, p)) .
```

Notice the use of ad-hoc polymorphism in Listf: Elem is not a subsort of List, but f is declared both on elements and on lists. This makes sense, since in many applications the same name is used for a function on elements and its canonical extension to words, lists, etc. It is easily checked that the signatures of ELEMf and LISTf are coherent and that the inclusion σ1 of ELEMf into LISTf is a regular embedding. As {Elem, Par} is downward closed in the poset of sorts in LISTf, σ1 is also a strongly regular single inheritance extension. Furthermore, it preserves maximal sorts and hence is locally upward dense by Lemma 1.

As actual parameter we consider a specification of graphical elements which is inspired by an example given in [Bre91]. Graphical elements consist of points, lines (given by the coordinates of their start and end points) and rectangles whose sides are parallel to the axes (given by one corner and the lengths of the sides). On graphical elements a subtype-polymorphic move-operation is specified. The specification is based on a specification COORDINATE of cartesian coordinates of pairs of integers containing amongst others the sorts Pos < Int, where Pos denotes the set of non-zero positive numbers, and a coordinate addition add : Coordinate Coordinate -> Coordinate.

```
GRAPHICS = COORDINATE +
  sorts GraphicElement, Point, Line, Rectangle .
  subsorts Point < Line < GraphicElement, Rectangle < GraphicElement .
  ops
    mkPoint : Coordinate -> Point,
    mkLine : Coordinate Coordinate -> Line,
    mkRect : Coordinate Pos Pos -> Rectangle,
    move : GraphicElement Coordinate -> GraphicElement,
    move : Point Coordinate -> Point,
    move : Line Coordinate -> Line,
    move : Rectangle Coordinate -> Rectangle.
  vars c, c1, c2, v : Coordinate, n, m: Pos .
  eqns
    mkPoint(c) = mkLine(c, c),
    move( mkLine(c1, c2), v) = mkLine( add(c1, v), add(c2, v)),
    move( mkRect (c, n, m), v ) = mkRect( add(c, v), n, m) .
```

As parameter passing morphism σ2 : ELEMf → GRAPHICS we use ([Elem -> GraphicElement, Par -> Coordinate], [f -> move]). It is easily checked that σ2 is a regular single inheritance extension. Therefore by Theorem 5, a pushout of σ1 and σ2 exists and hence the actualization is well-defined. The result is a specification of pictures as lists of graphical elements where   move : List Coordinate -> List   is an operation that moves an entire picture.   ◆

4. Conclusions

In this paper we have investigated the existence of pushouts in the category of order-sorted specifications and specification morphisms preserving overloading. As the existence of pushouts of specifications depends on the existence of pushouts of the underlying signatures and the preservation of coherence by these pushouts we started by investigating pushouts of signatures. In section 3.1, we showed that pushouts in the category of order-sorted signatures and signature morphisms preserving overloading always exist, and, in sections 3.2-3.4, we gradually established conditions on signature morphisms which guarantee that the pushout preserves monotonicity, regularity and coherence of signatures. Then, in section 3.5, we used these results to establish the main result that the existence of pushouts of specifications can be guaranteed by imposing certain conditions on the specification morphisms. Finally, in section 3.6, we investigated the applicability of the results. The results are important as pushouts are used to combine specifications in some specification languages, such as OBJ. Our investigations so far have shown that the conditions in most realistic cases are easy to satisfy. The only exception is the embedding condition on parameter passing morphisms. An interesting topic for future work could therefore be to investigate whether it would be possible to do without this condition by strengthening the conditions on the other morphism.

Acknowledgements

We wish to thank the anonymous referees for their valuable comments.

References

[BG85] R.M. Burstall and J.A. Goguen. *The Semantics of Clear, a Specification Language.* In: Advanced Course on Abstract Software Specifications, Springer LNCS 86, 1985.

[Bre91] R. Breu. *Algebraic Specification Techniques in Object Oriented Programming Environments.* Springer LNCS 562, 1991.

[EM85] H. Ehrig and B. Mahr. *Fundamentals of Algebraic Specification 1, Equations and Initial Semantics.* EATCS Monographs on Theoretical Computer Science, vol. 6. Springer-Verlag, 1985.

[EM90] H. Ehrig and B. Mahr. *Fundamentals of Algebraic Specification 2, Module Specifications and Constraints.* EATCS Monographs on Theoretical Computer Science, vol. 21. Springer-Verlag, 1990.

[FGJM85] K. Futatsugi, J.A. Goguen, J. Jouannaud, and J. Meseguer. *Principles of OBJ2.* In: 12th Symposium of POPL. Association for Computing Machinery, 1985.

[GB85] J.A. Goguen and R.M. Burstall. *Institutions: Abstract model theory for computer science.* Technical report, Center for Study of Language and Information, Stanford University, 1985.

[GD94] J.A. Goguen and R. Diaconescu. *An Oxford Survey of Order Sorted Algebra.* In: Mathematical Structures in Computer Science, 1994.

[GM92] J.A. Goguen and J. Meseguer. *Order-Sorted Algebra I: Equational Deduction for Multiple Inheritance, Overloading, Exceptions and Partial Operations.* Theoretical Computer Science, 105(2), 1992.

[GWMFJ92] J.A. Goguen, T. Winkler, J. Meseguer, K. Futatsugi, and J. Jouannaud. *Introducing OBJ.* Technical Report SRI-CSL-92-03, SRI Int., 1992. Draft.

[Hax88] A.E. Haxthausen. *Structuring Mechanisms in Algebraic Specification Languages.* PhD thesis, Department of Computer Science, the Technical University of Denmark,1988.

[HN94] R. Hennicker and F. Nickl. *A Behavioural Algebraic Framework for Modular System Design with Reuse.* In: F. Orejas (ed.): Recent Trends in Data Type Specification, Springer LNCS 785, pp. 220-234, 1994.

[HN96] A.E. Haxthausen and F. Nickl. *Pushouts of Order-Sorted Algebraic Specifications.* Technical Report, Institut für Informatik, Ludwig-Maximilians-Universität München, 1996.

[NN95] M. Nenninger and F. Nickl. *Implementing Data Structures by Composition of Reusable Components: A Formal Approach.* In: M. Wirsing (ed.): Formal Methods Applications in Software Engineering Practice, Proceedings of the ICSE-17 Workshop, Seattle, April 1995, pp. 134-142.

[Poi90] A. Poigné. *Parametrization for Order-Sorted Algebraic Specification.* Journal of Computer and System Sciences 40, pp. 229 - 268 (1990).

[ST85] D. Sannella and A. Tarlecki. *Specifications in an Arbitrary Institution.* Technical Report CSR-184-85, Department of Computer Science, University of Edinburgh, 1985.

[Wir90] M. Wirsing. *Algebraic specification.* In: J. van Leeuwen (ed.): Handbook of Theoretical Computer Science, 675-788, Elsevier Science Publishers B. V., 1990.

A Formal Framework for Modules with State*

Davide Ancona and Elena Zucca

DISI - Università di Genova
Via Dodecaneso, 35, 16146 Genova (Italy)
email: {davide, zucca}@disi.unige.it

1 Introduction

In this paper, we address the problem of formal foundations for module manipulation within an imperative context. A *module* in a programming language is a part of a program viewed as a whole (often a compilation unit), having an *interface* specifying the set of services offered to the outside, while the actual implementation is usually hidden to users (*encapsulation*). A modular language supports a variety of ways for composing modules. These combinators form what we call in this paper a *module language*, as opposed to the *core* language used for defining single components inside a module (this terminology was first introduced in Standard ML [13]). These two levels of language are quite independent, both from the syntactic and semantic point of view.

An appealing intuition about the semantics of a module language, already suggested by the ML terminology (ground modules are called "structures", their types are called "signatures" and parameterized modules are called "functors"), is that the denotation of a module should be a structure (model) over a signature in (the model part of) an appropriate institution, in the sense of [8].

That approach allows one to integrate in a pleasantly uniform way a (programming) module language with a specification module language, where modules do not define implementations of the features in the interface, but requirements (sentences in the underlying institution). An example of a wide-spectrum language obtained in this way is Extended ML ([14]). In a specification language, a module typically denotes a class of structures; composition of modules in specification languages has been extensively studied (see e.g. [4, 10]), and there exists a small set of combinators with clean semantics which are widely used.

Anyway, on the side of programming languages, a well-established theory of modules with state is missing. Existing programming languages are poor from the point of view of module manipulation (see [6]), there is no evidence about a minimal set of module combinators and, from the semantic point of view, as far as we now there is no semantic definition of a modular language in which the intuition "module = structure" is fully exploited in a compositional way, i.e. with module combinators interpreted as functions over structures. Moreover, imperative features are usually handled by a global store which is orthogonal to module composition.

---

* This work has been partially supported by WG n.6112 COMPASS, Murst 40% - Modelli della computazione e dei linguaggi di programmazione and CNR, Italy.

In this paper, we present the formal definition of a kernel module language which is a first attempt at solving these problems. We introduce, at the semantic level, a notion of *object structure* intended to be the natural denotation of a module with state. An object structure consists, roughly speaking, of a class of *states* and a family of *methods* (operations which change the current state, modeling procedures in imperative languages or methods in object oriented languages). Formally, a state is a data-type in the usual sense (an algebra), and methods are operations which handle algebras (the "state-as-algebra" approach, see e.g. [12]). Object structures are a variant of *d-oids* (see [3]). The framework of object structures we propose is somehow "institution-independent", in the sense that it is parameterized by the framework we choose for algebras representing states.

At the syntactic level, we introduce a small set of basic module operators which should be a minimal one allowing one to express operators commonly used (even implicitly) in programming languages. They are *renaming, sum* and *export*. These operators are independent of the underlying core language. In addition, we assume that the module language is parameterized by a family of *state* and *method definitions* for building basic modules, to be instantiated depending on the core language, and we give some concrete examples. Operations of composing modules are interpreted as functions over dynamic structures, giving a truly compositional semantics of the language.

The module language we present can be thought of as a paradigmatic representative for the class of *object based* languages following Wegner's widely accepted classification ([15]). Indeed a module with state is an object in the sense of this terminology. That covers for example Modula modules and Ada packages. In [2], we show how to deal with languages where objects (modules) can be handled as first-class values (*class-based* languages in Wegner's classification) by means of a *meta-module* operator.

The paper is organized as follows. In Sec. 2 we give some definitions and results about signatures with inclusions that will be needed in what follows.

In Sec. 3 we introduce object signatures and structures. In Sec. 4 we give the syntax and semantics of our module language (each subsection is devoted to an operator). In the conclusion we discuss some aspects of further work. An extended presentation of the ideas in this paper, including proofs and more significant examples, is given in [2].

2 Technical preliminaries

In this section, we introduce an abstract notion of *signature*. Basically we require that a signature has a set of *sorts* and that there is a notion of inclusion between signatures – needed for modeling the relation from the *visible* to the *internal* state signature of a module (including hidden components). We first define what is a distributive inclusive category (our definition is largely based on [10]).

If C is a category, then we denote the class of its objects by $|C|$.

Definition 1. A *distributive inclusive category* is a pair of categories $<C, \mathcal{I}>$, with $\mathcal{I}$ subcategory of C and $|\mathcal{I}| = |C|$, s.t.

– $\mathcal{I}$ is a distributive lattice; we call the morphisms in $\mathcal{I}$ *inclusions* and use the notation $A \hookrightarrow B$ or $i_{A,B}$ for the (unique) inclusion from A into B, if any; moreover, we call *union* (denoted by $A \cup B$) and *intersection* (denoted by $A \cap B$), respectively, the join and the meet of A and B in $\mathcal{I}$;

– every morphism $f: A \to B$ in **C** can be uniquely factored as $i_{fA,B} \circ f\!\!\downarrow$, with $f\!\!\downarrow: A \to fA$ an epimorphism; we call fA the *image* of A w.r.t. f;

– for each pair of objects A and B, the pair of inclusions $<A \hookrightarrow A \cup B, B \hookrightarrow A \cup B>$ is a pushout (in **C**) of the pair $<X \hookrightarrow A, X \hookrightarrow B>$ iff $X = A \cap B$. □

In the following we denote $<\mathbf{C}, \mathcal{I}>$ simply by **C**, when there is no ambiguity.

Example 1. The category **Set** of small sets, with $\mathcal{I}$ the set inclusions, trivially forms a distributive inclusive category.

Proposition 2. *Let $<\mathbf{C}, \mathcal{I}>$ be a distributive inclusive category. Then*

1. *every inclusion is a monomorphism in **C**;*
2. *if **C** is balanced, then for any monomorphism f, $f\!\!\downarrow$ is an isomorphism.* □

Definition 3. *Pushouts preserve inclusions* in a distributive inclusive category iff whenever a pair of arrows $<A \hookrightarrow A', A \to B>$ has a pushout, then it has also a pushout of the form $<B \hookrightarrow B', A' \to B'>$. □

Note that if pushouts preserve inclusions, then, whenever a pair of inclusions $<A \hookrightarrow B, A \hookrightarrow C>$ has a pushout, it has also a pushout D s.t. $B \hookrightarrow D$ and a pushout D' s.t. $C \hookrightarrow D'$ (but not necessarily a pushout where both the injections are inclusions). Since any inclusion is a monomorphism, it follows also that the injections of any pushout of $<A \hookrightarrow B, A \hookrightarrow C>$ are monomorphisms.

Definition 4. Let $<\mathbf{C}, \mathcal{I}>$ and $<\mathbf{C}', \mathcal{I}'>$ be two distributive inclusive categories. Then a *distributive inclusive category morphism* is a functor $F: \mathbf{C} \to \mathbf{C}'$ which preserves inclusions, intersection and union. □

We define now a signature category as a particular kind of distributive inclusive category. The main new features we introduce are *sorts* and a *difference* operator.

Definition 5. A *signature category* is a pair $<\mathbf{Sig}, Sorts: \mathbf{Sig} \to \mathbf{Set}>$, where **Sig** is a balanced and cocomplete distributive inclusive category and *Sorts* is a morphism of distributive inclusive categories s.t.

– pushouts in **Sig** preserve inclusions;
– for any $S \in |\mathbf{Set}|$, there exists an object $\emptyset_S \in |\mathbf{Sig}|$ s.t.
  • $Sorts(\emptyset_S) = S$;
  • for any $\Sigma \in |\mathbf{Sig}|$, if $S \hookrightarrow Sorts(\Sigma)$ then $\emptyset_S \hookrightarrow \Sigma$;
– for any $\Sigma_1, \Sigma_2 \in |\mathbf{Sig}|$ s.t. $\Sigma_1 \hookrightarrow \Sigma_2$, there exists an object $\Sigma_2 \backslash \Sigma_1$ s.t.

$$\Sigma_1 \cup (\Sigma_2 \backslash \Sigma_1) = \Sigma_2; \tag{1}$$
$$\Sigma_1 \cap (\Sigma_2 \backslash \Sigma_1) = \emptyset_{Sorts(\Sigma_1)}. \tag{2}$$

If $\Sigma \in |\mathbf{Sig}|$ with $Sorts(\Sigma) = S$, then we say that Σ is a *signature over* the set of *sorts* S. $\qquad\square$

The following proposition justifies the notation $\Sigma_2 \backslash \Sigma_1$.

Proposition 6. *In a signature category* $\mathbf{Sig}$, *for any* $\Sigma_1, \Sigma_2 \in |\mathbf{Sig}|$ *s.t.* $\Sigma_1 \hookrightarrow \Sigma_2, \Sigma_2 \backslash \Sigma_1$ *is unique.* $\qquad\square$

Note that in our definition of difference between signatures, the intersection between Σ_1 and $\Sigma_2 \backslash \Sigma_1$ (with $\Sigma_1 \hookrightarrow \Sigma_2$) is not the bottom element $\emptyset_\emptyset$, as is the case for sets. Indeed in usual cases such as algebraic many-sorted signatures it is not true that $Sorts(\Sigma_2 \backslash \Sigma_1) = Sorts(\Sigma_2) \backslash Sorts(\Sigma_1)$, since operations which are not in Σ_1 may be over sorts in $Sorts(\Sigma_1)$. Hence we keep all the sorts of Σ_2 in $\Sigma_2 \backslash \Sigma_1$. As a consequence, Σ_2 is not the disjoint sum of Σ_1 and $\Sigma_2 \backslash \Sigma_1$, as happens for sets, but the disjoint sum with sharing of the sorts of Σ_1, as formally defined below.

Definition 7. Let Σ_1 and Σ_2 be two signatures, $S \hookrightarrow Sorts(\Sigma_1 \cap \Sigma_2)$. Then we denote by $\Sigma_1 +_S \Sigma_2$ the pushout (up to isomorphisms) of the pair of arrows $<\emptyset_S \hookrightarrow \Sigma_1, \emptyset_S \hookrightarrow \Sigma_2>$. $\qquad\square$

Proposition 8. *For any pair of signatures* Σ_1 *and* Σ_2 *s.t.* $\Sigma_1 \hookrightarrow \Sigma_2$, $\Sigma_1 +_{Sorts(\Sigma_1)} (\Sigma_2 \backslash \Sigma_1) = \Sigma_2$. $\qquad\square$

Example 2. The category of algebraic many-sorted signatures (a signature over S is a $S^* \times S$-family of symbols), with the obvious definitions of inclusions, empty signature and difference, is a signature category.

3 Object signatures and structures

In this section, we present object structures as semantic counterpart of modules with state. We introduce our formal notion by a simple example: a circle in the Cartesian plain with variable position and radius, whose interface to the outside offers three features: $grow(r)$, growing the circle's radius by r, *isOrigIn*, testing whether the circle contains the origin, and $move(x, y)$, moving the circle horizontally by x and vertically by y. Formally, we describe the operational interface of the module by the following *object signature*:

$$O\Sigma_C =$$
$\qquad$ **sorts** $real, bool, posReal$
$\qquad$ **opns**
$\qquad\qquad$ $X, Y: real, R: posReal$
$\qquad$ **methods**
$\qquad\qquad$ $grow: posReal \Rightarrow , isOrigIn: \Rightarrow bool, move: real\ real \Rightarrow$

As shown by the example, an object signature is a pair consisting of an ordinary signature (the *state signature*) and a *method signature*. Methods have general form $m: s_1 \ldots s_n \Rightarrow [s]$ (where $[\ ]$ denotes optionality) and their interpretations are functions with a side-effect on the state. In the example, a circle state can be defined to be an algebra C over the signature

$<\{real, posReal\}, \{X, Y: real, R: posReal\}>$

s.t. C_{real} and $C_{posReal}$ are the sets of real numbers and positive real numbers, respectively. Let C be the class of such algebras. The interpretation of a method (say *grow*) can be seen consequently as a function which associates with each pair $<C, r>$, where $C \in C$, $r \in C_{posReal}$, the algebra C' in C s.t. $X^{C'} = X^C$, $Y^{C'} = Y^C$, $R^{C'} = R^C * r$.

We now give the formal definitions. Since we do not want to fix the algebraic framework for the static part (e.g. total, partial, order sorted algebras ...), we consider a general notion of *static framework*. Basically, we require that, for any signature Σ over S, a Σ-algebra is an S-sorted set enriched by some structure.

Definition 9. A *static framework* is a 4-tuple $<\mathbf{Sig}, Sorts, Alg, |-|>$ where

- $<\mathbf{Sig}, Sorts>$ is a signature category;
- Alg is a functor, $Alg: \mathbf{Sig}^{op} \to \mathbf{Cat}$; for any signature Σ, objects in $Alg(\Sigma)$ are called *algebras* over Σ or Σ-*algebras*; for any signature morphism $\sigma: \Sigma \to \Sigma'$, $Alg(\sigma)$ is called the *reduct* functor and denoted by $_{-|\sigma}$;
- $|-|$ is a natural transformation, $|-|: Alg \to SSet \circ Sorts^{op}$, s.t., for any Σ, the functor $|-|_\Sigma$ is faithful; for any Σ-algebra A, $|A|_\Sigma$ is called the *carrier* of A, and denoted by $|A|$ or even A when there is no ambiguity. □

Above and in what follows, $SSet$ denotes the functor giving, for any set of sorts S, the category of S-sorted sets. The assumption that $|-|_\Sigma$ is faithful (i.e. all the hom-set restrictions are injective) models the fact that Σ-morphisms are basically maps; in other words, for each signature Σ over S, $Alg(\Sigma)$ is an S-*concrete category* in the sense of [5, 1]. In particular an *inclusion* from A into B, denoted $i_{A,B}$ or $A \hookrightarrow B$, is the unique Σ-morphism, if any, s.t. $|i_{A,B}| = i_{|A|,|B|}$. If $\Sigma \hookrightarrow \Sigma'$ and A is a Σ'-algebra, then we write $A_{|\Sigma}$ instead of $A_{|i_{\Sigma, \Sigma'}}$.

Assume in what follows a fixed static framework $ST = <\mathbf{Sig}, Sorts, Alg, |-|>$. In the examples, ST is the static framework of partial algebras (see [7]). In the following, if S is a set, then $[S]$ denotes $S \cup \{\Lambda\}$ and $[s]$ stands for either an element of S or for the empty string.

Definition 10. If S is a set of sorts, then a *method signature* $M\Sigma$ over S is a $(S^* \times [S])$-family of symbols called *method symbols*; if $m \in M\Sigma_{w,[s]}$, then we write $m: w \Rightarrow [s]$. □

Intuitively, a method has a "hidden" argument (which is the current state), n explicit arguments and returns a transformed state (side effect, or hidden result) and, possibly, an explicit result.

Definition 11. Let S be a set of sorts; an *object signature over* S is a pair $O\Sigma = <\Sigma, M\Sigma>$ where Σ is a signature over S (called the *state signature*) and $M\Sigma$ is a method signature over S. Object signatures with the obvious component-wise definition of morphisms form a category. □

Definition 12. Let Σ be a signature over S. For every $w = s_1 \ldots s_n \in S^*$, set $Alg(\Sigma)_w = \{<A, \bar{a}> \mid A \in |Alg(\Sigma)|, a_i \in A_{s_i}, \forall i = 1, \ldots, n\}$. Then, for every $[s] \in [S]$, a *method* m over Σ of functionality $w \Rightarrow [s]$ is a partial map which associates with every $<A, \bar{a}> \in Alg(\Sigma)_w$:

- a Σ-algebra A', with $|A| \subseteq |A'|$;
- if $[s]$ is non-null, a value $a' \in A'_{[s]}$.

We denote by $Meth(\Sigma)$ the $S^* \times [S]$-family of classes of methods over Σ. □

The assumption $|A| \subseteq |A'|$ models the fact that the evolution from one state to another may involve the creation of new subcomponent objects. We forbid object deletion, since this assumption allows a simpler technical treatment.

Definition 13. If $O\Sigma = <\Sigma, M\Sigma>$ is an object signature, then an *object structure* over $O\Sigma$ is a pair $A = <i_{\Sigma, \Sigma^A}, \{m^A\}_{m \in M\Sigma}>$ where for each $m: w \Rightarrow [s]$, $m^A \in Meth(\Sigma^A)_{w[,s]}$. We call Σ and Σ^A the *visible* and the *internal state signature* of A, respectively. □

In the examples, we consider object structures over a fixed algebra V of basic values (like integers, booleans and so on) with signature Σ_V. Formally, we consider internal state signatures Σ^A s.t. $\Sigma_V \subseteq \Sigma^A$, and, instead of $Alg(\Sigma^A)$, the class of Σ^A-algebras

$$Alg_V(\Sigma^A) = \{A \mid A \in Alg(\Sigma^A), A_{|\Sigma_V} = V\}.$$

Example 3. The circle module informally introduced above can be formalized by the following object structure C over $O\Sigma_C$:

$$\Sigma^C = <\{real, posReal\}, \{X, Y: real, R: posReal\}> \cup \Sigma_V$$
$$isOrigIn^C(C) =_\perp <C, (X^C)^2 + (Y^C)^2 \le (R^C)^2>$$
$$grow^C(<C, r>) = C' \text{ where } X^{C'} =_\perp X^C, Y^{C'} =_\perp Y^C, R^{C'} =_\perp R^C * r$$
$$move^C(<C, x, y>) = C' \text{ where } X^{C'} =_\perp X^C + x, Y^{C'} =_\perp Y^P + y, R^{C'} =_\perp R^C.$$

Here and in what follows the symbol $=_\perp$ stands for strong equality, i.e. $e_1 =_\perp e_2$ means that either e_1, e_2 are both defined and equal, or both undefined.
In C the visible and internal state signatures coincide, but in general the internal one may be larger than the visible one. That models the fact that states are partly or completely "hidden" to the outside, and technically is needed for defining the reduct of an object structure w.r.t. a smaller object signature. To see this, consider the following object signature:

$$\overline{O\Sigma} =$$
> **sorts** *real, bool*
> **opns** X, Y: *real*
> **methods**
> > *isOrigIn*: $\Rightarrow$ *bool, move: real real* $\Rightarrow$

It is intuitively clear that the object structure $\mathcal{C}$ above can also be seen as an object structure over this restricted signature $\overline{O\Sigma}$, forgetting the operation R and the method *grow*. However, in this reduct structure, it is not possible to take as states $\overline{\Sigma}$-algebras, with $\overline{\Sigma} = <\{real\}, \{X, Y: real\}> \cup \Sigma_V$, since $isOrigIn^{\mathcal{C}}$ depends on R, and there is no way to derive from it a method over the $\overline{\Sigma}$. The solution is that states remain as before and only their "view from outside" changes.

Fact 14 Let $<\Sigma_1, M\Sigma_1>$ and $<\Sigma_2, M\Sigma_2>$ be two object signatures s.t. $\Sigma_1 \hookrightarrow \Sigma_2$, $M\Sigma_1 \hookrightarrow M\Sigma_2$, and let $\mathcal{A}$ be an object structure over $<\Sigma_2, M\Sigma_2>$. Then the pair $<i_{\Sigma_1, \Sigma^A}, \{m^{\mathcal{A}}\}_{m \in M\Sigma_1}>$ is an object structure over $<\Sigma_1, M\Sigma_1>$, called the *reduct of $\mathcal{A}$ w.r.t.* $<\Sigma_1, M\Sigma_1>$ and denoted by $\mathcal{A}_{|<\Sigma_1, M\Sigma_1>}$. □

We introduce now an equivalence relation between object structures, which captures the intuition that hidden components can be renamed without affecting the semantics of a module.
For any $<A, \overline{a}> \in Alg(\Sigma)_w$, let $<A, \overline{a}>_{|\sigma}$ denote the tuple $<A_{|\sigma}, \overline{a}>$.

Definition 15. Let $\mathcal{A}_1$ and $\mathcal{A}_2$ be object structures over $O\Sigma = <\Sigma, M\Sigma>$. Then $\mathcal{A}_1 \simeq_{O\Sigma} \mathcal{A}_2$ iff there exists an isomorphism $\sigma: \Sigma^{\mathcal{A}_1} \to \Sigma^{\mathcal{A}_2}$ s.t.

- $\sigma \circ i_{\Sigma, \Sigma^{\mathcal{A}_1}} = i_{\Sigma, \Sigma^{\mathcal{A}_2}}$;
- $\forall m \in M\Sigma_{w[,s]}, <A, \overline{a}> \in Alg(\Sigma^{\mathcal{A}_2})_w,$
  $m^{\mathcal{A}_2}(<A, \overline{a}>) =_{\perp} (m^{\mathcal{A}_1}(<A_{|\sigma}, \overline{a}>))_{|\sigma^{-1}}.$ □

Proposition 16. *For any object signature $O\Sigma$, $\simeq_{O\Sigma}$ is an equivalence.* □

In the following, for any object signature $O\Sigma$, $Obj(O\Sigma)$ denotes the class of the ($\simeq_{O\Sigma}$-equivalence classes of) object structures over $O\Sigma$.

4 An algebra of modules with state

In this section we present the syntax and semantics of our module language. Following the tradition of [4], we present the module language as a (partial) algebra $\mathcal{DM}$ (for "dynamic modules"), whose signature $\Sigma_{\mathcal{DM}}$ is given in Fig. 1. We assume that $\Sigma_{\mathcal{DM}}$ contains a family of constant operators indexed by a set *SDEF* of *state definitions* and a family of unary operators indexed by a set *MDEF* of *method definitions*; in other words, $\Sigma_{\mathcal{DM}}$ is parameterized over such sets, which depend on the underlying core language.
We associate with any module M a *type* (interface) which is the visible object signature of the object structure denoted by M; we write $M:O\Sigma$ for $Type(M) = O\Sigma$, and we give a typing rule for any module operator.
For any sort in $\Sigma_{\mathcal{DM}}$ we define a corresponding carrier: $\mathcal{DM}_{sort}$ is the universe of the sort symbols, $\mathcal{DM}_{signature}$ is the class of the object signatures, $\mathcal{DM}_{renaming}$ is the class of the isomorphisms of object signatures and $\mathcal{DM}_{module}$ is the class of all object structures.

sig $\Sigma_{\mathcal{D}\mathcal{M}} =$
    sorts *module, signature, sort, renaming*
    opns

$\{<Sdef>: \to module \mid Sdef \in SDEF\}$	(state definitions)
$\{<Mdef>: module \to module \mid Mdef \in MDEF\}$	(method definitions)
$\_ \star \_: renaming\ module \to module$	(renaming)
$\_ + \_: module\ module \to module$	(sum)
$\_\square\_: signature\ module \to module$	(export)
$Type: module \to signature$	(type)

Fig. 1. Signature of the algebra of modules with state

4.1 State definitions

We assume that the core language provides a set of *state definitions*, each one corresponding to a constant module. For instance, the case in which a state is a record, as happens in many object oriented languages, corresponds to having, for any signature $A\Sigma$ of only nullary operations (*attribute signature*), a module $<A\Sigma>$ with signature $<A\Sigma, Upd(A\Sigma)>$, where $Upd(A\Sigma)$ is the set of built-in methods for updating attributes defined as follows:

$$Upd(A\Sigma) = \{\, a \leftarrow \_: s \Rightarrow \mid a: s \text{ in } A\Sigma \,\}$$

The interpretation of a module constant of this kind is defined in Fig. 2.

$\forall A\Sigma$ attribute signature, $<A\Sigma>^{\mathcal{D}\mathcal{M}} \in Obj(<A\Sigma, Upd(A\Sigma)>) = \mathcal{A}$, where

- $\Sigma^{\mathcal{A}} = A\Sigma \cup \Sigma_V$
- for any $a: \to s$ in $A\Sigma$,

    $(a \leftarrow \_)^{\mathcal{A}}(<A, v>) = A[v/a]$

where $A[v/a]$ denotes the algebra equal to A except that $a^{A[v/a]} = v$.

Fig. 2. Interpretation of example module constants

Example 4. Recalling Ex. 3, let $A\Sigma$ be the attribute signature

    $<\{real, posReal\}, \{X, Y: real, R: posReal\}>,$

then $<A\Sigma>$ denotes the object structure $\mathcal{T}$ over $<A\Sigma, Upd(A\Sigma)>$ s.t. for any $A \in Alg_V(A\Sigma \cup \Sigma_V)$, $x, y \in A_{real}, r \in A_{posReal}$

    $(X \leftarrow \_)^{\mathcal{T}}(<A, x>) = A[x/X], (Y \leftarrow \_)^{\mathcal{T}}(<A, y>) = A[y/Y], (R \leftarrow \_)^{\mathcal{T}}(<A, r>) = A[r/R].$ $\square$

4.2 Method definitions

We assume that the core language provides a set of *method definitions*, each one, say *Mdef*, having a type of the form $<\Sigma, M\Sigma_1> \rightarrow <\Sigma, M\Sigma_1 \cup M\Sigma_2>$, with $M\Sigma_1 \cap M\Sigma_2 = \emptyset$, and corresponding to a unary module operator.

$$\frac{M:<\Sigma, M\Sigma_1>}{<Mdef>(M):<\Sigma, M\Sigma_1 \cup M\Sigma_2>} \qquad <Mdef>:<\Sigma, M\Sigma_1> \rightarrow <\Sigma, M\Sigma_1 \cup M\Sigma_2>$$

In the examples, we use a simple language for method definitions whose semantics should be obvious. We refer to [2] for a formal presentation of this language.

Example 5. Enrich the object structure $\mathcal{T}$ defined in Ex. 4 by the following method definition

> $CircleMdef =$
> $\quad isOrigIn{:}bool = sqr(X) + sqr(Y) \leq sqr(R)$
> $\quad grow(r{:}posReal) = R \leftarrow R * r$
> $\quad move(x, y{:}real) = X \leftarrow X + x; Y \leftarrow Y + y$

Then $(<CircleMdef>^{\mathcal{DM}}(\mathcal{T}))_{|O\Sigma_c}$, i.e. the object structure obtained enriching $\mathcal{T}$ and then hiding the built-in methods for updating attributes, is the object structure $\mathcal{C}$ defined in Ex. 3. $\qquad\square$

4.3 Renaming

Renaming is defined only for object signature morphisms that are isomorphisms (otherwise we could have, roughly speaking, either two conflicting interpretations or no interpretation for one symbol).

$$\frac{M:O\Sigma}{<\sigma, \mu> \star M:O\Sigma'} \qquad <\sigma, \mu>:O\Sigma \rightarrow O\Sigma' \text{ is an isomorphism}$$

We first analyze what should be the internal state signature of an object structure obtained from another by renaming. It turns out that hidden names must be renamed too, in order not to introduce name clashes. Consider, for example, the following signatures:

$\Sigma = <real, \{X{:}real\}>, \Sigma^{\mathcal{A}} = <real, \{X, Y{:}real\}>$
$\Sigma' = <real, \{Y{:}real\}>.$

Assume that Σ and $\Sigma^{\mathcal{A}}$ are the visible and the internal state signature, respectively, of an object structure $\mathcal{A}$ and apply to $\mathcal{A}$ a renaming whose first component is the unique isomorphism σ from Σ to Σ'. In the internal state signature $\Sigma^{\mathcal{A}'}$ of the object structure $\mathcal{A}'$ we obtain, X must be replaced by Y; the hidden symbol Y, however, must be replaced by a symbol not in Σ', for instance $\Sigma^{\mathcal{A}'} = <real, \{Y, Z{:}real\}>$. The situation is sketched by the diagram in Fig. 3. In the category of many-sorted algebraic signatures, $\Sigma^{\mathcal{A}'}$ turns out to be a pushout of $<i_{\Sigma,\Sigma^{\mathcal{A}}}, \sigma>$. The construction can be applied in a generic signature category, as stated below.

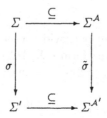

Fig. 3. Diagram for the renaming operator

Proposition 17. *If $\sigma: \Sigma \to \Sigma'$ is an isomorphism and $\Sigma \hookrightarrow \Sigma^A$ in **Sig**, then there exists a pushout of the pair $<i_{\Sigma, \Sigma^A}, \sigma>$ of the form $<\tilde{\sigma}, i_{\Sigma', \Sigma^{A'}}>$. Moreover $\tilde{\sigma}$ is an isomorphism.* □

We consider now what should be the interpretation of method symbols in an object structure obtained from another by renaming. It is easy to see that, since there is an isomorphism between the two internal state signatures, methods can be lifted in a natural way along this isomorphism, via reduct. The interpretation of the renaming operator can hence be defined as in Fig. 4. Note that Prop. 17 ensures the existence of $<\tilde{\sigma}, i_{\Sigma', \Sigma^{A'}}>$, but not the uniqueness (in fact it should be clear from the example above that $<\tilde{\sigma}, i_{\Sigma', \Sigma^{A'}}>$ is not unique); anyway, the following proposition states that the semantics of renaming is well-defined.

$\forall A \in Obj(<\Sigma, M\Sigma>), \forall <\sigma, \mu>: <\Sigma, M\Sigma> \to <\Sigma', M\Sigma'>$ isomorphism,
$<\sigma, \mu> \star^{DM} A \in Obj(<\Sigma', M\Sigma'>) = A'$ where

- $<i_{\Sigma', \Sigma^{A'}}, \tilde{\sigma}>$ pushout for $<i_{\Sigma, \Sigma^A}, \sigma>$, with $\tilde{\sigma}$ isomorphism;
- $\forall m \in M\Sigma_{w[,s]}, <A, \overline{a}> \in Alg(\Sigma^{A'})_{Sorts(\sigma)(w)}$,

$$\mu(m)^{A'}(<A, \overline{a}>) =_\perp (m^A(<A_{|\tilde{\sigma}}, \overline{a}>))_{|\tilde{\sigma}^{-1}}.$$

Fig. 4. Interpretation of the renaming operator

Proposition 18. *The definition in Fig. 4 does not depend on the choice of $<i_{\Sigma', \Sigma^{A'}}, \tilde{\sigma}>$.* □

4.4 Sum

The sum of two modules M_1 and M_2 is defined only if their method signatures are disjoint (the coexistence of two different definitions for the same method is not acceptable in a programming language). In this case, the visible components of the sum are exactly all the visible components of M_1 and M_2:

$$\frac{M_1:<\Sigma_1, M\Sigma_1> \qquad M_2:<\Sigma_2, M\Sigma_2>}{M_1 + M_2:<\Sigma_1 \cup \Sigma_2, M\Sigma_1 \cup M\Sigma_2>} \qquad M\Sigma_1 \cap M\Sigma_2 = \emptyset$$

Note that we allow sharing of static components (duplication can be obtained by renaming).

As explained for the renaming, the sum operator may cause name clashes, therefore renaming of hidden names is necessary. More precisely, if Σ_1 and Σ^{A_1} (respectively, Σ_2 and Σ^{A_2}) are the visible and the internal state signature of A_1 (respectively A_2), then the internal signature Σ^A of the object structure $A = A_1 + A_2$ must be a colimit of the diagram in Fig. 5, with the injection from $\Sigma_1 \cup \Sigma_2$ into Σ^A an inclusion. This is ensured by the following proposition.

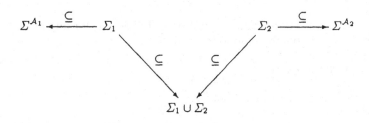

Fig. 5. Diagram for the sum operator

Proposition 19. *If $\Sigma_1 \hookrightarrow \Sigma^{A_1}$ and $\Sigma_2 \hookrightarrow \Sigma^{A_2}$ in* **Sig**, *then there exists a colimit Σ^A of the diagram in Fig. 5 with the injection from $\Sigma_1 \cup \Sigma_2$ an inclusion. Moreover the injections σ_1 and σ_2 from Σ^{A_1} and Σ^{A_2}, respectively, are monomorphisms.* $\square$

We consider now the interpretation of method symbols in $A_1 + A_2$. If A_1 and A_2 have method signatures $M\Sigma_1, M\Sigma_2$, respectively, then $A_1 + A_2$ must provide an interpretation for each method symbol in $M\Sigma_1 \cup M\Sigma_2$, and we expect this interpretation to be "inherited" from the interpretation in either A_1 or A_2. Hence we must be able to *lift* a method m over Σ along a monomorphism $\sigma: \Sigma \to \Sigma'$, getting a method m' over Σ'. The intuition suggests that this lifting must be

1. *conservative*, i.e. the effect of m' on the $\sigma\Sigma$-part of algebras must be the effect of m on Σ-algebras;
2. *minimal*, i.e. the new part of algebras cannot be affected by m.

Note that, for the condition 1 to make sense, σ must be a monomorphism. More formally, if m transforms A into B, then m' should transform any Σ'-algebra A' s.t. $A'|_\sigma = A$ into a Σ'-algebra B' s.t.

1. $B'|_\sigma = B$;
2. $B'|_{\Sigma' \setminus \sigma\Sigma} = A'|_{\Sigma' \setminus \sigma\Sigma}$.

Anyway, this formulation is only adequate in the case $|A| = |B|$ (recall that, by definition of method, $|A| \subseteq |B|$); if $|B|\backslash|A| \neq \emptyset$, 2 must be replaced by the requirement that $B'_{|\Sigma'\backslash\sigma\Sigma}$ is an algebra obtained from $A'_{|\Sigma'\backslash\sigma\Sigma}$ "extending" its carrier to $|B|$. This is formalized below.

Definition 20. Let $\mathcal{ST} = \langle\mathbf{Sig}, Sorts, Alg, |-|\rangle$ be a static framework. A *carrier extension* $\mathcal{E}$ for $\mathcal{ST}$ is a $|\mathbf{Sig}|$-family of maps s.t., for any signature Σ over S, $\mathcal{E}_\Sigma$ associates with any pair $\langle A, \tilde{B}\rangle$ where $A \in |Alg(\Sigma)|$, $\tilde{B} \in |SSet(S)|$ and $|A| \hookrightarrow \tilde{B}$, a Σ-algebra $B = \mathcal{E}_\Sigma(A, \tilde{B})$ s.t. $A \hookrightarrow B$ and $|i_{A,B}| = i_{|A|,\tilde{B}}$. We denote B by $A[\tilde{B}/|A|]$. □

The notation $A[\tilde{B}/|A|]$, even if redundant, is chosen to suggest that B is obtained from A by replacing its carrier by $\tilde{B}$.

Example 6. In the static framework of partial algebras, for any signature Σ, we can define $B = A[\tilde{B}/|A|]$ as follows:

for any $op \in \Sigma_{w,s}$, $\bar{a} \in \tilde{B}_w$,
$$op^B(\bar{a}) =_\perp \begin{cases} op^A(\bar{a}) & \text{if } \bar{a} \in A_w \\ \text{undefined} & \text{otherwise.} \end{cases}$$

This corresponds to the intuition that, in the case new subcomponent objects are created, operations are by default undefined over them. □

Finally, in order to interpret 1 and 2 above as a definition of B', we need a property of *regularity* of the static framework.

Definition 21. Let $\mathcal{ST} = \langle\mathbf{Sig}, Sorts, Alg, |-|\rangle$ be a static framework. Then $\mathcal{ST}$ is *regular* iff

1. for any $S \in |\mathbf{Set}|$, $|-|_{\emptyset_S}$ is an embedding;
2. for any $A_1 \in |Alg(\Sigma_1)|$, $A_2 \in |Alg(\Sigma_2)|$, whenever $A_{1|\Sigma_1\cap\Sigma_2} = A_{2|\Sigma_1\cap\Sigma_2}$, there exists a unique $A \in |Alg(\Sigma_1 \cup \Sigma_2)|$ s.t. $A_{|\Sigma_i} = A_i, i = 1, 2$. □

Note that A is what is usually called the *amalgamated union* of A_1 and A_2 [11]; i.e., a regular static framework must satisfy the amalgamation property restricted to inclusions.

Proposition 22. *Let* $\langle\mathbf{Sig}, Sorts, Alg, |-|\rangle$ *be a regular static framework with carrier extension. For any monomorphism* $\sigma: \Sigma \to \Sigma'$ *in* $\mathbf{Sig}$, $A' \in |Alg(\Sigma')|$, $B \in |Alg(\Sigma)|$ *s.t.* $|A'|_{|Sorts(\sigma)} \hookrightarrow |B|$, *there exists a unique* $B' \in |Alg(\Sigma')|$ *s.t.*

1. *(conservative)* $B'_{|\sigma} = B$;
2. *(minimal)* $B'_{|\Sigma'\backslash\sigma\Sigma} = A'_{|\Sigma'\backslash\sigma\Sigma}[\tilde{B}/|A'_{|\Sigma'\backslash\sigma\Sigma}|]$ *where,* $\forall s' \in Sorts(\Sigma')$ $\tilde{B}_{s'} =$
$$\begin{cases} B_s & \text{if } s' = Sorts(\sigma)(s) \\ A'_{s'} & \text{otherwise} \end{cases}$$

We denote B' *by* $A'[B/A'_{|\sigma}]$. □

Again the redundant notation $A'[B/A'|_\sigma]$ suggests that B' is obtained from A' by replacing its σ-reduct by B.

The interpretation of the sum operator is defined in Fig. 6. Analogously to the case of renaming, the following proposition states that the semantics of sum is well defined.

$\forall A_1 \in Obj(<\Sigma_1, M\Sigma_1>), \forall A_2 \in Obj(<\Sigma_2, M\Sigma_2>)$, with $M\Sigma_1 \cap M\Sigma_2 = \emptyset$,
$A_1 +^{DM} A_2 \in Obj(<\Sigma_1 \cup \Sigma_2, M\Sigma_1 \cup M\Sigma_2>) = A$, where

- Σ^A colimit of the diagram of Fig. 5 s.t. $\Sigma_1 \cup \Sigma_2 \hookrightarrow \Sigma^A$; let σ_1 and σ_2 denote the injections from Σ^{A_1} and Σ^{A_2}, respectively, into Σ^A;
- $\forall m \in (M\Sigma_1 \cup M\Sigma_2)_{w[,s]}$,

$\forall <A, \overline{a}> \in Alg(\Sigma^A)_w$, $m^A(<A, \overline{a}>) = \perp$

$$\begin{cases} <A[B/A_{|\sigma_1}][,b]> \text{ if } m \in M\Sigma_{1\,w[,s]}, \ m^{A_1}(<A_{|\sigma_1}, \overline{a}>) = <B[,b]> \\ <A[B/A_{|\sigma_2}][,b]> \text{ if } m \in M\Sigma_{2\,w[,s]}, \ m^{A_2}(<A_{|\sigma_2}, \overline{a}>) = <B[,b]> \\ \text{undefined} \qquad\qquad \text{otherwise} \end{cases}$$

Fig. 6. Interpretation of the sum operator

Proposition 23. *The definition in Fig. 6 does not depend on the choice of Σ^A, σ_1 and σ_2.* □

Example 7. Consider the following object signature

$O\Sigma_P =$
   sorts *real*
   opns X, Y, θ: *real*
   methods
      translate: real $\Rightarrow$, *rotate: real* $\Rightarrow$.

We define an object structure P over $O\Sigma_P$ modelling an "oriented" point, which can be translated along its current direction, given by θ, and rotated.

$\Sigma^P = <\{real\}, \{X, Y, \theta: real\}> \cup \Sigma_V$
$rotate^P(<P,t>) = P'$ where $X^{P'} =_\perp X^P$, $Y^{P'} =_\perp Y^P$, $\theta^{P'} =_\perp \theta^P + t$
$translate^P(<P,l>) = P'$ where $X^{P'} =_\perp X^P + l * \cos(\theta^P)$,
$\qquad\qquad\qquad\qquad\qquad\quad Y^{P'} =_\perp Y^P + l * \sin(\theta^P), \theta^{P'} =_\perp \theta^P$.

We can now define an oriented circle OC as the sum $P + C$, where C is the object structure of Ex. 3, obtaining an object structure over $O\Sigma_P \cup O\Sigma_C$. In this case the colimit Σ^{OC} is simply $\Sigma^P \cup \Sigma^C$, since there are no hidden components; also the lifting of methods is trivial: for example *translate*^{P} becomes

$translate^{OC}(<C,l>) = C'$ where $X^{C'} =_\perp X^C + l * \cos(\theta^C)$, $\theta^{C'} =_\perp \theta^C$,
$\qquad\qquad\qquad\qquad\qquad Y^{C'} =_\perp Y^C + l * \sin(\theta^C), R^{C'} =_\perp R^C$.

For more significant examples of sum, involving carrier extension in lifting methods, see [2].

4.5 Export

If M is a module and $O\Sigma$ is an object signature, then $O\Sigma\square M$ is obtained from M by hiding the components which are not in $O\Sigma$.

$$\frac{M:<\Sigma, M\Sigma>}{<\Sigma', M\Sigma'>\square M:<\Sigma\cap\Sigma', M\Sigma\cap M\Sigma'>}$$

The interpretation of the export operator is given in Fig. 7.

$$\forall\mathcal{A}\in Obj(<\Sigma, M\Sigma>),$$

$$<\Sigma', M\Sigma'>\square^{\mathcal{DM}}\mathcal{A} = \mathcal{A}_{|<\Sigma\cap\Sigma', M\Sigma\cap M\Sigma'>}$$

Fig. 7. Interpretation of the export operator

5 Conclusion and further work

The work presented in this paper is a first step towards the definition of a language of "modules with state" driven from the model of object structures. The aim is twofold: first, to define a "paradigmatic" representative of the class of object based languages (i.e. languages which support modules with state), thus clarifying the meaning of modules and their combinators in these languages; second, to have a (programming) language which can be naturally integrated with a specification language based on the same framework.

The main aspects which we have not considered up to now are subtyping, overriding and recursive module definitions.

Subtyping at the level of the core language looks quite orthogonal to our treatment (it corresponds to choosing an order-sorted underlying static framework). At the level of modules, we leave as further work the development of a language based on an explicit subtyping relation, even if we have a natural relation between types of modules (signatures) which is the inclusion. Moreover the core and the module type system should be related when modules become first-class values.

Overriding is a feature introduced together with inheritance in the object oriented approach, which means getting a new module from an old one by substituting some components (typically, the definition of a method). We prefer to keep distinct the two ideas for sake of clarity. Thus we call inheritance *by enrichment* the operation of getting a new module from an old one adding some features, without affecting the old part. Inheritance by enrichment is modeled in our framework by the sum operator. Inheritance by overriding cannot be modeled in a compositional way assuming that denotations of modules are just structures. Indeed, usually in the core language module components are defined in a mutually recursive way, hence changing a component actually requires one to "evaluate again" all the components. In the context of object oriented programming, this has been called the "self-reference" problem, and solved by interpreting a class (module) as a function from objects into objects; an instance is then obtained as the fixed point of the class (see [9]). This technique seems in principle to still work in our framework, and should allow recursive definitions to be included too.

References

1. J. Adámek, H. Herrlich, and G. Strecker. *Abstract and Concrete Categories*. Pure and Applied Mathematics. Wiley Interscience, New York, 1990.
2. D. Ancona and E. Zucca. A theory of programming modules with state. In preparation.
3. E. Astesiano and E. Zucca. D-oids: a model for dynamic data-types. *Mathematical Structures in Computer Science*, 5:257–282, 1995.
4. J.A. Bergstra, J. Heering, and P. Klint. Module algebra. *Journ. of the ACM*, 37(2):335–372, 1990.
5. M. Bidoit and A. Tarlecki. Behavioural satisfaction and equivalence in concrete model categories. In *Proc. CAAP '96*, LNCS. Springer Verlag, 1996. To appear.
6. G. Bracha. *The Programming Language JIGSAW: Mixins, Modularity and Multiple Inheritance*. PhD thesis, Dept. of Comp. Sci., Univ. of Utah, 1992.
7. M. Broy and M. Wirsing. Partial abstract types. *Acta Informatica*, 18, 1982.
8. R.M. Burstall and J.A. Goguen. Institutions: Abstract model theory for specification and programming. *Journ. of the ACM*, 39(1):95–146, January 1992.
9. W.R. Cook. *A Denotational Semantics of Inheritance*. PhD thesis, Dept. of Comp. Sci., Brown University, 1989.
10. R. Diaconescu, J. Goguen, and P. Stefaneas. Logical support for modularisation. In Gerard Huet and Gordon Plotkin, editors, *Logical Environments*, pages 83–130, Cambridge, 1993. University Press.
11. H. Ehrig and B. Mahr. *Fundamentals of Algebraic Specification 1. Equations and Initial Semantics*, volume 6 of *EATCS Monograph in Computer Science*. Springer Verlag, 1985.
12. H. Ehrig and F. Orejas. Dynamic abstract data types: An informal proposal. *Bull. of EATCS*, 53, June 1994.
13. R. Milner, M. Tofte, and R. Harper. *The Definition of Standard ML*. The MIT Press, Cambridge, Massachussetts, 1990.
14. D. Sannella and A. Tarlecki. Extended ML: an institution-independent framework for formal program development. In *Proc. Workshop on Category Theory and Computer Programming*, number 240 in LNCS, pages 364–389, Berlin, 1986. Springer Verlag.
15. P. Wegner. Dimensions of object based language design. In *Proc. OOPSLA '87*, pages 168–182, 1987.

Object-Oriented Implementation
of Abstract Data Type Specifications

Rolf Hennicker*, Christoph Schmitz**

*Institut für Informatik, Ludwig-Maximilians-Universität München
Oettingenstr. 67, D-80538 München, GERMANY
**Wilhelm-Schickard-Institut, Universität Tübingen,
Sand 13, D-72076 Tübingen, GERMANY

Keywords: Object-orientation; Axiomatic semantics; Observability; Implementation; Verification.

Abstract. We present a method for implementing abstract data type specifications by object-oriented programs and for proving implementation correctness. The method uses an algebraic description of the semantics of object-oriented programs which allows one to relate an abstract data type specification and its object-oriented implementation within a common formal framework. On this algebraic level the correctness of an implementation can be proved using the notion of observational implementation and its associated proof techniques.

1 Introduction

According to Bertrand Meyer object-oriented design is "the construction of software systems as structured collections of abstract data type implementations" (cf. [Mey 87]). Thus an object-oriented module (i.e. a class) is regarded as an implementation of an abstract data type. In this paper we establish a formal basis for this view and provide a method for proving the correctness of an object-oriented implementation with respect to an abstract data type specification.

The underlying programming language of our approach is a subset of R. Breu's language OP (cf. [Breu 91]) which is an object-oriented programming language in the style of Eiffel (cf. [Mey 92]). In order to relate object-oriented classes and abstract data type specifications we develop an algebraic specification of the semantics of object-oriented programs which incorporates a full description of object states, object environments and the execution of commands and method calls. (A related specification, however not based on our central concept of term execution, has been considered in [BZ 90].) Thus, given an abstract data type specification SP-ADT and a class C which is supposed to provide an implementation of C, we can formally define the correctness of the implementation by means of the algebraic specification framework.

For this purpose we adopt the implementation notion of [BH 95] which is based on a behavioural approach to algebraic specifications (see also e.g. [GM 82], [R 87], [ST 88], [NO 88]). Since behavioural implementations take into account only the observable input/output behaviour of programs, this approach is particularly suited for object-oriented implementations where it is necessary to abstract from internal object states and from object environments and to consider only the observable effects of method invocations (cf. also [MG 94]). Thereby all values of the basic data types like Booleans, Integers, etc. are considered to be observable. Having provided a formal definition of the correctness of object-oriented implementations, a major task is to prove the correctness in practical examples. For this purpose we apply the proof techniques for behavioural implementations presented in [BH 95].

The connection and integration of algebraic specification techniques and object-oriented programming is a rapidly developing area of research. Both approaches have been integrated, for instance, in languages like TROLL (cf. [JSHS 91]), Maude (cf. [Mes 93]) and FOOPS (cf. [GM 87]). The language TROLL stems from the field of information system modeling and takes into account the special need of this area. It uses templates, i.e. object types, to describe the static and dynamic properties of objects. The abstract data types used in such a description are specified by algebraic specifications and the behaviour of objects is specified using temporal logic. The languages FOOPS and Maude unify the paradigms of functional and object-oriented programming. FOOPS is based on hidden sorted specifications and the language Maude is based on rewriting logic which is a logic for reasoning about concurrent systems that evolve by state transitions.

In contrast to these approaches our aim was not the development of a specification (and/or) programming language but to focus strictly on implementation relations and their verification which is not incorporated in the above languages. In [MG 94] a behavioural approach to refinements of FOOPS specifications is considered but there refinements are performed on the specification level and do not connect specifications and concrete programs of some programming language which in our approach is possible due to the given axiomatization of the semantics of the programming language. A further advantage of this axiomatization is that implementation proofs can be performed using standard proof calculi as implemented in theorem provers like LP (cf. [GH 93]). This is a major difference to R. Breu's approach (cf. [Breu 91]) where the correctness of an OP program w.r.t. a given specification is proved on the model level using so-called state based homomorphisms.

The paper is organized as follows: In Section 3, we give an overview of our general method, introduce the languages for writing specifications and object-oriented programs and define the underlying implementation notion. In Section 4, a simple transformation schema for specifications is presented and, in Section 5, the specification of the semantics of the object-oriented programming language is given. Then, in Section 6, we provide proof techniques for implementations and study an example. Finally, in Section 7 we end with some concluding remarks.

2 Algebraic Preliminaries

We assume the reader to be familiar with the basic notions of algebraic specifications (cf. e.g. [EM 85]) like the notions of (many sorted) *signature* $\Sigma = (S, F)$, *signature morphism* $\sigma: \Sigma \to \Sigma'$, *total Σ-algebra* $A = ((A_s)_{s \in S}, (f^A)_{f \in F})$, *$\Sigma$-term algebra* $T_\Sigma(X)$, *valuation* $\alpha: X \to A$ and *interpretation* $I_\alpha: T_\Sigma(X) \to A$. Terms which contain no variables are called *ground terms*. Throughout this paper we assume that the carrier sets A_s of a Σ-algebra A are not empty and that $X = (X_s)_{s \in S}$ is a family of countably infinite sets X_s of variables of sort $s \in S$. A *Σ-congruence* on a Σ-algebra A is (as usual) a family $\approx_A = (\approx_{A,s})_{s \in S}$ of equivalence relations $\approx_{A,s}$ on A_s compatible with the operations of Σ. The *reduct* of a Σ-algebra A to a subsignature $\Sigma 1 \subseteq \Sigma$ is denoted by $A|_{\Sigma 1}$ and, more generally, if $\sigma: \Sigma \to \Sigma'$ is a signature morphism then $A|_\sigma$ denotes the reduct of A along σ. If C is a class of Σ-algebras then the reduct of C to a subsignature $\Sigma 1 \subseteq \Sigma$ is the class $C|_{\Sigma 1} = \{A|_{\Sigma 1} \mid A \in C\}$. The class of all Σ-algebras is denoted by $\text{Alg}(\Sigma)$.

The set of *first-order Σ-formulas* is defined as usual from equations $t = r$ (with $t, r \in T_\Sigma(X)$), the logical connectives $\neg, \wedge, \ldots$ and the quantifiers $\forall, \exists$ We will also use infinitary Σ-formulas of the form $\bigvee_{i \in I} \phi_i$ or $\bigwedge_{i \in I} \phi_i$ where ϕ_i is a countable set of Σ-formulas. A *Σ-sentence* is a *Σ-formula* which contains no free variables. The *(standard) satisfaction* of a Σ-formula ϕ by a Σ-algebra A, denoted by $A \models \phi$, is defined as usual in the first-order predicate calculus (with a straightforward extension to infinitary conjunctions and disjunctions).[1] The notation $A \models \phi$ is extended in the usual way to classes of algebras, specifications and sets of formulas.

---

[1] Due to the requirement of non-empty carrier sets no pathological situations can occur w.r.t. the satisfaction relation (cf. [KK 67]).

3 A Formal Framework for Object-Oriented Implementations

3.1 The General Method: An Overview

Let us first provide an overview of the proposed approach. Given an algebraic specification SP-ADT of an abstract data type and an object-oriented program, represented by a class C of our programming language, the aim is to prove that C is a correct implementation of SP-ADT. A difficulty stems from the fact that the abstract data type specification is given in a purely functional style while the notions of "state" and "dynamic behaviour" are inherent to object-oriented programs. Our basic assumption is that the difference between the functional and the imperative level is reflected by the different roles of a *term*. While in the functional view a term denotes a value which is obtained by term evaluation, in the imperative view a term denotes a command which can be executed and returns a result..

To relate these two views it is technically necessary first to transform the given specification SP-ADT into a similar specification SP'. This transformation is only related to a change of signature needed since basic values in SP-ADT will be implemented by commands which return these basic values as results. In the next step we transform the class C into a specification Sem$_C$ that provides an algebraic description of the semantics of C by specifying the effect of term executions. Now the implementation relation can be established by relating SP' and Sem$_C$ which both are algebraic specifications. For the formal implementation notion we use the concept of observational implementation where the basic values like the Booleans and the Integers are considered as observable. The implementation proof can then be carried out using observational proof techniques. The following picture summarizes the approach.

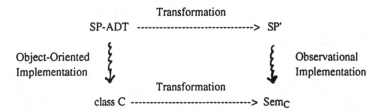

In the next sections we introduce the necessary formal ingredients of our approach which are: The underlying algebraic specification language (based on the ASL language and the loose semantics approach, cf. [W 86]), the object-oriented programming language (which is a subset of R. Breu's language OP, cf. [Breu 91]) and the concept of observational implementation and its associated proof techniques (cf. [BH 95]).

3.2 Algebraic Specifications

Algebraic specifications provide a means for specifying data structures and programs in an abstract, property-oriented and implementation independent way. We will use here the following constructs for writing specifications (for more operators see e.g. [W 86], [ST 88]):

Basic specification: A basic specification SP = ⟨Σ, Ax⟩ consists of a signature Σ = (S, F) and a set Ax of (possibly infinitary) Σ-sentences, called *axioms* of SP. The *model class* of SP is defined by Mod(SP) =$_{def}$ {A ∈ Alg(Σ) | A |= Ax}.

Sum: If SP1 and SP2 are specifications with signatures $\Sigma1$ and $\Sigma2$ respectively then SP1+SP2 is a specification, called the *combination (or sum)* of SP1 and SP2, with signature $\Sigma1\cup\Sigma2$ and with model class Mod(SP1+SP2) $=_{def}$ {A $\in$ Alg($\Sigma1\cup\Sigma2$) | A$|_{\Sigma1}$ $\in$ Mod(SP1) and A$|_{\Sigma2}$ $\in$ Mod(SP2)}.

Bijective Renaming: If SP is a specification with signature Σ and σ: $\Sigma \rightarrow \Sigma'$ is a bijective signature morphism then **rename SP by** σ is a specification with signature Σ' and with model class Mod(**rename SP by** σ) $=_{def}$ {A $\in$ Alg(Σ') | A$|_{\sigma}$ $\in$ Mod(SP)}.

As a derived operator we define the *enrichment* of a specification SP1 with signature $\Sigma1 = (S1, F1)$ by a set S of sorts, a set F of function symbols and a set Ax of axioms by

enrich SP1 **by sorts** S **operations** F **axioms** Ax $=_{def}$ SP1+$\langle$(S1$\cup$S, F1$\cup$F), Ax$\rangle$

We use the following notations for specifications SP with signature $\Sigma = (S, F)$: Sig(SP) $=_{def} \Sigma$, Sorts(Σ) $=_{def}$ S, Opns(Σ) $=_{def}$ F.

In the definition of basic specifications we have allowed infinitary sentences to be used as axioms. This allows us to require reachability constraints for the models of a specification which can be expressed by special infinitary formulas induced by a set $S_{\mathcal{R}}$ of constrained sorts and a set $F_{\mathcal{R}}$ of constructor symbols. (For more details see [BHW 95].)

Example 3.1   The following specification SET-ADT is a usual specification of finite sets over the integers. The operations "empty" and "insert" are onstructors for sets.

```
spec SET-ADT = enrich Bool + Int by
    constrained sorts {SET}
    constructors {empty: → SET, insert: SET, int → SET}
    opns   {is_empty: SET → bool, is_elem: SET, int → bool}
    axioms
           {is_empty(empty) = true, is_empty(insert(s, x)) = false,
           is_elem(empty, x) = false, is_elem(insert(s, y), x) = equal_int(y, x) or is_elem(s, x),
           insert(insert(s, x), x) = insert(s, x), insert(insert(s, x), y) = insert(insert(s, y), x) }
endspec ◆
```

Here and in the following examples variables without explicit quantification are assumed to be universally quantified. We also assume that there are given specifications Bool and Int of the standard data structures of the Booleans and Integers resp. with sorts "bool" and "int" and with the usual operations whereby the constants "true" and "false" are constructors for the Booleans and "zero", "succ" and "pred" are constructors for the Integers.

3.3 The Object-Oriented Programming Language

For writing programs we use a subset of the object-oriented programming language OP defined in [Breu 91]. The programming units in OP are classes (as usual in object-oriented programming) and there are structuring operators for clientship, inheritance and subclass construction. In this section we summarize the constructs of OP apart from the inheritance and subclass relation which will not be considered in this paper.

Example 3.2   This example shows a class SET which is intended to provide an implementation of the abstract data type specification of sets (cf. Example 3.1).

```
class SET is
    attributes
            first: int,
            rest: SET
    methods
            create empty,
            insert (X: int),
            is_empty return bool,
            is_elem (X: int) return bool
    implementations
            create empty is standard,
            insert (X: int) is
                if is_empty  then first:= X; rest:= empty else rest.insert(X) fi end,
            is_empty return bool is rest.is_void end,
            is_elem (X: int) return bool is
                if is_empty  then false else if equal_int(first, X) then true else rest.is_elem(X) fi fi end
end class  ♦
```

As we can see in the example a class has a class name, it declares a set of attributes which describe the internal states of the objects of the class and a set of methods which operate on the objects of the class and it contains method implementations. In general a class C has the following form where $U_1, ..., U_n$ are classes used by C (i.e C is a "client" of $U_1, ..., U_n$ and each U_i is a "server" of C).

```
class C is
    uses U1, ..., Un
    attributes A
    methods M
    implementations MI
end class
```

We generally assume that any class may use values and operations of the basic data types specified by the given specifications Bool and Int (cf. Section 3.2). The attributes occurring in A are of the form a:s where s is either a class name or s is the sort "bool" or "int". The methods (more precisely method declarations) occurring in M are of the form

(i)	$f(X_1:s_1, ..., X_n:s_n)$ return s	*(function)*
(ii)	$f(X_1:s_1, ..., X_n:s_n)$	*(procedure)*
(iii)	**create** $f(X_1:s_1, ..., X_n:s_n)$	*(create method)*

where $s_1, ..., s_n$, s are class names or the sorts "bool" or "int". All kinds of methods may have side effects, i.e. may change the state and/or the environment of the object for which the method is called. Methods with an explicit result type are called functions and return a basic value or (a reference to) an object of the given result type. Methods without explicit result type are called procedures. In OP procedures are considered as particular functions which return the identity of the active object. Invoking a create method results in the dynamic creation of a new object of the class. Although the declared functions and procedures operate on objects of the class C (i.e. may be called for an active object of C) the class name C is, as usual in object-oriented languages, surpressed in the declarations. The full type informations of the methods of a class C are recorded in the class signature Sig(C) which is defined as follows:

To each method declaration of the form (i) we associate a function symbol f: C, $s_1, ..., s_n \rightarrow s$, to each method declaration of the form (ii) we associate a function symbol f: C, $s_1, ..., s_n \rightarrow C$ and to each method declaration of the form (iii) we associate a function symbol f: $s_1, ..., s_n \rightarrow C$. The set of function symbols associated to the methods of C is denoted by Methods(C). Then Sig(C) is the union of the following signatures:

$$Sig(C) =_{def} Sig(Bool+Int) \cup Sig(U_1) \cup ... \cup Sig(U_n) \cup (\{bool, int, U_1, ..., U_n, C\}, Methods(C))$$

Each method implementation of MI has the form "f-decl is f-body end" where f-decl is a method declaration as defined above and f-body is a command determining the effect of the method invocation for an active object.[2]

In OP a command performs a transition on the object environment and delivers a result which is a basic value or a reference to an object. Since, in general, commands contain program variables, the transition depends on a given valuation of the program variables (by object identifiers or basic values). Commands are either standard commands or method calls. Standard commands are defined by the following constructs:

- $t_1 ; t_2$ *(sequential composition of two commands t_1 and t_2)*
- if t_b then t_1 else t_2 fi   *(conditional statement)*
- t.is_void   *(test for the void reference)*
- $t_1 == t_2$ *(test of equality of object identities)*
- a:= t   *(value assignment to an attribute)*
- a(t)   *(accessing the value of an attribute)*
- X   *(X is a program variable)*

The sequential composition $t_1 ; t_2$ composes the state transitions determined by t_1 and t_2. The effect of the conditional statement is obvious where t_b is assumed to deliver a boolean value. The commands t.is_void and $t_1 == t_2$ do not change the object environment and deliver a boolean value. Thereby t, t_1 and t_2 are commands which return an object identifier as result. The assignment a:= t changes the state of the active object where the result of t is assigned to the attribute a. The command a(t) delivers the current value of the attribute a of the object referenced by the result of t. Moreover, any program variable X is also considered as a command which does not change the object environment and delivers the value of X according to a given valuation of program variables. It is assumed that there exists a special program variable "Self" (denoting the reference to the active object of a class).

Commands may also be method calls. A method call is of the form $f(t_0, ..., t_n)$ where $f \in$ Opns(Sig(C)) is a function symbol of the signature of the class C and $t_0, ..., t_n$ are commands which provide results of appropriate type.[3] If f is a function symbol associated to a function with implementation $f(X_1:s_1, ..., X_n:s_n)$ return s is f-body end then a method call $f(t_0, ..., t_n)$ first executes the commands $t_0, ..., t_n$ in the given sequential order and then the body of f is executed where the special variable Self (occurring in f-body) is actualized by the result of t_0 (which is just the identity of the active object) and the formal parameter variables $X_1, ..., X_n$ are actualized by the results of $t_1, ..., t_n$. If f is a function symbol associated to a procedure with implementation $f(X_1:s_1, ..., X_n:s_n)$ is f-body end then f is handled as a function with body "f-body; Self". If f is a function symbol associated to a create method with implementation create $f(X_1:s_1, ..., X_n:s_n)$ is f-body end then a method call $f(t_1, ..., t_n)$ executes first sequentially the commands $t_1, ..., t_n$, then creates a new object of the class and finally executes the body of f where the variable Self is

---

[2] Note that f-body may contain recursive method calls. Since our algebraic framework is restricted to total functions we implicitly assume the termination of recursively defined functions.

[3] This is a slight extension of the form of method calls in OP where a method call consists only of function symbols and program variables. Since there is no need for this restriction we consider here the more general form of method calls which leads to a simplification of the specification of the semantics of commands given in Section 5.

actualized by the reference to the new object and the formal parameter variables $X_1, ..., X_n$ are actualized by the results of $t_1, ..., t_n$. Note that method calls are also defined for function symbols f which are basic operations of the specifications Int and Bool. In these cases the result of a method call is determined by the meaning of the corresponding basic operations.

According to common object-oriented notation the following abbreviations are used in concrete programs if f is an attribute or a method (different from a create method):
If f is called for the active object then we write $f(t_1, ..., t_n)$ for $f(Self, t_1, ..., t_n)$. For instance, in the method bodies of SET, is_empty = is_empty(Self), rest = rest(Self) and hence rest.is_void = rest(Self).is_void. More generally, if f is called for an arbitrary object which is the result of a command t_0 then we write $t_0.f(t_1, ..., t_n)$ for $f(t_0, ..., t_n)$. For instance, in the method bodies of SET, rest.insert(X) = insert(rest, X) = insert(rest(Self), X) and similarly rest.is_elem(X) = is_elem(rest(Self), X). As a further abbreviation there are predifined standard create methods in OP of the form **create f is standard** which denote the method implementation **create f is Self end**.

3.4 Observational Implementations

The observational implementation relation considered in this paper is a special instance of the notion of behavioural implementation studied in [BH 95]. It allows one to establish a relationship between two specifications, an "abstract" specification SP and a "concrete" specification SP-I which intuitively expresses that SP-I fulfills the intended observable behaviour of SP with respect to some observational equality. Before giving the definition of observational implementation let us first consider observational equalities.

An observational equality is a relation between the elements of a Σ-algebra which intuitively says that two elements are observationally equal if they cannot be distinguished by observable computations. Formally, observable computations are represented by observable contexts which are defined according to a set Obs of "observable sorts". The observable sorts determine the (carrier sets of the) observable values.

Definition 3.3 *(Observational equality)*   Let $\Sigma = (S, F)$ be a signature and $Obs \subseteq S$ be a set of observable sorts.

(1)   The set of observable Σ-contexts is defined as follows:
Let $X = (X_s)_{s \in S}$ be the generally assumed family of countably infinite sets X_s of variables of sort s. Let $Z = (\{z_s\})_{s \in S}$ be a disjoint S-sorted family of singleton sets. An *observable Σ-context* is a Σ-term $c \in T_\Sigma(X \cup Z)$ of observable sort which contains, besides variables in X, one or many occurrences of exactly one variable $z_s \in Z$, called the *context variable* of c. By exception, Var(c) will denote the set of variables occurring in c apart from the context variable of c. The application of a context c with context variable z_s to a term t of sort s, denoted by c[t], is the term obtained by substituting the term t for z_s. The set of the observable Σ-contexts is denoted by $C(\Sigma)^{Obs}$.

(2)   For any Σ-algebra $A \in Alg(\Sigma)$ the *observational equality* of elements w.r.t. the observable sorts Obs is the relation $\approx_{Obs,A}$ defined as follows:
Two elements $a, b \in A_s$ are observationally equal, i.e. $a \approx_{Obs,A} b$, if and only if for all observable Σ-contexts $c \in C(\Sigma)^{Obs}$ containing z_s and for all valuations $\alpha : X \to A$, we have $I_{\alpha_a}(c) = I_{\alpha_b}(c)$ where $\alpha_a, \alpha_b : X \cup \{z_s\} \to A$ are the unique extensions of α defined by $\alpha_a(z_s) =_{def} a$, $\alpha_b(z_s) =_{def} b$. Obviously, if s is an observable sort, then for all $a, b \in A$, $a \approx_{Obs,A} b$ is equivalent to $a = b$. ◆

It is easy to show that for any Σ-algebra A, $\approx_{Obs,A}$ is a Σ-congruence on A. The family $(\approx_{Obs,A})_{A \in Alg(\Sigma)}$ of observational equalities will be denoted in the following by $\approx_{Obs}$. It coincides with the observational equality used e.g. in [R 87].[4]

Definition 3.4   Let A be a Σ-algebra, $C \subseteq Alg(\Sigma)$ be a class of Σ-algebras, ϕ be a Σ-formula and let SP be a specification with signature Σ.

(1) The *behaviour of* A w.r.t. $\approx_{Obs}$ is given by the quotient algebra $A/\approx_{Obs,A}$.

(2) The *observational behaviour class* of C w.r.t. $\approx_{Obs}$ is the class
$$Beh_{\approx_{Obs}}(C) =_{def} \{ A \in Alg(\Sigma) \mid A/\approx_{Obs,A} \in C \}.$$
In particular, the *observational behavioural semantics* of SP is given by $Beh_{\approx_{Obs}}(Mod(SP))$.

(3) We write $A \models_{\approx_{Obs}} \phi$ if and only if $A/\approx_{Obs,A} \models \phi$. If $A \models_{\approx_{Obs}} \phi$ for all $A \in C$ we write $C \models_{\approx_{Obs}} \phi$ (or similarly SP $\models_{\approx_{Obs}} \phi$ if C is the model class of SP). Then ϕ is called *observational theorem* over C (over SP resp.). $\blacklozenge$

Remark 3.5

(1) The behaviour $A/\approx_{Obs,A}$ of a Σ-algebra A identifies all elements which are indistinguishable "from the outside". Hence $A/\approx_{Obs,A}$ can be considered as a "black box view" of A.

(2) The observational behaviour class $Beh_{\approx_{Obs}}(C)$ consists of all algebras whose behaviour belongs to C. In particular, for any specification SP, $Beh_{\approx_{Obs}}(Mod(SP))$ consists of all algebras whose behaviour fulfills the given specification SP. Thereby SP is interpreted as a specification of intended behaviours.

(3) The notation $A \models_{\approx_{Obs}} \phi$ expresses that the behaviour of A satisfies the formula ϕ, i.e. ϕ is satisfied by A up to the identification of indistinguishable elements. This can be equivalently defined using an explicit notion of *behavioural satisfaction* of formulas where instead of the set theoretic equality the observational equality is used for the interpretation of the equality symbol "=" (cf. [BHW 95]). $\blacklozenge$

We are now prepared to define formally observational implementations using the observational behaviour operator $Beh_{\approx_{Obs}}$[5]:

Definition 3.6 Let SP, SP-I be specifications with signatures $\Sigma = (S, F)$, Σ-I resp. such that $\Sigma \subseteq \Sigma$-I and let Obs $\subseteq S$ be a set of observable sorts.
SP-I is called *observational implementation of* SP w.r.t. Obs (written SP $\overset{\approx Obs}{\sim\sim\sim\sim>}$ SP-I) if $Mod(SP-I)|_{\Sigma} \subseteq Beh_{\approx_{Obs}}(Mod(SP))$. $\blacklozenge$

Due to the definition of $Beh_{\approx_{Obs}}(Mod(SP))$, SP-I is an observational implementation of SP w.r.t. Obs if and only if for any model A-I $\in$ Mod(SP-I) the following holds: If we first forget all sorts and operations of the "concrete" signature Σ-I which do not belong to the "abstract" signature Σ (i.e. if we construct the Σ-algebra A-I$|_{\Sigma}$) and if we then identify all elements w.r.t. the observational equality then we obtain a model of SP. Hence, if SP = $\langle \Sigma, Ax \rangle$ is a flat specification then we have directly the following characterization of observational implementations:

---

[4] In practice it is sometimes necessary to consider a more liberal indistinguishability relation where, for instance, only observable input is allowed for observable computations. Such equalities (which are not needed here due to the use of reachability constraints in the translation of class implementations) are partial Σ-congruences (cf. [BHW 95]).

[5] A related idea was formalized in [Hen 91] and for hidden order-sorted algebras in [MG 94]. Both approaches are, however, restricted to flat specifications with equational axioms.

Fact 3.7   Let SP = ⟨Σ, Ax⟩ be a basic specification and let SP-I be a specification with signature Σ-I ⊇ Σ. Then: SP $\overset{\neg Obs}{\leadsto}$ SP-I if and only if Mod(SP-I)$|_\Sigma$ $\models_{\approx_{Obs}}$ Ax. ♦

3.5 Object-Oriented Implementations

In Section 5 we will show how an object-oriented program given by a class C is transformed into an algebraic specification of the semantics of C using a transformation function Trans$_{class}$: CLASS → SPEC (where CLASS denotes our language of class expressions). Moreover, in the next section we define a transformation function Trans$_{spec}$: SPEC → SPEC (where SPEC denotes the language of all specification expressions) which performs some necessary adaptations on an abstract data type specification SP-ADT. Assuming given both transformation functions we can already define the implementation relation between abstract data type specifications and object-oriented programs. Thereby we assume as a general requirement that any abstract data type specification SP-ADT contains the basic specifications Bool and Int (cf. Section 3.2) for the Booleans and Integers which are considered to be observable. (Of course the approach can be extended to the case where further basic data types (e.g. Characters etc.) are given. Then the sorts of these data types are also considered as observable.)

Definition 3.8   Let SP-ADT be an algebraic specification of an abstract data type and let C be a class of our programming language.
C is called *object-oriented implementation* of SP-ADT (written SP-ADT $\overset{\infty}{\leadsto}$ C) if Trans$_{spec}$(SP-ADT) $\overset{\approx Obs}{\leadsto}$ Trans$_{class}$(C) where Obs = {bool, int}. ♦

4   Transformation of an Abstract Data Type Specification

Given an abstract data type specification SP-ADT and a class C which is supposed to provide an implementation of SP-ADT our task is to prove the correctness of the implementation. In the specification of the semantics of the class C (ground) terms will be interpreted as commands which can be executed and deliver a result. In particular, any ground term of basic sort is interpreted as a command which returns a basic (observable) value as result. In order to relate the class C and the specification SP-ADT the distinction between commands returning basic values and the basic values themselves must be reflected in the abstract signature. Technically this is done by transforming SP-ADT (which, by assumption, contains Bool and Int) into a similar specification SP' which contains a copy of Bool and Int where the basic sorts and operations are written in capital letters. Later on we will see that the sorts "BOOL" and "INT" will be implemented by (the sets of) commands of basic type while the sorts "bool" and "int" denote (the sets of) basic values. The relationship between both is defined by functions obs$_{BOOL}$: BOOL → bool and obs$_{INT}$: INT → int which map the constructors of "BOOL" and "INT" to the corresponding constructors of "bool" and "int". Formally, this leads to the following definition:

Definition 4.1 The transformation function Trans$_{spec}$: SPEC → SPEC is defined by: For any abstract data type specification SP-ADT, Trans$_{spec}$(SP-ADT) $=_{def}$ SP' where

```
spec SP' =
    enrich ((rename SP-ADT by τ) + Bool + Int) by
    opns  {obsBOOL : BOOL → bool, obsINT : INT → int}
    axioms
            {obsBOOL(TRUE) = true, obsBOOL(FALSE) = false, obsINT(ZERO) = zero,
             obsINT(SUCC(x)) = succ(obsINT(x)), obsINT(PRED(x)) = pred(obsINT(x))}
endspec
```

Thereby τ is a renaming mapping any sort and operation symbol of the signatures of Bool and Int to the same name written in capital letters. ♦

5 Transformation of a Class

In this section we show how a class C of our programming language is transformed into a corresponding algebraic specification by constructing a specification of the semantics of the class. The construction is guided by the model-theoretic semantics of OP given in [Breu 91]. However, in contrast to [Breu 91] and also to the class specification in [BZ 90], the central concept of our semantics specification is the execution of terms. Our basic intuition is that a class is an object-oriented system whose behaviour is determined by executing admissible experiments and that the admissible experiments are represented by ground terms over the signature of the class (cf. Section 3.3). An experiment provides an observable result if the corresponding term is of basic sort. Hence the results of the execution of terms of a basic sort characterize the observable behaviour of the system. Since we consider only experiments represented by ground terms their observable results are independent of a particular system state.

As a consequence of the above considerations our aim is to specify the execution of ground terms which are particular commands whose effect is determined by the implementations of the single methods associated to the function symbols occurring in a given term. For instance, executing the term "is_empty(insert(5, empty))" first creates a new object according to the create method "empty" then performs the "insert" method on the created object and finally returns the result of the "is_empty" method for this object.

In the sequel we assume that C is a class which has the form as described in Section 3.3. The following picture shows the hierarchy of the specifications used for specifying the semantics of C. Thereby we assume given specifications $Command_{U_i}$ which describe the commands associated to the classes U_i that are used by C.

$$Bool + Int + Command_{U_1} + \ldots + Command_{U_n}$$

$$Obj\text{-}Id_C$$

$$Obj\text{-}State_C \qquad Valuation_C$$

$$Environment_C$$

$$Standard\text{-}Command_C$$

$$Command_C$$

$$Sem_C$$

For lack of space we can present in the following only a summary of the single specifications. The complete specifications are given in [HS 96].

5.1 Object States, Object Environments and Valuations

The specification $Obj\text{-}Id_C$ specifies a set of object identities (also called references) for objects of the class C. It contains the sort "id_C" for object identities and a special constant $void_C: \rightarrow id_C$ denoting the void reference. The specification $Obj\text{-}State_C$ describes the states of objects of the class C (which may be considered as records with one field for any attribute of C) together with usual update and lookup operations. The specification $Environment_C$ specifies object environments where object identities are associated with object states. It contains a sort "env" for the environments and for any attribute "a" of C there exist operations "set_a_C" and "get_a_C" for actualizing and delivering the attribute value of an object (represented by its object identity) in an actual environment. The specification Environment$_C$ contains also an operation create$_C$: env → env, id$_C$ which creates a new object identity and changes the environment such that a special initial object state is associated to the new identity.

Remark 5.1   We sometimes use product sorts of the form s_1, s_2 as result sorts of operation symbols and projection functions $\_{}_{s_i}$: s_1, s_2 → s_i. Product sorts denote tuples of elements.

In the specification Valuation$_C$ we specify valuations of program variables where every program variable (of appropriate type) is associated with either a basic value or an object identity. It contains the sort "valuation" for the valuations and the sorts "var$_C$", "var$_{int}$" and "var$_{bool}$" for program variables of the corresponding types. In particular there is a constant Self$_C$: → var$_C$. For each s ∈ {C, bool, int} there is an update operation "$\_$ ($\_$ →$_s$ $\_$)" which assigns an object identity or a basic value to a program variable and there are corresponding lookup operations denoted by "$\_$ ($\_$)$_s$".

5.2 Specification of Standard Commands

We are now able to specify standard commands and their execution according to the constructs of standard commands described in Section 3.3. As already discussed in Section 3.3 a command transforms the object environment and yields a result which is either an object identity, a boolean value or an integer. The three kinds of commands are distinguished by the sorts "com$_C$", "com$_{bool}$" and "com$_{int}$". For the execution of commands we use functions "exec$_s$" (for s ∈ {C, bool, int}) which can be applied to a command, a valuation of the program variables and an object environment and deliver the new environment and the result of the command.

spec Standard-Command$_C$ = **enrich** Environment$_C$ + Valuation$_C$ **by**
    sorts {com$_C$, com$_{bool}$, com$_{int}$}
    opns
        {$\_$;$_{s_i \cdot s_j}$ $\_$: com$_{s_i}$, com$_{s_j}$ → com$_{s_j}$ | s_i, s_j ∈ Sorts(Sig(C))} ∪
        {if $\_$ then $\_$ else $\_$ fi$_s$: com$_{bool}$, com$_s$, com$_s$ → com$_s$ | s ∈ {C, bool, int}} ∪
        {$\_$ .is_void$_C$: com$_C$ → com$_{bool}$, $\_$ ==$_C$ $\_$: com$_C$, com$_C$ → com$_{bool}$} ∪
        {a:= $\_$: com$_s$ → com$_C$, a($\_$): com$_C$ → com$_s$ | a:s is an attribute of C} ∪
        {makecom$_s$: var$_s$ → com$_s$ | s ∈ {C, bool, int}} ∪
        {exec$_C$: com$_C$, valuation, env → env, id$_C$, exec$_{bool}$: com$_{bool}$, valuation, env → env, bool ,
          exec$_{int}$: com$_{int}$, valuation, env → env, int}
    axioms
        {exec$_{s_j}$(t$_1$, v, ρ) = (ρ',x$_1$) ⇒ exec$_{s_j}$(t$_1$;$_{s_i \cdot s_j}$ t$_2$, v, ρ) = exec$_{s_j}$(t$_2$, v, ρ')|s_i, s_j ∈ Sorts(Sig(C))} ∪
        {exec$_s$(t, v, ρ) = (ρ', x) ⇒ exec$_C$(a:= t, v, ρ) = (set_a$_C$(ρ',v(Self$_C$)$_C$, x), v(Self$_C$)$_C$),
          exec$_C$(t, v, ρ) = (ρ', x) ⇒ exec$_s$(a(t), v, ρ) = (ρ',get_a$_C$(ρ', x) | a:s is an attribute of C} ∪
        {exec$_s$(makecom$_s$(X), v, ρ) = (ρ, v(X)$_s$) | s ∈ {C, bool, int}} ∪
        ... etc. for the other command constructs
endspec

5.3 Specification of Method Calls

Up to now the given specifications are independent of the methods and the method implementations of the class C. In a next step the specification of standard commands has to be extended to a specification Command$_C$ which incorporates also method calls. Remember that a method call is of the form f(t$_0$, ..., t$_n$) where f ∈ Opns(Sig(C)) is a function symbol of the signature of the class C and t$_0$, ..., t$_n$ are commands which provide results of appropriate type. In the specification Command$_C$ a method call is represented by a term $f_{com}(t_0, ..., t_n)$ where f_{com}: $com_{s_0}, ..., com_{s_n} \rightarrow com_s$ is a new function symbol associated to f: $s_0, ..., s_n \rightarrow s \in Opns(Sig(C))$ and $t_0, ..., t_n$ are terms of sort $com_{s_0}, ..., com_{s_n}$. The execution of method calls is informally described in Section 3.3 and formally specified in Command$_C$ (cf. [HS 96]). We will present here as an example the specification Command$_{SET}$ for commands over the class SET (cf. Example 3.2) hoping that this is sufficient for illustrating the general idea.

In the specification Command$_{SET}$ we assume given a syntactic translation schema, called "trans", which translates method bodies written in the syntax of OP into corresponding terms of sort "com_s" (with appropriate sort s) over the signature of Command$_{SET}$. The translation schema replaces any occurrence of a method name f by the corresponding function symbol f_{com} and any occurrence of a program variable X of type s by the term $makecom_s(X)$. Note that before applying the translation schema the abbreviations used in method bodies (cf. end of Section 3.3) have to be replaced appropriately.

spec Command$_{SET}$ = **enrich** Standard-Command$_{SET}$ **by**
    opns {empty$_{com}$: $\rightarrow$ com$_{SET}$, insert$_{com}$: com$_{SET}$, com$_{int}$ $\rightarrow$ com$_{SET}$,
          is_empty$_{com}$: com$_{SET}$ $\rightarrow$ com$_{bool}$,
          is_elem$_{com}$: com$_{SET}$, com$_{int}$ $\rightarrow$ com$_{bool}$, true$_{com}$: com$_{bool}$, ... }
    axioms
    { create$_{SET}$(ρ) = (ρ', x$_0$) $\Rightarrow$
exec$_{SET}$(empty$_{com}$, v, ρ) = exec$_{SET}$(makecom$_{SET}$(Self$_{SET}$), v(Self$_{SET}$ $\rightarrow$$_{SET}$ x$_0$), ρ'),
    exec$_{SET}$(t$_0$, v, ρ) = (ρ_0, x$_0$) $\wedge$ exec$_{int}$(t$_1$, v, ρ_0) = (ρ_1, x$_1$) $\Rightarrow$
exec$_{SET}$(insert$_{com}$(t$_0$, t$_1$), v, ρ) = exec$_{SET}$(trans(insert-body; Self), v(Self$_{SET}$ $\rightarrow$$_{SET}$ x$_0$)(X$_1$ $\rightarrow$$_{int}$ x$_1$), ρ_1),
    exec$_{SET}$(t$_0$, v, ρ) = (ρ_0, x$_0$) $\Rightarrow$
exec$_{bool}$(is_empty$_{com}$(t$_0$), v, ρ) = exec$_{bool}$(trans(is_empty-body), v(Self$_{SET}$ $\rightarrow$$_{SET}$ x$_0$), ρ_0),
    exec$_{SET}$(t$_0$, v, ρ) = (ρ_0, x$_0$) $\wedge$ exec$_{int}$(t$_1$, v, ρ_0) = (ρ_1, x$_1$) $\Rightarrow$
exec$_{bool}$(is_elem$_{com}$(t$_0$, t$_1$), v, ρ) = exec$_{bool}$(trans(is_elem-body), v(Self$_{SET}$ $\rightarrow$$_{SET}$ x$_0$)(X $\rightarrow$$_{int}$ x$_1$), ρ_1),
    exec$_{bool}$(true$_{com}$, v, ρ) = (ρ, true), ... }
  endspec

where

trans(insert-body; Self) =
    if is_empty$_{com}$(makecom$_{SET}$(Self$_{SET}$)) then first:=makecom$_{int}$(X) ;$_{SET,SET}$ rest:=empty$_{com}$
      else insert$_{com}$(rest(makecom$_{SET}$(Self$_{SET}$)), makecom$_{int}$(X)) fi$_{SET}$;$_{SET,SET}$ makecom$_{SET}$(Self$_{SET}$)
trans(is_empty-body) = rest(makecom$_{SET}$(Self$_{SET}$)).is_void$_{SET}$
trans(is_elem-body) =
    if is_empty$_{com}$(makecom$_{SET}$(Self$_{SET}$)) then false$_{com}$
    else if equal_int$_{com}$(first(makecom$_{SET}$(Self$_{SET}$)), makecom$_{int}$(X)) then true$_{com}$
        else is_elem$_{com}$(rest(makecom$_{SET}$(Self$_{SET}$)), makecom$_{int}$(X)) fi$_{bool}$ fi$_{bool}$ $\blacklozenge$

5.4 Specification of Ground Term Executions

Finally, we can specify the execution of ground terms which provides the full specification Sem$_C$ of the semantics of a class C. Principially ground terms are special commands which are built only by function symbols of the signature of C and do not involve any program variable (or any other command). Therefore we have to introduce new sorts for ground term commands and new operation symbols for their construction. We will adopt a simple solution here where the sorts of the signature of the class C are used for denoting ground term commands and the function symbols in Sig(C) are used as ground term constructors. We have to be careful with respect to basic sorts and operations since "bool" and "int" and the basic function symbols like "true", "not" etc. are already used to denote basic values and their operations. Therefore the sorts for ground terms of a basic sort are written in capital letters, i.e. "BOOL", "INT", and similarly we use capital letters for the constructors "TRUE", "NOT" etc. of ground terms of basic sort.

Instead of the general specification Sem_C we present as an example the specification Sem_{SET} which describes the semantics of the class SET. All ground terms over the signature of SET are embedded into commands of appropriate sort by the operation symbols "in_s" for $s \in \{SET, BOOL, INT\}$. Then we can simply observe the result of the execution of a ground term t of basic sort if we first embed t into a command, then execute the command under an arbitrary valuation of the program variables and under an arbitrary object environment and finally consider the result value of the execution (obtained by the projection to the second component, denoted by $(\_)_{bool}$ or $(\_)_{int}$, since the execution of a command yields a pair consisting of a new environment together with a result value). The observation of the result values of executions of ground terms of basic sort is specified by the operations "obs_s" for $s \in \{BOOL, INT\}$. Note that these result values are independent of valuations and object environments. (Intuitively this follows from the fact that any ground term ecxecution generates a new local environment which is not connected to other parts of the environment.) Hence the variables v, ρ occurring in the axioms of the following specification Sem_{SET} can be assumed to be universally quantified (like all other variables).

spec Sem_{SET} = enrich $Command_{SET}$ by
    constrained sorts $\{SET, BOOL, INT\}$
    constructors
        $\{empty: \rightarrow SET, insert: SET, INT \rightarrow SET, is\_empty: SET \rightarrow BOOL,$
          $is\_elem: SET, INT \rightarrow BOOL, TRUE: \rightarrow BOOL, ...\}$
    opns
        $\{in_{SET} : SET \rightarrow com_{SET}, in_{BOOL} : BOOL \rightarrow com_{bool}, in_{INT} : INT \rightarrow com_{int},$
          $obs_{BOOL} : BOOL \rightarrow bool, obs_{INT} : INT \rightarrow int\}$
    axioms
        $\{in_{SET}(empty) = empty_{com}, in_{SET}(insert(s, x)) = insert_{com}(in_{SET}(s), in_{INT}(x)),$
        $in_{BOOL}(is\_empty(s)) = is\_empty_{com}(in_{SET}(s)),$
        $in_{BOOL}(is\_elem(s, x)) = is\_elem_{com}(in_{SET}(s), in_{SET}(x)), in_{BOOL}(TRUE) = true_{com}, ... ,$
        $obs_{BOOL}(is\_empty(s)) = exec_{bool}(in_{BOOL}(is\_empty(s)), v, \rho)_{bool},$
        $obs_{BOOL}(is\_elem(s, x)) = exec_{bool}(in_{BOOL}(is\_elem(s, x)), v, \rho)_{bool},$
        $obs_{BOOL}(TRUE) = exec_{bool}(in_{BOOL}(TRUE), v, \rho)_{bool}, ... \}$
endspec

It may be helpful to remark that considering the semantics of the class SET the ground term commands "$in_{BOOL}(is\_empty(empty))$" and "$in_{BOOL}(TRUE)$" are different because the execution of the first term changes the environment by creating a new object while the second term does not change the environment. However, both terms yield the same observable result namely the value "true", i.e. $obs_{BOOL}(is\_empty(empty)) = obs_{BOOL}(TRUE)$. Therefore the equation is_empty(empty) = TRUE (required by SET') is behaviourally valid in the implementation. This points out the importance of the observational approach for the formulation of the correctness concept for object-oriented implementations.

The construction of the specification Sem_{SET} extends in an obvious way to specifications Sem_C of arbitrary classes C (cf. [HS 96]). It gives rise to a general transformation of classes into algebraic specifications:

Definition 5.2 The transformation function $Trans_{class}$: CLASS $\rightarrow$ SPEC is defined by:
For any class C of our programmig language, $Trans_{class}(C) =_{def} Sem_C$.

6 Implementation Proofs

In this section we will consider the important issue how to prove the correctness of an object-oriented implementation SP-ADT $\overset{OO}{\leadsto}$ C. By definition, this means that one has to prove that $\text{Trans}_{\text{spec}}$(SP-ADT) $\overset{\approx Obs}{\leadsto}$ $\text{Trans}_{\text{class}}$(C) is an observational implementation where Obs = {bool, int}. For this purpose we apply the proof techniques for behavioural implementations presented in [BH 95].

6.1 Observational Proof Techniques

We will consider in the following only proof techniques for observational implementations of flat specifications (for modular proof rules see [BH 95]). As we have seen in Fact 3.7, a specification SP-I is an observational implementation of a flat specification SP = $\langle\Sigma, \text{Ax}\rangle$ w.r.t. a set Obs of observable sorts if and only if all axioms $\phi \in$ Ax are observational theorems over Mod(SP-I)$|_\Sigma$, i.e. Mod(SP-I)$|_\Sigma \models_{\approx Obs}$ Ax. Hence, for proving the correctness of observational implementations it is essential to be able to prove observational theorems. In order to reduce proofs of observational theorems to proofs of standard first-order theorems the first idea is to introduce an explicit denotation for the observational equality by corresponding predicate symbols.[6]

Definition 6.1 *(Axiomatization of the observational equality)* Given a signature $\Sigma = (S, F)$, $\mathcal{L}(\Sigma)$ is the signature Σ enriched by a binary predicate symbol $\sim_s$ for each sort $s \in S$, i.e. $\mathcal{L}(\Sigma) =_{\text{def}}$ $\Sigma \cup \{ \sim_s : s, s \mid s \in S \}$. Let $(\text{Beh}_s(x_s, y_s))_{s \in S}$ be a family of finitary first-order Σ-formulas with exactly two free variables x_s, y_s (both of sort s) and let BEH be the following $\mathcal{L}(\Sigma)$-sentence:

$$\text{BEH} =_{\text{def}} \bigwedge_{s \in S} \forall x_s, y_s : s. [\text{Beh}_s(x_s, y_s) \Leftrightarrow x_s \sim_s y_s].^7$$

$(\text{Beh}_s(x_s, y_s))_{s \in S}$ is called a (finitary) axiomatization of the observational equality $\approx_{Obs}$ w.r.t. a class C of Σ-algebras if for any Σ-algebra $A \in$ C and all elements $a, b \in A_s$ ($s \in S$), $a \sim_s^{\mathcal{E}(A)} b$ if and only if $a \approx_{Obs,A} b$ where $\mathcal{E}(A)$ is the unique extension of A to a model of $\langle\mathcal{L}(\Sigma), \text{BEH}\rangle$.[8] ♦

Having given an axiomatization of the observational equality the equivalence "(1) $\Leftrightarrow$ (3)" of the next theorem provides a proof method for observational implementations. It results from the combination of Fact 3.7 (which is just the equivalence "(1) $\Leftrightarrow$ (2)" of the theorem) together with Theorem 5.5 of [BH 95a] (which corresponds to the equivalence "(2) $\Leftrightarrow$ (3)" of the theorem).

Theorem 6.2 Let SP = $\langle\Sigma, \text{Ax}\rangle$ be a basic specification, let SP-I be a specification with signature Σ-I $\supseteq \Sigma$ and let $(\text{Beh}_s(x_s, y_s))_{s \in S}$ be an axiomatization of the observational equality $\approx_{Obs}$ w.r.t. Mod(SP-I)$|_\Sigma$. Let $\mathcal{L}(\text{Ax})$ be the set of $\mathcal{L}(\Sigma)$-formulas obtained from Ax by replacing each equality symbol "=" occurring in Ax by "$\sim_s$" (with appropriate sort s). Then the following conditions are equivalent:
(1) SP $\overset{\approx Obs}{\leadsto}$ SP-I,
(2) Mod(SP-I)$|_\Sigma \models_{\approx Obs}$ Ax,
(3) SP-I + $\langle\mathcal{L}(\Sigma), \text{BEH}\rangle \models \mathcal{L}(\text{Ax})$. ♦

---

[6] We assume the reader to be familiar with the usual notions of predicate symbols and their interpretations.

[7] We use an infix notation for the binary predicate symbols $\sim_s$.

[8] Such an extension (with the same carriers as A) exists since BEH defines unambiguously the interpretation of the predicate symbols $\sim_s$.

In general, it may be not easy to find an appropriate axiomatization of the observational equality. In simple cases, however, this can be done using the following criterion which is a special case of Corollary 7.6 in [BH 95a].

Proposition 6.3 Let $C_0 \subseteq C(\Sigma)^{Obs}$ be a finite subset of observable Σ-contexts such that, for any observable sort $s \in Obs$, $z_s \in C_0$. The set C_0 induces the following finitary Σ-formulas (for all $s \in S$): $Beh_s(x_s, y_s) =_{def} \bigwedge_{c \in C_0(s)} \forall Var(c). c[x_s] = c[y_s]$

where $C_0(s)$ denotes the subset of all the contexts in C_0 with context variable of sort s.
Let SP-I be a specification with signature $\Sigma\text{-}I \supseteq \Sigma$. Then:
$(Beh_s(x_s, y_s))_{s \in S}$ is an axiomatization of the observational equality $\approx_{Obs}$ with respect to $Mod(SP\text{-}I)|_\Sigma$ if and only if SP-I + $\langle \mathcal{L}(\Sigma), BEH \rangle \models CONG_\Sigma(\sim)$ where $CONG_\Sigma(\sim)$ is a finitary $\mathcal{L}(\Sigma)$-sentence requiring that the family $(\sim_s)_{s \in S}$ is a Σ-congruence.[9] ◆

6.2 Example: Proving the Object-Oriented Implementation of Sets

In this section we will apply the above proof technique for proving that the class SET is an object-oriented implementation of the abstract data type specification SET-ADT, i.e. we will show:

$$\text{SET-ADT} \stackrel{OO}{\text{~~~>}} \text{SET}.$$

By definition this means that we have to prove the correctness of the observational implementation SET' $\stackrel{\approx Obs}{\text{~~~>}}$ Sem$_{SET}$ where SET' is obtained by the transformation of SET-ADT (cf. Section 4), Sem$_{SET}$ is obtained by the transformation of the class SET (cf. Section 5) and the observable sorts are given by the set Obs = {bool, int}.

The implementation proof

We will consider SET' as a flat specification with the following set of axioms (which are implicitly assumed to be universally quantified):[10]

axioms(SET')=$_{def}$
{is_empty(empty) = TRUE, is_empty(insert(s, x)) = FALSE, is_elem(empty, x) = FALSE,
is_elem(insert(s, y), x) = EQUAL_INT(y, x) OR is_elem(s, x)),
insert(insert(s, x), x) = insert(s, x), insert(insert(s, x), y) = insert(insert(s, y), x),
NOT(TRUE) = FALSE, ... }

In the following let Σ_{SET} = Sig(SET'). We start by constructing an axiomatization of $\approx_{Obs}$ w.r.t. $Mod(Sem_{SET})|_{\Sigma_{SET}}$. Let C_0 be the following set of observable contexts:

$C_0 =_{def} \{z_{bool}, z_{int}, obs_{BOOL}(z_{BOOL}), obs_{INT}(z_{INT}), obs_{BOOL}(is\_elem(z_{SET}, N)) \}$.

The set C_0 induces the following formulas $(Beh_s(x_s, y_s))_{s \in S}$ (cf. Proposition 6.3):
$Beh_s(x_s, y_s) =_{def} x_s = y_s$ (for $s \in \{bool, int\}$)
$Beh_{BOOL}(BL, BR) =_{def} obs_{BOOL}(BL) = obs_{BOOL}(BR)$
$Beh_{INT}(NL, NR) =_{def} obs_{INT}(NL) = obs_{INT}(NR)$
$Beh_{SET}(SL, SR) =_{def} \forall N:INT. obs_{BOOL}(is\_elem(SL, N)) = obs_{BOOL}(is\_elem(SR, N))$

---

[9] A concrete example will be considered in Section 6.2.

[10] It is indeed easy to prove that SET' is semantically equivalent to a basic specification with this set of axioms.

We want to show that $(Beh_s(x_s, y_s))_{s \in S}$ is an axiomatization of $\approx_{Obs}$ w.r.t. $Mod(Sem_{SET})|_{\Sigma_{SET}}$ by applying the criterion of Proposition 6.3. But before we note that we can apply an obvious simplification. Since on observable sorts the observational equality coincides with the set-theoretic equality it is not necessary to introduce predicate symbols $\sim_{bool}$ and $\sim_{int}$. Hence it is sufficient to use the following definitions:

$\mathcal{L}(\Sigma_{SET}) =_{def} \Sigma_{SET} \cup \{\sim_{BOOL} : BOOL, BOOL, \sim_{INT} : INT, INT, \sim_{SET} : SET, SET\}$,

BEH-SET' $=_{def}$
$\forall BL, BR : BOOL. [obs_{BOOL}(BL) = obs_{BOOL}(BR) \Leftrightarrow BL \sim_{BOOL} BR] \land$
$\forall NL, NR : INT. [obs_{INT}(NL) = obs_{INT}(NR) \Leftrightarrow NL \sim_{INT} NR] \land$
$\forall SL, SR : SET. [\forall N:INT. obs_{BOOL}(is\_elem(SL, N)) = obs_{BOOL}(is\_elem(SR, N)) \Leftrightarrow SL \sim_{SET} SR]$

and $CONG_{\Sigma_{SET}}(\sim)$ is the conjunction of the following sentences:

$\quad \forall BL, BR:BOOL. [(BL \sim_{BOOL} BR) \Rightarrow$
$(\forall B:BOOL. NOT(BL) \sim_{BOOL} NOT(BR) \land OR(BL, B) \sim_{BOOL} OR(BR, B) \land ...] \land$
$\quad \forall NL, NR:INT. [(NL \sim_{INT} NR) \Rightarrow$
$(\forall N:INT, S:SET. insert(S, NL) \sim_{SET} insert(S, NR) \land is\_elem(S, NL) \sim_{BOOL} is\_elem(S, NR) \land ...] \land$
$\quad \forall SL, SR:SET. [(SL \sim_{SET} SR) \Rightarrow$
$(\forall N:INT. insert(SL, N) \sim_{SET} insert(SR, N) \land is\_empty(SL) \sim_{BOOL} is\_empty(SR) \land$
$is\_elem(SL, N) \sim_{BOOL} is\_elem(SR, N)]$

According to Proposition 6.3 we know that $(Beh_s(x_s, y_s))_{s \in S}$ is an axiomatization of $\approx_{Obs}$ w.r.t. $Mod(Sem_{SET})|_{\Sigma_{SET}}$ if we have discharged the following proof obligation:

Proof Obligation 1   Prove $Sem_{SET} + \langle\mathcal{L}(\Sigma_{SET}), BEH-SET'\rangle \models CONG_{\Sigma_{SET}}(\sim)$

Given the axiomatization of the observational equality we can now apply Theorem 6.2 which says that $SET' \stackrel{Obs}{\sim\sim\sim>} Sem_{SET}$ holds if we have discharged the next proof obligation:

Proof Obligation 2   Prove $Sem_{SET} + \langle\mathcal{L}(\Sigma_{SET}), BEH-SET'\rangle \models \mathcal{L}(axioms(SET'))$.

The verification of the proof obligations is not simple but all of them can be discharged using standard proof techniques.

7 Conclusion

We have studied a formal framework for object-oriented implementations and provided proof techniques based on an observational approach to algebraic specifications. It is an important step of future research to extend the proof method by taking into account also inheritance hierarchies and to apply our proof techniques to the verification of (reusable) components, for instance of the Eiffel library. Another interesting topic of future research is the combination of our method with approaches that formalize refinements of concurrent object-oriented systems (cf. [LLW 95]).

Acknowledgements   We would like to thank Michel Bidoit and Martin Wirsing for many important discussions. Martin Wirsing put our attention to the subject of this paper and the concepts and proof techniques for behavioural implementations were developed in a close cooperation with Michel Bidoit. We are grateful to anonymous referees of a previous version of this paper for helpful and interesting remarks.

References

[BH 95] M. Bidoit, R. Hennicker: Modular correctness proofs of behavioural implementations. Available by WWW: http://www.pst.informatik.uni-muenchen.de/~hennicke/, 1995. A short version appeared as: Proving the correctness of behavioural implementations. Proc. AMAST '95, Springer Lecture Notes in Computer Science 936, 152-168, 1995.

[BH 95a] M. Bidoit, R. Hennicker: Behavioural theories and the proof of behavioural properties. To appear in Theor. Comp. Science. Previous version in: Report LIENS-95-5, Ecole Normale Supérieure, 1995.

[BHW 95] M. Bidoit, R. Hennicker, M. Wirsing: Behavioural and abstractor specifications. Science of Computer Programming 25 (2-3), 149-186, 1995.

[Breu 91] R. Breu: Algebraic Specification Techniques in Object Oriented Programming Environments. Springer Lecture Notes in Computer Science 562, 1991.

[BZ 90] R. Breu, E. Zucca: An Algebraic Compositional Semantics of an Object Oriented Notation with Concurrency. In: C. E. Veni Madhavan (ed.): Proc. 9th Conf. on Foundations of Software Technology and Theoretical Computer Science, Springer Lecture Notes in Computer Science 405, 131-142, 1990.

[EM 85] H. Ehrig, B. Mahr: Fundamentals of algebraic specification 1, EATCS Monographs on Theoretical Computer Science 6, Springer, 1985.

[GH 93] J. Guttag, J. Horning: Larch: Languages and Tools for Formal Specification. Texts and Monographs in Computer Science, Springer, 1993.

[GM 82] J. A. Goguen, J. Meseguer: Universal realization, persistent interconnection and implementation of abstract modules. In Proc. ICALP '82, Springer Lecture Notes in Computer Science 140, 265-281, 1982.

[GM 87] J. A. Goguen, J. Meseguer: Unifying functional, object-oriented and relational programming with logical semantics. In: B. Shriver, P. Wegner (eds.): Research Directions in Object-Oriented Programming, 417-477, MIT Press, 1987.

[Hen 91] R. Hennicker: Context induction: a proof principle for behavioural abstractions and algebraic implementations. Formal Aspects of Computing 3 (4), 326-345, 1991.

[HS 96] R. Hennicker, C. Schmitz: Object-oriented implementation of abstract data type specifications. Extended version of this paper. Available by WWW: http://www.pst.informatik.uni-muenchen.de/~hennicke/, 1996.

[JSHS 91] R. Jungclaus, G. Saake, T. Hartmann and C. Sernadas: Object-oriented specification of information systems: The TROLL language. Informatik-Bericht 91-04, Technische Universität Braunschweig, 1991.

[KK 67] G. Kreisel, J. L. Krivine: Eléments de Logique Mathematique. Dunod (Paris), 1967.

[LLW 95] U. Lechner, C. Lengauer and M. Wirsing: An object-oriented airport: specification and refinement in Maude. In: E. Astesiano, G. Reggio, A. Tarlecki (eds.): Recent Trends in Data Type Specification, Springer Lecture Notes in Computer Science 906, 351-367, 1995.

[Mes 93] J. Meseguer: A logical theory of concurrent objects and its realization in the Maude language. In: G. Agha, P. Wegner and A. Yonezawa (eds.): Research Directions in Object-Based Concurrency, MIT Press, 314-390, 1993.

[Mey 87] B. Meyer: Programming for reusability and extendibility. Sigplan Notices 22 (2), 85-94, 1987.

[Mey 92] B. Meyer: Eiffel: the language. Prentice Hall International, 1992.

[MG 94] G. Malcolm, J. A. Goguen: Proving correctness of refinement and implementation. Technical Monograph PRG-114, Oxford University Computing Laboratory, 1994.

[NO 88] P. Nivela, F. Orejas: Initial behaviour semantics for algebraic specifications. In: D. T. Sannella, A. Tarlecki (eds.): Proc. 5th Workshop on Algebraic Specifications of Abstract Data Types, Springer Lecture Notes in Computer Science 332, 184-207, 1988.

[R 87] H. Reichel: Initial computability, algebraic specifications, and partial algebras. International Series of Monographs in Computer Science No. 2, Oxford: Clarendon Press, 1987.

[ST 88] D. T. Sannella, A. Tarlecki: Toward formal development of programs from algebraic specifications: implementation revisited. Acta Informatica 25, 233-281, 1988.

[W 86] M. Wirsing: Structured algebraic specifications: a kernel language. Theoretical Computer Science 42, 123-249, 1986.

On the Completeness of the Equations for the Kleene Star in Bisimulation

Wan Fokkink

Utrecht University, Department of Philosophy
Heidelberglaan 8, 3584 CS Utrecht, The Netherlands
fokkink@phil.ruu.nl

Abstract. A classical result from Redko [20] says that there does not exist a complete finite equational axiomatization for the Kleene star modulo trace equivalence. Fokkink and Zantema [13] showed, by means of a term rewriting analysis, that there does exist a complete finite equational axiomatization for the Kleene star up to strong bisimulation equivalence. This paper presents a simpler and shorter completeness proof. Furthermore, the result is extended to open terms, i.e., to ω-completeness. Finally, it is shown that the three equations for the Kleene star are all essential for completeness.

1 Introduction

Kleene [15] defined a binary operator x^*y in the context of finite automata, which denotes the iterate of x on y. Intuitively, the expression x^*y can choose to execute either x, after which it evolves into x^*y again, or y, after which it terminates. An advantage of the Kleene star is that on the one hand it can express recursion, while on the other hand it can be captured in equational laws. Hence, one does not need meta-principles such as the Recursive Specification Principle from Bergstra and Klop [8]. Kleene formulated several equations for his operator, notably $x^*y = x(x^*y) + y$.

Redko [20] (see also Conway [10]) proved that there does not exist a complete finite equational axiomatization for the Kleene star in language theory. We observe that Redko's proof can be transposed to the binary Kleene star in Basic Process Algebra, denoted by BPA*, modulo trace equivalence. This observation is not immediate because Redko studies the Kleene star in the presence of the special constants 0 and 1 from language theory, which are not present in BPA*. However, Redko's proof does not use these constants; the basic idea is that x^* is trace equivalent with $(x^n)^*(x + x^2 + \ldots + x^{n-1})$ for each $n \geq 2$, and this infinite number of equivalences cannot be expressed in finitely many equations. This reasoning is also valid in BPA* modulo trace equivalence.

Bergstra, Bethke and Ponse [7] studied BPA* modulo bisimulation equivalence, and they suggested a finite equational axiomatization for it. Fokkink and Zantema [13] proved that this axiomatization is complete, by means of a sophisticated term rewriting analysis. The completeness proof in [13] is deplorably long and complicated. Therefore, the completeness result itself was presented in the recent handbook chapter of Baeten and Verhoef [6], but its proof was omitted because it was considered beyond the scope of that paper. Here, a simpler completeness proof is proposed, which is based on induction on the structure of process terms. This proof is better suited for presentation in a handbook, or at an advanced process algebra course. Also, the proof method employed here is a general strategy, which can be applied to other iteration constructs just as well, see [3, 2].

Following [17, 14, 3], the preliminaries and the completeness proof focus on open terms, so that we obtain not only completeness, but also ω-completeness of the axioms. This last result is new.

Finally, it is shown that the completeness result is lost if either one of the three equations for the Kleene star is removed from the axiomatization. The proof strategy is to find a model for the axioms minus one of the equations for the Kleene star.

Sewell [22] proved that if the deadlock δ is added to BPA*, then a complete finite equational axiomatization does not exist. Milner [16] formulated an axiomatization for BPA* together with the deadlock δ and the empty process ϵ, which includes a conditional axiom which stems from Salomaa [21] in the setting of language theory. He asked whether his axiomatization is complete with respect to bisimulation. The proof that is presented here stems from an, up to now unsuccessful, attempt to solve this problem. However, the proof in this paper may constitute a first step towards solving Milner's problem. For example, in the setting of BPA* with the deadlock δ, the cases that are not yet covered by this proof can all be reduced to the form $p^*\delta \leftrightarrow q^*\delta$.

Acknowledgements. Luca Aceto and Rob van Glabbeek taught me how to deal with ω-completeness. Alban Ponse provided useful comments.

2 BPA with Binary Kleene Star

2.1 The Syntax

We assume a non-empty alphabet A of atomic actions, with typical elements a, b, c, and a countably infinite set Var of variables, with typical elements x, y, z. We shall use α, β to range over $A \cup$ Var. Furthermore, we have three binary operators: alternative composition $+$, sequential composition $\cdot$, and the Kleene star *. The language of Basic Process Algebra with the binary Kleene star, denoted by $\mathbb{T}(\text{BPA}^*(A))$, with typical elements P, Q, R, S, T, U, V, consists of all the open terms that can be constructed from the atomic actions and the three binary operators. That is, the BNF grammar for the collection of process terms is as follows:

$$P ::= \alpha \mid P + P \mid P \cdot P \mid P^*P.$$

In the sequel the operator $\cdot$ will often be omitted, so PQ denotes $P \cdot Q$. As binding convention, * and $\cdot$ bind stronger than $+$.

$T(\text{BPA}^*(A))$ denotes the subset of closed process terms in $\mathbb{T}(\text{BPA}^*(A))$, that is, the process terms which do not contain any variables.

2.2 Operational Semantics

Table 1 presents an operational semantics for $\mathbb{T}(BPA^*(A))$ in Plotkin style [19], where variables are taken to be atomic actions, that is, variable x can execute x and then terminate; the special symbol $\sqrt{}$ represents (successful) termination.

$$\alpha \xrightarrow{\alpha} \sqrt{}$$

$$\frac{P \xrightarrow{\alpha} \sqrt{}}{P+Q \xrightarrow{\alpha} \sqrt{} \xleftarrow{\alpha} Q+P} \qquad \frac{P \xrightarrow{\alpha} P'}{P+Q \xrightarrow{\alpha} P' \xleftarrow{\alpha} Q+P}$$

$$\frac{P \xrightarrow{\alpha} \sqrt{}}{P \cdot Q \xrightarrow{\alpha} Q} \qquad \frac{P \xrightarrow{\alpha} P'}{P \cdot Q \xrightarrow{\alpha} P' \cdot Q}$$

$$\frac{P \xrightarrow{\alpha} \sqrt{}}{P^*Q \xrightarrow{\alpha} P^*Q} \qquad \frac{P \xrightarrow{\alpha} P'}{P^*Q \xrightarrow{\alpha} P'(P^*Q)}$$

$$\frac{Q \xrightarrow{\alpha} \sqrt{}}{P^*Q \xrightarrow{\alpha} \sqrt{}} \qquad \frac{Q \xrightarrow{\alpha} Q'}{P^*Q \xrightarrow{\alpha} Q'}$$

Table 1. Action rules for $\mathbb{T}(BPA^*(A))$

Process terms are considered modulo bisimulation equivalence from Park [18]. Intuitively, process terms are bisimilar if they have the same branching structure.

Definition 1. Two processes P and Q are *bisimilar*, denoted by $P \leftrightarrow Q$, if there is a symmetric binary relation B on processes which relates P and Q such that:

- if $R \, B \, S$ and $R \xrightarrow{\alpha} R'$, then there is a transition $S \xrightarrow{\alpha} S'$ such that $R' \, B \, S'$,
- if $R \, B \, S$ and $R \xrightarrow{\alpha} \sqrt{}$, then $S \xrightarrow{\alpha} \sqrt{}$.

The action rules in Table 1 are in the 'path' format of Baeten and Verhoef [5]. Hence, bisimulation equivalence is a congruence with respect to all the operators, which means that if $P \leftrightarrow P'$ and $Q \leftrightarrow Q'$, then $P+Q \leftrightarrow P'+Q'$ and $PQ \leftrightarrow P'Q'$ and $P^*Q \leftrightarrow P'^*Q'$. See [5] for the definition of the path format, and for a proof of this congruence result. Their proof uses the extra assumption that the rules are well-founded; Fokkink and Van Glabbeek [12] showed that this requirement can be dropped.

Note that we give operational semantics to open terms, following [17, 14] for process algebra with abstraction, and [3] for process algebra with the prefix iteration operator from [11], which is a restricted version of the Kleene star. This approach deviates from the standard approach, which prescribes to give operational semantics to closed terms only, and to give meaning to open terms by defining $P \leftrightarrow Q$ if $P\sigma \leftrightarrow Q\sigma$ for all substitutions $\sigma : \text{Var} \to T(BPA^*(A))$. The next lemma implies that both approaches yield the same notion of bisimulation equivalence on $\mathbb{T}(\text{BPA}^*(A))$, that is, in our setting, two open terms are bisimilar if and only all their closed instantiations are bisimilar.

Lemma 2. $P \leftrightarrow Q$ if and only if $P\sigma \leftrightarrow Q\sigma$ for all substitutions $\sigma :$ Var $\rightarrow T(\text{BPA}^*(A))$.

This lemma can be proved following the strategy that was employed in [3] for prefix iteration, although in the case of the binary Kleene star the technical details are considerably more complicated [1]. An easy way out is offered by Sewell [22][Theorems 4 and 5], where this type of result is proved in the more general setting of a simply typed lambda calculus, which captures iteration.

According to Lemma 2, if an axiomatization $\mathcal{E}$ for $\mathbb{T}(\text{BPA}^*(A))$ is sound and complete modulo bisimulation, then it is ω-complete for $T(\text{BPA}^*(A))$ modulo bisimulation. Namely, if $\mathcal{E} \vdash P\sigma = Q\sigma$ for all $\sigma :$ Var $\rightarrow T(\text{BPA}^*(A))$, then soundness yields $P\sigma \leftrightarrow Q\sigma$ for all $\sigma :$ Var $\rightarrow T(\text{BPA}^*(A))$, so Lemma 2 implies $P \leftrightarrow Q$. Then completeness yields $\mathcal{E} \vdash P = Q$.

2.3 The Axioms

Table 2 contains an axiom system for $\mathbb{T}(\text{BPA}^*(A))$. It consists of the standard axioms A1-5 together with three axioms BKS1-3 for the binary Kleene star. The most advanced axiom BKS3 originates from Troeger [23]. In the sequel, $P = Q$ will mean that this equality can be derived from the axioms.

This axiomatization is sound for $\mathbb{T}(\text{BPA}^*(A))$ with respect to bisimulation equivalence, i.e., if $P = Q$ then $P \leftrightarrow Q$. Since bisimulation equivalence is a congruence, this can be verified by checking soundness for each axiom separately, which is left to the reader. The purpose of this paper is to prove that the axiomatization is complete with respect to bisimulation, i.e., if $P \leftrightarrow Q$ then $P = Q$.

A1	$x + y = y + x$
A2	$(x + y) + z = x + (y + z)$
A3	$x + x = x$
A4	$(x + y)z = xz + yz$
A5	$(xy)z = x(yz)$
BKS1	$x(x^*y) + y = x^*y$
BKS2	$(x^*y)z = x^*(yz)$
BKS3	$x^*(y((x + y)^*z) + z) = (x + y)^*z$

Table 2. Axioms for $\mathbb{T}(\text{BPA}^*(A))$

In the sequel, terms are considered modulo associativity and commutativity of the $+$, and we write $P =_{\text{AC}} Q$ if P and Q can be equated by axioms A1,2. As usual, $\sum_{i=1}^{n} P_i$ represents $P_1 + \ldots + P_n$. In the sequel, we will take care to avoid empty sums (where $\sum_{i \in \emptyset} P_i + Q$ is not considered empty).

For each process term P, its collection of possible transitions is non-empty and finite, say $\{P \xrightarrow{\alpha_i} P_i \mid i = 1, ..., m\} \cup \{P \xrightarrow{\beta_j} \sqrt{} \mid j = 1, ..., n\}$. We call

$$\sum_{i=1}^{m} \alpha_i P_i + \sum_{j=1}^{n} \beta_j$$

the *expansion* of P. The terms $\alpha_i P_i$ and β_j are called the *summands* of P.

Lemma 3. *Each process term is provably equal to its expansion.*

Proof. Straightforward, by structural induction, using axioms A4,5 and BKS1. $\blacksquare$

3 A New Completeness Proof

In this section we present a new proof for the fact that the axioms A1-5+BKS1-3 completely axiomatize $\mathbb{T}(\mathrm{BPA}^*(A))$ modulo bisimulation.

We start with determining a collection of normal forms such that for each infinite derivation $P_0 \xrightarrow{a_0} P_1 \xrightarrow{a_1} P_2 \xrightarrow{a_2} \cdots$ with P_0 a normal form, there is a normal form R^*S and a natural N such that each P_n for $n > N$ is of the form either R^*S or $R'(R^*S)$. Thus, the completeness proof boils down to checking the following three cases: $R^*S \leftrightarrow T^*U$ and $R'(R^*S) \leftrightarrow T^*U$ and $R'(R^*S) \leftrightarrow T'(T^*U)$. Such pairs of bisimilar terms are shown to be provably equal by structural induction with respect to a subtle ordering on terms.

3.1 A Lemma for Normed Processes

Process terms in $\mathbb{T}(\mathrm{BPA}^*(A))$ are *normed*, which means that they are able to terminate in finitely many transitions. The *norm* of a process yields the length of the shortest termination trace of this process; this notion stems from [4]. Norm can be defined inductively as follows.

$$|\alpha| = 1$$
$$|P + Q| = \min\{|P|, |Q|\}$$
$$|PQ| = |P| + |Q|$$
$$|P^*Q| = |Q|.$$

Note that bisimilar processes have the same norm.

Definition 4. P' is a *derivative* of P if P can evolve into P' by zero or more transitions. A derivative P' of P is *proper* if P can evolve into P' by one or more transitions.

The following lemma is typical for normed processes.

Lemma 5. *Let $PQ \leftrightarrow RS$. By symmetry we may assume $|Q| \leq |S|$. We can distinguish two cases:*

- *either $P \leftrightarrow R$ and $Q \leftrightarrow S$,*
- *or there is a proper derivative P' of P such that $P \leftrightarrow RP'$ and $P'Q \leftrightarrow S$.*

Proof. We prove this lemma from the following facts A and B. Fact B originates from Caucal [9].

A. If $PQ \leftrightarrow RS$ and $|Q| \leq |S|$, then either $Q \leftrightarrow S$, or there is a proper derivative P' of P such that $P'Q \leftrightarrow S$.

Proof. We apply induction on $|P|$. First, let $|P| = 1$. Then $P \xrightarrow{\alpha} \sqrt{}$ for some α, so $PQ \xrightarrow{\alpha} Q$. Since $PQ \leftrightarrow RS$, we have two options:
- $R \xrightarrow{\alpha} \sqrt{}$ and $Q \leftrightarrow S$. Then we are done.
- $R \xrightarrow{\alpha} R'$ and $Q \leftrightarrow R'S$. This leads to a contradiction: $|Q| \leq |S| < |R'S| = |Q|$.

Next, suppose that we have proved the case for $|P| \leq n$, and let $|P| = n+1$. Then there is a P' with $|P'| = n$ and $P \xrightarrow{\alpha} P'$, which implies $PQ \xrightarrow{\alpha} P'Q$. Since $PQ \leftrightarrow RS$, we have two options:
- $R \xrightarrow{\alpha} \sqrt{}$ and $P'Q \leftrightarrow S$. Then we are done.
- $R \xrightarrow{\alpha} R'$ and $P'Q \leftrightarrow R'S$. Since $|P'| = n$, induction yields either $Q \leftrightarrow S$ or $P''Q \leftrightarrow S$ for a proper derivative P'' of P'. Again, we are done.

B. If $PQ \leftrightarrow RQ$, then $P \leftrightarrow R$.

Proof. Define a binary relation B on process terms by $T \ B \ U$ if $TQ \leftrightarrow UQ$. We show that B constitutes a bisimulation relation between P and R:
- Since $\leftrightarrow$ is symmetric, so is B.
- $PQ \leftrightarrow RQ$, so $P \ B \ R$.
- Suppose that $T \ B \ U$ and $T \xrightarrow{\alpha} T'$. Then $TQ \xrightarrow{\alpha} T'Q$, so $TQ \leftrightarrow UQ$ implies that this transition can be mimicked by a transition from UQ. This cannot be a transition $UQ \xrightarrow{\alpha} Q$ because $|T'Q| > |Q|$, so apparently there is a transition $U \xrightarrow{\alpha} U'$ with $T'Q \leftrightarrow U'Q$. Hence, $T' \ B \ U'$.
- Similarly, we find that if $T \ B \ U$ and $T \xrightarrow{\alpha} \sqrt{}$, then $U \xrightarrow{\alpha} \sqrt{}$.

Finally, we show that facts A and B together prove the lemma. Let $PQ \leftrightarrow RS$ with $|Q| \leq |S|$. According to fact A we can distinguish two cases:

- $Q \leftrightarrow S$. Then $PQ \leftrightarrow RS \leftrightarrow RQ$, so fact B yields $P \leftrightarrow R$.
- $P'Q \leftrightarrow S$ for some proper derivative P' of P. Then $PQ \leftrightarrow RS \leftrightarrow RP'Q$, so fact B yields $P \leftrightarrow RP'$. $\square$

3.2 Basic Terms

We construct a set $\mathbb{B}$ of *basic* process terms, such that each process term is provably equal to a basic term. We will prove the completeness theorem by showing that bisimilar basic terms are provably equal.

Table 3 presents a rewrite system $\mathcal{R}$, which consists of directions of the axioms A4,5 and BKS2, pointing from left to right. The rules in $\mathcal{R}$ are to be interpreted modulo AC of the +. $\mathcal{R}$ is terminating, which means that there are no infinite

$$(x + y)z \longrightarrow xz + yz$$
$$(xy)z \longrightarrow x(yz)$$
$$(x^*y)z \longrightarrow x^*(yz)$$

Table 3. The rewrite system $\mathcal{R}$

reductions. This follows from the following weight function w in the natural numbers.

$$w(\alpha) = 2$$
$$w(P + Q) = w(P) + w(Q)$$
$$w(PQ) = w(P)^2 w(Q)$$
$$w(P^*Q) = w(P) + w(Q).$$

It is easy to see that if $\mathcal{R}$ reduces P to Q, then $w(P) > w(Q)$. Since the ordering on the natural numbers is well-founded, we can conclude that $\mathcal{R}$ is terminating. Let $\mathbb{G}$ denote the collection of *ground normal forms* of $\mathcal{R}$, i.e., the collection of process terms that cannot be reduced by rules in $\mathcal{R}$. Since $\mathcal{R}$ is terminating, and since its rules are directions of axioms, it follows that each process term is provably equal to a process term in $\mathbb{G}$. The elements in $\mathbb{G}$ are defined by:

$$P ::= \alpha \mid P + P \mid \alpha P \mid P^*P.$$

$\mathbb{G}$ is not yet our desired set of basic terms, due to the fact that there exist process terms in $\mathbb{G}$ which have a derivative outside $\mathbb{G}$. We give an example.

Example 1. Let $A = \{a, b, c\}$. Clearly, $(a^*b)^*c \in \mathbb{G}$, and

$$(a^*b)^*c \stackrel{a}{\longrightarrow} (a^*b)((a^*b)^*c).$$

However, the derivative $(a^*b)((a^*b)^*c)$ is not in $\mathbb{G}$ because the third rule in $\mathcal{R}$ reduces this term to $a^*(b((a^*b)^*c))$.

In order to overcome this complication, we introduce the following collection of process terms:

$$\mathbb{H} = \{P^*Q, \ P'(P^*Q) \mid P^*Q \in \mathbb{G} \land P' \text{ proper derivative of } P\}.$$

We define an equivalence relation $\cong$ on $\mathbb{H}$ by putting $P'(P^*Q) \cong P^*Q$ for proper derivatives P' of P, and taking the reflexive, symmetric, transitive closure of $\cong$.
    The set $\mathbb{B}$ of *basic* terms is the union of $\mathbb{G}$ and $\mathbb{H}$.

Lemma 6. *If $P \in \mathbb{B}$ and $P \stackrel{\alpha}{\longrightarrow} P'$, then $P' \in \mathbb{B}$.*

Proof. We apply induction on the structure of P.
    If $P \in \mathbb{H}\backslash\mathbb{G}$, then it is of the form $Q'(Q^*R)$ for some normal form Q^*R. So P' is of the form either Q^*R or $Q''(Q^*R)$ for some proper derivative Q'' of Q'. In both cases, $P' \in \mathbb{B}$.

If $P \in \mathbb{G}$, then it is of the form $\sum_i \alpha_i Q_i + \sum_j R_j^* S_j + \sum_k \beta_k$, where the Q_i and R_j and S_j are normal forms. So P' is of the form either Q_i or $R_j^* S_j$ or $R_j'(R_j^* S_j)$ or S_j', which are all basic terms (in the last case, this follows by structural induction). $\square$

3.3 An Ordering on Basic Terms

Norm does not constitute a nice ordering on process terms, because it does not respect term size, for example, $|aa + a| < |aa|$. L-value, from Fokkink and Zantema [13], induces an ordering which does not have this drawback. It is defined as follows:

$$L(P) = \max\{|P'| \mid P' \text{ proper derivative of } P\}.$$

Note that $L(P) < L(PQ)$ because for each proper derivative P' of P, $P'Q$ is a proper derivative of PQ. Even so, $L(P) < L(P^*Q)$. Since norm is preserved under bisimulation, it follows that the same holds for L-value, that is, if $P \leftrightarrow Q$ then $L(P) = L(Q)$.

We define an ordering on $\mathbb{B}$ as follows:

- $P < Q$ if $L(P) < L(Q)$,
- $P < Q$ if P is a derivative of Q but Q is not a derivative of P,

and we take the transitive closure of $<$.

Note that if $P, Q \in \mathbb{H}$ with $P \cong Q$, then P and Q have the same proper derivatives, and so $L(P) = L(Q)$. These observations imply that the ordering $<$ on $\mathbb{B}$ respects the equivalence $\cong$ on $\mathbb{H}$, that is, if $P \cong Q < R \cong S$, then $P < S$.

Lemma 7. $<$ *is a well-founded ordering on* $\mathbb{B}$.

Proof. If P is a derivative of Q, then all proper derivatives of P are proper derivatives of Q, so $L(P) \leq L(Q)$. Hence, if $P < Q$ then $L(P) \leq L(Q)$.

Suppose that $<$ is not well-founded, so there exists an infinite chain $P_0 > P_1 > P_2 > \cdots$. Then $L(P_n) \geq L(P_{n+1})$ for all n, so there is an N such that $L(P_N) = L(P_n)$ for all $n > N$. Since $P_N > P_n$ for $n > N$, it follows that P_n is a derivative of P_N for $n > N$. Each process term has only finitely many derivatives, so there are $m, n > N$ with $m < n$ and $P_m =_{AC} P_n$. Then $P_m \not> P_n$, so we have found a contradiction. Hence, $<$ is well-founded. $\square$

In the next two lemmas, we need a weight function g in the natural numbers, which is defined inductively as follows:

$$\begin{aligned}
g(\alpha) &= 0 \\
g(P + Q) &= \max\{g(P), g(Q)\} \\
g(PQ) &= \max\{g(P), g(Q)\} \\
g(P^*Q) &= \max\{g(P), g(Q) + 1\}
\end{aligned}$$

It is not hard to see, by structural induction, that if $P \xrightarrow{\alpha} P'$, then $g(P) \geq g(P')$.

Lemma 8. *Let $P^*Q \in \mathbb{B}$. If Q' is a proper derivative of Q, then $Q' < P^*Q$.*

Proof. Since Q' is a derivative of Q, it follows that $g(Q') \leq g(Q)$. Hence, $g(Q') < g(P^*Q)$, so P^*Q cannot be a derivative of Q'. On the other hand, Q' is a derivative of P^*Q, so then $Q' < P^*Q$. $\square$

Lemma 9. *If $P \in \mathbb{B}$ and $P \xrightarrow{\alpha} P'$, then either $P' < P$, or $P, P' \in \mathbb{H}$ and $P \cong P'$.*

Proof. We will use the following two facts A and B.

A. If $P \in \mathbb{B}$ and $P' \notin \mathbb{H}$ and $P \xrightarrow{\alpha} P'$, then P' has smaller size than P.
   Proof. We apply induction on the structure of P. If $P \in \mathbb{H}\backslash\mathbb{G}$ then it follows that $P' \in \mathbb{H}$, so then we are done. Hence, we may assume that $P \in \mathbb{G}$:

$$P =_{\text{AC}} \sum_i \alpha_i Q_i + \sum_j R_j^* S_j + \sum_k \beta_k.$$

   Since $P \xrightarrow{\alpha} P'$, we find that P' is of one of the following forms:
   - $P' =_{\text{AC}} Q_i$ for some i. In this case we are done because the Q_i have smaller size than P.
   - $P' =_{\text{AC}} R_j'(R_j^* S_j)$ or $P' =_{\text{AC}} R_j^* S_j$ for some j. These cases contradict the assumption that $P' \notin \mathbb{H}$.
   - $S_j \xrightarrow{\alpha} P'$ for some j. In this last case, induction yields that P' has smaller size than S_j, and thus P' has smaller size than P.
B. If $P \in \mathbb{H}$ and $P \xrightarrow{\alpha} P'$, then either $g(P) > g(P')$, or $P' \in \mathbb{H}$ and $P \cong P'$.
   Proof. Since $P \in \mathbb{H}$, either $P =_{\text{AC}} Q'(Q^*R)$ or $P =_{\text{AC}} Q^*R$ for some Q and R. Hence, either $P' =_{\text{AC}} Q''(Q^*R)$ or $P' =_{\text{AC}} Q^*R$ or $P' =_{\text{AC}} R'$ for a proper derivative R' of R. In the first two cases $P' \in \mathbb{H}$ and $P \cong P'$, and in the last case $g(P') = g(R') \leq g(R) < g(Q^*R) = g(P)$.

Now, we are ready to prove the lemma. Let $P \xrightarrow{\alpha} P'$ with $P' \not< P$; we prove that $P, P' \in \mathbb{H}$ and $P \cong P'$.

Since P' is a derivative of P and $P' \not< P$, apparently P is a derivative of P'. So there exists a derivation

$$P_0 \xrightarrow{\alpha_1} P_1 \xrightarrow{\alpha_2} \cdots \xrightarrow{\alpha_n} P_n =_{\text{AC}} P_0, \qquad n \geq 1.$$

where $P_0 =_{\text{AC}} P$ and $P_1 =_{\text{AC}} P'$ and $P_n =_{\text{AC}} P'$.

Suppose that $P_k \notin \mathbb{H}$ for all k. Then according to fact A, P_{k+1} has smaller size than P_k for $k = 0, ..., n-1$, so $P_n =_{\text{AC}} P_0$ has smaller size than P_0; contradiction. Hence, $P_l \in \mathbb{H}$ for some l.

Since each P_k is a derivative of each $P_{k'}$, we have $g(P_k) \leq g(P_{k'})$ for k and k', so $g(P_k)$ must be the same for all k. Then it follows from fact B, together with $P_l \in \mathbb{H}$, that $P_k \in \mathbb{H}$ for all k and $P_0 \cong P_1 \cong \cdots \cong P_n$. $\square$

Elements of $\mathbb{B} \times \mathbb{B}$ are considered modulo commutativity. The well-founded ordering $<$ on $\mathbb{B}$ is extended to a well-founded ordering on $\mathbb{B} \times \mathbb{B}$ as expected: $(P, Q) < (R, S)$ if $P < R$ and $Q \cong S$.

3.4   The Main Theorem

Now we are ready to prove the desired completeness result.

Theorem 10. *If $P \leftrightarrow Q$, then* A1-5+BKS1-3 $\vdash P = Q$.

Proof. Each process term is provably equal to a basic term, so it is sufficient to show that bisimilar basic terms are provably equal. Assume $P, Q \in \mathbb{B}$ with $P \leftrightarrow Q$; we show that $P = Q$, by induction on the ordering $<$ on $\mathbb{B} \times \mathbb{B}$. So suppose that we have already dealt with pairs of bisimilar basic terms that are smaller than (P, Q).

First, assume that P or Q is not in $\mathbb{H}$, say $P \notin \mathbb{H}$. Since $P \leftrightarrow Q$, by using axiom A3 we can adapt the expansions of P and Q to the following forms:

$$P = \sum_{i=1}^{m} \alpha_i P_i + \sum_{j=1}^{n} \beta_j, \qquad Q = \sum_{i=1}^{m} \alpha_i Q_i + \sum_{j=1}^{n} \beta_j,$$

where $P_i \leftrightarrow Q_i$ for $i = 1, ..., m$. Since $P \notin \mathbb{H}$, Lemma 9 says that $P_i < P$ for $i = 1, ..., m$. Furthermore, Lemma 9 says that either $Q_i < Q$ or $Q_i \cong Q$ for $i = 1, ..., m$. Then $(P_i, Q_i) < (P, Q)$, so induction yields $P_i = Q_i$ for $i = 1, ..., m$. Hence, $P = Q$.

Next, assume $P, Q \in \mathbb{H}$. We distinguish three cases.

1. Let $P =_{AC} R^*S$ and $Q =_{AC} T^*U$. We prove $R^*S = T^*U$.
   We spell out the expansions of R and T:

$$R = \sum_{i \in I} R_i, \qquad T = \sum_{j \in J} T_j,$$

   where the R_i and the T_j are of the form either αV or α.
   Clearly, the summands of T^*U are the summands of $T(T^*U)$ together with the summands of U. Hence, since $R^*S \leftrightarrow T^*U$, each term $R_i(R^*S)$ for $i \in I$ is bisimilar either to $T_j(T^*U)$ for a $j \in J$ or to a summand of U. We distinguish these two cases.
   (a) $R_i(R^*S) \leftrightarrow T_j(T^*U)$ for a $j \in J$. Then $R_i(R^*S) \leftrightarrow T_j(R^*S)$ because $R^*S \leftrightarrow T^*U$, so Lemma 5 implies $R_i \leftrightarrow T_j$.
   (b) $R_i(R^*S) \leftrightarrow \alpha U'$ for a $U \xrightarrow{\alpha} U'$.
   Thus, I can be divided into the following, not necessarily disjoint, subsets.

$$I_0 = \{i \in I \mid \exists j \in J \ (R_i \leftrightarrow T_j)\}$$
$$I_1 = \{i \in I \mid \exists U \xrightarrow{\alpha} U' \ (R_i(R^*S) \leftrightarrow \alpha U')\}$$

Similarly, J can be divided:

$$J_0 = \{j \in J \mid \exists i \in I \ (T_j \leftrightarrow R_i)\}$$
$$J_1 = \{j \in J \mid \exists S \xrightarrow{\alpha} S' \ (T_j(T^*U) \leftrightarrow \alpha S')\}$$

If both I_1 and J_1 are not empty, then $U' \leftrightarrow R^*S$ for a proper derivative U' of U and $S' \leftrightarrow T^*U$ for a proper derivative S' of S, and so $U' \leftrightarrow S'$. Then induction yields $R^*S = U' = S' = T^*U$, and we are done. Hence, we may assume that either I_1 or J_1 is empty, say $J_1 = \emptyset$.

$$\sum_{i \in I_1} R_i(R^*S) + S = U. \tag{1}$$

In order to derive Equation 1, we show that each summand at the left-hand side of the equality sign is provably equal to a summand of U, and vice versa. By definition of I_1, for each $R_i(R^*S)$ with $i \in I_1$ there is a summand $\alpha U'$ of U such that $R_i(R^*S) \leftrightarrow \alpha U'$. According to Lemma 8 $U' < T^*U$, so induction yields $R_i(R^*S) = \alpha U'$.
Consider a summand $\alpha S'$ of S. Since $R^*S \leftrightarrow T^*U$, and $J_1 = \emptyset$, it follows that $\alpha S'$ is bisimilar with a summand $\alpha U'$ of U, so induction yields $\alpha S' = \alpha U'$. Finally, summands α of S correspond with summands α of U.
By the converse argument it follows that each summand of U is provably equal to a summand at the left-hand side of the equality sign.

We continue with the proof of $R^*S = T^*U$. Since $J_1 = \emptyset$, it follows that $J_0 \neq \emptyset$, so clearly also $I_0 \neq \emptyset$. Put $R_0 = \sum_{i \in I_0} R_i$.

$$R_0 = T. \tag{2}$$

In order to prove this equation, note that by definition of I_0 and $J_0 = J$, each R_i for $i \in I_0$ is bisimilar to a T_j with $j \in J$. Since $L(R_i) \leq L(R) < L(R^*S)$, induction yields $R_i = T_j$. Conversely, each T_j for $j \in J$ is provably equal to a R_i with $i \in I_0$. Hence, $R_0 = T$.

Since $I_0 \cup I_1 = I$, we have $R \stackrel{\text{A3}}{=} R_0 + \sum_{i \in I_1} R_i$. Finally, we can derive $R^*S = T^*U$:

$$\begin{aligned}
R^*S &\stackrel{\text{A3}}{=} (R_0 + \sum_{i \in I_1} R_i)^*S \\
&\stackrel{\text{BKS3}}{=} R_0^*(\sum_{i \in I_1} R_i((R_0 + \sum_{i \in I_1} R_i)^*S) + S) \\
&\stackrel{\text{A3}}{=} R_0^*(\sum_{i \in I_1} R_i(R^*S) + S) \\
&\stackrel{\text{Eq.1,2}}{=} T^*U.
\end{aligned}$$

2. Let $P =_{\text{AC}} R'(R^*S)$ and $Q =_{\text{AC}} T^*U$. We prove $R'(R^*S) = T^*U$.
   $|U| = |T^*U| = |R'(R^*S)| \geq 2$, so U does not have atomic summands, so its expansion is of the form $\sum_i \alpha_i U_i$. Since $R'(R^*S) \leftrightarrow T^*U$, each U_i is bisimilar to R^*S or to a term $R''(R^*S)$. According to Lemma 8 $U_i < T^*U$, and $R^*S \cong R'(R^*S)$ or $R''(R^*S) \cong R'(R^*S)$, so induction yields $U_i = R^*S$ or $U_i = R''(R^*S)$ respectively. This holds for all i, so $U = \sum_i \alpha_i U_i = V(R^*S)$ for some term V. Then $R'(R^*S) \leftrightarrow T^*U \leftrightarrow (T^*V)(R^*S)$, so Lemma 5 implies $R' \leftrightarrow T^*V$. Since $L(R') < L(R'(R^*S))$ and $L(T^*V) < L(T^*U)$, induction yields $R' = T^*V$. Hence, $R'(R^*S) = (T^*V)(R^*S) \stackrel{\text{BKS2}}{=} T^*(V(R^*S)) = T^*U$.
3. Let $P =_{\text{AC}} R'(R^*S)$ and $Q =_{\text{AC}} T'(T^*U)$. We prove $R'(R^*S) = T'(T^*U)$.
   By symmetry we may assume $|R^*S| \leq |T^*U|$. Lemma 5 distinguishes two possible cases.

Either $R' \leftrightarrow T'$ and $R^*S \leftrightarrow T^*U$. Since $L(R') < L(R'(R^*S))$, induction yields $R' = T'$, and Case 1 applied to $R^*S \leftrightarrow T^*U$ yields $R^*S = T^*U$.

Or $R' \leftrightarrow T'R''$ and $R''(R^*S) \leftrightarrow T^*U$ for a proper derivative R'' of R'. Since $L(R') < L(R'(R^*S))$, induction yields $R' = T'R''$. Furthermore, Case 1 applied to $R''(R^*S) \leftrightarrow T^*U$ yields $R''(R^*S) = T^*U$. Hence, $R'(R^*S) = (T'R'')(R^*S) \overset{\text{BKS2}}{=} T'(R''(R^*S)) = T'(T^*U)$. □

Lemma 2 implies the following corollary.

Corollary 11. *The axiomatization A1-5+BKS1-3 is complete and ω-complete for $T(\text{BPA}^*(A))$ modulo bisimulation.*

3.5 An Example

We give an example as to how the construction in the completeness proof acts on a particular pair of bisimilar process terms.

Example 2. Let $A = \{a_1, b\}$, and consider the two bisimilar closed process terms:

$$a_1^*b \leftrightarrow a_1^*(a_1^*b).$$

We show how the construction in the proof of Theorem 10 applied to this pair produces a derivation of $a_1^*b = a_1^*(a_1^*b)$.

Clearly both terms are in $\mathbb{H}$, and we are dealing with the first of the three possible cases for bisimilar terms in $\mathbb{H}$ that were distinguished in the completeness proof. Following the notations that were introduced there, we have $I = I_0 = I_1 = \{1\}$ and $J = J_0 = \{1\}$ and $J_1 = \emptyset$. Hence, Equation 1 takes the form $a_1(a_1^*b) + b = a_1^*b$, which is an instantiation of BKS1, and Equation 2 takes the trivial form $a_1 = a_1$. Thus, the derivation at the end of the first case for pairs in $\mathbb{H}$ here takes the following form:

$$
\begin{aligned}
a_1^*b \;\overset{\text{A3}}{=}\;& (a_1 + a_1)^*b \\
\overset{\text{BKS3}}{=}\;& a_1^*(a_1((a_1 + a_1)^*b) + b) \\
\overset{\text{A3}}{=}\;& a_1^*(a_1(a_1^*b) + b) \\
\overset{\text{Eq.1}}{=}\;& a_1^*(a_1^*b).
\end{aligned}
$$

3.6 A Comparison of Proof Strategies

We discuss the strategy of the original completeness proof for $T(\text{BPA}^*(A))$ from Fokkink and Zantema [13] . That proof is based on a standard rewriting technique, which means a quest for unique ground normal forms. It is noted that this strive cannot be fulfilled for the Kleene star, so this operator is replaced by $x^{\oplus}y$, which represents $x(x^*y)$, and the axioms BKS1-3 are adopted for this new operator. These axioms are turned into conditional rewrite rules, which are applied modulo AC of the $+$. Four rewrite rules are added to make the rewrite system weakly confluent, that is, if there are one-step reductions from a term P to terms P' and P'', then both P' and P'' can be reduced to a term Q.

The next aim is to prove that the resulting conditional rewrite system is terminating, which means that there are no infinite reductions. In this particular case, deducing termination is a complicated matter, due to the occurrence of a rewrite rule where the left-hand side can be obtained from the right-hand side by the elimination of function symbols. Termination is obtained by means of the advanced technique of semantic labelling from Zantema [24]. Hence, each process term is provably equal to a ground normal form, which cannot be reduced by the conditional rewrite system.

Finally, a painstaking case analysis learns that if two ground normal forms are bisimilar, then they are the same modulo AC of the $+$. This observation yields the desired completeness result.

In this paper, we presented a completeness proof for $\mathbb{T}(\text{BPA}^*(A))$, based on induction on term structure. This strategy turns out to be much more convenient than the term rewriting analysis sketched above. Moreover, this approach is more general, in the sense that it can be applied to variants of iteration, see for example [3, 2].

4 The Axioms BKS1-3 are Essential for Completeness

Experience learns that axiom systems can contain embarrassing redundancies; see [14] for an example in branching bisimulation. Therefore, we conclude this paper by addressing the issue of the relative independence of the equations for the Kleene star. That is, we show that each of the axioms BKS1-3 for the binary Kleene star is essential for the obtained completeness result.

Theorem 12. *If one of the axioms BKS1-3 is skipped from A1-5+BKS1-3, then this axiomatization is no longer complete for $T(\text{BPA}^*(A))$ modulo bisimulation.*

Proof. We apply a standard technique for proving that an equation e cannot be derived from an equational theory $\mathcal{E}$, which prescribes to define a model for $\mathcal{E}$ in which e is not valid.

In order to show that BKS1 cannot be derived from A1-5+BKS2,3, we define the following interpretation function ϕ of open terms in the natural numbers. It captures the intuition that BKS1 is the only equality that enables to expand the Kleene star. Namely, it does not take into account terms that occur at the right-hand side of a multiplication.

$$\phi(\alpha) = 0$$
$$\phi(x) = 0$$
$$\phi(P + Q) = \max\{\phi(P), \phi(Q)\}$$
$$\phi(P \cdot Q) = \phi(P)$$
$$\phi(P^*Q) = \max\{\phi(P) + 1, \phi(Q) + 1\}$$

It is easy to see that this interpretation is a model for A1-5+BKS2,3. However, $\phi(a(a^*a)+a) = 0$, while $\phi(a^*a) = 1$. Hence, the equality $a(a^*a)+a = a^*a$ cannot be derived from A1-5+BKS2,3.

In order to show that BKS2 cannot be derived from A1-5+BKS1,3, we define the following interpretation function ψ of open terms in the natural numbers.

$$\psi(\alpha) = 0$$
$$\psi(x) = 0$$
$$\psi(P + Q) = \max\{\psi(P), \psi(Q)\}$$
$$\psi(P \cdot Q) = \psi(Q)$$
$$\psi(P^*Q) = \max\{\psi(P) + 1, \psi(Q)\}$$

It is easy to see that this interpretation is a model for A1-5+BKS1,3. However, $\psi((a^*a)a) = \psi(a) = 0$, while $\psi(a^*(aa)) = \max\{\psi(a) + 1, \psi(aa)\} = 1$. Hence, the equality $(a^*a)a = a^*(aa)$ cannot be derived from A1-5+BKS1,3.

In order to show that BKS3 cannot be derived from A1-5+BKS1,2, we define the following interpretation function η of open terms in sets of natural numbers. It captures the intuition that BKS3 is the only equality to change the interpretation at the left-hand side of a Kleene star. Namely, $\eta(P)$ collects the norms of subterms that occur as arguments at the left-hand side of a Kleene star.

$$\eta(\alpha) = \emptyset$$
$$\eta(x) = \emptyset$$
$$\eta(P + Q) = \eta(P) \cup \eta(Q)$$
$$\eta(P \cdot Q) = \eta(P) \cup \eta(Q)$$
$$\eta(P^*Q) = \eta(P) \cup \eta(Q) \cup \{|P|\}$$

It is easy to see that this interpretation is a model for A1-5+BKS1,2. However, $\eta((aa)^*(a((aa + a)^*a) + a)) = \{|aa|, |aa + a|\} = \{1, 2\}$ while $\eta((aa + a)^*a) = \{|aa + a|\} = \{1\}$. Hence, the equality $(aa)^*(a((aa + a)^*a) + a) = (aa + a)^*a$ cannot be derived from A1-5+BKS1,2. $\square$

References

1. L. Aceto. Personal communication, December 1995.
2. L. Aceto and W.J. Fokkink. A complete axiomatization for multi-exit iteration. In preparation.
3. L. Aceto, W.J. Fokkink, R.J. van Glabbeek, and A. Ingólfsdóttir. Axiomatizing prefix iteration with silent steps. Report RS-95-56, BRICS, University of Aalborg, 1995. To appear in *Information and Computation*.
4. J.C.M. Baeten, J.A. Bergstra, and J.W. Klop. Decidability of bisimulation equivalence for processes generating context-free languages. *Journal of the ACM*, 40(3):653–682, 1993.
5. J.C.M. Baeten and C. Verhoef. A congruence theorem for structured operational semantics with predicates. In E. Best, ed., *Proceedings CONCUR'93*, Hildesheim, LNCS 715, pp. 477–492. Springer, 1993.

6. J.C.M. Baeten and C. Verhoef. Concrete process algebra. In S. Abramsky, D.M. Gabbay, and T.S.E. Maibaum, eds., *Handbook of Logic in Computer Science, Volume IV*, pp. 149–268. Oxford University Press, 1995.

7. J.A. Bergstra, I. Bethke, and A. Ponse. Process algebra with iteration and nesting. *The Computer Journal*, 37(4):243–258, 1994.

8. J.A. Bergstra and J.W. Klop. Verification of an alternating bit protocol by means of process algebra. In W. Bibel and K.P. Jantke, eds., *Proceedings Mathematical Methods of Specification and Synthesis of Software Systems*, Wendisch-Rietz, LNCS 215, pp. 9–23. Springer, 1985.

9. D. Caucal. Graphes canoniques et graphes algébriques. *Theoretical Informatics and Applications*, 24(4):339–352, 1990.

10. J.H. Conway. *Regular algebra and finite machines*. Chapman and Hall, 1971.

11. W.J. Fokkink. A complete equational axiomatization for prefix iteration. *Information Processing Letters*, 52(6):333–337, 1994.

12. W.J. Fokkink and R.J. van Glabbeek. Ntyft/ntyxt rules reduce to ntree rules. Technical Note CS-95-17, Stanford University, 1995. To appear in *Information and Computation*.

13. W.J. Fokkink and H. Zantema. Basic process algebra with iteration: completeness of its equational axioms. *The Computer Journal*, 37(4):259–267, 1994.

14. R.J. van Glabbeek. A complete axiomatization for branching bisimulation congruence of finite-state behaviours. In A.M. Borzyszkowski and S. Sokołowski, eds., *Proceedings MFCS'93*, Gdansk, LNCS 711, pp. 473–484. Springer, 1993.

15. S.C. Kleene. Representation of events in nerve nets and finite automata. In *Automata Studies*, pages 3–41. Princeton University Press, 1956.

16. R. Milner. A complete inference system for a class of regular behaviours. *Journal of Computer and System Sciences*, 28:439–466, 1984.

17. R. Milner. A complete axiomatisation for observational congruence of finite-state behaviors. *Information and Computation*, 81(2):227–247, 1989.

18. D.M.R. Park. Concurrency and automata on infinite sequences. In P. Deussen, editor, *Proceedings 5th GI Conference*, Karlsruhe, LNCS 104, pp. 167–183. Springer, 1981.

19. G.D. Plotkin. A structural approach to operational semantics. Report DAIMI FN-19, Aarhus University, 1981.

20. V.N. Redko. On defining relations for the algebra of regular events. *Ukrainskii Matematicheskii Zhurnal*, 16:120–126, 1964. In Russian.

21. A. Salomaa. Two complete axiom systems for the algebra of regular events. *Journal of the ACM*, 13(1):158–169, 1966.

22. P. Sewell. Bisimulation is not finitely (first order) equationally axiomatisable. In *Proceedings LICS'94*, Paris, pp. 62–70. IEEE Computer Society Press, 1994.

23. D.R. Troeger. Step bisimulation is pomset equivalence on a parallel language without explicit internal choice. *Mathematical Structures in Computer Science*, 3:25–62, 1993.

24. H. Zantema. Termination of term rewriting by semantic labelling. *Fundamenta Informaticae*, 24(1,2):89–105, 1995.

An Equational Axiomatization of Observation Congruence for Prefix Iteration

Luca Aceto*   Anna Ingólfsdóttir

BRICS**
Department of Mathematics and Computer Science
Aalborg University
Fredrik Bajersvej 7E
9220 Aalborg Ø, Denmark
Email: {luca,annai}@iesd.auc.dk

Abstract. Fokkink ((1994) *Inf. Process. Lett.* **52**: 333–337) has recently proposed a complete equational axiomatization of strong bisimulation equivalence for $MPA^*_\delta(A_\tau)$, i.e., the language obtained by extending Milner's basic CCS with prefix iteration. Prefix iteration is a variation on the original binary version of the Kleene star operation p^*q obtained by restricting the first argument to be an atomic action. In this paper, we extend Fokkink's results to a setting with the unobservable action τ by giving a complete equational axiomatization of Milner's observation congruence over $MPA^*_\delta(A_\tau)$. The axiomatization is obtained by extending Fokkink's axiom system with two of Milner's standard τ-laws, and three equations that describe the interplay between the silent nature of τ and prefix iteration. Using a technique due to Groote, we also show that the resulting axiomatization is ω-complete, i.e., complete for equality of open terms.

1 Introduction

The research literature on process theory has recently witnessed a resurgence of interest in the study of Kleene star-like operations (cf., e.g., the papers [10, 3, 7, 6, 18, 5, 9]). Some of these papers, notably [3], have studied the expressive power of variations on standard process description languages in which infinite behaviours are defined by means of Kleene's star operation [13] rather than by means of systems of recursion equations. Some others (see, e.g., [10, 18, 7, 8, 9]) have investigated the possibility of giving finite equational axiomatizations of bisimulation-like equivalences [16] over simple process algebras that include variations on Kleene's star operation. De Nicola and his co-workers have instead focused on the study of tree-based models for what they call "nondeterministic Kleene algebras", and on the proof systems these models support to reason about regular expressions and more expressive languages built on top of those; see, e.g., [6, 5] for details on this line of research.

---

* On leave from the School of Cognitive and Computing Sciences, University of Sussex, Brighton BN1 9QH, UK. Partially supported by HCM project EXPRESS.

** Basic Research in Computer Science, Centre of the Danish National Research Foundation.

This paper aims at giving a contribution to the study of complete equational axiomatizations for Kleene star-like operations from the point of view of process theory. Our starting point is the work presented in [7]. In that reference, Fokkink has proposed a complete equational axiomatization of strong bisimulation equivalence for $\mathrm{MPA}^*_\delta(A_\tau)$, i.e., the language obtained by extending the fragment of Milner's CCS [15] containing the basic operations needed to express finite synchronization trees with prefix iteration. Prefix iteration is a variation on the original binary version of the Kleene star operation p^*q [13] obtained by restricting the first argument to be an atomic action. Intuitively, at any time the process term μ^*p can decide to perform action μ and evolve to itself, or an action from p, by which it exits the μ-loop. The behaviour of μ^*p is captured very clearly by the rules that give its Plotkin-style structural operational semantics:

$$\frac{}{\mu^*p \xrightarrow{\mu} \mu^*p} \qquad \frac{p \xrightarrow{\gamma} p'}{\mu^*p \xrightarrow{\gamma} p'}$$

As shown by Fokkink, such an operation can be completely characterized in strong bisimulation semantics by the following two natural laws:

$$\mu.(\mu^*x) + x = \mu^*x$$
$$\mu^*(\mu^*x) = \mu^*x$$

The reader familiar with Hennessy's work on complete axiomatizations for the delay operation of Milner's SCCS [12] will have noticed the similarity between the above laws and those presented *ibidem*. This is not surprising as such a delay operation is an instance of the prefix iteration construct studied by Fokkink.

In this paper, we extend Fokkink's results to a setting with the unobservable action τ by giving a complete equational axiomatization of Milner's observation congruence [15] over $\mathrm{MPA}^*_\delta(A_\tau)$. The axiomatization is obtained by extending Fokkink's axiom system with two of Milner's standard τ-laws and the following three laws that describe the interplay between the silent nature of τ and prefix iteration:

$$\tau.x = \tau^*x$$
$$a^*(x + \tau.y) = a^*(x + \tau.y + a.y)$$
$$\tau.(a^*x) = a^*(\tau.a^*x) \ .$$

The first of these equations was introduced in [3] under the name of *Fair Iteration Rule*, and expresses a fundamental property of observation congruence, namely the abstraction from τ-loops, that underlies the soundness of *Koomen's Fair Abstraction Rule* [4]. The other two equations are, to the best of our knowledge, new. They describe a rather subtle interplay between prefix iteration and τ, and will play a crucial role in the proof of our completeness theorem. Using a technique due to Groote [11], we also show that the resulting axiomatization is ω-complete, i.e., complete for equality of open terms over the signature of $\mathrm{MPA}^*_\delta(A_\tau)$.

The paper is organized as follows. Section 2 introduces the language of minimal process algebra with prefix iteration, $\mathrm{MPA}^*_\delta(A_\tau)$, and its operational semantics. In that section we also review the definition of observation congruence, and present several properties of this relation that will be used in the remainder of the paper.

The set of equations that will be shown to completely characterize observation congruence over $\mathrm{MPA}_\delta^*(A_\tau)$ is analyzed in Sect. 3. A detailed proof of the completeness of our axiom system with respect to observation congruence over $\mathrm{MPA}_\delta^*(A_\tau)$ is given in Sect. 4. The structure of the proof the completeness theorem (Thm. 16) follows standard lines in the process algebra literature and bears strong connections with the proofs of results in Hennessy's paper [12]. The details, however, are very different and rather involved. Finally, we prove in Sect. 5 that our axiomatization is also strong enough to completely characterize observation congruence of open terms over the signature of $\mathrm{MPA}_\delta^*(A_\tau)$.

Acknowledgements: We are most grateful to Wan Fokkink for his careful proof-reading of [2] and for his support.

2 Minimal Process Algebra with Iteration

We assume a countably infinite set A of observable actions not containing the distinguished symbol τ. Following Milner [15], the symbol τ will be used to denote an internal, unobservable action of a system. We define $A_\tau \triangleq A \cup \{\tau\}$, and use a, b to range over A and μ, γ to range over A_τ. We also assume a countable set of process variables Var, ranged over by x, y, w, z.

The language $\mathrm{MPA}_\delta^*(A_\tau)$ of minimal process algebra with prefix iteration is given by the following BNF grammar:

$$P ::= x \mid \delta \mid \mu.P \mid P + P \mid \mu^*P$$

where $x \in$ Var and $\mu \in A_\tau$. We shall use P, Q, T (possibly subscripted and/or superscripted) to range over $\mathrm{MPA}_\delta^*(A_\tau)$. In writing terms over the above syntax, we shall always assume that the operations μ^* and $\mu.\_$ bind stronger than $+$. We shall use the symbol $\equiv$ to stand for syntactic equality of terms. The set of closed terms, i.e., terms that do not contain occurrences of process variables, generated by the above grammar will be denoted by $\mathrm{MPA}_\delta^*(A_\tau)$. We shall use p, q, r, t, u (possibly subscripted and/or superscripted) to range over $\mathrm{MPA}_\delta^*(A_\tau)$.

The operational semantics for the language $\mathrm{MPA}_\delta^*(A_\tau)$ is given by the labelled transition system [17] $(\mathrm{MPA}_\delta^*(A_\tau), \{ \overset{\mu}{\to} \mid \mu \in A_\tau \})$, where the transition relations $\overset{\mu}{\to}$ are the smallest subsets of $\mathrm{MPA}_\delta^*(A_\tau) \times \mathrm{MPA}_\delta^*(A_\tau)$ satisfying the rules in Fig. 1. We say that a term $p \in \mathrm{MPA}_\delta^*(A_\tau)$ is *stable* iff $p \overset{\tau}{\to} q$ for no $q \in \mathrm{MPA}_\delta^*(A_\tau)$.

$$\frac{}{\mu.p \overset{\mu}{\to} p} \qquad \frac{p \overset{\mu}{\to} p'}{p+q \overset{\mu}{\to} p'} \qquad \frac{q \overset{\mu}{\to} q'}{p+q \overset{\mu}{\to} q'}$$

$$\frac{}{\mu^*p \overset{\mu}{\to} \mu^*p} \qquad \frac{p \overset{\mu}{\to} p'}{\gamma^*p \overset{\tau}{\to} p'}$$

Fig. 1. Transition Rules for $\mathrm{MPA}_\delta^*(A_\tau)$

Following Milner [15], we shall use $\hat{\mu}$ to stand for ε if $\mu = \tau$, and for μ otherwise. The derived transition relations $\overset{s}{\Rightarrow}$ and $\overset{\mu}{\Rightarrow}$ are defined in the standard way as follows:

$p \overset{s}{\Rightarrow} q \Leftrightarrow p \overset{\tau}{\rightarrow}^* q$, where $\overset{\tau}{\rightarrow}^*$ stands for the reflexive, transitive closure of $\overset{\tau}{\rightarrow}$

$p \overset{\mu}{\Rightarrow} q \Leftrightarrow \exists p_1, p_2 : p \overset{s}{\Rightarrow} p_1 \overset{\mu}{\rightarrow} p_2 \overset{s}{\Rightarrow} q$.

The notion of equivalence over process terms in $\mathrm{MPA}^*_\delta(A_\tau)$ that will be considered in this study is that of observation congruence [15]. This we now proceed to define for the sake of completeness.

Definition 1. A binary relation $\mathcal{R}$ over $\mathrm{MPA}^*_\delta(A_\tau)$ is a *bisimulation* iff it is symmetric and, whenever $p \, \mathcal{R} \, q$,

if $p \overset{\mu}{\rightarrow} p'$ then $q \overset{\hat{\mu}}{\Rightarrow} q'$ for some q' such that $p' \, \mathcal{R} \, q'$.

Two process terms p, q are *observation equivalent*, denoted by $p \approx q$, iff there exists a bisimulation $\mathcal{R}$ such that $p \, \mathcal{R} \, q$.

As it is well-known [15], $\approx$ is an equivalence relation over $\mathrm{MPA}^*_\delta(A_\tau)$. However, for the standard reasons explained at length in, e.g., Milner's textbook [15], observation equivalence is not a congruence with respect to the summation operation of $\mathrm{MPA}^*_\delta(A_\tau)$. In fact, it is also the case that $\approx$ is *not* preserved by the prefix iteration operation. As a simple example of this phenomenon, consider the terms $b.\delta$ and $\tau.b.\delta$. As it is well-known, $b.\delta \approx \tau.b.\delta$; however, it is not difficult to check that $a^*(b.\delta) \not\approx a^*(\tau.b.\delta)$. The largest congruence over $\mathrm{MPA}^*_\delta(A_\tau)$ contained in $\approx$, denoted by $\approx^c$, will be referred to as *observation congruence*. The following standard characterization of $\approx^c$ will be useful in what follows. The interested reader is invited to consult [15, Chapter 7] for details.

Fact 2 *For all $p, q \in \mathrm{MPA}^*_\delta(A_\tau)$, $p \approx^c q$ iff for all $\mu \in A_\tau$,*

1. *if $p \overset{\mu}{\rightarrow} p'$, then $q \overset{\mu}{\Rightarrow} q'$ for some q' such that $p' \approx q'$;*
2. *if $q \overset{\mu}{\rightarrow} q'$, then $p \overset{\mu}{\Rightarrow} p'$ for some p' such that $p' \approx q'$.*

Observation congruence can be naturally extended to open terms as follows:

Definition 3. For all $P, Q \in \mathrm{MPA}^*_\delta(A_\tau)$, $P \approx^c Q$ iff $P\sigma \approx^c Q\sigma$ for every substitution $\sigma : \mathrm{Var} \rightarrow \mathrm{MPA}^*_\delta(A_\tau)$.

In the remainder of this paper, we shall make use of several basic properties of the relations of observation congruence and observation equivalence that may be found in [15, Chapter 7]. For ease of reference, we collect these properties in the following lemma.

Lemma 4. *For every $p, q \in \mathrm{MPA}^*_\delta(A_\tau)$, the following statements hold:*

1. [HENNESSY'S THEOREM] *$p \approx q$ iff $p \approx^c q$ or $\tau.p \approx^c q$ or $p \approx^c \tau.q$.*
2. *$p \approx q$ implies $\mu.p \approx^c \mu.q$, for all $\mu \in A_\tau$.*
3. *If $p \approx q$ and p, q are stable, then $p \approx^c q$.*

The following result about the expressiveness of the language $\mathrm{MPA}^*_\delta(A_\tau)$ will be useful in the proof of the main result of this paper. We present it in this extended abstract for its intrinsic interest, albeit it will not be used in the fragment of the proof of Thm. 16 we detail.

Proposition 5. *For all* $p, q \in \mathrm{MPA}^*_\delta(A_\tau)$, $a, b \in \mathsf{Act}$, $a^*p \approx b^*q$ *implies* $a = b$.

3   Axiomatization and Soundness

The main aim of this study is to provide a complete equational axiomatization of the relation of observation congruence over the language $\mathrm{MPA}^*_\delta(A_\tau)$. In this section, we present the axiom system that will be shown to completely characterize observation congruence over the language $\mathrm{MPA}^*_\delta(A_\tau)$, and establish its soundness.

Consider the set $\mathcal{E}$ of equations in Fig. 3. This axiom system contains all of the equational theory $\mathcal{F}$ in Fig. 2. Apart from the law

$$\tau^*(\tau^*x) = \tau^*x$$

which is derivable in the presence of the other equations, the axiom system $\mathcal{F}$ is the one that was shown in [7] to characterize strong bisimulation over $\mathrm{MPA}^*_\delta(A_\tau)$. In addition, the axiom system $\mathcal{E}$ includes equations which express the unobservable nature of the τ action. Two of these laws, namely (T1) and (T3), are well-known from the theory of observation congruence over CCS-like languages (cf., e.g., [15]). The remaining three laws, namely (FIR) and (MT1)-(MT2), describe the interplay between τ and prefix iteration. Equation (FIR) was introduced in [3] under the name of (FIR$_1$) (*Fair Iteration Rule*). In [3] it is also noted that this law is an equational formulation of *Koomen's Fair Abstraction Rule* [4][3]. Together with the laws in the axiom system $\mathcal{F}$, this equation can be used to derive, for instance, Milner's second τ-law, namely

$$\mathrm{T2} \qquad \tau.x = \tau.x + x \ .$$

Equations (MT1)–(MT2) are, to the best of our knowledge, new. They express a rather subtle interplay between prefix iteration and τ, and will play a crucial role in reducing terms to normal forms (cf. Lem. 14) and in our completeness proof, respectively.

Notation 6 *We write* $\mathcal{E} \vdash P = Q$ *iff the equation* $P = Q$ *is provable from the axiom system* $\mathcal{E}$ *using the rules of equational logic. We also write* $P =_{AC} Q$ *iff the terms* P, Q *are identical modulo commutativity and associativity of* $+$, *i.e., iff the equality* $P = Q$ *can be proved from the equations* (A1)-(A2).

First of all, we establish the soundness of the axiom system $\mathcal{E}$.

Proposition 7. *For all* $P, Q \in \mathrm{MPA}^*_\delta(A_\tau)$, $\mathcal{E} \vdash P = Q$ *implies* $P \approx^c Q$.

---

[3] To be precise, Koomen's Fair Abstraction Rule is a general name for a family of proof rules KFAR$_n$, $n \geq 1$. FIR corresponds to KFAR$_1$.

$$
\begin{array}{ll}
\text{A1} & x + y = y + x \\
\text{A2} & (x + y) + z = x + (y + z) \\
\text{A3} & x + x = x \\
\text{A4} & x + \delta = x \\
\text{MI1} & \mu.(\mu^*x) + x = \mu^*x \\
\text{MI2} & a^*(a^*x) = a^*x
\end{array}
$$

Fig. 2. Fokkink's axiom system $\mathcal{F}$

$$
\begin{array}{ll}
\text{T1} & \mu.\tau.x = \mu.x \\
\text{T3} & a.(x + \tau.y) = a.(x + \tau.y) + a.y \\
\text{FIR} & \tau.x = \tau^*x \\
\text{MT1} & a^*(x + \tau.y) = a^*(x + \tau.y + a.y) \\
\text{MT2} & \tau.(a^*x) = a^*\bigl(\tau.(a^*x)\bigr)
\end{array}
$$

Fig. 3. The axiom system $\mathcal{E}$ is $\mathcal{F}$ plus the above equations

We conclude this section by addressing the issue of the irredundancy of the axiom system $\mathcal{E}$. We recall that a collection $\mathcal{T}$ of equations is said to be *irredundant* iff for every proper subset $\mathcal{T}'$ of $\mathcal{T}$, there exists an equation which is derivable from $\mathcal{T}$, but not from $\mathcal{T}'$.

Proposition 8. *The axiom system $\mathcal{E}$ is irredundant.*

4 Completeness

This section is entirely devoted to a detailed proof of the completeness of the axiom system $\mathcal{E}$ with respect to observation congruence over the language $\mathrm{MPA}^*_\delta(A_\tau)$. Before tackling the proof of completeness, we present several intermediate results that will be most useful in the technical developments to follow.

The following lemma is a standard tool in proofs of completeness theorems for process algebras (cf., e.g., [12, 15]), and we shall use it heavily in the proof of our main result.

Lemma 9. *For all $p, q \in \mathrm{MPA}^*_\delta(A_\tau)$, $\mu \in A_\tau$, if $p \overset{\mu}{\Rightarrow} q$ then $\mathcal{E} \vdash p = p + \mu.q$.*

We now establish a decomposition property of prefix iteration with respect to the relation of observation congruence that will find application in the main result of this paper. A similar decomposition property for the delay operation of Milner's SCCS with respect to a notion of strong bisimulation preorder was, to our knowledge, first shown by Hennessy in [12].

Definition 10. A term p is said to be *initially μ-saturated* iff for all $q \in \mathrm{MPA}^*_\delta(A_\tau)$, $p \overset{\mu}{\Rightarrow} q$ implies $p \overset{\mu}{\to} q$.

Lemma 11. Let $p, q \in \mathrm{MPA}^*_\delta(A_\tau)$ and $\mu \in A_\tau$. Suppose that $\mu^* p$ and $\mu^* q$ are both initially μ-saturated. Then $\mu^* p \approx^c \mu^* q$ iff $\mu^* p \approx^c q$ or $p \approx^c \mu^* q$ or $p \approx^c q$.

It is interesting to note that the above lemma does *not* hold for terms that are not initially μ-saturated. Consider, for example, the terms $p \equiv a^*(\tau.\delta + a.\delta)$ and $q \equiv a^*(\tau.\delta)$. It is not hard to see that $p \approx^c q$. However, none of the possible decompositions of this equality afforded by Lem. 11 applies. Note that q is not initially a-saturated, whereas p is. The rôle of axiom (MT1) in the completeness proof is to make sure that every sub-term of the form $a^* t$ of a normal form be initially a-saturated. This will allow us to use Lem. 11 to reason about equalities between such terms.

The proof of the completeness theorem relies, as usual, on the isolation of some notion of normal form for terms. This is introduced in the following definition.

Definition 12. A term $p \in \mathrm{MPA}^*_\delta(A_\tau)$ is τ^*-*free* iff it does not contain occurrences of the τ^* operation.

A τ^*-free term p is a *normal form* iff every sub-term of p of the form $a^* q$ is initially a-saturated.

For example, the term $a^*(\tau.\delta + a.\delta)$ is a normal form, while $a^*(\tau.\delta)$ is not.

The following result collects some elementary, but extremely useful, properties of normal forms that we state for the sake of clarity.

Fact 13 Let $p \in \mathrm{MPA}^*_\delta(A_\tau)$ be a normal form. Then:

1. Every sub-term of p is also a normal form.
2. For every $q \in \mathrm{MPA}^*_\delta(A_\tau)$, $\mu \in A_\tau$, if $p \overset{\mu}{\to} q$, then q is a normal form.

We now show that, using the axiom system $\mathcal{E}$, every term is provably equal to a normal form. Not surprisingly, axioms (FIR) and (MT1) play a vital role in the proof of the following result.

Lemma 14. For every $p \in \mathrm{MPA}^*_\delta(A_\tau)$ there exists a normal form $\mathrm{nf}(p)$ such that $\mathcal{E} \vdash p = \mathrm{nf}(p)$.

For example, the normal form associated with the term $a^*(\tau.\delta)$ is, modulo $=_{AC}$, the term $a^*(\tau.\delta + a.\delta)$.

In the proof of the completeness result to come, we shall make use of a weight function on terms $w : \mathrm{MPA}^*_\delta(A_\tau) \to \mathbb{N}$. This is defined by structural recursion on terms as follows:

$$w(\delta) = 1$$
$$w(\mu.p) = 1 + w(p)$$
$$w(p + q) = 1 + w(p) + w(q)$$
$$w(\mu^* p) = 2 + w(p)$$

The following lemma collects some basic facts about the interplay between the above weight function and the operational semantics for processes.

Lemma 15. For all $p, q \in \mathrm{MPA}^*_\delta(A_\tau)$, the following statements hold:

1. *for every* $\mu \in A_\tau$, $p \xrightarrow{\mu} q$ *implies* $w(q) \leq w(p)$;
2. *if p is τ^*-free and* $p \xrightarrow{\tau} q$, *then* $w(q) < w(p)$;
3. *if* $p \xrightarrow{\mu} q$ *and* $w(q) + 1 = w(p)$, *then* $p \equiv \mu.q$;
4. *if* $p \xrightarrow{\mu} q$ *and* $w(p) = w(q)$, *then* $p \equiv q \equiv \mu^*r$ *for some* $r \in \mathrm{MPA}^*_\delta(A_\tau)$;
5. *if* $p \equiv a^*t \xrightarrow{a} q$ *and* $w(q) + 2 > w(p)$, *then* $p \equiv q$.

We are now in a position to prove our main result of the paper, namely that the set of equations $\mathcal{E}$ in Fig. 3 is complete with respect to $\approx^c$ over the language $\mathrm{MPA}^*_\delta(A_\tau)$. This is the import of the following result. Unfortunately, the proof of the completeness theorem is combinatorial in nature and consists of the examination of a fairly large number of cases. For this reason, we have chosen to present the proof in a structured style following the spirit, albeit not the letter, of the proposal in [14]. We hope that this type of presentation will help the reader judge the correctness of the proof, in much the same way as it has helped us convince ourselves that the proof is, to the best of our knowledge, correct.

Theorem 16. *For all $p, q \in \mathrm{MPA}^*_\delta(A_\tau)$, $p \approx^c q$ implies $\mathcal{E} \vdash p = q$.*

Proof. In view of Lem. 14, it is sufficient to prove the claim for normal forms in $\mathrm{MPA}^*_\delta(A_\tau)$. In fact, it is even sufficient to prove that

$$\text{for all normal forms } p, q \in \mathrm{MPA}^*_\delta(A_\tau), \ p \approx^c p + q \text{ implies } \mathcal{E} \vdash p = p + q \ . \quad (1)$$

In fact, let us assume that we have established the above claim and that p and q are normal forms such that $p \approx^c q$. For such terms, both the equivalences $p \approx^c p + q$ and $q \approx^c q + p$ hold. Then claim (1) and (A1) give $\mathcal{E} \vdash p = p + q = q + p = q$, and we are done.

We now proceed to prove (1). The proof proceeds by complete induction on $w(p) + w(q)$. Let us assume, as inductive hypothesis, that p, q are normal forms in $\mathrm{MPA}^*_\delta(A_\tau)$, that $p \approx^c p + q$ and that (1) holds for all pairs of normal forms $p', q' \in \mathrm{MPA}^*_\delta(A_\tau)$ such that $p' \approx^c p' + q'$ and $w(p') + w(q') < w(p) + w(q)$. We show that, under these assumptions, $\mathcal{E} \vdash p = p + q$. Note that, by a reasoning similar to the one in the previous paragraph, the inductive hypothesis gives that, for all normal forms $p', q' \in \mathrm{MPA}^*_\delta(A_\tau)$:

$$p' \approx^c q' \text{ and } w(p') + w(q') < w(p) + w(q) \ \Rightarrow \ \mathcal{E} \vdash p' = q' \ . \quad (2)$$

We shall make use of the above fact repeatedly in the proof below. The proof of (1) proceeds by a case analysis on the form q takes. For lack of space, we shall only present the detailed proof for the case $q \equiv a^*r$, for some normal form r. (The complete proof may be found in full detail in [2].) Throughout the proof, we shall make repeated use, without further mention, of the fact that, by Fact 13, the set of normal forms is closed under transitions and taking sub-terms. The following equation, which may be derived using MI1 and T3, will also be useful:

$$\text{MT3} \ a^*(x + \tau.y) = a^*(x + \tau.y) + a.y$$

– CASE: $q \equiv a^*r$.

First of all, let us note that, as $p \approx^c p + q$ and $q \equiv a^*r$, it follows that:

$$p \approx^c p + r \ . \tag{3}$$

In fact,

$$p \approx^c p + a^*r$$
$$\approx^c p + a^*r + r$$
$$\approx^c p + r$$

As $w(r) < w(q)$, we may apply the inductive hypothesis to (3) to derive that:

$$\mathcal{E} \vdash p = p + r \ . \tag{4}$$

We shall repeatedly make use of this fact to show that $\mathcal{E} \vdash p = p + a^*r$. As $p \approx^c p + a^*r$ and $p + a^*r \xrightarrow{a} a^*r$, there exists a term p' such that:

$$p \xrightarrow{a} p' \text{ and } p' \approx a^*r \ . \tag{5}$$

By Lem. 4(1), $p' \approx a^*r$ implies

$$p' \approx^c a^*r \text{ or } \tau.p' \approx^c a^*r \text{ or } p' \approx^c \tau.a^*r \ . \tag{6}$$

We now proceed by examining the relationship between $w(p')$ and $w(p)$. We know, by Lem. 15(1), that $w(p') \leq w(p)$. We consider two possibilities, depending on whether $w(p') + 2 \leq w(p)$ or not.

1. CASE: $w(p') + 2 \leq w(p)$.

   In this case, we may apply (2) to each of the disjuncts in (6) to obtain that:

   $$\mathcal{E} \vdash p' = a^*r \text{ or } \mathcal{E} \vdash \tau.p' = a^*r \text{ or } \mathcal{E} \vdash p' = \tau.a^*r \ .$$

   By possibly applying equation (T1), in each case we derive that:

   $$\mathcal{E} \vdash \tau.p' = \tau.a^*r \ . \tag{7}$$

   We now reason as follows:

   $$
   \begin{aligned}
   \mathcal{E} \vdash \quad p &= p + a.p' & &\text{(Lem. 9, as } p \xrightarrow{a} p') \\
   &= p + a.\tau.p' & &\text{(T1)} \\
   &= p + a.\tau.a^*r & &\text{(7)} \\
   &= p + a.a^*r & &\text{(T1)} \\
   &= p + r + a.a^*r & &\text{(4)} \\
   &= p + a^*r & &\text{(A1 and MI1)}
   \end{aligned}
   $$

   and we are done.

2. CASE: $w(p') + 2 > w(p)$.

   In this case, p must consist of a single summand, otherwise the a-transition leading from p to p' would have to discard other summands and $w(p') + 2 \leq w(p)$ would then follow. As $p \xrightarrow{a} p'$ by (5) and p is τ^*-free, such a p can only take one of the following forms:

   (a) $p \equiv \tau.t$ for some $t \in \mathrm{MPA}^*_\delta(A_\tau)$ such that $t \xrightarrow{a} p'$; or
   (b) $p \equiv a.t$ for some $t \in \mathrm{MPA}^*_\delta(A_\tau)$ such that $t \xrightarrow{\epsilon} p'$; or

(c) $p \equiv a^*t$ for some $t \in \mathrm{MPA}_\delta^*(A_\tau)$. Note that the case $p \equiv b^*t$ for some $b \neq a$ does not apply here. In fact, if $b \neq a$ and $p \equiv b^*t \stackrel{a}{\Rightarrow} p'$, it would have to be the case that $t \stackrel{a}{\Rightarrow} p'$. In this case, we would be able to infer that $w(p') + 2 \leq w(p)$ because $w(p') \leq w(t)$ and $w(t) + 2 = w(p)$.

We proceed by examining the three cases above separately.

(a) CASE: $p \equiv \tau.t$ for some t such that $t \stackrel{a}{\Rightarrow} p'$.

To proceed with the proof, note, first of all, that, as we are assuming that $w(p') + 2 > w(p)$, it can only be the case that $w(p') = w(t)$. In fact, if $w(p') < w(t)$, then

$$w(p') < w(t) \text{ and } w(t) + 1 = w(p)$$

would hold, i.e., $w(p') + 2 \leq w(p)$. Hence, let us assume that $w(p') = w(t)$. As $t \stackrel{a}{\Rightarrow} p'$, by Lem. 15(2) and Lem. 15(4), this is only possible if $t \equiv p' \equiv a^*t'$ for some $t' \in \mathrm{MPA}_\delta^*(A_\tau)$. Instantiating (6), we obtain that:

$$a^*t' \approx^c a^*r \text{ or } \tau.a^*t' \approx^c a^*r \text{ or } a^*t' \approx^c \tau.a^*r . \tag{8}$$

If $t \equiv a^*t' \approx^c a^*r$, then, as $w(t) < w(p)$, we may apply (2) to derive that

$$\mathcal{E} \vdash a^*t' = a^*r . \tag{9}$$

Thus:
$$\mathcal{E} \vdash \quad p \equiv \tau.a^*t' = \tau.a^*t' + a^*t' \ (\mathrm{T2})$$
$$= p + a^*r \qquad (9)$$

and we are done.

Otherwise, we have that $a^*t' \approx a^*r$, but $a^*t' \not\approx^c a^*r$. This can only be because either:

A.1 $t \equiv a^*t' \stackrel{\tau}{\rightarrow} t''$ for some $t'' \approx a^*r$ which is inequivalent to every τ-derivative of a^*r; or, symmetrically,

A.2 $a^*r \stackrel{\tau}{\rightarrow} r'$ for some $r' \approx a^*t' \equiv t$ which is inequivalent to every τ-derivative of $a^*t' \equiv t$.

We examine these two cases in turn.

A.1 CASE: $t \equiv a^*t' \stackrel{\tau}{\rightarrow} t''$ for some $t'' \approx a^*r$ which is inequivalent to every τ-derivative of a^*r.

As $a^*t' \stackrel{\tau}{\rightarrow} t''$, it must be the case that $t' \stackrel{\tau}{\rightarrow} t''$. Therefore, as t' is τ^*-free, Lem. 15(3) gives $w(t'') < w(t')$. Moreover,

$$w(t') + 2 = w(a^*t')$$
$$< w(p) \quad (p \equiv \tau.a^*t') .$$

As $t'' \approx a^*r$, it follows by Lem. 4(2) that

$$\tau.t'' \approx^c \tau.a^*r . \tag{10}$$

By the above considerations on the relationship between $w(t'')$ and $w(p)$, we may apply (2) to (10) to derive that

$$\mathcal{E} \vdash \tau.t'' = \tau.a^*r . \tag{11}$$

Therefore,

$$
\begin{aligned}
\mathcal{E} \vdash \quad p &= \tau.a^*t' && (p \equiv \tau.a^*t') \\
&= p + a^*t' && (\text{T2}) \\
&= p + a^*(t' + \tau.t'') && (\text{Lem. 9, as } t' \xrightarrow{\tau} t'') \\
&= p + a^*(t' + \tau.t'') + a.t'' && (\text{MT3}) \\
&= p + a.\tau.t'' && (\text{T1}) \\
&= p + a.\tau.a^*r && (11) \\
&= p + a.a^*r && (\text{T1}) \\
&= p + r + a.a^*r && (4) \\
&= p + a^*r && (\text{A1 and MI1})
\end{aligned}
$$

and we are done.

A.2 CASE: $a^*r \xrightarrow{\tau} r'$ for some $r' \approx a^*t' \equiv t$ which is inequivalent to every τ-derivative of $a^*t' \equiv t$.

As $a^*r \xrightarrow{\tau} r'$, it must be the case that $r \xrightarrow{\tau} r'$. Thus, reasoning as in the previous case, we may apply (2) to infer that, as $p \equiv \tau.a^*t' \approx^c \tau.r'$ and $w(r') + 2 < w(a^*r) = w(q)$,

$$
\mathcal{E} \vdash p = \tau.r' \ . \tag{12}
$$

We now reason as follows:

$$
\begin{aligned}
\mathcal{E} \vdash \quad p &= \tau.a^*t' && (p \equiv \tau.a^*t') \\
&= \tau.a^*t' + \tau.a^*t' && (\text{A3}) \\
&= \tau.a^*t' + a^*(\tau.a^*t') && (\text{MT2}) \\
&= p + a^*(p + r) && (p \equiv \tau.a^*t' \text{ and } (4)) \\
&= p + a^*(\tau.r' + r) && (12) \\
&= p + a^*r && (\text{Lem. 9, as } r \xrightarrow{\tau} r')
\end{aligned}
$$

and we are done.

The proof for this case is then complete.

(b) CASE: $p \equiv a.t$ for some $t \in \mathrm{MPA}^*_\delta(A_\tau)$ such that $t \xrightarrow{\varepsilon} p' \approx a^*r \equiv q$.

First of all, note that, as $p \approx^c p + r$ by (3), it must be the case that r is stable. Therefore, as $p' \approx a^*r$, any τ-transition from p' must be matched by a^*r standing still, i.e., by the transition $a^*r \xrightarrow{\varepsilon} a^*r$. As p' is τ^*-free and τ-transitions decrease the weight of τ^*-free terms, there exists a term p'' such that

$$
p' \xrightarrow{\varepsilon} p'' \text{ and } p'' \approx a^*r \text{ and } p'' \text{ is stable} \ .
$$

By Lem. 4(3), it follows that

$$
p'' \approx^c a^*r \ . \tag{13}
$$

As $w(p'') \le w(p') < w(p)$, we may now apply (2) to (13) to derive that:

$$
\mathcal{E} \vdash p'' = a^*r \ . \tag{14}
$$

Therefore,

$$
\begin{aligned}
\mathcal{E} \vdash \quad p &= p + a.p'' & \text{(Lem. 9, as } p \overset{a}{\Rightarrow} p'') \\
&= p + a.(a^*r) & (14) \\
&= p + r + a.(a^*r) & (4) \\
&= p + a^*r & \text{(A1 and MI1)}
\end{aligned}
$$

and we are done.

(c) CASE: $p \equiv a^*t$ for some $t \in \mathrm{MPA}^*_\delta(A_\tau)$ and $p \overset{a}{\Rightarrow} p' \approx a^*r$.

First of all, note that, as we are assuming that $w(p') + 2 > w(p)$, by Lem. 15(5) the transition $p \overset{a}{\Rightarrow} p'$ must in fact be of the form $p \equiv a^*t \overset{a}{\to} a^*t \equiv p'$. Thus $p \equiv a^*t \approx a^*r \equiv q$. Note further that, as $p \approx^c p + q$, any τ-transition emanating from $q \equiv a^*r$ must be matched by a τ-transition from $p \equiv a^*t$. If the converse is also true, then, in fact, $p \equiv a^*t \approx^c a^*r \equiv q$ holds. In this case, as p and q are normal forms and, a fortiori, initially a-saturated, we may apply Lem. 11, to derive that

$$
t \approx^c r \text{ or } a^*t \approx^c r \text{ or } t \approx^c a^*r \ .
$$

In each of the above cases, we may apply (2) to obtain that

$$
\mathcal{E} \vdash t = r \text{ or } \mathcal{E} \vdash t = a^*r \text{ or } \mathcal{E} \vdash a^*t = r \ .
$$

In each case, after possibly applying (MI2), we derive that

$$
\mathcal{E} \vdash p \equiv a^*t = a^*r \equiv q
$$

from which $\mathcal{E} \vdash p = p + q$ follows immediately by (A3).

Otherwise, $p \equiv a^*t \not\approx^c a^*r \equiv q$ because there exists a term t' such that $p \overset{\tau}{\to} t'$, $t' \approx q$ and t' is inequivalent to every τ-derivative of q. By applying Lem. 4(1) to $t' \approx a^*r$, we infer that

$$
t' \approx^c a^*r \text{ or } \tau.t' \approx^c a^*r \text{ or } t' \approx^c \tau.a^*r \ . \tag{15}
$$

Note now that, as $p \equiv a^*t \overset{\tau}{\to} t'$, it must be the case that $t \overset{\tau}{\to} t'$. As $w(t') + 3 \leq w(p)$, we may apply (2) to each one of the disjuncts in (15) to derive that:

$$
\mathcal{E} \vdash t' = a^*r \text{ or } \mathcal{E} \vdash \tau.t' = a^*r \text{ or } \mathcal{E} \vdash t' = \tau.a^*r \ .
$$

In each one of these cases, after possibly applying (T1), we have that

$$
\mathcal{E} \vdash \tau.t' = \tau.a^*r \ . \tag{16}
$$

Therefore,

$$
\begin{aligned}
\mathcal{E} \vdash \quad p &= a^*t & (p \equiv a^*t) \\
&= a^*(t + \tau.t') & \text{(Lem. 9, as } t \overset{\tau}{\to} t') \\
&= a^*(t + \tau.t') + a.t' & \text{(MT3)} \\
&= p + a.\tau.t' & \text{(T1)} \\
&= p + a.\tau.a^*r & (16) \\
&= p + a.a^*r & \text{(T1)} \\
&= p + r + a.a^*r & (4) \\
&= p + a^*r & \text{(A1 and MI1)}
\end{aligned}
$$

and we are done.

The proof for the case $q \equiv a^*r$ is now complete.

An alternative proof of the previous theorem can be given by reducing the completeness problem for observation congruence to that for branching congruence. This alternative argument is reported in [1], where a comparison between the two proof strategies may also be found.

5 ω-Completeness

In the previous section we showed that the equational theory $\mathcal{E}$ is complete with respect to observation congruence over the language $\mathrm{MPA}^*_\delta(A_\tau)$. We shall now prove that $\mathcal{E}$ is in fact ω-complete, i.e., that for all $P, Q \in \mathrm{MPA}^*_\delta(A_\tau)$,

$$P \approx^c Q \;\Rightarrow\; \mathcal{E} \vdash P = Q \;. \tag{17}$$

This we show by using a technique based on inverted substitutions which is due to Groote [11], and that can often be used to give elegant, model-independent proofs of ω-completeness results.

Before applying Groote's technique to prove (17), we outline its general ideas in the setting of this study. Assume that $P, Q \in \mathrm{MPA}^*_\delta(A_\tau)$ are observation congruent, i.e., that

for every substitution $\sigma : \mathrm{Var} \to \mathrm{MPA}^*_\delta(A_\tau)$, $P\sigma \approx^c Q\sigma$.

Theorem 16 then gives that, for every substitution $\sigma : \mathrm{Var} \to \mathrm{MPA}^*_\delta(A_\tau)$,

$$\mathcal{E} \vdash P\sigma = Q\sigma \;. \tag{18}$$

We show that (18) implies that:

$$\mathcal{E} \vdash P = Q \;. \tag{19}$$

The result presented by Groote in [11, Thm. 3.1] allows us to infer (19) from (18) provided we can find a substitution $\rho : \mathrm{Var} \to \mathrm{MPA}^*_\delta(A_\tau)$ and a function $R : \mathrm{MPA}^*_\delta(A_\tau) \to \mathrm{MPA}^*_\delta(A_\tau)$ satisfying the following conditions:

1. For $T \equiv P$ and $T \equiv Q$,
$$\mathcal{E} \vdash R(T\rho) = T \;. \tag{20}$$

2. For all $p_1, q_1 \in \mathrm{MPA}^*_\delta(A_\tau)$ and $\mu \in A_\tau$:
$$\mathcal{E} \cup \{p_1 = q_1, R(p_1) = R(q_1)\} \vdash R(\mu.p_1) = R(\mu.q_1) \tag{21}$$

and
$$\mathcal{E} \cup \{p_1 = q_1, R(p_1) = R(q_1)\} \vdash R(\mu^*p_1) = R(\mu^*q_1) \;. \tag{22}$$

3. For all $p_i, q_i \in \mathrm{MPA}^*_\delta(A_\tau)$ $(i = 1, 2)$:
$$\mathcal{E} \cup \{p_i = q_i, R(p_i) = R(q_i) \mid i = 1, 2\} \vdash R(p_1 + p_2) = R(q_1 + q_2) \;. \tag{23}$$

4. For each axiom $(P_1 = Q_1) \in \mathcal{E}$ and substitution $\sigma : \mathrm{Var} \to \mathrm{MPA}^*_\delta(A_\tau)$,
$$\mathcal{E} \vdash R(P_1\sigma) = R(Q_1\sigma) \;. \tag{24}$$

If for every pair of terms $P, Q \in \text{MPA}^*_\delta(A_\tau)$ for which (18) holds we may find such a ρ and R, then Thm. 3.1 in [11] gives that:

Theorem 17. $\mathcal{E}$ is ω-complete, i.e., for all $P, Q \in \text{MPA}^*_\delta(A_\tau)$, $P \approx^c Q$ implies $\mathcal{E} \vdash P = Q$.

Therefore, all we need to do to show the ω-completeness of our axiomatization is to devise appropriate functions ρ and R for each pair of observation congruent terms $P, Q \in \text{MPA}^*_\delta(A_\tau)$, and prove that conditions (20)–(24) are satisfied by them. This we now proceed to do.

Let $P, Q \in \text{MPA}^*_\delta(A_\tau)$ be terms for which (18) holds. We define $\rho : \text{Var} \to \text{MPA}^*_\delta(A_\tau)$ by:

$$\rho(x) \triangleq a_x.\delta \tag{25}$$

where, for each $x \in \text{Var}$, a_x is a distinguished action in A which occurs neither in P nor in Q. (Note that such an injective assignment of actions in A to variables can always be found because A is countably infinite and the set of actions occurring in P or Q is, of course, finite.) The function $R : \text{MPA}^*_\delta(A_\tau) \to \text{MPA}^*_\delta(A_\tau)$ is instead defined by structural recursion on closed terms as follows:

$$R(\delta) \triangleq \delta \tag{26}$$

$$R(\mu.p) \triangleq \begin{cases} x & \text{if } \mu = a_x \text{ for some } x \in \text{Var} \\ \mu.R(p) & \text{otherwise} \end{cases} \tag{27}$$

$$R(p + q) \triangleq R(p) + R(q) \tag{28}$$

$$R(\mu^* p) \triangleq \begin{cases} x + R(p) & \text{if } \mu = a_x \text{ for some } x \in \text{Var} \\ \mu^* R(p) & \text{otherwise} \end{cases} \tag{29}$$

Note that R is well-defined because the assignment of actions to variables is injective.

We now show that conditions (20)–(24) are met by such a ρ and R, thus establishing the ω-completeness of the equational theory $\mathcal{E}$.

Lemma 18. Statements (20)–(24) hold for ρ and R.

For each pair of observation congruent terms $P, Q \in \text{MPA}^*_\delta(A_\tau)$ we have thus shown how to construct mappings ρ and R that, by the above lemma, satisfy Groote's conditions (20)–(24). By Thm. 3.1 of [11], we have therefore proven Thm. 17.

References

1. L. ACETO, W. FOKKINK, R. VAN GLABBEEK, AND A. INGÓLFSDÓTTIR, *Axiomatizing prefix iteration with silent steps*, Research Report RS-95-56, BRICS (Basic Research in Computer Science, Centre of the Danish National Research Foundation), Department of Mathematics and Computer Science, Aalborg University, November 1995. To appear in *Information and Computation*. Available by anonymous ftp at the address ftp.brics.aau.dk in the directory pub/BRICS/RS/95/56.

2. L. ACETO AND A. INGÓLFSDÓTTIR, *A complete equational axiomatization for prefix iteration with silent steps*, Research Report RS-95-5, BRICS (Basic Research in Computer Science, Centre of the Danish National Research Foundation), Department of Mathematics and Computer Science, Aalborg University, Jan. 1995. Available by anonymous ftp at the address ftp.brics.aau.dk in the directory pub/BRICS/RS/95/5.

3. J. BERGSTRA, I. BETHKE, AND A. PONSE, *Process algebra with iteration and nesting*, Computer Journal, 37 (1994), pp. 243–258.

4. J. BERGSTRA AND J. KLOP, *Process algebra for synchronous communication*, Information and Computation, 60 (1984), pp. 109–137.

5. F. CORRADINI, R. DE NICOLA, AND A. LABELLA, *Fully abstract models for nondeterministic Kleene algebras (extended abstract)*, in Proceedings CONCUR 94, Philadelphia, PA, USA, I. Lee and S. Smolka, eds., vol. 962 of Lecture Notes in Computer Science, Springer-Verlag, 1995, pp. 130–144.

6. R. DE NICOLA AND A. LABELLA, *A completeness theorem for nondeterministic Kleene algebras*, in Proceedings of MFCS '94, vol. 841 of Lecture Notes in Computer Science, Springer-Verlag, 1994.

7. W. FOKKINK, *A complete equational axiomatization for prefix iteration*, Inf. Process. Lett., 52 (1994), pp. 333–337.

8. ——, *A complete axiomatization for prefix iteration in branching bisimulation*, Logic Group Preprint Series 126, Dept. of Philosophy, Utrecht University, Jan. 1995. To appear in *Fundamenta Informaticae*. Available by anonymous ftp from phil.ruu.nl as logic/PREPRINTS/preprint126.ps.

9. ——, *On the completeness of the equations for the Kleene star in bisimulation*, 1996. In this volume. A full version of the paper is available by anonymous ftp from phil.ruu.nl as logic/PREPRINTS/preprint141.ps.

10. W. FOKKINK AND H. ZANTEMA, *Basic process algebra with iteration: Completeness of its equational axioms*, Computer Journal, 37 (1994), pp. 259–267.

11. J.F. GROOTE, *A new strategy for proving ω–completeness with applications in process algebra*, in Proceedings CONCUR 90, Amsterdam, J. Baeten and J. Klop, eds., vol. 458 of Lecture Notes in Computer Science, Springer-Verlag, 1990, pp. 314–331.

12. M. HENNESSY, *A term model for synchronous processes*, Information and Control, 51 (1981), pp. 58–75.

13. S. KLEENE, *Representation of events in nerve nets and finite automata*, in Automata Studies, C. Shannon and J. McCarthy, eds., Princeton University Press, 1956, pp. 3–41.

14. L. LAMPORT, *How to write a proof*, Research Report 94, Digital Equipment Corporation, Systems Research Center, Feb. 1993.

15. R. MILNER, *Communication and Concurrency*, Prentice-Hall International, Englewood Cliffs, 1989.

16. D. PARK, *Concurrency and automata on infinite sequences*, in 5th GI Conference, Karlsruhe, Germany, P. Deussen, ed., vol. 104 of Lecture Notes in Computer Science, Springer-Verlag, 1981, pp. 167–183.

17. G. PLOTKIN, *A structural approach to operational semantics*, Report DAIMI FN-19, Computer Science Department, Aarhus University, 1981.

18. P. SEWELL, *Bisimulation is not finitely (first order) equationally axiomatisable*, in Proceedings 9th Annual Symposium on Logic in Computer Science, Paris, France, IEEE Computer Society Press, 1994, pp. 62–70.

Finite Axiom Systems for Testing Preorder and De Simone Process Languages

Irek Ulidowski*

Research Institute for Mathematical Sciences, Kyoto University, Japan.
Email: irek@kurims.kyoto-u.ac.jp.

Abstract. We propose a procedure for generating finite axiomatisations of testing preorder of De Nicola and Hennessy for De Simone process language. We also prove that testing preorder is preserved by all De Simone process operators. The usefulness of our results is illustrated in specification and verification of a (small) multi-media system. The important features of the system are suspension, resumption and alternation of execution of its components. We argue that the ability to use specially tailored De Simone operators allows to write clear and intuitive specifications. Moreover, the automatically generated axioms for such operators make the verification straightforward.

1 Introduction

Process languages, for example CCS of Milner and CSP of Hoare, together with their semantic theories are reasonably successful in specification and verification of concurrent systems. Both specifications, of varying level of abstractness, and the implementation of a given system are represented by processes—the terms in a process language. The task of proving that a more concrete specification refines an abstract one, and that the implementation meets some specification is then performed. There is a number of different proof methods which can be employed. One can define a denotational meaning of processes and then argue that the abstract specifications, concrete specifications and the implementation have increasingly better (in some sense) denotations. Alternatively, an operational preorder may be defined which relates the abstract with concrete specifications and the concrete specifications with the implementation. The third method, which is solely based on the syntax of processes, uses equational reasoning within some axiom system.

There are four major references [Hoa85, Mil89, Hen88, BW90], where somewhat different process languages and their theories were presented and where the above described approach to specification and verification was originated and developed. More recently, due to Plotkin style *structured operational semantics* (SOS) [Plo81], these process languages and their numerous extensions were generalized to whole classes of process languages. Moreover, the theories for

---

* On leave from the School of Computing, University of North London, England. This work was partially supported by a grant from The Nuffield Foundation.

these languages and specification and verification techniques were extended to apply to such classes of languages. For example, a number of important preorders and equivalences on processes were shown to be congruences for certain classes of languages [BIM88, GV90, Vaa91, Uli92, Blo93, Uli94]. Axiomatic systems and denotational models for certain classes were proposed in [ABV92, Ace94, Uli95a] and [AI95] respectively. Also, two classes of languages were used in [Blo95] as general specification languages.

This paper continues the research related to general process languages. We consider a class of process languages generated by the De Simone format with silent actions. This class, denoted by τDeS, was defined in [Uli95a]. Out of many preorders (equivalences) proposed in the concurrency literature we consider *testing preorder* of De Nicola and Hennessy [NH84, Hen88], which is based on an intuitive notion of comparing responses of processes to tests.

As our first contribution we argue that (a characterisation of) testing preorder is a precongruence for all τDeS languages. This result is vital in the verification as it allows to split a verification of a complex system into verification of its components. In this paper we employ equational reasoning as the method of proof for verification.

Since, in our specifications, we will use arbitrary τDeS operators we require a general procedure for deriving axioms for such operators. Our second contribution is such a procedure. It generates sound and complete axiomatisations of testing preorder for arbitrary τDeS languages. In contrast to axiomatisations of refusal simulation preorder for τDeS languages proposed in [Uli95a] the present axiomatisations are *finite*, except for one infinitary induction rule required for non-finite processes.

We support the argument of Bloom in [Blo95] that classes of process languages, where one can use any operators within the class, are more superior for specification purposes than the standard languages like CCS and CSP. This is because simpler and easier to understand specifications can be written using both newly invented, specially tailored operators and the standard operators. As our third contribution we present two specifications of a simple multi-media system, where *suspension* and *resumption* of execution is important. We give both abstract and concrete specifications. Equational reasoning based on axiomatisation generated by our procedure is then used to show that the specifications are equivalent.

The paper is organized as follows. We recall, in Section 2, the definitions of τDeS process languages, labelled transition systems and testing preorder. Also, we show that a characterisation of testing preorder is a precongruence for any τDeS language. In Section 3 we restate the completeness result for the basic language and testing preorder. Then, we present a procedure for generating sound and head normalising axiomatisations for τDeS language. Our completeness result concludes the section. In Section 4 we present an example illustrating the application of our results. The last section contains conclusions and a discussion of related work. Due to space limitations, all the proofs are omitted. They can be found in [Uli95b].

2 Basic Concepts

In this section we repeat the definitions of τDeS process languages, labelled transition systems and testing preorder. We also define other notions in order to make the paper self-contained. Full definitions and the results concerning the above can be found, for example, in [Uli95a, Uli92, NH84, Hen88].

Let Var be a countable set of variables ranged by $X, Y, \ldots$. A signature Σ is a set process operators (f, n), where $f \notin$ Var and $n \in \mathbb{N}$ is an arity of f. Often, when the arity is clear from the context, the operator is simply abbreviated by its name, for example f. The set of open terms over Σ with variables in V is denoted by $\mathbb{T}(\Sigma, V)$. $\mathbb{T}(\Sigma, \text{Var})$, abbreviated by $\mathbb{T}(\Sigma)$, is ranged by $P, Q, \ldots$. The set of closed terms $\mathbb{T}(\Sigma)$ is ranged by $p, q, t, \ldots$. A Σ context with n holes $C[X_1, \ldots, X_n]$ is a member of $\mathbb{T}(\Sigma, \{X_1, \ldots, X_n\})$ in which $X_i, 1 \leq i \leq n$, occurs at most once. If $t_1, \ldots, t_n$ are Σ terms then $C[t_1, \ldots, t_n]$ is a term obtained by substituting X_i by $t_i, 1 \leq i \leq n$. A preorder $\sqsubseteq$ on $\mathbb{T}(\Sigma)$ is a precongruence if for all Σ contexts $C[X]$ we have $t \sqsubseteq t'$ implies $C[t] \sqsubseteq C[t']$. In such a case we often say that $\sqsubseteq$ is preserved by all Σ operators (or contexts). A (closed) *substitution* ρ is a mapping from Var to $(\mathbb{T}(\Sigma))$ $\mathbb{T}(\Sigma)$. The substitution ρ extends to a mapping $\mathbb{T}(\Sigma) \to \mathbb{T}(\Sigma)$ in a standard way. We will write $Q[P_1/X_1, \ldots, P_n/X_n]$ to denote the substitution which assigns each X_i to P_i. Vis $\cup \{\tau\}$, ranged by $\alpha, \ldots$, is a countably infinite set of actions, where Vis consists of visible actions $a, b, \ldots$, and $\tau \notin$ Vis is a silent, internal action.

2.1 τDeS Languages and Labelled Transition Systems

The τDeS format is a modification of the original De Simone format [dS85] in which silent actions are treated as unobservable and independent of the environment actions.

Definition 1. [Uli95a] A De Simone rule for (f, n) has the following form:

$$\frac{\{ X_i \xrightarrow{a_i} X_i' \}_{i \in I}}{f(X_1, \ldots, X_n) \xrightarrow{\alpha} C[Y]} \tag{1}$$

where X_i, X_i' are all different variables and $I \subseteq \{1, \ldots, n\}$. $C[Y]$ contains at most the variables $Y_1, \ldots, Y_n$, where $Y_i = X_i'$ if $i \in I$ and $Y_i = X_i$ otherwise. f is the *operator* of the rule, α is the *action*, $X_i \xrightarrow{a_i} X_i'$ are the *antecedents* and $f(X_1, \ldots, X_n) \xrightarrow{\alpha} C[Y]$ is the *consequent*. The *trigger* of rule (1) is a n-tuple $(\lambda_1, \ldots, \lambda_n)$, where $\lambda_i = a_i$, if $i \in I$, and $\lambda_i = *$ otherwise. The α trigger for f is the trigger of one of De Simone rules for f with action α. We say that i-th argument of f is *active* if there is a De Simone rule for f with the antecedent $X_i \xrightarrow{a_i} X_i'$, for some a_i.

A τ-rule for the above rule is any of the following rules for $i \in I$:

$$\frac{X_i \xrightarrow{\tau} X_i'}{f(X_1, \ldots, X_i, \ldots, X_n) \xrightarrow{\tau} f(X_1, \ldots, X_i', \ldots, X_n)}$$

A set of all τ-rules for the operator f is called its set of *associated* τ-rules. A set of rules is in the De Simone format, written as τDeS, if it consists of De Simone rules and their associated τ-rules. A process operator is τDeS if the set of its defining rules is in τDeS. A τDeS process language is a triple $(\Sigma, \Lambda \cup \{\tau\}, R)$, where Σ is a finite set of operators, $\Lambda \subseteq_{fin}$ Vis and R is a finite set of τDeS rules.

We will need more notation. For $(f, n) \in \Sigma$, $active(f)$ is the set of all i such that the ith argument of f is active. Also, $trig_\alpha(f)$ is the set of all α triggers for f.

Most of the operators in process algebras are τDeS except, for example, the CCS and ACP choice operator + and the ACP left-merge and communication merge operators, which do not have the associated τ-rules.

Throughout this work we will use a basic τDeS language B which is essentially the language considered in [Hen88]. It has two choice operators $\boxplus$ and $\oplus$, the *external* and *internal* choice operators respectively, instead of the CCS choice operator + and prefixing with τ. B is a τDeS process language $(\Sigma, \Lambda \cup \{\tau\}, R)$, where $\Sigma = \{(\mathbf{0}, 0), (\Omega, 0)\} \cup \{(a, 1) \mid a \in \Lambda\} \cup \{(\boxplus, 2), (\oplus, 2)\}$, $\Lambda \subseteq_{fin}$ Vis and R is given below. As usual, $(\mathbf{0}, 0)$ and $(\Omega, 0)$, abbreviated by $\mathbf{0}$ and Ω, are the deadlocked and divergent process operators respectively. The precedence of operators is given by $a. > \boxplus > \oplus$.

$$a.X \xrightarrow{a} X \qquad X \oplus Y \xrightarrow{\tau} X \qquad X \oplus Y \xrightarrow{\tau} Y$$

$$\frac{X \xrightarrow{a} X'}{X \boxplus Y \xrightarrow{a} X'} \qquad \frac{Y \xrightarrow{a} Y'}{X \boxplus Y \xrightarrow{a} Y'} \qquad \frac{X \xrightarrow{\tau} X'}{X \boxplus Y \xrightarrow{\tau} X' \boxplus Y} \qquad \frac{Y \xrightarrow{\tau} Y'}{X \boxplus Y \xrightarrow{\tau} X \boxplus Y'}$$

Next, we introduce labelled transition systems.

Definition 2. Let $G = (\Sigma_G, \Lambda \cup \{\tau\}, R_G)$ be a τDeS language. The *labelled transition system with divergence* for G is a structure $(\mathrm{T}(\Sigma_G), \Lambda \cup \{\tau\}, \rightarrow_G, \uparrow_G)$, where $\mathrm{T}(\Sigma_G)$ is a set of *process terms* or *processes*, $\rightarrow_G \subseteq \mathrm{T}(\Sigma_G) \times \Lambda \cup \{\tau\} \times \mathrm{T}(\Sigma_G)$ is the unique *transition relation* generated by G^2 and $\uparrow_G \subseteq \mathrm{T}(\Sigma_G)$ is the (postfix) *divergence predicate*. $\uparrow_G$ is defined as the least relation satisfying $\Omega \uparrow_G$ if $\Omega \in \Sigma_G$, and $f(\mathbf{p}) \uparrow_G$, for any $f \in \Sigma_G$, if $p_i \uparrow_G$ for some active i-th argument of f.

We will often call this transition system the basic transition system for G, and omit the subscript G if it is clear from the context. A derived transition system which abstracts away silent actions is defined below.

Definition 3. Given the basic transition system for G a structure $(\mathrm{T}(\Sigma), \Lambda \cup \{\varepsilon\}, \Rightarrow, \Uparrow)$ is the *derived* transition system with divergence, where the the transition relation $\Rightarrow \subseteq \mathrm{T}(\Sigma) \times \Lambda \cup \{\varepsilon\} \times \mathrm{T}(\Sigma)$ and $\Uparrow \subseteq \mathrm{T}(\Sigma) \times \Lambda^*$ are as follows, where $\xrightarrow{\tau^*}$ is reflexive and transitive closure of $\xrightarrow{\tau}$,

$$p \xrightarrow{\varepsilon} q \equiv p \xrightarrow{\tau^*} q, \qquad \qquad p \xrightarrow{a} q \equiv p \xrightarrow{\tau^*} \xrightarrow{a} \xrightarrow{\tau^*} q,$$

$$p \Uparrow \varepsilon \equiv \exists q.(p \xrightarrow{\tau^*} q \wedge q \uparrow) \vee p \xrightarrow{\tau^\omega}, \qquad p \Uparrow as \equiv p \Uparrow \varepsilon \vee \exists q.(p \xrightarrow{a} q \wedge q \Uparrow s).$$

---

[2] Full details of the construction of transition relation for a process language defined by a general format of rules can be found in, for example, [BIM88, GV90].

We say 'p converges on s', written as $p{\Downarrow}s$, if $\neg\, p{\Uparrow}s$. We will use some standard notation: $p \xrightarrow{a} q$ for $(p,a,q) \in \rightarrow$, $p \xrightarrow{a}$ for $\exists q \in \mathrm{T}(\Sigma)$. $p \xrightarrow{a} q$ and if $t = a_1 \dots a_n \in \Lambda^*$ then we write $p \xrightarrow{t}$ for $p \xrightarrow{a_1} \dots \xrightarrow{a_n}$. Expressions $p \Rightarrow$ and $p \xRightarrow{s}$ are defined correspondingly as $p \xrightarrow{a}$ and $p \xrightarrow{t}$ respectively. Also, let $\mathcal{L}(p) \equiv \{s \mid p \xRightarrow{s}\}$ and $\mathcal{S}(p) \equiv \{a \mid p \xRightarrow{a}\}$.

B generates the basic transition system $B = (\mathrm{T}(\Sigma), \Lambda \cup \{\tau\}, \rightarrow, \uparrow)$. Note that all processes in $\mathrm{T}(\Sigma)$ are *finite*. We have $\Omega\uparrow$, $(p \boxplus q)\uparrow$ and $(q \boxplus p)\uparrow$ if $p\uparrow$. But, for example, *not* $(p \oplus q)\uparrow$ if $p\uparrow$. Given B the derived transition system $(\mathrm{T}(\Sigma), \Lambda \cup \{\tau\}, \Rightarrow, \Uparrow)$ can be defined. One can check that divergence predicate $\Uparrow$ is the least relation satisfying the following: $\Omega\Uparrow$ and if $p\Uparrow$ then $(p \boxplus q)\Uparrow$, $(q \boxplus p)\Uparrow$, $(p \oplus q)\Uparrow$ and $(q \oplus p)\Uparrow$.

2.2 Testing Preorder

Testing was introduced by De Nicola and Hennessy in [NH84, Hen88]. Testing preorder, the preorder based on testing, is defined in terms of the responses of processes to tests, which themselves are processes with the set of actions containing a *success* action w not in Vis. The responses of a process to a test are determined by observing the computations of a system consisting of the test 'applied' to the process.

In this paper, we will consider testing in τDeS languages which are certain disjoint extensions of B. (A τDeS language H is a *disjoint extension* of a τDeS language G, written as $G \le H$, if the signature and rules of H include those of G, and H introduces no new rule for the operators in G.) Let B_w be the disjoint extension of B with the prefixing operator $(w, 1)$ and let $B_w \le G$. Thus, processes are the terms over G which do not contain actions w and tests, varied by t, are the terms over G which contain w.

The application of a test t to a process p is expressed by $p \mid t$, where the 'application' operator $\mid$ is defined as follows. It is clear that $\mid$ is τDeS.

$$\frac{X \xrightarrow{a} X' \quad Y \xrightarrow{a} Y'}{X \mid Y \xrightarrow{\tau} X' \mid Y'} \qquad \frac{X \xrightarrow{\tau} X'}{X \mid Y \xrightarrow{\tau} X' \mid Y} \qquad \frac{Y \xrightarrow{\tau} Y'}{X \mid Y \xrightarrow{\tau} X \mid Y'}$$

Sequence $p_0 \mid t_0 \xrightarrow{\tau} p_1 \mid t_1 \dots \xrightarrow{\tau} p_k \mid t_k \dots$ is a *computation* if it is maximal, that is infinite or it is finite with last element $p_k \mid t_k$ such that $p_k \mid t_k \xrightarrow{\tau} p' \mid t'$ for no pair p', t'. When we consider testing for a τDeS language G we assume that $B_T \le G$, where B_T is the disjoint extension of B_w with the operator $\mid$.

Next, we restate the definitions of 'may satisfy' and 'must satisfy' relations and of testing preorder $\sqsubseteq$ from [NH84, Hen88].

Definition 4. For processes p, q and a test t,

1. $p\,\mathrm{may}\,q$ if $p \mid t \xrightarrow{\tau^*} p' \mid t'$ and $t' \xrightarrow{w}$,
2. $p\,\mathrm{must}\,q$ if whenever $(p \mid t =)p_0 \mid t_0 \xrightarrow{\tau} p_1 \mid t_1 \xrightarrow{\tau}$ is a computation then (a) $\exists n \ge 0$ such that $t_n \xrightarrow{w}$, and (b) if $(p_k \mid t_k)\uparrow$ then $t_{k'} \xrightarrow{w}$, for some $k' \le k$.

3. $p \subsetsim q$ if p may t implies q may t and p must t implies q must t, for all tests t.

Instead of working directly with $\subsetsim$, we will employ one of its alternative characterisations, namely $\ll$, as defined in [NH84, Hen88].

Definition 5. For $p, q \in T(\Sigma)$, let $p \ll q$ if

  1. $\mathcal{L}(p) \subseteq \mathcal{L}(q)$

  2. $\forall s \in \Lambda^*$. $p \Downarrow s$ implies $q \Downarrow s \wedge$

$$\forall q'. \ q \overset{s}{\Rightarrow} q' \text{ implies } \exists p'. \ p \overset{s}{\Rightarrow} p' \wedge \mathcal{S}(p') \subseteq \mathcal{S}(q').$$

Note that $\ll$ is defined somewhat differently in [Hen88] (Definition 4.4.5). The main difference is that instead of the last line of our definition the condition $\mathcal{A}(q, s) \subset\subset \mathcal{A}(p, s)$ is used in [Hen88]. We remind that $\mathcal{A}(q, s)$ is $\{\mathcal{S}(p') \mid p \overset{s}{\Rightarrow} p'\}$ and $\mathcal{A} \subset\subset \mathcal{B}$ if for every $A \in \mathcal{A}$ there is some $B \in \mathcal{B}$ such that $B \subseteq A$. A simple inspection shows that the last line in Definition 5 and $\mathcal{A}(q, s) \subset\subset \mathcal{A}(p, s)$ are logically equivalent.

It is easily checked that $\ll$ is a preorder. Testing equivalence, written as $\simeq$, is defined by $p \simeq q \equiv p \ll q \wedge q \ll p$.

Finally, we have a generalisation of a characterisation result from [Hen88].

Theorem 6. For processes p, q over G such that $B_T \leq G$, $p \subsetsim q$ iff $p \ll q$.

The theorem follows similarly as Lemma 4.4.9 and Lemma 4.4.13 in [Hen88]. Thus, this characterisation is language-independent provided that the considered language is at least as expressive as B_T and the labelled transition system for the language is finitely branching[3].

The next theorem is the foundation on which our results are based.

Theorem 7. $\ll$ is a precongruence for all τDeS process languages.

As an immediate consequence we deduce that $\subsetsim$ is a precongruence for all τDeS process languages which disjointly extend B_T.

In the rest of the paper we will need the following. We will use $\text{Test}(G)$ to denote the quotient algebra of elements of $T(\Sigma)$ factored by $\ll$ and write $\text{Test}(G) \vDash P \sqsubseteq Q$ to mean $\rho(P) \ll \rho(Q)$, for all P, Q and ρ over G. Since we will talk about axioms which are preserved by taking disjoint extensions of τDeS languages we will need $\text{TEST}(G)$: a class of all algebras $\text{Test}(G')$, where G' is a disjoint extension of G. $\text{TEST}(G) \vDash P \sqsubseteq Q$ has the expected meaning.

3 Finite Axioms Systems for τDeS Languages

In this section we show how to produce a sound and complete axiomatisation an arbitrary τDeS language. The strategy is as follows. Firstly, we propose a number of general and sound laws (axiom schemas) for arbitrary τDeS operators which

---

[3] This is valid since every τDeS language is also GSOS language and transition systems generated by GSOS languages are finitely branching [BIM88].

Fig. 1. Axiomatization of testing preorder.

$$X \boxplus 0 = X$$
$$X \boxplus X = X \qquad\qquad\qquad X \oplus X = X$$
$$X \boxplus Y = Y \boxplus X \qquad\qquad X \oplus Y = Y \oplus X$$
$$X \boxplus (Y \boxplus Z) = (X \boxplus Y) \boxplus Z \qquad X \oplus (Y \oplus Z) = (X \oplus Y) \oplus Z$$

$$a.X \boxplus a.Y = a.X \oplus a.Y$$
$$a.X \boxplus a.Y = a.(X \oplus Y) \qquad\qquad X \oplus Y \sqsubseteq X \boxplus Y$$

$$X \boxplus (Y \oplus Z) = (X \boxplus Y) \oplus (X \boxplus Z) \qquad \Omega \sqsubseteq X$$
$$X \oplus (Y \boxplus Z) = (X \oplus Y) \boxplus (X \oplus Z) \qquad X \boxplus \Omega \sqsubseteq X \oplus \Omega$$

are not members of the basic process language B. Then, given any τDeS language G we disjointly extend it with B and thus obtain G'. The instances of the above mentioned laws for all the operators of G' (which are not B operators) together with the axioms for B make up a sound axiomatisation of G'. For finite processes this axiomatisation is also complete. We prove this by showing that terms over G can be rewritten into terms in head normal form (over B) by using the axiom system. Hence, the problem of completeness for finite processes over G is reduced to the already known completeness result for B. In order to achieve completeness for arbitrary processes we introduce an infinitary induction rule.

We start by recalling the axiom system T for $\ll$ and B. T consists of equations and inequations given in Figure 1 as well as the usual properties of precongruences (for example, if $p \sqsubseteq q$ then $f(p) \sqsubseteq f(q)$, and $\Omega \sqsubseteq X$) as in [Hen88]. We will write $S \vdash P \sqsubseteq Q$, $(P = Q)$ to mean that $P \sqsubseteq Q$, $(P = Q)$ can be derived from the axiomatic theory S.

Lemma 8. [Hen88] $T \vdash P \sqsubseteq Q$ if and only if $\text{Test}(B) \vDash P \sqsubseteq Q$.

Since $\boxplus$ and $\oplus$ are associative we will use the following summation notations $\sum_{i \in I} X_i$ and $\bigoplus_{j \in J \neq \emptyset} Y_j$. Finally, following [Hen88] we define *head normal forms*, hnf for short. If A is a saturated set of subsets of Λ then $\bigoplus_{A \in \mathcal{A}} \sum_{a \in A} ap_a$ is in hnf, and if A is a subset of Λ then $\sum_{a \in A} ap_a \boxplus \Omega$ is in hnf. Hence, 0, Ω, $(ap \boxplus bq) \oplus cr$ and $ap \boxplus \Omega$ are in hnf but $(ap \boxplus \Omega) \oplus cr$ is not.

3.1 Deriving Head Normalising Axioms

This subsection introduces a number of *laws* which allow rewriting process terms into hnf. We define a procedure which uses these laws to generate axiomatisations of arbitrary τDeS languages. As an example of axiomatisations generated by our procedure we present finite axiom systems for the CSP hiding and the CCS parallel composition operators.

We will need to distinguish several subclasses of τDeS operators. A τ-DeS operator f is *distinctive* [ABV92], written as $D(f)$, if for each argument i either all non-τ-rules or none of them have an active ith argument, and also for each pair of different non-τ-rules for f there is an argument for which both rules have the same antecedents but with a different action. A τDeS operator f is τ-*introducing* (Vis-*introducing*, written as Vis(f)) if the action of one of its defining non-τ-rules is τ ($a \in$ Vis). Moreover, the relation $Cycle$, which identifies τ cycles of terms, will be used in the condition of the divergence laws. Let $Tau(f(\boldsymbol{P}), g(\boldsymbol{Q}))$ iff there is a τ-introducing rule r with the consequent $f(\boldsymbol{X}) \xrightarrow{\tau} C[\boldsymbol{Y}]$ and a substitution ρ such that $\rho(f(\boldsymbol{X}) \xrightarrow{\tau} C[\boldsymbol{Y}]) = f(\boldsymbol{P}) \xrightarrow{\tau} g(\boldsymbol{Q})$ and the antecedents of r are valid under ρ. Next, define $\leadsto_1 : \mathbb{T}(\Sigma_G) \times \mathbb{T}(\Sigma_G)$ as $f(\boldsymbol{P}) \leadsto_1 g(\boldsymbol{Q})$ iff $D(f)$, $D(g)$ and $Tau(f(\boldsymbol{P}), g(\boldsymbol{Q}))$. Finally, $Cycle(f(\boldsymbol{P})$ iff $f(\boldsymbol{P}) \leadsto_1^+ f(\boldsymbol{P})$.

Lemma 9. [Uli95a] (**Action Laws**). Let a τDeS language G be a disjoint extension of B. Let (f, n) be a distinctive operator of G with a rule of the form (1). Also assume $P_i \equiv a_i.X_i'$ for $i \in I$ and $P_i \equiv X_i$ otherwise. If $\alpha \in \Lambda$ then, for an appropriate $\boldsymbol{P}'$, we have

$$\mathsf{TEST}(G) \vDash f(\boldsymbol{P}) = \alpha.C[\boldsymbol{P}'] \tag{2}$$

else (i.e. f is τ-introducing), for some $\boldsymbol{P}'$, we have

$$\mathsf{TEST}(G) \vDash f(\boldsymbol{P}) = C[\boldsymbol{P}']. \tag{3}$$

(**Inaction Laws**). Let (f, n) be an operator of G such that for each rule for f of the form (1) there is an index $i \in I$ such that either $P_i \equiv \boldsymbol{0}$ or $P_i \equiv a.X_i'$, for some $a \neq a_i$. Then

$$\mathsf{TEST}(G) \vDash f(\boldsymbol{P}) = \boldsymbol{0}. \tag{4}$$

(**Divergence Laws**). Let (f, n) be an operator of G. Suppose there is a rule for f of the form (1) such that for some $i \in I$ we have $P_i \equiv \Omega$, and, for all other rules for f of the form $\dfrac{\{ X_i \xrightarrow{c_i} X_i' \}_{i \in I'}}{f(X_1,...,X_n) \xrightarrow{a} C'[\boldsymbol{Y}]}$, there is an index $i \in I'$ such that $P_i \equiv \boldsymbol{0}$, $P_i \equiv \Omega$ or $P_i \equiv a.X_i'$, for some $a \neq c_i$. Or, suppose $Cycle(f(\boldsymbol{P}))$. Then

$$\mathsf{TEST}(G) \vDash f(\boldsymbol{P}) \sqsubseteq \Omega. \tag{5}$$

Using law (5) we deduce $g \sqsubseteq \Omega$, where g is defined by $g \xrightarrow{\tau} g$. Consider h defined by $h \xrightarrow{\tau} h$ and $h \xrightarrow{a} h$. As h is not distinctive law (5) cannot be used to approximate its behaviour. After we introduce the distributivity laws and the laws for non-distinctive operators we will extend the definition of $Cycle$ so that the behaviour of terms like h can be deduced using law (5) and other laws.

Lemma 10. (**Distributivity over $\oplus$ laws**). Let a τDeS language G be a disjoint extension of B. Let (f, n) be an operator of G such that its ith argument is active. If $X_i \equiv X \oplus Y$ then

$$\mathsf{TEST}(G) \vDash f(\boldsymbol{X}) = f(\boldsymbol{X})[X/X_i] \oplus f(\boldsymbol{X})[Y/X_i]. \tag{6}$$

Notice that by left-to-right application of $\oplus$ laws and the derived axiom $X \boxplus \Omega = X \oplus \Omega$ a process $f(\boldsymbol{p})$ with active arguments in hnf can be rewritten as $\bigoplus_I f(\boldsymbol{p}_i)$, where all active components of each $\boldsymbol{p}_i$ are either Ω or of the form $\sum_A a.p_a$, where $A \subseteq \Lambda$. This suggests that the distributivity over $\boxplus$ laws need only be given for $f(\boldsymbol{X})$ with all active arguments of the form $\sum_A a.X_a$ or Ω. This is, as will be explained later, one of two reasons why our axiomatisations are finite. In contrast, the $\boxplus$ laws for refusal simulation preorder $\sqsubseteq_{RS}$ in [Uli95a] require that all active arguments have the form $\sum_A a.X_a$ or $\sum_A a.X_a \boxplus \Omega$, where A is a multiset of visible actions. The reason for this difference is that terms like $\sum_A a.X_a$ can be transformed to equivalent terms of the form $\sum_A a.Y_a$ by using the axiom system for $\ll$ but not by the axiom system for $\sqsubseteq_{RS}$.

We will use the following notation to express the form of active arguments in terms like $f(\boldsymbol{Y})$. Let $\boldsymbol{A}$ be an n-ary vector whose i-th element A_i is $*$ if $i \notin active(f)$ and it is $*$ or $A_i \subset \Lambda$ otherwise. Then, $\boldsymbol{AX}$ (as in $f(\boldsymbol{AX})$ below) denotes an n-ary vector of open terms such that its i-th element, written as $A_i \boldsymbol{X}_i$, is any term if $i \notin active(f)$. Otherwise $A_i \boldsymbol{X}_i$ is Ω if $A_i = *$ and $\sum_{a_j \in A_i} a_j.X_{ij}$ if $A_i \subset \Lambda$. In the last two cases we will write $(A_i \boldsymbol{X}_i)_j$ to denote Ω if $A_i = *$ and $a_j.X_{ij}$ otherwise. Moreover, given trigger χ we say $\chi \in \boldsymbol{A}$ or χ *fires* from $\boldsymbol{A}$ if whenever χ_i, the ith element of χ, is not $*$ then $A_i \neq *$ and $\chi_i \in A_i$. Also, let $\Omega(f(\boldsymbol{AX}))$ be true if one of the active arguments of $f(\boldsymbol{AX})$ is Ω.

Lemma 11. (Distributivity over $\boxplus$ laws) Let (f, n) be an operator of a τDeS language G which is a disjoint extension of B, and suppose that i is such that each rule for f has an antecedent X_i. Then the following laws are valid in TEST(G), where C_i^m denotes the minimal set:

$$f(\boldsymbol{AX}) = \sum_j f(\boldsymbol{AX})[(A_i \boldsymbol{X}_i)_j / A_i \boldsymbol{X}_i]$$

$$\text{if } \Omega(f(\boldsymbol{AX})) \vee$$
$$\neg\Omega(f(\boldsymbol{AX})) \wedge \forall \chi \in trig_\tau(f).\ \chi \notin \boldsymbol{A} \qquad (7)$$

$$f(\boldsymbol{AX}) = \sum_{A_i} f(\boldsymbol{AX})[a_j.X_{ij}/A_i \boldsymbol{X}_i] \oplus \bigoplus_{C_i^m} f(\boldsymbol{AX})[c_j.X_{ij}/A_i \boldsymbol{X}_i]$$

$$\text{if } \neg\Omega(f(\boldsymbol{AX})) \wedge trig_\tau(f) \neq \emptyset \wedge$$
$$\exists C_i^m \subseteq A_i, \forall \chi \in trig_\tau(f).\ \text{if } \chi \in \boldsymbol{A} \text{ then } \chi \in \boldsymbol{A}[C_i^m/A_i]) \qquad (8)$$

Next, we briefly explain the syntactic conditions of the laws. The condition for law (7) is clear: one of the active arguments is Ω, or none of the active arguments is Ω and no τ triggers for f, if any, can fire from $\boldsymbol{A}$. The last two conjuncts of the condition for law (8) say that f is τ-introducing and there exists the minimal (non-empty) $C_i \subseteq A_i$ such that whenever any τ trigger for f can fire from $\boldsymbol{A}$ then it can fire from $\boldsymbol{A}[C_i/A_i]$.

We notice that there are only finitely many different instances of laws (7) and (8), up to a change of variable names. This is because there is only a finite

Fig. 2. Axioms for hiding.

$$(\sum_{b \in B} b.X_b) \backslash a = \sum_{b \in B} (b.X_b) \backslash a \qquad\qquad \text{if } a \notin B$$

$$(\sum_{b \in B} b.X_b \boxplus a.X) \backslash a = (\sum_{b \in B} (b.X_b) \backslash a \boxplus (a.X) \backslash a) \oplus (a.X) \backslash a \qquad \text{if } a \notin B$$

$$(X \oplus Y) \backslash a = X \backslash a \oplus Y \backslash a$$

$$(b.X) \backslash a = b.(X \backslash a) \qquad\qquad \text{if } b \neq a$$

$$(a.X) \backslash a = X \backslash a$$

$$0 \backslash a = 0$$

$$\Omega \backslash a \sqsubseteq \Omega$$

number of different A we can use in $f(AX)$: A_i is either $*$ or Ω or one of the subsets of (finite) Λ. Thus, laws (7) and (8) produce finite sets of axioms.

Next, consider the CSP hiding operator $\backslash a$ defined by the following rules:

$$\frac{X \xrightarrow{a} X'}{X \backslash a \xrightarrow{\tau} X' \backslash a} \qquad\qquad \frac{X \xrightarrow{b} X'}{X \backslash a \xrightarrow{b} X' \backslash a} \ b \neq a \qquad\qquad \frac{X \xrightarrow{\tau} X'}{X \backslash a \xrightarrow{\tau} X' \backslash a.}$$

Since $\backslash a$ is a distinctive operator it clearly satisfies the condition in Lemma 11. The axioms obtained by the last lemma are given in Figure 2. Note that the second axiom *does not* hold without the side condition. Each of the first two equations is an axiom schema but, as Λ is finite, it represents a finite set of axioms—one for each subset B of Λ. Hence, the axiomatisation is *finite*. Similarly, the axiomatisations of other distinctive operators, e.g restriction or renaming of CCS, will be finite.

The next lemma show how non-distinctive operators can be axiomatised. We use auxiliary distinctive operators which, as explained above, always have finite axiom systems. This is the second reason why our axiomatisations are finite.

Lemma 12. Let (f, n) be a non-distinctive operator of a τDeS language G which is a disjoint extension of B. Then there is a disjoint extension G' of G with (possibly zero) n-ary distinctive non-τ-introducing operators f_k, where $k \in K \subset_{fin} \mathbb{N}$, and (possibly zero) n-ary distinctive τ-introducing operators f^l, $l \in L \subset_{fin} \mathbb{N}$, such that G' is a τDeS language and the following laws hold in TEST(G):

$$f(AX) = \sum_K f_k(AX) \boxplus \sum_L f^l(AX)$$

$$\text{if } \Omega(f(AX)) \vee$$
$$\neg \Omega(f(AX)) \wedge \forall \chi \in trig_\tau(f). \ \chi \notin A \qquad\qquad (9)$$

$$f(AX) = (\sum_K f_k(AX) \boxplus \sum_L f^l(AX)) \oplus \bigoplus_N f^n(AX)$$

$$\text{if } \neg\Omega(f(\boldsymbol{AX})) \wedge \ trig_\tau(f) \neq \emptyset \wedge$$
$$\exists N \subseteq L, \forall \chi \in trig_\tau(f). \text{ if } \chi \in \boldsymbol{A} \text{ then } \exists n \in N.\chi \in trig_\tau(f^n) \ (10)$$

For the lack of space we cannot precisely describe how operators f_k and f^l are constructed, but in most cases the following method will work. Split the set of all non-τ-rules for f into subsets consisting of rules with the same active arguments. Call the subsets with non-τ-introducing rules R_k and let K be the set of all such k. Similarly, call the subsets of τ-introducing rules Q_l and let L be the set of all such l. Then, replace the operator symbol on the right side of the consequent in each of the sets R_k and Q_l with the symbol f_k and f^l respectively. Finally, add the required τ rules to each of the sets.

The condition of (9) is the same as the one for (7). The condition of (10) says that none of the active arguments of $f(\boldsymbol{AX})$ is Ω, f is τ-introducing and there exists a (non-empty since f is τ-introducing) subset N of L such that whenever a τ trigger for f fires from $\boldsymbol{A}$ then this trigger is a τ trigger for some $f^n, n \in N$. For the same reason as for laws (7) and (8), each of the laws (9) and (10) give rise to a finite set of instances. Thus, arbitrary non-distinctive τDeS operators have finite axiomatisations.

Next, we extend the definition of the relation $Cycle$. Let $L(f,g)$ iff f is τ-introducing and g is one of the τ-introducing f^i's generated for f by Lemma 12. We define $\leadsto_2, \leadsto_3$ over $\mathbb{T}(\Sigma_{G'}) \times \mathbb{T}(\Sigma_{G'})$, where G' is the disjoint extension of G obtained by applying Lemma 12 to all non-distinctive operators in Σ_G. Let $f(P) \leadsto_2 g(Q)$ iff either $D(f)$ and $Tau(f(P), g(Q))$ or $\neg D(f)$, $\neg\mathsf{Vis}(f)$, $L(f,g)$ and $P = Q$. Moreover, let $f(P) \leadsto_3 g(Q)$ iff either $f(P) \leadsto_i g(Q)$, for $i = 1, 2$, or $\neg D(f)$, $\mathsf{Vis}(f)$, $L(f,g)$ and $P = Q$. Finally, the extended version of $Cycle$ is

$$Cycle(f(P)) \text{ iff } f(P) \leadsto_1^+ f(P)$$
$$\vee \ (f(P) \leadsto_2^+ f(P) \wedge \exists g \in \Sigma_{G'}. \ L(g,f))$$
$$\vee \ (f(P) \leadsto_3^+ f(P) \wedge \exists g \in \Sigma_{G'}. \ L(g,f) \wedge \mathsf{Vis}(g)).$$

Now we can deduce $h \sqsubseteq a.h \boxplus \Omega$. Below, we give algorithm A for generating axiomatisations of $\ll$ for any τDeS language.

1. If G is not a disjoint extension of B then add disjointly to G a copy of B. Call the result G''.
2. For each operator $f \in \Sigma_{G''} \setminus \Sigma_B$ add to T, the axiom system for B, all the instances of law (6) and call the resulting system T''.
3. For each non-distinctive operator $f \in \Sigma_{G''} \setminus \Sigma_B$ apply the construction of Lemma 12 to obtain the resulting language G'. Add to T'' all the resulting instances of axioms (9) and (10) and call the resulting system T'.
4. For each distinctive operator $f \in \Sigma_{G''} \setminus \Sigma_B$ add to T' the following axioms: an action law (2) or (3) for each rule for f; all the inaction laws (4); all the divergence laws (5) (using the new version of $Cycle$); for each active argument of f the distributivity over $\boxplus$ laws (7)–(8). Call the resulting system T.

Theorem 13. Let G be a τDeS process language and G' be a disjoint extension of G produced by algorithm A. Moreover, let T be the axiom system produced by algorithm A. Then $\mathsf{TEST}(G) \models T$ and T is head normalising.

As an example of axiomatisation of a non-distinctive and τ-introducing operator we consider the CCS parallel composition operator $\|$. For this we assume that for each $a \in \Lambda$ we have $\bar{a} \in \Lambda$, and $\bar{\bar{a}} = a$ for all a. The auxiliary operators required by Lemma 12 are defined below (although their τ-rules are not listed). The operators are the left-merge, $\|$, the right-merge, $\|$, and the communication merge, $|$. Note that unlike their original versions in [BW90] the operators are τDeS, i.e. they have their associated τ-rules.

$$\frac{X \overset{a}{\to} X'}{X \| Y \overset{a}{\to} X' \| Y} \qquad \frac{Y \overset{a}{\to} Y'}{X \| Y \overset{a}{\to} X \| Y'} \qquad \frac{X \overset{a}{\to} X' \quad Y \overset{\bar{a}}{\to} Y'}{X | Y \overset{\tau}{\to} X' \| Y'}$$

Let AX and BY stand for $\sum_{a \in A} aX_a$ and $\sum_{b \in B} bX_b$ respectively, where $A, B \neq \emptyset$. Due to the lack of space we only give the two axioms for Ω-free processes. The axiomatisation of the CCS parallel is finite for the same reason as for hiding.

$$AX \| BY = AX \| BY \boxplus BY \| AX \boxplus AX | BY \qquad \text{if } A \cap \bar{B} = \emptyset$$
$$AX \| BY = AX \| BY \boxplus BY \| AX \oplus AX | BY \qquad \text{if } A \cap \bar{B} \neq \emptyset$$

3.2 Completeness

Algorithm A produces, for any τDeS language G, a disjoint extension G' with the axiom system T which allows conversion of process terms into hnf. If G is *well-founded*, i.e. all terms have finite derivations, then T is complete for $\ll$. This is because all the operators not in B can be eliminated from any term over G by applying the reduction to hnf a finite number of times.

In order to obtain the completeness result for non-well-founded languages we need the following infinitary conditional rule taken from [Uli95a]:

$$\frac{X/b^n\Omega \sqsubseteq Y/b^n\Omega \qquad \text{(for all } n)}{X \sqsubseteq Y} \tag{11}$$

where $b^n\Omega$ denotes $b \ldots b.\Omega$ with n occurrences of b and $\cdot/\cdot$ is the De Simone version of auxiliary operator defined in [ABV92]. For any τDeS language G let $G_/$ denote G extended with $\cdot/\cdot$.

Theorem 14. Let G be τDeS process language. Let G' and T denote the disjoint extension of $G_/$ and the axiom system for it produced by algorithm A respectively. Then for all $p, q \in \mathsf{T}(\Sigma_{G'})$ if $\mathsf{Test}(G') \vDash p \sqsubseteq q$ then $\mathsf{T}, (11) \vdash p \sqsubseteq q$.

The induction rule (11) is very strong and in many cases (for example, the systems to be discussed in the next section) a weaker form of induction would be sufficient. It is expected that for a suitably defined class of *regular* τDeS languages the techniques described in [Ace94], which do not rely on infinitary rules, would be applicable. Moreover, weaker but effective induction rules, for example those discussed in [Hen88], might be sufficient for some interesting subclasses of τDeS languages. This will be considered elsewhere.

4 Applications

The features of concurrent systems we will concentrate on are the interruption or abortion, suspension and resumption of activity of a system and the execution of two systems where the control alternates between the systems either by control seizing or control releasing actions.

Imagine a multi-media player which offers an interactive video performance. A viewer can *start* the performance, view the offered items, suspend and resume the performance by using the *pause* function and *choose* one of two alternatives. The viewer controls the player by a remote control, which has the buttons *start* (to start or restart the performance), *pause* and the buttons 1 and 2 for making a choice. We can specify the system by representing its states by the nullary operators, then we can define the transitions between the states by some τDeS rules and, finally, we can derive the equation(s) for the operators. However, we omit the details and only present the equations below. Let M and RC represent the multi-media player and the remote control systems respectively.

$$M = s.M'$$
$$M' = c_1.(c_2.M'' \boxplus M) \boxplus M$$
$$M'' = choice.(one.m_1 \boxplus two.m_2 \boxplus M) \boxplus M$$

$$RC = start.s.r.RC \boxplus pause.pause.RC \boxplus$$
$$1.one.r.RC \boxplus 2.two.r.RC$$

s is a signal of RC by which M starts the performance afresh and c_1, c_2 and m_1, m_2 stand for commercials and movies respectively. Actions *one* and *two* are choice signals and r is the actions by which RC returns the control to M.

M and RC make up subsystem P with the following intended behavior:

$$P = start.s.r.P' \boxplus pause.pause.P$$
$$P' = c_1.(c_2 P'' \boxplus P) \boxplus P$$
$$P'' = choice.(1.one.r.m_1 \boxplus 2.two.r.m_2 \boxplus P) \boxplus P$$

The whole system consists of viewer V together with M and RC. A concrete specification of the system could be $V \parallel_D op(M, RC)$, where $\parallel_D$ is parallel composition operator which requires synchronisation on actions in set $D = \{start, c_1, c_2, choice, 1, 2, pause, m_1, m_2\}$ and op is such that $op(M, RC)$ behaves as P above. Instead of defining a particular op we introduce a general operator $_{A})_{B})_C$ called *controlled parallel* composition, which has three parameters $A, B, C \subset_{fin} V$ is satisfying $(A \cup C) \cap B = \emptyset$. The defining rules are given below (but τ-rules are omitted). $_{A})_{B})_C$ binds weaker than the prefixing but stronger than the choice operators.

$$\frac{X \xrightarrow{a} X'}{X \,_{A})_{B})_C\, Y \xrightarrow{a} X' \,_{A})_{B})_C\, Y} \; a \notin A \qquad \frac{X \xrightarrow{a} X'}{X \,_{A})_{B})_C\, Y \xrightarrow{a} Y \,_{A})_{B})_C\, X'} \; a \in A$$

$$\frac{X \xrightarrow{b} X' \quad Y \xrightarrow{b} Y'}{X \,_{A})_{B})_C\, Y \xrightarrow{b} X' \,_{A})_{B})_C\, Y'} \; b \in B \qquad \frac{Y \xrightarrow{c} Y'}{X \,_{A})_{B})_C\, Y \xrightarrow{c} Y' \,_{A})_{B})_C\, X} \; c \in C$$

Next, we briefly explain the above rules. In P $_{A}\rangle_{B}\rangle_{C}$ Q the control of execution is with the first argument: see the first rule. Parameter A contains the actions by which the first argument transfers the control to the second argument: the second rule. Parameter B contains the actions on which both the arguments must synchronize: the third rule. Parameter C consists of all the actions by which the second argument takes over the control from the first one: the fourth rule.

The set of axioms for $_{A}\rangle_{B}\rangle_{C}$ can be easily generated using algorithm A. Similarly as for the CCS parallel operator the axiomatisation of $_{A}\rangle_{B}\rangle_{C}$ uses three auxiliary operators. Using the generated axioms, it is routine to show the following;

$$M \ _{A}\rangle_{B}\rangle_{C} RC \ = start.s.r.(M' \ _{A}\rangle_{B}\rangle_{C} RC) \ \boxplus \ pause.pause.(M \ _{A}\rangle_{B}\rangle_{C} RC)$$
$$M' \ _{A}\rangle_{B}\rangle_{C} RC \ = c_1.(c_2.(M'' \ _{A}\rangle_{B}\rangle_{C} RC) \ \boxplus \ M \ _{A}\rangle_{B}\rangle_{C} RC) \ \boxplus \ M \ _{A}\rangle_{B}\rangle_{C} RC$$
$$M'' \ _{A}\rangle_{B}\rangle_{C} RC = choice.(1.one.r.m_1 \boxplus 2.two.r.m_2 \ \boxplus \ M \ _{A}\rangle_{B}\rangle_{C} RC) \boxplus M \ _{A}\rangle_{B}\rangle_{C} RC$$

where $A = \{choice, pause, r\}$, $B = \{s, one, two\}$ and $C = \{start, pause, r\}$. Finally, by rule (11), we prove $P = M \ _{A}\rangle_{B}\rangle_{C} RC$.

5 Conclusions and Related Work

We have proposed a procedure for generating finite axiomatisations of testing preorder for De Simone process language. We have also proved that testing preorder is preserved by all De Simone process operators. The usefulness of our results have been demonstrated in the specification and verification of a small multi-media system.

Related work. The idea of generating axiomatisations of arbitrary process languages from their operational specifications (given by SOS rules) is due to Aceto, Bloom and Vaandrager [ABV92, Ace94]. They defined two procedures for obtaining axiomatisations of (strong) bisimulation for arbitrary GSOS languages. However, if one tries to adapt their procedure to any of weak equivalences one finds that the introduced auxiliary operators do not preserve many of weak equivalences. In [Blo93] this difficulty is overcome by considering *rooted* versions of weak equivalences and further restricting the (GSOS) format of rules. An alternative approach is presented in [Uli95a], where a general procedure is defined for deriving axiomatisations of refusal simulation preorder and coarser (weak) preorders. The procedure from [Uli95a] can be adjusted, by adding a number of extra axioms, to produce axiomatisations of testing preorder. But, the procedure presented in this paper has a number of important advantages over the adjusted procedure: (1) it is shorter since it uses only nine simpler laws instead of twenty of the adjusted procedure and (2) it always produces finite axiomatisations.

Acknowledgements

I would like to thank Matthew Hennessy and the anonymous referees for their comments and suggestions. Also, I wish to thank Reiji Nakajima for his continuous support. Thanks are also due to Paul Taylor for his LaTeX macros.

References

[ABV92] L. Aceto, B. Bloom, and F.W. Vaandrager. Turning SOS rules into equations. In *Proceedings of the 7th Annual IEEE Symposium on Logic in Computer Science*, Santa Cruz, California, 1992.

[Ace94] L. Aceto. Deriving complete inteference systems for a class of GSOS languages generating regular behaviours. In *Proceedings of the 5th International Conference* CONCUR'94, Uppsala, Sweden, 1994. LNCS 789.

[AI95] L. Aceto and A. Ingólfdóttir. CPO models for a class of GSOS languages. In P.D. Mosses, M. Nielsen, and M.I. Schwartzbach, editors, *Proceedings of TAPSOFT '95*. Springer-Verlag, 1995. LNCS 915.

[BIM88] B. Bloom, S. Istrail, and A.R. Meyer. Bisimulation can't be traced: preliminary report. In *Conference Record of the 15th ACM Symposium on Principles of Programming Languages*, San Diego, California, 1988.

[Blo93] B. Bloom. Structural operational semantics for weak bisimulations. Technical Report TR 93-1373, Cornell, 1993. To appear in Theoretical Computer Science.

[Blo95] B. Bloom. Stuctured operational semantics as a specification language. In *Conference Record of the 22nd ACM Symposium on Principles of Programming Languages*, San Francisco, California, 1995.

[BW90] J.C.M Baeten and W.P Weijland. *Process Algebra*. Cambridge Tracts in Theoretical Computer Science, 1990.

[dS85] R. de Simone. Higher-level synchronising devices in MEIJE-SCCS. *Theoretical Computer Science*, Vol. 37, pp. 245–267, 1985.

[GV90] J.F. Groote and F. Vaandrager. Structured operational semantics and bisimulation as a congruence. *Information and Computation*, Vol. 100, pp. 202–260, 1990.

[Hen88] M. Hennessy. *An Algebraic Theory of Processes*. The MIT Press, 1988.

[Hoa85] C.A.R. Hoare. *Communicating Sequential Processes*. Prentice Hall, 1985.

[Mil89] R. Milner. *Communication and Concurrency*. Prentice Hall, 1989.

[NH84] R. De Nicola and M. Hennessy. Testing equivalences for processes. *Theoretical Computer Science*, Vol. 34, pp. 83–133, 1984.

[Plo81] G. Plotkin. A structural approach to operational semantics. Technical Report DAIMI FN-19, Aarhus University, 1981.

[Uli92] I. Ulidowski. Equivalences on observable processes. In *Proceedings of the 7th Annual IEEE Symposium on Logic in Computer Science*, Santa Cruz, California, 1992.

[Uli94] I. Ulidowski. *Local Testing and Implementable Concurrent Processes*. PhD thesis, Imperial College, University of London, 1994.

[Uli95a] I. Ulidowski. Axiomatisations of weak equivalences for De Simone languages. In I. Lee and S.A. Smolka, editors, *Proceedings of the 6th International Conference on Concurrency Theory* CONCUR'95, Philadelphia, 1995. Springer-Verlag. LNCS 962.

[Uli95b] I. Ulidowski. Finite axiom systems for testing preorder and De Simone process languages. Technical report, RIMS, Kyoto University, 1995. Available at http://www.kurims.kyoto-u.ac.jp/~irek/.

[Vaa91] F.W. Vaandrager. On the relationship between process algebra and input/output automata. In *Proceedings of the 6th Annual IEEE Symposium on Logic in Computer Science*, Amsterdam, 1991.

Constructive Semantics of Esterel: From Theory to Practice (Abstract)

G. Berry

Ecole des Mines, BP 207, F-06904 Sophia-Antipolis CDX

INRIA, Route des Lucioles, F-06565 Sophia-Antipolis

berry@cma.cma.fr

http://cma.cma.fr/Personnel/Berry.html

Esterel is a synchronous language dedicated to reactive systems: software or hardware controllers, embedded systems, communication protocols, etc. The language is imperative and well-adapted to control-dominated applications. Conceptually, Esterel processes evolve synchronously and communicate using zero-delay signal broadcasting. The language primitives include sequencing, concurrency, and process preemption mechanisms. The semantics is defined in a mathematical way. Software or hardware implementation is based on the finite-state character of control in the language: the generated code or circuit is composed of a FSM that possibly drives a table of data computing action. The FSM can be either represented explicitly as a state graph or implicitly as a boolean circuit. Formal verification tools operate on the control FSM to automatically verify safety properties.

The synchronous model is very powerful and convenient to program reactive applications. However, zero-delay broadcasting has a drawback: one can write nonsensical programs such as "emit S if and only if S is not received". Detecting such causally incorrect programs and reporting good error-messages for them is the most difficult problem in Esterel. The former compilers Esterel v2, v3, and v4 each involved sufficient correctness conditions. However, the conditions were not clear enough and not tolerant enough for our industrial partners, who considered that they could not really use the language for large applications unless the problem was solved.

The right solution has been discovered only recently, and it is implemented in the Esterel v5 compiler. Theoretically speaking, the solution is to use a constructive approach to the semantics of Esterel programs and boolean circuits. The main theorem roots the constructive approach in physics: we show that a circuit is constructive if and only if it is electrically stable for all gate and wire delays, and that the same property holds for the hardware implementation of an Esterel program. On the practical side, we have developed algorithms for constructiveness checking: a linear-time interpreter and a BDD-based compiler that performs the full constructiveness analysis of a cyclic circuit or Esterel program and yields back an equivalent acyclic version in case of success. The algorithms marry well with symbolic debugging, which makes it possible to report causality errors in a user-friendly visual form. We discuss the performance of the algorithms on industrial examples.

Using Ghost Variables to Prove Refinement*

M. Marcus and A. Pnueli

Department of Computer Science,
Weizmann Institute of Science, Rehovot 76100, Israel.
e-mail: monica@wisdom.weizmann.ac.il

Abstract. We propose a method for proving refinement between programs, based on augmenting the program by ghost (auxiliary) variables and statements that assign values to these variables. We show that, in many cases, this augmentation can replace the need for an explicit refinement mapping from the variables of one system to the private variables of the other system. A novel feature of the proposed methodology is that the expressions assigned to the ghost variables may depend on the future. This may replace the need for prophecy variables that are defined by a decreasing induction and require some version of finite-image hypothesis. We believe that proving refinement by program augmentation leads to a more natural style of refinement and is easier to design and comprehend. Allowing future-dependent expressions in a program requires extensions to the temporal methodology for proving properties of programs. These extensions are explained and discussed in the paper.

1 Introduction

A rigorous development of a complex reactive system often proceeds through several intermediate stages on the way from a top-level abstract specification to a final efficient running version.

$$S_0 \sqsupseteq S_1 \sqsupseteq \cdots S_{k-1} \sqsupseteq S_k$$

In this development sequence, each system S_{i+1} *refines* its predecessor S_i (using the symbol $\sqsupseteq$ to denote the relation of refinement). In our linear semantics framework, refinement means that the set of behaviors allowed by S_{i+1} is a subset of the behaviors allowed by S_i. Behaviors of the two systems are compared by projecting the detailed computations of each of them on a set of *observable variables* which are common to both systems.

Many formalisms have been proposed for proving refinement between systems. We refer the reader to the collection [dBdRR90] for a comprehensive coverage of the main approaches to refinement proofs. The paper [AL91] presents a semantic framework for the study of refinement and proves, under some assumptions, completeness of a proof method based on refinement mapping. The note

---

* This research was supported in part by a basic research grant from the Israeli Academy of Sciences, and by the European Community ESPRIT Basic Research Action Project 6021 (REACT).

[Lam92] shows how these semantic ideas can be worked out within the TLA framework. In [KMP94], we showed how to prove simulation and refinement within the framework of the temporal logic of [MP91b], using the proof systems presented in [MP91a] and [MP91b].

Let $S^{\mathcal{A}}$ and $S^{\mathcal{C}}$ denote an abstract and a concrete system, and consider the problem of proving that system $S^{\mathcal{C}}$ refines system $S^{\mathcal{A}}$, which we can write as

$$S^{\mathcal{C}} \sqsubseteq S^{\mathcal{A}}.$$

One of the main problems in establishing such a refinement relation is in the case that $S^{\mathcal{A}}$ contains system variables that are not present in $S^{\mathcal{C}}$. To show that every observation of $S^{\mathcal{C}}$ corresponds to some observation of $S^{\mathcal{A}}$, it is necessary to identify the values assumed by the private $S^{\mathcal{A}}$ variables in such an observation. This requires the ability to map $S^{\mathcal{C}}$-states onto $S^{\mathcal{A}}$-states. We refer to such a mapping as a *refinement mapping* and its construction has been identified as one of the central tasks in proving refinements between systems.

In the simplest case the necessary mapping is a simple state-to-state transformation. However, as pointed out in [AL91], this may be impossible in some cases, and the mapping may depend on the prefix of the observation up to the present (which calls for the use of *history variables* in the terminology of [AL91]) and, in even more complicated cases, may also depend on the infinite suffix of the observation from the mapped state on (which calls for the use of *prophecy variables* in the terminology of [AL91]).

In [KMP94], we proposed a single proof rule for establishing refinement relation between two systems. This proof rule allowed the refinement mapping to be an arbitrary temporal function which may refer to the complete observation to determine the local concrete-to-abstract state mapping. This most general license covers the history and prophecy references as special cases. While, in principle, this single rule is adequate for proving all interesting refinement relations, it's overwhelming generality does not provide useful guidance to the user about how to make the first steps in establishing a refinement.

In this paper, we take an opposite approach. Instead of presenting a single monolithic rule that can do everything, we list a tool suite consisting of several smaller rules, each applicable in certain situations. It is fair to say that the proposed approach has a more algebraic proof style in which we establish $S^{\mathcal{C}} \sqsubseteq S^{\mathcal{A}}$ in a sequence of small steps of the form

$$S^{\mathcal{C}} = S_1 \sqsubseteq S_2 \sqsubseteq \cdots \sqsubseteq S_k = S^{\mathcal{A}},$$

where, typically, different rules may be applied in different steps.

An important contribution to the conceptual simplification of the refinement task is that, in many cases, we replaced the abstract notion of refinement mapping, which many practitioners find difficult to design correctly, by the more familiar concept of augmentation with auxiliary variables (e.g. [OG76]). It is not difficult to see how history variables, which are usually defined by an ascending inductive definition, can be viewed or implemented as auxiliary variables which are modified by assignments augmenting the program. What is less obvious is that a similar thing can be done with prophecy variables which are defined by a descending inductive definition. To do this, we extended the programming language and allow statements which assign future-dependent temporal expressions to auxiliary variables. This requires some extension of the proof rules for establishing invariants over a program.

The general strategy for proving refinement by program augmentation can be simplistically described as follows. Starting with system S^C, we add the private variables of S^A as auxiliary variables. This leads us to a combined system, let us call it S_2, in which assignments to the private variables of S^C and S^A co-exist side-by-side but the observable variables are assigned values depending only on the variables of S^C. Next, we prove some invariants for the combined system S_2 whose main role is to establish some relations between the private S^A variables and the S^C variables. As the next step, we use these relations to replace the assignments to the observable variables by assignments which refer only to S^A variables. This leads us to the next version of the system, say S_3. At this point, the private S^C variables no longer affect the observables and they may be considered as auxiliary variables, not essential to the observed behavior of the system. As the final step, we de-augment these variables from the system, reproducing system S^A.

Auxiliary variables are used by Reynolds [Rey81] in the development of data representation structuring for sequential programs. Their role is to help proving invariants about the program, which are used in the process of replacing the abstract variables by concrete ones. In [Rey81] the definition of auxiliary variables is attributed to Owicki and Gries [OG76] but it is said that the basic concept can be found already in [Luc68].

The general idea of constructing a joint cross product system that runs S^C and S^A together, establishing some invariants for the combined system and using them to simplify or transform the system into a version of S^A was already suggested in [Jon87]. Our main extension of this method is the introduction of future-dependent auxiliary variables, and treating them as any other program variables.

The rest of the paper is organized as follows. In Section 2, we present the basic model of fair transition systems and show how distributed programs can be represented in this model. In Section 3 we define the refinement relation between fair transition systems and present a verification rule for refinement. In Section 4, two types of equivalence transformations of programs are defined, namely spacing congruence and safe augmentation. Section 5 shows how to modify the proof rules for invariance properties of programs such that future-dependent temporal expressions are allowed in assignment statements. In Section 6, the proposed proof method is illustrated by examples. The final Section 7 contains discussions and conclusions.

2 Basic Concepts and Definitions

We assume a universal set of typed variables $\mathcal{V}$, called *vocabulary*. A *state* s is a type-consistent interpretation of $\mathcal{V}$, assigning to each variable $u \in \mathcal{V}$ a value $s[u]$ over its domain. The set of all states is denoted by Σ.

The specification language used in this paper is that of *linear quantified temporal logic* whose syntax and semantics can be found in [MP91b]. Temporal logic is constructed out of state formulas (to which we refer as *assertions*) to which we apply boolean and temporal operators.

A *model* for a temporal formula is an infinite sequence of states

$$\sigma: \quad s_0, s_1, \dots \ .$$

Model σ': $s'_0, s'_1, \dots$ is said to be a *stuttering variant* of model σ: $s_0, s_1, \dots$, if σ' can be obtained from σ by the duplication of some states and the deletion of some duplicate states.

The computational model for reactive systems is given by a *fair transition system* (FTS) $S = \langle V, \Theta, \mathcal{T}, \mathcal{J}, \mathcal{C} \rangle$ consisting of:

- $V = \{u_1, ..., u_n\}$: A finite set of *system variables*.
- Θ : The *initial condition*. A satisfiable assertion characterizing the initial states.
- $\mathcal{T}$: A finite set of *transitions*. Each transition $\tau \in \mathcal{T}$ is a function

$$\tau : \Sigma \mapsto 2^{\Sigma},$$

  mapping each state $s \in \Sigma$ into a (possibly empty) set of τ-*successor* states $\tau(s) \subseteq \Sigma$.
  The function associated with a transition τ is represented by an assertion $\rho_\tau(V, V')$, called the *transition relation*, which relates a state $s \in \Sigma$ to its τ-successor $s' \in \tau(s)$ by referring to both unprimed and primed versions of the system variables. An unprimed version of a system variable refers to its value in s, while a primed version of the same variable refers to its value in s'. For example, the assertion $x' = x + 1$ states that the value of x in s' is greater by 1 than its value in s.
- $\mathcal{J} \subseteq \mathcal{T}$: A set of *just* transitions. The requirement of justice for $\tau \in \mathcal{J}$ disallows a computation in which τ is continually enabled beyond a certain point but taken only finitely many times.
- $\mathcal{C} \subseteq \mathcal{T}$: A set of *compassionate* transitions. The requirement of compassion for $\tau \in \mathcal{C}$ disallows a computation in which τ is enabled infinitely many times but taken only finitely many times.

The enableness of a transition τ can be expressed by the formula

$$En(\tau): \ \exists V' \, \rho_\tau(V, V'),$$

which is true in s iff s has some τ-successor.

To ensure that every state $s \in \Sigma$ has at least one transition enabled on it, we standardly include in $\mathcal{T}$ the *idling* transition τ_I, whose transition relation is $\rho_I : V' = V$.

A *computation* of a fair transition system S is a model $\sigma : s_0, s_1, s_2, \ldots$, satisfying the following requirements:

- *Initiation:* s_0 satisfies Θ.
- *Consecution:* For each position $j > 0$, the state s_{j+1} is a τ-successor of the state s_j, for some $\tau \in \mathcal{T}$. In this case, we say that the transition τ is *taken* at position j in σ.
- *Justice:* For each $\tau \in \mathcal{J}$, there is no position $j \geq 0$ such that τ is continually enabled but not taken beyond j.
- *Compassion:* For each $\tau \in \mathcal{C}$, it is not the case that τ is enabled at infinitely many positions of σ but taken at only finitely many.

Let $S: \langle V, \Theta, \mathcal{T}, \mathcal{J}, \mathcal{C} \rangle$ be a system, and let $\mathcal{O} \subseteq V$ be a subset of the system variables of S, to which we refer as the *observable variables*. We say that the model $\tilde{\sigma}$ is an $\mathcal{O}$-observation of S if it can be obtained from a computation of S by finitely many stuttering and $\mathcal{O}$-preserving transformations. In the case that $\mathcal{O}$ is understood from the context, we refer to $\tilde{\sigma}$ simply as an *observation* of S.

For the presentation of programs we use the SPL programming language introduced in [MP95]. We refer the reader to [MP95] for the syntax and the semantics of SPL. Here, we shall only illustrate the interpretation of an SPL program as an FTS through an example.

Every program P is associated with a fair transition system S_P, which defines the semantics of P.

Consider program 2INC1 presented in Figure 1. The fair transition system

$$x, y : \textbf{integer where } x = y = 0$$
$$\begin{bmatrix} \ell_0: \textbf{ loop forever do} \\ \quad \begin{bmatrix} \ell_1: & y := x + 1 \\ \ell_2: & x := y + 1 \end{bmatrix} \end{bmatrix}$$

Fig. 1. Program 2INC1.

(FTS) associated with program 2INC1 is given by $S_P = \langle V, \Theta, \mathcal{T}, \mathcal{J}, \mathcal{C} \rangle$, where

- *System Variables:* $V = \{x, y, \pi\}$,
  where π is the control variable. The domain of π consists of the set of indices of the locations occurring in 2INC1, i.e., $\{0, 1, 2\}$.
- *Initial Condition:* $\Theta : \quad x = 0 \wedge y = 0 \wedge at\_\ell_0$,
  where at_ℓ_0 stands for the assertion $\pi = 0$.
- *Transitions:* $\mathcal{T} = \{\tau_0, \tau_1, \tau_2, \tau_I\}$. The transition relations are :
  $$\rho_{\tau_0} : \quad at\_\ell_0 \wedge at'\_\ell_1 \wedge x' = x \wedge y' = y$$
  $$\rho_{\tau_1} : \quad at\_\ell_1 \wedge at'\_\ell_2 \wedge x' = x \wedge y' = x + 1$$
  $$\rho_{\tau_2} : \quad at\_\ell_2 \wedge at'\_\ell_0 \wedge x' = y + 1 \wedge y' = y$$
  $$\rho_{\tau_I} : \quad \pi' = \pi \wedge x' = x \wedge y' = y,$$
  where, at_ℓ_i stands for $\pi = i$ and at'_ℓ_j stands for $\pi' = j$.

- *Justice:* $\mathcal{J} = \{\tau_0, \tau_1, \tau_2\}$
- *Compassion:* $\mathcal{C} = \emptyset$

If P is a program and φ a formula, we say that φ is P-valid if every computation of P satisfies φ. If φ is an assertion, we say that φ is P-state valid if every state that appears in a computation of P satisfies φ. An assertion φ is said to be an *invariant* of program P if it is P-state valid.

3 Refinement of Fair Transition Systems

Let S^A and S^C be two fair transition systems, and let $\mathcal{O} \subseteq V^A \cap V^C$ be a set of observable variables common to both. We say that S^C *refines* S^A *relative to* $\mathcal{O}$ (equivalently, S^C $\mathcal{O}$-*refines* S^A) and write $S^C \sqsubseteq_{\mathcal{O}} S^A$, if every $\mathcal{O}$-observation of S^C is an $\mathcal{O}$-observation of S^A.

Usually, when we compare two systems, we assume that $\mathcal{O} = V^A \cap V^C$. This can always be achieved by renaming some of the non-observable variables of the two systems.

Two systems S_1 and S_2 such that $S_1 \sqsubseteq_{\mathcal{O}} S_2$ and $S_2 \sqsubseteq_{\mathcal{O}} S_1$, are said to be $\mathcal{O}$-*equivalent*. The equivalence relation is denoted by $\sim_{\mathcal{O}}$. The relation of refinement is reflexive and transitive. That is, for every system S, $S \sqsubseteq_{\mathcal{O}} S$, and if $S_1 \sqsubseteq_{\mathcal{O}} S_2$ and $S_2 \sqsubseteq_{\mathcal{O}} S_3$, then $S_1 \sqsubseteq_{\mathcal{O}} S_3$. When the set of observable variables is understood from the context, e.g. $\mathcal{O} = V^A \cap V^C$, we write $\sqsubseteq_{\mathcal{O}}$ and $\sim_{\mathcal{O}}$, simply as $\sqsubseteq$ and $\sim$.

Let $L^C = V^C - \mathcal{O}$ and $L^A = V^A - \mathcal{O}$ denote the sets of *private* variables of the concrete and abstract systems, respectively. Let

$$\alpha \colon L^A \mapsto \mathcal{E}(V^C)$$

be a *substitution* that assigns to each private abstract variable $x \in L^A$ an expression over the concrete variables. We denote the expression assigned to x by $x_\alpha(V^C)$, or simply x_α. For an assertion φ, we denote by $\varphi[\alpha]$ the assertion obtained by replacing each occurrence of a private abstract variable x occurring in φ by x_α and each primed variable x' by $x_\alpha((V^C)')$. Such substitution α induces a mapping m_α on states as follows:

Let s^C be a state which appears in a computation of S^C. We refer to s^C as a concrete state. The abstract state $s^A = m_\alpha(s^C)$ corresponding to the concrete state s^C is such that the value of each private abstract variable $x \in L^A$ in s^A is the value of the expression x_α when evaluated in s^C. For the observable variables, on which S^C and S^A agree, $s^A[y] = s^C[y]$, for each $y \in \mathcal{O}$. We say that m_α is a *state mapping* from S^C to S^A, induced by α, with respect to the set $\mathcal{O}$ of observable variables.

The mapping m_α can be extended to a mapping between models. Thus, if $\sigma \colon s_0, s_1, \ldots$ is a model, then its image under m_α is $m_\alpha(\sigma) \colon m_\alpha(s_0), m_\alpha(s_1), \ldots$.

A state mapping m_α from S^C to S^A is called a *refinement mapping* if it maps computations of S^C to computations of S^A.

The existence of a refinement mapping from S^C to S^A is a sufficient condition for S^C to be a refinement of S^A.

The purpose of the refinement mapping is to represent the values of the private abstract variables in terms of the concrete system variables.

In some cases, we can identify a mapping $\kappa : T^C \mapsto T^A$, which maps each concrete transition to a corresponding abstract transition. The intended meaning of the mapping is that, when transforming a computation of S^C into a computation of S^A, we can always mimic the effect of τ^C in the concrete computation, by taking the corresponding abstract transition $\kappa(\tau^C)$ in the abstract computation. The *transition mapping* κ may also depend on the state.

In Figure 2 we present proof rule REF [KMP94], which can be used to prove that system S^C refines system S^A, given a substitution $\alpha: L^A \mapsto \mathcal{E}(V^C)$ and a transition mapping $\kappa : T^C \mapsto T^A$. All premises of the rule are interpreted as

SF1.	Θ^C	$\rightarrow$	$\Theta^A[\alpha]$	
SF2.	ρ_{τ^C}	$\rightarrow$	$\rho_{\kappa(\tau^C)}[\alpha]$	for every $\tau^C \in T^C$
SF3.	$En(\tau^A)[\alpha]$	$\Rightarrow$	$\Diamond(\neg En(\tau^A) \lor taken(\tau^A))[\alpha]$	for every $\tau^A \in \mathcal{J}^A$
SF4.	$\Box \Diamond En(\tau^A)[\alpha]$	$\Rightarrow$	$\Diamond taken(\tau^A)[\alpha]$	for every $\tau^A \in C^A$

$$S^C \sqsubseteq S^A$$

Fig. 2. Rule REF.

S^C-state valid (SF1 and SF2) or S^C-valid (SF3 and SF4). This means that in proving the premises, we are allowed to add any invariant assertion established for system S^C to the left-hand side of the implication or entailment.

Premise SF1 requires that the concrete initial condition Θ^C implies the substituted abstract initial condition $\Theta^A[\alpha]$. Premise SF2 guarantees that any concrete transition τ^C can be mimicked by the corresponding abstract transition $\kappa(\tau^C)$, after substitution. Premise SF3 requires that all abstract just transitions are treated with justice. That is, every abstract transition which is enabled at some position, must be disabled or taken at a later position. Under the substitution α this is a requirement that only refers to the concrete system variables V^C, and can therefore be posed as a requirement that concrete computations must satisfy. In a similar way, premise SF4 requires that compassionate abstract transitions be treated with compassion. That is, any abstract compassionate transition which is enabled infinitely many times, must be taken at least once beyond every position, and hence must be taken infinitely many times.

Without loss of generality, we may assume that the justice and compassion sets of transitions are disjoint. This implies that every abstract transition appears in at most one premise of the form SF3 or SF4.

Let τ^A be an abstract transition such that, for every S^C-accessible state, there exists precisely one concrete transition τ^C such that $\kappa(\tau^C) = \tau^A$. For such a transition, we may replace premises SF3 or SF4 for this transition by the following simplified premise:

EF3. $En(\tau^A)[\alpha] \quad \rightarrow \quad En(\kappa^{-1}(\tau^A))$

In [KMP94], rule REF was proposed as the only rule necessary for proving refinement. To support this, we considered substitutions α, in which the right-hand-side expressions assigned to private variables of S^A were general temporal functions. In the approach promoted here, we will use rule REF as only one of a larger assortment of rules, and then only for the special case that $V^A = \mathcal{O} \subseteq V^C$. Note that, for such cases, the substitution α becomes empty.

4 Equivalence Transformations of Programs

The definitions of refinement and of equivalence between fair transition systems can be transferred to programs in the obvious way.

4.1 Congruence and Equivalence Transformations

Let $P[S]$ be a program containing the statement S. We refer to $P[\,\cdot\,]$ as a *context* for statement S. Statements S_1 and S_2 are defined to be *congruent*, written

$$S_1 \approx S_2 \qquad \text{iff} \qquad P[S_1] \sim P[S_2], \quad \text{for every context } P[\,\cdot\,].$$

Obviously, any congruence between statements, gives rise to refinement transformations. Following are two useful congruences, called the *spacing* congruences:

- $[S] \approx [S; \textbf{skip}]$
- $y := e \approx [\textbf{skip}; y := e]$

The first congruence allows us to introduce a *skip* statement following any statement in the program. The second congruence allows to introduce a *skip* statement before an assignment. It can be shown that $[\textbf{skip}; S]$ is not congruent to S for a general S^2.

A third useful equivalence can be stated as follows:

- If $at\_\ell \to e_1 = e_2$ is an invariant of program $P[\ell: y := e_1]$, then
$$P[\ell: y := e_1] \sim P[\ell: y := e_2]$$

This equivalence allows us to replace the assignment $y := e_1$ by the assignment $y := e_2$ if we have previously established that $e_1 = e_2$ whenever we visit this statement in the program.

---

^{2} A typical counter-example is the program
$$\textbf{skip or } [\textbf{await F}] \qquad \text{compared to} \qquad \textbf{skip or } [\textbf{skip}; \textbf{await F}]$$
The two programs are not equivalent because the first program always terminate, while the second may get blocked in front of the **await** F statement

4.2 Safe Augmentation

Let $S^A = \langle V^A, \Theta^A, T^A, J^A, C^A \rangle$ and $S^C = \langle V^C, \Theta^C, T^C, J^C, C^C \rangle$ be two fair transition systems. Let $\mathcal{O} = V^A \cap V^C$ be the set of observable variables common to the two systems.

Let us consider again the question of proving that system S^C $\mathcal{O}$-refines system S^A. Instead of looking for a refinement mapping, one might augment the concrete system S^C with some *auxiliary (ghost) variables* to obtain a new system $\widehat{S}$, such that $S^C \sqsubseteq \widehat{S}$ and $\widehat{S} \sqsubseteq S^A$. The definition of augmentation will ensure that the first refinement always holds and the second can often be proved with rule REF and the trivial substitution. The transitivity of the refinement relation will then permit us to conclude that $S^C \sqsubseteq S^A$.

The method of using auxiliary variables to prove that a lower level specification implements a higher level specification was discussed, among others, in [AL91].

System $\widehat{S}$: $\langle \widehat{V}, \widehat{\Theta}, \widehat{T}, \widehat{J}, \widehat{C} \rangle$ is defined to be a *safe augmentation* of system S: $\langle V, \Theta, T, J, C \rangle$, if the following hold:

- $\widehat{V} = V \cup U$, for some set of auxiliary variables $U = \{u_1, \ldots, u_m\}$ disjoint from V;
- $\Theta \leftrightarrow \exists U : \widehat{\Theta}$ is state-valid;
- $\widehat{T} = \{\widehat{\tau} | \tau \in T\} \cup \{\tau_I\}$ such that for every transition τ, $\rho_\tau \leftrightarrow \exists U' : \rho_{\widehat{\tau}}$ is state-valid;
- $\widehat{J} = \{\widehat{\tau} | \tau \in J\}$ and $\widehat{C} = \{\widehat{\tau} | \tau \in C\}$.

The following theorem states that a safe augmentation of system S is equivalent to S.

Theorem 1. *Let S be a system with system variables V and let $\widehat{S}$ be a safe augmentation of S. The set of V-observations of $\widehat{S}$ coincides with the set of observations of S. It follows that S and $\widehat{S}$ are V-equivalent.*

Proof: First we show how to obtain, for any computation $\sigma : s_0, s_1, \ldots$ of S, a corresponding computation $\widehat{\sigma} : \widehat{s}_0, \widehat{s}_1, \ldots$ of $\widehat{S}$, such that the two computations agree on the interpretation of V.

According to the definition of computation of a fair transition system, $s_0 \models \Theta$. According to the definition of safe augmentation, $s_0 \models \exists U : \widehat{\Theta}$. Thus, there exists some state $\widehat{s}_0$ that might differ from s_0 only by the interpretation of the variables in U, such that $\widehat{s}_0 \models \widehat{\Theta}$. Assume that for some $n \geq 0$, $\widehat{s}_0, \ldots, \widehat{s}_n$ have been defined, such that for every j, $0 \leq j \leq n$, $\widehat{s}_j$ agrees with s_j on the interpretation of V. Let $\tau \in T$ be the transition taken between states s_n and s_{n+1} of σ, i.e., $\langle s_n, s_{n+1} \rangle \models \rho_\tau(V, V')$ holds. Since s_n and $\widehat{s}_n$ coincide on V, we have also that $\langle \widehat{s}_n, s_{n+1} \rangle \models \rho_\tau(V, V')$ holds. According to the definition of $\widehat{S}$, $\langle \widehat{s}_n, s_{n+1} \rangle \models \exists U' : \rho_{\widehat{\tau}}(\widehat{V}, \widehat{V}')$ holds, hence there exists some state $\widehat{s}_{n+1}$, agreeing with s_{n+1} on the interpretation of V, such that $\langle \widehat{s}_n, \widehat{s}_{n+1} \rangle \models \rho_{\widehat{\tau}}(\widehat{V}, \widehat{V}')$ holds.

Clearly, for every $n \geq 0$, if $\widehat{\tau}$ is enabled in state $\widehat{s}_n$ then τ is enabled in state s_n and if τ is taken in state s_n then $\widehat{\tau}$ is taken in state $\widehat{s}_n$. Therefore $\widehat{\sigma}$ is a computation of $\widehat{S}$ which agrees with σ on the interpretation of V.

In the other direction, it is straightforward to show that every computation of $\widehat{S}$ is, without any changes, a computation of S.

It follows that the set of V-observations of S and of $\widehat{S}$ coincide.   □

Applied to programs, a safe augmentation $\widehat{P}$ of a program P can be obtained by

- Declaring auxiliary variables $U = \{u_1, \ldots, u_k\}$ in the program. The declarations can specify initial values.
- Assignments to auxiliary variables of the form $u_i := e$ may be added to P by grouping them together with existing statements.

The grouping may be done either by explicitly grouping an auxiliary assignment with an existing statement or, if the existing statement is an assignment, by transforming the assignment into a multiple assignment with additional entries for the auxiliary variables.

For example, in Figure 3, we present program **B**, which is a safe augmentation of program **A**.

$$x : \textbf{integer where } x = 0$$
$$\begin{bmatrix} m_0\text{:} \ \ \textbf{loop forever do} \\ \begin{bmatrix} m_1\text{:} \ \ \textbf{skip} \\ m_2\text{:} \ \ x := x + 2 \end{bmatrix} \end{bmatrix}$$

$$-- \text{Program } \textbf{A} --$$

$$x, y : \textbf{integer where } x = y = 0$$
$$\begin{bmatrix} m_0\text{:} \ \ \textbf{loop forever do} \\ \begin{bmatrix} m_1\text{:} \ \ y := x + 1 \\ m_2\text{:} \ \ (x, y) := (x + 2, y + 1) \end{bmatrix} \end{bmatrix}$$

$$-- \text{Program } \textbf{B} --$$

Fig. 3. Example of safe augmentation.

A unique feature of our approach is that the expression e appearing on the right-hand-side of an augmenting assignment may refer to future values of all the variables in V. We allow two forms of future-dependent expressions:

- An assignment of the form
$$u := \textbf{if } \varphi \textbf{ then } e_1 \textbf{ else } e_2,$$
  where φ is a future temporal formula and e_1, e_2 are normal (future-independent) expressions. To evaluate this expression, we check whether φ holds at the current position of the computation and accordingly select the current value of e_1 or the current value of e_2.
- An assignment of the form
$$u := e@\varphi,$$
  where φ is a future temporal formula and e is a normal expression. The value of this expression is the value of e at the first position following the current one at which φ holds. If φ holds at no future position, $e@\varphi$ is taken to be some default value which, in the case of integer variables, is 0.

5 Proof Rules for Invariance Properties of Programs

Proving that the conditions of rule REF hold might require some additional invariance properties. Usually, by an invariance property of a program P we mean a P-valid formula $\Box p$ where p is an assertion. Since our augmentation allows assigning future-dependent expressions to auxiliary, the notion of invariance property must be extended to allow p to be a future temporal formula.

Rule INV of Figure 4 can be used to prove invariance properties of programs.

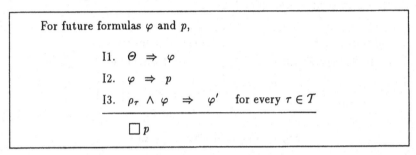

For future formulas φ and p,

> I1. $\Theta \Rightarrow \varphi$
>
> I2. $\varphi \Rightarrow p$
>
> I3. $\rho_\tau \wedge \varphi \Rightarrow \varphi'$ for every $\tau \in \mathcal{T}$
>
> ---
>
> $\Box p$

Fig. 4. Rule INV (invariance).

In establishing instances of the verification conditions required by premise I3, it is necessary to relate φ to its primed version φ'. For the simple case that φ is an assertion, φ' is obtained simply by priming each occurrence of a variable appearing in φ. For the extended cases considered here, φ may be a future formula. In this case, we may be helped by the following expansion formulas:

$$\Box \varphi \quad \Leftrightarrow \quad \varphi \wedge (\Box \varphi)'$$
$$\Diamond \varphi \quad \Leftrightarrow \quad \varphi \vee (\Diamond \varphi)'$$
$$\varphi_1 \, \mathcal{U} \, \varphi_2 \quad \Leftrightarrow \quad \varphi_2 \vee (\varphi_1 \wedge (\varphi_1 \, \mathcal{U} \, \varphi_2)')$$

The following entailments (implications holding at every position) can be used for simplifying future expressions of the form $e@\varphi$:

$$\Box \neg \varphi \quad \Rightarrow \quad e@\varphi = 0$$
$$\neg \varphi \quad \Rightarrow \quad e@\varphi = (e@\varphi)'$$
$$\varphi \quad \Rightarrow \quad e@\varphi = e$$

Rule C-INV in Figure 5 can be used to prove invariance properties of the form $p \Rightarrow \Box q$. All the formulas occurring as premises of the verification rules are

For future formulas p and q,

> C1. $p \Rightarrow q$
>
> C2. $\rho_\tau \wedge q \Rightarrow q'$ for every $\tau \in \mathcal{T}$
>
> ---
>
> $p \Rightarrow \Box q$

Fig. 5. Rule C-INV (invariance with precondition).

meant to be P-valid formulas.

6 Examples

In this section, we will illustrate the proposed proof methods by establishing equivalences of pairs of programs of increasing complexities.

6.1 Incrementation by 1 and 2

Consider programs 1INC2 and 2INC1, presented in Figure 6. We wish to show that these two programs are equivalent.

$$x : \textbf{integer where } x = 0$$
$$\begin{bmatrix} m_0: \textbf{ loop forever do} \\ \quad \begin{bmatrix} m_1: & x := x + 2 \end{bmatrix} \end{bmatrix}$$
$$-- \; 1\textsc{inc}2 \; --$$

$$x : \textbf{integer where } x = 0$$
$$y : \textbf{integer where } y = 0$$
$$\begin{bmatrix} \ell_0: \textbf{ loop forever do} \\ \quad \begin{bmatrix} \ell_1: & y := x + 1 \\ \ell_2: & x := y + 1 \end{bmatrix} \end{bmatrix}$$
$$-- \; 2\textsc{inc}1 \; --$$

Fig. 6. Two equivalent programs.

In Figure 7, we present a sequence of equivalence transformations leading from 1INC2 to 2INC1 and back.

$$x : \textbf{integer where } x = 0$$
$$\begin{bmatrix} m_0: \textbf{ loop forever do} \\ \quad \begin{bmatrix} m_1: & x := x + 2 \end{bmatrix} \end{bmatrix}$$
$$-- \; 1\textsc{inc}2 \; --$$

$\sim$

$$x : \textbf{integer where } x = 0$$
$$\begin{bmatrix} \ell_0: \textbf{ loop forever do} \\ \quad \begin{bmatrix} \ell_1: & \text{skip} \\ \ell_2: & x := x + 2 \end{bmatrix} \end{bmatrix}$$
$$-- \; A_1 \; --$$

$\sim$

$$x : \textbf{integer where } x = 0$$
$$y : \textbf{integer where } y = 0$$
$$\begin{bmatrix} \ell_0: \textbf{ loop forever do} \\ \quad \begin{bmatrix} \ell_1: & y := x + 1 \\ \ell_2: & x := x + 2 \end{bmatrix} \end{bmatrix}$$
$$-- \; A_2 \; --$$

$\sim$

$$x : \textbf{integer where } x = 0$$
$$y : \textbf{integer where } y = 0$$
$$\begin{bmatrix} \ell_0: \textbf{ loop forever do} \\ \quad \begin{bmatrix} \ell_1: & y := x + 1 \\ \ell_2: & x := y + 1 \end{bmatrix} \end{bmatrix}$$
$$-- \; 2\textsc{inc}1 \; --$$

Fig. 7. Transformation sequence.

The transformation from 1INC2 to program A_1 is a spacing transformation. The transformation from A_1 to A_2 is justified by safe augmentation. The equivalence between A_2 and 2INC1 is justified by the invariance of the assertion
$$at\_\ell_2 \quad \rightarrow \quad y = x + 1,$$
which is invariant for both programs.

6.2 Non-Deterministic Assignment

The second example proves equivalence between programs P_3 and P_4, presented in Figure 8. Program P_3 is an infinite loop, whose body consists of nondeterministically choosing a value from the set $\{-1, +1\}$ and assigning it to the observable variable x. This is done in one step, by the statement $x :\in \{-1, +1\}$. Program P_4 first chooses nondeterministically a value from $\{-1, +1\}$ and assigns it to the local variable y. Only in the next step, the chosen value is assigned to x.

$$x : \textbf{integer where } x = 1$$

$$\begin{bmatrix} m_0: & \textbf{loop forever do} \\ & \begin{bmatrix} m_1: & x :\in \{-1, +1\} \end{bmatrix} \end{bmatrix}$$

– Program P_3 –

$$x : \textbf{integer where } x = 1$$
$$y : \textbf{integer where } y = 1$$

$$\begin{bmatrix} \ell_0: & \textbf{loop forever do} \\ & \begin{bmatrix} \ell_1: & y :\in \{-1, +1\} \\ \ell_2: & x := y \end{bmatrix} \end{bmatrix}$$

– Program P_4 –

Fig. 8. Programs P_3 and P_4.

As a first step, we apply a spacing transformation to program P_3, obtaining program P_5 of Figure 9. We proceed to show that P_4 is equivalent to P_5. To

$$x : \textbf{integer where } x = 1$$

$$\begin{bmatrix} \ell_0: & \textbf{loop forever do} \\ & \begin{bmatrix} \ell_1: & \textbf{skip} \\ \ell_2: & x :\in \{-1, +1\} \end{bmatrix} \end{bmatrix}$$

Fig. 9. Program P_5, a spaced version of P_3.

show that P_4 refines P_5, i.e.

$$P_4 \sqsubseteq P_5,$$

we establish first the invariance of the assertion

$$\varphi_1: \quad at\_\ell_2 \ \rightarrow \ y \in \{-1, +1\}.$$

We then apply rule REF with no substitution. The only nontrivial verification condition involves transition ℓ_2, where we have to show the implication

$$x' = y \ \rightarrow \ x' \in \{-1, +1\}$$

This is implied by the invariant assertion φ_1.

To prove the other refinement $P_5 \sqsubseteq P_4$, we first construct P_6 (presented in Figure 10), a safe augmentation of P_5. Program P_5 is augmented with an

$$x : \textbf{integer where } x = 1$$
$$y : \textbf{integer where } y = 1$$

$$\begin{bmatrix} \ell_0: & \textbf{loop forever do} \\ & \begin{bmatrix} \ell_1: & y := x@at\_\ell_0 \\ \ell_2: & x :\in \{-1, +1\} \end{bmatrix} \end{bmatrix}$$

Fig. 10. Program P_6: a safe augmentation of P_5

auxiliary variable y which has to guess the value assigned to x in the next step. Thus, y is defined using the @ operator, in terms of *future values* of the observable variable x.

As a first step in showing that P_6 refines P_4, we establish for program P_6 the invariant

$$at\_\ell_2 \ \Rightarrow \ y = x@at\_\ell_0.$$

To do so, we use rule INV with the appropriate simplifications of the primed value of $x@at\_\ell_0$.

Next, we apply rule REF with the trivial substitution to prove that program P_6 refines P_4. The only nontrivial verification condition involves premise SF2 for transition l_2. For this, the invariant $at\_\ell_2 \Rightarrow y = x@at\_\ell_0$ and the property $\neg at\_\ell_0 \wedge at'\_\ell_0 \Rightarrow x' = x@at\_\ell_0$ of the @ operator are necessary.

Due to space limitations, we do not present here a more advanced example, comparing two versions of a buffer which may lose messages. For detailed presentation of this example, we refer the reader to [MP96].

7   Discussion

Two important questions require further discussion. The first is an assessment of the proving power of the proposed method. In particular, it would be useful if we can establish some completeness result for the method. A second interesting question is a more detailed comparison with the methods proposed by Abadi and Lamport in [AL91], and a reexamination of our initial claim that our future-dependent augmentation can be used to eliminate prophecy variables as they are introduced in [AL91]. The two questions are strongly related.

In Section 4, we introduced two restricted types of future-dependent expressions that may appear in augmentations. They were the expressions

$$\textbf{if } \varphi \textbf{ then } e_1 \textbf{ else } e_2 \qquad \text{and} \qquad e@\varphi,$$

where φ is a future temporal formula. We do not know yet whether completeness of the method can be established when only these two types of expressions are allowed. On the other hand, we may consider a more general future-dependent expression of the form

$$\min v. \, \varphi(v),$$

where v is a rigid variable and $\varphi(v)$ is a future temporal formula that may refer to v. Without loss of generality, we will only consider the case that v ranges over the naturals. The value of this expression at position j of a model σ is defined as follows:

$$\min v. \, \varphi(v) = \begin{cases} \text{minimal } v \text{ such that } (\sigma, j) \vDash \varphi(v) & \text{if } (\sigma, j) \vDash \exists v. \varphi(v) \\ 0 & \text{otherwise} \end{cases}$$

The *min* expression is at least as expressive as the two special cases considered in Section 4. The conditional expression (**if** φ **then** e_1 **else** e_2) can be expressed as

$$\min v. (\varphi \, \wedge \, v = e_1) \, \vee \, (\neg \varphi \, \wedge \, v = e_2).$$

Similarly, the expression $e@\varphi$ can be represented by a *min* expression of the form

$$\min v. (\neg \varphi) \, \mathcal{U} \, (\varphi \, \wedge \, v = e).$$

In a related way, also Abadi & Lamport's prophecy variables can be expressed using an appropriate *min* expression. Recall that the essence of prophecy variables is given by a state function f and the search for a flexible variable y satisfying

$$\Box(y = f(\bigcirc y)).$$

That is, an infinite sequence of values satisfying the descending recurrence rule

$$y_i = f(y_{i+1}),$$

for every $i = 0, 1, \ldots$. The requirement that f has the finite-image property is necessary in order to ensure that there exists at least one such sequence y. It is obvious that we can use a *min* expression to represent this special case as

$$\min v. \exists y \left(v = y \wedge \Box(y = f(\bigcirc y)) \right).$$

Using *min* expressions for augmentation, we can establish the following result:

Theorem 2 (Completeness). *The combination of rule* REF *of Figure 2 for the case of empty substitutions and safe augmentation, using min expressions, is complete for proving refinements between fair transition systems.*

We refer the reader to [MP96] for a proof of this theorem.

References

[AL91]   M. Abadi and L. Lamport. The existence of refinement mappings. *Theoretical Computer Science*, 82(2):253–284, May 1991.

[dBdRR90]   J.W. de Bakker, W.-P. de Roever, and G. Rozenberg, editors. *Stepwise Refinement of Distributed Systems: Models, Formalism, Correctness*. Lecture Notes in Computer Science 430. Springer-Verlag, 1990.

[Jon87]   B. Jonsson. Modular verification of asynchronous networks. In *Proc. 6th ACM Symp. Princ. of Dist. Comp.*, pages 152–166, 1987.

[KMP94]   Y. Kesten, Z. Manna, and A. Pnueli. Temporal verification of simulation and refinement. In J.W. de Bakker, W.-P. de Roever, and G. Rozenberg, editors, *A Decade of Concurrency*, volume 803 of *Lect. Notes in Comp. Sci.*, pages 273–346. Springer-Verlag, 1994.

[Lam92]   L. Lamport. The existence of refinement mapping. TLA Note 92-03-19, March 1992.

[Luc68]   P. Lucas. Two constructive realizations of the block concept and their equivalences. Technical Report Technical Report TR 25.085, IBM Laboratory Vienna, 1968.

[MP91a]   Z. Manna and A. Pnueli. Completing the temporal picture. *Theor. Comp. Sci.*, 83(1):97–130, 1991.

[MP91b]   Z. Manna and A. Pnueli. *The Temporal Logic of Reactive and Concurrent Systems: Specification*. Springer-Verlag, New York, 1991.

[MP95]   Z. Manna and A. Pnueli. *Temporal Verification of Reactive Systems: Safety*. Springer-Verlag, New York, 1995.

[MP96]   M. Marcus and A. Pnueli. Using ghost variables to prove refinement. Technical report, Weizmann Institute, 1996.

[OG76]   S. Owicki and D. Gries. An axiomatic proof technique for parallel programs. *Acta Informatica*, 6:319–340, 1976.

[Rey81]   J.C. Reynolds. *The Craft of Programming*. Prentice-Hall, Engelwood Cliffs, NJ, 1981.

Tracing the Origins of Verification Conditions

Ranan Fraer

INRIA, 2004 Route des Lucioles, 06902 Sophia-Antipolis, France
rfraer@sophia.inria.fr

Abstract. The typical program verification sytem is a batch tool that accepts as input a program annotated with Floyd-Hoare assertions, performs syntactic and semantic analysis on it, and generates a list of verification conditions that is subsequently submitted to a theorem prover. When a verification condition cannot be proved, this may be due to an error in the program or an inconsistency in the annotations. Unfortunately, it is very difficult to relate a failing proof attempt to a particular piece of code or assertion. We propose a solution to this problem using the technique of origin tracking.

1 Introduction

Since the late sixties, when Floyd and Hoare [Flo66, Hoa69] set up the basis of a method for proving programs correct, several program verification systems have appeared. Usually the main component of such a system is a verification condition generator (VCG) that takes as input an imperative program and a specification (under the form of pre/post-conditions and loop invariants) and outputs a list of logical conditions. These conditions are supposed to be proved manually or mechanically (using a theorem prover), and their satisfiability ensures the correctness of the program. As examples of tools that work this way we can cite the Stanford Pascal Verifier [ILL75], Gypsy [Goo85], EVES [KPS+92] or Penelope [GMP90]. Verification condition generators are also used in formal methods based on stepwise refinement like VDM [Jon86] or B [Abr95], as each refinement step has to be validated by proving the corresponding set of verification conditions.

However, if one verification condition cannot be proved this means that either the program does not satisfy its specification, or the specification does not state correctly the intended meaning of the program. In both cases the user is supposed to modify the program or the specification and the system does not give any hint on where this modification should occur. Even when trying to prove a true condition, stated as an ordinary first order logic formula, it is quite difficult to understand what one is trying to prove, and in which way this condition is related to a possible execution of the program. In other words, the absence of links between the source program and the verification conditions is a serious lack to the task of formal verification. To compensate, users do some kind of mental processing for retrieving the origin of terms that appear in a condition. For instance, by recognizing in a condition the negation of the test of an `if` statement, they deduce that this condition is generated by the **else** branch of this statement.

This paper proposes a way of mechanizing this process by instrumenting a verification condition generator with origin tracking facilities. This technique, proposed by Bertot in [Ber91a, Ber92, Ber93], has beeen initially applied in implementing source-level debugging of programming languages by establishing a relation between the current instruction and a position in the source program. Given a natural semantics description of the language, it is possible to integrate this relation in the semantics and the integration is shown to be systematic and semi-automatizable. Related work on origin tracking in the framework of algebraic specifications is reported by Van Deursen, Klint and Tip in [DKT93].

As origin tracking has been proved useful for interpreters, it is sensible to apply it to verification conditions generators. Indeed, both kinds of tools are similar in that they perform syntactic and semantic analysis on the input program and generate some output, be it the current state of an execution machine, or verification conditions. If debugging is considered essential in understanding program execution, there is no counterpart in program verification systems that could help understanding verification conditions. Our work represents an attempt to progress in this area.

We have applied these ideas in a verification condition generator built with the programming environment generator Centaur [Jac94]. We have benefited of the facilities of manipulating syntactic structures and of the built-in mechanisms of selection and highlighting. Alternative approaches could use other programming environment generators like the Synthesizer Generator [RT88], or ASF+SDF [Kli93].

The paper is organized as follows. Section 2 presents the algorithm of verification condition generation. In the section 3 we exemplify the problem to solve on a specific program and its conditions. Sections 4 and 5 introduce origin functions as a data structure well suited to represent descendance information. In section 6 we describe the integration of origin functions in the verification conditions generator and the complexity of the new algorithm is analyzed in section 7. Section 8 explains the particularities of the Centaur implementation. Section 9 studies the extensibility of this work to real program verification systems. We conclude in section 10 by some remarks on the connections with program slicing.

2   Verification condition generators

We will concentrate on a small imperative programming language with assignments, conditionals and loops. Programs are annotated with loop invariants and optional assertions can be placed before instructions. A BNF syntax of the language is given below. Variable declarations, expressions and first-order assertions are defined in the usual way.

\<program\> ::= **decl** \<decls\> **in** \{\<assert\>\} \<inst\> \{\<assert\>\}

<inst> ::= skip | <id> := <exp> | <annot_inst> ; <annot_inst> |
     if <exp> then <annot_inst> else <annot_inst> |
     while <exp> inv {<assert>} do <annot_inst>

<annot_inst> ::= {<assert>} <inst> | <inst>

The algorithm to generate verification conditions from an annotated program is based on Dijkstra's weakest-precondition calculus [Dij76]. Let $wp(I, Q)$ denote the *weakest precondition that should be satisfied before execution of I, for the postcondition Q to be true after execution of I*. The algorithm performs a backwards traversal of the instruction I starting from the postcondition Q, and computes the missing assertions at each intermediary point. When reaching a user provided assertion P, it generates a verification condition of the form $P \Rightarrow wp(I, Q)$, and it restarts with P as the new postcondition.

We introduce the relation[1] $Post \vdash I \rightarrow Pre, Conds$ with the meaning: *the postcondition Post is true after a terminating execution of the instruction I if the precondition Pre is true before executing I, and if the list of verification conditions Conds contains only valid formulas*. We restrict our presentation to partial correctness, but the same considerations apply to total correctness as well. In what follows, we use $[]$ to denote the empty list, $[a, b]$ for a list with two elements a and b, and $L_1.L_2$ for the concatenation of lists L_1 and L_2. The algorithm is described using inference rules:

$$Q \vdash \textbf{skip} \rightarrow Q, []$$

$$\frac{x, E \vdash Q \rightarrow Q'}{Q \vdash x := E \rightarrow Q', []}$$

$$\frac{Q \vdash I_2 \rightarrow P_2, Conds_2 \quad P_2 \vdash I_1 \rightarrow P_1, Conds_1}{Q \vdash I_1 ; I_2 \rightarrow P_1, Conds_1.Conds_2}$$

$$\frac{Q \vdash I_1 \rightarrow P_1, Conds_1 \quad Q \vdash I_2 \rightarrow P_2, Conds_2}{Q \vdash \textbf{if } B \textbf{ then } I_1 \textbf{ else } I_2 \rightarrow (B \Rightarrow P_1) \wedge (\neg B \Rightarrow P_2), Conds_1.Conds_2}$$

$$\frac{Inv \vdash S \rightarrow P, Conds}{Q \vdash \textbf{while } B \textbf{ inv } \{Inv\} \textbf{ do } S \rightarrow Inv, [Inv \wedge B \Rightarrow P, Inv \wedge \neg B \Rightarrow Q].Conds}$$

$$\frac{Q \vdash S \rightarrow P, Conds}{Q \vdash \{A\} S \rightarrow A, [A \Rightarrow P].Conds}$$

---

[1] The convention followed here is to separate inputs and outputs of the relation by an arrow "$\Rightarrow$". The input term preceded by a turnstyle "$\vdash$" is also distinguished as the *subject* of the relation, while the other inputs form the evaluation context.

The relation $x, E \vdash Q \to Q'$ stands for $Q' = Q[E/x]$ where the substitution $Q[E/x]$ is formalized in the usual way avoiding the capture of free variables in quantifications. We present below two typical substitution rules:

$$\frac{x, E \vdash P \to P' \qquad x, E \vdash R \to R'}{x, E \vdash P \wedge R \to P' \wedge R'} \tag{1}$$

$$x, E \vdash x \to E \tag{2}$$

Finally, we need a rule for computing the conditions for the whole program. The notation $\vdash Prog \to Conds$ stands for: $Conds$ is the set of verification conditions generated from the annotated program $Prog$.

$$\frac{Q \vdash I \to P', Conds}{\vdash \texttt{decl } Decls \texttt{ in } \{P\} \ I \ \{Q\} \to [P \Rightarrow P'].Conds} \tag{3}$$

3 An example

As an example, consider the following program computing the quotient q and the remainder r of the integer division of x by y. We have purposedly introduced a bug in the program: the test of the loop is $r > y$ instead of $r \geq y$. This way, if x is an exact multiple of y the program stops with r equal to y and not to 0.

```
decl
var x, y, q, r:integer
in
{x ≥ 0}
q := 0 ;
r := x ;
while r > y
inv { x = q * y + r ∧ r ≥ 0}
do
      q := q + 1 ;
      r := r − y ;
{x = q * y + r ∧ r ≥ 0 ∧ r < y}
```

$x \geq 0 \Rightarrow$
$\qquad x = 0 * y + x \wedge x \geq 0$

$x = q * y + r \wedge r \geq 0 \wedge r > y \Rightarrow$
$\qquad \boxed{x = (q+1) * y + r - y} \wedge r - y \geq 0$

$x = q * y + r \wedge r \geq 0 \wedge \boxed{\neg \boxed{r > y}} \Rightarrow$
$\qquad x = q * y + r \wedge r \geq 0 \wedge r < y$

☐ - existing term with no modified subterms.

⬭ - newly created term.

⊡ - existing term with modified subterms.

Fig. 1. An integer division program and its verification conditions

In the figure 1 the program is shown on the left-hand side and the verification conditions on the right-hand side. The three conditions state in order that the invariant is satisfied at the entry of the loop, the invariant is preserved by each loop iteration, and the postcondition is satisfied at the exit of the loop. The error appears in the last verification condition, that cannot be satisfied since $\neg(r > y)$

does not imply $r < y$. A system based on the technique proposed in this paper automatically highlights the origin of $r > y$ in the source program, when the user selects this expression in the verification condition.

Note also that the origin of $r > y$ is exactly the same expression in the program. This is not always the case. We distinguish two other cases:

- there are expressions like $\neg\ (r > y)$ that have no origin, although some of their subexpressions might have an origin. They represent new terms that have been constructed from already existing expressions during the generation process.
- more subtly, an expression like $x = (q + 1) * y + r - y$ has its origin in the subexpression $x = q * y + r$ of the loop invariant, but some of its subexpressions, like $q + 1$ and $r - y$, have their origins in the right-hand sides of the assignments in the loop body.

We will propose a representation of origin informations that takes into account these differences by avoiding to store the origins of all subterms of a term that was not changed during the condition generation.

4   Origin functions

In order to understand how parts of the source program appear at different positions in the verification conditions, let us consider a very simple program decl D in $\{P\}\ x := E\ \{x > 0\}$ which generates only one verification condition: $P \Rightarrow E > 0$. Considering the program and the condition as trees the descendance relation can be depicted as in the figure 2.

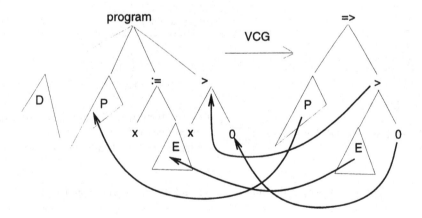

Fig. 2. The descendance relation

It is obvious that a node at any position in area P in the condition descends from the node at the same position in area P in the program. The same goes for the area E, while individual nodes like ">" and "0" descend from their counterparts in the program.

Occurrences are the most natural way to denote positions in trees. For every natural number k, we consider the function s_k which maps any tree, $op(t_1, \ldots, t_k, \ldots, t_n)$, to its child of rank k, i.e, t_k. We call an *occurrence* any function obtained by composing an arbitrary number of times the functions s_k. The composition operation is denoted $\circ$, we denote its neutral element id, and $\mathcal{O}$ is the set of all the occurrences. For any tree T we call its *domain*, denoted $\mathcal{D}(T)$, the set of occurrences that are valid on this tree.

For example, if we consider the tree $T = f(g(1, 2), 3)$, we have $s_2(T) = 3$, $s_1(T) = g(1, 2)$, and $s_2 \circ s_1(T) = 2$. The domain of the tree T is the set $\mathcal{D}(T) = \{id, s_1, s_2, s_1 \circ s_1, s_2 \circ s_1\}$.

There are two reasons for preferring this unusual representation of occurrences. First, ascending paths are well-suited for top-down recursive computations (as in the VCG algorithm), as from the occurrence of a node one can compute in constant time the occurrence of a son. of a son can be computed in constant time. Second, projections are more flexible to manipulate than lists of integers. For instance, the subterm at a given occurrence is obtained by simple function application.

Following [Ber93], we remark that the relation of descendance is simply a relation between occurrences in the final term and occurrences in the initial term. We also notice that the converse of this descendance relation is a function (called the *origin function*) from $\mathcal{D}(Conds)$ to $\mathcal{D}(Prog)$. The origin function is partial as there might be some nodes in $Conds$ newly created during the generation, thus with no origin in $Prog$. In order to make this function total we associate a special value nil to all the nodes that have no origin. Denoting by $\mathcal{O}_{nil}$ the set $\mathcal{O} \cup \{nil\}$, we let $Orig = \mathcal{O}_{nil} \to \mathcal{O}_{nil}$ be the type of origin functions. The occurrence composition $\circ$ can be extended to $\mathcal{O}_{nil}$ as follows:

$$u \circ nil = nil \circ u = nil, \ u \in \mathcal{O}_{nil}$$

For instance, the origin function O corresponding to the figure 2 is given by:

$$O(id) = nil$$
$$O(u \circ s_1) = u \circ s_2, \ u \in \mathcal{D}(P)$$
$$O(s_2) = s_4$$
$$O(v \circ s_1 \circ s_2) = v \circ s_2 \circ s_3, \ v \in \mathcal{D}(E)$$
$$O(s_2 \circ s_2) = s_2 \circ s_4$$
$$O(w) = nil, \ w \in \mathcal{O}_{nil} \setminus \mathcal{D}(Conds)$$

5 Representing origin functions

Our problem being to compute the origin function relating occurrences in $Conds$ to occurrences in $Prog$, we have to choose first a suitable representation for origin functions. As explained in this section, we end up with a non-trivial data structure motivated by the need of mixing implicit and explicit informations.

A natural idea is to label each node of *Conds* with the occurrence of the corresponding node in *Prog* if there is such a node, and with *nil* otherwise. The representation of the origin function can follow the recursive structure of terms: suppose we want to describe the labels carried by a term $M = op(t_1, \ldots, t_n)$. These labels will be completely described once we have given the label u carried by the head of the term, and the origin functions $f_1, \ldots, f_n$ for the terms $t_1, \ldots, t_n$. The functions $f_1, \ldots, f_n$ may in turn be defined in the same way recursively.

Denoting $Orig^*$ the set of tuples $[f_1, \ldots, f_n]$ of origin functions, we introduce the mapping $c : (Orig^* \times \mathcal{O}_{nil}) \to Orig$ that maps a tuple of origin functions over occurrences and an occurrence to an origin function defined by the following properties:

$$c([f_1, \ldots, f_n], u)(id) = u \tag{4}$$

$$c([f_1, \ldots, f_n], u)(v \circ s_i) = f_i(v), \ i \leq n \tag{5}$$

$$c([f_1, \ldots, f_n], u)(w) = nil, \ w \in \{nil\} \cup \{v \circ s_i \mid i > n\} \tag{6}$$

Note that in the case of a leaf the tuple $[f_1, \ldots, f_n]$ is empty, the corresponding origin function having the form $c([], u)$. The operator c gives the possibility to describe *extensionally* the labeling of a term as it permits to construct a tree isomorphic to the labeled term, carrying all the labels. Obviously, this notation is powerful enough to represent all origin functions.

However, as discussed in [Ber93], this representation would be highly redundant. Let $T = u(Prog)$ be a term that gets translated without modifications from *Prog* to *Conds* (as is the case for P or E in the figure 2). The origin function f associated to T is a very regular one: $f(v) = v \circ u$ for any occurrence $v \in \mathcal{D}(T)$. An informal explanation of this statement (see figure 3) is: if t is the subterm of T at the occurence v then

$$t = v(T) = v(u(Prog)) = (v \circ u)(Prog)$$

This suggests interpreting occurrences as origin functions in the following way. We introduce a mapping $\mu : \mathcal{O} \to Orig$ defined by the property:

$$\mu(u)(v) = v \circ u, \ u \in \mathcal{O}, \ v \in \mathcal{O}_{nil} \tag{7}$$

Now, for each term $T = u(Prog)$ as above, its origin function would be simply denoted by u, being interpreted by the function $\mu(u)$. This way we pass from an *extensional* representation, demanding an explicit labeling of each node, to an *intensional* one. The operator μ will be systematically omitted in practical manipulations, as it is always possible to infer from the context, when u should be interpreted as an occurrence or as the corresponding origin function.

Considering again the example of the figure 2, the origin function O can be represented by $O = c([s_2, c([s_2 \circ s_3, s_2 \circ s_4], s_4)], nil)$. The tree representation in figure 4 is easier to understand, as it shows the correspondence between nodes in

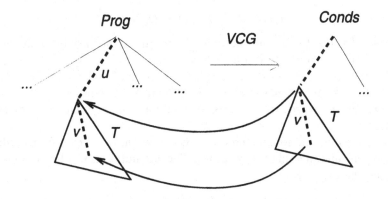

Fig. 3. A regular origin function

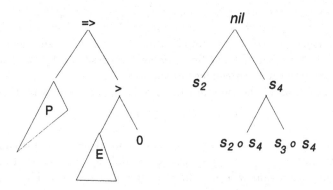

Fig. 4. A tree representation of the origin function

the syntactic tree of the conditions and their labels in the origin function. It is interesting to remark that due to the intensionality this representation holds for arbitrary values of P and E. This property will be essential when instrumenting the generation algorithm with origin computations.

6 Computing origin functions

In this section we show how to integrate origin functions in the VCG algorithm, by adding them as new parameters to each rule. This way, every term t will be annotated with its origin function O_t relative to the initial term of the computation $Prog$. First, the relation $\vdash Prog \to Conds$ will be extended to a new relation $\vdash Prog \to O_{Conds} : Conds$ that computes not only $Conds$ but also its origin function O_{Conds}. In turn, this requires corresponding extensions of the other relations, as shown below:

$$O_{Post} : Post \vdash O_{Inst} : Inst \to O_{Pre} : Pre, O_{Conds} : Conds$$

$$x, O_E : E \vdash O_Q : Q \to O_{Q'} : Q'$$

The reason for not taking into account the origin of the variable x in the last relation, is that x only acts as a binder here, and it will not appear in the result of the substitution Q'. This shows that the extension of each relation with origin functions is not as systematic as one might think. It requires in particular a data-flow analysis to see which parts of the input could actually appear in the output.

In order to accommodate these extensions we have to modify accordingly the inference rules defining the relations. The computation will be initialised by modifying the rule (3) to:

$$\frac{s_4 : Q \vdash s_3 : I \to O_{P'} : P', O_{Conds} : Conds}{\vdash \texttt{decl } Decls \text{ in } \{P\}\ I\ \{Q\} \to c([s_2, O_{P'}], nil).O_{Conds} : [P \Rightarrow P'].Conds}$$

The fact that s_4 is the origin functions of Q follows from $Q = s_4(Prog)$. In the same way s_3 and s_2 are the origin functions of I and P. The origin function of $P \Rightarrow P'$ is $c([s_2, O_{P'}], nil)$ as the implication "$\Rightarrow$" has no origin itself. Note also that the origin function of a list like $Conds$ is represented by the list of origin functions associated to each element of the list.

The modification of the rule for skip needs no further explanation:

$$O_Q : Q \vdash O_I : \texttt{skip} \to O_Q : Q, [] : []$$

The only difficulty in the assignment rule (shown below) is proving that the origin function of E is $O_E = O_I \circ s_2$, where $\circ$ stands for the composition of origin functions (operation that will be defined in the next section). This follows from $E = s_2(I)$:

Let v be an arbitrary occurrence in $\mathcal{D}(E)$.
Then the subterm at the occurrence v in E is

$$v(E) = v(s_2(I)) = (v \circ s_2)(I)$$

so the origin of this subterm in $Prog$ is given by:

$$O_E(v) = O_I(v \circ s_2) = O_I(s_2(v)) = (O_I \circ s_2)(v)$$

By extensionality we infer $O_E = O_I \circ s_2$.

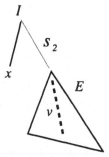

$$\frac{x, O_I \circ s_2 : E \vdash O_Q : Q \to O_{Q'} : Q'}{O_Q : Q \vdash O_I : x := E \to O_{Q'} : Q', [] : []}$$

One can already see that the integration of origin functions in each rule is systematic as it respects the following general principle:

- Compute the origins of inputs in premises and the origins of outputs in the conclusion as a function of already computed origins (of inputs in the conclusion or of outputs in premises). In this respect, we remark the analogy with the evaluation of synthesized and inherited attributes in Attribute Grammars.

– The computed origins have to be coherent with the structure of terms, and also satisfy the property of *common variables*: each occurrence of a same variable in a rule has to be annotated with the same origin function.

For the sake of completeness, we present below the modifications of the other rules of the VCG algorithm:

$$\frac{O_Q : Q \vdash O_I \circ s_2 : I_2 \to O_{P_2} : P_2, O_{Conds_2} : Conds_2 \quad O_{P_2} : P_2 \vdash O_I \circ s_1 : I_1 \to O_{P_1} : P_1, O_{Conds_1} : Conds_1}{O_Q : Q \vdash O_I : I_1 \; ; \; I_2 \to O_{P_1} : P_1, O_{Conds_1}.O_{Conds_2} : Conds_1.Conds_2}$$

$$\frac{O_Q : Q \vdash O_I \circ s_2 : I_1 \to O_{P_1} : P_1, O_{Conds_1} : Conds_1 \quad O_Q : Q \vdash O_I \circ s_3 : I_2 \to O_{P_2} : P_2, O_{Conds_2} : Conds_2}{\begin{array}{l} O_Q : Q \vdash O_I : \text{if } B \text{ then } I_1 \text{ else } I_2 \to \\ \quad c([c([O_I \circ s_1, O_{P_1}], nil), c([c([O_I \circ s_1]), nil), O_{P_2}], nil)], nil) : \\ \quad (B \Rightarrow P_1) \wedge (\neg B \Rightarrow P_2), O_{Conds_1}.O_{Conds_2} : Conds_1.Conds_2 \end{array}}$$

$$\frac{O_I \circ s_2 : Inv \vdash O_I \circ s_3 : S \to O_P : P, O_{Conds} : Conds}{\begin{array}{l} O_Q : Q \vdash O_I : \text{while } B \text{ inv } \{Inv\} \text{ do } S \to O_I \circ s_2 : Inv, \\ \quad [c([c([O_I \circ s_2, O_I \circ s_1], nil), O_P], nil), \\ \quad c([c([O_I \circ s_2, c([O_I \circ s_1], nil)], nil), O_Q], nil)].O_{Conds} : \\ \quad [Inv \wedge B \Rightarrow P, Inv \wedge \neg B \Rightarrow Q].Conds \end{array}}$$

$$\frac{O_Q : Q \vdash O_I \circ s_2 : S \to O_P : P, O_{Conds} : Conds}{\begin{array}{l} O_Q : Q \vdash O_I : \{A\} \; S \to O_I \circ s_1 : O_A, \\ \quad [c([O_I \circ s_1, O_P], nil)].O_{Conds} : [A \Rightarrow P].Conds \end{array}}$$

This shows that the manipulation of origin functions becomes quite tedious in the case of more complex rules, but it is still systematic. For instance, in the if rule $c([c([O_I \circ s_1, O_{P_1}], nil), c([c([O_I \circ s_1], nil), O_{P_2}], nil)], nil)$ is the origin function of $(B \Rightarrow P_1) \wedge (\neg B \Rightarrow P_2)$ where $c([O_I \circ s_1, O_{P_1}], nil)$ is the origin function of $B \Rightarrow P_1$, etc.

Given the difficulty of hand-writing such complex rules, it is sensible to investigate the possibility of automatizing the derivation of the new algorithm from the initial one. This automatization is possible for most of the rules, but there are still some delicate cases as exemplified by the substitution rules:

$$\frac{x, O_E : E \vdash O_Q \circ s_1 : P \to O_{P'} : P' \quad x, O_E : E \vdash O_Q \circ s_2 : R \to O_{R'} : R'}{x, O_E : E \vdash O_Q : P \wedge R \to c([O_{P'}, O_{R'}], O_Q(id)) : P' \wedge R'} \quad (8)$$

$$x, O_E : E \vdash O_Q : x \to O_E : E$$

We use the occurrence $O_Q(id)$ in the rule (8) to indicate that the operator $\wedge$ in $P' \wedge R'$ descends from the same operator in $P \wedge R$. Unfortunately, this information cannot be derived automatically from the syntactic form of the rule (1). It is this kind of semantic reasoning that prevents us from having an automatic instrumentation of the initial algorithm with origin computations.

Van Deursen, Klint and Tip [DKT93] propose some useful heuristics for dealing with such cases. For instance, an heuristic that will solve the problem above considers that the top symbol of the output tree descends from the top symbol of the input tree. However, this approach is still limited as there are examples where the heuristics will fail to establish some descendance relations.

As an alternative, we can envision a semi-automatic approach where an approximate version of each modified rule is generated automatically. This version will only take into account the 'syntactic descendance' information given by the property of *common variables*, and might be further adjusted by the user to accommodate 'semantic descendance' information.

7 The complexity of the modified algorithm

In this section we prove that the additional overhead of computing origin functions does not modify the global time complexity of the VCG algorithm. The proof is based on a complexity analysis of the two new operations used in the algorithm: the application of an origin function to an occurrence, and the composition of two origin functions.

Lemma 1. *If f is an origin function and v an occurrence, then the time required to compute $f(v)$ is $\mathcal{O}(size_O(v))$, where:*

$$size_O(v \circ s_i) = 1 + size_O(v)$$
$$size_O(id) = 0$$

Proof By induction on the structure of v using the equations (4)-(7). □

Lemma 2. *If f and g are two origin functions, then the time complexity of computing $f \circ g$ is $\mathcal{O}(size_{Orig}(g))$ where:*

$$size_{Orig}(c[f_1, \ldots, f_n], u) = 1 + size_O(u) + size_{Orig}(f_1) + \ldots + size_{Orig}(f_n)$$
$$size_{Orig}(\mu(v)) = size_O(v)$$

Proof The composition of two origin functions can be defined recursively on the structure of the second function, as follows:

$$f \circ c([f_1, \ldots, f_n], u) = c([f \circ f_1, \ldots, f \circ f_n], f(u))$$
$$c([f_1, \ldots, f_n], u) \circ \mu(v \circ s_i) = f_i \circ \mu(v)$$
$$f \circ \mu(id) = f$$
$$\mu(v) \circ \mu(u) = \mu(u \circ v)$$

All the equalities above can be verified easily, by applying each side of an equality to an arbitrary occurrence w. The proof follows by structural induction on g.□

Proposition 3. *The modified VCG algorithm has the same time complexity as the initial one (modulo a multiplying constant).*

Proof The complexity of each algorithm is given by the number of inference steps. The new algorithm takes the same steps as the initial one, but each step might take some additional time to compute occurrences like $O_Q(id)$ or origin functions like $O_I \circ s_2$. But according to the two lemmas above these additional computations can be done in constant time. □

The price of intensionality When a variable x has no free occurrence in an expression Q, the result of the substitution is still Q, but the corresponding origin function has a completely extensional representation instead of a more concise, intensional one. This is due to rules like (8) that systematically use the operator c for constructing origin functions. If we really want to exploit the advantages of an intensional representation, we have to distinguish explicitly the case when no substitution effectively occurs. This can be done by the means of the following normalization rule (whose validity can be proved by applying both sides of the equality to an arbitrary occurrence w):

$$c([f \circ s_1, \ldots, f \circ s_n], f(id)) = f, \ f \in Orig \tag{9}$$

Applying this rule in (8) we obtain that if $O_P = O_{P'}$ and $O_R = O_{R'}$ then $O_{Q'} = c([O_{P'}, O_{R'}], O_Q(id)) = O_Q$.

However, the complexity of the equality tests on origin functions is proportional to the size of the functions, so we loose the property of constant time overhead for computing origin functions. Instead of equality tests we might use a boolean that records for the current subtree if a substitution has actually occurred or not. Although this solution is less elegant, it preserves the essential property of a constant time overhead for computing origin functions.

8 Implementation in Centaur

The VCG algorithm is written in the Typol formalism [Des84], that allows one to specify natural semantics in an inference-rule style. This style of specification is well suited to execution, as it can easily be related with Prolog, Attribute Grammars or functional evaluation.

After computing *Conds* and O_{Conds} the next step is to descend recursively in the two trees by labeling each node of *Conds* with its origin given by the corresponding node in O_{Conds}. As the two trees are not really isomorphic (due to the intensionality) a leaf in O_{Conds} might correspond to an entire subtree in *Conds*. In this case we do not descend further in that subtree, as the origin information is implicit for the nodes below.

Using Centaur, we benefit from the facilities of a syntax directed editor like selection and highlight mechanisms. Thus when selecting a term t in a verification condition, we obtain a pointer to the corresponding node in the syntactic tree of *Conds*. If t is not labeled, we have to compute its implicit origin by going upwards in the tree until we reach a labeled ancestor T of t. If T is labeled with the occurrence u and $t = v(T)$ then t descends from the occurrence $v \circ u$ in *Prog* (see figure 3).

Once the origin of t has been computed, if it different from *nil* we want to send this value from the window containing the verification conditions to the one containing the source program. This is done using Sophtalk [JMBC93] with the two windows declared as nodes of a network, the communication being asynchronous and event-driven. When receiving the occurence denoting the origin of t, the corresponding subtree is highlighted in the window of *Prog*.

9   Scaling up to real verification condition generators

We have described in this paper the instrumentation of a program verification system with origin informations relating terms in the verification conditions to terms in the source program. Of a particular importance is that the the modified algorithm has the same time complexity as the initial one. The use of an intensional representation makes it possible to reduce memory consumption.

However, real verification condition generators are more complicated than the one presented in this paper. In this section we investigate the application of the method proposed in this paper to these generators.

In the case of complex programming languages, there is a normalization phase reducing all the constructs of the language to some set of normal forms (for example, transforming `repeat` and `for` loops in `while` loops). There is also a simplifier, whose task is to discharge automatically some trivial verification conditions and simplify the remaining ones. As origin tracking follows a general principle that applies to arbitrary tree manipulations, origin informations can be propagated throughout the various pre/post-processing steps. Note also that our approach has the pleasant property of being language-independent, as the representation of origin functions does not interfere with the particular syntax of annotated programs.

In the case of formal methods based on stepwise refinement like B [Abr95], when proving that a concrete implementation is compatible with an abstract specification, the terms appearing in a verification condition might have their origins in the specification or in the implementation. Although our method assumes that the computation has a single input, it can be trivially extended to multiple inputs. It is enough to consider the forest formed by the trees of all inputs as a single tree with a fictive root.

The semi-automatic approach of generating the modified program from the initial one suggested in the section 6 may be of great help when dealing with large generators. It becomes essential if the generator makes use of *adaptive* proof rules, as is the case for the Stanford Pascal Verifier [ILL75] or EVES [KPS+92]. One needs a formal representation of the language in which the generation program is written, in order to be able to describe transformations on the programs of this language. It is also important to have a clear semantics of this language (or at least of the subset of the language used in the generation algorithm) as the transformations require precise data-flow analysis on the initial program. These requirements are satisfied by most of the verification condition generators as they are written in a symbolic processing language like Lisp, ML or Prolog.

10   Future work

Until now we have explained how to retrieve the origins of various subexpressions of a verification condition. However, this only gives a local understanding, but does not solve the problem of relating a verification condition to a corresponding loop-free execution path in the program. A way of doing this is to associate to the condition the union of the origins of all subexpressions of this condition. The union will contain the occurrences of right-hand sides of assignments, and tests of conditionals and loops that appear in the condition.

Although this approach gives only a rough approximation, it could be worked out such as to identify exactly the corresponding execution path. In fact, it is even more selective, as it gives only the instructions that contribute effectively to the generation of the condition. This relates our work to program slicing techniques [Wei84]. Informally, a program slice contains the parts of a program that affect the values computed at some designated point of interest.

Further work will exploit this connection. Instead of proving that a conjunct of assertions is true at a point in the program, one can prove that each assertion is true on the corresponding slice of the program, and regroup the proofs of the separate slices together to obtain a proof of the whole program.

Acknowledgements. I am very grateful to Yves Bertot for many useful comments and helpful suggestions.

References

[Abr95]   J-R. Abrial. *The B-Book. Assigning Programs to Meanings*. Cambridge University Press, 1995. (to appear).

[Ber91a]   Y. Bertot. Occurrences in Debugger Specifications. In *ACM SIGPLAN Conference on Programming Language Design and Implementation*, 1991.

[Ber91b]   Y. Bertot. *Une Automatisation du Calcul des Résidus en Sémantique Naturelle*. PhD thesis, Université de Nice-Sophia Antipolis, 1991.

[Ber92]   Y. Bertot. Origin Functions in λ-calculus and Term Rewriting Systems. In *CAAP'92*, 1992. Springer Verlag LNCS 581.

[Ber93]   Y. Bertot. A Canonical Calculus of Residuals. In G. Huet and G. Plotkin, editors, *Logical Frameworks*, pages 147–163. Cambridge University Press, 1993. (also appears as INRIA Report no. 1542, Oct. 1991).

[Des84]   T. Despeyroux. Executable Specifications of Static Semantics. In *International Symposium on Semantics of Data Types*, 1984. Springer-Verlag LNCS 173.

[Dij76]   E.W. Dijkstra. *A Discipline of Programming*. Prentice-Hall, 1976.

[DKT93]   A.V. Deursen, P. Klint, and F. Tip. Origin Tracking. In *Journal of Symbolic Computation*, volume 15, pages 523–545, 1993.

[Flo66]   R.W. Floyd. Assigning Meanings to Programs. In J.T. Schwartz, editor, *Mathematical Aspects of Computer Science : Proceedings of the 19th Symposium in Applied Mathematics*, pages 19–32, Providence, United States, 1966.

[GMP90] D. Guaspari, C. Marceau, and W. Polak. Formal Verification of Ada Programs. In *IEEE Transactions on Software Engineering*, volume 16, pages 1058–1075, September 1990.

[Goo85] D.I. Good. Mechanical Proofs about Computer Programs. In C.A.R. Hoare and J.C. Sheperdson, editors, *Mathematical Logic and Programming Languages*. Prentice Hall, 1985.

[Hoa69] C.A.R. Hoare. An Axiomatic Basis for Computer Programming. In *Communications of the ACM*, October 1969.

[ILL75] S. Igarashi, R.L. London, and D.C. Luckham. Automatic Program Verification: A Logical Basis and its Implementation. In *Acta Informatica*, volume 4, pages 145–182, 1975.

[Jac94] I. Jacobs. The Centaur Reference Manual. Technical report, INRIA, Sophia-Antipolis, 1994.

[JMBC93] I. Jacobs, F. Montagnac, J. Bertot, and D. Clement. The Sophtalk Reference Manual. Technical Report 150, INRIA, Sophia-Antipolis, 1993.

[Jon86] C. Jones. *Systematic Software Development using VDM*. Prentice-Hall, 1986.

[Kli93] P. Klint. A Meta-environment for Generating Programming Environments. In *ACM Transaction on Software Engineering and Methodology*, volume 2, pages 176–201, 1993.

[KPS$^+$92] S. Kromodimoeljo, B. Pase, M. Saaltink, D. Craigen, and I. Meisels. The EVES System. In *Proceedings of the International Lecture Series on Functional Programming, Concurrency, Simulation and Automated Reasoning*, 1992.

[RT88] T. Reps and T. Teitelbaum. *The Synthesizer Generator: a System for Constructing Language Based Editors*. Springer Verlag, 1988. (third edition).

[Wei84] M. Weiser. Program Slicing. In *IEEE Transactions on Software Engineering*, volume 10, page 352, 1984.

Preprocessing for Invariant Validation[1]

E. Pascal Gribomont

University of Liège (Belgium)

Topics : *formal verification of concurrent systems, theorem proving systems*

Abstract. Hoare's logic and Dijkstra's predicate transformer calculus have proved adequate for reducing the correctness problem for programs to the validity problem for logical formulas. However, the size of the logical formulas to be validated grows faster than the size of the program, and, even in the propositional case, the validation problem is NP-complete and becomes practically intractable for large programs. We introduce a strategy for dealing with this problem. The principle is to write the formulas in the form $(h_1 \wedge \cdots \wedge h_n) \Rightarrow c$, and to use efficiently computable criteria to select a small subset $I \subset \{1, \dots, n\}$ such that c remains a logical consequence of $H_I = \{h_i : i \in I\}$. These criteria are motivated and the efficiency of the method is investigated.

1 Introduction

A classical method for proving that some concurrent system S is correct with respect to some safety property J, when initial condition A holds, is the invariant method. In this case, an invariant is a formula I satisfying three conditions :

1. $\models (A \Rightarrow I)$;
2. $\{I\}\, \tau\, \{I\}$, for all atomic actions τ of S;
3. $\models (I \Rightarrow J)$.

The notation $\sigma \models B$ means that formula (or assertion) B is true in state σ, and $\models B$ means that B is true in every program state.

Condition 1 expresses that I is true initially, condition 2 means that I is respected by each transition τ of the program, that is, if state σ satisfies I and if transition τ leads from state σ to state ρ, then state ρ also satisfies I. When these three conditions hold, it is clear that all states of all computations (whose initial state satisfies A) do satisfy the safety requirement J; otherwise stated, J holds throughout the computation.

This method is reputed to have three drawbacks :

1. Only safety properties are within the scope of the method.
2. Invariant design is often a subtle task.

---

[1] *Correspondence to :*

P. Gribomont   Phone :   +32 41 66 26 67
Institut Montefiore   Fax :   +32 41 66 29 84
ULg, Sart-Tilman, B 28   e-mail :   gribomon@montefiore.ulg.ac.be
B – 4000 Liège (Belgium)

3. Invariant validation becomes intractable for large programs.

The first point is of little practical significance, since the liveness properties of a program (the most relevant kind of non-safety properties) usually are consequences of previously established safety properties, joined with a fairness assumption. (This has been demonstrated many times in the literature, for instance in [7].) The second drawback is more real, but the discovery of adequate invariants is made easier by using an incremental methodology (more about this later). The third drawback is more serious. Most invariant design methodologies, including the incremental one just mentioned, are in fact trial-and-error methods: "promising candidate invariants" are rather easily produced, but have to be checked for invariance. Even for programs of moderate size, a complete verification is an awfully long and tedious work. The purpose of this paper is to contribute to solve this problem.

It should be noted first that the verification conditions associated with a program and an invariant are not "difficult" formulas, in so far only elementary mathematical results about data models (integers, arrays, and so on) are needed to validate them. The only problem is the size of the formulas. A straightforward approach is to use an automatic theorem prover. Many successful experiments with theorem provers, and especially with the well-known Boyer-Moore prover, have been reported in the literature (see e.g. [13, 25, 26]). In fact, this prover can deal with far deeper mathematical formulas than verification conditions, but it is not able to deal quickly with very long formulas, for an obvious reason. Even in the pure propositional case (and we are seldom in this case) the validity problem is NP-complete, so no *general* algorithm for validity checking can be practically efficient in all cases.[2] We intend to take advantage of the very specific structure of invariant verification conditions to produce a practically efficient validation system; for now, only "nearly finite-state" systems are considered, i.e., systems for which nearly all variables have finite range [17].

The sequel of this paper is as follows. Section 2 recalls briefly the invariant method with an example; the specific structure of verification conditions is described. Our algorithm is introduced and investigated in Section 3. Section 4 is devoted to a worked-out example and Section 5 contains comparison with related work and the conclusion.

2 Structure of invariant verification conditions

2.1 Construction of the invariant and verification conditions

The procedure is best recalled on a short example (see e.g. [16] for more details) of a simple algorithm for mutual exclusion.

---

[2] It is well-known that some NP-complete problems allow algorithms which behave efficiently for most instances occurring in practice but, until now, this is not the case for the propositional validity problem, although rather recent techniques like connection-based methods and the use of ordered binary decision diagrams have led to substantial improvement.

We consider a resource shared by n distributed computing stations. The resource is directed by a controller which must provide access in mutual exclusion. A station p is initially in a non-critical section (state p_n). It performs internal computation until access to the shared resource becomes necessary, that is, until an internal condition, denoted rcs_p, becomes true. At this moment, a request (REQ_p) is sent to the controller. The access can be delayed (waiting state p_w). When the permission has been granted by the controller (OK_p), the station may use the resource (state p_c), until the internal condition rcs_p becomes false; at this time, the station releases the resource (END_p) and returns to its non-critical section (state p_n). At every time, the station p is in one and only one of its three possible states: exactly one of the place predicates $at\ p_n$, $at\ p_w$ and $at\ p_c$ holds.

The controller deals with a variable $INCS$ and a waiting queue E. $INCS$ is intended to record the name of the station currently lying in its critical section; its value will be $\bot$ when no station performs its critical section. Variable E is intended to record the names of the waiting stations. The controller is ready to receive a message when $at\ C$ is true; at C'_p (at C''_p) means that the controller has just received a request (a release) from station p, and has to react to this message before receiving any other.

It is not difficult to translate this informal description into code:

$$(p_n, \neg rcs_p \longrightarrow [\,], p_n),$$
$$(p_n, rcs_p \longrightarrow REQ_p := 1, p_w),$$
$$(p_w, OK_p = 1 \longrightarrow OK_p := 0, p_c),$$
$$(p_c, rcs_p \longrightarrow [\,], p_c),$$
$$(p_c, \neg rcs_p \longrightarrow END_p := 1, p_n),$$

$$(C, REQ_p = 1 \longrightarrow REQ_p := 0, C'_p),$$
$$(C'_p, INCS = \bot \longrightarrow (INCS, OK_p) := (p, 1), C),$$
$$(C'_p, INCS \neq \bot \longrightarrow E := E \cup \{p\}, C),$$
$$(C, END_p = 1 \longrightarrow END_p := 0, C''_p),$$
$$(C''_p, q \in E \longrightarrow (INCS, E, OK_q) := (q, E \setminus \{q\}, 1), C),$$
$$(C''_p, E = \emptyset \longrightarrow INCS := \bot, C),$$

where p and q are the names of arbitrary distinct stations.[3]

However, even for such a short program, it is not so easy to discover the appropriate invariant, establishing that two stations p and q cannot be at the same time in their critical section (in formula: $\forall p, q\,[\neg at\ p_c \vee \neg at\ q_c]$). The incremental method consists in considering first an abstract version of the program, where synchronization problems have been removed. For instance, we can consider that every communication is instantaneous, and further that any reaction to a message is also instantaneous. As a result, intermediate states of the controller (i.e., C'_p and C''_p, for each station p) disappear. The abstract version is quite a lot simpler:[4]

---

[3] The code should be self-explanatory. For instance, transition $(C''_p, q \in E \longrightarrow (INCS, E, OK_q) := (q, E \setminus \{q\}, 1), C)$ can be executed when the controller has received a release from station p while the waiting set is not empty. The specified reaction of the controller is the selection of an arbitrary waiting station q, which receives the OK-message and the access to the shared resource; q is also removed from the waiting set.

[4] In the abstract version, some transitions involve process synchronisation. For instance, transition $(p_c q_w C, \ldots, p_n q_c C)$ involves stations p and q and the controller; it is enabled only in states satisfying $at\ p_c q_w C$, that is, $at\ p_c \wedge at\ q_w \wedge at\ C$.

$$(p_n, \neg rcs_p \longrightarrow [\,], p_n),$$
$$(p_n C, \ rcs_p \wedge INCS = \bot \longrightarrow INCS := p, p_c C),$$
$$(p_n C, \ rcs_p \wedge INCS \neq \bot \longrightarrow E := E \cup \{p\}, p_w C),$$
$$(p_c, \ rcs_p \longrightarrow [\,], p_c),$$
$$(p_c q_w C, \neg rcs_p \wedge q \in E \longrightarrow (INCS, E) := (q, E \setminus \{q\}), p_n q_c C),$$
$$(p_c C, \neg rcs_p \wedge E = \emptyset \longrightarrow INCS := \bot, p_n C).$$

and an adequate invariant is now readily found:

$$\forall p \, (at \ p_w \equiv p \in E) \qquad (E \text{ is the waiting set})$$
$$\wedge \ \forall p \, (INCS = p \equiv at \ p_c) \quad (INCS \text{ records the station within its C.S., if any})$$
$$\wedge \ (INCS = \bot \ \Rightarrow \ E = \emptyset) \quad (\text{resource is free only when waiting set is empty}).$$

In fact, the intuitive meaning of each line is obvious.

Comment. Appropriate initial conditions are

$$\forall p \, (at \ p_n) \ \wedge \ INCS = \bot \ \wedge \ E = \emptyset.$$

We can now adapt the invariant of the abstract program in order to get an invariant of the real program.[5] For instance, assertion

$$at \ p_w \equiv p \in E$$

has to be replaced by the following set of assertions:

$$(at \ p_w \equiv [at \ C'_p \vee REQ_p = 1 \vee OK_p = 1 \vee p \in E])$$
$$\wedge \ at \ C'_p \Rightarrow [REQ_p = OK_p = 0 \wedge p \notin E]$$
$$\wedge \ REQ_p = 1 \Rightarrow [\neg at \ C'_p \wedge OK_p = 0 \wedge p \notin E]$$
$$\wedge \ OK_p = 1 \Rightarrow [\neg at \ C'_p \wedge REQ_p = 0 \wedge p \notin E]$$
$$\wedge \ p \in E \Rightarrow [\neg at \ C'_p \wedge REQ_p = OK_p = 0].$$

Comment. If we view *false* as 0 and *true* as 1, a more concise form is available:
$at \ p_w = (at \ C'_p + REQ_p + OK_p + p \in E).$

2.2 Structural properties of the verification conditions

The invariant appears as a conjunctive set of assertions, say

$$I =_{def} \bigwedge_{k \in K} a_k.$$

For realistic programs, the size of the set can be quite large, but typically most individual assertions remain small; the sizes of I and of S are roughly the same.

The set of verification conditions associated with the program S and the invariant I is defined as

$$V =_{def} \bigwedge_{k \in K} \bigwedge_{\tau \in S} (I \Rightarrow wlp[\tau; a_k]).$$

---

[5] In this paper, we are not concerned with the incremental adaptation procedure but only with the validation of the "candidates" produced by this procedure (see e.g. [20, 16] for an introduction to the procedure).

Comments. We take into account that wlp is $\wedge$-additive: $wlp[\tau; (a_k \wedge a_\ell)]$ is equivalent to $wlp[\tau; a_k] \wedge wlp[\tau; a_\ell]$, and also that $(A \Rightarrow \bigwedge_k B_k)$ is equivalent to $\bigwedge_k (A \Rightarrow B_k)$. The notation wlp stands for "weakest liberal precondition". In practice, the size of V is quadratic in the size of $\mathcal{S}$.[6]

We do not recall here the $w(l)p$-calculus (see [10] for an introduction to the wp-calculus, and [15] for the detail of the notation used here), but an example is given to point out a useful fact. Let

$$\tau =_{def} (C, REQ_p = 1 \longrightarrow REQ_p := 0 , C'_p),$$
$$a_k =_{def} at\ q_w \equiv [at\ C'_q \vee REQ_q = 1 \vee OK_q = 1 \vee q \in E].$$

If q and p denote distinct stations, then $wlp[\tau; a_k]$ reduces to

$$at\ C \Rightarrow (REQ_p = 1 \Rightarrow (at\ q_w \equiv [false \vee REQ_q = 1 \vee OK_q = 1 \vee q \in E]));$$

otherwise $(p = q)$, $wlp[\tau; a_k]$ reduces to

$$at\ C \Rightarrow (REQ_p = 1 \Rightarrow (at\ p_w \equiv [true \vee 0 = 1 \vee OK_p = 1 \vee p \in E])),$$

which simplifies into

$$at\ C \Rightarrow (REQ_p = 1 \Rightarrow at\ p_w).$$

The point here is that the canonical form of a verification condition is

$$(a_1 \wedge \cdots \wedge a_n) \Rightarrow (c \Rightarrow a'_k), \tag{1}$$

for some k, where a'_k is $wlp[\tau; a_k]$ for some τ. Besides, for large programs, a transition τ usually alters few of the assertions. When τ does not evoke any entity occurring in a_k, then $a'_k = a_k$ and the condition reduces to *true*; otherwise, few other hypotheses a_j can be relevant to the conclusion $(c \Rightarrow a'_k)$, but nevertheless most of them are irrelevant and therefore could be omitted.[7] The next section proposes a way to discover the few useful hypotheses.

3 A classification algorithm

3.1 Introduction

We have seen that, except for small, abstract programs, the number of assertions in an invariant can be large. However, each assertion is rather short and mentions only few program variables and, similarly, each program transition alters only few variables. As a result, although the antecedent of the implication (1) usually contains a lot of assertions, only a few one are really needed; recognizing them is a critical step of the (human) process of invariant validation.[8]

---

[6] This is not a formal result; in fact, the size of $\mathcal{S}$, and still more the sizes of I and V depend on the kind of notations used to write them. Canonical forms exist, but their use often leads to longer formulas than more specific notation.

[7] This problem has been formalized in [21].

[8] The same holds for theorem proving in general; knowing which (already proved) mathematical truths will be useful to prove a new conjecture is as difficult as combining these truths into a formal proof of the conjecture.

The algorithm we propose orders the set $\{a_1, a_2, \ldots, a_n\}$ of assertions into a sequence $(a_{j_1}, a_{j_2}, \ldots)$. Afterwards, the theorem prover attempts to reduce successively formulas

$$(c \Rightarrow a'_k),$$
$$a_{j_1} \Rightarrow (c \Rightarrow a'_k),$$
$$a_{j_2} \Rightarrow (a_{j_1} \Rightarrow (c \Rightarrow a'_k)),$$
$$\ldots$$

until a formula is successfully reduced to *true*, or some limit is reached (failure).

3.2 Type, reduced type, rank and polarity

In the sequel of this section, we assume that all formulas belong to propositional logic. This hypothesis is realistic for finite-state systems, and for many other systems like n-process mutual exclusion algorithms, data transfer protocols and other communication and synchronization problems. (We also see in the next section how this hypothesis can be relaxed.) We also assume that the connectives are $\neg$, $\wedge$, $\vee$ and $\Rightarrow$ (no equivalence).

Every subformula (more precisely: every occurrence of every subformula) of a formula has a *type*, which is a word of the language $(c \cup d \cup n)^*$. Let B be a formula. The type of B as a subformula in any formula A is defined inductively as follows:

- The type of B in B is λ (empty word).
- If the type of B in A is w, then
  - its type in $\neg A$ is nw,
  - its type in $(A \wedge X)$ or $(X \wedge A)$ is cw,
  - its type in $(A \vee X)$, $(X \vee A)$ or $(X \Rightarrow A)$ is dw,
  - its type in $(A \Rightarrow X)$ is dnw.

Comment. Implication $(p \Rightarrow q)$ is viewed as $(\neg p \vee q)$; "n", "c" and "d" are for negation, conjunction and disjunction, respectively.

Let B_A be a subformula occurrence in A, with type w. The *reduced type* of B_A is obtained by applying to w first the rewriting rule

$$c \longrightarrow ndn,$$

and then the rewriting rule

$$nn \longrightarrow \lambda.$$

Let us consider a propositional formula A and a subformula B of A. The *rank* of an occurrence B_A of B in A is the number of "d"'s preceded (immediately or not) by an even number of "n"'s in the reduced type of B_A. The *polarity* of the occurrence B_A of B in A is positive if the type (or the reduced type) of B_A contains an even number of "n"'s; it is negative otherwise.

Comment. A subformula can have several occurrences in a formula, with distinct types and polarities.

The occurrence B_A of B in A is *purely disjunctive* if its reduced type w belongs to $(d^* \cup d^* n)$; the rank of B_A is then the number of "d"'s in w.

Examples. Let A be $(p \Rightarrow q) \vee \neg(r \wedge (\neg s \Rightarrow \neg(t \Rightarrow u)))$. The types, reduced types, ranks and polarities of propositions occurring in A are as follows:

occurrence	p	q	r	s	t	u
type	*ddn*	*dd*	*dnc*	*dncdnn*	*dncdndn*	*dncdnd*
reduced type	*ddn*	*dd*	*ddn*	*ddnd*	*ddndndn*	*ddndnd*
purely disjunctive?	yes	yes	yes	no	no	no
rank	2	2	2	2	3	3
polarity	−	+	−	−	−	+

Rank lemma. Let B_A be a purely disjunctive occurrence of subformula B in formula A. If v is an interpretation such that $v(A) = false$, then $v(B) = false$ if B_A is positive, and $v(B) = true$ if B_A is negative.

Proof. Let w and k be the reduced type and the rank of B_A. We proceed by induction on k. If $k = 0$, then either $w = \lambda$ and A is logically equivalent to B, with $v(B) = v(A) = false$, or $w = n$ and A is logically equivalent to $\neg B$, with $v(B) = v(\neg A) = true$. If $k > 0$, then formulas A' and X exist such that A is $(A' \vee X)$, $(X \vee A')$, $\neg(\neg A' \wedge X)$, $\neg(X \wedge \neg A')$, $(\neg A' \Rightarrow X)$ or $(X \Rightarrow A')$, and the rank of B_A in A' is $k - 1$.[9] We consider only the implication cases (the other cases are similar).

Let us suppose A is $(\neg A' \Rightarrow X)$. From $v(A) = false$ we deduce $v(A') = false$ and $v(X) = false$. The reduced type of B_A in A' is w', where $w = dw'$. If B_A is positive (resp. negative) in A, then it is positive (resp. negative) in A' and, due to the induction hypothesis, from $v(A') = false$ we deduce $v(B) = false$ (resp. $v(B) = true$). Similarly, if A is $(X \Rightarrow A')$, then from $v(A) = false$ we deduce $v(A') = false$ and $v(X) = true$. If B_A is positive (resp. negative) in A, then it is positive (resp. negative) in A' and, due to the induction hypothesis, from $v(A') = false$ we deduce $v(B) = false$ (resp. $v(B) = true$).

3.3 Polarized interpolation

Let us now recall a classical result. An *interpolant* of two formulas H and C is a formula J such that every proposition occurring in J has also occurrences in both H and C, and $(H \Rightarrow J)$ and $(J \Rightarrow C)$ are tautologies. A *polarized interpolant* of two formulas H and C is an interpolant J such that every proposition p occurring in J also occurs in both H and C, with the same polarity.

Craig-Lyndon interpolation lemma. If $(H \Rightarrow C)$ is a tautology, then H and C have a polarized interpolant.

Comments. This theorem generalizes to predicate logic; see [8] (pp. 84-90), or [12] for statements and proofs. We only need the propositional case, for which an elementary proof can be given. First, if no proposition occurs with the same polarity in both H and C, then either $\neg H$ or C is a tautology (if not, some interpretation would make H true and C false, contradicting the hypothesis).

---

[9] To see this, we observe that any other form for A would give rise to an incorrect reduced type. For instance, $\neg(A' \Rightarrow X)$ leads to *ndn*, indicating that neither A' nor its components are purely disjunctive.

Second, if the theorem holds for at most $n-1$ common occurrences, it holds also for n, since a polarized interpolant for $H(p)$ and $C(p)$ is easily obtained from polarized interpolants of $H(true)$ and $C(true)$, and of $H(false)$ and $C(false)$.

Example. Let $H =_{def} r \wedge p \wedge a$ and $C =_{def} r \vee \neg p \vee b$. Formulas $J_1 =_{def} r \wedge p$ and $J_2 =_{def} r \vee \neg p$ are (unpolarized) interpolants, and r is a polarized interpolant of H and C.

The notion of polarized interpolant is used in the section 3.5.

3.4 Relevance and the elimination rule

Definition. Let Π be a set of propositional variables and H and C be formulas on Π. Formula H is *relevant to* C *with respect to* Π if an interpretation v on Π exists such that $v(H) = v(C) = false$.

Comments. This definition does not capture exactly the intuitive notion of relevance but a larger relation. However, the following theorem indicates that irrelevant hypotheses can be omitted (and so really are irrelevant in the intuitive sense). We also note that relevance is a symmetrical relation, and that members of Π are mutually relevant. In practice, the set Π is not mentioned explicitly.

Relevance theorem (direct). If h_1 is not relevant to C w.r.t. Π, then formulas

$$\phi_1 =_{def} (h_1 \wedge h_2 \wedge \cdots \wedge h_n) \Rightarrow C,$$
$$\phi_2 =_{def} \quad\quad (h_2 \wedge \cdots \wedge h_n) \Rightarrow C,$$

are logically equivalent, for any formulas $h_2, \ldots, h_n$.

Proof. Formula $\phi_2 \Rightarrow \phi_1$ is clearly valid. If formula $\phi_1 \Rightarrow \phi_2$ is not, then a Π-interpretation v exists such that $v(\phi_1) = true$ and $v(\phi_2) = false$; as a consequence, $v(h_2) = \cdots = v(h_n) = true$, $v(h_1) = v(C) = false$ and h_1 is relevant to C w.r.t. Π.

A partial converse of this theorem can be proved:

Relevance theorem (converse). If h_1 is relevant to C w.r.t. Π, then formulas $h_2, \ldots, h_n$ exist such that ϕ_1 (see above) is valid, whereas ϕ_2 is not.

Proof. We choose $n = 2$ and $h_2 =_{def} (h_1 \Rightarrow C)$. Clearly enough, formula $(h_1 \wedge (h_1 \Rightarrow C)) \Rightarrow C$ is valid. However $h_2 \Rightarrow C$ is not valid; if v is such that $v(h_1) = v(C) = false$, then $v(h_2 \Rightarrow C) = v((h_1 \Rightarrow C) \Rightarrow C) = false$.

Elimination rule. Let A be a common subformula of H and C, and A_H and A_C be the corresponding occurrences. If A_H and A_C are purely disjunctive and have opposite polarities, then H is not relevant to C.

Proof. Suppose that A_H is positive and A_C is negative. If an interpretation v such that $v(H) = v(C) = false$ exists, then the rank lemma applies to A_H, leading to $v(A) = false$, and also to A_C, leading to $v(A) = true$ and a contradiction.

Example. Let $H =_{def} a \vee (b \Rightarrow c)$ and $C =_{def} a \vee (c \Rightarrow d)$. Proposition c is purely disjunctive in both H and C, positive in H and negative in C. So H is not relevant to C.

Comment. The elimination rule is useful because it can be applied systematically and in polynomial time, and because its application discards only provably useless hypotheses.

3.5 Direct relevance

Elimination of *provably* useless hypotheses is important, but not sufficient, since many useless hypotheses cannot be recognized as such in isolation. For instance, if q is the conclusion, p is theoretically relevant, but practically useful only if $p \Rightarrow q$ can be inferred from other hypotheses. It is therefore appropriate to quantify relevance, that is, potential usefulness. Intuitively, p can be useful for establishing q but not "directly", that is, only if an adequate intermediate hypothesis, say $p \Rightarrow q$, is also available. In this paragraph, we introduce the notion of *direct relevance*.

A formula H is *directly relevant* to a formula C (w.r.t. Π) if it is relevant and if H and C admit a common subformula, with the same polarity.
Comment. Direct relevance is a symmetrical relation.
Examples. $p \Rightarrow q$ is directly relevant to $p \Rightarrow r$ since these formulas are mutually relevant and p occurs negatively in both of them. On the contrary, $p \Rightarrow q$ is not directly relevant to p, nor to $q \Rightarrow r$.

Directly relevant formulas are not necessarily more useful than other relevant formulas for establishing some conclusion C. For instance, p is not directly relevant to $C =_{def} (q \Rightarrow r)$, while $p \vee r$ is; as far as $p \vee r$ is weaker than p, it cannot be more useful. Nevertheless, we have the following result.

Direct relevance theorem. Let $\mathcal{H}$ be a consistent set of formulas (hypotheses) and C be an invalid formula (conclusion). If C is a logical consequence of $\mathcal{H}$, then $\mathcal{H}$ contains a formula h such that h is directly relevant to C.
Proof. It is not a restriction to assume $\mathcal{H}$ is minimal, that is, C is not a logical consequence of any proper subset of $\mathcal{H}$; so, $\mathcal{H}$ contains only non-valid, relevant formulas; besides, $\mathcal{H}$ is not empty. Let $H =_{def} \bigwedge \mathcal{H}$. As an application of Craig-Lyndon's lemma, a formula J exists which contains only propositions occurring both in H and C, with identical polarities and such that $(H \Rightarrow J)$ and $(J \Rightarrow C)$ are tautologies. As J cannot reduce to *true* (C is not valid) nor to *false* (H is consistent), it does contain a proposition p, which has occurrences both in H and C, with the same polarity. As H is the conjunction of the elements of $\mathcal{H}$, at least one of these elements, say h, contains p with the right polarity and is therefore directly relevant to C.

This result shows that at least one directly relevant hypothesis is needed to establish a conclusion. As a result, hypotheses which share common subformula(s) with the conclusion are promising, *provided that the polarity is the same in the hypothesis and in the conclusion*. However, not all directly relevant hypotheses have the same degree of usefulness. For instance, if p occurs positively in C, then $h_1 =_{def} p$, $h_2 =_{def} (p \wedge Y)$, $h_3 =_{def} (p \vee X)$ and $h_4 =_{def} (Y \Rightarrow (p \vee X))$ may be all directly relevant through variable p (for short, formulas h_1, h_2, h_3 and h_4 are said p-*directly relevant* to C) but h_1 and h_2 are more promising, since they *guarantee* that p is true. An appropriate measure of p-direct relevance of h for C is the rank of p in h; low rank indicates high direct relevance. The rank of p is 0 in h_1 and in h_2; it is 1 in h_3 and 2 in h_4.

Let p and q be two propositions occurring in C (say positively) and let h_p and h_q be two directly relevant hypotheses for C. Assume that p (q) occurs positively in h_p (h_q) with rank k_p (k_q). The relation $k_p = k_q$ does not mean that the potential usefulness of h_p and h_q is the same. For instance, if C is $p \vee (q \wedge r)$, then h_p is potentially more useful; indeed, if p is true, then C is true, whereas if q is true, then C may be false if r is false. This means that, in order to quantify direct relevancy, we have to take into account not only the rank of some proposition p in the hypothesis, but also the rank of p in the *negation* of the conclusion. For instance, the rank of p is 0 in $\neg C$, and the rank of q is 1 in $\neg C$. This leads to the following definition.

Definition. If h and C are p-directly relevant due to some similarly polarized occurrences p_h and p_C, then the *degree of p-direct relevance* of h to C is the sum of the rank of p_h in h and the rank of p_C in $\neg C$.

3.6 The classification algorithm

Let $\mathcal{H}$ be a set of hypotheses and C be a conclusion. Our purpose is to discover as small as possible a subset $\mathcal{R}$ of $\mathcal{H}$ (if any) such that $(\bigwedge \mathcal{R}) \Rightarrow C$ is a tautology. A preliminary step consists in eliminating irrelevant members of $\mathcal{H}$, which can be done in polynomial time. A second step consists in computing for each hypothesis $h \in \mathcal{H}$, and for each proposition p occurring with the same polarity in h and C, the sum $\rho_h(p) + \rho^C(p)$ of the ranks of p in h and in $\neg C$, respectively, which can also be done in polynomial time.

A naïve algorithm consists in ordering the relevant members of $\mathcal{H}$ according to the following relation:

$$h_i \prec h_j \quad \text{iff} \quad \inf_{p \in \Pi} \{\rho_{h_i}(p) + \rho^C(p)\} < \inf_{p \in \Pi} \{\rho_{h_j}(p) + \rho^C(p)\}.$$

This algorithm is not acceptable since only *direct* relevance is considered. Let us consider the following case:

$$C =_{def} p, \quad \mathcal{H} =_{def} \{q, q \Rightarrow p, (p \vee r_1), \ldots, (p \vee r_n)\}.$$

Every hypothesis but q is directly relevant to the conclusion. As a result, the naïve algorithm will classify q at the very last position, although q is quite mandatory to establish the conclusion, together with only one directly relevant hypothesis (i.e., $q \Rightarrow p$).

In order to prevent this, we can use the naïve algorithm to select the k most promising hypotheses, say $h_1, \ldots, h_k$, and then use it again, with $\mathcal{H}$ replaced by $\mathcal{H} \setminus \{h_1, \ldots, h_k\}$ and C replaced by $(h_1 \wedge \cdots \wedge h_k) \Rightarrow C$, in order to select k' new hypotheses. These hypotheses are not necessarily directly relevant to the conclusion, but directly relevant to an already selected hypothesis that is directly relevant to the conclusion. This iteration process can go on, but experimentation shows that, for invariant validation, few iterations are needed.[10]

---

[10] This is not surprising since invariants may involve a lot of variables, but each assertion contains few of them; besides, a variable usually occurs in few assertions. A good rule of thumb is as follows. If the invariant contains n assertions, $k \simeq \sqrt{n}$ is a good choice, and more often than not, two iterations are enough. This means that the length of verification conditions is reduced from $O(n)$ to $O(\sqrt{n})$.

4 A worked-out example

4.1 Verifying Ricart and Agrawala's algorithm

The mutual exclusion algorithm introduced in Section 2 is very elementary, so a recent verification program would validate it quickly, without preprocessing. The situation is more interesting with Ricart and Agrawala's more sophisticated mutual exclusion algorithm, introduced in [24], which does not require a centralized controller and/or shared memory between the stations.

It is not useful to give here the code of the algorithm, and the full invariant to be verified (see [16, 17]). As for the elementary example introduced in Section 2, the invariant is a universally quantified formula, i.e., $\forall p \forall q \neq p [I(p, q)]$. When coded in propositional calculus, formula $I(p, q)$ is the conjunction of 20 assertions and contains 41 literals. There are 14 transitions for each couple of distinct stations.

Elimination of quantification is possible. Due to the symmetry between processes, we can consider only the transitions about an arbitrary couple (p, q), and then check that these transitions respect the 7 assertions listed below:
$$I(p, q), I(q, p), I(p, r), I(q, r), I(r, p), I(r, q), I(r, s),$$
where p, q, r, s denote four distinct stations.[11]

Besides, for any transition τ, instead of verifying the Hoare triple
$$\{\forall p \forall q \neq p [I(p, q)]\} \, \tau \, \{J\},$$
where J is one of the seven assertions listed above, we can verify the triple
$$\{K\} \, \tau \, \{J\},$$
where K is the conjunction of the seven assertions.

Recall that each J is the conjunction of 20 smaller assertions. The total number of triples to be verified is therefore $7 \times 20 \times 14 = 1\,960$, and each corresponding verification condition $K \Rightarrow wp[\tau; j]$ contains around $7 \times 41 = 287$ literals. The specific tool CAVEAT introduced in [17] is not able to cope with such a big set of propositional formulas, neither is the recent version NQTHM of Boyer and Moore.[12] However, both tools succeeded quite quickly for the two-process case (only 560 verification conditions, each of them involving roughly 80 literals).

We have applied preprocessing to the general case, and observed that for most assertions, only directly relevant hypotheses were needed. Even for the few cases where not directly relevant assertions where needed, the system succeeded in deriving the conclusion from at most one third of the available hypotheses, so CAVEAT was able to validate the Ricart and Agrawala's algorithm in less than 20 minutes.

---

[11] These seven assertions reduce to six if there are only three stations, and to two if there are only two stations.
[12] Both tools runned for more than 24 h without producing answers.

4.2 Propositional coding of predicates

Many concurrent systems involve mostly boolean variables. However, some other variables can be used; in this case, a propositional coding is needed to apply the classification algorithm. Ricart and Agrawala's algorithm use a "time stamp" SN[p] for each station p, that is, an integer variable that records the time (an abstract version of it) when station p has applied for access to its critical section, in order to fix priorities among stations: first come, first served. These variables are only used for comparison purpose, and, although SN[p] is not a boolean variable, the predicate SN[p]<SN[q] is. So, our system considers predicates like SN[p]<SN[q] as boolean variables. However, our system is based on *connections* (see [28]), that is, contradictions between boolean variables. They can be detected syntactically, as assertions that some variable r is both true and false, which is represented as { T: r, F: r }.

This is not true for predicates, so our system requires that connection schemes for predicates are given explicitly. For the language based on = and <, the connections are

{T: x<y, T: x=y}, {T: x<y, T: y<x}, {F: x<y, F: x=y, F: y<x}

We also need explicitly given connection schemes for variables recording station names. Ricart and Agrawala's algorithm deals with N stations, and each station p has to broadcast messages to each other station q≠p. A boolean array XP is used for that purpose,[13] together with a variable XPcard, which records the number of true components in XP. As a station does not send messages to itself, XP[p] is always true, so XPcard range of values is 1,...,N. Explicitly given connections are

{T: XP[q], T: XPcard=1}, {F: XP[q], T: XPcard=N}

The intuitive meaning is clear: if XP[q] is true, then XPcard cannot be 1 (it is at least 2); if XP[q] is false, then XPcard cannot be N (it is at most N−1).
Last, we use place predicates. If at_pi (i = 1,...,R) are the place predicates of process p, exactly one of them is true at every time, so

{T: at_pi, T: at_pj} ,   {F: at_p1, ..., F: at_pR}

are connections.

This simple technique is sufficient to perform the validation of Ricart and Agrawala's algorithm in a purely propositional framework.

4.3 An example of classification

As an example, let us see the only verification condition in Ricart and Agrawala's algorithm, for which the preprocessing technique was only moderately efficient. The conclusion to be established was

---

[13] XP[q] means "the message from p has already been sent to q".

```
(RDP[q] => time<SN[q])
```

and 68 hypotheses were available.[14] Hypotheses were automatically ordered as follows:

```
...
 9. RDP[q] => RCS[p]
...
19. not RCS[p]
...
```

In fact, out of 68 hypotheses, only 2 are really useful. The first one appears in position 9 and is directly relevant: atom RCS[p] appears negatively in the hypothesis and in the conclusion. The second useful hypothesis appears only in position 19; it is not directly relevant to the conclusion, but directly relevant to the hypothesis not RCS[p]. This rather poor performance of the ordering procedure comes from the fact that there are many directly relevant hypotheses, but only one of them is needed; besides, few hypotheses were discarded as irrelevant, due to the occurrence of a predicate (time<SN[q]) in the conclusion.[15]

4.4 Summary of statistical results

The case introduced above was the worst case for our version Ricart-Agrawala's algorithm, as indicated in Figure 1.

0-4	76	favourable cases
5-9	19	acceptable cases
10-14	11	acceptable cases
15-29	3	not really acceptable
30-68	0	
total	109	

Fig. 1. Number of selected hypotheses vs. number of assertions

The verification of our version of Ricart-Agrawala's algorithm involved the validation of 109 assertions (of approximately the same size as the one considered in the preceding paragraph, that is, a full page); poor results (at least 15 selected hypotheses, leading to lengthy validation time) occurred only for three assertions. We noticed in [17] that CAVEAT, our implementation of the connection method, although very promising, was not able to deal with this example in a practical way (more than 24h were needed for the full version, whereas 10 minutes were enough for the two-process version). The elementary preprocessing introduced in this paper allowed us to obtain a full validation in less than an hour.

---

[14] The list is rather long and therefore omitted here.

[15] As a result, all hypotheses containing = or < are relevant; for instance, $a < b$ is relevant to $c < d$, since additional hypotheses $c < a$ and $b < d$ might exist.

5 Comparison and conclusion

The technique introduced here cannot be viewed as a way to improve tautology checking in general, but only as a way to improve the verification of propositional invariants, that is, invariants of finite-state systems. It may also prove useful for the (semi-)automatic design of invariants as fixpoints (see e.g. [5, 9]); recent improvement in hardware and software tools might turn fixpoint approaches into practically feasible methods (see [2, 3, 14, 18, 23]). In fact, several techniques have been developed to validate properties (not restricted to invariants) of finite-state concurrent systems. Early examples are reported in [4, 6]; besides, many efficient tools have been produced. However, these techniques based on model-checking in temporal logic are strictly restricted to finite-state systems, and exclude "parameters", like N (the number of stations) in mutual exclusion algorithms. Such algorithms can therefore be verified by model-checking only for fixed (and quite small) values of N. In spite of some attempts to extend the scope of automatic model checking (see [19, 27]), there are theoretical limitations [1], and the preprocessing verification technique avoids the problem since it is fully automatic only in the purely propositional case, without parameter; the user has to give explicitly the connection schemes as soon as non-propositional variables and/or parameters are used. This drawback is a small price to pay for substantial improvement in validation time.

Another approach is to use a theorem prover for predicate logic. This technique is not restricted to finite-state systems, but as we have already mentioned, available tools cannot deal efficiently with very large formulas, so only small concurrent systems can be realistically checked in this way. Nevertheless, good results can be obtained with a little interaction between the theorem prover and the user (see e.g. [23]). It is also possible to combine finite-state methods with automated theorem proving (see e.g. [21, 22]).

References

1. K.R. Apt and D.C. Kozen, Limits for Automatic Program Verification, *Inform. Process. Letters* **22** (1986) 307-309.
2. S. Bensalem, Y. Lakhnech and H. Saidi, Powerful techniques for the automatic generation of invariants, Proc. 8th Int. Conf. on Computer-Aided Verification, to appear in *Lect. Notes in Comput. Sci.* (1996).
3. N. Bjorner, A. Browne and Z. Manna, Automatic Generation of Invariants and Intermediate Assertions, *Lect. N. in Comp. Sc.* **976** (1995) 589-623.
4. J.R. Burch et al., Symbolic Model Checking: 10^{20} States and Beyond, *Proc. 5th. Symp. on Logic in Computer Science* (1990) 428-439.
5. E. Clarke, Program invariants as fixed points, Proc. 18th IEEE Symp. on Foundations of Comput. Sci. (1977) 18-29.
6. E. Clarke, E. Emerson and A. Sistla, Automatic Verification of Finite-State Concurrent Systems Using Temporal Logic Specifications, *ACM Trans. Programming Languages Syst.* **8** (1986) 244-263.

7. K.M. Chandy and J. Misra, *Parallel Program Design: A Foundation* (Addison-Wesley, Reading, MA, 1988).
8. C.C. Chang and H.J. Keisler, *Model Theory* (North-Holland, Amsterdam, 1973).
9. P. Cousot and N. Halbwachs, Automatic Discovery of Linear Restraints Among Variables of a Program, Proc. 5th ACM Symp. on Principles of Programming Languages (1978) 84-96.
10. E.W. Dijkstra, *A discipline of programming* (Prentice Hall, New Jersey, 1976)
11. M. Fitting, *First-order logic and automated theorem proving* (Springer, 1990).
12. J.-Y. Girard, *Proof theory and logical complexity* (Bibliopolis, Napoli, 1966).
13. D.M. Goldschlag, Mechanically Verifying Concurrent programs with the Boyer-Moore prover, *IEEE Trans. on Software Engineering* **16** (1990) 1005-1023.
14. S. Graf and H. Saidi, Verifying invariants using theorem proving, Proc. 8th Int. Conf. on Computer-Aided Verification, to appear in *Lect. Notes in Comput. Sci.* (1996).
15. E.P. Gribomont, A Programming Logic for Formal Concurrent Systems, *Lect. Notes in Comput. Sci.* **458** (1990) 298-313.
16. E.P. Gribomont, Concurrency without toil: a systematic method for parallel program design, *Sci. Comput. Programming* **21** (1993) 1-56.
17. E.P. Gribomont and D. Rossetto, CAVEAT: technique and tool for Computer Aided VErification And Transformation, *Lect. N. in Comp. Sc.* **939** (1995) 70-83.
18. B. Jonsson and L. Kempe, Verifying safety properties of a class of infinite-state distributed algorithms, *Lect. N. in Comp. Sc.* **939** (1995) 42-53.
19. R.P. Kurshan and L. Lamport, Verification of a Multiplier: 64 Bits and Beyond, *Lect. Notes in Comput. Sci.* **697** (1993) 166-179.
20. L. Lamport, An Assertional Correctness Proof of a Distributed Algorithm, *Sci. Comput. Programming* **2** (1983) 175-206.
21. K. Larsen, B. Steffen and C. Weise, A constraint oriented proof methodology based on modal transitions systems, *Lect. Notes in Comput. Sci.* **129** (1995) 17-40.
22. K. Larsen, B. Steffen and C. Weise, Fisher's protocol revisited: a simple proof using modal constraints, Proc. 4th DIMACS Workshop on Verification and Control of Hybrid Systems. New Brunswick, New Jersey, 22-24 October, 1995.
23. Z. Manna et al., STEP: the Stanford Temporal Prover (Draft), June 1994.
24. G. Ricart and A.K. Agrawala, An optimal algorithm for mutual exclusion, *Comm. ACM* **24** (1981) 9-17 (corrigendum: *Comm. ACM* **24** (1981) 578).
25. D.M. Russinoff, A Verification System for Concurrent Programs Based on the Boyer-Moore Prover, *Formal Aspects of Computing* **4** (1992) 597-611.
26. D.M. Russinoff, A Mechanically Verified Incremental Garbage Collector, *Formal Aspects of Computing* **6** (1994) 359-390.
27. P. Wolper and V. Lovinfosse, Verifying Properties of large Sets of Processes with Network Invariants, CAV'89, *Lect. Notes in Comput. Sci.* **407** (1990) 68-80.
28. L. Wallen, *Automated Deduction in Nonclassical Logics* (MIT Press, 1990).

Formal Verification of SIGNAL Programs: Application to a Power Transformer Station Controller[*]

Michel Le Borgne, Hervé Marchand, Éric Rutten
IRISA / INRIA - Rennes
F-35042 RENNES, France
e-mail:{leborgne,hmarchan,rutten}@irisa.fr

Mazen Samaan
EDF/DER, EP, dept. CCC
6 quai Watier, 78401 CHATOU, France
e-mail: Mazen.Samaan@der.edf.fr

Abstract. We present a methodology for the verification of reactive systems, and its application to a case study. Systems are specified using the synchronous data flow language SIGNAL. As this language is based on an equational approach (*i.e.* SIGNAL programs are constraint equations between signals), it is natural to translate its Boolean part into a system of polynomial equations over three values denoting *true*, *false* and *absent*. Using operations in algebraic geometry on the polynomials, it is possible to check properties concerning the system, such as liveness, invariance, reachability and attractivity. We apply this method to the verification of the automatic circuit breaking control system of an electric power transformer station. This system handles the reaction to electrical defects on high voltage lines.

Keywords: Reactive systems, synchronous language, verification, case study.

1 Introduction

This paper presents a formal method for the verification of reactive real-time systems and its application to the case study of the controller of a power transformer station. The specification of the controller is made in the real-time synchronized data-flow language SIGNAL[10]. Its declarative style is based on equations defining the values and the synchronizations of flows of data called signals. Schematically, processes are systems of equations, and the compilation of a SIGNAL program involves transforming the specification into an executable code solving this system of equations at each reaction. Compilation performs the checking of the causal and temporal consistency of the specification. Some statical properties can thus be proved by the compiler (this part of the verification is only briefly mentioned in this paper; see [2] and [10] for details). The original equational nature of SIGNAL makes that it relies on a formal model in terms of polynomial dynamical equations systems, and the proof method is based on the theory of algebraic geometry. This way, it is possible to prove a wide variety of dynamical properties, such as *liveness, invariance, reachability* or *attractivity* [9, 5]. This paper focuses on the method for verification, based on this model, and on its application to a case study.

The formal method is applied to the verification of the automatic circuit-breaking controller of an electric power transformer station. It concerns the response to electric

---

[*] This work is supported by Électricité de France (EDF).

defects on the lines traversing it. The functionality of the controller is to handle the interruption of current, the redirection of supply sources, and the re-establishment of current following an interruption. The objective is double: protecting the components of the transformer itself, and minimizing the defect in the distribution of power in terms of duration and size of the interrupted sub-network. This system has been specified in SIGNAL and SIGNALGTi, which is a extension of the language, with the notion of time intervals and preemptive tasks [11].

The remainder of this paper is organized as follows: Section 2 presents an outline of the data-flow language SIGNAL, and of its model in polynomial dynamical systems. The algebraic method dedicated to the verification of SIGNAL programs is described in Section 3. Their application to the verification of the controller of a transformer station is described in Section 4. Discussion on results and related work is given in Section 5.

2 The SIGNAL language and its model

2.1 The SIGNAL equational language

SIGNAL [10] is built around a minimal kernel of operators. It manipulates *signals* X, which denote unbounded series of typed values $(x_t)_{t \in T}$, indexed by time t in a time domain T. An associated clock determines the set of instants at which values are present. A particular type of signals called **event** is characterized only by its presence, and always has the value *true* (hence, its negation by not is always *false*). The clock of a signal X is obtained by applying the operator **event** X. The constructs of the language can be used in an equational style to specify the relations between signals i.e., between their values and between their clocks. Systems of equations on signals are built using a composition construct, thus defining *processes*. Data flow applications are activities executed over a set of instants in time. At each instant, input data is acquired from the execution environment; output values are produced according to the system of equations considered as a network of operations.

Kernel of the SIGNAL language. It is based on four operations, defining primitive processes or equations, and a composition operation to build more elaborate processes in the form of systems of equations.

- **Functions** are transformations on data at an instant t. For example, the definition of a signal Y_t by the function f: $\forall t$, $Y_t = f(X_{1_t}, X_{2_t}, \ldots, X_{n_t})$ is encoded in SIGNAL: Y := f{ X1, X2,..., Xn}. The signals Y, X1,..., Xn are constrained to have the same clock.
- **Selection** of a signal X according to a boolean condition C is: Y := X when C. If C is present and *true*, then Y has the presence and value of X. The clock of Y is the *intersection* of (*i.e., included* in) that of X and that of C at the value *true*.
- **Deterministic merge** noted: Z:= X default Y has the value of X when it is present, or otherwise that of Y if it is present and X is not. Its clock is the *union* of (*i.e., includes*) or *contains* those of X and Y.
- **Delay** gives access to past values of a signal. *e.g.*, the equation $ZX_t = X_{t-1}$, with initial value V_0 defines a *dynamical process*. It is encoded by: ZX := X$1 with initialization ZX init V0. X and ZX have equal clocks.

 – **Composition** of processes is noted "|" (for processes P_1 and P_2, with parentheses: ($|\ P_1\ |\ P_2\ |$)). It consists in the composition of the systems of equations; it is associative and commutative. It can be interpreted as parallelism between processes; communication between them is carried by the broadcasting of signals.

Derived processes have been defined on the base of the primitive operators, providing programming comfort and modularity, *e.g.*, the instruction synchro{X,Y} specifies that signals X and Y are synchronous (*i.e.*, have equal clocks); **when** B gives the clock of *true*-valued occurrences of logical signal B; X cell B memorizes values of X and also outputs them when B is true. Arrays of signals and of processes have been introduced as well. Hierarchy and re-use of the definition of processes are supported by the possibility of defining process models that can be invoked by instantiation.

Time intervals and preemptive tasks. A recent extension to SIGNAL (SIGNAL*GTi*) handles tasks executing on time intervals and their sequencing and preemption [13]. The notion of *time interval* has been introduced: it is entered (takes the value inside) upon the occurrence of the start event, and is exited (takes the value outside) upon the occurrence of an end event, and can then be entered again, iteratively. Intervals have an initial state given by declaration. An interval is constructed by the statement: I:=]B,E] init I0 with initial value I0 (inside or outside). With this extension, we can define the notion of *task* on an interval, which is a SIGNAL process active when the interval is inside, and inactive outside. A *suspensive task* is written P on I: it re-starts at its current state when re-entering I. An *interruptible task* is written P each I: it re-starts at its *initial state* (as defined by the declarations of its state variables). Processes can themselves be decomposed into sub-tasks: this way, the specification of *hierarchies* of preemptive behaviors is possible.

This extension is implemented as a pre-processor to the SIGNAL compiler, and is fully compatible with the environment, including the verification tools. In particular, the intervals are coded by a boolean state variable, true when the interval is inside and false when outside. Occurrences of a signal X inside an interval I are coded by X when I. The specification of the power transformer station uses this extension [11]. This kind of specification, using tasks and intervals, is useful to specify properties such as "two process are not active at the same time". An example is given in Section 4.2.

Verification tools for SIGNAL programs. The verification of a SIGNAL program can concern invariant properties (to be satisfied at all instants of its execution) or dynamical properties (to be satisfied on the histories of the program). The first kind is addressed by the compiler, which checks the consistency of constraints between the clocks and proves these statical properties. Different phases occur during the compilation of a SIGNAL program. One of these consists in the resolution of a system of boolean equations, coding the constraints among the different clocks. This clock calculus relies on an algebra on sets of instants detailed in [2]. In fact, the compiler has to check the consistency on the constraints on the clocks of the different signals of a SIGNAL program. This way, by composing the specification with the expression in SIGNAL of a statical property (*i.e.*, *temporally invariant* property), the compiler checks if they are consistent w.r.t. each other. If so, their composition constitutes a correct controller that satisfies the property. An example is given in Section 4.2.

The second kind of properties is addressed by a formal method, based on a model of the behavior of the program presented in Section 2.2, and with which dynamical properties of the system can be proved.

2.2 An equational model of the behaviors of SIGNAL programs

The equational nature of the SIGNAL language leads naturally to the use of a method based on systems of polynomial dynamical equations over $\mathbb{Z}/3\mathbb{Z}$ as a formal model of programs behavior. The systems of polynomial equations characterize sets of solutions, which are states and events. The method consists in manipulating the equation systems instead of the solutions sets, avoiding the enumeration of the state space. This paper makes an overview presentation of results without recalling details and proofs (see [9, 5, 8]).

Signals. In order to model its behaviors, a SIGNAL process is translated into a system of polynomial equations over $\mathbb{Z}/3\mathbb{Z}$, *i.e.* integers modulo 3: $\{-1,0,1\}$ [8]. The principle is to code the three possible states of a boolean signal X (*i.e.*, *present* and *true*, or *present* and *false*, or *absent*) in a *signal variable* x by:

$$\begin{cases} present \wedge true & \rightarrow +1 \\ present \wedge false & \rightarrow -1 \\ absent & \rightarrow 0 \end{cases}$$

For the non-boolean signals, we only code the fact that the signal is *present* or *absent*: $\begin{cases} present & \rightarrow \pm 1 \\ absent & \rightarrow 0 \end{cases}$. Note that the square of a *present* signal is 1, whatever its value. Hence, for a signal X, its clock can be coded by x^2. Thus, two synchronous signals X and Y satisfy the constraint equation: $x^2 = y^2$. This fact will be used extensively in the following.

Primitive processes. Each of the primitive processes of SIGNAL can be encoded in a polynomial equation. For example C := A when B, which means "*if b = 1 then c = a else c = 0*" can be rewritten in $c = a(-b - b^2)$: the solutions of this equation are the set of possible behaviors of the primitive process when.

The delay $, which is a dynamical operator, is different because it requires memorizing the past value of the signal into a *state variable* ξ. In order to encode Y := X$1 init Y0, we have to introduce the three following equations:

$$\begin{cases} \xi' = x + (1 - x^2)\xi & (1) \\ y = \xi x^2 & (2) \\ \xi_0 = y_0 & (3) \end{cases}$$

Equation (1) describes what will be the next value ξ' of the state variable. If x is *present*, ξ' is equal to x (because $(1 - x^2) = 0$), otherwise ξ' is equal to the last value of x, memorized by ξ. Equation (2) gives to y the last value of x (*i.e.* the value of ξ) and constrains the clocks y and x to be equal. Indeed, $y^2 = \xi^2 x^4$, and in $\mathbb{Z}/3\mathbb{Z}$ we have $x^3 = x$, *i.e.* $x^4 = x^2$, so this leads to $y^2 = \xi^2 x^2$; as $\xi^2 = 1$ (because ξ is always present), we finally get $y^2 = x^2$. Equation (3) corresponds to the initial value of ξ, which is the initial value of y.

Table 1 shows how all the primitive operators are translated into polynomial equations.

Boolean instructions	
Y := not X	$y = -x$
Z := X and Y	$z = xy(xy - x - y - 1)$ $x^2 = y^2$
Z := X or Y	$z = xy(1 - x - y - xy)$ $x^2 = y^2$
Z := X default Y	$z = x + (1 - x^2)y$
Z := X when Y	$z = x(-y - y^2)$
Y := X \$1 (init y_0)	$\xi' = x + (1 - x^2)\xi$ $y = x^2\xi$ $\xi_0 = y_0$
non-boolean instructions	
Y := $f(X_1, \ldots, X_n)$	$y^2 = x_1^2 = \cdots = x_n^2$
Z := X default Y	$z^2 = x^2 + y^2 - x^2y^2$
Z := X when Y	$z^2 = x^2(-y - y^2)$
Y := X \$1 (init y_0)	$y^2 = x^2$

Table 1. Translation of the primitive operators.

Processes. By composing the equations representing the elementary processes, any SIGNAL specification can be translated into a set of equations called polynomial dynamical system. Using this encoding, the reaction events of the program, *i.e.* the value of each of the m *signal variables* and n *state variables*, are represented by a vector in $(\mathbb{Z}/3\mathbb{Z})^{n+m}$. Formally, a polynomial dynamical system can be reorganized into three sub-systems of polynomial equations of the form:

$$\begin{cases} Q(X, Y) = 0 \\ X' = P(X, Y) \\ Q_0(X) = 0 \end{cases}$$

where:

- X is a set of n variables, called *state variables*, represented by a vector in $(\mathbb{Z}/3\mathbb{Z})^n$;
- Y is a set of m variables, called *event variables*, represented by a vector in $(\mathbb{Z}/3\mathbb{Z})^m$;
- $X' = P(X, Y)$ is the *evolution equation* of the system; it can be considered as a vectorial function $[P_1, \ldots, P_n]$ from $(\mathbb{Z}/3\mathbb{Z})^{n+m}$ to $(\mathbb{Z}/3\mathbb{Z})^n$. It groups all the equations on the state variables, and characterizes the dynamical aspect of the system ;

- $Q(X, Y) = 0$ is the *constraints equation* of the system. it is a vectorial equation $[Q_1, \ldots, Q_l]$. It groups all the equations characterizing the statical aspect of the system (invariant for all instants t) ;
- $Q_0(X) = 0$ is the *initialization equation* of the system, it is a vectorial equation $[Q_{0_1}, \ldots, Q_{0_n}]$. It groups all the equations characterizing the initialization of the system.

For example the following small process in SIGNAL,

```
process altern =
{? event A,B
 !}
(| X := not ZX
 | ZX := X$1
 | synchro{A,when X}
 | synchro{B,when ZX}
 |)
where
logical X, ZX init false
end
```

is translated in the polynomial dynamical system with variable a, b, X and zx corresponding to the events A, B and the logical signals X and ZX and a state variable *state* introduced by the delay. The system consist of

- an initialization equation : $state = -1$,
- an evolution equation : $state' = x + (1 - x^2) * state$
- and a system of constraint equation

$$x = -zx, zx = state * x^2, a^2 = when\ x, b^2 = when\ zx$$

A polynomial dynamical system can be seen as a finite transition system. The initial states of this automaton are the solutions of the equation $Q_0(X) = 0$. When the system is in a state $x \in (\mathbb{Z}/3\mathbb{Z})^n$, any event $y \in (\mathbb{Z}/3\mathbb{Z})^m$ such that $Q(x, y) = 0$ can fire a transition. In this case, the system evolves to a state x' such that $x' = P(x, y)$.

Using this kind of representation and the operations explained in the next section, we hope for the reduction of combinatoric explosion experienced with automata composition. The number of states of the resulting automata is the product of the number of states of each automaton. In contrast, the composition of two polynomial dynamical systems is simply obtained by putting the equation together.

We thus have a mathematical model characterizing the behavior of dynamical systems. In the perspective of analyzing these behaviors by the evaluation of the satisfaction of properties, we need operations on polynomial systems, which correspond to the manipulation of the sets of their solutions. This way we can express ourselves about sets of behaviors, states and transitions, while still remaining in the domain of polynomial functions, and not having to enumerate them.

3 Verifying SIGNAL programs

3.1 Operations on the polynomial dynamical systems

The theory of polynomial dynamical systems uses operations in algebraic geometry such as varieties, ideals and morphisms. They are used to define the properties of systems such as liveness, invariance and invariance under control. This section presents the essential results of an extensive study [9, 8].

Description of the basic objects and operations. Let us define the quotient ring of polynomial functions $A[X, Y] = \mathbb{Z}/3\mathbb{Z}[X, Y]/(X^3 - X, Y^3 - Y)$ [2]: it is the set of polynomials in $\mathbb{Z}/3\mathbb{Z}$ for which the degree in each variable is ≤ 2 because of the fact that $X^3 = X$. Let E be a set of event and state variables in $(\mathbb{Z}/3\mathbb{Z})^{n+m}$. The following set of polynomials:

$$I(E) = \{p \in A[X, Y] \; / \; \forall (x, y) \in E, \; p(x, y) = 0\}$$

is called the *ideal* of E in $A[X, Y]$. This set represents all the polynomials, for which the set E is a solution. In terms of dynamical systems, it represents the set of equations characterizing the states and events in E.

Reciprocally, to any set of polynomials G, we can associate a set in $(\mathbb{Z}/3\mathbb{Z})^{n+m}$, called the *variety* of G, defined as follows:

$$V(G) = \{(x, y) \in (\mathbb{Z}/3\mathbb{Z})^{n+m} \; / \; \forall p \in G, \; p(x, y) = 0\}$$

This set represents all the solutions for a given set of polynomials. In terms of dynamical systems, it represents the set of states and events admissible by the dynamical systems in G.

The advantage of using ideals is that there exists a direct correspondence between an ideal and the associated variety. In fact, we can easily prove that, in the quotient ring $A[X, Y]$:

$$V(I(E)) = E \text{ and } I(V(<G>)) = <G>$$

where, for a set of polynomials G, $< G >$ is the set of all linear combinations of polynomials in G: this means that their solutions include those of G. This way, we can translate properties of sets into equivalent properties of associated ideals of polynomials. Hence, instead of manipulating explicitly and enumerating the states, this approach manipulates the polynomial functions characterizing their sets. An other important aspect is that an ideal can be represented by a single polynomial, called *the principal generator*. This particularity is used in the practical implementation of the algorithms on ideals [5].

For example, for the constraint equation Q of a polynomial dynamical system: the equation $Q(X, Y) = 0$ represents a set of polynomial equations, decomposed as follows:

$$\begin{cases} Q_1(X, Y) = 0 \\ \quad \cdots \\ Q_l(X, Y) = 0 \end{cases}$$

---

[2] $X^3 - X$ (resp. $Y^3 - Y$) denotes all the polynomials $X_i^3 - X_i$ (resp. $Y_i^3 - Y_i$).

If E is the set of solutions of this system of equations, it is clear that

$$E = V(< Q_1, ..., Q_l >) \text{ and } I(E) = < Q_1, ..., Q_l > .$$

So instead of manipulating the set of solutions E of the constraint equation, represented in our case by a variety, we can easily convert it into an ideal $I(E)$, which can be represented by a single polynomial. Thus, the relations between different sets (*e.g.* inclusion or projection), can be translated into operations on polynomials.

Operations on dynamical behaviors. To capture the dynamical aspect of a polynomial dynamical system, we introduce the notion of morphism and comorphism. A *morphism* (often called in other community *post-condition*) is a polynomial function P from $(\mathbb{Z}/3\mathbb{Z})^{n+m}$ to $(\mathbb{Z}/3\mathbb{Z})^n$ (the *evolution equation* $X' = P(X, Y)$ of the system, for example).

With the morphism P, there is an associated *comorphism* P^* from $\mathbb{Z}/3\mathbb{Z}[X]$ to $\mathbb{Z}/3\mathbb{Z}[X, Y]$, defined by:
for a polynomial $p \in \mathbb{Z}/3\mathbb{Z}[X]$:

$$P^*(p(X)) = P^*(p(X_1, ..., X_n))$$
$$= p(P_1(X, Y), ..., P_n(X, Y))$$

where $P_1, ..., P_n$ are the components of P. In other words $P^*(p(X))$ is obtained by substituting every X_i in p with the corresponding $P_i(X, Y)$. In fact, the comorphism (which is often called *pre-condition*) can be seen as a map computing the states *from which* we can reach the states that are solutions of the *evolution equations*; it can be used to take the transitions backwards.

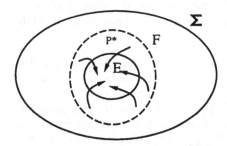

Fig. 1. Representation of the comorphism P^*

In Figure 1, F represents all the states from which all the states of E can be reached with only one transition (F represents the set obtained by the application of the comorphism on E), where Σ represents the set of states of the system.

This is the basic tool for analyzing transitions between states. But, we do not have to compute this transition map, which has a very high computing complexity. There are relations between varieties and ideals using morphisms and comorphisms that are used to perform calculations on the properties of polynomial dynamical systems.

3.2 Properties on the polynomial dynamical systems

Various properties of systems can be evaluated on such models using these operations; in this subsection we define several properties and give their expression in terms of algebraic operators, such as they are established in [5].

Liveness. We say that a system is *alive* if and only if it can not be in a state from which no transition can be taken, *i.e.* no deadlock can occur. This property states that every trajectory of the system is infinite. In terms of polynomial dynamical systems, this definition can be formalized as follows:

Definition 1. – A *state* x is alive if there exists a signal y such that $Q(x, y) = 0$ (*i.e.*a transition can be taken) ;
 – A *set of states* V is alive if and only if every state of V is alive ;
 – A *system* is alive, if and only if $\forall (x, y)$ such that $Q(x, y) = 0$, $P(x, y)$ is an alive state (*i.e.*, from live states, only live states can be reached).

Using this definition, it can be proved [5] that the property of liveness of a system can be stated as follows: $P^*(< Q > \cap \ \mathbb{Z}/_{3\mathbb{Z}}[X]) \subseteq < Q >$

Safety. Informally, whereas a liveness property stipulates that some *good things* do happen, a safety property stipulates that some *bad things* do not happen during any execution of the program [1]. In our case this kind of property covers the class of properties, describing the set of good states which remains invariant. The definition of an invariant set of states is as follows:

Definition 2. A subset E of states is *invariant* for a dynamical system, if and only if for every state $x \in E$ and for *every event* y admissible in the state x, the state $x' = P(x, y)$ is in E.

This way, if we describe a property by an equivalent set of states which verify it, the property is always verified if and only if this equivalent set of states is invariant for the dynamical system.

Using this definition, it has been proved [5] that the invariance of a property, represented by a set of states E, considering a polynomial dynamical system, can be stated as: $< P^*(I(E)) > \subseteq < Q > + I(E)\mathbb{Z}/_{3\mathbb{Z}}[X, Y]$. This notion is illustrated in Figure 2(a). Σ is the set of the states of the system; the set E_0 is the set of initial states, and E represents the set of states, which verify the property. The arrows correspond to the different possible trajectories of the system, which remain inside the set E, because it is invariant.

It may happen that the property, represented by an equivalent set of states is not invariant. In this case, it is interesting to compute the largest invariant subset included in the set of states E . This property is evaluated using a fix-point computation.

Definition 3. A subset E of states is control-invariant for a dynamical system, if and only if for every state $x \in E$, there exists an event y admissible in the state x, the state $x' = P(x, y)$ is in E.

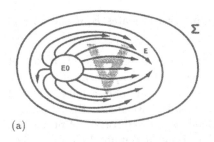 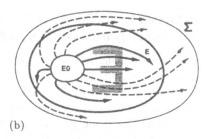

(a) (b)

Fig. 2. Invariance (a) and invariance under control (b) of E (from E_0)

Using Definition 3, it has been proved [5] that a sub-set E is control-invariant for a dynamical system, if and only if: $(<Q> + P^*(I(E))) \cap \mathbb{Z}/_{3\mathbb{Z}}[X] \subseteq I(E)$. This notion is illustrated in Figure 2(b). The dotted arrows correspond to the trajectories of the system, which should be forbidden or inhibited by a controller in order to obtain invariance. It is also possible to compute the largest control invariant sub-set included in a given set E of states.

Other kinds of properties may be derived from the liveness, invariance and control invariance properties.

Reachability and attractivity.

Definition 4. A subset F of states is reachable for a dynamical system, if and only if every state $x \in F$ can be reached from the initial states E_0 of the considered dynamical system *i.e.*, there exists a trajectory initialized in E_0 that reaches x.

To prove this property, we use the largest invariant sub-set of a set, as described before. Thus, a set of states F is reachable from the initial states of a polynomial dynamical system if and only if the initial states are *not* included in the largest invariant sub-set of the *complement* of F (*i.e.*, from the initial states, one is not compelled to stay in states not verifying the property).

This notion is illustrated in Figure 3(b). The black arrows represent the trajectories of the system, which reach the set of states F, whereas the dotted arrows correspond to the trajectories, which never reach the set of states F.

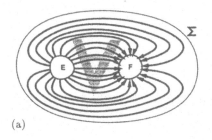 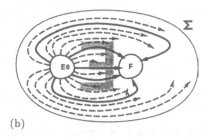

(a) (b)

Fig. 3. Attractivity (a) and reachability (b) and of F w.r.t. E

Definition 5. A set of states F is attractive for a set of states E, if and only if, every trajectory initialized in E reaches F.

Using the definition above, we can prove that F is attractive for E if the set E is not included in the greatest control-invariant of the *complement* of F (*i.e.*, a trajectory can not lead to an invariant set, which does not contain the set F, and from which it is impossible to reach F). This notion is illustrated in Figure 3(a).

This section made an overview of the method for the verification of properties, with its basic operators: set theoretic operators, fix-point computation, quantifiers elimination. Using the algebraic methods, explained before, it is also possible to express CTL formulae. The reader interested in the theoretical foundation of this approach is referred to [9, 5, 8].

4 Application to a power transformer station

4.1 Specification of the power transformer station

The transformer stations on the power network. The French national power network, operated by *Électricité de France* (EDF), counts a large number of transformer stations. For each high voltage line, a transformer lowers the voltage, so that it can be distributed in urban centers to end-users [11]. In the course of exploitation of this system, several kinds of electrical defects can occur, due to causes internal or external to the station. Three types of electrical defects are considered: phase (PH), homopolar (H), or wattmetric (W). In order to protect the device and the environment, several circuit breakers are placed in different parts of the station. These circuit breakers are alerted by sensors at different locations, and controlled by local control systems called *cells* (arrival cell, link cells, and departure cells, see Figure 4) and by an operator in a remote control center.

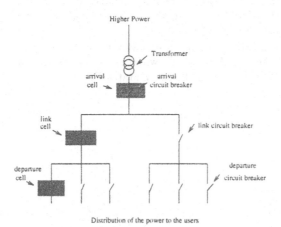

Fig. 4. Topology of a power transformer station

Functional description of a departure cell. We will focus on one of these types of cell: the departure cell, because it features all the interesting aspects of the controllers behavior. It is decomposed in a confirmation process, which sequentially tests for the different types of defect, followed by a treatment phase, consisting in attempts at making the defect disappear. These behaviors feature sub-tasks which are interrupted, in a nested way, and are repeated on series of activity intervals; their specification makes use of the corresponding constructs of SIGNAL *GTi* [11]. We only describe here the details necessary for the understanding of the verification presented further.

The *confirmation phase* consists in detecting the first defect occurrence (event First_Defect) and from then on, for each of the defect types (PH, H, or W), and in taking the time to let transient defects cease naturally, or else assess their persistent presence. They are tested in sequence: from First_Defect, interval I_PH is entered. Associated with this interval, the confirmation task first waits until Delay_PH is elapsed, and then enters interval I_H in which a task first waits until Delay_H is elapsed, and then enters interval I_W in which a task waits until Delay_W is elapsed. If in the meantime a defect is confirmed (*i.e.*, PH, H or W is present at the end of the corresponding delay), the sequence is interrupted (interval I_PH is ended), and the defect is confirmed by emission of the boolean Def_Conf with value true. It is also exited if the defect disappears: the last delay elapses without defect (with Def_Conf at value false)emission of event Ext_Def)A first property to be verified is that if a defect is detected after the end of its corresponding delay then the defect is actually confirmed (*i.e.*, in the example of a PH-defect, if PH is present in the interval I_H, then Def_Conf is actually emitted). A second property is that the confirmation is never active at the same time as the treatment (*i.e.* the controller can not be in states where both intervals I_PH and I_Treat are inside). A third property is that if a defect appears then the controller will necessarily evolve in such a way that either the defect is confirmed, or it disappears, or an external defect occurs (*i.e.* the controller necessarily evolves towards states where one of these is true).

The *treatment phase* begins when the defect is confirmed: the interval I_Treat is entered on the occurrence of Def_Conf. The task alternates breaking the circuit during varying delays, and closing it again to check whether the defect has disappeared, for a certain number of cycles. At the end of the last cycle, if the defect is present the circuit breaker is definitely cut off: the signal Def_Break is emitted, and the management is left to a remote control operator. A property to be verified here is that if a defect is confirmed, then either it disappears and the circuit-breaker is closed, or it does not and Def_Break is emitted.

4.2 Formal verification of the power transformer station

In this section, we apply the differents tools we have presented to check various properties on our SIGNAL implementation of the power transformer station. After the translation of our SIGNAL program, we obtain a dynamical system (This translation has been made in 10s. During this same time, we have also checked the causal and temporal concurrency of our program and produced an executable code). The polynomial dynamical system obtained is represented by 12 state variables and 22 event variables; that is to say, our system can be represented by an automaton of

500.000 possibles states. In fact, we must just consider the number of reachable states. For that, we just have to compute the orbit of the system, corresponding to the set of all the states which can be reached from the initial states. Using our representation in ideals and varieties, this set is represented by a single polynomial. Then to obtain the number of different states, we have to count the number of solutions of our polynomial.In our case, the system can involve in 7000 different reachable states.

We will now describe the different properties, which have been proved.

1. *if a defect* PH *is detected after the end of its corresponding delay, in interval* I_H, *then the defect is confirmed by the emission of* Def_Conf.

   To check this property, we use the SIGNAL compiler, which proves statical properties (*i.e.*, invariant over time instants) as explained in Section 2. We express the property in SIGNAL as an inclusion between clocks as follows:

   synchro{(when PH when I_H), ((when PH when I_H) when Def_Conf)}

   (where $A \subset B$ is expressed in the form $A = A \cap B$, with when as intersection, and synchro as equality for clocks). We compose this constraint with the controller. The compilation of the whole checks the consistency of all the constraints on clocks in the specification. The fact that our composed specification is consistent means that this new constrained controller verifies the property.

2. *the controller can not be in states where both intervals* I_PH *and* I_Treat *are* inside.

   This property can be established by proving that the set of states corresponding to the situation where the treatment phase and the confirmation phase are both active, can not be reached from the initial states of the controller (given by the declarations in the program).

   For that, we consider the two intervals I_Treat and I_PH, encoded by logicals which are true when the system is in the treatment phase, respectively in the confirmation phase. After the translation of the SIGNAL program into the corresponding polynomial dynamical system over $\mathbb{Z}/3\mathbb{Z}$, we compute the set of states where I_Treat=1 and I_PH=1. Then, the method consists in verifying that this set of states is not reachable from the initial states of the polynomial dynamical system. Reachability can be computed as described in Section 3.2 by a function of the proof system: in our example the result obtained is *false*.

3. *If* First_Defect *occurs,then the controller will necessarily evolve in such a way that:*

   (a) either Def_Conf *will be emitted with value* true

   (b) or Def_Conf *will be emitted with value* false.

   (c) or event Ext_Def *occurs.*

   The method for verifying this property is to build an observer, which is a process composed with the controller, and which evaluates a boolean signal OUT, which is *present* when one of these possibilities occurs, true when the conditions (a) or (c) are verified, and false, when the condition (b) is verified. The property can be proved by checking the attractivity of the set of states F, where OUT is present, from the set of states E, where the defect appears (*i.e.* there is an occurrence of the event First_Defect: First_Defect=1). By applying the proof system function computing attractivity as described by Definition 5, we prove that F is attractive from E (*i.e.* when a defect appears, all the trajectories of the system lead to the state where OUT is present).

4. *If* Def_Conf *occurs, then the controller will necessarily evolve in such a way that:*

   (a) either the defect does not disappear and the signal Def_Break *will be emitted,*

   (b) or the defect does disappear, with the circuit-breaker closed.

The method used to prove this property is the same as that used to prove the property (3). We compute the set of states E, where the defect is confirmed (*i.e.* Def_Conf=1), and the set of states F, corresponding to the union of the states where the condition (a) is verified and the states where the condition (b) is verified. Using the function computing attractivity, we prove that F is an attractive set of states from the set of states E.

5 Conclusion

This paper presents the verification method associated with the SIGNAL reactive language, and its application to the controller of a power transformer station, that was specified and implemented in SIGNAL and its extention with nested preemptive tasks SIGNAL*GTi* [11]. The verification is based on the model underlying SIGNAL, *i.e.* systems of polynomial dynamical equations over $\mathbb{Z}/3\mathbb{Z}$ [9]. The systems of polynomial equations characterize a set of solutions which encode states and events. The techniques used in the method consist in manipulating the equation systems instead of the solutions sets, which can avoid the enumeration of the state space. Operations used on equations systems belong to the theory of algebraic geometry, such as varieties, ideals and morphisms. They enable the treatment of properties of *safety*, *liveness*, *reachability* and *attractivity*. The SIGNAL approach to the verification of control systems has also been experimented on other applications, such as a robotic production cell [3].

The equational nature of the SIGNAL language makes it natural to use an equational framework for modeling behaviors and proving properties on them. This description of dynamical systems using equations is quite common in the fields of control theory and digital circuits, but not in verification and model-checking. This aspect is an originality of the SIGNAL approach compared to others using transition systems. For example, the reactive languages ESTEREL [4] and LUSTRE [7] are compiled into finite state automata; hence they naturally interface with tools based on these formalisms like AUTO and AUTOGRAPH. In principle the two methods are equivalent, but in practice they might be better suited each to a certain class of problems; in particular, the compactness of the implicit representation by a system of equations can help avoiding the combinatorial explosion of explicit state-based representations. Both models support verification by the methods of model-checking and comparison (bisimulation or behavioral equivalence), and as in the case of LUSTRE, some properties or observers can be specified in the language. Given that polynomial dynamical systems are an implicit description of transition systems, it is possible to give a semantics of temporal logic formulae (for example the Computational Tree Logic CTL) in terms of the algebraic operators [5], and perform symbolic model checking by evaluating them on a polynomial model. We can notice that the language LUSTRE uses the same methodology for the verification of their programs, using Binary Decisions Diagrams to encode their formulas [7].

A perspective for a different use of the polynomial model is the automated synthesis of controllers, where algebraic methods are used for the derivation, from a model of a system, of a controller statisfying given properties and objectives such as invariance or attractivity [6, 12]. In our application, the method will be used for the synthesis of the controller of the interactions between the various cells composing the transformer station controller. Another perspective concerns the possibility of proving properties that depend on the behavior of numerical variables, or in general on data other than presence/absence and Boolean which are handled currently.

References

1. B. Alpern and F. B. Schneider. – Recognizing safety and liveness. – Technical Report 86-727, Departement of Computer Science Cornell University, Ithaca, New York, January 1986.

2. T. A. Amabegnon, L. Besnard, and P. Le Guernic. – Arborescent canonical form of booelan expressions. – Technical Report 2290, INRIA, June 1994. – (ftp: **ftp.inria.fr**, file **/INRIA/publications/RR/RR-2290.ps.Z**).

3. T. Amagbegnon, P. Le Guernic, H. Marchand, and E. Rutten. – SIGNAL – *the specification of a generic, verified production cell controller*, volume 891 of *LNCS (Lecture Notes in Computer Science)*, chapter VII, pages 115 – 129. – Springer Verlag, January 1995.

4. F. Boussinot and R. de Simone. – The ESTEREL language. – *Proc. of the IEEE*, 9(79):1293–1304, September 1991.

5. B. Dutertre. – *Spécification et preuve de systèmes dynamiques: Application à* SIGNAL. – Thèse, Université de Rennes, December 1992. – (In French).

6. B. Dutertre and M. Le Borgne. – Control of polynomial dynamic systems: an example. – Technical Report 2193, INRIA, January 1994. – ftp: **ftp.inria.fr,** file **/INRIA/publications/RR/RR-2193.ps.Z**.

7. N. Halbwachs, F Lagnier, and C. Ratel. – Programming and verifying real-time systems by means of the synchronous data-flow programming language LUSTRE. – In *IEEE Transactions on Software Engineering, Special issue on the Specification and Analysis of Real-Time Systems*, September 1992.

8. M. Le Borgne. – *Systèmes dynamiques sur des corps finis*. – Thèse, Université de Rennes I, September 1993. – (In French).

9. M. Le Borgne, A. Benveniste, and P. Le Guernic. – Dynamical systems over galois fields and deds control problems. – In *Proc. of 33rd IEEE Conf. on Decision and Control*, volume 3, pages 1505–1509, 1991.

10. P. Le Guernic, M. Le Borgne, T. Gautier, and C. Le Maire. – Programming real time application with SIGNAL. – *Proc. of the IEEE*, 79(9):1321–1336, September 1991.

11. H. Marchand, E. Rutten, and Samaan M. – Specifying and verifying a transformer station in SIGNAL and SIGNAL*GTi*. – Technical Report 2521, inria, March 1995. – (ftp: **ftp.inria.fr**, file **/INRIA/publications/RR/RR-2521.ps.Z**).

12. P.J. Ramadge and W.M. Wonham. – The control of discrete events systems. – *Proc. of the IEEE*, 77(1):81–97, January 1989.

13. E. Rutten and P. Le Guernic. – The sequencing of data flow tasks in SIGNAL. – In *Proceedings of the ACM SIGPLAN Workshop on Language, Compiler and Tool Support for Real-Time Systems*, Orlando, Florida, June 1994. –

The Discrete Time TOOLBUS

J.A. Bergstra[1,2] and P. Klint[3,1]

[1] Programming Research Group, University of Amsterdam
P.O. Box 41882, 1009 DB Amsterdam, The Netherlands
[2] Department of Philosophy, Utrecht University
Heidelberglaan 8, 3584 CS Utrecht, The Netherlands
[3] Department of Software Technology
Centre for Mathematics and Computer Science
P.O. Box 4079, 1009 AB Amsterdam, The Netherlands

Abstract. The notion of "time" plays an important role when coordinating large, heterogeneous, distributed software systems. We present a generic coordination architecture that supports relative and absolute, discrete time. First, we briefly sketch the TOOLBUS coordination architecture. Next, we give a major example of its use: a distributed auction. Finally, we present the theory underlying our notion of discrete time.

1 Introduction

1.1 Motivation

Building large, heterogeneous, distributed software systems poses serious problems for the software engineer. Systems grow *larger* because the complexity of the tasks we want to automate increases. They become *heterogeneous* because large systems may be constructed by re-using existing software as components. It is more than likely that these components have been developed using different implementation languages and run on different hardware platforms. Systems become *distributed* because they have to operate in the context of local area networks.

It is fair to say that the *interoperability* of software components is essential to solve these problems. The question how to connect a number of independent, interactive, tools and integrate them into a well-defined, cooperating whole has already received substantial attention in the literature and it is easy to understand why:

- by connecting existing tools we can reuse their implementation and build new systems with lower costs;
- by decomposing a single monolithic system into a number of cooperating components, the modularity and flexibility of the systems' implementation can be improved.

We refer to our paper [BK96] for further motivation and and a survey of related work.

1.2 Our approach

Requirements and points of departure. Before explaining our approach to component interconnection in more detail, it is useful to make a list of our requirements and state our points of departure.

To get control over the possible interactions between software components ("tools") we forbid direct inter-tool communication. Instead, all interactions are controlled by a "script" that formalizes all the desired interactions among tools. This leads to a communication architecture resembling a hardware communication bus, and therefore we will call it a "TOOLBUS". Ideally speaking, each individual tool can be replaced by another one, provided that it implements the same protocol as expected by other tools. The resulting software architecture should thus lead to a situation in which tools can be combined with each other in many fashions. We replace the classical procedure interface (a named procedure with typed arguments and a typed result) by a more general *behaviour description*.

A "T script" should satisfy a number of requirements:

- It has a formal basis and can be formally analyzed.
- It is simple, i.e., it only contains information directly related to the objective of tool integration.
- It exploits a number of predefined communication primitives, tailored towards our specific needs. These primitives are such, that the common cases of deadlock can be avoided by adhering to certain styles of writing specifications.
- The manipulation of *data* should be completely transparent, i.e., data can only be received from and send to tools, but inside the TOOLBUS there are no operations on them.
- There should be no bias towards any implementation language for the tools to be connected. We are at least interested in the use of C, Lisp, Tcl, and ASF+SDF for constructing tools.
- It can be mapped onto an efficient implementation.

The TOOLBUS. The TOOLBUS coordination architecture can integrate and coordinate a fixed number of existing tools. We approach the problem of tool integration as follows:

Data integration: Instead of providing a general mechanism for representing the data in arbitrary applications, we will use a single, uniform, data representation based on term structures.

Control integration: the control integration between tools is achieved by using process-oriented "T scripts" that model the possible interactions between tools.

User-interface integration: we will *not* address user-interface integration as a separate topic, but we want to investigate whether our control integration mechanism can be exploited to achieve user-interface integration as well.

A consequence of this approach is that *existing* tools will have to be encapsulated by a small layer of software that acts as an "adapter" between the tool's internal dataformats and conventions and those of the TOOLBUS.

Compared with other approaches, the most distinguishing features of the TOOLBUS approach are:

- The prominent role of primitives for process control in the setting of tool integration. The major advantage being that complete control over tool communication can be achieved.
- The absence of built-in datatypes. Compare this with the abstract datatypes in, for instance, LOTOS [Bri87], PSF [MV90, MV93], and μCRL [GP90]. We only depend on a free algebra of terms and use matching to manipulate data. Transformations on data can only be performed by tools, giving opportunities for efficient implementation.

In [BK94] (see [BK96] for an extended abstract) we have applied a number of established techniques (i.e., process algebra [BK84, BW90], algebraic specification using ASF+SDF [BHK89, HHKR89, vDHK96], and C implementation) to approach the design of the TOOLBUS at various levels of abstraction. This has given rise to—even mutual—feedback between different levels. Experiences with this first design were reported in [BK96]. A redesign of the TOOLBUS is fully described in [BK95]. In this contribution (an extended abstract of [BK95]), we concentrate on the time-related features of the new TOOLBUS design. A large application of the TOOLBUS is described in [Oli96a, Oli96b]. A guide to TOOLBUS programming can be found in [Kli96].

1.3 Plan of the paper

We will now first give an overview of the TOOLBUS coordination architecture including an annotated example not involving time features (Section 2). Next, we discuss a major example that makes essential use of time: a distributed auction (Section 3). Then we present a description of the discrete time process algebra needed to define the notion of time in the TOOLBUS (Section 4). A discussion (Section 5) completes the paper.

2 Overview of the TOOLBUS coordination architecture

The global architecture of the TOOLBUS is shown in figure 1. The TOOLBUS serves the purpose of defining the cooperation of a variablenumber of *tools* T_i ($i = 1, ..., m$) that are to be combined into a complete system. The internal behaviour or implementation of each tool is irrelevant: they may be implemented in different programming languages, be generated from specifications, etc. Tools may, or may not, maintain their own internal state. Here we concentrate on the external behaviour of each tool. In general an *adapter* will be needed for each tool to adapt it to the common data representation and message protocols imposed by the TOOLBUS.

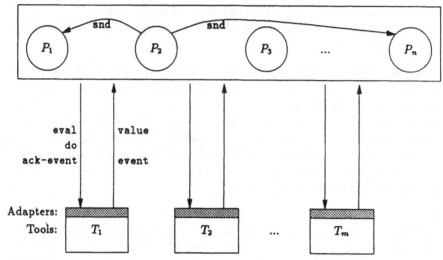

Fig. 1. Global organization of the TOOLBUS

The TOOLBUS itself consists of a variable number of processes P_i ($i = 1, ..., n$). The parallel composition of the processes P_i represents the intended behaviour of the whole system. Although a one-to-one correspondence between tools and processes seems simple and desirable, we do not enforce this and permit tools that are being controlled by more than one process as well as clusters of tools being controlled by a single process.

Inside the TOOLBUS, there are two communication mechanisms available. First, a process can send a *message* (using snd-msg) which should be received, synchronously, by one other process (using rec-msg). Messages are intended to request a service from another process. When the receiving process has completed the desired service it may inform the sender, synchronously, by means of another message (using snd-msg). The original sender can receive the reply using rec-msg. By convention, the original message is contained in the reply.

Second, a process can send a *note* (using snd-note) which is broadcasted to other, interested, processes. The sending process does not expect an answer while the receiving processes read notes asynchronously (using rec-note) at a low priority. Notes are intended to notify others of state changes in the sending process. Sending notes amounts to *asynchronous selective broadcasting*. Processes will only receive notes to which they have *subscribed*.

The communication between TOOLBUS and tools is based on handshaking communication between a TOOLBUS process and a tool. A process may send messages in several formats to a tool (snd-eval, snd-do, and snd-ack-event) while a tool may send the messages event and value to a TOOLBUS process.

Primitive	Description
delta	inaction ("deadlock")
+	choice between two alternatives (P_1 or P_2)
.	sequential composition (P_1 followed by P_2)
*	iteration (zero or more times P_1 followed by P_2)
create	process creation
snd-msg	send a message (binary, synchronous)
rec-msg	receive a message (binary, synchronous)
snd-note	send a note (broadcast, asynchronous)
rec-note	receive a note (asynchronous)
no-note	no notes available for process
subscribe	subscribe to notes
unsubscribe	unsubscribe from notes
snd-eval	send evaluation request to tool
rec-value	receive a value from a tool
snd-do	send request to tool (no return value)
rec-event	receive event from tool
snd-ack-event	acknowledge a previous event from a tool
if ... then ... fi	guarded command
if ... then ... else ... fi	conditional expressions
||	communication-free merge (parallel composition)
let ... in ... endlet	local variables
:=	assignment
delay	relative time delay
abs-delay	absolute time delay
timeout	relative timeout
abs-timeout	absolute timeout
rec-connect	receive a connection request from a tool
rec-disconnect	receive a disconnection request from a tool
execute	execute a tool
snd-terminate	terminate the execution of a tool
shutdown	terminate TOOLBUS
attach-monitor	attach a monitoring tool to a process
detach-monitor	detach a monitoring tool from a process

Fig. 2. Overview of TOOLBUS primitives.

There is no direct communication possible between tools.

2.1 Overview of T scripts

First, we address the data integration problem by introducing a notion of *terms* as follows:

– An integer *Int* is a term.

- A string *String* is a term.
- A variable *Var* is a term.
- A single identifier *Id* is a term.
- $Id(Term_1, Term_2, \ldots)$ is a term, provided that $Term_1$, $Term_2$, ... are also terms.
- A list $[Term_1, Term_2, \ldots]$ is a term, provided that $Term_1$, $Term_2$, ... are also terms.

Examples of terms are: 747 and departure(flight(123), "12:35"). It is important to stress that terms provide a simple, but versatile, mechanism for representing arbitrary data.

We distinguish two kinds of *occurrences of variables*:

- *Value occurrences* of the form V whose value is obtained from the context in which they are used.
- *Result occurrences* of the form V? which get a value assigned depending on the context in which they occur; this may be either as a result of a successful match with another term, or as a result of an assignment.

For instance, in a context where variable X has value 3, the term f(X) is equivalent to f(3). When, on the other hand, the terms f(X?) and f(3) are matched, the value 3 will be assigned to variable X as a result of this successful match.

A "T script" describes the complete behaviour of a system and consists of a number of definitions (for processes and tools) followed by one "TOOLBUS configuration".

A process definition is a named processes expression (see Figure 2 for an overview of the primitives used in process expressions). It has the form:

process *Pname(Formals)* is *P*

Formals are optional and contain a list of formal parameter names. *P* is a process expression.

A TOOLBUS *configuration* is an parallel composition of processes and has the form:

toolbus($Pname_1(Formals_1), \ldots, Pname_n(Formals_n)$)

It describes the initial configuration of processes in the TOOLBUS. During execution, new processes can be created using the create primitive. Each process is identified by a unique, dynamically generated, process identifier.

We will explain many of the primitives in Figure 2 while presenting examples later on. In particular, we will explain the relation between time primitives and other primitives in Section 3.

2.2   Example: a calculator

Informal description. Consider a calculator capable of evaluating expressions, showing a log of all previous computations, and displaying the current time.

Concurrent with the interactions of the user with the calculator, a batch process is reading expressions from file, requests their computation, and writes the resulting value back to file.

The calculator is defined as the cooperation of six processes:

- The user-interface process UI1 can receive the external events button(calc) and button(showLog).
  After receiving the "calc" button, the UI process is requested to provide an expression (probably via a dialogue window). This may have two outcomes: cancel to abort the requested calculation or the expression to be evaluated. After receiving the "showLog" button all previous calculations are displayed.
- The user-interface process UI2 can receive the event button(showTime) which displays the current time. The user-interface has the property that the "showTime" button can be pushed at any time, i.e. even while a calculation is in progress. That is why the control over the user-interface is split in the two parallel processes UI1 and UI2.
- The actual calculation process CALC.
- A process BATCH that reads expressions from file, calculates their value, and writes the result back on file.
- A process LOG that maintains a log of all calculations performed. Observe that LOG explicitly subscribes to "calc" notes.
- A process CLOCK that can provide the current time on request.

Note on the use of time primitives. The calculator example does *not* use the time-related primitives of the Discrete Time TOOLBUS. However, the example does contain a tool clock that deals with time. It turns out that for the detailed control of the timing aspects of distributed applications built-in primitives at the level of the T scripts are mandatory. Their use is shown in Section 3.

TOOLBUS *script for the calculator.*

```
process CALC is
  let Tid : calc, E : str, V : int
  in
      execute(calc, Tid?) .
    ( rec-msg(compute, E?) . snd-eval(Tid, expr(E)) .
      rec-value(Tid, V?) .
      snd-msg(compute, E, V) . snd-note(compute(E, V))
    ) * delta
  endlet
```

We take a closer look at the definition of the CALC process. First, three typed variables are introduced: Tid (of type calc, a tool identifier representing the calc-tool, see below), E (a string variable representing the expression whose value is to be computed), and V (an integer variable representing the computed value of expressions). The first atom,

```
    execute(calc, Tid?)
```

executes the calc-tool using the command (and optionally also the desired host computer) as defined in calc's tool definition. The result variable Tid gets as value a descriptor of this particular execution of the calc-tool. All subsequent atoms (e.g., snd-eval, rec-event) that communicate with this tool instance will use this descriptor as first argument. Next, we encounter a construct of the form

(rec-msg(compute, E?) ...) * delta

describing an infinite repetition of all steps inside the parentheses. Note that inaction (delta) will be avoided as long as there are other steps possible. Next, we see the atom

rec-msg(compute, E?)

for receiving a computation request from another process. Here, compute is a constant, and the variable E will get as value a string representing the expression to be computed. Next, an evaluation request goes to the calc-tool as a result of

snd-eval(Tid, expr(E))

The resulting value is received by

rec-value(Tid, V?)

Observe the combination of an ordinary variable Tid and a result variable V. Clearly, this atom should *only* match with a value event coming from the calc-tool that was executed at the beginning of the CALC process. It is also clear that V should get a value as a result of the match. A reply to the original request rec-msg(compute, E?) is then given by

snd-msg(compute, E, V)

and this is followed by the notification

snd-note(compute(E, V))

that will be used by the LOG process.
The definition for the calc tool is:

```
tool calc is {command = "./calc"}
```

The string value given for command is the operating system level command needed to execute the tool. It may contain additional arguments as can be seen in the definition of the ui-tool below.

The user-interface is defined by the process UI. First, it executes the ui-tool and then it handles three kinds of buttons. Note that the buttons "calc" and "log" exclude each other: either the "calc" button or the "log" button may be pushed but not both at the same time. The "time" button is independent of the other two buttons: it remains enabled while any of the other two buttons has been pushed.

```
process UI is
  let Tid : ui
  in
     execute(ui, Tid?) .
     ( ( CALC-BUTTON(Tid) + LOG-BUTTON(Tid) ) * delta
     ||
        TIME-BUTTON(Tid) * delta
     )
  endlet
```

```
tool ui is {command = "wish-adapter -script ui-calc.tcl"}
```

The treatment of each button is defined in a separate, auxiliary, process definition. They have a common structure:

- Receive an event from the user-interface.
- Handle the event (either by doing a local computation or by communicating with other TOOLBUS processes that may communicate with other tools).
- Send an acknowledgement to the user-interface that the handling of the event is complete.

```
process CALC-BUTTON(Tid : ui) is
  let  N : int, E : str, V : int
  in
     rec-event(Tid, N?, button(calc)) .
     snd-eval(Tid, get-expr-dialog).
     ( rec-value(Tid, cancel)
     + rec-value(Tid, expr(E?)) .
       snd-msg(compute, E) . rec-msg(compute, E, V?) .
       snd-do(Tid, display-value(V))
     ) . snd-ack-event(Tid, N)
  endlet
```

```
process LOG-BUTTON(Tid : ui) is
  let N : int, L : term
  in
     rec-event(Tid, N?, button(showLog)) .
     snd-msg(showLog) .  rec-msg(showLog, L?) .
     snd-do(Tid, display-log(L)) .
     snd-ack-event(Tid, N)
  endlet
```

```
process TIME-BUTTON(Tid : ui) is
  let N : int, T : str
  in
     rec-event(Tid, N?, button(showTime)) .
     snd-msg(showTime) . rec-msg(showTime, T?) .
     snd-do(Tid, display-time(T)) .
     snd-ack-event(Tid, N)
  endlet
```

The BATCH process executes the batch tool, reads expressions from file, computes their value by exchanging messages with process CALC and writes an (expression, value) pair back to a file.

```
process BATCH is
  let Tid : batch, E : str, V : int
  in
      execute(batch, Tid?) .
      ( snd-eval(Tid, fromFile). rec-value(Tid, expr(E?)) .
        snd-msg(compute, E). rec-msg(compute, E, V?).
        snd-do(Tid, toFile(E, V))
      ) * delta
  endlet

tool batch is {command = "./batch"}
```

The LOG process subscribes to notes of the form compute(<str>,<int>), i.e., a function compute with a string and an integer as arguments.

```
process LOG is
  let Tid : log, E : str, V : int, L : term
  in
      subscribe(compute(<str>,<int>)) .
      execute(log, Tid?) .
      ( rec-note(compute(E?, V?)) . snd-do(Tid, writeLog(E, V))
      + rec-msg(showLog) . snd-eval(Tid, readLog) .
        rec-value(Tid, L?) . snd-msg(showLog, L)
      ) * delta
  endlet

tool log is {command = "./log"}
```

There are alternatives for the way in which the process definitions in this example can be defined. The LOG process can, for instance, be defined without resorting to a tool in the following manner:

```
process LOG1 is
  let TheLog : list, E : str, V : int
  in
      subscribe(compute(<str>,<int>)) .
      TheLog := [] .
      ( rec-note(compute(E?, V?)) . TheLog := join(TheLog, [[E, V]])
      + rec-msg(showLog) .  snd-msg(showLog, TheLog)
      ) * delta
  endlet
```

Instead of storing the log in a tool we can use a variable (TheLog) for this purpose in which we maintain a list of pairs. We use the function "join" (list concatenation) to append a new pair to the list. Note that join operates on lists, hence we concatenate a singleton list consisting of the pair as single element. The process CLOCK executes the clock tool and answers requests for the current time.

```
process CLOCK is
  let Tid : clock, T : str
  in
     execute(clock, Tid?) .
     ( rec-msg(showTime) .
       snd-eval(Tid, readTime) .
       rec-value(Tid, T?) .
       snd-msg(showTime, T)
     ) * delta
  endlet

tool clock is {command = "./clock"}
```

Finally, we define one of the possible TOOLBUS configurations that can be defined using the above definitions:

```
toolbus(UI, CALC, LOG1, CLOCK, BATCH)
```

3   A distributed auction

3.1   Preliminaries

Before turning our attention to an example where the use of time at the level of the T script is essential, we need to explain how the time primitives interact with other primitives.

The following attributes can be attached to atomic processes, in order to define their behaviour in time:

− delay: relative execution delay.
− abs-delay: absolute execution delay.
− timeout: relative timeout for execution.
− abs-timeout: absolute timeout for execution.

We only permit the following combinations of these attributes:

− relative time: delay, delay/timeout, timeout.
− absolute time: abs-delay, abs-delay/abs-timeout, abs-timeout.

Other combinations, e.g., mixtures of relative and absolute time are forbidden. Note that time is determined by the actual clock time of the TOOLBUS and not by the clocks of the tools, since these may be executing on different computers and their clocks are likely to be in conflict with each other.

A typical example is

```
rec-msg(compute, E?) delay(sec(10))
```

which becomes enabled after 10 seconds and is then identical to

```
rec-msg(compute, E?)
```

```
┌─────────────────────────────────────────────────────────────────────┐
│ if b then X else Y fi = if b then X fi + if not(b) then Y fi        │
│ if true then X fi     = X                                            │
│ if false then X fi    = delta                                        │
└─────────────────────────────────────────────────────────────────────┘
```

Fig. 3. Axioms for conditionals in **T** scripts.

More complex behaviour can be defined by combining time primitives and conditionals. The behaviour of the conditional constructs in **T** scripts is defined in Figure 3. Now consider the fragment

```
if not(or(Final, Sold)) then
    snd-note(any-higher-bid) delay(sec(10))
fi
```

In this example, the snd-note can only become enabled when the test of the conditional yields true *and* at least 10 seconds have passed. In the auction example, we will see the use of several choices between conditionals of the above form, each with its own Boolean and timing constraints.

3.2 Informal description

Consider a completely distributed auction in which the auction master (auction-eer) and the bidders are cooperating via a workstation in their own office. The problem is how to synchronize bids, how to inform bidders about higher bids, and how to decide when the bidding is over. In addition, bidders may connect and disconnect from the auction whenever they want.[4]

The auction is defined by the following processes:

- The auction is initiated by the process Auction which executes the "master" tool (the user-interface used by the auction master) and then handles connections and disconnections of new bidders, introduction of a new item for sale to the auction, and the actual bidding process. A delay is used to determine the end of the bidding activity per item.
- A Bidder process is created for each new bidder that connects to the auction; it describes the possible behaviour of the bidder.

This example illustrates the dynamic connection/disconnection of tools and the use of time.

---

[4] This example is an extension of the example given in [Yel94], where it was used in the context of protocol conversion and the generation of protocol adapters. We have added certain features, e.g., dynamic connection and disconnection of bidders and time considerations, to approximate the behaviour of a "real" auction.

3.3 T script for auction

The overall steps performed during an auction are described by the process Auction.

```
process Auction is
  let Mid : master, Bid : bidder
  in
        execute(master, Mid?) .        %% execute the master tool
        ( ConnectBidder(Mid, Bid?)     %% repeat:  add new bidder
                                       %%              between sales,
        +                              %%          or
          OneSale(Mid)                 %%              perform one sale
        ) *
        rec-event(Mid, quit) .         %% until auction master quits
        shutdown("Auction is closed")  %% close the auction
  endlet
```

```
tool master is { command = "wish-adapter -script master.tcl" }
```

The auxiliary process ConnectBidder handles the connection of a new bidder to the auction. It takes the following steps:

- Receive a connection request from some bidder. This may occur when someone executes a bidder tool outside the TOOLBUS (may be even on another computer). As part of its initialization, the bidder tool will attempt to make a connection with some TOOLBUS (the particular TOOLBUS is given as a parameter when executing the bidder tool).
- Create an instance of the process Bidder that defines the behaviour of this particular bidder.
- Ask the bidder for its name and send that to the auction master.

```
process ConnectBidder(Mid : master, Bid : bidder?) is
  let Pid : int, Name : str
  in
      rec-connect(Bid?) .              %% receive connection request from
                                       %% new bidder
      create(Bidder(Bid), Pid?) .      %% create a new Bidder process
      snd-eval(Bid, get-name) .        %% ask bidder for its name, and send
      rec-value(Bid, Name?) .          %% it to the master tool
      snd-do(Mid, new-bidder(Bid, Name))
  endlet
```

The auxiliary process OneSale handles all steps needed for the sale of one item:

- Receive an event from the master tool announcing a new item for sale.
- Broadcast this event to all connected bidders and perform one of the following steps as long as the item is not sold:
  - receive a new bid;
  - connect a new bidder;

- ask for a final bid if no bids were received during the last 10 seconds;
- declare the item sold if no new bids arrive within 10 seconds after asking for a final bid.

The process definition is:

```
process OneSale(Mid : master) is
  let Descr : str,      %% Description of item for sale
      InAmount : int,   %% Initial amount for item
      Amount : int,     %% Current amount
      HighestBid : int, %% Highest bid so far
      Final : bool,     %% Did we already issue a final call for bids?
      Sold : bool,      %% Is the item sold?
      Bid : bidder      %% New bidder tool connected during sale
  in
      rec-event(Mid, new-item(Descr?, InAmount?)) .
      HighestBid := InAmount .
      snd-note(new-item(Descr, InAmount)) .
      Final := false . Sold := false .
      ( if not(Sold) then
            rec-msg(bid(Bid?, Amount?)) .
            snd-do(Mid, new-bid(Bid, Amount)) .
            if less-equal(Amount, HighestBid) then
                snd-msg(Bid, rejected)
            else
                HighestBid := Amount .
                snd-msg(Bid, accepted) .
                snd-note(update-bid(Amount)) .
                snd-do(Mid, update-highest-bid(Bid, Amount)) .
                Final := false
            fi
        fi
      +
        if not(or(Final, Sold)) then
            snd-note(any-higher-bid) delay(sec(10)) .
            Final := true
        fi
      +
        if and(Final, not(Sold)) then
            snd-note(sold(HighestBid)) delay(sec(10)) .
            Sold := true
        fi
      +
        ConnectBidder(Mid, Bid?) . %% add new bidder during a sale
        snd-msg(Bid, new-item(Descr, HighestBid)) .
        Final := false
      ) *
      if Sold then snd-ack-event(Mid, new-item(Descr, InAmount)) fi
  endlet
```

The Bidder process defines the behaviour of one bidder.

```
process Bidder(Bid : bidder) is
  let Descr : str,      %% Description of current item for sale
      Amount : int,     %% Current amount
      Acceptance : term %% Acceptance/rejection of our last bid
  in
      subscribe(new-item(<str>, <int>)) . subscribe(update-bid(<int>)) .
      subscribe(sold(<int>)) . subscribe(any-higher-bid) .
      ( ( rec-msg(Bid, new-item(Descr?, Amount?))
        +
          rec-note(new-item(Descr?, Amount?))
        +
          rec-disconnect(Bid) . delta
        ) .
        snd-do(Bid, new-item(Descr, Amount)) .
        ( rec-event(Bid, bid(Amount?)) .
          snd-msg(bid(Bid, Amount)) . rec-msg(Bid, Acceptance?) .
          snd-do(Bid, accept(Acceptance)) .
          snd-ack-event(Bid, bid(Amount))
        +
          rec-note(update-bid(Amount?)) . snd-do(Bid, update-bid(Amount))
        +
          rec-note(any-higher-bid) . snd-do(Bid, any-higher-bid)
        +
          rec-disconnect(Bid) . delta
        ) *
        rec-note(sold(Amount?)) . snd-do(Bid, sold(Amount))
      )
      * delta
  endlet

tool bidder(Name : str) is
  { command = "wish-adapter -script bidder.tcl -script-args -name Name" }
```

The complete auction is, finally, defined by the TOOLBUS configuration:

```
toolbus(Auction)
```

4 Discrete time process algebra for the TOOLBUS

4.1 Preliminaries

Following [BB96] we assume that time is divided in a countably infinite number of discrete slices. In the case of the TOOLBUS, the unit is a second and the first slice ranges from 0 to 1. With $a^v(n+1)$ we denote a process that may perform the action a during the course of time slice number $n+1$ or, alternatively, it may idle indefinitely. The $n+1$-th time slice takes time from $time = n$ to $time = n+1$. Within a slice actions take place in interleaved fashion.

We follow discrete time process algebra in [BB96] in our explanation. In the syntax used there, we have $a^\vee(n+1) = \underline{a}(n+1) + \delta$ where $\underline{a}(n+1)$ is a process that *must* perform a in time slice $n+1$ and δ is a process that idles forever.

To model **T** scripts, it suffices to work in a subalgebra of the parametric time process algebra of [BB96]. This subalgebra is the *time-stop-free parametric time process algebra* and is is generated by time-stop-free actions $a^\vee(n)$ rather than $\underline{a}(n)$. Parametric discrete time processes allow initialisation at any time $t \in N$. With $n \gg P$ we denote the process that P develops into after initialization at n. $n \gg P$ itself is a so called absolute discrete time process. Its actions are all timed with reference to the same initial time 0

Using time spectrum abstraction we introduce parametric time processes: $P = \sqrt{}_d x.F$. When initialised at n this P behaves as $P[n/x]$ (or, more precisely, as $n \gg P[n/x]$). Time spectrum abstraction in the real time case was introduced in [BB93]. The discrete time case occurs in [BB92, BB96].

Two parametric time processes are equal (in absolute time) if they are equal after all possible initializations. In this way equality is reduced to the simple notion of strong bisimulation for absolute discrete time transition systems. The Extensionality for Parametric Discrete Time rule

$$\frac{\text{for all } n : n \gg X = n \gg Y}{X = Y} \quad \text{(EPDT)}$$

embodies this version of process equality in parametric time. Notice that relative time notation is easily obtained on the basis of time spectrum abstraction: $a^\vee[n] = \sqrt{}_d x.a^\vee(n+x)$. Hence, $a^\vee[n]$ can perform a in slice "n after initialization" or idle.

Using $a^\vee(x)$, time spectrum abstraction, and infinite sums $\sum_{i \in N} P_i$ we can define the meaning of the actions $script(a)$ (excluding the time primitives) that occur in the TOOLBUS by

$$script(a) = \sum_{i \in N} a^\vee(i+1).$$

This means that to explain a as an action in a **T** script in the discrete time setting, we replace it by an infinite sum of $a^\vee$'s. We will write a for $script(a)$ when no confusion arises.

a absdelay(e)	$= \sqrt{}_d n. \sum_{i \in N} (i \geq e[n/time]) :\to a^\vee(i)$	
a abstimeout(e)	$= \sqrt{}_d n. \sum_{i \in N} (i < e[n/time]) :\to a^\vee(i)$	
a absinterval(e_1, e_2)	$= \sqrt{}_d n. \sum_{i \in N} (i \geq e_1[n/time]) \wedge (i < e_2[n/time]) :\to a^\vee(i)$	
a delay(e)	$= \sqrt{}_d n. \sum_{i \in N} (i \geq e[n/time] + n) :\to a^\vee(i)$	
a timeout(e)	$= \sqrt{}_d n. \sum_{i \in N} (i < e[n/time] + n) :\to a^\vee(i)$	
a interval(e_1, e_2)	$= \sqrt{}_d n. \sum_{i \in N} (i \geq e_1[n/time] + n) \wedge (i < e_2[n/time] + n) :\to a^\vee(i)$	

Fig. 4. Timed atoms

Basic Process Algebra (BPA)		Encapsulation operator	
$x + y = y + x$	A$_1$	$\partial_H(a) = a$, if $a \notin H$	D$_1$
$(x + y) + z = x + (y + z)$	A$_2$	$\partial_H(a) = \delta$, if $a \in H$	D$_2$
$x + x = x$	A$_3$	$\partial_H(x + y) = \partial_H(x) + \partial_H(y)$	D$_3$
$(x + y).z = x.z + y.z$	A$_4$	$\partial_H(x.y) = \partial_H(x).\partial_H(y)$	D$_4$
$(x.y).z = x.(y.z)$	A$_5$		

Deadlock (BPA$_\delta$)

$x + \delta = x$	A$_6$
$\delta.x = \delta$	A$_7$

Renaming operator

$\rho_f(\delta) = \delta$	RN$_0$
$\rho_f(a) = f(a)$	RN$_1$
$\rho_f(x + y) = \rho_f(x) + \rho_f(y)$	RN$_2$
$\rho_f(x.y) = \rho_f(x).\rho_f(y)$	RN$_3$
$\rho_{id}(x) = x$	RR$_1$
$\rho_f \circ \rho_g(x) = \rho_{f \circ g}(x)$	RR$_2$

Free merge operator

$x \parallel y = x \lfloor\!\lfloor y + y \lfloor\!\lfloor x$	M$_1$
$a \lfloor\!\lfloor (n \gg x) = a.(n \gg x)$	M$_2$
$a.x \lfloor\!\lfloor (n \gg y) = a.(x \parallel (n \gg y))$	M$_3$
$(x + y) \lfloor\!\lfloor z = x \lfloor\!\lfloor z + y \lfloor\!\lfloor z$	M$_4$

Process creation operator

$E_\phi(a) = a$, if $a \notin cr(D)$	CR$_1$
$E_\phi(cr(d)) = \overline{cr}(d).E_\phi(\phi(d))$	
for $d \in D$	CR$_2$
$E_\phi(a.x) = a.E_\phi(x)$, if $a \notin cr(D)$	CR$_3$
$E_\phi(cr(d).x) = \overline{cr}(d).E_\phi(\phi(d) \parallel x)$	
for $d \in D$	CR$_4$
$E_\phi(x + y) = E_\phi(x) + E_\phi(y)$	CR$_5$

Merge operator

$a \mid b = \gamma(a, b)$, if γ defined	CF$_1$
$a \mid b = \delta$, otherwise	CF$_2$

State operator

$\lambda_S(\delta) = \delta$	SO$_1$
$\lambda_S(a) = a(S)$	SO$_2$
$\lambda_S(a.x) = a(S).\lambda_{S(a)}(x)$	SO$_4$
$\lambda_S(x + y) = \lambda_S(x) + \lambda_S(y)$	SO$_5$

$x \parallel y = x \lfloor\!\lfloor y + y \lfloor\!\lfloor x + x \mid y$	CM$_1$
$a \lfloor\!\lfloor (n \gg x) = a.(n \gg x)$	CM$_2$
$a.x \lfloor\!\lfloor (n \gg y) = a.(x \parallel (n \gg y))$	CM$_3$
$(x + y) \lfloor\!\lfloor z = x \lfloor\!\lfloor z + y \lfloor\!\lfloor z$	CM$_4$
$a.x \mid b = (a \mid b).x$	CM$_5$
$a \mid b.x = (a \mid b).x$	CM$_6$
$a.x \mid b.y = (a \mid b).(x \parallel y)$	CM$_7$
$(x + y) \mid z = x \mid z + y \mid z$	CM$_8$
$x \mid (y + z) = x \mid y + x \mid z$	CM$_9$

Iteration operator

$x \,{}^* y = x.(x \,{}^* y) + y$	I

Conditional control

$T :\to x = x$	C$_1$
$F :\to x = \delta$	C$_2$

Fig. 5. Untimed Process Algebra axioms

$$
\begin{aligned}
a^\vee(0) &= \delta \\
\delta^\vee(k) &= \delta \\
a^\vee(k + 1).x &= a^\vee(k + 1).k \gg x
\end{aligned}
$$

Fig. 6. Timed atoms (primitives)

$k \gg a$	$= a^{\vee}(k+1) + (k+1) \gg a$
$k \gg a^{\vee}(l)$	$= a^{\vee}(l)$ if $k < l$, otherwise δ
$k \gg (x+y)$	$= k \gg x + k \gg y$
$k \gg (x.y)$	$= (k \gg x).y$
$k \gg (x \parallel y)$	$= (k \gg x) \parallel (k \gg y)$
$k \gg (x \lfloor\!\lfloor y)$	$= (k \gg x) \lfloor\!\lfloor (k \gg y)$
$k \gg (x \mid y)$	$= (k \gg x) \mid (k \gg y)$
$k \gg \partial_H(x)$	$= \partial_H(k \gg y)$
$k \gg \rho_f(x)$	$= \rho_f(k \gg x)$
$k \gg \lambda_S(x)$	$= \lambda_S(k \gg x)$
$k \gg E_\phi(x)$	$= E_\phi(k \gg x)$
$k \gg l \gg x$	$= l \gg x$ if $k \leq l$
$k \gg l \gg m \gg x$	$= max(k,l) \gg m \gg x$
$k \gg a\ absdelay(e)$	$= max(k, e[k/time]) \gg a$
$k \gg a\ abstimeout(e)$	$= e[k/time] > k :\rightarrow$
	$\quad (a^{\vee}(k+1) + (k+1) \gg a\ abstimeout(e[k/time]))$
$k \gg a\ absinterval(ae_1, e_2)$	$= max(k, e_1[k/time]) \gg a\ abstimeout(e_2[k/time])$
$k \gg a\ delay(e)$	$= (k + e[k/time]) \gg a$
$k \gg a\ timeout(e)$	$= e[k/time] > 0 :\rightarrow$
	$\quad (a^{\vee}(k+1) + (k+1) \gg a\ timeout(e[k/time] - 1))$
$k \gg a\ interval(e_1, e_2)$	$= (k + e_1[k/time]) \gg a\ timeout(e_2[k/time])$

Fig. 7. Initialization

Timed atoms are described in table 4. Note that e is an expression with free variable *time*, and the empty sum equals δ.

In the axiomatization below we will avoid time spectrum abstraction and infinite sums, thus obtaining equations that are closer to an implementation though (perhaps) less intuitive.

4.2 Untimed process algebra axioms

For reference purposes, we include here first in Figure 5 the standard (untimed) process algebra axioms as given in [BK94]. Note that in this table:

- a ranges over all possible time-stop-free atomic actions (both $script(a)$ and $a^{\vee}(n)$).
- BPA consists of A1 ... A5.
- PA consists of BPA plus free merge operator.
- ACP consists of BPA$_\delta$ plus merge and encapsulation.
- Axioms M1, M2, (CM2), M3 (CM3) have been modified using $n \gg x$ instead of x. Here, $n \gg x$ denotes the initialization of x in n. In the absence of time bound actions, $n \gg x$ is just x. This modification guarantees consistency with the setting involving time bounds.

In Figures 6, 7 and 8 we extend the above table with additional axioms for discrete time process algebra. In the definition of the state operator, $a(S)^{\vee}(k)$ is

$$
\begin{array}{ll}
a^{\vee}(k) \mid b^{\vee}(l) & = \delta \text{ if } k \neq l \\
a^{\vee}(k) \mid b^{\vee}(k) & = (a|b)^{\vee}(k) \\
\partial_H(a^{\vee}(k)) & = a^{\vee}(k) \text{ if } a \notin H \\
\partial_H(a^{\vee}(k)) & = \delta \text{ if } a \in H \\
\rho_f(a^{\vee}(k)) & = (f(a))^{\vee}(k) \\
\lambda_S(a^{\vee}(k)) & = a(S)^{\vee}(k) \\
\lambda_S(a^{\vee}(k).x) & = a(S)^{\vee}(k).\lambda_{S(a)}(x) \\
E_\phi(a^{\vee}(k)) & = a^{\vee}(k) \quad \text{if } a \notin \text{cr}(D) \\
E_\phi(\text{cr}(d)^{\vee}(k)) & = \overline{\text{cr}}(d)^{\vee}(k).E_\phi(\phi(d)) \\
E_\phi(\text{cr}(d)^{\vee}(k).x) & = a^{\vee}(k).E_\phi(x) \\
E_\phi(\text{cr}(d)^{\vee}(k).x) & = \overline{\text{cr}}(d)^{\vee}(k).E_\phi(x \parallel \phi(d))
\end{array}
$$

Fig. 8. Axioms for other operators that modify atoms

the action that takes place if within the scope of λ_S a takes place in time slice k. $S(a)$ is the new state after performing a in state S during time slice k. Observe that all axioms where some operator distributes over + can also be applied to infinite sums, e.g.,

$$
(\sum_i X_i).Y = \sum_i (X_i.Y)
$$

This is helpful to rewrite the expressions that emerge if **T** scripts are assigned a meaning by means of the definitions given in Section 4.1.

5 Discussion

The Discrete Time TOOLBUS is a satisfactory extension of the original, untimed, TOOLBUS, but many further extensions can be imagined, such as:

- Capturing the influence of monitoring and debugging on the time behaviour of a system.
- Describing time behaviour with arbitrary precision ("Real Time TOOLBUS"): this is both conceptually and technically an open problem and constitutes an interesting research area.
- Which security concepts are needed in a coordination architecture?
- How can transaction monitoring and crash recovery be incorporated in a coordination architecture?

References

[BB92]   J.C.M. Baeten and J.A. Bergstra. Discrete time process algebra (extended abstract). In *Proceedings of CONCUR'92*, LNCS 630. Springer Verlag, 1992.

[BB93]   J.C.M. Baeten and J.A. Bergstra. Real space process algebra. *Formals Aspects of Computing*, 5(6):481–529, 1993.

[BB96]   J.C.M. Baeten and J.A. Bergstra. Discrete time process algebra. *Formal Aspects of Computing*, 1996. To appear.

[BHK89]   J.A. Bergstra, J. Heering, and P. Klint, editors. *Algebraic Specification*. ACM Press Frontier Series. The ACM Press in co-operation with Addison-Wesley, 1989.

[BK84]   J.A. Bergstra and J.W. Klop. Process algebra for synchronous communication. *Information & Control*, 60:82–95, 1984.

[BK94]   J.A. Bergstra and P. Klint. The TOOLBUS—a component interconnection architecture. Technical Report P9408, Programming Research Group, University of Amsterdam, 1994.

[BK95]   J.A. Bergstra and P. Klint. The Discrete Time TOOLBUS. Technical Report P9502, Programming Research Group, University of Amsterdam, 1995.

[BK96]   J.A. Bergstra and P. Klint. The TOOLBUS coordination architecture. In P. Ciancarini and C. Hankin, editors, *Coordination Languages and Models (COORDINATION'96)*, volume 1061 of *Lecture Notes in Computer Science*, pages 75–88. Springer-Verlag, 1996.

[Bri87]   E. Brinksma, editor. *Information processing systems–open systems interconnection–LOTOS–a formal description technique based on the temporal ordering of observational behaviour*. 1987. ISO/TC97/SC21.

[BW90]   J.C.M. Baeten and W.P. Weijland. *Process Algebra*. Cambridge University Press, 1990.

[GP90]   J.F. Groote and A. Ponse. The syntax and semantics of μCRL. Technical Report CS-R9076, CWI, 1990.

[HHKR89]   J. Heering, P.R.H. Hendriks, P. Klint, and J. Rekers. The syntax definition formalism SDF - reference manual. *SIGPLAN Notices*, 24(11):43–75, 1989.

[Kli96]   P. Klint. A guide to TOOLBUS programming. Technical report, Programming Research Group, University of Amsterdam, 1996. to appear.

[MV90]   S. Mauw and G.J. Veltink. A process specification formalism. *Fundamenta Informaticae*, pages 85–139, 1990.

[MV93]   S. Mauw and G.J. Veltink, editors. *Algebraic specification of communication protocols*, volume 36 of *Cambridge Tracts in Theoretical Computer Science*. Cambridge University Press, 1993.

[Oli96a]   P. Olivier. Embedded system simulation – testdriving the TOOLBUS. Technical Report P9601, Programming Research Group, University of Amsterdam, 1996.

[Oli96b]   P. Olivier. A simulator framework for embedded systems. In *Coordination Languages and Models (COORDINATION'96)*, volume 1061 of *Lecture Notes in Computer Science*, pages 436–439, 1996.

[vDHK96]   A. van Deursen, J. Heering, and P. Klint, editors. *Language Prototyping, An Algebraic Approach*, volume 5 of *AMAST Series in Computing*. World Scientific Publishing Co., 1996. To appear.

[Yel94]   D.M. Yellin. Interfaces, protocols and the semi-automatic construction of software adaptors. Technical Report RC19460, IBM T.J. Watson Research Center, 1994.

Note. The citations [BK94, BK95, BK96] contain an extensive list of references to related work. This paper is an extended abstract of [BK95].

A Study on the Specification and Verification of Performance Properties* (Extended Abstract)

Xiao Jun Chen[1], Flavio Corradini[2], Roberto Gorrieri[3]

[1] Dipartimento di Scienze dell'Informazione, Università "La Sapienza"
e-mail: chen@dsi.uniroma1.it
[2] School of Cognitive and Computing Sciences, University of Sussex
e-mail: flavioc@cogs.sussex.ac.uk
[3] Dipartimento di Scienze dell'Informazione, Università di Bologna
e-mail: gorrieri@cs.unibo.it

Abstract. The process algebra expressing *nets of automata* is provided with a new operational semantics, that allows us to reason about performance properties of concurrent systems. Based on the idea that actions are durational and execution is asynchronous, performance equivalence and performance preorder are introduced as extensions of *interleaving bisimulation*. They turn out to be a congruence and a precongruence, respectively, w.r.t. the operators of the language we study. The equivalence (preorder) is also characterized by Hennessy-Milner logic (and its positive form), with natural numbers as propositional constants. Furthermore, we show how to apply modal μ-calculus to specify and verify performance-oriented properties.

1 Introduction

The analysis of system efficiency can be done in process algebras by way of suitable notions of equivalences and preorders [1, 3, 13, 18]. Some of them [1, 2, 8, 9, 11, 12, 13] use the time consumed for process execution as a measure of the efficiency: they rely on the assumption that the actions have a *static duration*, chosen on the basis of the features of the abstract machine. Precisely, systems are distributed over the space where each sequential component is associated with a *local clock* whose elapsing is set dynamically during the execution of the actions by the corresponding component. Whenever an action a is executed by a sequential component E, the value n of the clock of E is incremented to n plus the duration of a, whilst the local clocks of those sequential components not involved in the execution of a are unaffected. By incorporating the duration of actions into the notion of process equivalence/preorder, we are able to discriminate processes not only according to the *functionality* (what actions a process can do), but also according to their *performance*.

---

* This work has been partially founded by EEC within the HCM Project EXPRESS, and by CNR.

In [2, 13], *performance equivalences* are introduced, based on the standard notion of *bisimulation* [17]: processes are performance equivalent whenever they perform the same actions in the same amount of time. The approach of [2], however, is rather strict because it requires a very stringent synchronization rule, preventing possible synchronizations that need some busy waiting from one of the communicating partners. Moreover, some synchronizations that are possible in the interleaving "untimed" case are actually prevented; thus, performance equivalence on the resulting transition system is not a refinement of interleaving behavioural equivalences. Another approach, relaxing the synchronization rule to allow any form of busy waiting in a synchronization, is taken in [13]; the resulting semantics is comparable with the interleaving untimed semantics, but has the unfortunate effect of loosing compositionality. Both proposals assume urgency on actions (unless in a synchronization context for the latter proposal) and both admit the phenomenon of the so-called "well-caused but ill-timed" executions [2].

In this paper, we present a new operational semantics for a process algebra expressing nets of automata. Differently from the above, we allow actions to be executed in delay in any context (as in [7]), resulting in a rather simple operational semantics for the synchronization among processes. However, actions cannot be delayed at will, but there is an upper bound due to the maximum local clock value, representing the value of the global clock. This essentially guarantees that the resulting labelled transition system is *finitely branching*. Thus, our point of view lies between *eager* systems [1, 2, 8, 9, 11, 12, 13], where actions have to be performed as soon as possible,[4] and *lazy* systems [7] where systems can delay the execution of actions arbitrarily long. Our approach has also the effect of forbidding the generation of ill-timed traces, where the "observation time" (the order of transitions generation) agrees with the "execution time" (the number occurring in the label of a transition); in other words, execution time in a computation always increases. Finally, no interleaving (untimed) synchronization is prevented, so that performance equivalence is in our case more discriminating than interleaving bisimulation equivalence. Based on this new transitional semantics, (i) performance equivalence is a congruence; (ii) moreover, performance preorder, which *orders processes with respect to speed*, is a precongruence. Intuitively, a process E_1 is faster than another process E_2 iff they are bisimilar (i.e. they have the same functional behaviour), and E_1 is at least as fast as E_2. This preorder extends the notion in [8, 9] to deal with communicating processes under the hypothesis of lazyness of actions.

Equivalences and preorders can also be characterized by means of modal and temporal logics: two processes are equivalent iff they are not distinguishable by formulas of the logic, and a process q is finer than p iff q satisfies all formulas that p does. As it is well-known, interleaving bisimulation equivalence is fully characterized by Henessy-Milner logic [14] (HML for short). In this paper, we show that performance equivalence (as defined above) can be logically charac-

---

[4] In [12, 13] actions may be delayed at will only if they are involved in a synchronization with a late partner.

terized by suitably extending HML with an additional set of propositions, i.e. the natural numbers. Intuitively, these numbers are used to test the passing of the time during the possible computations of running systems. We give interpretation of these propositions on labelled transition systems, and show that with this interpretation, the equivalence deduced by this logic coincides with performance equivalence. Furthermore, the positive form of HML is also extended with natural numbers (together with a new suitable interpretation for them), based on which the performance preorder mentioned above can be fully characterized.

In comparison with process algebras, logics have the advantage of not always requiring to specify the full behavior of a system: they can be used to focus on specific interesting properties of systems, like safety or fairness. As the expressivity of HML is rather limited, we adopt modal μ-calculus [15] to specify performance properties; essentially, we consider HML extended by fixed point operators. As above, the natural numbers are taken as propositional constants.

If the process is finite state, properties expressed in modal μ-calculus can be verified in polynomial time [5] and the verification can be done automatically by means of tools like the Concurrency Workbench [6]. In our approach the number of states of labelled transition system for a process is infinite in general, because states contain clocks, the value of which increases as the computation proceeds. We present a technique for reducing the check of a property ϕ on an infinite state labelled transition system TS to the check of a different property $F(\phi)$ on a finite state approximation TS' of TS, thus allowing to exploit existing verification tools on finite state processes.

The paper is organized as follows: section 2 presents the syntax, the operational semantics of the language and the notions of performance equivalence/preorder; section 3 shows the logical characterizations of the performance equivalence/preorder, and section 4 discusses the way to specify and verify performance properties using modal μ-calculus.

2 The Language and its Behavioural Semantics

In this section, we present the algebraic description of the processes with durational actions, including the syntax, the operational semantics, and the notions of performance equivalence/preorder.

2.1 The Language

We consider *timed processes* as *nets of automata* equipped with clocks. Nets are obtained by composing regular processes (sequential and non-deterministic processes) by means of the static operators of CCS [17]. Thus, the number of states the classic interleaving semantics associates to each net is finite.

Let A (ranged over by a, b, ...) be a set of atomic actions, $\bar{A}$ (ranged over by $\bar{a}$, $\bar{b}$, ...) its complementation, and Act (ranged over by α, β, ...) defined as $Act = A \cup \bar{A}$. Complementation is extended to Act by $\bar{\bar{\alpha}} = \alpha$. As usual, τ

($\tau \notin Act$) denotes the invisible or internal action, and we use Act_τ to denote $Act \cup \{\tau\}$.

Let V (ranged over by $v, v', v'', ...$) denote a set of variables. The set of regular processes $\mathcal{P}$ ($p, q \in \mathcal{P}$) over Act and V, is the set of closed (i.e., without free variables) and guarded (i.e., variables appear within a $a._-$ or wait $n._-$ context) terms generated by the following grammar:

$$p ::= nil \mid \alpha.p \mid \text{wait } n.\, p \mid p + p \mid v \mid \text{rec } v.\, p$$

Process *nil* denotes a terminated process. By prefixing a term p with an action α, we get a process term $\alpha.p$ which can do an action α and then behaves like p. wait $n.\, p$ denotes a process which waits for at least $n \in N^+$ time units and then behaves like process p. $p_1 + p_2$ denotes the alternative composition of p_1 and p_2, while rec $v.\, p$ is used for recursive definitions.

The set $\mathcal{E}$ of *nets of automata* ($E, E' \in \mathcal{E}$) is defined by the following grammar:

$$E ::= p \mid E|E \mid E[\varPhi] \mid E\backslash\{\alpha\}$$

$E_1|E_2$, the parallel composition of E_1 and E_2, is the process which can perform any interleaving of the actions of E_1 and E_2 or synchronizations whenever E_1 and E_2 can perform complementary actions. $E[\varPhi]$ is a process which behaves like E but its actions are relabelled according to function $\varPhi$. Finally, $E\backslash\{\alpha\}$ is a process which behaves like E but actions $\alpha, \bar{\alpha}$ are forbidden.

The states of the labelled transition system we are going to define are processes enriched with local clocks which record the local view of the elapsing of time together with the value of the global clock (corresponding to the maximum of local views). Formally, we introduce extended processes, obtained by *nets of automata* with a *local clock prefixing* operator, $n \Rightarrow \_$:

$$d ::= n \Rightarrow p \mid d|d' \mid d\backslash\{\alpha\} \mid d[\varPhi].$$

with $p \in \mathcal{P}$, $n \in N$. We use $\mathcal{D}$ (ranged over by $d, d' \ldots$) to denote the set of terms generated by this grammar. The *clock distribution equations*

$$n \Rightarrow (E \mid E') = (n \Rightarrow E) \mid (n \Rightarrow E')$$
$$n \Rightarrow (E\backslash\{\alpha\}) = (n \Rightarrow E)\backslash\{\alpha\}$$
$$n \Rightarrow (E[\varPhi]) = (n \Rightarrow E)[\varPhi]$$

show that a term $n \Rightarrow E$ can be reduced canonically to an extended process, when interpreting these equations as rewrite rules from left to right.

A *timed process* (or state) $d \triangleright n$ is an extended process d, equipped with a global clock n. The global clock represents the global observation time for the execution. The explicit use of a global clock allows us to define a semantics that avoids the system to stay idle. This will be clearer in the next subsection. Here, we require that $n \geq maxclock(d)$, where $maxclock(d)$ gives the maximum of clock values m occurring in subterms of d of the form $m \Rightarrow p$. We use $\mathcal{S}$ (ranged over by $s, t, \ldots$) to denote the set of timed processes.

The amount of time needed for the execution of a particular action is fixed once for all on the basis of the chosen machine. As the duration of actions can be different for different machines, we should take this parameter into account in our semantic description. One possibility is to introduce *duration functions* (ranged over by f, g) which associate to each action a the positive integer $f(a)$ of time units needed for its execution. In the following, we choose a duration function f to fix this parameter.

2.2 The Operational Semantics

The *timed processes* are interpreted on *timed labelled transition systems* $\langle S, M, T \rangle$, where S is the set of *timed processes*, M a set of *timed actions*. Here, the *timed action* has form (μ, n) where $\mu \in Act_\tau$ and $n \in N^+$. Intuitively, a label (μ, n) means that action $\mu \in Act_\tau$ has been completed exactly n time units after the computation began. $T = \{\stackrel{\mu}{\longrightarrow} \subseteq S \times S \mid \mu \in M\}$ is the *transition relation*. We will write $s \stackrel{\mu}{\longrightarrow} s'$ instead of $\langle s, s' \rangle \in \stackrel{\mu}{\longrightarrow}$.

As usual, the transition relation is given through a set of inference rules, listed in Table 1. It is worthwhile observing that these rules are parametric w.r.t. the chosen duraction function f. Hence, we should write $\rightarrow_f$. For the sake of simplicity, the subscript will be omitted as clear from the context.

A few comments on the rules in Table 1 are now in order. The rule for action prefixing Act states that action α can only be completed at a time greater than or equal to the global clock, but less than or equal to the global clock plus the duration of α. This guarantees that the system *as a whole* never stays idle. Moreover, an obvious constraint on the local clock is imposed: the time of completion is greater than (or equal to) the sum of the local clock value with the duration of α. For the last rebelling rule, we confine ourselves in this paper to duration-preserving relabellings, i.e. $f(\alpha) = f(\Phi(\alpha))$. The other rules are self explanatory.

Some properties of the operational semantics immediately follow. First we show that the time increases as the computation proceeds, so that only "well timed traces" are taken into account. Moreover, we show that the system as a whole never idles. Then we give a few examples in order to show how process computations proceed. Finally, we prove that our semantics never gets an infinitely branching transition system.

In a derivation $d \triangleright n \xrightarrow{(\mu, t)} d' \triangleright n'$, $duration(\mu) = f(a)$ if μ is a visible action a; if $\mu = \tau$, then $duration(\mu) = f(a)$ if an $(a, \bar{a})$-communication is performed; $duration(\mu) = m$ if a *wait m* is performed. Clearly, in these two latter cases, an inspection of the proof of the derivation is needed in order to solve ambiguities.

Proposition 1. *Let* $d \triangleright n \xrightarrow{(\mu, t)} d' \triangleright n'$ *be derivable. Then, the following hold:*

(i) $t = n'$ *and* $n \le t$ *(no ill-timed); and*
(ii) $n' \le n + duration(\mu)$ *(no idling, as a whole).*

$$Act \quad \frac{t \geq n + f(\alpha) \text{ and } n' \leq t \leq n' + f(\alpha)}{(n \Rightarrow \alpha.p) \triangleright n' \xrightarrow{(\alpha,t)} (t \Rightarrow p) \triangleright t}$$

$$Wait \quad \frac{t \geq n + n'', \text{ and } n' \leq t \leq n' + n''}{(n \Rightarrow \text{wait } n''.p) \triangleright n' \xrightarrow{(\tau,t)} (t \Rightarrow p) \triangleright t}$$

$$Alt_1 \quad \frac{(n \Rightarrow p_1) \triangleright n' \xrightarrow{(\mu,t)} (t \Rightarrow p'_1) \triangleright t}{(n \Rightarrow p_1 + p_2) \triangleright n' \xrightarrow{(\mu,t)} (t \Rightarrow p'_1) \triangleright t}$$

$$Alt_2 \quad \frac{(n \Rightarrow p_2) \triangleright n' \xrightarrow{(\mu,t)} (t \Rightarrow p'_2) \triangleright t}{(n \Rightarrow p_1 + p_2) \triangleright n' \xrightarrow{(\mu,t)} (t \Rightarrow p'_2) \triangleright t}$$

$$Rec \quad \frac{(n \Rightarrow p[\text{rec } v. \, p/v]) \triangleright n' \xrightarrow{(\mu,t)} (t \Rightarrow p') \triangleright t}{(n \Rightarrow \text{rec } v. \, p) \triangleright n' \xrightarrow{(\mu,t)} (t \Rightarrow p') \triangleright t}$$

$$Par_1 \quad \frac{d_1 \triangleright n \xrightarrow{(\mu,t)} d'_1 \triangleright t}{(d_1 \mid d_2) \triangleright n \xrightarrow{(\mu,t)} (d'_1 \mid d_2) \triangleright t}$$

$$Par_2 \quad \frac{d_2 \triangleright n \xrightarrow{(\mu,t)} d'_2 \triangleright t}{(d_1 \mid d_2) \triangleright n \xrightarrow{(\mu,t)} (d_1 \mid d'_2) \triangleright t}$$

$$Synch \quad \frac{d_1 \triangleright n \xrightarrow{(a,t)} d'_1 \triangleright t, \qquad d_2 \triangleright n \xrightarrow{(\bar{a},t)} d'_2 \triangleright t}{(d_1 \mid d_2) \triangleright n \xrightarrow{(\tau,t)} (d'_1 \mid d'_2) \triangleright t}$$

$$Res \quad \frac{d \triangleright n \xrightarrow{(\mu,t)} d' \triangleright t \text{ and } \mu \notin \{\alpha, \bar{\alpha}\}}{d \backslash \{\alpha\} \triangleright n \xrightarrow{(\mu,t)} d' \backslash \{\alpha\} \triangleright t}$$

$$Rel \quad \frac{d \triangleright n \xrightarrow{(\mu,t)} d' \triangleright t}{d[\Phi] \triangleright n \xrightarrow{(\Phi(\mu),t)} d'[\Phi] \triangleright t}$$

Table 1. The Structural Rules for the Operational Semantics.

Example 1. Let $f(\alpha) = 2$, $f(\beta) = 3$ for α, $\beta \in Act$ and consider process $\alpha|\beta$.

(i) The fastest terminating computation performed by $(0 \Rightarrow \alpha|0 \Rightarrow \beta) \triangleright 0$ is the one in which action α is observed at time $f(\alpha)$ and then action β is observed at time $f(\beta)$. This is possible when the two processors in which the two components are located start their execution at time 0. This corresponds to having two processors available from the beginning.

(ii) The slowest terminating computations are the two in which the two actions are sequentialized in time. These computations take $f(\alpha) + f(\beta)$ time units to be performed. This corresponds to having only one processor available.

(iii) Between these two ($f(\beta)$ and $f(\alpha) + f(\beta)$) extreme performance limits, there are some other possible computations. An interesting one is that when action β starts at time 0 and then a new processor is available from time 2, permitting to overlap for one time unit the execution of the two actions. Then the whole process ends at time 4.

Proposition 2. *Let $d \triangleright n$ be any timed process. Then, set*

$$\{d' \triangleright n' | d \triangleright n \xrightarrow{(\mu, n')} d' \triangleright n'\} \text{ is finite.}$$

The following example shows that we are not taking the so-called "maximal progress" approach, according to which an immediately executable action always takes precedence over actions with a later enabling time.

Example 2. Consider net $(\alpha.\beta.\delta|(\bar{\beta}+\gamma))\backslash\{\beta\}$. According to the maximal progress approach, if $f(\alpha) \geq f(\gamma)$, then action δ will never be performed. In our approach, instead, because actions are lazy, γ is not forced to be performed starting at time 0. Thus we allow an α-labelled transition at completing time $f(\alpha)$, then a communication is possible that leads to the execution of action δ at completing time $f(\alpha) + f(\beta) + f(\delta)$.

2.3 Behavioural Semantics

The observational semantics we are interested in is based on the branching-time semantics of bisimulation. We first define our notion of *performance equivalence* that relates two systems whenever they perform the same actions at the same time. Then we define *performance preoder* that allows us to order processes with respect to speed.

Definition 3. *(Performance Equivalence)*

Let Rel denote the set of binary relations over S. The functional $R : Rel \rightarrow Rel$ is defined, for each $\Re \in Rel$, as follows: $(d_1 \triangleright n, d_2 \triangleright n) \in R(\Re)$ if, for each $\mu \in Act_\tau$,

i) $d_1 \triangleright n \xrightarrow{(\mu, n')} d'_1 \triangleright n'$ implies $d_2 \triangleright n \xrightarrow{(\mu, n')} d'_2 \triangleright n'$ such that $(d'_1 \triangleright n', d'_2 \triangleright n') \in \Re$;

ii) $d_2 \rhd n \xrightarrow{(\mu,n')} d_2' \rhd n'$ implies $d_1 \rhd n \xrightarrow{(\mu,n')} d_1' \rhd n'$ such that
$(d_1' \rhd n', d_2' \rhd n') \in \Re$.

A relation $\Re \in Rel$ will be called a *R-bisimulation* if $\Re \subseteq R(\Re)$. We say that two timed processes s_1 and s_2 are *f-performance equivalent*, notation $s_1 \sim^f s_2$, iff there exists a *R-bisimulation* $\Re$ such that $(s_1, s_2) \in \Re$. We say that two processes E_1, $E_2 \in \mathcal{E}$ are *f-performance equivalent*, notation $E_1 \sim_p^f E_2$, iff $(0 \Rightarrow E_1) \rhd 0 \sim^f (0 \Rightarrow E_2) \rhd 0$. When f is clear from the context, we omit the superscript f, as in $d_1 \rhd n \sim d_2 \rhd n$ and $E_1 \sim_p E_2$.

Proposition 4. *Let* p_1, p_2, $p \in \mathcal{P}$, E_1, E_2, $E \in \mathcal{E}$, $n \in N^+$ *and* $p_1 \sim_p p_2$. *If* $E_1 \sim_p E_2$ *then the following holds:*

$$\alpha.p_1 \sim_p \alpha.p_2 \qquad wait\ n.p_1 \sim_p wait\ n.p_2 \qquad p_1 + p \sim_p p_2 + p$$
$$E_1 \mid E \sim_p E_2 \mid E \qquad E_1[\varPhi] \sim_p E_2[\varPhi] \qquad E_1\backslash\{\alpha\} \sim_p E_2\backslash\{\alpha\}$$

Moreover, like in [17], it can be proved that $\sim_p$ is a congruence for recursion as well, on automata.

While performance equivalence asks whether two processes can do the same action at the same time, performance preorder allows us to express whether two processes have the same functional behaviors but one is faster than another according to duration function f.

Definition 5. *(Performance Preorder)*

Let *Rel* denote the set of binary relations over $\mathcal{S}$. The functional $G : Rel \to Rel$ is defined, for each $\Re \in Rel$, as follows: $(d_1 \rhd n', d_2 \rhd n'') \in G(\Re)$ if, for each $\mu \in Act_\tau$,

i) $d_1 \rhd n' \xrightarrow{(\mu,n)} d_1' \rhd n$ implies $d_2 \rhd n'' \xrightarrow{(\mu,m)} d_2' \rhd m$ with $n \leq m$ and $(d_1' \rhd n,\ d_2' \rhd m) \in \Re$;

ii) $d_2 \rhd n'' \xrightarrow{(\mu,m)} d_2' \rhd m$ implies $d_1 \rhd n' \xrightarrow{(\mu,n)} d_1' \rhd n$ with $n \leq m$ and $(d_1' \rhd n,\ d_2' \rhd m) \in \Re$;

A relation $\Re \in Rel$ will be called a *G-bisimulation* if $\Re \subseteq G(\Re)$. We say that two timed processes s_1 and s_2 are in the relation of *f-performance preorder* (denoted by $s_1 \sqsubseteq^f s_2$) iff there exists a *G-bisimulation* $\Re$ such that $(s_1, s_2) \in \Re$. We say that $E_1 \sqsubseteq_p^f E_2$ iff $0 \Rightarrow E_1 \rhd 0 \sqsubseteq^f 0 \Rightarrow E_2 \rhd 0$. Whenever clear from the context we will omit the superscript duration function.

Example 3. $\alpha \mid \beta \sqsubseteq_p \alpha.\beta + \beta.\alpha$ but not $\alpha.\beta + \beta.\alpha \sqsubseteq_p \alpha \mid \beta$. In other words, $\alpha \mid \beta$ is faster than its interleaving explanation $\alpha.\beta + \beta.\alpha$. To show $\alpha \mid \beta \sqsubseteq_p \alpha.\beta + \beta.\alpha$, it is sufficient to observe that relation:

$$\Re = \{ \; \langle (0 \Rightarrow \alpha | 0 \Rightarrow \beta) \triangleright 0, (0 \Rightarrow \alpha.\beta + \beta.\alpha) \triangleright 0 \rangle,$$
$$\langle (0 \Rightarrow \alpha.\beta + \beta.\alpha) \triangleright 0, (0 \Rightarrow \alpha | 0 \Rightarrow \beta) \triangleright 0 \rangle,$$
$$\langle (n \Rightarrow nil | 0 \Rightarrow \beta) \triangleright n, (n \Rightarrow \beta) \triangleright n \rangle,$$
$$\langle (n \Rightarrow \beta) \triangleright n, (n \Rightarrow nil | 0 \Rightarrow \beta) \triangleright n \rangle,$$
$$\langle (0 \Rightarrow \alpha | m \Rightarrow nil) \triangleright m, (m \Rightarrow \alpha) \triangleright m \rangle,$$
$$\langle (m \Rightarrow \alpha) \triangleright m, (0 \Rightarrow \alpha | m \Rightarrow nil) \triangleright m \rangle,$$
$$\langle (n \Rightarrow nil | m \Rightarrow nil) \triangleright max\{n, m\}, (m + n \Rightarrow nil) \triangleright n + m \rangle,$$
$$\langle (m + n \Rightarrow nil) \triangleright n + m, (n \Rightarrow nil | m \Rightarrow nil) \triangleright max\{n, m\} \rangle \}$$

is a *G-bisimulation*. To prove that $\alpha.\beta + \beta.\alpha \not\sqsubseteq_p \alpha \mid \beta$, it is sufficient to observe that the two transitions

$$(0 \Rightarrow \alpha \mid 0 \Rightarrow \beta) \triangleright 0 \xrightarrow{(\alpha, f(\alpha))} (f(\alpha) \Rightarrow nil \mid 0 \Rightarrow \beta) \triangleright f(\alpha)$$

$$(f(\alpha) \Rightarrow nil \mid 0 \Rightarrow \beta) \triangleright f(\alpha) \xrightarrow{(\beta, t)} (f(\alpha) \Rightarrow nil \mid t \Rightarrow nil) \triangleright t$$

with $t = max\{f(\alpha), f(\beta)\}$ cannot be matched by system $(0 \Rightarrow \alpha.\beta + \beta.\alpha) \triangleright 0$.

Now we establish a precongruence result for our performance preorder.

Proposition 6. *Let p_1, p_2, $p \in \mathcal{P}$, $n \in N^+$ and $p_1 \sqsubseteq_p p_2$. Let E_1, E_2, $E \in \mathcal{E}$, Φ be a duration preserving relabelling function, and assume $E_1 \sqsubseteq_p E_2$. Then, the following holds:*

$$\alpha.p_1 \sqsubseteq_p \alpha.p_2 \qquad wait\ n.p_1 \sqsubseteq_p wait\ n.p_2 \qquad p_1 + p \sqsubseteq_p p_2 + p$$
$$E_1 \mid E \sqsubseteq_p E_2 \mid E \qquad E_1[\Phi] \sqsubseteq_p E_2[\Phi] \qquad E_1 \backslash \{\alpha\} \sqsubseteq_p E_2 \backslash \{\alpha\}$$

We finish this section by observing that performance semantics is consistent with classic untimed interleaving strong bisimulation. Let $\sim$ denote strong bisimulation equivalence [17] over the transition system of net of automata (label τ is used for prefixes of the form wait n).

Proposition 7. *Let E_1, E_2, $E \in \mathcal{E}$. Then, the following hold:*

(i) $E_1 \sim_p E_2$ implies $E_1 \sim E_2$;
(ii) $E_1 \sqsubseteq_p E_2$ implies $E_1 \sim E_2$.

3 Logical Characterizations

Temporal and modal logics offer another way to characterize equivalences and preorders [4, 14]: (i) two processes are equivalent if they are not distinguishable by formulas of the logical language under consideration. For example, HML gives a logical characterization of bisimulation [14], while the equivalence deduced by HML+Until coincides with branching bisimulation [19]. (ii) process Q is finer/better than P if Q satisfies all formulas that P satisfies.

In this section, we extend HML (and its positive form) with natural numbers as propositional constants. We give proper interpretations of these propositional constants on timed labelled transition systems, so that together with these constants, the equivalence deduced by HML (and its positive form), coincides with performance equivalence (performance preorder).

3.1 Characterizing Performance Equivalence

We consider the following HML formulas with natural numbers as propositional letters ($\alpha \in Act$, $n \in N^+$). For convenience, we use L_t to denote this set of formulae.

$$\phi ::= tt \mid \neg\phi \mid \phi \wedge \phi \mid \langle\alpha\rangle\phi \mid n$$

Here $\langle\alpha\rangle$ is the *next* modality as in HML, except that it is interpreted on timed labelled transition systems:

$$s \models \langle\alpha\rangle\phi \text{ iff } \exists n, s'. \text{ such that } s \xrightarrow{(\alpha,n)} s' \text{ and } s' \models \phi$$

Remark. Formally, the satisfaction relation $\models$ is defined between a pair (TS, s) (composed of a transition system TS and a state s) and a logical formula φ. In the following, when there is no confusion, we will simply use $s \models \varphi$ instead of $(TS, s) \models \varphi$.

The propositional constants are used to identify the global clock in a state:

$$d \triangleright n' \models n \text{ iff } n' = n$$

The equivalence deduced by L_t coincides with performance equivalence:

Proposition 8. *Let s_1, $s_2 \in \mathcal{S}$. $s_1 \sim_p s_2$ iff $(\forall\phi \in L_t,\ s_1 \models \phi$ iff $s_2 \models \phi)$.*

Immediately from this proposition, we have

Theorem 9. *Let E_1, $E_2 \in \mathcal{P}$. $E_1 \sim_p E_2$ iff*

$$(\forall\phi \in L_t,\ 0 \Rightarrow E_1 \triangleright 0 \models \phi \text{ iff } 0 \Rightarrow E_2 \triangleright 0 \models \phi).$$

3.2 Characterizing Performance Preorder

To characterize preorders, the positive form of the logic languages are usually adopted. In the following, we will use L_t^p to denote the set of positive HML formulas, with propositional constants. This logic is generated by the following grammar ($\alpha \in Act$, $n \in N$):

$$\phi ::= tt \mid ff \mid \phi \wedge \phi \mid \phi \vee \phi \mid \langle\alpha\rangle\phi \mid [\alpha]\phi \mid n$$

Here ff ($\neg tt$) is the dual of tt, and $[\alpha]\phi$ ($\neg\langle\alpha\rangle\neg\phi$) is the dual of $\langle\alpha\rangle\phi$. So, the satisfaction relation of $[\alpha]\phi$ on timed labelled transition systems is

$$s \models [\alpha]\phi \text{ iff } \forall n, s'.\ s \xrightarrow{(\alpha,n)} s' \text{ implies } s' \models \phi$$

However, with the interpretation of the propositional constants previously defined for L_t, we have that L_t^p does not characterize performance preorder, as the following example shows.

Example 4. From Example 3, we know that $\alpha \mid \beta \sqsubseteq_p \alpha.\beta + \beta.\alpha$. But using the previous interpretation of L_t, let $\varphi = \langle \alpha \rangle \langle \beta \rangle max\{f(\alpha), f(\beta)\}$, we have $\alpha \mid \beta \models \varphi$ but $\alpha.\beta + \beta.\alpha \not\models \varphi$.

At this point, we propose the following new interpretation of propositional constants in L_t^p, based on which the preorder deduced by L_t^p coincides with performance preorder: $d \triangleright n' \models n$ iff $n' \geq n$

Proposition 10. *Let* s_1, $s_2 \in \mathcal{S}$. $s_1 \sqsubseteq s_2$ *iff* $\forall \phi \in L_t^p$, $s_1 \models \phi$ *implies* $s_2 \models \phi$.

Immediately from this proposition, we have

Theorem 11. *Let* E_1, $E_2 \in \mathcal{E}$. $E_1 \sqsubseteq E_2$ *iff*

$$(\forall \phi \in L_t^p, (0 \Rightarrow E_1) \triangleright 0 \models \phi \text{ implies } (0 \Rightarrow E_2) \triangleright 0 \models \phi).$$

4 Specifying and Verifying Performance Properties

Many temporal and modal logics have been proposed in the literature for abstract specifications of concurrent systems [10, 14, 16], since they can be used to describe system properties, such as necessity, possibility, eventuality, etc. The logics we have discussed previously (L_t and L_t^p), can be used to express local capabilities and necessities, but they can not express safety properties (something bad will never happen) or liveness properties (something good will eventually happen), which are very useful abstract descriptions of systems behaviour.

Modal μ-calculus [15] has been recognized as a powerful logic language to describe safety and liveness properties. Furthermore, techniques have been provided to verify the truth of a formula in a given process [5, 6, 20]. What we consider here is, in fact, HML extended by fixpoint operators, denoted by $\mathcal{M}_\mu$. The formulas are generated by

$$\varphi ::= \neg\varphi \mid \varphi_1 \wedge \varphi_2 \mid \langle \alpha \rangle \varphi \mid n \mid Z \mid \mu Z.\varphi$$

where the constants n are interpreted as in L_t, and

$$s \models \mu Z.\phi \quad iff \quad \exists n. \ s \models (\mu Z. \ \phi)^n$$

Here $(\mu Z. \ \phi)^n$ is used for the n-th approximations of the least fixpoint formula:

$$s \models (\mu Z. \ \phi)^0 \quad \text{always holds}$$
$$s \models (\mu Z. \ \phi)^{n+1} \quad iff \quad s \models \phi[Z/(\mu Z. \ \phi)^n]$$

and $[Z/\phi]$ denotes the syntactic substitution of ϕ for the free occurrences of Z. We will also use $[\alpha]$ and $\nu Z. \ \varphi$ as the duals of $\langle \alpha \rangle$ and $\mu Z. \ \varphi$ respectively:

$$[\alpha]\varphi = \neg\langle \alpha \rangle \neg\varphi \qquad \nu Z. \ \varphi = \neg\mu Z. \ \neg(\varphi[Z := \neg Z])$$

with $\varphi[Z := \neg Z]$ the result of replacing all free occurrences of Z in φ with $\neg Z$.

The constant formula tt is definable as $\nu Z. \ Z$, and we will use it directly for convenience. As the usual syntactic restriction on $\mu Z. \ \varphi$, we require that all free occurrences of Z in φ lie within the scope of an even number of negations.

The least fixpoint is useful for expressing *eventual* properties, while the greatest one is useful to describe *invariance*. For instance,

$$\mu Z.(\varphi \vee (\overset{\alpha \in A}{\bigvee} \langle \alpha \rangle tt \wedge \underset{\alpha \in A}{\bigwedge} [\alpha]Z))$$

expresses that property φ is eventually satisfied along any computations, while

$$\nu Z. (\varphi \wedge \underset{\alpha \in A}{\bigwedge} [\alpha]Z)$$

expresses that φ is satisfied by all states along all the computations.

Example 5. Note that formula $\langle \alpha_0 \rangle 10$ states that it is possible to do an α_0 action ending at time 10; $\langle \alpha_0 \rangle \bigvee_{n \leq 10} n$ states that it is possible to do an α_0 action ending before time 10. Thus, formula

$$\mu Z.(((\langle \alpha_0 \rangle \overset{n \leq 10}{\bigvee} n) \vee (\overset{\alpha \in A}{\bigvee} \langle \alpha \rangle tt \wedge \underset{\alpha \in A}{\bigwedge} [\alpha]Z))$$

expresses that along all computations, it is possible to do an α_0 action at some point before time limit 10.

The verification of a particular property expressed in $\mathcal{M}_\mu$ can be done for finite state processes, even automatically [6], in polynomial time [5]. However, the number of states in the timed transition system is in fact infinite, due to the increase of the clock values.

Now we explain how to exploit existing model checkers on finite state processes, to verify performance properties in the infinite structures we generate. The observation we use is that the timed transition system TS could be cut into a finite state transition system TS' in a way such that for any s not in the states of TS', the verification for $(TS, s) \models \varphi$ can be reduced into the one for $(untimed(TS), untimed(s)) \models \mathcal{F}(\varphi)$ where $untimed(TS)$ denotes the underlying (untimed and *finite state*) transition system of TS, and $\mathcal{F}(\varphi)$ is the untimed formula of φ defined by

$$\mathcal{F}(\varphi) = \begin{cases} tt & \varphi = tt \\ \neg \mathcal{F}(\varphi') & \varphi = \neg \varphi' \\ \mathcal{F}(\varphi_1) \wedge \mathcal{F}(\varphi_2) & \varphi = \varphi_1 \wedge \varphi_2 \\ \langle \alpha \rangle \mathcal{F}(\varphi') & \varphi = \langle \alpha \rangle \varphi' \\ \neg tt & \varphi = n \\ Z & \varphi = Z \\ \mu Z. \mathcal{F}(\varphi') & \varphi = \mu Z. \varphi' \end{cases}$$

The states s having the above property are those that have the global clocks greater than the maximum time appeared in φ. This fact is stated in Theorem

13. Let $T(\varphi)$ denote the maximum time appeared in φ:

$$T(\varphi) = \begin{cases} 0 & \varphi = tt \\ T(\varphi') & \varphi = \neg\varphi' \\ max\{T(\varphi_1), T(\varphi_2)\} & \varphi = \varphi_1 \wedge \varphi_2 \\ T(\varphi') & \varphi = \langle\alpha\rangle\varphi' \\ n & \varphi = n \\ 0 & \varphi = Z \\ T(\varphi') & \varphi = \mu Z.\varphi' \end{cases}$$

and given $TS = \langle S, A, \rightarrow, s_0 \rangle$ and number n, we use $H(TS, n)$ to denote the set of states with global clocks greater than n: $H(TS, n) = \{d \triangleright n' \in S \mid n' > n\}$

Lemma 12. $\forall n \geq T(\varphi)$, $s \in H(TS, n)$: $(TS, s) \models \varphi$ iff $(TS, s) \models \mathcal{F}(\varphi)$

Theorem 13. $\forall s \in H(TS, T(\varphi))$:

$(TS, s) \models \varphi$ iff $(untimed(TS), untimed(s)) \models \mathcal{F}(\varphi)$.

Now we show how this theorem can be used to define a verification strategy for performance properties. We first need to define – for a given formula φ – the relevant (finite state) "prefix" $TS|_\varphi$ of the timed transition system TS, and its underlying untimed transition system. Obviously, the finite prefix should contain all those states s such that $s \notin H(TS, T(\varphi))$.

Definition 14. Given timed transition system $TS = \langle S, A, \rightarrow, s_0 \rangle$, and $\mathcal{M}_\mu$ formula φ, define $TS|_\varphi = \langle S' \cup Leaves(TS, \varphi), A, \rightarrow', s_0 \rangle$, where

$S' = S - H(TS, T(\varphi))$

$Leaves(TS, \varphi) = \{r \in H(TS, T(\varphi)) \mid \exists \alpha, n, s \in S' \text{ such that } s \xrightarrow{(\alpha,n)} r\}$

$\rightarrow' = \{(s, (\alpha, n), r) \mid s \in S', (s, (\alpha, n), r) \in \rightarrow\}$

To make easier the definition of the verification strategy, we introduce a new notion of satisfaction relation $\models'$. Given two transition systems $TS_1 = \langle S_1, A, \rightarrow_1, s_0 \rangle$ and TS_2, a set of states S where $S \subseteq S_1$, and a state $s \in S_1$, we define a satisfaction relation $\models'$ between a quadruple (TS_1, TS_2, S, s) and a formula φ, with the intuitive meaning that the verification is done in TS_1, but during the procedure, whenever it is necessary to verify the truth of a subformula φ' of φ in a state $s' \in S$, it should be changed into verifying $\mathcal{F}(\varphi')$ in TS_2.

$$
\begin{array}{ll}
s \in S, (TS_1, TS_2, S, s) \models' \varphi & \text{iff } (TS_2, s) \models \mathcal{F}(\varphi) \\
s \notin S, (TS_1, TS_2, S, s) \models' \neg\varphi & \text{iff } (TS_1, TS_2, S, s) \not\models' \varphi \\
s \notin S, (TS_1, TS_2, S, s) \models' \varphi_1 \wedge \varphi_2 & \text{iff } (TS_1, TS_2, S, s) \models' \varphi_1 \text{ and} \\
& \qquad (TS_1, TS_2, S, s) \models' \varphi_2 \\
s \notin S, (TS_1, TS_2, S, s) \models' \langle\alpha\rangle\varphi & \text{iff } \exists r, n. \ s \xrightarrow{(\alpha,n)}_1 r \text{ and} \\
& \qquad (TS_1, TS_2, S, r) \models' \varphi \\
s \notin S, (TS_1, TS_2, S, s) \models' \mu Z.\varphi & \text{iff } \exists n. (TS_1, TS_2, S, s) \models' (\mu Z. \varphi)^n
\end{array}
$$

The existing tools for verifying $\models$ could be easily extended to verify this $\models'$, if both TS_1 and TS_2 are finite.

As an important fact formally stated in Proposition 1(i), our new operational semantics avoids the computations that are well-caused but ill-timed. Thus, the global clock keeps increasing along the computations. This guarantees that $TS|_\varphi$ is finite, with $Leaves(TS, \varphi)$ the set of leaves, containing exactly all states reachable from S' in one step of transition. So according to the definition of $\models'$ and Theorem 13, we have

$$(TS, s_0) \models \varphi \quad \textit{iff} \quad (TS|_\varphi, untimed(TS), Leaves(TS, \varphi), s_0) \models' \varphi$$

5 Conclusion

In this paper we have proposed a new version of timed semantics for nets of automata where actions are patient, but not too lazy. The resulting equivalence and preorder have nice mathematical properties and possess simple logic characterizations which can be easily exploited to check performance related properties.

The kinds of performance analysis we can do are related to the hypoteses on action executions we have taken. Actions can be delayed but with an upper bound given by the current global clock. This means that the system as a whole is anyway urgent, i.e., never stays idle. Two systems are equated if, considering the whole range of their executions going from the hypothesis of maximal parallelism (best urgent well-timed case) to the hypothesis of having just one processor (worst urgent well-timed case), they perform the same actions in the same amount of time. In other words, if $P \sim Q$ in our approach, then P and Q are executed urgently in equivalent ways on any kind of architecture (= number of processors) they can be actually implemented, even if the allocation of processes to processors can vary during the execution (see Example 1).

Among other approaches to time, we would like to mention [21], developing a theory of timed processes within Petri net theory. Even if in a different context, Vogler's work presents some analogies with ours, at least because both approaches assume a non-interleaving point of view. Further work will be devoted to study the relationships between the two approaches.

References

1. L. Aceto and D. Murphy. On the ill-timed but well-caused. In E. Best, editor, *CONCUR'93, LNCS 715*, pages 97-111. Springer-Verlag, 1993.
2. L. Aceto and D. Murphy. Timing and causality in process algebra. Technical Report 9/93, University of Sussex, 1993. To appear in Acta Informatica.
3. S. Arun-Kumar and M. Hennessy. An efficient preorder for processes. *Acta Informatica*, 29:737-760, 1992.
4. S. Brooks and W. Rounds. Behavioural equivalence relations induced by programming logics. In *LNCS 154*, pages 97-108. Springer-Verlag, 1983.
5. R. Cleaveland. Tableau-based model checking in the propositional μ-calculus. *Acta Informatica*, 27:725-747, 1990.

6. R. Cleaveland, J. Parrow, and B. Steffen. The concurrency workbench: A semantics-based tool for the verification of concurrent systems. *ACM Transaction on Programming Languages and Systems*, 15:36–72, 1993.

7. F. Corradini. Compositionality for processes with durational actions. In *Proc. Fifth Italian Conference on Theoretical Computer Science*, 1995.

8. F. Corradini, R. Gorrieri, and M. Roccetti. Performance preorder and competitive equivalence. Technical Report 95/01, University of Bologna, 1995.

9. F. Corradini, R. Gorrieri, and M. Roccetti. Performance preorder: Ordering processes with respect to speed. In *MFCS'95, LNCS 969*, pages 444–453, 1995.

10. E.A. Emerson and J.Y. Halpern. "Sometimes" and "Not Never" revisited: on branching time versus linear time temporal logic. *Journal of ACM*, 33(1):151–178, 1986.

11. G-L. Ferrari and U. Montanari. Dynamic matrices and the cost analysis of concurrent programs. In *AMAST'95*, 1995.

12. R. Gorrieri and M. Roccetti. Towards performance evaluation in process algebras. In *AMAST'93*, pages 289–296. Springer-Verlag, 1993.

13. R. Gorrieri, M. Roccetti, and E. Stancampiano. A theory of processes with durational actions. *Theoretical Computer Science*, 140(1):73–94, 1995.

14. M. Hennessy and R. Milner. Algebraic laws for nondeterminism and concurrency. *J. of ACM*, 32(1):137–161, 1985.

15. D. Kozen. Results on the propositional μ-calculus. *Theoretical Computer Science*, 27:333–354, 1983.

16. Z. Manna and A. Pnueli. The anchored version of the temporal framework. In J. de Bakker, P. de Roever, and G. Rozenberg, editors, *Linear Time, Branching Time and Partial Order in Logics and Models for Concurrency, LNCS 354*, pages 201–284. Springer-Verlag, 1989.

17. R. Milner. *Communication and Concurrency*. Prentice Hall International, 1989. International Series on Computer Science.

18. F. Moller and C. Tofts. Relating processes with respect to speed. In *CONCUR'91, LNCS 527*, pages 424–438, 1991.

19. R. De Nicola and V. Vaandrager. Three logics for branching bisimulation. *Journal of ACM*, 42(2):458–487, 1995.

20. C. Stirling. Modal and temporal logics. In *Handbook of Logic in Computer Science, Volume 2*, pages 477–563. Oxford University Press, 1992.

21. W. Vogler. Faster asynchronous systems. In *Proc. CONCUR'95, LNCS 962*, pages 299–312. Springer, 1995.

Symbolic Bisimulation for Timed Processes*

Michele Boreale

Università di Roma "La Sapienza"

Abstract

Basing on symbolic transition systems, we propose a novel approach to the semantics of timed processes. A process algebra in which actions may occur within specified time intervals is introduced, together with a notion of bisimulation equivalence, based on standard transition systems.

The language is also equipped with a new, symbolic operational semantics. The latter, contrary to standard operational semantics, gives rise to transition systems which are finitely branching and, for a large class of processes, finite. On top of the symbolic operational semantics, we introduce a notion of symbolic bisimulation, for which a tractable proof technique exists. We then prove that symbolic and standard bisimulations coincide for our processes. A proof system to reason about bisimilarity is also presented. The soundness and completeness proofs for the system take great advantage of the symbolic characterization of bisimilarity.

1 Introduction

The treatment of timing aspects is often a delicate issue in concurrent systems, particularly if they must react in real-time to stimuli from the external environment. When describing a system that controls a dangerous industrial process, we should be able to specify that, after the detection of some error, a certain recovery action must take place within a given time interval. Several attempts have been made to incorporating timing aspects in classical process algebras, such as CCS and CSP: among the many, [8, 3, 2]. Here, we focus on a specific approach, taken e.g. in [3, 2]: it is based on attaching *time-stamps* to standard actions, to record their time of occurrence. For example, in the notation of [3], the expression

$$\int_{t \in [0,5]} a(t).P \tag{1}$$

represents a non-deterministic process that may engage action a at any real time between 0 and 5, and that then behaves like P.

A central goal of a theory of timed systems should be that of providing feasible reasoning techniques, perhaps amenable to mechanization. In this respect, a first,

---

*Work done while the author was at Istituto per Elaborazione dell'Informazione - CNR, Pisa. The work has been partially supported by EEC, HCM Project Express and by CNR within the project "Specifica ad Alto Livello e Verifica di Sistemi Digitali". Author's e-mail address: michele@dsi.uniroma1.it.

obvious difficulty is encountered if trying (as in [3]) to model time by means of real numbers, which cannot have a finite representation. A reasonable solution to this is restricting to rational numbers, which, for all applicative purposes, are the best possible approximation of reals. Even so, formulating a tractable theory remains problematic. The standard way of modelling the operational behaviour of (1) is to use a transition system having a transition labelled by $a(r)$ for each value r allowed in the interval $[0,5]$ (see e.g. [3]). In other words, the temporal parameter t is instantiated in all possible manners. This leads typically to transition systems which are infinite-branching (*infinitary*), even in very simple cases like (1). Usual behavioural relations, like bisimilarity [7], can be defined in a familiar way over such structures, but reasoning with them is generally quite difficult. In particular, the fact that the considered transition systems are infinitary prevents us from applying usual reasoning techniques of process algebras: the existence of complete proof systems, for example, is problematic in this setting, or relies on very ad-hoc techniques [5]. For similar reasons, there seems to be no obvious way of extending known automatic verification methods to this setting.

In the present paper, we try to address some of the above issues, focusing on a specific behavioural equivalence, bisimilarity, written $\sim$. We introduce a language of rational-timed processes, equipped with a notion of bisimilarity based on a standard infinitary transition system. The language we consider is quite expressive (more than, e.g., Wang's timed CCS [8]). For example, our language naturally permits describing time-outs or specifying that one action must take place within a certain time interval after another (relative delays). In this timed setting, we then develop a theory of *symbolic bisimulation*, in the style of Hennessy's and Lin's theory for value-passing processes [6]. Our theory yields an alternative, finitary representation of processes behaviours and a more tractable characterization of bisimilarity. For the latter, in particular, "exhibiting symbolic bisimulation relations" turns out to be a feasible reasoning technique. We also propose a sound and complete proof system for reasoning about $\sim$. A more detailed account of our work is as follows.

Our approach can be explained in two steps. First, besides the standard infinitary one, a new *symbolic* operational semantics is introduced. There, the infinitely many standard transitions raised by expressions like (1) are reduced to a single, symbolic transition. In the latter, no instantiation of the temporal parameter t is performed; rather, the temporal constraints on t are recorded via a logical formula. Thanks to this fact, the resulting symbolic transition system is finite-branching, and, for a large class of timed processes (including all those without recursion), is even finite. To clarify these points, let us write expression (1) in the more conventional form $a(t, 0 \leq t \leq 5).P$. According to our approach, the latter gives rise to the single symbolic transition:

$$a(t, 0 \leq t \leq 5).P \xmapsto{a(t),(0 \leq t \leq 5)} P.$$

In general, our logical formulae are built, via the usual boolean connectives, from temporal variables, rational values, operator $+$ and predicates $<$ and $=$. As a second step, on top of the symbolic transition system, a new, symbolic equivalence is defined. Intuitively, two timed processes P and Q are symbolically equivalent if for every symbolic move $P \xmapsto{a(t)\,\phi} P'$ of P, we can find a decomposition in sub-cases of the formula ϕ, such that each subcase "entails", in a logical sense, a matching transition for Q (and vice-versa for Q, P). As a simple example, consider the processes:

$$P \stackrel{def}{=} a(t, 0 \le t \le 10).P' \qquad \text{and}$$
$$Q \stackrel{def}{=} a(t, 0 \le t \le 5).P' + a(t, 5 < t < 10).P'$$

where $+$ is the operator of non-deterministic choice. Proving the equivalence of P and Q by relying on the definition of $\sim$ would imply exhibiting an infinite binary relation of processes, due to the necessity of instantiating the parameter t. On the contrary, the symbolic equivalence of P and Q is readily established by noting that the formula $(0 \le t \le 10)$, attached to the only symbolic transition of P, can be decomposed into the set of subcases $\{(0 \le t \le 5), (5 < t < 10)\}$, each of which implies a formula in a symbolic transition of Q (the vice-versa for Q, P is obvious). It is worth noting that the decompositions can always be taken *finite*.

Our main theorem shows that the symbolic equivalence, $\simeq$, can be used to establish the standard one, $\sim$. More precisely, we prove that standard and symbolic bisimilarities coincide on processes not containing free temporal parameters. This makes "exhibiting symbolic bisimulation relations" a feasible proof technique for $\sim$ and lays the basis for the development of automatic verification tools. For the latter, in particular, it should be possible to adapt to our setting Hennessy's and Lin's algorithms for checking value-passing symbolic equivalence [6]: but this point remains to be fully worked out.

For processes without recursion, we also prove decidability of timed bisimilarity and put forward a sound and complete proof system. The corresponding proofs take great advantage of the symbolic characterization of $\sim$ and are themselves examples of application of the proposed techniques.

A few words about the "local-time vs. global-time" issue are in order. Like in [2], we adopt for our language the local-time point of view. However, we will argue that this choice is not critical for the development of our theory.

The rest of the paper is organized as follows. Section 2 describes the language of timed processes and standard bisimulation over it. Symbolic transitional semantics and symbolic bisimulation are introduced and discussed in Section 3. In Section 4, after having established some technical properties, the main theorems, stating the correspondence between symbolic and standard bisimulation, are discussed. The proof system is described in Section 5. Finally, Section 6 contains comparison with related work and a few conclusive remarks.

2 The Language

2.1 Syntax

To manipulate temporal constraints in processes, we use a simple language of boolean formulae, BF. We introduce BF below, and then describe the syntax and the standard semantics of timed processes.

2.1.1 Expressions and boolean formulae

We assume a countable set Var of *variables* ranged over by $t, t', \ldots$. The letters $r, r' \ldots$ range over the non-negative rationals, $\mathbf{Q}^{\ge 0}$. Letters $p, p', \ldots$ range over $Var \cup \mathbf{Q}^{\ge 0}$.

Expressions e are given by $e := p \mid p + r$. The set of rational values and the set of variables occurring in e are denoted, respectively, by $val(e)$ and $var(e)$. The language of *boolean formulae* BF, ranged over by $\phi, \psi, \ldots$, is given by the following grammar:

$$\phi := true \mid p < e \mid p = e \mid \phi \wedge \phi \mid \neg \phi.$$

In the sequel, standard abbreviations such as $false$ for $\neg true$, $\phi \vee \psi$ for $\neg(\neg \phi \wedge \neg \psi)$, $p \leq e$ for $(p < e) \vee (p = e)$ and so on, will be freely used. We denote by $var(\phi)$ (resp. $val(\phi)$) the set variables (resp. rational values) occurring in ϕ.

Environments, ranged over by $\sigma, \rho, \ldots$, are finite partial maps from Var to $\mathbf{Q}^{\geq 0}$; $[r_1/t_1, \ldots, r_n/t_n]$, $n \geq 0$, denotes the environment mapping t_i to r_i, for $1 \leq i \leq n$, and undefined elsewhere. For a given σ, $\sigma[r/t]$ denotes the environment which maps t to r and behaves like σ elsewhere. The domain of σ is denoted by $dom(\sigma)$. For any expression or formula h, $h\sigma$ denotes the result of substituting each $x \in var(h) \cap dom(\sigma)$ by $\sigma(x)$.

An expression or a formula is *ground* if it does not contain variables. Given a ground expression e, its *evaluation* $[\![e]\!]$ is the non-negative rational value obtained by evaluating e in the expected way (once the operator symbol $+$ is interpreted as the standard summation over $\mathbf{Q}^{\geq 0}$). Given a ground formula ϕ, the evaluation of ϕ into the set $\{true, false\}$, $[\![\phi]\!]$, is inductively defined in the expected way, once we set that: $[\![true]\!] = true$, $[\![r < e]\!] = true$ iff $r < [\![e]\!]$ and $[\![r = e]\!] = true$ iff $r = [\![e]\!]$. Some basic (somewhat standard) notions on environments and formulae are summarized below.

- $\sigma \models \phi$ (σ *satisfies* ϕ), holds if $dom(\sigma) \supseteq var(\phi)$ and $[\![\phi\sigma]\!] = true$. A formula ϕ is *satisfiable* if there exists σ s.t. $\sigma \models \phi$.

- $\phi \models \psi$ (ϕ *logically implies* ψ) holds if for every σ s.t. $dom(\sigma) \supseteq var(\phi) \cup var(\psi)$, $\sigma \models \phi$ implies $\sigma \models \psi$. We say that ϕ and ψ are *equivalent* if $\phi \models \psi$ and $\psi \models \phi$.

- $\bigvee D$, where $D = \{\phi_1, \ldots, \phi_n\} \subseteq_{fin} BF$, $n > 0$, is the boolean formula $\phi_1 \vee \ldots \vee \phi_n$. A similar notation will be used for $\bigwedge D$. Furthermore, we let $\bigvee \emptyset$ denote $false$ and $\bigwedge \emptyset$ denote $true$.

2.1.2 Timed processes

As in CCS, we assume a countable set A of *actions* and a bijection $\_ : A \longrightarrow \overline{A}$, giving the complementary action for each action a, with the property that $\overline{\overline{a}} = a$; Act is $A \cup \overline{A}$ and is ranged over by $a, b, \ldots$. Each action in A is assigned positive *duration*, given by a function $\Delta : A \longrightarrow \mathbf{Q}^+$; the latter is extended to Act by letting $\Delta(\overline{a}) = \Delta(a)$. A family of labels $T = \{\tau_\delta \mid \delta \in \mathbf{Q}^+ \}$ disjoint from Act, to be used for internal actions of processes, is also assumed. Letters $c, c', \ldots$ range over $Act \cup T$. A countable set of *agent identifiers*, ranged over by $A, B, \ldots$ and each having a non-negative arity, is presupposed. The language of *agent terms*, $\mathcal{P}$, ranged over by $P, Q, \ldots$, is built from the operators of *inaction, action prefix, summation, boolean guard, parallel composition, restriction* and *agent identifier*.

$$P := \mathbf{0} \mid \alpha.P \mid P + P \mid \phi P \mid P | P \mid P \backslash a \mid A(e_1, \ldots e_k)$$

where k is the arity of the identifier A and $\alpha := wait_\delta \mid a(t, \phi)$, with $\delta \in \mathbf{Q}^+$ and $\phi \models t \leq e$, for some expression e not containing t. The prefix $a(t, \phi)$. is intented to be a *binder* for t in $a(t, \phi).P$, thus the notions of *free variables* $fvar(.)$, *bound variables* $bvar(.)$ and *α-equivalence* over agent terms are the expected ones. We shall consider agent terms up to α-equivalence: thus terms differing only in the choice of the bound names will be identified. We will sometimes use $a(e).P$ as a shorthand for $a(t, t = e).P$, whenever $t \notin fvar(P, e)$. We sometimes abbreviate $a(t, \phi).0$ simply as $a(t, \phi)$. We assume an arbitrarily fixed *finite* set $\mathcal{D}$ of guarded identifiers definitions, each having the form $A(t_1, \ldots, t_n) \Leftarrow P$, with the t_i's distinct and $fvar(P) \subseteq \{t_1, \ldots, t_n\}$. A *process* is a closed agent term, i.e. a P such that $fvar(P) = \emptyset$. The set of processes is denoted by $\mathcal{P}_c$.

Some intuitive explanation on the operators of our language is in order. Inaction, summation, parallel composition and restriction have essentially the same meaning as in CCS. The meaning of the other constructs is as follows. In $a(t, \phi).P$, action a can be engaged starting at a certain time t and then last for a time $\Delta(a)$; the time t must satisfy a certain temporal constraint, expressed by the formula ϕ. E.g., the action a in $a(t, 5 \leq t \leq 8).P$ can start at any time between 5 and 8. Note that we require that ϕ determine some upper-bound to the value of t: for example, $a(t, true)$. is a forbidden action prefix. In other words, actions cannot delay arbitrarily long. This assumption can be fulfilled in many practical situations and greatly simplifies the theory of symbolic bisimulation, as we shall see in later sections. The action $wait_\delta$ represents an internal activity that takes time δ. Process ϕP behaves like P if ϕ is true and like 0 otherwise. Finally, agent identifiers allow us to specify recursive behaviours, using a set of temporal parameters. The following example shows that the language $\mathcal{P}_c$ is indeed quite expressive.

Example 2.1 Let us describe a simple communication protocol supporting time-out. Starting at time t_0, a communication $\overline{com}$ occurs, after which an acknowledgment ack is awaited for a time T; if this time elapses without receiving any ack, a recovery procedure $\overline{recov}$ is invokated (we assume for simplicity that the duration of actions $\overline{com}$, ack and $\overline{recov}$ is 1):

$$A(t_0) \Leftarrow \overline{com}(t_0).\big(ack(t, t < t_0 + T).A(t+1) + \overline{recov}(t', t' = t_0 + T).A(t'+1)\big).$$

2.1.3 Configurations

In order to describe standard operational semantics, we follow [2] and use *configurations* to keep track of the time of occurrence of actions. The idea is that of associating with each process P a "clock", $\bullet e$, recording the current time, thus obtaining a configuration $P \bullet e$. A process P is then viewed as a configuration starting at time 0, $P \bullet 0$. The syntax of configurations $\mathcal{C}$, ranged over by $S, R, \ldots$, is as follows:

$$S := 0 \mid P \bullet e \mid \phi S \mid S + S \mid S \,|\, S \mid S \backslash a \,.$$

Following [2], we will consider configurations in canonical form with respect to the clock $\bullet e$, which is assumed to be distributive over all operators different from α. and identifiers. Formally, let $\equiv$ be defined as the least congruence generated by the axioms below:

$$
\begin{array}{ll}
(P + Q) \bullet e = (P \bullet e) + (Q \bullet e) & (\phi P) \bullet e = \phi(P \bullet e) \\
(P \,|\, Q) \bullet e = (P \bullet e) \,|\, (Q \bullet e) & (P \backslash a) \bullet e = (P \bullet e) \backslash a \\
\multicolumn{2}{c}{0 \bullet e = 0\,.}
\end{array}
$$

Applying these axioms as left-to-right rewriting rules, it is easy to see that each configuration S is reducible to a $\equiv$-congruent canonical configuration generated by the grammar:

$$\textbf{Act}\frac{\overline{\qquad\qquad\qquad\qquad\qquad\qquad\qquad\qquad}}{(a(t,\phi).P)\bullet e\xrightarrow{a(r)}(P[^r\!/t])\bullet(r+\Delta(a))},\ r\geq[e]\ \text{and}\ [\![\phi[^r\!/t]]\!]=true$$

$$\textbf{Wait}\frac{\overline{\qquad\qquad\qquad\qquad\qquad\qquad}}{(wait_\delta.P)\bullet e\xrightarrow{\tau_\delta([e])}P\bullet([e]+\delta)}$$

$$\textbf{Sum}\frac{S_1\xrightarrow{\mu}S_1'}{S_1+S_2\xrightarrow{\mu}S_1'}\qquad\textbf{Guard}\frac{S\xrightarrow{\mu}S'}{\phi S\xrightarrow{\mu}S'},\ [\phi]=true\qquad\textbf{Res}\frac{S\xrightarrow{\mu}S'}{S\backslash a\xrightarrow{\mu}S'\backslash a},\ a,\bar{a}\ \text{not in}\ \mu$$

$$\textbf{Par}\frac{S_1\xrightarrow{\mu}S_1'}{S_1\,|\,S_2\xrightarrow{\mu}S_1'\,|\,S_2}\qquad\textbf{Com}\frac{S_1\xrightarrow{a(r)}S_1',\ S_2\xrightarrow{\bar{a}(r)}S_2'}{S_1\,|\,S_2\xrightarrow{\tau_{\Delta(a)}(r)}S_1'\,|\,S_2'}$$

$$\textbf{Ide}\frac{(P\{e_1/t_1,\ldots,e_n/t_n\})\bullet e\xrightarrow{\mu}S'}{A(e_1,\ldots,e_n)\bullet e\xrightarrow{\mu}S'}\ \text{if}\ A(t_1,\ldots,t_n)\Leftarrow P\ \text{is in}\ \mathcal{D}$$

Table 1: Concrete operational semantics over closed configurations $\mathcal{C}_c$.

$$S:=0\ \mid\ (\alpha.P)\bullet e\ \mid\ A(e_1,\ldots,e_k)\bullet e\ \mid\ \phi S\ \mid\ S+S\ \mid\ S\backslash a\ \mid\ S\,|\,S.$$

In the rest of the paper, we will always consider configurations in canonical form w.r.t. $\equiv$. The notions of free and bound variables extend to configurations in the expected way. When giving the standard, "concrete" operational semantics, we will be interested in closed configurations, i.e. the set of those S s.t. $fvar(S)=\emptyset$, which is referred to by $\mathcal{C}_c$.

2.2 Standard operational semantics

We are now set to introduce the standard "concrete" operational semantics over closed configurations, $\mathcal{C}_c$. In the sequel, for H an agent term or a configuration, we let $H\sigma$ denote the result of substituting each $x\in fvar(H)\cap dom(\sigma)$ by $\sigma(x)$. Furthermore, the notation $P\{e_1/t_1,\ldots,e_n/t_n\}$ is used to indicate the simultaneous substitution of the variables t_i's with the expressions e_i's (this may involve renaming of bound names in P); in order to keep the result of this operation within our syntax, we assume that formulae are suitably normalized. (E.g., $\big(a(t,t<t_1+5).0\big)\{t'+4/t_1\}=a(t,t<t'+9).0$). Operational semantics of $\mathcal{C}_c$ is presented in Table 1. There, the symmetrical rules of Sum and Par have been omitted, e is confined to ground expressions and μ ranges over transition labels.

Some comments on the operational semantics are in order. Our rules are related to the operational semantics of [2]. In the latter, all actions are assumed to be "eager", in the sense that they occur as soon as they are allowed. This assumption permits modelling processes behaviour by means of finitary transition systems. Our rule Act is the obvious adaption of the corresponding rule in [2] to a more general setting, where actions may also delay. The meaning of Guard should be obvious. The other rules of Table 1 are formally identical to rules in [2]. In particular, rule Par says that, in a configuration $P\bullet e\,|\,Q\bullet e'$, e and e' are the local clocks at P and Q. These clocks never interact, except when a sinchronization between P and Q takes place (rule Com); this also causes clocks to be synchronized (this view is adopted, for example, in certain communication protocols, in which agents use local clocks to time-stamp messages, but periodically synchronize clocks).

On top of closed configurations operational semantics, we define bisimilarity in the standard way.

Definition 2.2 (Bisimilarity) *A symmetric binary relation $\mathcal{R}$ over $\mathcal{C}_c$ is a bisimulation iff whenever $S \mathcal{R} R$ and $S \xrightarrow{\mu} S'$, there exists R' such that $R \xrightarrow{\mu} R'$ and $S' \mathcal{R} R'$. We say that S is bisimilar to R, and write $S \sim R$ iff there exists a bisimulation $\mathcal{R}$ such that $S \mathcal{R} R$. Given two processes P and Q, we say that P and Q are bisimilar, and write $P \sim Q$, iff $P \bullet 0 \sim Q \bullet 0$.*

It is easy to show that the relation $\sim$, over $\mathcal{P}_c$, is preserved by all operators different from $a(t, \phi)$. The binding nature of latter operator raises a little problem: if we want to deduce that $a(t, \phi).P \sim a(t, \phi).Q$ from the equivalence of P and Q, which are in general open terms (as may contain free occurrences of t), we have to extend the relation $\sim$ over such terms. This can be done by "closing" $\sim$ under all possible environments. The congruence properties of $\sim$ will be further discussed in Section 5.

From now on, we will freeely use such abbreviations as $fvar(P, S, \phi, t)$ to mean $fvar(P) \cup fvar(S) \cup var(\phi) \cup \{t\}$. Furthermore, $v(\cdot)$ stands for $val(\cdot) \cup fvar(\cdot)$.

3 Symbolic Semantics

First symbolic operational semantics and then symbolic bisimulation will be introduced over the set of configurations (either closed or open), $\mathcal{C}$.

The rules for operational symbolic semantics over configurations, $\xrightarrow{c(t), \phi}$, are reported in Table 2. Rules symmetrical to S – Sum and S – Par have been omitted to save space. In any symbolic transition $S \xrightarrow{c(t), \phi} S'$, the formula ϕ collects all conditions, on the values and the free variables of S and on the time t itself, necessary for the action c to take place at time t. Note that each symbolic rule is the counter-part of a concrete one. In S – Act and S – Guard, the side-conditions of the corresponding concrete rules have been, so to speak, moved on the transitions. Here, the side-conditions on the variable t are of syntactic nature, they just ensure that t is taken "fresh", i.e. different from any other free variable in the configuration.

Note that, since we are working up to α-equivalence, α-equivalent configurations are deemed to have the same transitions. Thus, the symbolic transition system is actually finite-branching up to α-equivalence, while the concrete one has an infinite branching factor.

We are now ready to introduce symbolic bisimulation. In a value-passing setting, this notion was first introduced by Hennessy and Lin [6]. It is convenient to define a *family* of symbolic equivalences $\simeq^\phi$, each depending on a formula ϕ (equivalence under ϕ), instead of a single relation. The intuitive idea is as follows: S and R are symbolically equivalent under ϕ, $S \simeq^\phi R$, if for every symbolic transition of S, say $S \xrightarrow{c(t) \psi} S'$, one can find a decomposition of the formula $\phi \wedge \psi$ into a *finite* set of sub-conditions, each of which "entails" (in a logical sense) a matching transition for

$$S - Act \frac{\overline{}}{(a(t,\phi).P) \bullet e \xrightarrow{a(t),\phi \wedge (t \geq e)} P \bullet (t + \Delta(a))}, \; t \notin var(e)$$

$$S - Wait \frac{\overline{}}{(wait_\delta.P) \bullet e \xrightarrow{\tau_\delta(t), t = e} P \bullet (t + \delta)}, \; t \notin fvar(P) \cup var(e)$$

$$S - Sum \frac{S_1 \xrightarrow{c(t),\phi} S_1'}{S_1 + S_2 \xrightarrow{c(t),\phi} S_1'} \qquad S - Guard \frac{S \xrightarrow{c(t),\psi} S'}{\phi S \xrightarrow{c(t),\psi \wedge \phi} S'}, t \notin var(\phi) \qquad S - Res \frac{S \xrightarrow{c(t),\phi} S'}{S \backslash a \xrightarrow{c(t),\phi} S' \backslash a}, c \neq a, \bar{a}$$

$$S - Par \frac{S_1 \xrightarrow{c(t),\phi} S_1'}{S_1 \mid S_2 \xrightarrow{c(t),\phi} S_1' \mid S_2}, t \notin fvar(S_2) \qquad S - Com \frac{S_1 \xrightarrow{a(t),\phi} S_1', \; S_2 \xrightarrow{\bar{a}(t),\psi} S_2'}{S_1 \mid S_2 \xrightarrow{\tau_{\Delta(a)}(t),\phi \wedge \psi} S_1' \mid S_2'}$$

$$S - Ide \frac{(P\{e_1/t_1, \ldots, e_n/t_n\}) \bullet e \xrightarrow{c(t),\phi} S'}{A(e_1, \ldots, e_n) \xrightarrow{c(t),\phi} S'}, \; \text{if } A(t_1, \ldots, t_n) \Leftarrow P \text{ is in } \mathcal{D}$$

Table 2: Symbolic operational semantics over configurations $\mathcal{C}$.

R. We will now give the formal definitions and shortly after that explain the necessity of this decomposition.

Definition 3.1 (ϕ-decomposition) *Given ϕ and a finite set of formulae $D = \{\phi_1, \ldots, \phi_n\}$, we say that D is a ϕ-decomposition if ϕ is equivalent to $\bigvee D$.*

Definition 3.2 (Symbolic bisimulation)

- *A family $\mathcal{F} = \{\mathcal{R}^\phi \mid \phi \in BF\}$ of symmetric binary relations over configurations, indexed over the set BF of boolean formulae, is a family of symbolic bisimulations (FSB) iff for each ϕ and $(S, R) \in \mathcal{R}^\phi$, whenever $S \xrightarrow{c(t),\psi} S'$ with $t \notin fvar(S, R, \phi)$ then:*

    there exists a $\phi \wedge \psi$-decomposition D, such that for all $\zeta \in D$, there is a transition $R \xrightarrow{c(t),\chi} R'$ with $\zeta \models \chi$ and $(S', R') \in \mathcal{R}^\zeta$.

- *$S \simeq^\phi R$ iff there exists a FSB $\{\mathcal{R}^\psi \mid \psi \in BF\}$ such that $(S, R) \in \mathcal{R}^\phi$.*

To check symbolic equivalence, it is not necessary to consider all the cases corresponding to the (infinitely many) instantiations of the parameter t in prefixes $a(t, \phi)$. Rather, it is sufficient to consider the single symbolic transition which $a(t, \phi)$. gives rise to. The infinitary "case-analysis" on the value of the time-stamp, implicitly present in the standard definition of bisimilarity, is here embodied in the decomposition D, which can be always taken finite. Furthermore, by choosing D appropriately, the number of cases to deal with can often be kept small. A simple example will help to clarify these points.

Example 3.3 Consider the processes

$$P \stackrel{def}{=} a(t, t \leq 10).b(t + \Delta(a)) \qquad \text{and}$$
$$Q \stackrel{def}{=} a(t, t \leq 10).P' \qquad \qquad \text{where:}$$
$$P' \stackrel{def}{=} (t < 5)b(t + \Delta(a)) + (t \geq 5)b(t + \Delta(a)) + (t = 3)b(3 + \Delta(a)).$$

It should be immediate to establish that P and Q are equivalent, in that both of them can engage action a at any time $t \in [0, 10]$, after which action b is immediately executed. We show that $P \bullet 0 \simeq^{true} Q \bullet 0$, by exhibiting an appropriate family of relations. Consider the family of relations $\{\mathcal{R}^\phi \cup (\mathcal{R}^\phi)^{-1} \,|\, \phi \in BF\}$, where the relations $\mathcal{R}^\phi$ are defined as follows:

$$\begin{aligned}
\mathcal{R}^{true} &= \{(P \bullet 0, Q \bullet 0)\} \\
\mathcal{R}^{(t<5)} &= \{\left(P' \bullet (t + \Delta(a)),\ b(t + \Delta(a)) \bullet (t + \Delta(a))\right)\} \\
\mathcal{R}^{(t \geq 5)} &= \mathcal{R}^{(t<5)} = \mathcal{R}^{(t=3)} = \mathcal{R}^{(t<5)} \\
\mathcal{R}^\phi &= \{(0, 0)\} \text{ for any other different } \phi.
\end{aligned}$$

This corresponds to decomposing the condition $(t \leq 10)$, present in the symbolic transition of P, into the set $\{(t < 5), (t \geq 5), (t = 3)\}$. Indeed, each of these conditions is sufficient to establish that $P' \bullet (t + \Delta(a))$ is equivalent to $b(t + \Delta(a)) \bullet (t + \Delta(a))$.

Note that if want to establish the equivalence of P and Q using the concrete equivalence $\sim$, then we have to exhibit the infinite relation $S \cup S^{-1}$, where S is:

$$\{(P \bullet 0, Q \bullet 0)\} \cup \{\left(P[r/t]' \bullet (r + \Delta(a)),\ b(r + \Delta(a)) \bullet (r + \Delta(a))\right) | r \in [0, 10]\} \cup$$
$$\{(0, 0)\}.$$

In [6], Hennessy and Lin present an algorithm that, taken two generic finite symbolic transition systems T and T', produces a formula ψ, which is the weakest formula under which T and T' are symbolically equivalent. Thus, checking the symbolic equivalence under ϕ of T and T' reduces to the problem of checking whether $\phi \models \psi$. Now, modulo the different language, our definition of symbolic bisimulation is formally the same as the one given by Hennessy and Lin [6]. Thus, it should not be too difficult to adapt their algorithm for checking symbolic equivalence to our setting. We want also point out that, as we shall see, the relation $\models$ is decidable for our language. This could lay the basis for automatic verification of timed systems. For processes not containing recursion (agent identifiers), a direct proof of the decidability of symbolic bisimulation can be given, by relying on the existence of a "canonical" decomposition.

4 Consistency and Adequacy of Symbolic Bisimulation

In order to establish the correspondence between symbolic and standard semantics, we have to develop a few technical properties.

4.1 Fundamental properties

In what follows, the symbol V will range over finite subsets of $Var \cup \mathbf{Q}^{\geq 0}$, unless otherwise stated. Furthermore, we say that ρ is an environment *on* V if $dom(\rho) \supseteq V \cap Var$.

A central role in our theory is played by the concept of *complete formula*. In the standard sense, a formula ϕ is complete if for *every* formula ψ either $\phi \models \psi$ or $\phi \models \neg\psi$. This notion is however too strong for our purposes. Intuitively, we will always deal with some fixed, finite set of variables and non-negative rational values (those occurring in the two configurations being compared). Therefore we are only interested in completeness relatively to those formulae whose variables and values are in this set. For technical reasons, also the "closure" of the given set of values, under the arithmetical operations $+$ and $-$, must be considered. These considerations lead to the following definitions.

Definition 4.1 (Closure under $+$ and $-$) *For any $W \subseteq_{fin} \mathbf{Q}^{\geq 0}$ the closure of W is the set $\Sigma(W) \subseteq \mathbf{Q}^{\geq 0}$ defined as*
$$\{r \geq 0 \mid r = \textstyle\sum_{r' \in W \cup \{1\}} (q_{r'} * r') \text{ for some integers } q_{r'}, \text{ with } r' \in W \cup \{1\} \}.$$

Note that, given any $r \in \mathbf{Q}^{\geq 0}$, the set $\Sigma(W) \cap [0, r]$ is finite[1]. We denote by $\Sigma(V)$ the set $\Sigma(V \cap \mathbf{Q}^{\geq 0}) \cup V$.

Definition 4.2 (Completeness for formulae) *A formula ϕ is complete over V if for each ψ with $v(\psi) \subseteq \Sigma(V)$, either $\phi \models \psi$ or $\phi \models \neg\psi$.*

The next result ensures that, under certain conditions, a formula can be decomposed into a finite set of formulae, each of which is complete, in the sense of Definition 4.2. In the sequel, given a set $Z \subseteq_{fin} Var$, we say that a formula ϕ is *bounding for Z* if there exists a rational r such that $\phi \models \bigwedge_{t \in Z} t \leq r$. By slight abuse of notation, we sometimes say that ϕ is bounding for V, meaning that ϕ is bounding for $V \cap Var$.

Lemma 4.3 (Existence of finite decomposition) *Suppose that ϕ is bounding for V. Then there exists a finite set D of formulae s.t.*

1. *D is a ϕ-decomposition;*

2. *each $\zeta \in D$ is satisfiable, complete over V and bounding for V.*

The next lemma is important as far as decidability of symbolic bisimulation is concerned.

Lemma 4.4 *The relation $\models \subseteq BF \times BF$ is decidable.*

We now come to some important properties of operational semantics. The following proposition is crucial, since it relates symbolic and standard operational semantics. It can be easily shown by transition induction.

Proposition 4.5 (Operational correspondence) *Let ρ be an environment on $fvar(S)$.*

1. *Given any $t \notin fvar(S)$, $S\rho \xrightarrow{c(r)} S_1$ implies $S \xrightarrow{c(t),\phi} S'$ for some ϕ and S' s.t. $\rho[r/t] \models \phi$ and $S_1 = S'\rho[r/t]$.*

---

[1]It can be shown that this property would *not* hold in general if W contained non-rational real numbers.

2. $S \xrightarrow{c(t),\phi} S'$ and $\rho[^{r}/t] \models \phi$ imply $S\rho \xrightarrow{c(r)} S_1$, with $S_1 = S'\rho[^{r}/t]$.

The following definition introduce the concept of "closing" bisimilarity under a family of environments. This notion is useful for stating the next theorem and the theorem of correspondence between symbolic and standard bisimulation.

Definition 4.6 (Closure of $\sim$ under ϕ) *Given any boolean formula ϕ, the relation $\sim^\phi$ is defined as: $S_1 \sim^\phi S_2$ iff for each environment ρ on $fvar(S_1, S_2, \phi)$ s.t. $\rho \models \phi$, it holds that $S_1\rho \sim S_2\rho$.*

Note, over closed configurations (hence over processes), $\sim^{true}$ is the same as $\sim$. In general, when checking $S \sim^\phi R$, one has to check bisimilarity of S and R under all the (possibly infinitely many) environments satisfying ϕ. The next theorem states that considering just one such environment is sufficient when ϕ is complete over $fvar(S, R)$. This is crucial for proving the correspondence between symbolic and standard bisimulation.

Theorem 4.7 *Consider S, R and ζ s.t. ζ is complete over $v(S, R)$. Suppose that for some ρ on $fvar(S, R, \zeta)$ it holds that $\rho \models \zeta$ and $S\rho \sim R\rho$. Then $S \sim^\zeta R$.*

4.2 Main results

In order to prove that standard, "concrete" bisimulation $\sim$ coincides with $\simeq^{true}$ over closed configurations, and hence over processes, it is convenient to show a more general correspondence on open configurations. The proof of the latter can be naturally split into two parts, consistency and adequacy.

Theorem 4.8 (Consistency of symbolic bisimulation) *Let S and R be configurations. Then $S \simeq^\phi R$ implies $S \sim^\phi R$.*

PROOF: (Sketch). The relation
$$\mathcal{R} = \{(S\sigma, R\sigma) \mid \sigma \text{ is on } fvar(S, R) \text{ and there exists } \phi \text{ with } \sigma \models \phi \text{ and } S \simeq^\phi R \}$$
is a bisimulation. The thesis is a consequence of this fact, which can be shown by exploiting Proposition 4.5. □

Theorem 4.9 (Adequacy of symbolic bisimulation) *Let ϕ be bounding for $fvar(S, R)$ and suppose that $S \sim^\phi R$. Then $S \simeq^\phi R$.*

PROOF: We prove that the family of relations given by
$$\mathcal{R}^\phi = \{(S, R) \mid S \sim^\phi R \text{ and } \phi \text{ is bounding for } fvar(S, R) \}$$
for each $\phi \in BF$, is a family of symbolic bisimulations. This fact implies the thesis.

Suppose that $S \mathcal{R}^\phi R$ and assume that $S \xrightarrow{c(t),\psi} S'$, for some fresh t. We have to show that there exists a $\phi \wedge \psi$-decomposition D s.t. for each $\zeta \in D$ there is a transition $R \xrightarrow{c(t),\chi} R'$ such that $\zeta \models \chi$ and $S'\mathcal{R}^\zeta R'$. Let $V = v(S, R)$.

Since every action prefix imposes a bound to its variable, it holds that $\psi \models t \leq e$ for some e with $var(e) \subseteq V$. Since ϕ is bounding for V, it easily follows that $\phi \wedge \psi$ is bounding for $V \cup \{t\}$. Therefore, by Lemma 4.3, there exists a $\phi \wedge \psi$-decomposition D such that each $\zeta \in D$ is satisfiable and is complete and bounding for $V \cup \{t\}$. Fix now a generic $\zeta \in D$ and let ρ be any environment on $var(\phi) \cup V \cup \{t\}$ such that $\rho \models \zeta$. Since $\rho \models \bigvee D$, it must be $\rho \models \phi \wedge \psi$, hence $\rho \models \psi$. From this, applying Proposition 4.5.2 to the transition $S \stackrel{c(t),\psi}{\longmapsto} S'$ we get $S\rho \stackrel{c(r)}{\longrightarrow} S'\rho$, where $r = \rho(t)$. Since it also holds that $\rho \models \phi$ and $S \sim^\phi R$, it follows that $S\rho \sim R\rho$, hence for some R_1 we have

$$R\rho \stackrel{c(r)}{\longrightarrow} R_1 \sim S'\rho. \tag{2}$$

Applying Proposition 4.5.1 to the above transition, we get a symbolic transition

$$R \stackrel{c(t),\chi}{\longmapsto} R', \text{ where } R_1 = R'\rho \text{ and } \rho \models \chi. \tag{3}$$

We now show that (a) $\zeta \models \chi$, and that (b) $S'\mathcal{R}^\zeta R'$, which will conclude the proof. As to (a), first note that $v(\chi) \subseteq \Sigma(V) \cup \{t\}$; since ζ is complete for $V \cup \{t\}$ and ρ satisfies both ζ and χ (from (3)), it follows that $\zeta \models \chi$. As to (b), from (2) and (3), we deduce that $S'\rho \sim R'\rho$; hence, noting that ζ is complete over $v(S', R')$ (indeed it is $v(S', R') \subseteq_{fin} \Sigma(V) \cup \{t\}$), and that $\rho \models \zeta$, we can apply Theorem 4.7 and deduce that $S' \sim^\zeta R'$. Finally, by hypothesis ζ is bounding for $fvar(S', R') \subseteq fvar(S, R) \cup \{t\}$. These facts imply that $S'\mathcal{R}^\zeta R'$. □

Putting together the two preceding theorems, we obtain the result we are most interested in, the symbolic characterization of $\sim$:

Corollary 4.10 (Symbolic characterization of $\sim$) *Given two closed configuration S and R, $S \sim R$ if and only if $S \simeq^{true} R$.*

As a corollary of consistency and adequacy and of Theorem 4.7, it is not hard to prove decidability of $\sim$ over finite configurations.

Corollary 4.11 *Let S and R be closed configurations without agent identifiers. Then it is decidable whether $S \sim R$.*

We want to argue that the obtained symbolic characterization of $\sim^\phi$ is independent of any specific syntax and local/global-clock assumption for timed processes. The proofs of Theorems 4.8 and 4.9 depend only on the logic BF and the properties of the operational semantics stated in Proposition 4.5 and Theorem 4.7. The proof of the latter theorem depends, in turn, only on BF and Proposition 4.5. Therefore, Theorems 4.8 and 4.9 would still hold for any pair of (bounded-delay) rational-timed and symbolic transition systems, T and ST, for which the statement of Proposition 4.5 is true (this of course implies that T and ST are equipped with reasonable notions of free variables and environments).

5   A Proof System

We present a proof system for reasoning about $\simeq^\phi$ on finite (not containing agent identifiers) configurations. The system is based on a syntax of *extended* configurations, $\mathcal{EC}$, which may involve an new kind of action prefix, $c(t, \phi)$:, with $c \in Act \cup \{\tau_\delta \mid \delta \in Q^+\}$ and $\phi \models t \leq e$ for some e not containing t. The latter prefix is used to express

Axioms

Summation Laws

(S1)	$S + 0$	$=$	S
(S2)	$S + S$	$=$	S
(S3)	$S + R$	$=$	$R + S$
(S4)	$S + (R + T)$	$=$	$(S + R) + T$

Restriction Laws

(R1)	$(S + R) \backslash a$	$=$	$S \backslash a + R \backslash a$
(R2)	$(c(t, \phi) : P) \backslash a$	$=$	$c(t, \phi) : (P \backslash a)$, if $a \neq c$
(R3)	$(a(t, \phi) : P) \backslash a$	$=$	0

Clock Laws

(C1) $(a(t, \phi).P) \bullet e = a(t, \phi \wedge t \geq e) : (P \bullet (t + \Delta(a)))$, if $t \notin var(e)$

(C2) $(wait_\delta.P) \bullet e = \tau_\delta(t, t = e) : (P \bullet (t + \delta))$, for t fresh

Boolean Guard Law

(G) $\phi\, c(t, \psi) : S = c(t, \psi \wedge \phi) : S$, if $t \notin var(\phi)$

Expansion Law

Let $S \equiv \sum_{i \in I} \mu_i : S_i$, $R \equiv \sum_{j \in J} \nu.R_j$ and, for each i, j, $bvar(\mu_i) = bvar(\nu_j) = t$ fresh:

(E) $S \mid R = \sum_{i \in I} \mu_i : (S_i \mid R) + \sum_{j \in J} \nu_j : (S \mid R_j) + \sum_{\mu_i = a(t, \phi_i),\ \nu_j = \bar{a}(t, \psi_j)} \tau_{\Delta(a)}(t, \phi_i \wedge \psi_j) : (S_i \mid R_j)$

Table 3: Axioms of the proof system on finite extended configurations.

a convenient form of expansion theorem. The operational, concrete and symbolic, rules for the new prefix are, respectively:

$$\text{Pre}\frac{}{c(t, \phi) : S \xrightarrow{c(r)} S[r/t]}, \quad [\![\phi[r/t]]\!] = true \qquad \text{and} \qquad \text{S} - \text{Pre}\frac{}{c(t, \phi) : S \overset{c(t),\phi}{\longmapsto} S}.$$

All notions and definitions that hold for $\mathcal{C}$, including standard and symbolic bisimulation, conservatively extend to $\mathcal{EC}$ in the expected manner. The consistency and adequacy theorems of symbolic bisimulation of Section 4 are still valid in the new more general setting. In a different timed setting, configurations similar to ours were considered in [2].

In the sequel, $R, S, \ldots$ will range over finite extended configurations. The proof system consists of a set of axioms and inference rules, presented in Table 3 and 4 (standard rules for reflexivity, symmetry and transitivity of $=$ omitted to save space). The statements derivable within the proof system are of the form $\phi \vdash S = R$, to be read as: *under ϕ, S equals R*. The notation $c : S$ is used to denote the configuration $c(t, t = 0) : S$, whenever $t \notin fvar(S)$ (the specific value 0 is not actually relevant). We will also use $\equiv$ to denote syntactical equality, as opposed to proof-theoretic equality $=$.

Correctness and completeness of the system are proven by exploiting the consistency and adequacy theorems (Th. 4.8 and 4.9). The proofs are not too different from the corresponding proofs for the value-passing case in [6]. However, additional complications are introduced here by the fact that the instantiation of the parameter t in a prefix $a(t, \phi)$ is constrained by ϕ, whereas in a value-passing setting the instantiation is not constrained (prefixes are of the form $a(t)$). We omit our proofs due to lack of space.

Theorem 5.1 (Correctness and completeness of the proof system) *Let ϕ be a bounding formula for $fvar(S, R)$. Then $\phi \vdash S = R$ if and only if $S \simeq^\phi R$.*

Inference Rules

$(Congr)$ $\dfrac{\phi \vdash S = R}{\phi \vdash S' = R'}$ where $S' = R'$ stands for either of: $c : S = c : R$, $\psi S = \psi R$, $S + T = R + T$, $S|T = R|T$, $S \backslash a = R \backslash a$.

(Pre) $\dfrac{\phi \wedge (t \leq r_0) \vdash \sum_{i \in I} \phi_i c : S_i = \sum_{j \in J} \psi_j c : R_j}{\phi \vdash \sum_{i \in I} c(t, \phi_i) : S_i = \sum_{j \in J} c(t, \psi_j) : R_j}$ if $t \notin var(\phi)$ and for each i and j: $\phi \wedge \phi_i \models t \leq r_0$ and $\phi \wedge \psi_j \models t \leq r_0$

$(Guard)$ $\dfrac{\phi \wedge \psi \vdash S = R,\ \phi \wedge \neg\psi \vdash R = 0}{\phi \vdash \psi S = R}$ $\qquad (False)$ $\dfrac{-}{false \vdash S = R}$

(Cut) $\dfrac{\phi_1 \vdash S = R,\ \phi_2 \vdash S = R}{\phi \vdash S = R}$ if $\phi \models \phi_1 \vee \phi_2$ $\qquad (Axiom)$ $\dfrac{-}{true \vdash S = R}$ for each axiom $S = R$

Table 4: Inference rules of the proof system on finite extended configurations.

6 Conclusions an Related Work

We have proposed a theory of symbolic bisimulation for an algebra of timed processes, that yields a more tractable characterization of bisimilarity. For future work, we regard as very promising the development of verification algorithms for timed symbolic bisimulation, in the style of the algorithms for value-passing of [6].

Our work is mainly related to [6] and [2]. In [6], a theory of symbolic bisimulation has been developed in a setting where values on transitions represent input/output data, rather than time-stamps. Technically, the basic difference between our work and [6], is as follows. Hennessy and Lin work within a general framework, with no specific language for formulae and values. However, in order to find a suitable decomposition when proving their adequacy theorem, they assume the existence of a very powerful logic. Here, we had to deal with a *specific* and non-trivial logic (BF), which lacks the property required in [6]. As a consequence, a substantially different development has to be undertaken to prove, e.g., that a suitable decomposition always exists. Additional care (such as restricting to rationales and to bounded-delay actions) is needed to ensure that the decomposition can always be chosen finite.

In [2], Aceto and Murphy put forward a timed process algebra with "eager" actions, which must occur as soon as possible. As a consequence, finitary transition systems are obtained; this makes it possible to re-use familiar techniques and devise, for instance, complete axiomatizations of equivalences.

Our work is also related to a series of papers (mainly [3, 5, 8, 4]), where the notion of occurrence of an action within a time interval is considered. In [3], Baeten and Bergstra introduces a timed version of ACP that incorporates real-time actions, a global-clock assumption and also relative delays. Bisimilarity over this language has been given an effective axiomatization by Fokkink and Klusener [5]. The problem of devising a finitary representation of process behaviours is not tackled though, and the proof relies therefore on rather ad-hoc techniques. One of the first timed versions of

CCS has been proposed in [8]. Conditional axiomatizations of bisimilarity for (variants of) Wang's language have been obtained by Chen [4]. The languages by considered by Chen are less expressive than ours: for example, relative delays are not expressible.

Alur and Dill have proposed *timed automata* [1], whose transitions are equipped with time constraints on "clock variables". Their setting is quite different from ours, in that automata are compared on the basis of the (timed) traces they accept, and fairness requirements are imposed on the accepted traces.

Acknowledgments

I would like to thank Flavio Corradini for discussions on the topics of the paper and Giuseppe Melfi and Luca Trevisan for technical suggestions. Rocco De Nicola read a preliminary draft, suggesting several improvements. Two anonymous referees provided valuable comments.

References

[1]   R. Alur and D.L. Dill. A theory of timed automata. *Theoretical Computer Science*, 126(2):183–235, 1994.

[2]   L. Aceto and D. Murphy. On the ill-timed – but well-caused. In E. Best, editor, *Proceedings of CONCUR '93, LNCS 715*. Springer-Verlag, Berlin, 1993. Full version to appear in *Acta Informatica*.

[3]   J.C.M. Baeten and A. Bergstra. Real time process algebra. *Formal Aspects of Computing*, 3:142–188, 1991.

[4]   L. Chen. Axiomatizing real-timed processes. In S. Brooks, M. Main, A. Melton, M. Mislove, and D. Schmidt, editors, *Proceedings of MFPS'93, LNCS 802*, pages 215–229. Springer-Verlag, Berlin, 1993.

[5]   W.J. Fokkink and S. Klusener. An effective axiomatization for real time ACP. Technical Report CS-R9542, CWI, Computer Science, 1995. To appear in *Information and Computation*.

[6]   M. Hennessy and H. Lin. Symbolic bisimulations. *Theoretical Computer Science*, 138:353–389, 1995.

[7]   R. Milner. *Communication and Concurrency*. Prentice-Hall, 1989.

[8]   Y. Wang. Real time behaviour of asynchronous agents. In J.C.M. Baeten and J.W. Klop, editors, *Proc. 1st Conference on Concurrency Theory (CONCUR'90), LNCS 458*. Springer-Verlag, Berlin, 1990.

Approximative Analysis by Process Algebra with Graded Spatial Actions

Yoshinao ISOBE, Yutaka SATO, Kazuhito OHMAKI

Electrotechnical Laboratory
1-1-4 Umezono, Tsukuba, Ibaraki 305, Japan
E-mail:{ isobe|ysato|ohmaki }@etl.go.jp

Abstract. In this paper we propose a process algebra, $CCSG$, in which we can *approximately* analyze processes by neglecting unimportant distant actions. Although many kinds of process algebra have already been proposed, there is a common problem that the number of feasible action sequences explosively increases with the number of concurrent processes. Therefore, an approximative approach is useful for large systems.
We assume that each action has a *grade* which represents the importance. In CCSG, processes can be distributed in a space, and grades of observed actions decrease with distance. Hence observations of a system depend on the positions of observers. In this paper we give *shift-(s) equivalence* to relate observations at different positions, and give *level-(r) equivalence* to relate an approximative observation and the complete observation.

1 Introduction

Concurrent processes are more complex than sequential processes, because actions of concurrent processes can be independently performed and sometimes synchronize with each other. Process algebra is a mathematical tool to analyze concurrent processes. Actions of processes are described as *(process) expressions* in a process algebra, then equality between the actions of two processes can be checked by rewriting their expressions according to algebraic laws of the process algebra. A real problem of analysis of concurrent processes is that the number of feasible action sequences explosively increases by interleaving of actions [1].

We propose a process algebra $CCSG$ (a Calculus of Communicating Systems with Graded spatial actions) to *approximately* analyze processes. In CCSG each action has a *grade* which represents the importance and a *position* where the action occurs, thus unimportant distant actions can be neglected by observers.

Distributed processes are connected through *routers* with *loss* of grades. Each router consists of a name a and a loss r, then has the form $a\langle r \rangle$. Grades of actions observed through a router $a\langle r \rangle$ decrease by the loss r. Routers are connected in a star structure as shown in Fig.1(a). Branches represent routers and nodes represent processes. Routers can be hierarchically connected as shown in Fig.1(b).

CCSG is an extension of CCS [2]. CCS is a well known fundamental process algebra. A new combinator @ called *Route combinator* is introduced in CCSG as compared with CCS. For example, the system of Fig.1(a) is described as S_0

$$S_0 \equiv P_0 | (P_1@a_1\langle 6 \rangle) | (P_2@a_2\langle 4 \rangle) | (P_3@a_3\langle 1 \rangle)$$

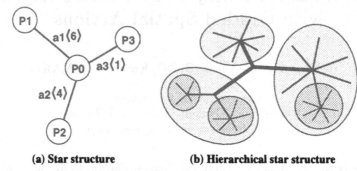

(a) Star structure   **(b) Hierarchical star structure**

Fig. 1. Connection examples of routers

by an observer standing at the position of P_0. $\equiv$ represents syntactic identity and $|$ is a composition combinator. Notice that observations depend on positions of observers. For example, the system of Fig.1(a) is also described as S_2 and S_3

$$S_2 \equiv P_2|((P_0|(P_1@a_1\langle 6\rangle)|(P_3@a_3\langle 1\rangle))@a_2\langle 4\rangle)$$
$$S_3 \equiv P_3|((P_0|(P_1@a_1\langle 6\rangle)|(P_2@a_2\langle 4\rangle))@a_3\langle 1\rangle)$$

by observers standing at the positions of P_2 and P_3, respectively.

We give *shift-(s) equivalence* $\stackrel{\backprime}{\sim}_{(s)}$ to relate processes observed at different positions, where s is a parameter which represents the difference between the positions. Namely s is the *route* from the position of the left-side observer to the position of the right-side observer. The route between two points is a sequence of routers between them. For example, S_2 and S_3 are shift-$(a_2\langle 4\rangle a_3\langle 1\rangle)$ equivalent, $S_2 \stackrel{\backprime}{\sim}_{(a_2\langle 4\rangle a_3\langle 1\rangle)} S_3$, because the route from P_2 to P_3 is $(a_2\langle 4\rangle a_3\langle 1\rangle)$. Particularly $\stackrel{\backprime}{\sim}_{(\varepsilon)}$ is identical with strong equivalence in [2], where ε is the empty sequence.

An action of CCSG consists of a label α, a grade r, and a route s, then has the form $\alpha\langle r\rangle@s$. This @ is not the combinator over processes previously introduced. We use the same symbol @ for actions and processes, because their roles are the same and they can be distinguished by grammar. $\alpha\langle r\rangle@s$ represents that an action named α with the grade r occurs at the position pointed to by the route s. The grade r is a real number. Positive grades are assigned to important actions and negative grades are assigned to unimportant actions. s is the route from the position where the action occurs to the position of the observer. The empty route is sometimes omitted, and thus $\alpha\langle r\rangle$ is used for representing $\alpha\langle r\rangle@\varepsilon$. For example, in Fig.1(a), an action α with a grade 7 which occurs at P_1 is observed as the action $\alpha\langle 7\rangle@(a_1\langle 6\rangle a_2\langle 4\rangle)$ by an observer at P_2.

The total sum of losses of routers between two points is called the *loss distance* between them. For example, the loss distance between the positions of P_1 and P_2 is $(6+4 =)$ 10. It is important that the grade of $\alpha\langle 7\rangle@(a_1\langle 6\rangle a_2\langle 4\rangle)$ is actually observed as $(7 - (6 + 4) =) - 3$. This decreased grade -3 by the loss distance is called the *actual grade* of $\alpha\langle 7\rangle@(a_1\langle 6\rangle a_2\langle 4\rangle)$.

In CCSG the following condition of synchronization is very important.

| Two actions can synchronize only if the sum of their grades is not less than the loss distance between them. | **(Condition 1)** |

For example, a graded action $\alpha\langle 9 \rangle$ which occurs at P_1 can synchronize with a graded action $\overline{a}\langle 3 \rangle$ which occurs at P_2, because the sum $(9 + 3 =)$ 12 of their grades is greater than the loss distance $(6 + 4 =)$ 10 between P_1 and P_2.

It is possible to approximately analyze processes by neglecting low actual graded actions in CCSG. We give a relation called *level-$\langle r \rangle$ equivalence* $=_{\langle r \rangle}$ for such approximative analysis. r is a parameter which represents a level of similarity. Level-$\langle r \rangle$ equivalence bases on the following *level-$\langle r \rangle$ observation*.

Actions which have lower actual grades (at the position of the observer) than $-r$, can not be observed.	(**Assumption 1**)

Intuitively, r represents the radius of the observable area in level-$\langle r \rangle$ observation. Particularly level-$\langle \infty \rangle$ equivalence $=_{\langle \infty \rangle}$ corresponds to observation congruence $=$ defined in [2]. For example, the following relations hold.

$$(\alpha\langle 1 \rangle @ a\langle 4 \rangle).P =_{\langle 2 \rangle} \tau.P, \quad (\alpha\langle 1 \rangle @ a\langle 2 \rangle).P \neq_{\langle 2 \rangle} \tau.P,$$

$(\alpha\langle 1 \rangle @ a\langle 4 \rangle).P$ is a process which can perform the action $(\alpha\langle 1 \rangle @ a\langle 4 \rangle)$, and thereafter behaves like the process P. τ is an internal action which can not be observed. The action $(\alpha\langle 1 \rangle @ a\langle 4 \rangle)$ need not be observed in level-$\langle 2 \rangle$ observation, because its actual grade $(1 - 4 =) -3$ is less than the minus level, thus $-3 < -2$.

An important property is that level-$\langle r \rangle$ equivalence is preserved by Composition combinator $|$. Therefore we can check level-$\langle r \rangle$ equivalence part by part.

The outline of this paper is as follows: In Section 2, we define the syntax and the semantics of CCSG. In Section 3, shift-(s) equivalence and level-$\langle r \rangle$ equivalence are defined. Then, we give a sound and complete axiom system for level-$\langle r \rangle$ equivalence of finite sequential processes. In Section 4, an example of approximative analysis in CCSG is shown. In Section 5, we discuss space process algebra already proposed. In Section 6, we conclude this paper.

2 Definition of CCSG

In Subsection 2.1, various sets used in CCSG are given. In Subsection 2.2, three operators over routes are defined, and their properties are shown. In Subsection 2.3 and 2.4, the syntax and the semantics of CCSG are defined, respectively.

2.1 Actions of CCSG

We assume that an infinite set of *names* $\mathcal{N}$ is given. The set of routers Ω, ranged over by ω, is given as the Cartesian product $\{a\langle r \rangle : a \in \mathcal{N}, r \in \mathcal{R}^+\}$ of the set of names $\mathcal{N}$ and the set of non-negative real numbers $\mathcal{R}^+$. Two routers $a_1\langle r_1 \rangle$ and $a_2\langle r_2 \rangle$ are not distinct if $a_1 = a_2$ and $r_1 = r_2$. We assume that:

All routers connected to a node are distinct from each other.	(**Assumption 2**)

As shown in Fig.2, if P_2 and P_4 are connected to P_0 through two indistinct routers $a_2\langle 4 \rangle$, then it is interpreted that P_2 and P_4 are positioned in the same place. Namely, the route between P_2 and P_4 in Fig.2 is not $(a_2\langle 4 \rangle a_2\langle 4 \rangle)$ but ε. Thus any route between two points is expressed with no adjacent indistinct routers. Therefore the set of routes Ψ can be defined as $\{s \in \Omega^* | No\text{-}adjacent(s)\}$, where Ω^* is the set of finite router sequences, and $No\text{-}adjacent(s)$ expresses that s does not have two adjacent routers. For example, $(a_2\langle 4 \rangle a_2\langle 4 \rangle) \notin \Psi$.

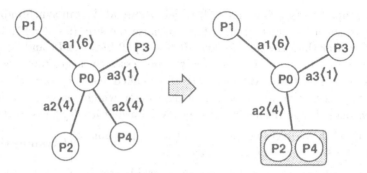

Fig. 2. The interpretation of indistinct connections

The set of *co-names* $\overline{\mathcal{N}}$ is given as $\{\overline{a} : a \in \mathcal{N}\}$, where the overbar represents a bijection such that $\overline{\overline{a}} = a$ for all $a \in \mathcal{N}$. Then the union of $\mathcal{N}$ and $\overline{\mathcal{N}}$ is called the set of *label* $\mathcal{A}(= \mathcal{N} \cup \overline{\mathcal{N}})$ ranged over by α. The set of *observable actions Act* is the Cartesian product $\{\alpha \langle r \rangle @s : \alpha \in \mathcal{A}, r \in \mathcal{R}, s \in \Psi\}$ of $\mathcal{A}$, the set of real numbers $\mathcal{R}$, and Ψ. Finally the set of *actions Act_τ*, ranged over by μ, is given as $Act \cup \{\tau\}$, where τ is called an internal action.

The sets given in this subsection are summarized in Table 1.

Table 1. The sets used in CCSG

Sets	Elements	Variables	Sets	Elements	Variables
$\mathcal{N}$	name	$a, a', a_1, \cdots$	Ω	router	$\omega, \omega', \omega_1, \cdots$
$\overline{\mathcal{N}}$	co-name	$\overline{a}, \overline{a'}, \overline{a_1}, \cdots$	Ψ	route	$s, s', s_1, \cdots$
$\mathcal{R}$	real number	$r, r', r_1, \cdots$	Act	observable action	$\nu, \nu', \nu_1, \cdots$
$\mathcal{A}$	label	$\alpha, \alpha', \alpha_1, \cdots$	Act_τ	action	$\mu, \mu', \mu_1, \cdots$

2.2 Operators over Routes

In Fig.1(a), the route s_{12} from P_1 to P_2 is $(a_1\langle 6 \rangle a_2 \langle 4 \rangle)$ and the route s_{23} from P_2 to P_3 is $(a_2 \langle 4 \rangle a_3 \langle 1 \rangle)$. In this case, the *sum* of s_{12} and s_{23} is expected to be the route $(a_1 \langle 6 \rangle a_3 \langle 1 \rangle)$ from P_1 to P_3 by considering **Assumption 2**. The sum of routes is not a simple concatenation of two routes such as $(a_1 \langle 6 \rangle a_2 \langle 4 \rangle a_2 \langle 4 \rangle a_3 \langle 1 \rangle)$.

In this subsection, three operators over routes are defined, then their properties are shown. One of them is *Sum operator* $\circ$. The sum of two routes s_1 and s_2 is a route produced by connecting the terminal point of s_1 to the initial point of s_2, and it is denoted by $(s_1 \circ s_2)$. The initial point of $(s_1 \circ s_2)$ is the initial point of s_1 and the terminal point of $(s_1 \circ s_2)$ is the terminal point of s_2.

Definition 2.1 *Sum operator* $\circ : \Psi \times \Psi \to \Psi$ *is inductively defined by*

$$s_1 \circ s_2 = \begin{cases} s_1' \circ s_2' & (s_1 = s_1'\omega, s_2 = \omega s_2') \\ s_1 s_2 & (otherwise) \end{cases}$$

$\square$

We explain how to calculate the sum of routes by using Fig.3. Each ω_i is a router and each s_i is a route such as $s_1 = \omega_1 \omega_2 \omega_3 \omega_4$, $s_2 = \omega_4 \omega_3 \omega_5$, and $s_3 = \omega_1 \omega_2 \omega_5$. In this case s_3 is the sum route of s_1 and s_2 as follows:

$$s_1 \circ s_2 = \omega_1 \omega_2 \omega_3 \omega_4 \circ \omega_4 \omega_3 \omega_5 = \omega_1 \omega_2 \omega_3 \circ \omega_3 \omega_5 = \omega_1 \omega_2 \circ \omega_5 = \omega_1 \omega_2 \omega_5 = s_3$$

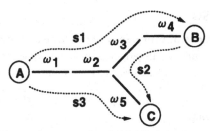

Fig. 3. An example of calculation of routes

The next operator is *Reverse operator* rev to reverse the direction of a route.

Definition 2.2 *Reverse operator* $\mathrm{rev} : \Psi \to \Psi$ *is inductively defined by*

$$\mathbf{rev}(s) = \begin{cases} \mathbf{rev}(s_2)\mathbf{rev}(s_1) & (s = s_1 s_2) \\ \omega & (s = \omega) \\ \varepsilon & (s = \varepsilon) \end{cases}$$

$\square$

The last operator is *Difference operator* ◁. The difference of two routes s_1 and s_2 is a route produced by connecting the terminal point of s_1 to the terminal point of s_2, and it is denoted by $(s_1 \triangleleft s_2)$. The initial point of $(s_1 \triangleleft s_2)$ is the initial point of s_1 and the terminal point of $(s_1 \triangleleft s_2)$ is the initial point of s_2. Difference operator is defined by using Sum and Reverse operators.

Definition 2.3 *Difference operator* $\triangleleft : \Psi \times \Psi \to \Psi$ *is defined by*

$$s_1 \triangleleft s_2 = s_1 \circ \mathbf{rev}(s_2)$$

$\square$

For example, s_1 is the difference route of s_3 and s_2 in Fig.3 as follows:

$$s_3 \triangleleft s_2 = s_3 \circ \mathbf{rev}(s_2) = \omega_1 \omega_2 \omega_5 \circ \omega_5 \omega_3 \omega_4 = \omega_1 \omega_2 \circ \omega_3 \omega_4 = \omega_1 \omega_2 \omega_3 \omega_4 = s_1$$

It is needed to evaluate the loss distance of a route to check whether **Condition 1** is satisfied or not. The function π is given to evaluate the loss distance.

Definition 2.4 *The function* $\pi : \Psi \to \mathcal{R}^+$ *is defined by*

$$\pi(s) = \begin{cases} \pi(s_1) + \pi(s_2) & (s = s_1 s_2) \\ r & (s = a\langle r \rangle) \\ 0 & (s = \varepsilon) \end{cases}$$

$\square$

It is often needed to evaluate the loss distance between the two terminal points of two routes whose initial points are the same. For example, the loss distance between A and B is evaluated by $\pi(s_3 \triangleleft s_2)$ in Fig.3.

Calculus of routes is similar to calculus of vectors. Some equations of routes are shown in Proposition 2.1. The proofs are omitted because of lack of space.

Proposition 2.1 *For any* $s, s_i \in \Psi$, *the following equations hold.*

(1) $s \circ \varepsilon = \varepsilon \circ s = s$
(2) $s \triangleleft s = \varepsilon$
(3) $(s_1 \circ s_2) \circ s_3 = s_1 \circ (s_2 \circ s_3)$
(4) $(s_1 \triangleleft s_2) \triangleleft s_3 = s_1 \triangleleft (s_3 \circ s_2)$
(5) $(s_1 \circ s_2) \triangleleft s_3 = s_1 \circ (s_2 \triangleleft s_3)$

(6) $(s_1 \circ s_2) \triangleleft s_3 = s_1 \triangleleft (s_3 \triangleleft s_2)$
(7) $s_1 \triangleleft s_2 = (s_1 \circ s) \triangleleft (s_2 \circ s)$
(8) $s_1 \circ s_2 = s_3$ iff $s_1 = s_3 \triangleleft s_2$
(9) $\pi(s_1 \circ s_2) \geq |\pi(s_1) - \pi(s_2)|$
(10) $\pi(s_1 \circ s_2) \leq \pi(s_1) + \pi(s_2)$

$\square$

2.3 Syntax of CCSG

In process algebra, actions of processes are described as *process expressions*. We introduce a set of *Variables* $\mathcal{X}$ ranged over by X and a set of *Constants* $\mathcal{K}$ ranged over by A. We define the set of process expressions $\mathcal{E}$ ranged over by $E, F, \cdots$.

Definition 2.5 *The set of process expressions $\mathcal{E}$ is the smallest set including the following expressions:*

X : *Variable* $(X \in \mathcal{X})$	$E|F$: *Composition*
A : *Constant* $(A \in \mathcal{K})$	$E[f]$: *Relabelling* (f : *a relabelling function*)
$\mathbf{0}$: *Inaction*	$E\backslash^{L}_{\langle r \rangle(s)}$: *Restriction* $(r \in \mathcal{R}, s \in \Psi, L \subseteq \mathcal{A})$
$\mu.E$: *Prefix* $(\mu \in Act_\tau)$	$E@s$: *Route* $(s \in \Psi)$
$E + F$: *Choice*	

where E and F are already in $\mathcal{E}$. □

The relabelling function f is a function from $\mathcal{A}$ to $\mathcal{A}$ such that $f(\overline{\alpha}) = \overline{f(\alpha)}$. We practically extend f over Act_τ by decreeing that $f(\alpha\langle r \rangle @s) = f(\alpha)\langle r \rangle @s$ and $f(\tau) = \tau$. Notice that names of routers can not be changed by Relabelling.

A *process* is a process expression with no Variables. The set of processes is denoted by $\mathcal{P}$ and is ranged over by $P, Q, R, \cdots$. A *Constant* is a process whose meaning is given by a defining equation. In fact, we assume that for every Constant $A \in \mathcal{K}$, there is a defining equation of the form $A \stackrel{\text{def}}{=} P$, where $P \in \mathcal{P}$.

We informally explain roles of each combinator and relations of positions of an expression and subexpressions as follows:

- $\mu.E$ can perform the action μ, and thereafter behaves like E. $\mu.E$ and E are positioned at the same place. If $\mu = \alpha\langle r \rangle @s$, then the graded action $\alpha\langle r \rangle$ occurs the route s away from E.
- $E + F$ represents a choice between E and F. The choice is made by an action of E or F. $E + F$, E, and F are positioned at the same place.
- $E|F$ represents a concurrent composition of E and F. $E|F$, E, and F are positioned at the same place.
- $E[f]$ behaves like E except that actions of E are relabelled by f. $E[f]$ and E are positioned at the same place.
- $E\backslash^{L}_{\langle r \rangle(s)}$ locally restricts actions in the *restriction area* decided by r and s. s is the route from the center of the restriction area to E. r is the *restriction power* at the center, and the restriction power decreases with loss distance. Thus, the *actual restriction power* for an action which occurs the loss distance r' away from the center, is $(r - r')$. If the absolute value of the grade of the action is less than the actual restriction power and the label of the action is included in L, then the action can not occur. We will explain this local restriction at the end of Subsection 2.4 by using an example. $E\backslash^{L}_{\langle r \rangle(s)}$ and E are positioned at the same place.
- $E@s$ behaves like E, but $E@s$ is the route s away from E.

To avoid too many parentheses, combinators have binding power in the following order: {Restriction, Relabelling, Route} >Prefix>Composition>Choice.

$$\textbf{Act}\frac{}{\mu.E \xrightarrow{\mu} E}\qquad\qquad \textbf{Con}\frac{P \xrightarrow{\mu} P'}{A \xrightarrow{\mu} P'}(A \stackrel{\text{def}}{=} P)$$

$$\textbf{Choice}_1\frac{E \xrightarrow{\mu} E'}{E + F \xrightarrow{\mu} E'}\qquad\qquad \textbf{Choice}_2\frac{F \xrightarrow{\mu} F'}{E + F \xrightarrow{\mu} F'}$$

$$\textbf{Com}_1\frac{E \xrightarrow{\mu} E'}{E|F \xrightarrow{\mu} E'|F}\qquad\qquad \textbf{Com}_2\frac{F \xrightarrow{\mu} F'}{E|F \xrightarrow{\mu} E|F'}$$

$$\textbf{Com}_3\frac{E \xrightarrow{\alpha\langle r_1\rangle @ s_1} E' \quad F \xrightarrow{\overline{\alpha}\langle r_2\rangle @ s_2} F'}{E|F \xrightarrow{\tau} E'|F'}(r_1 + r_2 \geq \pi(s_1 \vartriangleleft s_2))$$

$$\textbf{Res}_1\frac{E \xrightarrow{\alpha\langle r_1\rangle @ s_1} E'}{E\backslash^L_{\langle r_2\rangle(s_2)} \xrightarrow{\alpha\langle r_1\rangle @ s_1} E'\backslash^L_{\langle r_2\rangle(s_2)}}\left(\begin{array}{l}\alpha, \overline{\alpha} \notin L \text{ or} \\ |r_1| > r_2 - \pi(s_1 \vartriangleleft s_2)\end{array}\right)$$

$$\textbf{Res}_2\frac{E \xrightarrow{\tau} E'}{E\backslash^L_{\langle r\rangle(s)} \xrightarrow{\tau} E'\backslash^L_{\langle r\rangle(s)}}\qquad \textbf{Rel}\frac{E \xrightarrow{\mu} E'}{E[f] \xrightarrow{f(\mu)} E'[f]}$$

$$\textbf{Rou}_1\frac{E \xrightarrow{\alpha\langle r\rangle @ s_1} E'}{E@s_2 \xrightarrow{\alpha\langle r\rangle @ (s_1 \circ s_2)} E'@s_2}\qquad \textbf{Rou}_2\frac{E \xrightarrow{\tau} E'}{E@s \xrightarrow{\tau} E'@s}$$

Fig. 4. The operational semantics

2.4 Semantics of CCSG

The semantics is given by the labelled transition system $(\mathcal{E}, Act_\tau, \{\xrightarrow{\mu}: \mu \in Act_\tau\})$. $E \xrightarrow{\mu} E'$ indicates that E may perform μ and thereafter behaves like E'.

Definition 2.6 *The transition relation $\xrightarrow{\mu}$ over process expressions is the smallest relation satisfying the inference rules in Fig.4. Each rule is read as follows: if the transition relation(s) above the line are inferred and the side condition(s) are satisfied, then the transition relation below the line can be also inferred.* ☐

The five rules, $\textbf{Rou}_{1,2}$, $\textbf{Com}_3$, $\textbf{Res}_{1,2}$, are different from the rules for CCS.

For $\textbf{Rou}_1$, the action $\alpha\langle r\rangle$ occurs the route s_1 away from E. Therefore the action occurs the route $(s_1 \circ s_2)$ away from $E@s_2$.

$\textbf{Com}_3$ infers a synchronization of two actions with complementary labels. The side condition represents **Condition 1**. Namely, the sum $(r_1 + r_2)$ of their grades is not less than the loss distance $\pi(s_1 \vartriangleleft s_2)$ between their positions.

The side condition $(|r_1| > r_2 - \pi(s_1 \vartriangleleft s_2))$ of $\textbf{Res}_1$ means that the action $(\alpha\langle r_1\rangle @ s_1)$ with the grade r_1, whose absolute value $|r_1|$ is greater than the actual restriction power $(r_2 - \pi(s_1 \vartriangleleft s_2))$ for the action, is not restricted even though the label α of the action is included in L. $\pi(s_1 \vartriangleleft s_2)$ is the loss distance between the center of the restriction area and the position where the action occurs. We explain this local restriction by using the following example.

$$SYS \equiv (P@s_1)\backslash^{\{\alpha\}}_{\langle 7\rangle(s_2)}, \quad P \equiv (\alpha\langle 5\rangle @ \varepsilon).\mathbf{0}$$

where $s_1 = a_2\langle 1\rangle a_1\langle 4\rangle$ and $s_2 = a_3\langle 2\rangle a_1\langle 4\rangle$. The process P is the route s_1 away from SYS, and SYS locally restricts α. The route from the center of the restriction area to SYS is s_2, and the restriction power at the center is 7. Then the loss distance between the action and the center is evaluated as follows:

$$\pi(s_1 \lhd s_2) = \pi(s_1 \circ \mathrm{rev}(s_2)) = \pi((a_2\langle 1\rangle a_1\langle 4\rangle) \circ (a_1\langle 4\rangle a_3\langle 2\rangle)) = \pi(a_2\langle 1\rangle a_3\langle 2\rangle) = 3$$

Thus the action $\alpha\langle 5\rangle$ is not restricted, because the actual restriction power for the action is $(7 - 3 =)$ 4.

3 Equality in CCSG

In Subsection 3.1, we define *shift-(s) equivalence* $\overset{\backsim}{\sim}_{(s)}$, introduced in Section 1. In Subsection 3.2, *weak level-$\langle r\rangle$ equivalence* $\approx_{\langle r\rangle}$ is defined before *level-$\langle r\rangle$ equivalence* $=_{\langle r\rangle}$, because level-$\langle r\rangle$ equivalence is defined based on weak level-$\langle r\rangle$ equivalence. In Subsection 3.3, we define level-$\langle r\rangle$ equivalence, which is the largest equivalence relation preserved by Choice $+$ and included in $\approx_{\langle r\rangle}$. In Subsection 3.4, we give a sound and complete axiom system for level-$\langle r\rangle$ equivalence of finite sequential processes. In Subsection 3.5, we discuss a strong version of weak level-$\langle r\rangle$ equivalence, where the number of transitions by τ must be matched.

3.1 Shift-(s) Equivalence

We define shift-(s) equivalence by using *shift-(s) bisimulations*, in order to cancel the difference s between positions of two observers.

Definition 3.1 *Let $s \in \Psi$. A binary relation $S \subseteq \mathcal{P} \times \mathcal{P}$ over processes is a shift-(s) bisimulation if $(P,Q) \in S$ implies, for all $\alpha\langle r\rangle @s' \in Act$, that*

(i) *whenever $P \xrightarrow{\alpha\langle r\rangle @s'} P'$ then, for some $Q', Q \xrightarrow{\alpha\langle r\rangle @(s' \circ s)} Q'$ and $(P',Q') \in S$,*

(ii) *whenever $P \xrightarrow{\tau} P'$ then, for some $Q', Q \xrightarrow{\tau} Q'$ and $(P',Q') \in S$,*

(iii) *whenever $Q \xrightarrow{\alpha\langle r\rangle @s'} Q'$ then, for some $P', P \xrightarrow{\alpha\langle r\rangle @(s' \lhd s)} P'$ and $(P',Q') \in S$,*

(iv) *whenever $Q \xrightarrow{\tau} Q'$ then, for some $P', P \xrightarrow{\tau} P'$ and $(P',Q') \in S$.* □

Definition 3.2 *P and Q are shift-(s) equivalent, written $P \overset{\backsim}{\sim}_{(s)} Q$, if $(P,Q) \in S$ for some shift-(s) bisimulation S.* □

Although shift-(s) equivalence is not an equivalence relation, *parameterized* reflexive, symmetric, and transitive laws hold as shown in Proposition 3.1.

Proposition 3.1 (1) $P \overset{\backsim}{\sim}_{(\varepsilon)} P$

(2) *If $P \overset{\backsim}{\sim}_{(s)} Q$, then $Q \overset{\backsim}{\sim}_{(\mathrm{rev}(s))} P$*

(3) *If $P \overset{\backsim}{\sim}_{(s_1)} Q$ and $Q \overset{\backsim}{\sim}_{(s_2)} R$, then $P \overset{\backsim}{\sim}_{(s_1 \circ s_2)} R$* □

Therefore the total union of $\overset{\backsim}{\sim}_{(s)}$ over $s \in \Psi$ is an equivalence relation.

The differences of shift-(s) equivalence $\overset{\backsim}{\sim}_{(s)}$ from strong equivalence $\sim$ are only $(s' \circ s)$ and $(s' \lhd s)$ in (i) and (iii) of Definition 3.1. Thus shift-(ε) equivalence $\overset{\backsim}{\sim}_{(\varepsilon)}$ is strong equivalence, because $(s' \circ \varepsilon = s' \lhd \varepsilon = s')$. We also conventionally use the symbol $\sim$ for $\overset{\backsim}{\sim}_{(\varepsilon)}$. The following equations for Route @ hold.

Proposition 3.2 (1) $((\alpha\langle r\rangle @s).P)@s' \sim (\alpha\langle r\rangle @(s \circ s')).(P@s')$

(2) $(P_1|P_2)@s \sim (P_1@s)|(P_2@s)$

(3) $(P@s_1)@s_2 \sim P@(s_1 \circ s_2)$ □

For (1), the action $\alpha\langle r\rangle$ occurs the route s away from P. Thus $\alpha\langle r\rangle$ is the route $(s \circ s')$ away from $P@s'$, because $P@s'$ is the route s' away from P. For (2), the route between P_1 and P_2 of the left-side is clearly ε. And the route between P_1 and P_2 of the right-side is also ε by **Assumption 2**.

The following proposition shows properties of shift-(s) equivalence very well.

Proposition 3.3 (1) *If* $P \overset{\prec}{\sim}_{(s)} Q$, *then* $P \overset{\prec}{\sim}_{(s \circ s')} Q@s'$

(2) *If* $P \overset{\prec}{\sim}_{(s)} Q$, *then* $P@\mathrm{rev}(s') \overset{\prec}{\sim}_{(s' \circ s)} Q$ □

Shift-(s) equivalence is preserved by Composition combinator | as follows.

Proposition 3.4 *If* $P_i \overset{\prec}{\sim}_{(s)} Q_i$ $(i \in \{1, 2\})$, *then* $P_1|P_2 \overset{\prec}{\sim}_{(s)} Q_1|Q_2$. □

3.2 Weak Level-$\langle r\rangle$ Equivalence

In this subsection, *weak level-$\langle r\rangle$ equivalence* is defined based on **Assumption 1**.

First we give the sequential transition relations. The set Act_r^*, ranged over by $t, t', \cdots$, is the set of action sequences including the empty sequence ε, and if $E \overset{\mu_1}{\longrightarrow} \cdots \overset{\mu_n}{\longrightarrow} E'$ for some $t = \mu_1 \cdots \mu_n \in Act_r^*$, then we write $E \overset{t}{\longrightarrow} E'$.

Secondly, we define a (single) threshold function to neglect unobservable actions which have lower actual grades than $-r$, considering **Assumption 1**.

Definition 3.3 *The single threshold function* $\phi : Act_r^* \times \mathcal{R} \to Act^*$ *is defined by*

$$\phi(t, r) = \begin{cases} \phi(t_1, r)\phi(t_2, r) & (t = t_1 t_2, t_1 \neq \varepsilon, t_2 \neq \varepsilon) \\ a\langle r'\rangle @s & (t = a\langle r'\rangle @s, r' - \pi(s) \geq -r) \\ \varepsilon & (otherwise) \end{cases}$$
□

It is important to notice that too high graded actions are *ambiguous*, because they can synchronize with unobservable actions. More exactly, in level-$\langle r\rangle$ observation, if an action occurs the route s away from the observer and has higher grades than $(r - \pi(s))$, then it is ambiguous, because observable level decreases with loss distance. Thus we define a *double* threshold function as follows:

Definition 3.4 *The double threshold function* $\theta : Act_r^* \times \mathcal{R} \to Act^*$ *is defined by*

$$\theta(t, r) = \begin{cases} \theta(t_1, r)\theta(t_2, r) & (t = t_1 t_2, t_1 \neq \varepsilon, t_2 \neq \varepsilon) \\ a\langle r'\rangle @s & (t = a\langle r'\rangle @s, |r'| \leq r - \pi(s)) \\ \varepsilon & (otherwise) \end{cases}$$
□

For example, the following applications show properties of ϕ and θ very well.

$\phi(\alpha\langle -2\rangle @\varepsilon, 1) = \varepsilon$, $\quad \phi(\alpha\langle 0\rangle @\varepsilon, 1) = \alpha\langle 0\rangle @\varepsilon$, $\quad \phi(\alpha\langle 2\rangle @\varepsilon, 1) = \alpha\langle 2\rangle @\varepsilon$

$\theta(\alpha\langle -2\rangle @\varepsilon, 1) = \varepsilon$, $\quad \theta(\alpha\langle 0\rangle @\varepsilon, 1) = \alpha\langle 0\rangle @\varepsilon$, $\quad \theta(\alpha\langle 2\rangle @\varepsilon, 1) = \varepsilon$

In level-$\langle 1\rangle$ observation, $(\alpha\langle -2\rangle @\varepsilon)$ is unobservable since $(-2 < -1)$, and $(\alpha\langle 2\rangle @\varepsilon)$ is ambiguous since $(2 > 1)$.

We define the new labelled transition system $(\mathcal{E}, Act_r^*, \{\overset{t}{\Longrightarrow}_{\langle r\rangle} : t \in Act_r^*\})$ for any $r \in \mathcal{R}$, in which the transition relations $\overset{t}{\Longrightarrow}_{\langle r\rangle}$ implicitly includes transitions through unobservable actions and ambiguous actions in level-$\langle r\rangle$ observation.

Definition 3.5 *Let* $r \in \mathcal{R}$. *If* $\theta(t, r) = \varepsilon$ *and* $E \xrightarrow{t} E'$ *for some* $t \in Act_r^*$, *then* $E \overset{\varepsilon}{\Longrightarrow}_{\langle r \rangle} E'$ *(also written* $E \Longrightarrow_{\langle r \rangle} E'$). *If* $E \Longrightarrow_{\langle r \rangle} \xrightarrow{\mu_1} \Longrightarrow_{\langle r \rangle} \cdots \Longrightarrow_{\langle r \rangle} \xrightarrow{\mu_n} \Longrightarrow_{\langle r \rangle}$ E' *for some* $t = \mu_1 \cdots \mu_n \in Act_r^*$, *then* $E \overset{t}{\Longrightarrow}_{\langle r \rangle} E'$. □

We define weak level-$\langle r \rangle$ equivalence by using *level-$\langle r \rangle$ bisimulations*.

Definition 3.6 *Let* $r \in \mathcal{R}$. *A binary relation* $\mathcal{S} \subseteq \mathcal{P} \times \mathcal{P}$ *over processes is a* level-$\langle r \rangle$ *bisimulation if* $(P, Q) \in \mathcal{S}$ *implies, for all* $\mu \in Act_r$, *that*

(*i*) *whenever* $P \xrightarrow{\mu} P'$ *then, for some* Q', $Q \overset{\phi(\mu, r)}{\Longrightarrow}_{\langle r \rangle} Q'$, *and* $(P', Q') \in \mathcal{S}$,

(*ii*) *whenever* $Q \xrightarrow{\mu} Q'$ *then, for some* P', $P \overset{\phi(\mu, r)}{\Longrightarrow}_{\langle r \rangle} P'$, *and* $(P', Q') \in \mathcal{S}$. □

Definition 3.7 *P and Q are weakly level-$\langle r \rangle$ equivalent, written* $P \approx_{\langle r \rangle} Q$, *if* $(P, Q) \in \mathcal{S}$ *for some level-$\langle r \rangle$ bisimulation $\mathcal{S}$.* □

Notice that ϕ is used on $\Longrightarrow_{\langle r \rangle}$ in Definition 3.6, because ambiguous actions can be observed. Proposition 3.5 shows the basic properties of $\approx_{\langle r \rangle}$.

Proposition 3.5 (1) *$\approx_{\langle r \rangle}$ is an equivalence relation.*
(2) *If* $r \geq r'$, *then* $\approx_{\langle r \rangle} \subseteq \approx_{\langle r' \rangle}$. □

If the level is high enough that no action is neglected, then unobservable actions are only τ. Particularly $\approx_{\langle \infty \rangle}$ corresponds to weak equivalence $\approx$ defined in [2]. $\approx_{\langle r \rangle}$ is preserved by Composition combinator $|$, and conditionally preserved by Restriction combinator $\backslash$ as shown in Proposition 3.6.

Proposition 3.6 *Let* $P_1 \approx_{\langle r \rangle} P_2$. *Then*
(1) $P_1 | Q \approx_{\langle r \rangle} P_2 | Q$
(2) $P_1 \backslash_{\langle r' \rangle (s')}^{L} \approx_{\langle r \rangle} P_2 \backslash_{\langle r' \rangle (s')}^{L}$ *if* $r' + \pi(s') \leq r$
(3) $P_1 @ s' \approx_{\langle r \rangle} P_2 @ s'$ *if* $r' + \pi(s') \leq r$ □

Intuitively the condition of (2) shows that the restriction area, inside the circle whose center is $\pi(s')$ away from the observer and whose radius is r', must not be overlapped on the unobservable area, outside the circle whose radius is r.

3.3 Level-$\langle r \rangle$ Equivalence

Weak level-$\langle r \rangle$ equivalence $\approx_{\langle r \rangle}$ is not preserved by Choice combinator $+$ like weak equivalence $\approx$. In this subsection, we define a relation called *level-$\langle r \rangle$ equivalence* preserved by $+$. First, a binary relation over actions is defined.

Definition 3.8 *Let* $r \in \mathcal{R}$. *Level-$\langle r \rangle$ substitution* $\trianglerighteq_{\langle r \rangle} (\subset Act_r \times Act_r)$ *is a binary relation over actions defined by*

$$\trianglerighteq_{\langle r \rangle} = \{(\mu, \mu) : \mu \in Act_r\} \cup \{(\mu, \mu') : \mu, \mu' \in Act_r, \phi(\mu, r) = \theta(\mu', r) = \varepsilon\}$$ □

$(\mu \trianglerighteq_{\langle r \rangle} \mu')$ implies that μ' can be substituted for μ in level-$\langle r \rangle$ observation. For example the following relations show properties of $\trianglerighteq_{\langle r \rangle}$.

$\tau \trianglerighteq_{\langle 1 \rangle} (\alpha \langle -2 \rangle @ \varepsilon)$, $(\alpha \langle -2 \rangle @ \varepsilon) \trianglerighteq_{\langle 1 \rangle} \tau$, $\tau \trianglerighteq_{\langle 1 \rangle} (\alpha \langle 2 \rangle @ \varepsilon)$, $(\alpha \langle 2 \rangle @ \varepsilon) \ntrianglerighteq_{\langle 1 \rangle} \tau$

In level-$\langle 1 \rangle$ observation, $(\alpha \langle -2 \rangle @\varepsilon)$ is unobservable and $(\alpha \langle 2 \rangle @\varepsilon)$ is ambiguous. Unobservable actions correspond to internal actions τ, while ambiguous actions do not correspond to τ. Ambiguous actions can be substituted for internal actions, but internal actions can not be substituted for ambiguous actions.

Then we define level-$\langle r \rangle$ equivalence.

Definition 3.9 *Let $r \in \mathcal{R}$. P and Q are level-$\langle r \rangle$ equivalent, written $P =_{\langle r \rangle} Q$, if for all $\mu \in Act_\tau$, that*

(i) whenever $P \overset{\mu}{\longrightarrow} P'$ then, for some (Q', μ'), $Q \overset{\mu'}{\Longrightarrow}_{\langle r \rangle} Q', P' \approx_{\langle r \rangle} Q', \mu \trianglerighteq_{\langle r \rangle} \mu'$,

(ii) whenever $Q \overset{\mu}{\longrightarrow} Q'$ then, for some (P', μ'), $P \overset{\mu'}{\Longrightarrow}_{\langle r \rangle} P', P' \approx_{\langle r \rangle} Q', \mu \trianglerighteq_{\langle r \rangle} \mu'$ $\square$

For $=_{\langle r \rangle}$, each *initial* action must be matched by a substitutive action unlike $\approx_{\langle r \rangle}$. Particularly $=_{\langle \infty \rangle}$ corresponds to observation congruence. Proposition 3.7 show that $=_{\langle r \rangle}$ is the largest relation preserved by $+$ and included in $\approx_{\langle r \rangle}$.

Proposition 3.7 *(A characterization of $=_{\langle r \rangle}$)*
1. *If $P_1 =_{\langle r \rangle} P_2$, then $P_1 + R =_{\langle r \rangle} P_2 + R$, for any R.*
2. *Let $\mathcal{Q} \subseteq \approx_{\langle r \rangle}$ such that $(P_1 + R, P_2 + R) \in \mathcal{Q}$ for any R, if $(P_1, P_2) \in \mathcal{Q}$. Then if $(P_1, P_2) \in \mathcal{Q}$ and $\mathcal{L}(P_1) \cup \mathcal{L}(P_2) \neq \mathcal{A}^1$, then $P_1 =_{\langle r \rangle} P_2$.*

Proof *We show only a proof of 2. We choose that R is $A \overset{def}{=} (a_0 \langle r_0 \rangle @\varepsilon).A$ such as $a_0 \notin \mathcal{L}(P_1) \cup \mathcal{L}(P_2)$ and $r_0 \geq -r$. Let $P_1 \overset{\mu}{\longrightarrow} P'$. By **Choice₁**, $P_1 + A \overset{\mu}{\longrightarrow} P'$.*

Since $P_1 + A \approx_{\langle r \rangle} P_2 + A$, for some Q', $P_2 + A \overset{\phi(\mu, r)}{\Longrightarrow}_{\langle r \rangle} Q'$ and $P' \approx_{\langle r \rangle} Q'$. If μ is $(a_1 \langle r_1 \rangle @s_1)$ such as $(r_1 \geq \pi(s_1) - r)$, then $\phi(a_1 \langle r_1 \rangle @s_1, r) = a_1 \langle r_1 \rangle @s_1$. In this case, we easily obtain that $P_2 \overset{\mu}{\Longrightarrow}_{\langle r \rangle} Q'$, $P' \approx_{\langle r \rangle} Q'$, and $\mu \trianglerighteq_{\langle r \rangle} \mu$.

Otherwise, $\phi(\mu, r) = \varepsilon$. Therefore, $P_2 + A \Longrightarrow_{\langle r \rangle} Q'$. Now we show that $Q' \not\equiv P_2 + A$ by inconsistency. Suppose that $Q' \equiv P_2 + A$. In this case Q' has $(a_0 \langle r_0 \rangle @\varepsilon)$-derivations, because $\phi(a_0 \langle r_0 \rangle @\varepsilon, r) = a_0 \langle r_0 \rangle @\varepsilon$ since $r_0 \geq -r$. Thus P' must also have $(a_0 \langle r_0 \rangle @\varepsilon)$-derivations, since $P' \approx_{\langle r \rangle} Q'$, but it is impossible, because $a_0 \notin \mathcal{L}(P') \subseteq \mathcal{L}(P)$. Hence $Q' \not\equiv P_2 + A$, namely, $P_2 + A \overset{\mu'}{\Longrightarrow}_{\langle r \rangle} Q'$ for some μ' such as $\theta(\mu', r) = \varepsilon$. This transition must be caused by P_2, because P' has no $(a_0 \langle r_0 \rangle @\varepsilon)$-derivation. Hence $P_2 \overset{\mu'}{\Longrightarrow}_{\langle r \rangle} Q'$ and $\mu \trianglerighteq_{\langle r \rangle} \mu'$, since $\phi(\mu, r) = \varepsilon = \theta(\mu', r)$. $\square$

$\approx_{\langle r \rangle}$ is not a congruence relation, because it is not always preserved by Restriction and Route combinators. Proposition 3.6 for $\approx_{\langle r \rangle}$ also holds for $=_{\langle r \rangle}$.

3.4 Axiom System $\mathcal{A} \langle r \rangle$

In order to compare level-$\langle r \rangle$ equivalence $=_{\langle r \rangle}$ and observation congruence $=$, we give an axiom system $\mathcal{A} \langle r \rangle$ for finite sequential processes which consist only of Inaction '0', Prefix '.', and Choice '+'. The set of finite sequential processes is denoted by $\mathcal{P}_{seq}(\subset \mathcal{P})$, and is ranged over by $P, Q, \cdots$.

$=_{\langle r \rangle}$ is a congruence relation for $\mathcal{P}_{seq}$, because it is preserved by Prefix and Choice combinators. A sound and complete axiom system $\mathcal{A}_\infty$ for observation congruence of $\mathcal{P}_{seq}$ has already been given in [2] as follows.

---

[1] $\mathcal{L}(P)$ is the set of labels of all actions which P can perform in the future.

Definition 3.10 *We write $\mathcal{A}_\infty \vdash P = Q$ if the equality of two processes P and Q can be proven by equational reasoning from the axiom system $\mathcal{A}_\infty$, which consists of the following equations:*

M1 $P_1 + P_2 = P_2 + P_1$	**T1** $\mu.\tau.P = \mu.P$
M2 $(P_1 + P_2) + P_3 = P_1 + (P_2 + P_3)$	**T2** $P + \tau.P = \tau.P$
M3 $P = P + P$	**T3** $\mu.(P + \tau.Q) + \mu.Q = \mu.(P + \tau.Q)$
M4 $P = P + 0$	□

Theorem 3.8 *Let $P, Q \in \mathcal{P}_{seq}$. Then $P = Q$ iff $\mathcal{A}_\infty \vdash P = Q$.* □

We define an axiom system $\mathcal{A}\langle r \rangle$ for any $r \in \mathcal{R}$ as follows.

Definition 3.11 *Let $r \in \mathcal{R}$. We write $\mathcal{A}\langle r \rangle \vdash P = Q$ if the equality of two processes P and Q can be proven by equational reasoning from the axiom system $\mathcal{A}\langle r \rangle$, which consists of the equations in $\mathcal{A}_\infty$ and the following equations:*

$$\mathbf{A1}\langle r \rangle \ (\alpha\langle r' \rangle @s).P = \tau.P \qquad \qquad \text{if } r' < -(r - \pi(s))$$
$$\mathbf{A2}\langle r \rangle \ (\alpha\langle r' \rangle @s).P = (\alpha\langle r' \rangle @s).P + \tau.P \quad \text{if } r' > r - \pi(s) \qquad □$$

$\mathbf{A1}\langle r \rangle$ and $\mathbf{A2}\langle r \rangle$ are equations for unobservable actions and ambiguous actions, respectively. We define a standard form to prove completeness of $\mathcal{A}\langle r \rangle$.

Definition 3.12 *P is a level-$\langle r \rangle$ standard form, or is in level-$\langle r \rangle$ standard form, if [2]*
   (i) $P \equiv \sum_{i=1}^{m} \mu_i.P_i$ where each P_i is also in level-$\langle r \rangle$ standard form,
   (ii) $P \xrightarrow{\ \ a\langle r' \rangle @s\ \ }\!\!\!\!\!/ \ \ $ such as $r' < -(r - \pi(s))$,
   (iii) whenever $P \xrightarrow{\ a\langle r' \rangle @s\ } P'$ such as $r' > r - \pi(s)$, then $P \xrightarrow{\ \tau\ } P'$. □

(ii) means that all unobservable actions except τ can not occur. *(iii)* means that all ambiguous actions must be bypassed through τ.

Proposition 3.9 strengthens relations between processes.

Proposition 3.9 *Let P and Q be in level-$\langle r \rangle$ standard form. Then,*
$$P \approx_{\langle r \rangle} Q \text{ implies } P \approx Q, \text{ and } P =_{\langle r \rangle} Q \text{ implies } P = Q.$$
Proof *(Key points) Let P be in level-$\langle r \rangle$ standard form. It is important to prove that if $P \xrightarrow{\ \mu\ } P'$ and $\theta(\mu, r) = \varepsilon$ then $P \xrightarrow{\ \tau\ } P'$. $\theta(\mu, r) = \varepsilon$ implies $\mu = \tau$ or $\mu = (\alpha\langle r' \rangle @s')$ such as $|r'| > \pi(s') - r$. Then, $P \xrightarrow{\ \tau\ } P'$ is easily obtained by the conditions (ii) and (iii) of level-$\langle r \rangle$ standard form.* □

Lemma 3.10 is used for the proof of completeness of $\mathcal{A}\langle r \rangle$ for $=_{\langle r \rangle}$ of $\mathcal{P}_{seq}$.

Lemma 3.10 *For any $P \in \mathcal{P}_{seq}$, there is a level-$\langle r \rangle$ standard form P' of equal depth, such that $\mathcal{A}\langle r \rangle \vdash P = P'$.*
Proof *(ii) and (iii) are satisfied by $\mathbf{A1}\langle r \rangle$ and $\mathbf{A2}\langle r \rangle$, respectively.* □

Finally we give Theorem 3.11 which shows that $\mathcal{A}\langle r \rangle$ is sound and complete for level-$\langle r \rangle$ equivalence of finite sequential processes.

Theorem 3.11 *Let $P, Q \in \mathcal{P}_{seq}$. Then $P =_{\langle r \rangle} Q$ iff $\mathcal{A}\langle r \rangle \vdash P = Q$.*
Proof *($\Leftarrow$) A level-$\langle r \rangle$ bisimulation for each equation can be found.*
   ($\Rightarrow$) By Lemma 3.10, Proposition 3.9, and Theorem 3.8. □

---

[2] If $m \geq 1$, then $\sum_{i=1}^{m} P_i$ is the short notation of $P_1 + P_2 + \cdots + P_m$, otherwise it is **0**.

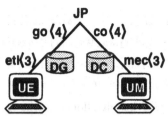

Fig. 5. A communicating system with deadlocks

3.5 Strong Level-$\langle r \rangle$ Equivalence

In [2] *strong* equivalence $\sim$ is considered before *weak* equivalence $\approx$, because $\sim$ is simpler than $\approx$. In this subsection we discuss a *strong version* $\sim_{\langle r \rangle}$ of $\approx_{\langle r \rangle}$.

Strong level-$\langle r \rangle$ bisimulation may be defined by using the condition that
(i) whenever $P \xrightarrow{\mu} P'$ then, for some (Q', μ'), $Q \xrightarrow{\mu'} Q'$, $(P', Q') \in \mathcal{S}$, $\mu \unrhd_{\langle r \rangle} \mu'$, instead of (i) in Definition 3.6, and (ii) is symmetric. $P \sim_{\langle r \rangle} Q$ implies $P \approx_{\langle r \rangle} Q$, and a sound and complete axiom system for $\sim_{\langle r \rangle}$ of $\mathcal{P}_{seq}$ is given from **M1-M4**, **A1$\langle r \rangle$**, **A2$\langle r \rangle$**. Unfortunately, $\sim_{\langle r \rangle}$ is not preserved by Composition $|$. For example, consider the following three processes: $P_1 \equiv \alpha \langle -2 \rangle . 0$, $P_2 \equiv \tau . 0$, $P_3 \equiv \alpha \langle 2 \rangle . 0$. P_1 and P_2 are strongly level-$\langle 1 \rangle$ equivalent, because $\alpha \langle -2 \rangle$ is unobservable, but $P_1 | P_3$ and $P_2 | P_3$ are *not* strongly level-$\langle 1 \rangle$ equivalent, because $P_1 | P_3$ can reach a stop process through an internal action τ by **Com$_3$**, while $P_2 | P_3$ can not do so.

4 An Example of Approximative Analysis

We show an example of approximative analysis in CCSG by using the system in Fig.5. DG and DC are databases of government and corporations, respectively. UE and UM are interfaces of the national laboratory ETL and the corporation MEC, respectively. They are connected through the four routers as shown in Fig.5. This system is described by an observer at JP as follows:

$$SYS \stackrel{\text{def}}{=} ((GO@go\langle 4 \rangle) | (CO@co\langle 4 \rangle)) \backslash^L_{\langle 18 \rangle(\varepsilon)} \quad \Big| \quad GO \stackrel{\text{def}}{=} DG | (UE@etl\langle 3 \rangle)$$
$$L = \{lk_1, lk_2, ul_1, ul_2\} \quad \Big| \quad CO \stackrel{\text{def}}{=} DC | (UM@mec\langle 3 \rangle)$$

We assume that locks are needed for access to databases, and each interface trys to lock the near database at first and another one after that, when it accepts the action ac_i. Each component process is described as follows:

$$UE \stackrel{\text{def}}{=} ac_1 . \overline{lk_1} \langle 3 \rangle . \overline{lk_2} \langle 11 \rangle . su_1 . \overline{ul_2} \langle 11 \rangle . \overline{ul_1} \langle 3 \rangle . UE \quad \Big| \quad DG \stackrel{\text{def}}{=} lk_1 . ul_1 . DG$$
$$UM \stackrel{\text{def}}{=} ac_2 . \overline{lk_2} \langle 3 \rangle . \overline{lk_1} \langle 11 \rangle . su_2 . \overline{ul_1} \langle 11 \rangle . \overline{ul_2} \langle 3 \rangle . UM \quad \Big| \quad DC \stackrel{\text{def}}{=} lk_2 . ul_2 . DC$$

where the empty route ε and the zero grade $\langle 0 \rangle$ are omitted. su_i is used to inform success of locking. The grades of ac and su are set to 0, because they are local at their interfaces. lk and ul are used for locking and unlocking, respectively. lk and ul of interfaces have grades high enough to synchronize with databases. For example, the grade 11 of $\overline{lk_2} \langle 11 \rangle$ is the loss distance between UE and DC. These lk and ul are restricted from environment. The restriction power 18 of SYS is the minimal to restrict $\overline{lk_i} \langle 11 \rangle$ and $\overline{ul_i} \langle 11 \rangle$ the loss distance 7 away from JP.

In order to understand the behavior of SYS, we give the sequential process SP which is observation congruent to SYS, written $SYS = SP$, as follows:

$$SP \overset{\text{def}}{=} ac_1@s_1.R_1 + ac_2@s_2.R_2, \qquad s_1 = etl\langle 3\rangle go\langle 4\rangle, \quad s_2 = mec\langle 3\rangle co\langle 4\rangle$$

$$R_1 \overset{\text{def}}{=} \tau.(\tau.(su_1@s_1.SP + ac_2@s_2.su_1@s_1.R_2) + ac_2@s_2.O_{12}) + ac_2@s_2.O$$

$$R_2 \overset{\text{def}}{=} \tau.(\tau.(su_2@s_2.SP + ac_1@s_1.su_2@s_2.R_1) + ac_1@s_1.O_{21}) + ac_1@s_1.O$$

$$O \overset{\text{def}}{=} \tau.O_{12} + \tau.O_{21}, \quad O_{12} \overset{\text{def}}{=} \tau.su_1@s_1.R_2 + \tau.0, \quad O_{21} \overset{\text{def}}{=} \tau.su_2@s_2.R_1 + \tau.0$$

SP *explicitly* shows that SYS has deadlocks. Although SP has useful information, but it is somewhat complex even for the simple example SYS.

We often stay in ETL and are interested only in the situation near ETL. Thus actions of UM are unobservable. First, the position of the observer is shifted from JP to ETL by $SYS \overset{\cdot}{\approx}_{(s)} SYS@s$, where s is the route $(go\langle 4\rangle etl\langle 3\rangle)$ from JP to ETL. Let $SP_{ETL} \overset{\text{def}}{=} ac_1.(\tau.su_1.SP_{ETL} + \tau.0)$, then the equation

$$SYS \overset{\cdot}{\approx}_{(s)} SYS@s =_{\langle r\rangle} \tau.SP_{ETL} \approx_{\langle r\rangle} SP_{ETL}$$

holds, where r is less than 14 which is the loss distance between ETL and MEC. The τ of $\tau.SP_{ETL}$ is needed for matching unobservable actions in MEC. SP_{ETL} shows that SYS may fall to a deadlock after ac_1 while it never falls just after su_1.

5 Related Work

Several process algebras considering space have already been proposed, for example [3, 4, 5] as extensions of CCS and [7] as an extension of ACP [6].

An advantage of [7] is that time and space are integrated. For example, the possibility of communication between distributed processes can be checked by considering the velocity of communication. The main purpose of CCSG is approximative analysis, while [7] is not interested in such analysis. Although CCSG has no notion of time yet, we are interested in introducing the notion of time [8] to CCSG. The velocity of communication may be expressed by routers with *delay*.

In [3, 4, 5], equality of processes is checked by considering locations of actions. For example, $P_1 \equiv (\alpha_1.0|\alpha_2.0)$ and $P_2 \equiv (\alpha_1.\alpha_2.0 + \alpha_2.\alpha_1.0)$ are not *location equivalent* [3], because the locations of α_1 and α_2 are independent of each other in P_1, while they are dependent in P_2, as shown in the *location transitions*:

$$P_1 \xrightarrow[u_1]{\alpha_1} (u_1 :: 0)|(\alpha_2.0) \xrightarrow[u_2]{\alpha_2} (u_1 :: 0)|(u_2 :: 0),$$

$$P_2 \xrightarrow[u_1]{\alpha_1} u_1 :: \alpha_2.0 \xrightarrow[u_1 u_2]{\alpha_2} u_1 u_2 :: 0.$$

where u of $\xrightarrow[u]{\alpha}$ represents the location of α. In the transitions of P_2, the location $u_1 u_2$ of α_2 depends on u_1 of α_1. Location transitions *automatically* assign locations. Thus, concurrent processes are distinct from sequential processes.

In CCSG positions of actions are *explicitly* described, and concurrent processes are not always distinct from sequential processes. For example, the following processes P_1' and P_2' are level-$\langle \infty\rangle$ equivalent (i.e. observation congruent).

$$P_1' \equiv (\alpha_1.0)@s_1|(\alpha_2.0)@s_2, \qquad P_2' \equiv (\alpha_1@s_1).(\alpha_2@s_2).0 + (\alpha_2@s_2).(\alpha_1@s_1).0$$

It is not recommended to apply location transitions into CCSG, because locations automatically assigned to actions by location transitions may be inconsistent with the explicitly described positions. The purpose of location equivalence is different from ours. We introduce the positions for estimating the loss distance.

6 Conclusion

We have proposed CCSG by introducing *grades* and *routes* to CCS. The grades represent the importance of actions and the routes point to positions where actions occur. An advantage of CCSG is to approximately analyze systems under assumption that unimportant distant actions can not be observed. We have given an approximative equivalence relation called level-$\langle r \rangle$ equivalence. The difference of level-$\langle r \rangle$ equivalence from observation congruence is shown by $\mathbf{A1}\langle r \rangle$ and $\mathbf{A2}\langle r \rangle$ in the axiom system $\mathcal{A}\langle r \rangle$.

The most interesting and urgent future work is to modify the connection of routers to *graph structure* from the hierarchical star structure.

MBone [11] is known as a communication style where a value assigned to each message restricts the receivable area of the message. In MBone each router has a threshold, and messages with values less than the threshold can not pass the router. Although CCSG hsa a similar communication style to MBone, CCSG has point-to-point communication, while MBone has broadcast communication. CBS [9] and CCB [10] have already been proposed as process algebra with broadcast communication. We want to extend CCSG with broadcast communication.

Acknowledgement

The authors wish to express our gratitude to Dr. Kimihiro Ohta, Director of Computer Science Division, ETL. They also thank Dr. Yoshiki Kinoshita in Computer Language Section and all our colleagues in Information Base Section for their helpful discussions.

References

1. M.Tsujigao, T.Hikita, and J.Ginbayashi, "Process Composition and Interleave Reduction in Parallel Process Specification", Proc. of JCSE'93, pp.218-225, 1993.
2. R.Milner, *"Communication and Concurrency"*, Prentice-Hall, 1989.
3. G.Boudol, I.Castellani, M.Hennessy, and A.Kiehn, "Observing localities", *Theoretical Computer Science*, Vol.114, pp.31-61, 1993.
4. P.Krishnan,"Distributed CCS", CONCUR'91, LNCS 527, Springer-Verlag, pp.393-407, 1991
5. Ugo Montanari and Daniel Yankelevich, "A Parametric Approach to Localities", ICALP'92, LNCS 623, Springer-Verlag, pp.617 - 628, 1992
6. J.C.M.Baeten and W.P.Weijland, *"Process Algebra"*, Cambridge Tracts in Theoretical Computer Science 18, Cambridge University Press, 1990.
7. J.C.M.Baeten and J.A.Bergstra, "Real Space Process Algebra", CONCUR'91, LNCS 527, Springer-Verlag, pp.96 - 110, 1991
8. F.Moller and C.Tofts,"An overview of TCCS", Proc. of EUROMICRO'92, 1992.
9. K.V.S.Prasad, "A Calculus of Broadcasting Systems", TAPSOFT'91, Vol.1:CAAP, LNCS 493, Springer-Verlag, pp.338 - 358, 1991
10. Y.Isobe, Y.Sato, and K.Ohmaki, "A Calculus of Countable Broadcasting Systems", AMAST'95, LNCS 936, Springer-Verlag, pp.489-503, 1995.
11. "The MBONE Information Web", http://www.eit.com/techinfo/mbone/mbone.html.

Boolean Formalism and Explanations

Eric C. R. Hehner

University of Toronto

Abstract

Boolean algebra is simpler than number algebra, with applications in programming, circuit design, law, specifications, mathematical proof, and reasoning in any domain. So why is number algebra taught in primary school and used routinely by scientists, engineers, economists, and the general public, while boolean algebra is not taught until university, and not routinely used by anyone? A large part of the answer may be in the terminology of logic, in the symbols used, and in the explanations of boolean algebra found in textbooks. The subject has not yet freed itself from its history and philosophy. This paper points out the problems delaying the acceptance and use of boolean algebra, and suggests some solutions.

Introduction

This is not a mathematically deep talk. It does not contain any new mathematical results. It is about the symbols and notations of boolean algebra, and about the way the subject is explained. It is about education, and about putting boolean algebra into general use and practice. To make the scope clear, by "boolean algebra" I mean the usual algebra whose expressions are boolean, where "boolean" is a type. I mean to include propositional logic and predicate calculus. I shall say "boolean algebra", "boolean calculus", or "logic" interchangeably, and call its expressions "boolean expressions". Analogously, I say "number algebra", "number calculus", or "arithmetic" interchangeably, and call its expressions "number expressions".

Boolean algebra is the basic algebra for much of computer science. Other applications include digital circuit design, law, reasoning about any subject, and any kind of specifications, as well as providing a foundation for all of mathematics. Boolean algebra is inherently simpler than number algebra. There are only two boolean values and a few boolean operators, and they can be explained by a small table. There are infinitely many number values and number operators, and even the simplest, counting, is inductively defined. So why is number algebra taught in primary school, and boolean algebra in university? Why isn't boolean algebra better known, better accepted, and better used?

One reason may be that, although boolean algebra is just as useful as number algebra, it isn't as necessary. Informal methods of reckoning quantity became intolerable several thousand years ago, but we still get along with informal methods of specification, design, and reasoning. Other reasons may be accidents of educational history, and still others may be our continuing mistreatment of boolean algebra.

Historical Perspective

To start to answer these questions, I'm going to look briefly at the history of number algebra. Long after the invention of numbers and arithmetic, quantitative reasoning was still a matter of trial and error, and still conducted in natural language. If a man died leaving his 3 goats and 20 chickens to be divided equally between his 2 sons, and it was agreed that a goat is worth 8 chickens, the solution was determined by iterative approximations, probably using the goats and chickens themselves in the calculation. The arithmetic needed for verification was well understood long before the algebra needed to find a solution.

The advent of algebra provided a more effective way of finding solutions to such problems, but it was a difficult step up in abstraction. The step from constants to variables is as large as the step from chickens to numbers. In English 500 years ago, constants were called "nombers denominate" [concrete numbers], and variables were called "nombers abstracte". Each step in an abstract calculation was accompanied by a concrete justification. For example, we have the Commutative Law [0]:

> When the chekyns of two gentle menne are counted, we may count first the chekyns of the gentylman having fewer chekyns, and after the chekyns of the gentylman having the greater portion. If the nomber of the greater portion be counted first, and then that of the lesser portion, the denomination so determined shall be the same."

This version of the Commutative Law includes an unnecessary case analysis, and it has missed a case: when the two gentlemen have the same number of chickens, it does not say whether the order matters. The Associative Law [0]:

> When thynges to be counted are divided in two partes, and lately are found moare thynges to be counted in the same generall quantitie, it matters not whether the thynges lately added be counted together with the lesser parte or with the greater parte, or that there are severalle partes and the thynges lately added be counted together with any one of them.

One of the simplest, most general laws, sometimes called the Transparency Law, or "substitution of equals for equals",

$$x=y \implies fx=fy$$

seems to have been discovered a little at a time. Here is one special case [1]:

"In the firste there appeareth 2 nombers, that is $14x + 15y$ equalle to one nomber, whiche is $71y$. But if you marke them well, you maie see one denomination, on bothe sides of the equation, which never ought to stand. Wherfore abating [subtracting] the lesser, that is $15y$ out of bothe the nombers, there will remain $14x = 56y$ that is, by reduction, $1x = 4y$.

Scholar. I see, you abate $15y$ from them bothe. And then are thei equalle still, seyng thei wer equalle before. According to the thirde common sentence, in the patthewaie: If you abate even [equal] portions, from thynges that bee equalle, the partes that remain shall be equall also.

Master. You doe well remember the firste grounds of this arte."

And then, a paragraph later, another special case:

"If you adde equalle portions, to thynges that bee equalle, what so amounteth of them shall be equalle."

As you can imagine, the distance from $2x + 3 = 3x + 2$ to $x=1$ was likely to be several pages. The reason for all the discussion in between formulas was that algebra was not yet fully trusted. Algebra replaces meaning with symbol manipulation; the loss of meaning is not easy to accept. The author had to constantly reassure those readers who had not yet freed themselves from thinking about the objects represented by numbers and variables. Those who were skilled in the art of informal reasoning about quantity were convinced that thinking about the objects helps to calculate correctly, because that is how they did it. As with any technological advance, those who are most skilled in the old way are the most reluctant to see it replaced by the new.

Today, of course, we expect a quantitative calculation to be conducted entirely in algebra, without reference to thynges. Although we justify each step in a calculation by reference to an algebraic law, we do not have to justify the laws anymore. We can go farther, faster, more succinctly, and with much greater certainty. The following proof of Wedderburn's Theorem (a finite division ring is a commutative field) is typical of today's algebra; I have taken it from the text used when I studied algebra [2]. You needn't read it; I quote it only so that I can comment on it after.

(start of typical modern proof)

Let D be a finite division ring and let Z be its center. By induction we may assume that any division ring having fewer elements than D is a commutative field.

We first remark that if $a, b \in D$ are such that $b^t a = a b^t$ but $ba \neq ab$ then $b^t \in Z$. For, consider $N(b^t) = \{x \in D \mid b^t x = x b^t\}$. $N(b^t)$ is a subdivision ring of D; if it were not D, by our induction hypothesis, it would be commutative. However, both a and b are in $N(b^t)$ and these do not commute; consequently, $N(b^t)$ is not commutative so must be all of D. Thus $b^t \in Z$.

Every nonzero element in D has finite order, so some positive power of it falls in Z. Given $w \in D$ let the order of w relative to Z be the smallest positive integer $m(w)$ such that $w^{m(w)} \in Z$. Pick an element a in D but not in Z having minimal possible order relative to Z, and let this order be r. We claim that r is a prime number for if $r=pq$ with $1<p<r$ then a^p is not in Z. Yet $(a^p)^q = a^r \in Z$, implying that a^p has an order relative to Z smaller than that of a.

By the corollary to Lemma 7.9 there is an $x \in D$ such that $xax^{-1} = a^i \neq a$; thus $x^2ax^{-2} = x(xax^{-1})x^{-1} = xa^ix^{-1} = (xax^{-1})^i = (a^i)^i = a^{i^2}$. Similarly, we get $x^{r-1}ax^{-(r-1)} = a^{i^{(r-1)}}$. However, r is a prime number thus by the little Fermat theorem (corollary to Theorem 2.a), $i^{r-1} = 1 + ur$, hence $a^{i^{(r-1)}} = a^{1+ur} = aa^{ur} = \lambda a$ where $\lambda = a^{ur} \in Z$. Thus $x^{r-1}a = \lambda azx^{r-1}$. Since $x \notin Z$, by the minimal nature of r, x^{r-1} cannot be in Z. By the remark of the earlier paragraph since $xa \neq ax$, $x^{r-1}a \neq ax^{r-1}$ and so $\lambda \neq 1$. Let $b = x^{r-1}$; thus $bab^{-1} = \lambda a$; consequently, $\lambda^r a = (bab^{-1})^r = ba^rb^{-1} = a^r$ since $a^r \in Z$. This relation forces $\lambda^r = 1$.

We claim that if $y \in D$ then whenever $y^r = 1$, then $y = \lambda^i$ for some i, for in the field $Z(y)$ there are at most r roots of the polynomial $u^r - 1$; the elements $1, \lambda, \lambda^2, ..., \lambda^{r-1}$ in Z are all distinct since λ is of the prime order r and they already account for r roots of $u^r - 1$ in $Z(y)$, in consequence of which $y = \lambda^i$.

Since $\lambda^r = 1$, $b^r = \lambda^r b^r = (\lambda b)^r = (a^{-1}ba)^r = a^{-1}b^r a$ from which we get $ab^r = b^r a$. Since a commutes with b^r but does not commute with b, by the remark made earlier, b^r must be in Z. By Theorem 7.b the multiplicative group of nonzero elements of Z is cyclic; let $\gamma \in Z$ be a generator. Thus $a^r = \gamma^j$, $b^r = \gamma^k$; if $j = sr$ then $a^r = \gamma^{sr}$; whence $(a/\gamma^s)^r = 1$; this would imply that $a/\gamma^s = \lambda^i$, leading to $a \in Z$, contrary to $a \notin Z$. Hence, r does not divide j; similarly r does not divide k. Let $a_1 = a^k$ and $b_1 = b^j$; a direct computation from $ba = \lambda ab$ leads to $a_1b_1 = \mu b_1a_1$ where $\mu = \lambda^{-jk} \in Z$. Since the prime number r which is the order of λ does not divide j or k, $\lambda^{jk} \neq 1$ whence $\mu \neq 1$. Note that $\mu^r = 1$.

Let us see where we are. We have produced two elements a_1, b_1 such that:

(1) $a_1^r = b_1^r = \alpha \in Z$.

(2) $a_1b_1 = \mu b_1a_1$ with $\mu \neq 1$ in Z.

(3) $\mu^r = 1$.

We compute $(a_1^{-1}b_1)^r$; $(a_1^{-1}b_1)^2 = a_1^{-1}b_1a_1^{-1}b_1 = a_1^{-1}(b_1a_1^{-1})b_1 = a_1^{-1}(\mu a_1^{-1}b_1)b_1 = \mu a_1^{-2}b_1^2$. If we compute $(a_1^{-1}b_1)^3$ we find it equal to $\mu^{1+2}a_1^{-3}b_1^3$. Continuing we obtain $(a_1^{-1}b_1)^r = \mu^{1+2+...+(r-1)}a_1^{-r}b_1^r = \mu^{1+2+...+(r-1)} = \mu^{r(r-1)/2}$. If r is an odd prime, since $\mu^r = 1$, we get $\mu^{r(r-1)/2} = 1$, whence $(a_1^{-1}b_1)^r = 1$. Being a solution of $y^r = 1$, $a_1^{-1}b_1 = \lambda^i$ so that $b_1 = \lambda^ia_1$; but then $\mu b_1a_1 = a_1b_1 = b_1a_1$, contradicting $\mu \neq 1$. Thus if r is an odd prime number, the theorem is proved.

We must now rule out the case $r=2$. In that special situation we have two elements $a_1, b_1 \in D$ such that $a_1^2 = b_1^2 = \alpha \in Z$, $a_1b_1 = \mu b_1a_1$ where $\mu^2 = 1$ and $\mu \neq 1$. Thus $\mu = -1$ and $a_1b_1 = -b_1a_1 \neq b_1a_1$; in consequence, the characteristic of D is not 2. By Lemma 7.7 we can find elements $\zeta, \eta \in Z$ such that $1 + \zeta^2 - \alpha\eta^2 = 0$. Consider $(a_1 + \zeta b_1 + \eta a_1b_1)^2$; on computing this out we find that $(a_1 + \zeta b_1 + \eta a_1b_1)^2 = \alpha(1 + \zeta^2 - \alpha\eta^2) = 0$. Being in a division ring this yields that $a_1 + \zeta b_1 + \eta a_1b_1 = 0$; thus $0 \neq 2a_1^2 = a_1(a_1 + \zeta b_1 + \eta a_1b_1) + (a_1 + \zeta b_1 + \eta a_1b_1)a_1 = 0$. This contradiction finishes the proof and Weddderburn's theorem is established.

(end of typical modern proof)

Before we start to feel pleased with ourselves at the improvement, let me point out that there are two kinds of calculation in this text. One kind occurs in formulas, such as

$$\lambda^r a' = (bab^{-1})^r = ba^r b^{-1} = a'$$

$$b^r = \lambda^r b' = (\lambda b)^r = (a^{-1}ba)^r = a^{-1}b^r a$$

$$(a_1^{-1}b_1)^2 = a_1^{-1}b_1 a_1^{-1}b_1 = a_1^{-1}(b_1 a_1^{-1})b_1 = a_1^{-1}(\mu a_1^{-1}b_1)b_1 = \mu a_1^{-2}b_1^2$$

$$(a_1^{-1}b_1)^r = \mu^{1+2+\ldots+(r-1)}a_1^{-r}b_1^r = \mu^{1+2+\ldots+(r-1)} = \mu^{r(r-1)/2}$$

This kind uses algebra well. The other kind occurs in the English text between the formulas. A proof is a boolean calculation, and in the current state of mathematics, as in the example, it is usually conducted mostly in natural language. Words like "consequently", "implying", "there is/are", "however", "thus", "hence", "since", "forces", "if...then", "in consequence of which", "from which we get", "whence", "would imply", "contrary to", "so that", "contradicting" suggest boolean operators; all the bookkeeping sentences suggest the structure of a boolean expression. A formal proof is a boolean calculation using boolean algebra; when we learn to use it well, it will enable us to go farther, faster, more succinctly, and with much greater certainty. But there is a great resistance in the mathematical community to formal proof, especially from those who are most expert at informal proof. They complain that formal proof loses meaning, replacing it with symbol manipulation. The current state of boolean algebra, not as an object of study but as a tool for use, is very much the same as number algebra was 5 centuries ago.

Traditional Terminology

Formal logic has developed a traditional terminology that its students are required to learn. There are terms which are said to have values. There are formulas, also known as propositions or sentences, which are said not to have values, but instead to be true or false. Operators $(+, -)$ join terms, while connectives $(\wedge, \vee)$ join formulas. Some terms are boolean, and they have the value *true* or *false*, but that's different from being true or false. It is difficult to find a definition of predicate, but it seems that a boolean term like $x=y$ stops being a boolean term and mysteriously starts being a predicate when we admit the possibility of using quantifiers $(\exists, \forall)$. Does $x+y$ stop being a number term if we admit the possibility of using summation and product (Σ, Π)? There are at least three different equal signs: $=$ for terms, and then $\Leftrightarrow$ and $\equiv$ for formulas and predicates, with one of them carrying an implicit universal quantification. We can even find a peculiar mixture in some textbooks, such as the following:

$$a+b = a \ \vee \ a+b = b$$

Here, a and b are boolean variables, $+$ is a boolean operator (disjunction), $a+b$ is a boolean term (having value *true* or *false*), $a+b = a$ and $a+b = b$ are formulas (so they are true or false), and finally $\vee$ is a logical connective.

Fortunately, in the past few decades there has been a noticeable shift toward erasing the distinction between being true or false and having the value *true* or *false* . It is a shift toward the calculational style of proof. But we have a long way to go yet, as I find whenever I ask my beginning students to prove something. If I ask them to prove something of the form $a=b$ they happily try to do so. If I ask them to prove something of the form $a{\lor}b$, they take an unwittingly constructivist interpretation, and suppose I want them to prove a or prove b ; they cannot understand the phrase "prove $a{\lor}b$ " otherwise, because "or" isn't a verb! Here is an even more blatant example: prove $a{\oplus}b$ where $\oplus$ is pronounced "exclusive or". They cannot even start because they need something that looks grammatically like a proposition or sentence. If I change it to either $(a{\oplus}b) \equiv true$ or to $a{\neq}b$ they are happy. The same lack of understanding can be found in many introductory programming texts where boolean expressions are not taught in their generality but as comparisons because comparisons have verbs!

> **while** *flag=true* **d** o *something*

Our dependence on natural language for the understanding of boolean expressions is a serious impediment.

Traditional Notations

Arithmetic notations are reasonably standard throughout the world. The expression

$$738 + 45 = 783$$

is recognized and understood by schoolchildren almost everywhere. But there are no standard boolean notations. Even the two boolean constants have no standard symbols. Symbols in use include

true	t	𝔱	T	1	0	1=1
false	f	𝔣	F	0	1	1=2

Quite often the boolean constants are written as 1 and 0 , with $+$ for disjunction, juxtaposition for conjunction, and perhaps $-$ for negation. With this notation, here are some laws.

$$x(y+z) = xy + xz$$
$$x + yz = (x+y)(x + z)$$
$$x + -x = 1$$
$$x(-x) = 0$$

The overwhelming reaction of algebraists is: it doesn't matter which symbols are used. Just introduce them, and get on with it. But to apply an algebra, one must recognize the patterns, matching laws to the expression at hand. The laws have to be familiar. The first law above coincides with number algebra, but the next three clash with number algebra. It takes an extra moment to think which algebra I am using as I apply a law. The logician

R.L. Goodstein [3] chose to use 0 and 1 the other way around, which slows me down a little more. A big change, like using + as a variable and x as an operator, would slow me down a lot. I think it matters even to algebraists because they too have to recognize patterns. To a larger public, the reuse of arithmetic symbols with different meanings is an insurmountable obstacle. And when we mix arithmetic and boolean operators in one expression, as we often do, it is impossible to disambiguate.

The most common notations for the two boolean constants found in programming languages and in programming textbooks seem to be *true* and *false* . I have two objections to these symbols. The first is that they are clumsy. Number algebra could never have advanced to its present state if we had to write out words for numbers.

seven three eight + four five = seven eight three

is just too clumsy, and so is

true ∧ false ∨ true ≡ true

Clumsiness may seem minor, but it can be the difference between success and failure in a calculus.

My second, and more serious, objection is that the words *true* and *false* confuse the algebra with an application. One of the primary applications of boolean algebra is to formalize reasoning, to determine the truth or falsity of some statements from the truth or falsity of others. In that application, we use one of the boolean values to represent an arbitrary true statement, and the other to represent an arbitrary false statement. So for that application, it seems reasonable to call them *true* and *false* . The algebra arose from that application, and it is so much identified with it that many people cannot separate them. But of course boolean expressions are useful for describing anything that comes in two kinds. We apply boolean algebra to circuits in which there are two voltages. We sometimes say that there are 0s and 1s in a computer's memory, or that there are *true*s and *false*s. Of course that's nonsense; there are neither 0s and 1s nor *true*s and *false*s in there; there are low and high voltages. We need symbols that can represent truth values and voltages equally well.

Boolean expressions have other applications, and the notations we choose should be equally appropriate for all of them. Computer programs are written to make computers work in some desired way. Before writing a program, a programmer should know which ways are desirable and which are not. That divides computer behavior into two kinds, and we can use boolean expressions to represent them. A boolean expression used this way is called a specification. We can specify anything, not just computer behavior, using boolean expressions. For example, if you would like to buy a table, then tables are of two kinds:

those you find desirable and are willing to buy, and those you find undesirable and are not willing to buy. So you can use a boolean expression as a table specification. Acceptable and unacceptable human behavior is specified by laws, and boolean expressions have been proposed as a better way than legal language for writing laws.

For symbols that are independent of the application, I propose the lattice symbols $\top$ and $\bot$, pronounced "top" and "bottom". Since boolean algebra is the mother of all lattices, I think it is appropriate, not a misuse of those symbols. They can equally well be used for true and false statements, for high and low voltages (power and ground), for satisfactory and unsatisfactory tables, for innocent and guilty behavior, or any other opposites.

We seem to be settling on the symbols $\wedge$ and $\vee$ for conjunction and disjunction, although they are still not universal. They are explained by the use of the words "and" and "or"; even when they are explained by their "truth tables" we remember them by the fact that $x \wedge y$ is $\top$ exactly when both x <u>and</u> y are $\top$, and similarly for $\vee$.

We are less settled on a symbol for implication. Symbols in use include

$$\rightarrow \quad \Rightarrow \quad \therefore \quad \supset$$

The usual explanation says it means "if then", followed by a discussion about the meaning of "if then". Apparently, people find it difficult to understand an implication whose antecedent is *false*. Such an implication is called "counter-factual". For example, Charles Navarre declared [4]: "If my mother had been a man, I'd be the king of France.". Some people are uneasy with the idea that *false* implies anything, so some researchers in Artificial Intelligence have proposed a new definition of implication. The following truth table shows both the old and new definitions.

a	b	old $a \Rightarrow b$	new $a \Rightarrow b$
true	*true*	*true*	*true*
true	*false*	*false*	*false*
false	*true*	*true*	*unknown*
false	*false*	*true*	*unknown*

where *unknown* is a third boolean value. When the antecedent is *false*, the result of the new kind of implication is *unknown*. This is argued to be more intuitive. I believe this proposal betrays a serious misunderstanding of the use of logic. When someone makes a statement, they are saying that the statement is *true*. Even if the statement is "if a then b" and a is known to be *false*, nonetheless we are being told that "if a then b" is *true*. It is the consequent b that is unknown. And that is represented perfectly by the old implication: there are two rows in which a is *false* and $a \Rightarrow b$ is *true*; on one of these rows, b is *true*, and on the other b is *false*.

There are two other symbols

————— ⊢

that mean something like implication. We are told that these are not implication, but you must admit that the distinction is subtle. The explanations sound similar: if the left (or top) side is a theorem, then the right (or bottom) side is too. And the Deduction Theorem says that ⊢ coincides with implication for a large part of logic. It is just such complications that keep logic out of use, even by mathematicians.

In case you think that confusion is just for beginners or philosophers, consider the explanation of implication in *Contemporary Logic Design*, 1994 [5]:

> "As an example, let's look at the following logic statement:
>
> IF the garage door is open
>
> AND the car is running
>
> THEN the car can be backed out of the garage
>
> It states that the conditions — the garage is open and the car is running — must be true before the car can be backed out. If either or both are false, then the car cannot be backed out. If we determine that the conditions are valid, then mathematical logic allows us to infer that the conclusion is valid."

Even a Berkeley electrical engineering professor can't get implication right.

Implication is best presented as an ordering, and for primary school students, all the explanation necessary can be carried by its name. If we are still calling the boolean values "true" and "false" then we can call it "falser than or equal to", or if you prefer, "as false as". It is easy to see that *false* is falser than or equal to *true* , and that *false* is falser than or equal to *false* . As we get into boolean expressions that use other types, this explanation remains good: $x>6$ is falser than or equal to $x>3$, as a sampling of evaluations illustrates. If we are calling the boolean values "top" and "bottom", we can say "lower than or equal to" for implication. With this new pronunciation and explanation, three other neglected boolean operators become familiar and usable; they are "higher than or equal to", "lower than", and "higher than". For lack of a name and symbol, the last two operators have been treated like shameful secrets, and shunned. Even implication has often been defined as a "secondary" operator in terms of the "primary" operators negation and disjunction:

$$(a{\Rightarrow}b) \equiv \neg a \vee b$$

This avoids the philosophical explanation, but it makes an unsupportable distinction between "primary" and "secondary" operators, and hides the fact that it is an ordering. If we present implication as an ordering, as I prefer, then we face the problem of how to use this ordering in the formalization of natural language reasoning. Philosophers and linguists can help, or indeed dominate in this difficult and important area. But we shouldn't let the complexities of this application of boolean algebra complicate the algebra, any more than we let the complexities of the banking industry complicate the definition of arithmetic.

That implication is the boolean ordering, with $\top$ and $\bot$ at the extremes, is not known to all who use boolean algebra. In the specification language Z, boolean expressions are used as specifications. Specification A refines specification B if all behavior satisfying A also satisfies B. Although increasing satisfaction is exactly the implication ordering, the designers of Z defined a different, complicated ordering for refinement where $\top$ is <u>not</u> satisfied by all computations, only by terminating computations, and $\bot$ <u>is</u> satisfied by some computations, namely nonterminating computations. When even they can get it wrong, logic is not well understood or used.

Symmetry and Duality

In choosing binary infix symbols, there is a simple principle that really helps our ability to calculate: we should choose symmetric symbols for symmetric operators, and asymmetric symbols for asymmetric operators, and choose the reverse of an asymmetric symbol for the reverse operator. The benefit is that we get a lot of laws for free: we can write an expression backwards and get an equivalent expression. For example, $x + y < z$ is equivalent to $z > y + x$. By this principle, the arithmetic symbols $+ \times < > =$ are well chosen but $-$ and $\neq$ are not. The boolean symbols $\wedge \vee \Rightarrow \Leftarrow \equiv \oplus$ are well chosen, but $\not\equiv$ is not.

Duality can be put to use, just like symmetry, if we use vertically symmetric symbols for self-dual operators, and vertically asymmetric operators for non-self-dual operators with the vertical reverse for their duals. The laws we get for free are: to negate an expression, turn it upside down. For example, $(\top \wedge -\bot) \vee \bot$ is the negation of $(\bot \vee -\top) \wedge \top$ if you allow me to use the vertically symmetric symbol $-$ for negation, which is self-dual. There are two points that require attention when using this rule. One is that parentheses may need to be added to maintain the precedence; but if we give dual operators the same precedence, there's no problem. The other point is that variables cannot be flipped, so we negate them instead (since flipping is equivalent to negation). The well-known example is deMorgan's law: to negate $a \vee b$, turn it upside down and negate the variables to get $-a \wedge -b$. By this principle, the symbols $\top \bot - \wedge \vee$ are well chosen, but $\Rightarrow \Leftarrow \equiv \not\equiv \oplus$ are not. By choosing better symbols we can let the symbols do some of the work of calculation, moving it to the level of visual processing.

Booleans and Numbers

I have long thought it was a mistake to identify booleans with numbers, even if just by the reuse of symbols. It's a type error. The C language continues the mistake. Thus we can write (1 && 1) + 1 and get 2. I have recently changed my mind. I now think the association —even the identification— between booleans and numbers is right, but not the association we are used to.

I like to prove things about the execution time of programs, and for that purpose I use a number system extended with an infinity (because that's the execution time of some programs). For some purposes I use integers extended with infinity, and for others I use reals extended with infinity. For a list of axioms of this arithmetic, please see the appendix; for more detail, please see [6]. Here I mention only that infinity is maximum $x \leqslant \infty$ and it absorbs additions $\infty + 1 = \infty$. For my purposes, I have not needed a lot of infinite cardinalities; a single infinity is enough. The association I want to make between booleans and numbers is the following.

	boolean		number	
top	$\top$	∞		infinity
bottom	$\bot$	$-\infty$		minus infinity
negation	$\neg$	$-$		negation
conjunction	$\wedge$	$\downarrow$		minimum
disjunction	$\vee$	$\uparrow$		maximum
"nand"	$\Uparrow$	$\updownarrow$		negation of minimum
"nor"	$\Downarrow$	$\updownarrow$		negation of maximum
implication	$\Rightarrow$	$\leqslant$		order
reverse implication	$\Leftarrow$	$\geqslant$		reverse order
strict implication	$\triangleright$	$<$		strict order
strict reverse implication	$\triangleleft$	$>$		strict reverse order
equivalence	$\equiv$	$=$		equality
exclusive or	$\oplus$	$\neq$		inequality

I have temporarily invented a few symbols to fill in some gaps. The remaining three unary operators and six binary operators are degenerate, so I have not included them. With this association, all number laws employing only these operators correspond to boolean laws. For example,

boolean law	number law
$\top \equiv \neg\bot$	$\infty = --\infty$
$a \equiv \neg\neg a$	$x = --x$
$a \lor \top \equiv \top$	$x \uparrow \infty = \infty$
$a \land \bot \equiv \bot$	$x \downarrow -\infty = -\infty$
$a \lor \bot \equiv a$	$x \uparrow -\infty = x$
$a \land \top \equiv a$	$x \downarrow \infty = x$
$a \Rightarrow \top$	$x \leq \infty$
$\bot \Rightarrow a$	$-\infty \leq x$
$a \lor (b \land c) \equiv (a \lor b) \land (a \lor c)$	$x \uparrow (y \downarrow z) = (x \uparrow y) \downarrow (x \uparrow z)$
$a \land (b \lor c) \equiv (a \land b) \lor (a \land c)$	$x \downarrow (y \uparrow z) = (x \downarrow y) \uparrow (x \downarrow z)$
$a \lor b \equiv \neg(\neg a \land \neg b)$	$x \uparrow y = -(-x \downarrow -y)$
$a \land b \equiv \neg(\neg a \lor \neg b)$	$x \downarrow y = -(-x \uparrow -y)$

There are, however, boolean laws that do not correspond to number laws. For example,

boolean law	number non-law
$\top$	∞
$\neg\bot$	$--\infty$
$a \lor \neg a \equiv \top$	$x \uparrow -x = \infty$
$a \land \neg a \equiv \bot$	$x \downarrow -x = -\infty$
$(\top \Rightarrow a) \equiv a$	$(\infty \leq x) = x$
$(\top \equiv a) \equiv a$	$(\infty = x) = x$

Number algebra has developed by the desire to solve equations, or more generally, to solve boolean expressions. This has resulted in an increasing sequence of domains, from naturals to integers to rationals to reals to complex numbers. As we gain solutions, we lose laws.

small domain	$\longleftrightarrow$	large domain
more laws	$\longleftrightarrow$	fewer laws
fewer solutions	$\longleftrightarrow$	more solutions

This is because a law is essentially a universal quantification, and a boolean expression to be solved is essentially an existential quantification.

law: $\forall$*variables*: *domains*· *boolean expression*

solution: $\exists$*variables*: *domains*· *boolean expression*

As the domain of an operation or function grows, we do not change its symbol; addition is still denoted $+$ as we go from naturals to complex numbers. I will not argue whether the naturals are a subset of the complex numbers or just isomorphic to a subset; for me the question has no meaning. But I do argue that it is important to use the same notation for natural 1 and complex 1 because they behave the same way, and for natural + and complex + because they behave the same way on their common domain. To be more precise, all laws of complex arithmetic that can be interpreted over the naturals are laws of natural arithmetic, and all equations (or more generally, boolean expressions) over the naturals retain the same solutions over the complex numbers. The reason we must use the same symbols is so that we do not have to relearn all the laws and solutions as we enlarge or shrink the domain.

I have been hammering on a point that I expect is not contentious. If I have your agreement, then you must conclude, as I must, that the symbols of boolean algebra and arithmetic must be unified. The question whether boolean is a different type from number is no more relevant than the question whether natural and integer are different types. What's important is that laws and solutions are learned once, in a unified system, not twice in conflicting systems. And that matters both to professional mathematicians who must apply laws and solve, and to primary school students who must struggle to learn what will be useful to them.

Unified Algebra

Here is my proposal for the symbols of a unified algebra.

		unified
top	$\top$	infinity
bottom	$\bot$	minus infinity
negation	$-$	negation
conjunction	$\wedge$	minimum
disjunction	$\vee$	maximum
"nand"	$\triangle$	negation of minimum
"nor"	$\triangledown$	negation of maximum
implication	$\leq$	order
reverse implication	$\geq$	reverse order
strict implication	$<$	strict order
strict reverse implication	$>$	strict reverse order
equivalence	$=$	equality
exclusive or	$\neq$	inequality

The symbols $- \leq \geq < > =$ are world-wide standards, used by school children in all countries, so I dare not suggest any change to them. The symbol $\neq$ for inequality is the next best known, but I have dared to stand up the slash so that all symmetric operators have symmetric symbols and all asymmetric operators have asymmetric symbols. (Although it was not a consideration, $\neq$ also looks more like $\oplus$.) There are no standard symbols for minimum and maximum, so I have used the boolean conjunction and disjunction symbols. The "nand" symbol is a combination of the "not" and "and" symbols, and similarly for "nor". Duality has been sacrificed to standards; the pair $\leqslant$ $<$ are duals, so they ought to be vertical reflections of each other; similarly the pair $\geqslant$ $>$, and also $=$ $\neq$. Since we now have a unified boolean and number algebra, I might mention that addition and subtraction are self-dual, and happily $+$ and $-$ are vertically symmetric; multiplication is not self-dual, but $\times$ is unfortunately vertically symmetric.

Having unified the symbols, I suppose we should also unify the terminology. I vote for the number terminology in the right column, except that I prefer to call $\top$ and $\bot$ "top" and "bottom".

In the unified algebra, the fact that $x=-x$ has no boolean solution but does have an integer solution is no more bothersome than that $x^2=2$ has no integer solution but does have a real solution. The fact that $x \neq -x$ is a boolean law but not an integer law is no more bothersome than that $x^2 \neq 2$ is an integer law but not a real law.

Quantifiers

I am told that the symbols $\forall$ and $\exists$ send engineers running, and I don't blame them. For me, the problem with these symbols is that they are associated with the words "all" and "exist". I am truly sorry the word "existence" was ever used in mathematics. We can certainly apply mathematics to problems concerning the existence of something in the application area, and then I once again leave it to philosophers or linguists to determine how best to apply it, and how well the mathematical expressions can represent the existence of some application objects. But I don't want any debate about existence within mathematics; to me, mathematical existence is meaningless.

The nicest, simplest presentation of quantifiers, perhaps due to Curry, begins with the treatment of functions due to Church. I write a function, or local scope, according to the following example:

$\langle n: nat \cdot n+1 \rangle$

Originally, instead of angle brackets, Church used a long hat over the expression to denote the scope of the variable. Due to the obvious typesetting difficulty, Church was persuaded to write the hat in front of the expression rather than over it, and the most similar available character was λ ; thus the lambda calculus was born. Following van de Snepscheut, I have returned to the original spirit, and use angle brackets to delimit scope. Next, I want to get rid of the idea that all possible variables (infinitely many of them) already "exist", and the function notation (λ or $\langle \rangle$) is said to "bind" variables, and any variable that is not bound remains "free". I prefer the programmer's terminology of "local" and "global" variables. Variables do not automatically "exist"; they are introduced (rather than bound) by the function notation.

A local variable can be instantiated, in other words a function can be applied to an argument, but at the moment I am interested in applying operators to functions. If the body of a function is a number expression, then we can apply $+$ to obtain the sum of the function results. For example,

$$+\langle n: nat \cdot 1/2^n \rangle$$

There is no syntactic ambiguity caused by this use of $+$, so no need to employ another symbol Σ for addition. The introduction of the dummy variable and its domain are exactly the job of the function notation, so no need to employ another notation for variable introduction with quantifiers. And the notation generalizes to other binary associative symmetric operators, such as

$$\times\langle n: nat \cdot 1/2^n \rangle$$
$$\wedge\langle n: nat \cdot n>5 \rangle$$
$$\vee\langle n: nat \cdot n>5 \rangle$$

There are no scary symbols. We talk about a maximum, not existence, because it <u>is</u> a maximum, not existence. By applying $=$ and $\neq$ to functions we obtain the two independent parity quantifiers. Even set formation, limits, and integrals can be treated this way.

The sum of two rationals is rational; the sum of infinitely many rationals may not be rational. Nonetheless, we continue to use the word "sum" and symbol $+$. Similarly, I see no need to switch teminology from "maximum" to "least upper bound" as we generalize $\vee$ from two operands to infinitely many; we just have to learn that the maximum of a set may not be in the set.

If function f has domain D , then $f = \langle x: D \cdot fx \rangle$, so quantifications traditionally written

$$\Sigma x: D \cdot fx \qquad\qquad \forall x: D \cdot Px$$

which we can now write as

$$+\langle x: D \cdot fx \rangle \qquad\qquad \wedge\langle x: D \cdot Px \rangle$$

can be written even more succinctly as

$$+f \qquad\qquad \wedge P$$

Using juxtaposition for composition, deMorgan's laws

$$\neg(\forall x: D \cdot Px) \equiv (\exists x: D \cdot \neg Px) \qquad \neg(\exists x: D \cdot Px) \equiv (\forall x: D \cdot \neg Px)$$

become

$$-\wedge P = \vee - P \qquad\qquad -\vee P = \wedge - P$$

or even more succinctly

$$(-\wedge) = (\vee-) \qquad\qquad (-\vee) = (\wedge-)$$

The Specialization and Generalization laws say that if $y: D$,

$$(\forall x: D \cdot Px) \Rightarrow Py \qquad\qquad Py \Rightarrow (\exists x: D \cdot Px)$$

They now become

$$\wedge P \leqslant Py \qquad\qquad Py \leqslant \vee P$$

which say that the minimum item is less than or equal to any item, and any item is less than or equal to the maximum item. These laws hold for all numbers, not just for the boolean subset.

To define quantifiers formally, we have to say, for each domain constructor, how they apply to functions with such domains. The axioms follow a pattern:

$$\wedge \langle x: \{\,\} \cdot e \rangle = \mathsf{T}$$
$$\wedge \langle x: \{y\} \cdot e \rangle = \langle x: \{y\} \cdot e \rangle \, y$$
$$\wedge \langle x: A \cup B \cdot e \rangle = \wedge \langle x: A \cdot e \rangle \wedge \wedge \langle x: B \cdot e \rangle$$

$$\vee \langle x: \{\,\} \cdot e \rangle = \bot$$
$$\vee \langle x: \{y\} \cdot e \rangle = \langle x: \{y\} \cdot e \rangle \, y$$
$$\vee \langle x: A \cup B \cdot e \rangle = \vee \langle x: A \cdot e \rangle \vee \vee \langle x: B \cdot e \rangle$$

$$+ \langle x: \{\,\} \cdot e \rangle = 0$$
$$+ \langle x: \{y\} \cdot e \rangle = \langle x: \{y\} \cdot e \rangle \, y$$
$$+ \langle x: A \cup B \cdot e \rangle + + \langle x: A \cap B \cdot e \rangle = + \langle v: A \cdot e \rangle + + \langle v: B \cdot e \rangle$$

$$\times \langle x: \{\,\} \cdot e \rangle = 1$$
$$\times \langle x: \{y\} \cdot e \rangle = \langle x: \{y\} \cdot e \rangle \, y$$
$$\times \langle x: A \cup B \cdot e \rangle \times \times \langle x: A \cap B \cdot e \rangle = \times \langle x: A \cdot e \rangle \times \times \langle x: B \cdot e \rangle$$

If there are other domain constructors, there are other axioms. A domain can even be defined by saying how a quantifier applies to functions with that domain. For example, *nat* can be defined by

$$\wedge \langle x: nat \cdot Px \rangle = P0 \wedge \wedge \langle x: nat \cdot Px \leqslant P(x+1) \rangle$$

or dually (renaming P as its negation)

$$\vee \langle x: nat \cdot Px \rangle = P0 \vee \vee \langle x: nat \cdot Px < P(x+1) \rangle$$

Those who dislike formal definitions may have a desire to say in natural language how $\wedge$ applies to all boolean functions, regardless of how the domain was constructed. They may want to say that the result is $\top$ exactly when all range elements are $\top$. The word "all" sounds clear and unambiguous, but we have enough experience to know that it is far from clear and unambiguous. (Are so-called "undefined" range elements included?) Natural language definitions lead to a lot of arguments, and I have lost patience with them. Only a formal definition, equivalent to an automated theorem prover, is clear and unambiguous.

Here's an interesting experiment: ask a colleague if $(\forall x \cdot Px) \Rightarrow (\exists y \cdot Qy)$ is equivalent to $\exists x \cdot \exists y \cdot (Px \Rightarrow Qy)$ and then listen to their efforts to find the answer. They probably don't find it obvious. Those who reason informally say things like "suppose all x have property P", and "suppose some y has property Q". They are led into case analyses by treating $\forall$ and $\exists$ as abbreviations for "for all" and "there exists" (as they originally were). Of the very few who reason formally, most don't know many laws; perhaps they start by getting rid of the implications in favor of $\neg$ and $\vee$, then use deMorgan's laws. Let me rewrite the question in the new notations.

$$(\wedge P \le \vee Q) \;=\; \vee\langle x \cdot \vee\langle y \cdot Px \le Qy \rangle\rangle$$

On the left, it says the minimum P is at most the maximum Q. On the right it says that some P is at most some Q. Now it's more obviously a theorem, not just for booleans but for all numbers. To prove it, one should know (or prove) laws like

$$(\wedge P \le q) \;=\; \vee\langle x \cdot Px \le qy \rangle$$

(the minimum P is less than or equal to q if and only if some P is less than or equal to q), and dually

$$(p \le \vee Q) \;=\; \vee\langle y \cdot p \le Qy \rangle$$

(p is less than or equal to the maximum Q if and only if p is less than or equal to some Q). The proof is then

$$\quad\quad \vee\langle x \cdot \vee\langle y \cdot Px \le Qy \rangle\rangle$$
$$=\quad \vee\langle x \cdot Px \le \vee Q \rangle$$
$$=\quad (\wedge P \le \vee Q)$$

It is not the presence of quantifiers that moves us up from zero-order logic to first-order logic, but the presence of functions, with domains restricted to zero-order expressions. With unrestricted domains, we move up again to higher-order logic. Logicians seem to like to settle the question "which logic are we in" before they do any reasoning. Can you imagine asking a working mathematician or engineer to decide whether they will be using functions, and if so, what will be their domains, before beginning their work? The answer would be: I'll use whatever I need when I need it.

Metalogic

Almost always, number algebra is presented without a metanotation, while logic is presented with one. The distinction between the metanotation and the object notation is not easily appreciated by students, or by many teachers.

Logicians study logic. There are no applied logicians who use logic to study something else. In the study of logic, at or near the beginning, logicians present the very important symbol $\vdash$ to represent theoremhood. I ask you to put yourself in the place of a beginning student. This symbol is applied to a boolean expression just like the boolean operators; but we know all the boolean operators and this isn't one of them. To say that it is a "meta-operator" just labels it, and doesn't explain it. Saying that it applies to the form, rather than the meaning, is confusing too, since the entire point of the algebra is to enable us to work with the form and ignore the meaning. In my opinion, the use of meta-level operators is unnecessary and ill-conceived.

To apply an operator to the form of an expression, we do not need any new kind of operator. Rather, we need to do exactly what Gödel did when he encoded expressions, but we can use a better encoding. We need to do exactly what programmers do: distinguish program from data. One person's program may be a compiler writer's data, but when it is data, it is a character string. We should apply $\vdash$ to character strings. The character string "$a \vee -a$" can be used as a code for the expression $a \vee -a$. We define $\vdash s$ according to the structure of boolean expressions so that $\vdash s$ is a theorem when the boolean expression represented by string s is a theorem. We could also define another operator $\dashv$ that serves a dual role to $\vdash$: it applies to character strings so that $\dashv s$ is an antitheorem when the boolean expression represented by string s is an antitheorem. By "antitheorem" I mean those boolean expressions that can be simplified (proven equal) to $\bot$. In some logics, those having negation and an appropriate proof rule, "antitheorem" means "negation of a theorem", but not in all. It deserves a name and symbol just as much as $\bot$ does. It's surprising that the dual of theorem has not been invented before.

I propose that logicians can improve metalogic in another way, by taking another lesson from programming. Instead of $\vdash$ and $\dashv$, we need only one operator to serve both purposes. It is called an interpreter. I want $\mathcal{I}\, s$ to be a theorem if and only if s represents a theorem, and an antitheorem if and only if s represents an antitheorem. It is related to $\vdash$ and $\dashv$ by the two implications.

$$\vdash s \ \leqslant \ \mathcal{I}\, s \ \leqslant \ -\dashv s$$

In fact, if we have defined $\vdash$ and $\dashv$, those implications define $\mathcal{I}$. But I want $\mathcal{I}$ to replace ⊢ and ⊣ so I shall instead define it by showing how it applies to every form of boolean expression. Here is the beginning of its definition.

$$\mathbf{I}\text{``T''} = \text{T}$$
$$\mathbf{I}\text{``}\perp\text{''} = \perp$$
$$\mathbf{I}(\text{``--''}\,s) = -\mathbf{I}\,s$$
$$\mathbf{I}(s\,\text{``}\wedge\text{''}\,t) = \mathbf{I}\,s \wedge \mathbf{I}\,t$$
$$\mathbf{I}(s\,\text{``}\vee\text{''}\,t) = \mathbf{I}\,s \vee \mathbf{I}\,t$$

And so on. In a vague sense $\mathbf{I}$ acts as the inverse of quotation marks; it "unquotes" its operand. That is what an interpreter does: it turns passive data into active program. It is a familiar fact to programmers that we can write an interpreter for a language in that same language, and that is just what we are doing here. Interpreting (unquoting) is exactly what logicians call Tarskian semantics. In summary, an interpreter is a better version of ⊢, and strings make meta-level operators unnecessary.

Proof Rules

You cannot learn a programming language by reading an interpreter for it written in that same language. And you cannot learn logic, or a logic, by reading an interpreter for it written in logic. Not only is it inscrutable to a novice, but also it may be subject to more than one interpretation. We can, of course, present one formalism with the aid of another, a metanotation. But my goal is to teach boolean algebra to a wide audience, and for that purpose I do not think it is profitable to require them to learn another formalism first. I think it should be presented as number algebra is presented, with a little natural language and a lot of axioms, because axioms don't use any extra notations.

Here are the proof rules I am using. The rules place boolean expressions into two classes: theorems and antitheorems. In an incomplete logic, some boolean expressions will remain unclassified. Note that the rules never mention any boolean operators.

Axiom Rule   If a boolean expression is an axiom, then it is a theorem. If a boolean expression is an antiaxiom, then it is an antitheorem.

Evaluation Rule   If all the boolean subexpressions of a boolean expression are classified, then it is classified according to the evaluation tables (truth tables).

Completion Rule	If a boolean expression contains unclassified boolean subexpressions, and all ways of classifying them place it in the same class, then it is in that class.
Consistency Rule	If a classified boolean expression contains boolean subexpressions, and exactly one way of classifying them is consistent, then they are classified that way.
Instance Rule	If a boolean expression is classified, then all its instances have that same classification.

There can be both axioms and antiaxioms; $\top$ is an axiom and $\bot$ is an antiaxiom. If the logic includes both negation and the Consistency Rule, we can dispense with the words "antiaxiom" and "antitheorem", but I suggest we keep them for the sake of duality. The boolean operators all enter together with equal status via the Evaluation Rule. The Completion Rule includes, as a special case, that $a \vee \neg a$ is a theorem; constructivists will omit this rule. Consistency means that no boolean expression is classified both as a theorem and as an antitheorem; the Consistency Rule includes modus ponens as a special case. The Instance Rule refers to expressions obtained by replacing variables with expressions. In addition to these rules, we need only axioms (and perhaps antiaxioms), and the usual substitution rules.

Terms of Honor

My final comment concerns mathematical terminology intended to honor mathematicians. In some parts of mathematics it is standard: Lie algebra, Stone algebra, Jordan decomposition, Cayley transform, Hilbert space, Banach space, Hausdorff space, Borel measure, Lebesgue integration, Fredholm index, and so on. It is well known that the person so honored is sometimes the wrong person; often it is only one of many who equally deserve to have their names attached to the idea. I suspect that sometimes the intention is not so much to honor a person as to use the person's prestige to lend respectability to a subject. Even when the intention is to honor, the effect is to obscure and make the mathematics forbidding and inaccessible. It may be argued that this is good, keeping the uninitiated from thinking they understand when they don't. I know what nand and nor are, but I forget which is the Scheffer stroke and which the Pierce arrow. To say that an operator is symmetric or commutative is much more descriptive and understandable than calling it Abelean. DeMorgan's laws would be better named duality laws. We who are used to the terms forget what a barrier they pose to beginners.

The term "boolean algebra" honors George Boole. It is popularly thought that the word "algebra" honors someone, but according to scholars, that's a myth; it comes from an arabic word meaning "the reintegration and reunion of broken parts". In any case, the word is now standard, known by average people everywhere. I revere George Boole and I want to honor him. The greatest honor I can think of is to make the algebra that he created a well known and well used tool, and to do that we might have to remove his name from it, and give it a more descriptive and accessible name, like "binary algebra".

Conclusions

Logic has been well studied and is now well understood, but it is not well used. Programmers learn that logic is a foundation of programming, but they don't often use it to program. Mathematicians study about logic, but they don't often use it in their proofs. Logic is a tool, like a knife. People have looked at it from every angle; they've described how it works at great length; now it's time to pick it up and use it. To use logic well, one must learn it early, and practice a lot. Fancy versions of logic, such as three-valued logic, temporal logic, and metalogic, can be left to university study, but there is a simple basic algebra that can be taught early and used widely.

Number algebra is used by scientists and engineers everywhere. It is used by economists and architects. It is taught first to 6-year olds, very concretely as addition and subtraction of numbers. Then variables and equations are introduced, and always the applications are emphasized. As a result of that early and long education, scientists and engineers and mathematicians are comfortable with it. Boolean algebra, or logic, can be equally useful if it is taught the same way. At present, it is not in a good state for presentation to a wide audience. We need to simplify the terminology, choose some good symbols, adopt the view that proof is calculation, detach it from its dominant application in which the boolean values represent true and false statements, free it from philosophy and explain it as algebra.

There is a small advantage to choosing uniquely boolean symbols: we can give them a precedence.after the arithmetic operators, which reduces the need for parentheses. On the other hand, there is a large advantage to uniting boolean and number symbols in the way I have suggested: the laws and solutions are familiar and can be interpreted either as booleans or numbers. In addition, by placing booleans in the same context as numbers, we move quickly away from philosophical explanations, and we are less likely to introduce strange kinds of implication or strange kinds of logic. The fact that the booleans can be embedded in the extended integers just as smoothly as the integers are embedded in the rationals seems a compelling reason to do so.

Quantifiers can be simplified, made uniform, and generalized by treating them as operators on functions. We should stop speaking about "existence", and speak instead about the maximum of a function. Similarly, we should stop speaking about "all", and speak instead about the minimum of a function.

An interpreter serves the same purpose as the meta-level theoremhood operator with the added advantage that it gives antitheoremhood as well as theoremhood. And by applying it to strings, we don't need to introduce a separate meta-level of operators. Metalogic is an advanced topic, not a good introduction to logic for those who are new to the subject.

Appendix

Let d be a sequence of (zero or more) digits, let x, y, and z be any expressions. Then the following axioms are a unified boolean and number theory. The transitive operators $=\ <\ \leq$ are used in a continued (conjunctional) syntax. In addition to these axioms, we need proof rules (presented earlier), substitution rules, and evaluation tables (truth tables). Minimality is not claimed.

$$\top$$
$$-\bot$$

$x = x$	reflexivity
$(x=y) = (y=x)$	symmetry
$(x=y) \wedge (y=z) \leq (x=z)$	transitivity
$(x \neq y) = -(x=y)$	
$-(x<x)$	irreflexivity
$-((x<y) \wedge (y<x))$	antisymmetry
$(x<y) \wedge (y<z) \leq (x<z)$	transitivity
$-((x<y) \wedge (x=y))$	exclusivity
$(x \leq y) = (x<y) \vee (x=y)$	
$(x>y) = (y<x)$	
$(x \geq y) = (y \leq x)$	
$(x<y) \vee (x=y) \vee (x>y)$	totality, trichotomy
$d0+1 = d1$	counting
$d1+1 = d2$	counting
$d2+1 = d3$	counting
$d3+1 = d4$	counting
$d4+1 = d5$	counting
$d5+1 = d6$	counting

$d6+1 = d7$ — counting

$d7+1 = d8$ — counting

$d8+1 = d9$ — counting

$d9+1 = (d+1)0$ — counting

$+x = x$ — identity

$x+0 = x$ — identity

$x+y = y+x$ — symmetry

$x+(y+z) = (x+y)+z$ — associativity

$(\bot < x < \top) \leqslant ((x+y = x+z) = (y=z))$ — cancellation

$--x = x$ — self-inverse

$-(x+y) = -x + -y$ — distributivity

$-(x \times y) = -x \times y$ — semi-distributivity

$x-y = x + -y$

$(\bot < x < \top) \leqslant (x-x = 0)$ — inverse

$(\bot < y < \top) \leqslant (x - y + y = x)$ — inverse

$(\bot < x < \top) \leqslant (x \times 0 = 0)$ — base

$x \times 1 = x$ — identity

$x \times y = y \times x$ — symmetry

$x \times (y+z) = x \times y + x \times z$ — distributivity

$x \times (y \times z) = (x \times y) \times z$ — associativity

$(\bot < x < \top) \wedge (x \neq 0) \leqslant ((x \times y = x \times z) = (y=z))$ — cancellation

$(\bot < y < \top) \wedge (y \neq 0) \leqslant (x/y \times y = x)$ — inverse

$(\bot < x < \top) \leqslant (x^0 = 1)$ — base

$x^1 = x$ — identity

$x^{y+z} = x^y \times x^z$

$x^{y \times z} = (x^y)^z$

$\bot < 0 < 1 < \top$ — direction

$(\bot < x < \top) \leqslant ((x+y < x+z) = (y<z))$ — cancellation, translation

$(0 < x < \top) \leqslant ((x \times y < x \times z) = (y<z))$ — cancellation, scale

$(x<y) = (-y<-x)$ — reflection

$\bot \leqslant x \leqslant \top$ — extremes

$\top+1 = \top$ — additive absorption

$(0<x) \leqslant (x \times \top = \top)$ — multiplicative absorption

$(0<x) \leqslant (x/0 = \top)$

$(\bot < x < \top) \leqslant (x/\top = 0)$

Acknowledgment

Theo Norvell provided the Navarre quotation and the example from the Katz text.

References

[0]   Unfortunately, 500 year old algebra texts are hard to find. This is not a quotation, but my own creation. I think it is representative of the work of the time.

[1]   Robert Recorde: *the Whetstone of Witte*, London 1557, reprinted by Da Capo Press Amsterdam 1969

[2]   I.N. Herstein: *Topics in Algebra*, Blaisdell 1964 p.323

[3]   R.L. Goodstein: *Development of Mathematical Logic*, Springer-Verlag 1971

[4]   quoted in Barbara W. Tuchman: *a Distant Mirrror: the Calamitous Fourteenth Century*, Knopf 1978

[5]   Randy H. Katz: *Contemporary Logic Design*, Benjamin Cummings 1994 p.10

[6]   E.C.R. Hehner: *a Practical Theory of Programming*, Springer-Verlag 1993

Proving Existential Termination of Normal Logic Programs

Massimo Marchiori

Dept. of Pure and Applied Mathematics, University of Padova
Via Belzoni 7, 35131 Padova, Italy
max@hilbert.math.unipd.it

Abstract. The most important *open problem* in the study of termination for logic programs is that of *existential termination*. In this paper we present a powerful transformational methodology that provides necessary (and, under some conditions, sufficient) criteria for existential termination. The followed approach is to develop a suitable transformation from logic programs to Term Rewriting Systems (TRSs), such that proving termination of the obtained TRS implies existential termination of the original logic program. Thus, all the extensive amount of work on termination for TRSs can be automatically used in the logic programming setting. Moreover, the approach is also able to cope with the dual notion of universal termination: in fact, a whole spectrum of termination properties, said *k*-termination, is investigated, of which universal and existential termination are the extremes. Also, a satisfactory treatment to the problem of termination for logic programming with *negation* is achieved. This way we provide a unique, uniform approach covering all these different notions of termination.

1 Introduction

The study of program termination is a fundamental topic in computer science. In the field of logic programming, however, the power of the paradigm, together with the way in which it is implemented (e.g. in Prolog), make the study of termination extremely hard. Two kinds of termination are distinguished for logic programs: existential and universal.

The key property of *existential termination* is the natural notion of termination from the programmer's viewpoint: if the program is run with an input, it must stop (finding a solution to the problem or saying there are not solutions).

Unfortunately, existential termination is still the most important *open problem* (see [13]) in the field of termination for logic programs. Very few works so far tried to shed some light on the problem, namely [9, 18, 6], without giving satisfactory results (cf. [13]): all of them give results of expressibility nature, saying that the Prolog operational semantics can be in principle codified into some formalism, like first-order logic for instance, and thus termination and other properties could be studied by trying to use some kind of inductive reasoning or the like.

On the other hand, the 'dual' notion of *universal termination* is the much stronger property that says a program must terminate not only existentially, but *for every* further invocation, by the user, of backtracking, and moreover that the number of solutions to the problem must be finite.

This property has been the subject of a great number of works (cf. [13]) but, due to the intrinsic complexity of the problem, even in this much more restrictive case, most of the works are only of theoretical nature and extremely difficult to implement.

A noticeable exception is given by the so-called 'transformational approach' started by Rao, Kapur and Shyamasundar in [26] and further investigated in [19, 1, 8, 23, 5], consisting in giving a transformation from logic programs into TRSs such that to prove the universal termination of a logic program it suffices to prove the termination of the transformed term rewriting system.

This transformational approach has several advantages. The main one is that for TRSs the study of termination, in sharp contrast to the logic programming case, is much easier, being available plenty of powerful criteria and many automatic or semi-automatic implementations to test termination: for instance path orderings, polynomial orderings, semantic labelling, general path orderings and many others (see e.g. [15, 17, 16]). The reader is referred to [27] for a nice application of the transformational approach to compiler verification.

Another advantage of this approach is that giving such a translation we do not obtain only *one* criterion but a bunch of: every (present or future) criterion of termination for TRSs becomes automatically a criterion for logic programs

In this paper, we address the open problem of existential termination by developing a suitable powerful transformational approach able to cope with this fundamental property. This way, we also gain all the aforementioned benefits proper of this kind of approach.

In fact, we will tackle a much more general problem, introducing and studying the more expressive property of *k-termination*: roughly speaking, given an ordinal k a program k-terminates if its first k derivations are finite. k-termination generalizes both existential and universal termination (corresponding respectively to 1-termination and $\omega + 1$-termination), providing a hierarchy of intermediate properties.

We also show how the presented method can cope without difficulties even with the corresponding *strong* versions of termination (cf. [13]), i.e. termination not only w.r.t. one input but w.r.t. all the possible inputs.

This way, we provide a unique, *uniform* way to cope with all these different notions of termination.

Moreover, we do not limit to definite logic programming, but we cover also termination of *normal logic programming*, i.e. programs with the important feature of *negation*, as implemented in Prolog. The primary importance of negation for applications in non-monotonic reasoning and in artificial intelligence is well-known. However, even in the restricted ambit of universal termination a fully satisfactory treatment of termination of programs with negation has been so far out of scope, since the problem is tightly related to existential termination: for instance, a program universally terminates w.r.t. a ground literal *not A* if and only if it existentially terminates w.r.t. A.

The analysis is taken even further: it is carefully studied to what extent we get not only *sufficient* criteria for all these kinds of termination, but even *necessary* ones, thus allowing to formally state what is the 'minimum power' of the method.

So, for instance, the presented method, when restricted to universal termination only, is *by far* more powerful than all the other works based on the transformational approach.

Another point is that, unlike the other works based on the transformational approach, here we followed a modular technique: Instead of presenting a very complicated transformation for a main class of logic programs, we built the transformation as a composition of two smaller submodules. This way we split the complexity of a big transformation into a composition of two easier sub-transformations, making the analysis easier; also, subsequent improvements can be obtained separately enhancing one of the submodules, without having to rebuild a whole transformation from the scratch.

The work is organized as follows. First, we develop a transformation to TRSs for a core subclass of logic programs, that of *Regularly Typed* programs (RT for short). This core transformation is proven to completely preserve k-termination, hence giving a *necessary and sufficient* criterion for k-termination (or, better, plenty of them, for what we said earlier). We then show how this subclass can be extended to the bigger class of *Safely Typed* programs (ST), via a suitable transformation (which is of independent interest) from ST logic programs to RT logic programs. Then, all the results are extended to normal logic programming, thus covering *negation*. Finally, an accurate comparison with the related work is presented.

2 Preliminaries

We assume basic knowledge of logic programming and term rewriting systems. For standard logic programming terminology, we will mainly follow [21], whilst for TRSs we use standard notations from [17]. Logic programs will be considered as executed with leftmost selection rule and depth-first search rule, that is the standard way in which logic programming is implemented (for example, in Prolog). Also, we will consider in full generality conditions that can constrain both the logic program and the goal: so, for notational convenience we will talk by abuse of a *class of logic programs* meaning a collection both of logic programs and of goals.

2.1 Notation

We assume that the logic program is written using the (infinite) set of variables VAR and a signature $\Sigma = \{p_0, p_1, ..; f_0, f_1, ..\}$ where p_i are the predicate symbols and f_i the function symbols (constants are nullary functions). Usually, the employed Σ will be just the minimal signature in which the considered logic program can be written, hence a finite one.

Given a substitution ϑ, $Dom(\vartheta)$ and $Ran(\vartheta)$ indicates, respectively, its domain and range; ϑ^{-1} denotes its inverse mapping, and $\vartheta|_V$ its restriction to some set of variables V. Composition of two functions f and g will be indicated with $f \circ g$. Sequences of terms will be written in vectorial notation (e.g. $\bar{t}$). Sequences in formulae should be seen just as abbreviations: for instance, $[\bar{t}]$, with $\bar{t} = t_1, .., t_m$, denotes the string $[t_1, .., t_m]$. Accordingly, given two sequences $\bar{s} = s_1, .., s_n$ and $\bar{t} = t_1, .., t_m$, $\bar{s}, \bar{t}$ stands for the sequence $s_1, .., s_n, t_1, .., t_m$.

Given a family S of objects (terms, atoms, etc.), Var(S) is the set of all the variables contained in it; moreover, S is said to be *linear* if no variable occurs more than once in it. For every term (or sequence) t, a *linearization* of t (via σ) is a linear term (sequence) t' such that, for some substitution σ, $t'\sigma = t$, $Dom(\sigma) = \text{Var}(t')$, Var($t'$) $\cap$ Var(t) $= \emptyset$, and $Ran(\sigma) \subseteq$ VAR (i.e., we simply replace repeated variables with different fresh ones to make the term linear: for instance, if $t = f(X, g(X, Y))$ we could take $t' = f(Z, g(V, W))$ and $\sigma = \{Z/X, V/X, W/Y\}$).

To make formulae more readable, we will sometimes omit brackets from the argument of unary functions (e.g. $f(g(X))$ may be written fgX). Also, given a sequence $\bar{t} = t_0, .., t_n$ and a unary function f, we use $f\bar{t}$ as a shorthand for $f(t_0), .., f(t_n)$.

2.2 Goals as Clauses

Being goals and clauses different objects, when describing a class of logic programs one usually has to provide different descriptions both for the goal and for the clauses. In this paper we will overcome this difficulty using the following definition:

Definition 2.1 A class $\mathcal{P}$ is said *regular* if $P \cup \{ \leftarrow A_1, .., A_m \} \in \mathcal{P} \Leftrightarrow P \cup \{ goal \leftarrow A_1, .., A_m \} \in \mathcal{P}$ (where *goal* is a new nullary predicate symbol). $\square$

Using regular properties allows to define a class of logic programs and goal giving only the definition for programs, hence making definitions much shorter.

Assumption 1 All the classes we consider in this paper are understood to be regular.

In the context of this paper, this will be even more useful: since we are going to introduce transformations that translate logic programs (possibly together with a goal) into logic programs (possibly with a goal) or into TRSs (possibly together with a term), we can again shorten the definitions of such transformations by defining them only on logic programs: goals G are identified with the clause $goal \leftarrow G$ (and analogously, for TRSs terms t are identified with a produced 'rule' of the form $goal \rightarrow t$). This automatically gives a translation for the goal(s) eventually present.

3 The Program Classes

Definition 3.1 A *mode* for a n-ary predicate p is a map from $\{1, .., n\}$ to $\{in, out\}$. A *moding* is a map associating to every predicate p a mode for it. A *moded program* is a program endowed with a moding. An argument position of a moded predicate is called input (resp. output) if it is mapped by the mode into *in* (resp. *out*). $\square$

Multiple modings can be defined by renaming the predicates.

$p(\bar{s}; \bar{t})$ denotes a moded atom p having its input positions filled in by the sequence of terms $\bar{s}$, and its output positions filled in by $\bar{t}$. We denote with $in(p)$ and $out(p)$ respectively the number of input and output positions of p.

A moded predicate should be roughly seen as a function from its input arguments to its output ones. For instance, a predicate p with moding (in, in, out) should be viewed as a function having two inputs (the first two arguments) and one output (the third one).

The programs that we will consider are typed. Any type system can be used, provided only it satisfies the following:

Assumption 2 Every type is closed under substitutions.

We denote with *Types* the set of types used in the chosen type system. For example, possible types are *Any* (all the terms), *Nat* (the terms 0, $s(0)$, $s(s(0))$, ..), *Ground* (all the ground terms), *List* (all the lists), *NatList* (all the lists of *Naturals*) and so on. In the following examples we will assume these basic types are in the type system. Also, we say a type is ground if it is contained in *Ground*.

A term t of type T will be indicated with $t : T$. If $\bar{t} = t_1, .., t_n$ and $\bar{T} = T_1, .., T_n$ are respectively a sequence of terms and types, $\bar{t} : \bar{T}$ is a shorthand for $t_1 : T_1, .., t_n : T_n$.

Just like modes, types can be associated to predicates as well:

Definition 3.2 A *type* for an n-ary predicate p is a map from $\{1, .., n\}$ to *Types*. A *typing* is a map associating to every predicate p a type for it. A *typed program* is a program endowed with a typing. An argument position of a typed predicate is said of type T if it is mapped by the type into T. $\square$

We write $p(m_1 : T_1, .., m_n : T_n)$ to indicate that a predicate p has moding $(m_1, .., m_n)$ and typing $(T_1, .., T_n)$.

To reason about types, we employ the standard concept of *type checking*: an expression of the form $\bar{s} : \bar{S} \models \bar{t} : \bar{T}$ indicates that from the fact that $\bar{s}$ has type $\bar{S}$ we can infer that $\bar{t}$ has type $\bar{T}$. More formally, $\bar{s} : \bar{S} \models \bar{t} : \bar{T}$ if for every substitution θ, $\bar{s}\theta \in \bar{S}$ implies $\bar{t}\theta \in \bar{T}$. For instance, $X : Any, Y : List \models [X|Y] : List$.

Another concept we need is the following:

Definition 3.3 A term t is a *generic expression* of the type T if every $s \in T$ having no common variables with t and unifying with it is an instance of t (i.e. $\exists \theta . t\theta = s$). $\square$

For example, variables are generic expressions of *Any*, every term is a generic expression of *Ground*, $[], [X], [X|X], [X|Y], [X, Y|Z]$ etc. are generic expressions of *List*.

We will use types and generic expression in such a way that during a program execution unification behaves in a more regular way, that is to say it can be performed using repeated applications of pattern matching (see [3, 24]). So, we now introduce the main class studied in the paper:

Definition 3.4 A program is said to be *Safely Typed* (ST) if for each of its clauses $p_0(\bar{t}_0 : \bar{T}_0; \bar{s}_{n+1} : \bar{S}_{n+1}) \leftarrow p_1(\bar{s}_1 : \bar{S}_1; \bar{t}_1 : \bar{T}_1), .., p_n(\bar{s}_n : \bar{S}_n; \bar{t}_n : \bar{T}_n)$ we have:
- $\bar{t}_0 : \bar{T}_0, .., \bar{t}_{j-1} : \bar{T}_{j-1} \models \bar{s}_j : \bar{S}_j \quad (j \in [1, n+1])$
- each term in $\bar{t}_i$ is filled in with a generic expression for its corresponding type in $\bar{T}_i$
- if a variable X occurs twice in $\bar{t}_0, .., \bar{t}_n$, then there is a $\bar{t}_i$ $(0 \le i \le n)$ s.t. $X \in \text{Var}(\bar{t}_i)$, $X \notin \text{Var}(\bar{t}_0, .., \bar{t}_{i-1})$, and every term $r \in \bar{t}_i$ has a corresponding ground type. $\square$

For example, the program quicksort using difference lists (see Example 6.2) is Safely Typed. The scope of the class ST is quite large: it is comparable to the class of *Well Typed* programs introduced in [7]; for instance, the great majority of the programs in [29] and [10] are safely typed. Finding whether a program is ST or not is a problem that can be addressed using one of the many existing tools to find moding and typing information of a logic program (e.g. [14, 28, 2]). Moreover, the syntactical nature of the class makes it suitable to be used just as a strongly typed logic programming language on its own. This is the direction followed in many recent systems: in many cases the moding/typing information can be optionally supplied; in others, like the state-of-the-art fastest compiler, Mercury (cf. [12]), modes and types are just the adopted syntax.

We note how, when the type system contains only the type *Ground*, the ST class collapses into the well-known class of *Well Moded* programs (cf. [7]).

Definition 3.5 A program is said to be *Regularly Typed* (RT) if it is Safely Typed and for each of its clauses $p_0(\bar{s}_0; \bar{t}_0) \leftarrow p_1(\bar{s}_1; \bar{t}_1), .., p_n(\bar{s}_n; \bar{t}_n)$ we have that $\bar{t}_1, .., \bar{t}_n$ is a linear sequence of variables and $\forall i \in [1, n]$. $\text{Var}(\bar{t}_i) \cap \bigcup_{j=0}^{i} \text{Var}(\bar{s}_j) = \emptyset$. $\square$

Example 3.6 The usual program to add two numbers

$$add(0, X, X) \leftarrow \qquad\qquad add(s(X), Y, s(Z)) \leftarrow add(X, Y, Z)$$

with moding/typing $add(in : Ground, in : Any, out : Any)$ is regularly typed.

Also, the standard basic programs *append*, *reverse*, *quicksort*, *member* etc. are (with suitable modings/typings) all in RT. $\square$

It is interesting to notice that many parts of logic programming codes are written, more or less consciously, in the form given by the RT class. Indeed, this class properly contains the class of simply moded and well typed (SWT) programs introduced in [3], and that class has already been shown to be quite expressive (see for instance the list of programs presented in [3]).

We remark how the above definitions concern *definite* logic programs only (i.e. programs without negation). In Section 8 these classes will be extended to *normal* logic programs (i.e. programs with negation).

4 k-termination

Suppose a logic program P is run with goal G. Let us denote with $answer_{P,G}(1)$ the first obtained answer: it is equal to

1. ϕ if the computation terminates successfully giving ϕ as computed answer substitution.
2. Fail if the computation terminates with failure.
3. $\perp$ if the computation does not terminate.
(here, Fail and $\perp$ are special symbols used to denote failure and nontermination respectively).

In case 1, the user can activate backtracking to look for the second answer $answer_{P,G}(2)$, and so on till for some $k \geq 1$ $answer_{P,G}(k)$ returns Fail or $\perp$ (in case of infinite answers, we assume $k = \omega$ and $answer_{P,G}(\omega) = \perp$).

Now, the *answer semantics* $\alpha_P(G)$ of a logic program P w.r.t. a goal G is defined as the (possibly infinite) sequence

$$\alpha_P(G) = answer_{P,G}(1), .., answer_{P,G}(k)$$

We can now provide a formal definition of termination:

Definition 4.1 Given a program P and a goal G, suppose its answer semantics is $\alpha_P(G) = \phi_0, .., \phi_m$. Then P is said to *existentially (resp. universally) terminate* w.r.t. G if $\phi_0 \neq \perp$ (resp. if $\phi_m \neq \perp$). $\square$

Hence, a program existentially terminates if its first answer is different from $\perp$ (i.e. it is not an infinite derivation), and universally terminates if it does not give $\perp$ answers at all (i.e. the program returns a finite number of answers and then halts with a failure).

There is however a more general concept of termination, that encompasses the previous two:

Definition 4.2 Given a program P and a goal G, suppose its answer semantics is $\alpha_P(G) = \phi_0, .., \phi_m$. Then, for every ordinal k, P is said to k-*terminate* w.r.t. G if $\forall i < k. \phi_i \neq \perp$. $\square$

k-termination provides a complete spectrum of termination properties, with intermediate degrees between the two extremes consisting of existential and universal termination. Indeed, it is immediate to see that existential termination corresponds to 1-termination, whereas universal termination corresponds to $\omega + 1$-termination. Note that for every ordinal $k > \omega + 1$, k-termination coincides with $\omega + 1$-termination, hence universal termination is the strongest termination property in this hierarchy. Observe also that every program trivially 0-terminates, and hence we can without loss of generality restrict our attention to k-termination with $1 \leq k \leq \omega + 1$.

Example 4.3 The termination property closest to universal termination in the k-termination hierarchy is ω-termination, that says a program cannot enter an infinite derivation (but might perform an infinite number of finite derivations). $\square$

4.1 Strong k-termination
In this paper we will also investigate strong k-termination, that is k-termination not only for a single goal, but for all the goals in the given class:

Definition 4.4 Given a class $\mathcal{P}$ of logic programs, and an ordinal k, a program $P \in \mathcal{P}$ is said to *strongly k-terminate* w.r.t. $\mathcal{P}$ if P k-terminates w.r.t. G for every goal $G \in \mathcal{P}$. $\square$

The big difference with the previous case of k-termination w.r.t. a goal is given by this result (to be precise, we remark that it holds under the assumption of *persistent classes* (i.e. closed via resolution, see [24]), an assumption always satisfied in this paper):

Theorem 4.5 *Strong existential termination and strong ω-termination coincide.*

That is to say, in the strong termination case the k-termination hierarchy *collapses* into two properties only (plus the trivial strong 0-termination): strong existential and strong universal termination.

In the sequel, when talking about strong termination w.r.t. some class $\mathcal{P}$, we will usually omit mentioning $\mathcal{P}$: it will be clear from the context what class is meant.

5 The Basic Transformation

In this section we provide the transformation $\mathcal{E}_{RT}$ from regularly typed program to TRSs that will be the core of the subsequent transformations. Before giving the formal definition, we need some preliminary notions.

In the corresponding TRS we will utilize, besides the symbols of the original logic program, some new symbols.

We will employ so-called $\Diamond$-*lists*, that is lists where the constructors are the binary symbol c and the constant $\Diamond$: we will use the notation $\langle t_1, .., t_n \rangle$ to denote such lists (e.g. $\langle t_1, t_2 \rangle = c(t_1, c(t_2, \Diamond))$).

The unary symbol $\mathcal{M}$ will be used as a marker to indicate that its argument is, roughly speaking, a 'result' (i.e. a datum that doesn't need to be processed further). Also, we will make use of symbols of the form $\lambda_{t_1}^{t_2}$, that can be roughly seen as the function $\lambda t_1.t_2$ (i.e. it expects a datum of the form t_1 and gives as output t_2): the exact formalization of this 'lambda operator' will be given later.

Definition 5.1 Take a regularly typed clause $C = p_0(\bar{t}_0; \bar{s}_{n+1}) \leftarrow p_1(\bar{s}_1; \bar{t}_1), .., p_n(\bar{s}_n; \bar{t}_n)$. Then FLOW($C$) is defined as

$$\lambda_{[\mathcal{M} V(n), \mathcal{M} \bar{t}_n]}^{[\mathcal{M} \bar{s}_{n+1}]} \lambda_{[\mathcal{M} V(n-1), \mathcal{M} \bar{t}_{n-1}]}^{[\mathcal{M} V(n) | p_n [\mathcal{M} \bar{s}_n]]} \cdots \lambda_{[\mathcal{M} V(0), \mathcal{M} \bar{t}_0]}^{[\mathcal{M} V(1) | p_1 [\mathcal{M} \bar{s}_1]]} [\mathcal{M} \bar{t}_0]$$

where $V(k) = \cup_{i=0}^{k-1} \mathrm{Var}(\bar{t}_i)$. $\qquad\qquad\Box$

The idea behind the FLOW definition is that every clause $p_0(\bar{t}_0; \bar{s}_{n+1}) \leftarrow ..$ provides a way to calculate $p_0[\mathcal{M} \bar{t}_0]$ (i.e. p_0 applied to its input arguments). Its output value $[\mathcal{M} \bar{s}_{n+1}]$ is obtained in the following way.

Informally, $V(k)$ denotes the *V*ariables of $p_1, .., p_{k-1}$ that could be needed for the input arguments of $p_{k+1}, .., p_n$ and for the output argument of the head predicate p_0 (i.e. $\bar{s}_{k+1}, .., \bar{s}_{n+1}$).

We start with the input data $[\mathcal{M} \bar{t}_0]$. Then, applying the first operator $\lambda_{[\mathcal{M} V(0), \mathcal{M} \bar{t}_0]}^{[\mathcal{M} V(1) | p_1 [\mathcal{M} \bar{s}_1]]}$ we calculate $p_1[\mathcal{M} \bar{s}_1]$ (that gives its output values for $\mathcal{M} \bar{t}_1$), together with the values from $\mathcal{M} \bar{t}_0$ that are needed in the sequel to calculate some other $p_i[\mathcal{M} \bar{s}_i]$ or the final output $[\mathcal{M} \bar{s}_{n+1}]$ (i.e. $V(1)$). The process goes on till all the $p_1, .., p_n$ have been processed, and the last operator $\lambda_{[\mathcal{M} V(n), \mathcal{M} \bar{t}_n]}^{[\mathcal{M} \bar{s}_{n+1}]}$ simply passes to the final output $[\mathcal{M} \bar{s}_{n+1}]$ the values previously computed (present in $[\mathcal{M} V(n), \mathcal{M} \bar{t}_n]$).

Example 5.2 After Example 3.6, let C be the clause $add(s(X), Y, s(Z)) \leftarrow add(X, Y, Z)$ (recall the moding/typing was $add(in: Ground, in: Any, out: Any)$). Then

$$\mathsf{FLOW}(C) = \lambda_{[\mathcal{M} X, \mathcal{M} Y, \mathcal{M} Z]}^{[\mathcal{M} s(Z)]} \lambda_{[\mathcal{M} s(X), \mathcal{M} Y]}^{[\mathcal{M} X, \mathcal{M} Y | add[\mathcal{M} X, \mathcal{M} Y]]} [\mathcal{M} s(X), \mathcal{M} Y] \qquad\Box$$

Definition 5.3 The map $\mathcal{V}$ from terms to terms is inductively defined this way:

$$\begin{aligned} \mathcal{V}(f(t_1, .., t_k)) &= f(\mathcal{V}(t_1), .., \mathcal{V}(t_k)) &&(f \in \Sigma) \\ \mathcal{V}(X) &= \mathsf{v} &&(X \in \mathrm{VAR}) \end{aligned}$$

where v is a special new constant. $\qquad\qquad\Box$

Hence, the map $\mathcal{V}$ simply replaces every variable of a term with the special constant v: for instance, $\mathcal{V}(f(X, g(Y, a))) = f(\mathsf{v}, g(\mathsf{v}, a))$.

Definition 5.4 (Unification Engine)
For every term t, its unification engine $UNIFY_t$ is defined as follows. Let t' be a linearization of t (via σ). Then the rules defining $UNIFY_t$ are:

$$UNIFY_t(X) \to \mathcal{U}_t(X, \mathcal{L}(\mathcal{V}(t), X))$$
$$\mathcal{U}_t(t', true) \to \bigwedge_{\substack{X \in Var(t) \\ \{X_1, .., X_k\} = \sigma^{-1}(X)}} \bigwedge_{i=1.. k-1} \mathcal{L}(X_i, X_{i+1})$$
$$\mathcal{U}_t(X, false) \to false$$

$$\mathcal{L}(\mathsf{v}, X) \to true$$
$$\mathcal{L}(f(X_1, .., X_m), f(Y_1, .., Y_m)) \to \bigwedge_{i=1..m} \mathcal{L}(X_i, Y_i) \qquad (f \in \Sigma)$$
$$\mathcal{L}(f(X_1, .., X_m), g(Y_1, .., Y_n)) \to false \qquad (f, g \in \Sigma, \ f \not\equiv g)$$

$$true \wedge true \to true$$
$$X \wedge false \to false$$
$$false \wedge X \to false$$

(note that we write $\bigwedge_{i \in \emptyset}$ as a synonymous for $true$). $\qquad\qquad\square$

The unification engine of a term t formalizes in the TRS the concept of unification: it tests whether or not a given term is unifiable with t.

Informally, the behaviour of $UNIFY_t$ can be summarized as follows. The $\mathcal{L}$ test performs a kind of restricted Martelli-Montanari algorithm, as can be easily seen looking at the rewrite rules defining it: roughly speaking, it performs unification of $\mathcal{L}$inear terms. The only rule not immediate to understand is $\mathcal{L}(\mathsf{v}, X) \to true$: it simply says that whenever the first argument is a variable (denoted by the special constant v), then everything unifies with it. This is the reason why the $\mathcal{V}$ operator was introduced (Definition 5.3): it performs the 'is-a-variable' test at a syntactic level.

$UNIFY_t$ invokes $\mathcal{L}$ several times, since it must also face the problem of all the repeated variables (i.e. non-linear terms): this is done in the rules defining $\mathcal{U}_t$, where repeated variables are in sequence, via an 'and' operator (written infix for easier readability) imposed to have a common unifier.

Note that the unification engine is built to work with the terms produced by the transformation only (i.e. when invoked in the transformation it properly performs the unification test, but it does not work in general for all the terms).

Example 5.5 Take the term $t = f(X, g(X, Y))$, and a corresponding linearization $t' = f(Z, g(V, W))$. Then the first two rules defining $UNIFY_{f(X, g(X, Y))}$ are:

$$UNIFY_{f(X, g(X,Y))}(Z) \to \mathcal{U}_{f(X, g(X,Y))}(Z, \mathcal{L}(f(\mathsf{v}, g(\mathsf{v}, \mathsf{v})), Z))$$
$$\mathcal{U}_{f(X, g(X,Y))}(f(Z, g(V, W)), true) \to \mathcal{L}(Z, V) \wedge true \qquad\qquad\square$$

We are now ready to provide the formal definition of $\mathcal{E}_{RT}$: its explanation will be given soon afterwards.

Definition 5.6 (Transformation $\mathcal{E}_{RT}$)
The transformation $\mathcal{E}_{RT}(P)$ of a regularly typed logic program P is defined this way.
1) For every predicate $p \in \Sigma$, take the definition of p in P:

$$\begin{cases} p(\bar{t}_0^{(1)}; \bar{s}_{n_1+1}^{(1)}) \leftarrow \cdots & (C_1) \\ \quad\vdots & \quad\vdots \\ p(\bar{t}_0^{(k)}; \bar{s}_{n_k+1}^{(k)}) \leftarrow \cdots & (C_k) \end{cases}$$

Then produce the following rewrite rules $(i = 1..k)$, plus the corresponding unification engines:

$$p[\mathcal{M}X_1,..,\mathcal{M}X_{\text{in}(p)}] \rightarrow \mathcal{B}\,\langle ENC_p^{(1)}[\mathcal{M}X_1,..,\mathcal{M}X_{\text{in}(p)}],..,ENC_p^{(k)}[\mathcal{M}X_1,..,\mathcal{M}X_{\text{in}(p)}]\rangle$$
$$\mathcal{B}\,ENC_p^{(i)}[\mathcal{M}X_1,..,\mathcal{M}X_{\text{in}(p)}] \rightarrow TRY_p^{(i)}([\mathcal{M}X_1,..,\mathcal{M}X_{\text{in}(p)}], UNIFY_{[\bar{t}_0^{(i)}]}[X_1,..,X_{\text{in}(p)}])$$
$$TRY_p^{(i)}([\mathcal{M}\bar{t}_0^{(i)}], true) \rightarrow \mathsf{FLOW}(C_i) \qquad\qquad TRY_p^{(i)}(X, false) \rightarrow \Diamond$$

2) For every $\lambda_{t_1}^{t_2}$ so far introduced, produce:

$$\lambda_{t_1}^{t_2} t_1 \rightarrow t_2 \qquad\qquad \lambda_{t_1}^{t_2}\Diamond \rightarrow \Diamond \qquad\qquad \mathcal{B}\,\lambda_{t_1}^{t_2} X \rightarrow \lambda_{t_1}^{t_2}\mathcal{B}\,X$$

$$\lambda_{t_1}^{t_2}\langle[\mathcal{M}X_1,..,\mathcal{M}X_{\text{in}(p)}]|Y\rangle \rightarrow \langle\lambda_{t_1}^{t_2}[\mathcal{M}X_1,..,\mathcal{M}X_{\text{in}(p)}]|\lambda_{t_1}^{t_2}Y\rangle \qquad (p \in \Sigma)$$

3) Finally, produce:

$$\mathcal{B}\,\langle X|Y\rangle \rightarrow \langle\mathcal{B}\,X|Y\rangle \qquad\qquad \mathcal{B}\,\Diamond \rightarrow \Diamond$$
$$\mathcal{B}\,\mathcal{B}\,X \rightarrow \mathcal{B}\,X \qquad\qquad \langle\Diamond|Y\rangle \rightarrow \mathcal{B}\,Y \qquad\qquad \square$$

Observe that in Point 1 in case p is not defined in P, i.e. $k = 0$, the transformation simply produces $p[\mathcal{M}X_1,..,\mathcal{M}X_{\text{in}(p)}] \rightarrow \mathcal{B}\,\Diamond$.

The behaviour of $\mathcal{E}_{\text{RT}}$ can be intuitively illustrated as follows.

We said earlier every clause defining a predicate p provides a way to calculate p applied to its input values. In Point 1 of the transformation the first rule says that in order to calculate p we have at our disposal the definition given in the first clause (encoded via $ENC_p^{(1)}(\cdots)$), till that in the last clause ($ENC_p^{(k)}(\cdots)$). All these different choices are grouped together, in left to right order, using a $\Diamond$-list.

The $\mathcal{B}$ symbol present in the rule before this $\Diamond$-list represents the 'backtracking command' which activates a computation.

This backtracking command can penetrate into the possibly complicated structures it encounters, via the rules (produced in Points 2 and 3 respectively) $\mathcal{B}\,\lambda_{t_1}^{t_2} X \rightarrow \lambda_{t_1}^{t_2}\mathcal{B}\,X$ and $\mathcal{B}\,\langle X|Y\rangle \rightarrow \langle\mathcal{B}\,X|Y\rangle$.

Also, the backtracking command is idempotent (rule $\mathcal{B}\,\mathcal{B}\,X \rightarrow \mathcal{B}\,X$).

As soon as $\mathcal{B}$ finds an ENC operator (encoding a certain clause), it tries to activate it via the second rules produced in Point 1: It must be checked that the (representation in the TRS of the) selected atom in the goal and the (representation of the) head of the clause unify, and this is performed via the test $UNIFY_{[\bar{t}_0^{(i)}]}[X_1,..,X_{\text{in}(p)}]$.

In case the test succeeds, the rule $TRY_p^{(i)}([\mathcal{M}\bar{t}_0^{(i)}], true) \rightarrow \mathsf{FLOW}(C_i)$ applies the clause; in case it does not, the rule $TRY_p^{(i)}(X, false) \rightarrow \Diamond$ says that no result (i.e. $\Diamond$) has been produced.

The rule (produced in Point 3) $\langle\Diamond|Y\rangle \rightarrow \mathcal{B}\,Y$ says that whenever in a group of choices (contained in a $\Diamond$-list) the first argument produced no results (i.e. $\Diamond$), then it is discarded and another 'backtracking command' $\mathcal{B}$ is generated and applied to the remaining choices ($\mathcal{B}\,Y$). Note that if, instead, a result is produced, no backtracking command is generated, and so the execution stops.

Eventually, if $\mathcal{B}$ finds no results it gives no results as well (rule $\mathcal{B}\,\Diamond \rightarrow \Diamond$).

The last thing that remains to consider is the behaviour of the $\lambda_{t_1}^{t_2}$ operators.

As said at the beginning of the section, $\lambda_{t_1}^{t_2}$ is supposed to act roughly like the function $\lambda t_1.t_2$: this is expressed by the rule $\lambda_{t_1}^{t_2} t_1 \rightarrow t_2$. The difference is that it has also to deal with the other kinds of structures that can crop up: in case it finds no results, it produces no results (rule $\lambda_{t_1}^{t_2} \Diamond \rightarrow \Diamond$), and in case it finds more choices (grouped in a $\Diamond$-list), it applies itself to all of them via the last rules produced in Point 2.

Observation 5.7 An useful shorthand is to consider only *atomic* goals, i.e. goals of the form $G = \leftarrow p(\bar{s}; \bar{t})$. This way we can simply define the translation $\mathcal{E}_{RT}(G)$ of the goal as $p[\mathcal{M}\bar{s}]$ (hence without using the convention of Subsection 2.2). From now on, for brevity, we will only consider examples with atomic goals. As an aside, note that in general this is not restrictive since, e.g., a regularly typed goal of the form $\leftarrow p_1(\bar{s}_1; \bar{t}_1), .., p_n(\bar{s}_n; \bar{t}_n)$ can be split into a goal $\leftarrow p(\bar{s}_1; \bar{t}_1, .., \bar{t}_n)$ and a clause $p(\bar{s}_1; \bar{t}_1, .., \bar{t}_n) \leftarrow p_1(\bar{s}_1; \bar{t}_1), .., p_n(\bar{s}_n; \bar{t}_n)$ (where p is a new predicate) that are both regularly typed, giving an equivalent program. □

Example 5.8 Consider the program defining the integers ([29]):

$$int(0) \leftarrow \qquad\qquad int(s(X)) \leftarrow int(X)$$

and the goal $\leftarrow int(X)$ (where the moding/typing is $int(out: Any)$).

Its translation via $\mathcal{E}_{RT}$ is ($i = 1, 2$):

$$int[] \rightarrow \mathcal{B} \langle ENC_{int}^{(1)}[], ENC_{int}^{(2)}[] \rangle$$

$$\mathcal{B}\, ENC_{int}^{(i)}[] \rightarrow TRY_{int}^{(i)}([], UNIFY_{[]}[]) \qquad TRY_{int}^{(1)}([], true) \rightarrow \lambda_{[]}^{[\mathcal{M}0]}[]$$
$$TRY_{int}^{(2)}([], true) \rightarrow \lambda_{[\mathcal{M}X]}^{[\mathcal{M}s(X)]} \lambda_{[]}^{int[]}[] \qquad TRY_{int}^{(i)}(X, false) \rightarrow \Diamond$$

and the term $int[]$ (plus the rules of the unification engine and of steps 2 and 3 of the $\mathcal{E}_{RT}$ Definition). The corresponding reduction of the term in the TRS is:

$$int[] \rightarrow \mathcal{B} \langle ENC_{int}^{(1)}[], ENC_{int}^{(2)}[] \rangle \rightarrow^* \langle TRY_{int}^{(1)}([], UNIFY_{[]}[]), ENC_{int}^{(2)}[] \rangle \rightarrow^*$$
$$\langle TRY_{int}^{(1)}([], true), ENC_{int}^{(2)}[] \rangle \rightarrow \langle \lambda_{[]}^{[\mathcal{M}0]}[], ENC_{int}^{(2)}[] \rangle \rightarrow \langle [\mathcal{M}0], ENC_{int}^{(2)}[] \rangle \qquad □$$

The TRSs produced by $\mathcal{E}_{RT}$ have a quite regular structure:

Lemma 5.9 *For every regularly typed program P, $\mathcal{E}_{RT}(P)$ is weakly confluent. If $\mathcal{E}_{RT}(P)$ is terminating, then it is also confluent.*

We now state what existential termination properties $\mathcal{E}_{RT}$ enjoys:

Theorem 5.10 *Let P and G be respectively a regularly typed program and goal: then P existentially terminates w.r.t. G iff $\mathcal{E}_{RT}(P)$ terminates w.r.t. $\mathcal{E}_{RT}(G)$.*

Theorem 5.11 *Let P be a regularly typed program: then P strongly existentially terminates iff $\mathcal{E}_{RT}(P)$ terminates.*

Hence via the above two theorems we obtain a characterization of existential termination for the class of regularly typed programs.

Example 5.12 Graph structures are used in many applications, such as representing relations, situations or problems. Consider the program *CONNECTED*, that finds whether two nodes in a graph are connected:

$$connected(X, Y) \leftarrow arc(X, Y) \qquad connected(X, Y) \leftarrow arc(X, Z), connected(Z, Y)$$

with moding/typing $connected(in: Ground, out: Ground)$, $arc(in: Ground, out: Ground)$. Suppose the graph G is defined via the facts

$$arc(a, b) \leftarrow \qquad\qquad arc(b, c) \leftarrow \qquad\qquad arc(c, a) \leftarrow$$

When the graph is cyclic (like in this case), the program *CONNECTED* $\cup\, G$ does not strongly universally terminate. However, using Theorem 5.11, we can prove that it is strongly existentially terminating. □

Example 5.13 Reconsider the integer program of Example 5.8. This program does not strongly universally terminates, as it is trivial to see. However, the obtained TRS can be proven to be terminating, hence showing, via Theorem 5.11, that the integer program strongly existentially terminates. □

6 From ST to RT

In this section we show how to extend the previous results to the whole class of safely typed programs, using a transformation which is of independent interest.

Given a safely typed clause $C = p_0(\bar{t}_0; \bar{s}_{n+1}) \leftarrow p_1(\bar{s}_1; \bar{t}_1), .., p_n(\bar{s}_n; \bar{t}_n)$, define $\mu(C)$ as the number of $\bar{t}_i$'s that do not satisfy the RT condition. Thus, $\mu(C)$ is somehow a measure of how much of C does not belong to RT, viz. how many atoms in a clause are 'bad' ones (note that $\mu(C) = 0$ iff $C \in$ RT).

Extend μ to a program P in the obvious way: $\mu(P) = \sum_{C \in P} \mu(C)$.

Now we can define a transformation C that translates a safely typed program into a regularly typed one.

Definition 6.1 (Transformation C)
Let P be a safely typed program. If P is already regularly typed, then C leaves it unchanged ($C(P) = P$).

So, suppose that P is not RT, i.e. that $\mu(P) > 0$. Take a clause C of P with $\mu(C) > 0$:
$$C = p_0(\bar{t}_0; \bar{s}_{n+1}) \leftarrow p_1(\bar{s}_1; \bar{t}_1), .., p_n(\bar{s}_n; \bar{t}_n)$$

Take an $i > 0$ such that $\bar{t}_i$ makes the RT condition fail (i.e. $p_i(\bar{s}_i; \bar{t}_i)$ is a 'bad' atom of the body). Then, replace C with the following two clauses:

$$p_0(\bar{t}_0; \bar{s}_{n+1}) \leftarrow p_1(\bar{s}_1; \bar{t}_1), .., p_{i-1}(\bar{s}_{i-1}; \bar{t}_{i-1}),$$
$$p_i(\bar{s}_i; X_1, .., X_{\text{out}(p_i)}),$$
$$\text{EQ}_{C,p_i}(X_1, .., X_{\text{out}(p_i)}, \text{Var}(\bar{t}_i) \cap \bigcup_{j=0}^{i-1} \text{Var}(\bar{t}_j); \text{Var}(\bar{t}_i) \setminus \bigcup_{j=0}^{i-1} \text{Var}(\bar{t}_j)),$$
$$p_{i+1}(\bar{s}_{i+1}; \bar{t}_{i+1}), .., p_n(\bar{s}_n; \bar{t}_n)$$

$$\text{EQ}_{C,p_i}(\bar{t}_i, \text{Var}(\bar{t}_i) \cap \bigcup_{j=0}^{i-1} \text{Var}(\bar{t}_j); \text{Var}(\bar{t}_i) \setminus \bigcup_{j=0}^{i-1} \text{Var}(\bar{t}_j)) \leftarrow$$

where $X_1, .., X_{\text{out}(p_i)}$ are fresh variables and EQ_{C,p_i} is a new predicate symbol: note its mode and type is given implicitly by the above clauses.

It is not difficult to prove that this new program P' so obtained is still safely typed, and moreover $\mu(P') = \mu(P) - 1$.

Hence, repeating this process, we finally get a program Q with $\mu(Q) = 0$ (therefore regularly typed), and let $C(P) = Q$. □

The intuition is that we patch the bad atoms in a program: if $p_i(\bar{s}_i; \bar{t}_i)$ is bad, we force it back to RT by inserting in place of $\bar{t}_i$ new fresh variables: next we check that these variables have been instantiated to something unifiable with $\bar{t}_i$ via the introduction of the new EQ predicate.

Example 6.2 Take the *QUICKSORTDL* program using difference lists (after [29, page 244]):

C_1 $quicksort(Xs, Ys) \leftarrow quicksort\_dl(Xs, Ys, [])$
C_2 $quicksort\_dl([X|Xs], Ys, Zs) \leftarrow partition(Xs, X, Littles, Bigs), quicksort\_dl(Littles, Ys, [X|Ys1]), quicksort\_dl(Bigs, Ys1, Zs)$
C_3 $quicksort\_dl([], Xs, Xs) \leftarrow$

(plus the rules for *partition*), with moding/typing $quicksort(\text{in}: NatList, \text{in}: NatList)$, $quicksort\_dl(\text{in}: NatList, \text{in}: NatList, \text{out}: NatList)$, $partition(\text{in}: NatList, \text{in}: Nat, \text{out}:$

$NatList, out: NatList$). This program is safely typed but not regularly typed because of the first and second clause: the atom $quicksort\_dl(Xs, Ys, [\,])$ in C_1 and the atom $quicksort\_dl(Littles, Ys, [X|Ys1])$ in C_2 are the only 'bad' ones ($\mu(QUICKSORTDL) = 2$). Applying C, we obtain in place of C_1 and C_2 the clauses:

C_1' $quicksort(Xs, Ys) \leftarrow quicksort\_dl(Xs, Ys, X_1), EQ_1(X_1)$
C_1'' $EQ_1([\,]) \leftarrow$
C_2' $quicksort\_dl([X|Xs], Ys, Zs) \leftarrow partition(Xs, X, Littles, Bigs), quicksort\_dl(Littles,$
$\qquad\qquad\qquad\qquad\qquad\qquad Ys, X_1), EQ_2(X_1, X, Ys1), quicksort\_dl(Bigs, Ys1, Zs)$
C_2'' $EQ_2([X|Ys1], X, Ys1) \leftarrow$

where EQ_1 is moded/typed ($in: NatList$) and EQ_2 ($in: NatList, in: Nat, out: NatList$).
$\qquad\qquad\qquad\qquad\qquad\qquad\qquad\qquad\qquad\qquad\qquad\qquad\qquad\qquad\qquad\qquad\square$

Observe that the transformation C can in general introduce some extra computations since it delays the test on the output arguments (via EQ). However, it somehow retains the original structure of the program, since it preserves the logical meaning in the following sense:

Theorem 6.3 *Let P and G be a safely typed program and goal. Then ϑ is an SLD computed answer substitution for $C(P \cup \{G\})$ iff $\vartheta|_{Var(G)}$ is an SLD computed answer substitution for $P \cup \{G\}$.*

The proof of the above theorem makes use of fold/unfold techniques.

As far as termination is concerned, the following result holds:

Lemma 6.4 *Let P and G be a safely typed program and goal. For every ordinal k, if $C(P)$ k-terminates w.r.t. $C(G)$ then P k-terminates w.r.t. G, and if $C(P)$ strongly k-terminates then P strongly k-terminates.*

Hence we can analyze the termination behaviour of a safely typed program by applying the compound transformation

$$\mathcal{E}_{ST} = \mathcal{E}_{RT} \circ C$$

Theorem 6.5 *Let P and G be respectively a safely typed program and goal: then P existentially terminates w.r.t. G if $\mathcal{E}_{ST}(P)$ terminates w.r.t. $\mathcal{E}_{ST}(G)$.*

Theorem 6.6 *Let P be a safely typed program: then P strongly existentially terminates if $\mathcal{E}_{ST}(P)$ terminates.*

7 The k-termination case

So far, we have presented only criteria on existential termination. In this section, we provide more general results to cope with the whole spectrum of k-termination.

Through this section, $\mathcal{A}$ and $\mathcal{S}$ denote two new fresh symbols.

Theorem 7.1 *Let P and G be a regularly typed (resp. safely typed) program and goal. Then for every k s.t. $0 < k < \omega$, P k-terminates w.r.t. G iff (resp. if) $\mathcal{E}_{ST}(P) \cup \{\mathcal{A}(\mathcal{S}(X), \langle[\,]|W\rangle) \rightarrow \mathcal{A}(X, B\,W), \mathcal{A}(\mathcal{S}(X), \langle[Y|Z]|W\rangle) \rightarrow \mathcal{A}(X, B\,W)\}$ terminates w.r.t. $\mathcal{A}(\underbrace{\mathcal{S}\cdots\mathcal{S}}_{k-1}\Diamond, \mathcal{E}_{ST}(G))$.*

The intuition is that we consider reductions in the TRS not of the original term $\mathcal{E}_{ST}(G)$, but of the term $\mathcal{A}(\mathcal{S}\cdots\mathcal{S}\Diamond, \mathcal{E}_{ST}(G))$ that 'counts' how many answers have been so far produced. The counter is stored in the first argument of $\mathcal{A}$, initially set to a unary representation of $k - 1$. Each time one answer has been found, one of the two added rules defining $\mathcal{A}$ is applied, forcing a new backtracking ($B\,W$) and decrementing the counter by one, till all the k answers have been found.

As far as ω-termination is concerned, it is so close to universal termination that there seems to be no way to provide a specific criterion for ω-termination: to infer ω-termination once can nevertheless use a criterion for universal termination (see later).

Example 7.2 Consider the following program *PATH* computing paths in a graph (the goal asks for paths from a_1 to b):

$$\leftarrow path(a_1, b, X)$$

$$path(X, Y, [X, Y]) \leftarrow arc(X, Y)$$
$$path(X, Y, [X|Xs]) \leftarrow arc(X, Z), \, path(Z, Y, Xs)$$

With moding/typing $path(in : Ground, in : Ground, out : List)$, $arc(in : Ground, in : Ground)$ (in the first clause) and $arc(in : Ground, out : Ground)$ (in the second clause), it is regularly typed.

Suppose the graph G_k is defined via the facts

$$arc(a_1, b) \leftarrow, .., arc(a_k, b) \leftarrow, \ arc(a_1, a_2) \leftarrow, .., arc(a_k, a_{k+1}) \leftarrow, \ arc(a_{k+1}, a_{k+1}) \leftarrow$$

Using the above Theorem 7.1, we can prove that for every $0 < k < \omega$, the program $PATH \cup G_k$ is k-terminating. Note also that all these programs do not universally terminate: $PATH \cup G_k$ is not $k+1$-terminating. Incidentally, this also provides a proof that, unlike in the strong termination case, in the case of termination w.r.t. a goal the k-termination hierarchy does not collapse. $\square$

Theorem 7.3 *Let P and G be a regularly typed (resp. safely typed) program and goal. Then P universally terminates w.r.t. G iff (resp. if) $\mathcal{E}_{ST}(P) \cup \{A(\langle[]\|Z\rangle) \rightarrow A(B\,Z), A(\langle[X|Y]\|Z\rangle) \rightarrow A(B\,Z)\}$ terminates w.r.t. $A(\mathcal{E}_{ST}(G))$.*

We turn now our attention towards strong k-termination.

Since, by Theorem 4.5, strong k-termination with $1 \leq k \leq \omega$ coincides with strong existential termination, Theorem 6.6 suffices in all these cases. The only remaining case is strong universal termination:

Theorem 7.4 *Let P be a regularly typed (resp. safely typed) program. Then P strongly universally terminates iff (resp. if) $\mathcal{E}_{ST}(P) \cup \{A(\langle[]\|Z\rangle) \rightarrow A(B\,Z), A(\langle[X|Y]\|Z\rangle) \rightarrow A(B\,Z)\}$ terminates.*

Example 7.5 Consider the program *QUICKSORTDL* seen in Example 6.2: via the above theorem we can prove that it is strongly universally terminating.

Analogously, we can prove for instance that the program to solve the Hanoi towers problem (cf. [29, pp. 64–65]) with moding/typing $hanoi(in : List, out : List)$, the usual quicksort program ([29, page 56]) with $quicksort(in : List, out : List)$, and the English sentences parser ([29, pp. 256–258]) with $sentence(in : Ground, out : Ground)$ are all strongly universally terminating. $\square$

8 Normal Logic Programs

After having analyzed definite logic programming, we extend the results previously obtained to normal logic programming, that is allowing usage of *negation*. As usual in Prolog, negated atoms are solved using the negation as finite failure procedure, i.e. they succeed if and only if they finitely fail. Since we have already defined classes of definite logic programs, we can give the definition of their extensions to normal logic programs inductively on the number of negative literals:

Definition 8.1 A clause is normal safely typed iff either it is safely typed, or: if the clause is of the form $p_0(\bar{t}_0; \bar{s}_{n+1}) \leftarrow p_1(\bar{s}_1; \bar{t}_1), .., not\,(p_k(\bar{s}_k; \bar{t}_k)), .., p_n(\bar{s}_n; \bar{t}_n)$, then both both $p_0(\bar{t}_0; \bar{s}_{n+1}) \leftarrow p_1(\bar{s}_1; \bar{t}_1), .., p_k(\bar{s}_k; \bar{t}_k)$ and $p_0(\bar{t}_0; \bar{s}_{n+1}) \leftarrow p_1(\bar{s}_1; \bar{t}_1), .., p_{k-1}(\bar{s}_{k-1}; \bar{t}_{k-1}), p_{k+1}(\bar{s}_{k+1}; \bar{t}_{k+1}), .., p_n(\bar{s}_n; \bar{t}_n)$ are normal safely typed.
A program is *Normal Safely Typed* (NST) if each of its clauses is.
The class of *Normal Regularly Typed* (NRT) logic programs is defined analogously. $\square$

Example 8.2 Suppose p and q have both moding/typing $(in: Any, out: Any)$. Then the clause $p(X, f(Z)) \leftarrow q(X, Y), not\ (p(Y, Z)), q(Y, Z)$ is normal regularly typed since both $p(X, f(Z)) \leftarrow q(X, Y), p(Y, Z)$ and $p(X, f(Z)) \leftarrow q(X, Y), q(Y, Z)$ are regularly typed. □

Now we have to extend the definition of $\mathcal{E}_{RT}$ to cope with negation. The modification is quite simple. The definition of FLOW (cf. Def. 5.1) is extended this way: it acts like before, only that if a predicate p_i in the body of the clause is negated, i.e. of the form $not\ p_i(\cdots)$, then in the produced term it appears as the compound function $not \circ p_i$, where not is defined as follows:

$$not\ \Diamond \rightarrow \langle[]\rangle \qquad not\ \langle[]|X\rangle \rightarrow \Diamond \qquad not\ \langle[X|Y]|Z\rangle \rightarrow \Diamond$$

The explanation of these rules is perfectly natural: since $not\ p_i(\cdots)$ succeeds iff $p_i(\cdots)$ finitely fails, in the TRS we first calculate $p_i(\cdots)$ and then apply to it the not operator: if no answers are returned $(\Diamond)$, it outputs a result $[]$ via the rule $not\ \Diamond \rightarrow \langle[]\rangle$ ($[]$ corresponds to the fact that a successful negative literal produces no bindings), whereas if a result is returned, it outputs no result (via the other two rules).

This way we obtain a new basic transformation $\mathcal{E}_{NRT}$ that extends $\mathcal{E}_{RT}$ from regularly typed to normal regularly typed programs. Hence, all the transformations previously defined (and their results) extend to normal logic programs, with the correspondence RT↝NRT, and ST↝NST.

For brevity, we only cite the cases of strong existential and universal termination: all the others are similarly obtained using the above syntactic correspondence.

Theorem 8.3 *Let P be a normal regularly typed (resp. normal safely typed) program: then P strongly existentially terminates iff (resp. if) $\mathcal{E}_{NST}(P)$ terminates.*

Theorem 8.4 *Let P be a normal regularly typed (resp. normal safely typed) program. Then P strongly universally terminates iff (resp. if) $\mathcal{E}_{NST}(P) \cup \{\mathcal{A}(\langle[]|Z\rangle) \rightarrow \mathcal{A}(B\ Z),$ $\mathcal{A}(\langle[X|Y]|Z\rangle) \rightarrow \mathcal{A}(B\ Z)\}$ terminates.*

Example 8.5 Consider the following normal program

$$p \leftarrow not\ q \qquad\qquad q \leftarrow \qquad\qquad q \leftarrow q$$

Via Theorem 8.3, we can prove this program is strongly existentially terminating. Nevertheless, it is not universally terminating. □

Example 8.6 A much more complicated example of normal program is given by the Block-World Planner of [29, pp. 221–224], that with moding/typing $transform(in : State, in : State, out : Plan)$ ($State$ and $Plan$ are suitable types) can be proven via Theorem 8.3 to be strongly existentially terminating. □

Example 8.7 The normal program to solve efficiently the n-queens problem, after [29, page 211], moded/typed $queens(in: Ground, out: List)$, can be proven via Theorem 8.4 to be strongly universally terminating. □

9 Relations with previous work

As said, the main contribution of the paper is aimed towards the open problem of existential termination: indeed, as mentioned in the introduction, the very few works on the subject ([9, 18, 6]) give only expressibility results and are, presently, of no practical use (cf. [13]). Also, they do not cope with the intermediate degrees of k-termination $(2 \leq k \leq \omega)$. Very recently, other two works have addressed the subject, namely [25, 20]. The first work [25] has introduced the concept of k-termination, and shown how it can be studied using functional programming techniques. However, the class of normal logic programs to which this analysis can be applied is rather limited, since the main goal of the work is completely different, namely to identify what part of logic programming is just functional programming in disguise. The second work is [20], but besides do not treating negation, its practical importance is at the moment unclear.

Thus, in order to make a comparison with other works we have to *restrict* our approach to the *universal termination* case only. A first point that can be made is that our approach is able to satisfactorily cope with *negation*: the only works that manage to cover some aspects of negation are, to the best of our knowledge, very few.

In [4] a theoretical criterion (acceptable programs) is given: however, this result is considered as a main theoretical foundation, rather than an effective methodology: no practical way to automate or semi-automate the criterion is known, since it heavily relies on semantical information (e.g. it must be provided a model of the program which is also a model of the completion of its 'negative part'). Recently, a novel methodology that overcomes some of the difficulties of this method due to the use of the semantic information, has been introduced in [22].

In [30] a sufficient criterion for termination of normal logic programs is presented. This criterion suffers from the same drawback of [4]: it is far from being easily implemented being exclusively semantically-based (in addition, it requires its main semantical information to be provided by some other proof method). Also, treatment of negation is coped with by assuming that every negated literal *will always succeed*, which readily limits by far the usefulness of the approach to negation.

Another recent work is [11]: the importance of this work is that it manages to treat not only logic programming, but the whole class of (normal) constraint logic programming, even in the presence of delays. Moreover, it also provides a characterization of termination when negation is not present. A limitation is that the treatment of negation is analogous to the aforementioned [30].

Theoretically, comparing the power of all these approaches with ours gives the result that they overlap but no one is strictly more powerful than the other.

Turning to all the other works on the subject, *which do not cover negation*, we have already discussed in the introduction what are the advantages of the transformational approach towards all the other methods (for a panoramic, see [13]). Hence, it remains to ask how our approach fits w.r.t. all the other papers based on the transformational approach (cf. [26, 19, 1, 8, 23, 5]).

First, all the cited works only cover the 'strong universal termination' case.

Second, all the works (but for [23]) can only treat *well moded* programs (i.e., cf. Section 3, the class obtained from ST when the unique type allowed is *Ground*), hence restricting by far the applicability scope.

Third, call a transformation T_1 *at least as powerful as* T_2 (notation $T_1 \geq T_2$) if, for every logic program P, $T_2(P)$ terminates implies that $T_1(P)$ terminates (i.e., every program that can be proven terminating by T_2 can be proven terminating even by T_1). Call T_1 *strictly more powerful than* T_2 if $T_1 \geq T_2$ and $T_1 \not\leq T_2$. Then, with the exception of one of the two transformations of [23] (T_{fwm}), which seems to be only of theoretical interest, we have the following result:

Theorem 9.1 *Even when restricting to a type system with the only type Ground, our transformation is strictly more powerful than all the transformations in [26, 19, 1, 8, 23, 5].*

References

[1] G. Aguzzi and U. Modigliani. Proving termination of logic programs by transforming them into equivalent term rewriting systems. *FST&TCS*, LNCS 761, pp. 114–124. 1993.

[2] A. Aiken and T.K. Lakshman. Directional type checking of logic programs. In *Proc. of SAS*, LNCS 864, pages 43–60, 1994.

[3] K.R. Apt and S. Etalle. On the unification free Prolog programs. *Proc. MFCS*, LNCS 711, pp. 1–19. Springer, 1993.

[4] K.R. Apt and D. Pedreschi. Proving termination of general Prolog programs. In *Proc. TACS*, LNCS 526, pages 265–289. Springer–Verlag, 1991.

[5] T. Arts and H. Zantema. Termination of logic programs using semantic unification. In *Proc. 5th LoPSTr*, LNCS. 1996. To appear.

[6] M. Baudinet. Proving termination properties of Prolog programs: a semantic approach. *Journal of Logic Programming*, 14:1–29, 1992.

[7] F. Bronsard, T.K. Lakshman, and U.S Reddy. A framework of directionality for proving termination of logic programs. *Proc. JICSLP*, pp. 321–335. The MIT Press, 1992.

[8] M. Chtourou and M. Rusinowitch. Méthode transformationnelle pour la preuve de terminaison des programmes logiques. Manuscript, 1993.

[9] K.L. Clark and S.-Å. Tärnlund. A first order theory of data and programs. In B. Gilchrist, editor, *Proc. IFIP Congress on Information Processing*, pp. 939–944, 1977.

[10] H. Coelho and J.C. Cotta. *Prolog by Example*. Springer–Verlag, 1988.

[11] L. Colussi, E. Marchiori, and M. Marchiori. On termination of constraint logic programs. In *Proc. CP'95*, LNCS 976, pp. 431–448. Springer, 1995.

[12] T. Conway, F. Henderson, and Z. Somogyi. Code generation for Mercury. In *Proc. International Logic Programming Symposium*, pp. 242–256. The MIT Press, 1995.

[13] D. de Schreye and S. Decorte. Termination of logic programs: The never-ending story. *Journal of Logic Programming*, 19,20:199–260, 1994.

[14] S.K. Debray. Static inference of modes and data dependencies in logic programs. *ACM TOPLAS*, 11(3):418–450, July 1989.

[15] N. Dershowitz. Termination of rewriting. *J. of Symbolic Computation*, 3:69–116, 1987.

[16] N. Dershowitz and C. Hoot. Topics in termination. In *Proceedings of the Fifth RTA*, LNCS 690, pp. 198–212. Springer, 1993.

[17] N. Dershowitz and J. Jouannaud. Rewrite systems. *Handbook of Theoretical Computer Science*, vol. B, chapter 6, pp. 243–320. Elsevier – MIT Press, 1990.

[18] N. Franchez, O. Grumberg, S. Katz, and A. Pnueli. Proving termination of Prolog programs. In R. Parikh, editor, *Logics of programs*, pp. 89–105. Springer, 1985.

[19] H. Ganzinger and U. Waldmann. Termination proofs of well-moded logic programs via conditional rewrite systems. *CTRS'92*, LNCS 656, pp. 216–222. Springer, 1993.

[20] G. Levi and F. Scozzari. Contributions to a theory of existential termination for definite logic programs. *GULP-PRODE'95*, pp. 631–642. 1995.

[21] J.W. Lloyd. *Foundations of Logic Programming*. Springer–Verlag, second edition, 1987.

[22] E. Marchiori. Practical methods for proving termination of general logic programs. *The Journal of Artificial Intelligence Research*, 1996. To appear.

[23] M. Marchiori. Logic programs as term rewriting systems. *Proc. 3rd Int. Conf. on Algebraic and Logic Programming*, LNCS 850, pp. 223–241. Springer, 1994.

[24] M. Marchiori. Localizations of unification freedom through matching directions. *Proc. International Logic Programming Symposium*, pp. 392–406. The MIT Press, 1994.

[25] M. Marchiori. The functional side of logic programming. In *Proc. ACM FPCA*, pages 55–65. ACM Press, 1995.

[26] K. Rao, D. Kapur, and R.K. Shyamasundar. A transformational methodology for proving termination of logic programs. *5th CSL*, LNCS 626, pp. 213–226, Springer, 1992.

[27] K. Rao, P.K. Pandya, and R.K. Shyamasunder. Verification tools in the development of provably correct compilers. FME'93, LNCS 670, pp. 442–461. Springer, 1993.

[28] Y. Rouzaud and L. Nguyen-Phoung. Integrating modes and subtypes into a Prolog type checker. In *Proc. JICSLP*, pages 85–97. The MIT Press, 1992.

[29] L. Sterling and E. Shapiro. *The Art of Prolog*. The MIT Press, 1986.

[30] B. Wang and R.K. Shyamasundar. A methodology for proving termination of logic programs. *Journal of Logic Programming*, 21(1):1–30, 1994.

Programming in Lygon: An Overview

James Harland[1]   David Pym[2]   Michael Winikoff[3]

[1] RMIT, GPO Box 2476V, Melbourne 3001, Australia
[2] Queen Mary & Westfield College, University of London, UK
[3] University of Melbourne, Parkville 3052, Australia

Abstract. For many given systems of logic, it is possible to identify, via *systematic* proof-theoretic analyses, a fragment which can be used as a basis for a logic programming language. Such analyses have been applied to linear logic, a logic of *resource-consumption*, leading to the definition of the linear logic programming language *Lygon*. It appears that (the basis of) Lygon can be considered to be the largest possible first-order linear logic programming language derivable in this way. In this paper, we describe the design and application of Lygon. We give examples which illustrate the advantages of resource-oriented logic programming languages.

1 Introduction

Logic programming languages are based upon the observation that certain sequents can be interpreted as a program together with a goal: if Γ is a set of program clauses and $\exists x . \phi$ is a goal clause, the existentially bound variable x being a "logical variable", then the sequent $\Gamma \vdash \exists x . \phi$ is interpreted as a request to search for a term t, *i.e.*, an answer substitution, together with a proof of the sequent $\Gamma \vdash \phi[t/x]$.

In order to identify the fragment of a given system of logic which can form the basis of a logic programming language, one must have an independent notion of what is meant by a logic programming language. Whilst any definition should include the use of Horn clauses in classical logic as a special case, it is not clear exactly what characterizes a logic programming language. For example, precisely how does a logic programming system differ from a theorem prover ? An obvious point of departure is a consideration of the amount of non-determinism inherent in the search for a proof. Implementations of (logic) programming languages must be tolerably efficient: roughly speaking, the lesser the non-determinism, the greater the efficiency. Furthermore, the requirement of "minimal" non-determinism is also motivated by certain "definiteness" requirements (see, for example, [16]). So it is appropriate to consider design principles that limit the non-determinism in the search for proofs.

One such principle is that of *goal-directed provability*, in which the search strategy is determined by the structure of the goal and which the program supplies the context of the (putative) proof. Once we have determined an appropriate notion of goal-directed provability, we can look for classes of formulae for which goal-directed provability is complete for the given consequence relation. Such classes of formulae then form logic programming languages. The analysis of logic programming languages based on this criterion has been carried out for various logics and classes of formulae, including intuitionistic logic [16], higher-order logics [16] and linear logic [7, 17, 12, 19]. Logic programming languages based on linear logic allow a notion of *resource-oriented* programming: by default, a clause in such a program must be used exactly once. This makes the writing of many programs simpler and more intuitive than in a language, such as Prolog, based on classical logic. For example, the resource-sensitive nature of linear logic means that path-problems in graphs can be solved simply and elegantly even in the presence of cycles in the graph. Moreover, the standard transitive closure predicate can be used, with a very minor modification, which will find any path in a graph, whether it is cyclic or not.

In this paper we give an overview of the linear logic programming language *Lygon*. Lygon is based on a fragment of classical linear logic [7] (of which we assume a basic knowledge) identified as a basis for logic programming via a systematic proof-theoretic analysis [17].

In common with other linear logic programming languages, Lygon allows clauses to be used exactly once in a computation, thereby avoiding the need for the explicit resource-counting often necessary in Prolog-like languages. Just as linear logic is a strict extension of classical logic, Lygon is a strict extension of (pure) Prolog: all (pure) Prolog programs can be executed by the Lygon system. Hence all the features of classical pure logic programs are available in Lygon, together with new ones based on linear logic. These include a theoretically transparent notion of *state*, a notion of resources and a form of concurrency. All of these follow from the basis of Lygon in linear logic and *do not require* extra-logical features for their definition.

2 Goal-directedness and resolution in linear logic

In order to obtain a logic programming language based on linear logic, we must, according to the criteria of § 1, identify a class of formulae for which an appropriate notion of resolution proof is complete. Our analysis, presented in detail in [17], appears to provide as broad as possible an interpretation of goal-directedness and thereby appears to allow the broadest possible linear logic programming language. Although the details are beyond the scope of this paper, we briefly review the key ideas.

In the cut-free (linear) sequent calculus, goal-directed proof can be achieved via *uniform proof* [16, 17]. The basic idea, introduced in [16], is to use the left- and right-rules of the sequent calculus as *reduction operators* (in the sense of [13]) and proceed as follows: if, at any stage, some right-rules are applicable, then one of them must be applied; otherwise, *i.e.*, if all goal-formulae are atomic, proceed to apply a left-rule. In linear logic with multiple conclusions, this basic notion is not quite adequate. A slightly weaker notion of goal-directedness, characterized by *simple locally LR proofs* [17], is required. In simple locally LR proofs, certain, highly restricted, occurrences of $\multimap$L are permitted below occurrences of right rules.[4]

Resolution proof is a refinement of uniform (simple locally LR) proof so that only one left-rule, the resolution rule, is required. Completeness of uniform proof depends on a restriction to hereditary Harrop formulae, *i.e.*, just definite-formulae on the left and just

---

[4] In [17], uniform proofs are defined to be simple locally LR proofs.

goal-formulae on the right. Completeness of resolution depends on definite formulae being expressed in a suitable *clausal form*. Full detail of the resolution rule and its proof-theoretic properties can be found in [17]; a sketch is provided below.

2.1 Definite formulae and goal formulae

Goal-directed (uniform [17]) proof is sound and complete for linear hereditary Harrop sequents, $\Gamma \vdash \Delta$, in which Γ and Δ are composed, respectively, of the following classes of D-formulae and G-formulae:

$$D ::= A \mid 1 \mid \bot \mid D \,\&\, D \mid D \otimes D$$
$$\mid D \,\aleph\, D \mid \forall x . D \mid\, ! D$$
$$\mid G \multimap A \mid G \multimap \bot \mid G \multimap 1$$

$$G ::= A \mid 1 \mid \bot \mid \top \mid G \,\&\, G \mid G \otimes G$$
$$\mid G \,\aleph\, G \mid G \oplus G \mid \forall x . G \mid \exists x . G$$
$$\mid\, ! G \mid ? G \mid D \multimap G$$

where A ranges over atomic formulae.[5][6] This class of formulae is compared the language Forum [15] in § 5.

---

[5] Slight extensions to this class are possible. Note that definite formulae of the form $G \multimap (D_1 \,\aleph\, D_2)$ are equivalent to $(G \multimap \bot) \,\aleph\, D_1 \,\aleph\, D_2$. If D_1 and D_2 are atomic, then the equivalence is goal-directed. Weaker notions of goal-directedness, parameterized on classes of definite formulae, are possible. For example, we can choose not to enforce the reduction of a tensor product of atomic formulae, so obtaining goal-directedness "up to $A_1 \otimes A_2$". Under such a choice, the equivalence above is goal-directed even if D_1 and D_2 are permitted to be of the form $A_1 \otimes A_2$. See also Footnote 12.

[6] $D ::= G^\perp$ and $G ::= D^\perp$ are implicit.

For single-conclusioned sequents, the goal-directed interpretation of linear hereditary Harrop formulae is determined by the right-rules of the linear sequent calculus and is explained in detail in [17]. We review a few important cases. (Note that for multiple-conclusioned sequents, which are forced by the presence of $\aleph$ in goals, the situation is complicated by the need to consider locally LR proofs [17].)

- $G_1 \otimes G_2$ is a consequence of Γ *only if* G_1 is a consequence of Γ_1, G_2 is a consequence of Γ_2 and $\Gamma = \Gamma_1, \Gamma_2$. The resources in Γ must be divided into those available to solve G_1 and those available to solve G_2.[7]

- $G_1 \,\&\, G_2$ is a consequence of Γ *only if* G_1 and G_2 are consequences of Γ. The resources in Γ must be used to solve each of G_1 and G_2.

- $D \multimap G$ is a consequence of Γ *only if* G is a consequence of $\Gamma, [D]$. The clausal form $[D]$ of the formula D must be added to the program Γ. The definition of the mapping $[-]$ is related to our definition of resolution: it is discussed below.

- $G_1 \,\aleph\, G_2$ is a consequence of Γ *only if* G_1, G_2 is a consequence of Γ. The program must have sufficient resources to solve both G_1 and G_2 simultaneously. For example, Γ includes a clause of the form $D_1 \,\aleph\, D_2$, then a resolution step (see below) driven by such a clause will cause both program (and goal) to be split, thereby dividing the program into those resources available

---

[7] In general, for multiple-conclusioned sequents, we must divide the resources in the succedent (other than $G_1 \otimes G_2$) as well, but we omit this for simplicity here.

to solve each of G_1 and G_2. A similar splitting is required for the formulae in the succedent.

Discussions of the remaining connectives can be found in [17, 22].

So the right-rules of the linear sequent calculus provide us with an operational interpretation of goal formulae. For resolution proof, we must also provide an operational account of definite formulae.

Essentially, in goal-directed proof, we invoke a left-rule only if no right-rule is applicable, with an exception in the case of $\multimap$L. Consider, then, $\multimap$L,

$$\frac{\Gamma_1 \vdash \phi, \Delta_1 \quad \Gamma_2, \psi \vdash \Delta_2}{\Gamma_1, \Gamma_2, \phi \multimap \psi \vdash \Delta_1, \Delta_2}.$$

In resolution proof, we require a special case of this rule in which the right-hand premiss is an axiom,

$$\frac{\Gamma \vdash \phi, \Delta \quad \overline{\psi \vdash \psi}}{\Gamma, \phi \multimap \psi \vdash \psi, \Delta}.$$

Note that although resolution proof requires that ψ be atomic, non-atomic formulae are permitted in Δ. In this sense, resolution proof is characterized by locally LR proof.

We also require that resolution be the only left-rule required. This is achieved by restricting formulae in the antecedent to be *clausal*. In our setting, the resolution rule codes up instances of $\multimap$L, $\wp$L, &L, $\forall$L and !L, as well as contraction on the left (via !) that can occur in locally LR proofs. Note that $\otimes$L is absent from this list. Outermost occurrences of $\otimes$ on the left are removed by the mapping $[-]$ which reduces (multisets of) linear definite formulae to clausal form in such a way that logical consequence is preserved.

Briefly, the general form of the resolution rule is

$$\frac{\Gamma_1 \vdash \Delta_1 \dots \Gamma_m \vdash \Delta_m}{\Gamma \vdash \Delta},$$

where $\bigcup_{i=1}^{m} \{ \Gamma_i \vdash \Delta_i \}$ is a *resolvant* of $\Gamma \vdash \Delta$, a resolvant being a multiset of sequents that decomposes the structure of the conclusion of the resolution rule according to the structure of a *selected clause*. Propositionally, the basic units of clauses are atomic formulae and the implicational definite formulae, e.g., $G \multimap A$. However, in order for resolution to code up the required instances of &L and $\wp$L, these basic units must be combined by certain instances of &, $\wp$ and $\otimes$. For example, if we let c denote the clause $!((p \multimap r) \wp ((q_1 \otimes q_2) \multimap s))$, then

$$\frac{c, p, p \multimap r \vdash r \quad c, q_1, q_2 \vdash q_1 \otimes q_2}{p, q_1, q_2, !((p \multimap r) \wp ((q_1 \otimes q_2) \multimap s)) \vdash r, s}$$

is an instance of resolution, in which c is the selected clause. In this case, the resolvant has two components, i.e., $m = 2$ because the clause c has as subformulae two basic clauses, $p \multimap r$ and $(q_1 \otimes q_2) \multimap s$, combined by a $\wp$. In this instance of resolution, the basic clause $(q_1 \otimes q_2) \multimap s$ has driven the rule, by matching its head s with the s in the succedent. Since this basic clause is connected in c by a $\wp$ to the basic clause $p \multimap r$, this latter must now also be used. In this example, it is available for use on the left-hand branch. Since c has a ! as its outermost connective, it can continue to be available on both branches, i.e., resolution builds in contractions. The details of clauses and resolution can be found in [17].

To understand the mapping $[-]$, defined fully in in [17], consider a few examples. Firstly, $[p \otimes q] =_{\text{def}} \{ p, q \}$, so that when querying the program $p \otimes q$ with the goal $p \otimes q$, we search for a proof of the sequent $p, q \vdash p \otimes q$, which has a goal-directed proof. Secondly, $[(\forall x \,.\, (p \multimap q(x))) \otimes (r \multimap s)]$ $=_{\mathrm{def}} \{\, p \multimap q(x), r \multimap s \,\}$. Finally, $[!D]$ $=_{\mathrm{def}} \{\, ! \bigotimes_{C \in [D]} C \,\}$.

Resolution proof is complete for consequences of the form $[\mathcal{D}] \vdash \mathcal{G}$. [8]

2.2 Searching for resolution proofs

Whilst resolution proofs provide a basic strategy for finding proofs for the above class of formulae, there is still a significant amount of non-determinism in them. In particular, the problem of "splitting" programs, as specified by the following rule for introducing $\otimes$ on the right, when read as a reduction operator from conclusion to premisses, is not addressed:

$$\frac{\Gamma_1 \vdash G_1, \Delta_1 \quad \Gamma_2 \vdash G_2, \Delta_2}{\Gamma_1, \Gamma_2 \vdash G_1 \otimes G_2, \Delta_1, \Delta_2}.$$

The main problem here is how to "split" a program and goal along the lines specified by this rule. As there is an exponential number of sub-multisets of a given multiset, an exhaustive approach is not feasible. Hodas and Miller [12] have proposed a *lazy sequential* approach to this problem, in which the first conjunct is given all the resources, and those which are not consumed are passed to the second, which must consume all remaining resources. [9]

In the input/output model, the constraint that each formula must appear in exactly one branch is maintained by evaluating the conjuncts sequentially. As the class of formulae considered by Hodas and Miller is somewhat more restrictive than the class of formulae above, it is not obvious how this technique can be systematically applied to the class of formula used in Lygon. It turns out that this approach requires some significant revisions to the proof system. A full description of this process, which is beyond the scope of this paper, can be found in [22]. A brief summary can also be found in [10].

An important point to note that this method of implementation provides us with a method of "state-passing", in that we can think of the passage of "excess" resources from one branch to another as a means of state transition. As we shall see, there are some restrictions placed on this process, in accordance with the rules of the logic, but nonetheless this process has many interesting and useful applications.

3 Programming techniques and examples

In this section, we discuss various programming techniques which distinguish Lygon from Prolog (see also [9, 23, 22, 21]), including several examples of Lygon programs. We begin with brief remarks on Lygon syntax [22].

3.1 Lygon syntax

The current implementation of Lygon (Version 0.4) is an interpreter written in BinProlog[10] The interpreter com-

---

[8] The current Lygon interpreter [22] implements resolution proofs via one-sided sequents [7].

[9] The so-called "input/output model of resource consumption".

[10] Version 0.4 of Lygon is available from the authors by email or via the World Wide Web [21].

prises about 500 lines of code, including comments and whitespace. Version 0.4 supports a limited form of program: clauses are limited to the forms atoms, $\forall \overline{x} . (G \multimap A)$ and $!(\forall \overline{x} . (G \multimap A))$. Universal quantifiers are excluded from goals. Universal and existential quantifiers in programs and goals, respectively, need not be written explicitly, Prolog-style (upper case) logical variables being acceptable. We use the following mapping $\Rightarrow$ between logical connectives and ASCII:

$\otimes \Rightarrow$	*	$\& \Rightarrow$	&	$\bindnasrepma \Rightarrow$	#
$\oplus \Rightarrow$	@	$\multimap \Rightarrow$	->	$-^{\perp} \Rightarrow$	neg -
$\mathbf{1} \Rightarrow$	one	$\top \Rightarrow$	top	$\perp \Rightarrow$	bot

Predicates are as in Prolog. The Lygon equivalent of the Prolog :- is <-.

3.2 Resource allocation

It can be useful sometimes to ignore certain resources, so that rather than requiring that they be used *exactly* once, we only require that they be used *at most* once. Whilst in general this would require a different logic (known as *affine logic*, i.e., linear logic with an unrestricted weakening rule), the effect of this less restrictive approach can be simulated in linear logic. For example, to ensure that the clause C can be used at most once, we can write $C \& \mathbf{1}$. Then we can either use C as normal, or instead use the linear constant $\mathbf{1}$, which we can interpret as the empty clause. Note that this is similar to allowing the weakening rule but not contraction, so that we refer to this as *affine mode*.

A similar trick can be used to specify that a goal need not consume all of the available resources. Consider a program $\mathcal{P}$ and the goal $G \otimes \top$. In order

for this goal to succeed, we must be able to divide up the program so that $\mathcal{P} = \mathcal{P}_1 \cup \mathcal{P}_2$, $\mathcal{P}_1 \vdash G$ and $\mathcal{P}_2 \vdash \top$. Now as the latter sequent is provable for any program $\mathcal{P}_2$ (including the empty program), the goal G need not consume all of the resources of $\mathcal{P}$, as any "leftovers" will be accounted for by $\top$.

An important application of this notion of resource allocation is graph problems. Graphs are an important data structure in computer science. Indeed, there are many applications of graph problems, such as laying cable networks, evaluating dependencies, designing circuits and optimization problems. The ability of Lygon to naturally state and satisfy constraints, such as that every edge in a graph can be used at most once, means that the solution to these problems in Lygon is generally simpler than in a language such as Prolog. The solutions presented are, we consider, concise and lucid.

One of the simplest problems involving graphs is finding paths. The standard Prolog program for path finding is the following one, which simply and naturally expresses that the predicate path is the transitive closure of the predicate edge, in a graph.

```
path(X,Y) :- edge(X,Y).
path(X,Y) :- edge(X,Z),
             path(Z,Y).
```

Whilst this is a simple and elegant program, there are some problems with it. For example, the order of the predicates in the recursive rule is important, as due to Prolog's computation rule, if the predicates are in the reverse order, then goals such as path(a,Y) will loop forever. This problem can be avoided by using a memoing system such as XSB [20], or a bottom-up system such as Aditi [18]. However, it is common to re-write the program above so that the path found is returned as part of the answer. In such cases, systems such as XSB and Aditi will only work for graphs which are acyclic. For example, consider the program below.

```
path(X,Y,[X,Y]) :- edge(X,Y).
path(X,Y,[X|Path]) :-
    edge(X,Z), path(Z,Y,Path).
```

If there are cycles in the graph, then Prolog, XSB and Aditi will all generate an infinite number of paths, many of which will traverse the cycle in the graph more than once.

The main problem is that edges in the graph can be used an arbitrary number of times, and hence we cannot mark an edge as used, which is what is done in many imperative solutions to graph problems. However, in a linear logic programming language such as Lygon, we can easily constrain each edge to be used at most once on any path, and hence eliminate the problem with cycles causing an infinite number of paths to be found.

The code is simple; the main change to the above is to load a "linear" copy of the edge predicate, and use the code as above, but translated into Lygon. Most of this is mere transliteration, and is given below.

```
graph <-
 neg edge(a,b) # neg edge(b,c)
# neg edge(c,d) # neg edge(d,a).

trip(X,Y,[X,Y]) <- edge(X,Y).
trip(X,Y,[X|P]) <-
    edge(X,Z) * trip(Z,Y,P).

path(X,Y,P) <- top * trip(X,Y,P).
```

The extra predicate trip is introduced so that not every path need use every edge in the graph. As written above, trip will only find paths which use every edge in the graph (and so trip can used directly to find Eulerian circuits, i.e., circuits which use every edge in the graph exactly once). However, the path predicate can ignore certain edges, provided that it does not visit any edge more than once, and so the path predicate may be considered the affine form of the predicate trip.

The goal graph is used to load the linear copy of the graph, and as this is a non-linear rule, we can load as many copies of the graph as we like; the important feature is that within each graph no edge can be used twice. We can then find all paths, cyclic or otherwise, starting at node a in the graph with the goal

```
graph # path(a,_,P).
```

This goal yields the solutions below. Note that in the following and in other interactions with the Lygon system we elide irrelevant system responses such as More? (y/n).

```
P = [a,b,c,d,a]    P = [a,b,c,d]
P = [a,b,c]        P = [a,b]
```

We can also find all cycles in the graph with a query such as

```
graph # path(X,X,P).
```

which yields the solutions:

```
X = c, P = [c,d,a,b,c]
X = d, P = [d,a,b,c,d]
X = b, P = [b,c,d,a,b]
X = a, P = [a,b,c,d,a]
```

Note that we are not restricted to only one copy of the graph; if we wanted to do some further graph processing we could use a goal such as (graph # (q1 * top)) & (graph # (q2 * top))..

This provides one copy of the graph to the subgoal q1., and a separate, independent copy to the other subgoal q2..

This example suggests that Lygon is an appropriate vehicle for finding "interesting" cycles, such as Hamiltonian cycles, *i.e.*, those visiting every node in the graph exactly once, which involve counting. We can write such a program in a "generate and test" manner by using the **path** predicate above, and writing a test to see if the cycle is Hamiltonian. The key point to note is that we can delete any edge from a Hamiltonian cycle and we are left with an acyclic path which includes every node in the graph exactly once. Assuming that the cycle is represented as a list, then the test routine will only need to check that the "tail" of the list of nodes in the cycle (*i.e.*, the returned list minus the node at the head of the list) is a permutation of the list of nodes in the graph. Hodas and Miller [12] have shown that such permutation problems can be solved simply in linear logic programming languages by "asserting" each element of each list into an appropriately named predicate, such as list1 and list2, and testing that list1 and list2 have exactly the same solutions.

The full Lygon program for finding Hamiltonian cycles is given below.

```
go(P) <- graph # (top *
         (nodes # hamilton(P))).

graph <- neg edge(a,b) #
 neg edge(b,c) # neg edge(c,d) #
 neg edge(d,a).
nodes <- neg node(a) #
 neg node(b) # neg node(c) #
 neg node(d).

trip(X,Y,[X,Y]) <- edge(X,Y).
trip(X,Y,[X|P]) <- edge(X,Z) *
```

```
         trip(Z,Y,P).

all_nodes([]).
all_nodes([Node|Rest]) <-
    node(Node) * all_nodes(Rest).

hamilton(Path) <- trip(X,X,Path)
 * eq(Path,[_|P]) * all_nodes(P).

eq(X,X).
```

The rôle of the **top** in **go** is to make the **edge** predicate affine (*i.e.*, not every edge need be used). Given the query **go(P)**, the program gives the solutions:

```
P = [c,d,a,b,c]   P = [d,a,b,c,d]
P = [b,c,d,a,b]   P = [a,b,c,d,a]
```

A problem related to the Hamiltonian path is that of the travelling salesman. In the travelling salesman problem we are given a graph as before. However each edge now has an associated *cost*. The solution to the travelling salesman problem is the (or a) Hamiltonian cycle with the minimal total edge cost. Given a facility for finding aggregates, such as **findall** or **bagof** in Prolog, which will enable all solutions to a given goal to be found, we can use the given program for finding Hamiltonian cycles as the basis for a solution to the travelling salesman problem. This would be done by simply finding a Hamiltonian cycle and computing its cost. This computation would be placed within a **findall**, which would have the effect of finding all the Hamiltonian cycles in the graph, as well as the associated cost of each. We would then simply select the minimum cost and return the associated cycle. Note that as this is an NP-complete problem, there is no better algorithm known than one which exhaustively searches through all possibilities.

In order to directly implement the solution described above, aggregate operators in Lygon are needed. As these are not yet present (but their effect can be simulated by some more lengthy code), we do not give the code for this problem here.

3.3 Representing states and actions

When attempting to find a proof of $\mathcal{P} \vdash G_1 \otimes G_2, \mathcal{G}$, we use the technique of passing the unused resources from one conjunct to the other. This can be used as a kind of state-mechanism, in that the first conjunct can pass on information to the second. In particular, we can use this feature to simulate a memory. For example, consider a memory of just two cells, represented by two instances of the predicate m, the first argument being the address and the second the contents of the cell. The state in which these two cells contain the values t_1 and t_2 would then be represented by the multiset of clauses $\{m(1, t_1), m(2, t_2)\}$. A (non-destructive) read for cell 2, say, would be given by the goal $m(2, x) \otimes (m(2, x) \multimap G)$, where G is to be executed after the read. The states in this computation are (i) that $m(2, x)$ is unified with $m(2, t_2)$, (ii) that the latter atom is deleted from the program, and then (iii) added again via the $\multimap$ connective, before G is executed. Note that a similar sequence occurs for the goal $m(2, x) \otimes m^{\perp}(2, x)$.[11] Similarly, writing the value t' into the memory can be done using the goal $m(2, x) \otimes (m(2, t') \multimap G)$, where it is possible that t' can contain x, so that either the new value can be dependent on the old,

or t' can be totally independent of the old value. In this way we can use the "delete after use" property of the linear system to model a certain form of destructive assignment.

Using a continuation passing style to encode sequentiality, with a predicate call to invoke continuations, we can create an abstract data type for memory cells using the operations newcell/3, lookup/3 and update/3.

```
newcell(Id,Value,Cont) <-
 neg m(Id,Value) # call(Cont).
lookup(Id,Value,Cont) <-
 m(Id,Value) * (neg m(Id,Value)
 # call(Cont)).
update(Id,NewValue,Cont) <-
 m(Id,_) * (neg m(Id,NewValue)
 # call(Cont)).
```

For example, consider summing a list using a variable which is updated: the top in the second clause is needed to consume the cell once it is no longer needed.

```
sum(List,Result) <-
 newcell(sum,0,
       sumlist(List,Result)).
sumlist([],Result) <-
 lookup(sum,Result,top).
sumlist([N|Ns],Result) <-
 lookup(sum,S,(is(S1,S+N) *
 update(sum,S1,
       sumlist(Ns,Result)))).
```

We can then run the program using a goal such as sum([1,5,3,6,7],X) which yields the solution X = 22.

The notion of state present in Lygon can also be applied in planning type problems where there is a notion of a state and operators which change the state.

The Yale shooting problem [8] is a prototypical example of a problem

---

[11] We write $m^{\perp}(2, x)$, rather than $m(2, x) \multimap \perp$, for brevity.

involving actions. The main technical challenge in the Yale shooting problem is to model the appropriate changes of state, subject to certain constraints. In particular:

1. Loading a gun changes its state from unloaded to loaded;
2. Shooting a gun changes its state from loaded to unloaded;
3. Shooting a loaded gun at a turkey changes its state from alive to dead.

To model this in Lygon, we have predicates alive, dead, loaded, and unloaded, representing the given states, and predicates load and shoot, which, when executed, change the appropriate states. The initial state is to assert alive and unloaded, as initially the turkey is alive and the gun unloaded. The actions of loading and shooting are governed by the following rules:

```
load <- unloaded * neg loaded.
shoot <- alive * loaded *
(neg dead # neg unloaded).
```

Hence given the initial resources alive and unloaded, the goal shoot # load will cause the state to change first to alive and loaded, as shoot cannot proceed unless loaded is true, and then shoot changes the state to dead and unloaded, as required.

Note that the rules for load and shoot can be written in the following manner:[12]

```
load # loaded <- unloaded.
shoot # (dead * unloaded) <-
alive * loaded.
```

Written in this way, the rules above can be considered as stating that if the state is unloaded, then on a request to load, the state is updated to loaded; that if the state is alive and loaded, then on a request to shoot, update the state to dead and unloaded. Hence this way of writing the rules makes the state changes a little more explicit than the previous one, and provides the possibility of a more flexible execution strategy, such as determining the order into which to change the state of the gun from unloaded to loaded, it is necessary to perform a load action.

Note that this program makes essential use of the possibility afforded by Lygon of positive occurrences of # in clauses. In languages, such as Lolli [12], lacking this facility, the second clause, shoot # (dead * unloaded) <- alive * loaded., would have to be written as two special cases. Although the language Forum [15] can represent the first clause, load # loaded <- unloaded., directly, its representation of the second clause would necessarily be more complex and less transparent than Lygon's. Similar remarks obtain for the language LO [2].

A (slightly) less artificial planning problem is the blocks world. The blocks world consists of a number of blocks sitting either on a table or on another block and a robotic arm capable of picking and moving a single block at a time. We seek to model the state of the world and of operations on it.

The predicates used to model the world in the Lygon program below are the following:

- empty: the robotic arm is empty;
- hold(A): the robotic arm is holding block A;
- clear(A): block A does not sup-

---

[12] The first clause load # loaded <- unloaded. can be considered an abbreviation for (bot <- unloaded) # loaded # load.. See Footnote 5.

port another block;

- ontable(A): block A is supported by the table;
- on(A,B): block A is supported by block B.

There are a number of operations that change the state of the world. We can **take** a block. This transfers a block that does not support another block into the robotic arm. It requires that the arm is empty.

```
take(X) <- (empty * clear(X) *
ontable(X)) * neg hold(X).
```

We can **remove** a block from the block beneath it, which must be done before picking up the bottom block.

```
remove(X,Y) <-
(empty * clear(X) * on(X,Y))
* (neg hold(X) # neg clear(Y)).
```

We can also **put** a block down on the table or **stack** it on another block.

```
put(X) <- hold(X) * (neg empty #
neg clear(X) # neg ontable(X)).
stack(X,Y) <- (hold(X) *
clear(Y)) * (neg empty #
neg clear(X) # neg on(X,Y)).
```

Finally, we can describe the initial state of the blocks.

```
initial <- neg ontable(a) #
neg ontable(b) # neg on(c,a)
# neg clear(b) # neg clear(c)
# neg empty.
```

```
Lygon (initial # take(c) # put(c)
    # take(a) # stack(a,b)
    # showall(R)).
[empty,on(a,b),clear(a),clear(c),
ontable(c), ontable(b)]
Succeeded.
```

The order of the instructions **take**, **put** *etc.* is not significant: there are actions, specified by the rules, such as put(c), which cannot take place from the initial state, and others, such as take(b) which can. It is the problem of the implementation to find an appropriate order in which to execute the instructions, so giving the final state.

By allowing clause heads to contain multiple formulae (in the manner of LO [2]), the rules describing state transitions become more clearly stated and allow the possibility of more flexible execution. For example, the **put** rule becomes

```
put(X) # (empty * clear(X) *
ontable(X)) <- hold(X).
```

This rule can be read as "given that we are holding block X, we can do a **put**; the resulting state has the **hold** fact deleted and contains the facts **empty**, clear(X) and ontable(X)".

3.4 Concurrency

Our next example is the classical dining philosophers (or logic programmers) problem and illustrates the use of Lygon to model concurrent behaviour.[13] This solution is adapted from [4].

For N logic programmers there are $N - 1$ "room tickets". Before entering the room each logic programmer must take a roomticket from a shelf beside the door. This prevents all of the programmers from being in the room at the same time.

The program uses a number of linear predicates: **rm** represents a roomticket, log(X) represents the Xth programmer and ch(X) the Xth chopstick.

---

[13] This problem is particularly apt — Lygon's name is of gastronomic origin.

Since the Lygon implementation is basically unfair, one of the logic programmers dominates the action. It is a simple matter (five lines of code) to modify the Lygon interpreter to use a fairer strategy which allows all of the programmers a chance to dine.

```
go <-  log(a) # neg ch(a)
# neg rm # log(b) # neg ch(b)
# neg rm # log(c) # neg ch(c)
# neg rm # log(d) # neg ch(d)
# neg rm # log(e) # neg ch(e).


log(N) <- hack(N) * rm *
 succmod(N,N1) * ch(N) * ch(N1)
 * eat(N) * (neg ch(N) #
 neg ch(N1) # neg rm # log(N)).
```

Procedurally, this code is read as: get a room ticket; get the chopsticks in sequence; eat; return the chopsticks and room ticket; go back to hacking.

```
succmod(a,b).    succmod(d,e).
succmod(b,c).    succmod(e,a).
succmod(c,d).
```

```
eat(N) <- print('log(')
 * print(N) * print(')')
 eating') * nl.
hack(N) <- print('log(')
 * print(N) * print(')')
 hacking') * nl.
```

We have the following interaction with the modified system:

```
Lygon ['phil.lyg'].
.............................
Lygon go.
log(e) hacking    log(e) eating
log(d) hacking    log(d) eating
```

3.5 Counting clauses

Another problem, in which the properties of linear logic make a significant

simplification and which has been discussed as a motivation for the use of embedded implications in the presence of Negation-as-Failure [3, 5], is the following: given a number of clauses $r(1)$, $\ldots r(n)$, how can we determine whether n is odd or even ? The program below has been used for this purpose.

```
even :- not odd.
odd :- select(X),
       (mark(X) => even).
select(X) :- r(X), not mark(X).
```

Note the dependence on the co-existence of Negation-as-Failure and embedded implications. In the linear case, there is no need to do the explicit marking, as this will be taken care of by the Lygon system. This can be thought of as a simple aggregate problem; a good solution to this would indicate potential for more involved problems (and possibly some meta-programming possibilities). Clearly the marking step can be subsumed by the linear properties of Lygon, resulting in a conceptually simpler program, which is given below.

```
check(Y) <-
 r(X) * (toggle # check(Y)).
check(X) <- count(X).


toggle <- (count(even) *
 neg count(odd)) @ (count(odd)
 * neg count(even)).
```

The goal

```
neg count(even) # neg r(1)
# neg r(2) # check(X).
```

returns the answer X = even.

4 Other techniques

We briefly review the possibility of programming in Lygon with notions of *glo-*

bal variables, *mutual exclusion* and *preserving context*. Other possible notions, not considered here but briefly discussed in [9], include "soft" deletes and additions.

4.1 Global variables

In linear logic, formulae cannot be copied unless they commence with a !, variables which appear outside the scope of a ! cannot be standardized apart; hence variable names can persist across clauses. Consequently, we denote any universally quantified variable which appears in a clause outside the scope of any occurrence of ! as a *global variable*. Such a variable can occur in more than one clause and, in contrast to Prolog, such occurrences cannot be standardized apart. This is because in linear logic the universal quantifier does not distribute over $\otimes$, *i.e.*, that the two formulae $\forall x.\,(p(x) \otimes q(x))$ and $(\forall x.\,p(x)) \otimes (\forall x.\,q(x))$ are not equivalent. This contrasts with the case in classical logic, in which the formulae $\forall x.\,(p(x) \wedge q(x))$ and $(\forall x.\,p(x)) \wedge (\forall x.\,q(x))$ are equivalent. So in linear logic, the substitution generated by a unification must sometimes be propagated to other clauses.

Thus when a global variable is involved in a unification, the resulting substitution must be applied to other parts of the program. In programming terms, this property can be interpreted as a (restricted) form of a pointer.

Another possible application of global variables is to message passing. In this case, the variable would be instantiated to a non-ground term, usually a list, with the ground parts of the instantiating term being interpreted as a message. The last element of the list

would always be a variable, thus ensuring that the message-list can always have a further message appended to it. In this way different clauses can communicate by means of this shared message-list.

A mixture of global and local variables can have some interesting effects. For example, consider the definite formulae $\forall x.\,!\forall y.\,p(x, y)$, corresponding to the clause $!\,p(x, y)$, in which x is global and y is local. For the formula $p(t_1, t_2) \otimes p(u_1, u_2)$ to be provable, we must have that $t_1 = u_1$; but there is no restriction on t_2 and u_2. Hence we have that $!\,p(x, y) \vdash p(a, b) \otimes p(a, c)$ but not $!\,p(x, y) \vdash p(a, b) \otimes p(c, d)$.

4.2 Mutual exclusion

The connective $\&$ can be thought of as specifying internal choice; in other words, when faced with a linear program clause such as $C_1 \,\&\, C_2$, one can replace it with either C_1 or C_2. However, it is not (generally) possible to replace it with *both* subformulae. Thus $\&$ can be interpreted as a mutual exclusion operator — the use of one formulae precludes the use of the other. Logically, this arises from the form of the $\&L$ rule, read as a reduction operator. For example, in

$$\frac{\Gamma, G_i \multimap A_i \vdash \Delta}{\Gamma, (G_1 \multimap A_1) \,\&\, (G_2 \multimap A_2) \vdash \Delta} \quad i = 1, 2,$$

once we have chosen one of the basic clauses $G_i \multimap A_i$, the other is no longer available.

Operationally, it seems most natural to implement this via backtracking, which means that $\&$ behaves in a similar manner to pruning operators. For example, given the formula $C_1 \,\&\, C_2$ and the goal G, we first try to prove G using the formula C_1. If we find that G succeeds, we are done. If G fails, then we can backtrack and use C_2 instead. However, at no time are both C_1 and C_2 available.

4.3 Preserving context

As noted above, one of the key features of Lygon is the linear context that must be maintained, *i.e.*, the current resources. These resources are generally updated by one goal and passed to another. However, if it is desired to maintain the same resources, then & in goals can be used. For example, to determine if G_1 succeeds and then restore the same original context for the goal G_2, we need only ask the goal $G_1 \& G_2$. In general, it can be better to use the goal $(G_1 \otimes \top) \& G_2$, so that not all resources need be consumed by the test.

5 Other linear logic programming languages

As well as Lygon, there are various other logic programming languages based on linear logic. These include LO [2], LinLog [1], ACL [14], $\mathcal{LC}$ [19], Lolli [12, 11] and Forum [15].

An adequate comparison of Lygon with these languages is beyond the scope of this paper. However, we emphasize the following points: (i) Lygon is the result of a systematic proof-theoretic analysis of linear logic with respect to the goal-directed account of logic programming [17, 16]; (ii) Consequently, Lygon is (based on) the largest fragment of linear logic of all the languages given above. Although Forum is described (in [15]) as a logic programming language for all of linear logic, only a

fragment of Forum is a logic programming language according to the goal-directed account of logic programming [16, 17], the rest of linear logic being obtained via equivalences which lack goal-directed proofs.[14] J. Hodas and J. Polakow have recently made similar observations.

6 Discussion

One of the main lessons that we have learnt from writing programs in Lygon is that the programming methodology seems to have some significant differences from Prolog. In particular, resource-sensitivity is critical. For example, in the blocks world program in § 3.3, the information that we wish to extract from the computation is the final state of the blocks. This is given explicitly by the state of the linear predicates rather than by any particular answer substitution. This suggests that programming in Lygon would seem to be *resource-oriented* rather than just *substitution-oriented* — it is easy to envisage input and output as formulae, rather than just as terms.

More examples in which the linear logic basis of Lygon facilitates elegant solutions to problems are given in [21]. Included are modelling exceptions, parsing visual diagrams using multiset grammars and solving bin-packing problems. Other possibilities for further investigation include the use of Lygon as an object-oriented language (*cf.* [2]) and the use of Lygon for agent-based applications which combine planning and concurrency.

The operational model on which the current implementation [22, 21] of Lygon is based represents only one choice

---

[14] See also Footnotes 5 and 12.

among many. For example, many variations on the basic input/output model are possible. One possibility would be a concurrent model in which different multiplicative branches of a search, e.g., created by a $\otimes R$, would have access to the same collection of resources, thereby necessitating explicit communication between branches as resources be consumed. Other variations would include ones motivated entirely by efficiency concerns.

Acknowledgements

We thank the referees and many colleagues for their comments this work. The partial support of the Australian Research Council, the Collaborative Information Technology Research Institute, the Centre for Intelligent Decision Systems and the UK EPSRC is gratefully acknowledged. Michael Winikoff is supported by an Australian Postgraduate Award.

References

1. J.-M. Andreoli. Logic Programming with Focusing Proofs in Linear Logic. *J. Logic Computat.* 2(3), 1992.
2. J.-M. Andreoli and R. Pareschi. Linear objects: Logical processes with built-in inheritance. *New Gen. Comp.*, 9:445-473, 1991.
3. A. Bonner and L. McCarty. Adding Negation-as-Failure to Intuitionistic Logic Programming. Proc. NACLP, 681-703, Austin, October, 1990.
4. N. Carriero and D. Gelernter. Linda in context. *CACM*, 32(4):444-458, 1989.
5. P. Dung. Hypothetical Logic Programming. Proc. 3rd. International Workshop on Extensions of Logic Programming 61-73, LNCS, Springer, 1992.
6. M. van Emden and R. Kowalski. The Semantics of Predicate Logic as a Programming Language. *J.ACM* 23:4:733-742, 1976.
7. J.-Y. Girard. Linear Logic. *Theoret. Comp. Sci.* 50, 1-102, 1987.
8. S. Hanks and D. MacDermott. Nonmonotonic Logic and Temporal Projection. *Artif. Intell.* 33:3:379-412, 1987.
9. J. Harland and D. Pym. A note on the implementation and applications of linear logic programming languages. *Australian Computer Science Communications* 16(1), 647-658, 1994.
10. J. Harland, D. Pym and M. Winikoff. Programming in Lygon: a system demonstration. This volume.
11. J. Hodas. *Logic Programming in Intuitionistic Linear Logic: Theory, Design and Implementation.* PhD thesis, University of Pennsylvania, 1994.
12. J. Hodas and D. Miller. Logic Programming in a Fragment of Intuitionistic Linear Logic. *Inform. and Computat.* 110:2:327-365, 1994.
13. S.C. Kleene. *Mathematical Logic.* Wiley and Sons, 1968.
14. N. Kobayash and A. Yonezawa. ACL - A Concurrent Linear Logic Programming Paradigm. Proc. ILPS'93, D. Miller (ed.), 279-294, MIT Press, 1993.
15. D. Miller. A multiple-conclusion metalogic. Proc. *LICS'94*, 272-281, IEEE, 1994.
16. D. Miller, G. Nadathur, F. Pfenning and A. Ščedrov. Uniform Proofs as a Foundation for Logic Programming. *Ann. Pure Appl. Logic* 51 (1991) 125-157.
17. D. Pym and J. Harland. A Uniform Proof-theoretic Investigation of Linear Logic Programming. *J. Logic Computat.* 4:2:175-207, 1994.
18. J. Vaghani, K. Ramamohanarao, D. Kemp, Z. Somogyi, P. Stuckey, T. Leask and J. Harland. *The Aditi Deductive Database System.* VLDB J. 3:2:245-288, 1994.
19. P. Volpe. Concurrent Logic Programming as Uniform Linear Proofs. In: G. Levi and M. Rodríguez-Artalejo (eds.), *Algebraic and Logic Programming*, 133-149. Springer, 1994.
20. D.S. Warren. Programming the PTQ Grammar in XSB. in *Applications of Logic Databases*, Raghu Ramakrishna (ed.), Kluwer Academic, 1994.
21. M. Winikoff. Lygon home page (subject to alteration). http://www.cs.mu.oz.au/~winikoff/lygon/lygon.html.
22. M. Winikoff and J. Harland. Implementing the linear logic programming language Lygon. In: J. Lloyd (ed.), *Proc. ILPS'95*, 66-80, MIT Press, 1995.
23. M. Winikoff and J. Harland. Some applications of the linear logic programing language Lygon. *Australian Computer Science Communications*, 18(1), Kotagiri Romamohanarao (editor), 1996.

Some Characteristics of
Strong Innermost Normalization

M. R. K. Krishna Rao*

Max-Planck-Institut für Informatik
Im Stadtwald
66123 Saarbrücken, GERMANY
e-mail: **krishna@mpi-sb.mpg.de**

Abstract. A term rewriting system is *strongly innermost normalizing* if every innermost derivation of it is of finite length. This property is very important in the integration of functional and logic programming paradigms. Unlike termination, strong innermost normalization is not preserved under subsystems, i.e., every subsystem of a strongly innermost normalizing need not be strongly innermost normalizing. Preservation of a property under subsystems is important in analyzing systems in a modular fashion. In this paper, we identify a few classes of TRSs which enjoy this property. These classes are of particular interest in studying modularity of composable and hierarchical combinations. It is also proved that the choice of the innermost redex to be reduced at any step has no bearing on termination (finiteness) of innermost derivations. It may be noted that such selection invariance does not hold for outermost derivations. The proof techniques used are novel and involve oracle based reasoning –which is very sparsely used in the rewriting literature.

1 Introduction

In the last few decades, term rewriting systems (TRS, for short) have played a fundamental role in the analysis and implementation of abstract data type specifications, decidability of word problems, theorem proving, computability theory, design of functional programming languages (e.g. Miranda), integration of functional programming and logic programming paradigms, etc.

Termination and confluence are two fundamental properties of TRSs. When termination of each and every computation cannot be ensured, specialized termination properties such as termination under some reduction strategy are very useful. The innermost reduction strategy –which closely corresponds to call-by-value evaluations– is an important strategy. A TRS is *strongly innermost normalizing* (also called, innermost terminating) if every innermost derivation is of finite length. Strong innermost normalization (SIN) property of TRSs is important in

---

* On leave from Tata Institute of Fundamental Research, Bombay. The work was partially carried out at TIFR.

studying termination of logic programs by transforming them into TRSs [6] and implementation of functional logic programming languages [4] etc. A logic program terminates for a class of queries if the derived TRS innermost terminates (not necessarily terminate under all reduction strategies) [1]. In the functional logic programming, innermost reduction strategy is used for both narrowing as well as rewrite steps. In this paper, we study about the strong innermost normalization property of TRSs.

If a rewrite system terminates, every subsystem of it terminates as well. This nice property is useful in analyzing TRSs in an incremental (modular) fashion using the divide-and-conquer approach. Unfortunately strong innermost normalization lacks this property as can be seen from the following simple example. The system {f(a) → f(a); a → b} is a strongly innermost normalizing system but its subsystem {f(a) → f(a)} is not strongly innermost normalizing. This raises a question 'for what classes of systems strong innermost normalization is preserved under subsystems?'. In this paper, we provide some answers to this question by identifying a few classes of systems with this nice property.

It is proved that every subsystem of a strongly innermost normalizing overlay system is strongly innermost normalizing. Then a (somewhat surprising) observation is made through a counterexample: an independent subsystem (which does not create any new redeces of the rules omitted) of a strongly innermost normalizing system need not be strongly innermost normalizing. The independent subsystems play a very crucial role in studying modularity of composable and hierarchical combinations, where two systems sharing some defined symbols and rewrite rules are combined (see a.o. [7, 8, 9, 11]). Two sufficient conditions for strong innermost normalization of independent subsystems are proposed: (i) the subsystem is non-duplicating or (ii) the omitted rules do not overlap the rules in the chosen subsystem. These two results are tight in the sense that violation of both these conditions leads to a counterexample.

In the second part of the paper, we establish that the choice of the innermost redex to be reduced at any step has no bearing on termination (finiteness) of innermost derivations. That is, if a TRS is innermost terminating under a particular (e.g., leftmost innermost) reduction strategy, it is innermost terminating under any other strategy. For simplicity, we consider leftmost innermost strategy and show that every leftmost innermost normalizing system is strongly innermost normalizing. Then, we show that this selection invariance result is very handy in proving strong innermost normalization property, by presenting a straightforward proof for one of the main results of [7], i.e., modularity of strong innermost normalization property for a class of hierarchical combinations. In general, this selection invariance does not hold for outermost normalization (see Example 3).

2 Preliminaries

We assume that the reader is familiar with the basic terminology of term rewriting systems and give definitions only when they are required. The notations not defined in the paper can be found in Dershowitz and Jouannaud [2], or Klop [5].

In the following, $T(\mathcal{F}, \mathcal{X})$ denotes the set of terms constructed from a set of function symbols $\mathcal{F}$ and a set of variables $\mathcal{X}$, and $F(t)$ denotes the set of function symbols occurring in term t. The root of a term t is defined as: $root(t) = f$ if $t \equiv f(s_1, \ldots, s_n)$, and $root(t) = t$ if $t \in \mathcal{X}$.

Definition 1 (critical pairs)
Let $l_1 \to r_1$ and $l_2 \to r_2$ be renamed versions of rules in a rewrite system $\mathcal{R}(\mathcal{F}, R)$ such that they have no variables in common. Suppose $l_{1|p}$ is not a variable for some position p and $l_{1|p}$ unifies with l_2 through a most general unifier σ. *The pair of terms* $\langle l_1[r_2]_p\sigma, r_1\sigma \rangle$ *is called a critical pair*[2] *of* $\mathcal{R}(\mathcal{F}, R)$. If $l_1 \to r_1$ and $l_2 \to r_2$ are renamed versions of the same rewrite rule, we do not consider the case $p = \epsilon$. A critical pair $\langle l_1[r_2]_p\sigma, r_1\sigma \rangle$ with $p = \epsilon$ is called an *overlay*, and a critical pair $\langle s, t \rangle$ is *trivial* if $s \equiv t$.

The following definition defines the classes of overlay systems.

Definition 2 *A term rewriting system* $\mathcal{R}(\mathcal{F}, R)$ *is an* overlay system *if all its critical pairs are overlays.*

The following definition defines the notion of innermost normalization.

Definition 3 A reduction step $C[l\sigma] \Rightarrow C[r\sigma]$ with rewrite rule $l \to r$ is an *innermost* reduction step if no proper subterm of $l\sigma$ is reducible. We denote the innermost rewrite relation by $\Rightarrow_i$. A TRS is strongly innermost normalizing (SIN) if it has no infinite innermost derivation $t_1 \Rightarrow_i t_2 \Rightarrow_i \cdots$. A TRS is weakly innermost normalizing (WIN) if every term can be reduced to a normal form through an innermost rewriting derivation.

3 Innermost Normalization of Overlay Systems

In this section, we establish that strong innermost normalization is preserved under subsystems for the class of overlay systems. In the following, we consider a TRS $\mathcal{R}$ and its subsystem $\mathcal{R}'$. The innermost rewrite relation of $\mathcal{R}$ is denoted by $\Rightarrow_{i_\mathcal{R}}$ and that of $\mathcal{R}'$ by $\Rightarrow_{i_{\mathcal{R}'}}$. Further, $s \Rightarrow_{i_\mathcal{R}}^k t$ indicates that s reduces to t through an innermost derivation of length k. The set of innermost redex positions of $\mathcal{R}$ in a term t is denoted by $INP(t)$ and the set of innermost redex positions of $\mathcal{R}'$ in t is denoted by $INP'(t)$.

We essentially show that there is an infinite innermost derivation of $\mathcal{R}$ whenever there is an infinite innermost derivation of $\mathcal{R}'$. For any innermost derivation S' of $\mathcal{R}'$ starting with a term s, we exhibit an innermost derivation S of $\mathcal{R}$ starting with s such that all the reductions in S' are done in S with the same rules as in S' and the other reductions in S are done with some discipline. Some discipline is enforced to take care of the non-left-linear rules by reducing a normal form of $\mathcal{R}'$ using one particular rule whenever that term is reduced in S (any number of times). This is achieved by keeping the *history* of reductions which only occur in S but not in S'.

The following lemmas are needed.

[2] $t_{|p}$ denotes the subterm of t at position p and $t[u]_p$ denotes the term obtained from t by replacing the subterm $t_{|p}$ with u.

Lemma 1 If $l \to r$ is a rule in a weakly innermost normalizing overlay system $\mathcal{R}$ and $s \equiv l\sigma$ is not an innermost redex, then *there exists a term s' such that* $s \Rightarrow^*_{i_\mathcal{R}} s'$ *and s' is an innermost redex.*

Proof: Since $\mathcal{R}$ is weakly innermost normalizing, every term can be reduced to a normal form through an innermost derivation. So σ can be reduced to an irreducible substitution σ' by reducing $X\sigma$ to a normal form through innermost reduction, for each variable $X \in Var(l)$. Since $\mathcal{R}$ is an overlay system, $s' \equiv l\sigma'$ is an innermost redex. $\qquad\qquad\square$

Lemma 2 Let $l \to r$ be a rule in an overlay system $\mathcal{R}$ and $s \equiv l\sigma \Rightarrow^* t$ be a derivation such that no reduction step took place at the root and $s \equiv C[s_1, \cdots, s_m]$ and $t \equiv C[t_1, \cdots, t_m]$ such that $s_i \equiv s_j$ if and only if $t_i \equiv t_j$. Then *there exists a term t' such that $t \Rightarrow^* t'$ and $t' \equiv l\sigma'$ for some substitution σ'. Further if $\mathcal{R}$ is weakly innermost normalizing and $s \equiv l\sigma \Rightarrow^* t$ is an innermost derivation, then $s \Rightarrow^*_i t \Rightarrow^*_i l\sigma''$ and $l\sigma''$ is an innermost redex.*

Proof: Without loss of generality, we assume that C is the maximal context such that no reduction in $s \Rightarrow^* t$ took place in C, i.e., at least one step in $s_i \Rightarrow^* t_i$ took place at root for each $i \in [1, m]$. Since $\mathcal{R}$ is an overlay system, each s_i must be a subterm of $X\sigma$ for some variable $X \in Var(l)$. Now, let σ' be a substitution such that $X\sigma' \equiv X\sigma$ if no occurrence of $X\sigma$ is reduced in $s \Rightarrow^* t$ and $X\sigma' \equiv u$ if an occurrence of $X\sigma$ is reduced to u in $s \Rightarrow^* t$. The condition $s_i \equiv s_j$ if and only if $t_i \equiv t_j$ ensures that every reduced occurrence of $X\sigma$ is reduced to u in $s \Rightarrow^* t$. It is easy to see that t can be reduced to $l\sigma'$ by reducing each occurrence of $X\sigma$ in C to $X\sigma'$ for each variable X in l. The second part of the lemma can be proved on similar lines using the above lemma. $\qquad\qquad\square$

The following theorem exhibits an innermost derivation S of $\mathcal{R}$ corresponding to an innermost derivation S' of $\mathcal{R}'$ starting with a term.

Theorem 1 Let $\mathcal{R}'$ be a subsystem of a strongly innermost normalizing overlay TRS $\mathcal{R}$. Then $s \Rightarrow^k_{i_{\mathcal{R}'}} t$ implies that there exits a term w such that

(i) $s \Rightarrow^{k'}_{i_\mathcal{R}} w$,

(ii) $k' \geq k \geq 0$,

(iii) $INP(w) = INP'(t)$ and for each $p \in INP'(t)$ the sequence of function symbols occurring from root to p is the same in both t and w,

(iv) if $t_{|p} \equiv l\sigma$ for some $p \in INP'(t)$ then $w_{|p} \equiv l\sigma'$, where σ' is a substitution obtained by innermost normalizing (w.r.t. $\mathcal{R}$) $X\sigma$ for each variable $X \in Var(l)$ and

(v) $w_{|q} \equiv w_{|q'}$ if $t_{|q} \equiv t_{|q'}$ for any two positions q and q' occurring in both t and w.

Proof (sketch): Induction on k.

Basis: $k = 0$. In this case $t \equiv s$. If $INP(s) = INP'(s)$, we can take $w \equiv s$. Otherwise, we can obtain w from s by reducing redeces which are innermost redeces w.r.t. R but not w.r.t. R' using the following **while** loop with initial values $History = \phi$; $u = s$; $v = s$.

while $INP(u) \neq INP'(v)$ and u is not a normal form of $\mathcal{R}$ **do**
begin
    Let $p \in INP(u) - INP'(v)$;
    if $u_{|p}$ occurs in the first column of $History$
        then Reduce $u_{|p}$ to w using the rule associated with this term
        else begin
                Reduce $u_{|p}$ to w using any applicable rule $l \to r \in \mathcal{R}$;
                Place a pair $\langle u_{|p}, \ l \to r \rangle$ in $History$.
            end;
    $u := u[w]_p$
end

We take the final value of u as our w. The **while** loop terminates as $\mathcal{R}$ is strongly innermost normalizing. We show that it terminates with $INP(u) = INP'(v)$.

It is clear that no position in $INP(s)$ is above any position in $INP'(s)$. So each position in $INP(s)$ is either below some position in $INP'(s)$ or disjoint from all the positions in $INP'(s)$. We can normalize all the redeces in s not below any position in $INP'(s)$ to get a term s'. Now consider a redex position $p \in INP'(s) = INP'(s')$ and let $s'_{|p} \equiv l\sigma$. By Lemma 1, we have $l\sigma \Rightarrow^*_{i_\mathcal{R}} l\sigma'$, where σ' is an irreducible substitution derived from σ by reducing each $X\sigma$ to a normal form. Further, $l\sigma'$ is an innermost redex. Repeating the same process at every position in $INP'(s')$ we get a term w such that $s \Rightarrow^*_{i_\mathcal{R}} w$ and $INP'(s) = INP(w)$ ensuring statements (i)-(iv) of the theorem. We do all these normalizations using the above **while** loop and $History$ ensures the statement (v) of the theorem.

Induction step : $k = m + 1$. Let $s \Rightarrow^m_{i_{\mathcal{R}'}} t' \Rightarrow_{i_{\mathcal{R}'}} t$. By induction hypothesis, $s \Rightarrow^{m'}_{i_\mathcal{R}} w'$ such that $m' \geq m$ and $INP'(t') = INP(w')$. Let $l \to r$ be the rule and σ be the substitution applied in $t' \Rightarrow_{i_{\mathcal{R}'}} t$ (say at position p), that is, $t_{|p} \equiv r\sigma$. By induction hypothesis, $w'_{|p} \equiv l\sigma'$, where σ' is a substitution obtained by innermost normalizing (w.r.t. $\mathcal{R}$) $X\sigma$ for each variable $X \in Var(l)$ and hence we get $w' \Rightarrow_{i_\mathcal{R}} w'[r\sigma']_p \equiv u$. That is, $t_{|p} \equiv r\sigma$ and $u_{|p} \equiv r\sigma'$. Now, we exhibit a term w such that $INP'(t) = INP(w)$. Consider a position $p' \in INP'(t)$ and assume that $t_{|p'} \equiv l_1\theta_1$. By induction hypothesis, $t'_{|p'} \Rightarrow^*_{i_\mathcal{R}} w'_{|p'}$. If p' is disjoint from p, it is obvious that $p' \in INP'(t') = INP(w')$ and we only have to consider p' above/at/below p. Since σ is irreducible, p' must be either (a) in r or (b) above p.

Case (a): Since $r\sigma \Rightarrow^*_{i_\mathcal{R}} r\sigma'$, it is obvious that $t_{|p'} \Rightarrow^*_{i_\mathcal{R}} u_{|p'}$ and none of these reductions took place at p' as these reductions involve reduction of $X\sigma$ to $X\sigma'$. By Lemma 2, $u_{|p'} \Rightarrow^*_{i_\mathcal{R}} l_1\theta'_1$ such that $l_1\theta'_1$ is an innermost redex. We reduce u to a term w using the above **while** loop with the $History$ of the derivation $s \Rightarrow^{m'}_{i_\mathcal{R}} w'$ such that $INP'(t) = INP(w)$ and other statements of the theorem hold. It is easy to see from the proof of Lemma 2 that the reductions in $u_{|p'} \Rightarrow^*_{i_\mathcal{R}} l_1\theta'_1$ are indeed the ones enforced by the **while** loop.

Case (b): p' is above p. We show that for every non-variable position q in l_1, the function symbol is the same in both t and u at position $p'.q$. This ensures that we can reduce u to a term w using the above **while** loop with the $History$ of the derivation $s \Rightarrow_{i_{\mathcal{R}}}^{m'} w'$ such that $INP'(t) = INP(w)$ and other statements of the theorem hold.

Subcase (1): $p'.q$ lies in $r\sigma$ in t. If the function symbols at position $p'.q$ in t and u are different, $p'.q$ must occur inside $X\sigma$ in t and there should be at least one reduction step above $p'.q$ in the derivation $X\sigma \Rightarrow^* X\sigma'$. Since $\mathcal{R}$ is an overlay system this is impossible.

Subcase (2): $p'.q$ lies outside $r\sigma$ in t (and hence outside $l\sigma$ in t'). If $p'.q$ lies above p, it follows from induction hypothesis that the function symbol at $p'.q$ is the same in both t and u. Now consider the case that $p'.q$ is disjoint from p. If the function symbol at $p'.q$ is not the same in both t and u (and hence in both t' and w'), a reduction must have taken place in $s \Rightarrow_i^* w'$ at/above $p'.q$ (which did not take place in $s \Rightarrow_{i_{\mathcal{R}'}}^* t'$). This is not possible as $\mathcal{R}$ is an overlay system and q is a non-variable position in l_1.

Therefore, for every non-variable position q in l_1, the function symbol is the same in both t and u at position $p'.q$. This completes the proof. $\square$

The following theorem presents the main result of this section.

Theorem 2 Every subsystem $\mathcal{R}'$ of a strongly innermost normalizing overlay system $\mathcal{R}$ is strongly innermost normalizing.

Proof: Follows from the above theorem. $\square$

If the rules in $\mathcal{R} - \mathcal{R}'$ do not overlap with the rewrite rules in $\mathcal{R}'$ at a non-root position, one may conjecture that strong innermost normalization of $\mathcal{R}$ implies strong innermost normalization of the subsystem $\mathcal{R}'$. The following counterexample refutes this conjecture.

Example 1 The following system $\mathcal{R}$ is strongly innermost normalizing.

$$\mathbf{f(g(x))} \rightarrow \mathbf{f(g(h(a)))}$$
$$\mathbf{g(a)} \rightarrow \mathbf{b}$$
$$\mathbf{h(x)} \rightarrow \mathbf{x}$$

But the independent subsystem $\mathcal{R}'$ containing the first two rules is not strongly innermost normalizing as the following innermost derivation of $\mathcal{R}'$ loops: $\mathbf{f(g(x))} \Rightarrow_{i_{\mathcal{R}'}} \mathbf{f(g(h(a)))} \Rightarrow_{i_{\mathcal{R}'}} \mathbf{f(g(h(a)))}$. $\square$

The following result of Gramlich [3] is related to the above results.

Theorem 3 Every locally confluent strongly innermost normalizing overlay system is *both confluent and terminating*.

This result says that a (locally) confluent overlay system is terminating if it is strongly innermost normalizing. Since every subsystem of a terminating system is terminating and hence strongly innermost normalizing, we have the following corollary.

Corollary 1 Every subsystem of a (locally) confluent strongly innermost normalizing overlay system is strongly innermost normalizing.

Theorem 2 is more general than this result as Theorem 2 does not need confluence.

4 Innermost Normalization of Independent Subsystems

In the example given in the previous section, $\mathcal{R}'$ can create a new redex which can be reduced by the rule in $\mathcal{R} - \mathcal{R}'$ and this leads to the anomaly that there is an infinite innermost derivation of $\mathcal{R}'$ while there is no infinite innermost derivation of $\mathcal{R}$. In this section, we consider subsystems R' which do not create redeces that can be reduced by the rules in $\mathcal{R} - \mathcal{R}'$. The following notion of dependency relation captures the creation of redeces. Note that the systems considered in this section need not be overlay systems.

Definition 4 The set $D_{\mathcal{R}}$ of *defined* symbols of a term rewriting system $\mathcal{R}(\mathcal{F}, R)$ is defined as $\{root(l) \mid l \to r \in R\}$ and the set $C_{\mathcal{R}}$ of *constructor* symbols of $\mathcal{R}(\mathcal{F}, R)$ is defined as $\mathcal{F} - D_{\mathcal{R}}$.

To show the defined and constructor symbols explicitly, we often write the above rewrite system as $\mathcal{R}(D_{\mathcal{R}}, C_{\mathcal{R}}, R)$ and omit the subscript when such omission does not cause any confusion.

Definition 5 (dependency relation $\succeq_d$ over defined symbols)
The dependency relation of a rewrite system $\mathcal{R}(D, C, R)$ is the smallest quasi-order $\succeq_d$ over D satisfying the following conditions:

- $f \succeq_d f$ for each $f \in D$ **(reflexivity)**
- $f \succeq_d h$ if $f \succeq_d g$ and $g \succeq_d h$ **(transitivity)**
- $f \succeq_d g$ if there is a rewrite rule $l \to r \in R$ such that $f \equiv root(l)$ and $g \in F(r)$.

We say that a defined symbol $f \in D$ *depends on* a defined symbol $g \in D$ if $f \succeq_d g$. The set of symbols depending on a set of symbols S is defined as $\{f \mid f \succeq_d g \text{ and } g \in S\}$. Intuitively, $f \succeq_d g$ means that an evaluation of the defined function f for some arguments *may* involve an evaluation of the defined function g for some arguments (i.e., the definition of f depends in some sense on that of g). It also means that an appearance of f in a derivation might lead to a creation of g in the later part of the derivation.

Definition 6 Let $\mathcal{R}(\mathcal{F}, R)$ be a rewrite system and t be a term in $\mathcal{T}(\mathcal{F}, \mathcal{X})$. A set of function symbols $S \subseteq \mathcal{F}$ is *unreachable* (in $\mathcal{R}$) from t if $S \cap F(t') = \phi$ whenever $t \Rightarrow_{\mathcal{R}}^* t'$.

Lemma 3 Let $\mathcal{R}(\mathcal{F}, R)$ be a rewrite system, $S \subseteq \mathcal{F}$ be a set of function symbols and t be a term in $\mathcal{T}(\mathcal{F}, \mathcal{X})$. Then, S *is unreachable from t if no function symbol in t depends on S.*

Now, we define the notion of independent subsystems.

Definition 7 A subsystem $\mathcal{R}'$ of a rewrite system $\mathcal{R}$ is *independent* if $f \not\succeq_d g$ for every pair of defined symbols in $\mathcal{R}$ such that f is a defined symbol of $\mathcal{R}'$ and g is a defined symbol of $\mathcal{R} - \mathcal{R}'$.

The defined symbols of $R - R'$ do not occur in the right-hand sides of rules in R' but they can occur in the left-hand sides of rules in R' if R' is an independent subsystem of R. The defined symbols of R' can occur in both left- and right-hand sides of rules in $R - R'$. Essentially, an application of rules in R' does not create new redeces of $R - R'$. This may raise a hope that every independent subsystem of a strongly innermost normalizing system is strongly innermost normalizing. But the following counterexample refutes this conjecture.

Example 2 The following system R is strongly innermost normalizing.

$$f(g(x,y), w) \to f(w, w)$$
$$g(x, y) \to x$$

But the independent subsystem R' containing just the first rule is not strongly innermost normalizing as the following innermost derivation of R' loops:
$$f(g(x,y), g(x,y)) \Rightarrow_{i_{R'}} f(g(x,y), g(x,y)) \qquad \square$$

In the above example, (i) R' is a duplicating system –a TRS is duplicating if some variable occurs more often in the right-hand side than in the left-hand side of rule– and (ii) the left-hand side of the rule in $R - R'$ unifies with a proper subterm of the left-hand side of the rule in R'. We prove in the following that these two properties are essential for the counterexample. In other words, we prove that

1. every non-duplicating independent subsystem of a strongly innermost normalizing system is strongly innermost normalizing and

2. any independent subsystem R' of a strongly innermost normalizing system R is strongly innermost normalizing if the rules in $R - R'$ do not overlap the rules in R'.

To prove these two results, we need the following lemmas.

Lemma 4 If D' is the set of defined symbols of R', D'' is the set of defined symbols of $R - R'$ and R' is an independent subsystem of R, then $D' \cap D'' = \phi$.

Proof: Follows from the definition of independent subsystems. $\qquad \square$

Lemma 5 If D'' is the set of defined symbols of $R - R'$ and R' is an independent subsystem of a strongly innermost normalizing system R, then *there is no infinite innermost derivation of R' starting from any term $t \in \mathcal{T}(F, X)$ such that $F \cap D'' = \phi$.*

Proof: From the definition of independent subsystems and Lemma 3 it follows that the symbols in D'' are not reachable from t. Hence only the rules in R' are applicable in any derivation starting from t. That is, any innermost derivation of R' starting from t is also an innermost derivation of R. By strong innermost normalization of R, such a derivation cannot be infinite. $\qquad \square$

Notation: In the following, $\mathcal{R}'$ denotes an independent subsystem of a system $\mathcal{R}$ and D'' denotes the set of defined symbols of $\mathcal{R} - \mathcal{R}'$. For a term t, (i) $\#(t)$ is defined as $\#(t) = |P_o(t)| + |P_i(t)|$, where $P_o(t)$ and $P_i(t)$ respectively denote the sets of positions (ii) $P_o(t) = \{\, p \mid root(t_{|_p}) \in D''$ and $t_{|_p}$ is reducible by $\mathcal{R}'\, \}$ and (iii) $P_i(t) = \{\, p \mid root(t_{|_p}) \in D''$ and $t_{|_p}$ is not reducible by $\mathcal{R}'\}$. Further, $\#_o(t) = |P_o(t)|$ and $\#_i(t) = |P_i(t)|$.

The following lemma is very useful.

Lemma 6 If $\mathcal{R}'$ is an independent subsystem of $\mathcal{R}$ and $t \Rightarrow_{i_{\mathcal{R}'}} t'$, then $\#_o(t) \geq \#_o(t')$.

Proof: If the reduction took place at position disjoint from the positions in $P_o(t)$, it is obvious that $P_o(t) = P_o(t')$. In the other case, the reduction must have taken place below some position $p \in P_o(t)$ as it is an innermost reduction step. We can write t as $t[u]_p$ and t' as $t[v]_p$. It is easy to see that $\#_o(t[v]_p) = \#_o(t[u]_p) - 1$ if v is a normal form of $\mathcal{R}'$ and $\#_o(t[v]_p) = \#_o(t[u]_p)$ otherwise. The lemma holds in either case. $\qquad\square$

4.1 Non-duplicating Independent Subsystems

In this subsection, we establish that every non-duplicating independent subsystem of a strongly innermost normalizing system is strongly innermost normalizing.

The following lemma plays a very crucial role.

Lemma 7 If $\mathcal{R}'$ is a non-duplicating independent subsystem of $\mathcal{R}$ and $t \Rightarrow_{i_{\mathcal{R}'}} t'$, then $\#_i(t) \geq \#_i(t')$ and $\#(t) \geq \#(t')$.

Proof: If the reduction took place at position disjoint from the positions in $P_i(t)$, it is obvious that $P_i(t) = P_i(t')$. In the other case, the reduction must have taken place above some positions in $P_i(t)$ as $t_{|_p}$ is irreducible for each $p \in P_i(t)$. Let p' be the position in t at which the reduction took place, that is, $t \equiv t[u]_{p'}$ and $t' \equiv t[v]_{p'}$. Since D''-symbols do not occur in right-hand sides of rules in $\mathcal{R}'$ and $\mathcal{R}'$ is non-duplicating, it follows that the number of occurrences of D''-symbols in v is no more than that in u and hence $\#_i(t) \geq \#_i(t')$. From this and the above lemma, it follows that $\#(t) \geq \#(t')$. $\qquad\square$

The following lemma gives an instance of $\#_i(t) > \#_i(t')$.

Lemma 8 If $\mathcal{R}'$ is a non-duplicating independent subsystem of $\mathcal{R}$, $l\sigma \Rightarrow_{i_{\mathcal{R}'}} r\sigma$ and a D''-symbol occurs in l, then $\#_i(l\sigma) > \#_i(r\sigma)$.

Proof: Follows from the facts that (i) D''-symbols do not occur in the right-hand sides of $\mathcal{R}'$, (ii) $\mathcal{R}'$ is non-duplicating and (iii) a D''-symbol occurs in l. $\qquad\square$

Now, we are in position to prove the main result of this subsection.

Theorem 4 *Every non-duplicating independent subsystem of a strongly inner-most normalizing system is strongly innermost normalizing.*

Proof: Assume to the contrary that there is an infinite innermost derivation $t_1 \Rightarrow_{i_{\mathcal{R}'}} t_2 \Rightarrow_{i_{\mathcal{R}'}} \cdots$ of $\mathcal{R}'$. Since $\#(t)$ is finite for any term t, there exists a k such that $\#_i(t_k) = \#_i(t_{k+j})$ and $\#_o(t_k) = \#_o(t_{k+j})$ for all $j \geq 1$ by lemmas 6 and 7. By lemma 5, there can only be a finitely many reductions at positions which are not below any position in $P_o(t_k)$. Now, it follows from the fact $\#_o(t_k) = \#_o(t_{k+j})$ for all $j \geq 1$ and König's lemma that there is an infinite innermost derivation of $\mathcal{R}'$ from $t_{k|p}$ for some position $p \in P_o(t_k)$.

The fact $\#_i(t_k) = \#_i(t_{k+j})$ for all $j \geq 1$ and Lemma 8 imply that no left-hand side of a rule applied in $t_k \Rightarrow_{i_{\mathcal{R}'}} t_{k+1} \Rightarrow_{i_{\mathcal{R}'}} t_{k+2} \Rightarrow_{i_{\mathcal{R}'}} \cdots$ contains any D''-symbols. Therefore, there must be an infinite innermost derivation of $\mathcal{R}'$ from a term $u \in \mathcal{T}(F, X)$ such that $F \cap D'' = \phi$, where u is the term obtained from $t_{k|p}$ by replacing the subterms $\{u_1, \cdots, u_n\}$ at positions in $P_i(t_k)$ by fresh variables $\{X_1, \cdots, X_n\}$ such that $X_i \equiv X_j$ if and only if $u_i \equiv u_j$. But by lemma 5, there cannot be any infinite innermost derivation of $\mathcal{R}'$ from u, a contradiction. $\square$

4.2 Duplicating Independent Subsystems

In this subsection, we establish that any independent subsystem $\mathcal{R}'$ of a strongly innermost normalizing system $\mathcal{R}$ is strongly innermost normalizing if the rules in $\mathcal{R} - \mathcal{R}'$ do not overlap the rules in $\mathcal{R}'$.

Theorem 5 *Let $\mathcal{R}'$ be an independent subsystem of a strongly innermost normalizing system $\mathcal{R}$ such that for any rule $l \to r \in (\mathcal{R} - \mathcal{R}')$, l does not unify with a non-variable subterm of any rule $l' \to r' \in \mathcal{R}'$. Then $\mathcal{R}'$ is strongly innermost normalizing too.*

Proof: Assume to the contrary that there is an infinite innermost derivation $t_1 \Rightarrow_{i_{\mathcal{R}'}} t_2 \Rightarrow_{i_{\mathcal{R}'}} \cdots$ of $\mathcal{R}'$. Since $\#(t)$ is finite for any term t, there exists a k such that $\#_o(t_k) = \#_o(t_{k+j})$ for all $j \geq 1$ by Lemma 6. As in Theorem 4, this implies that there is an infinite innermost derivation of $\mathcal{R}'$ from $t_{k|p}$ for some position $p \in P_o(t_k)$. Since for any rule $l \to r \in (\mathcal{R} - \mathcal{R}')$, l does not unify with a non-variable subterm of any rule $l' \to r' \in \mathcal{R}'$ the following holds: if $l\sigma$ is a subterm of an innermost redex $l'\sigma'$ reduced in the innermost derivation of $\mathcal{R}'$ from $t_{k|p}$ such that $l \to r \in (\mathcal{R} - \mathcal{R}')$ and $l' \to r' \in \mathcal{R}'$, then $l\sigma$ is a subterm of $X\sigma'$ for some variable $X \in Var(l')$. Therefore there is an infinite innermost derivation of $\mathcal{R}'$ from a term u, where u is the term obtained from $t_{k|p}$ by replacing its $(\mathcal{R} - \mathcal{R}')$-redeces $\{u_1, \cdots, u_n\}$ by fresh variables $\{X_1, \cdots, X_n\}$ such that $X_i \equiv X_j$ if and only if $u_i \equiv u_j$. Since $\mathcal{R}'$ is independent subsystem, no new redeces of $(\mathcal{R} - \mathcal{R}')$ are created and hence the derivation from u is an (infinite) innermost derivation of $\mathcal{R}$ as well, contradicting the strong innermost normalization of $\mathcal{R}$. This completes the proof. $\square$

Corollary 2 *Let $\mathcal{R}'$ be an independent subsystem of a strongly innermost normalizing system $\mathcal{R}$ such that no defined symbol of $(\mathcal{R} - \mathcal{R}')$ occurs in left-hand-sides of $\mathcal{R}'$. Then $\mathcal{R}'$ is strongly innermost normalizing too.*

5 Selection Invariance in Innermost Normalization

In this section, we show that the choice of innermost redex to be reduced at any step has no bearing on termination (finiteness) of innermost derivations. That is, if a TRS is innermost terminating under a particular reduction strategy, it is innermost terminating under any other strategy. For simplicity, we consider leftmost innermost strategy.

Definition 8 A reduction step $C[l\sigma] \Rightarrow C[r\sigma]$ with rewrite rule $l \to r$ is a *leftmost innermost* reduction step if $l\sigma$ is the leftmost innermost redex in $C[l\sigma]$. A TRS is leftmost innermost normalizing (LIN) if it has no infinite leftmost innermost derivation.

In the following we show that every leftmost innermost normalizing (LIN) system is strongly innermost normalizing (SIN). From an arbitrary innermost derivation IND starting with a term s, we construct a leftmost innermost derivation IND' starting with s such that every reduction in IND also takes place in IND'. So, from an infinite (arbitrary) innermost derivation we get an infinite leftmost innermost derivation, which is not possible for any leftmost innermost normalizing (LIN) system. Hence there cannot be an infinite (arbitrary) innermost derivation, that's, the system is strongly innermost normalizing.

We construct the leftmost innermost derivation IND' starting with s using an oracle as follows. At every step reducing the leftmost innermost redex (say, t) in the current term $C[t]$ at position p, we ask the oracle whether an innermost redex t is reduced in IND. If the answer is negative, we normalize t to a normal form using any leftmost innermost derivation. If the answer is positive, the oracle gives the rewrite rule $l \to r$ applied in that step (and marks that step) and we reduce t using $l \to r$ in IND'. At every step the oracle is given as input (1) the leftmost innermost redex position p, (2) the sequence of function symbols occurring from the root to p and (3) the subterm t at that position. The oracle looks for the **first** reduction $C'[t] \Rightarrow C'[t']$ in IND satisfying the following conditions: (a) $C'[t] \Rightarrow C'[t']$ is not yet marked by the oracle, (b) t occurs at position p in $C'[t]$, (c) the sequence of function symbols occurring from the root to p in $C'[t]$ is same as the input sequence (given in (2) above) and (d) $t \equiv l\sigma$ and $t' \equiv r\sigma$ for some substitution σ. The oracle gives an answer **no** if there is no such reduction step in IND. Otherwise it marks the reduction step $C'[t] \Rightarrow C'[t']$ and outputs the rule $l \to r$.

Theorem 6 *Every leftmost innermost normalizing (LIN) system is strongly innermost normalizing (SIN).*

Proof: Assume to the contrary that there is infinite an innermost derivation $t_1 \Rightarrow_{i_R} t_2 \Rightarrow_{i_R} \cdots$ of a leftmost innermost normalizing (LIN) system $\mathcal{R}$. From this derivation (call IND), we construct a leftmost innermost derivation IND' using the following **while** loop such that $redeces(IND) \subseteq redeces(IND')$, where $redeces(IND)$ (resp. $redeces(IND')$) is the multiset of redeces reduced in the derivation IND (resp. IND').

$u := t_1$

while u is not a normal form of $\mathcal{R}$ **do**
begin

    Let $v \equiv u_{|p}$ be the leftmost innermost redex in u and F be the sequence of
        function symbols occurring in u from the root to p;
    Call $Oracle(p, F, v)$;
    if the answer is **no**
        then Normalize v to w using any leftmost innermost derivation
        else if the answer is $l \to r \in \mathcal{R}$ **then** Reduce v to w using $l \to r$;
    $u := u[w]_p$

end

This **while** loop terminates as the system $\mathcal{R}$ is leftmost innermost normalizing. Let IND' be the leftmost innermost derivation constructed by the **while** loop. Now, we show that $redeces(IND) \subseteq redeces(IND')$ arriving at a contradiction that IND is an infinite derivation but the multiset of redeces reduced in it is finite. We establish this through induction by showing that the reduction step $t_j \Rightarrow t_{j+1}$, $j \geq 1$ in IND is marked by the oracle.

Basis : $j = 1$. The redex reduced in the first step in IND eventually becomes the leftmost innermost redex in any leftmost innermost derivation from t as the system is leftmost innermost normalizing. Hence the reduction step $t_1 \Rightarrow t_2$ in IND is marked by the oracle.

Induction hypothesis : Assume that every reduction step $t_j \Rightarrow t_{j+1}$ in IND is marked by the oracle for each $1 \leq j < k$.

Induction step : $j = k$. Let $l\sigma$ be the innermost redex reduced in t_k at position p. Let S be the reduction steps in IND leading to the creation of this redex $l\sigma$. Note that S is empty if $l\sigma$ is the subterm of t_1 at position p. By induction hypothesis these reductions are done in IND' (marked by the oracle) and from the **while** loop, it is easy see that these reductions are done in IND' applying the same rules as in IND. Therefore $l\sigma$ is an innermost redex in IND' at position p of some term. And this redex eventually becomes the leftmost innermost redex in IND' (and the oracle marks the reduction step $t_k \Rightarrow t_{k+1}$ in IND) as $\mathcal{R}$ is leftmost innermost normalizing. This completes the proof. $\qquad\square$

In the next section, using this result we give a straightforward proof for one of the main results of [7].

The following example shows that the selection invariance does not hold for outermost normalization. The main reason is that an outermost redex may no longer be an outermost redex after another outermost redex is reduced.

Example 3 The following system $\mathcal{R}$ is leftmost outermost normalizing.

$$c(a) \rightarrow d(a, c(a))$$
$$a \rightarrow c(a)$$
$$d(x, e) \rightarrow e$$
$$d(x, x) \rightarrow e$$

But this system is not strongly outermost normalizing as the following outermost derivation from a is nonterminating: $a \Rightarrow_o c(a) \Rightarrow_o d(a, c(a)) \Rightarrow_o d(a, d(a, c(a))) \Rightarrow_o d(a, d(a, d(a, c(a)))) \Rightarrow_o \cdots$

In a leftmost outermost derivation, a is forced to be reduced to $c(a)$ in $d(a, c(a))$, that is, $d(a, c(a))$ reduces to $d(c(a), c(a))$ which in turn reduces to the normal form e. The outermost redex $c(a)$ in $d(a, c(a))$ is no longer an outermost redex in $d(c(a), c(a))$. This leads to the termination of leftmost outermost derivations. Whereas in the rightmost outermost derivation, the outermost redex $c(a)$ gets reduced repeatedly producing a new rightmost outermost redex $c(a)$. □

6 Application of Selection Invariance

In this section, we give a straightforward proof for one of the main results of [7], using the selection invariance result of the previous section. In [7], modularity of *completeness* is established for a class of hierarchical combinations generalizing the main result of [10]. The main step in proving that result is the proof of strong innermost normalization of $\mathcal{R}_0 \cup \mathcal{R}_1$ when $\mathcal{R}_0$ and $\mathcal{R}_1$ are complete. From this and Theorem 3 follows the modularity of completeness for the following class of hierarchical combinations.[3] The proof given in [7] is somewhat contrived and we need to consider a special set of terms and use quasi-commutation, whereas the proof given below is straightforward and intuitive.

Definition 9 Constructor system $\mathcal{R}_1(D_1, C_1, R_1)$ is a *nice extension* of another constructor system $\mathcal{R}_0(D_0, C_0, R_0)$ if the following conditions are true:

1. $\mathcal{R}_0 \cup \mathcal{R}_1$ is a constructor system.
2. $D_0 \cap D_1 = C_0 \cap D_1 = \phi$
3. Each rewrite rule $l \rightarrow r \in \mathcal{R}_1$ satisfies the following condition:
   (H) : For every subterm s of r, if $root(s) \in D_1$ then s contains no function symbol depending on D_0 except at the outermost level (of s).

Notation: Henceforth, we deal with nice extensions and assume that the two constituent systems $\mathcal{R}_0$ and $\mathcal{R}_1$ are complete. We denote the set of constructors $C_0 \cup C_1 - D_0$ of the combined system by $\overline{Constr}$. $\mathcal{T}_i$ denotes $\mathcal{T}(D_i \cup Constr, \mathcal{X})$ and $\mathcal{C}_i$ denotes the set of contexts of $D_i \cup Constr$ i.e., terms in $\mathcal{T}(D_i \cup Constr \cup \{\Box\}, \mathcal{X})$ and $NF_i(t)$ denotes the normal form of term t under $\mathcal{R}_i$.

The following two theorems relate innermost $\mathcal{R}_1$-derivations innermost $\mathcal{R}_0$-derivations with innermost derivations of $\mathcal{R}_0 \cup \mathcal{R}_1$. See full version of the paper for proofs.

---

[3] In [7], a slightly larger class is considered. Here, we consider a simpler class as our main purpose is just to illustrate the application of selection invariance.

Theorem 7 *If $t \in \mathcal{T}_1$ is an innermost redex of $\mathcal{R}_1$ and $t \Rightarrow_{\mathcal{R}_1} t_1 \Rightarrow_{\mathcal{R}_1} \cdots \Rightarrow_{\mathcal{R}_1} t_m$ is an innermost derivation then $t \Rightarrow_{\mathcal{R}_1 \cup \mathcal{R}_0} t_1 \Rightarrow_{\mathcal{R}_1 \cup \mathcal{R}_0} \cdots \Rightarrow_{\mathcal{R}_1 \cup \mathcal{R}_0} t_m$ is also an innermost derivation. Further, $NF_1(t)$ is of the form $C[s_1, \cdots, s_n]$ such that $C \in \mathcal{C}_0$ and $s_i \in \mathcal{T}_1$ for all $i \in [1, n]$.*

Theorem 8 *Let $t \equiv C[s_1, \cdots, s_n]$ be a term such that $C \in \mathcal{C}_0$ and $root(s_i) \in D_1$ and s_i is normal form of $\mathcal{R}_0 \cup \mathcal{R}_1$ for all $i \in [1, n]$. If $t \Rightarrow_{\mathcal{R}_0} t_1 \Rightarrow_{\mathcal{R}_0} \cdots \Rightarrow_{\mathcal{R}_0} t_m$ is an innermost derivation then $t \Rightarrow_{\mathcal{R}_0 \cup \mathcal{R}_1} t_1 \Rightarrow_{\mathcal{R}_0 \cup \mathcal{R}_1} \cdots \Rightarrow_{\mathcal{R}_0 \cup \mathcal{R}_1} t_m$ is also an innermost derivation.*

Using the above two theorems, we prove that $\mathcal{R}_0 \cup \mathcal{R}_1$ is strongly innermost normalizing if $\mathcal{R}_0$ and $\mathcal{R}_1$ are complete. We use multiset-extension $\ll$ of prefix ordering $<$ over the set of positions [2, 5].

Theorem 9 *The combined system $\mathcal{R}_0 \cup \mathcal{R}_1$ is strongly innermost normalizing if $\mathcal{R}_0$ and $\mathcal{R}_1$ are complete.*

Proof: By Theorem 6, it is enough to prove leftmost innermost normalization (LIN) of $\mathcal{R}_0 \cup \mathcal{R}_1$. Consider a term t in $\mathcal{T}(D_0 \cup D_1 \cup Constr, \mathcal{X})$. Let $IP(t)$ be the set of innermost redex positions (w.r.t. $\mathcal{R}_0 \cup \mathcal{R}_1$) in t. We prove that t reduces to a term t' after a finite number of leftmost innermost $\mathcal{R}_0 \cup \mathcal{R}_1$-reduction steps such that $IP(t') \ll IP(t)$. Leftmost innermost normalization of $\mathcal{R}_0 \cup \mathcal{R}_1$ follows from this and well-foundedness of multiset-ordering $\ll$.

Now consider the leftmost innermost redex s (say at position p) in t. There are two cases: (a) s is reducible by $\mathcal{R}_0$ or (b) s is reducible by $\mathcal{R}_1$.

Case (a): s is of the form $C[s_1, \cdots, s_n]$ such that $C \in \mathcal{C}_0$ and $root(s_i) \in D_1$ and s_i is normal form of $\mathcal{R}_0 \cup \mathcal{R}_1$ for all $i \in [1, n]$ ($n \geq 0$). Since $\mathcal{R}_0$ is complete, s has unique normal and every leftmost innermost derivation ends in it (in finite number of reduction steps). By Theorem 8, any leftmost innermost $\mathcal{R}_0$-derivation from s to its normal form $NF_0(s)$ is a leftmost innermost $(\mathcal{R}_0 \cup \mathcal{R}_1)$-derivation and $NF_0(s)$ is a normal form of $\mathcal{R}_0 \cup \mathcal{R}_1$. Let t' be the term obtained from t by replacing s by its normal form. It is clear that $IP(t') \ll IP(t)$.

Case (b): s is of the form $C[s_1, \cdots, s_n]$ such that $C \in \mathcal{C}_1$ and $root(s_i) \in D_0$ and s_i is normal form of $\mathcal{R}_0 \cup \mathcal{R}_1$ for all $i \in [1, n]$ ($n \geq 0$). Now replace the subterms $s_1, \cdots, s_n$ in s by new variables $X_1, \cdots, X_n$ to get a term $s' \in \mathcal{T}_1$ such that $X_i \equiv X_j$ if and only if $s_i \equiv s_j$. Since $\mathcal{R}_1$ is complete, s' has unique normal and every leftmost innermost derivation ends in it (in finite number of reduction steps). By Theorem 7, any leftmost innermost $\mathcal{R}_1$-derivation from s' to its normal form $NF_1(s')$ is a leftmost innermost $(\mathcal{R}_0 \cup \mathcal{R}_1)$-derivation and $NF_1(s')$ is of the form $C'[v_1, \cdots, v_m]$ such that $C' \in \mathcal{C}_0$ and $v_i \in \mathcal{T}_1$ for all $i \in [1, m]$. Let s'' be the term obtained from $NF_1(s')$ by replacing the variables $X_1, \cdots, X_n$ by terms $s_1, \cdots, s_n$. As in case (a), s'' can be reduced to a normal form of s w.r.t. $\mathcal{R}_0 \cup \mathcal{R}_1$ through a leftmost innermost $\mathcal{R}_0$-derivation and that derivation is a leftmost innermost $(\mathcal{R}_0 \cup \mathcal{R}_1)$-derivation as well. Let t' be the term obtained from t by replacing s by this normal form. It is clear that $IP(t') \ll IP(t)$. $\square$

7 Conclusion

In this paper, we study certain characteristics of strong innermost normalization of term rewrite systems. First we consider the question *when is strong innermost normalization preserved under subsystems ?* This question arises very naturally while studying modularity of composable and hierarchical combinations. We identified three classes of systems for which strong innermost normalization is preserved under subsystems. Then it is shown that if every innermost derivation of a TRS under a particular reduction strategy is of finite length, then every innermost derivations of it is of finite length under any other strategy. To demonstrate the practical implications of this selection invariance, we present a straightforward and intuitive proof for one of the main results of [7]. We believe that this selection invariance result is very handy in proving strong innermost normalization of TRSs as this allows us to prove innermost termination under one particular strategy and conclude strong innermost normalization.

References

1. T. Arts and H. Zantema (1994), *Termination of logic programs via labelled term rewrite systems*, Tech Rep. Utrecht University.
2. N. Dershowitz and J.-P. Jouannaud (1990), *Rewrite Systems*, in J. van Leeuwen (ed.), *Handbook of Theoretical Computer Science*, Vol. B, pp. 243-320, North-Holland.
3. B. Gramlich (1995), *Abstract relations between restricted termination and confluence properties of rewrite systems*, Fundamenta Informaticae 24, pp. 3-23.
4. M. Hanus (1994), *The integration of functions into logic programming: a survey*, J. Logic Prog. 19/20, pp. 583-628.
5. J.W. Klop (1992), *Term Rewriting Systems*, in S. Abramsky, D. Gabbay and T. Maibaum (ed.), *Handbook of Logic in Computer Science*, Vol. 2, Oxford Press.
6. M.R.K. Krishna Rao, D. Kapur and R.K. Shyamasundar (1991), *A Transformational methodology for proving termination of logic programs*, Proc. of Computer Science Logic, CSL'91, LNCS 626, pp. 213-226, Springer-Verlag.
7. M.R.K. Krishna Rao (1993), *Completeness of hierarchical combinations of term rewriting systems*, Proc. of FST&TCS'93, LNCS 761, pp. 125-138, Springer-Verlag. Revised version appears as *Modular proofs for completeness of hierarchical systems*, Theoretical Computer Science 151, pp. 487-512.
8. M.R.K. Krishna Rao (1994), *Simple termination of hierarchical combinations of term rewriting systems*, Proc. of TACS'94, LNCS 789, pp. 203-223, Springer-Verlag.
9. M.R.K. Krishna Rao (1995), *Semi-completeness of hierarchical and super-hierarchical combinations of term rewriting systems*, Proc. of TAPSOFT'95, LNCS 915, pp. 379-393, Springer-Verlag.
10. A. Middeldorp and Y. Toyama (1993), *Completeness of combinations of constructor systems*, J. Symb. Comp. 15, pp. 331-348.
11. E. Ohlebusch (1994), *Modular properties of composable term rewriting systems*, Ph.D. Thesis, Univ of Bielefeld.

On the Emergence of Properties in Component-Based Systems[(*)]

J.L.Fiadeiro

Department of Informatics
Faculty of Sciences, University of Lisbon,
Campo Grande, 1700 Lisboa, PORTUGAL
llf@di.fc.ul.pt

Abstract. When several components are interconnected to form a complex system, they may exhibit more properties (individually) than they had when considered in isolation. When we consider a category SPEC of component specifications taken as theories in some logic, properties are expressed as sentences of the underlying logic, and emergence of properties can be characterised by the fact that the morphisms that connect component specifications to the system specification are not conservative. Depending on the relationship that can be established between SPEC and a corresponding category PROG of programs, we show that such emergence phenomena can be interpreted in more than one way: (1) considering an individual component, the rest of the system is acting as a "regulator" for that component which, therefore, has a more constrained behaviour and exhibits more properties; (2) the overall good behaviour of the system requires co-operation of the components (some sort of sociability with regard to the rest of the system) which gives rise to the emergence of new properties. Some of these forms of sociability are characterised and related to well known properties of concurrent systems such as fairness and, more generally, to the assumptions that are made on the environment in rely-guarantee styles of specification.

1 Introduction

In the early 70's, J. Goguen proposed the use of categorical techniques in *General Systems Theory* for unifying a variety of notions of system behaviour and their composition techniques [Goguen 71, 73, Goguen and Ginali 78]. His approach has been summarised in a very simple but far reaching principle: "given a category of widgets, the operation of putting a system of widgets together to form a super-widget corresponds to taking a colimit of the diagram of widgets that shows how to interconnect them".

These principles were originally formulated in the context of mathematical models of system behaviour. Similar principles were later applied in the context of program development as a means of modularising the specification of abstract data types. The seminal paper of Burstall and Goguen – "Putting theories together to make specifications" [Burstall and Goguen 77] – and subsequent work on the theory of institutions [Goguen and Burstall 92], shows that theories (or theory presentations) of a logic (institution) can be used as building blocks in the construction of structured specifications, category theory providing the mathematical framework in which operations on specifications are formalised [Sannella and Tarlecki 88].

[(*)]   This work was partially supported by the Esprit WG 8319 (MODELAGE), the HCM Scientific Network CHRX-CT92-0054 (MEDICIS), and contract PRAXIS XXI 2/2.1/MAT/46/94 (ESCOLA).

The same principles have been applied to the algebraic specification of reactive systems by using typical logics for concurrent system specification, such as temporal logic [Manna and Pnueli 91]. In this approach [Fiadeiro and Maibaum 92], the specification of a system of interconnected components is given as a diagram showing how the specifications of the individual components are interconnected, the colimit of this diagram providing a specification of their joint behaviour.

In [Fiadeiro and Maibaum 92], we further showed how some typical phenomena of concurrent system behaviour, such as *starvation*, can be given an algebraic characterisation in terms of the conservativeness of the morphisms that connect each object to the system of which it is a component. Basically, we showed that the *emergence* of properties in the language of a component as theorems of the system could be diagnosed as a lack of co-operation between the components of the system and, hence, as a source of conflicts in their implementations.

In this paper, we resume the study of such emergence phenomena and investigate the relationships that may exist between the structural properties of specification logics and of the programming languages that are chosen to realise them, reflecting the fact that any categorical formalisation of modularity in system development has to take into account the relationship between these two levels – specifications and their realisations. More precisely, we show that compositionality, the key property for achieving modularity and incrementality in system development, can be characterised, algebraically, through the existence of a functor relating two development levels. Finally, we show how rely-guarantee styles of specification result from weaker structural relationships between two such levels.

Having this in mind, the paper proceeds as follows. In section 2, we revise the categorical approach to reactive system specification proposed in [Fiadeiro and Maibaum 92] and illustrate the phenomenon of emergence of properties. In section 3, adapting from [Fiadeiro and Maibaum 95, 96], we introduce programs in the language COMMUNITY and formalise their parallel composition in a categorical framework. Finally, in section 4, we formalise the notion of compositionality in this categorical framework and relate certain emergence phenomena with the lack of compositionality and rely/guarantee styles of specification.

2 Interconnections of Specifications and Emergence

We shall use linear temporal logic as a specification formalism. We define this logic in the style of institutions [Goguen and Burstall 92]:

Definition 2.1: The linear temporal logic institution LTL is defined as follows:

- its category of signatures is SET.
- the grammar functor defines, for every signature Σ, the set of *linear temporal propositions* LTL(Σ) as follows:

$$\phi ::= a \mid (\neg \phi) \mid (\phi \supset \psi) \mid \textbf{beg} \mid (\phi \textbf{U} \psi)$$

for $a \in \Sigma$. A signature morphism $f: \Sigma \to \Sigma'$ induces the translation $\underline{f}$: LTL(Σ)$\to$LTL(Σ') defined as follows:

$$\underline{f}(\phi) ::= f(a) \mid \neg \underline{f}(\phi) \mid \underline{f}(\phi) \supset \underline{f}(\psi) \mid \textbf{beg} \mid \underline{f}(\phi) U \underline{f}(\psi).$$

- the model functor is defined as follows: for every signature Σ, a Σ-model consists of a mapping M: $\Sigma \rightarrow 2^{\omega}$. We denote by Mod($\Sigma$) the set of all Σ-models. Given a signature morphism f:$\Sigma \rightarrow \Sigma'$, for every M$\in$Mod($\Sigma'$) we define M|$_f \in$Mod($\Sigma$) by M|$_f$(a)=M(f(a)).

- the satisfaction relation is defined as follows: a Σ-proposition ϕ is said to be true in a Σ-model M at instant i$\in \omega$ (which we write (M,i)$\vDash_\Sigma \phi$) iff:
  - for all a$\in \Sigma$, (M,i)$\vDash_\Sigma$a iff i$\in$M(a);
  - (M,i)$\vDash_\Sigma \neg \phi$ iff (M,i)$\nvDash_\Sigma \phi$;
  - (M,i)$\vDash_\Sigma \phi \supset \psi$ iff (M,i)$\vDash_\Sigma \phi$ implies (M,i)$\vDash_\Sigma \psi$;
  - (M,i)$\vDash_\Sigma$**beg** iff i=0;
  - (M,i)$\vDash_\Sigma \phi U\psi$ iff there exists j>i such that (M,j)$\vDash_\Sigma \psi$ and, for all k such that i<k$\leq$j, (M,k)$\vDash_\Sigma \phi$.

A Σ-proposition ϕ is said to be true in M, which we denote by M$\vDash_\Sigma \phi$, iff (M,i)$\vDash_\Sigma \phi$ for every i$\in \omega$. Given $\Phi \subseteq$LTL(Σ) and $\phi \in$LTL(Σ), $\Phi \vDash_\Sigma \phi$ iff, for every Σ-model M, M$\vDash_\Sigma \phi$ whenever M$\vDash_\Sigma \psi$ for every $\psi \in \Phi$. ∎

Some remarks seem to be in order:

- each signature provides a set of propositional symbols;
- every signature has an associated language generated from the propositional symbols, the usual propositional connectives, the propositional constant **beg** (denoting the initial instant of time) and the temporal operator **U** ("until");
- propositions are interpreted over the natural numbers; that is, a linear, discrete temporal structure is chosen;
- the interpretation of the temporal operator **U** ("until") is different from other uses that can be found in the literature, e.g. [Goldblatt 87]: it is "strict", i.e. it does not include the present, and $\phi U\psi$ requires ϕ to be satisfied when ψ becomes satisfied;
- the following operators can be defined as abbreviations:
  - $\textbf{F}^+\phi \approx$ (true **U** ϕ), "sometime in the future ϕ but not necessarily now"
  - $\textbf{F}\phi \approx (\textbf{F}^+\phi \vee \phi)$, "sometime in the future ϕ"
  - $\textbf{G}^+\phi \approx (\neg\textbf{F}^+(\neg\phi))$, "always in the future ϕ but not necessarily now"
  - $\textbf{G}\phi \approx (\neg\textbf{F}(\neg\phi))$, "always in the future ϕ"
  - $\phi\textbf{W}\psi \approx (\phi U\psi) \vee \textbf{G}^+(\phi \wedge \neg\psi)$, "$\phi$ until ψ but, possibly, never ψ"

Proposition 2.2: LTL as defined above is an institution, i.e. the satisfaction condition is satisfied: given a signature morphism f:$\Sigma_1 \rightarrow \Sigma_2$, M$\in$Mod($\Sigma_2$) and $\phi \in$LTL(Σ_1), M$\vDash_{\Sigma_2}\underline{f}(\phi)$ iff M|$_f \vDash_{\Sigma_1}\phi$. ∎

Specifications are taken as theory presentations in this logic:

Definition 2.3: The objects of the category $\mathcal{SPEC}$ of specifications are the pairs $\langle\Sigma,\Phi\rangle$, where Σ is a signature and $\Phi \subseteq$LTL(Σ). A morphism f: $\langle\Sigma_1,\Phi_1\rangle \rightarrow \langle\Sigma_2,\Phi_2\rangle$ is a signature morphism f:$\Sigma_1 \rightarrow \Sigma_2$ such that, for every $\phi \in \Phi_1$, $\Phi_2 \vDash_{\Sigma_2}\underline{f}(\phi)$. ∎

In a specification, the signature indicates what is the language of the component being specified and the axioms correspond to the properties that the component is required to satisfy. Specification morphisms are translations between the languages of the two theory presentations such that the axioms of the first specification are translated to theorems of the second. This implies that all the theorems of the first specification are translated to theorems of the second. Notice that the axioms are propositions that are required to be satisfied at every instant of time.

As an example, consider the following specification of a vending machine:

specification vending machine **is**
sign   coin, cake, cigar, reset
axioms   **beg** $\supset$ ($\neg$cake$\land\neg$cigar$\land\neg$reset) $\land$ (coin $\lor$ ($\neg$cake$\land\neg$cigar$\land\neg$reset)Wcoin)
        coin $\supset$ ($\neg$coin $\land$ $\neg$reset)W(cake $\lor$ cigar)
        (cake $\lor$ cigar) $\supset$ ($\neg$cake $\land$ $\neg$cigar $\land$ $\neg$coin)Wreset
        reset $\supset$ ($\neg$cake $\land$ $\neg$cigar $\land$ $\neg$reset)Wcoin
        cake $\supset$ ($\neg$cigar)

That is to say, the machine is initialised so as to accept only coins. Once it accepts a coin it can deliver either a cake or a cigar (but not both). After delivering a cake or a cigar it can only be reset, after which it is ready to accept more coins.

In order to illustrate the categorical approach to composition, assume now that it becomes politically incorrect for cigars to be sold by vending machines. Instead of throwing away the machines, it is probably cheaper to *reuse* them by blocking the cigar option. This can be done *incrementally* by coupling machines with *regulators*. The specification of a regulator is quite simple:

specification regulator **is**
sign   trigger, action
axioms   trigger $\supset$ $G^{+}\neg$action

That is to say, a regulator can perform two actions, *trigger* and *action*. After performing *trigger*, *action* can no longer occur.

It remains to show how to connect a regulator to a vending machine. Intuitively, we want *action* to be synchronised with *cigar* and *trigger* with *pay* so that the action of accepting a coin triggers the cigar option to be blocked. In the categorical approach, interconnections are established through diagrams. For the purpose at hand, we need a communication channel between *vending machine* and *regulator*. This channel is specified as having two ports with no required properties:

specification channel **is**
sign   a, b
axioms

The configuration of the required system can be given by the following diagram:

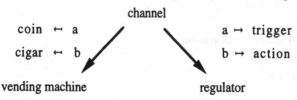

The properties of the resulting system can be obtained by the colimit of its configuration diagram:

Property 2.4: The category $\mathcal{SPEC}$ is finitely cocomplete. Its initial object is $\langle\emptyset,\emptyset\rangle$ and the pushout of $f_1:\langle\Sigma,\Phi\rangle\rightarrow\langle\Sigma_1,\Phi_1\rangle$ and $f_2:\langle\Sigma,\Phi\rangle\rightarrow\langle\Sigma_2,\Phi_2\rangle$ is given by $g_1:\langle\Sigma_1,\Phi_1\rangle\rightarrow\langle\Sigma',\Phi'\rangle$ and $g_2:\langle\Sigma_2,\Phi_2\rangle\rightarrow\langle\Sigma',\Phi'\rangle$, where g_1 and g_2 result from the pushout of f_1 and f_2 as signature morphisms (the resulting signature Σ' is the amalgamated sum of Σ_1 and Σ_2 relative to f_1 and f_2) and $\Phi'=f_1(\Phi_1)\cup f_2(\Phi_2)$. ∎

This is a property of any institution [Goguen and Burstall 92]. It tells us that the set of axioms of the resulting specification consists of the union of the translations of the axioms of the components. Because the union of sets of formulae has the same logical value as their conjunction, the categorical approach complies with the "composition as conjunction" idea put forward in [Abadi and Lamport 93] for parallel composition of reactive systems. However, we should stress that our approach is more "structured" in the sense that formulae are not being considered individually as units of construction but are organised into modules (theories) that have a meaning in terms of the structure of the system – hence the use of morphisms for establishing interconnections through the language of these theories, something that cannot be achieved at the level of individual formulae.

Hence, the specification of the system that results from interconnecting the vending machine and the regulator as above is given below, assuming that the morphisms that connect *vending machine* and *regulator* to the new specification are the identity and (trigger ↦ coin, action ↦ cigar), respectively:

specification regulated vending machine **is**
sign   coin, cake, cigar, reset
axioms   **beg** ⊃ (¬cake∧¬cigar∧¬reset) ∧ (coin ∨ (¬cake∧¬cigar∧¬reset)Wcoin)
          coin ⊃ (¬coin ∧ ¬reset)W(cake ∨ cigar)
          (cake ∨ cigar) ⊃ (¬cake ∧ ¬cigar ∧ ¬coin)Wreset
          reset ⊃ (¬cake ∧ ¬cigar ∧ ¬reset)Wcoin
          cake ⊃ (¬cigar)
          coin ⊃ G^+¬cigar

Consider now the following derivation:

1. **beg** ⊃ ¬cigar
   from the first axiom
2. **beg** ⊃ coin ∨ (¬cigarWcoin)
   from the first axiom
3. G(coin ⊃ G^+¬cigar)
   necessitation over the last axiom
4. (¬cigarWcoin) ∧ G(coin ⊃ G^+¬cigar) ⊃ G^+¬cigar
   temporal theorem
5. **beg** ⊃ G^+¬cigar
   from 2, 4, and the last axiom
6. **beg** ⊃ G¬cigar
   from 1 and 5
7. ¬cigar
   from 6 and the properties of beg

The theorem (¬cigar) provides a simple example of emergence: it is a property in the language of one of the components (vending machine) that is a theorem of the interconnected system but not of that component. That is to say, within the system, the vending machine satisfies more properties than what it did in isolation. The explanation for the emergence of this property is quite simple: because, due to the interconnections, the action *coin* triggers the blocking of action *cigar*, and *coin* was already specified to be the first action to occur in *vending machine*, the action *cigar* will never occur.

Technically, this phenomenon is characterised by the fact that the morphism relating the specification of the component to that of the system is not conservative:

Definition 2.5: A morphism f: $<\Sigma_1,\Phi_1> \rightarrow <\Sigma_2,\Phi_2>$ is *conservative* iff, for every $\phi \in LTL(\Sigma_1)$, $\Phi_2 \vDash_{\Sigma_2} f(\phi)$ implies $\Phi_1 \vDash_{\Sigma_1} \phi$. ∎

The emergence of this property is a good indication of the "success" of the construction operated on the vending machine: as a property of the regulated vending machine we can prove that cigars cannot be sold. Indeed, systems (software or not) evolve quite often through increments whose goal is to induce new forms of behaviour on "old" components. In such circumstances, emergence of properties is an intended goal of the design and configuration decisions.

However, it is not always so simple to interpret the emergence of properties. Consider the following specification of a costumer of the vending machine:

specification costumer **is**
sign   pay, eat
axioms   Feat

That is to say, a customer can pay and eat but is simply required to eat!

Given the configuration diagram

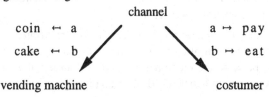

channel

coin ← a   a ↦ pay

cake ← b   b ↦ eat

vending machine   costumer

the specification of the joint behaviour of the customer and vending machine is given by the following presentation, assuming that the pushout morphisms for the vending machine and the costumer are (coin ↦ pay_coin, cake ↦ eat_cake, cigar ↦ cigar, reset ↦ reset) and (pay ↦ pay_coin, eat ↦ eat_cake), respectively:

specification served customer **is**
sign   pay_coin, eat_cake, cigar, reset
axioms   **beg** ⊃ (¬eat_cake∧ ¬cigar ∧ ¬reset)
                ∧ (pay_coin ∨ (¬eat_cake ∧ ¬cigar ∧ ¬reset)Wpay_coin)
         pay_coin ⊃ (¬pay_coin ∧ ¬reset)W(eat_cake ∨ cigar)
         (eat_cake ∨ cigar) ⊃ (¬eat_cake∧ ¬cigar ∧ ¬pay_coin)Wreset
         reset ⊃ (¬eat_cake ∧ ¬cigar ∧ ¬reset)Wpay_coin
         eat_cake⊃ (¬cigar)
         Feat_cake

Consider now the following derivation:

1. Feat_cake ⊃ ¬G(¬eat_cake ∧ ¬cigar ∧ ¬pay_coin ∧ ¬reset)
   temporal logic tautology
2. ¬G(¬eat_cake ∧ ¬cigar ∧ ¬pay_coin ∧ ¬reset)
   from 1 and the last axiom
3. eat_cake ⊃ (¬eat_cake ∧ ¬cigar ∧ ¬pay_coin)Ureset
   *from 2, the third axiom, and the definition of **W***
4. eat_cake ⊃ Freset
   temporal consequence of 3 (until implies eventually)
5. reset ⊃ (¬eat_cake ∧ ¬cigar ∧ ¬reset)Upay_coin
   *from 2, the fourth axiom, and the definition of **W***
6. reset ⊃ Fpay_coin
   temporal consequence of 5 (until implies eventually)
7. eat_cake ⊃ Fpay_coin
   *from 4 and 6 (transitivity of **F**)*
8. Fpay_coin
   temporal consequence of 7 and the last axiom

That is to say, after each consumption of a cake, the vending machine will be reset (4), and the customer will have to pay, recurrently, one more coin (8). These two theorems provide further examples of emergence of properties.

On the one hand, (4) is the translation of a sentence of *vending machine* – (cake ⊃ Freset). This sentence is not a theorem of *vending machine* (there are no liveness properties of the vending machine). The emergence of this property can be explained as follows: because, after serving the customer, the machine needs to be reset before serving him/her again, in order to satisfy the customer's greed, the machine will have to be reset after each service.

On the other hand, 8 is the translation of a sentence of *customer* – (Fpay). This sentence is clearly not a theorem of *customer*. The emergence of this property can be explained as follows: because the customer can only be served after he/she pays, in order for him/her to keep eating he/she needs to keep paying.

There is no formal difference between these two cases of emergence and the one before (no cigar). However, from a conceptual point of view, they seem to have completely different interpretations: whereas the first case is a natural result of having connected a regulator to a vending machine, the second cases seem to be the unexpected emergence of a property that results from the need to ensure "co-operation" between the components. Whereas the first case is a sign of "success" of the construction, the second seems to be a "symptom" of potential *starvation!*

From the point of view of *requirement specification*, these phenomena illustrate situations in which the interconnections impose additional requirements on the behaviour of the components, suggesting that not all possible implementations of the component specifications can be put together to build the required system. Indeed, the difference between the situations of emergence illustrated above seems to be related to the notion of realisation of specifications by means of programs.

Underlying the use of diagrams and category theory for specification is the intended ability to build systems in an incremental and modular way. That is to say, given a diagram in the category of specifications, we would expect that, by choosing programs that satisfy the component specifications and interconnecting them in a way that is consistent with the interconnections of their specifications, the composed program would satisfy the composed specification. This property is known as *compositionality*.

Intuitively, emergence of properties is not a symptom of potential malfunctioning if the specification language is *compositional* wrt the envisaged programming language. If we can ensure that the composition of realisations of the component specifications is a realisation of the composed specification, then the emergence of properties at the specification level can be accounted for in terms of the chosen programs.

However, it is not always possible to achieve compositionality. The second two cases of emergence studied above seem to suggest lack of compositionality. Indeed, what is baffling in the cases discussed above is that if the costumer is not realised by a program that ensures that it pays after having eaten, it seems strange that this behaviour can emerge when it is interconnected with the vending machine. If the vending machine is not realised by a program that ensures that it is reset after each service, and the costumer plays no part in the action of resetting the machine, it seems strange that this behaviour can emerge when it is interconnected with the customer. Situations like these seem to suggest that some components need to be redesigned (costumers must be programmed to pay) and new components need to be added (that reset the vending machine). But how can we account for these different diagnoses and solutions in a formal way?

Being a property of the relationship between a specification and a programming formalism, compositionality cannot be discussed before the programming language and the notion of realisation of a specification by a program are defined. That is to say, emergence phenomena cannot be evaluated at the specification level alone. Hence, in the rest of the paper, we are going to show how compositionality can be formally characterised in a categorical framework of programs and specifications, how the absence of compositionality explains why the emergence of certain properties indicates that the good overall behaviour of the system relies of forms of "co-operation" that are not ensured locally at the level of the components and their interconnections, and how rely/guarantee styles of specification arise naturally in those circumstances and suggest revisions to be made to the system to ensure that it meets the composed specification.

3 Parallel Program Design in a Categorical Framework

In order to illustrate the role of programs in interpreting emergence of properties and formalise compositionality in a categorical framework, we shall use a subset of the language COMMUNITY introduced in [Fiadeiro and Maibaum 95] for supporting parallel program design. This language is similar to UNITY [Chandy and Misra 88],

Action Systems [Back and Kurki-Suonio 88] and IP [Francez and Forman 90]. The simplification consists in working with Boolean attributes and omitting external attributes. On the other hand, fairness requirements have been added to the language.

A COMMUNITY program P in this simplified version has the following structure:

$$P \equiv \quad var \quad V$$

$$init \quad I$$

$$do \quad \underset{g \in \Gamma}{[\!]} \quad g: [B(g) \rightarrow \underset{a \in D(g)}{\|} a:=F(g,a)]$$

$$fair \quad C$$

where

- V is the set of attributes used by the program (i.e. the program "variables");
- Γ is the set of *action names*; each action name has an associated statement (see below) and can act as a *rendez-vous* point for program synchronisation;
- I is a condition on the attributes – the initialisation condition;
- for every action $g \in \Gamma$, $B(g)$ is a condition on the attributes – the *guard* of the action;
- for every action $g \in \Gamma$, $D(g) \subseteq V$ is the set of attributes that action g can change; we also denote by $D(a)$, where $a \in V$, the set of actions that can change a;
- for every action $g \in \Gamma$ and attribute $a \in D(g)$, $F(g,a)$ is a proposition;
- C is the subset of actions on whose execution fairness (compassion) applies.

As an example, consider the following program corresponding to the vending machine specified in the previous section (the correspondence will be formalised later on):

program vending machine **is**
var   ready, served_cake, served_cigar
init   ready $\wedge$ (served_cake $\vee$ served_cigar)
do   coin : [ready $\wedge$ (served_cake $\vee$ served_cigar)
                    $\rightarrow$ ready:=false $\|$ served_cake:=false $\|$ served_cigar:=false]
     $[\!]$ cake : [$\neg$ready $\wedge$ $\neg$(served_cake $\vee$ served_cigar)
                    $\rightarrow$ served_cake:=true]
     $[\!]$ cigar: [$\neg$ready $\wedge$ $\neg$(served_cake $\vee$ served_cigar)
                    $\rightarrow$ served_cigar:=true]
     $[\!]$ reset: [$\neg$ready $\wedge$ (served_cake $\vee$ served_cigar)
                    $\rightarrow$ ready:=true]
fair

Formally,

Definition 3.1: A *program signature* is a tuple (V,Γ) where

- V is a set.
- Γ is a 2^V-indexed family of sets.

All these sets of symbols are assumed to be finite and mutually disjoint.   ∎

Definition 3.2: Given a signature $\theta = <V,\Gamma>$, the language of propositions is defined as follows:

$$\phi ::= a \mid (\phi_1 \supset \phi_2) \mid (\phi_1 \vee \phi_2) \mid (\phi_1 \wedge \phi_2) \mid (\neg\phi)$$

for $a \in V$.   ∎

Definition 3.3: Given a signature $<V,\Gamma>$, and a subset $V' \subseteq V$, a V'-command F maps to every attribute a∈ V' a proposition.　　　　　　　　　　　■

Commands model multiple assignments. The proposition F(a) denotes the value that is assigned to a. If V' is empty, the only available command is the empty one: *skip*.

Definition 3.4: A *program* is a pair $<\theta,\Delta>$ where θ is a signature $<V,\Gamma>$ and Δ, the *body* of the program, is a triple (I,F,B,C) where

- I is a θ-proposition (constraining the initial values of the attributes);
- F assigns to every action g∈ Γ a D(g)-command;
- B assigns to every action g∈ Γ a proposition (its guard);
- C⊆Γ is the compassion set.　　　　　　　　　　　　　　　■

It is easy to recognise in this definition the basic features of parallel programs, namely guarded simultaneous assignments. Fairness requirements – compassion – are imposed on the actions included in the set C.

We shall work with a trace-based semantic interpretation of programs:

Definition 3.5: An interpretation structure for a signature $\theta=<V,\Gamma>$ is a pair $S=(\mathcal{A}:V\rightarrow 2^{\omega}, \mathcal{G}:\Gamma\rightarrow 2^{\omega})$ (trajectory). The interpretation of propositions over a trajectory is defined as follows:

- $(S,i) \vDash a$ iff $i\in \mathcal{A}(a)$;
- $(S,i) \vDash (\phi_1 \supset \phi_2)$ iff $(S,i) \vDash \phi_1$ implies $(S,i) \vDash \phi_2$;
- $(S,i) \vDash (\phi_1 \vee \phi_2)$ iff $(S,i) \vDash \phi_1$ or $(S,i) \vDash \phi_2$;
- $(S,i) \vDash (\phi_1 \wedge \phi_2)$ iff $(S,i) \vDash \phi_1$ and $(S,i) \vDash \phi_2$;
- $(S,i) \vDash (\neg\phi)$ iff $(S,i) \nvDash \phi$

A θ-formula ϕ is *true* in a θ-interpretation structure S, written $S\vDash\phi$, iff $(S,i) \vDash \phi$ at every instant i. A formula ϕ is *valid*, written $\vDash\phi$, iff it is true in every interpretation structure.　　　　　　　　　　　　　　　　　　　　　　■

Definition 3.6: A trajectory for a signature $\theta=<V,\Gamma>$ is a model of a program $<\theta,\Delta>$ where $\Delta=(I,F,B,C)$ iff

- $(S,0) \vDash I$;
- if i∈ $\mathcal{G}(g)$ and a∈ D(g), then (i+1)∈ $\mathcal{A}(a)$ iff $(S,i) \vDash F(g,a)$;
- if i∈ $\mathcal{G}(g)$, then $(S,i) \vDash B(g)$;
- if, for every g∈ D(a), i∉ $\mathcal{G}(g)$, then i∈ $\mathcal{A}(a)$ iff (i+1)∈ $\mathcal{A}(a)$

The trajectory is said to be *live* iff, for every g∈ C and i∈ ω, if $(S,j) \vDash B(g)$ for infinitely many j≥i, then there is k≥i such that k∈ $\mathcal{G}(g)$.　　　　　　　■

That is to say, a *model* of a program is an interpretation structure for which the initial state satisfies the initialisation constraint, the assignments are enforced, actions only occur when their guards are true, and only the actions in the domain of an attribute can change the value of that attribute. A *live* model is one in which every action in the compassion set occurs infinitely often if its guard is true infinitely often.

A categorical formalisation of program interconnection and composition can also be given based on a notion of morphism that captures what in the literature is known as superposition or superimposition [e.g. Bougé and Francez 88, Chandy and Misra 88, Kurki-Suonio and Järvinen 89, Francez and Forman 90, Katz 93].

Definition 3.7: Given program signatures $\theta_1=<V_1,\Gamma_1>$ and $\theta_2=<V_2,\Gamma_2>$, a *signature morphism* σ from θ_1 to θ_2 consists of a pair $(\sigma_\alpha:V_1\rightarrow V_2, \sigma_\gamma:\Gamma_1\rightarrow\Gamma_2)$ of (total) functions such that, for every action $g\in\Gamma$, $\sigma_\alpha(D_1(g))\subseteq D_2(\sigma_\gamma(g))$. ∎

Proposition 3.8: Program signatures and morphisms constitute a category $\mathcal{SIG}$. ∎

Signature morphisms provide us with the means for relating a program with its superpositions. However, superposition is more than just a relationship between signatures, i.e. more than "syntax". To capture its semantics, we have to analyse the bodies of the two programs involved. That is, given two programs $<\theta_1,\Delta_1>$ and $<\theta_2,\Delta_2>$ and a signature morphism $\sigma: \theta_1\rightarrow\theta_2$, we have to look for relationships between Δ_1 and Δ_2 such that $<\theta_2,\Delta_2>$ can be considered to be a superposition of $<\theta_1,\Delta_1>$ via σ, i.e. for σ to be considered as a superposition morphism.

Signature morphisms define translations between the languages associated with each signature in the obvious way:

Definition 3.9: Given a signature morphism $\sigma: \theta_1 \rightarrow \theta_2$,

$$\sigma(\phi) ::= \sigma(a) \mid (\sigma(\phi_1)\supset\sigma(\phi_2)) \mid (\sigma(\phi_1)\vee\sigma(\phi_2)) \mid (\sigma(\phi_1)\wedge\sigma(\phi_2)) \mid \neg\sigma(\phi)$$ ∎

Definition 3.10: Given a signature morphism $\sigma: \theta_1 \rightarrow \theta_2$ and a θ_2-interpretation structure $S=(\mathcal{A}, \mathcal{G})$, its σ-*reduct*, $S|_\sigma$, is the θ_1-interpretation structure $(\mathcal{A}|_\sigma, \mathcal{G}|_\sigma)$ where $\mathcal{A}|_\sigma(a) = \mathcal{A}(\sigma(a))$, and $\mathcal{G}|_\sigma(g) = \mathcal{G}(\sigma(g))$. ∎

That is, we interpret attribute and action symbols in the reduct of a model in the same way as their images are interpreted in the original model. Reducts provide us with the means for relating the behaviour of a program with that of the superposed one. The following proposition establishes that properties of reducts are characterised by translation of properties:

Proposition 3.11: Given a θ_1-formula ϕ and a θ_2-interpretation structure $S=(\mathcal{A}, \mathcal{G})$, we have for every $i\in\omega$: $(S,i) \vDash \sigma(\phi)$ iff $(S|_\sigma,i) \vDash \phi$. ∎

Definition/Proposition 3.12: A *superposition morphism* $\sigma:<\theta_1,\Delta_1>\rightarrow<\theta_2,\Delta_2>$ is a signature morphism $\sigma: \theta_1\rightarrow\theta_2$ such that

1. For all $g_1\in\Gamma_1$, $a_1\in D_1(g_1)$, $\vDash_{\theta_2} B_2(\sigma(g_1)) \supset \sigma(F_1(g_1,a_1))\equiv F_2(\sigma(g_1),\sigma(a_1))$.
2. $\vDash_{\theta_2} (I_2 \supset \sigma(I_1))$.
3. For every $g_1\in\Gamma_1$, $\vDash_{\theta_2} (B_2(\sigma(g_1)) \supset \sigma(B_1(g_1)))$.
4. For every $a_1\in V_1$, $D_2(\sigma(a_1))\subseteq\sigma(D_1(a_1))$.
5. $\sigma(C_1)\subseteq C_2$.

Programs and superposition morphisms form a category $\mathcal{PROG}$. ∎

Requirements 1 and 2 correspond to the preservation of the functionality of the base program: (1) the effects of the instructions are preserved and (2) so are the initialisation conditions. Requirement 3 allows guards to be strengthened but not to be weakened. Requirement 4 corresponds to a locality condition: new actions cannot be added to the domains of attributes of the source program. That is to say, no new actions can change the old attributes. Together with the fact that signature morphisms preserve the domains of actions, it implies that the domains of the attributes remain the same up to translation, i.e. $D_2(\sigma(a_1))=\sigma(D_1(a_1))$ for every $a_1\in V_1$. Requirement 5 means that fairness is preserved by the morphism.

Proposition 3.13: Let σ: $<\theta_1,\Delta_1> \to <\theta_2,\Delta_2>$ be a superposition morphism. Then, the reduct of every model of $<\theta_2,\Delta_2>$ is also a model of $<\theta_1,\Delta_1>$. ∎

Notice, however, that the reduct of a live model is not necessarily live. Indeed, because guards are allowed to be strengthened, the fact that the image of the guard of an action is satisfied at a given state does not imply that the guard of the image of the action is satisfied at that state. We shall see some examples later on.

We shall now describe how complex programs can be put together from components in much the same way as we proposed for specifications:

Proposition 3.14: The category $\mathcal{PROG}$ is finitely cocomplete. ∎

The proof of this result can be found in [Fiadeiro and Maibaum 96]. Basically, pushouts work as follows:

- actions are synchronised according to the rendez-vous points established by the actions of the middle program (channel) and morphisms; the resulting joint actions have the following properties:
  - their domain is the union of the domains of the joined actions;
  - they perform the parallel composition of the assignments of the joined actions;
  - if the interconnecting morphisms are injective (which is usually the case), they are guarded by the conjunction of the guards of the joined actions; otherwise, see [Fiadeiro and Maibaum 95];
- the initialisation condition of the resulting program is given by the conjunction of the initialisation conditions of the component programs;
- the compassion set of the resulting program is the union of the translations of the compassion sets of the components.

As an example, consider the program:

program regulator **is**
var   set
init   ¬set
do   trigger: [true → set:=true] [] action: [¬set → *skip*]
fair

We are going to interconnect it with *vending machine* using the following channel:

program channel **is**
var
init   true
do   a: [true → *skip*] [] b: [true → *skip*]
fair

The configuration of the required system is the following:

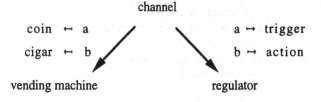

channel

coin ← a   a ↦ trigger
cigar ← b   b ↦ action

vending machine   regulator

The colimit of this diagram returns the program:

program regulated vending machine **is**
var   ready, served_cake, served_cigar, set
init   ready ∧ (served_cake ∨ served_cigar) ∧ ¬set
do   coin : [ready ∧ (served_cake ∨ served_cigar)
           → ready:=false ‖ served_cake:=false ‖ served_cigar:=false ‖ set:=true]
      [] cake : [¬ready ∧ ¬(served_cake ∨ served_cigar)
                → served_cake:=true]
      [] cigar: [¬set ∧ ¬ready ∧ ¬(served_cake ∨ served_cigar)
                → served_cigar:=true]
      [] reset: [¬ready ∧ (served_cake ∨ served_cigar)
                → ready:=true]
fair

together with the identity morphism and the morphism (trigger ↦ coin, action ↦ cigar) connecting *vending machine* and *regulator* to *regulated vending machine*, respectively.

This program is a simple superposition of *vending machine* – it strengthens the guard of the action *cigar* with the guard of *action* – (¬set). Hence, this action will never be undertaken after *coin* occurs.

Consider now the interconnection of the costumer:

program costumer **is**
var
init   true
do   pay: [true → *skip*] [] eat: [true → *skip*]
fair   eat

The configuration diagram of the system is as follows:

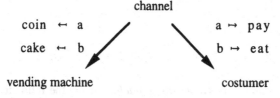

$$\text{channel}$$

$$\begin{array}{ccc} \text{coin} \leftarrow a & & a \mapsto \text{pay} \\ \text{cake} \leftarrow b & & b \mapsto \text{eat} \end{array}$$

vending machine   costumer

Its pushout is given, up to isomorphism, by

program served customer **is**
var   ready, served_cake, served_cigar
init   ready ∧ (served_cake ∨ served_cigar)
do   pay_coin : [ready ∧ (served_cake ∨ served_cigar)
                    → ready:=false ‖ served_cake:=false ‖ served_cigar:=false]
      [] eat_cake : [¬ready ∧ ¬served_cake ∧ ¬served_cigar
                → served_cake:=true]
      [] cigar: [¬ready ∧ ¬served_cake ∧ ¬served_cigar
                → served_cigar:=true]
      [] reset: [¬ready ∧ (served_cake ∨ served_cigar)
                → ready:=true]
fair   eat_cake

together with (coin ↦ pay_coin, cake ↦ eat_cake, cigar ↦ cigar, reset ↦ reset, ready ↦ ready, served_cake ↦ served_cake, served_cigar ↦ served_cigar) and (pay ↦ pay_coin, eat ↦ eat_cake) as morphisms connecting *vending machine* and *costumer* to *served customer*, respectively.

4 Compositionality

In order to define a notion of satisfaction between programs and specifications, we need to be able to relate their syntax and semantics.

Definition/Proposition 4.1: Every program signature $<V,\Gamma>$ defines the temporal signature $V \cup \Gamma$. Because V and Γ are disjoint, this mapping extends to a functor, i.e. every morphism of program signatures extends to a morphism of temporal signatures. ∎

Definition/Proposition 4.2: Given a program signature $<V,\Gamma>$, every interpretation structure $(\mathcal{A}, \mathcal{G})$ can be mapped to the model $\mathcal{A} \cup \mathcal{G}$ of $V \cup \Gamma$ defined by $(\mathcal{A} \cup \mathcal{G})(a) = \mathcal{A}(a)$ for every $a \in V$ and $(\mathcal{A} \cup \mathcal{G})(g) = \mathcal{G}(g)$ for every $g \in \Gamma$. ∎

Definition 4.3: Given a program $<\theta,\Delta>$ where $\theta = <V,\Gamma>$ and $\Delta = <I,F,B,C>$, and a proposition $\phi \in LTL(V \cup \Gamma)$, we say that $<\theta,\Delta>$ satisfies ϕ, $<\theta,\Delta> \vDash \phi$, iff, for every model $(\mathcal{A}, \mathcal{G})$ of $<\theta,\Delta>$, $(\mathcal{A} \cup \mathcal{G}) \vDash \phi$. We say that $<\theta,\Delta>$ satisfies a specification $<V \cup \Gamma, \Phi>$ iff $<\theta,\Delta>$ satisfies every $\phi \in \Phi$. ∎

Consider now the extension LTX of the linear temporal logic defined in 2.1 with the operator **X** (next) defined by:

$$(M,i) \vDash_\Sigma \mathbf{X}\phi \text{ iff } (M,i+1) \vDash_\Sigma \phi$$

Proposition 4.4: Given a program $<\theta,\Delta>$ where $\theta = <V,\Gamma>$ and $\Delta = <I,F,B,C>$, and a proposition $\phi \in LTX(V \cup \Gamma)$, $<\theta,\Delta> \vDash \phi$ iff $Spec(<\theta,\Delta>) \vDash \phi$ where $Spec(<\theta,\Delta>)$ is the following set of propositions in the language of $V \cup \Gamma$:

- the proposition $(\mathbf{beg} \supset I)$;
- for every action $g \in \Gamma$, the proposition $(g \supset B(g) \wedge (\bigwedge_{a \in D(g)} \mathbf{X}a \equiv F(g,a)))$;
- for every $a \in V$, the propositions $a \supset ((\bigvee_{g \in D(a)} g) \vee a\mathbf{W}(\bigvee_{g \in D(a)} g))$
  and $(\neg a) \supset ((\bigvee_{g \in D(a)} g) \vee (\neg a)\mathbf{W}(\bigvee_{g \in D(a)} g))$ ∎

These propositions do capture the semantics of a program: the first axiom establishes that I is an initialisation condition; the second set of axioms formalises the assignment – if g is about to occur, the next value of attribute a is the current value of $F(g,a)$ – and establishes $B(g)$ as a necessary condition for the occurrence of g; the last set of axioms (the locality axioms) capture locality of attributes: if, in a given state, none of the actions of the domain of an attribute occurs, that attribute remains invariant until the next state transition performed by an action in the domain of the attribute.

Proposition 4.5: The mapping $Spec: \mathcal{PROG} \rightarrow \mathcal{SPEC}$ can be extended to a functor.

proof: It is important to give a sketch of the proof of this result. Because $Spec$ is a lifting of the corresponding functor on signatures, it is only necessary to prove that, given a program morphism $\sigma: <\theta_1,\Delta_1> \rightarrow <\theta_2,\Delta_2>$, $Spec(\sigma)$ is a specification morphism $Spec(<\theta_1,\Delta_1>) \rightarrow Spec(<\theta_2,\Delta_2>)$. According to definition 2.3, we have to prove that the translation of each of the axioms of $Spec(<\theta_1,\Delta_1>)$ is a theorem of $Spec(<\theta_2,\Delta_2>)$.

- the proposition (**beg** $\supset \sigma(I_1)$) can be derived from the axiom (**beg** $\supset I_2$) and the property ($I_2 \supset \sigma(I_1)$) of the program morphism;

- for every $g \in \Gamma_1$ and $a \in D_1(g)$, the proposition ($\sigma(g) \supset X\sigma(a) \equiv \sigma(F_1(g,a))$) can be derived from the axiom ($\sigma(g) \supset X\sigma(a) \equiv F_2(\sigma(g),\sigma(a))$), the axiom ($\sigma(g) \supset B_2(\sigma(g))$) and the property ($B_2(\sigma(g)) \supset \sigma(F_1(g,a)) \equiv F_2(\sigma(g),\sigma(a))$) of the program morphism;

- for every $g \in \Gamma_1$, the proposition ($\sigma(g) \supset \sigma(B_1(g))$) can be derived from the axiom ($\sigma(g) \supset B_2(\sigma(g))$) and the property ($B_2(\sigma(g)) \supset \sigma(B_1(g))$) of the program morphism.

- for every $a \in V_1$, the propositions $\sigma(a) \supset ((\bigvee_{g \in D_1(a)} \sigma(g)) \vee \sigma(a)W(\bigvee_{g \in D_1(a)} \sigma(g)))$ can be derived from $D_2(\sigma(a))=\sigma(D_1(a))$ as implied by the program morphism and $\sigma(a) \supset ((\bigvee_{g' \in D_2(\sigma(a))} g') \vee \sigma(a)W(\bigvee_{g' \in D_2(\sigma(a))} g'))$. The same can be proved for the other set of propositions. ∎

For instance, the program *regulator* is mapped to the following specification:

sign   set, trigger, action

axioms   **beg** $\supset \neg$set

          trigger $\supset$ **X**set

          action$\supset \neg$set

          set $\supset$ trigger $\vee$ set**W**trigger

          ($\neg$set) $\supset$ trigger $\vee$ ($\neg$set)**W**trigger

The proof that the program *regulator* satisfies the specification given in section 2 cannot go through because the signature of the specification is not the image of the signature of the program. We can, however, generalise the definition of satisfaction as follows:

Definition 4.6: A *realisation* of a specification S is a pair $<\sigma,P>$ such that $P:PROG$ and σ is a specification morphism $S \rightarrow Spec(P)$. ∎

Realisations generalise the notion of satisfaction by allowing the program and the specification to be over different signatures. More concretely, the program is allowed to have features that are not relevant to the specification (like the attributes). Hence the morphism from S to $Spec(P)$ corresponds to the way in which P realises S, i.e., intuitively, it records the *design decisions* (namely the choice of attributes) that lead from S to P (seen as a design exercise carried out in *SPEC*).

As an example, we can now prove that the program *regulator* is a realisation of the specification given in section 2 by means of the obvious inclusion morphism. In order to do so, we just have to prove that the property (trigger $\supset$ **G**$^+\neg$action) is a theorem of $Spec(regulator)$:

1. set $\supset$ **G**set

    from the second and fourth axioms

2. set $\supset$ **G**($\neg$action)

    from 1 and the third axiom

3. trigger $\supset$ **$G^+\neg$action**
    from 2 and the second axiom

Compositionality can now be defined as the property according to which whatever interconnection of specifications we have as a specification of a complex system, we can pick up arbitrary realisations of these specifications, interconnect them as specified, and obtain a composite program that is a realisation of the composite specification.

The following theorem proves that compositionality is a consequence of the functorial nature of the relationship between programs and specifications:

Theorem 4.7: Consider the *SPEC* diagram given by φ_1 and φ_2, interconnecting specifications S_1 and S_2 via a channel S. Let $<\eta,P>$, $<\eta_1,P_1>$, $<\eta_2,P_2>$ be realisations of S, S_1 and S_2, respectively (i.e. $\eta: S \to Spec(P)$, $\eta_i: S_i \to Spec(P_i)$), interconnected in a way that is consistent with the interconnection of the specifications, i.e. $\mu_i: P \to P_i$ are such that $\eta;Spec(\mu_i)=\varphi_i;\eta_i$. Then, there is a unique way in which the pushout program P' is a realisation of the pushout specification S', i.e. there is a unique $\eta':S' \to Spec(P')$ s.t. $\beta_i;\eta'=\eta_i;Spec(\sigma_i)$.

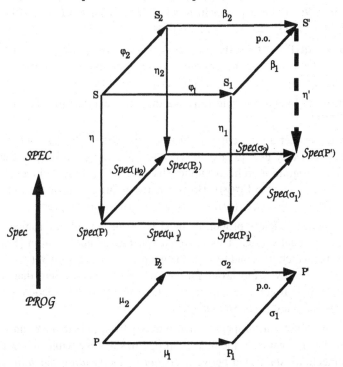

proof (sketch): because *Spec* is a functor, the image of the commutative diagram at the program level is a commutative diagram at the specification level. The rest follows from the universal property of the pushout and the compatibility of the interconnections. ∎

We should point out that this theorem holds for any functor *Spec* between categories of programs and of specifications. That is to say, it does not depend on the nature of the program design language (as long as it can be defined as a category) and of the specification logic (as long as it can be defined as an institution).

Hence, if programs are related to specifications through a functor, the emergence of properties at the specification level (e.g. β_2 is not conservative) is accounted for at the program level through the morphism η' (i.e. the composed program P' is strong enough to realise the emergent properties).

In terms of the examples analysed in sections 2 and 3, we can prove that the interconnection of the programs *vending machine* and *regulator* is a realisation of the interconnection between the specifications given in section 2. Hence, as expected, the emergence of the property ($\neg$cigar) is accounted for.

However, it is easy to see that the program *costumer* is not a realisation of the specification given in section 2. Indeed, the functor *Spec* does not account for liveness properties. Consider, then, the following extension of *Spec*:

Definition 4.8: Given a program $<\theta,\Delta>$, we define the specification $Live(<\theta,\Delta>)$ over $\theta \cup \Delta$ as follows: $Live(<\theta,\Delta>) = Spec(<\theta,\Delta>) \cup \{(\mathbf{GFB}(g) \supset \mathbf{F}g) \mid g \in C\}$. ∎

Proposition 4.9: Given a proposition $\phi \in LTX(\theta \cup \Delta)$, $Live(<\theta,\Delta>) \vDash \phi$ iff, for every *live* model $(\mathcal{A}, \mathcal{G})$ of $<\theta,\Delta>$, $(\mathcal{A} \cup \mathcal{G}) \vDash \phi$. ∎

That is to say, $Live(P)$ captures the properties that are true in every live model of the program P. In the case of the program *costumer*, this mapping generates the axiom (Feat) and, hence, the program satisfies the given specification.

However, it is no longer possible to prove that $Live$ extends to a functor between $PROG$ and $SPEC$.

Indeed, if we consider a program morphism $\sigma: <\theta_1,\Delta_1> \rightarrow <\theta_2,\Delta_2>$, we would have to prove that, for every $g \in C_1$, $Live(<\theta_2,\Delta_2>) \vDash (\mathbf{GFB}_1(g)) \supset \mathbf{F}\sigma(g))$. Because the fact that σ is a program morphism implies that $\sigma(g) \in C_2$, we have in $Live(<\theta_2,\Delta_2>)$ the axiom $(\mathbf{GFB}_2(\sigma(g)) \supset \mathbf{F}\sigma(g))$. However, the requirement of the morphism on the guards – $(B_2(\sigma(g)) \supset \sigma(B_1(g)))$ – does not contribute to the proof.

This is why, when liveness properties need to be preserved, a stronger notion of superposition is usually used. This is called spectative superposition [Francez and Forman 90], for which the condition on the guards is $B_2(\sigma(g)) \equiv \sigma(B_1(g))$. Spectative superposition is, however, too strong for the kind of interconnections that are usually involved in parallel program design, namely the ones we used in section 3, because it does not allow for guards to be strengthened.

The loss of the functorial property when moving from *Spec* to *Live* can be used to explain why the emergence of the liveness properties that we witnessed as a result of the interconnection established between *costumer* and *vending machine* seemed to indicate that not all realisations of the component specifications might be used for implementing the interconnected system.

We can easily see that the program morphism $\sigma_{costumer}$ that relates *costumer* to *served customer* does not map through $Live$ to a specification morphism. For instance, the guard of the action *eat* is strengthened from *true* to ($\neg$ready $\wedge$

¬served_cake ∧ ¬served_cigar). Hence, the property (Feat_cake) cannot be derived. In order to be able to do so, we would have to rely on a theorem of the form **GF**(¬ready ∧ ¬served_cake ∧ ¬served_cigar). Indeed, the fairness axiom of *eat_cake* – (**GF**(¬ready ∧ ¬served_cake ∧ ¬served_cigar) ⊃ Feat_cake) – would then guarantee (Feat_cake).

The proposition **GF**(¬ready ∧ ¬served_cake ∧ ¬served_cigar) expresses a liveness requirement. Liveness properties are usually proved by showing that certain actions eventually occur. In the case above, the action of interest is *pay_coin*. Indeed, under the assumption (Fpay_coin), we can derive:

1. **GF**pay_coin
   necessitation
2. (pay_coin ⊃ **X**¬ready ∧ **X**¬served_cake ∧ **X**¬served_cigar)
   effects of pay_coin
3. Fpay_coin ⊃ **F**(¬ready ∧ ¬served_cake ∧ ¬served_cigar)
   temporal consequence of 2
4. **GF**pay_coin ⊃ **GF**(¬ready ∧ ¬served_cake ∧ ¬served_cigar)
   temporal consequence of 3
5. **GF**(¬ready ∧ ¬served_cake ∧ ¬served_cigar)
   from 1 and 4

Hence, for the translation *Live* from programs to specifications, (Fpay_coin) can be explained in terms of the need to ensure that the guard of *eat_cake* becomes true.

We can conclude that $\sigma_{costumer}$ is mapped through *Live* to a specification morphism provided that (Fpay_coin) is added to *served customer*. This suggests that the program configuration be revised so as to enforce that property. There are, of course, many ways of doing so. The "incremental" way is to add a new component to the system with the responsability of ensuring that property. For instance,

program reminder **is**
var
init   true
do   wake_up: [true → *skip*]
fair   wake_up

This program would then be interconnected to *costumer* by synchronising *wake-up* with *pay*. The resulting *paying_costumer* would indeed have the property (Fpay). Incremental revisions like this one seem to be the most "economical": they promote reuse, are monotonic, etc. But they do not necessarily provide optimal solutions and the designer may opt, instead, for revising one or more components of the system.

Notice, however, that after connecting the paying costumer to the vending machine, we would still have to account for the new fairness requirement imposed on *pay*. Indeed, we would now need to ensure that the guard of the new joint live action *pay_coin*, which is strengthened to (ready ∧ (served_cake ∨ served_cigar)), becomes true. Again, this would lead us to the revision of the program with the addition of a new reminder, this time connected to the action *reset* thus explaining again the role of the emergent property (Freset) in the context of the mapping *Live*!

When, then, should we stop? And which emergent properties should we actually take into account? We shall now demonstrate that this process of revision can be rationalised and made systematic.

Recall that the source of the problem is that *Live* is not a functor. We know, however, why it is not a functor. More precisely, we know which conditions have to be required on a program morphism so that it gives rise to a specification morphism:

Proposition 4.10: Given a program morphism $\sigma: <\theta_1,\Delta_1> \rightarrow <\theta_2,\Delta_2>$, $Spec(\sigma)$ is a specification morphism $Live(<\theta_1,\Delta_1>) \rightarrow Live(<\theta_2,\Delta_2>)$ iff the following condition holds: for every $g \in C_1$, $Live(<\theta_2,\Delta_2>) \vDash (\mathbf{GF}\sigma(B_1(g)) \supset \mathbf{GFB}_2(\sigma(g)))$.

proof: we already know from proposition 4.5 that the axioms of $Spec(<\theta_1,\Delta_1>)$ are translated to theorems of $Spec(<\theta_2,\Delta_2>)$ and, hence, of $Live(<\theta_2,\Delta_2>)$. Therefore, it remains to prove that $Live(<\theta_2,\Delta_2>) \vDash (\mathbf{GF}\sigma(B_1(g)) \supset \mathbf{F}\sigma(g))$ for every $g \in C_1$. But this is an immediate consequence of the axiom $(\mathbf{GFB}_2(\sigma(g)) \supset \mathbf{F}\sigma(g))$ of $Live(<\theta_2,\Delta_2>)$ and the given assumption $(\mathbf{GF}\sigma(B_1(g)) \supset \mathbf{GFB}_2(\sigma(g)))$. The fact that this is also a necessary condition results from the axiom $\sigma(g) \supset B_2(\sigma(g))$. ∎

Proposition 4.10 tells us that, although *Live* is not a functor, it is a "conditional" functor. It "relies" on certain conditions of the target program of a morphism to map that program morphism to a specification morphism. Because a program morphism $\sigma: P \rightarrow P'$ can be seen as describing how a program P is part of a bigger environment P', this resembles rely/guarantee styles of specification [e.g. Abadi and Lamport 93, Collette 93].

Indeed, if we take the general case of two categories $\mathcal{PROG}$ (of programs) and $\mathcal{SPEC}$ (of specifications in some institution) linked by a mapping *Spec* on their object classes, and $R(\sigma: P \rightarrow P')$ is a set of propositions in the language of $Spec(P')$ such that $Spec(P') \vDash R(\sigma)$ implies that $Spec(\sigma)$ is a morphism $Spec(P) \rightarrow Spec(P')$, we are in a rely/guarantee style of specification where $Spec(P)$ are the conditions that are guaranteed to hold in any environment σ that satisfies the conditions $R(\sigma)$.

To have a satisfactory specification framework, however, it is essential that the specification style be incremental in the following sense: if we have proved that some system satisfies the rely conditions on its components, we should no longer have to prove them when we extend that system to a bigger one in a such a way that the rely conditions on the old system are satisfied. That is to say, the following property should be satisfied:

if $\sigma_1: P_1 \rightarrow P_2$ and $\sigma_2: P_2 \rightarrow P_3$ are program morphisms, then

$Spec(P_3) \vDash R(\sigma_1;\sigma_2)$ provided that $Spec(P_2) \vDash R(\sigma_1)$ and $Spec(P_3) \vDash R(\sigma_2)$.

A sufficient condition for this to happen is that

$R(\sigma_2), \sigma_2(R(\sigma_1)) \vDash R(\sigma_1;\sigma_2)$.

On the other hand, any program should satisfy the rely conditions of the identity (i.e. when the program is closed):

$Spec(P) \vDash R(id_P)$

We can prove that this is the case for COMMUNITY and the temporal logic defined in section 2, taking $R(\sigma_1: P_1 \rightarrow P_2)$ to be $\{(\mathbf{GF}\sigma(B_1(g)) \supset \mathbf{GFB}_2(\sigma(g))) \mid g \in C_1\}$ as seen in 4.10. Indeed, if $\sigma_1: P_1 \rightarrow P_2$ and $\sigma_2: P_2 \rightarrow P_3$, given $g \in C_1$ we have

1. $GF\sigma_2(B_2(\sigma_1(g))) \supset GFB_3(\sigma_2(\sigma_1(g)))$ in $R(\sigma_2)$
2. $GF\sigma_2(\sigma_1(B_1(g))) \supset GF\sigma_2(B_2(\sigma_1(g)))$ in $\sigma_2(R(\sigma_1))$
3. $GF(\sigma_1;\sigma_2)(B_1(g)) \supset GFB_3((\sigma_1;\sigma_2)(g))$ from 1 and 2

On the other hand, given $g \in C$, the condition in $R(id)$ is $GFB(g) \supset GFB(g)$, which is a tautology.

Hence, although the existence of a functorial relationship between $\mathcal{PROG}$ and $\mathcal{SPEC}$ implies compositionality, there are weaker relationships that still give us some control on the modular and incremental development of programs. These weaker relationships reflect rely/guarantee styles of specification and account for emergent properties that require forms of co-operation between the components of the system that are not enforced locally at the level of their specifications and interconnections. These rely conditions act as proof obligations on the programs that are chosen to realise the component specifications. If these proof obligations cannot be discharged, either the programs have to be revised or new programs have to be interconnected as illustrated above.

It is very important to notice that the nature of these rely conditions depends on the mapping from programs to specifications. Intuitively, this mapping defines what the "operating system" guarantees about the execution of programs. For instance, in the examples above, the nature of proof obligations (rely conditions) depends on the fact that the semantics of the set C (fairness requirements) is of strong fairness (compassion). Other notions of fairness would lead to conditions of a different nature. In particular, program morphisms may satisfy the proof obligations for one such notion but not for another. Hence, revisions to the realisations of given specifications are always subject to the nature of these rely conditions. A change of "operating system" may remove the need for any revision or addition to the programs.

For instance, an even stronger notion of fairness, called *politeness* in [Barreiro et al 95], would not require the realisations of the *costumer* and *vending machine* to be revised. According to this notion of fairness, execution of an action is guaranteed if it is always *possible* to grant it permission: it is always possible for the costumer to pay after he has consumed, and it is always possible for the vending machine to be reset after it dispenses the goods. The formalisation of this notion requires a branching time logic – $(GEFB(g) \supset Fg)$. This is a very strong notion of fairness because it requires an active operating system, capable of making components move in order to grant permission to joint actions. Such notions of fairness are not uncommon in social contexts, i.e. when we are modelling systems composed of "living" entities.

5 Concluding Remarks

In this paper, we resumed previous work on the categorical approach to reactive system specification [Fiadeiro and Maibaum 92] to provide a formal account of emergence phenomena during interconnection of component specifications. Capitalising in recent work [Fiadeiro and Maibaum 95, 96] on the integration of parallel program design techniques within the "categorical paradigm", we showed that, if specifications are *compositional* wrt programs, emergence of properties of components in the interconnected system is accounted for in terms of whatever programs and interconnections between programs are chosen as realisations of the configuration of specifications. Compositionality was formulated in this categorical framework in terms of the existence of a functor from the category of programs to the category of specifications. In fact, we showed that the critical issue in the existence of such a functor is the property that program morphisms are mapped to specification morphisms. That is to say, and because the morphisms characterise the structural properties of the domain being formalised as a category, compositionality is a property of structure preservation between two levels in the development process.

The absence of compositionality was shown to be the critical factor in diagnosing potential mismatches between specifications and their realisations from the emergence of certain properties. Indeed, we showed that certain emergent properties can be interpreted as complementing the component specifications with the functionality that is necessary for compensating the lack of compositionality, namely that program morphisms are not strong enough to induce specification morphisms. Naturally, this interpretation is not absolute and cannot be given without knowing what programming language is used for realising specifications and what "operating system" controls the execution and co-operation between programs.

This notion of "operating system" is captured by the mapping that relates the objects of the category of programs with the objects of the category of specifications. It provides the set of properties that each program "guarantees" about its execution. Situations in which the mapping does not induce a functor (i.e. compositionality fails) can be interpreted as indicating that such guarantees "rely" on properties of the environment in which the program executes, therefore leading us in the direction of rely/guarantee styles of specification [e.g. Abadi and Lamport 93, Collette 93]. Because a program morphism $\sigma:P \rightarrow P'$ can be seen as describing how a program P is part of a bigger environment P', it is only natural that such "rely" conditions be defined relative to morphisms like σ and formulated in the language of P'. Indeed, we showed that if the set of rely properties satisfies some structural properties, the functorial relationship between programs and specifications can be weakened while preserving modularity and incrementality in an essential way.

Rely properties act as proof obligations on the realisations chosen for component specifications and interconnections. Upon failure to discharge them, revisions have to be made to the chosen programs and program interconnections. We gave examples of how revisions can be made in an incremental way by adding new components, but a systematic study of incremental revision is still missing.

Further work is also going on exploring such weak, or conditional, functorial relationships, namely in conjunction with different fairness requirements. The whole categorical approach to system development is, in fact, being revised in order to accommodate weaker functorial relationships such as those illustrated in the paper, namely those that arise from rely/guarantee styles of specification.

Acknowledgements

This work "emerged" from many fruitful interactions with Tom Maibaum. The characterisation of non-conservative extensions as representing emergence phenomena was suggested by Félix Costa. Nuno Barreiro and Antónia Lopes have also provided much valuable input in discussions on compositionality. Finally, special thanks to Martin Wirsing for the opportunity to present this work at AMAST.

References

[Abadi and Lamport 93]
M.Abadi and L.Lamport, "Composing Specifications", *ACM TOPLAS* 15(1), 1993, 73-132.
[Back and Kurki-Suonio 88]
R.Back and R.Kurki-Suonio, "Distributed Cooperation with Action Systems", *ACM TOPLAS* 10(4), 1988, 513-554.
[Barreiro et al 95]
N.Barreiro, J.Fiadeiro and T.Maibaum, "Politeness in Object Societies", in R.Wieringa and R.Feenstra (eds) *Information Systems – Correctness and Reusability*, World Scientific Publishing Company 1995, 119-134.
[Bougé and Francez 88]
L.Bougé and N.Francez, "A Compositional Approach to Superimposition", in *Proc. 15th ACM Symposium on Principles of Programming Languages"*, ACM Press 1988, 240-249.
[Burstall and Goguen 77]
R.Burstall and J.Goguen, "Putting Theories together to make Specifications", in R.Reddy (ed) *Proc Fifth International Joint Conference on Artificial Intelligence*, 1977, 1045-1058.
[Chandy and Misra 88]
K.Chandy and J.Misra, *Parallel Program Design - A Foundation*, Addison-Wesley 1988.
[Collette 93]
P.Collette, "Application of the Composition Principle to UNITY-like Specifications", in M.C.Gaudel and J.P.Jouannaud (eds) *TAPSOFT'93*, LNCS 668, Springer-Verlag 1993, 230-242.
[Fiadeiro and Maibaum 92]
J.Fiadeiro and T.Maibaum, "Temporal Theories as Modularisation Units for Concurrent System Specification", *Formal Aspects of Computing* 4(3), 1992, 239-272.
[Fiadeiro and Maibaum 95]
J.Fiadeiro and T.Maibaum, "Interconnecting Formalisms: supporting modularity, reuse and incrementality", in G.E.Kaiser (ed) *Proc. 3rd Symp. on Foundations of Software Engineering*, ACM Press 1995, 72-80.
[Fiadeiro and Maibaum 96]
J.Fiadeiro and T.Maibaum, *Categorical Semantics of Parallel Program Design*, Technical Report, available at http://www.di.fc.ul.pt/~llf
[Francez and Forman 90]
N.Francez and I.Forman, "Superimposition for Interacting Processes", in *CONCUR'90*, LNCS 458, Springer-Verlag 1990, 230-245.

[Goguen 71]
> J.Goguen, "Mathematical Representation of Hierarchically Organised Systems", in E.Attinger (ed) *Global Systems Dynamics*, Krager 1971, 112-128.

[Goguen 73]
> J.Goguen, "Categorical Foundations for General Systems Theory", in F.Pichler and R.Trappl (eds) *Advances in Cybernetics and Systems Research*, Transcripta Books 1973, 121-130.

[Goguen and Burstall 92]
> J.Goguen and R.Burstall, "Institutions: Abstract Model Theory for Specification and Programming", *Journal of the ACM* 39(1), 1992, 95-146.

[Goguen and Ginali 78]
> J.Goguen and S.Ginali, "A Categorical Approach to General Systems Theory", in G.Klir (ed) *Applied General Systems Research*, Plenum 1978, 257-270.

[Goldblatt 87]
> R.Goldblatt, *Logics of Time and Computation*, CSLI 1987.

[Katz 93]
> S.Katz, "A Superimposition Control Construct for Distributed Systems", *ACM TOPLAS* 15(2), 1993, 337-356.

[Kurki-Suonio and Järvinen 89]
> R.Kurki-Suonio and H.Järvinen, "Action System Approach to the Specification and Design of Distributed Systems", in *Proc. 5th Int. Workshop on Software Specification and Design*, IEEE Press 1989, 34-40.

[Manna and Pnueli 91]
> Z.Manna and A.Pnueli, *The Temporal Logic of Reactive and Concurrent Systems*, Springer-Verlag 1991.

[Sannella and Tarlecki 88]
> D.Sannella and A.Tarlecki, "Building Specifications in an Arbitrary Institution", *Information and Control* 76, 1988, 165-210.

Algebraic View Specification*

Barbara Paech

Institut für Informatik, Technische Universität München
Arcisstr.21, D-80290 München
paech@informatik.tu-muenchen.de

Abstract. The application of algebraic specification techniques in the early phases of software development requires a means for specifying *views*. In this paper we argue for algebraic view specification based on an *algebraic concept model*. The concept model consists of two parts: a meta model defining the concepts of different views and the relationships between them, and a system model defining the system behaviour. We show how to derive an algebraic concept model from a semi-formal one given usually as an entity relationship diagram. This gives the rigour of formality to pragmatic view specifications and allows for an easy translation between formal and pragmatic specifications.

1 Introduction

Using algebraic methods in industrial software development means introducing an algebraic specification at some point of the development process and exploiting the mathematical semantics for code generation, refinement, verification and the like. There is some evidence that introducing formal specifications very early in the development process is most profitable [SH95]. This is due to the fact that errors in requirement analysis and design are the most costly, making the expenses for precise specification and thorough validation worthwhile. In the following, *algebraic view specifications* based on an *algebraic concept model* are introduced as a means of making algebraic specifications better applicable to requirements analysis and definition.

Views

In the process of requirements analysis *several views* of the required software system and its environment are specified. The reason is that in the early stages there is not enough information to describe the system as a whole. Instead, seperated in several views, information is gathered which later on must be integrated in a design satisfying all the views. Pragmatic development methods like FUSION [CAB+94], OMT [RBP+91], OOSE [Jac92], SSADM [DCC92] offer description techniques for theses views. Mostly, only the notation is defined together with an informal semantics. Consequently, CASE tools often only support editing and syntactic checks of these description.

---

* This work was carried out within the project SysLab, supported by Siemens Nixdorf and by the Deutsche Forschungsgemeinschaft under the Leibniz program

Meta Model

More powerful CASE tools are based on a *repository* in which information about all the objects relevant to the software development is stored [HL93]. Following the ANSI standard for *information resource dictionary systems* [ANS89] there are four levels of such objects:

1. the real world objects relevant to the software system (e.g. `Miss Marple`),
2. the types and relationships of the real world objects (e.g. `detective`, `crime`, `worksOn`), often called *model level*,
3. the concepts used to describe these types and relationships (e.g. `entity`, `process`), often called *meta model level*, and
4. the concepts used to describe the meta model.

From the point of view of a method designer the meta model level is particularly interesting. On this level the general concepts used to model the application and the software system are fixed. Interestingly, most books on software engineering methods do not make this meta model explicit. It is, however, becoming increasingly popular for method comparison (e.g. [Gil93]). In the tradition of semantic data modelling usually entity relationship or object diagrams are used to define the meta model. Thus the modelling concepts are characterized through their attributes and relationships (and operations - in case of an object diagram). Each view corresponds to a certain part of the meta model. Relationships between concepts of different views determine *consistency conditions* between different views. These consistency condition can be enforced by a CASE tool to give support to the *integration* of the views.

Concept Model

To allow for *algebraic* view specification the meta model can be formalized in an algebraic specification language. This idea is worked out in the first part of the paper. However, from the point of view of algebraic specification, traditional meta models are not sufficient. They do not provide a semantics of the modelling concepts in terms of *system behaviour*. Therefore, in the second part of the paper the *system model* is introduced and combined with the meta model. The combined model is called *concept model*. Different parts of this model determine different views together with their mathematical semantics. The relationships between the concepts give rise to very powerful consistency conditions.

This paper is structured as follows. As an example we introduce part of the meta model of the method FUSION and the corresponding views. Then we discuss their formalization. In section 4 we define a system model for FUSION and show how to combine the two models to give a precise semantics to the views. Related work is discussed in the conclusions.

2 Views and the Meta Model - An Example

As an example we discuss the simplified meta model of the analysis phase of
FUSION (see figure 1). The notation used for this and the following models is
explained in the legend. We only show the most important attributes.

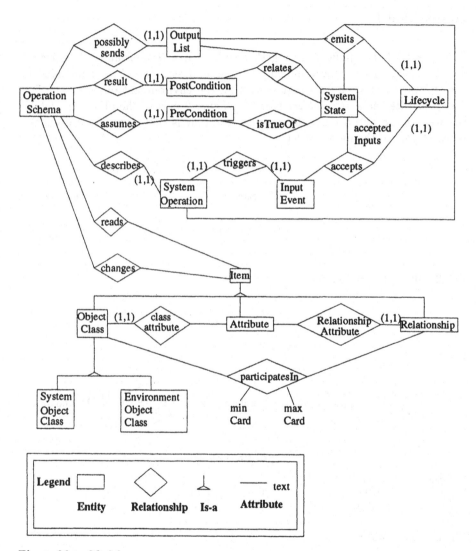

Fig. 1. Meta Model

This meta model is not given explicitly in [CAB+94]. The model given here
covers all concepts necessary to explain the description techniques for the views

developed in the analysis phase. After explanation of the model along with the description techniques for the different views some modelling alternatives are discussed.

FUSION offers three views: the object model, the operation model and the lifecycle model.

Object Model

The *objects* of the application, together with their *attributes* and *relationships*, are described in the object model[2]. In a second step the objects included in the software system are distinguished from the environment objects. The former consitute the *system object model*. In figure 2 part of the object model for the well-known automatic teller machine example is shown. Figure 3 gives the relevant part of the meta model.

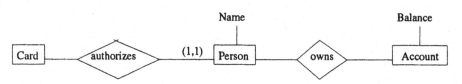

Fig. 2. Object Model Example

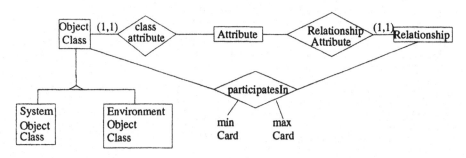

Fig. 3. Object Model

---

[2] For the sake of simplicity we omit further structuring facilities like generalization and aggregation here.

Operation Model

System operations are *described* in one or more *operation schemata*. Each schema covers the items *read* or *changed*, the output events *possibly sent*, the *precondition* and *the postcondition*. The precondition characterizes the set of *system states* enabling the operation. The postcondition characterizes a set of pairs of system states and a *list of output events* such that the application of the operation in the first state yields the second state together with the list of output events. As example the system operation **dispenseCash** of the automatic teller machine is given in figure 4[3]. The relevant part of the meta model is shown in figure 5.

Operation	dispenseCash(amount)
reads	Account
changes	Account
sends	Person: {overdraw, newAmount?, cash, ejectCard}
assumes	Card inserted and Account owned by Person who is authorized through Card
result	If amount available on the Account, subtract amount from Account balance, send cash and ejectCard. Otherwise send overdraw and newAmount?.

Fig. 4. Operation Model Example

Lifecycle Model

The *lifecycle* model determines when input events are *accepted* (depending on the history of accepted events) and what output events may be *emitted*. In FUSION lifecycles are denoted as regular expressions, where output events are prefixed by #. An example describing the lifecycle of the automatic teller machine is given in figure 6. Figure 7 shows the corresponding part of the meta model.

As is most evident in the lifecycle meta model, the concrete syntax of the description technique and the concepts defined in the meta model may be quite different. This only mirrors the fact that different description techniques can be used for the same view. Therefore the meta model is much more adequate for method comparison than the description techniques themselves. Also, the meta model makes it easier to understand the description techniques.

---

[3] We have simplified the parameterization mechanism of FUSION here.

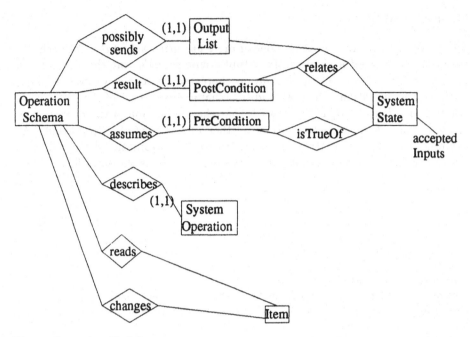

Fig. 5. Operation Model

```
(insertCard.(#rejectCard |
          #amount?. (dispenseCash.#overdraw.#newAmount? |
          dispenseCash.#cash.#newAmount?)*. eject.#ejectCard))*
```

Fig. 6. Lifecycle Example

This finishes the explanation of the meta model. As mentioned before, this model is not unique. It is adequate for method description. For implementation in a CASE repository it is too general. For example, it is not possible to keep a list of all system states. Therefore only a simplified version of the relationships involving SystemState will be supported. E.g. instead of the accepts relationship all input events referred to in the lifecycle could be recorded.

3   Algebraic Meta Model and Algebraic Views

As shown in [Het95] entity relationship diagrams can be formalized in an algebraic specification language. For each entity a sort is introduced, for each

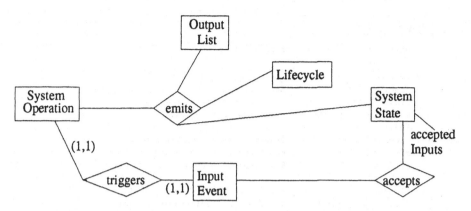

Fig. 7. Lifecycle Model

attribute an operation and a predicate for each relationship. Cardinalities are expressed as constraints. In the following the meta model of figure 1 is translated into the algebraic specification language SPECTRUM [BFG+93]. The translation is shown in figure 8. The numbers (i) are reference points for the following explanation.

(1) This specification is based on the specification of natural numbers, of sets, of the attribute sorts and polymorphic lists. All functions are strict and total.

(2) For each entity of the meta model a sort is introduced. EQ means that for all the introduced sorts equality is decidable.

(3) The attributes are mapped into strict and total functions from the entity sorts to the attribute sorts:

(4) The relationships are mirrored in general by predicates. One-one relationships are translated into functions (see for example the **triggers** relationship).

(5) The cardinality constraints are captured by axioms. These axioms use the function **card** defined in the specification of sets. For a relationship **rel**: Sort1 × ... × Sortn a cardinality constraint for **Sorti** determines the number of instances of the relationship where the entities of the other sorts are fixed. As an example consider the relationship **accepts** between **Lifecycle**, **SystemState** and **InputEvent**.

(6) As discussed in [Het95] there are many constraints not expressible with entity relationship diagrams. They can be expressed in SPECTRUM and added as further axioms to the algebraic meta model. One example is a stronger cardinality constraint for **Lifecycle** in **accepts**. There is just one lifecycle for the whole system. Another example is the consistency between the output list characterized by **relates** and the one characterized by **emits**.

Figure 10 gives an example of an algebraic view specification. It specifies the equivalent of the lifecycle of figure 6 based on the concepts defined in

```
META MODEL = {

(1) enriches Nat + Set + AttrSort + List;
    strict total;
(2) sort InputEvent, SystemOp, OpSchema, OutputEvent, SystemState,
    Precondition, Postcondition, Lifecycle, Attribut, ObjectClass,
    SystemObjectClass, EnvironmentObjectClass, Relationship;
    sort Item = Attribute ⊌ Relationship ⊌ Object;
    EQ;
(3) acceptedInputs          : SystemState → List InputEvent;
    minCard                 : Relationship × ObjectClass → Nat;
    maxCard                 : Relationship × ObjectClass → Nat;

(4) classAttribute          : Attribute× ObjectClass → Bool;
    relationshipAttribute   : Attribute × Relationship → Bool;
    participatesIn          : ObjectClass × Relationship → Bool;
    describes               : OpSchema → SystemOp;
    possiblySends           : OpSchema → List OutputEvent;
    triggers                : InputEvent → SystemOp;
    reads                   : OpSchema × Item → Bool;
    changes                 : OpSchema × Item → Bool;
    assumes                 : OpSchema → Precondition;
    result                  : OpSchema → PostCondition;
    isTrueOf                : Precondition × SystemState → Bool;
    relates                 : Postcondition × SystemState × SystemState
                              × List OutputEvent → Bool;
    accepts                 : Lifecycle × SystemState × InputEvent → Bool;
    emits                   : Lifecycle × SystemState × SystemOp
                              × List OutputEvent → Bool;

(5) axioms
    ...
    ∀ l: LifeCycle. ∀ st: SystemState. ∃ acceptsSet: Set (LifeCycle ×
    SystemState × InputEvent). ∀ in: InputEvent.
    ((l,st,in) ∈ acceptsSet ⇔ accepts(l,st,in)) ∧
    1 ≤ card(acceptsSet);
    ∀ l : LifeCycle. ∀ in:InputEvent. ∃ acceptsSet: Set (LifeCycle ×
    SystemState × InputEvent). ∀ st: SystemState.
    ((l,st,in) ∈ acceptsSet ⇔ accepts(l,st,in)) ∧
    1 ≤ card(acceptsSet);
    ∀ in: InputEvent. ∀ st: SystemState. ∃ acceptsSet: Set (LifeCycle ×
    SystemState × InputEvent). ∀ l: Lifecycle.
    ((l,st,in) ∈ acceptsSet ⇔ accepts(l,st,in)) ∧
    1 ≤ card(acceptsSet) ∧ card(acceptsSet) ≤ 1);
(6) ........
    ∀ l,l': lifecycle. ∀ st,st': SystemState. ∀ in,in': InputEvent.
    (accepts(l,st,in) ∧ accepts(l',st',in')) ⇒ l = l';
    ∀ st: SystemState. ∀ op: SystemOp. ∀ out: List OutputEvent.
    (∃ l: Lifecycle. emits(l,st,op,out)) ⇔
    (∃ st': SystemState. ∀ sch: OpSchema . ∀ cond1: Precondition. ∀
    cond2: Postcondition. (describes (sch) = op ∧ assumes(sch)= cond1 ∧
    isTrueOf(cond1,st) ∧ result(sch) = cond2) →
    relates(cond2,st,st',out));
    endaxioms;

}
```

Fig. 8. Formal Meta Model

the algebraic meta model. First, for the sorts **InputEvent**, **OutputEvent** and **Lifecycle** the relevant elements are introduced. Then the relationships **accepts** and **emits** are specified by axioms. Essentially, these axioms characterize an Mealy-automaton corresponding to the lifecycle expression. This automaton is shown in figure 9.

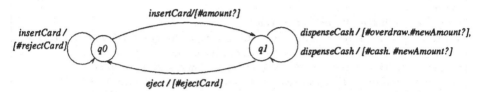

Fig. 9. Lifecycle Automaton

Automaton state q_0 characterizes all system states where the sequence of **acceptedInputs** is empty or ends with *eject*. Automaton state q_1 characterizes system states reached by accepting *insertCard* or *dispenseCash*. So the axioms for **accepts** first describe the set of accepted **InputEvents**. *insertCard* is accepted in system states characterized by q_0 and *dispenseCash* and *eject* are accepted in system states characterized by q_1. The axioms for **emits** first describe the set of **OutputEvents**. Then the **OutputEvent** is specified in dependency of the **InputEvent**. This corresponds to the transition labels of the automaton of figure 9.

Discussion

The algebraic meta model and view specification combines elements of pragmatic and formal software engineering methods.

From the point of view of pragmatic software engineering methods, formally specified views are not of *direct* use because of the skills required to apply mathematical specifications in general. However, mirroring the meta model in the algebraic meta model allows for an easy translation between the pragmatic view description and the algebraic view description. This translation supports the *indirect use* of formal methods as characterized in [Huß95]. The algebraic specification can be used for an analysis of the corresponding views yielding precise rules for transformation and consistency checks to be used by the software developer. If required, e.g. in the case of safety-critical system properties, a large part of the algebraic specification can be generated from the informal one.

From the point of view of algebraic specifications, views introduce a new structuring principle. The meta model introduces a new level of indirection into the specifications making the modelling concepts explicit. While this lengthens the specifications, it makes the process of specifying more flexible. Because of the

```
ATM LIFE = {
enriches META MODEL;
insertCard, dispenseCash, eject : InputEvent;
#rejectCard, #amount?, #overdraw, #newAmount?, #cash,
#ejectCard : OutputEvent;
atmLife : Lifecycle;

axioms
∀ st: SystemState. ∀ in: InputEvent.
accepts(atmLife,st,in) ⇒ (in = insertCard ∨ in = dispenseCash ∨ in = eject) ∧
accepts(atmLife,st,insertCard) ⇔ (acceptedInputs(st) = [] ∨
(δlast(acceptedInputs(st)) ∧ last(acceptedInputs(st)) = eject)) ∧
(accepts(atmLife,st,dispenseCash) ∨ accepts(atmLife, st, eject)) ⇔
(δlast(acceptedInputs(st)) ∧
( last(acceptedInputs(st)) = insertCard ∨ last(acceptedInputs (st)) =
dispenseCash));

∀ st:SystemState. ∀ out: List OutputEvent. ∀ x: OutputEvent.
∀ op: SystemOp.
(emits(atmLife,st,op,out) ∧ isEl(x,out)) ⇒ (x = #rejectCard
∨ x = #amount? ∨ x = #overdraw ∨ x = newAmount? ∨ x = #cash
∨ x = #ejectCard) ∧
emits(atmLife,st,op,out) ⇒ (op = triggers(insertCard)
∨ op = triggers(dispenseCash) ∨ op = triggers(eject)) ∧
emits(atmLife,st,triggers(insertCard),out) ⇔
(out = [#rejectCard] ∨ out = [#amount?]) ∧
emits(atmLife,st,triggers(dispenseCash),out) ⇔
(out = [#overdraw. #newAmount?] ∨ out = [#cash.#newAmount?]) ∧
emits(atmLife,st,triggers(eject),out) ⇔ (out = [#ejectCard]);
endaxioms
```

Fig. 10. Algebraic Lifecycle Specification

common vocabulary different views can be specified and refined by different people at different times. The consistency constraints between the views are made explicit through the axioms relating concepts of different views. One example of such a consistency condition is the second formular in (6) of figure 8. It relates the lifecycle and the operation view.

However, the semantics of the concepts given in the algebraic meta model is not complete. Nothing is said about the relationship between system states and objects. Nothing is said about the transition between two system states in general. The meta model is lacking the concepts necessary to define *system behaviour*. Of course, we could have included them in the meta model from the beginning. However, this is not necessary, if the meta model is used to charcterize the views. Also, meta models of pragmatic methods do not cover these concepts. Thus we prefer to introduce another model collecting all the concepts relating to system behaviour in one place: the *system model*. The system model of FUSION, its integration with the meta model, and its formalization is discussed in the following sections.

4 System Model and Concept Model

In this section the system model of FUSION is given. For reasons of space, we only give the semi-formal version denoted as an entity relationship-diagram. The derivation of the algebraic version follows the approach discussed above.

FUSION only considers *sequential systems*. These can be modelled as state transition systems, where the state determines the set of existing objects, the values of attributes and of relationships. Since FUSION distinguishes between input events received and the ones accepted, in each state the list of accepted input events leading to this state is included. Also, for each transition the list of emitted output events is recorded. Altogether, figure 11 shows the system model. Entities depicted as dashed boxes (**SystemObjectClass** in the figure) are just introduced for layout reasons to avoid crossing lines.

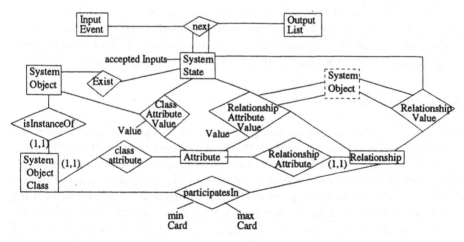

Fig. 11. System Model

The meta model and the system model can be joined by identifying common concepts. We call the combined model the *concept model*. On the algebraic side this corresponds to a specification combination using +. Again, there are a lot of consistency constraints between the concepts of the joined models which are not expressed in the entity relationship diagram. In the algebraic concept model these can (and have to) be expressed with further axioms. The most important one is the connection between **next** and the concepts of the operation schema (see figure 12).

```
∀ st1,st2: SystemState. ∀ in : InputEvent. ∀ out: List OutputEvent.
next( st1,in,st2,out) ⇔
∃ life: Lifecycle. ∃ op: SystemOp. ∀ sch: OpSchema.
∀ cond1 : PreCondition. ∀ cond2: PostCondition.
(¬ accepts( st1,in,life) ∧ st1 = st2 ∧ out = []) ∨
(accepts(st1,in,life) ∧ triggers( in) = op ∧
((assumes (sch) = cond1 ∧ isTrueOf( cond1,st1) ∧ result( sch) = cond2)
⇒ relates( cond2,st1,st2,out)) )
```

Fig. 12. Concept Model Axiom

The concept model gives a semantics to all modelling concepts in terms of the system behaviour. Some of the concepts are directly reflected in the syntax of the description techniques (e.g. the concepts of the object model), while others are only indirectly reflected (e.g. the concepts of the lifecycle model). Also, some concepts are exclusively related to views or the system model, while others are common to some view and the system model. Thus the purpose of the concepts within the method is made explicit in the concept model. Structuring formal specifications along these lines makes them easier to comprehend.

5 Conclusions

Altogether we advocate the following combination of algebraic specification and pragmatic software development methods. The views supported by the pragmatic method are captured in the meta model. Together with the system model underlying the pragmatic method it constitutes the pragmatic concept model. The concept model is directly translated to an algebraic concept model using the ideas of [Het95]. This specification has to be completed with axioms for the constraints not expressible in the entity-relationship-diagram. The resulting specification can be structured as follows:

Basic View Specification All sorts, functions and axioms which refer to concepts of one view or the system model specify the semantics of that view.

Consistency All axioms which refer to concepts of different views specify the consistency constraints between the views..

Based on this specification the concrete syntax of the description techniques supported in the pragmatic method is given a semantics in terms of the algebraic concept model. Thus every pragmatic view specification can directly be translated to an algebraic one. Following the paradigma of indirect use, the algebraic view specification is hidden to the everyday system developer. It is exploited as much as possible within CASE-tools for the pragmatic method. One example is the automatic check of consistency constraints between views. Another example is support of a refinement notion for views based on the algebraic semantics. An expert system developer might use the algebraic semantics for semi-automatic proofs of complex and critical properties.

Related Work

There are two sides two our approach. On one hand it is related to the efforts to give a formal foundation to pragmatic software development methods. In this respect our work is most influenced by [Huß94] where an algebraic semantics to SSADM is given. There also an algebraic system model is used to give semantics to the description techniques of SSADM. However, this is not related to an explicit meta model.

On the other hand our approach extends the work on algebraic system specification. Approaches for the algebraic specification of concurrent systems, for example SMoLCS [AMRW85], also include a system model. However, this work is not extended to views. In [GH95] the language TROLL *light* is given an algebraic semantics. TROLL *light* offers a template to specify different aspects of the system. However, this template does not give the full flexibility of views, since all aspects have to be specified at the same time. So this language is more suited for the design than for requirements analysis.

Future Work

In this paper we have argued for an algebraic concept model allowing for the algebraic specification and integration of views. On one hand this introduces the flexibility of views into algebraic specifications making them better applicable to the early phases of software development. On the other hand this gives the rigour of formality to pragmatic view specification. A great challenge is to extend these ideas to the specification of distributed systems. Within the SYSLAB-project a powerful system model for distributed systems has been given [RKB95] . In a next step this will be related to a meta model supporting an adequate set of views. Because of the additional complexity of distributed systems it is even more important to integrate the views using an algebraic concept model.

Acknowledgement

Thanks are due to the SYSLAB-group for stimulating discussions and to the anonymous referees for many helpful comments.

References

[AMRW85] E. Astesiano, G.F. Mascari, R. Reggio, and M. Wirsing. On the parameterized algebraic specification of concurrent systems. In *TAPSOFT,LNCS 185*, pages 342–358. Springer Verlag, 1985.

457

[ANS89]   ANSI. *American National Standard X3.138-1988: Information Resource Dictionary System (IRDS)*. American National Standard Institute, 1989.

[BFG⁺93]   M. Broy, C. Facchi, R. Grosu, R. Hettler, H. Hußmann, D. Nazareth, F. Regensburger, O. Slotosch, and K. Stølen. The Requirement and Design Specification Language SPECTRUM, An Informal Introduction, Version 1.0. Technical Report TUM-I9312, Technische Universität München, 1993.

[CAB⁺94]   D. Coleman, P. Arnold, S. Bodoff, C. Dollin, H. Gilchrist, F. Hayes, and P. Jeremaes. *Object-Oriented Development - The FUSION method*. Prentice Hall, 1994.

[DCC92]   E. Downs, P. Clare, and I. Coe. *Structured systems analysis and design method: application and context*. Prentice-Hall, 1992.

[GH95]   M. Gogolla and R. Herzig. An algebtraic development technique for information systems. In *AMAST,LNCS 936*, pages 446–460. Springer Verlag, 1995.

[Gil93]   M. Gilpin. A comparison of object-oriented analysis and design methods. Technical report, INTERSOLV at CASE World, 1993.

[Het95]   R. Hettler. *Entity/Relationship-Datenmodellierung in axiomatischen Spezifikationssprachen, Ph.D. thesis*. Reihe Softwaretechnik, FAST. Tectum Verlag, 1995.

[HL93]   H. Habermann and F. Leymann. *Repository*. R. Oldenbourg Verlag, 1993.

[Huß94]   H. Hußmann. Formal foundation for pragmatic software engineering methods. In B. Wolfinger, editor, *Innovationen bei Rechen- und Kommunikationssystemen*, pages 27–34, 1994.

[Huß95]   H. Hußmann. Indirect use of formal methods in software engineering. In M.Wirsing, editor, *ICSE-17 Workshop on Formal Methods Applications in Software Engineering Practice*, pages 126–133, 1995.

[Jac92]   I. Jacobson. *Object-Oriented Software Engineering*. Addison-Wesley, 1992.

[RBP⁺91]   J. Rumbaugh, M. Blaha, W. Premerlani, F. Eddy, and W. Lorensen. *Object-oriented Modeling and Design*. Prentice-Hall, 1991.

[RKB95]   B. Rumpe, C. Klein, and M. Broy. Ein strombasiertes mathematisches modell verteilter informationsverarbeitender systeme - SYSLAB Systemmodell. Technical Report TUM-I9510, Technische Universität München, 1995.

[SH95]   H. Saiedian and M. Hinchey. Issues surrounding the transfer of formal methods technology into the actual workplace. In M.Wirsing, editor, *ICSE-17 Workshop on Formal Methods Applications in Software Engineering Practice*, pages 69–76, 1995.

Towards Heterogeneous Formal Specifications

Gilles Bernot[1] and Sophie Coudert[1] and Pascale Le Gall[1]

L.a.M.I., Université d'Évry, Cours Monseigneur Roméro, 91025 Evry Cedex, France
{bernot,coudert,legall}@lami.univ-evry.fr

Abstract. We believe that big software systems could be more easily formally specified if several specification approaches were allowed within a single system specification. We propose a notion of heterogeneous framework where the specifier can choose a dedicated specification framework for each specification module. We show how the resulting heterogeneous modular specifications can get semantics, and how modular proofs can still be performed on these specifications. Our contribution is mainly focussed on a sort of interoperability between heterogeneous specification modules and we retrieve, as much as possible, classical notions of "meta-formalisms," modularity for structured specifications, or inference systems, as they are well known in the algebraic specification community. With this respect, our work can be regarded as an attempt to unify frameworks, by accepting and formalizing heterogeneity.

Keywords: heterogeneous specifications, modularity, formal specifications, logical frameworks, inference systems, algebraic specifications, theorem proving.

Introduction

The huge size of software systems requires more and more rigorous approaches for their design, maintenance, reuse, etc. It is in particular especially important to take care of the specification methods and techniques for such systems. *Formal specifications* are more and more often used for critical parts of such systems, and to face the complexity and the variety of the requirements to be specified, several specification languages or dialects will probably be used in the future, each of them being dedicated to specific areas (nuclear plants, public transportation, telecommunications, hardware, etc.) Unfortunately, the wide variety of academic formal specification languages is rather understood as a handicap for formal specifications instead of a flexibility advantage. People need to know how to compare formal specification languages. For this reason, great efforts are devoted to *unifying frameworks*. Some of these efforts are made via "meta-formalisms," following the institution approach [GB84], where specification formalisms can be compared via some kind of institution morphisms. The institution-like approaches have the advantage to keep the flexibility of "tuning" a specification framework according to the project under development [Mes89] [AC92] [SS92] [CM93] [EGR94] [CR94] [Wol95]. Other recent efforts tend to propose a unique common framework, as simple as possible, containing only the indispensable aspects (e.g., within the ESPRIT Basic Research Working Group COMPASS or the IFIP Working Group on

Foundations of Systems Specification). A common framework has the advantage to provide a pragmatic way to mix several existing specification languages together, or at least to identify their intersection.

Heterogeneity *inside* a specification is not addressed by these unifying frameworks. The explosive growth of wide systems induces a cooperation of several subsystems which have been *a priori* made to fulfill very heterogeneous needs. They have been specified and developed according to heterogeneous specification and programming languages. Thus, it becomes very convenient to choose a dedicated specification framework for *each component* of a system, in a similar way than programming languages are chosen at the present time according to the component under development (and the skills of the man-power). In this article, we define heterogeneous specifications where each specified module can have its own underlying specification framework. Owing to this granularity the flexibility is maximal, since the specification language has not to be the same for all components of a huge system.

To define a *heterogeneous framework* for heterogeneous specifications, we have carefully avoided the approach which consists in embedding the whole specification into a big logic that would be a sort of "union" of all the logics appearing in the specification modules. It would have produced a framework far too rich, complex, and possibly inconsistent. Our choice has been to privilege the top level module of a structured specification. The semantics of a specification are made of models in the sense of the framework of the top level module, and the expressible sentences about the specification belong to this framework as well. Nevertheless it remains possible to prove sentences by using lemmas issued from the imported frameworks, and proved within them. Such an approach reduces to one the number of specification frameworks to understand in order to reuse a software part: it is sufficient to understand the top level module specification framework. For reusability purposes, such an approach could as well simplify the management of a library of heterogeneously specified softwares; it suffices to identify the top level framework.

We have also tried, as much as possible, to follow classical ideas from the algebraic specification community for usual (homogeneous) modular specifications. Our contribution is mainly focussed on a sort of *interoperability* between formal specifications, at the proof level via a heterogeneous inference bridge, and at the semantic level via extraction functors.

In the first section, we define the notion of *homogeneous framework*, which is slightly weakened with respect to general logics [Mes89] in order to directly accept inference relations containing structural induction principles. In the second section, we define a notion of *heterogeneous framework* which allows to properly define *heterogeneous specifications*, their *semantics*, and an associated *heterogeneous inference system*. Then, we show how some previous works on institution-like frameworks can be reused in order to build heterogeneous frameworks for free; lastly we provide a toy *example* of heterogeneous specification, and develop a typical example of *heterogeneous proof* which delegates the proof of a lemma to a heterogeneously imported module.

1 Homogeneous frameworks

Let *Set* and *Cat* respectively denote the category of sets[1] and the category of categories [ML71] [BW90]. We call "homogeneous framework" a slightly weakened notion of general logic [Mes89].

Definition 1 *A* homogeneous framework *is a quintuple* $(Sig, sen, mod, \vdash, \models)$ *where:*

- *Sig is a category whose objects are called* signatures

- *sen is a (covariant) functor from Sig to Set associating to each signature a set of* sentences

- *mod is a contravariant functor from Sig to Cat associating to each signature a category of* models

- $\vdash$, *called* inference system, *is a* $|Sig|$-*indexed family such that for each signature* Σ, $\vdash_\Sigma$ *is a binary relation included in* $\mathcal{P}(sen(\Sigma)) \times sen(\Sigma)$

- $\models$, *called* satisfaction relation, *is a* $|Sig|$-*indexed family such that for each signature* Σ, $\models_\Sigma$ *is a binary relation included in* $mod(\Sigma) \times sen(\Sigma)$

and the following properties are satisfied:

- $\vdash$ *is reflexive, monotonic and transitive, i.e., respectively*

  - $\forall \Sigma \in Sig, \forall \varphi \in sen(\Sigma), \{\varphi\} \vdash_\Sigma \varphi$

  - $\forall \Sigma \in Sig, \forall \Gamma \subseteq sen(\Sigma), \forall \Gamma' \subseteq sen(\Sigma), \forall \varphi \in sen(\Sigma), \ \Gamma \vdash_\Sigma \varphi \text{ and } \Gamma \subseteq \Gamma' \implies \Gamma' \vdash_\Sigma \varphi$

  - $\forall \Sigma \in Sig, \forall \Gamma \subseteq sen(\Sigma), \forall \Gamma' \subseteq sen(\Sigma), \forall \varphi \in sen(\Sigma), \ \Gamma \vdash_\Sigma \Gamma' \text{ and}^2 \ \Gamma \cup \Gamma' \vdash_\Sigma \varphi \implies \Gamma \vdash_\Sigma \varphi$

- (weak) $\vdash$-translation: *for any isomorphism between two signatures* $\sigma : \Sigma \to \Sigma'$, *any* $\Gamma \subseteq sen(\Sigma)$ *and any* $\varphi \in sen(\Sigma)$, $\Gamma \vdash_\Sigma \varphi$ *if and only if* $sen(\sigma)(\Gamma) \vdash_{\Sigma'} sen(\sigma)(\varphi)$

- (weak) satisfaction condition: *for any isomorphism between two signatures* $\sigma : \Sigma \to \Sigma'$, *any* $M' \in mod(\Sigma')$ *and any* $\varphi \in sen(\Sigma)$, $M' \models_{\Sigma'} sen(\sigma)(\varphi)$ *if and only if* $mod(\sigma)(M') \models_\Sigma \varphi$

- soundness: *for any* $\Gamma \subseteq sen(\Sigma)$ *and any* $\varphi \in sen(\Sigma)$, *if* $\Gamma \vdash_\Sigma \varphi$ *then*[3]

$$\forall M \in mod(\Sigma), \ (M \models_\Sigma \Gamma) \implies (M \models_\Sigma \varphi)$$

In the remainder of this article, by notation abuse, $sen(\sigma)$ will still be denoted σ, and $mod(\sigma)$ will often be denoted U_σ by analogy with the usual notation for "the forgetful functor."

---

[1] with *total functions* as morphisms

[2] $\Gamma \vdash_\Sigma \Gamma'$ means $\forall \psi \in \Gamma', \Gamma \vdash_\Sigma \psi$

[3] $M \models_\Sigma \Gamma$ means $\forall \psi \in \Gamma, \ M \models_\Sigma \psi$

Homogeneous frameworks are logics as defined by Meseguer in [Mes89] except that the ⊢-translation and the satisfaction condition are restricted to signature isomorphisms only. It means that properties are preserved by renaming of operations and variables (since these notions are hidden behind signatures and sentences). Our motivation for such a weakening is:

– Without these restrictions to isomorphisms, it would not be possible to consider inference systems with structural induction. If we consider for example a (first order) signature morphism $\Sigma_1 \to \Sigma_2$ which is not surjective, then a proof by structural induction on Σ_1 has no reason to remain valid in Σ_2. Moreover, in such a case, the functor *mod* should concern only finitely generated models and similarly, the satisfaction condition is not always satisfied.

– Of course, to solve such situations, it is often argued that it is possible to tune the notions of signature, sentence or model to fulfill the definition of general logic. We do not encourage such modifications of homogeneous frameworks. Indeed, the more the homogeneous frameworks are tuned in order to fit a unifying presentation of frameworks, the more the relationships between heterogeneous specification modules are difficult to establish and the more their meaning become obscure (see e.g., partial-to-total translation in Section 3.2). It is also often argued that induction and finitely generated models consideration belong to a specification language level and has not to be captured directly in the logic. In computer science, the proof of non-trivial properties requires structural induction. Thus, we want to take into account the fundamental theoretical problems raised by structural induction.

However, to deal with the lack of satisfaction condition, we give the following definition which formalizes usual encapsulation principles of programming languages. It will be used in Section 2.2 to define semantics of heterogeneous specifications (Definition 6).

Definition 2 *A homogeneous framework* $(Sig, sen, mod, \vdash, \models)$ *being given, let* $\delta : \Sigma_{imp} \to \Sigma$ *be a signature morphism and* $\mathcal{I}mport$ *a subcategory of* $mod(\Sigma_{imp})$. *A functor* $F : \mathcal{I}mport \to mod(\Sigma)$ *is said* δ-*encapsulated if and only if*

$$\forall \varphi \in sen(\Sigma_{imp}), \forall M \in \mathcal{I}mport, \quad M \models_{\Sigma_{imp}} \varphi \iff F(M) \models_{\Sigma} \delta(\varphi).$$

Most of the time (e.g., [BB91] [BEPP87] [NOS95]), instead of δ-encapsulated functors, authors consider functors such that $U_\delta \circ F = Id$ and the δ-encapsulation results from the satisfaction condition (see Section 3.1).

Definition 3 *A homogeneous framework* $(Sig, sen, mod, \vdash, \models)$ *being given:*

– *A (flat) presentation is a tuple* $P = (\Sigma, \Gamma)$ *such that* Σ *is a signature and* $\Gamma \subseteq sen(\Sigma)$. *The elements of* Γ *are often called the* axioms *of P. We define presentation morphisms* $\sigma : (\Sigma, \Gamma) \to (\Sigma', \Gamma')$ *as signature isomorphisms* $\sigma : \Sigma \to \Sigma'$ *such that* $\Gamma' \vdash_{\Sigma'} \sigma(\Gamma)$. *Let Pres denote the category of presentations, and* $sign : Pres \to Sig$ *denote the forgetful functor.*

– *The semantics of presentations is by definition the contravariant functor Mod from Pres to Cat such that $Mod(\Sigma, \Gamma)$ is the full subcategory of $mod(\Sigma)$ whose objects satisfy Γ with respect to $\models$.*[4]

– *a* specification module *is a tuple $\Delta P = (\delta, \Delta\Gamma)$ such that $\delta : \Sigma_{imp} \to \Sigma$ is a signature morphism and $\Delta\Gamma \subseteq sen(\Sigma)$. The signature Σ_{imp} is called the* imported signature *of the module.*

– *in the homogeneous case,* structured specifications *can be recursively defined as follows: any presentation $P \in Pres$ is a* structured specification *and its flattened signature is $sign(P)$; if SP_{imp} is a structured specification whose flattened signature is Σ_{imp}, and $\Delta P = (\delta : \Sigma_{imp} \to \Sigma, \Delta\Gamma)$ is a specification module, then they form a structured specification denoted $SP = SP_{imp} + \Delta P$, whose flattened signature is Σ.*

Intuitively, in most cases, $\Delta\Gamma$ contains sentences specifying only the new operations introduced by the signature morphism δ (belonging to $\Sigma \setminus \delta(\Sigma_{imp})$). Our structured specifications are defined in a similar way as [NOS95] [BEPP87] for simple enrichment. Let us note that usually, authors define multiple import of modules as a simple extension of the simple import defined above. They simply use unions of modules which are rather easy to define in an homogeneous framework (provided that Sig has pushouts, or that specifications have amalgamation [EGR94].

2 Heterogeneous frameworks

2.1 Definitions

Intuitively, we define a heterogeneous framework in order to provide a family of "bridges" between homogeneous frameworks. Let a specification module, written according to a homogeneous framework o, import another module, written according to a homogeneous framework i. We need to know how to transpose signatures from i to o, how to extract models from i to o and how to heterogeneously infer sentences from i to o. This is defined as follows.

Definition 4 *A* heterogeneous framework *is a quadruple $(\mathcal{B}, Tr, Ext, \Vdash)$ where:*

– *$\mathcal{B}$ is a set of homogeneous frameworks (Definition 1) whose elements are called* basic frameworks

– *Tr is a family indexed by a subset $\mathcal{D}$ of $\mathcal{B} \times \mathcal{B}$, such that for each (i, o) in $\mathcal{D}$, Tr_i^o is a functor from Sig_i to Sig_o, called* signature transposition functor *(from the input framework i to the output framework o)*

– *Ext is a family, also indexed by $\mathcal{D}$, such that Ext_i^o is a natural transformation from the functor mod_i to the functor $mod_o \circ Tr_i^o$, each $Ext_{i,\Sigma}^o : mod_i(\Sigma) \to mod_o(Tr_i^o(\Sigma))$ (for $\Sigma \in Sig_i$) is called* model

---

[4] *Mod is actually a functor owing to the $\vdash$-translation and the satisfaction condition.*

extraction functor

- $\Vdash$ *is a family indexed by the set* $\{(i,o,\Sigma) \mid (i,o) \in \mathcal{D} \text{ and } \Sigma \in Sig_i\}$, *such that* $\Vdash^o_{i,\Sigma}$ *is a binary relation included in* $\mathcal{P}(sen_i(\Sigma)) \times sen_o(Tr^o_i(\Sigma))$, *called* heterogeneous inference bridge

and the following properties are satisfied:

- *the domain* $\mathcal{D}$ *contains the diagonal* $\{(b,b) \mid b \in \mathcal{B}\}$

- $\forall b \in \mathcal{B}$, $Tr^b_b = Id_{Sig_b}$

- $\forall b \in \mathcal{B}$, $Ext^b_b = Id_{mod_b}$

- *diagonal reflexivity: for any* $b \in \mathcal{B}$, *any* $\Sigma \in Sig_b$, *and any* $\Gamma \subseteq sen_b(\Sigma)$, $(\Gamma \Vdash^b_{b,\Sigma} \varphi \iff \varphi \in \Gamma)$

- $\Vdash$ *is monotonic*

- $\Vdash$*-translation: for any* $(i,o) \in \mathcal{D}$, *any isomorphism* $\sigma : \Sigma \to \Sigma'$ *in* Sig_i, *any* $\Gamma \subseteq sen_i(\Sigma)$, *and any* $\varphi \in sen_o(Tr^o_i(\Sigma))$, $\Gamma \Vdash^o_{i,\Sigma} \varphi$ *if and only if* $\sigma(\Gamma) \Vdash^o_{i,\Sigma'} Tr^o_i(\sigma)(\varphi)$

- *heterogeneous soundness: for any* $(i,o) \in \mathcal{D}$, *for any* $\Gamma \subseteq sen_i(\Sigma)$, *for any* $\varphi \in sen_o(Tr^o_i(\Sigma))$, *if* $\Gamma \Vdash^o_{i,\Sigma} \varphi$ *then for all* $M \in mod_i(\Sigma)$, *we have* $[M \models_i \Gamma \implies Ext^o_{i,\Sigma}(M) \models_o \varphi]$

Since we want an inference bridge as elementary as possible, we generally prefer for $\Vdash$ to be a recursive set. Expressing this constraint is not easy [Mes89] [SS95].

Transitivity would be meaningless for $\Vdash$ because a sentence according to the framework o cannot be introduced back in the framework i in general. $\Vdash$ should be understood as an unique inference step (a "bridge") in the heterogeneous proof process. However, the whole heterogeneous proof process (Definition 7) will be transitive.

The syntax of structured specifications composed of modules from different frameworks can be defined as follows.

Definition 5 *A heterogeneous framework* $(\mathcal{B}, Tr, Ext, \Vdash)$ *being given, the set Spec of all* heterogeneous structured specifications *is recursively defined as follows:*

- *Any presentation* $(\Sigma, \Gamma) \in Pres_o$ *for some basic framework* $o \in \mathcal{B}$ *is a heterogeneous structured specification. Its* flattened signature *is* Σ *(which belongs to the basic framework* o*).*

- *If* SP_i *is a heterogeneous structured specification whose flattened signature* Σ_i *belongs to some basic framework* $i \in \mathcal{B}$, *and if* $\Delta P = (\delta : \Sigma_{imp} \to \Sigma, \Delta\Gamma)$ *is a specification module belonging to some basic framework* $o \in \mathcal{B}$ *such that* $(i,o) \in \mathcal{D}$ *and* $Tr^o_i(\Sigma_i) = \Sigma_{imp}$, *then* SP_i *and* ΔP *form a structured specification denoted* $SP = SP_i + \Delta P$, *whose flattened signature is* Σ *(which belongs to the basic framework* o*).*

Moreover, with the previous notations,

- *ΔP is called the top level, or leading module of SP,*

- *o is called the* leading basic framework *of SP,*

- *and we extend sign to Spec by $sign(SP) = \Sigma$ (the flattened signature).*

2.2 Heterogeneous semantics

In Definition 6 below, we follow an idea similar to [BB91] in order to give modular semantics to our heterogeneous structured specifications. The semantics of a structured specification SP is supposed to represent a set of "acceptable programs" for SP. We assume moreover that the modularity of the considered programs matches the structure of SP. Then, the semantics of a program module can be represented by a δ-encapsulated functor. As in [BB91], if the semantics of a program module is correct with respect to the corresponding specification module ΔP, then it means that necessarily, it is independent of the chosen implementation of the imported module.

Definition 6 *The* modular semantics *of a heterogeneous structured specification SP, denoted Het(SP), is the category recursively defined as follows:*

- *If SP is reduced to a homogeneous presentation $P \in Pres_o$, then[5] $Het(SP) = Mod_o(P)$*

- *If $SP = SP_i + \Delta P$, where the leading basic framework of SP_i is i and the leading module $\Delta P = (\delta : \Sigma_{imp} \to \Sigma, \Delta\Gamma)$ belongs to the basic framework o, let $\mathcal{F}$ be the class of all δ-encapsulated functors F from $Ext^o_{i,\Sigma_i}(Het(SP_i))$ to $Mod_o(\Sigma, \Delta\Gamma)$, then $Het(SP)$ is the class of all $F(Ext^o_{i,\Sigma_i}(M))$ such that M belongs to $Het(SP_i)$.*

Let us notice that $Het(SP)$ is included in $mod_o(sign(SP))$. Thus, the basic framework of the top module of SP "hides" all the other imported modules. We choose this approach in order to avoid the "complexity explosion" of semantics carrying more or less the union of the frameworks appearing in the specification. From a methodological point of view, our approach has the advantage to allow the user of a heterogeneous specification to only take care about one formalism, the leading basic formalism. This will facilitate reuse purposes and the management of heterogeneous specification libraries.

Remark   The class of functors $\{ F \circ Ext^o_{i,\Sigma_i}|_{Het(SP_i)} : Het(SP_i) \to Het(SP) \mid F \in \mathcal{F} \}$ is called "the semantics of the module ΔP over SP_i." Notice that $\mathcal{F}$ can be empty, in which case $Het(SP)$ is also empty and the structured specification SP is said *inconsistent*.

---

[5] In [BB91] the authors prefer to restrict the semantics of basic cases to initial or minimal models only. It would not be difficult to follow a similar approach here, however the heterogeneous dimension of our approach allows to have dedicated basic frameworks in B in order to reach such features.

2.3 Heterogeneous proofs

Definition 7 *A heterogeneous framework* $(B, Tr, Ext, \Vdash)$ *being given, the corresponding heterogeneous inference system is the least binary relation* $\Vvdash \subseteq Spec \times \coprod_{b \in B} sen_b(Sig_b)$ *such that, for any* $SP \in Spec$ *(with leading framework o):*

- $\Vvdash$ *is compatible with* $\vdash_o$: *when SP is of the form* $SP_i + (\delta, \Delta\Gamma)$ *(resp.* (Σ, Γ) *), for any* $\varphi \in sen_o(sign(SP))$ *if* $\Delta\Gamma \vdash_o \varphi$ *(resp.* $\Gamma \vdash_o \varphi$ *) then* $SP \Vvdash \varphi$.

- $\Vvdash$ *is compatible with* $\Vdash$: *when SP is of the form* $SP_i + (\delta, \Delta\Gamma)$, *for any* $\Gamma' \subseteq sen_i(sign(SP_i))$, *and for any* $\varphi \in sen_o(Tr_i^o(sign(SP_i)))$, *if* $SP_i \Vvdash \Gamma'$ *and* $\Gamma' \Vdash_i^o \varphi$ *then* $SP \Vvdash \delta(\varphi)$.

- $\Vvdash$ *is transitive: when SP is of the form* $SP = SP_i + (\delta, \Delta\Gamma)$, *for any* $\Gamma' \subseteq sen_o(sign(SP))$, *and for any* $\varphi \in sen_o(sign(SP))$, *if* $SP \Vvdash \Gamma'$ *and* $(SP_i + (\delta, \Delta\Gamma \cup \Gamma')) \Vvdash \varphi$ *then* $SP \Vvdash \varphi$.

Notice that $SP \Vvdash \varphi$ implies that the leading basic framework of SP is the framework of φ, and the flattened signature of SP is the underlying signature of φ. The leading basic framework given by the top level module masks all the subspecification frameworks. Properties inherited from subspecifications are filtered by the leading basic framework. These properties recursively come up through the specification structure.

To prove from SP a sentence φ by means of our heterogeneous proof process ($SP \Vvdash \varphi$), we have to find a set of lemmas Γ_o (possibly empty) which, added to the axioms of the top level module, infers φ in the leading basic framework o (via $\vdash_o$). Then for each lemma ψ in Γ_o, we look for a set of lemmas Γ_i in the leading basic framework of the direct subspecification such that $\Gamma_i \Vdash_i^o \psi$. Then we recursively prove each sentence of Γ_i in the same way.

Theorem 8 *For every heterogeneous framework, the corresponding heterogeneous inference system is sound. This means that for any heterogeneous structured specification SP and for any sentence φ belonging to the leading basic framework o of SP, we have:*

$$SP \Vvdash \varphi \implies (\forall M \in Het(SP), \ M \models_o \varphi)$$

Proof: By induction on the proofs. If the last proof step comes from the first property of Definition 7 (compatibility with $\vdash_o$), then $SP \Vvdash \varphi$ comes from $\Delta\Gamma \vdash_o \varphi$ (resp. $\Gamma \vdash_o \varphi$). Since $\vdash_o$ is sound and $Het(SP) \subseteq Mod_o(\Sigma, \Delta\Gamma)$ (resp. $Het(SP) \subseteq Mod_o(\Sigma, \Gamma)$) we have $Het(SP) \models_o \varphi$. For a step using the compatibility with $\Vdash$, the heterogeneous soundness of $\Vdash$ and the δ-encapsulation property ensure the soundness of $\Vvdash$. For a $\Vvdash$ transitivity step, $SP \Vvdash \varphi$ comes from $SP \Vvdash \Gamma'$ and $(SP_i + (\delta, \Delta\Gamma \cup \Gamma')) \Vvdash \varphi$ with $SP = SP_i + (\delta : \Sigma_i \to \Sigma, \Delta\Gamma)$.

Let $\mathcal{F} = \{F : Ext_{i,\Sigma_i}^o(Het(SP_i)) \to Mod_o(\Sigma, \Delta\Gamma) \mid F \text{ is a } \delta\text{-encapsulated functor}\}$

let $\mathcal{F}' = \{F : Ext^o_{i,\Sigma_i}(Het(SP_i)) \to Mod_o(\Sigma, \Delta\Gamma \cup \Gamma') \mid F$ is a δ-encapsulated functor $\}$

by induction hypothesis, $SP \Vdash \Gamma'$ is sound, then $\forall F \in \mathcal{F}, \forall M \in F(Ext^o_{i,\Sigma_i}(Het(SP_i)))$, $M \models_\Sigma \Gamma'$, so we have $\mathcal{F} = \mathcal{F}'$, and then $Het(SP_i + (\delta, \Delta\Gamma \cup \Gamma')) = Het(SP)$. By induction hypothesis, $(SP_i + (\delta, \Delta\Gamma \cup \Gamma')) \models_\Sigma \varphi$. It results that $SP \models_\Sigma \varphi$. $\qquad\qquad\square$

The heterogeneous soundness property ensures that properties inherited via the heterogeneous inference bridge are also transmitted through the model extraction. Conversely, we can define a property of "local heterogeneous completeness" which ensures that each sentence preserved by model extraction can be inferred via the heterogeneous bridge [Cou95]. Unfortunately, when all the homogeneous inference systems $\vdash$ are complete, this local heterogeneous completeness is not sufficient to ensure the completeness of the heterogeneous inference system $\Vdash$ (except if the specification contains at most one heterogeneous bridge).

3 Examples

3.1 Homogeneous modular semantics

A specification where all the modules are expressed in a unique basic framework b obviously corresponds to a structured specification in the homogeneous framework b as defined in Definition 1. Our heterogeneous framework gives modular semantics for such homogeneous structured specifications.

Of course, the resulting semantics for such homogeneous specifications meet the classical requirements for modular design of software [BB91], [NOS95]. All the authors share a common principle expressing that a module preserves the import part. More precisely, the semantics of a module is such that the application of the forgetful functor to any model of the global specification gives a model of the subspecification. If the underlying homogeneous framework is an institution, then the satisfaction condition and this semantic conservativity property ensures the δ-encapsulation. This allows to perform structured proofs accordingly to the structure of the specification (as we do in Section 7). As seen in Section 1, our definition of homogeneous framework admits institutions as a particular case.

3.2 Using maps between formalisms

To face the multiplicity of specification formalisms, many previous works contributed to give an unifying presentation of these formalisms. They abstract details which are specific to each specification formalism. For example, institutions, pre-institutions, specification frameworks or general logics are such "meta-formalisms." They are used to characterize some general properties of specification formalisms and to relate different specification formalisms. These relations are given by means of some kinds of translations between two formalisms. Their purpose is to be able either to compare their expressive power or to take benefit, for the second formalism, of results or tools already available in the first formalism (e.g., a theorem prover). For this aim, they characterize different kinds of translation between formalisms defined according to their underlying meta-formalism. Depending on the context, these translations are called morphisms, transformations, simulations or maps. They share some common properties. First, these translations are expressed in term of natural transformation in order to ensure a certain compatibility with the signature category. They also impose an equivalence between the two satisfaction relations involving models and sentences corresponding each other by the translation.

This provides means to combine two specification formalisms, but it does not really correspond to our notion of heterogeneousness since they do not look for integrating heterogeneous specification modules inside a unique global specification. Nevertheless, if we choose two formalisms related by a translation, it gives us examples for free of tuples $(i, o) \in \mathcal{D}$ for our heterogeneous framework (even if it may need some adaptations). Intuitively, their satisfaction conditions are very close to our heterogeneous soundness (Definition 4). We sketch below how to make use of their works, provided that, from a technical point of view, the considered specification formalisms fit our homogeneous framework definition[6] :

- Our first example concerns institutions and institution morphisms defined in [GB84]. (It could also be relevant for semi-institution morphisms as in [ST88], provided that we add a translation of sentences.) Let $\mathcal{I} = (Sign, sen, mod, \models)$ and $\mathcal{I}' = (Sign', sen', mod', \models')$ two institutions and an institution morphism $\mu : \mathcal{I} \to \mathcal{I}'$. By definition, μ consists of a functor $\mu_{Sign} : Sign \to Sign'$, a natural family of functions $\mu_{sen\Sigma} : sen'(\mu_{Sign}(\Sigma)) \to sen(\Sigma)$ and a natural family of functors $\mu_{mod\Sigma} : mod(\Sigma) \to mod'(\mu_{Sig}(\Sigma))$ such that:

$$\forall \Sigma \in Sign, \forall \varphi' \in sen'(\Sigma), \forall M \in mod(\Sigma), M \models_\Sigma \mu_{sen\Sigma}(\varphi') \iff \mu_{mod\Sigma}(M) \models_{\mu_{Sig}(\Sigma)} \varphi'$$

It suffices to let $Tr_{\mathcal{I}}^{\mathcal{I}'} = \mu_{Sign}$, $Ext_{\mathcal{I},\Sigma}^{\mathcal{I}'} = \mu_{mod\Sigma}$ and $\Vdash_{\mathcal{I},\Sigma}^{\mathcal{I}'}$ is defined by: $\forall \varphi' \in sen'(\mu_{Sign}(\Sigma)), \forall \Gamma \subseteq \mathcal{P}(sen(\Sigma)), (\mu_{sen\Sigma}(\varphi') \in \Gamma \Leftrightarrow \Gamma \Vdash_{\mathcal{I},\Sigma}^{\mathcal{I}'} \varphi')$. With these definitions, the heterogeneous soundness condition is obviously satisfied.

  From a technical point of view, such uses of institution morphisms prove to be very suitable for our purpose because they directly give the property of heterogeneous soundness.

- The second example concerns institutions and simulations defined in [AC92]. Let us consider again two institutions $\mathcal{I}$ and $\mathcal{I}'$ and a simulation $\mu : \mathcal{I} \to \mathcal{I}'$. By definition, μ consists of a functor $\mu_{Sign} : Sign \to Sign'$, a natural family of functions $\mu_{sen\Sigma} : sen(\Sigma) \to sen'(\mu_{Sign}(\Sigma))$ and a natural family of partial representative[7] functors $\mu_{mod\Sigma} : mod'(\mu_{Sign}(\Sigma)) \to mod(\Sigma)$ such that: $\forall \Sigma \in Sign, \forall \varphi \in sen(\Sigma), \forall M' \in mod'(\mu_{Sign}(\Sigma)), \mu_{mod\Sigma}(M') \models_\Sigma \varphi \iff M' \models_{\mu_{Sig}(\Sigma)} \mu_{sen\Sigma}(\varphi)$. It suffices to let $Tr_{\mathcal{I}}^{\mathcal{I}'} = \mu_{Sign}$, to choose $Ext_{\mathcal{I},\Sigma}^{\mathcal{I}'}$ in such a way that $\mu_{mod\Sigma} \circ Ext_{\mathcal{I},\Sigma}^{\mathcal{I}'} = Id_{mod(\Sigma)}$ (it is possible thanks to the surjectivity condition on $\mu_{mod\Sigma}$) and $\Vdash_{\mathcal{I},\Sigma}^{\mathcal{I}'}$ is defined by: $\forall \varphi \in sen(\Sigma), \forall \Gamma \subseteq sen(\Sigma), (\varphi \in \Gamma \iff \Gamma \Vdash_{\mathcal{I},\Sigma}^{\mathcal{I}'} \mu_{sen\Sigma}(\varphi))$. As for the previous case, the heterogeneous soundness condition still holds.

---

[6] if necessary, by taking the satisfaction relation for defining the inference system as in the example of institutions

[7] It means surjective both on the objects and the arrows

- An example very similar is the one of logics and maps of logics defined in [Mes89]. Let us consider two logics $\mathcal{L} = (Sign, sen, mod, \vdash, \models)$ and $\mathcal{L}' = (Sign', sen', mod', \vdash', \models')$ and a map of logics $\mu : \mathcal{L} \to \mathcal{L}'$. This map is built from a functor $\mu_{Th_o} : Th_o \to Th'_o$ where Th_o denotes the category whose objects are theories (Σ, Γ) with $\Gamma \subset sen(\Sigma)$ and morphisms $\sigma : (\Sigma, \Gamma) \to (\Xi, \Delta)$ define a signature morphism $\sigma : \Sigma \to \Xi$ and are axiom-preserving ($\sigma(\Gamma) \subseteq \Delta$). The map μ also comprises two natural families $\mu_{sen(\Sigma,\Gamma)} : sen((\Sigma, \Gamma)) \to sen'(\mu_{Th_o}((\Sigma, \Gamma)))$ and $\mu_{mod(\Sigma,\Gamma)} : mod'(\mu_{Th_o}((\Sigma, \Gamma))) \to mod((\Sigma, \Gamma))$ verifying that the functor μ_{Th_o} is μ_{sen}-sensible[8]. Moreover, with the notation $\mu_{Th_o}((\Sigma, \emptyset)) = (\Sigma', \Gamma'_\Sigma)$, the two following properties are satisfied : for any $\Gamma \subseteq sen(\Sigma)$, and for any $\varphi \in sen(\Sigma)$, $\Gamma \vdash_\Sigma \varphi \Longrightarrow$ $\mu_{sen\Sigma}(\Gamma) \cup \Gamma'_\Sigma \vdash_{\Sigma'} \mu_{sen\Sigma}(\varphi)$ and for any model $M' \in mod'((\Sigma', \Gamma'_\Sigma))$, $M' \models_{\Sigma'} \mu_{sen\Sigma}(\varphi) \Longleftrightarrow$ $\mu_{mod(\Sigma,\emptyset)}(M') \models_\Sigma \varphi$. If we assume that the functors $\mu_{mod(\Sigma,\emptyset)}$ are representative, we can define heterogeneous use as above with simulations : it suffices to let $Tr_\mathcal{L}^{\mathcal{L}'}(\Sigma) = sign'(Th_o((\Sigma, \emptyset)))$, to choose $Ext_{\mathcal{L},\Sigma}^{\mathcal{L}'}$ in such a way that $\mu_{mod(\Sigma,\emptyset)} \circ Ext_{\mathcal{L},\Sigma}^{\mathcal{L}'} = Id_{mod(\Sigma)}$ and $\Vdash_{\mathcal{L},\Sigma}^{\mathcal{L}'}$ is defined by: $\forall \varphi \in sen'(\Sigma'), \forall \Gamma \subseteq sen(\Sigma)((\varphi \in \mu_{sen\Sigma}(\Gamma) \vee \varphi \in \Gamma'_\Sigma) \Longleftrightarrow \Gamma \Vdash_{\mathcal{L},\Sigma}^{\mathcal{L}'} \varphi)$. Once again, the heterogeneous correction condition holds.

- The last example concerns pre-institutions and pre-institutions transformations defined in [SS92]. Let $\mathcal{I} = (Sign, sen, mod, \models)$ and $\mathcal{I}' = (Sign', sen', mod', \models')$ two pre-institutions and a pre-institution transformation $\mu : \mathcal{I} \to \mathcal{I}'$. By definition, μ consists of a functor $\mu_{Sign} : Sign \to Sign'$, a family of natural functions $\mu_{sen\Sigma} : \mathcal{P}(sen(\Sigma)) \to \mathcal{P}(sen'(\mu_{Sig}(\Sigma)))$ and a family of natural functions $\mu_{mod\Sigma} : mod(\Sigma) \to \mathcal{P}(mod'(\mu_{Sig}(\Sigma)))$ ($\mu_{mod\Sigma}(M)$ being nonempty) such that: $\forall \Sigma \in Sign, \forall \Gamma \subseteq sen(\Sigma), \forall M \in mod(\Sigma), M \models_\Sigma \Gamma \Longleftrightarrow (\forall M' \in \mu_{mod\Sigma}(M), M' \models_{\mu_{Sig}(\Sigma)} \mu_{sen\Sigma}(\Gamma))$. It suffices to let $Tr_\mathcal{I}^{\mathcal{I}'} = \mu_{Sign}$, to choose when it is possible $Ext_{\mathcal{I},\Sigma}^{\mathcal{I}'}(M)$ among $\mu_{mod\Sigma}(M)$ in such a way that $Ext_\mathcal{I}^{\mathcal{I}'}$ defines a functor and to define $\Vdash_{\mathcal{I},\Sigma}^{\mathcal{I}'}$ by: $\forall \Sigma \in Sign, \forall \Gamma \subseteq sen(\Sigma), \forall M \in mod(\Sigma), \forall \varphi' \in sen(\mu_{Sig}(\Sigma)), (\varphi' \in \mu_{sen\Sigma}(\Gamma) \Leftrightarrow \Gamma \Vdash_{\mathcal{I},\Sigma}^{\mathcal{I}'} \varphi')$. Once again, the heterogeneous soundness condition is obviously satisfied.

Using examples of the translations mentioned above and adapting them with the translation schemes developed above, we inherit numerous examples for our heterogeneous framework. However, these examples are not all as intuitive as each other. One should be aware of some "semantic shift" introduced by heterogeneity.

- The first example which can be brought up for our purpose is the one of the heterogeneous use of first order logic with equality $\mathcal{FOEQ}$ by equational logic $\mathcal{EQ}$ defined by means of institution morphism (this example is given in [GB84]). Intuitively, this case is convenient for us because this heterogeneous use just amounts to forget extra-informations. Thanks to this heterogeneous use, one can benefit in a somehow low-level specification module of properties inherited from high-level specification module.
- Another example which clearly exhibits what we call "semantic shift," is the one of heterogeneous

---

[8] It means that their natural transformations $\mu_{sen(\Sigma,\Gamma)}$ only depend on the signatures . They are now denoted by $\mu_{sen\Sigma}$.

use of partial algebras with predicates ($\mathcal{PAP}$) by total algebras with predicates ($\mathcal{TAP}$) defined by means of simulations (this example is given in [AC92]). The principle is well-known and consists in introducing a special constant denoted $\perp_s$ per sort s and a particular predicate D_s. The extracted total algebras are such that the predicate D_s exactly characterizes the definition domain for the sort s, the value of $\perp_s$ being the only one undefined. When translating sentences of $\mathcal{PAP}$, the predicates D_s are used to reduce the scope of sentences to the defined values.

Let us remind that our purpose when defining heterogeneous modular semantics is to encapsulate the imported specification by the higher level module in order to only filter properties expressible in the leading formalism. Here, such an ulterior heterogeneous use would consider $\perp_s$ and D_s as any constant or predicate, forgetting the intuition which has motivated their introduction. In particular, there is no obligation to continue to propagate bottom values. Thus, the specifiers of the higher level module have to explicitly manage the bottom values.

As a conclusion, we share with all these works on meta-formalisms a common technical background and thus, we take advantage of their numerous results. However, before extracting a result from these works for our purpose, we should look at the accordance with the intuition of what heterogeneous modularity should be.

3.3   An example of heterogeneous proof

Let us consider a simple example where $B = \{\mathcal{E}, \mathcal{O}\}$ and $\mathcal{D} = B^2$, $\mathcal{E}$ being the classical first order logic with equality $\mathcal{FOEQ}$ [EM85], ($\mathcal{E}$ for short), and $\mathcal{O}$ being the simple theory of equational observational data types with sort observation (for $\mathcal{O}$, a signature is a triple (S, F, Obs) such that $Obs \subseteq S$, see e.g., [BBK94]).

For the tuple $(\mathcal{E}, \mathcal{O})$, we can define $Tr_{\mathcal{E}}^{\mathcal{O}}((S, F)) = (S, F, S)$, which meets the intuition that all imported sorts defined in $\mathcal{E}$ can be considered as observable. Then, the model extraction is the identity and the heterogeneous bridge is defined by " $\Gamma \Vdash_{\mathcal{E}}^{\mathcal{O}} \varphi$ if and only if $\varphi \in \Gamma \cap sen_{\mathcal{O}}(\Sigma)$," which makes sense because the set of the $\mathcal{O}$-sentences is included in the one of the $\mathcal{E}$-sentences. It just amounts to relate the equality predicates symbols of the two formalisms. Intuitively, this heterogeneous bridge is sound because the semantics of the equality for the observable sorts is the same as in $\mathcal{E}$.

Conversely, for the tuple $(\mathcal{O}, \mathcal{E})$, we can define $Tr_{\mathcal{O}}^{\mathcal{E}}((S, F, Obs)) = (S, F)$. The heterogeneous bridge can be defined by " $\Gamma \Vdash_{\mathcal{O}}^{\mathcal{E}} \varphi$ if and only if $\varphi \in \Gamma$ ". The model extraction is a little bit more complex. The identity would not suffice because values which are different but observationally equal have to become actually equal with respect to $\mathcal{E}$. The solution is to quotient the imported observational model with the observational equivalence, so that for all observational model M, $Ext_{\mathcal{O}}^{\mathcal{E}}(M) = M/_{\approx_{\mathcal{O}}}$. This is well defined because $\approx_{\mathcal{O}}$ is a congruence [BHW95] and the quotient as extraction ensures that the heterogeneous bridge is sound.

Now, let us consider the specification *SP* which consists of a Stack module according to $\mathcal{E}$, which imports a Set module according to $\mathcal{O}$. Booleans and elements are supposed to be specified in sub-specifications (according to $\mathcal{E}$ or $\mathcal{O}$ indifferently).

Module: Set	Module: Stack
Framework: $\mathcal{O}$	Framework: $\mathcal{E}$
Use: Elem	Use: Set with δ the inclusion of Σ_{Set} in Σ_{Stacks}
with δ the inclusion of Σ_{Elem} in Σ_{Set}	Sorts: *stack*
Sorts: *set*	Operations:
Observable: *elem, bool*	$empty\ :\ \to stack$
Operations:	$push\ \_\_\ :\ set\ stack \to stack$
$\emptyset\ :\ \to set$	...
$ins\ \_\_\ :\ elem\ set \to set$	$monopush\ \_\_\ :\ set\ stack \to stack$
$\_ \in \_\ :\ elem\ elem \to bool$	Axioms $\Delta\Gamma_{Stack}$:
Axioms $\Delta\Gamma_{Set}$:	...
$x \in \emptyset = false$	$X = Y \Rightarrow monopush(X, push(Y, P)) = push(Y, P)$
$x \in (ins\ y\ X) = (eq\ x\ y)\ or\ (y \in X)$	$X \neq Y \Rightarrow monopush(X, push(Y, P)) = push(X, push(Y, P))$
where $x, y : elem, X : set$	where $X, Y : set, P : stack$

Let us prove the sentence φ from the specification Stack :

(φ) $\quad monopush(ins(a, ins(b, \emptyset)), push(ins(b, ins(a, \emptyset)), empty) = push(ins(b, ins(a, \emptyset)), empty)$

From the before last axiom of Stack, it suffices to prove the sentence ψ :

(ψ) $\quad ins(a, ins(b, \emptyset)) = ins(b, ins(a, \emptyset))$

Via the heterogeneous bridge $\Vdash_{\mathcal{O}}^{\mathcal{E}}$, it suffices to prove $\Delta\Gamma_{Set} \vdash_{\mathcal{O}} \psi$. The only operation which allows to distinguish sets is the membership operation "$\in$" and it is easy to prove ψ by context induction (see [Hen91]).

This example of heterogeneous proof is an illustration that our heterogeneous proof system is built in such a way that the proof of lemmas concerning imported data types are delegated to the proof systems of the subspecifications. Moreover, this example shows that besides the compatibility between model extraction and provability, we endeavour to give a solution which cope with the intuition.

Conclusion

We have proposed a definition of heterogeneous framework which is, roughly speaking, a family of "homogeneous frameworks" together with relationships that allow to define heterogeneous structured specifications. In a heterogeneous specification, each module can be written according to its own homogeneous framework. Moreover, the heterogeneous specification inherits the formalism of its top level module. This approach limits the number of "visible" formalisms and avoids using the union of all frameworks appearing in the specification. We also give a heterogeneous proof principle where properties inherited from imported specifications can be translated as lemmas in order to prove sentences in the top level formalism. Lastly, a small typical example has been developed.

Our approach is clearly a nice way to unify numerous specification formalisms. Moreover, this unification faithfully preserves all the specificities of each formalism. The relationships between formalisms remain as simple as possible in a heterogeneous framework because we combine them only two by two. It allows a local solving of difficulties, with minimal loss of information from a module to another one.

Nevertheless, our approach is only a first proposal for heterogeneity within specifications. Some improvements can be studied:

- To only consider heterogeneous soundness is not sufficient. A notion of heterogeneous *completeness* is missing. It is not difficult to define a notion of "local heterogeneous completeness" (which ensures that $\Vdash_i^\circ$ is as powerful as Ext_i°). Unfortunately, this local completeness is not sufficient to ensure the completeness of $\Vdash$ in general. We will steadily work on this problem.
- In the homogeneous case, *multiple imports* in a module are rather easily defined as an extension of the single import, using pushouts of specifications. Pushouts of specifications which do not belong to the same homogeneous formalism are more complicated to apprehend, thus multiple imports (where the Tr_i° are taken into account) have to be studied in more details.
- Our weakening of the notion of general logic (by restricting $\vdash$-translation and the satisfaction condition to signature isomorphisms only) is rather *ad hoc* (in order to capture proofs with structural induction). It is not directly the purpose of our work, however we would like to find a better solution, without distorting the meaning of Tr, Ext and $\Vdash$.
- Lastly, we are looking for a good definition of a category of heterogeneous structured signatures Sig_B (e.g., similar to [DR94]), as well as sen_B and $\models_B$, in order to turn $(Sig_B, sen_B, Het, \Vdash, \models_B)$ into a homogeneous framework (Definition 1) itself. But it is indeed a rather esthetic consideration for the time being.

Acknowledgments: We would like to thank Marc Aiguier for a proofreading of the draft version of this article. This work has been partly supported by CEC under ESPRIT-III WG6112 COMPASS, and by the French "GDR de programmation."

References

[AC92]   E. Astesiano and M. Cerioli. Relationships between logical frameworks. In LNCS, editor, *Recent Trends in Data Type Specification*, volume 655, pages 101–126, Dourdan, 1992.

[BB91]   G. Bernot and M. Bidoit. Proving the correctness of algebraically specified software modularity and observability issues. In *Proc. of AMAST-2, Second Conference of Algebraic Methodology and Software Technology*, May 1991. Iowa City, Iowa, USA.

[BBK94] G. Bernot, M. Bidoit, and T. Knapik. Observational approaches to algebraic specifications: A comparative study. *Acta Informatica*, 31:651–671, 1994.

[BEPP87] E.K. Blum, H Ehrig, and F. Parisi-Pressicce. Algebraic specification of modules and their basic interconnections. *Journal of Computer Systems Science*, 34:293–339, 1987.

[BHW95] M. Bidoit, R. Hennicker, and M. Wirsing. Behavioural and abstractor specifications. *Science of Computer Programming*, 25:149–186, 1995.

[BW90] M. Barr and C. Wells. *Category Theory for Computer Science*. Prentice Hall, 1990.

[CM93] M. Cerioli and J. Meseguer. Can I borrow your logic ? In *Proc. Int. Mathematical Foundations of Computer Science, MFC'93, Gdansk*, pages 342–351, 1993.

[Cou95] S. Coudert. Vers une sémantique des spécifications hétérogènes. Université d'Evry, Rapport de DEA, 1995.

[CR94] M. Cerioli and G. Reggio. Institutions for very abstract specifications. In LNCS, editor, *Recent Trends in Data Type Specification, Caldes de Malavella*, volume 785, pages 113–127, 1994.

[DR94] E. David and C. Roques. An institution for modular specifications. *Proc. of the 10th British Colloquium on Theoretical Computer Science*, Bristol, 1994.

[EGR94] H. Ehrig and M. Grosse-Rhode. Functorial theory of parameterized specifications in a general specification framework. *Theoretical Computer Science*, pages 221–266, 1994. Elsevier Science Pub. B.V. (North-Holland).

[EM85] H. Ehrig and B. Mahr. *Fundamentals of Algebraic Specification 1. Equations and initial semantics*, volume 6. Springer-Verlag,EATCS Monographs on Theoretical Computer Science, 1985.

[GB84] J.A. Goguen and R.M. Burstall. Introducing institutions. In Springer-Verlag LNCS 164, editor, *Proc. of the Workshop on Logics of Programming*, pages 221–256, 1984.

[Hen91] R. Hennicker. Context induction: a proof principle for behavioural abstractions and algebraic implementations. *Formal Aspects of Computing*, 3(4):326–345, 1991.

[Mes89] J. Meseguer. General logics. In North-Holland, editor, *Proc. Logic. Colloquium '87*, Amsterdam, 1989.

[ML71] S. Mac Lane. *Categories for the working mathematician*, volume 5 of *Graduate texts in mathematics*. Springer-Verlag, 1971.

[NOS95] M. Navarro, F. Orejas, and A. Sanchez. On the correctness of modular systems. *Theoretical Computer Science*, 140:139–177, 1995.

[SS92] A. Salibra and G. Scollo. A soft stairway to institutions. In LNCS, editor, *Recent Trends in Data Type Specification*, volume 655, pages 320–329, Dourdan, 1992.

[SS95] A. Sernadas and C. Sernadas. Theory spaces. Technical report, IST, Lisboa, 1995.

[ST88] D. Sannella and A. Tarlecki. Toward formal development of programs from algebraic specifications: Implementations revisited. *Acta Informatica*, 25:233–281, 1988.

[Wol95] U. Wolter. Institutional frames. In LNCS, editor, *Recent Trends in Data Type Specification*, volume 906, pages 469–482, 1995.

A Categorical Characterization of Consistency Results

Christel Baier, Mila Majster-Cederbaum

Fakultät für Mathematik und Informatik
Universität Mannheim, Germany
{baier,mcb}@pi1.informatik.uni-mannheim.de

Abstract. It is meaningful that a language is provided with several semantic descriptions: e.g. one which serves the needs of the implementor, another one that is suitable for specification and yet another one that will be used to explain the language to the user. In this case one has to guarantee that the various semantics are 'consistent'. The attempt of this paper is to clarify the notion 'consistency' and to give categorical characterizations of consistency results. Applications to verification as well as compositional semantics are considered.

1 Introduction

Various methods to define the semantics of languages that allow for parallelism, communication and synchronisation have been proposed in the last years. They can be classified by several criteria as e.g. operational versus denotational versus axiomatic methods, interleaving versus true parallelism approaches, branching time versus linear time models, event versus action based models, choice of mathematical discipline to assist the handling of recursion and the solution of domain equations.

The semantics of a (nondeterministic) program P should give a description of the (possible) behaviours of P which provides the possibility to prove that P satisfies its specification, i.e. to verify P. There are different ways to give specifications for programs: In process algebra the language for specification and implementation coincide and satisfaction usually means either some kind of equivalence $\equiv$ (e.g. strong or weak bisimulation equivalence [26] or failure equivalence [9]) or some kind of preorder $\sqsubseteq$ (e.g. partial bisimulation [15] or some kind of testing preorder [28]). Then a program P satisfies a specification S iff $P \equiv S$ resp. $P \sqsubseteq S$ or equivalently iff $P \in E_S$ where E_S means the equivalence class of S resp. the set of predecessors of S. In the logical approach a specification is a logical formula (or a set of formulas). The usual way to define what is meant by 'a program P satisfies a formula S (or a set of formulas)' is to fix a semantics α such that the meaning $\alpha(P)$ of P yields an interpretation for the underlying logic. P satisfies S iff $\alpha(P)$ is a model of S, i.e. S evaluates to true under the interpretation $\alpha(P)$. For instance, transition system semantics yield interpretations of modal logic [16], string semantics can be used to interpret linear time temporal logics [21, 31], computation tree semantics for interpreting branching time temporal logics [10], petri net semantics to interpret concurrent temporal logics [33]. Regardless the formalism in which the specification is given a specification S can be considered as a subset E_S of the set of programs $\mathcal{P}$ which is under consideration:

$$E_S = \{ P \in \mathcal{P} : P \text{ satisfies } S \}$$

Given a specification S for a program P verification of P means proving $P \in E_S$. In the following we assume that for the set $\mathcal{P}$ of programs under consideration there is a collection $Prop$ of interesting properties which a given program can fulfill or not and a specification is an intersection of such properties. We say a semantics $\alpha : \mathcal{P} \to A$ is 'suitable for checking a property E' iff for all $P \in \mathcal{P}$: $\alpha(P) \in \alpha(E)$ implies $P \in E$ or equivalently iff $\alpha^{-1}(\alpha(E)) = E$. Then instead of proving $P \in E$ one proves $\alpha(P) \in \alpha(E)$ which might be easier since $\alpha(P)$ is an abstraction of P. In this sense 'suitable for checking property E' does not mean that the semantics α really offers a method for testing whether program P has property E or not. This is because it might be the case that the problem whether a given element $a \in A$ is contained in the set $\alpha(E)$ is undecidable. It only ensures that α distinguishes programs satisfying property E from those programs not satisfying property E. This a necessary (but not sufficient) condition for the capability to test property E with help of the semantics α.

By the 'consistency' of two semantics $\alpha_1 : \mathcal{P} \to A_1$, $\alpha_2 : \mathcal{P} \to A_2$ w.r.t. the set $Prop$ of properties we mean the equivalence of α_1, α_2 w.r.t. the capability of proving that a program satisfies its specification: We say that α_1, α_2 are consistent w.r.t. $Prop$ iff both α_1, α_2 are suitable for checking the properties $E \in Prop$. One can show (Theorem 9) that this notion of consistency is equivalent to the existence of a semantics $\beta : \mathcal{P} \to B$ which is suitable for checking the properties $E \in Prop$ and functions $f_i : A_i \to B$ such that $f_1 \circ \alpha_1 = f_2 \circ \alpha_2 = \beta$. It is interesting that this kind of consistency of semantics via a more abstract semantics β was already mentioned in [18] in a special case. A variety of results in the literature can be interpreted as consistency results in this sense, e.g. [2, 7, 8, 13, 14, 32]. Another group of consistency results, e.g. [3, 5, 6, 11, 13, 18, 19, 20, 24, 27, 29, 34], relates two semantics $\alpha_1 : \mathcal{P} \to A_1$ and $\alpha_2 : \mathcal{P} \to A_2$ via a function $f : A_1 \to A_2$ and the equation $f \circ \alpha_1 = \alpha_2$. In this case we say that α_2 is an abstraction of α_1 and that α_1 and α_2 are weakly consistent.

The purpose of this paper is to clarify the notion of consistency of two (or more) semantics and to derive a categorical characterization of consistency. Section 2 introduces the several notions of consistency (weak and strong consistency, consistency w.r.t. a specification formalism, consistency relative to a more abstract semantics) where no restrictions on the syntax of the language $\mathcal{P}$ in which the programs are written or on the semantics are made. We consider the category $Sem(\mathcal{P})$ of semantics (as objects) and abstractions between them (as morphisms). Theorem 4 shows that for a given specification formalism (i.e. a set of properties $Prop$) there exists a semantics which identifies exactly those programs which cannot be distinguished by any of the given properties. This semantics is the final object in the subcategory $Sem(\mathcal{P}, Prop)$ of semantics suitable for proving the correctness of programs whose specifications are given in this specification formalism $Prop$. Theorem 5, 6 and 7 show the existence of products and coproducts in the category *Sem(P)* and *Sem(P, Prop)*. The coproduct can be considered as the most concrete common abstractions. It combines the different views which are given by the semantics since it identifies exactly those programs which are identified by each of the semantics. The product represents the most abstract common refinement. It can be used to check properties which can be checked by at least one of the semantics. Section 3 shows how weak consistency results can help to verify programs which are generated by stepwise refinement. Section 4 deals with compositional semantics where the existence of semantic operators is required but no additional structure like metric or partial order is assumed. In section 5 we show the relationship between weak consistency and adequacy and full abstractness.

2 Several notions of consistency

This section defines the notions strong and weak consistency, consistency w.r.t. a set of properties, consistency relative to a semantics β and presents conditions for establishing consistency results. We assume a fixed set of programs $\mathcal{P}$ where we do not make any restriction on the programming language in which the programs are written. The semantics under consideration are arbitrary surjections $\alpha : \mathcal{P} \to A$. In order to guarantee the surjectivity of a function $\alpha : \mathcal{P} \to A$ we identify α with the induced surjection $\alpha | \mathcal{P} \to \alpha(\mathcal{P})$.

A property E is any subset of $\mathcal{P}$. A program P has property E iff $P \in E$. A semantics $\alpha : \mathcal{P} \to A$ is suitable for checking E iff $\alpha^{-1}(\alpha(E)) = E$. In this case we write $\alpha \models E$. A specification formalism means a set *Prop* of properties and a specification (in this specification formalism) is an intersection of properties in *Prop*. A semantics α is suitable for the specification formalism *Prop* iff $\alpha \models E$ for all $E \in Prop$. Then α is suitable for *Prop* if and only if α identifies only those programs which cannot be distinguished by any property of *Prop*. An abstraction from a semantics $\alpha : \mathcal{P} \to A$ to a semantics $\beta : \mathcal{P} \to B$ is a function $f : A \to B$ with $f \circ \alpha = \beta$. In this case β is called an abstraction of α and α a refinement of β. Often a property is described in terms of a semantics $\alpha : \mathcal{P} \to A$, i.e. it is of the form $\alpha^{-1}(A_0)$ where A_0 is a subset of A. In this case the semantics α is suitable for checking the property $\alpha^{-1}(A_0)$. For instance the termination property E for a *CCS*-like language can easily be defined by a tree semantics: We put $E = \alpha^{-1}(A_0)$ where A_0 is the set of trees of finite height and α a tree semantics in the sense of [26] or [35].

Notation 1. *Sem(P) denotes the category whose objects are semantics for $\mathcal{P}$ and whose morphisms $\alpha \to \beta$ are abstractions from α to β. Sem(P, Prop) denotes the subcategory of semantics which are suitable for the specification formalism Prop.*

If β is an abstraction of α then there is a unique abstraction from α to β. This is because we assume the surjectivity of α. Hence in *Sem(P)* there is at most one arrow $\alpha \to \beta$. As mentioned in the introduction a variety of authors have established consistency results of the form that one semantics is an abstraction of the other one. This is what we call weak consistency:

Definition 2. Let $\alpha : \mathcal{P} \to A$ and $\beta : \mathcal{P} \to B$ be semantics. α and β are called **weakly consistent** iff α is an abstraction of β or β an abstraction of α. α and β are called **strongly consistent** iff α is an abstraction of β and β an abstraction of α.

Establishing weak consisteny results means looking for an arrow in the category $Sem(\mathcal{P})$. If α and β are strongly consistent then there exists a bijection $f : A \to B$ such that f is an abstraction from α to β and f^{-1} an abstraction from β to α. I.e. strong consistent semantics are isomorphic objects in the category $Sem(\mathcal{P})$. The simplest form of strong consisteny results is the equality of semantics. E.g. [5, 6, 11, 20] contain strong consistency results of the form $\mathcal{O} = \mathcal{D}$ where $\mathcal{O}$ is an operational, $\mathcal{D}$ a denotational semantics. A strong consistency result for different semantics is established in [34].

Lemma 3. Let $\alpha : \mathcal{P} \to A$ and $\beta : \mathcal{P} \to B$ be semantics. The following are equivalent:

(a) β is an abstraction of α.
(b) For all $P, Q \in \mathcal{P}$: $\alpha(P) = \alpha(Q)$ implies $\beta(P) = \beta(Q)$.
(c) For all properties E: $\beta \models E$ implies $\alpha \models E$.

We conclude by Lemma 3 that strongly consistent semantics are fully equivalent w.r.t. the capability of testing properties (independently of any specification formalism).

Theorem 4. Let Prop be a specification formalism. Then $Sem(\mathcal{P}, Prop)$ has a final object.

In other words, for each specification formalism Prop there exists a most abstract semantics α such that α is suitable for Prop. The construction of such a semantics α is as follows: Take $\equiv$ to be the equivalence relation on $\mathcal{P}$ which identifies exactly those programs which cannot be distinguished by any property $E \in Prop$. I.e.

$$P \equiv Q \quad :\Longleftrightarrow \quad \forall E \in Prop \ (P \in E \text{ if and only } Q \in E)$$

Let $\alpha : \mathcal{P} \to \mathcal{P}/\!\equiv$ be the canonical function which maps each program to its equivalence class. Then α is the final object in $Sem(\mathcal{P}, Prop)$.

In the situation where for the same language several semantic descriptions are given (e.g. one serving the needs of the implementation, one that is suitable for the verification and another one that explains the language to the user) it might be useful to combine all the different views, i.e. to look for the properties which can be checked by all semantics or to look for the properties which can be checked by at least one the semantics. This can be done by examination of the (co-)product:

Theorem 5. *Sem($\mathcal{P}$) has products for arbitrary families of semantics.*

The construction of the product $\prod \alpha_i$ of a family $(\alpha_i)_{i \in I}$ of semantics is as follows: If A_i is the range of α_i then we take A to be the product of the sets A_i and $\prod \alpha_i : \mathcal{P} \to A$ to be the function which assigns to each program P the family $(\alpha_i(P))_{i \in I}$. The product can be considered as the most abstract common refinement: $\prod \alpha_i$ is the unique semantics α (uniqueness up to strong consistency) which is a refinement of each of the semantics α_i and whenever β is also a common refinement of $\alpha_i, i \in I$, then α is an abstraction of β. With Lemma 3: If $\alpha_i \models E$ for some $i \in I$ then $\prod \alpha_i \models E$. I.e. $\prod \alpha_i$ is suitable to check all those properties which can be checked by some of the semantics α_i. Hence it can be used to prove additional properties that cannot be expressed by the specification formalism which in general only provides the possibility to describe what a program has to do but not how it has to be done. For instance the product might be suitable to verify properties which assert something about how the program is implemented (e.g. time and space complexity of the implementation).

Theorem 6. *Sem($\mathcal{P}$) has coproducts for arbitrary families of semantics.*

The coproduct $\coprod \alpha_i$ of a family $(\alpha_i)_{i \in I}$ of semantics is as follows: If A_i is the range of α_i then we take A to be the disjoint union of A_i factored by the smallest equivalence relation which identifies the elements $\alpha_i(P)$, $i \in I$. Then $\coprod \alpha_i : \mathcal{P} \to A$ assigns to each program P the equivalence class of $\alpha_i(P)$. $\coprod \alpha_i$ can be considered as the most concrete common abstraction: $\coprod \alpha_i$ is the unique semantics α (uniqueness up to strong consistency) such that α is an abstraction of each of the semantics α_i, $i \in I$, and whenever β is also a common abstraction then β is an abstraction of α. It can be shown that:

$$\coprod \alpha_i \models E \quad \Longleftrightarrow \quad \forall i \in I : \alpha_i \models i$$

Hence $\coprod \alpha_i$ is suitable to check **exactly** those properties which can be checked by each of the semantics α_i. It can be used to test whether each of the semantics α_i is suitable for a given specification: One has to check whether each property of the specification formalism can be checked by $\coprod \alpha_i$.

If each of the semantics α_i is suitable for a given specification formalism then also their product and coproduct is suitable for the specification formalism. Hence $\prod \alpha_i$ and $\coprod \alpha_i$ are the product resp. coproduct in *Sem($\mathcal{P}$, Prop)*. Hence:

Theorem 7. *Sem($\mathcal{P}$, Prop) has products and coproducts for arbitrary families of semantics which are suitable for Prop.*

In order to compare two (or more) semantics with regard to their capability of verifying the correctness of the programs we have to look for the properties E which can be checked by them. If both semantics are suitable to check all properties E of a given specification formalism we consider them as consistent w.r.t. to this specification formalism. [18] proposes a notion of consistency relative to a denotational semantics. We generalize this notion and define consistency of two or more semantics α_i relative to another semantics β (not necessary a denotational one) and show that the consistency w.r.t. a specification formalism $Prop$ is equivalent to the consistency relative to a semantics β which is suitable for $Prop$ (Theorem 9).

Definition 8. Let $Prop$ be a set of properties and $\beta : \mathcal{P} \to B$ a semantics. A family $(\alpha_i)i \in I$ of semantics is called **consistent w.r.t.** $Prop$ iff $\alpha_i \models E$ for all $E \in Prop$, $i \in I$. $(\alpha_i)_{i \in I}$ is called β-**consistent** iff β is an abstraction of α_i, $i \in I$.

Weak consistency results that assert that a semantics β is an abstraction of another semantics α are special cases of β-consistency results. A list of publications which establish β-consistency in the form of weak consistency results is given in introduction. Other consistency results establish some form of equivalence between two semantic descriptions, e.g. [2, 7, 8, 14, 13, 32]. This type of results can be viewed as β-consistency results.

Example 1. [13] and [2] show the 'consistency' of the operational transition system semantics $\mathcal{O}$ of [29] and a denotational prime event structure semantics $\mathcal{D}$ for guarded $TCSP$ in the following sense:

$$\mathcal{O}(P) \approx trans(\mathcal{D}(P))$$

Here *trans* means a function which assigns a transition system to each prime event structure and $\approx$ means weak bisimulation equivalence in the sense of [26]. Let f be the function which maps each transition system to its weak bisimulation equivalence class then the result of [2, 13] says $f \circ \mathcal{O} = f \circ trans \circ \mathcal{D}$ which is a consistency result in our sense: Let $\beta = f \circ \mathcal{O}$. Then $\mathcal{O}$ and $\mathcal{D}$ are β-consistent. □

Each family $(\alpha_i)_{i \in I}$ of semantics α_i is β-consistent where β is the final object in $Sem(\mathcal{P})$, i.e. $\beta : \mathcal{P} \to B$ is a semantics which maps $\mathcal{P}$ into a one-element domain B. Hence the 'quality' of β-consistency depends on the 'quality' of the semantics β (i.e. the set of properties E with $\beta \models E$). By Lemma 3 we get: $(\alpha_i)_{i \in I}$ is β-consistent if and only if for each property E: $\beta \models E$ implies $\alpha_i \models E$ for all $i \in I$. I.e. the set of properties which can be checked by β gives a measure for the quality of a β-consistency result.

Theorem 9. *Let Prop be a specification formalism and $(\alpha_i)_{i \in I}$ a family of semantics. Then the following are equivalent:*

(a) $(\alpha_i)_{i \in I}$ is consistent w.r.t. Prop.

(b) There exists a semantics β which is suitable for Prop (i.e. $\beta \models E$ for all $E \in Prop$) such that $(\alpha_i)_{i \in I}$ is β-consistent.

(c) $\coprod \alpha_i \models E$ for all $E \in Prop$.

As strong consistency is a special case of weak consistency and weak consistency a special case of consistency relative to a more abstract semantics the above theorem also clarifies the connection between our four notions of consistency. The following diagram shows the hierarchy of consistency results where the arrows denote implication:

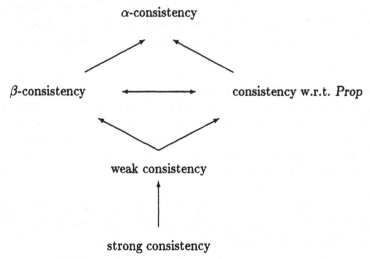

where β is a most abstract semantics suitable for checking all properties in *Prop* (Theorem 4) and α an abstraction of β. β-consistency is a weaker notion than weak consistency. E.g. one can provide a pomset semantics α_1 and a synchronization tree semantics α_2 for a language which includes nondeterministic choice and parallel composition that are β-consistent where β maps a process to a set of traces. α_1 and α_2 cannot be weakly consistent as α_1 is a linear time true concurrency model and α_2 a branching time interleaving model.

3 Application: Verification and stepwise refinement

Weak consistency results can help to prove the correctness of implementations which are generated by stepwise refinement. We show that under the assumption that a given program P which is written in a high-level language $\mathcal{P}$ meets the specification it can be concluded that its refinement $i(P)$ (which is written in a lower-level language $\mathcal{P}'$) also meets the specification. The programs $P \in \mathcal{P}$ are considered as algorithms. We assume a mapping $i : \mathcal{P} \to \mathcal{P}'$ which assigns to each $P \in \mathcal{P}$ a program $i(P) \in \mathcal{P}'$ which we call the implementation of P.

We assume semantics $\alpha : \mathcal{P} \to A$ and $\alpha' : \mathcal{P}' \to A'$ and a 'consistency result' of the form $\alpha = f \circ \alpha' \circ i$ where $f : A' \to A$ is a function. The reason why we assume that f maps A' to A and not vice versa is that in general $i(P)$ (and then also $\alpha'(i(P))$) contains more details. E.g. it might be the case that in $\mathcal{P}$ there is an atomic statement a which stands for the sorting of a finite sequence of natural numbers. The function i might map this atomic statement to a program which implements Quicksort (or another sorting algorithm). The assumption

$\alpha = f \circ \alpha' \circ i$ can be considered as a weak consistency result for the semantics α and $\alpha' \circ i$ for the language $\mathcal{P}$.

Lemma 10. *Let $\alpha : \mathcal{P} \to A$ and $\alpha' : \mathcal{P}' \to A'$ be semantics and $f : A \to A'$ a function such that $\alpha = f \circ \alpha' \circ i$. Then:*

(a) For each property $E \subseteq \mathcal{P}$ with $\alpha \models E$: If the algorithm P has property E then its implementation $i(P)$ has property $i(E)$.

(b) If $E = \alpha^{-1}(A_0)$ where $A_0 \subseteq A$ and $E' = \alpha'^{-1}(A'_0)$ where $A'_0 \subseteq A'$ and $f^{-1}(A_0) \subseteq A'_0$ then:

> *If the algorithms P has property E then its implementation $i(P)$ has property E'.*

This result can be used to verify the correctness of the implementation w.r.t. a specification written in some logic. In addition to the assumptions of above we assume that the specifications are given as a set of logical formulas of some logic L.

Lemma 11. *Let $\alpha : \mathcal{P} \to A$ and $\alpha' : \mathcal{P}' \to A'$ be semantics, $f : A \to A'$ a function such that $\alpha = f \circ \alpha' \circ i$ and let $F : A \to I$, $F' : A' \to I'$ be functions where I, I' are sets of interpretations for some logic L such that for all $a' \in A'$ and all formulas φ of L:*

> *If $F(f(a'))$ is a model of φ then $F'(a')$ is a model of φ.*

Here we say $P \in \mathcal{P}$ satisfies φ iff $F(\alpha(P))$ is a model of φ and similary, $P' \in \mathcal{P}'$ satisfies φ iff $F'(\alpha'(P'))$ is a model of φ. Then:

> *If the algorithm P satisfies φ then the implementation $i(P)$ satisfies φ.*

Hence under the assumptions of above the verification problem is reduced to prove that the algorithm meets the specification and whenever if $F(f(a'))$ is a model of φ then $F'(a')$ is a model of φ. The simplest case in which the second condition is satisfied is $I' = I$, $F \circ f = F'$.

4 Compositional semantics

In compositional semantics the meaning of a program $P = \omega(P_1, \ldots, P_n)$ can be computed by composing the meanings of the modules $P_1, \ldots, P_n$ via a semantic operator ω_A on the underlying semantic domain A. Compositionality yields tools to compute the semantics and for modular verification. Modular verification means that in order to prove the correctness of a program each of the program modules is verified separately and then one proves the correctness of the composite program using the specifications of the modules but without using any knowledge about how the modules are implemented. This implies that also the specifications should be modular: For each property E of the specification formalism and each n-ary operator ω of the underlying language there exists a set $\mathcal{E}_{E,\omega}$ consisting of n-tuples $(E_1,\ldots,E_n)$ of properties E_i such that the composite program $\omega(P_1,\ldots,P_n)$ has property E if and only if P_i has property E_i, $i = 1,\ldots,n$ for such a n-tuple $(E_1,\ldots,E_n) \in \mathcal{E}_{E,\omega}$. In this case, if α is a compositional semantics suitable for checking all properties of the underlying specification formalism then

$$\alpha(P) \in \alpha(E) \iff \exists (E_1,\ldots,E_n) \in \mathcal{E}_{E,\omega} : \alpha(P_i) \in \alpha(E_i),\ i = 1,\ldots,n.$$

Hence in order to show the correctness of P one shows that $\alpha(P_i) \in E_i$ for some of these n-tuples $(E_1,\ldots,E_n)$, i.e. α is suitable for modular verification.

In this and the following section we deal with a language $\mathcal{P}$ with abstract operator symbols and recursion (modelled by declarations). The syntax is as in [3]: By a symbol-algebra (or signature) we mean a pair $\Sigma = (Op, |\cdot|)$ consisting of a set Op of operator symbols and a function $|\cdot| : Op \to I\!N_0$ which assigns the arity $|\omega|$ to each operator symbol ω. Operator symbols of arity 0 are called constant symbols. The set $\mathcal{L}(\Sigma, Idf)$ of statements over Σ and Idf (where Idf is a fixed set of variables) is given by the production system

$$s \ ::= \ a \ | \ x \ | \ \omega(s_1,\ldots,s_n)$$

where a is a constant symbol, $x \in Idf$, ω an operator symbol with $|\omega| = n \geq 1$, $s_1,\ldots,s_n \in \mathcal{L}(\Sigma, Idf)$. A declaration is a mapping $\sigma : Idf \to \mathcal{L}(\Sigma, Idf)$. A program over (Σ, Idf) is a pair $< \sigma, s >$ consisting of a declaration σ and a statement s. The behaviour of a program $< \sigma, s >$ is given by s where each occurrence of a variable x in s is interpreted as a recursive call of the procedure $\sigma(x)$. In the following we fix a declaration σ and we define $\mathcal{P}$ to be the set of programs $< \sigma, s >$ where $s \in \mathcal{L}(\Sigma, Idf)$. The operator symbols are considered as operators on $\mathcal{P}$ where we put

$$\omega(<\sigma, s_1>, \ \ldots, \ <\sigma, s_n>) = < \sigma, \omega(s_1,\ldots,s_n) >.$$

We write x to denote the recursive program $< \sigma, x >$, $\sigma(x)$ instead of $< \sigma, \sigma(x) >$ and a instead of $< \sigma, a >$ for each constant symbol a.

As usual interpretations of symbol-algebras are given by Σ-algebras. If $\Sigma = (Op, |\cdot|)$ is a symbol-algebra then a Σ-algebra is a pair (A, Op_A) consisting of a set A and a set Op_A of operators $Op_A = \{\omega_A : \omega \in Op\}$ such that $\omega_A : A^n \to A$ is a function where $|\omega| = n$. (In the case $n = 0$ $\omega_A \in A$.) In the following we omit the operator set Op_A of a Σ-algebra and we shortly write A instead of (A, Op_A). If A and B are Σ-algebras then a function $f : A \to B$ is called a homomorphism iff

$$f(\ \omega_A(\xi_1,\ldots,\xi_n) \ ) = \omega_B (\ f(\xi_1),\ldots,f(\xi_n) \ )$$

for each $\omega \in Op$, $|\omega| = n$. A compositional semantics for $\mathcal{P}$ is a function $\alpha : \mathcal{P} \to A$ where A is a Σ-algebra which satisfies the following conditions:

(I) $\alpha(\omega(P_1,\ldots,P_n)) = \omega_A (\alpha(P_1),\ldots,\alpha(P_n))$
(II) α satisfies the recursion condition: $\alpha(x) = \alpha(\ \sigma(x) \ )$ for all $x \in Idf$.

Notation 12. *CompSem($\mathcal{P}$) denotes the category of compositional semantics (as objects) and abstractions (as morphisms). If Prop is a specification formalism then CompSem($\mathcal{P}$, Prop) denotes the subcategory of compositional semantics which are suitable for Prop.*

The following lemma shows that the morphisms in *CompSem($\mathcal{P}$)* are homomorphisms. Hence establishing a weak consistency result for compositional semantics means establishing a homomorphism between the underlying Σ-algebras (see also [22]).

Lemma 13. *Let $\alpha : \mathcal{P} \to A$, $\beta : \mathcal{P} \to B$ be compositional semantics and $f : A \to B$ an abstraction from α to β. Then f is a homomorphism.*

The following theorem extends the result of Theorem 4 and presents a condition for the existence of a compositional semantics which is suitable to verify the correctness of programs w.r.t. a given specification formalism. The condition which is needed is the modularity of the properties:

Definition 14. Let *Prop* be a set of properties. *Prop* is called **modular** iff the following conditions are satisfied:

1. For each property $E \in Prop$ and each n-ary operator symbol ω $(n \geq 1)$ there exists a set $\mathcal{E}_{E,\omega}$ consisting of n-tuples of properties in *Prop* such that for all $P_1, \ldots, P_n \in \mathcal{P}$:

$$\omega(P_1, \ldots, P_n) \in E \quad \Longleftrightarrow \quad \exists\, (E_1, \ldots, E_n) \in \mathcal{E}_{E,\omega} : P_i \in E_i, \ i = 1, \ldots, n$$

2. For all variables $x \in \mathcal{P}$ and all properties $E \in Prop$:

$$x \in E \quad \Longleftrightarrow \quad \sigma(x) \in E$$

If a specification formalism is modular then the first condition asserts the soundness and completeness of modular verification: the implication $\Leftarrow$ reflects the soundness of modular verification (if the modules fulfill certain properties then the composite program satisfies its specification), the implication $\Rightarrow$ stands for the completeness of modular verification (if the composite program is correct then the correctness can be shown by proving that its modules have certain properties). The second condition is needed to ensure that the recursive program x which is assumed to consist of a recursive call of $\sigma(x)$ cannot be distinguished from $\sigma(x)$ by any property.

Lemma 15. *Let Prop be a set of properties satisfying condition 2 of Definition 14 and let $\equiv$ be the induced equivalence relation, i.e.*

$$P \equiv Q \quad \Longleftrightarrow \quad \forall\, E \in Prop : P \in E \text{ iff } Q \in E.$$

Then:

(a) *If Prop is modular then $\equiv$ is a congruence relation on $\mathcal{P}$, i.e. for every n-ary operator symbol ω: $P_i \equiv Q_i$, $i = 1, \ldots, n$, implies $\omega(P_1, \ldots, P_n) \equiv \omega(Q_1, \ldots, Q_n)$.*

(b) *If $\equiv$ is a congruence relation on $\mathcal{P}$ and $Prop = \mathcal{P}/\equiv$ then Prop is modular.*

By Lemma 15(b), every congruence relation on a process algebra induces a modular specification formalism. For instance, bisimulation equivalence $\sim$ is a congruence on CCS [26] and hence the specification formalism $Prop = CCS/\sim$ a modular specification formalism.

The next lemma shows that for every modular specification formalism $Prop$ there exists a most abstract compositional semantics which is suitable for checking all properties of $Prop$, i.e. which is suitable for modular verification.

Theorem 16. *Let Prop be a modular set of properties. Then $CompSem(\mathcal{P}, Prop)$ has a final object.*

If $Prop$ is modular then the range of the final object α in $Sem(\mathcal{P}, Prop)$ can be equipped with suitable semantic operators which turn α into a compositional semantics. Hence the final object in $CompSem(\mathcal{P}, Prop)$ is the final object in $Sem(\mathcal{P}, Prop)$. It is the unique compositional semantics α (uniqueness up to strong consistency) which is suitable for $Prop$ such that whenever β is a (not necessary compositional) semantics also suitable for $Prop$ then α is an abstraction of β.

The most concrete common abstraction and most abstract common refinement of compositional semantics are compositional. Hence:

Theorem 17. *$CompSem(\mathcal{P})$ and $CompSem(\mathcal{P}, Prop)$ have products and coproducts.*

The (co-)product of a family of compositional semantics α_i can be endowed with suitable semantic operators which turn $\prod \alpha_i$ and $\coprod \alpha_i$ into compositional semantics: Let ω be an n-ary operator symbol and ω_{A_i} a semantic operator on the range A_i of α_i. Then the operator

$$(\xi_1, \ldots, \xi_n) \mapsto (\omega_{A_i}(f_i(\xi_1), \ldots, f_i(\xi_n)))_{i \in I}$$

models ω on the product where f_i denotes the unique abstraction from $\prod \alpha_i$ to α_i. Dealing with the coproduct ω is modelled by the semantic operator which assigns to each n-tuple $(\xi_1, \ldots, \xi_n)$ of elements ξ_j in the range of $\coprod \alpha_i$ the equivalence class of $\omega_{A_i}(a_1, \ldots, a_n)$ where i is an arbitrary index and $a_j \in A_i$ a representant of ξ_j.

5 Adequacy and full abstractness

Often when relating an operational with a denotational semantics of a language $\mathcal{P}$ as in section 4 the notions of adequacy and full abstraction are employed. We extend these notions to arbitrary semantics α and β.

Definition 18. A semantics α is called *adequate* w.r.t. a semantics β iff for all programs P, Q:

$$\alpha(P) = \alpha(Q) \text{ implies } \forall\, C[\cdot] \;:\; \beta(\, C[P]\,) \;=\; \beta(\, C[Q]\,).$$

α is called *fully abstract* w.r.t. β iff

$$\forall\, C[\cdot] \;:\; \beta(\, C[P]\,) \;=\; \beta(\, C[Q]\,) \text{ implies } \alpha(P) = \alpha(Q).$$

Here $C[\cdot]$ ranges over the set of contexts for $\mathcal{P}$, i.e. the set of 'programs' in $\mathcal{P}$ containing one or more holes. $C[P]$ is the program which is obtained by substituting P for the holes in $C[\cdot]$.

Having a weak consistency result $\beta = f \circ \alpha$ where α is a compositional semantics then it can be shown by structural induction that α is adequate w.r.t. β. Vice versa, if α is adequate w.r.t. β then $\alpha(P) = \alpha(Q)$ implies $\beta(P) = \beta(Q)$. Hence by Lemma 3: β is an abstraction of α. Hence we get:

Theorem 19. *Let α be a compositional semantics. Then: α is adequate w.r.t. β if and only if β is an abstraction of α.*

If α and α' are semantics which are adequate and fully abstract w.r.t. β then α and α' identify exactly the same programs. Hence α and α' are strongly consistent. The next theorem shows the existence of a compositional semantics which is adequate and fully abstract w.r.t. a given semantics β under the assumption that β does not distinguish between a procedure name x and its body $\sigma(x)$ in every context.

Theorem 20. *For each semantics β there exists a unique (up to strong consistency) semantics α which is adequate and fully abstract w.r.t. β.*
If $\beta(C[x]) = \beta(C[\sigma(x)])$ for all variables x and all contexts $C[\cdot]$ then α is compositional.

This semantics α can be constructed with help of Theorem 4: Let α be the final object in the category $Sem(Prop_\beta)$ where $Prop_\beta = \mathcal{P}/\equiv_\beta$ and

$$P \equiv_\beta Q \quad\Longleftrightarrow\quad \forall\, C[\cdot] \;:\; \beta(C[P]) = \beta(C[Q]).$$

Then $\alpha(P)$ is the equivalence class of P w.r.t. $\equiv_\beta$. Hence α identifies two programs P and Q if and only if $P \equiv_\beta Q$, i.e. α is adequate and fully abstract w.r.t. β. The semantic operators on the range $A = \mathcal{P}/\equiv_\beta$ of α are given by:

$$\omega_A(\, [P_1]_{\equiv_\beta}, \ldots, [P_n]_{\equiv_\beta}\,) \;=\; [\, \omega(P_1, \ldots, P_n)\,]_{\equiv_\beta}$$

where ω is an n-ary operator symbol. It is easy to see that α is the most abstract semantics which is adequate w.r.t. β (i.e. it is the final object in the subcategory of semantics which are adequate w.r.t. β) and it is the most concrete semantics which is fully abstract w.r.t. β (i.e. it is the initial object in the subcategory of semantics which are fully abstract w.r.t. β).

6 Conclusion

We introduced the notions of weak, strong and β-consistency and consistency w.r.t. a specification formalism, i.e. a set *Prop* of properties. It is shown that the various 'consistency' results from the literature fit into our framework. The connection between β-consistency and consistency w.r.t. a specification formalism is studied (Theorem 9). We showed that there is always a unique most abstract semantics suitable for verification (Theorem 4). Under the assumption that the underlying specification formalism allows for modular verification this semantics is compositional (Theorem 16). We also gave special attention to compositionality and verification of programs that are built by stepwise refinement. Finally we showed that each (operational) semantics β with $\beta(C[x]) = \beta(C[\sigma[x]])$ possesses a unique denotational semantics which is adequate and fully abstract w.r.t. β (Theorem 20).

References

1. S. Abramsky, A. Jung: Domain Theory, In S. Abramsky, D.M. Gabbay and T.S.E. Maibaum, (ed.), Handbook of Logic in Computer Science, Vol. 3, Clarendon Press, 1994.
2. C. Baier, M.E. Majster-Cederbaum: The Connection between an Event Structure Semantics and an Operational Semantics for $TCSP$, Acta Informatica 31, 1994.
3. C. Baier, M.E. Majster-Cederbaum: Denotational Semantics in the CPO and Metric Approach, Theoretical Computer Science, Vol. 135, 1994.
4. C. Baier, M.E. Majster-Cederbaum: Construction of a CMS on a given CPO, Techn. Report 28/95, Universität Mannheim, 1994, submitted for publication to Acta Informatica.
5. J.W. de Bakker, J.J.Ch. Meyer: Metric Semantics for Concurrency, Report CS-R8803, Centre for Mathematics and Computer Science, Amsterdam, 1988.
6. J.W. de Bakker, J.H.A. Warmerdam: Metric Pomset Semantics for a Concurrent Language with Recursion, Report CS-R9033, Centre for Mathematics and Computer Science, Amsterdam, July 1990.
7. G. Boudol, I.Castellani: Concurrency and Atomicity, Theoretical Computer Science, Vol. 59, 1988.
8. G. Boudol, I.Castellani: Three Equivalent Semantics for CCS, Lecture Notes in Computer Science 469, Springer-Verlag, 1990.
9. S.D. Brookes, C.A.R. Hoare, A.W. Roscoe: A Theory of Communicating Sequential Processes, Journal of the ACM, Vol. 31, No. 3, July 1984.
10. E.M. Clarke, E.A. Emerson: Design and Synthesis of Synchronization Skeletons using Branching Time Temporal Logic, Proc. Workshop on Logics of Programs, Lecture Notes in Computer Science 131, 1981.
11. P. Degano, R. De Nicola, U. Montanari: On the Consistency of 'Truly Concurrent' Operational and Denotational Semantics, Proc. Symposium on Logic in Computer Science, Edinburgh, 1988.
12. G. Gierz, H. Hofmann, K. Keimel, J. Lawson, M. Mislove, D. Scott: A Compendium of Continuous Lattices, Springer-Verlag, 1980.
13. U. Goltz, R. Loogen: Modelling Nondeterministic Concurrent Processes with Event Structures, Fundamenta Informaticae, Vol. 14, No.1, 1991.

14. U. Goltz, A. Mycroft: On the Relationship of CCS and Petri Nets, Proc. ICALP 84, Lecture Notes in Computer Science 172, Springer-Verlag, 1984.
15. M. Hennessy: Axiomatising Finite Delay Operators, Acta Informatica, Vol. 21, 1984.
16. M. Hennessy, R. Milner: On Observing Nondeterminism and Concurrency, in Automata, Languages and Programming, Lecture Notes in Computer Science 85, 1980.
17. C.A.R. Hoare: Communicating Sequential Processes, Prentice Hall, 1985.
18. C.A.R. Hoare, P.E. Lauer: Consistent and Complementary Formal Theories of the Semantics of Programming Languages, Acta Informatica, Vol. 3, 1974.
19. E. Horita: A Fully Abstract Model for a Nonuniform Concurrent Language with Parametrization and Locality, in Proc. REX Workshop '92, Lecture Notes in Computer Science 666, Springer-Verlag 1993.
20. J.N. Kok, J.J.M.M. Rutten: Contractions in Comparing Concurrency Semantics, Report CS-R8755, Centre for Mathematics and Computer Science, November 1987.
21. L. Lamport: Specifying Concurrent Program Modules, ACM Transactions on Programming Languages and Systems, Vol. 5, No. 2, 1983.
22. M. Majster-Cederbaum: General Properties of Semantics, Habilitation Thesis, Technische Universität München, 1983.
23. M. Majster-Cederbaum, C. Baier: Metric Completion versus Ideal Completion, to appear in Theoretical Computer Science, Vol. 170.
    (Extended abstract in Proc. STRICT 95, J. Desel (ed.), Springer-Verlag.)
24. M. Majster-Cederbaum, F. Zetzsche: The comparison of a CPO-Based with a CMS-Based Semantics for CSP, Theoretical Computer Science, Vol. 124, 1994.
25. R. Milner: A Calculus of Communicating Systems, Lecture Notes in Computer Science 92, Springer-Verlag, 1980.
26. R. Milner: Communication and Concurrency, Prentice Hall, 1989.
27. M.W. Mislove, F.J. Oles: Full Abstraction and Unnested Recursion, in Proc. REX Workshop '92, Lecture Notes in Computer Science 666, Springer-Verlag, 1993.
28. R. de Nicola, M. Hennessy: Testing Equivalences for Processes, Theoretical Computer Science, Vol. 34, 1984.
29. E.R. Olderog: $TCSP$: Theory of Communicating Sequential Processes, Advances in Petri-Nets 1986, Lecture Notes in Computer Science 255, Springer-Verlag, 1987.
30. E.R. Olderog: Operational Petri-Net Semantics for $CCSP$, Advances in Petri-Nets 1987, Lecture Notes in Computer Science 266, Springer-Verlag, 1987.
31. A. Pnueli: The Temporal Logic of Programs, 18th Ann. Symp. on Foundations of Computer Science, Providence, 1977.
32. W. Reisig: Partial Order Semantics versus Interleaving Semantics for CSP-like Languages and its Impact on Fairness, Proc. ICALP 84, Lecture Notes in Computer Science 172, Springer-Verlag, 1984.
33. W. Reisig: Elements of a Temporal Logic Coping with Concurrency, SFB-Bericht 342/23, 92A, Techn. Universität München, 1992.
34. M. Spanier: Vergleich zweier Theorien nebenläufiger Prozesse, Ph.D.Thesis, Universität Mannheim, 1993.
35. G. Winskel: Synchronisation Trees, Theoretical Computer Science, Vol. 34, 1984.

Algebraic Specification of Reactive Systems[*]

Manfred Broy

Institut für Informatik, Technische Universität München
D-80290 München

Abstract. We present an algebraic method for the specification of reactive distributed systems. We introduce basic operators on specifications making the set of specifications into a specification algebra. This allows us to work with an algebra of system specifications in analogy to the process algebras that provide algebras of reactive programs. However, in contrast to process algebras we work with a concrete representation (a mathematical system model) of specifications and use algebaric equations to specify components and not programming languages. A specification is represented by a predicate that describes a set of behaviors. A deterministic component has exactly one behavior. A behavior is represented by a stream processing function. We introduce operations on behaviors and lift them to specifications. We show how algebraic system specifications can be used as an algebraic and logical basis for state automata specifications and state transition diagrams.

1 Introduction

There are many approaches to the formal description and specification of distributed interactive systems. We follow the idea of functional system modeling as it is explained in detail for instance under the keyword FOCUS in [FOCUS 94] or in [Broy 93] (for the theoretical background see also [Broy 86] and [Broy 87b]). There the basic idea is to describe the input/output relationship called the *black box behavior* of a system component by specifying predicates that characterize sets of deterministic behaviors. A deterministic behavior is represented by a stream processing function.

In the following, we extend and complement the functional approach by algebraic specification concepts. We specify a number of basic operations on specifications. This allows us to write elegant algebraic equations to characterize specifications.

Our motivation is to extend the functional approach to system specification by concepts and notations that provide the most simple and suggestive way of writing specifications for certain types of components. Algebraic specification techniques for reactive systems allow us to describe reactive systems by specifying equations very much along the line of algebraic specification techniques for data structures.

We show, in particular, the close relationship between finite automata and extended finite automata and algebraic techniques. Extended finite automata are automata with a finite control but an infinite data space. There are a number of system description concepts such as state transition diagrams that are used in practice (such as for instance in SDL, see [SDL 88]) that are based on this idea. Our approach provides an algebraic and logical foundation for these concepts.

There are components for which it is much easier and more elegant to describe their behavior by algebraic equations for their specification than by classical predicate logic. We introduce, in particular, a tuned notation for the algebraic specification of reactive systems.

Our paper is organized as follows. Section 2 briefly introduces the basic notion of component that we use. Section 3 introduces operations on behaviors called input and output transition. Section 4 defines the algebra of specifications based on transitions. Section 5 defines recursion for specifications. Section 6 considers the fundamental forms

---

[*] This work was partially sponsored by the Sonderforschungsbereich 342 "Werkzeuge und Methoden für die Nutzung paralleler Rechnerarchitekturen" and the industrial research project SysLab sponsored by Siemens Nixdorf and by the DFG under the Leibniz program.

of compositions for building systems. Section 7 gives the algebraic laws for the algebra of transitions and system composition operations. Section 8 illustrates the relationship of this algebra to state transition diagrams. Section 9 outlines an extension of our approach to time dependent systems. An appendix repeats the basic notions of streams.

2 Components, Interfaces, Behaviors, Specifications

The concept of a *component* is fundamental in software and systems engineering. Distributed systems are composed of components that are connected in a way that allows them to exchange information and to cooperate. We use a very simple, but powerful, abstract, general, mathematical concept of a component.

A component has an interface described by a family of named input channels as well as a family of named output channels. By the channels a component communicates with its environment. By I we denote the set of input channel identifiers and by O we denote the set of output channel identifiers. Each channel has assigned a sort. For simplicity throughout this paper all channels carry messages of the same sort M. An extension to individually sorted channels is straightforward. Fig 1 shows a component with individually sorted channels as a data flow node.

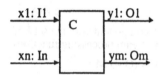

Fig. 1 Graphical representation of component C with sorted and named channels

Semantically, a component C is represented by a predicate defining a set of deterministic behaviors. A *deterministic behavior* is represented by a stream processing function

$$f : (I \rightarrow M^\omega) \rightarrow (O \rightarrow M^\omega)$$

that maps every input history onto an output history. An input or output history is given by a valuation of the channels by streams. Here M^ω denotes the set of streams over the set M. It is defined by $M^\omega = M^* \cup M^\infty$. It consists of the finite and infinite sequences of elements from M. The concatenation of two sequences s and t is denoted by $s^\frown t$. A detailed introduction to streams and stream processing functions is given in the appendix.

A component then is described by a predicate

$$C: ((I \rightarrow M^\omega) \rightarrow (O \rightarrow M^\omega)) \rightarrow \mathbb{B}$$

that specifies a set of deterministic behaviors. Given such a component C we denote by In(C) its set I of input channels and by Out(C) its set O of output channels.

In many applications, it is useful to work with specifications that are parameterized. Mathematically, this means that we deal with a function

$$Q: \Xi \rightarrow (((I \rightarrow M^\omega) \rightarrow (O \rightarrow M^\omega)) \rightarrow \mathbb{B})$$

where Ξ is an arbitrary set. For every element $\sigma \in \Xi$ we obtain by $Q(\sigma)$ a component specification. One way to think about Ξ is to see it as a state space.

Throughout this paper we write f.x for the function application f(x) whenever appropriate.

3 The Algebra on Behavior Functions

In this section we introduce a mathematical concept of operations applied to the black box behavior of deterministic components. We start with the introduction of a basic operation on streams. Let $x \in M^\omega$ be a stream and $m \in M$ be a message. We write

$$m \triangleleft x$$

for the stream $\langle m \rangle\hat{\ }x$ that starts with message m and then continues with the stream x of messages. We extend this notation to finite sequences $s \in M^*$ and write

$$s \triangleleft x$$

for the stream $s\hat{\ }m$ that starts with the messages in s and continues with the stream x.

We extend this notion also to families of named streams. Let A be a set of names for streams which we call *channels*. Let $x \in A \rightarrow M^\omega$ be a family of streams with names from A, $c \in A$ be a channel and $m \in M$ be a message. We extend the concatenation on streams to valuations x: $A \rightarrow M^\omega$ and y: $A \rightarrow M^\omega$ elementwise by the definition

$$(x\hat{\ }y).a = (x.a)\hat{\ }(y.a)$$

We specify the family of streams

$$c:m \triangleleft x$$

by the following equations:

$$(c:m \triangleleft x).c' = x.c' \qquad \Leftarrow c \neq c',$$

$$(c:m \triangleleft x).c = \langle m \rangle\hat{\ }(x.c),$$

$$c:m \triangleleft x = x \qquad \Leftarrow c \notin A.$$

The behavior of a deterministic component with the set I of input channels and the set O of output channels is described by stream processing functions

$$f : (I \rightarrow M^\omega) \rightarrow (O \rightarrow M^\omega)$$

mapping each valuation of the input channels I by streams over M onto valuations of the output channels O by streams from M^ω.

We define for messages $m \in M$, channels $c \in I$ and input histories $x \in I \rightarrow M^\omega$ the following operation on the stream processing function f:

$$f \triangleleft c:m$$

By this term we denote the stream processing function that behaves like the function f on the communication history $x \in (I \rightarrow M^\omega)$ after we add the message m as the first message on channel c to the input x. Formally, this explanation can be expressed by an equation as follows:

$$(f \triangleleft c:m).x = f(c:m \triangleleft x)$$

For every output channel $c \in O$ we define in a similar way the stream processing function denoted by

$$c:m \triangleleft f$$

as the function that represents the same behavior as the function f but always adds the message m as its first output on channel c to the output produced by the function f. Again we can express this description formally by an equation as follows:

$$(c:m \triangleleft f).x = c:m \triangleleft (f.x)$$

These operations on functions are called *input transitions* and *output transitions*. They can easily be generalized from stream processing functions to sets of stream processing functions and therefore to specifications.

With the transition operators introduced so far we can already specify behaviors by algebraic equations.

Example: Simple Memory Component

A memory component that can store data values has one input channel i and one output channel o. Let D be a set of data and ® denote the request signal. We define a behavior f for such a component with one input channel i and one output channel o of sort

$$M = D \cup \{®\}$$

by the equations (let e, d ∈ D):

$$f \triangleleft i{:}d \triangleleft i{:}® = o{:}d \triangleleft f \triangleleft i{:}d \qquad \text{(Read value equation)}$$

$$f \triangleleft i{:}d \triangleleft i{:}e = f \triangleleft i{:}e \qquad \text{(Write value equation)}$$

By these algebraic equations the behavior function f is only loosely specified since nothing is fixed about the behavior of the function

$$f \triangleleft i{:}®.$$

A state diagram description of our example is given in Fig. 2. The node of the state transition diagram denotes a state represented by the behavior f ◁ i:d. Each equation corresponds to a transition with an input pattern separated by the symbol "/" from the corresponding output pattern followed by a statement that specifies the associated state change. A more detailed explanation of state transition diagrams will be given in section 8. □

$$i{:}e \, / \, - \, \{d := e\}$$

$$f \triangleleft i{:}d$$

$$i{:}® \, / \, o{:}d$$

Fig. 2 State diagram description of the memory component

The example shows a classical algebraic specification style for the description of reactive systems.

4 The Algebra of Specifications

A system behavior is specified by a predicate Q that characterizes a set of behaviors represented by stream processing functions. Formally, we have

$$Q : ((I \to M^\omega) \to (O \to M^\omega)) \to \mathbb{B}$$

We can think about the predicate Q in the following also as a set of functions. As it is well-known, all operations on functions can be extended to sets of functions and therefore to specifications by applying them pointwise to the elements in this set. We write

$$Q \triangleleft x{:}m$$

for the specification of the set of functions that we obtain from the set of functions described by the predicate Q by applying the operation to each of these functions. This corresponds to the following formal definition of the predicate

$$Q \triangleleft x{:}m \equiv \lambda f : \exists f' : Q.f' \wedge f = f' \triangleleft x{:}m$$

According to this definition the specification

$$Q \triangleleft x{:}m$$

characterizes all behaviors f for which there is a behavior f' with Q.f' such that f behaves like f' after it has received the message m on channel x.

In analogy we write

$$x{:}m \triangleleft Q$$

for the specification (the predicate) characterized by the following equation:

$$x{:}m \triangleleft Q \equiv \lambda f : \exists f' : Q.f' \wedge f = x{:}m \triangleleft f'$$

According to this definition the specification

$$x{:}m \triangleleft Q$$

characterizes all behaviors f for which there is a behavior f' with Q.f' such that f behaves like the function f' after producing the message m on the output channel x.

The transitions

$$\lambda Q: Q \triangleleft x{:}m$$

and

$$\lambda Q: x{:}m \triangleleft Q$$

define algebraic operators on specifications. We call these operators again *input* and *output transitions*.

If a component described by a specification has only one input and one output channel (which need not be named by channel identifiers then) we write

$$Q \triangleleft m$$

and

$$m \triangleleft Q$$

without explicitly referring to the channel with the meaning as explained above[1].

Our notation of input and output transitions is simply extended from messages $m \in M$ to finite nonempty sequences $s \in M^*$ of messages by the definitions

$$Q \triangleleft (\langle m \rangle {}^{\frown} s) = (Q \triangleleft m) \triangleleft s$$

$$Q \triangleleft c{:}(\langle m \rangle {}^{\frown} s) = (Q \triangleleft c{:}m) \triangleleft c{:}s$$

$$Q \triangleleft \langle\rangle = Q \triangleleft c{:}\langle\rangle = Q$$

where $m \in M$. In analogy we extend our notation to sequences of output transitions and write $s \triangleleft Q$ and $c{:}s \triangleleft Q$ resp.

5 Recursive Equations for Specifications

Using the operators on specifications introduced above we can write axiomatic equations for specifications. Besides the operators introduced explicitly above we can also use all logical connectors for composing specifications since specifications formally are nothing but predicates. Since the set of predicates forms a complete lattice the treatment of recursion is straightforward.

Often we are interested in recursive specifications for predicates Q using equations like

$$Q \equiv \psi(Q)$$

where ψ is an implication monotonic (inclusion monotonic if we think about predicates as sets) operator on specifications. Then we can work with well-known concepts from μ-calculus.

We write

$$Q: [\,\psi(Q)\,]$$

for the weakest specification (the weakest predicate) called Q that fulfills the equation

$$Q \equiv \psi(Q).$$

This property of the specification of Q can be formally expressed by the following two axioms:

---

[1] This notation can also be used in cases of sorted channels for messages the sorts of which identify the channel uniquely.

$$Q: [\psi(Q)] \Rightarrow Q \equiv \psi(Q) \qquad \text{(fixpoint property)}$$

$$Q: [\psi(Q)] \wedge (R \Rightarrow \psi(R)) \Rightarrow (R \Rightarrow Q) \qquad \text{(least fixpoint)}$$

These two axioms can be used to prove properties about the specification of the predicate Q by Q: $[\psi(Q)]$. In classical λ-notation the proposition

$$Q: [\psi(Q)]$$

stands for

$$Q = \mathbf{fix}\ \lambda\ Q: \psi(Q)$$

Now we are ready to give a first example of a specification using our algebraic specification formalism.

Example: Unbounded Buffer
We describe the buffer by a specification. A buffer has one input line and one output line. It receives data messages that are to be buffered and request signals ® that indicate that a buffered data element is to be sent back. A buffer (an interactive queue) is specified by Q as described in the following formula:

$$Q: [\forall\ x \in D^*, d \in D: Q \triangleleft d \triangleleft x \triangleleft ® = d \triangleleft Q \triangleleft x]$$

The specification essentially expresses that if a buffer receives the data message d and afterwards a finite number of data messages x and then the request signal ® this is equivalent to a buffer that sends at first the data message d and then receives the sequence of messages x.

Note the difference between the specification above and the following one which works with an equation for the deterministic behaviors:

$$R.f \equiv \forall\ x \in D^*, d \in D: f \triangleleft d \triangleleft x \triangleleft ® = d \triangleleft f \triangleleft x$$

Of course, we have

$$R \Rightarrow Q$$

since

$$R.f \Rightarrow \forall\ x \in D^*, d \in D: f \triangleleft d \triangleleft x \triangleleft ® = d \triangleleft f \triangleleft x$$

and by the least fixpoint property of Q we obtain Q.f. However, we do not have

$$Q \Rightarrow R$$

since there exist functions f with Q.f for which we do not have

$$f \triangleleft d \triangleleft ® \triangleleft ® = d \triangleleft f \triangleleft ®$$

which certainly holds for all functions in R. So R is less underspecified than Q is. A specification R' more liberal than R is obtained by the declaration

$$R': [R'.f \equiv \forall\ x \in D^*, d \in D: f \triangleleft d \triangleleft x \triangleleft ® \in d \triangleleft R' \triangleleft x]$$

The weakest predicate that fulfills this specification is equivalent to Q. However, the description of R' is again recursive, while the specification of R is not. □

To demonstrate the flexibility of our specification method we also describe a stack using algebraic techniques.

Example: A Reactive Stack
A stack is specified by the specification S defined by the following formula:

$$S: [\forall\ x \in D^*, d \in D: S \triangleleft x \triangleleft d \triangleleft ® = d \triangleleft S \triangleleft x] \qquad □$$

Both specifications S and Q of the examples above are highly underspecified[2], since nothing is said about the behavior in cases where the input does not conform to the given

---

[2] A component with specification Q is called *underspecified* or *nondeterministic* if there exist more than one function that fulfills Q.

input pattern. Thus in both cases the behavior is not fixed when the input stream starts with a request. In such cases the component may show any behavior. We speak of a *chaotic behavior*, which is an extreme case of underspecification.

It is more difficult to specify nondeterministic systems that do not have a chaotic but a more specific but nevertheless highly nondeterministic behavior for certain input by our algebraic specification technique. For instance, for a given input, a component may react by sending one of two possible messages. Let us study this in a small example.

Example: Unreliable Lossy Buffer with Acknowledgments
If we send a message to the unreliable buffer it answers with an acknowledgment that may be positive (indicated by the signal @) or negative (indicated by the signal ®). If it is negative this expresses that the message was lost. This behavior is described by the following equations:

$$Q \triangleleft d \equiv \circledR \triangleleft Q \vee @ \triangleleft R(d)$$

$$R(d) \triangleleft \circledR \equiv \circledR \triangleleft R(d) \vee d \triangleleft Q$$

Here R(d) is an auxiliary specification of a component parameterized by d. We do not express any fairness assumptions that way, however.   □

So far, we have worked with equations between specifications defining sets of behaviors. Sets of behaviors are used to model nondeterminism as well as underspecification. Through an execution one behavior is selected. There are two extreme techniques to select such a behavior. One extreme is to choose one behavior in advance before the first input arrives. The other extreme is to do the nondeterministic choices step by step only when reaction by output enforces such choices. This second strategy may be called *delayed choice* while the first one is called a *prophecy strategy*.

The prophecy technique can also be used in specifications. Then we write formulas that refer to single deterministic behaviors.

Example: Fairness Specified with the Help of Prophecies
We may express the fairness conditions for the unreliable buffer using prophecies by negative conditions as follows:

$$Q.f \Rightarrow \neg \forall \ i \in \mathbb{1}: f \triangleleft d^i \in \circledR^i \triangleleft Q$$

$$R(d).f \Rightarrow \neg \forall \ i \in \mathbb{1}: f \triangleleft \circledR^i \in \circledR^i \triangleleft R(d)$$

These two equations express that the buffer cannot always react with a reject signal to input but eventually accepts input. These negative condition can be replaced by positive conditions using an existential quantifier:

$$Q.f \Rightarrow \exists \ i \in \mathbb{1}: f \triangleleft d^{i+1} \in \circledR^i \triangleleft @ \triangleleft R(d)$$

$$R(d).f \Rightarrow \exists \ i \in \mathbb{1}: f \triangleleft \circledR^{i+1} \in \circledR^i \triangleleft d \triangleleft Q$$

This is, in combination with the equations above for Q and R(d), logically equivalent to the formulation of the fairness properties above with the negative conclusion.   □

The problem of fairness occurs only when describing underspecified or nondeterministic components, of course. In the case of nondeterministic behaviors, we do not only use equations but also implications. We demonstrate this technique by specifying a lossy one element buffer.

Example: Specification of the Unreliable Buffer by Implication
The unreliable buffer can be specified with the help of an implication as follows:

$$\tilde{Q}: [\forall \ d \in D: \exists \ i, j \in \mathbb{1}: Q \triangleleft d^{i+1} \triangleleft \circledR^{j+1} \Leftarrow \circledR^i \triangleleft @ \triangleleft \circledR^j \triangleleft d \triangleleft \tilde{Q}] \ (*)$$

Unfortunately this specification does not really express what we intend to. Let us consider $Q \triangleleft d^{i+1} \triangleleft \circledR^{j+1}$; for some behaviors of Q we actually get $\circledR^i \triangleleft @ \triangleleft \circledR^j \triangleleft d$ as output for this specification but for other behaviours this is not true. So the specifying formula (*) is too narrow. We have to use prophecies, again.

For every behavior f with Q.f we assume that there exist numbers $i, j \in \mathbb{1}$ such that

$$f \cdot d^{i+1} \cdot \textcircled{R}^{j+1} \in \textcircled{R}^i \cdot @ \cdot \textcircled{R}^j \cdot d \cdot Q$$

This is perhaps the most concise specification of Q if we in addition specify that every input triggers exactly one output. From this specification we can conclude the equations for Q and R(d) used in the specification above by the prefix monotonicity of the functions involved. □

Using logical operators we may compose a specification of a number of specifications expressing the required properties. Of course, all logical operators are understood to be applied pointwise.

Example: Unreliable Buffer and Driver
In the following F(d) is a parameterized auxiliary specification. We combine equational behavior specifications and prophecies as described above and get the following specification.

$$Q: \quad [\exists F: F: [\forall d \in D: Q \cdot d \equiv @ \cdot F(d) \vee \textcircled{R} \cdot Q \wedge$$
$$F(d) \cdot \textcircled{R} \equiv (d \cdot Q \vee \textcircled{R} \cdot F(d)) \wedge$$
$$\textcircled{R}^\infty \notin Q \cdot d^\infty \wedge$$
$$\textcircled{R}^\infty \notin F(d) \cdot \textcircled{R}^\infty]]$$

Another example for the usage of algebraic techniques is the specification of a driver component V. The driver has two input channels x and y. On x it receives data messages that it repeatedly sends on its output channel as long as it gets on its input line y the negative acknowledgment ®. If it gets a positive acknowledgment @ it continues by sending the next message received on the channel x:

$$V: [\exists W: W: [\forall m \in M: \quad V \cdot x{:}m \equiv m \cdot W(m)$$
$$W(m) \cdot y{:}\textcircled{R} \equiv m \cdot W(m)$$
$$W(m) \cdot y{:}@ \equiv V]$$

For the driver, we need no fairness assumptions. □

As we demonstrated, we can express fairness with the help of prophecies and negative conditions that rule out certain unintended behaviors. Of course, negative conditions are more difficult to handle. In particular, they may lead to inconsistencies. To avoid such inconsistencies, we may also include fairness by encoding prophecies into the state. However, this is much more difficult to express in all details and less abstract.

Example: Fairness by Prophecies as Part of the State
To express fairness conditions we add prophecy parameters to our specifications. As an example we specify the unreliable one element buffer. We specify the component P(k) that formalizes the behavior of the empty buffer. Here k is the prophecy that determines how often the buffer replies by the reject signal ® to data input. R(d, n) denotes the one-element buffer that is full. It contains the data element d. The number n determines how often the buffer responds to a read signal ® by the reject signal until it produces the data element d as output.

$$P(0) \cdot d \equiv \exists n: R(d, n)$$
$$P(n+1) \cdot d \equiv \textcircled{R} \cdot P(n)$$
$$R(d, 0) \cdot \textcircled{R} \equiv d \cdot \exists n: P(n)$$
$$R(d, n+1) \cdot \textcircled{R} \equiv \textcircled{R} \cdot R(d, n)$$

Here n is the prophecy part of the state that fixes the number of reject signals that are sent. We can hide the prophecy n in the specification P(n) by existential quantification. By

$$\exists n: P(n)$$

we denote the specification of the empty unreliable one element buffer. □

We have to choose a specific mechanism to encode fairness by prophecies in any case. This is demonstrated by the example above. We have basically three options to deal with fairness. The first two work with prophecies. We either include prophecies into the state or talk about deterministic behaviors. In both cases we use existential quantification. The third option is to work with negation.

Example: Merge component
Using the algebraic specification technique the specification of the nondeterministic merge that has two input channels x and y and one output channel and maps its input stream onto an output stream can be written as follows

$$Q ‹ x{:}m ‹ y{:}n \equiv n ‹ Q ‹ x{:}m \lor m ‹ Q ‹ y{:}n$$

This equation does not introduce any fairness conditions. We can express fairness for channels x by an additional property

$$f \in Q \Rightarrow \forall s \in M^\infty{:} \exists i \in \mathbb{N}{:} \; f ‹ x{:}m ‹ y{:}s \in s[1{:}i] ‹ m ‹ Q ‹ y{:}s[i{+}1{:}\infty[$$

Here for $s \in M^\infty$ we denote by $s[i{:}j]$ the sequence of elements $s_i, s_{i+1}, ..., s_j$. This way nonfair behaviors are excluded. □

The examples above show the power and the flexibility of the algebraic specification technique for reactive systems.

6 Composition

So far we have studied basic operations on specifications that correspond to communication (input and output transitions) and to the logical connectives that allow us to combine properties. In this section, we define two basic operations on components, namely *parallel composition* and *feedback* (for a more careful treatment of these forms of composition see [Broy 87a]). These operations are sufficient to form all kinds of data flow nets. Although we consider these operations rather as combining forms for components but as connectors for combining properties, they can nevertheless be defined by logical connectors on the predicates representing the specifications.

Besides parallel composition and feedback, we introduce a hiding operator for the channels of a component. Formally, it is also an operation on predicates.

So far we have only used classical logical connectives such as conjunction, disjunction, implication and quantification besides the basic operations on components that work with message exchange as introduced above. Now we show how we may compose components by parallel composition. Given two components C_1 and C_2 with (recall that Out was defined in section 2 and denotes the set of output channels of a component) disjoint sets of output channels as indicated by the formula

$$Out(C_1) \cap Out(C_2) = \emptyset$$

we denote their *parallel composition* by the formula:

$$C_1 \parallel C_2$$

The requirement that the sets of output channels are disjoint simplifies the algebraic treatment of components. In a more sophisticated approach we can drop this restriction. Then we assume that in the parallel composition of components with overlapping sets of output channels the output on those channels is merged.

We define the input and output channel of the component obtained by parallel composition by the following equations:

$$Out(C_1 \parallel C_2) \quad = \quad Out(C_1) \cup Out(C_2)$$
$$In(C_1 \parallel C_2) \quad = \quad In(C_1) \cup In(C_2)$$

Besides parallel composition we work with feedback. It allows us to use the output of a component on its output channel y as input for its input channel x. For channels $x \in In(C)$

and $y \in Out(C)$ we write

$$\mu_x^y C$$

for the *feedback* of the output from the channel y to the input channel x (without hiding the channel y, but of course hiding the channel x). A graphical explanation of feedback is given in Fig. 3.

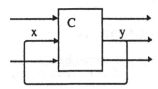

Fig. 3 Feedback for the component C from the output channel y to the input channel x

We define therefore

$$In(\mu_x^y C) \quad = \quad In(C) \setminus \{x\}$$
$$Out(\mu_x^y C) \quad = \quad Out(C)$$

We may drop an input or output line x by hiding the corresponding channel. To do that we write

$$C \setminus \{x\}$$

We define

$$In(C\setminus\{x\}) = In(C) \setminus \{x\}$$
$$Out(C\setminus\{x\}) = Out(C) \setminus \{x\}$$

Sometimes it is useful to rename channels. We write $\rho_y^x C$ to rename the channel y in the component described by C to x. We define

$$In(\rho_y^x C) = (In(C) \setminus \{y\}) \cup \{x\}$$
$$Out(\rho_y^x C) = (Out(C) \setminus \{y\}) \cup \{x\}$$

If $x \in In(C)$ then

$$\rho_y^x C$$

is a component which "contains the input channel x twice". In other words, it takes two copies of the stream x as input. This is no problem as long as the sorts of the channels coincide. If $x \in Out(C)$ then

$$\rho_y^x C$$

is a component with two different output channels with the same name. This leads to an inconsistency and is therefore forbidden.

The algebraic laws of renaming are very simple and straightforward: Let z, z', y, x be pairwise distinct channel identifiers and $x \notin Out(C) \cup Out(C_1) \cup Out(C_2)$:

$$\rho_y^x C = C \qquad\qquad\qquad \Leftarrow x \notin In(C) \cup Out(C)$$
$$(\rho_y^x C) \langle z{:}m = \rho_y^x (C \langle z{:}m)$$
$$\rho_y^x (z{:}m \langle C) = z{:}m (\rho_y^x C)$$
$$\rho_y^x (C_1 \| C_2) = (\rho_y^x C_1) \| (\rho_y^x C_2)$$
$$(\rho_y^x C) \langle x{:}m = \rho_y^x (C \langle y{:}m) \qquad \Leftarrow x \notin In(C)$$
$$(\rho_y^x C) \langle x{:}m = \rho_y^x (C \langle x{:}m \langle y{:}m) \qquad \Leftarrow x \in In(C)$$

$$\rho_y^x (y{:}m \triangleleft C) = x{:}m \triangleleft \rho_y^x C$$
$$\rho_y^x \mu_z^y C = \mu_z^x \rho_y^x C$$
$$\rho_y^x \mu_y^z C = \mu_x^z \rho_y^x C$$
$$\rho_y^x \mu_{z'}^z C = \mu_{z'}^z \rho_y^x C$$

These rules are rather straightforward. Therefore we do not explain and motivate them.

7 The Calculus of Specifications

Algebraic formalisms can nicely be described by equational axioms. We use the following rules (let x, y and z be distinct identifiers for channels and C_1 and C_2 have disjoint sets of output channels) as axioms:

$C \triangleleft x{:}m$	$=$	$C \quad \Leftarrow x \notin In(C)$
$(C_1 \parallel C_2) \triangleleft x{:}m$	$=$	$(C_1 \triangleleft x{:}m) \parallel (C_2 \triangleleft x{:}m)$
$(x{:}m \triangleleft C_1) \parallel C_2$	$=$	$x{:}m \triangleleft (C_1 \parallel C_2)$
$C_1 \parallel C_2$	$=$	$C_2 \parallel C_1$
$(\mu_x^y C) \triangleleft z{:}m$	$=$	$\mu_x^y (C \triangleleft z{:}m)$
$\mu_x^y (z{:}m \triangleleft C)$	$=$	$z{:}m \triangleleft \mu_x^y C$
$\mu_x^y y{:}m \triangleleft C$	$=$	$y{:}m \triangleleft \mu_x^y (C \triangleleft x{:}m)$
$\mu_y^x (Q \parallel D)$	$=$	$(\mu_y^x Q) \parallel D$ if $x \notin In(D)$ and $y \notin Out(D)$
$C \triangleleft x{:}m_1 \triangleleft z{:}m_2$	$=$	$C \triangleleft z{:}m_2 \triangleleft x{:}m_1$
$x{:}m_1 \triangleleft z{:}m_2 \triangleleft C$	$=$	$z{:}m_2 \triangleleft x{:}m_1 \triangleleft C$

The last two equations are called the rules of *asynchrony*. There is no causal relationship for messages on different channels. These rules of asynchrony have to be dropped as laws if we consider timed streams where the timing of the messages and thus the relative timing of messages on different input streams can be expressed.

The equations define a process algebra. We do not give a more careful analysis of this algebra. Such an analysis can be found in [Broy, Stefanescu 95]. The algebraic laws give an axiomatization of our operations in terms of communication actions. They allow us to do proofs about specifications. Furthermore they can be used as a basis for an operational semantics and therefore for an interpreter that executes such specifications.

8 Relation to State Transition Diagrams

State transition systems are a well-known and well-accepted concept for describing the behavior of components in systems engineering (see for instance [Lynch, Tuttle 87] and [Lynch, Stark 89]). Every algebraic equation or logical implication as introduced above can be seen as the description of a transition of a state machine. It is interesting that in a state machine, equations and implications are represented both by one arc. It is helpful in the understanding of systems to visualize equations by clear means. Therefore we represent for instance the transition equation

$$Q \triangleleft m \equiv y_1 \triangleleft Q_1 \vee y_2 \triangleleft Q_2$$

by the multitarget arc as shown in Fig. 4. Vice versa we may translate diagrams into equations by this correspondence.

Using this technique of interacting state transition diagrams we may translate algebraic specifications of reactive systems into state transition diagrams and vice versa. The translation of state transition diagrams to algebraic equations is straightforward according to the rules mentioned above.

In diagrams we use states represented by little circles that correspond to specifications. Therefore we label states by specifications. We label arrows by input and output events corresponding to channels and messages.

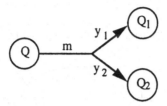

Fig. 4 Multitarget Arc

It is more common to represent the transitions by two independent arcs in this case as shown in Fig. 5.

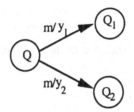

Fig. 5 State Transition Diagram with Two Transitions

This state transition diagram corresponds rather to two specifying formulas that have to be written by implications instead of equations

$$Q \cdot m \Leftarrow y_1 \cdot Q_1$$

$$Q \cdot m \Leftarrow y_1 \cdot Q_2$$

Note, however, that a state transition diagram always includes a closed world assumption corresponding to the statement "and no further transitions".

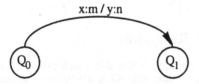

Fig. 6 State Transition

The state transition given in Fig. 6 corresponds to the specification

$$Q_0 \cdot x{:}m \Leftarrow y{:}n \cdot Q_1$$

or expressed with the help of prophecies:

$$\forall f_1 : Q_1.f_1 \Rightarrow \exists f_0 : Q_0.f_0 \wedge f_0 \cdot x{:}m = y{:}n \cdot f_1$$

If we know, in addition, that there is no other arrow labeled by x:m as input we even work with the equation

$$Q_0 \cdot x{:}m = y{:}n \cdot Q_1$$

This expresses basically the closed world assumption that for the input m on the channel x only one reaction is possible.

Example: One-element Buffer

The algebraic specification of the one-element buffer is given in section 5 by the equations

$$Q \cdot d \equiv R(d)$$

$$R(d) \cdot ® \equiv d \cdot Q$$

This corresponds to the state transition diagram given in Fig. 7.　　　　　　　　□

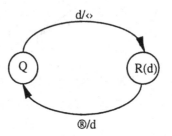

Fig. 7 Transition Diagram

If there are several transitions labeled with the input pattern x:m we may translate the transitions into the equation:

$$Q_0 \cdot x{:}m \equiv \bigwedge_{i=1}^{k} y_i{:}m_i \cdot Q_i \qquad (*)$$

If for an input pattern a transition is missing, the behavior is unspecified for such an input. Therefore it is not appropriate to interpret transitions by the formula

$$\bigwedge_{i=1}^{k} (Q_0 \cdot x{:}m \Leftarrow y_i.m_i \cdot Q_i)$$

Since in the case of this formula the weakest specification for Q_0 is true. This does not hold for the interpretation above. This illustrates that a state transition description always corresponds to a number of implications and a closed world assumption. A more detailed treatment is given in [Broy 96].

9 Incorporation of Real Time

In this section, we extend our approach to the specification of real time properties by using a specific message $\sqrt{}$ called a time tick. Since we assume a global time for all channels we assume that a time tick message comes "at the same time" on all channels. For a specification Q we write

$$Q \cdot \sqrt{}$$

to denote the behavior described by the predicate Q provided in the first time interval (the end of which is indicated by the time tick $\sqrt{}$) there do not arrive any messages. In analogy, we use the notation

$$\sqrt{} \cdot Q$$

If we write

$$Q \cdot c{:}m \cdot \sqrt{}$$

this denotes the behavior of the component where in the first interval only on channel c the message m is received and no further messages.

Example: Timer

A timer is a component $T(k)$ that receives the messages set(n) with k, $n \in \mathbb{N}$ to set the timer and the message ® to reset the timer. $T(0)$ is the unset timer. If the time set is over, the timer sends a timeout message:

$$T(0) \cdot \sqrt{} = \sqrt{} \cdot T(0)$$

$$T(n) \cdot set(k) = T(k)$$

$$T(1) \cdot \sqrt{} = \sqrt{} \cdot timeout \cdot T(0)$$

$$T(k+1) \cdot \sqrt{} = \sqrt{} \cdot T(k) \qquad \Leftarrow k > 0$$

$$T(k) \cdot \circledR = T(0) \qquad\qquad\qquad\qquad \Box$$

Since we assume that time tick signal $\sqrt{}$ arrives on all channels the rule of asynchrony does not hold for messages separated by $\sqrt{}$. In other words, in general, we have

$$Q \cdot x{:}m_1 \cdot \sqrt{} \cdot y{:}m_2 \neq Q \cdot y{:}m_2 \cdot \sqrt{} \cdot x{:}m_1$$

even in cases where x and y denote different channels. We show by a second example how to specify time dependent components.

Example: Time Out

A component with one input channel and one output channel that transmits a message provided it arrives twice before a timeout occurs is specified by the following equations (let $m \neq \sqrt{}$)

$$Q \cdot m \cdot m \cdot \sqrt{} = \sqrt{} \cdot m \cdot Q$$

$$Q \cdot m \cdot \sqrt{} = Q \cdot \sqrt{}$$

$$Q \cdot \sqrt{} = \sqrt{} \cdot Q$$

So far nothing is said what happens if other patterns of input occur. They are covered by (let m_1, m_2, $m_3 \neq \sqrt{}$) the following equations

$$Q \cdot m_1 \cdot m_2 \cdot \sqrt{} = \sqrt{} \cdot \circledR \cdot Q \qquad \Leftarrow m_1 \neq m_2$$

$$Q \cdot m_1 \cdot m_2 \cdot m_3 = Q \cdot m_1 \cdot m_3$$

The second equation indicates that a message is also forwarded if the last message that is received before the time tick repeats it. $\qquad\qquad\qquad\qquad\qquad\qquad \Box$

Of course we need additional assumptions about the time flow to get a proper formalization of time properties. We do not go deeper into the question of formalizing time. For a more careful treatment see [Broy 83] and [Broy 93].

10 Conclusion

Algebraic equations for components provide a powerful and useful technique for the specification of systems. They can be used in addition to the specification techniques of FOCUS that are based on predicate logic. They complement and extend these specification techniques that are based on classical higher order predicate logic. They, on the other hand, are the mathematical basis for state transition diagram descriptions.

Algebraic equations for specifications of reactive systems can often be interpreted as recursive definitions of systems. This gives some operational flavor and allows us to express and even to generate algorithmic executions. In addition, algebraic techniques form a bridge to state transition systems and state transition diagrams.

The approach that we have introduced above can be extended to treat dynamic systems with channel creation and channel deletion and with component ("object") creation and deletion along the lines of [Milner et al. 92], [Grosu 94], [Broy 95] and [Grosu et al. 95].

FOCUS provides a powerful theory and method of refinement (see [Broy, Stølen 94]) which has a very algebraic flavor that can be combined with the algebraic specification techniques.

Appendix A0: Mathematical Basis

Throughout this paper interactive systems are supposed to communicate asynchronously through unbounded FIFO channels. Streams are used to denote histories of communications on channels. Given a set M of messages, a *stream* over M is a finite or infinite sequence of elements from M. By M^* we denote the finite sequences over M. M^* includes the empty stream that is denoted by ◇.

By M^∞ we denote the infinite streams over the set M. M^∞ can be represented by the total mappings from the natural numbers $I\!I$ into M. We denote the set of all streams over the set M by M^ω. Formally we have

$$M^\omega = M^* \cup M^\infty.$$

We introduce a number of functions on streams that are useful in system descriptions.

A classical operation on streams is the *concatenation* that we denote by ˆ. The concatenation is a function that takes two streams (say s and t) and produces a stream sˆt as result, starting with the stream s and continuing with the stream t. Formally the concatenation has the following functionality:

$$\hat{\ } : M^\omega \times M^\omega \to M^\omega .$$

If the stream s is infinite, then concatenating the stream s with a stream t yields the stream s again:

$$s \in M^\infty \Rightarrow s\hat{\ }t = s .$$

Concatenation is associative and has the empty stream ◇ as its neutral element:

$$r\hat{\ }(s\hat{\ }t) = (r\hat{\ }s)\hat{\ }t, \qquad\qquad ◇\hat{\ }s = s = s\hat{\ }◇ .$$

For any message $m \in M$ we denote by ‹m› the one element stream consisting of the element m.

On the set M^ω of streams we define a *prefix ordering* ⊑. We write s ⊑ t for streams s and t if s is a *prefix* of t. Formally we have

$$s \sqsubseteq t \quad \text{iff} \quad \exists r \in M^\omega : s\hat{\ }r = t .$$

The prefix ordering defines a partial ordering on the set M^ω of streams. If s ⊑ t, then we also say that s is an *approximation* of t. The set of streams ordered by ⊑ is complete in the sense that every directed set $S \subseteq M^\omega$ of streams has a *least upper bound* denoted by lub S. A nonempty subset S of a partially ordered set is called *directed*, if

$$\forall\, x, y \in S: \exists z \in S: x \sqsubseteq z \wedge y \sqsubseteq z .$$

By least upper bounds of directed sets of finite streams we may describe infinite streams. Infinite streams are also of interest as (and can also be described by) fixpoints of prefix monotonic functions. The streams associated with feedback loops in interactive systems correspond to such fixpoints.

A *stream processing function* is a function

$$f: M^\omega \to N^\omega$$

that is *prefix monotonic* and *continuous*. Stream processing functions model data flow components (see [Kahn, MacQueen 77], [Park 80] and [Park 83]). The function f is called *prefix monotonic*, if for all streams s and t we have

$$s \sqsubseteq t \ \Rightarrow\ f.s \sqsubseteq f.t .$$

For better readability we often write for the function application f.x instead of f(x). A prefix monotonic function f is called *prefix continuous*, if for all directed sets $S \subseteq M^\omega$ of streams we have

$$\text{f.lub } S = \text{lub } \{f.s: s \in S\} .$$

If a function is prefix continuous, then its results for infinite input can be already determined from its results on all finite approximations of the input.

We denote the function space of (n,m)-ary prefix continuous stream processing functions by

$$[(M^\omega)^n \to (M^\omega)^m]$$

The operations ft and rt are prefix monotonic and continuous, whereas concatenation $\hat{}$ as defined above is prefix monotonic and continuous only in its second argument.

References

[Broy 83]
M. Broy: Applicative Real Time Programming. In: Information Processing 83, IFIP World Congress, Paris 1983, North Holland Publ. Company 1983, 259-264

[Broy 85]
M. Broy: Specification and Top Down Design of Distributed Systems. In: H. Ehrig et al. (eds.): Formal Methods and Software Development. Lecture Notes in Computer Science 186, Springer 1985, 4-28, Revised version in JCSS 34:2/3, 1987, 236-264

[Broy 86]
M. Broy: A Theory for Nondeterminism, Parallelism, Communication and Concurrency. Habilitation, Fakultät für Mathematik und Informatik der Technischen Universität München, 1982, Revised version in: Theoretical Computer Science 45 (1986) 1-61

[Broy 87a]
M. Broy: Semantics of Finite or Infinite Networks of Communicating Agents. Distributed Computing 2 (1987), 13-31

[Broy 87b]
M. Broy: Predicative Specification for Functional Programs Describing Communicating Networks. Information Processing Letters 25 (1987) 93-101

[Broy 93]
M. Broy: Functional Specification of Time Sensitive Communicating Systems. ACM Transactions on Software Engineering and Methodology 2:1, Januar 1993, 1-46

[Broy 95]
M. Broy: Equations for Describing Dynamic Nets of Communicating Systems. In: E. Astesiano, G. Reggio, A. Tarlecki (eds): Recent Trends in Data Types Specification, 10th Workshop on Specification of Abstract Data Types joint with the 5th COMPASS Workshop, S.Margherita, Italy, May/June 1994, Lecture Notes in Computer Science 906, Springer 1995, 170-187

[Broy 96]
M. Broy: The Specification of System Components by State Transition Diagrams. Technical Memo 1996

[Broy, Stefanescu 95]
M. Broy, G. Stefanescu: Algebra of Stream Processing Functions. Forthcoming paper

[Broy, Stølen 94]
M. Broy, K. Stølen: Specification and Refinement of Finite Dataflow Networks – a Relational Approach. In: Langmaack, H. and de Roever, W.-P. and Vytopil, J. (eds): Proc. FTRTFT'94, Lecture Notes in Computer Science 863, 1994, 247-267

[Dybier, Sander 88]
P. Dybier, H. Sander: A Functional Programming Approach to the Specification and

503

Verification of Concurrent Systems. Chalmers University of Technology and University of Göteborg, Department of Computer Sciences 1988

[FOCUS 94]
M. Broy, M. Fuchs, T. F. Gritzner, B. Schätz, K Spies, K Stølen: Summary of Case Studies in FOCUS - a Design Method for Distributed Systems. Technische Universität München, Institut für Informatik, TUM-I9423, Juni 1994

[Grosu 94]
R. Grosu: A Formal Foundation for Concurrent Object Oriented Programming. Ph. D. Thesis, Technische Universität München, Fakultät für Informatik, 1994

[Grosu et al. 95]
R. Grosu, K. Stølen, M. Broy: A Denotational Model for Mobile Data Flow Networks. To appear

[Kahn, MacQueen 77]
G. Kahn, D. MacQueen: Coroutines and Networks of Processes, Proc. IFIP World Congress 1977, 993-998

[Lynch, Stark 89]
N. Lynch, E. Stark: A Proof of the Kahn Principle for Input/Output Automata. Information and Computation 82, 1989, 81-92

[Lynch, Tuttle 87]
N. A. Lynch, M. R. Tuttle: Hierarchical Correctness Proofs for Distributed Algorithms. In: Proceedings of the Sixth ACM Symposium on Principles of Distributed Computing, 1987

[Milner et al. 92]
R. Milner, J. Parrow, D. Walker: A Calculus of Mobile Processes. Part i + ii, Information and Computation, 100:1 (1992) 1-40, 41-77

[Park 80]
D. Park: On the Semantics of Fair Parallelism. In: D. Björner (ed.): Abstract Software Specification. Lecture Notes in Computer Science 86, Berlin-Heidelberg-New York: Springer 1980, 504-526

[Park 83]
D. Park: The "Fairness" Problem and Nondeterministic Computing Networks. Proc. 4th Foundations of Computer Science, Mathematical Centre Tracts 159, Mathematisch Centrum Amsterdam, (1983) 133-161

[SDL 88]
Specification and Description Language (SDL), Recommendation Z. 100. Technical Report, CCITT 1988

A Model for Mobile Point-to-Point Data-flow Networks without Channel Sharing

Radu Grosu, Ketil Stølen*

Institut für Informatik, TU München, Postfach 20 24 20, D-80290 München
email:grosu,stoelen@informatik.tu-muenchen.de

Abstract. We present a fully abstract, denotational model for mobile, timed, nondeterministic data-flow networks whose components communicate in a point-to-point fashion. In this model components and networks of components are represented by sets of stream processing functions. Each stream processing function is required to be strongly guarded, generic and point-to-point. A stream processing function is strongly guarded if it is contractive with respect to the metric on streams. This property guarantees the existence of unique fix-points. Genericity is a privacy requirement specific to mobile systems. It guarantees that a function never accesses, depends on or sends a port whose name it does not already know. The point-to-point property guarantees that no port is known to more than two components: the sender and the receiver. Our model allows the description of a wide variety of networks — in particular, the description of mobile, unbounded nondeterministic networks. We demonstrate some features of our model by specifying a communication central.

1 Introduction

One of the most prominent theories for interactive computation is the theory of data-flow networks. In this theory, an interactive system is represented by a network of autonomous components communicating solely by asynchronous transmission of messages via directed channels.

A very elegant model for static, deterministic data-flow networks, whose components communicate in a point-to-point fashion, was given by Kahn in [Kah74]. Despite of its elegant foundation, this class of networks is, however, too restrictive for many practical applications. In this paper we extend Kahn's model in two directions.

Firstly, contrary to [Kah74], we model *nondeterministic* behavior. Like Park [Par83], Broy [Bro87] and Russell [Rus90], we represent nondeterministic data-flow networks by sets of stream processing functions. However, in contrast with [Par83] and [Bro87], our model is fully abstract. This is achieved by considering only sets of functions which are closed with respect to the external observations.

---

* Address of Ketil Stølen from September 1, 1996: Institute for Energy Technology, P.O.Box 173, 1751 Halden, Norway. Email:Ketil.Stoelen@hrp.no

The closure idea was used by [Rus90] for the same purpose. However, contrary to [Rus90], we use a timed model and a different notion of observation. This allows us to describe a considerably greater class of networks which includes all the fair merge components described in [PS92]. In fact, we can describe any liveness property that can be expressed in standard property-oriented specification languages for distributed systems [CM88, Lam91, BDD⁺93]. Moreover, since our model is fully abstract, we obviously avoid the expressiveness problem known as the Brock/Ackermann anomaly [BA81].

Secondly, contrary to [Kah74], and also contrary to [Par83], [Bro87] and [Rus90], we describe *dynamically reconfigurable* or *mobile* networks. The formal modeling of mobility has been a very popular research direction in recent years. However, most models published so far have been formalized mainly in operational terms. Examples of such models are the Actor Model [HBS73], the π–Calculus [EN86, MPW92], the Chemical Abstract Machine [BB90], the Rewriting Logic [Mes91] and the Higher Order CCS [Tho89]. On the contrary, our model gives a denotational formalization of mobility. As in the above models, this formalization is based on two assumptions. Firstly, ports are allowed to be passed between network components. Secondly, the components preserve privacy: their behavior cannot depend on ports they do not know. Although it is well understood how to express privacy operationally, there is less denotational understanding. Our solution is to require each stream processing function to be *generic*. This requirement can be thought of as an invariant satisfied by any mobile system. Informally speaking, the genericity property makes sure that a function never receives on, sends along or sends a port whose name "it does not already know". By "the ports it does not already know" we basically mean any port which is not in its initial interface, it has not already received, and it has not already created itself. Any port created by the function itself is assigned a "new" name taken from a set that is "private" to the component in question.

Our semantic framework is powerful enough to allow the modeling of both *point-to-point* and *many-to-many* communication. In [GS96a] we model many-to-many communication. In this paper we concentrate on point-to-point communication. By point-to-point communication we mean that no port is known to more than two components: the sender and the receiver. Some readers may wonder why we at all find point-to-point communication interesting. After all, point-to-point communication is only a special case of many-to-many communication. The main reason is that point-to-point communication allows a tight control of channel interference. In a point-to-point model the default situation is no interference at all or a very restricted form of interference. Unrestricted interference is only simulated by introducing explicit fair merge components for those channels where this is desirable. In a many-to-many model there is unrestricted interference by default. The tight control of interference in a point-to-point setting simplifies both specification (programming) and formal reasoning. Thus, our interest in point-to-point communication is methodological: we want to combine the power of nondeterminism and mobility with the simplicity of point-to-point communication.

There are basically two different variants of point-to-point communication. In the first case, the sender and the receiver of a channel remain the same during the whole lifetime of the channel. In the second case, the sender and the receiver of a channel may change. However, at any point in time a channel has not more than one sender and one receiver. In the first case there is no interference at all — two different components cannot send along the same channel. In the second case only a restricted type of interference may occur — two different components may send on the same channel, but never simultaneously. The advantage of the first alternative is its simplicity with respect to formal reasoning and understanding. The advantage of the second alternative is that many things can be expressed more directly. However, the price to pay is a more complicated model. In this paper we concentrate on the first alternative. The second alternative is investigated in [GS96b].

To keep the model simple components are not allowed to forward ports they receive on their input channels. Thus, we cannot change the communication partners of a component. However, we can build up new connections between components that are already connected. These new connections can be in the opposite directions of the already existing ones. In our opinion, this facility of building up new connections is the basic building block of mobility. It allows us to dynamically change the interfaces of components.

Although we could have formulated our semantics in a cpo context, we decided to base it on the topological tradition of *metric spaces* [dBZ82]. Firstly, we wanted to understand the exact relationship between our approach and those based on metric spaces. Secondly, the use of metric spaces seems more natural since our approach is based on infinite streams, and since our strong guardedness constraint, guaranteeing the existence of a unique fix-point, corresponds straightforwardly to contractivity.

Because of the space limitations, we assume basic knowledge of metric spaces. For more details on metric spaces we refer to the full version of the paper [GS95]. The full version also provides detailed proofs.

The rest of the paper is organized as follows. Section 2 introduces basic notions like communication histories and stream processing functions. Section 3 formalizes the privacy invariants of mobile point-to-point systems. Section 4 introduces mobile components. Section 5 is devoted to composition. Section 6 gives an example. Section 7 contains a discussion. Finally, there is a short appendix containing a metric formalization of streams and named stream tuples.

2 Basic Notions

We model interactive systems by networks of autonomous components communicating via directed channels in a *time-synchronous* and *message-asynchronous* way. Time-synchrony is achieved by using a global clock splitting the time axis into discrete, equidistant time units. Message-asynchrony is achieved by allowing arbitrary, but finitely many messages to be sent along a channel in each time unit.

2.1 Communication Histories

We model the *communication histories* of directed channels by infinite streams of finite streams of messages. Each finite stream represents the communication history within a time unit. The first finite stream contains the messages transmitted within the first time unit, the second the messages transmitted within the second time unit, and so on. Since time never halts, any complete communication history is infinite.

A message is either a *port* or a *data element*. A port is a *channel name* together with an *access right*, which is either a receive right, represented by ?, or a send right, represented by !. Let N be the set of all channel names and let $C \subseteq N$. Then $?C = \{?c \mid c \in C\}$ is the corresponding set of receive ports and $!C = \{!c \mid c \in C\}$ is the corresponding set of send ports. We also write $?!C$ for $?C \cup !C$. A data element is any message not contained in $?!N$. Let D be the set of all data elements. The set of all complete[2], and partial communication histories for a channel are then characterized by $[(D \cup ?!C)^*]$ and $((D \cup ?!C)^*)^*$, respectively. When no ambiguity occurs we use $[C^*]$ and $(C^*)^*$ as short-hands. This is justified by the convention that D is fixed.

Since ports are exchanged dynamically between network components, each component can in principle access any channel in N. For that reason we model the complete and partial input and output histories of a component by named stream tuples contained in $N \to [C^*]$ and $N \to (C^*)^*$, respectively. In the sequel we refer to named stream tuples of these signatures as *named communication histories*. Thus, each named communication history assigns a communication history to each channel name in N. The use of named communication histories is inspired by [BD92].

2.2 Guarded Functions

A *mobile, deterministic component* is modeled by a stream processing function

$$f \in (N \to [C_1^*]) \to (N \to [C_2^*])$$

mapping complete named communication histories for its input channels to complete named communication histories for its output channels. Note that if no message is communicated along an input channel within a time unit then the empty stream, represented by ϵ, occurs in the communication history for that channel. The lack of this information causes the fair merge anomaly [Kel78].

The functions process their input *incrementally* — at any point in the time, their output is not allowed to depend on future input. Functions satisfying this constraint are called *weakly guarded*. If the output they produce in time unit t, is not only independent of future input, i.e., the input received during time unit $t + 1$ or later, but also of the input received during time unit t, then they are called *strongly guarded*. Intuitively, the strongly guarded functions introduce a

---

[2] For an arbitrary set S, S^* denotes the set of all finite streams over S, and $[S]$ denotes the set of all infinite streams over S. See also the appendix.

delay of at least one time unit between input and output. The weakly guarded functions allow in addition zero-delay behavior.

For any named communication history θ, let $\theta\downarrow_j$ represent the prefix of θ of length j, i.e., the result of cutting θ after the jth time unit. Then weak and strong guardedness can be formalized as below.

Definition 1. (Guarded functions) A function $f \in (N \to [C_1{}^*]) \to (N \to [C_2{}^*])$ is weakly guarded if

$$\forall \theta, \varphi \in (N \to [C_1{}^*]), j \in \mathbb{N}: \quad \theta\downarrow_j = \varphi\downarrow_j \quad \Rightarrow \quad f(\theta)\downarrow_j = f(\varphi)\downarrow_j$$

and strongly guarded if

$$\forall \theta, \varphi \in (N \to [C_1{}^*]), j \in \mathbb{N}: \quad \theta\downarrow_j = \varphi\downarrow_j \quad \Rightarrow \quad f(\theta)\downarrow_{j+1} = f(\varphi)\downarrow_{j+1}$$

We use the arrow $\to$ to characterize sets of strongly guarded functions. The actual formulation of guardedness has been taken from [Bro95a].

A weakly guarded function is *non-expansive* and a strongly guarded function is *contractive* with respect to the metric on stream-tuples. This metric is defined in the appendix. As a consequence, by Banach's fix-point theorem, strong guardedness not only replaces the usual monotonicity and continuity constraints of domain theory but also guarantees unique fix-points of feedback loops.

In the following sections we introduce two important operators on named communication histories.

2.3 Sum

A *sum* operator takes two named communication histories as input and delivers their "sum" as output. We define both a *partial* "disjoint" sum and a *total* sum. For any $\varphi \in (N \to [C^*])$, let

$$\mathsf{act}(\varphi) = \{i \in N \mid \varphi(i) \neq \epsilon^\infty\}$$

be the set of *active* channels of φ. The partial sum $\varphi + \psi$ is defined if $\mathsf{act}(\varphi)$ is disjoint from $\mathsf{act}(\psi)$.

Definition 2. (Partial sum) Given two named stream tuples $\varphi \in (N \to [C_1{}^*])$ and $\psi \in (N \to [C_2{}^*])$ such that $\mathsf{act}(\varphi) \cap \mathsf{act}(\psi) = \emptyset$. We define their *partial sum* $\varphi + \psi$ to be the element of $N \to [(C_1 \cup C_2)^*]$ such that for all $i \in N$

$$(\varphi + \psi)(i) = \begin{cases} \psi(i) & \text{if } i \notin \mathsf{act}(\varphi) \\ \varphi(i) & \text{if } i \in \mathsf{act}(\varphi) \end{cases}$$

Note that the partial sum has no syntactic conditions assuring its well-definedness. We therefore also define a total version $\varphi \mathbin{+\mkern-8mu+} \psi$. This simplifies the use of Banach's fix-point theorem. Totalisation is achieved by defining $(\varphi \mathbin{+\mkern-8mu+} \psi)(i)$ to consist of only ϵ's from the first moment in which both $\varphi\downarrow_n$ and $\psi\downarrow_n$ are active, i.e., different from ϵ^n, the stream consisting of n ϵ's. For any stream s, by $s(n)$ we denote its nth element.

Definition 3. (Total sum) Given two named stream tuples $\varphi \in (N \to [C_1{}^*])$ and $\psi \in (N \to [C_2{}^*])$. We define their *total sum* $\varphi \mathbin{+\!\!\!+} \psi$ to be the element of $N \to [(C_1 \cup C_2)^*]$ such that for all $i \in N, n \in \mathbb{N}$

$$(\varphi \mathbin{+\!\!\!+} \psi)(i)(n) = \begin{cases} \psi(i)(n) & \text{if } \varphi(i){\downarrow}_n = \epsilon^n \\ \varphi(i)(n) & \text{if } \varphi(i){\downarrow}_n \neq \epsilon^n \wedge \psi(i){\downarrow}_n = \epsilon^n \\ \epsilon & \text{if } \varphi(i){\downarrow}_n \neq \epsilon^n \wedge \psi(i){\downarrow}_n \neq \epsilon^n \end{cases}$$

Note that $\varphi \mathbin{+\!\!\!+} \psi$ has a hiding effect if $\text{act}(\varphi) \cap \text{act}(\psi) \neq \emptyset$, and that $\varphi \mathbin{+\!\!\!+} \psi$ is equal to $\varphi + \psi$, otherwise.

Theorem 4. *The total sum operator is weakly guarded.*

Proof. The sum $(\varphi \mathbin{+\!\!\!+} \psi)(i)(n)$ depends only on $\varphi{\downarrow}_n$ and $\psi{\downarrow}_n$.

2.4 Projection

The domain of any named communication history $\theta \in N \to [C^*]$ is N, the set of all channel names. However, in connection with generic functions and network composition, we often need to restrict the visible messages in θ with respect to a history of known channel names $O \in [\mathcal{P}(N)]$. To achieve this we introduce a projection operation $\theta|_O$ which, for each time unit k, replaces the finite stream of messages received during time unit k on each channel contained in $N \setminus O(k)$ by ϵ.

Definition 5. (Projection) For any named communication history $\theta \in (N \to [C^*])$, we define its *projection* $\theta|_O$ on $O \in [\mathcal{P}(N)]$ to be the element of $N \to [C^*]$ such that for all $i \in N, k \in \mathbb{N}$

$$\theta|_O(i)(k) = \begin{cases} \theta(i)(k) & \text{if } i \in O(k) \\ \epsilon & \text{otherwise} \end{cases}$$

Theorem 6. *The projection operator is weakly guarded.*

Proof. $\theta|_O(i)(k)$ depends only on $\theta{\downarrow}_k$ and $O{\downarrow}_k$.

3 Privacy Invariants

A stream processing function $f \in (N \to [C_1{}^*]) \to (N \to [C_2{}^*])$ used to model a component is not only required to be strongly guarded, but also to be *generic* and *point-to-point*. In this section we formalize these additional properties. As already explained, they can be thought of as privacy invariants satisfied by any mobile point-to-point system.

3.1 Genericity

The *genericity* constraint requires a function to access only ports contained in the function's initial, static interface; ports already created by the function itself or ports already received by the function. Genericity can be described with respect to Figure 1, as follows.

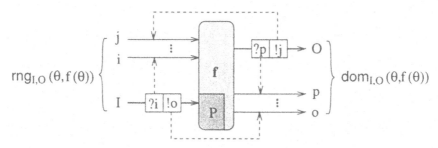

Fig. 1. Generic Stream Processing Function

Initially, each generic function receives on a designated set of input channels I and sends along a designated set of output channels O, disjoint from I. These two sets name the *static* channels or the initial wiring. To make sure that the *dynamic* channels *created* by the different components in a network have different names, each generic function is assigned a set of *private names* P. Obviously, this set should be disjoint from the static interface. Thus, we require that $(I \cup O) \cap P = \emptyset$.

During computation the sets of accessible ports gradually grow. For example, if the function receives a receive port $?i$ then it may receive on the channel i, and if it receives a send port $!o$ then it may send along the channel o. Similarly, whenever the function sends a send port $!j$, whose channel $j \in P$ it has created itself, it may later receive what is sent along j, and whenever it sends a receive port $?p$, whose channel $p \in P$ it has created itself, it may itself send messages along p which eventually are received by the component which receives the receive port.

For a given point in time n and a named input history θ, the sets of accessible input and output channels are represented by respectively $\mathrm{dom}_{I,O}(\theta, f(\theta))(n)$ and $\mathrm{rng}_{I,O}(\theta, f(\theta))(n)$. The functions $\mathrm{dom}_{I,O}$ and $\mathrm{rng}_{I,O}$ are formally defined at the end of the next section.

3.2 Point-to-Point Communication

To ensure the form of point-to-point communication investigated in this paper, the networks have to maintain the following invariant: each channel is used by *at most* two components, the *sender* and the *receiver*. As a consequence, the sender and the receiver of a channel cannot change during the lifetime of channel. This type of point-to-point communication can be captured by a few simple constraints given that we do not allow forwarding of ports. Firstly, the creator of a channel is allowed to send only one of the channel's ports. If it sends a receive port then it keeps the send port, and the other way around. Secondly, we also insist that the same port is not sent more than once. Since we also restrict received ports from being forwarded, and different components to have disjoint sets of private channels, there is no way in which more than two components can gain access to the same channel.

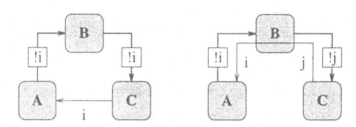

Fig. 2. Forwarding and Point-to-Point Privacy

To explain why we do not allow forwarding, let us have a careful look at a small example. Given a mobile system consisting of three components A, B and C. Assume there is a channel connecting A to B and a channel connecting B to C, but no channel connecting C to A. Now, suppose the component A creates a channel i; it keeps the receive port and sends the send port $!i$ to the component B, which again forwards $!i$ to C. We then obtain the network on the left-hand side of Figure 2. In [GS96b], where we model the more general form of point-to-point communication, we allow forwarding by constraining the functions to "forget" ports as soon as they are sent. A similar technique could have been used here. However, this would make the model more complicated. In fact, the whole advantage gained through the very restrictive communication paradigm would be lost. Since the emphasis in this paper is on a *simple* model we have chosen not to include forwarding. Nevertheless, we are able to express a nontrivial class of mobile networks.

Forwarding can be simulated *straightforwardly*, as indicated by the network on the right-hand side of Figure 2. The component B does not forward $!i$, but a send port $!j$ for a new channel j created by B. Thereafter, any data element B receives on j is forwarded along i. Hence, B "does not receive or send on i itself" — it only forwards the data elements sent by C along j. The component B in the network to the right simulates the "forget-constraint" required for the component B in the network to the left.

One may ask, how do we impose the point-to-point requirement in our model? We do that by imposing an invariant on the named communication histories. The important point to realize is that in a network, where all components have disjoint sets of private names, and where all components behave in accordance with the communication constraints imposed above, we may restrict ourselves to named communication histories in which the same port occurs only once and where two different ports are assigned different channel names. We use the arrow $\overset{u}{\to}$ to distinguish named communication histories satisfying these two *port uniqueness* constraints from other named communication histories.

Port uniqueness is preserved by projection and summation on stream tuples whose sets of channel names are disjoint. More precisely, for $\theta \in N \overset{u}{\to} [C^*]$, $\varphi \in N \overset{u}{\to} [C_1^*]$ and $\psi \in N \overset{u}{\to} [C_2^*]$ such that $C_1 \cap C_2 = \emptyset$, we have that $\theta|_O \in N \overset{u}{\to} [C^*]$ and that $\varphi \!+\!\!+ \psi \in N \overset{u}{\to} [(C_1 \cup C_2)^*]$.

As a consequence of the forwarding restriction, any port sent by a function has to belong to a channel created by the function. Moreover, since static channels are used for the initial wiring, their corresponding ports cannot be transmitted. For simplicity we split the set of names N into two disjoint sets — a set of *static* channel names S and a set of *dynamic* channel names A. Because of the above restrictions, it is enough to consider functions of the following signature

$$(N \overset{u}{\to} [\overline{P}^*]) \to (N \overset{u}{\to} [P^*])$$

where $P \subseteq A$ and $\overline{P} = A \setminus P$.

We are now ready to give the formal definitions of $\mathrm{dom}_{I,O}$ and $\mathrm{rng}_{I,O}$. In this definition, the operator $\in$ is overloaded to test for containment in a list

Definition 7. (Domain and range) Given $(I, O) \subseteq S \times S$, $P \subseteq A$, $I \cap O = \emptyset$, $\theta \in (N \overset{u}{\to} [\overline{P}^*])$ and $\delta \in (N \overset{u}{\to} [P^*])$. We define

$D_1 = I$
$R_1 = O$
$D_{n+1} = D_n \cup \bigcup_{i \in D_n} \{p \in A \mid ?p \in \theta(i)(n)\} \cup \bigcup_{i \in R_n} \{p \in A \mid !p \in \delta(i)(n)\}$
$R_{n+1} = R_n \cup \bigcup_{i \in D_n} \{p \in A \mid !p \in \theta(i)(n)\} \cup \bigcup_{i \in R_n} \{p \in A \mid ?p \in \delta(i)(n)\}$

The definitions of $\mathrm{dom}_{I,O}(\theta, \delta)$ and $\mathrm{rng}_{I,O}(\theta, \delta)$ follow immediately

$$\mathrm{dom}_{I,O}(\theta, \delta)(n) = D_n, \quad \mathrm{rng}_{I,O}(\theta, \delta)(n) = R_n$$

Theorem 8. *The functions* $\mathrm{dom}_{I,O}$ *and* $\mathrm{rng}_{I,O}$ *are strongly guarded.*

Proof. $\mathrm{dom}_{I,O}(\theta, \delta)(n)$, $\mathrm{rng}_{I,O}(\theta, \delta)(n)$ depend only on $\theta\!\downarrow_{n-1}$ and $\delta\!\downarrow_{n-1}$.

Theorem 9. *The functions* $\mathrm{dom}_{I,O}$ *and* $\mathrm{rng}_{I,O}$ *have the following properties*

$$\mathrm{dom}_{I,O}(\theta, \delta) = \mathrm{dom}_{I,O}(\theta|_{\mathrm{dom}_{I,O}(\theta, \delta)}, \delta) = \mathrm{dom}_{I,O}(\theta, \delta|_{\mathrm{rng}_{I,O}(\theta, \delta)})$$
$$\mathrm{rng}_{I,O}(\theta, \delta) = \mathrm{rng}_{I,O}(\theta|_{\mathrm{dom}_{I,O}(\theta, \delta)}, \delta) = \mathrm{rng}_{I,O}(\theta, \delta|_{\mathrm{rng}_{I,O}(\theta, \delta)})$$

Proof. By induction on the recursive definitions of $\mathrm{dom}_{I,O}$ and $\mathrm{rng}_{I,O}$.

Genericity can then be formalized as below.

Definition 10. (Generic functions) A function $f \in (N \overset{u}{\to} [\overline{P}^*]) \to (N \overset{u}{\to} [P^*])$ is *generic* with respect to the initial wiring (I, O) iff

$$\forall \theta : f(\theta) = f(\theta|_{\mathrm{dom}_{I,O}(\theta, f(\theta))}) = f(\theta)|_{\mathrm{rng}_{I,O}(\theta, f(\theta))}$$

We use the decorated arrow $\overset{I,O}{\rightarrow}$ to denote sets of strongly guarded functions that are generic with respect to the initial wiring (I, O). In the following we refer to such functions as *mobile*.

4 Mobile Components

We model a *mobile, nondeterministic component* by a set of mobile functions F. Any pair $(\theta, f(\theta))$, where $f \in F$, is a possible *behavior* of the component. Intuitively, for any input history each mobile function $f \in F$ represents one possible nondeterministic behavior. For any set of functions F we define $\mathcal{O}(F)$ to be the set of all behaviors of F, i.e., $\mathcal{O}(F) = \{(x, f(x)) \mid f \in F\}$.

Different sets of mobile functions may have the same set of behaviors. The reason is that for some sets of mobile functions we may find additional mobile functions which can be understood as combinations of the functions already in the set. For example, we may find a mobile function g which for one input history behaves as the function $f \in F$ and for another input history behaves as the function $f' \in F$, and so on. This means, a model in which a nondeterministic component is represented by an arbitrary set of mobile functions, is too distinguishing and, consequently, not fully abstract. To achieve *full abstraction* we consider only closed sets, i.e., sets F, where each combination of functions in F, which gives a mobile function, is also in F.

Definition 11. (Mobile components) A *mobile component*, with initial wiring $(I, O) \subseteq S \times S$ and private names $P \subseteq A$, where $I \cap O = \emptyset$, is a *nonempty* set of mobile functions

$$F \subseteq (N \overset{u}{\rightarrow} [\overline{P}^*]) \overset{I,O}{\rightarrow} (N \overset{u}{\rightarrow} [P^*])$$

that is *closed* in the sense that for any mobile function $f \in (N \overset{u}{\rightarrow} [\overline{P}^*]) \overset{I,O}{\rightarrow} (N \overset{u}{\rightarrow} [P^*])$

$$(\forall \theta \in N \overset{u}{\rightarrow} [\overline{P}^*] : \exists f' \in F : f(\theta) = f'(\theta)) \Rightarrow f \in F$$

It follows straightforwardly that if F_1 and F_2 are mobile components then $F_1 = F_2$ iff $\mathcal{O}(F_1) = \mathcal{O}(F_2)$. Thus, our notion of a component is fully abstract with respect to the corresponding set of behaviors. Note the relationship to [Rus90]. That our semantics is fully abstract with respect to $\mathcal{O}$ is of course trivial. Nevertheless, this notion of observation characterizes the expectations we have to a semantics dealing with time.

5 Point-to-Point Composition

We now introduce a *composition operator* $\otimes$ which allows us to compose mobile components into networks of mobile components. When observed from the outside these networks can themselves be understood as mobile components.

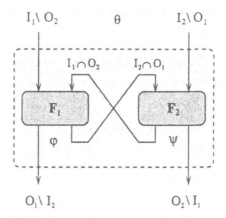

Fig. 3. Point-to-Point Composition

In the formal definition given below we use the operator for total sum. This operator allows us to exploit Banach's fix-point theorem. We later show that this operator can be replaced by the operator for partial sum.

Definition 12. (Point-to-point composition) Given two mobile components

$$F_1 \subseteq (N \xrightarrow{u} [\overline{P_1}^*]) \xrightarrow{I_1, O_1} (N \xrightarrow{u} [P_1^*]), \qquad F_2 \subseteq (N \xrightarrow{u} [\overline{P_2}^*]) \xrightarrow{I_2, O_2} (N \xrightarrow{u} [P_2^*])$$

such that $I_1 \cap I_2 = O_1 \cap O_2 = P_1 \cap P_2 = \emptyset$. Let

$$I = (I_1 \setminus O_2) \cup (I_2 \setminus O_1), \quad O = (O_1 \setminus I_2) \cup (O_2 \setminus I_1), \quad P = P_1 \cup P_2$$

The *point-to-point composition* of F_1 and F_2 is defined as follows

$$F_1 \otimes F_2 = \{f \in (N \xrightarrow{u} [\overline{P}^*]) \xrightarrow{I, O} (N \xrightarrow{u} [P^*]) \mid \forall \theta : \exists f_1 \in F_1, f_2 \in F_2 :$$
$$f(\theta) = (\varphi \leftHarpoon \psi)|_{\mathsf{rng}_{I,O}(\theta, \varphi \leftHarpoon \psi)} \text{ where}$$
$$\varphi = f_1(\delta \leftHarpoon \psi), \quad \psi = f_2(\delta \leftHarpoon \varphi), \quad \delta = \theta|_{\mathsf{dom}_{I,O}(\theta, \varphi \leftHarpoon \psi)}\}$$

Note the close correspondence between this definition and Figure 3. Any input channel of F_1 which is also an output channel of F_2, and any input channel of F_2 which is also an output channel of F_1, are connected and hidden.

Note also the role of $\mathsf{dom}_{I,O}$ and $\mathsf{rng}_{I,O}$ in maintaining privacy. If F_1 sends a private port $!p$ on a feedback channel, then only F_2 should send along p and only F_1 should receive on p. F_1 can receive on p because dom_{I_1,O_1} is automatically enlarged with p. Only F_1 can receive on p because $\mathsf{rng}_{I,O}$ automatically hides from the environment what F_2 sends along p. F_2 can send along p because rng_{I_2,O_2} is automatically enlarged with p. Only F_2 can influence F_1 via p because $\mathsf{dom}_{I,O}$ automatically hides what the environment sends along p.

Similarly, if F_1 sends a private port $?p$ on a feedback channel, then only F_2 should receive on p and only F_1 should send along p. F_2 can receive on p because dom_{I_2, O_2} is automatically enlarged with p. Only F_2 can receive on p because $rng_{I,O}$ automatically hides from the environment what F_1 sends along p. F_1 can send along p because rng_{I_1, O_1} is automatically enlarged with p. Only F_1 can influence F_2 via p because $dom_{I,O}$ automatically hides what the environment sends along p.

Theorem 13. $F_1 \otimes F_2$ *is a mobile component.*

Proof. That $F_1 \otimes F_2 \neq \emptyset$ follows from Banach's fix-point theorem and Theorem 9. Closedness follows straightforwardly.

The definition of $\otimes$ depends on the operator for total sum. This operator is a bit strange since it results in hiding when the arguments are active on the same channels. Our composition operator $\otimes$, on the other hand, should only hide the feedback channels. This means that all messages sent or received by the components along the external channels should be visible also after the composition. As a consequence, in the definition of $\otimes$ it should be possible to replace the operator for total sum by the partial one.

Theorem 14. *The operator* $\uplus$ *can be replaced by* $+$ *in the definition of* $\otimes$.

Proof. With respect to Definition 12, we have to show that

$$\mathsf{act}(\varphi) \cap \mathsf{act}(\psi) = \mathsf{act}(\varphi) \cap \mathsf{act}(\delta) = \mathsf{act}(\psi) \cap \mathsf{act}(\delta) = \emptyset$$

Since the genericity of f_1 and f_2 implies that

$$\varphi = \varphi|_{rng_{I_1, O_1}(\delta \uplus \psi, \varphi)}, \quad \psi = \psi|_{rng_{I_2, O_2}(\delta \uplus \varphi, \psi)}$$

it is enough to show that the sets $rng_{I_1, O_1}(\delta \uplus \psi, \varphi)(n)$, $rng_{I_2, O_2}(\delta \uplus \varphi, \psi)(n)$ and $dom_{I,O}(\theta, \varphi \uplus \psi)(n)$ are mutually disjoint, for all $n \in \mathbb{N}$. The proof is by induction on the recursive definition of $dom_{I,O}$ and $rng_{I,O}$. The induction hypothesis requires both the above disjointness condition and the mutual disjointness of $dom_{I_1, O_1}(\delta \uplus \psi, \varphi)(n)$, $dom_{I_2, O_2}(\delta \uplus \varphi, \psi)(n)$ and $rng_{I,O}(\theta, \varphi \uplus \psi)(n)$.

6 Communication Central

As an example we specify a communication central (see Figure 4). Its task is to build up connections between station$_1$ and station$_2$. The initial "wires" are a_1 and a_2. Station$_1$ can send ports to be connected (both receive and send) along a_1; station$_2$ can send ports to be connected (both receive and send) along a_2.

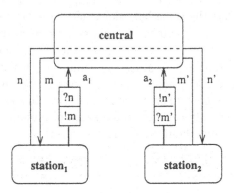

Fig. 4. Communication Central

Let $?n$ be the jth receive port sent along a_1 by station$_1$. The central is allowed to receive on n as soon as this port is received. Moreover, let $!n'$ be the jth send port sent along a_2 by station$_2$. The central is allowed to send along n' as soon as this port is received. The central "connects" these two channels by forwarding each data element in D it receives on the channel n along the channel n'. Symmetrically, if $?m'$ is the kth receive port sent along a_2 by station$_2$, and $!m$ is the kth send port sent along a_1 by station$_1$, then the data elements in D received on m' are forwarded along m.

In order to model this component, we introduce three basic operators. The first one is a *filter* operator: for any set of messages M and stream of messages s, $M \circledS s$ denotes the stream we obtain by removing any message in s that is not contained in M. The second one is a *length* operator: for any stream s, $\#s$ yields its length. This means that $\#s = \infty$ if s is infinite. Finally, we need a *time abstraction operator*: for any named communication history β, $\widehat{\beta}$ denotes the result of removing all time information in β. For any i, this is achieved by concatenating all the finite streams in $\beta(i)$ into one stream. Thus, each communication history consisting of infinitely many finite streams of messages is replaced by the result of concatenating its finite streams into one stream of messages. The timing information is thereby abstracted away.

$$\text{Central} = \{ f \in (N \xrightarrow{u} [A^*]) \xrightarrow{\{a_1,a_2\},\emptyset} (N \xrightarrow{u} [\emptyset^*]) \mid$$

$\quad \forall \alpha : f(\alpha) = \beta \quad$ where

$\qquad \forall (n,n') \in acon : \widehat{\beta}(n') = D \circledS \widehat{\alpha}(n) \quad$ -- the forwarding mechanism

$\qquad acon = con(a_1,a_2) \cup con(a_2,a_1) \quad$ -- the set of all connections

$\qquad con(a,b) = \{(n,n') \mid \quad$ -- the connections from "a to b"

$\qquad\qquad \exists k \in [1..\min\{\#\mathrm{rr}(a), \#\mathrm{wr}(b)\}] :$

$\qquad\qquad\quad \mathrm{rr}(a)(k) = ?n \ \wedge \ \mathrm{wr}(b)(k) = !n'\}$

$\qquad \mathrm{rr}(a) = ?N \circledS \widehat{\alpha}(a) \quad$ -- the set of receive ports from a

$\qquad \mathrm{wr}(b) = !N \circledS \widehat{\alpha}(b) \quad$ -- the set of send ports from b

$\}$

Note that this expression does not say anything about the timing of the output. It may be argued that the same behavior could have been obtained in a static network, where an infinite number of channels connect the stations with the central. However, in that case both the central and the stations would be allowed to observe anything that is sent along the channels. This should be contrasted with our model, where the components are allowed to access only the channels whose ports they have received or created themselves. In our opinion, it is exactly this privacy that, not only captures the essence of mobility, but also simplifies the conceptual reasoning about mobile reconfiguration.

7 Discussion

The main contribution of this paper is that we have extended a denotational model for timed, point-to-point, nondeterministic data-flow networks to handle a notion of *mobility*. Our model is fully compositional. It allows us to reason about mobility at a very abstract level. In fact, we believe our semantics is well-suited as a foundation for a method for the specification and development of mobile systems. The exact relationship between our model and other models like for instance the π-calculus [MPW92] and actor-based approaches [AMST92] is a interesting area for future research. For example, we believe that the model for many-to-many communication [GS96a] can be used to give a denotational semantics for the asynchronous π-calculus. We also believe that the actor languages can be smoothly integrated within our formalism.

Our approach is related to the work of Kok [Kok87, Kok89]. The major difference is that Kok does not deal with mobility. Moreover, his handling of nondeterminism differs from ours. In [Kok89], where he uses a metric on relations, he can basically handle only bounded nondeterminism. In [Kok87], which is not based on metric spaces, an automaton is used to generate the behaviors of basic agents. This guarantees the existence of fix-points. We use sets of strongly guarded functions for the same purpose.

[Gro94, Bro95b] give equational characterizations of dynamic reconfiguration with respect to stream processing functions.

8 Acknowledgments

The authors would like to thank Manfred Broy for many inspiring discussions on this and related topics. The first author has been financially supported by the Syslab project. The second author has been financially supported by the Sonderforschungsbereich 342 "Werkzeuge und Methoden für die Nutzung paralleler Rechnerarchitekturen".

References

[AMST92] G. Agha, I. A. Mason, S. F. Smith, and C. L. Talcott. Towards a theory of actor computation. In *Proc. CONCUR'92, Lecture Notes in Computer Science 630*, pages 565–579, 1992.

[BA81]   J. D. Brock and W. B. Ackermann. Scenarios: A model of non-determinate computation. In *Proc. Formalization of Programming Concepts, Lecture Notes in Computer Science 107*, pages 252–259, 1981.

[BB90]   G. Berry and G. Boudol. The chemical abstract machine. In *Proc. POPL'90*, pages 81–94, 1990.

[BD92]   M. Broy and C. Dendorfer. Modelling operating system structures by timed stream processing functions. *Journal of Functional Programming*, 2:1–21, 1992.

[BDD+93] M. Broy, F. Dederichs, C. Dendorfer, M. Fuchs, T. F. Gritzner, and R. Weber. The design of distributed systems — an introduction to Focus (revised version). Technical Report SFB 342/2/92 A, Technische Universität München, 1993.

[Bro87]   M. Broy. Semantics of finite and infinite networks of concurrent communicating agents. *Distributed Computing*, 2:13–31, 1987.

[Bro95a]   M. Broy. Advanced component interface specification. In *Proc. TPPP'94, Lecture Notes in Computer Science 907*, pages 369–392, 1995.

[Bro95b]   M. Broy. Equations for describing dynamic nets of communicating systems. In *Proc. 5th COMPASS Workshop, Lecture Notes in Computer Science 906*, pages 170–187, 1995.

[CM88]   K. M. Chandy and J. Misra. *Parallel Program Design, A Foundation*. Addison-Wesley, 1988.

[dBZ82]   J. W. de Bakker and J. I. Zucker. Denotational semantics of concurrency. In *Proc. 14 ACM Symposium on Theory of Computing*, pages 153–158, 1982.

[EN86]   U. Engberg and M Nielsen. A calculus of communicating systems with label-passing. Technical Report DAIMI PB-208, University of Aarhus, 1986.

[Eng77]   R. Engelking. *General Topology*. PWN — Polish Scientific Publishers, 1977.

[Gro94]   R. Grosu. *A Formal Foundation for Concurrent Object Oriented Programming*. PhD thesis, Technische Universität München, 1994. Also available as report TUM-I9444, Technische Universität München.

[GS95]   R. Grosu and K. Stølen. A denotational model for mobile point-to-point dataflow networks. Technical Report SFB 342/14/95 A, Technische Universität München, 1995.

[GS96a]   R. Grosu and K. Stølen. A denotational model for mobile many-to-many dataflow networks. To appear as technical report, Technische Universität München, 1996.

[GS96b]   R. Grosu and K. Stølen. A denotational model for mobile point-to-point dataflow networks with channel sharing. To appear as technical report, Technische Universität München, 1996.

[HBS73]   C. Hewitt, P. Bishop, and R. Steiger. A universal modular actor formalism for artificial intelligence. In *Proc. IJCAI'73*, pages 235–245, 1973.

[Kah74]   G. Kahn. The semantics of a simple language for parallel programming. In *Proc. Information Processing 74*, pages 471–475. North-Holland, 1974.

[Kel78]   R. M. Keller. Denotational models for parallel programs with indeterminate operators. In *Proc. Formal Description of Programming Concepts*, pages 337–366. North-Holland, 1978.

[Kok87]   J. N. Kok. A fully abstract semantics for data flow nets. In *Proc. PARLE'87, Lecture Notes in Computer Science 259*, pages 351–368, 1987.

[Kok89]   J. N. Kok. An iterative metric fully abstract semantics for nondeterministic dataflow. In *Proc. MFCS'89, Lecture Notes in Computer Science 379*, pages 321–331, 1989.

[Lam91] L. Lamport. The temporal logic of actions. Technical Report 79, Digital, SRC, Palo Alto, 1991.

[Mes91] J. Meseguer. Conditional rewriting logic as a unified model of concurrency. Technical Report SRI-CSL-91-05, SRI, 1991.

[MPW92] R. Milner, J. Parrow, and D. Walker. A calculus of mobile processes, part I. *Information and Computation*, 100:1–40, 1992.

[Par83] D. Park. The "fairness" problem and nondeterministic computing networks. In *Proc. 4th Foundations of Computer Science, Mathematical Centre Tracts 159*, pages 133–161. Mathematisch Centrum Amsterdam, 1983.

[PS92] P. Panangaden and V. Shanbhogue. The expressive power of indeterminate dataflow primitives. *Information and Computation*, 98:99–131, 1992.

[Rus90] J. R. Russell. On oraclizable networks and Kahn's principle. In *Proc. POPL'90*, pages 320–328, 1990.

[Tho89] B. Thomsen. A calculus of higher order communicating systems. In *Proc. POPL'89*, 1989.

A Streams and Named Stream Tuples

A *stream* is a finite or infinite sequence of elements. For any set of elements E, we use E^* to denote the set of all finite streams over E, and $[E]$ to denote the set of all infinite streams over E. For any infinite stream s, we use $s\!\downarrow_j$ to denote the prefix of s containing exactly j elements. We use ϵ to denote the empty stream.

We define the metric of streams generically with respect to an arbitrary discrete metric (E, ρ).

Definition 15. (The metric space of streams) The metric space of streams $([E], d)$ over a discrete metric (E, ρ) is defined as follows

$$[E] = \prod_{i \in \mathbb{N}} E$$
$$d(s,t) = inf\{2^{-j} \mid s\!\downarrow_j = t\!\downarrow_j\}$$

This metric is also known as the Baire metric [Eng77].

Theorem 16. *The metric space of streams $([E], d)$ is complete.*

Proof. See for example [Eng77].

A *named stream tuple* is a mapping $\theta \in (I \to [E])$ from a set of names to infinite streams. $\downarrow$ is overloaded to named stream tuples in a point-wise style, i.e., $\theta\!\downarrow_j$ denotes the result of applying $\downarrow_j$ to each component of θ.

Definition 17. (The metric space of named stream tuples) The metric space of *named stream tuples* $(I \to [E], d)$ with names in I and elements in (E, ρ) is defined as follows

$$d(s,t) = inf\{2^{-j} \mid s\!\downarrow_j = t\!\downarrow_j\}$$

where $I \to [E]$ is the set of functions from the countable set I to the metric $[E]$.

Theorem 18. *The metric space of named stream tuples $(I \to [E], d)$ is complete.*

Proof. This metric is equivalent to the Cartesian product metric $\prod_{i \in I}[E]$ which is complete because $[E]$ is [Eng77].

Coalgebraic Specifications and Models of Deterministic Hybrid Systems

Bart Jacobs

CWI, Kruislaan 413, 1098 SJ Amsterdam, The Netherlands.

Email: bjacobs@cwi.nl   Tel ++31 – 20 – 592.4008   Fax ++31 – 20 – 592.4199

Abstract. *Coalgebraic specification and semantics, as used earlier for object-oriented programming, is extended with temporal aspects. The (non-temporal) expression* s.meth *expressing that method* meth *is applied in state* s *is extended to an expression* s.meth@α, *where* α *is a time parameter. It means: in state* s *let the state evolve for* α *units of time, and then apply method* meth. *With this formalism we specify various (elementary) deterministic hybrid systems (and give a few simulations). We also define a notion of model for such a specification, and define what it means for a model to be terminal. Terminal models are "optimal" in the sense that they involve a minimal set of states, as will be illustrated in a number of examples. This shows that standard model theory can be applied to temporal (coalgebraic) specifications.*

1 Introduction

Hybrid systems combine discrete and continuous dynamics. They involve a combination of automata theory and differential equations. A typical hybrid system is a thermostat keeping the temperature in a room close to a goal temperature that can be set by a user. There are different control laws describing the temperature in the room as a function of time, depending on whether the heater is switched on or off. And if the temperature rises above the goal temperature then the heater will be switched off, and if the temperature falls below the goal, then the heater will be switched on. These discontinuities in the control law through internal actions are based on internal pre-programmed decisions. Further, the user can set a new goal temperature, causing a discontinuity as a result of an external action. Such a hybrid system can be seen as a kind of automaton, with different differential equations describing the continuous behaviour in different discrete states.

In this paper we propose a temporal specification format for (deterministic) hybrid systems that grew out of earlier work on object-oriented programming (see [16, 8, 10, 9]). This format is called "coalgebraic", because the underlying models are based on "coalgebras". These are the formal duals of algebras, in which one only has "destructors" (or "observers") as operations, instead of "constructors" in algebras. Coalgebras may be seen as abstract machines, consisting of a state space together with certain operations acting on this space. But typically, we have no means for constructing elements of the state space. Cofree coalgebras are used in [9] to describe inheritance. Here we extend this coalgebraic specification format as used for object-oriented programming with temporal aspects. We introduce a notation which allows us to indicate that a method (object-oriented terminology for operation) will be applied after a certain time delay. The new specification format of "temporal" coalgebraic specification contains assertions for reasoning both about states and about time. Thus we combine object-oriented specification with time, but we do not consider non-determinism or parallelism (at this stage). And we use assertional methods (in contrast to process algebraic methods) to describe and reason about these systems.

The additional time component in specification asks for an extension at the semantic level. We shall describe the influence of the elapse of time on a state space via a so-called "monoid action", acting on the state space. And the monoids we use are the monoids $\langle \mathbb{N}, 0, + \rangle$ and $\langle \mathbb{R}_{\geq 0}, 0, + \rangle$ of discrete and real time. Monoid actions are fundamental in system theory see e.g. [11, Definition 1.1] (the "consistency" and "composition" conditions for the state transition function of a dynamical system). They occur in the form of an "evolution function" in [13, Definition 2.1]. These monoid actions arise naturally via (unique) solutions of differential equations. A model of a temporal coalgebraic specification will consist of a coalgebra together with a monoid action. The monoid action captures the continuous dependence of attributes on time, and also the internal actions, but the external (input and output) actions are described by the coalgebra. A subtle point is what definition should be taken for "homomorphism of models". The obvious notion of both a homomorphism of monoid actions (also called an equivariant mapping, see e.g. [3, 3.2.1 and 3.2.2]) and a homomorphism of coalgebras does not work (in the sense that it does not yield the terminal characterization of the intended models). Therefore we introduce a different notion, see Definition 5.1 below. It tells us what a "terminal model" is: it is characterized by the property—dual to the property that determines initial models—that from an arbitrary model there is a unique homomorphism to the terminal model. We will show in various examples that terminal models are "optimal" models in the sense that they have the minimal set of states. They form minimal realizations, in the terminology of [5]. And the terminal model is usually the intended model of a specification. Terminal models are special because they identify all observationally indistinguishable (bisimilar) states (see e.g. [17]). We find that forcing oneself to identify the terminal model is a great way to get one's specification right. In writing out the details of the terminal model it often became clear (in our experience) that the specification was incomplete, and that extra assertions had to be added.

Since we have a clear separation between specification and implementation, our work falls under the "two-language approach" distinguished in [15]. In the coalgebraic approach that we introduce below, invariance conditions form part of specifications (and need not be derived), since they describe essential aspects of models. Also, in contrast to the descriptions of hybrid systems as used in [13, 1], coalgebraic specifications are somewhat verbose, and contain many details. But with these details one can easily compute the values of attributes (see for example the computation after the REACT$_A$ specification below). What we see as advantages of the coalgebraic framework are: it is intuitively clear, easy to manipulate, has a precise semantics, and offers the perspective of incorporating useful object-oriented notions like inheritance (for incremental specification and implementation, see [18, 9]) into the study of hybrid systems (see also [2]).

2 Monoids of time, and monoid actions

We recall that a monoid is a 3-tuple $\langle M, 0, + \rangle$ consisting a set M with a distinguished "zero" element $0 \in M$, and with a binary operation $+: M \times M \to M$ which is associative: $\alpha + (\beta + \gamma) = (\alpha + \beta) + \gamma$ and has $0 \in M$ as neutral element: $\alpha + 0 = \alpha$ and $0 + \alpha = \alpha$. Often we write M for the 3-tuple $\langle M, 0, + \rangle$ when $0, +$ are understood from the context. We shall mainly use the (commutative) monoids $\langle \mathbb{N}, 0, + \rangle$ of discrete time and $\langle \mathbb{R}_{\geq 0}, 0, + \rangle$ of real time, where $\mathbb{R}_{\geq 0} = \{\alpha \in \mathbb{R} \mid \alpha \geq 0\}$ is the set of positive reals. Actually we shall also use that these are ordered monoids (i.e. monoids in the category of posets).

Let $\langle M, 0, + \rangle$ be an arbitrary monoid. An action of this monoid on a set U consists of a function $\mu: U \times M \to U$ satisfying the following two requirements.

$$\mu(x, 0) = x \quad \text{and} \quad \mu(x, \alpha + \beta) = \mu(\mu(x, \alpha), \beta).$$

In the examples below, the set U will be the set of states of a certain abstract machine, and the function $\mu: U \times M \to U$ may be seen as giving for a state $x \in U$ and amount of time $\alpha \in M$ a new state $\mu(x, \alpha) \in U$ obtained by letting the machine run for α units of time starting in state x. The above two conditions express a certain linearity of this action: $\mu(x, 0) = x$ says that letting the machine run for 0 units of time does not change the state, and $\mu(x, \alpha + \beta) = \mu(\mu(x, \alpha), \beta)$ expresses that the effect of letting the machine run $\alpha + \beta$ units of time is the same as first letting it run α units of time, and then β units of time. But there are many more (non-temporal) instances of monoid-actions: for example, modules and vector spaces are monoid-actions, given by the application $(a, v) \mapsto a \cdot v$ of a scalar a to a vector v; it satisfies $1 \cdot v = v$ and $(ab) \cdot v = a \cdot (b \cdot v)$ and is thus a monoid action with respect to the (multiplicative) monoid structure on the scalars. Also, for a deterministic automaton with alphabet A and transition function $\delta: X \times A \to X$ there is (by induction) an extended transition function $\delta^*: X \times A^* \to X$ forming a monoid action with respect to the (free) monoid A^* of words. Finally, unique solutions to differential equations give rise to monoid actions, see e.g. [7, 8.7] (where they are called flows).

We mention a paradigmatic (temporal) example of a monoid action. It involves the "monus" function $\stackrel{.}{-}$ (also called truncated subtraction) defined as follows.

$$x \stackrel{.}{-} y = \max(0, x - y) = \begin{cases} x - y & \text{if } x \geq y \\ 0 & \text{otherwise.} \end{cases}$$

This monus will be used as a function $\mathbf{N} \times \mathbf{N} \to \mathbf{N}$, and also as a function $\mathbb{R}_{\geq 0} \times \mathbb{R}_{\geq 0} \to \mathbb{R}_{\geq 0}$. Let $U = \{s \in \mathbb{R}_{\geq 0} \mid s \leq 10\}$ be the set of states of a (real-time) timer, where the state $s \in U$ indicates that the timer will give a signal in s units of time. There is then an action $\mu: U \times \mathbb{R}_{\geq 0} \to U$ given by $\mu(s, \alpha) = s \stackrel{.}{-} \alpha$. Thus, if we have a state $5 \in U$ indicating that a signal will be given in 5 units of time, then the state $\mu(5, 3)$ obtained by letting the timer run for 3 units of time, is $2 \in U$. It is not hard to see that μ satisfies the two equations of a monoid action.

3 Coalgebraic specification

What distinguishes coalgebraic specification from algebraic specification is the use of "destructors" instead of "constructors" as atomic function symbols. Typically, if X is an unknown type that we are specifying and A is a constant set, then a map of the form $A \longrightarrow X$ is a constructor, since it tells us how to form elements of X, and a map $X \longrightarrow A$ is a destructor since it gives us some observations about what is in X. In the coalgebraic specification format in this paper we shall restrict ourselves to two kinds of destructors, of the form at: $X \longrightarrow A$, and proc: $X \times B \longrightarrow X$. The first of these is an attribute giving us some information about X, and the second one is a procedure which allows us to produce a new state (from a given one and a parameter element in a constant set B). Attributes correspond to (instance) variables, whose values may be changed by procedures, see the example below. We mostly use the object-oriented dot-notation instead of the functional notation. Hence for a state $s \in X$ we write s.at for at(s) and s.proc(b) for proc(s, b). Thus s.proc(b).at is the result of applying in state s the procedure proc with parameter b, and then applying the attribute at to its outcome. Functionally this would be written as at(proc(s, b)).

Here is a typical example of a coalgebraic specification, provided with some comments after the #-sign.

class spec: FF	#	'FF' is the name of the specification; it stands for 'flip-flop'
methods:	#	object-oriented terminology for function symbols
val: $X \longrightarrow \{0, 1\}$	#	this is an attribute, with output values 0 or 1.
on: $X \longrightarrow X$	#	this a procedure without parameter, giving a new state.
off: $X \longrightarrow X$	#	same thing
assertions:	#	statements imposing some behavioural restrictions, where s $\in X$
s.on.val = 1	#	thus, after 'on' in a state s the value is 1
s.off.val = 0	#	now the end result is 0
creation:	#	requirement for the initial state new
new.val = 0	#	hence newly created instances of FF have value 0.
end class spec		

The typically coalgebraic aspect of such a specification is that it tells nothing about what is inside X; it only describes the operations on X, and the constraints that they satisfy. We restrict equations (here and below) to be exclusively between attribute values, and not between states. This is in line with the coalgebraic philosophy in which states are not directly accessible. More examples may be found in [10, 9], giving coalgebraic specifications and models for classes in object-oriented languages.

A model of such a flip-flop specification consists of three parts. First, it consists of an interpretation $U = [\![X]\!]$ of the unknown type X as a set (of states). Secondly, the methods are interpreted as functions $[\![\text{val}]\!]: U \to \{0, 1\}$, $[\![\text{on}]\!]: U \to U$ and $[\![\text{off}]\!]: U \to U$ acting on the state space U, which should be such that the above assertions are satisfied. Usually we omit these interpretation braces

⟦−⟧. Thirdly, there should be an initial state $u_0 \in U$ satisfying the creation condition, i.e. satisfying $\mathsf{val}(u_0) = 0$. The three (interpretations of the) methods can be combined into a single function $U \to \{0,1\} \times U \times U$, giving us a **coalgebra** on U of the functor $X \mapsto \{0,1\} \times X \times X$.

Such a model $\langle U \to \{0,1\} \times U \times U, u_0 \in U \rangle$ is called **terminal** if for every model $\langle V \to \{0,1\} \times V \times V, v_0 \in V \rangle$ there is a unique function $f : V \to U$ preserving the operations and the initial state:

$$\mathsf{val}_U \circ f = \mathsf{val}_V, \qquad \mathsf{on}_U \circ f = f \circ \mathsf{on}_V, \qquad \mathsf{off}_U \circ f = f \circ \mathsf{off}_V, \qquad f(u_0) = v_0.$$

Terminal models form "minimal realizations" (in the terminology of [5]): they consist of the minimal set of states needed to perform the required behaviour. For example, the terminal model of the above flip-flop specification is the set $U = \{0,1\}$ of attribute values, with operations:

$$\{0,1\} \overset{\mathsf{val}}{\longrightarrow} \{0,1\} \qquad \{0,1\} \overset{\mathsf{on}}{\longrightarrow} \{0,1\} \qquad \{0,1\} \overset{\mathsf{off}}{\longrightarrow} \{0,1\}$$
$$x \longmapsto x \qquad\qquad x \longmapsto 1 \qquad\qquad x \longmapsto 0$$

and with $0 \in \{0,1\}$ as initial state. Indeed, for every model $\langle V \to \{0,1\} \times V \times V, v_0 \in V \rangle$ there is a unique homomorphism $f : V \to \{0,1\}$ satisfying the above requirements, namely $f = \mathsf{val}_V$. There are plenty of other models of this specification; for example, any set V with at least two elements can be turned into a model of this specification. But terminal models of coalgebraic specifications distinguish themselves as "optimal" models, in the same sense that initial (term) models of algebraic specifications are "optimal". See [4] for more information on the semantics of algebraic specifications.

Although we have described the notion of model only for a particular coalgebraic specification, it should be clear what a model is for an arbitrary coalgebraic specification: a carrier set together with functions acting on it which interpret the attributes and procedures, and satisfy the assertions, together with an initial state satisfying the creation conditions.

4 Temporal coalgebraic specification

In this section we extend coalgebraic specifications as above, with temporal aspects, and present a number of examples of the resulting "temporal coalgebraic specifications", together with a few simulations, using the OmSim simulator of OMOLA [2]. Semantics will be postponed until the next section.

A "temporal" coalgebraic specification is, like before, given by a collection of methods consisting of attributes and procedures, but the crucial difference lies in the formulations of the assertions. They will contain temporal information. For an arbitrary method meth and a state s we shall use the new notation

s.meth@α for the result of applying method meth in state s after a delay of α units of time.

Or, more operationally, s.meth@α means: in state s, wait α units of time and then apply method meth. We shall consider examples where α ranges over $\mathbf{N}$ (discrete time) and also over $\mathbb{R}_{\geq 0}$ (real time). We allow α to be 0, so that meth$_1$@α.meth$_2$@0 means that meth$_2$ is applied immediately after meth$_1$ (which is applied after a delay of α time units). We assume that messages arrive in sequential order: if we write s.meth@α, then it is assumed that meth is the first method to be applied in state s (after α units of time), and that no other method was applied in the meantime. If meth is a method that takes a parameter $b \in B$ we shall write s.meth(b)@α for the result of applying meth(b) after α units of time.

Let us consider an elementary example, building on the flip-flops from the previous section. Suppose we wish to specify flip-flops which can be switched on, and will automatically switch off after 10 units of discrete time. We specify these as follows.

> **DT-class spec:** DTFF   #   'DT' for 'discrete time'; name 'DTFF' for
> **methods:**   #   'discrete time flip-flop'
> $\quad$ val: $X \longrightarrow \{0,1\}$
> $\quad$ on: $X \longrightarrow X$ #   (the method off is not used)

assertions: # as before $s \in X$; and $\alpha, \beta \in \mathbb{N}$ (discrete time)
s.val@$\alpha = 0 \vdash$ s.val@$(\alpha + \beta) = 0$ # "monotony", forming an invariant
$\beta \geq 10 \vdash$ s.val@$\beta = 0$ # also an invariant
$\beta < 10 \vdash$ s.on@α.val@$\beta = 1$
creation:
new.val@$0 = 0$
end class spec

We explain the meaning of the assertions. We use the turnstile $\vdash$ to describe conditional assertions. The first "monotony" assertion tells that if at some time α the value in state s is 0, then this value is still 0 at some later time $\alpha + \beta$. Hence the flip-flop does not simply switch on (get value 1) by itself. In this temporal coalgebraic format we have to indicate explicitly what the values of attributes are as a function of time. The second assertion tells us that no matter in what state our flip-flop is, if we wait at least 10 units of time, then its value will be 0. And finally, if we switch it on at some time α, and then inspect it at some time β less than 10 units later, then it will have value 1. This formally captures our informally described timer. Finally, the creation clause tells us that newly created instances have value 0 immediately after their creation. Then we can deduce new.val@$\alpha = 0$ for any α, from the first assertion.

In order to familiarize the reader with this formalism, we consider some variations. Notice that a timed flip-flop satisfying the above specification can be switched on (again) if it has value 1. In this way we can keep it with value 1 for a longer time than 10. Suppose we wish to alter this and stipulate that the flip-flop can only be switched on if it has value 0. We can achieve this by taking the following two assertions, instead of the above third assertion.

s.val@$\alpha = 0, \beta < 10 \vdash$ s.on@α.val@$\beta = 1$
s.val@$\alpha = 1 \vdash$ s.on@α.val@$\beta =$ s.val@$(\alpha + \beta)$.

The first new assertion is like above, except that it now has an extra assumption that the value is 0 at the moment α that the 'on-event' happens. This reflects our modification. And the second assertion tells us that at a moment α when the value is 1, an 'on-event' has no effect on the value: looking at the value β time later is the same as looking at the value $\alpha + \beta$ time after the original state. For example, if we have a state s with s.val@$2 = 0$, then if we switch it on 2 units after s, switch it on again 5 units later, and inspect 7 seconds later, then the value will be 0, although the inspection took place less than 10 units after an on-event. Formally:

$$s.on@2.on@5.val@7 \; = \; s.on@2.val@12 \quad \text{since s.on@2.val@}5 = 1,$$
$$\text{since s.val@}2 = 0 \text{ and } 5 < 10$$
$$= \; 0 \quad \text{since } 12 \geq 10.$$

We can further modify this example by requiring that after the timer has had value 1, it must remain with value 0 for at least 20 units (say) of time. This comes close to the (single) traffic light specification for pedestrians in [6] with value 0 standing for "red light" and 1 for "green light". We need an auxiliary (possibly private) attribute waiting: $X \longrightarrow \{$yes, no$\}$ telling us if we have waited long enough in a state with value 0 (to switch the flip-flop on again). Details of such a specification are left to the reader. Another variation on the above discrete-time flip-flop DTFF is a corresponding real-time RTFF, which will be discussed in Example 5.3 below. Similarly one can coalgebraically specify more standard examples from the literature—like a railway crossing explicitly taking account of the times needed to open and close the gate, or a watch-dog surveying a number of processes and expecting signals that everything is all-right at regular intervals (see e.g. [12, 19]).

We turn to some examples from chemistry, showing the interaction between the discrete structure of method-events and the continuous structure associated with the elapse of time, typical of hybrid systems. Assume we have control over a confined reaction space into which we can inject a chemical substance A. In this space, A will start reacting and transforming itself to another substance, with a reaction speed proportional to the available amount of A. If we write this amount as a function $A = A(\alpha)$ depending on a time parameter $\alpha \in \mathbb{R}_{\geq 0}$, then we have a differential equation

$$\frac{dA}{d\alpha} = -kA \qquad \text{where } k \in \mathbb{R}_{\geq 0} \text{ is a reaction constant.}$$

The solution of this equation is the function $A(\alpha) = A(0) \cdot e^{-k\alpha}$. It is used in the following specification.

> **RT-class spec: REACT$_A$**
>   **methods:**
>   amount$_A$: $X \longrightarrow \mathbb{R}_{\geq 0}$
>   add$_A$: $X \times \mathbb{R}_{\geq 0} \longrightarrow X$
>   clear: $X \longrightarrow X$
>   **assertions:**
>   s.add$_A(x)$@α.amount$_A$@0 = (s.amount$_A$@α) + x
>   s.clear@α.amount$_A$@0 = 0
>   s.amount$_A$@$(\alpha + \beta)$ = (s.amount$_A$@α) $\cdot e^{-k\beta}$
>   **creation:**
>   new.amount$_A$@0 = 0
> **end class spec**

Hence the amount$_A$ attribute tells us how much A there is (in our confined reaction space). And with the two procedures add$_A$ and clear we can inject a certain amount of A (using the parameter of the method), and clear the space in which we are working. This explains the first two assertions. The third assertion incorporates the solution of the differential equation: it tells what at any time β after α the amount of A is, in terms of the amount of A at α and the elapsed time β.

For example, we can do the following. In arbitrary state s, we first clear our working space, 1 time unit later we inject 10 units of A, then 8 time units later we decide to inject another 5 units of A, and then we check 3 time units later. The result can be computed as:

$$\begin{aligned}
&\text{s.clear@0.add}_A(10)\text{@1.add}_A(5)\text{@8.amount}_A\text{@3} \\
={}& \text{s.clear@0.add}_A(10)\text{@1.add}_A(5)\text{@8.amount}_A\text{@}(0+3) \\
={}& (\text{s.clear@0.add}_A(10)\text{@1.add}_A(5)\text{@8.amount}_A\text{@0}) \cdot e^{-3k} \\
={}& (\text{s.clear@0.add}_A(10)\text{@1.amount}_A\text{@8} + 5) \cdot e^{-3k} \\
={}& ((\text{s.clear@0.add}_A(10)\text{@1.amount}_A\text{@0}) \cdot e^{-8k} + 5) \cdot e^{-3k} \\
={}& ((\text{s.clear@0.amount}_A\text{@1} + 10) \cdot e^{-8k} + 5) \cdot e^{-3k} \\
={}& (((\text{s.clear@0.amount}_A\text{@0}) \cdot e^{-k} + 10) \cdot e^{-8k} + 5) \cdot e^{-3k} \\
={}& (10 \cdot e^{-8k} + 5) \cdot e^{-3k} \\
={}& 10 \cdot e^{-11k} + 5 \cdot e^{-3k}.
\end{aligned}$$

The first factor shows the amount of A after inserting 10 units of A and waiting 11 time units, whereas the second factor shows the amount after waiting 3 time units starting from 5 units of A. This shows that one can actually calculate with a coalgebraic specification.

A more interesting example arises when we can (independently) insert two substances A and B, which can engage in reactions $A \leftrightarrows B$, both with reaction speed proportional to the amount of transforming substance, and such that an x-amount of A (resp. B) is transformed into an x-amount of B (resp. A). This leads to the differential equation

$$\frac{dA}{d\alpha} = -kA + \ell B \qquad \text{where} \qquad A(\alpha) + B(\alpha) = A(0) + B(0).$$

In the first equation, k, ℓ are constants (in $\mathbb{R}_{\geq 0}$). The second equation tells that the total amount of A plus B must be constant (and equal to the sum at initiation). The solution of this equation is

$$\begin{aligned}
A(\alpha) &= \frac{1}{k+\ell}\left((kA(0) - \ell B(0)) \cdot e^{-(k+\ell)\alpha} + \ell(A(0) + B(0))\right) \\
B(\alpha) &= A(0) + B(0) - A(\alpha).
\end{aligned}$$

This leads to the following specification.

RT-class spec: REACT$_{A \rightleftharpoons B}$
  methods:
    amount$_A$: $X \longrightarrow \mathbb{R}_{\geq 0}$
    add$_A$: $X \times \mathbb{R}_{\geq 0} \longrightarrow X$
    amount$_B$: $X \longrightarrow \mathbb{R}_{\geq 0}$
    add$_B$: $X \times \mathbb{R}_{\geq 0} \longrightarrow X$
    clear: $X \longrightarrow X$
  assertions:
    s.add$_A(x)$@α.amount$_A$@0 = (s.amount$_A$@α) + x
    s.add$_B(x)$@α.amount$_A$@0 = s.amount$_A$@α
    s.clear@α.amount$_A$@0 = 0
    s.amount$_A$@$(\alpha + \beta) = \frac{1}{k+\ell}\Big((k(\text{s.amount}_A@\alpha) - \ell(\text{s.amount}_B@\alpha)) \cdot e^{-(k+\ell)\beta}$
                                       $+\ell((\text{s.amount}_A@\alpha) + (\text{s.amount}_B@\alpha))\Big)$
    s.add$_B(x)$@α.amount$_B$@0 = (s.amount$_B$@α) + x
    s.add$_A(x)$@α.amount$_B$@0 = s.amount$_B$@α
    s.clear@α.amount$_B$@0 = 0
    s.amount$_B$@$(\alpha + \beta)$ = (s.amount$_A$@α) + (s.amount$_B$@α) $-$ (s.amount$_A$@$(\alpha + \beta)$)
  creation:
    new.amount$_A$@0 = 0
    new.amount$_B$@0 = 0
  end class spec

Let s be an arbitrary state, and put t = s.clear@0.add$_A(10)$@0. Then one can show that, as the time β goes to infinity, the amount t.amount$_A$@β of A in state t at time β goes to $\frac{\ell}{k+\ell} \cdot 10$, and the amount t.amount$_B$@β of B goes to $\frac{k}{k+\ell} \cdot 10$. What we have is an abstract description of a mini-chemical plant, in which two substances can be put together at controlled times and quantities, and their presence over time can be monitored. We have a "passive" hybrid system, because control is on the outside. See Figure 1 for the output of a simulation in OmSim [2].

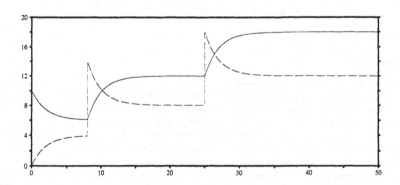

Figure 1: Initially: $A = 10, B = 0$. Additions of B: 10 at time = 8, and again 10 at time = 25. (The values of the constants in this simulation are: $k = 0.2$ and $\ell = 0.3$. Hence the eventual ratio $\frac{A}{B}$ is $\frac{3}{2}$.)

Our final hybrid example in this section involves a thermostat, and is adapted from [14, 1] (and put in coalgebraic format). We shall describe a "passive" and an "active" version. The passive thermostat PTHERM lets the user regulate the temperature in a room, via 'on' and 'off' switches of a heater (like for the earlier flip-flops). There are two attributes, namely 'val' describing whether the heater is on or off, and 'temp' describing the temperature in the room. We have to consider the following two cases.

- When the heater is off, the temperature in the room is determined by "Newton's law of cooling": the rate of change $\frac{dT}{d\alpha}$ of the temperature $T = T(\alpha)$ in the room is proportional to the difference between the temperature T in the room and the temperature of its surroundings. For convenience we assume the latter to be constantly 0, so that we have a differential equation

$$\frac{dT}{d\alpha} = -kT, \quad \text{with solution} \quad T(\alpha) = T(0) \cdot e^{-k\alpha}.$$

- If the heater is switched on, we assume that the change of temperature due to heating is constant. Hence we have an extra constant ℓ in our differential equation:

$$\frac{dT}{d\alpha} = -kT + \ell, \quad \text{with solution} \quad T(\alpha) = \left(T(0) - \frac{\ell}{k}\right) \cdot e^{-k\alpha} + \frac{\ell}{k}.$$

(These solutions are also used in [14, 1].) We thus arrive at the following specification.

RT-class spec: PTHERM
  methods:
    val: $X \longrightarrow \{0, 1\}$
    temp: $X \longrightarrow \mathbb{R}_{\geq 0}$
    on: $X \longrightarrow X$
    off: $X \longrightarrow X$
  assertions:
    s.val@$(\alpha + \beta)$ = s.val@α
    s.on@α.val@0 = 1
    s.off@α.val@0 = 0
    s.on@α.temp@0 = s.temp@α
    s.off@α.temp@0 = s.temp@α
    s.val@α = 0 $\vdash$ s.temp@$(\alpha + \beta)$ = (s.temp@α) $\cdot e^{-k\beta}$
    s.val@α = 1 $\vdash$ s.temp@$(\alpha + \beta)$ = ((s.temp@α) $- \frac{\ell}{k}$) $\cdot e^{-k\beta} + \frac{\ell}{k}$
  creation:
    new.val@0 = 1
    new.temp@0 = 0
end class spec

What is interesting about this example is that different states have different dynamic control laws: different formulas are used for the temperature in the room (as a function of the elapsed time) whether the heater is on (value 1) or off (value 0). In the last case only the natural loss of temperature is described: if $\beta \to \infty$, then the temperature at time $\alpha + \beta$ goes to 0. But if the heater is on there is an extra factor raising the temperature: if $\beta \to \infty$, then the temperature at $\alpha + \beta$ goes to the ratio $\frac{\ell}{k}$; this is the highest temperature that we can achieve by heating the room: it forms an equilibrium between heating and cooling. Notice that newly created thermostats have their heater on, and have a temperature equal to 0 (which is the temperature of the environment).

As an example, assume we have an arbitrary state s in which the value is 0 (heater is off), then if we switch the heater on after α time units, and then read the temperature β units later we get:

$$
\begin{aligned}
\text{s.on@}\alpha\text{.temp@}\beta &= \text{s.on@}\alpha\text{.temp@}(0 + \beta) \\
&= ((\text{s.on@}\alpha\text{.temp@0}) - \tfrac{\ell}{k}) \cdot e^{-k\beta} + \tfrac{\ell}{k} \quad \text{since s.on@}\alpha\text{.val@0} = 1 \\
&= ((\text{s.temp@}\alpha) - \tfrac{\ell}{k}) \cdot e^{-k\beta} + \tfrac{\ell}{k} \\
&= (\text{s.temp@}(0 + \alpha) - \tfrac{\ell}{k}) \cdot e^{-k\beta} + \tfrac{\ell}{k} \\
&= ((\text{s.temp@0}) \cdot e^{-k\alpha} - \tfrac{\ell}{k}) \cdot e^{-k\beta} + \tfrac{\ell}{k} \quad \text{since s.val@0} = 0 \\
&= (\text{s.temp@0}) \cdot e^{-k(\alpha+\beta)} + \tfrac{\ell}{k} \cdot (1 - e^{-k\beta}).
\end{aligned}
$$

We call this a "passive" hybrid system because the heater will be switched on or off only as a result of an action of a client. A more user-friendly system allows a client to set the goal temperature, whereupon the system "actively" regulates the temperature. We shall specify such a system in which the temperature (after some time for adjustment) is kept in the interval $[z - 1, z + 1] \subseteq \mathbb{R}_{\geq 0}$ around the clients choice z. Therefore we assume that the highest possible temperature $\frac{\ell}{k}$ in the room is bigger than 2, and that the clients choice z lies in the open interval $(1, \frac{\ell}{k} - 1) \subseteq \mathbb{R}_{\geq 0}$.

The specification below has three attributes val, temp, goal for respectively the value of the heater (0=off, 1=on), the actual temperature in the room, and the goal temperature as set by the client. (Initially this goal will be set to $\frac{\ell}{2k}$, i.e. to half of the maximal temperature.) There is one procedure set, which allows a client to feed the desired temperature into the system. We shall use the abbreviations

$$\uparrow(s, \alpha) \overset{\text{def}}{=} \sup \{\beta \mid ((\text{s.temp@}\alpha) - \tfrac{\ell}{k}) \cdot e^{-k\beta} + \tfrac{\ell}{k} < (\text{s.goal@}\alpha) + 1\}$$
$$= \frac{1}{k} \ln \left(\frac{\ell - k(\text{s.temp@}\alpha)}{\ell - k((\text{s.goal@}\alpha) + 1)} \right)$$
$$\downarrow(s, \alpha) \overset{\text{def}}{=} \sup \{\beta \mid (\text{s.temp@}\alpha) \cdot e^{-k\beta} > (\text{s.goal@}\alpha) - 1\}$$
$$= \frac{1}{k} \ln \left(\frac{\text{s.temp@}\alpha}{(\text{s.goal@}\alpha) - 1} \right)$$

for the time $\uparrow(s, \alpha)$ needed in state s at α to reach the maximum $(\text{s.goal@}\alpha) + 1$ by heating, and the time $\downarrow(s, \alpha)$ needed to reach the minimum $(\text{s.goal@}\alpha) - 1$. These abbreviations will be used for "time can proceed" (tcp) predicates—like in [13]—in the following specification.

RT-class spec: ATHERM
  methods:
    val: $X \longrightarrow \{0, 1\}$
    temp: $X \longrightarrow \mathbb{R}_{\geq 0}$
    goal: $X \longrightarrow (1, \frac{\ell}{k} - 1)$
    set: $X \times (1, \frac{\ell}{k} - 1) \longrightarrow X$
  assertions:
    $\text{s.temp@}\alpha < \frac{\ell}{k}$
    $\text{s.goal@}(\alpha + \beta) = \text{s.goal@}\alpha$
    $\text{s.temp@}\alpha < (\text{s.goal@}\alpha) - 1 \vdash \text{s.val@}\alpha = 1$
    $\text{s.temp@}\alpha > (\text{s.goal@}\alpha) + 1 \vdash \text{s.val@}\alpha = 0$
    $\text{s.temp@}\alpha \geq a \vdash \text{s.set}(a)\text{@}\alpha.\text{val@}0 = 0$
    $\text{s.temp@}\alpha < a \vdash \text{s.set}(a)\text{@}\alpha.\text{val@}0 = 1$
    $\text{s.set}(a)\text{@}\alpha.\text{temp@}0 = \text{s.temp@}\alpha$
    $\text{s.set}(a)\text{@}\alpha.\text{goal@}0 = a$
    $\text{s.val@}\alpha = 1, \beta < \uparrow(s, \alpha) \vdash \text{s.val@}(\alpha + \beta) = 1$
    $\text{s.val@}\alpha = 1, \beta < \uparrow(s, \alpha) \vdash \text{s.temp@}(\alpha + \beta) = ((\text{s.temp@}\alpha) - \tfrac{\ell}{k}) \cdot e^{-k\beta} + \tfrac{\ell}{k}$
    $\text{s.val@}\alpha = 1 \vdash \text{s.val@}(\alpha + \uparrow(s, \alpha)) = 0$
    $\text{s.val@}\alpha = 1 \vdash \text{s.temp@}(\alpha + \uparrow(s, \alpha)) = (\text{s.goal@}\alpha) + 1$
    $\text{s.val@}\alpha = 0, \beta < \downarrow(s, \alpha) \vdash \text{s.val@}(\alpha + \beta) = 0$
    $\text{s.val@}\alpha = 0, \beta < \downarrow(s, \alpha) \vdash \text{s.temp@}(\alpha + \beta) = (\text{s.temp@}\alpha) \cdot e^{-k\beta}$
    $\text{s.val@}\alpha = 0 \vdash \text{s.val@}(\alpha + \downarrow(s, \alpha)) = 1$
    $\text{s.val@}\alpha = 1 \vdash \text{s.temp@}(\alpha + \downarrow(s, \alpha)) = (\text{s.goal@}\alpha) - 1$
  creation:
    $\text{new.val@}0 = 1$ # in fact, this can be deduced
    $\text{new.temp@}0 = 0$
    $\text{new.goal@}0 = \frac{\ell}{2k}$
  end class spec

We leave it to the reader to verify that for a state s with $(\text{s.goal@}\alpha) - 1 \leq \text{s.temp@}\alpha \leq (\text{s.goal@}\alpha) + 1$,

$$\text{s.temp@}\alpha = \text{s.temp@}(\alpha + \uparrow(\text{s.goal@}\alpha) + \downarrow(\text{s.goal@}\alpha))$$
$$\text{s.val@}\alpha = \text{s.val@}(\alpha + \uparrow(\text{s.goal@}\alpha) + \downarrow(\text{s.goal@}\alpha))$$

where $\uparrow z$ (resp. $\downarrow z$) is the time that is required for the temperature to rise from $z-1$ to $z+1$, (resp. to fall from $z+1$ to $z-1$). Hence, once the temperature has reached the required region around the goal temperature, it will oscillate around this goal with a periodicity of $\uparrow(\mathsf{s.goal@}\alpha) + \downarrow(\mathsf{s.goal@}\alpha)$, and it will stay within this region $[(\mathsf{s.goal@}\alpha) - 1, (\mathsf{s.goal@}\alpha) + 1]$. Further, the heater will be switched on and off with the same periodicity. See Figure 2 for an OmSim simulation.

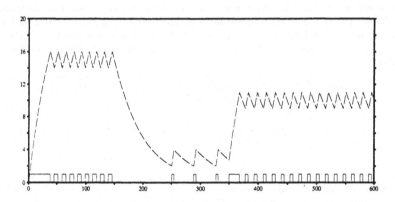

Figure 2: Initially: goal temperature = 15. Goal is set to 3 at time = 150, and to 10 at time = 350. The dashed line describes the resulting temperature, and the blocks at the bottom indicate whether the heater is on or off.

5 Models of temporal coalgebraic specifications

We now turn to semantics. In this section notions of "model" and of "terminal model" will be introduced for the temporal coalgebraic specifications from the previous section. Subsequently, terminal models will be identified for these example specifications.

First, we reconsider the specification DTFF of discrete-time flip-flops as described in the beginning of the previous section. A model of such a specification will first of all be a model of the "underlying" coalgebraic specification as in Section 4—obtained by ignoring aspects of time; that is, by taking the time parameters α, β equal to 0 in the specification. Thus we should have a carrier set U of states, together with operations $\mathsf{val}\colon U \to \{0,1\}$ and $\mathsf{on}\colon U \to U$, and an initial state $u_0 \in U$. What we further need (in this discrete time case) is an $\mathbf{N}$-action $\mu\colon U \times \mathbf{N} \to U$ describing the influence of time on the state space. Then we can interpret timed methods as:

$$\mathsf{s.val@}\alpha = \mathsf{val}(\mu(\mathsf{s}, \alpha)) \qquad \text{and} \qquad \mathsf{s.on@}\alpha = \mathsf{on}(\mu(\mathsf{s}, \alpha)).$$

This interpretation corresponds with our earlier operational explanation: $\mathsf{s.val@}\alpha$ means: first wait α units of time and take the resulting state $\mu(\mathsf{s}, \alpha)$ emerging after this period of time, then apply the val-method. Notice that $\mathsf{s.val@}0 = \mathsf{s.val}$, because μ is an action. Similarly for the procedure on.

In order to find concrete examples of models it is useful to think of elements of the carrier set U as internal states needed to display the specified behaviour. In this case we can take as internal states the elements $\mathsf{s} \in \mathbf{N}$ with $\mathsf{s} \leq 10$. Such a state s can be seen as the number of units of time before the value of the flip-flop becomes 0. This explains the maximum 10. We thus take $U = \{0, 1, \ldots, 10\} \subseteq \mathbf{N}$ as underlying state state space, with action

$$\mu\colon \{0, 1, \ldots, 10\} \times \mathbf{N} \longrightarrow \{0, 1, \ldots, 10\} \qquad \text{given by} \qquad (\mathsf{s}, \alpha) \longmapsto \mathsf{s} \doteq \alpha.$$

The interpretations of the methods are then:

$$\{0, 1, \ldots, 10\} \xrightarrow{\mathsf{val}} \{0, 1\} \text{ is } \mathsf{s} \mapsto \begin{cases} 0 & \text{if } \mathsf{s} = 0 \\ 1 & \text{else} \end{cases} \quad \text{and} \quad \{0, 1, \ldots, 10\} \xrightarrow{\mathsf{on}} \{0, 1, \ldots, 10\} \text{ is } \mathsf{s} \mapsto 10.$$

And as initial state in this model we take $0 \in \{0, 1, \ldots, 10\}$. We verify that the assertions of the DTFF specification hold in this model.

(i) The first assertion s.val@$\alpha = 0 \vdash$ s.val@$(\alpha + \beta) = 0$ holds since

$$\text{s.val@}\alpha = 0 \Rightarrow \mu(s, \alpha) = s \doteq \alpha = 0 \Rightarrow \alpha \geq s \Rightarrow \alpha + \beta \geq s \Rightarrow \text{s.val@}(\alpha + \beta) = 0.$$

(ii) The second assertion $\beta \geq 10 \vdash$ s.val@$\beta = 0$ obviously holds, since for $s \in \{0, 1, \ldots, 10\}$ and $\beta \geq 10$ one has $s \doteq \beta = 0$.

(iii) And the last assertion $\beta < 10 \vdash$ s.on@α.val@$\beta = 1$ holds since

$$\beta < 10 \Rightarrow 10 \doteq \beta > 0 \Rightarrow (\text{s.on@}\alpha) \doteq \beta > 0 \Rightarrow \text{s.on@}\alpha\text{.val@}\beta = 1.$$

(iv) Finally, the initial state $0 \in \{0, 1, \ldots, 10\}$ satisfies the creation condition, because 0.val@0 = 0, since $\mu(0, 0) = 0 \doteq 0 = 0$.

There are other models of this DTFF specification besides $\{0, 1, \ldots, 10\} \subseteq \mathbb{N}$. One can also take the closed intervals $[0, 10] \subseteq \mathbb{Q}$ and $[0, 10] \subseteq \mathbb{R}$ of (positive) rational and real numbers below 10. The definitions of the action and methods are as above. But in these models of rationals and reals there are "too many" states[1]. The minimality of the model $\{0, 1, \ldots, 10\} \subseteq \mathbb{N}$ can be expressed mathematically using terminality. This will be formulated next.

5.1. Definition. Consider a (discrete or real time) specification S as above, with attributes $X \longrightarrow A_1, \ldots, X \longrightarrow A_n$ and procedures $X \times B_1 \longrightarrow X, \ldots, X \times B_m \longrightarrow X$.

(i) A **model** of this specification consists of four parts:

(a) a "state space" or "carrier set" U, serving as interpretation $U = [\![X]\!]$ of the unknown type X in the specification S; elements of U will be called states;

(b) a monoid action $\mu: U \times M \to U$, where M is the monoid of discrete or real time (in accordance with whether S is a discrete or real time specification);

(c) functions $U \to A, U \times B \to U$, where $A = A_1 \times \cdots \times A_n$ is the product of the sets of attribute values and $B = B_1 + \cdots + B_m$ is the coproduct (disjoint union) of the procedure parameter sets, giving combined interpretations $U \to A_i$ of the attributes and of the procedures $U \times B_j \to U$, in such a way that the assertions of the specification S are satisfied;

(d) An initial state $u_0 \in U$ satisfying the creation conditions in the specification S.

We notice that the interpretations of the attributes and of the procedures form a *coalgebra* $U \to A \times U^B$ on the state space U. Hence we are describing coalgebraic models of temporal specifications.

(ii) Such a model $\langle U \xrightarrow{\text{at}} A, U \times B \xrightarrow{\text{proc}} U, U \times M \xrightarrow{\mu} U, u_0 \in U \rangle$ is called **terminal** if for every model $\langle V \xrightarrow{\text{at}} A, V \times B \xrightarrow{\text{proc}} V, V \times M \xrightarrow{\nu} V, v_0 \in V \rangle$ there is a unique function $f: V \to U$ making the following three diagrams commute.

$$
\begin{array}{ccc}
V \times M \xrightarrow{\nu} V \xrightarrow{\text{at}} A & (V \times M) \times B \xrightarrow{\nu \times id} V \times B \xrightarrow{\text{proc}} V & 1 \xrightarrow{v_0} V \\
\downarrow{f \times id} \quad \| & \downarrow{(f \times id) \times id} \qquad \downarrow{f} & \| \qquad \downarrow{f} \\
U \times M \xrightarrow{\mu} U \xrightarrow{\text{at}} A & (U \times M) \times B \xrightarrow{\mu \times id} U \times B \xrightarrow{\text{proc}} U & 1 \xrightarrow{u_0} U
\end{array}
$$

That is, f satisfies for $v \in V$, $\alpha \in M$ and $b \in B$:

$$f(v).\text{at@}\alpha = v.\text{at@}\alpha \quad \text{and} \quad f(v).\text{proc}(b)@\alpha = f(v.\text{proc}(b)@\alpha) \quad \text{and} \quad f(v_0) = u_0.$$

A function f satisfying these three requirements will sometimes be called a **homomorphism** (of models).

In the notion of homomorphism used in the definition, the internal time steps are not preserved directly, but only indirectly via their observable effect. As an aside we mention that every model $\langle V \xrightarrow{\text{at}} A, V \times B \xrightarrow{\text{proc}} V, V \times M \xrightarrow{\nu} V, v_0 \in V \rangle$ yields a coalgebra $V \to A^M \times V^{B \times M}$

---

[1] But for a client who can only use the specified methods, these differences of implementation are not noticeable.

by $v \mapsto \langle \lambda \alpha. v.\text{at}@\alpha, \lambda(b, \alpha). v.\text{proc}(b)@\alpha \rangle$. The notion of homomorphism used in this definition corresponds to a morphism of coalgebras for the functor $X \mapsto A^M \times X^{B \times M}$. And associated with this functor is a notion of *bisimulation* relation. It is a relation $R \subseteq V \times V$ on the carrier of a model V such that for all x, y with $R(x, y)$ one has $R(\nu(x, \alpha), \nu(y, \alpha))$ and $x.\text{at}@\alpha = y.\text{at}@\alpha$ and $R(x.\text{proc}(b)@\alpha, y.\text{proc}(b)@\alpha)$, for all $\alpha \in M$ and $b \in B$. By a standard result, bisimilar elements become equal when mapped to the terminal model.

We have already seen examples of models. We now present an example of a terminal model.

5.2. Example (Discrete-time flip-flop). Consider the discrete time flip-flop specification DTFF, with its model $U = \{0, 1, \ldots, 10\} \subseteq \mathbb{N}$ as described in the beginning of this section. This model can be characterized as terminal model of the specification. And this formalizes our earlier intuition that it involves the minimal set of states (or: forms a "minimal realization"). For any model with carrier set V, action $\nu: V \times \mathbb{N} \to V$, methods val: $V \to \{0, 1\}$, on: $V \to V$ and initial state $v_0 \in V$, there is a function

$$f: V \longrightarrow \{0, 1, \ldots, 10\} \qquad \text{given by} \qquad f(v) = \inf \{\beta \in \{0, 1, \ldots, 10\} \mid v.\text{val}@\beta = 0\}.$$

Thus f maps a state $v \in V$ to the first unit of time where the value of state v is 0. We show that f is a homomorphism.

(i) Commutation with val:

$$
\begin{aligned}
f(v).\text{val}@\alpha = 0 \quad &\Leftrightarrow \quad \mu(f(v), \alpha) = f(v) \dot{-} \alpha = 0 \\
&\Leftrightarrow \quad \alpha \geq f(v) = \inf \{\beta \in \{0, 1, \ldots, 10\} \mid v.\text{val}@\beta = 0\} \\
&\Leftrightarrow \quad v.\text{val}@\alpha = 0.
\end{aligned}
$$

The direction ($\Leftarrow$) of the last step is easy, by definition of infimum. For ($\Rightarrow$), assume $\alpha \geq f(v)$, say $\alpha = f(v) + \beta$. Since $v.\text{val}@f(v) = 0$—because $f(v)$ is the first time that the value is 0—we get $v.\text{val}@(f(v) + \beta) = v.\text{val}@\alpha = 0$ by the monotony assertion in the DTFF specification.

(ii) Commutation with on:

$$
\begin{aligned}
f(v.\text{on}@\alpha) &= \inf \{\beta \in \{0, 1, \ldots, 10\} \mid v.\text{on}@\alpha.\text{val}@\beta = 0\} \\
&= \inf \{\beta \in \{0, 1, \ldots, 10\} \mid \mu(v.\text{on}@\alpha, \beta) = (v.\text{on}@\alpha) \dot{-} \beta = 10 \dot{-} \beta = 0\} \\
&= \inf \{\beta \in \{0, 1, \ldots, 10\} \mid \beta \geq 10\} \\
&= 10 \\
&= f(v).\text{on}@\alpha.
\end{aligned}
$$

(iii) Preservation of the initial state:

$$f(v_0) = \inf \{\beta \in \{0, 1, \ldots, 10\} \mid v_0.\text{val}@\beta = 0\} = \inf \{\beta \in \{0, 1, \ldots, 10\} \mid \beta \geq 0\} = 0.$$

Finally we have to show that f is unique with these properties. If also $g: V \to \{0, 1, \ldots, 10\}$ satisfies $g(v).\text{val}@\alpha = v.\text{val}@\alpha$, $g(v).\text{on}@\alpha = g(v.\text{on}@\alpha)$ and $g(v_0) = 0$, then $g(v) = f(v)$ since:

- $g(v) \leq f(v)$ because $g(v)$ is a lower bound of the set $\{\beta \in \{0, 1, \ldots, 10\} \mid v.\text{val}@\beta = 0\}$:

$$v.\text{val}@\beta = 0 \Rightarrow g(v).\text{val}@\beta = 0 \Rightarrow \mu(g(v), \beta) = g(v) \dot{-} \beta = 0 \Rightarrow g(v) \leq \beta.$$

- $g(v) \geq f(v)$ because $v.\text{val}@g(v) = 0$. This follows since $g(v).\text{val}@g(v) = 0$ since $\mu(g(v), g(v)) = g(v) \dot{-} g(v) = 0$.

5.3. Example (Real-time flip-flop). We now consider a real-time version of the above timed flip-flop. Its specification is the same as the discrete time specification (in the beginning of Section 4) except that in order to deal with boundary problems we add an extra "denseness" assertion

$$s.\text{val}@\alpha = 1 \vdash \exists \beta > 0 \, s.\text{val}@(\alpha + \beta) = 1.$$

It tells us that if the value at time α is 1, then we can always find a (possibly very small) non-zero positive real number β such that β units of time later the value is still 1. As a consequence, if $v.\mathrm{val}@\alpha = 1$, then the set $\{\beta \mid \mathrm{s.val}@(\alpha + \beta) = 1\}$ is an upwardly open interval $[0, \gamma) \subseteq \mathbb{R}_{\geq 0}$.

We claim that the terminal model satisfying this RTFF specification is the closed interval $[0, 10] \subseteq \mathbb{R}$ of positive reals less than or equal to 10. The idea is that a state $s \in [0, 10]$ represents the state of the flip-flop in which the value will be 0 in s units of time. The (real-time) action $\mu: [0, 10] \times \mathbb{R}_{\geq 0} \to [0, 10]$ is $(s, \alpha) \mapsto s \overset{.}{-} \alpha$. And the method interpretations are

$$\mathrm{val}: [0, 10] \longrightarrow \{0, 1\} \quad \text{is} \quad s \mapsto \begin{cases} 0 & \text{if } s = 0 \\ 1 & \text{else} \end{cases} \quad \text{and} \quad \mathrm{on}: [0, 10] \longrightarrow [0, 10] \quad \text{is} \quad s \mapsto 10.$$

with $0 \in [0, 10]$ as initial state—much as in the discrete case. We check the validity of the extra assertion $\mathrm{s.val}@\alpha = 1 \vdash \exists \beta > 0\ \mathrm{s.val}@(\alpha + \beta) = 1$. If for some state $s \in [0, 10]$ and time $\alpha \in \mathbb{R}_{\geq 0}$ we have $\mathrm{s.val}@\alpha = 1$, then $s \overset{.}{-} \alpha > 0$, so that $\alpha < s$. But then we can find a $\beta > 0$ with $\alpha + \beta < s$ because $\mathbb{R}_{\geq 0}$ is dense. This means that $\mathrm{s.val}@(\alpha + \beta) = 1$.

In order to show terminality of the model $[0, 10]$, assume another model consisting of a carrier set V, with action $\nu: V \times \mathbb{R}_{\geq 0} \to V$, method interpretations $\mathrm{val}: V \to \{0, 1\}$, $\mathrm{on}: V \to V$ and initial state $v_0 \in V$. Then we can define a function $f: V \to [0, 10]$ by $f(v) = \inf \{\beta \in [0, 10] \mid v.\mathrm{val}@\beta = 0\}$. We show that $f(v).\mathrm{val}@\alpha = v.\mathrm{val}@\alpha$. Indeed

$$f(v).\mathrm{val}@\alpha = 0 \Leftrightarrow f(v) \overset{.}{-} \alpha = 0 \Leftrightarrow \alpha \geq f(v) \overset{(*)}{\Leftrightarrow} v.\mathrm{val}@\alpha = 0.$$

The marked implication ($\Leftarrow$) is easy by definition of infimum. For ($\Rightarrow$) we use that $v.\mathrm{val}@f(v) = 0$. Suppose not, i.e. $v.\mathrm{val}@f(v) = 1$. Then we can find a $\gamma > 0$ with $v.\mathrm{val}@(f(v) + \gamma) = 1$, by the additional assertion mentioned above. But $f(v) + \gamma$ is a lower bound for the $\beta \in [0, 10]$ with $v.\mathrm{val}@\beta = 0$. Hence $f(v) + \gamma \geq f(v)$, because $f(v)$ is infimum. But this is impossible.

The remaining details that f is the unique homomorphism $V \to [0, 10]$ are as in the previous example, and are left to the reader.

5.4. Example (Chemical reactions). We consider the specifications REACT_A and $\mathrm{REACT}_{A \rightleftarrows B}$ from the previous section. In the first case a model has to keep track of the amount of the chemical substance A. This is done most economically by taking as state space the set $\mathbb{R}_{\geq 0}$ of positive reals, elements of which represent this amount of A. The associated action $\mu: \mathbb{R}_{\geq 0} \times \mathbb{R}_{\geq 0} \to \mathbb{R}_{\geq 0}$ sends a pair (x, α) consisting of the present amount x of A and the time α, to the amount $\mu(x, \alpha) = x \cdot e^{-k\alpha}$ after α time units. This is an action, since $\mu(x, 0) = x \cdot e^0 = x \cdot 1 = x$, and $\mu(\mu(x, \alpha), \beta) = \mu(x, \alpha) \cdot e^{-k\beta} = (x \cdot e^{-k\alpha}) \cdot e^{-k\beta} = x \cdot e^{-k(\alpha + \beta)} = \mu(x, \alpha + \beta)$. The interpretations of the methods amount_A, add_A and clear are then simply:

$$\begin{array}{ccc}
\mathbb{R}_{\geq 0} \times \mathbb{R}_{\geq 0} \xrightarrow{\mathrm{add}_A} \mathbb{R}_{\geq 0} & \mathbb{R}_{\geq 0} \xrightarrow{\mathrm{amount}_A} \mathbb{R}_{\geq 0} & \mathbb{R}_{\geq 0} \xrightarrow{\mathrm{clear}} \mathbb{R}_{\geq 0} \\
(x, y) \longmapsto x + y & x \longmapsto x & x \longmapsto 0.
\end{array}$$

As initial state we have to take $0 \in \mathbb{R}_{\geq 0}$. This is the terminal model, since for an arbitrary model V with action $\nu: V \times \mathbb{R}_{\geq 0} \to V$, attribute $\mathrm{amount}_A: V \to \mathbb{R}_{\geq 0}$, procedures $\mathrm{add}_A: V \times \mathbb{R}_{\geq 0} \to V$, $\mathrm{clear}: V \to V$ with initial state $v_0 \in V$, we get a unique homomorphism $f: V \to \mathbb{R}_{\geq 0}$, namely $f(v) = v.\mathrm{amount}_A@0$. Then

$$\begin{aligned}
f(v).\mathrm{amount}_A@\alpha \\
= \mu(f(v), \alpha) \\
= f(v) \cdot e^{-k\alpha} \\
= (v.\mathrm{amount}_A@0) \cdot e^{-k\alpha} \\
= v.\mathrm{amount}_A@(0 + \alpha) \\
= v.\mathrm{amount}_A@\alpha
\end{aligned}$$

$$\begin{aligned}
f(v).\mathrm{add}_A(x)@\alpha \\
= \mu(f(v), \alpha) + x \\
= v.\mathrm{amount}_A@\alpha + x \\
= v.\mathrm{add}_A(x)@\alpha.\mathrm{amount}_A@0 \\
= f(v.\mathrm{add}_A(x)@\alpha)
\end{aligned}$$

$$\begin{aligned}
f(v).\mathrm{clear}@\alpha \\
= 0 \\
= v.\mathrm{clear}@\alpha.\mathrm{amount}_A@0 \\
= f(v.\mathrm{clear}@\alpha).
\end{aligned}$$

And also $f(v_0) = v_0.\mathrm{amount}_A@0 = 0$. Uniqueness is obvious.

A model of the second specification $\mathrm{REACT}_{A \rightleftarrows B}$ must keep track of both the amounts of A and of B. This suggests $\mathbb{R}_{\geq 0} \times \mathbb{R}_{\geq 0}$ as carrier of the terminal model. We only define the action, and leave further details to the reader. This action $\mu\colon (\mathbb{R}_{\geq 0} \times \mathbb{R}_{\geq 0}) \times \mathbb{R}_{\geq 0} \to (\mathbb{R}_{\geq 0} \times \mathbb{R}_{\geq 0})$ is given by

$$\mu(\langle x_A, x_B \rangle, \alpha) = \langle \mu_A(\langle x_A, x_B \rangle, \alpha), x_A + x_B - \mu_A(\langle x_A, x_B \rangle, \alpha) \rangle$$

$$\text{where } \mu_A(\langle x_A, x_B \rangle, \alpha) = \frac{1}{k+\ell}\left((kx_A - \ell x_B) \cdot e^{-(k+\ell)\alpha} + \ell(x_A + x_B)\right)$$

Notice that $\mu_A(\langle x_A, x_B \rangle, 0) = \frac{1}{k+\ell}(\ell(x_A + x_B) + kx_A - \ell x_B) = \frac{1}{k+\ell}((\ell + k)x_A) = x_A$, and thus $\mu(\langle x_A, x_B \rangle, 0) = \langle x_A, x_A + x_B - x_A \rangle = \langle x_A, x_B \rangle$. The other action-equation $\mu(\mu(\langle x_A, x_B \rangle, \alpha), \beta) = \mu(\langle x_A, x_B \rangle, \alpha + \beta)$ is left to the interested reader.

5.5. Example (Thermostats). The passive and active thermostat PTHERM and ATHERM in the previous section also involve non-trivial actions. The terminal model in the passive case PTHERM has carrier set $\{0, 1\} \times \mathbb{R}_{\geq 0}$, where the first component describes whether the heater is on (1) or off (0), and the second component is the current temperature. This implementation contains all the information we need, and nothing more. The action $\mu\colon (\{0, 1\} \times \mathbb{R}_{\geq 0}) \times \mathbb{R}_{\geq 0} \to \{0, 1\} \times \mathbb{R}_{\geq 0}$ is given by

$$\mu(\langle 0, x \rangle, \alpha) = \langle 0, x \cdot e^{-k\alpha} \rangle \qquad \text{and} \qquad \mu(\langle 1, x \rangle, \alpha) = \langle 1, \left(x - \frac{\ell}{k}\right) \cdot e^{-k\alpha} + \frac{\ell}{k} \rangle$$

where k, ℓ are the constants as used in the PTHERM-specification. It is not hard to check that μ is an action. The interpretations of the methods on the state space $\{0, 1\} \times \mathbb{R}_{\geq 0}$ are given by

$$
\begin{array}{ll}
\{0, 1\} \times \mathbb{R}_{\geq 0} \stackrel{\mathrm{val}}{\longrightarrow} \{0, 1\} & \qquad \{0, 1\} \times \mathbb{R}_{\geq 0} \stackrel{\mathrm{temp}}{\longrightarrow} \mathbb{R}_{\geq 0} \\
\langle z, x \rangle \longmapsto z & \qquad \langle z, x \rangle \longmapsto x \\[2mm]
\{0, 1\} \times \mathbb{R}_{\geq 0} \stackrel{\mathrm{on}}{\longrightarrow} \{0, 1\} \times \mathbb{R}_{\geq 0} & \qquad \{0, 1\} \times \mathbb{R}_{\geq 0} \stackrel{\mathrm{off}}{\longrightarrow} \{0, 1\} \times \mathbb{R}_{\geq 0} \\
\langle z, x \rangle \longmapsto \langle 1, x \rangle & \qquad \langle z, x \rangle \longmapsto \langle 0, x \rangle.
\end{array}
$$

As initial state we take $\langle 1, 0 \rangle \in \{0, 1\} \times \mathbb{R}_{\geq 0}$, as prescribed by the specification. We leave it to the reader to verify that the assertions in the PTHERM-specification hold in this model.

If we have another PTHERM-model with carrier set V, action $V \times \mathbb{R}_{\geq 0} \to V$, method interpretations $\mathrm{val}\colon V \to \{0, 1\}$, $\mathrm{temp}\colon V \to \mathbb{R}_{\geq 0}$, $\mathrm{on}\colon V \to V$, $\mathrm{off}\colon V \to V$ and initial state $v_0 \in V$. Then there is a unique homomorphims $f\colon V \to \{0, 1\} \times \mathbb{R}_{\geq 0}$, namely $f(v) = \langle v.\mathrm{val}@0, v.\mathrm{temp}@0 \rangle$. We only check that f commutes with the temperature attributes. If $v.\mathrm{val}@0 = 0$, then

$$f(v).\mathrm{temp}@\alpha = \mathrm{snd}\mu(f(v), \alpha) = (\mathrm{snd}f(v)) \cdot e^{-k\alpha} = (v.\mathrm{temp}@0) \cdot e^{-k\alpha} = v.\mathrm{temp}@\alpha.$$

And if $v.\mathrm{val}@0 = 1$, then

$$f(v).\mathrm{temp}@\alpha = \left(\mathrm{snd}f(v) - \frac{\ell}{k}\right) \cdot e^{-k\alpha} + \frac{\ell}{k} = \left((v.\mathrm{temp}@0) - \frac{\ell}{k}\right) \cdot e^{-k\alpha} + \frac{\ell}{k} = v.\mathrm{temp}@\alpha.$$

We turn to the semantics of the active thermostat ATHERM. In a model of this specification one has to keep track of (1) whether the heater is on or off, (2) the current temperature in the room, and (3) the goal temperature. The minimal set of these data is

$$U = \{\langle x, y, z \rangle \in \{0, 1\} \times [0, \tfrac{\ell}{k}) \times (1, \tfrac{\ell}{k} - 1) \mid y < z - 1 \Rightarrow x = 1 \text{ and } y > z + 1 \Rightarrow x = 0\}.$$

The restriction in this definition deals with the states of adjustment, when the temperature y in the room is outside the region $[z - 1, z + 1]$ around the goal temperature z. The method interpretations on U are as follows.

$$
\begin{array}{ll}
U \stackrel{\mathrm{val}}{\longrightarrow} \{0, 1\} & \qquad U \stackrel{\mathrm{temp}}{\longrightarrow} [0, \tfrac{\ell}{k}) \\
\langle x, y, z \rangle \longmapsto x & \qquad \langle x, y, z \rangle \longmapsto y \\[2mm]
U \stackrel{\mathrm{goal}}{\longrightarrow} (1, \tfrac{\ell}{k} - 1) & \qquad U \times (1, \tfrac{\ell}{k} - 1) \stackrel{\mathrm{set}}{\longrightarrow} U \\
\langle x, y, z \rangle \longmapsto z & \qquad (\langle x, y, z \rangle, a) \longmapsto \begin{cases} \langle 0, y, a \rangle & \text{if } y \geq a \\ \langle 1, y, a \rangle & \text{if } y < a \end{cases}
\end{array}
$$

The action $\mu \times \mathbb{R}_{\geq 0} \to U$ is more difficult. We first define, for a goal temperature $z \in (1, \frac{\ell}{k} - 1)$, a history function $h_z : \mathbb{R}_{\geq 0} \to [0, \frac{\ell}{k})$ describing the periodic oscillation of the temperature in the room around the goal temperature z, as function of time $\alpha \in \mathbb{R}_{\geq 0}$. Therefore we first need the times

$$\uparrow z \overset{\text{def}}{=} \frac{1}{k} \ln \left(\frac{\ell - k(z-1)}{\ell - k(z+1)} \right) \quad \text{and} \quad \downarrow z \overset{\text{def}}{=} \frac{1}{k} \ln \left(\frac{z+1}{z-1} \right)$$

that it takes for the temperature in the room to rise from $z-1$ to $z+1$, respectively to fall from $z+1$ to $z+1$. The periodicity of h_z is then $\uparrow(z) + \downarrow(z)$, through the definition:

$$h_z(x) = \begin{cases} ((z-1) - \frac{\ell}{k}) \cdot e^{-kx} + \frac{\ell}{k} & \text{if } x \in [0, \uparrow z) \\ (z+1) \cdot e^{-kx} & \text{if } x \in [\uparrow z, \uparrow z + \downarrow z) \\ h_z(x - n(\uparrow z + \downarrow z)) & \text{otherwise, where } n \in \mathbb{N} \text{ is least with } x \geq n(\uparrow z + \downarrow z). \end{cases}$$

Now we define the action $\mu : U \times \mathbb{R}_{\geq 0} \to U$ as follows. We first deal with the adjustment phases: if $y < z - 1$, then

$$\mu(\langle x, y, z \rangle, \alpha) = \begin{cases} \langle x, (y - \frac{\ell}{k}) \cdot e^{-k\alpha} + \frac{\ell}{k}, z \rangle & \text{if } \alpha < \frac{1}{k} \ln(\frac{\ell - ky}{\ell - k(z-1)}) \\ \mu(\langle x, z-1, z \rangle, \alpha - \frac{1}{k} \ln(\frac{\ell - ky}{\ell - k(z-1)})) & \text{otherwise.} \end{cases}$$

And if $y > z + 1$, then

$$\mu(\langle x, y, z \rangle, \alpha) = \begin{cases} \langle x, y \cdot e^{-k\alpha}, z \rangle & \text{if } \alpha < \frac{1}{k} \ln(\frac{y}{z+1}) \\ \mu(\langle x, z+1, z \rangle, \alpha - \frac{1}{k} \ln(\frac{y}{z+1})) & \text{otherwise.} \end{cases}$$

Finally, if we are in the "stability" phase $z - 1 \leq y \leq z + 1$, then we can use the history function h_z to define μ.

$$\mu(\langle 0, y, z \rangle, \alpha) = \langle x, h_z(h_z^{-1}(y) + \alpha), z \rangle \quad \text{where}$$
$$h_z^{-1}(y) \in [\uparrow z, \uparrow z + \downarrow z) \text{ is unique with } h_z(h_z^{-1}(y)) = y,$$
and $x = 0$ if the derivative $h_z'(h_z^{-1}(y) + \alpha) < 0$, and $x = 1$ else.

$$\mu(\langle 1, y, z \rangle, \alpha) = \langle x, h_z(h_z^{-1}(y) + \alpha), z \rangle \quad \text{where}$$
$$h_z^{-1}(y) \in [0, \uparrow z) \text{ is unique with } h_z(h_z^{-1}(y)) = y,$$
and $x = 0$ if the derivative $h_z'(h_z^{-1}(y) + \alpha) < 0$, and $x = 1$ else.

It is laborious, but in essence straightforward, to check that U with this action is a model of the active thermostat specification ATHERM; and also that it is the terminal model: for an arbitrary model V there is a unique homomorphism $f : V \to U$ given by $f(v) = \langle v.\text{val}@0, v.\text{temp}@0, v.\text{goal}@0 \rangle$.

6 Final remarks

Terminal models play a special role in (coalgebraic) specification as minimal realizations in which all observationally indistinguishable states are identified. We have introduced (non-obvious) notions of model and of homomorphism of models for temporal coalgebraic specifications, and have shown in various examples that the resulting terminal models are the intended minimal models, thereby achieving the modest aim of this paper: to show that terminality applies in these situations as well.

We have not explained where the terminal models came from. We used the intuitive (and quite useful) heuristics that terminal models are "minimal realizations", i.e. consist of the minimal set of states needed for the specified behaviour. There is a more mathematical way to find these terminal models by following the recipe of [8]: first find the terminal model of operations only, and then carve out the appropriately universal submodel satisfying the assertions, using (temporal) mongruences. Due to lack of space, we only give a sketch: in a situation with attribute $X \longrightarrow A$, procedure $X \times B \longrightarrow X$ and monoid M, this terminal model has as carrier the function space $A^{(B \times M)^* \times M}$ of "sampling observations". And for the second step, one uses the greatest "temporal mongruence" which is contained in the subset determined by the equations, where a temporal mongruence is a subset of the carrier set of a model, which is closed under the monoid action and under the procedure.

References

1. R. Alur, C. Courcoubetis, N. Halbwachs, T.A. Henzinger, P.-H. Ho, X. Nicollin, A. Olivero, J. Sifakis, and S. Yovine. The algorithmic analysis of hybrid systems. *Theor. Comp. Sci.*, 138(1):3–34, 1995.

2. M. Andersson. *Object-Oriented Modeling and Simulation of Hybrid Systems*. PhD thesis, Dep. of Automatic Control, Lund Inst. of Techn., 1994.

3. M. Barr and Ch. Wells. *Category Theory for Computing Science*. Prentice Hall, 1990.

4. H. Ehrig and B. Mahr. *Fundamentals of Algebraic Specification I: Equations and Initial Semantics.* Number 6 in EATCS Monographs. Springer, Berlin, 1985.

5. J.A. Goguen. Realization is universal. *Math. Syst. Theor.*, 6(4):359–374, 1973.

6. T.A. Henzinger, Z. Manna, and A. Pnueli. Timed transition systems. In J.W. de Bakker, C. Huizing, W.P. de Roever, and G. Rozenberg, editors, *Real-Time: Theory in Practice*, number 600 in Lect. Notes Comp. Sci., pages 226–251. Springer, Berlin, 1992.

7. M.W. Hirsch and S. Smale. *Differential Equations, Dynamical Systems, and Linear Algebra*. Academic Press, New York, 1974.

8. B. Jacobs. Mongruences and cofree coalgebras. In V.S. Alagar and M. Nivat, editors, *Algebraic Methods and Software Technology*, number 936 in Lect. Notes Comp. Sci., pages 245–260. Springer, Berlin, 1995.

9. B. Jacobs. Inheritance and cofree constructions. CWI Techn. Rep. CS-R9564. To appear in *European Conference on object-oriented programming* (ECOOP 1996), Springer LNCS, 1996.

10. B. Jacobs. Objects and classes, coalgebraically. In B. Freitag, C.B. Jones, and C. Lengauer, editors, *Object-Orientation with Parallelism and Persistence.* Kluwer, 1996, to appear.

11. R.E. Kalman, P.L. Falb, and M.A. Arbib. *Topics in Mathematical System Theory*. McGraw-Hill Int. Series in Pure & Appl. Math., 1969.

12. R. Koymans, R. Kuiper, and E. Zijlstra. Paradigms for real-time systems. In M. Joseph, editor, *Formal Techniques in Real-Time and Fault-Tolerant Systems*, number 331 in Lect. Notes Comp. Sci., pages 159–174. Springer, Berlin, 1988.

13. X. Nicollin, A. Olivero, J. Sifakis, and S. Yovine. An approach to the description and analysis of hybrid systems. In R.L. Grossman, A. Nerode, A.P. Ravn, and H. Rischel, editors, *Hybrid Systems*, number 736 in Lect. Notes Comp. Sci., pages 149–178. Springer, Berlin, 1993.

14. X. Nicollin, J. Sifakis, and S. Yovine. From ATP to timed graphs and hybrid systems. In J.W. de Bakker, C. Huizing, W.P. de Roever, and G. Rozenberg, editors, *Real-Time: Theory in Practice*, number 600 in Lect. Notes Comp. Sci., pages 549–572. Springer, Berlin, 1992.

15. A. Pnueli. Development of hybrid systems. In H. Langmaack, W.P. de Roever, and J. Vytopil, editors, *Formal Techniques in Real-Time and Fault-Tolerant Systems*, number 863 in Lect. Notes Comp. Sci., pages 159–174. Springer, Berlin, 1994.

16. H. Reichel. An approach to object semantics based on terminal co-algebras. *Math. Struct. Comp. Sci.*, 5:129–152, 1995.

17. J. Rutten and D. Turi. Initial algebra and final coalgebra semantics for concurrency. In J.W. de Bakker, W.P. de Roever, and G. Rozenberg, editors, *A Decade of Concurrency*, number 803 in Lect. Notes Comp. Sci., pages 530–582. Springer, Berlin, 1994.

18. P. Wegner. The object-oriented classification paradigm. In B. Shriver and P. Wegner, editors, *Research Directions in Object-Oriented Programming*, pages 479–560. The MIT Press series in computer systems, 1987.

19. W. Yi. Real-time behaviour of asynchronous agents. In J.C.M. Baeten and J.W. Klop, editors, *CONCUR '90. Theory of Concurrency: unification and extension*, number 458 in Lect. Notes Comp. Sci., pages 502–520. Springer, Berlin, 1990.

A Bounded Retransmission Protocol for Large Data Packets

A Case Study in Computer Checked Algebraic Verification

Jan Friso Groote[1] & Jaco van de Pol

Dept. of Philosophy, Utrecht University, The Netherlands

e-mail: jfg@phil.ruu.nl, jaco@phil.ruu.nl

Abstract

A protocol is described for the transmission of large data packets over unreliable channels. The protocol splits each data packet and broadcasts it in parts. In case of failure of transmission, only a limited number of retries is allowed (*bounded* retransmission), hence the protocol may give up the delivery of a part of the packet. Both the sending and the receiving client are informed adequately. This protocol is used in one of Philips' products.

We used μCRL as formal framework, a combination of process algebra and abstract data types. The protocol and its external behaviour are specified in μCRL. The correspondence between these is shown using the proof theory of μCRL. The whole proof of this correspondence has been computer checked using the proof checker Coq. This provides an example showing that proof checking of realistic protocols is feasible within the setting of process algebras.

1 Introduction

Background and motivation. During the last 15 years the state-of-the-art in the description and analysis of parallel and distributed systems has advanced enormously. Still the field has not reached a state in which the results are applied frequently and routinely in industry. This situation is improved by carrying out small scale case studies into existing industrial distributed systems. The spin-off of these experiments is generally an assessment of the theory and some indications for further developments of the encountered shortcomings. It is our belief that such hints can steer the theory towards a situation where it can effectively be used at acceptable cost. Therefore, we have started to specify and verify instances of simple distributed systems, using process algebra.

Around 1990 it was realised that process algebraic languages [1, 14] lack a sufficiently precise treatment of data. Up till that moment it seemed sufficient for verification purposes to use standard data types and the generally accepted common sense knowledge about them. This route had already been abandoned by developers of specification languages as they had experienced that commonly accepted data types do not exist (see e.g. [11, 13]). Therefore, abstract data types were added to process algebra.

Given the additional requirement that specifications in such a language should be suited for handling by computer based tools, the language μCRL (micro Common Representation Language) was born. This is a simple, semantically clear and completely formally defined language based on process algebra that incorporates data [6]. The next step was to define a proof theory that enabled to prove distributed systems correct [7]. From this point on μCRL was ready for its usability test. Several distributed systems have now been proved correct [2, 3, 5, 12]. These experiments have revealed several problems. The most important is that proofs contain very many trivial steps. For human beings it is hard to guarantee that all these steps are correct. Therefore, we think it is necessary to check the correctness proofs with automated proof checkers [15, 16, 12, 2].

Verification of the BRP. The Bounded Retransmission Protocol of Philips is an example of a distributed system which relies heavily on data. It is a simplified variant of a telecommunication protocol that is used in one of Philips' products. The protocol allows to transmit large blocks of data within a limited amount of time. After transmission it indicates whether delivery was successful.

---

[1] Current Affiliation: CWI, Kruislaan 413, 1089 SJ Amsterdam, The Netherlands. E-mail: jfg@cwi.nl

The key features of the protocol are that data is transferred in small chunks, and that only a limited number of retransmissions are allowed for each chunk.

The protocol and its external behaviour are specified in μCRL (Sections 2 and 3) and proved equivalent using the proof system for μCRL (Theorem 4.1). The correctness proof for the BRP is rather typical, because proof principles of process algebra, abstract data types and inductive arguments cohere in an intricate way. This was one of the motivations for designing μCRL. Instead of assuming fairness, we exclude possibly diverging internal behaviour by induction on the bounded number of retries still allowed and the length of the data packet.

The creative part of the proof is to find a suitable system of recursive equations, that has the protocol as well as the external behaviour among its solutions. This is far from trivial; in Section 4 we explain the intuition behind this system. The desired equivalence then follows from the Recursive Specification Principle (RSP), which states that a system of guarded equations has a unique solution. The by far largest part of the proof consists of a proof that the protocol is indeed a solution. This proof (Section 5) is structured by induction on the number of retries still allowed. Within this induction, a large amount of purely algebraic manipulations are necessary, using the equations of process algebra and the axioms of our abstract data types. As we will show, this part lends itself very naturally to term rewriting and hence to automated proof checking.

Finally, the whole correctness proof has been proof checked using the system Coq [4] along the lines set out in [15, 16] (see also [2]). This guarantees the highest degree of correctness that can be reached nowadays. We think that we can safely claim that all lemmas and theorems in this document are correct and that they can be proved correct using only the axioms mentioned in this document.

In Section 6 we report on this verification process. It is explained which features of Coq were used, and which missing features would have been helpful. The algebraic part of the verification has been mechanized. Apart from a rigorous discipline, the verification yields a term rewriting system to compute the expansion of parallel processes in an optimal way. Large parts of the verification can be reused for other protocols.

Discussion. The same protocol has been studied in the setting of I/O-automata [10]. Several invariants, safety, deadlock freeness and liveness results are proven. Parts of these proofs are machine checked. A more recent approach can be found in [9]. Here an abstract interpretation is given, with the help of a theorem prover. The abstract protocol, which has a finite state space, could be verified by a model checker. Our work [8] precedes these two approaches.

We feel that our approach has several merits. The description of the protocol is very compact (it fits in one page, instead of eleven pages in [9]) and completely formal. Furthermore, we give a compact, perspicuous and intuitive correctness proof. Finally, the correctness criterion is highly informative, because the protocol is proved *equivalent* to a straightforward description, representing the external behaviour of the protocol. Here equivalence (branching bisimulation) means that there is no observable difference. Hence a simple process answers all possible questions about the external behaviour of the protocol (inclusive safety, deadlock freeness). Consequently, any user only needs to understand this description. This is a real advantage in the common situation that many people work on the same project, while only a few know about the particularities of the protocol.

Of course, we leave it to the interested reader to judge which approach is mostly suited to his purposes. The common conclusion is, that a formal specification and analysis of realistic distributed systems is possible. We amplify this statement for the algebraic approach.

Acknowledgements. Thanks go to Leen Helmink, Alex Sellink, Frits Vaandrager and Thijs Winter for working on and discussing this protocol. We also thank Doeko Bosscher and Jan Springintveld for reading a preliminary version of this paper.

2 Description of External Behaviour of the BRP

As any transmission protocol, the BRP behaves like a buffer, i.e. it reads data from one client, to be delivered at another one. There are two distinguishing features that make the behaviour much more complicated than a simple buffer. Firstly, the input is a *large data packet* (modeled as a list), which is delivered in small chunks. Secondly, there is a *limited amount of time* for each chunk to be delivered, so we cannot guarantee an eventually successful delivery within the given time bound. It is assumed that either an initial part of the list or the whole list is delivered, so the chunks will not be garbled or change order. Of course, both the sender and the receiver want an *indication* whether the whole list has been delivered successfully or not.

This section ends with a formal description of the external behaviour of the Bounded Retransmission Protocol (BRP) for large data packets. This behaviour is modeled as the process X_1, defined by a system of four recursive equations, written in the syntax of μCRL. Some standard data types are specified in Appendix A. We first give an informal description of the external behaviour, illustrated by Figure 1.

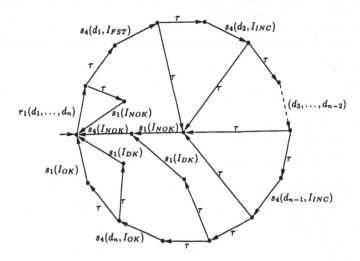

Figure 1: External behaviour of the BRP

The input is read on port 1, by the action $r_1(d_1, \cdots, d_n)$. Ideally, (the outer edge of Figure 1) each d_i is delivered on port 4. Each chunk is accompanied by an indication. This indication can be I_{FST}, I_{INC} or I_{OK}. I_{OK} is used if d_i is the last element of the list. I_{FST} is used if d_i is the first element of the list *and more will follow*. All other chunks are accompanied by I_{INC}.

However, when something goes wrong, a "not OK" indication is sent without datum, $s_4(I_{NOK})$. Note that the receiving client doesn't need a "not OK" indication before delivery of the first chunk, nor after delivery of the last one. This accounts for the irregularity before d_1 and after d_n in Figure 1. The τ-steps indicate that the choice between delivery or loss is decided by internal steps of the protocol.

The sending client is informed after transmission of the whole list, or when the protocol gives up. An indication is sent on port 1, $s_1(c)$. This indication can be I_{OK}, I_{NOK} or I_{DK}. After an I_{OK} or an I_{NOK} indication, the sender can be sure, that the receiver has the corresponding indication. A "don't know" indication I_{DK} may occur after delivery of the last-but-one chunk d_{n-1}. This situation arises, because no realistic implementation can make sure whether the last chunk got lost. The reason is that information about a successful delivery has to be transported back somehow over the same unreliable medium. In case the last acknowledgement fails to come, there is no way to know whether the last chunk d_n has been delivered or not. This explains the exception after d_{n-1} in Figure 1. After this indication, the protocol is ready to transmit a subsequent list.

The rest of this section is devoted to the formal description below. The language primitives are: basic actions ($r_i(d)$ and $s_i(d)$ stand for read and send datum d over port i, respectively), sequential composition ($x \cdot y$, or xy for short), choice over a data type ($\sum_{d:D} x(d)$), a then-if-else construction ($x \triangleleft b \triangleright y$) and choice between two processes ($x + y$). Furthermore, τ is a silent step. These operators are enumerated in order of binding strength (strongest first). See also Table 2 in Appendix B.

In X_1 (corresponding to the leftmost point in Figure 1) some list l is read, and forwarded to X_2, in order to transmit the elements one by one. To inform X_2 whether it is sending the first element of the initial list, it is provided with an extra bit b, which equals e_1 only if the list is fresh, and e_0 if some elements of the initial list have been sent already. X_2 itself is of the form $\tau x + \tau y$, where x and y correspond to loosing or delivering the first element of l. Note that just $x + y$ would mean that the user could refuse to accept failure and force the protocol to succeed. Always chosing the second summand of X_2 corresponds with the outer edge of Figure 1. Finally, X_3 or X_4 is called, depending on whether the receiver needs an indication.

The functions C_{ind} and I_{ind} compute the indications for the sending and receiving client, respectively. See Appendix A for the auxiliary function $indl$, which yields e_1 for empty and singleton lists and e_0 otherwise.

sort $\quad Ind$
func $\quad I_{FST}, I_{OK}, I_{NOK}, I_{INC}, I_{DK} :\rightarrow Ind$
$\qquad\quad C_{ind} : List \rightarrow Ind$
$\qquad\quad I_{ind} : Bit \times Bit \rightarrow Ind$
$\qquad\quad if : \mathbf{Bool} \times Ind \times Ind \rightarrow Ind$
var $\quad l : List, i_1, i_2 : Ind$
rew $\quad C_{ind}(l) = if(eq(indl(l), e_0), I_{NOK}, I_{DK})$
$\qquad\quad I_{ind}(e_0, e_0) = I_{INC}$
$\qquad\quad I_{ind}(e_0, e_1) = I_{OK}$
$\qquad\quad I_{ind}(e_1, e_0) = I_{FST}$
$\qquad\quad I_{ind}(e_1, e_1) = I_{OK}$
$\qquad\quad if(\mathrm{t}, i_1, i_2) = i_1$
$\qquad\quad if(\mathrm{f}, i_1, i_2) = i_2$
act $\quad r_1 : List$
$\qquad\quad s_1, s_4 : Ind$
$\qquad\quad s_4 : D \times Ind$
proc $\quad X_1 = \sum_{l:List} r_1(l) X_2(l, e_1)$

$\qquad\quad X_2(l{:}List, b{:}Bit) =$
$\qquad\qquad \tau(X_3(C_{ind}(l)) \triangleleft eq(b, e_1) \triangleright X_4(C_{ind}(l)))$
$\qquad\qquad + \tau s_4(head(l), I_{ind}(b, indl(l)))$
$\qquad\qquad\qquad ((\tau X_3(I_{OK}) + \tau X_3(I_{DK})) \triangleleft last(l) \triangleright (\tau X_2(tail(l), e_0) + \tau X_4(I_{NOK})))$

$\qquad\quad X_3(c{:}Ind) = s_1(c) X_1$
$\qquad\quad X_4(c{:}Ind) = s_1(c) s_4(I_{NOK}) X_1$

3 Description of the Protocol

We now describe the protocol itself. It consists of a sender S equipped with a timer T_1, and a receiver R equipped with a timer T_2 that exchange data via two unreliable channels K and L. See Figure 2 and also the defining equations below.

The protocol has an intricate timing behaviour. The timers use a new set of signals ($TComm$). A timer can only *signal* a time out, if it is *set*; *reset*ting a timer turns it off. Because we have no explicit time in our framework, we could not deal with explicit time bounds. The timers just have the choice to expire; we only cared about order of actions. Synchronization is enforced by two extra signals. These signals are *lost* and *ready*, to be sent over the links 9 and 10. These signals are understood as "elapse of time" and not as physical signals. The dashed lines in Figure 2 indicate that 9 and 10 don't model a physical medium.

It would be interesting to describe the protocol using explicit time delays, to be able to verify that the protocol terminates transmission within the required time bound.

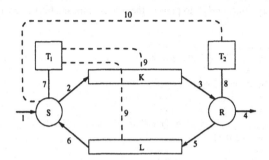

Figure 2: The structure of the BRP.

The sender reads a list at r_1 and sets the retry counter rn to 0 (equation S). Then it starts sending the elements of the list one by one in S_1. Timer T_1 is set ($s_7(set)$) and a frame is sent into channel K. This frame consists of three bits (e_0 or e_1) and a datum. The first bit indicates whether the datum is the first element of the list. The second bit indicates whether the datum is the last item of the list. The third bit is the so-called alternating bit, that is used to guarantee that data is not duplicated. After having sent the frame, the sender waits (in S_2) for an acknowledgement from the receiver, or for a time out. In case an acknowledgement arrives (r_6), the timer T_1 is reset and (depending on whether this was the last element of the list) the sending client is informed of correct transmission, or the next element of the list is sent.

If timer T_1 signals a time out, the frame is resent, (after the counter for the number of retries is incremented and the timer is set again), or the transmission of the list is broken off and timer T_2 is allowed to expire ($s_{10}(ready)$). This occurs if the retry counter exceeds its *max*imum value.

The receiver (initially equation R) waits for a first frame to arrive. This frame is delivered (in R_2) at the receiving client, timer T_2 is started and an acknowledgement is sent (s_5). Then the receiver simply waits for more frames to arrive (in R_1); the value of the alternating bit is stored.

The first bit of R_1 indicates whether the previous frame was the last element of the list; the second bit is the expected value of the alternating bit. Each frame is acknowledged, but it is handed over to the receiving client only if the alternating bit indicates that it is new. In this case timer T_2 is reset. Note that (only) if the previous frame was the last of the list, then a fresh frame will be the first of the subsequent list and a repeated frame will still be the last of the old list. This explains the double reuse of bit b.

This goes on until T_2 times out. This happens if for a long time no new frame is received, indicating that transmission of the list has been given up. The receiving client is informed, provided the last element of the list has not just been delivered. Note that if transmission of the next list starts before timer T_2 expires, the alternating bit scheme is simply continued. This scheme is only interrupted after a failure.

Timer T_1 times out if an acknowledgement does not arrive "in time" at the sender. It is set when a frame is sent and reset after this frame has been acknowledged. To avoid that a message arrives *after* the timer expires, we let the channels K and L send a signal $s_9(lost)$ to T_1, indicating that a time out may occur. This models the following meta-assumption: the total time to move a datum through K, to generate an acknowledgement in R and to transfer this via L is bounded by a fixed delay.

Timer T_2 is (re)set by the receiver ($s_8(set)$) at the arrival of each new frame. It times out if the transmission of a list has been interrupted by the sender. It is also used to model that the sender does not start reading and transmitting the next list before the receiver has properly reacted to the failure. This is necessary, because the receiver has not yet switched its alternating bit, so a new frame would be interpreted as a repetition. The time out ($s_8(signal)$) is preceded by a signal of the sender ($r_{10}(ready)$) to make sure that transmission of the current list has come to a standstill. It is followed by $r_8(ready)\, s_{10}(ready)$, to prevent the sender from sending a new list too early.

sort $TComm$

func $set, reset, signal, ready, lost : TComm$

act $r_2, s_2, c_2, s_3, r_3, c_3 : Bit \times Bit \times Bit \times D$
       $r_5, s_5, c_5, r_6, s_6, c_6$
       $r_7, s_7, c_7, r_8, s_8, c_8, r_9, s_9, c_9, r_{10}, s_{10}, c_{10} : TComm$

comm $r_2|s_2 = c_2$ $r_5|s_5 = c_5$ $r_7|s_7 = c_7$ $r_9|s_9 = c_9$
        $r_3|s_3 = c_3$ $r_6|s_6 = c_6$ $s_8|r_8 = c_8$ $r_{10}|s_{10} = c_{10}$

proc $K = \sum_{b,b',b'':Bit,d:D} r_2(b, b', b'', d)\, \big(\tau\, s_3(b, b', b'', d) + \tau\, s_9(lost)\big)\, K$
       $L = r_5\, (\tau\, s_6 + \tau\, s_9(lost))\, L$

$$S(b'':Bit, max:\mathbb{N}) = \sum_{l:List} r_1(l)\, S_1(l, e_1, b'', 0, max)$$

$$S_1(l:List, b, b'':Bit, rn, max:\mathbb{N}) = s_7(set)\, s_2(b, indl(l), b'', head(l))\, S_2(l, b, b'', rn, max)$$

$$S_2(l:List, b, b'':Bit, rn, max:\mathbb{N}) =$$
$$r_6\, s_7(reset)\, (s_1(I_{OK})\, S(inv(b''), max) \lhd last(l) \rhd S_1(tail(l), e_0, inv(b''), rn, max))$$
$$+ r_7(signal)\, S_3(l, b, b'', rn, max, C_{ind}(l))$$

$$S_3(l:List, b, b'':Bit, rn, max:\mathbb{N}, c:Ind) =$$
$$s_1(c)\, s_{10}(ready)\, r_{10}(ready)\, S(inv(b''), max) \lhd eq(rn, max) \rhd \delta$$
$$+ S_1(l, b, b'', s(rn), max) \lhd lt(rn, max) \rhd \delta$$

$$T_1 = r_7(set)\, \big(r_9(lost)\, s_7(signal) + r_7(reset)\big)\, T_1$$

$$R = \sum_{b',b'':Bit,d:D} r_3(e_1, b', b'', d)\, R_2(b', b'', d, I_{ind}(e_1, b'))$$

$$R_1(b, b'':Bit) =$$
$$\sum_{b':Bit,d:D} \big(r_3(b, b', b'', d)\, s_8(reset)\, R_2(b', b'', d, I_{ind}(b, b'))$$
$$+ r_3(b', b, inv(b''), d)\, s_5\, R_1(b, b''))$$
$$+ r_8(signal)\, \big(s_4(I_{NOK})\, s_8(ready)\, R \lhd eq(b, e_0) \rhd s_8(ready)\, R\big)$$

$$R_2(b', b'':Bit, d:D, i:Ind) = s_4(d, i)\, s_8(set)\, s_5\, R_1(b', inv(b''))$$

$$T_2 = \big(r_8(set)\, (r_{10}(ready)\, s_8(signal)\, r_8(ready)\, s_{10}(ready) + r_8(reset))$$
$$+ r_{10}(ready)\, s_{10}(ready)\big)\, T_2$$

The Bounded Retransmission Protocol for large data packets is obtained by putting these components together. To *enforce* communication, we encapsulate single occurrences of actions in the set $H := \{r_2, s_2, r_3, s_3, r_5, s_5, r_6, s_6, r_7, s_7, r_8, s_8, r_9, s_9, r_{10}, s_{10}\}$. The effect is that e.g. r_2 can only occur simultaneously with s_2; the resulting action is called c_2 by the **comm**-part above. Then the actions in the set $I := \{c_2, c_3, c_5, c_6, c_7, c_8, c_9, c_{10}\}$ are hidden, to indicate that the communications are internal. (See [1] for a good explanation of these concepts and cf. Table 3 in Appendix B). BRP is then specified as the parallel composition of its components, with the actions in H forbidden, and the actions in I hidden.

proc $BRP(max:\mathbb{N}) = \tau_I \partial_H(T_1 \parallel S(e_0, max) \parallel K \parallel L \parallel R \parallel T_2)$

4 The Correctness Proof

The main result to be established is that the internal and external descriptions of the BRP coincide. The rest of this section is devoted to a proof of the following theorem, where equality refers to the theory of μCRL (see Appendix B). Branching bisimulation (a stronger variant of weak bisimulation) is a model of this theory. The importance of this theorem is that a user of the BRP only needs to understand the definition of X_1. This answers all questions about the BRP, like "What happens when an empty list is sent?"[2] Note that the equation even holds when $max = 0$ and also when all signals in $TComm$ are equal, because it is not specified that they are pairwise different.

Theorem 4.1. *For all* $max : \mathbb{N}$ *we find* $\boxed{X_1 = BRP(max).}$

The heart of the correctness proof is as usually an application of RSP, which states that every guarded equation has a unique solution. So a suitable system of recursive equations is needed, having both the protocol and its external behaviour as a solution. Finding it is *the* creative step in the proof. For simple protocols, this system of equations is just the definition of the external behaviour, or a small variation of it.

In our case, the intermediate system of equations is less straightforward. The intuitive reason is that the protocol can start transmission of a list in two distinct modes. In the first mode, the receiver doesn't know what the toggle bit of the list will be; the receiver is in state R. This mode occurs after start up of the protocol and after termination due to a failure. The second mode arises after the successful transmission of a list. In this case, the receiver assumes that the alternating bit sequence is simply continued; the receiver is in state $R_1(e_1, b'')$, where b'' is the expected bit.

First, we define auxiliary processes, denoting the components of the BRP in some non-initial state:

$$K'(b, b', b'', d) := (\tau\, s_3(b, b', b'', d) + \tau\, s_9(lost))\, K$$
$$L' := (\tau\, s_6 + \tau\, s_9(lost))\, L$$
$$T_2' := (r_{10}(ready)\, s_8(signal)\, r_8(ready)\, s_{10}(ready) + s_8(reset))\, T_2$$
$$T_1' := (r_9(lost)\, s_7(signal) + r_7(reset))\, T_1$$

In the set of equations (I) below, Z_1 and Z_1' denote the two major modes described above. $Z_2, \ldots, Z_4''$ are inspired by $X_2, \ldots, X_4$ of the external behaviour, but the two modes are kept distinct. These equations can be read as the definition of processes $Z_1, \ldots, Z_4''$.

$$Z_1(b'', max) = \sum_{l:List} r_1(l)\, \tau_I \partial_H(T_1 \parallel S_1(l, e_1, b'', 0, max) \parallel K \parallel L \parallel R \parallel T_2)$$
$$Z_1'(b'', max) = \sum_{l:List} r_1(l)\, \tau_I \partial_H(T_1 \parallel S_1(l, e_1, b'', 0, max) \parallel K \parallel L \parallel R_1(e_1, b'') \parallel T_2')$$

$$Z_2(l, b'', max) =$$
$$(\tau\, Z_4(I_{DK}, b'', max) + \tau\, Z_3(l, b'', max))$$
$$\triangleleft last(l) \triangleright$$
$$(\tau\, Z_4(I_{NOK}, b'', max)$$
$$+ \tau\, s_4(head(l), I_{FST})\, (\tau\, Z_2'(tail(l), e_0, inv(b''), max) + \tau\, Z_4''(I_{NOK}, b'', max)))$$

(I) $$Z_2'(l, b, b'', max) =$$
$$(\tau\, (Z_4(I_{DK}, b'', max) \triangleleft eq(b, e_1) \triangleright Z_4''(I_{DK}, b'', max)) + \tau\, Z_3(l, b'', max))$$
$$\triangleleft last(l) \triangleright$$
$$(\tau\, (Z_4(I_{NOK}, b'', max) \triangleleft eq(b, e_1) \triangleright Z_4''(I_{NOK}, b'', max))$$
$$+ \tau\, s_4(head(l), I_{ind}(b, e_0))\, (\tau\, Z_2'(tail(l), e_0, inv(b''), max) + \tau\, Z_4''(I_{NOK}, b'', max)))$$

$$Z_3(l, b'', max) = s_4(head(l), I_{OK})\, (\tau\, Z_4'(I_{OK}, b'', max) + \tau\, Z_4(I_{DK}, b'', max))$$

---

[2] In this case one element is delivered, namely $head(empty)$.

$$Z_4(c, b'', max) = s_1(c) Z_1(inv(b''), max)$$
$$Z_4'(c, b'', max) = s_1(c) Z_1'(inv(b''), max)$$
$$Z_4''(c, b'', max) = s_1(c) s_4(I_{NOK}) Z_1(inv(b''), max)$$

At this point we need a large number of straightforward calculations, which are postponed to the next section for expository reasons. Using Lemma 5.1.17 and 5.1.18 (and axioms A5 and B1 from Appendix B), we get the following equalities:

$$Z_1(b'', max) = \sum_{l:List} r_1(l) Z_2(l, b'', max)$$
$$Z_1'(b'', max) = \sum_{l:List} r_1(l) Z_2'(l, e_1, b'', max)$$

The set of equations (II) is obtained, by replacing the first two equations in (I) by these two equations. (II) is clearly guarded, so by RSP it has a unique solution. Clearly, $Z_1, \ldots, Z_4''$ is a solution of (II). "Another" solution is found by applying the following substitution of (II). This can easily be verified from the equations defining $X_1, \ldots, X_4$ (use a case distinction on $last(l)$ for the equations with X_2).

$$X_1 \quad \text{for } Z_1(b'', max) \text{ and } Z_1'(b'', max)$$
$$X_2(l, e_1) \quad \text{for } Z_2(l, b'', max)$$
$$X_2(l, b) \quad \text{for } Z_2'(l, b, b'', max)$$
$$s_4(head(l), I_{OK}) (\tau X_3(I_{OK}) + \tau X_3(I_{DK})) \quad \text{for } Z_3(l, b'', max)$$
$$X_3(c) \quad \text{for } Z_4(c, b'', max) \text{ and } Z_4'(c, b'', max)$$
$$X_4(c) \quad \text{for } Z_4''(c, b'', max)$$

All solutions are equal, so $Z_1(b'', max) = X_1$. By Lemma 5.1.1 and the defining equation of $BRP(max)$ we find that $BRP(max) = Z_1(e_0, max)$. These two results imply the theorem. ☒

5 Algebraic Calculations

In this section we give the calculations that were needed in the correctness proof. All calculations fall within the proof theory developed in [7] including the branching τ-laws mentioned in [1].

Lemma 5.1 establishes the link between the Z_i, defined in the process equations (I) and the BRP protocol. The goals are item 17 and 18; all other items are needed in the proof. The proof is in fact by unfolding the equations. Although usually recursive equations specify infinite processes, we use the fact that for given max, rn and l, the equations in (I) contain no infinite loop. Eventually, we end up in Z_1 or Z_1'. The proof proceeds by induction on the number of retries still allowed ($minus(max, rn)$) and on list l.

Lemma 5.1. For all $b, \bar{b}, b'', b''' : Bit$, $max, rn : \mathbb{N}$, $i, c : Ind$ with $lt(rn, max)$ or $eq(rn, max)$, we find

1. $Z_1(b'', max) = \tau_I \partial_H(T_1 \parallel S(b'', max) \parallel K \parallel L \parallel R \parallel T_2)$

2. $Z_1'(b'', max) = \tau_I \partial_H(T_1 \parallel S(b'', max) \parallel K \parallel L \parallel R_1(e_1, b'') \parallel T_2')$

3. $Z_4(c, b'', max) = \tau_I \partial_H(T_1 \parallel S_3(l, b, b'', max, max, c) \parallel K \parallel L \parallel R \parallel T_2)$

4. $Z_4''(c, b'', max) = \tau_I \partial_H(T_1 \parallel S_3(l, \bar{b}, b'', max, max, c) \parallel K \parallel L \parallel R_1(e_0, b''') \parallel T_2')$

5. $Z_4(c, b'', max) = \tau_I \partial_H(T_1 \parallel S_3(l, \bar{b}, b'', max, max, c) \parallel K \parallel L \parallel R_1(e_1, b''') \parallel T_2')$

6. $Z_4'(c, b'', max) = \tau_I \partial_H(T_1 \parallel s_1(c) S(inv(b''), max) \parallel K \parallel L \parallel R_1(e_1, inv(b'')) \parallel T_2')$

7. $last(l) = f \rightarrow$
   $\tau (\tau Z_2'(tail(l), e_0, inv(b''), max) + \tau Z_4''(I_{NOK}, b'', max)) =$
   $\quad \tau \tau_I \partial_H(T_1' \parallel S_2(l, b, b'', rn, max) \parallel K \parallel L' \parallel R_1(e_0, inv(b'')) \parallel T_2')$

8. $last(l) = \mathsf{t} \to$
$\tau\,(\tau\,Z_4'(I_{OK}, b'', max) + \tau\,Z_4(I_{DK}, b'', max)) =$
$\quad \tau\tau_I\partial_H(T_1' \parallel S_2(l, b, b'', rn, max) \parallel K \parallel L' \parallel R_1(e_1, inv(b'')) \parallel T_2')$

9. $last(l) = \mathsf{t} \to$
$Z_3(l, b'', max) = \tau_I\partial_H(T_1' \parallel S_2(l, b, b'', rn, max) \parallel K \parallel L \parallel R_2(indl(l), b'', head(l), I_{OK}) \parallel T_2)$

10. $last(l) = \mathsf{t} \to$
$\tau\,(\tau\,Z_4'(I_{OK}, b'', max) + \tau\,Z_4(I_{DK}, b'', max)) =$
$\quad \tau\,\tau_I\partial_H(T_1' \parallel S_2(l, b, b'', rn, max) \parallel K'(b, indl(l), b'', head(l)) \parallel L \parallel R_1(e_1, inv(b'')) \parallel T_2')$

11. $last(l) = \mathsf{t} \to$
$\tau\,(\tau\,Z_4'(I_{OK}, b'', max) + \tau\,Z_4(I_{DK}, b'', max)) =$
$\quad \tau_I\partial_H(T_1 \parallel S_1(l, b, b'', rn, max) \parallel K \parallel L \parallel R_1(e_1, inv(b'')) \parallel T_2')$

12. $last(l) = \mathsf{f} \to$
$s_4(d, i)\,(\tau\,Z_2'(tail(l), e_0, inv(b''), max) + \tau\,Z_4''(I_{NOK}, b'', max)) =$
$\quad \tau_I\partial_H(T_1' \parallel S_2(l, b, b'', rn, max) \parallel K \parallel L \parallel R_2(e_0, b'', d, i) \parallel T_2)$

13. $last(l) = \mathsf{f} \to$
$\tau(\tau\,Z_2'(tail(l), e_0, inv(b''), max) + \tau\,Z_4''(I_{NOK}, b'', max)) =$
$\quad \tau\,\tau_I\partial_H(T_1' \parallel S_2(l, b, b'', rn, max) \parallel K'(b, indl(l), b'', head(l)) \parallel L \parallel R_1(e_0, inv(b'')) \parallel T_2')$

14. $last(l) = \mathsf{f} \to$
$\tau(\tau\,Z_2'(tail(l), e_0, inv(b''), max) + \tau\,Z_4''(I_{NOK}, b'', max)) =$
$\quad \tau_I\partial_H(T_1 \parallel S_1(l, b, b'', rn, max) \parallel K \parallel L \parallel R_1(e_0, inv(b'')) \parallel T_2')$

15. $\tau\,Z_2(l, b'', max) = \tau\,\tau_I\partial_H(T_1' \parallel S_2(l, e_1, b'', rn, max) \parallel K'(e_1, indl(l), b'', head(l)) \parallel L \parallel R \parallel T_2)$

16. $\tau\,Z_2'(l, b, b'', max) =$
$\quad \tau\,\tau_I\partial_H(T_1' \parallel S_2(l, b, b'', rn, max) \parallel K'(b, indl(l), b'', head(l)) \parallel L \parallel R_1(b, b'') \parallel T_2')$

17. $\tau\,Z_2(l, b'', max) = \tau_I\partial_H(T_1 \parallel S_1(l, e_1, b'', rn, max) \parallel K \parallel L \parallel R \parallel T_2)$

18. $\tau\,Z_2'(l, b, b'', max) = \tau\,\tau_I\partial_H(T_1 \parallel S_1(l, b, b'', rn, max) \parallel K \parallel L \parallel R_1(b, b'') \parallel T_2')$

Proof. In each step, the parallel processes at the right hand side have to be expanded, to see what steps they can perform. These expansions have been omitted, as they are completely standard. We only show how the inductive proof is structured, and which facts are used.

1,2 Straightforward expansion.

3,4,5 After an expansion, use 1.

6 After an expansion, use 2.

8,10,11 Simultaneous induction on $minus(max, rn)$, the number of retransmissions still allowed. For fixed max and rn, 11 is a consequence of 10. For the base case, first prove 8, using 5 and 6; this together with 5 is used for 10. For the step case, 8 uses 6 and the induction hypothesis for 11; 10 uses the just obtained result for 8, and the induction hypothesis for 11.

9 Use 8.

7,12,13,14,16,18 First, for fixed max, rn and l, $7 \Rightarrow 12$, $13 \Rightarrow 14$ and $16 \Rightarrow 18$ can be seen by expansions only. The proof proceeds by simultaneous induction on $minus(rn, max)$ and within that to the list l. If $l = empty$, then 7 and 13 are vacuously true, because then $last(empty) = \mathsf{t}$. For $rn = max$, 7 implies 16. To see this, we need 4 or 5 (depending on bit b) and 9 or 12 (depending on $last(l)$).

Case 0, add. For 7, use 4 and the innermost induction hypothesis of 18. This, together with 4 is used for 13.

Case s, empty. In this case, 16 can be proved with the help of 9, and the outer induction hypothesis for 18.

Case s, add. 7 uses the outer induction hypothesis of 14 and the inner induction hypothesis of 18. This instance of 7, together with the outer induction hypothesis of 14 is used to establish the induction step for 13. For 16, the outer induction hypothesis for 18 is used, and either 9 or 12 (which holds, because 7 has just been established), depending on $last(l)$.

15,17 By simultaneous induction on $minus(max, rn)$. First note that for fixed max and rn, 15 implies 17. The base case of 15 uses 3; the step case uses the induction hypothesis of 17. Furthermore, both cases use 9 or 12, depending on whether $last(l)$ holds or not. ⊠

6 Mechanical Proof Checking using Coq V5.8.2

About Coq. The verification of the correctness proof has been carried out in the theorem prover Coq V5.8.2 [4]. This system is designed as a proof checker and is not an automated theorem prover. The user can enter tactics (called *vernacular* code), which enable Coq to reproduce the proof. These tactics allow to introduce and unfold definitions, to apply previously proved theorems, to use (directed) equations and to perform induction. Moreover, such tactics can be combined by tacticals, like **Repeat** and **Orelse**. With the help of these tacticals, simple predicates (e.g. membership of lists) can be mechanized, and also a term rewriting system can be implemented within Coq.

Coq's logic is based on a powerful type theory, known as the Calculus of Inductive Constructions (i.e. higher order arithmetic). The main advantage of this strong theory is that all concepts can be defined without encoding. Although the largest part of the proof uses only first order equational logic, we benefited from Coq's expressive power. We used polymorphism to formulate schematic rules (like induction rules and RSP) as single rules. Note also that RSP quantifies over process operators (modeling the right hand of a recursive equation), which take a parametrized process $X(d)$ as argument, which in turn takes a first order datum as argument. So the RSP axiom is a fourth order object in Coq.

Reusable part of the verification. We refer to [15] for a detailed explanation how the syntax, axioms and rules of μCRL can be incorporated in Coq. We reused vernacular code from [2] for a lot of standard facts of process algebra. The files with vernacular commands are available and can be obtained by contacting the second author.

Recursive processes are defined by adding a constant for the process and putting the defining equation as an axiom. This is in fact a hidden appeal to the Recursive Definition Principle, which says that each equation has at least one solution.

Because Lemma 5.1 requires a large number of elementary calculations, we have automatized the computation of the expansion of parallel processes. Lemma 5.1.1 for instance needs the following equality:

$$\sum_{l:List} r_1(l)\, \tau_I \partial_H (T_1 \parallel S_1(l, e_1, b'', 0, max) \parallel K \parallel L \parallel R \parallel T_2) = \tau_I \partial_H (T_1 \parallel S(b'', max) \parallel K \parallel L \parallel R \parallel T_2),$$

which can be proved by expanding the right hand side once (i.e. by looking which steps this term can perform). By CM1, each pair x, y of the 6 processes put in parallel, gives rise to three scenarios: either x or y performs a first step, or they synchronize into a communication. The Handshaking axiom tells that at most two processes can synchronize. Hence, there are 36 scenarios to be considered (6 single steps, and $5 \cdot 6 = 30$ combinations), indicating a potential blow up.

However, the left hand side shows that only one scenario really occurs, namely S may perform a $r_1(l)$ step for some l. All other single steps are encapsulated by the ∂_H. Furthermore, immediate synchronizations are forbidden by the **comm** part in Section 3. In this way, the equality above can be proved by applying equations only.

We succeeded to mechanize these parts of the proof almost completely. To this end a term rewriting system was identified that computes the expansions. With outermost rewriting, the potential blow up is avoided, because the 36 scenarios are not generated at once. Before a new scenario is generated, it is tried to eliminate the old one by encapsulation and excluding synchronization. In vernacular code, the proof of the equation above has the following form: (certain details are replaced by ...)

```
Goal (b'':Bit)(max:Nat)<proc>
  (sum List [l:List] (seq (ia List r1 1) (hide IL (enc HL
    (mer T1 (mer (S1 l e1 b'' o max) (mer K (mer L (mer R T2)))))))))
=(hide IL (enc HL
    (mer T1 (mer (S b'' max) (mer K (mer L (mer R T2))))))).
Intros.
Pattern 2 T1; Rewrite <- hnf_T1. Rewrite <- Proc_S. ...
Load exp_tac.
Rewrite -> hnf_T1; Rewrite -> Proc_S; ...
Rewrite <- S_Lmer.
Load hide_strip.
Load equal_tac.
Save Exp_1.
```

First the equation is stated as a goal. Then we unfold the definitions of the processes in the right hand side. Now the term rewriting system is called (it is stored in the file **exp_tac**). The process definitions are folded back. At this point we need an auxiliary lemma, called S_Lmer. Finally, we compute the result of hiding, and call the tactic **equal_tac**, which compares left and right hand side modulo associativity and commutativity. The proof is stored as **Exp_1**.

Lacking features of Coq. Unfortunately, we could not mechanize all parts of the algebraic computation. In the example above, we used a lemma (S_Lmer) and we had to specify which abbreviations to unfold. A full mechanization of the algebraic part would be desirable. First of all, this saves a lot of time. More importantly, unmechanized parts of the proof are very sensitive to small changes. After the first verification, we made some changes in the protocol. This only invalidated parts of the proof, where mechanization had not been successful (e.g. the proof of lemma S_Lmer).

Below we identify some features that would enable us to complete the mechanization. These features are currently lacking in the Coq system.

- *Metavariables.* We had to compute the left hand side of the **Goal** above ourselves, before entering it. Ideally, one would type a metavariable for the left hand side. With a metavariable we mean a temporary unknown part of the proof. After the computation of the expansion, the theorem prover knows the value of the metavariable and can instantiate it accordingly. A metavariable could also be generated during the application of a theorem, whose premises contain variables that are not present in the conclusion (e.g. transitivity). This variable could get its value in the next proof step. Coq refuses such applications.

- *Full second order matching* is needed for instance in the application of SUM3 (Table 2) from right to left. In the current version, the user has to specify p and e, preventing the use of a general tactic.

- *Definition unfolding mechanism.* In the example above, definitions have to be unfolded (and refolded) by hand. Especially the **Pattern** construct is very sensitive to small changes in the formulae.

- *Extensible vernacular language.* This has been added to Coq 5.10. It allows to add for instance a term rewriter as a common vernacular command.

Specific part of the verification. We will not fully discuss the part of the verification that is specific to this protocol. We only mention two deviations of the proof in the previous sections. The first deviation is, that we didn't use RSP in the way indicated in Section 4. Instead of this, we encoded the system of recursive equations as one single recursive equation. This simplifies the formulation of RSP considerably.

The second deviation is that we implemented the sorts N, *Bit*, *List* and **Bool** as inductive sets, instead of as abstract data types. Functions on these sets have been defined with primitive recursion. The division between *free constructors* and *functions* was done by hand. In order to check that these definitions coincide with the algebraic specification, the equalities in the specification were proved with induction. Note that the proof theory of μCRL already incorporates induction. See also [16].

This approach is advantageous, as Coq highly supports induction and primitive recursion over inductively defined sets. Furthermore, equality between terms of these sorts coincides with Coq's meta-equality, and can be checked by the system immediately. For the other sorts ($D, TComm, Ind$) this approach was not possible, because the free constructors of them are not given.

We give some statistics, in order to show which fraction of the vernacular code can be reused. The total amount of vernacular code is about 123 Kb, divided over 4367 lines. 1172 lines comprise the definitions of μCRL prove the standard facts and set up the term rewriting system; these are reusable for other protocols. The definition of the protocol requires 468 lines (228 to specify actions, 240 for protocol and behaviour). Specification and proofs regarding data took 497 lines. For Lemma 5.1 we used 1706 lines (311 for auxiliary lemmas, 548 lines for the expansions and 847 lines for the inductive argumentation). The main proof needed 524 lines of code (mainly for the encoding of the system of equations into one equation). A Sparc Station 10-514 needed 11 hours to interpret these vernacular commands and to generate a concrete proof term; this proof term is about 15 Mb large.

Appendix A Standard Data Types

Standard data types used in the BRP are described in Table 1. The functions are fully self explaining. No other facts about data types have been used in the correctness proof of the BRP than those that are mentioned in the main text and in this appendix. Some of the functions, such as $\wedge, pred$ and *minus* have neither been used in the description of the external behaviour nor in the description of the BRP itself, but were instrumental in the correctness proof. We also used the usual rules for first order predicate logic with equality. Finally, the following induction schemata were incorporated.

$$\frac{P(e_0) \qquad P(e_1)}{\forall e{:}Bit\, P(e)} \qquad \frac{P(t) \qquad P(f)}{\forall b{:}\mathbf{Bool}\, P(b)} \qquad \frac{P(0) \qquad \forall x{:}\mathrm{N}\, P(x) \to P(s(x))}{\forall x{:}\mathrm{N}\, P(x)}$$

$$\frac{P(empty) \qquad \forall d{:}D\, \forall l{:}List\, P(l) \to P(add(d,l))}{\forall l{:}List\, P(l)}$$

Appendix B Axioms of μCRL

All the process algebra axioms used to prove the BRP can be found in Table 2–5. These axioms form the basic theory that has been provided to the theorem prover Coq. We do not explain the axioms (see [1, 7]) but only include them to give an exact and complete overview of the axioms that we used. The axiom SC4 is a direct consequence of SC3 and Handshaking. Axiom CD2 is implied by CD1 and SC3. Furthermore, the γ-function is defined as follows: $\gamma(a,b) = c$ if and only if $a|b = c$ or $b|a = c$ occur in the **comm** part of the specification in Section 3.

Besides the axioms we have used the RSP principle, saying that guarded recursive equations have at most one solution. In the following x, y denote parametrized processes that can be applied to a data parameter d of arbitrary sort D, and deliver a process. The symbol Ψ is a process operator, i.e. a process which is parametrized with a process $x(d)$ and a datum element d. It models the right hand side of a recursive equation.

$$\text{RSP} \qquad \frac{\Psi \text{ is guarded} \quad \forall d{:}D.\, x(d) = \Psi(x, d) \quad \forall d{:}D.\, y(d) = \Psi(y, d)}{\forall d : D.\, x(d) = y(d)}.$$

In the correctness proof in this paper we have used a strong notion of guardedness, namely: for guarded processes p' and p'', an arbitrary process q, boolean term b and action $a(d)$, the following processes are guarded: $a(d)$, δ, τ, $p' + p''$, $p' \triangleleft b \triangleright p''$, $\sum_{d:D} p'(d)$, $a(d)\, q$ and $\tau\, p'$.

sort	**Bool**	sort	*Bit*
func	f, t $:\to$ **Bool**	func	$e_0, e_1 :\to Bit$
	$\wedge$: **Bool** $\times$ **Bool** $\to$ **Bool**		$inv : Bit \to Bit$
var	b : **Bool**		$if : \mathbf{Bool} \times Bit \times Bit \to Bit$
rew	$t \wedge b = b$		$eq : Bit \times Bit \to \mathbf{Bool}$
	$f \wedge b = f$	var	$b, b_1, b_2 : Bit$
		rew	$inv(e_0) = e_1$
sort	$D, List$		$inv(e_1) = e_0$
func	$d_0 :\to D$		$if(t, b_1, b_2) = b_1$
	$if : \mathbf{Bool} \times D \times D \to D$		$if(f, b_1, b_2) = b_2$
	$eq : D \times D \to \mathbf{Bool}$		$if(eq(b_1, b_2), b_1, b_2) = b_2$
	$empty :\to List$		$eq(b, inv(b)) = f$
	$add : D \times List \to List$		$eq(b, b) = t$
	$head : List \to D$		
	$tail : List \to List$	sort	N
	$last : List \to \mathbf{Bool}$	func	$0 :\to \mathbf{N}$
	$indl : List \to Bit$		$s, pred : \mathbf{N} \to \mathbf{N}$
var	$d, d_1, d_2 :\to D$		$eq : \mathbf{N} \times \mathbf{N} \to \mathbf{Bool}$
	$l :\to List$		$lt : \mathbf{N} \times \mathbf{N} \to \mathbf{Bool}$
rew	$head(empty) = d_0$		$minus : \mathbf{N} \times \mathbf{N} \to \mathbf{N}$
	$head(add(d, l)) = d$	var	$n, n_1, n_2 :\to \mathbf{N}$
	$tail(empty) = empty$	rew	$eq(0, 0) = t$
	$tail(add(d, l)) = l$		$eq(0, s(n)) = f$
	$last(empty) = t$		$eq(s(n), 0) = f$
	$last(add(d, empty)) = t$		$eq(s(n_1), s(n_2)) = eq(n_1, n_2)$
	$last(add(d_1, add(d_2, l))) = f$		$lt(0, s(n)) = t$
	$indl(empty) = e_1$		$lt(n, 0) = f$
	$indl(add(d, empty)) = e_1$		$lt(s(n_1), s(n_2)) = lt(n_1, n_2)$
	$indl(add(d_1, add(d_2, l))) = e_0$		$pred(0) = 0$
	$if(t, d_1, d_2) = d_1$		$pred(s(n)) = n$
	$if(f, d_1, d_2) = d_2$		$minus(n, 0) = n$
	$eq(d, d) = t$		$minus(n_1, s(n_2)) = pred(minus(n_1, n_2))$
	$if(eq(d_1, d_2), d_1, d_2) = d_2$		

Table 1: Specification of standard data types used in the BRP

A1	$x + y = y + x$	SUM1	$\Sigma_{d:D} x = x$
A2	$x + (y + z) = (x + y) + z$	SUM3	$\Sigma_{d:D}\, p(d) = \Sigma_{d:D}\, p(d) + p(e)$
A3	$x + x = x$	SUM4	$\Sigma_{d:D}(p(d) + q(d)) = \Sigma_{d:D}\, p(d) + \Sigma_{d:D}\, q(d)$
A4	$(x + y) \cdot z = x \cdot z + y \cdot z$	SUM5	$\Sigma_{d:D}(p(d) \cdot x) = (\Sigma_{d:D}\, p(d)) \cdot x$
A5	$(x \cdot y) \cdot z = x \cdot (y \cdot z)$	SUM11	$(\forall d\, p(d) = q(d)) \rightarrow \Sigma_{d:D}\, p(d) = \Sigma_{d:D}\, q(d)$
A6	$x + \delta = x$		
		Bool1	$\neg(t = f)$
		Bool2	$\neg(b = t) \rightarrow b = f$
B1	$x \cdot \tau = x$	C1	$x \triangleleft t \triangleright y = x$
B2	$z \cdot (\tau \cdot (x + y) + x) = z \cdot (x + y)$	C2	$x \triangleleft f \triangleright y = y$

Table 2: pCRL axioms

SUM6	$\Sigma_{d:D}(p(d) \parallel z) = (\Sigma_{d:D}\, p(d)) \parallel z$	CF	$a(d)|b(e) = \begin{cases} \gamma(a,b)(d) & \text{if } d = e \text{ and} \\ & \gamma(a,b) \text{ defined} \\ \delta & \text{otherwise} \end{cases}$
SUM7	$\Sigma_{d:D}(p(d)|z) = (\Sigma_{d:D}\, p(d))|z$		
SUM8	$\Sigma_{d:D}(\partial_H(p(d))) = \partial_H(\Sigma_{d:D}\, p(d))$		
SUM9	$\Sigma_{d:D}(\tau_I(p(d))) = \tau_I(\Sigma_{d:D}\, p(d))$		
SUM10	$\Sigma_{d:D}(\rho_R(p(d))) = \rho_R(\Sigma_{d:D}\, p(d))$	CD1	$\delta|x = \delta$
		CD2	$x|\delta = \delta$
CM1	$x \parallel y = x \parallel\!\!\!\lfloor y + y \parallel\!\!\!\lfloor x + x|y$	CT1	$\tau|x = \delta$
CM2	$c \parallel\!\!\!\lfloor x = c \cdot x$	CT2	$x|\tau = \delta$
CM3	$c \cdot x \parallel\!\!\!\lfloor y = c \cdot (x \parallel y)$		
CM4	$(x + y) \parallel\!\!\!\lfloor z = x \parallel\!\!\!\lfloor z + y \parallel\!\!\!\lfloor z$	DD	$\partial_H(\delta) = \delta$
CM5	$c \cdot x|c' = (c|c') \cdot x$	DT	$\partial_H(\tau) = \tau$
CM6	$c|c' \cdot x = (c|c') \cdot x$	D1	$\partial_H(a(d)) = a(d)$ if $a \notin H$
CM7	$c \cdot x|c' \cdot y = (c|c') \cdot (x \parallel y)$	D2	$\partial_H(a(d)) = \delta$ if $a \in H$
CM8	$(x + y)|z = x|z + y|z$	D3	$\partial_H(x + y) = \partial_H(x) + \partial_H(y)$
CM9	$x|(y + z) = x|y + x|z$	D4	$\partial_H(x \cdot y) = \partial_H(x) \cdot \partial_H(y)$

Table 3: Primary μCRL axioms

TID	$\tau_I(\delta) = \delta$	
TIT	$\tau_I(\tau) = \tau$	
TI1	$\tau_I(a(d)) = a(d)$	if $a \notin I$
TI2	$\tau_I(a(d)) = \tau$	if $a \in I$
TI3	$\tau_I(x + y) = \tau_I(x) + \tau_I(y)$	
TI4	$\tau_I(x \cdot y) = \tau_I(x) \cdot \tau_I(y)$	

Table 4: Secondary μCRL axioms

SC1	$x \parallel\!\!\!\lfloor (y \parallel z) = (x \parallel\!\!\!\lfloor y) \parallel\!\!\!\lfloor z$
SC2	$x \parallel\!\!\!\lfloor \delta = x \delta$
SC3	$x \mid y = y \mid x$
SC4	$(x \mid y) \mid z = x \mid (y \mid z)$
SC5	$(x \mid y) \parallel\!\!\!\lfloor z = x \mid (y \parallel\!\!\!\lfloor z)$
Handshaking	$(x \mid y) \mid z = \delta$

Table 5: Standard Concurrency and Handshaking

References

[1] J.C.M. Baeten and W.P. Weijland. *Process Algebra*. Cambridge Tracts in Theoretical Computer Science 18. Cambridge University Press, 1990.

[2] M. Bezem, R. Bol, and J.F. Groote. Formalizing process algebraic verifications in the calculus of constructions. Technical Report 95-02, Eindhoven University of Technology, January 1995. To appear in Formal Aspects of Computing.

[3] M.A. Bezem and J.F. Groote. A correctness proof of a one-bit sliding window protocol in μCRL. *The Computer Journal*, 37(4):289–307, 1994.

[4] G. Dowek, A. Felty, H. Herbelin, G. Huet, C. Murthy, C. Parent, C. Paulin-Mohring, and B. Werner. The Coq proof assistant user's guide. Version 5.8. Technical report, INRIA – Rocquencourt, May 1993.

[5] J.F. Groote and H.P. Korver. A correctness proof of the bakery protocol in μCRL. In A. Ponse, C. Verhoef, and S.F.M. van Vlijmen, editors, *Proc. 1st Workshop on the Algebra of Communicating Processes (ACP'94)*, Utrecht, Workshops in Computing, pages 63–86. Springer-Verlag, 1994.

[6] J.F. Groote and A. Ponse. The syntax and semantics of μCRL. Technical Report CS-R9076, CWI, Amsterdam, December 1990.

[7] J.F. Groote and A. Ponse. Proof theory for μCRL: a language for processes with data. In D.J. Andrews, J.F. Groote, and C.A. Middelburg, editors, *Proc. of the Int. Workshop on Semantics of Specification Languages*, pages 232–251. Workshops in Computing, Springer Verlag, 1994.

[8] J.F. Groote and J.C. van de Pol. A bounded retransmission protocol for large data packets. Technical Report Logic Group Preprint Series No. 100, Utrecht University, Oct 1993.

[9] K. Havelund and N. Shankar. Experiments in theorem proving and model checking for protocol verification. Obtainable via http://www.csl.sri.com/~shankar/shankar.html, 1995.

[10] L. Helmink, M.P.A. Sellink, and F.W. Vaandrager. Proof-checking a data link protocol. In H.P. Barendregt and T. Nipkow, editors, *Proc. of the 1st International Workshop "Types for Proofs and Programs"*, May 1993, volume 806 of *LNCS*, pages 127–165, Nijmegen, 1994.

[11] ISO. *Information processing systems – open systems interconnection – LOTOS – a formal description technique based on the temporal ordering of observational behaviour* ISO IS 8807, 1989.

[12] H. Korver and J. Springintveld. A computer-checked verification of Milner's scheduler. In M. Hagiya and J.C. Mitchell, editors, *Proc. of the Int. Symp. on Theoretical Aspects of Computer Software*, volume 789 of *LNCS*, pages 161–178, Sendai, Japan, April 1994. Springer Verlag.

[13] S. Mauw. *PSF – A Process Specification Formalism*. PhD thesis, University of Amsterdam, December 1991.

[14] R. Milner. *Communication and Concurrency*. Prentice-Hall International, Englewood Cliffs, 1989.

[15] M.P.A. Sellink. Verifying process algebra proofs in type theory. In D.J. Andrews, J.F. Groote, and C.A. Middelburg, editors, *Proc. of the Int. Workshop on Semantics of Specification Languages, Utrecht 1993*, Workshops in Computing, pages 315–339. Springer-Verlag, 1994.

[16] M.P.A. Sellink. *Computer-Aided Verification of Protocols, The Type Theoretic Approach*. Phd thesis, Utrecht University, February 1996.

SPECWARE: An Advanced Environment for the Formal Development of Complex Software Systems

Demonstration Abstract

R. Juellig, Y. Srinivas, J. Liu
Kestrel Institute
3260 Hillview Ave.
Palo Alto, CA 94304

1. Introduction

SPECWARE is an advanced environment for the formal development of complex software systems. It supports the specification, design, and evolution of high-performance, correct-by-construction software. Software development using SPECWARE consists of the systematic transformation of formal specifications into executable programs, using high-level, parallel and sequentially composable design steps formally represented within and applied by the system.

The explicit representation of the structure of specifications, design steps, and target code is the most important new aspect that SPECWARE adds to the synthesis technology embodied in earlier Kestrel prototypes including KIDS [Smith], DTRE [Blaine], and Reacto [Gilham] (cf. also [Juellig]). The explicit representation and manipulation of structure is crucial to scaling program construction techniques to system development. SPECWARE combines the strength of CASE and OOP technology with the strengths of formal methods and automated program synthesis technology.

2. Foundation

SPECWARE is based on algebraic specifications [Wirsing], category theory, and sheaf theory [JS 95]. We believe that the use of such ``heavy'' formal machinery is well-justified. For instance, category theory seems ideally suited for describing the manipulation of richly detailed structures at various levels of granularity. Similarly, the sheaf-theoretic notion of compatible families seems fundamental to and pervasive in putting systems together from interdependent components. We will briefly overview some of the aforementioned concepts in the following.

Specifications and Morphisms An (algebraic) specification defines a language (i.e., a collection of types and operations on these types) and constrains its possible meanings via axioms. A specification morphism translates the language of a source specification into the language of a target specification in a way that preserves theorems.

Interpretations Interpretations are generalized specification morphisms by allowing the translation of a symbol (operator or sort name) to an expression (composite operation or sort expression). Interpretations are the primary concept for expressing data type refinement and algorithm design as an incremental process that constructs a series of interpretations.

Diagrams We can use morphisms to express a system as an interconnection of its parts. Then, a diagram is a directed multigraph in which the nodes are labeled by specifications or interpretations, and the edges by the corresponding morphisms (in a multigraph, there can be more than one edge between any two nodes). Diagrams are used in our environment to express system structure, and design consists of refining a diagram by refining its parts.

Composition (Colimit) By taking the colimit of a diagram, a single specification is obtained by combining the constituent components (nodes) and identifying their shared parts (expressed by morphisms). As a special case, the colimit operation can be used to instantiate parameterized specifications.

Algorithm Design Algorithm theories capture the common structure of a class of algorithms, e.g., search, divide-and-conquer, dynamic programming, etc. Each algorithm theory identifies the minimal structure needed in a domain to solve a given problem as an instance of the class of algorithms characterized by the theory. Given a collection of algorithm theories (organized in a refinement hierarchy) and a problem specification, algorithm design consists now in showing that the problem can be cast as an instance of the known algorithm classes.

3. SPECWARE System

This section is meant to give a "look and feel" of the current SPECWARE^{TM} system. In the current status, the main capabilities of SPECWARE are to define and edit specifications both graphically and textually, to type checking specifications, to compute colimits of specifications, and to refine specifications (e.g. data type refinement). Due to lack of space, we could not fully explain each step in the following formal development process.

The goal of the following development is to generate lisp code for bags of natural number with mod. This specification BAG-OF-NAT-MOD is constructed by using the colimit of bags (BAG) and natural numbers with mod (NAT-MOD). The subsequent development for generating lisp code for it will take advantage of this structured specification. All development interactions are supported by the SPECWARE graphical user interface.

3.1 The System Interface
The system interface consists of three parts, namely, system menu, display area and an emacs pane for system message and interactions, as shown below.

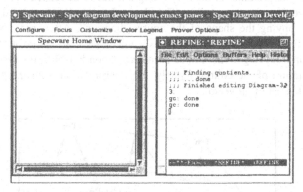

Through the system menu, one can change the interface configuration, enter knowledge base (editing, developing and creating objects). Then display window can be used to show graphical representation of any objects, for instance, specification diagram, diagram refinement. One can create other display windows as well. There is an emacs pane for recording system messages and similar things.

3.2 Diagram and Colimit

A specification diagram is composed of specifications as nodes and specification morphisms as arcs. There are various methods in the system to create a new diagram, change an existing diagram and visualize diagrams. The problem BAG-OF-NAT-MOD is composed by the colimit of the subdiagram in the cocone shown below.

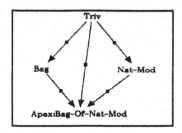

3.3 Sequential and Parallel Refinement

Refinement is represented by interpretations in SPECWARE. Two subsequent refinement can be put together by sequential composition. For instance, the following diagram shows that Bag is refined to List via Sequence. SPECWARE supports sequential composition as one of several interpretation methods, the system will compute the composition automatically, provided that each individual interpretation is given.

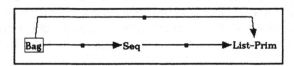

Moreover, parallel refinement supports refinement through exploring the structure of a specification (expressed via diagrams). It requires for each component an interpretation, and if two components in the source diagram are related by a specification morphism, their interpretation in the target diagram has to be related in such a way that two interpretations are compatible. The above diagram is constructed via a system command "copying the shape of the source diagram". Afterwards, one constructs needed interpretations, e.g., the previously via sequential composition constructed interpretation from Bag to List can be used here. Upon finishing, the system computes the interpretation of the colimit namely, the interpretation from the bag of natural numbers to the list of bit vector.

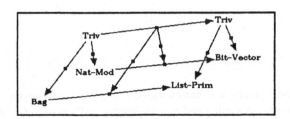

3.4 Code Generation

When finishing high-level refinement (algorithm design, data refinement, and other reformulations and optimizations), one can generate code from a sublangauge of SLANG to LISP. The code generation is based on a framework adapted from institution morphisms [Meseguer]. Basically, in the new framework, one can generate code in the specification-refinement style. For our problem, we can generate the lisp code for each of the components and put them together. The following diagrams show this process.

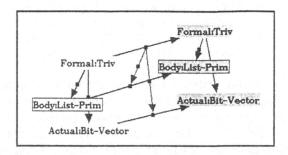

3.5 Applications

One of the Kestrel projects has focused on the synthesis of high-performance schedulers (e.g. transportation schedulers). The main step in the synthesis process is to develop a formal model of scheduling domain knowledge. We have successfully using the SPECWARE system built structured abstract scheduling domain theories and their instantiations to transportation scheduling domain.

4. Conclusions

SPECWARE supports the systematic construction of formal specifications and their stepwise refinement into programs. The fundamental operations in SPECWARE are that of composing specifications (via colimits), the corresponding refinement by composing refinements (via sheaves), and the generation of programs by composing code modules (via colimits). We believe that this formal basis will enable the scaling to system-level software construction.

5. References

[Gilham] Li-Mei Gilham and Allen Goldberg and T. C. Wang: Toward Reliable Reactive Systems, in Proceedings of the 5th International Workshop on Software Design. 1989, Pittsburgh,.

[Blaine] Lee Blaine and Allen Goldberg: DTRE -- A Semi-Automatic Transformation System, in Constructing Programs from Specifications (editor B. Moeller), North-Holland, 1991.

[Smith] Smith, D.R. KIDS-- a semi-automatic program development system. IEEE Transactions on Software Engineering 16, 9 (September 1990), 1024--1043.

[SJ 95],Y. V. Srinivas and Richard Juellig: SPECWARE^{TM}: Formal Support for Composing Software, in Proc. of the Conf. on Mathematics of Program Construction, Germany, July 1995.

[Meseguer] Meseguer, J. General logics. Logic Colloquium'87. H.-D. Ebbinghaus et. al., Eds. North-Holland, 1989, pp.~275--329.

[Wirsing] Wirsing, M. Structured algebraic specifications: A kernel language.Theoretical Comput. Sci. 42 (1986), 123--249.

ASSPEGIQUE+
An Integrated Specification Environment Providing Inter-Operability of Tools *

Michel Bidoit,[1] Christine Choppy[2,3] and Frédéric Voisin[3]

[1] LIENS, C.N.R.S. U.R.A. 1327 & Ecole Normale Supérieure
45 Rue d'Ulm, F–75230 Paris Cedex 05, France
[2] IRIN, Université de Nantes & Ecole Centrale
F–44072 Nantes Cedex 03, France
[3] LRI, C.N.R.S. U.R.A. 410 & Université de Paris-Sud
Bât. 490, F–91405 Orsay Cedex, France

ASSPEGIQUE+ is an integrated environment for the development of large algebraic specifications and the management of a specification data base. The aim of the ASSPEGIQUE+ specification environment is to provide the user with a "specification laboratory" where a large range of various tools supporting the use of algebraic specifications are closely integrated. While building this environment, we have also been motivated by the idea of providing a way to use tools for algebraic specifications built by our colleagues, and this led us firstly to work on building interfaces between ASSPEGIQUE and these tools (e.g. REVE [23] and SLOG [16]), and then to design a generic way to provide inter-operability between tools [7, 13, 20].

The main aspects adressed in the design of the tools in ASSPEGIQUE+ are the following : dealing with modularity and reusability, providing ease of use, flexibility of the environment and user-friendly interfaces. The ASSPEGIQUE+ specification environment supports the specification langage PLUSS[8, 4, 19]. The previous version of this environment, ASSPEGIQUE [6, 5, 9] supported only the enrichment primitive, while ASSPEGIQUE+ [11, 24] supports in addition renaming, parameterization and instantiation.

The tools available in the ASSPEGIQUE+ specification environment include browsing tools, a specification editing tool, a specification modules integrator, symbolic evaluation tools and interfaces to other tools or environments. Most of these tools use CIGALE [25, 26], a system for incremental grammar construction and parsing, which has been especially designed in order to cope with a flexible, user-oriented way of defining operators : mixfix operator names, coercion and overloading are supported.

The symbolic evaluation tools take conditional rewrite rules into account. There are three different possibilities for evaluation : (i) "standard" rewriting, with textual and graphic trace options, and choice of the rewriting strategy, (ii) eval-

* Work partially supported by the ESPRIT Basic Research Working Group 6112 COMPASS-II, by a CNRS/NSF grant, and by the C.N.R.S. G.D.R.-P.R.C. "Programmation".

uation with compiled rules [21], (iii) mixed evaluation (a combination of rewriting and user code) [22, 10, 14]. The mixed evaluation mode allows to perform computations where rewriting interacts with the execution of code. This code should include an implementation for constructor inverses and may be written by the user; it may be an implementation for some modules of the specification, or even for parts of modules of the specification. This facility is implemented in ASSPEGIQUE$^+$ in a very flexible way: the implemented modules may be any module in the specification (not necessarily the "bottom" ones), and for each module for which an implementation is provided, the user may choose to use either rewriting in the specification version or execution of the available code.

The principles we developed [7, 13] for designing a generic interfacing design between algebraic specification tools or environments comprise both issues concerning a common interchange format, and issues regarding interaction with the user, that is how to get and display information using the specification language known to the user. These ideas were used for developing interfaces with the proof checker LP [18, 17], and, within the SALSA project [20], interfaces with environments for the algebraic specification languages LPG [3, 2] and GLIDER [15]. It is hoped that further developments along these lines will be achieved in the scope of the Common Framework Initiative [1].

A case study [12] is used to present the use of these tools for testing and validating specifications.

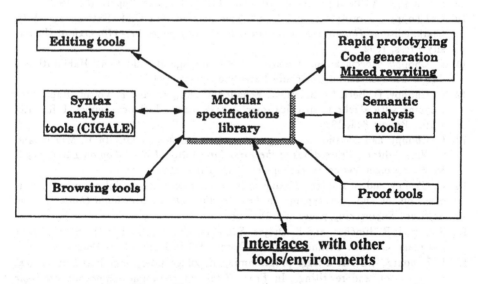

Fig. 1. The ASSPEGIQUE$^+$ environment

References

1. The Common Framework Initiative. Web home page available at the address http://www1.daimi.aau.dk/~pdm/Common/, 1995.
2. D. Bert, P. Drabik, and R. Echahed. Manuel de référence de LPG. Technical Report 17, IMAG-LIFIA, 1987.
3. D. Bert and R. Echahed. Design and implementation of a generic, logic and functional programming language. In *ESOP-86*, pages 119–132. Springer-Verlag L.N.C.S. 213, 1986.
4. M. Bidoit. PLUSS, un langage pour le développement de spécifications algébriques modulaires. Thèse d'Etat, Université Paris-Sud, 1989.
5. M. Bidoit and C. Choppy. ASSPEGIQUE: an integrated environment for algebraic specifications. In *Proc. of the 1st International Joint Conference on Theory and Practice of Software Development (TAPSOFT)*, pages 246–260. Springer-Verlag L.N.C.S. 186, 1985.
6. M. Bidoit, C. Choppy, and F. Voisin. The ASSPEGIQUE specification environment: Motivations and Design. In *Proc. of the 3rd Workshop on Theory and Applications of Abstract Data Types*, pages 54–72. Springer-Verlag I.F.B. 116, 1984.
7. M. Bidoit, C. Choppy, and F. Voisin. Interchange Format for Inter-Operability of Tools and Translation The SALSA and ASSPEGIQUE+/LP Experience. In *Recent Trends in Data Type Specifications - Proc. 11th Workshop on Abstract Data Type joint with 8th COMPASS Workshop - Selected Papers*. L.N.C.S. Springer Verlag, to appear.
8. M. Bidoit, M.-C. Gaudel, and A. Mauboussin. How to make algebraic specifications more understandable? An experiment with the PLUSS specification language. *Science of Computer Programming*, 12(1), 1989.
9. C. Choppy. ASSPEGIQUE: User's Manual. L.R.I. Research Report 452, 1988.
10. C. Choppy. Prototyping and formal specification. In C.M. Rattray and R.G. Clark, editors, *The unified computation laboratory*, pages 141–170. Oxford University Press, 1992.
11. C. Choppy. Spécifications algébriques: Prototypage et validation. Habilitation à diriger des recherches, Université Paris-Sud, Orsay, 1994.
12. C. Choppy, D. Bert, M. Bidoit, R. Echahed, C. Roques, and F. Voisin. Rapid prototyping with algebraic specifications: A case study. Technical report, L.R.I. Research Report 844, 1993.
13. C. Choppy and M. Bidoit. Integrating ASSPEGIQUE and LP. In U. Martin and J. Wing, editors, *Proceedings of the First International Workshop on Larch*, pages 69–85. Springer-Verlag Workshops in Computing, 1993.
14. C. Choppy and S. Kaplan. Mixing abstract and concrete modules : specification, development and prototyping. In *Proc. of the 12th International Conference on Software Engineering*, pages 173–184, 1990.
15. S. Clérici, R. Jiménez, and F. Orejas. Semantic Constructions in the Specification Language GLIDER. Technical Report Dissem-033-P, Icarus, June 1992.
16. L. Fribourg. SLOG: a logic programming language interpreter based on clausal superposition and rewriting. In *Proc. of the International Symposium on Logic Programming*, 1985.
17. S. Garland and J. Guttag. An overview of LP, the Larch Prover. In *Proc. of the Third International Conference on Rewriting Techniques and Applications*, pages 137–151. Springer-Verlag L.N.C.S. 355, 1989.

18. S. Garland and J. Guttag. A Guide to LP, The Larch Prover. Technical Report 82, DEC-SRC, 1991.
19. M.-C. Gaudel. Structuring and modularizing algebraic specifications : the PLUSS specification language, evolutions and perspectives. In *Proc. of the 9th Symposium on Theoretical Aspects of Computer Science (STACS)*, pages 3–23. Springer-Verlag L.N.C.S. 577, 1992.
20. SALSA (group composed of D.Bert, M. Bidoit, C. Choppy, R. Echahed, J.-M. Hufflen, J.-P. Jacquot, M. Lemoine, N. Levy, J.-C. Reynaud, C. Roques, and F. Voisin). Opération SALSA: Structure d'Accueil pour Spécifications Algébriques. Final report, 1994.
21. S. Kaplan. A compiler for conditional term rewriting systems. In *Proc. 2nd Conf. on Rewriting Techniques and Applications*, pages 25–41. Springer LNCS 256, 1987.
22. S. Kaplan and C. Choppy. Abstract rewriting with concrete operators. In *Proc. of the Third International Conference on Rewriting Techniques and Applications*, pages 178–186. Springer-Verlag L.N.C.S. 355, 1989.
23. P. Lescanne. Computer experiments with the REVE term rewriting system generator. In *Proc. 10th Symposium on Principles of Programming Languages*, pages 99–108. ACM, 1983.
24. C. Roques. *Modularité dans les spécifications algébriques, Théorie et application.* PhD thesis, Thèse de Doctorat, Université Paris-Sud, 1994.
25. F. Voisin. CIGALE: a tool for interactive grammar construction and expression parsing. *Science of Computer Programming*, 7(1):61–86, 1986.
26. F. Voisin. A bottom-up adaptation of Earley parsing algorithm. In *Proc. of the Int. Workshop on programming language implementation and logic programming*, pages 146–160. Springer-Verlag L.N.C.S. 348, 1988.

Towards Integrating Algebraic Specification and Functional Programming: the Opal System

Extended Abstract

Klaus Didrich, Carola Gerke, Wolfgang Grieskamp, Christian Maeder,
Peter Pepper

Technische Universität Berlin, Fachbereich Informatik, Institut für Kommunikations-
und Softwaretechnik, Franklinstr. 28/29, D – 10587 Berlin
opal@cs.tu-berlin.de, http://www.cs.tu-berlin.de/~opal

1 Introduction

We envisage a software engineering environment based on formal methods, that encompasses requirements capture and formal specification as well as efficient implementation in a functional style. The overall principles to be used in such an environment have been studied, for example, in the KORSO project [2] and in the KIDS project [8], in the tradition of projects such as CIP [1] and OBJ [6].

The OPAL project focusses on the design and implementation of a *functional language* that fits into the above context. Ideally, the project should comprise concepts for functional programming and algebraic specification, a methodology and a proof calculus for verification and synthesis and a suite of elaborate support tools. In this extended abstract we sketch the current state of the system.

2 The Opal Language

OPAL [3] is a strongly typed, higher-order, functional language with a distinctive algebraic flavour, as becomes apparent in the fact that specification constructs are available in the language, in the syntactical appearance of OPAL, and last but not least, in the semantics of OPAL. Additionally, the language introduces some novel features for the handling of overloading and parameterization.

Specifications consist of laws stating freely generated properties for types and first-order propositional theorems in general. The incorporation of specifications is orthogonal to the functional sublanguage, and the tools listed below are therefore also applicable to the specification constructs. However, it is not our intention to animate specifications, we concentrate on the generation of efficient executable code. Thus the implementation must be done entirely functionally.

The OPAL language encapsulates I/O side-effects with the so-called *command monad*, a concept quite similar to HASKELL's I/O monad, as now proposed for version 1.3 of the language[1]. The command monad has recently been extended to allow *concurrent functional programming*.

---

[1] The usage of the name "command" stems from long-standing local tradition.

3 The Opal System

The significance of a comfortable environment for a programming paradigm can hardly be overestimated. The environment we envisage for a language such as OPAL shall consist at least of the following tools:

- A *Language Checker*, which produces comprehensive diagnostics about errors in language use;

- A *Language Translator*, which translates functional programs into efficient executable code;

- An *Optimizer*, which automatically performs structural improvements on the functional source;

- An *Interpreter and Debugger*, which allows for prototypical evaluation and tracing of program execution;

- A *Proof Assistant*, which supports formal proofs;

- A *Library* of reusable software components;

- A *Librarian*, which provides navigation to sources and processes queries for library components;

- A *Documentation Generator*, which produces printable documentation of software;

- A *Project Repository Manager*, which records the documents of a software project and administers configurations and relations between the documents.

Many of these components have been implemented, some exist as prototypes, others are on the agenda. In the following, we sketch some of the individual tools.

Language Translator The OPAL translator takes an intermediate representation of an OPAL structure and translates it to standard C [7]. The decision to use C as a target language reflects a reasonable division of tasks in compiling functional languages: mapping a functional language to an imperative language with explicit memory and control flow, and mapping such an imperative language to a given machine architecture are mostly distinct problems.

The basic tasks of the OPAL translator are automatic memory management and the realization of higher-order values[2]. The translator uses an enhanced reference-counting approach to memory management, which in particular enables updates of monolithic arrays in constant time. As a recent comparison of many functional language implementations shows [4], OPAL programs are among the fastest world-wide. Individual benchmarks for comparable algorithms show that OPAL code can be as fast and even faster than handwritten C code.

---

[2]Lazy evaluation is realized as a special case of higher-order values which are represented as closures.

The performance of the generated code has convinced us "by experiment" that functional languages can indeed be compiled in reasonable time to fast code – a result which is corroborated at the present time by many other groups implementing functional languages.

Library A library of *reusable software components* is an integral part of a modern programming environment. Its function is to relieve the user of having to constantly "re-invent the wheel". Such a library, containing most data types and functions needed for everyday use, has been developed for OPAL over the last few years. It encompasses more then 40 data types, including types such as numbers, strings, sequences, arrays, sets, bags, finite mappings and so on, and supporting operating system facilities such as processes, files, group ids and more. The library incorporates modular extensions for *concurrent functional programming*, which has been used to provide a comprehensive library for window programming [5].

The power of the library is, as is to be expected, heavily supported by the algebraic concept of parameterization as available in OPAL. The purely functional parts of the library have been specified extensively. The possibility to easily incorporate *handcoded* structures – that is, structures which are coded totally or partially in C – simplifies the access to operating system resources and use of tools. So it is possible to use LEX and YACC in OPAL programs, or the ANTLR parser generator from PCCTS; most recently, an interface to an SQL database management system (INFORMIX) has been developed.

Documentation Generator Documentation of software is traditionally treated as a "step-child". The concept of *literate programming*, as introduced by Knuth, was intended to solve this problem by merging documentation and program code in a single document. For the OPAL environment we took the approach of embedding the documentation in special comments, so-called *documentaries*. This allows the integration of undocumented and fully documented program parts, because no special adaptation to the documentation generator is needed. The documentation integrates the views of the document as a sequential text and as a hypertext; we can thus produce a sequential documentation on paper and a hypertext documentation for online use. A prototypical documentation generator has been implemented on the basis of this concept.

Proof Assistant An environment for functional languages should also include some support for proving the correctness of given algebraic properties. This task consists of *generating the proof obligations, managing* them and the *interactive resolution* of these proof obligations.

A first prototype of such a system, called BOP, has been developed for the OPAL environment. Verification technology is a challenging research area of its own, but lies beyond our current focus. Hence, we intend to investigate the possibility of integrating existing verification machines into the OPAL proof support.

Repository Manager A loose collection of tools does not make up a programming environment. The minimal functionality a user expects from an environment is automatic *configuration management*. A maintenance driver based alternatively on the GNU `make` utility program or on the SHAPE configuration and version management tool kit has been designed for OPAL. It manages the version and configuration management of OPAL projects, which may consist of many subsystems and libraries provided by many developers.

4 Conclusion

The OPAL system has been used in teaching and research activities. The experience that we have gained from working on and with the OPAL system indicates that functional programming is indeed well suited for producing "real-life" software. This result coincides with the findings of other research teams working in this area. The integration of algebraic specification constructs into a functional language as it is done in the OPAL system helps in closing the gap between the two worlds of formal specification and efficient implementation. We feel confident that the functional paradigm, supported by formal methods, will eventually provide a basis for industrial software development.

References

1. F.L. Bauer, M. Broy, B. Möller, P. Pepper, M. Wirsing, et al. *The Munich Project CIP. Vol. I: The Wide Spectrum Language CIP-L*, volume I of *Lecture Notes on Computer Science*. Springer Verlag, Berlin, Heidelberg, New York, Berlin, 1985.

2. M. Broy and S. Jähnichen. *KORSO, Correct Software by Formal Methods*. Springer, 1994.

3. Klaus Didrich, Andreas Fett, Carola Gerke, Wolfgang Grieskamp, and Peter Pepper. OPAL: Design and Implementation of an Algebraic Programming Language. In Jürg Gutknecht, editor, *Programming Languages and System Architectures, International Conference, Zurich, Switzerland, March 1994*, LNCS 782, pages 228–244. Springer, 1994.

4. P. H. Hartel et al. Benchmarking implementations of functional languages with "pseudoknot", a Float-Intensive benchmark. *J. functional programming*, to appear, 1996.

5. Thomas Frauenstein, Wolfgang Grieskamp, Peter Pepper, and Mario Südholt. Concurrent functional programming of graphical user interfaces. Technical Report 95-19, TU Berlin, 1996. to appear.

6. Joseph A. Goguen and Timothy Winkler. Introducing OBJ3. Technical Report SRI-CSL-88-9, SRI International, 1988.

7. Wolfram Schulte and Wolfgang Grieskamp. Generating Efficient Portable Code for a Strict Applicative Language. In *Phoenix Seminar and Workshop on Declarative Programming*. Springer-Verlag, 1992.

8. Douglas R. Smith. KIDS: A semiautomatic program development system. *IEEE Transactions on Software Engineering*, 16(9):1024–1043, September 1990.

InterACT: An Interactive Theorem Prover for Algebraic Specifications

Robert Geisler*, Marcus Klar**, Felix Cornelius*

* Technische Universität Berlin, FB Informatik
Sekr. 6-1, Franklinstr. 28/29, D-10587 Berlin.

** Fraunhofer-Institut für Software- und Systemtechnik ISST
Kurstr. 33 D-10117 Berlin.

E-mail: {geislerr,mklar,felix}@cs.tu-berlin.de

Abstract. The *InterACT* tool is a theorem prover for algebraic specifications with conditional equations emphasizing user-friendliness and interaction. Its purpose is mainly educational, e.g. to support the teaching of formal methods. It already has been used successfully in universitary courses on formal specification of software systems. *InterACT* provides a graphical user interface that supports proving "by mouse".

1 Introduction

In order to communicate the benefits of formal methods in software engineering, e.g. formal specifications, tool support is required. The opportunity to prove theorems about a formal specification is one of the most important advantages of formal methods. Furthermore, in the field of educational tools, this mechanical proof support should resemble "pencil and paper proofs" as close as possible in order for the proof to be understandable and readable. Since nowadays, user interfaces are of growing importance for the evaluation and acceptance of theorem provers (see e.g. [6]), a sophisticated user interface allows the *InterACT* proof technique to be learned easily. *InterACT* is embedded in the ACT environment [1, 2]. The presented tool was developed in 1995 as a diploma thesis [3, 4]. It was designed and implemented using object oriented techniques. The implementation language is C++, the user interface was designed with Tcl/Tk.

2 A brief description

In Figure 1, the *InterACT* main window is shown, displaying the actual goal under attack, several rule buttons and the message window. *InterACT* supports the proof of universally and existentially quantified conditional equations, based on a sequent calculus. Term rewriting (paramodulation), structural induction, and Noetherian induction are the most important rules of *InterACT*.

The proofs are performed interactively step by step. Only very basic support for automating proof sequences is offered (the *simplifier* feature). This includes user definable strategies for term rewriting, leading to symbolical execution of

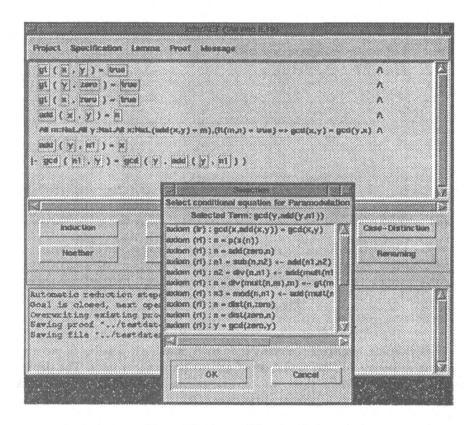

Fig. 1. The *InterACT* main window

specification parts. Proofs can be visualized as trees (see Figure 2). This proof tree allows for the performance of administrative operations, like undoing proof steps, changing or displaying the actual goal. At each proof step, all matching rules are offered to the user. Therefore we distinguish local rules (such as paramodulation), that are applied by clicking on an expression in the actual proof goal, and global rules (e.g. structural induction) that are invoked by clicking on a rule button. The opportunity to concentrate just on one part of the actual goal by using local rules resembles the so called *windowing* technique [5]. In case that the structural induction is not powerful enough, Noetherian induction is provided, giving the user the opportunity to specify the ordering and prove its termination within the *InterACT*-tool. Another important subject is to prove the completeness of an operation symbol w.r.t. the constructors of the specification. *InterACT* offers the operation symbols that might be proven to be complete in a user-dialogue and generates the desired completeness theorem. Completeness proofs are carried out using the abstract notion of a signature morphism.

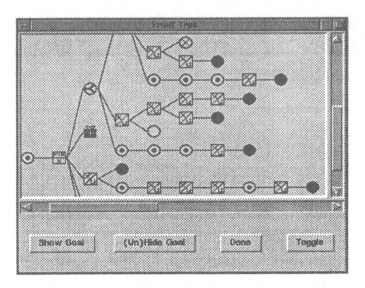

Fig. 2. The Proof Tree

The system is managing theorems and proofs, making it possible to presume lemmata necessary for the actual proof and to prove them later. The dependencies between different theorems are maintained, disabling cyclic proofs. A LaTeX-output of proofs is generated by *InterACT*.

3 Experiences

In order to demonstrate the kind of specifications that can be handled by *Inter-ACT* we give a snapshot of a well known generic list specification. Two operations for the reversal of lists are specified:

```
func reverse: List -> List;
    reverse(nil) = nil;
    reverse(ladd(d,l)) = radd(reverse(l),d);
func reverse_ac: List, List -> List;
    reverse_ac(nil,l) = l;
    reverse_ac(ladd(d,l),ll) = reverse_ac(l,ladd(d,ll));
```

Interesting questions about the specification which should be answered by formal proofs are for example:

- Is the data of sort List generated by the constructors nil and ladd, i.e. is the **reverse** operation complete (or reducible) wrt. nil and ladd?
- Do the two reverse operations always yield the same result?

The first statement can be formulated as the following, existentially quantified equation: $\exists l : List . reverse(\phi(l')) = \phi(l)$, where ϕ denotes the morphism from the signature consisting only of the constructors of the specification into the specification itself. l and l' are variables of the constructor signature. The theorem for **reverse_ac** looks similar. The second proposition is expressed by the equation $reverse(l) = reverse\_ac(l, nil)$. Both theorems can be shown by structural induction. Furthermore, by reverting a list with both functions using the simplifier feature, the time complexity of the two solutions for list reversal can be compared. Additionally, some more practical case studies have been performed with *InterACT*, for example the proof of safety requirements for a hydraulic press and a simple intersection light controller. For both case studies, interesting safety relevant properties could be proven, some of them clearly too complex in size (several hundred proof steps) to be shown by hand. The theorems and their proofs were not trivial, nevertheless, *InterACT* turned out to be able to deal also with such complex proofs.

4 Future Plans

Specification morphisms are a useful means to describe relations between different specifications, e.g. import or refinement relations. Giving explicit morphisms and proving properties about them would strengthen the reusability of specifications and of proofs. We will extend *InterACT* in order to support proofs on the basis of collections of specifications interrelated by morphisms. Because morphisms are already implemented in *InterACT* as they are used for completeness proofs, this should be a rather straightforward and conceptually clean task.

References

1. I. Claßen, H. Ehrig, and D. Wolz. *Algberaic Specification Techniques and Tools for Software Development - The ACT Approach*. AMAST Series in Computing Vol. 1. World Scientific, 1993.
2. H. Ehrig and B. Mahr. *Fundamentals of Algebraic Specification 1: Equations and Initial Semantics*, volume 6 of *EATCS Monographs on Theoretical Computer Science*. Springer, Berlin, 1985.
3. R. Geisler and M. Klar. Design and realisation of the interactive theorem- and completeness prover *interact* for algebraic specifications (in german). Master's thesis, Berlin University of Technology, June 1995.
4. M. Klar, R. Geisler, and F. Cornelius. *InterACT*: An interactive theorem and completeness prover for algebraic specifications with conditional equations. submitted to Proc. 11th WADT, Oslo, 1996.
5. P. Robinson and J. Staples. Formalizing a hierarchical structure of practical mathematical reasoning. *Journal of Logic and Computation*, 3(1), Feb. 1993.
6. L. Théry, Y. Bertot, and G. Kahn. Real theorem provers deserve real user-interfaces. *ACM Software Engineering Notes*, 17(5), 1992. Fifth ACM SIGSOFT Symposium on Software Development Environments.

A New Proof-Manager and Graphic Interface for the Larch Prover

Frédéric Voisin

C.N.R.S. U.R.A. 410 and Université de Paris-Sud,
L.R.I., Bât. 490, F-91405 Orsay Cedex, France

Abstract. We present PLP, a proof management system and graphic interface for the "Larch Prover" (LP). The system provides additional support for interactive use of LP, by letting the user control the order in which goals are proved. We offer improved ways to investigate, compare and communicate proofs by allowing independent attempts at proving a goal, a better access to the information associated with goals and an additional script mechanism. All the features are accessible through a graphic system that makes the proof structure accessible to the user.

1 Introduction

The "proof-debugger" LP is part of the Larch project. It has been designed to help reasoning about algebraic specifications written in the Larch specification language by making it easier to prove properties of such specifications [2]. LP has also been applied to other domains such as the proof of circuits, of software components or of distributed algorithms [1, 3]. Here we focus on proof management since our system does not add any new logical mechanism to the ones already present in LP. We shall only recall that LP supports multi-sorted first-order formulas and offers various proof mechanisms, usually applied on user's request. The main operational mechanism is term rewriting with additional commands on top of it. Proof commands in LP are split in two groups: the "forward-inference" commands, used to enrich the current logical system without modifying the goal to be proved (like in critical-pairing or quantifier elimination), and the "backward-inference" commands, used to decompose the proof of a goal into the proofs of several subgoals (as in proof by cases or by induction), usually with some hypotheses. Therefore each subgoal is proved in a specific logical system formed by the initial axiomatization and the hypotheses corresponding to the various proof commands at the origin of a particular subgoal. The original formulas can be altered as part of the proof process: orientation of equations into rewrite rules, inter-normalization of rewrite systems.

2 What's new with PLP

The preliminary objectives and design of our system are described in [4]. Our objective is to augment LP with additional support for the interactive work on proofs and also to provide better mechanisms to investigate and compare proofs. LP is guided by the "design, code, debug" approach and offers very efficient commands for running large proofs written as scripts, but we also need more interactive support for helping in completing unfinished proofs or in correcting failed ones. Part of the problem is that it is not easy to write a script from scratch and to guess the exact form of the subgoals to prove, or the associated rewrite systems, after a few proof commands. For a given subgoal, one can sometimes think of several ways to prove it and we would like to be able to compare them, their subgoals or the contexts in which they are proved, without having to discard one strategy for trying another one. Also, with LP, a subgoal is discarded once proved, and its logical system is no longer accessible to the user. When the user is blocked in the proof of some subgoal, there is no possibility of switching to another subgoal, for instance for gaining some experience on another subgoal, or to understand why the proof of some subgoal succeeds while the proof of another do not. This hinders the comparison of similar proofs and this is where our system can help !

User control on the order of proof steps: LP does not provide the user with the control over the order in which the subgoals are proved: Each subgoal must be proved as soon as it is introduced, and the relative order of the subgoals originating from a given command is imposed by the system. We use the same default ordering, but at any moment the user of PLP can switch to another subgoal without first completing the current goal. New conjecture can be introduced by the user, that rely on conjectures that have not yet been completed. Therefore a user can prove the subgoals in the order that is the most natural for he/her, skip parts of a long proof when wanting to focus on a subpart of it, or state a sequence of conjectures whose proofs are deferred to separate files. The system automatically records which goals are unproved and proposes a new goal when the current task is completed.

Multiple attempts at proving subgoals: We allow independent attempts at proving subgoals, using different proof strategies. Variants can be started, cancelled, left uncompleted and later resumed, and the user can switch back and forth among them. A variant at a node is logically compatible with any variant at a node in an independent subtree: The validity depends only on the formulas in the subgoals. All subgoals have a "current" variant, with respect to which commands are interpreted. Switching between variants is done only on user request to minimize the risk of confusion for the user.

Variants are also useful to "replay" part of a proof either to try to simplify it or to have a closer look at its execution. This may be more convenient than retrieving the corresponding part in the log file maintained by LP.

Better access to proof information: With PLP, proved subgoals are not discarded automatically and it is possible to re-enter them to inspect their logical systems or to perform some computation (like normalization). This gives an easier way to compare the proofs of independent subgoals. Part of the information is recorded within the interface part and is accessible by mouse clicking without interaction with the proof engine (that can be working on a different subgoal). This includes the basic information about subgoals: logical status, the formula as initially stated and its current form after processing by the proof engine, current hypothesis etc. The rest of the information for a subgoal, even proved, can be retrieved by selecting that subgoal as the current focus for LP. This gives access to additional information, like the associated rewrite system, that would be too large to record within the interface part. Being able to run a whole proof and later browse through it, while picking up local information easily, provides valuable help when trying to understand someone else's proof.

Graphical presentation of proofs: We provide an explicit view of the tree that is the natural representation of a proof, with a proof command connecting a goal to the list of its subgoals. The selection of goals is done by mouse clicking or by name. The tree structure is used for representing backward-inference commands, the only ones that introduce subgoals. Forward-inference commands, which are not undoable in LP and which do not introduce subgoals, are displayed with a square box whose opening lists all the commands issued for the subgoal. Different displays for completed and uncompleted subgoals make clear where unfinished parts are. Pointing at a node provides information about it (logical status, associated hypothesis, etc) while selecting it as the current focus for LP allows to (re-)enter the associated logical context and make it ready to accept new commands.

Variants can also be displayed in separate windows. This helps the comparison between different attempts at proving a goal. No proof action can be issued from the windows associated with variants, to prevent confusion about the node at which a proof action will take place. A variant must be selected as the current variant at a goal before one can issue a command for it. A "stack" display of commands for subgoals with variants makes explicit the presence of variants.

The tree structures can be dumped in Postscript format for later printing or inclusion into documents, in a form more readable than textual scripts.

New script mechanism: An additional script mechanism complements the one that exists in LP, which provides an on-line recording of all user's actions, even the ones that have no impact on the proof (displays, cancelled actions, errors, etc). The new mechanism traverses the proof tree structure and lists only the commands that are necessary to rebuild the tree structure (or a selected part of it), cleared of all superfluous commands.

3 Conclusion

The new prototype system runs on SUN workstations. It is based on a customized release of LP, built in collaboration with Steve Garland from MIT. The proof engine is in CLU, the proof-manager part is in C and uses Tcl/Tk for the graphic manipulation. This prototype can be viewed as a first step towards a "proof editor" that would take advantage of the explicit proof structure to provide additional facilities. Among them we can mention dynamic annotation

570

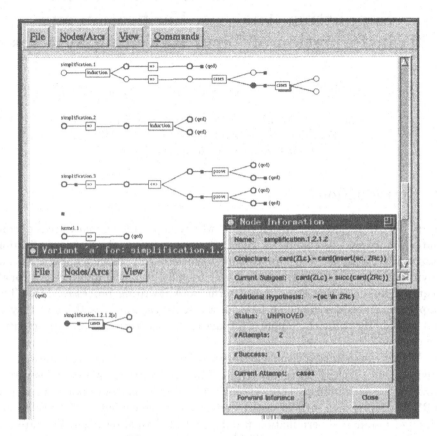

Fig. 1. A snapshot of the system

of scripts, scratch-pad facilities for performing computations at subgoals, a "re-play" mechanism for reusing a proof at some subgoal for another subgoal, or the dynamic reshaping of proofs like when moving lemmas higher in a proof tree to make them sharable by several subgoals.

References

1. S. Garland and J. Guttag. A Guide to LP, The Larch Prover. Technical Report 82, DEC-SRC, 1991.
2. J. V. Guttag and J. J. Horning. *Larch: Languages and Tools for Formal Specification.* Springer-Verlag, 1993.
3. U. Martin and J. M. Wing (Eds). *First International Workshop on Larch, Dedham, 1992.* Workshop in Computing, Springer Verlag, 1992.
4. F. Voisin. A new front-end for the larch prover. In *First International Workshop on Larch, Dedham, 1992*, pages 282–296. Springer Verlag, 1992.

TERSE : A Visual Environment for Supporting Analysis, Verification and Transformation of Term Rewriting Systems

Nobuo KAWAGUCHI   Toshiki SAKABE   Yasuyoshi INAGAKI

Department of Information Engineering, Nagoya University
Furo-cho, Chikusa-ku, Nagoya, 464-01 JAPAN
E-mail: kawaguti@nuie.nagoya-u.ac.jp

1 Introduction

Term rewriting systems(TRS)[1] can be widely applicable in many areas of computer science such as equational logics, theorem proving, algebraic specification, program verification, transformation and synthesis, etc. In such applications, an environment for term rewriting with user friendly graphical interface is strongly required for analyzing structure of terms and rewriting processes. Most TRS implementations developed so far[3, 4] are text-based ones, and hence they do not provide the sufficient supports for analyzing structure of terms nor rewriting sequences.

We have developed a visual environment for term rewriting computation. The environment (TERSE:TErm Rewriting Support Environment) provides various kinds of visualization to support analysis, verification and transformation of TRS. Currently, five sorts of visual viewers are implemented in TERSE. Several kinds of automated termination proof and transformation algorithms are also included in the environment. TERSE is implemented with CML(Concurrent ML[5]) with eXene[6] library. Using higher order features in CML makes it easy to modify and extend the environment.

2 Overview of TERSE

TERSE is composed of four parts, Core part and three Studios(Figure 1). Core part have the term rewriting engine and Main Window. Main Window can handle multiple terms, rewriting rules and rewriting strategies. The user can perform text-base term rewriting in Main Window and enter to any Studios for further analysis.

2.1 Visualization Studio

Visualization Studio is currently composed of four viewers(Term, Sequence, Relation, Statistics). Fig 2 shows Term Viewer. The structure of a term is displayed by a tree with information such as redex occurrence, sort of function symbols and subterm abbreviation. We call this special drawing method for terms as

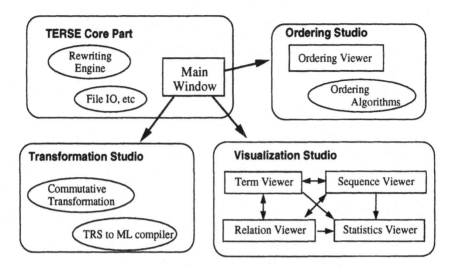

Fig. 1. Modules of TERSE

Term Visualization. One can call other three viewers from Term Viewer with the current displayed term.

Sequence Viewer shows the rewrite sequences of terms with Term Visualization. Visual analysis on rewrite sequence provides the insight of effective transformation.

Relation Viewer displays the graph of rewriting relations. Each node on the graph represents one term and the arcs represent the rewriting relation. The root node is starting point of rewriting. Visualization of rewriting relations can provide various information for evaluating rewriting strategies.

Statistics Viewer shows statistic information of the term by line-chart. Each line on the chart shows the size, length, width and number of redexes of the term. The functions for acquising for these statistic values can be exchanged with any user configured function.

2.2 Ordering Studio

Ordering Studio implements various kinds of termination algorithms[2]. It also has a Ordering Viewer for visualizing the recursive structure of path orderings.(Shown in Fig.3) Two terms are displayed at the same window and overlapped colored rectangles describe the comparison of subterms. This visualization helps to determine the precedence of function symbols and to analyze the ordering.

2.3 Transformation Studio

Transformation Studio has two transformation methods. Commutative transformation is an automated transformation algorithm for TRS optimization. TRS

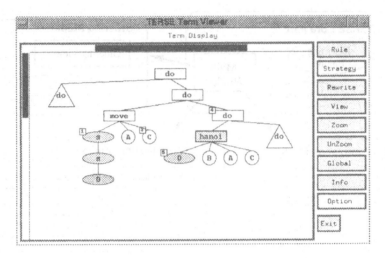

Fig. 2. Term Viewer

to ML compiler converts TRS rules into ML programs. The resulting program can be evaluated under the environment.

3   Implementation

TERSE is implemented on CML(Concurrent ML)[5] with eXene[6] Library. CML is a concurrent functional language and eXene is an X-window library built on CML. Implementation of TERSE is clearly modularized by MVC(Model, View, Controller)model. Powerful datatype facility makes ML as one of the most powerful and easy prototyping languages for symbolic computation(Model). Combination of CML and eXene makes GUI(View and Controller) programming on ML practically. The code size of TERSE is about 8000 lines

Currently, many (text-based) symbolic computation systems are well implemented in ML. Visualizing methods and GUIs provided in TERSE might be also applicable for those systems.

4   Concluding Remarks

We have proposed TERSE, a visual environment with GUI that supports design and analysis of TRS. TERSE provides various operations on visualized terms and TRSs such as customizing visualization style, controlling rewriting steps, analyzing rewriting processes, and so forth.

The implementation is modularized clearly by MVC model for the convenience of further refinements and reuses.

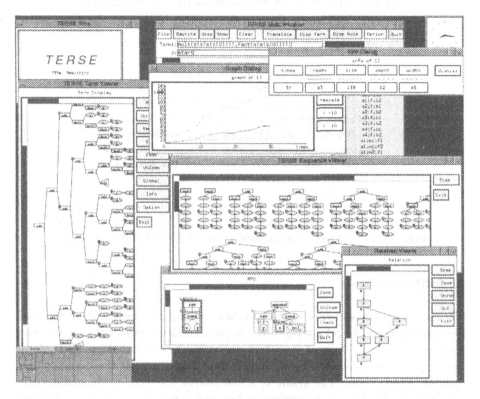

Fig. 3. A screen shot of TERSE

References

1. Huet, G. , "Confluent Reductions:Abstract Properties and Applications to Term Rewriting Systems", J.ACM, Vol.27, No.4, pp797-821 (1980).
2. Dershowitz, N. , "Termination of Rewriting" , J. Symbolic Computation, Vol.3, pp69-116 (1989).
3. Matthews,B. : MERILL: An Equational Reasoning System in Standard ML, *Rewriting Techniques and Applications*, Lecture Notes in Computer Science, No. 690, pp. 441-445(1993).
4. Bundgen,R. ,Reduce the Redex → ReDuX , Rewriting Techniques and Applications, Lecture Notes in Computer Science, No. 690, pp. 446-450(1993).
5. Reppy,J.H., "CML: A higer-order concurrent language", In Proceedings of the ACM SIGPLAN'91 on PLDI, pp293-305 (1991).
6. Reppy,J.H., Gansner,E.R., "The eXene Library Manual(Version 0.4)", AT&T Bell Laboratories (1993).
7. Kawaguchi,N., Sakabe,T. and Inagaki,Y. ,"TERSE: TErm Rewriting Support Environment" ,Proceedings of the 1994 ACM SIGPLAN Workshop on Standard ML and its Applications, pp91-100 (1994).
8. Kawaguchi,N., Sakabe,T. and Inagaki,Y. ,"Visual Support Methods for Analysis, Verification and Transformation of Term Rewriting Systems" ,JSSST Computer Software, Vol.13, No. 1, pp.23-36 (1996).(In Japanese)

The TOOLBUS Coordination Architecture
— A Demonstration —

P. Klint[1,2] and P. Olivier[2]

[1] Department of Software Technology
Centre for Mathematics and Computer Science
P.O. Box 4079, 1009 AB Amsterdam, The Netherlands
[2] Programming Research Group, University of Amsterdam
P.O. Box 41882, 1009 DB Amsterdam, The Netherlands

Abstract. The TOOLBUS is a generic software architecture for building heterogeneous, distributed, systems. We demonstrate several applications that have been implemented using the TOOLBUS technology.

1   Introduction

We show a generic software architecture for building heterogeneous, distributed software systems. To get control over the possible interactions between software components ("tools") direct inter-tool communication is forbidden. Instead, all interactions are controlled by a "script" that formalizes all the desired interactions among tools. The result is a component interconnection architecture resembling a hardware communication bus, and therefore we call it the "TOOL-BUS".

We describe the coordination of tools in process-oriented "T scripts" featuring, amongst others, (1) sequential composition, choice and iteration of processes; (2) handshaking (synchronous) communication of messages; (3) asynchronous communication of notes to an arbitrary number of processes; (4) subscription to notes; (5) dynamic process creation; (5) absolute and relative timeout and delay; (6) dynamic execution and termination of tools; (7) dynamic connection and disconnection of tools; (8) synchronous communication between TOOLBUS and tools; and (9) dynamic connection of monitoring tools.

Experience with the TOOLBUS coordination architecture and further references can be found in [BK96].

2   Motivation and background

The development of the TOOLBUS has primarily been motivated by the need to re-engineer the existing implementation of the ASF+SDF Meta-environment [Kli93, vDHK96]: given a formal description of some language (e.g., programming language, query language, mark up language, or other application language) the Meta-Environment generates an interactive programming environment for it. The need to make connections with other, existing, software (e.g., user-interfaces, editors, proof checkers) as well as the flexibility we needed for further development of our system, were the driving forces for designing a generic coordination architecture.

It is our aim to use the TOOLBUS as the interconnection technology for connecting the various components involved in generated programming environments (such as parser generators, syntax-directed editors, rewrite rule compilers, compiled specifications, and the like). Our main expectations of this approach are therefore:

- By decomposing a single monolithic system into a number of cooperating components, the modularity and flexibility of the systems' implementation can be improved:
  - For each component we can select the optimal re-engineering strategy (e.g., adapt the old component, re-implement it using the best tools available, buy it, etc.)
  - The components can be combined in new ways that were previously inconceivable; rather than using a fixed skeleton for each programming environment generated, it becomes possible to tailor it towards specific needs.
  - The system will be very extensible because of its open nature.
- By connecting existing tools we can reuse their implementation and build new systems with lower costs. Typical examples we have encountered so far are the integration of existing tools for constructing user-interfaces and for constraint solving, as well as implementations of various programming languages.
- The distributed nature of the system immediately opens up possibilities for a parallel implementation.
- Formal methods can be used to create executable prototypes of the components. In a later stage, individual components can be replaced by more efficiently implemented versions. Note that the presence of a "correct" (formally developed) version of each component makes it possible to use some form of automated regression testing when developing a more efficient implementation.

3 Characteristics of the TOOLBUS

Data integration. How can tools exchange and share data structures representing application specific information? Instead of providing a general mechanism for representing the data in arbitrary applications, we will use a single, fixed, data representation based on term structures. We do not allow the exchange of arbitrary data structures, but insist that all data are represented in the same term format before they can be exchanged between tools. A consequence of this approach is that *existing* tools will have to be encapsulated by a small layer of software that acts as an "adapter" between the tool's internal data formats and conventions and those of the TOOLBUS.

Control integration. How can tools communicate or cooperate with each other? The control integration between tools is achieved by using process-oriented "T scripts" that model the possible interactions between tools. The major difference with other approaches is that we use one, formal, description of *all* tool interactions. Coordination and computation are strictly separated: inside the TOOLBUS a varying number of parallel processes takes care of the coordination while all actual computation is performed in tools (and not in the TOOLBUS itself). We uncouple the coordination activities inside the TOOLBUS by using pattern matching to establish communication between processes rather than using explicitly named communication ports. We support heterogeneity, since tools implemented in different languages running on different machines can be coordinated by way of a single TOOLBUS.

4   A demonstration

We will show the feasibility of our approach by demonstrating several applications that have been implemented using the TOOLBUS technology:

- A small (calculator-like) example in order to explain the basic principles and show (a) integration of tools written in different languages (C, Tcl); (b) distributed execution of such tools; (c) interactive monitoring of distributed TOOLBUS applications.
- A distributed auction featuring (a) a single auction master and a dynamically varying set of bidders all communicating with the auction via different work stations; (b) the use of time and time outs to control the bidding process.
- The use of algebraic specifications (using ASF+SDF) to specify and prototype tools.
- A C development environment for embedded systems [Oli96].
- Parts of the ASF+SDF Meta-environment that have been re-engineered by means of the TOOLBUS.

5   Other applications

The TOOLBUS has been used for building other applications as well:

- Various simulators (traffic light control, platform allocation).
- Connection of a constraint solver to a graphical editor.
- Various distributed games (including Go Moku and Battleship).
- Connecting different symbolic algebra packackes.
- A toolbox for checking and simulating μCRL specifications [DG95].

6   Current status of the implementation

The TOOLBUS has been implemented in ANSI C and runs on a variety of platforms (SUN/SOLARIS, SGI/IRIX, IBM PC/LINUX, IBM SP1/AIX).

Tools written in C, C++, Tcl, Python, Perl, Prolog and ASF+SDF can at this moment be connected to the TOOLBUS. In addition, arbitrary executables can be encapsulated in a standard fashion and be used as a tool.

In the current implementation, the **T** script is executed by an interpreter that runs as a single (operating system level) process. Tools are executed as separate processes and they are connected to the interpreter by means of inter-process communication (using TCP/IP). Tools may run on different computers.

7 Discussion

The work presented here stresses the importance of a strict separation between coordination and computation and shows that:

- Coordination can be based on a firm theoretical foundation (Process Algebra) that at the same time yields a feasible implementation strategy.
- Computation should be based on a language paradigm that is most suited for the application at hand. Rather than striving for the integration of many language paradigms into a single linguistic framework, we keep the various paradigms apart and only integrate tools implemented with different paradigms at the coordination level. As a special case, we are investigating the use of algebraic specifications and term rewriting for building tools.
- Formal methods can be used to create an executable prototype of each component. The efficiency of individual components can be increased incrementally by replacing them by faster implementations.

References

[BK96]   J.A. Bergstra and P. Klint. The TOOLBUS coordination architecture. In P. Ciancarini and C. Hankin, editors, *Coordination Languages and Models (COORDINATION'96)*, volume 1061 of *Lecture Notes in Computer Science*, pages 75–88. Springer-Verlag, 1996.

[DG95]   D. Dams and J.F. Groote. Specification and implementation of components of a μCRL toolbox. Technical Report 152, Department of Philosophy, University of Utrecht, 1995.

[Kli93]   P. Klint. A meta-environment for generating programming environments. *ACM Transactions on Software Engineering and Methodology*, 2(2):176–201, 1993.

[Oli96]   P. Olivier. A simulator framework for embedded systems. In *Coordination Languages and Models (COORDINATION'96)*, volume 1061 of *Lecture Notes in Computer Science*, pages 436–439, 1996.

[vDHK96]   A. van Deursen, J. Heering, and P. Klint, editors. *Language Prototyping, An Algebraic Approach*, volume 5 of *AMAST Series in Computing*. World Scientific Publishing Co., 1996. To appear.

ASD: The Action Semantic Description Tools

Arie van Deursen[1] and Peter D. Mosses[2]

[1] CWI, P. O. Box 94079, 1090 GB Amsterdam, The Netherlands, arie@cwi.nl
[2] BRICS (Basic Research in Computer Science, Centre of the Danish National
Research Foundation), Computer Science Department, Aarhus University, Ny
Munkegade Bldg. 540, DK-8000 Aarhus C, Denmark, pdmosses@brics.dk

Introduction *Action Semantics* is a framework for describing the semantics of
programming languages [6, 9]. One of the main advantages of Action Semantics
over other frameworks is that it scales up smoothly to the description of larger
practical languages, such as Standard Pascal [7]. An increasing number of researchers and practitioners are starting to use action semantics in preference to
other frameworks, e.g., [8].

The ASD tools include facilities for parsing, syntax-directed (and textual)
editing, checking, and interpretation of action semantic descriptions. Such facilities significantly enhance accuracy and productivity when writing large specifications, and are also particularly useful for students learning about the framework.
The notation supported by the ASD tools is a direct ASCII representation of
the standard notation used for action semantic descriptions in the literature, as
defined in [6, Appendices B–F].

Action Semantic Descriptions The notation used in action semantic descriptions can be divided into four kinds:

Meta-Notation, used for introducing and specifying the other notations;
Action Notation, a fixed notation used for expressing so-called *actions*, which
represent the semantics of programming constructs;
Data Notation, a fixed notation used for expressing the data processed by
actions; and
Specific Notation, introduced in particular action semantic descriptions to
specify the abstract syntax of the programming language, the semantic functions that map abstract syntax to semantic entities, and the semantic entities
themselves (extending the fixed action and data notation with new sorts and
operations).

Compared with conventional frameworks for algebraic specification, the Meta-
Notation is unusual in that it allows operations on sorts, not only on individual
values. Its foundations are given by the framework of Unified Algebras [5]. Moreover, so-called *mix-fix* notation for operations is allowed, thus there is no fixed
grammar for terms. This is a crucial feature, because action notation includes
many infix combinators (e.g., A_1 and then A_2, which expresses sequencing of the
actions A_1, A_2) and mix-fix primitive actions (e.g., bind I to D). The specific
notation introduced by users tends to follow the same style.

The Meta-Notation's features include constructs for modularization, introduction of symbols, expressing functionalities, equations between sorts or individuals, and the definition of abstract syntax. These constructs can be given in arbitrary order; one module can both introduce mix-fix symbols and use them in equations.

The Platform The ASD tools are implemented using the ASF+SDF system [1, 4, 3]. In the ASF+SDF approach to tool generation, the syntax of a language is described using the Syntax Definition Formalism SDF, which defines context-free syntax and signature at the same time. Functions operating on terms over such a signature are defined using (conditional) equations in the algebraic specification formalism ASF. Typical functions describe type checking, interpreting, compiling, etc., of programs. These functions are executed by interpreting the algebraic specifications as term rewriting systems. Moreover, from SDF definitions, parsers can be generated, which in turn are used for the generation of syntax-directed editors. ASF+SDF modules allow hiding and mutual dependence. (The demonstration will start by explaining the basic features of ASF+SDF).

The ASF+SDF system currently runs on, e.g., Sparc (Solaris or SunOS) and Silicon Graphics workstations, and uses X-Windows. It is based on the Centaur system (developed by, amongst others, INRIA). Once one has installed the ASF+SDF system, all that is needed before using the ASD tools is to get a copy of the ASF+SDF modules implementing ASD and the user guide, together with a configuration file that specifies the effects of the various buttons in the ASD interface; these items are freely available by FTP.

The Implementation ASD modules written in the Meta-Notation are translated to ASF+SDF modules, using the ASF+SDF system itself. Concerning the unusual features of the Meta-Notation: The arbitrary mix-fix operations are catered for by a two-phase generation scheme. First, a very basic grammar (essentially recognizing key-words, lists of tokens, and well-balanced brackets) is used to parse Meta-Notation modules. Using this first parse, the Meta-Notation constructs introducing symbols, functionalities, and grammars are further processed and translated to ASF+SDF modules. These generated ASF+SDF modules are then used to analyse the complete ASD module again. Sort operations in the Meta-Notation are dealt with by generating (in some cases) extra sorts in the ASF+SDF module.

Main Features The main features of ASD are centered around a syntax-directed editor containing an ASD module. A user writing an ASD module can use the buttons in this editor to check this module or test the grammar and semantic functions contained in it. The features include:

SYMBOL Checking: By starting the SYMBOLS phase, it is checked whether all symbols used in the ASD module were indeed introduced, and whether their use conforms to the arity specified. In this SYMBOLS phase, an

ASF+SDF module is generated the signature of which contains all symbols introduced.

SORT Checking: By starting the SORTS phase, the functionalities — which specify the sort of the operands and the result — are taken into account as well. Since sort checking in Unified Algebras is undecidable, several heuristics are used. In this SORTS phase, an ASF+SDF module is generated containing all (auxiliary) sorts and function declarations.

Grammar Generation: ASD grammars can be used for two purposes: first to produce a context-free grammar that can be used to generate a parser recognizing programs in concrete syntax ("real" programs); and second to write abstract syntax trees in the format used in action semantic descriptions. These grammar declarations are translated to (1) an ASF+SDF module called ABSTRACT covering the ASD abstract syntax notation; and (2) an ASF+SDF module called CONCRETE containing the concrete notation, as well as a function (signature and defining equations) mapping the CONCRETE representation to the ABSTRACT one.

Rewriting: The semantic equations given in an action semantic description specify the mapping between ABSTRACT trees and Action Notation (generally extended with specific notation). The semantic function definitions are directly translated to ASF+SDF rewrite rules. Together with the ABSTRACT and CONCRETE steps, these can be used to translate actual program sources automatically to their action semantic denotation.

Further features (e.g., "pretty-printing") are currently being implemented, using the generator technology as described in [2].

The demonstration will be based on the newest version of the ASD Tools (2.5) which is not only approximately 10 times as fast as the version showed during AMAST'93, but also capable of handling much larger action semantic descriptions. Most likely, example semantic definitions will be shown of "Ad" (a large subset of Ada) and full ISO Pascal.

References

1. J.A. Bergstra, J. Heering, and P. Klint, editors. *Algebraic Specification*. ACM Press Frontier Series. The ACM Press in co-operation with Addison-Wesley, 1989.
2. M. van den Brand and E. Visser. Generation of formatters for context-free languages. Technical Report P9506, Programming Research Group, University of Amsterdam, 1995. To appear in ACM Transactions on Software Engineering Methodology.
3. A. van Deursen, J. Heering, and P. Klint (eds.). *Language Prototyping, An Algebraic Specification Approach*, volume 5 of *AMAST Series in Computing*. World Scientific Publishing Co., 1996. To Appear.
4. P. Klint. A meta-environment for generating programming environments. *ACM Transactions on Software Engineering and Methodology*, 2(2):176–201, 1993.
5. P.D. Mosses. Unified algebras and institutions. In *LICS'89, Proceedings 4th Annual Symposium on Logic in Computer Science*, pages 304–312. IEEE, 1989.

6. P.D. Mosses. *Action Semantics*, volume 26 of *Cambridge Tracts in Theoretical Computer Science*. Cambridge University Press, 1992.
7. P.D. Mosses and D.A. Watt. Pascal action semantics. Technical report, Aarhus University, 1993. Draft, version 0.6. Available by *ftp* from ftp.daimi.aau.dk: pub/action/pascal.
8. J. P. Nielsen and J. U. Toft. Formal specification of ANDF, existing subset. Technical Report 202104/RPT/19, issue 2, DDC International A/S, Lundtoftevej 1C, DK-2800 Lyngby, Denmark, 1994.
9. D.A. Watt. *Programming Language Syntax and Semantics*. Prentice Hall, 1991.

Hardware and Software Requirements

For installing and demonstrating the ASD system:

Disk Space

- 250 Mbytes needed to install and store ASD.

Workstation

- Minimum 64 Mbytes main memory needed for running the demonstration.
- Preferably Sparc Station running Solaris.
- Standard Unix software needed: X-Windows, twm.
- Colour screen desirable, but not essential.

Using Occurrrence and Evolving Algebras for the Specification of Language–Based Programming Tools

Arnd Poetzsch-Heffter
Institut für Informatik
Technische Universität
D–80290 München
poetzsch@informatik.tu-muenchen.de

1 Introduction

The specification of realistic programming languages is difficult and expensive. That is why such specifications should be used not only as formal language documentation, but as well as a starting point for the development of language specific software (interpreters, compilers, verification editors, browsers, etc.). The MAX system supports such developments in two ways: 1. It provides a formal, algebra-based specification framework. 2. It generates prototyping tools from such specifications and enables stepwise refinement of such tools (cf. [PH94] for an example). In the framework, static language aspects are defined by a very general attribution technique enabling e.g. the formal specification of flow graphs. Dynamic aspects are defined by evolving algebra rules, a technique that has been successfully applied to several realistic programming languages.

This extended abstract sketches the supported specification methods, the underlying formal approach, and experiences made so far by the MAX system.

2 Specification Methods

The MAX system supports operational language specifications. Conceptually, a MAX specification consists of two parts: the static language aspects, specified in a declarative way, and the dynamic aspects specified by transistion rules. Usually, the static aspects comprise context-free and context-dependent syntax, context conditions, basic data types of the language, and possibly further aspects that can be statically determined, like e.g. control flow information. Dynamic aspects usually deal with the operational behaviour of programs. Of course, there is no principle border between static and dynamic aspects. E.g. the relation between jumps and corresponding labels can be specified statically by edges in control flow graphs or dynamically by using continuation techniques. Essentially there are two reasons why MAX supports different techniques for specifying static and dynamic aspects:

1. Adequacy: Whereas declarative techniques are usually more compact and lead to simpler proof techniques, operational techniques are better suited for the specification of nondeterminism and parallelism.

2. Efficiency: Distinguishing between static and dynamic aspects in the specification allows for the generation of more efficient programming tools.

To demonstrate the specification techniques, we roughly sketch the main concepts used in a specification of a small imperative, parallel language, called SIMPL. The following SIMPL program computes the Fibonacci function of the initial value of the variable *input*[1]:

---

[1] If *input* is initially even, the result is contained in *v1*, otherwise in *v2*.

```
declare
   var  input, v1, v2 : int
begin
   (  v1 := 1  ||  v2 := 1  );
   while 1 < input  do
      (  v1:=v1+v2 ;  v2:=v1+v2 )  ||  input:=input-2
   end
end
```

Here, the operator || denotes parallel execution. The specification techniques for syntax and context conditions used in MAX are similar to techniques used with attribute grammars (cf. [DJL88]). The main difference is that in our approach attributes are ordinary functions of an algebra. This leads to a simpler formal model (cf. section 3) and provides more flexibility. In particular, it allows to specify control flow graphs in a declarative way as enrichment of syntax trees. The following figure visualizes how control flow graphs would look like for SIMPL programs using the example program from above. The nodes of the flow graph (dashed ellipses) correspond to the *atomic tasks* that have to be performed during program execution; Skip-tasks are only an auxiliary device to specify the control flow over the syntax tree:

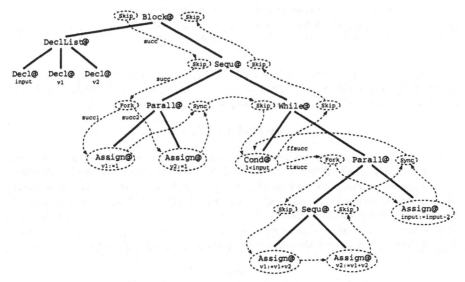

The dynamic semantics of SIMPL specifies the signature of states, possible initial states, and for each type of atomic task the corresponding state transitions. States for SIMPL have four components: a) a function *cont* mapping variables to values; b) a variable *curr_task* holding the task to be executed next; c) a set of active tasks *sat*; d) a predicate *waiting* recording the status of Sync-tasks. Initially, *cont* may be arbitrary, *curr_task* is the Skip-task before the root, *sat* is empty, and *waiting* yields false for all Sync-tasks. Transition rules specify how the atomic tasks modify the state. This will be explained at the end of the next section.

3   Formal Approach

In order to realize the sketched specification method in a formal framework, the framework should support a powerful attribution mechanism and a technique for specifying transition rules. This attribution mechanism has to enable in particular the declarative specification of flow information. For the specification of attributions, we developed occurrence algebras, an extension of order-sorted term algebras. For the specification of transition rules, we use evolving algebras developed by Gurevich (cf. [Bö95]). This section provides a first step introduction to both techniques. Beside these two techniques, MAX supports the specification of functions, i.e. in summary, a MAX specification consists of an occurrence algebra, a set of functions, and a set of evolving algebra rules.

3.1 Occurrence Algebras

Occurrence algebras can be considered as an extension of order-sorted term algebras. The universe of an occurrence algebra contains not only all terms that can be built by a set of constructors, but as well all occurrences[2] of subterms within these constructor terms. For the convenient specification of such an algebra, MAX provides a data construct similar to that of functional programming languages. As an example, let us consider part of the abstract syntax of SIMPL:

```
occdata
   Stm = Block  ( decls:    DeclList  body:     Stm )
       | While  ( cond:     Cond      lbody:    Stm )
       | Parall ( thread1:  Stm       thread2:  Stm )
       | Sequ   ( stm1:     Stm       stm2:     Stm )
       | Assign ( lhs:      Var       rhs:      Exp )
   end
```

This conctruct specifies sorts Stm, Block, While, Parall, Sequ, and Assign, specifies that Block, While, etc. are subsorts of Stm, specifies the constructors *Block*, *While*, *Parall*, *Sequ*, and *Assign*, and specifies selectors *decls*, *body*, etc.; i.e. we have axioms like:

$$body(Block(DL, S)) = S$$

In addition to that, the construct specifies for each sort a corresponding occurrence sort; e.g. Block@ is the sort of all subterm occurrences of sort Block in some term. And, it specifies a constructor *occ* yielding for each term the corresponding root occurrence, as well as a unary constructor for each selector, e.g. *body@*: Block@→Stm@. If BO is an occurrence of sort Block@, i.e. BO represents a subterm B of sort Block in some term T, then *body@(BO)* represents "the occurrence of *body(B)* in T". Finally, it specifies a function *term* yielding for each subterm occurrence the corresponding subterm. Typical axioms are:

$$term(occ(T)) = T$$

$$term(BO) = Block(DL, S) \iff term(decls@(BO)) = DL \land term(body@(BO)) = S$$

Now, attributes in the sense of attribute grammars are simply unary functions having an occurrence sort as domain. Moreover, we can define new sorts based on occurrence sorts. E.g. the Fork- and Sync-tasks illustrated in the example above can be specified as follows:

```
occdata
   Task = Fork( nodef:  Parall@ )
        | Sync( nodes:  Parall@ )
          . . .
   end
```

For a more detailed definition of occurrence algebras, we refer to [PH94].

---

[2]In some communities, subterm occurrences are called positions.

3.2 Evolving Algebras

Evolving algebras provide an elaborate specification framework used for a fairly broad range of applications (cf. [Bö95]). Essentially they allow to specify state transition systems where a state is modeled by an algebra. The MAX system uses the kernel notions of evolving algebras for the specification of transition rules. A rule essentially consists of a guard and a set of so-called updates. The meaning of a set of rules is as follows: Simultaneously perform all updates the guard of which evaluate to true in the current state. To give an idea of how such rules look like, we sketch the rules for SIMPL; for brevity, the rules for the Cond- and Sikp-tasks are omitted:

```
IF  isSchedule( curr_task )      THEN   curr_task := choose( sat )
IF  NOT isSchedule( curr_task ) THEN   curr_task := Schedule
IF  isAssign( curr_task )
  THEN  sat  := sat\{curr_task} U { succ(curr_task) }
        cont( var(lhs(curr_task)) ) := eval( rhs(curr_task), cont )
IF  isFork( curr_task )
  THEN  sat := sat\{curr_task} U { succ1(curr_task), succ2(curr_task) }
IF  isSync( curr_task )  AND  waiting(curr_task) = false
  THEN  waiting( curr_task ) := true
        sat  := sat\{curr_task}
IF  isSync( curr_task )  AND  waiting(curr_task) = true
  THEN  waiting( curr_task ) := false
        sat  := sat\{curr_task} U { succ(curr_task) }
```

A task is either the task Schedule or one of the tasks shown in the above figure. If the current task is the Schedule-task, only the first guard is true and the next current task is chosen from the set of active tasks. Otherwise the guard of the second rule and of some other rule is true and the corresponding updates specify the state transition.

4 Pragmatic Aspects and Experiences

The MAX System is implemented in ANSI C and runs under different UNIX versions including Linux, HPUX, Solaris, and SunOS. An important design aspect of the MAX implementation was the development of a simple and flexible interface to C. Whereas this is of minor importance from a specification point of view, it is of great importance for the construction of realistic systems from specifications, in particular to allow flexible interaction with the environment (graphical user interfaces, etc.) and to support implementation refinements leading to efficient tools even for huge language specifications.

Until now, the MAX System has been used for several applications of different sizes and in compiler construction courses. In particular, it was used for the bootstrap of the system itself, for the specification of a subset of the object-oriented language Sather, and for an almost complete specification of ANSI C.

References

[Bö95] E. Börger, editor. *Specification and Validation Methods.* Clarendon Press, 1995.

[DJL88] P. Deransart, M. Jourdan, and B. Lorho. *Attribute Grammars*, Springer–Verlag, 1988. (LNCS 323)

[PH94] A. Poetzsch-Heffter. Developing efficient interpreters based on formal language specifications. In P. Fritzson, editor, *Compiler Construction*, pages 233–247, Springer–Verlag, 1994. (LNCS 786)

ECHIDNA: A System for Manipulating Explicit Choice Higher Dimensional Automata

Richard Buckland and Michael Johnson *

School of Mathematics and Computing, Macquarie University,
Sydney, Australia, 2109

Abstract. We present a system (ECHIDNA) used to manipulate models of concurrent processes based on explicit choice higher dimensional automata. Such models are more suited to the full software engineering process than the older non-deterministic automata and higher dimensional automata, but manipulating them does require computer assistance. The conference presentation will include a detailed introduction to explicit choice higher dimensional automata as well as a description and demonstration of the system ECHIDNA.

1 Introduction

Explicit choice higher dimensional automata (ECHDA) are used as a model of concurrent computation (eg see [1]). Their principal advantages are that they are a graphical model, well suited to software engineering, and that by treating choice explicitly (unlike most graph based models of concurrency) they can be used in all phases of development from high level specification to implementation. Then a detailed theoretical treatment of refinement can be used to establish relative correctness between ECHDA models. In short, since choices must be made explicit in an implementation, a model which incorporates them is of great value in the development process because it can be used throughout the process.

ECHDA can be manipulated mechanically, and since their 1-dimensional skeletons are frequently the non-deterministic automata widely used in concurrent specification, they are easily understood by most software engineers familiar with more traditional concurrent specification techniques. However, their mechanistic manipulation can become quite complicated and where several processes are permitted to execute concurrently or where modules are integrated by choices in a nested fashion, the ECHDA can become quite high dimensional and computer assistance is usually needed.

We report here a system ECHIDNA which is designed to aid the software engineering process by performing the manipulations of ECHDA. In Section 2 we very briefly review ECHDA while Section 3 outlines the system's computational features. Section 4 makes a few remarks about the history of the tensor product of ECHDA which is used here to model concurrency and synchronisation.

* The authors gratefully acknowledge the Australian Research Council (ARC) and the Microsoft Research Institute (MRI).

2 Explicit Choice Higher Dimensional Automata

Buckland [1] has been modelling concurrent systems using pasting schemes [3] (certain high dimensional directed graphs). The work is inspired by Pratt's higher dimensional automata (HDA) [4, 2] which Pratt originally described as labelled pasting schemes with cubical cells. However Buckland's work differs from most treatments in that choices are modelled explicitly so the non-deterministic automata (or labelled transition systems) usually used to model concurrent processes and the non-deterministic HDA of Pratt are replaced by explicit choice higher dimensional automata.

An ECHDA is a labelled pasting scheme. In an ECHDA the points represent states (including start and end states), the 1-dimensional arrows represent events, and each cell of dimension greater than 1 is labelled with the circumstances under which its domain or codomain occur (these may include ordinary if ...else ... statements, probabilistically specified choices, explicitly non-deterministic internal and external choices and so on). Concurrent events are modelled by topological products (as in HDA [4]) and the cells of dimension greater than 1 which arise in the product are labelled by the concurrent choice (which indicates that either the domain or the codomain or any other interleaving or truly concurrent computation of the factors may occur).

A very simple example is provided by the following ECHDA in which three possible events can result in a transition from state S to state T, and two choices, α and β, will determine which event, if any, takes place.

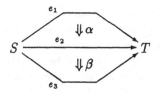

Note that the composite effect of α and β is determined in the same way as the composition of events $e : P \to Q$ and $f : Q \to R$ in which f only has the opportunity to occur if we have already reached state Q. Thus, in state S, β only has the opportunity to choose between e_2 and e_3 if α has already chosen that e_1 may *not* occur.

The system demonstration will include many other examples of ECHDA. Note also that all HDA and all non-deterministic automata are examples of ECHDA.

3 The ECHIDNA Engine

Representing and manipulating ECHDA of arbitrary size and dimension has previously posed computational difficulties because of the volume of information required to define complex objects of potentially high dimension. However the possibility of representing such objects as recursive terms led us to consider the use of Prolog which was found to tackle the problem with ease and with a surprisingly small amount of code and manageable data structures. The declarative nature of Prolog also helped in establishing confidence in the code, which was essential in developing a CASE tool which manipulates high dimensional shapes which can be difficult to visualise.

Since ECHDA are themselves models of (concurrent) processes, the basic manipulations of ECHDA which the system performs correspond to the basic operations on processes. These include:

- sequential composition of processes
- selection (choice) between two processes
- concurrent composition of processes
- synchronization of concurrently executing processes

and these correspond in turn to

- zero pasting of ECHDA (identifying the start and end states of two ECHDA)
- "plastering" of ECHDA to construct higher dimensional ECHDA (identifying the domains and codomains of two n-dimensional ECHDA and inserting a new $(n + 1)$-dimensional choice between them)
- the tensor product of ECHDA (based on the tensor product of pasting schemes originally developed by Street and Johnson)
- a subobject of the tensor product of ECHDA

Each of these is handled easily by taking advantage of Prolog's internal mechanisms. The mechanization of the last two is particularly important because even for relatively small schemes the tensor products are unwieldy.

In addition ECHIDNA provides an operation called "flattening" which replaces an ECHDA by an equivalent ECHDA of lower dimension, if necessary requesting further details about choices so that they can be combined. This operation depends on a detailed algebra of choice and is important in reducing high level specifications to implementations. A detailed example will be given in the conference presentation.

4 The Tensor Product of Pasting Schemes

This work depends crucially upon the tensor product of pasting schemes which, as noted above, was originally developed by Street and Johnson. Unfortunately their formulations were severely limited – although Pratt took up the tensor product and decided to use it to model the concurrent composition of processes, it was not long before Pratt and Johnson showed that pasting schemes as defined in [3] were not closed under the desired tensor product (their counterexample is six dimensional).

Nevertheless, the tensor product is important, and it has been used in a range of applications by, among others, Aitchison and Crans.

To resolve the difficulty Street [5] chose to restrict the schemes to obtain a class which is closed under the tensor product and he called those schemes *parity complexes*. Meanwhile Johnson aimed to widen the class of schemes to obtain a more complete collection which was also to be closed under tensor product.

Buckland has now obtained such a class, and the detailed definition of the *constructed pasting schemes* and a proof that they are closed under the tensor product appear in his forthcoming PhD thesis.

It is worth noting that the complete collection is essential here – parity complexes are not adequate for this work because they are not closed under the basic refinement notion of replacing a cell by a factorisation of it as a composition of two cells.

References

1. R. Buckland, Choice as a first class citizen. In Intensional Programming I, eds Orgun and Ashcroft, World Scientific, to appear
2. E. Goubault, Schedulers as abstract interpretations of HDA. ACM Proc. (1995) to appear
3. M. Johnson, The combinatorics of n-categorical pasting. Jour. Pure and Appl. Alg. **63** (1989) 211–225
4. V. Pratt, Modeling concurrency with geometry. in ACM Proc. POPL (1991) 311–322
5. R. Street, Parity complexes. Cahiers de Topol. et Geom. Categorique **32** (1991) 315–343

Verification Using PEP *

Stephan Melzer, Stefan Römer** and Javier Esparza

Institut für Informatik
Technische Universität München
Arcisstr. 21 D–80290 München
e-mail:{melzers, roemer, esparza}@informatik.tu-muenchen.de

Abstract. **PEP** is a tool for the design, analysis and the verification
of parallel programs. Two approaches are presented in this paper being
the underlying technique of the verification component of **PEP**.
KEY WORDS: Verification, Net Unfoldings, Linear Programming.

1   Introduction

PEP[1] (**P**rogramming **E**nvironment based on **P**etri Nets) is a tool for the verification of parallel programs which implements two of the main theoretical developments of the Esprit BRA DEMON [2] and its successor, the Esprit WG
CALIBAN [4]:

- the design of the Box Calculus, a rich process algebra with a compositional
  net semantics [3];
- the development of new verification techniques for the Petri net model [8, 9,
  14].

Typically, the user starts a **PEP** session by typing a finite-state concurrent program in an imperative, concurrent programming language called **Basic
Petri Net Programming Notation** B(PN)^2 [6]. The language contains control
instructions for sequential and (nested) parallel composition, iteration and nondeterministic choice. Different processes can communicate via both handshake
and buffered communication channels, as well as shared variables.

PEP automatically translates B(PN)^2 programs into Petri boxes, a particular class of 1-safe, labelled Petri nets. The translation is fully compositional,
i.e., in a first step elementary Petri boxes are generated for the atomic actions
of the program, and then these Petri boxes are joined using net operators corresponding to the different program constructs. The theoretical framework of this
translation is the Box Calculus.

---

* This work was supported by the Sonderforschungsbereich SFB-342 A3 – SAM.
** Partially this work was done while the author was a member of the University of
Hildesheim.
[1] **PEP** is supported by the Deutsche Forschungsgemeinschaft and was mainly developed by the University of Hildesheim [5].

Once the program has been typed, the user can express properties in a simple branching-time logic which extends propositional logic with a possibility operator. Typically, they are used for expressing safety and liveness properties, respectively. The atomic expressions of the two logics are of the form *the variable x has value n* or *the n-th process of the program is at location l*. These properties are automatically translated by **PEP** into properties of the underlying Petri net.

PEP offers the user two different model checking techniques for the verification of properties. They have been developed at the Technical University of Munich and the University of Hildesheim. They are described in sections 2 and 3, respectively. Here we only mention that the two have been developed with the goal of palliating the state explosion problem; in fact, none of them constructs the state space of the system.

2 Verification by Means of Linear Programming

The **PEP** tool offers a model-checking component that is based on a linear upper approximation of the state space of a program. The drawback of this model checker is the fact that the underlying method is only a semidecision method. On the other hand, the approximation is obtained from a structural analysis of the associated Petri box that does avoid the well-known state explosion problem.

Linear upper approximations of the set of reachable states have also been used by Cousot and Halbwachs and others in the field of abstract interpretation [7, 11]. The main difference with our approach is that we derive the linear approximation directly from the structure of the system, in one single step, and not by means of successive approximations, as in [7].

In the Petri net community several structural analysis techniques exist that represent necessary criteria for the reachability test of states [1]. One part of these techniques have an algebraic origin and thereby, can be easily expressed as a system of inequalities. Other techniques need nontrivial appropriate transformations yielding linear algebraic representation [14]. A linear approximation of the state space is obtained by the union of all these systems, denoted by $\mathcal{L}$.

Moreover, we can formulate linear inequalities $\mathcal{L}_\phi$ characterizing states that violate property ϕ. The infeasibility of the system $\mathcal{L}_\phi \cup \mathcal{L}$ implies that ϕ holds for every reachable state of the program. The feasibility is checked by means of a mixed integer programming solver. Properties that can be expressed in such a way belong to the class of safety properties, e.g. deadlock-freedom, mutual exclusion property, *etc.*

Unlike safety properties, liveness properties need the consideration of infinite occurrence sequences of a program. It also exists an upper approximation $\mathcal{L}'$ of those sequences by means of structural analysis. Furthermore this approximation can be restricted (specified) by Horn formulae q_i among variables of the program.

If $\mathcal{L}'$ contains a sequence that models the negation of a liveness property ϕ *and* satisfies all formulae q_i, then ϕ holds for all sequences of the program. This containment test is carried out using constraint programming [10], because its techniques combine Horn logic and linear programming.

In the near future we plan to implement a semidecision method for entire Propositional Linear Time Temporal Logic (PLTL). In this connection the negation of a PLTL-formula ϕ is translated into a Petri net [13], that behaves equivalent to an associated Büchi automaton. If the Petri Box of a program and this Petri net have no common occurrence sequences, then ϕ holds for the program. This check can be solved by the above-mentioned techniques of linear and disjunctive programming respectively.

3 Verification Based on Net Unfoldings

The second model checking technique, unlike the latter one, checks the satisfaction of temporal properties by means of an exact representation of the state space. Reduction methods are used again to avoid the state explosion problem.

One possibility to reduce the state space of the system is to use partial orders (acyclic nets). Several runs of a system can be modelled by net unfoldings, a special partial order structure.

For verification purposes, these unfoldings have the problem of being infinite even for systems with a finite number of states. In the **PEP** environment an improved version [9] of an algorithm introduced by McMillan [12] is used to construct a *finite prefix* of the unfolding that is large enough to represent all the reachable states of the system. Computation of this prefix is terminated by finding so–called *cut–off points* that produce states already contained in the constructed part of the finite prefix.

The unfold method allows a fully automatic verification of safety/liveness properties. A fast model checker [8] has been integrated in the **PEP** tool, which takes the unfolding and a formula as input to verify whether the formula holds for the corresponding program. The formula can be expressed in a simple branching time or linear time logic.

Another interesting problem is the question of detecting deadlocks, i. e. if there exists a reachable state in that no transition of the underlying net is enabled. Deadlock-freedom can be expressed by a temporal logic formula, while there exist more efficient algorithms for this purpose. In the **PEP** tool we have included a component that verifies the deadlock property of a given concurrent program using the finite prefix of its unfolding, based also on a procedure by McMillan [12]. The basic idea behind this algorithm is to find a configuration, a special kind of "path" containing the complete history needed for enabling a certain event (element) of the prefix, which is in conflict with all of the cut–off points. If such a configuration exists, the checked program contains no deadlock.

4 Conclusion

We have described the two verification techniques implemented in the **PEP** tool. The entire tool is embedded in a graphical user interface containing editors for programs, Petri nets, *etc.* The **PEP** tool – already containing the model checker based on unfoldings – is available via WWW[2] or for further information send an e-mail to pep_help@informatik.uni-hildesheim.de.

References

1. Bernd Baumgarten. *Petri-Netze. Grundlagen und Anwendungen.* BI-Wissenschaftsverlag, 1990.
2. Eike Best. Esprit Basic Research Action 3148 DEMON (Design Methods Based on Nets) – Aims, Scope and Achievements. In *Advances in Petri Nets*, volume 609 of *Lecture Notes in Computer Science*, pages 1–20. Springer Verlag, 1992.
3. Eike Best, Raymond Devillers, and Jon G. Hall. The Box Calculus: A new causal Algebra with multi-label Communication. In *Advances in Petri Nets 92*, volume 609 of *Lecture Notes in Computer Science*, pages 21 – 69. Springer-Verlag, 1992.
4. Eike Best, Raymond Devillers, Elisabeth Pelz, Arend Rensink, Manuel Silva, and Enrique Teruel. Caliban – Esprit Basic Research WG 6067. In *Structures in Concurrency Theory*, Workshops in Computing, pages 2 – 31, Berlin, May 1995. Springer Verlag.
5. Eike Best and Hans Fleischhack. PEP: Programming Environment Based on Petri Nets. Hildesheimer Informatik Bericht 14/95, Universtät Hildesheim, May 1995.
6. Eike Best and Richard Pinder Hopkins. B(PN)^2 – a Basic Petri Net Programming Notation. In *Proceedings of PARLE '93*, volume 694 of *Lecture Notes in Computer Science*, pages 379 – 390. Springer-Verlag, 1993.
7. P. Cousot and N.Halbwachs. Automatic discovery of linear restraints among variables of a program. In *5th ACM Symposium on Principles of Programming Languages*. ACM-Press, 1978.
8. Javier Esparza. Model checking using net unfoldings. Science of Computer Programming 23, pp. 151 – 195 (1994).
9. Javier Esparza, Stefan Römer, and Walter Vogler. An Improvement of McMillan's Unfolding Algorithm. Sonderforschungsbericht 342/12/95 A, Technische Universtät München, München, August 1995. (to appear in the proceedings of TACAS '96).
10. Thom Frühwirth, Alexander Herold, Volker Küchenhoff, Thierry Le Provost, Pierre Lim, Eric Monfroy, and Mark Wallace. Constraint Logic Programming – An Informal Introduction. ECRC–93–5, European Computer-Industry Research Centre, München, 1993.
11. N. Halbwachs. About synchronous programming and abstract interpretation. In *SAS '94: Static Analysis Symposium*, volume 864 of *Lecture Notes in Computer Science*, pages 179–192. Springer-Verlag, 1994.
12. K. L. McMillan. Using unfoldings to avoid the state explosion problem in the verification of asynchronous circuits. In *4th Workshop on Computer Aided Verification*, pages 164 – 174, Montreal, 1992.
13. Stephan Melzer. Büchi Nets – A Pendant to Büchi Automata. Sonderforschungsbericht, Technische Universität, 1996. (in preparation).
14. Stephan Melzer and Javier Esparza. Checking system properties via integer programming. Sonderforschungsbericht 342/13/95 A, Technische Universität München, August 1995. (to appear in the proceedings of ESOP '96).

---

[2] http://www.informatik.uni-hildesheim.de/~pep/HomePage.html

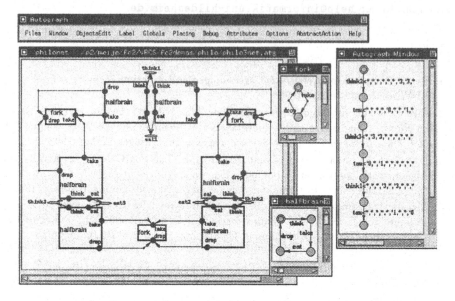

Fig. 1. AUTOGRAPH display

to maintain the set of already reached states, and new discovered states are given an integer reference and stored in a list of "states to explore".

Compositional Reductions: FC2EXPLICIT can perform automata minimisation with respect to *strong, weak* or *branching* bisimulation. When invoked on a multi-level network, the hierarchical model construction can be alternated with such reduction steps at intermediate stages. One retrieves then the *compositional model reduction* approach popularized through the original AUTO tool.

Model Abstraction: *Abstract Actions* allow us to define the atomicity level at which we want to observe an automaton. The idea is to consider terminated sequences of concrete behaviours as atomic and to call such a set abstract action. Reducing a global system w.r.t. a set of abstract actions results in a system conceptually simpler where meaningful activities have been isolated. As a simple subcase, a single abstract action indicating improper (rational) behaviour can be presented for refutation; this implements language inclusion (in the complement language of the abstract action), and is noticed in FC2EXPLICIT by the absence of transition in the resulting automaton. Example: `Abstract_Wrong =` `tau*.enter1.tau*.enter2` can specify lack of mutual exclusion property between two processes. We describe abstract actions as automata in the FC2 format, with specific terminal labels on states indicating completion of an abstract step.

The Fc2TOOLS Set*

Amar Bouali[1], Annie Ressouche[2], Valérie Roy[1], Robert de Simone[2]

[1] CMA/Ecole des Mines de Paris, B.P. 207, F-06904 Sophia-Antipolis cedex
[2] INRIA , B.P. 93, F-06902 Sophia-Antipolis cedex

Abstract. We describe a set of modular extensions to our Auto/Graph verification toolset for networks of communicating processes. These software additions operate from a common file exchange format for automata and networks, called FC2. Tool functionalities comprise graphical depiction of objects, global model construction from hierarchical descriptions, various types of model reductions and of verification of simple modal properties by observers, counterexample production and visualisation. We illustrate typical verification sessions conducted on usual academic examples. Based on previous experience of drastic state explosion problems we aim here at efficiency in implementation. We use both explicit representation techniques and implicit techniques such as BDDs, with functional overlap at places.

1 The Tool Set

1.1 AUTOGRAPH

Renamed ATG for its new C++ implementation, AUTOGRAPH is a graphical display system for both labeled transition graphs and networks of communicating systems. Lay-out is very much in the tradition of process algebra graphical depiction. Objects in AUTOGRAPH can also be extensively annotated so as to match the FC2 format standards. Figure 1 provides a simple example of the famous dining philosophers problem as directly drawn in AUTOGRAPH. It can also be used to visualise automata that were produced elsewhere, typically as an output of verification. Then, when reading an FC2 file AUTOGRAPH prompts the user for interactive unfolding and layout positioning of successive states. An automaton can also be automatically drawn using an algorithm based on spring-like attraction/repulsion between states, depending on connections.

1.2 FC2EXPLICIT

Global Automaton Generation: The construction algorithm is there rather straightforward. Target states are stored when reached together with the labeled transition reaching them as part of the source state description. Hash tables allow

---

* Available by ftp from `ftp://cma.cma.fr/pub/verif`. See also the WWW page `http://cma.cma.fr/Verification/verif-eng.html`

1.3 Fc2implicit

Global Automata Generation: Fc2implicit computes the (BDD characteristic formula given a proper boolean encoding of the) set of global reachable states of the system. Compositional speed-up method is in sight yet, so that the network is flattened to a single-level vector of individual automata. The reachable state space is of course evaluated in a breadth-first search strategy, applying event synchronisation vectors iteratively until fix-point, staring from initial state.

Fix-point reachable state computation can be refined to allow for on-line deadlock detection, and followed by livelock or divergent states detection on the result (a divergent state may perform infinite sequences of hidden τ actions, a livelock state can exhibit *only* such behaviour). Symbolic computation of bisimulation classes can also be applied from this BDD description of reachable states. following results from [1].

Bisimulation Checking: Symbolic computation of strong, weak or branching bisimulation equivalence classes was described in [1]. The quotient automaton can be produced in fc2 through symbolic projection functions to replace any (symbolic) state by a uniquely determined representative, and then providing integer representations of such representative to use in place of target states.

When checking for equivalence between two distinct networks, the synchronous product is built so that only couple of states reached in some way through a common path are challenged for bisimulation.

Verification by Observers and Comparisons: A great deal of practical verification is usually conducted by compiling an automaton-like structure from the property to establish, with possibly additional annotations on states and transitions of various sorts (*success, failure* or *recur* states, *don't care* transitions,...). Verification then starts by constructing a synchronised product of the (usually large) network state space with the (usually smaller) state space of the observer structure. One can attempt to introduce the actual verification algorithms in the middle of this construction, to get potential negative results as early as possible (known as "on the fly" or "local" techniques).

Analysis of Annotated Global States: Symbolic techniques based on implicit state space representations perform at their best when searching reachable state space forward, looking for success states to stop the search or failure states to indicate misbehaviours and generate retrospective counterexample paths. We have implemented a function which performs exactly this. When combined with other functions such as product constructions combining either subnetworks or networks with observers it can be applied on the fly, in the sense that a failure state can be reached way before the entire possible state space is reached.

2   An Example

We now illustrate the basic verification features on the famous *dining philosophers* problem graphically depicted (in the case of 3 philosophers) in figure 1.

2.1 Implicit evaluation of the global system

We first evaluate the global system to have an idea of the size of the state space. We use for that symbolic methods based on BDDs that allow easy evaluation of global state spaces.This academical problem is known to have deadlocks. We have a way to detect them and to extract an example path leading to a deadlock from the global initial state. Here is the session using fc2implicit:

```
0-duick$ fc2implicit -dead -fc2 philo.fc2 > deadpath.fc2
--- fc2tool: parsing fc2 file: philo.fc2.
--- fc2tool: file: philo.fc2 parsed successfuly
--- fc2implicit: Making reachable state space
--- fc2implicit: State space depth: 13
--- fc2implicit: First deadlock(s) detected at depth 7
--- fc2implicit: Reachable states: <<214>> -- BDD nodes: <<85>>
--- fc2implicit: Global automaton has 2 DEADLOCKS state(s)
```

The global automaton has 214 states. The BDD that represents it has 85 nodes only.The first detected deadlocks have been found at depth 7 in the global automaton, that is the shortest path leading to a deadlock has 7 states and 6 transitions. As we have set the option -fc2, an example path has been extracted and written in FC2 in deadpath.fc2.

Now we visualize back in ATG this result that we picture out in figure 1.

The deadlock corresponds to the case where each philosopher takes a fork (the τ action after each think action): then no action can be further enabled from any of them.

Now if -debug option was added to the FC2IMPLICIT command, further annotations were appended to the path example so as to allow source recovery. Then the path can be simulated as a run on FC2 files using FC2VIEW, or even visualised graphically on an original displayed network with AUTOGRAPH. In the latter case one needs only load the path in FC2 to AUTOGRAPH, and then selects the Debug:Edge button from the menu bar. Then each selection of an edge will highlight the source and target states at all components in their respective AUTOGRAPH windows, and active communications at ports in the synchronisation network (see figure 1).

References

1. A. Bouali and R. de Simone. Symbolic bisimulation minimisation. In *Fourth Workshop on Computer-Aided Verification*, volume 663 of *LNCS*, pages 96–108, Montreal, 1992. Springer-Verlag.
2. A. Bouali, A. Ressouche, V. Roy, and R. de Simone. The FCTOOLS user manual. In *final ESPRIT-BRA CONCUR2 deliverables*, Amsterdam, October 1995. Available by ftp from cma.cma.fr:pub/verif as file *fc2userman.ps*.
3. P.C. Kanellakis and S.A. Smolka. CCS expressions, finite state processes, and three problems of equivalence. *Information and Computation*, 86:43–68, 1990.
4. V. Roy and R. de Simone. AUTO and AUTOGRAPH. In R. Kurshan, editor, *proceedings of Workshop on Computer Aided Verification*, New-Brunswick, June 1990. AMS-DIMACS.

Programming in Lygon: A System Demonstration

James Harland[1]   David Pym[2]   Michael Winikoff[3]

[1] RMIT, GPO Box 2476V, Melbourne 3001, Australia
[2] Queen Mary & Westfield College, University of London, UK
[3] University of Melbourne, Parkville 3052, Australia

Introduction. The application of algebraic and logical techniques to programming is facilitated by the use of *declarative* languages. Such languages have simple semantics and programs in them are easy to reason about. However, declarative languages are often weak at expressing such important notions as *resource-allocation*, *state-manipulation* and *concurrency*.

Girard's *linear logic*,[4] provides an elegant framework for expressing these notions. For this and other reasons there has been significant interest recently in the design of logic programming languages based on linear logic.

Our demonstration is of the linear logic programming language *Lygon*. Intuitively, Lygon can be thought of as an extension of Prolog with (i) a linear context, and (ii) logical connectives manipulating this context.

A paper describing Lygon's design, together with example programs illustrating its expressive power in general, and its ability to handle state, resources and concurrency in particular, can be found elsewhere in this volume.[5]

On the interpreter. The operational rules of linear sequent calculus divide into *additive* and *multiplicative* groups. Typical of these groups, respectively, are the rules for & and $\otimes$:

$$\& \frac{\vdash \phi_1, \Delta \quad \vdash \phi_2, \Delta}{\vdash \phi_1 \& \phi_2, \Delta}; \quad \otimes \frac{\vdash \phi_1, \Delta_1 \quad \vdash \phi_2, \Delta_2}{\vdash \phi_1 \otimes \phi_2, \Delta_1, \Delta_2}.$$

For simplicity, the Δs here should be read as the linear context only. (Note that the interpreter is based on one-sided sequents.)

The interpreter must read these rules as reduction operators, from conclusion to premises. Under this interpretation, the conjunction & (ASCII for &, pronounced "with") makes a separate copy of the linear context for each of its two arguments. Thus, for example, given the context (*i.e.*, the negation of Δ) a(1) and program a(2), part of the unbounded context, the goal a(X) & a(Y) has the single solution X=1,Y=1. Note that neither variable can be 2 since each call to a gets a copy of the context and the formula in the context must be used.

The conjunction * (ASCII for $\otimes$, pronounced "tensor") *divides* the context between its arguments. Thus, given the same program and context, the goal a(X) * a(Y) succeeds with the two possible solutions being X=1, Y=2 and X=2, Y=1. Note that both variables cannot be 1 since there is only a single copy of a(1) in the context and we should need two copies (one for each call to a). Both variables cannot be 2 since formulae in the linear context cannot be arbitrarily deleted.

If the linear context is not used, then & and * both reduce to Prolog's conjunction (,).

The division of the context associated with a tensor product is, at the level of the logical definition of Lygon, *non-deterministic*. However, the interpreter must determine this dynamically. The solution adopted in the current implementation (see below) is a non-trivial development of the *input/output model of resource consumption* first introduced by Hodas and Miller.[6] The basic idea is that all resources are passed first to the left branch; upon completion of the left branch, the remaining resources are passed to the right branch. The (substantial) details have been presented by Winikoff and Harland.[7]

System availability. The current implementation of Lygon (Version 0.4) is an interpreter written in BinProlog and is available by email from the authors or via the World Wide Web from the URL http://www.cs.mu.oz.au/~winikoff/lygon/lygon.html. The system includes a debugger which extends the standard Prolog four port model with the ability to view the context.

One of the strengths of declarative languages is the support for formal reasoning tools: future work involves developing advanced debugging tools. Plans are afoot for a system which combines Lygon and Mercury to give a strongly typed and moded, compiled language.

[4] J.-Y. Girard, Linear Logic, *Theoret. Comp. Sci.*, 50:1–102, 1987.

[5] J. Harland, D. Pym, M. Winikoff. Programming in Lygon: an overview. This volume.

[6] J. Hodas and D. Miller. Logic Programming in a Fragment of Intuitionistic Linear Logic. *Inform. and Computat.* 110:2:327-365, 1994.

[7] M. Winikoff and J. Harland. Implementing the linear logic programming language Lygon. In: J. Lloyd (ed.), *Proc. ILPS'95*, 66–80, MIT Press, 1995.

CtCoq: A System Presentation

Janet Bertot and Yves Bertot

INRIA, 2004 Route des Lucioles, 06902 Sophia-Antipolis, France
{jmi,bertot}@sophia.inria.fr

Abstract. The CtCoq system is a graphical user-interface using a distributed architecture adapted to the Coq proof system [3]. Basic features provided by this graphical interface are direct manipulation of formulas and commands using the mouse, mathematical notations with an extended character set and colors, menus for guiding users in their manipulations of commands and formulas. More advanced features also include textual explanation of proofs, proof-by-pointing, and script management.

1 Introduction

Integrating proof systems in user-friendly environments is a crucial issue if software engineers are to use these tools on a daily basis. We have concentrated on the user-interface part of proof engine development, by developing this user-interface as a different process, communicating with a proof engine using a simple protocol. The user-interface itself has been developed using a program environment generator, the Centaur system [1, 2]. The proof engine is developed in an independent team. We believe this paradigm of independent development of programs integrated in a multi-process, possibly distributed system, has an impact on the future directions of research in the domain of interactive proof systems, as it allows for the fast integration of progress in both the automated deduction and man-machine interface domains.

2 Basic features

The basic elements of the graphical interface are editing windows where the commands and formulas are displayed and edited in a structured way. This means that the data is almost always considered as trees, where the tree structure reflects the syntax of the language. From a purely visual point of view, the data still looks like enriched text. But by comparison with plain textual editing, the structured approach makes it possible to have more contextual help during the editing process and more accurate notations, adapted to usual mathematical practice, with a wide variety of fonts and colors.

Instead of a notion of current position in a document represented by a single character cursor, the editing windows make it possible to have a whole sub-structure as a *current selection*. Editing operations are then related to this current selection. For instance, the position of the current selection is used to provide menu-guided context help. For this tool, a menu is provided to the user, whose content is updated every time the current selection moves, to propose syntactic constructs that are adapted to the syntactic context of this current selection.

The CtCoq user-interface also accommodates more traditional text editing. At any time, the user can select a structure and edit it as a text fragment, meanwhile forgetting the structure information. Coming back to a structured representation is then necessary, and can be done through a parse operation. This integration of textual editing also makes it possible to communicate with other X-Windows applications through the usual textual selection mechanism.

2.1   Pretty printing and notations

For pretty-printing matters, the CtCoq system relies on the Centaur display machinery, which has two important features. First, the notations are chosen through a tree pattern-matching mechanism, which is more powerful than what can be done with text editors as in the TkHOL or Emacs environments. Second, the layout is computed incrementally and it is still sensitive to the mouse, in the sense that it is possible to select sub-expressions of a formula, to copy, paste, or trigger commands with. This makes it more practical to use than layout approaches that use the LaTeX-xdvi chain, where the output is computed in a batch mode and is inert.

3   Advanced features

The CtCoq user-interface also provides elaborate solutions to problems often encountered in the usage of interactive proof systems. *Proof-by-pointing* is concerned with inputting the basic commands. It shows that in the domain of proof manipulation, the mouse can be used to guide a symbolic system in a much more clever way than a simple push-button user-interface. *Script management* is concerned with the support that can be given to a user who tries different solutions to a problem and wants to record his successful attempts. *Textual explanation of proof* provides support to a user who wants to produce documents from his proofs that any mathematician can read, even a mathematician who does not know the Coq system.

3.1   Proof-by-pointing

In the Coq system, most proofs are done interactively in a goal directed style. In this mode of operation, the user first states a goal to prove and then applies commands that reduce this goal to a number of simpler subgoals. Some of the commands have a very elaborate behavior, while others perform very simple logical bookkeeping. *Proof-by-pointing* is a method to ensure that the bookkeeping commands can be very easily triggered and composed, to make their use less tedious.

The idea of proof-by-pointing is that selecting a position in a goal formula can be interpreted as a command to bring the selected sub-formula to the surface of the goal. With this algorithm, the user of the CtCoq environment ends up performing a lot of proofs using mostly the mouse to select relevant parts of goals, and sometimes choosing a more elaborate command from a menu.

3.2 Script management

The CtCoq proof environment supports the activity of interactive proof search. In this mode, the user may try several possibilities before finding the right formalization and the right sequence of inference steps. His work is then a succession of steps forward and backward. Script management is a tool to keep only the successful attempts, discarding the failed ones.

Script management works by separating the window containing the commands sent to the proof system into several areas. One area (called the final area) contains the commands that have already been sent to the proof system, another (the buffer area) contains the command being executed, and a third (the scratch area) contains just the commands being edited by the user. When a command is undone, it is removed from the final area and returned to the scratch area.

The various areas are made visible by different colors. This way the user can see at a glance the current state of his work. This is especially useful when modifying the formalization of a problem and trying to recuperate large amounts of work that were valid in the formalization and that need to be checked again the new formalization.

3.3 Textual Explanation of Proofs

The proof scripts written to check a proof under Coq actually represent the proof but they are unreadable to people who don't have a good knowledge of the proof system's behavior. Fortunately, the Coq system also constructs a typed λ-term that represents the basic inferences used to prove a mathematical result. We are working on pretty-printing facilities that produce formalized English text from these proof terms. With a simple keystroke, it is thus possible to open a window containing the English text describing the proof of a theorem, or even a proof currently in progress.

4 Availability

The CtCoq system is available on Sun and Dec Alpha workstations. Information on how to retrieve this system is available at the following WWW address:

http://www.inria.fr/croap/ctcoq/ctcoq-eng.html

Fig. 1. A typical session with CtCoq

References

1. P. Borras, D. Clément, T. Despeyroux, J. Incerpi, G. Kahn, B. Lang, and V. Pascual. Centaur: the system. In *Third Symposium on Software Development Environments*, 1988. (Also appears as INRIA Report no. 777).

2. D. Clément. A distributed architecture for programming environments. *Software Engineering Notes*, 15(5), 1990. *Proceedings of the 4th Symposium on Software Development Environments*.

3. C. Cornes, J. Courant, J.-C. Filliâtre, G. Huet, P. Manoury, C. Muñoz, C. Murthy, C. Parent, C. Paulin-Mohring, A. Saïbi, and B. Werner. *The Coq Proof Assistant User's Guide*. INRIA, May 1995. Version 5.10.

The TYPELAB Specification and Verification Environment *

F.W. von Henke, M. Luther, H. Pfeifer, H. Rueß,
D. Schwier, M. Strecker, M. Wagner

Universität Ulm
D-89069 Ulm, Germany

1 Introduction

TYPELAB is an experimental environment that permits the specification of software and hardware systems in a modular fashion. Modules are first-class objects that can be manipulated in different ways, for example through refinement in a stepwise process. A high degree of abstraction and good reuse properties are achieved by genericity. The specification language of TYPELAB is based on a very expressive type theory, the *Extended Calculus of Constructions* [Luo94], which gives the system a sound semantic foundation. The pure type theory has been augmented by syntactic constructs that permit an intuitive handling of the entities managed by the system. TYPELAB comprises a proof assistant which is primarily thought to be used as an interactive proof checker. However, a sequent-style theorem prover has been developed for automatically solving medium-sized problems in restricted fragments of the logic. During a specification development activity or during a proof, a knowledge base can be consulted. This knowledge base contains previous developments and theorems that have either been added explicitly or which can be inferred by the system by a kind of "inheritance" mechanism.

2 The Specification Language

The TYPELAB specification language (see [vHDR+95] for a more detailed discussion) has properties that make it suitable both for small-scale and large-scale development and verification tasks. The type theory *ECC* on which TYPELAB is based has been enriched by constructs found in traditional specification languages. Thus, although the full expressiveness of the underlying logic and type system is made available to the user, no prior knowledge of type theory is required. Types not only serve the purpose offered by sorts in traditional algebraic specifications; they also permit to express semantic constraints, as for example restrictions on the domain of partial functions, and thus lead to a concise notation.

* This research has partly been supported by the "Deutsche Forschungsgemeinschaft" within the "Schwerpunktprogramm Deduktion"

The language can basically be perceived as a functional programming language with a strong type system. By the use of dependent function types, ML-style polymorphism can easily be expressed. As in the PVS system [OSR93], partial functions can be defined by means of semantic subtypes, which restrict the domain of a function to arguments satisfying certain properties. Semantic subtypes can be coded as dependent record types in the underlying type theory ECC. A higher-order logic is tightly integrated in the type system via the type-theoretic "propositions-as-types" paradigm.

Structuring in the large is achieved through a powerful module system which considers specifications (or theories, in mathematical parlance) as first-class objects. Specifications are interpreted as dependent record types of ECC and thus can be treated in a uniform manner with other objects of the software development process. In particular, parameterized specifications can be expressed as functions that map a parameter P of a specification type to a specification type depending on P. Similarly, a refinement of specifications can be understood as a function having a specification as its domain and a specification as range. The tight integration of the module system with the type system and the higher-order specification logic yield a language which is more expressive than the languages of most systems and formalisms propagating a style of "parameterized programming" [Gog84].

In recent years, implementations based on type theories have gained recognition, notably Alf [MN94], Coq [Cor95], Lego [LP92] and Nuprl [Con86]. These systems are dedicated very much to the underlying logical formalism, and program derivation is closely linked to a constructive proof of a formula which embodies the specification of the program. As opposed to this view, TYPELAB regards expressive type theories as an adequate foundational formalism, but otherwise tries to abstract from the particular type theory by offering a syntax that makes it similar to advanced verification environments like PVS [OSR93].

In particular, abstract datatypes can be specified in a familiar notation, i.e. by first declaring functions that make up the signature and then specifying axioms the functions have to fulfill. In addition, theorems can be stated in a specification. They give rise to proof obligation that may later be discharged with the aid of the proof assistant.

3 System Support

The TYPELAB system consists of a type checker, a proof assistant and, as an experimental feature, a knowledge base of developments and proofs. These components are closely integrated and are accessible through a uniform user interface.

The type checker ensures the type correctness of the objects manipulated by the system and generates proof obligations, if necessary. Proof obligations arise if a term is coerced to a semantic subtype, if theorems are stated in a specification, and if maps between specifications are given. In the latter case, a map specifies how the functions of an abstract specification can be implemented in a refined specification, without showing that the properties of the functions are preserved. The system then generates proof obligations derived from the appropriately instantiated axioms of the abstract specification.

The proof assistant can be started either with a system-generated proof obligation or with a proof goal issued by the user. Proof construction is to be understood in a large sense: Proofs are not limited to logical statements, but equally well permit the construction of a refinement map between specifications. The proof assistant is thought to be used primarily in an interactive mode, where proof goals can be decomposed by rules of a sequent-style calculus. Some automation is offered by search procedures which are complete for restricted fragments of the logic. Among them are a decision procedure for (intuitionistic) propositional logic and a complete proof procedure for the first-order fragment. Furthermore, the proof assistant provides a tactic language, which permits to define proof procedures for repeatedly occurring patterns of deduction. The proof assistant is further described in [Wag95].

Currently, a knowledge-based component is under construction, which aims at organizing mathematical entities and components of the software development process, such as conceptual vocabulary (for example terminology describing different kinds of orders) or (parameterized) specifications. These objects are arranged in a taxonomy which is structured by a subsumption relation. In the case of a terminology, this is a generalized implication (see [Lut95] for details). In the case of parameterized specifications, the subsumption relation is a covariant refinement relation. The construction of such a database not only has the advantage of making the relation between objects more perspicuous. It also permits to inherit statements made about certain objects in the taxonomy or theorems asserted in a specification, thus promoting reuse of proofs and developments in different contexts.

4 Future Extensions

A research prototype of the TYPELAB system has been implemented and is currently being tested on small examples drawn from the domains of program development and mathematics. Enhancements of the syntax and further automation of the prover are envisaged. They will permit to tackle more substantial examples from hardware and software design.

Currently, work is in progress to integrate specification operators in the style of ASL [Wir86] into the TYPELAB language, for example extension of a specification or renaming of the signature. These operators facilitate the construction of knowledge bases of specifications.

The knowledge-based component of TYPELAB will be further extended to allow not only inheritance of theorems, but also proof abstraction and analysis of applicability conditions of program transformations and refinement steps.

References

[Con86]   R.L. Constable et al. *Implementing Mathematics with the Nuprl Proof Development System*. Prentice-Hall, 1986.

[Cor95]   Cristina Cornes et al. *The Coq Proof Assistant Reference Manual*. INRIA Rocquencourt and CNRS-ENS Lyon, 1995.

[Gog84]   J.A. Goguen. Parameterized programming. *IEEE Transactions on Software Engineering*, SE-10(5), September 1984.

[LP92]   Zhaohui Luo and Robert Pollack. *LEGO Proof Development System: User's Manual*. University of Edinburgh, Department of Computer Science, 1992.

[Luo94]   Zhaohui Luo. *Computation and Reasoning*. Oxford University Press, 1994.

[Lut95]   Marko Luther. Wissensbasierte Methoden zur Beweisunterstützung in Typentheorie. Master's thesis, Universität Ulm, 1995. Available at URL http://www.informatik.uni-ulm.de/ki/Forschung/Deduktion /ml-diplomarbeit.html.

[MN94]   Lena Magnusson and Bengt Nordström. The ALF proof editor and its proof engine. In H. Barendregt and T. Nipkow, editors, *Types for Proofs and Programs*, volume 806 of *Springer LNCS*, pages 213–237, 1994.

[OSR93]   S. Owre, N. Shankar, and J.M. Rushby. *The PVS Specification Language*. Computer Science Lab, SRI International, Menlo Park CA 94025, March 1993.

[vHDR+95] F.W. von Henke, A. Dold, H. Rueß, D. Schwier, and M. Strecker. Construction and deduction methods for the formal development of software. In *KORSO: Methods, Languages, and Tools for the Construction of Correct Software*, Springer LNCS 1009. 1995.

[Wag95]   Matthias Wagner. Entwicklung und Implementierung eines Beweisers für konstruktive Logik. Master's thesis, Universität Ulm, 1995. Available at URL http://www.informatik.uni-ulm.de/ki/Forschung /Deduktion/mw-diplomarbeit.html.

[Wir86]   Martin Wirsing. Structured algebraic specifications: A kernel language. *Theoretical Computer Science*, 42:123–249, 1986.

Incremental Formalization

Bernhard Steffen, Tiziana Margaria, Andreas Claßen, Volker Braun

Lehrstuhl für Programmiersysteme
Universität Passau
D-94030 Passau (Germany)
{steffen,tiziana,classen,deepthou}@fmi.uni-passau.de

1 Motivation

In his invited talk at TAPSOFT'95, Joseph Goguen claimed that practical success of formal methods is bound to a *tool-supported domain specific* paradigm (cf. [1]), which he characterized as follows:

1. *a narrow, well defined, well understood problem domain is addressed; there may already be a successful library for this domain,*
2. *there is a community of users who understand the domain, have good communication among themselves, and have potential financial resources,*
3. *the tool has a graphical user interface that is intuitive to the user community, embodying their own language and conventions,*
4. *the tool takes a large grain approach; rather than synthesizing procedures out of statements, it synthesizes systems out of modules; it may use a library of components and synthesize code for putting them together,*
5. *inside the tool is a powerful engine that encapsulates formal methods concepts and/or algorithms; it may be a theorem prover or a code generator; users do not have to know how it works, or even that it is there.*

The METAFrame environment [7] developed in Passau arose exactly from the need for such tool support.[1] It helps high-level programming with whole subroutines and modules as elementary building blocks on the basis of a specifically instantiated *repository*. Originally, the need arose from the problem of the construction of application-specific heterogeneous analysis and verifications tools on the basis of a repository of elementary tools and algorithms [8]. In the meantime it turned out that METAFrame has a much wider application profile, as we illustrate in Sec. 3 by means of a completely different domain: the construction of intelligent network (IN) telecommunication services.

---

[1] Other systems fitting this description are, e.g., CAPS, ControlH and MetaH, AMPHION, Panel, and DSDL (see [1]).

2   The METAFrame Environment

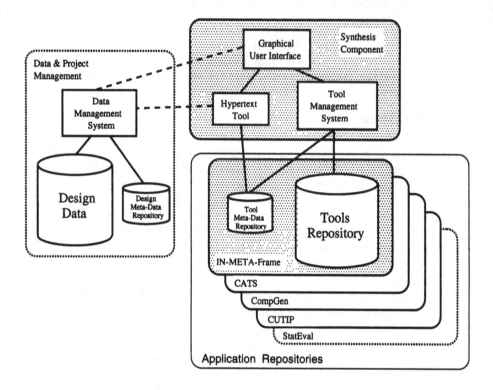

Fig. 1. The METAFrame Global Architecture

METAFrame is a *meta-level environment* for the flexible management of large repositories of complex objects which are best modelled and described at a coarse-grain level. It is designed to offer sophisticated support for the *systematic* and *structured* computer aided generation, analysis, verification, and testing of application-specific complex systems from collections of reusable components. Figure 1 shows its overall organization together with the current applications.

The METAFrame approach abstracts from implementation details by allowing designers a *high-level-development* of the programs. Specifications express constraints in a *temporal logic*, SLTL, that uniformly and elegantly captures an abstract view of the repository [8, 9]. Implementations are in a *high-level language* (HLL) tailored to express the combination of reusable library components stored in the repository, which are considered as atomic on this level. These components may well be written in different programming languages. Constructed programs are hierarchical, based on subcomponents, which may be written in different application languages (C, ML, C++) of different programming paradigms (imperative, functional, object-oriented). This allows a designer team the rapid and reliable realization of efficient application specific complex programs without a sophisticated user interaction, and is therefore an ideal means for a systematic investigation and construction of adequate large-to huge grain systems which solve specific problems.

METAFrame is currently available for UNIX systems, e.g. the Siemens Nixdorf RM line, and for PCs under LINUX. Its graphical interface as well as the hypertext browser are built on top of the Tcl/Tk graphics library [3]. Target language is the HLL, whose interpreter is implemented in C++.

3 Application: Definition of Intelligent Network Services

Intelligent Network (IN) Services are customized telephone services, like e.g., 1) 'Free-Phone', where the receiver of the call can be billed if some conditions are met, 2) 'Virtual Private Network', enabling groups of customers to define their own private net within the public net, or 3) 'Info Lines', where a number of menus lead a caller to the most convenient connection for information and services.

This application led to a very successful industrial cooperation with the Siemens Nixdorf Informationssysteme AG (SNI), aimed at the development of a new Service Creation Environment (SCE): an interactive environment responsible for the definition, modification, customization and provision of new IN services.

The realization of these services is in fact quite complex and error prone, thus it is till now carried out centrally, by teams of experts. However, the current trend in advanced IN services clearly evolves towards a *decentralization* of the service processing. This demands for quick customization of the offered services, and requires rapid availability of the modified or reconfigured services. As a consequence, decentralization imposes a simplification of the development process (currently, the construction of a single service may take several 'expert years') as well as drastic decentralization of the (major part of) the quality control.

Our METAFrame -based SCE environment is unique in featuring *formal verification* of global correctness and consistency as well as *abstract views* [5].

- Formal verification guarantees frame conditions for the design, concerning implementability, country specific standards, and network specific features. Frame conditions are formulated as constraints [6] in a temporal logic and verified via model checking.
- Abstract views focus the development process, and support error correction.

This approach provides an *incremental* use of formal methods: if no formal constraints are defined, our system behaves like standard systems for service definition. However, the more constraints are added, the more reliable are the created services. This provides a 'soft' entry into the world of formal methods avoiding drastic changes, which would be costly and lead to acceptance problems.

The major expected benefit is a drastic reduction of the development and testing time (and thus of the costs) of new IN services, since expert knowledge, usually being distributed over various sites, can now be formulated during the whole development process and made available even for non-experts.

4 Lesson Learned

The key to the acceptance of our underlying method in the industrial environment was the *incremental formalization*, ranging from 'no specification', which results in the old-fashioned development style, to 'detailed specification' with full tool support.[2] However other acceptance factors played an important role too: strong support of software reuse, enhanced flexibility, an intuitive specification language, graphical interface and hypertext support.

Indeed, one year after the project's start this SCE, which was developed in collaboration by five differents sites (two in Munich, Berlin, Vienna and Passau), has become an industrial product, has been presented by SNI at various international fairs (e.g. Ce-Bit, and TELECOM'95), and is already installed at a number of customers (e.g. Deutsche Telekom).

References

1. J.A. Goguen, Luqi: *"Formal Methods and Social Context in Software Development,"* (invited talk) 6th Int. Conf. on Theory and Practice of Software Development (TAPSOFT'95), Aarhus (Denmark), May 1995, LNCS N.915, pp.62-81.
2. C. Floyd: *"Theory and Practice of Software Development - Stages in a Debate",* (invited talk) 6th Int. Conf. on Theory and Practice of Software Development (TAPSOFT'95), Aarhus (Denmark), May 1995, LNCS N.915, pp.25-41.
3. J.K. Ousterhout: *"Tcl and the Tk Toolkit,"* Addison–Wesley, April 1994.
4. B. Steffen, T. Margaria, A. Claßen, V. Braun, M. Reitenspieß: *"An Environment for the Creation of Intelligent Network Services",* inv. contrib. to the *Annual Review of Communications,* IEC, Chicago (USA), 1996 - also in *The Advanced Intelligent Network: A Comprehensive Report",* IEC, Dec. 1995.
5. B. Steffen, T. Margaria, A. Claßen, V. Braun, M. Reitenspieß: *"A Constraint-Oriented Service Creation Environment,"* Proc. PACT'96, Int. Conf on Practical Applications of Constraint Technology, 24-26 Apr.1996, London (UK).
6. B. Steffen, A. Claßen, T. Margaria: *"The METAFrame : An Environment for Flexible Tool Management,"* Proc. TAPSOFT'95, Aarhus (DK), May 1995, LNCS N.915, pp.791-792.
7. B. Steffen, T. Margaria, A. Claßen: *Heterogeneous Analysis and Verification for Distributed Systems,* To appear in the Journal "SOFTWARE: Concepts and Tools", Springer Verlag, 1996.
8. B. Steffen, T. Margaria, B. Freitag: *"Module Configuration by Minimal Model Construction,"* Techn. Rep. MIP 93-13, Fak. für Mathematik und Informatik, Universität Passau (Germany), December 1993.

---

[2] This observation is in full correspondence with Christiane Floyd's statements at TAPSOFT'95 [2].

PROPLANE :
A Specification Development Environment

Jeanine Souquières and Nicole Lévy

CRIN—CNRS B.P. 239 Bâtiment LORIA, F-54506 Vandœuvre-lès-Nancy Cedex,
Jeanine.Souquieres@loria.fr, Nicole.Levy@loria.fr

Abstract. PROPLANE is an environment supporting formal specification activity by providing methodological assistance during the development process. The central key of the system is the notion of operator:
the development of a specification is defined as a sequence of steps in
which each step maps a development state to the next one by application of some operator. Operators separate the design concepts from
the technical details of how they are captured in the target specification
language.

Introduction

Experience has shown that the most critical and least supported phases of the
development process are requirement analysis and specification. Errors and mis-
conceptions contained in the requirements will be contained in the system specification, and all those contained in the specification will show up in the program.
A formal approach to specification could greatly help in reducing the amount of
error because of the non ambiguity of formal specifications and the availability of
powerful analysis techniques and prototyping tools. We believe that the effective
availability of tools supporting specification development could greatly help in
promoting the use of formal specifications by practitioners.

Is it possible to combine graphical notations and formal languages? Moreover
machine support should include book-keeping and guidance during the specification development process giving hints on what has to be done and in which
order. The specification development process should be problem oriented instead
of language oriented. For example, it is more important to choose to specify a
system by a global state and state transitions than to first select the specification
language. It should also be possible to check if existing specifications could be
combined.

In our prototype tool, PROPLANE, the development of a specification is defined as a sequence of steps in which each step maps some development state to
the next one by the application of some operator. A development state consists
of two consistent and linked viewpoints, a workplan and a product. When using
this tool, the specifier selects predefined operators in a library to make the specification evolve as needed; she or he is relieved from many humdrum activities
and can concentrate on creative aspects. The main benefits of the model are the
following [DFHs+94]:

- language-independence [LS94, Smi94]. The development process model can be used whatever the product to be built is, e.g. a specification, a program or a piece of documentation. Experiments with the languages Glider [Sou93], PLUSS [SL93], and Z [DS93] have been carried out and are still under progress with Lotos in the domain of communication protocols. It is to be noted that this work is complementary to specification language research.

- hierarchical structure of the process. The tree structure of the workplan makes it possible to distinguish abstract or method-related tasks and operators from concrete or language-dependent ones (often the former are applied before the latter).

- process documentation. All the design decisions taken during specification development are recorded in a tree-structured way. They make the specification easier to understand and help the incremental verification and refinement of the system.

- support for backtracking. Backtracking on decisions with undoing task side-effects is a basic construct of design processes which is rarely supported in existing meta-models. Backtracking is supported by starting new reductions at appropriate places in the workplan and recording the old version.

- support for guidance. For example, at any stage of the elaboration process, the developer knows what remains to be done [SD95] and has at his disposal a library of predefined operators.

- process reuse by replay. Typical patterns can be associated with specific methods, domains and languages [Dar95]. Recording such patterns and instantiating them to new situations make it possible to replay developments according to the methodological patterns defined.

A development state

Figure 1 shows an example of a development state for the Abracadabra communication protocol system. The left–hand side of the figure represents the workplan state. A workplan is a collection of tasks linked through a *reduction relation*. A *task*, for example *"Define 'ABRA'"*, denotes work to be done in order to produce a piece of specification or a product. A *reduction*, denoted by a circle, represents a decision taken for accomplishing the task. Subtasks can be introduced. The right–hand side of the figure represents a product state. The specification language used is Glider [CJO94] in which some undefined parts are meta-variables like $< OP\_UNIT1 >$. Similar structures are used to model the workplan and the product: *and/or*–trees. The workplan is related to the product: in the figure, the grey tint task *"Structure of 'KIND'"* is related to the grey tint part of the product *"ENUM [ConReq, Conlnd, C ...]"*. Development operators work in parallel on the workplan and the product to reduce tasks and construct or modify the product text. An operator menu is popped up in the middle of Figure 1 from which we can choose between two applicable operators written in bold characters, namely *Add a Component* and *Backtrack* for the selected task (because it is already reduced). If some parameters of the operators are needed,

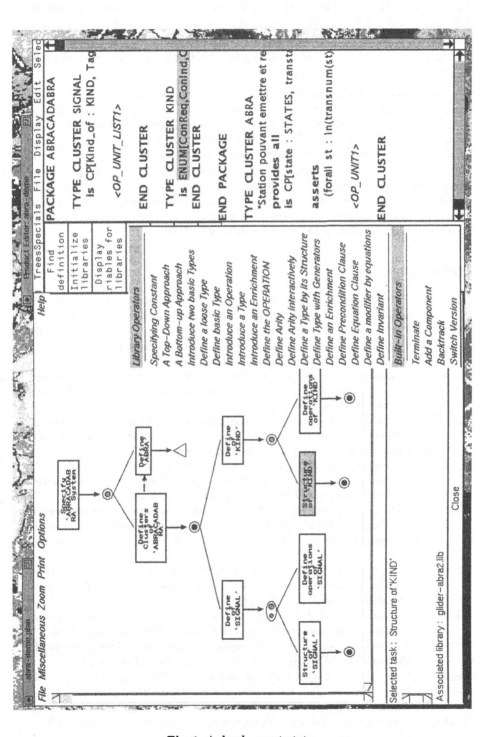

Fig. 1. A development state

they are interactively asked of the specifier or calculated from the current development state. A workplan is always incrementally developed top-down with possible backtracks to open new alternatives. Therefore, the description of the development is top-down but bottom-up, top-down or middle-out methodologies can be captured in our framework.

The prototype tool, PROPLANE, consists of a plan editor connected to a product manager [BS94]. The Centaur platform provides generic facilities to build development environments for specific languages. Its structural editor has been instantiated by the Glider, Z, Object-Z and Lotos languages. A companion workplan editor has been developed under Lucid Emacs (with Emacs Lisp as the programming language) and interfaced with Centaur so as to keep process-product links consistent throughout the development process. The tool has a graphical interface developed with TCL-TK and several libraries of development operators can be defined. At present, the prototype is under evolution in order to allow more powerful operators to be defined [Lév95].

References

[BS94]   G. Bosch and J. Souquières. Prototype Assistant: its Function and its Design. Esprit Project 2537 ICARUS, Deliverable #48, January 1994.

[CJO94]   S. Clerici, R. Jimenez, and F. Orejas. *Semantic Constructions in the GLIDER Specification Language*, volume Recent Trends in Data Type Specification of *LNCS 785*. Springer Verlag, 1994.

[Dar95]   R. Darimont. Process support for requirements elaboration. Phd thesis, Université catholique de Louvain, Faculté des Sciences Appliquées, Département d'Ingénierie Informatique, June 1995.

[DFHs⁺94] E. Dubois, J.-P. Finance, J. Hagelstein, A. van Lamsweerde, F. Orejas, J. Souquières, and P. Wodon. Icarus: Overview of the project. Technical report, Esprit2 Project, EEC, December 1994.

[DS93]   R. Darimont and J. Souquières. A Development Model: Application to Z Specifications. In *Proc. of the WG 8.1 Working Conference on Information System Development Process*, Como, Italy, 1993. North Holland.

[Lév95]   N. Lévy. Improving PROPLANE: a Specification Development Framework. In *Proc. Second IFAC Int. Workshop on Safety and Reliability in Emerging Control Technologies, Daytona Beach, Florida*, pages 229–240, November 1995.

[LS94]   N. Lévy and G. Smith. A language-independent approach to specification construction. In *Proceedings SIGSOFT'94: Symposium on the Foundations of Software Engineering, New Orleans, USA.*, December 1994.

[SD95]   J. Souquières and R. Darimont. La description du développement de spécifications. *Technique et Science Informatiques*, 14(9), novembre 1995.

[SL93]   J. Souquières and N. Lévy. Description of Specification Developments. In *Proceeding of RE'93*, pages 216–223. I.E.E.E. Press, January 1993.

[Smi94]   G. Smith. An Object-Oriented Development Framework for Z. In J.P. Bowen and J.A. Hall, editors, *Proc. of the 8th Z User Meeting (ZUM'94), Cambridge*. Springer-Verlag, Workshops in Computing, June 1994.

[Sou93]   J. Souquières. Aides au développement de spécifications. Thèse d'état, CRIN/Université de Nancy 1, Janvier 1993.

A Logic-Based Technology to Mechanize Software Components Reuse

System demonstration proposal

Patrick Parot

Institut National de Recherche en Informatique et Automatique
Domaine de Voluceau, B.P. 105, 78153 Le Chesnay, FRANCE

1 Introduction

A prototype system named SER has been developing and is used as a support for the experimentations we present. We have applied notions relative to module reuse to the area of software configuration management. We think that the obtained results encourage us to go deeper into the applications of our work in this domain. After introducing a few words about the prototype we will sketch a few simple experiments concerning automatic retrieval of first order modules of programs (described by their interface and property specifications), then we will consider some experiments about automatic system modelling from a library of *general-purpose software components*.

2 Realization, Experiments and Results

SER is a prototype system developed to achieve experiments whose results prove, in practice, design and theory viability. SER is written in the Caml functional language and the chosen external resolution system is the logic program evaluator DyALog because of the crucial importance of a good behaviour concerning the completeness and ending of the solution search process.

2.1 Retrieval of First Order Modules of Programs

Experiment 1 *A simple example: the query is an incomplete interface and property specification. The returned solutions are deduced from the library (lib1) by composing components whose implementations match query specifications. The underscore symbol denotes an anonymous variable.*

```
#              retrieve interface X ~ {
#                      + : self -> self -> self,  * : X -> _ }
#                  and properties {
#                      space = large } ;;
```

Solution set :

```
> solution:  Polynom (Church) --> component: C1_Polynom (C1_Church)
> solution:  Church           --> component: C1_Church
> solution:  Complex          --> component: C2_Complex
```

Experiment 2 *The* Lifo, Fifo, 1_Lifo, 1_Fifo, Queue *and* List *are polymorphic specifications.* V1, V2, ... *are polymorphic variables. Let consider the following query:*

```
#                     retrieve interface X ~ { insert: _ } ;;
```

Solution set :

```
> solution: (1_Lifo (List (V6, V5))) (V6)
  --> component: C1_1_Lifo (C2_List)
  --> component: C2_1_Lifo (C2_List)
  --> component: C1_1_Lifo (C1_List)
  --> component: C2_1_Lifo (C1_List)
> solution: (1_Fifo (List (V4, V5))) (V4)
> solution: Queue (V3)  --> component: C1_Queue
> solution: Lifo (V2)   --> component: C1_Lifo
> solution: Fifo (V1)   --> component: C1_Fifo
```

2.2 System Modelling by Software Components Reuse

The considered library (lib 2) stores specifications of a C executable compiler (cc1), the C source of an optimizing compiler (cc2), an executable linker (lk), some caml compilers (camlc1, camlc2) and the source of a sort module (Caml_sort).

Experiment 3 *The returned solutions are formulas that denote the way to create executable sort algorithms. The solutions are deduced from the library lib2 by applying compilers and linkers upon the* caml_sort *component.*

```
#             retrieve interface X ~ {
#                        written_in: exe, class: sort } ;;
```

Solution set :

```
--> component: lk ((lk (cc1 (camlc1))) (caml_sort))
--> component: lk ((lk ((lk (cc1 (cc2))) (camlc1))) (caml_sort))
--> component: lk ((lk ((lk (cc1 (camlc1))) (camlc2))) (caml_sort))
    ...
```

Experiment 4 *The retrieval system derives formulas which denote the derivation way to produce a* quick optimizing compiler *expressed by the following query:*

```
#             retrieve interface X ~ { written_in : exe }
#                   and properties ~ { object_code = optimized,
#                                      func = compiler,
#                                      speed = quick } ;;
```

Solution set :

```
--> component: lk ((lk (cc1 (cc2))) (cc2))
--> component: lk ((lk ((lk (cc1 (cc2))) (cc2))) (cc2))
    ...
```

3 Library lib1 (extract)

```
(****** Church  Integers *******)

interface Church ~ {
  int : int -> self ,
  one : self ,
  zero : self ,
  succ : self * self,
  + : self -> self -> self ,
  * : self -> self -> self,
  print: self -> unit } ;;

component C1_Church :: Church ;;
component C2_Church :: Church ;;

C1_Church :: properties ~ {
  speed = fast,
  space = large,
  code = optimized } ;;

C2_Church :: properties ~ {
  speed = very_fast,
  space = very_large,
  code = up_optimized } ;;

(***** Complex numbers *******)

interface Complex ~ {
  complex: float * float -> self ,
  float : float -> self,
  real : self -> float,
  + : self -> self -> self,
  - : self -> self -> self,
  * : self -> self -> self,
  = : self -> self -> bool,
  print : self -> unit } ;;

component C1_Complex :: Complex ;;
component C2_Complex :: Complex ;;

C1_Complex :: properties ~ {
  speed = slow,
  space = tiny,
  code = no_optimized } ;;

C2_Complex :: properties ~ {
  speed = fast,
  space = large,
  code = optimized } ;;
```

```
(********* Polynoms ***********)

interface Polynom [r] ~ {
  list: r list -> self ,
(* zero : self ,  Prevent infinite
                  application on itself *)
  one : self ,
  + : self -> self -> self ,
  - : self -> self -> self ,
  * : self -> self -> self ,
  scal : self -> r -> self,
  print : self -> unit }
where {
  interface r ~ {
            print: self -> unit,
            zero: self,
            one: self } }
  ;;

functor C1_Polynom :: Polynom ;;
functor C2_Polynom :: Polynom ;;

C1_Polynom [X] :: properties ~ {
  speed = fast if (X.speed = fast),
  space = large if (X.speed = fast
                    & X.space = large),
  code = no_optimized }
  ;;

(********* List **************)

interface (a, b) List ~ {
  hd : self -> a,
  tl : self -> self,
  nil : self,
  null : self -> bool,
  cons : a -> self -> self,
  list : a list -> self,
  length : self -> Int,
  nth : self -> Int -> a,
  ^ : self -> self -> self,
  mapper : (a -> b) -> self -> b list,
  do_all : (a -> unit) -> self -> unit }
  ;;

component C1_List :: List ;;
component C2_List :: List ;;
```

```
C1_List :: properties ~ {                    interface a l_Lifo [l] ~ {
    speed = fast,                                empty : self ,
    space = tiny,                                insert: a -> self -> self,
    code = optimized } ;;                        delete : self -> (a * self) }
                                             where {
                                               interface l ~ {
C2_List :: properties ~ {                          list: a list -> self,
    speed = very_fast,                             tl: self -> self,
    space = tiny,                                  hd: self -> a,
    code = up_optimized } ;;                       ons: a -> self -> self,
                                                   nil: self } }
(********* Queues ************)                     ;;

 interface a Lifo ~ {                        functor C1_l_Lifo :: l_Fifo ;;
    empty : self ,                           functor C2_l_Lifo :: l_Fifo ;;
    insert: a -> self -> self,
    delete : self -> (a * self) } ;;         C1_l_Lifo [x] :: properties ~ {
                                                 speed = slow,
component C1_Lifo :: Lifo ;;                      space = tiny,
                                                 code = optimized }
C1_Lifo :: properties ~ {                          ;;
    speed = slow,
    space = tiny,                            C2_l_Lifo [x] :: properties ~ {
    code = optimized }                           speed = fast,
      ;;                                          space = large
                                                       if (x.speed = very_fast),
 interface a Fifo ~ {                            code = no_optimized }
    empty : self,                                  ;;
    insert: a -> self -> self,
    delete : self -> (a * self) }            interface a l_Fifo [l] ~ {
      ;;                                          empty : self ,
                                                  insert: a -> self -> self,
component C1_Fifo :: Fifo ;;                      delete : self -> (a * self) }
                                             where {
C1_Fifo :: properties ~ {                      interface l ~ {
    speed = fast,                                  list: a list -> self,
    space = large,                                 cons: a -> self -> self,
    code = no_optimized }                          tl: self -> self,
      ;;                                            hd: self -> a,
                                                    nil: self,
 interface a Queue ~ {                              ~ : self -> self -> self } }
    empty : self ,                                  ;;
    insert: a -> self -> self,
    delete : self -> (a * self) }
      ;;

component C1_Queue :: Queue ;;

C1_Queue :: properties ~ {
    speed = average,
    space = average,
    code = no_optimized }
      ;;
```

4 Library lib2 (extract)

```
(******** Sort component *********)
interface a caml_sort ~ {
      written_in: caml,
      type: a list -> a list,
      class: sort } ;;

(******** Compilers, linker *******)
component camlc1 :: interface
   camlc1 ~ { written_in: c,
             type: caml -> o,
             class: translator } ;;

component camlc2 :: interface
   camlc2 ~ { written_in: caml,
             type: caml -> o,
             class: translator } ;;

component cc1 :: interface
   cc1 ~ { written_in: exe ,
          type: c -> o,
          class: translator } ;;

component cc2 :: interface
   cc2 ~ { written_in: c,
          type: c -> o,
          class: translator } ;;

component linker :: interface
      Linker ~ {
             written_in: exe,
             type: o -> exe,
             class: linker } ;;

(*** Meta rule parsing, linking ***)
functor parsing ::
   interface (S, T, C) parsing [F, X]
        ~ { written_in: o,
           type: T,
           class: C }
      where {
          interface F ~ {
                written_in: exe,
                type: S -> o,
                class: translator
                }
          and interface X ~ {
                written_in: S,
                type: T,
                class: C } } ;;
```

```
functor linking ::
   interface (O, T, C) linking [L, X]
        ~ { written_in: exe,
           type: T,
           class: C }
      where {
          interface L ~ {
                written_in: exe,
                type: O -> exe,
                class: linker
                }
          and interface X ~ {
                written_in: O,
                type: T,
                class: C } } ;;

(***** property specifications *******)
   camlc1 :: properties ~ {
             func = compiler,
             object_code = average } ;;

   camlc2 :: properties ~ {
             func = compiler,
             object_code = optimized } ;;

   cc1 :: properties ~ {
             func = compiler,
             object_code = average } ;;

   cc2 :: properties ~ {
             func = compiler,
             object_code = optimized } ;;

   linker :: property ~ { func = link } ;;

(****** Properties meta-rules *******)

parsing [F, X] :: properties ~ {
   func = X.func,
   object_code = optimized
      if (X.object_code = optimized
      & X.func = compiler
      & F.func = compiler),
   speed = quick
      if (F.object_code = optimized) }
   ;;
linking [L, X] :: properties ~ {
             func = X.func,
             speed = X.speed } ;;
```

TkGofer: A Functional GUI Library

Wolfram Schulte, Thilo Schwinn, Ton Vullinghs

Fakultät für Informatik, Universität Ulm, D-89069 Ulm, Germany
email: {wolfram, thilo, ton}@informatik.uni-ulm.de

Abstract. We present a constructor class based implementation of a graphical user interface library, named TkGofer. It provides a convenient way to develop window-based applications in the pure, functional programming language Gofer [1], which is a subset of Haskell. The principal contribution of the approach embodied in the library is that it offers a simple and type secure solution to specify the appearance and behaviour of individual and composed user interface components.

1 Motivation

Functional programming languages offer many advantages to programmers. Using functional languages often results in faster development times and shorter code compared with imperative languages. Furthermore, reasoning about and reusing programs is easier. Recent research in the field of functional programming resulted in new concepts such as monads to tame the imperative aspects of IO and state [7], and constructor classes to deal with higher order polymorphism [2].

Today, the specification of graphical user interfaces (GUIs) is an essential part of any realization of interactive systems. To avoid multi-paradigm programming, it is an obvious idea to incorporate GUI programming in functional languages. Due to intrinsic state-based properties of GUIs, monads are a natural choice for their implementation [4].

In this paper, we describe the structure of TkGofer. TkGofer consists of the standard Gofer interpreter and the TkGofer prelude file [5, 6]. The prelude file is a library of useful types and functions, which is automatically imported in every Gofer program. It includes all functions for creating and modifying user interfaces.

2 The Library

The library is structured using constructor classes. A constructor class serves to introduce overloading for sets of datatypes and type constructors (higher-order polymorphism). Constructor classes help us to develop an extendable hierarchy of widget classes to support type secure and flexible programming of GUIs. This hierarchy permits homogeneous access to typed widget options, and hides the low level details of window programming, such as layout definitions and naming conventions. Furthermore, usage of classes supports code reuse and the definition of new widgets.

The TkGofer Class Hierarchy. A GUI typically consists of building blocks like windows, menus and buttons. All these entities, each with their own particular behaviour and appearance, are called widgets.

Although a lot of differences between widgets exist, most properties that widgets may have are shared by some widgets or even by all widgets, e.g., the way in which they have to be accessed or the way in which we have to specify their outline. (Constructor) classes are used to express the common characteristics of a set of widgets. This leads to a hierarchy of classes as depicted in Fig. 1. The basic class is called `Widget`. In this class we define functions that

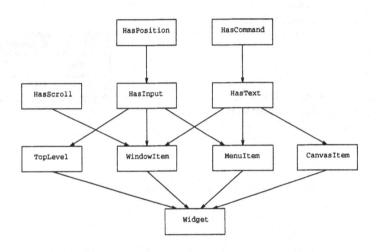

Fig. 1. *The TkGofer class hierarchy*

apply to every widget, e.g., the function `background` to change a widget's background colour, or the function `cset` to update a widget's configuration. To exploit the similarities among the widgets of a certain kind, the classes `TopLevel`, `WindowItem`, `MenuItem` and `CanvasItem` are introduced. To make programming GUIs even more convenient, several additional classes are provided. For example, class `HasText` includes all widgets that may have a static text, class `HasCommand` contains all static text widgets that additionally may be configured with a command. A typical instance of these classes is the type `Button`.

Layout Combinators. Widgets can be composed vertically and horizontally using layout combinators. The two basic associative combinators are `<<` for horizontal and `^^` for vertical composition. Furthermore, idempotent layout functions exist to specify the size of a widget, relative to the size of its neighbours. To combine the principles of sizing and positioning widgets, we introduce derived combinators, which are associative again. They glue interface-components in an abstract, precise and elegant way together. For example v `^-^` w indicates that widget w is placed underneath widget v and both widgets are aligned in length.

Example. We take a look at a simple decimal-octal-converter. Each time a value is entered in the decimal entryfield the octal one displays the converted value and vice versa, see Fig. 2. The root of the program has the monadic type IO().

```
main :: IO ()
main = start converter where
  converter =
    do { w <- window [title "Convert"]
       ; (f1,e1) <- input w "dec"
       ; (f2,e2) <- input w "oct"
       ; conv intToOct e1 e2
       ; conv octToInt e2 e1
       ; pack (f1 << f2)
       }

  input w s =
    do { l <- label w [text s]
       ; e <- entry w [width 9]
       ; result ((l ^-^ e),e)
       }

  conv f a b =
    cset a (on return (do {x <- get a; set b (f x)}))
```

Fig. 2. *The decimal-octal-converter application*

In our concept main calls the function start with an initial window setup. The function converter defines a window and two additional events to invoke the corresponding convert functions upon pressing the return key. The function input defines a small input mask, consisting of two widgets: a label with text s and an entry field to handle the decimal or octal input, respectively. As soon as the user presses the return button in one of the entryfields, the entered value is read and the converted value is written in the other entry field. The function pack returns the horizontally composed input masks to the GUI manager. Apart from the definition of the functions intToOct and octToInt, Fig. 2 lists all you have to write in TkGofer.

Implementation. The implementation of TkGofer is based on the graphical user interface toolkit Tcl/Tk [3]. This tool handles the events from the console and visualizes the user interface. Gofer is extended with a few primitives for communication with this toolkit. Actions that change the GUI are represented by executable scripts, which are send to the Tcl/Tk interpreter.

Thus, to perform graphical IO, it suffices to perform textual IO. This can be easily done using the monadic IO primitives, offered by Gofer. Furthermore, we need some proper datastructures to store global elements of the GUI, like the callback structure. To hide these details from the user, also this part of the implementation rests on a suitable combination of monads.

3 Conclusion

The here presented library represents a very smooth, type secure and high level interface to the application programmer — who can now fully concentrate on the core of the system instead of fuzzy details of window programming. The implementation of TkGofer is small, easily extendable, reasonably fast, and due to the robustness of Tcl/Tk, stable.

Using TkGofer, we were able to rapidly develop a large number of applications with attractive user interfaces, ranging from a lift simulator to a hypertext browser. The tool is freely available. For more information, please contact `ton@informatik.uni-ulm.de`.

References

1. M.P. Jones. *An introduction to Gofer (draft)*, 1993.
2. M.P. Jones. Functional programming with overloading and higher-order polymorphism. In J. Jeuring and E. Meijer, editors, *Advanced Functional Programming. First International Spring School on Advanced Functional Programming Techniques, Båstad, Sweden, May 1995*, volume 925 of *Lecture Notes in Computer Science*, pages 97–136. Springer-Verlag, 1995.
3. J.K. Ousterhout. *Tcl and the Tk toolkit*. Addison Wesley, 1994.
4. S.L. Peyton Jones and Ph. Wadler. Imperative functional programming. In *Proc. 20th ACM Symposium on Principles of Programming Languages*, Charlotte, North Carolina, January 1993.
5. T. Vullinghs, T. Schwinn, and W. Schulte. TkGofer User Manual. Technical report, University of Ulm, to appear, 1996.
6. T. Vullinghs, D. Tuijnman, and W. Schulte. Lightweight GUIs for functional programming. In M. Hermenegildo and S.D. Swierstra, editors, *Programming Languages: Implementations, Logics and Programs. 7th International Symposium, PLILP '95*, volume 982 of *Lecture Notes in Computer Science*, pages 341–356. Springer-Verlag, September 1995.
7. Ph. Wadler. Comprehending monads. In *Proc. 1990 ACM Conference on Lisp and Functional Programming*, 1990.

ALPHA – A Class Library for a Metamodel Based on Algebraic Graph Theory

Sebastian Erdmann* and Ingo Claßen**

Technical University of Berlin

Abstract. A class library supporting a metamodel based on algebraic graph theory is presented. The metamodel provides the basis for a representation of different modeling techniques and evolution of corresponding schemes. The library is intended to support the implementation of modeling and restructuring tools.

1 Introduction

Metamodels play an important role in CASE tools for graphical techniques like Entity–Relationship models, Petri nets, object–oriented models, etc. They represent information on different levels (e. g. models, schemes, instances) in a common way. In [CL95] we presented a metamodel based on algebraic graph theory [Löw93] where simultaneous modifications on different levels (e. g. simultaneous modification of a scheme and already existing instances) can be described by graph transformation rules. This metamodel based on the following attributed graph signature ALPHA

$$
\begin{aligned}
&\textbf{ags } \text{ALPHA} \\
&\quad \textbf{graph part sorts } \textit{Item} \\
&\qquad\qquad\quad \textbf{opns } r_i : \textit{Item} \to \textit{Item} \quad (i \in \mathbb{N}) \\
&\quad \textbf{data part} \quad \textbf{sorts } \textit{Data} \\
&\qquad\qquad\quad \textbf{opns } op_i^j : \textit{Data}^i \to \textit{Data} \, (i, j \in \mathbb{N}) \\
&\quad \textbf{attr part} \quad \textbf{opns } v_i : \textit{Item} \to \textit{Data} \quad (i \in \mathbb{N}) \\
&\quad \textbf{end}
\end{aligned}
$$

serves as a general frame for the formalization of evolution in software systems.

To support the implementation of modeling and restructuring tools, we designed and implemented a class library that represents our metamodel in form of C++ classes. It reduces the gap between a formal description and corresponding system support by providing software abstractions that mirror formal notions. To assist in the implementation of specialized tools, the library has been designed to be extensible and flexible.

---

* erdmann@cs.tu-berlin.de

** iclassen@cs.tu-berlin.de

2   Structure of the Class Library

The class library ALPHA provides concepts like ALPHA algebras and ALPHA homomorphisms. Moreover, it supports the application of (typed) graph transformation rules. This leads to classes representing diagrams and cocones in the sense of category theory, since a graph transformation step is given by a colimes construction in the category of ALPHA algebras (see [Löw93]). Additionally, correct typing of items can be described in terms of unique extensions induced by colimits.

Although the structure of ALPHA is primarily determined by the underlying theory, its realization with the goal of extensibility and flexibility requires important design decisions (see Sect. 3) that have no theoretical counterpart.

Figure 1 shows the general structure of the library, using the Booch notation [Boo94].

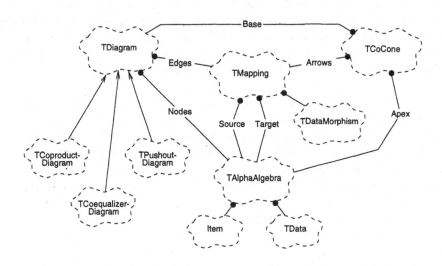

Fig. 1. The structure of the class library

ALPHA algebras consist of a graph part, an attribute part, and a data part. The data part is fixed,[1] whereas the graph and attribute parts can be modified dynamically. A minimal interface to the data part is defined by the class TData, from which user-defined data-type classes can be derived. The class TAlphaAlgebra is used to represent ALPHA algebras. It manages the elements of the carrier sets of sort $Item$ (class Item) as well as the references r_i and the attribute valuations v_i.

An ALPHA homomorphism consists of a partial homomorphism on the graph part and a total homomorphism on the data part. The former is represented by

---

[1] Transformation steps are not intended to modify data types like natural numbers.

class **TMapping** and the latter by class **TDataMorphism**.

Diagrams represent the application context for category-theoretic operations. The ALPHA library implements the colimes operation on arbitrary diagrams and provides special support for coproduct, coequalizer, and pushout diagrams.

The result of the colimes operation is a cocone, represented in the class **TCoCone**. A cocone on a diagram is an ALPHA algebra (the apex) together with, for each node in the diagram, a homomorphism from that node to the apex. Class **TCoCone** provides a method for calculating the unique extension between two cocones on the same diagram.

3 Special Design Issues

The main design goals for the class library ALPHA are extensibility and flexibility. In particular, it is possible to have several coexisting implementations of the same interface. For instance, there can be a persistent representation of algebras as well as a transient one (which is useful for calculating intermediate results). The differences between these implementations are mostly transparent to the user of the class library. To achieve this flexibility, the top-level classes of the library do not define a particular representation of their data. Instead, they only define abstract access methods which must be implemented in derived classes.

A concept that has no direct counterpart in the theory is that of an iterator (see Fig. 2). ALPHA provides standard iterators to represent (subsets of) carrier sets of sort *Item*, domains/codomains of mappings, and inverse images. Therefore, sets need not be constructed explicitly. Iterators are used to access algebras and homomorphisms as is necessary to construct, e. g. the greatest subalgebra of an ALPHA algebra that is contained within a given set of items. They are a well known concept to encapsulate knowledge of the representation of an aggregate.

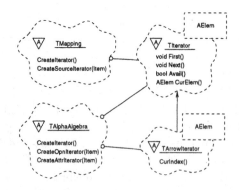

Fig. 2. Iterators on **TAlphaAlgebra** and **TMapping**

In order to separate interface and implementation, it is not sufficient to provide abstract base classes which do not enforce a particular data representation. The protocol of the base classes must be designed to allow the creation of derived objects (like iterators) on the level of abstract classes. ALPHA uses two design patterns for this purpose, *factory method* and *prototype* [GHJV95].

Factory methods are used to create iterators. For example, **TAlphaAlgebra** declares an abstract **CreateIterator** method which creates an iterator over the elements of the *Item* carrier set. Derived classes implement this method; they can therefore choose an iterator class according to their internal representation.

The *prototype* pattern also deals with object creation. In this pattern, new objects are created by copying a prototypical instance. This instance is passed to clients, which only access its abstract interface, so they are independent of the concrete type of the instance. Clients can be configured dynamically to use different prototypes, thereby letting them transparently work with different representations.

ALPHA uses the prototype pattern for creating cocones on diagrams and for creating the unique extension between two cocones. **TDiagram** has a **TAlpha-Algebra** prototype for creating apex objects and, for each node in the diagram, a **TMapping** prototype for creating homomorphisms from the nodes of the base diagram to the apex. **TCoCone** has a **TMapping** prototype for creating the unique extension.

4 Summary

In its present state [Erd95], ALPHA provides basic support for the construction of CASE tools based on our metamodel. Additional components are necessary (e. g. for the management of different description levels) for a more comprehensive assistance in tool implementation. The library consists of 46 classes comprising approximately 4600 lines of C++ code.

References

[Boo94]   G. Booch. *Object Oriented Analysis and Design with Applications*. Benjamin/Cummings, 2nd edition, 1994.

[CL95]   I. Claßen and M. Löwe. Scheme evolution in object–oriented models. In M. Wirsing, editor, *ICSE–17 Workshop on Formal Methods Application in Software Engineering Practice*, Seattle, Washington, April 1995.

[Erd95]   S. Erdmann. Konzeption und Realisierung einer Basisklassenbibliothek für Modellierungs- und Restrukturierungswerkzeuge. Master's thesis, Technical University of Berlin, 1995.

[GHJV95] E. Gamma, R. Helm, R. Johnson, and J. Vlissides. *Design Patterns: elements of reusable object-oriented software*. Addison-Wesley, 1995.

[Löw93]   M. Löwe. Algebraic approach to single-pushout graph transformation. *Theoretical Computer Science*, 109:181–224, 1993. Short version of Techn. Rep. 90/05, TU Berlin, Department of Computer Science, 1990.

Resolution of Goals with the Functional and Logic Programming Language LPG : Impact of Abstract Interpretation

Didier Bert, Rachid Echahed and Kamel Adi

IMAG-LSR, CNRS, BP 53, 38041 Grenoble cedex 9, France
e-mail: {bert, echahed}@imag.fr
http://thot.imag.fr/Les.Groupes/scop/

1 Introduction

LPG [1, 5] belongs to the class of languages designed for software specification, rapid prototyping and high-level programming. It allows one to define abstract data types, functions and predicates within one unified framework : Horn clause logic with equality. An implementation of LPG for SUN4/SunOS 4.1.3 is available by URL ftp://ftp.imag.fr/pub/SCOP/LPG. The LPG calculus, designed to solve goals à la Prolog, is mainly based on narrowing techniques. These techniques yield semi-decidable algorithms. Recently, we have shown in [2, 4] how abstract interpretation may help to improve the operational semantics of LPG-like languages. In this demonstration, we intend to present the specification and programming styles of LPG as well as the capabilities of the "solver" augmented with *abstract* term rewrite systems.

2 Examples of LPG specifications

In LPG, specifications are built up by composition of reusable modules. There are three kinds of specification modules, namely *properties, types* and *enrichments*. All the modules are composed of a signature part and an axiomatization part. The signature part is a many-sorted first-order signature $\Sigma = (S, \Omega, \Pi)$ where S is a set a sorts, Ω is a set of operator symbols and Π is a set of predicate symbols. The axiomatization of operators is achieved by conditional equations whereas the predicates definitions are provided by Horn clauses, where the bodies of the clauses may include classical literals, equations (t == t') and/or disequations (t =/= t'). The axiomatization is structured in two layers: the algebraic axiomatization of the operators, like in algebraic specification languages, without any reference to predicate symbols, and a second layer for the axiomatization of predicates which can mix all kinds of logical atoms. The *type* modules are intended to define new data types. The *constructors* of data types are explicitly given. In Figure 1, we define the data type of naturals with some operators. Figure 2, which defines the data type of binary trees, shows an example of a generic type module. The *enrichment* modules define new operators and/or new predicates over previously defined data types. An enrichment may be generic or not. In Figure 4, we give an example of a generic enrichment that defines an equality

```
type Naturals                    variables
sorts                              x, y : nat
  nat                            equations
constructors                       1: max (0, x) ==> x
  0 : → nat                        2: max (succ(x), 0) ==> succ(x)
  succ : nat → nat                 3: max (succ(x), succ(y)) ==> succ(max(x, y))
operators                          4: g (0) ==> 0
  max : (nat, nat) → nat           5: g (succ(x)) ==> g(x)
  g : nat → nat                  end Naturals
```

Fig. 1. Data type of natural numbers with some operators.

```
type Bin_Trees requires Formal_Sort [elem]
sorts tree
constructors
  empty: → tree[elem]
  node : (tree[elem], elem, tree[elem]) → tree[elem]
operators
  height : tree[elem] → nat
predicates
  balanced, not_balanced : tree[elem]
variables
  i : elem
  a,b : tree[elem]
equations
  1 : height (empty) ==> 0
  2 : height (node(a,i,b)) ==> succ(max(height(a), height(b)))
clauses
  1 : balanced (empty)
  2 : balanced (node(a,i,b)) <== height(a) == height(b), balanced(a), balanced(b)
  3 : not_balanced (node(a,i,b)) <== height(a) =/= height(b)
  4 : not_balanced (node(a,i,b)) <== not_balanced(a)
  5 : not_balanced (node(a,i,b)) <== not_balanced(b)
end Bin_Trees
```

Fig. 2. Data type of binary trees.

operator = : (tree[elem],tree[elem]) → bool over binary trees. The definition of this operator requires another equality operator over the formal sort elem. The specification of this formal operator is introduced by the statement requires Equality [elem operators eq].

The *property* modules are designed to specify first-order theories. Such modules are mainly used for specification purposes. They are used to characterize precisely the formal parameters of generic modules. Figures 3 and 4 give two examples of property modules. Formal_Sort specifies the class of sets and Equality characterizes algebras that consist of a set and a boolean operator which satisfies the axioms of "equivalence". More details about LPG may be found in [5, 3].

3 The LPG solver

In LPG system, one may either normalize terms using an abstract machine as in classical functional languages or solve goals à la Prolog. A goal is syntactically written as "$A_1, \ldots, A_m, \ldots, A_n$?" where every A_i is either an equation, a disequation or any other literal. The operational semantics of LPG [1, 6, 5]

```
property Formal_Sort
sorts t
end Formal_Sort
```

Fig. 3. Property of any data type.

```
property Equality
sorts t
operators
    =: (t,t) → bool
variables
    x,y,z: t
equations
    1: x = x == true
    2: x = y == y = x
    3: (x = y and y = z) ⇒ (x = z) == true
satisfies Formal_Sort [t]
end Equality
```

```
enrichment Eq_Tree
requires Equality [elem operators eq]
operators
    =: (tree[elem], tree[elem]) → bool
variables
    i, j: elem
    a, b, c, d: tree[elem]
equations
    1: empty = empty ==> true
    2: empty = node(a, i, b) ==> false
    3: node(a, i,b) = node(c, j, d) ==>
                      eq(i,j) and a = c and b = d
models
    Eq_tree: Equality[tree[elem] operators =]
end Eq_Tree
```

Fig. 4. Generic definition of equality of binary trees requiring the property of any data type with "equality" operator.

may be defined informally as an extension of the SLD-resolution where syntactic unification has been replaced by semantic unification, augmented with two algorithms for solving equations and disequations. The last two algorithms are based on narrowing. The current implementation always selects the leftmost atom for SLD-resolution and uses leftmost-innermost narrowing strategy. The searching tree may be constructed following the depth-first or breadth-first strategies according to user's indications. In Figure 5, we give a sample session. The reader familiar with narrowing-based algorithms might be surprised to see that our solver develops a finite search space for each of the considered goals. Actually, most narrowing-based algorithms will loop when solving these goals. Our current implementation of LPG solver uses a new procedure that cooperates with the classical narrowing-based algorithms. This new procedure, based on abstraction techniques, tries to verify the unsatisfiability or the validity of the considered goals. For each term t, it provides an approximation $A(t)$ of the set of possible normal forms of the ground instances of t. Then, the equation $t == t'$ is not satisfiable if $A(t)$ and $A(t')$ are *disjoint*. Such approximations are computed using abstract rewriting systems [4]. In Figure 6, we give an abstract rewriting system which is obtained automatically from the concrete specifications of the operators **height** and g given in Figures 1 and 2. In such abstract rewriting systems, the top operator, $\top : s$, is a constant that stands for all possible values of sort s.

References

1. D. Bert and R. Echahed. Design and implementation of a generic, logic and functional programming language. In *Proc. of ESOP-86, LNCS 213*, pp 119–132. Springer-Verlag, 1986.

```
{1} variables a:tree[nat] i,j:nat end

{2} max (g(i), g(j)) == 1 ?
No solution.

{3} max (g(i), g(j)) == 0 ?
for all j : nat
for all i : nat
more solutions?y
No more solution.

{4} height(a) <= 2 == true, balanced(a) ?
a == empty
more solutions? y
for all x_4 : nat
a == node(empty,x_4,empty)
more solutions? y
for all x_4 : nat
for all x_26 : nat
for all x_20 : nat
a == node(node(empty,x_20,empty),
          x_4,
          node(empty,x_26,empty))
more solutions? y
No more solution.
```

```
{5} height(a) <= 2 == true, not_balanced(a) ?
for all x_5 : nat
for all x_17 : nat
a == node(empty,x_5,node(empty,x_17,empty))
more solutions? y
for all x_5 : nat
for all x_37 : nat
a == node(node(empty,x_37,empty),x_5,empty)
more solutions? y
No more solution.

{6} height(a) == g(i) ?
for all i : nat
a == empty
more solutions? y
No more solution.

{7} end
```

Fig. 5. Sample session of LPG solver.

```
1: height(empty) → 0
2: height(node(empty,T:nat,empty)) → 1
3: height(node(node(T:(tree,nat,tree)),T:nat,empty)) → succ(succ(T:nat))
4: height(node(T:tree,T:nat,node(T:(tree,nat,tree)))) → succ(succ(T:nat))
5: height(node(node(T:(tree,nat,tree)),T:nat,node(T:(tree,nat,tree)))) → succ(succ(T:nat))
6: g(succ(0)) → 0
7: g(0) → 0
8: g(succ(succ(T:nat))) → 0
```

Fig. 6. Sample abstract term rewriting system.

2. D. Bert, R. Echahed, and B. M. Østvold. Abstract rewriting. In *Proceedings of the 3rd International Workshop on Static Analysis, WSA'93*, number 724 in Lecture Notes in Computer Science, pp 178–192. Springer-Verlag, 1993.
3. D. Bert, R. Echahed, and J.-C. Reynaud. Reference manual of the LPG specification language and environment. ftp://ftp.imag.fr/pub/SCOP/LPG, 1994.
4. D. Bert and R. Echahed. Abstraction of conditional term rewriting systems. In J. Lloyd, editor, *Proc. of the International Symposium on Logic Programming, ILPS-95*, pp 162–176, Portland, Oregon, 1995. MIT Press.
5. D. Bert and R. Echahed. On the operational semantics of the algebraic and logic language LPG. In *Recent Trends in Data Types Specification, LNCS 906*, , pp 132–152. Springer-Verlag, 1995.
6. R. Echahed. *Sur l'intégration des langages algébriques et logiques*. PhD thesis, INPG, Grenoble, 1990.

Combining Reductions and Computations in ReDuX

Reinhard Bündgen and Werner Lauterbach

Wilhelm-Schickard-Institut, Universität Tübingen
Sand 13, D-72076 Tübingen
⟨buendgen@informatik.uni-tuebingen.de⟩

ReDuX [1, 4] is a term rewriting laboratory mainly aimed at theorem proving and completion procedures. ReDuX comprises several variants of Knuth-Bendix completion including a version supporting associative commutative operators and an inductive completion procedure. Several term orderings are available as well as a random term generator and a program to automatically analyze the set of irreducible ground terms.

The goal of this work is to improve the rewrite machine of ReDuX. This is achieved by replacing part of the reductions by computations in appropriate data structures. Building in data structures should fulfill the following requirements. It should

- not pose any semantic restriction on the intended model of a rewrite specification,
- work for terms with free variables,
- preserve the confluence and the termination of the combined completion and reduction relation,
- be robust w. r. t. extensions of the specification, and
- it should be easily possible to augment a given rewrite specification by built-ins.

Evaluation domains offer a particular form of building-in data structures that for canonical term rewriting systems fulfill all of the above requirements. Hence they increase the efficiency of both rewrite proofs and rapid prototyping.

ReDuX has been extended to support evaluation domains and this extension has been successfully applied to the verification of a RISC processor [2].

Partial Evaluation Domains

Given a canonical rewrite specification $\Delta = (\mathcal{F}, \mathcal{R})$, then an algebra $E \in Mod(\Delta)$ that is free in $Mod(\Delta)$ on a countable set of generators is an *evaluation domain* if the following holds:

1. There is an implementation of E.
2. There is an isomorphism $\phi : T(\mathcal{F}, \mathcal{X})\!\downarrow_{\mathcal{R}} \rightarrow E$ that is uniquely defined by an isomorphism from the variables $\mathcal{X}$ to the generators of E where $T(\mathcal{F}, \mathcal{X})\!\downarrow_{\mathcal{R}}$ denotes the set of $\mathcal{R}$-irreducible terms.
3. ϕ^{-1} is effective.

Then $\phi^{-1}(\phi(t))$ computes the $\mathcal{R}$-normal form for each term t.

Example 1. Lists over $\mathbb{N}$ are evaluation domains for monoids, sets over $\mathbb{N}$ for Abelian idempotent monoids, reduced words over $\mathbb{Z}$ for groups, multivariate polynomials over $\mathbb{Z}$ for commutative rings with ones, and Stone polynomials [6] and FDDs [5] for Boolean rings. □

Evaluation domains can also be used to support canonical extensions of specifications for that evaluation domains are known. More precisely, let $\Delta' = (\mathcal{F}', \mathcal{R}')$ and let $\Delta = (\mathcal{F}, \mathcal{R})$ with evaluation domain E such that $\mathcal{F} \subseteq \mathcal{F}'$, $=_{\mathcal{R}} \subseteq =_{\mathcal{R}'}$, and $\mathcal{R} \cup \mathcal{R}'$ are terminating then E is a *partial evaluation domain* for Δ'. In this case ϕ must be defined by an isomorphism from $T(\mathcal{F}', \mathcal{X}) \setminus T(\mathcal{F})$ to the generators of E. For more details on theoretical aspects of evaluation domains see [3].

Evaluation Domains in ReDuX

ReDuX has been extended to support multiple independent partial evaluation domains. Figure 1 gives an example of such a specification. It shows parts of the specification of the Sparrow-0 processor, a 4-bit RISC processor with an 8-bit address space developed in a computer engeneering course at the University of Tübingen [7] and implemented on an FPGA. The base specification has been automatically generated from a hardware description at gate level in BLIF format [8][1] by the ReDuX tool *blif2rdx*. The base specification was then extended by further components describing the functions of the requirement specification and by information defining an evaluation domain.

An evaluation domain is declared as an external sort (here the external sort BPR denotes a Boolean polynomial ring) which must have two properties: XTERM, a function that implements ϕ^{-1} and XFG, a function that computes the i-th generator of the evaluation domain. Constants and operators that are interpretable by ϕ have their interpretation function stored as a property named after the associated evaluation domain (e. g., xor = BPRSUM). The specification can easily be changed to use FDDs as evaluation domain instead of Boolean polynomials by modifying the EXTERNAL and PROPERTY statements. So far the following evaluation domains have been prepared for the use with ReDuX: reduced words and reduced multisets over $\mathbb{Z}$, integral polynomials, Boolean polynomials and FDDs.

With the declaration of Boolean polynomials as evaluation domain, the rules (AXIOM) 1–8 in Figure 1 become redundant, but all other rules are still necessary. Redundant rules can be declared by the user to speed up the normalization of terms. Normalization then becomes a composition of calls to evaluation and reduction algorithms. ReDuX allows to experiment with different strategies for combining evaluation and reduction. In addition the result of normalizing a term may or may not be added as a new rule (lemma) to the term rewriting system.

Note that the specification of the Sparrow-0 is an example where the combination of evaluation and rewriting is really needed due to the definition of latches (e. g., like in

---

[1] BLIF specifications can be compiled into silicon.

```
%%   comment symbol
DATATYPE Sparrow0Processor-ev_bpr;
SORT        SIGNAL, TIME, SEL, VECTOR4, VECTOR8;
%% Boolean Polynomials as evaluation domains:
EXTERNAL  BPR: XTERM=TFIPRE,          XFG=IPRFG;
CONST     0, t0: TIME;
          L, H: SIGNAL;
%% ...
PROPERTY  %% interpretation to evaluation domain
          L:   BPR=PRZERO;     %% the zero-polynomial
          H:   BPR=IPRONE;     %% the one-polynomial
OPERATOR  %% base structures
          xor, and, or, imply, equal: SIGNAL, SIGNAL -> SIGNAL;
          neg, not: SIGNAL -> SIGNAL;
          S: TIME -> TIME;
THEORY    xor, and: AC;
PROPERTY  %% interpretation to evaluation domain
          xor: BPR=BPRSUM;     %% polynomial addition
          and: BPR=BPRPRO;     %% polynomial multiplication
          or:  BPR=BPROR;      %% "or" on Boolean polynomials
          not: BPR=BPRNOT;     %% "not" on Boolean polynomials
OPERATOR   %% hardware variables
%% ...
          V16: TIME -> SIGNAL
%% ...
VAR       t: TIME;
          O, P, Q, R: SIGNAL;
%% ...
AXIOM
   [1] or(P,Q) == xor(and(P,Q),xor(P,Q));
   [2] not(P) == xor(P,H);
   [3] xor(P,L) == P;
   [4] xor(P,P) == L;
   [5] and(P,H) == P;
   [6] and(P,P) == P;
   [7] and(P,L) == L;
   [8] and(P,xor(Q,R)) == xor(and(P,Q),and(P,R));
   [9] imply(P,Q) == xor(and(P,Q),xor(P,H));
   [10] equal(P,Q) == xor(P,xor(Q,H));
%% ...
   [21] V16(t) == and(not(V23(t)),not(V24(t)));
%% ...
  [263] V72(0) == L;            %% reset state of latch V72
  [264] V72(S(t)) == V97(t);  %% successor state of latch V72
%% ...
```

Fig. 1. A ReDuX specification for the Sparrow-0 Processor

AXIOMs 263 and 264) where the language of first order logic is essential. Thus the verification cannot be performed by some variant of a Boolean Gröbner base algorithm.

Using random inputs we observed speed-ups of more than 100 for finitely presented groups or rings using reduced words and integral polynomials respectively as evaluation domains. During the verification of Sparrow-0, we even encountered terms whose normalization with evaluation support lead to speed-ups greater than 1000 compared with the pure rewrite based normalization. The time for the whole verification dropped from 52 min to 10 min (normalization time) on an i486 DX100 based PC under Linux when we introduced Boolean polynomials (or FDDs) as evaluation domains. The verification of Sparrow-0 requires some 600 equations to be proved and over 8000 lemmas to be generated under different preconditions. The equations to be proved and used as preconditions are assembled automatically by Unix tools such that (an arbitrary part of) the proof can be performed automatically.

Conclusion

We think that in order to be useful for theorem proving and rapid prototyping on non-trivial examples rewrite based specifications must have support for efficient rewriting in standard structures like monoids, (multi) sets, commutative rings and Boolean rings. Evaluation domains form a very attractive solution to this requirement. Their implementation in ReDuX has been found to be extremely effective.

References

1. R. Bündgen. Reduce the redex → ReDuX. In C. Kirchner, editor, *Rewriting Techniques and Applications (LNCS 690)*, pages 446–450. Springer-Verlag, 1993.
2. R. Bündgen, W. Küchlin, and W. Lauterbach. Verification of the Sparrow processor. In *IEEE Symposium and Workshop on Engineering of Computer-Based Systems*. IEEE Press, 1996. (Proc. ECBS'96, to appear).
3. R. Bündgen and W. Lauterbach. Experiments with partial evaluation domains for rewrite specifications. In *11th Workshop on Abstract Data Types*, 1995. (submitted, presented at WADT'95, Oslo, N, September 1995).
4. R. Bündgen, C. Sinz, and J. Walter. ReDuX 1.5: New facets of rewriting. In H. Ganzinger, editor, *Rewriting Techniques and Applications*. Springer-Verlag, 1996. (to appear).
5. U. Kebschull, E. Schubert, and W. Rosenstiel. Multilevel logic synthesis based on functional decision diagrams. In *Proc. EDAC 1992*, 1992.
6. M. H. Stone. The theory of representations of Boolean algebras. *Trans. American Math. Society*, 40:37–111, 1936.
7. P. Thole, U. Kebschull, E. Schubert, and W. Rosenstiel. The design and implementation of an educational computer system based on FPGAs. In *Proc. 4th Eurochip Workshop on VLSI Design Training*, 1993.
8. University of California, Berkeley, CA. *Berkeley Logic Interchange Format (BLIF)*, July 1992.

Conditional Directed Narrowing[*]

Sébastien Limet and Pierre Réty

LIFO - Université d'Orléans B.P. 6759, 45067 Orléans cedex 2, France
e-mail : {limet, rety}@lifo.univ-orleans.fr

Abstract. We present an implementation of directed narrowing extended to the conditional framework, which is complete for two classes of conditional term rewrite systems : confluent and decreasing on one hand, level-confluent and terminating on the other hand.

1 Introduction

Narrowing was originally introduced for solving unification of terms modulo a theory represented by a term rewrite system (E-unification). Next it has been used as the operational semantics of functional logic programming languages (see [5] for a recent survey). In this framework, the program is often represented by a set of equational Horn clauses, i.e. a conditional term rewrite system (CTRS). However, conditional narrowing is inefficient for practical applications because the search space is huge and contains infinite branches. This is why many authors have proposed optimizations to the narrowing procedure : innermost, basic innermost, LSE, lazy, approximations, etc.... Many of them need some restrictions on the rewrite system to keep completeness, like left-linearity, non-ambiguity, constructor discipline.

Another idea consists in directing narrowing [3]. In the non-conditional case, this idea has led to the 'narrowing directed by a graph of terms' [2, 8]. A graph of terms is built from the rewrite system and the equation to be solved, and prevents from computing some narrowing steps that do not lead to solutions. Thus the search space is pruned and many infinite branches are cut. In comparison with [2], the implementation presented in this paper is both an extension to the conditional case and a refinement that directs narrowing in more cases, i.e. that cuts more branches. It is called conditional directed narrowing ($\mathcal{CDN}$). $\mathcal{CDN}$ is sound and complete for two different approaches of conditional rewriting : decreasing and confluent CTRS's [6] and on the other hand level-confluent and terminating CTRS's [4].

Example 1. Now let us explain the principle of the method using an example. Let R be the rewrite system :
$r_1 : g(x, 0) \quad \rightarrow 0$
$r_2 : h(0, y, x) \quad \rightarrow 0 \Leftarrow g(x, y) \doteq_R y$
$r_3 : h(1, x, s(y)) \rightarrow h(1, 0, y)$

This rewrite system is both level-confluent and decreasing. It is also left-linear, constructor based (the constructors are 0, 1, and s), and has no critical

---

[*] For a complete description of the method, see [7]

pairs. We want to solve $h(x, 0, z) \doteq_R 0$. With a naive strategy, we get a derivation that computes the solution $\{x \mapsto 0\}$:

$$h(x, 0, z) \doteq_R 0 \leadsto_{[1, r_2, \{x \mapsto 0, y_1 \mapsto 0, x_1 \mapsto z\}]} \underline{g(z, 0) \doteq_R 0} \quad \wedge 0 \doteq_R 0$$
$$\leadsto_{[1, r_1, \{x_2 \mapsto z\}]} \qquad 0 \doteq_R 0 \qquad \wedge 0 \doteq_R 0$$

But there is another derivation, infinite, which is at once lazy, basic, LSE:

$$h(x, 0, z) \doteq_R 0 \leadsto_{[1, r_3, \{\ldots, z \mapsto s(z_1)\}]} h(1, 0, z_1) \doteq_R 0$$
$$\leadsto_{[1, r_3, \{\ldots, z_1 \mapsto s(z_2)\}]} h(1, 0, z_2) \doteq_R 0 \leadsto \ldots$$

Therefore all these strategies have some infinite derivations in their search spaces.

When using directed narrowing, we first construct a graph of terms by considering the sides of the equation to be solved, the rewrite rules, and by adding arrows such that : if some term s of the graph narrows into some term t of the graph, then there is a path from the top of s to the top of t. From a mathematical point of view, the graph of terms is not a graph whose nodes are terms since there may be arrows between subterms. Even so, it can be easily transformed by replacing arrows between subterms by arrows between tops, labelled by occurrences. For this reason we will continue to speak of a 'graph of terms'.

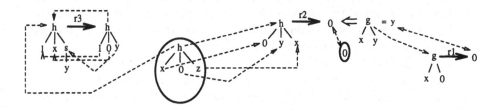

Fig. 1. the graph of terms

Recall we want to solve $h(x, 0, z) \doteq_R 0$ (the encircled terms in the graph, see figure 1). The only path on the tops between $h(x, 0, z)$ and 0 goes via r_2. [2] Therefore, we know that all the narrowing derivations from $h(x, 0, z)$ to 0 (i.e. that yield solutions) contain a step on the top using the rule r_2. Then (possibly infinite) derivations applying other rules on the top are useless. So, we have first to try r_2 on top, i.e. the subterms of $h(x, 0, z)$ have to be narrowed into the subterms of the lhs of r_2 (1) and the premise of r_2 have to R-unify (2). Then we have to R-unify the rhs of r_2 with 0 (3). It is the meaning of the following computation. For technical reasons, we transform $h(x, 0, z) \doteq_R 0$ into $h(x, 0, z) =_R z_1 \wedge 0 =_R z_1$, where z_1 is a new variable. By applying r_2 on the first equation we get :

$$\underbrace{x \doteq 0 \wedge 0 =_R y_1 \wedge z \doteq x_1}_{(1)} \wedge \underbrace{g(x_1, y_1) =_R y_1}_{(2)} \wedge \underbrace{0 =_R z_1}_{(3)} \wedge 0 =_R z_1$$

In the equation $0 =_R y_1$ the term 0 cannot be narrowed. Then we get $y_1 \doteq 0$, which can be merged with $g(x_1, y_1) =_R y_1$:

$$x \doteq 0 \wedge y_1 \doteq 0 \wedge z \doteq x_1 \wedge g(x_1, y_1) =_R 0 \wedge 0 =_R z_1 \wedge 0 =_R z_1$$

---

[2] The meaning of double arrows is explained in [7]

The graph shows that only r_1 can be applied to narrow $g(x_1, y_1)$ into 0:

$$x \doteq 0 \wedge y_1 \doteq 0 \wedge z \doteq x_1 \wedge x_1 \doteq x_2 \wedge y_1 \doteq 0 \wedge 0 =_R 0 \wedge 0 =_R z_1 \wedge 0 =_R z_1$$

By instantiating x_1 by x_2:

$$x_1 \doteq x_2 \wedge x \doteq 0 \wedge y_1 \doteq 0 \wedge z \doteq x_2 \wedge y_1 \doteq 0 \wedge 0 =_R 0 \wedge 0 =_R z_1 \wedge 0 =_R z_1$$

This gives: $x_1 \doteq x_2 \wedge x \doteq 0 \wedge y_1 \doteq 0 \wedge z \doteq x_2 \wedge 0 =_R z_1 \wedge 0 =_R z_1$

Since 0 cannot be narrowed, we get: $x_1 \doteq x_2 \wedge x \doteq 0 \wedge y_1 \doteq 0 \wedge z \doteq x_2 \wedge z_1 \doteq 0$

This equational system is in solved form and gives the solution. So, this method terminates whereas lazy, basic, LSE do not.

2 Implementation

$\mathcal{CDN}$ has been implemented in C as an extension of UREVEAL, a software written by J. Chabin that combined ordered basic completion and basic narrowing. User interaction is easy thanks to the graphic environment. Note that:

- The graph depends on the equation to be solved. When solving several equations, we can avoid building the whole graph several times by removing only the old equation as well as the arrows that deal with it, then adding the new one and building the arrows that deal with it.
- As in PROLOG, the selection rule, i.e. the choice of the equation to be solved within the current equational system, is crucial for the efficiency. Our experiments have shown that it is important to solve the syntactic equations as soon as they appear. To detect failures, equations that can be solved in finite time, i.e. that contain terms whose top symbols are constructors or are not recursively defined, must be selected at first. Concerning the other equations, the selection rule may be fair or not, as the user wants. We have noticed that, as in logic programming, fairness is important for termination, but seldom gives the most efficient procedure.

3 Experiments

The following experiments have been done on a SPARC Station 10, using a non fair selection rule. For these examples, $\mathcal{CDN}$ terminates while basic strategies (including LSE) loops.

Example 2. This problem comes from [1] and concerns the addition and multiplication of non-negative integers with the rewrite system

$$R_1 = \{0 + x \to x,\ s(x) + y \to s(x + y),\ 0 * x \to 0,\ s(x) * y \to y + x * y\}$$

where the goal is $x * x + y * y \doteq_R s(0)$.

According to [1], normalizing LSE-narrowing (which is an optimization of basic narrowing) computes 46 narrowing steps with the rewrite system R_1 if its infinite search space is cut at depth 7. Lazy narrowing (used in BABEL language) loops on this example too, it performs 30 narrowing steps at depth 7. On the other hand CDN has a finite search space of maximal depth 7 that contains 21 narrowing steps.

To have a significant running time, let us solve $x*x+y*y = s^{26}(0)$. CDN takes $7.4sec$ to construct the graph and solve the goal and computes 3780 narrowing steps.

Example 3. The second example is a program for solving the wolf, the goat and the cabbage problem; the rewrite system contains 46 rules and 31 function symbols. It is to illustrate that the construction of the graph of terms is not time costing. The construction takes about 0.7 milliseconds. The time for searching paths in the graph has not been evaluated but, it seems negligible wrt the gain that the graph provides. The overall problem is solved in 16.7 sec after 6092 narrowing steps.

Many other experiments have been done with various rewrite systems. We have remarked that CDN is quite efficient for examples coming from logic-functional programming, i.e. constructor-based systems without critical pairs because in such cases the graph of terms prunes large parts of the search tree. For this kind of rewrite systems, directed narrowing often even terminates. On the other hand, the graph is less efficient for non-constructor-based rewrite systems because there are too many relations between terms. Our non normalizing strategy is not adapted to overlapping rewrite systems but its performance seems to be equivalent to basic normalizing narrowing.

References

1. A. Bockmayr, S. Krischer, and A. Werner. Narrowing strategies for arbitrary canonical systems. *Fundamenta Informaticae*, 24(1,2):125 – 155, 1995.
2. J. Chabin and P. Réty. Narrowing Directed by a Graph of Terms. In R. V. Book, editor, *Proceedings 4th Conference on Rewriting Techniques and Applications, Como (Italy)*, volume 488 of *LNCS*, pages 112–123. Springer-Verlag, April 1991.
3. N. Dershowitz and G. Sivakumar. Solving Goals in Equational Langages. In S. Kaplan and J-P. Jouannaud, editors, *proceedings of the 1st International Workshop on Conditional and Typed Rewriting Systems*, volume 308 of *LNCS*, pages 45–55. Springer-Verlag, 1987.
4. E. Giovannetti and C. Moiso. A Completeness result for e-unification algorithms based on conditional narrowing. In *Proc. of Workshop on Foundation of Logic and Functional Programming*, volume 306 of *LNCS*, pages 157–167. Springer-Verlag, 1986.
5. M. Hanus. The Integration of Functions into Logic Programming: From Theory to Practice. *Journal of Logic Programming*, 19 & 20:583–628, May/July 1994.
6. S. Kaplan. Simplifying conditional term rewriting systems: Unification, termination and confluence. *Journal of Symbolic Computation*, 4(3):295–334, 1987.
7. S. Limet and P. Réty. Conditional Directed Narrowing (including proofs). Technical Report 95-11, Laboratoire d'Informatique Fondamentale d'Orléans, 1995. Available by anonymous ftp at ftp-lifo.univ-orleans.fr.
8. S. Limet and P. Réty. Directed Narrowing: An Optimization That More Often Terminates (including proofs). Technical Report 95-07, Laboratoire d'Informatique Fondamentale d'Orléans, 1995. Available by anonymous ftp at ftp-lifo.univ-orleans.fr.

Author Index

Lecture Notes in Computer Science

For information about Vols. 1–1029

please contact your bookseller or Springer-Verlag

Vol. 1064: B. Buxton, R. Cipolla (Eds.), Computer Vision – ECCV '96. Volume I. Proceedings, 1996. XXI, 725 pages. 1996.

Vol. 1065: B. Buxton, R. Cipolla (Eds.), Computer Vision – ECCV '96. Volume II. Proceedings, 1996. XXI, 723 pages. 1996.

Vol. 1066: R. Alur, T.A. Henzinger, E.D. Sontag (Eds.), Hybrid Systems III. IX, 618 pages. 1996.

Vol. 1067: H. Liddell, A. Colbrook, B. Hertzberger, P. Sloot (Eds.), High-Performance Computing and Networking. Proceedings, 1996. XXV, 1040 pages. 1996.

Vol. 1068: T. Ito, R.H. Halstead, Jr., C. Queinnec (Eds.), Parallel Symbolic Languages and Systems. Proceedings, 1995. X, 363 pages. 1996.

Vol. 1069: J.W. Perram, J.-P. Müller (Eds.), Distributed Software Agents and Applications. Proceedings, 1994. VIII, 219 pages. 1996. (Subseries LNAI).

Vol. 1070: U. Maurer (Ed.), Advances in Cryptology – EUROCRYPT '96. Proceedings, 1996. XII, 417 pages. 1996.

Vol. 1071: P. Miglioli, U. Moscato, D. Mundici, M. Ornaghi (Eds.), Theorem Proving with Analytic Tableaux and Related Methods. Proceedings, 1996. X, 330 pages. 1996. (Subseries LNAI).

Vol. 1072: R. Kasturi, K. Tombre (Eds.), Graphics Recognition. Proceedings, 1995. X, 308 pages. 1996.

Vol. 1073: J. Cuny, H. Ehrig, G. Engels, G. Rozenberg (Eds.), Graph Grammars and Their Application to Computer Science. Proceedings, 1994. X, 565 pages. 1996.

Vol. 1074: G. Dowek, J. Heering, K. Meinke, B. Möller (Eds.), Higher-Order Algebra, Logic, and Term Rewriting. Proceedings, 1995. VII, 287 pages. 1996.

Vol. 1075: D. Hirschberg, G. Myers (Eds.), Combinatorial Pattern Matching. Proceedings, 1996. VIII, 392 pages. 1996.

Vol. 1076: N. Shadbolt, K. O'Hara, G. Schreiber (Eds.), Advances in Knowledge Acquisition. Proceedings, 1996. XII, 371 pages. 1996. (Subseries LNAI).

Vol. 1077: P. Brusilovsky, P. Kommers, N. Streitz (Eds.), Mulimedia, Hypermedia, and Virtual Reality. Proceedings, 1994. IX, 311 pages. 1996.

Vol. 1078: D.A. Lamb (Ed.), Studies of Software Design. Proceedings, 1993. VI, 188 pages. 1996.

Vol. 1079: Z.W. Raś, M. Michalewicz (Eds.), Foundations of Intelligent Systems. Proceedings, 1996. XI, 664 pages. 1996. (Subseries LNAI).

Vol. 1080: P. Constantopoulos, J. Mylopoulos, Y. Vassiliou (Eds.), Advanced Information Systems Engineering. Proceedings, 1996. XI, 582 pages. 1996.

Vol. 1081: G. McCalla (Ed.), Advances in Artificial Intelligence. Proceedings, 1996. XII, 459 pages. 1996. (Subseries LNAI).

Vol. 1082: N.R. Adam, B.K. Bhargava, M. Halem, Y. Yesha (Eds.), Digital Libraries. Proceedings, 1995. Approx. 310 pages. 1996.

Vol. 1083: K. Sparck Jones, J.R. Galliers, Evaluating Natural Language Processing Systems. XV, 228 pages. 1996. (Subseries LNAI).

Vol. 1084: W.H. Cunningham, S.T. McCormick, M. Queyranne (Eds.), Integer Programming and Combinatorial Optimization. Proceedings, 1996. X, 505 pages. 1996.

Vol. 1085: D.M. Gabbay, H.J. Ohlbach (Eds.), Practical Reasoning. Proceedings, 1996. XV, 721 pages. 1996. (Subseries LNAI).

Vol. 1086: C. Frasson, G. Gauthier, A. Lesgold (Eds.), Intelligent Tutoring Systems. Proceedings, 1996. XVII, 688 pages. 1996.

Vol. 1087: C. Zhang, D. Lukose (Eds.), Distributed Artificial Intelliegence. Proceedings, 1995. VIII, 232 pages. 1996. (Subseries LNAI).

Vol. 1088: A. Strohmeier (Ed.), Reliable Software Technologies – Ada-Europe '96. Proceedings, 1996. XI, 513 pages. 1996.

Vol. 1089: G. Ramalingam, Bounded Incremental Computation. XI, 190 pages. 1996.

Vol. 1090: J.-Y. Cai, C.K. Wong (Eds.), Computing and Combinatorics. Proceedings, 1996. X, 421 pages. 1996.

Vol. 1091: J. Billington, W. Reisig (Eds.), Application and Theory of Petri Nets 1996. Proceedings, 1996. VIII, 549 pages. 1996.

Vol. 1092: H. Kleine Büning (Ed.), Computer Science Logic. Proceedings, 1995. VIII, 487 pages. 1996.

Vol. 1093: L. Dorst, M. van Lambalgen, F. Voorbraak (Eds.), Reasoning with Uncertainty in Robotics. Proceedings, 1995. VIII, 387 pages. 1996. (Subseries LNAI).

Vol. 1094: R. Morrison, J. Kennedy (Eds.), Advances in Databases. Proceedings, 1996. XI, 234 pages. 1996.

Vol. 1095: W. McCune, R. Padmanabhan, Automated Deduction in Equational Logic and Cubic Curves. X, 231 pages. 1996. (Subseries LNAI).

Vol. 1096: T. Schäl, Workflow Management Systems for Process Organisations. XII, 200 pages. 1996.

Vol. 1097: R. Karlsson, A. Lingas (Eds.), Algorithm Theory – SWAT '96. Proceedings, 1996. IX, 453 pages. 1996.

Vol. 1098: P. Cointe (Ed.), ECOOP '96 – Object-Oriented Programming. Proceedings, 1996. XI, 502 pages. 1996.

Vol. 1099: F. Meyer auf der Heide, B. Monien (Eds.), Automata, Languages and Programming. Proceedings, 1996. XII, 681 pages. 1996.

Vol. 1101: M. Wirsing, M. Nivat (Eds.), Algebraic Methodology and Software Technology. Proceedings, 1996. XII, 641 pages. 1996.

Vol. 1102: R. Alur, T.A. Henzinger (Eds.), Computer Aided Verification. Proceedings, 1996. XII, 472 pages. 1996.

Vol. 1103: H. Ganzinger (Ed.), Rewriting Techniques and Applications. Proceedings, 1996. XI, 437 pages. 1996.

Vol. 1105: T.I. Ören, G.J. Klir (Eds.), Computer Aided Systems Theory – CAST '94. Proceedings, 1994. IX, 439 pages. 1996.

Vol. 1106: M. Jampel, E. Freuder, M. Maher (Eds.), Over-Constrained Systems. X, 309 pages. 1996.